SO-DUT-926

Genealogies of
Connecticut Families

From The New England Historical
and Genealogical Register

Genealogies of CONNECTICUT FAMILIES

―――――❦―――――

From The New England Historical and Genealogical Register

Volume II

Geer – Owen

―――――❦―――――

Selected and Introduced by
GARY BOYD ROBERTS

With an Index by Elizabeth Petty Bentley

Baltimore
GENEALOGICAL PUBLISHING CO., INC.
1983

Excerpted and reprinted from *The New England
Historical and Genealogical Register,*
with added Table of Contents and Index.
Genealogical Publishing Co., Inc., Baltimore, 1983.
Copyright © 1983 by Genealogical Publishing Co., Inc.
Baltimore, Maryland. All Rights Reserved.
Library of Congress Catalogue Card Number 83-80639
International Standard Book Number, Volume II: 0-8063-1028-6
Set Number: 0-8063-1030-8
Made in the United States of America

Contents

―――――――――――――――⇒ﻬⲊⲊ⇐―――――――――――

v

xi

Genealogies of CONNECTICUT *F*AMILIES

From The New England Historical
and Genealogical Register

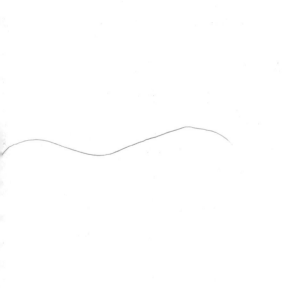

GEER NOTES.—Walter Geer in the *Geer Genealogy* (1923), p. 17, lists the children of Joseph[2] Geer (George[1]), born 14 Oct. 1664, died 10 Aug. 1743, married in Preston, Conn., 7 Jan. 1692, Sarah Howard as follows: Joseph, b. 17 Oct. 1692; Keziah, b. 23 Feb. 1710; Sarah, b. 17 Sept. 1712; Benajah, b. 31 May 1714; Joseph, b. 29 May 1719; Silas, b. 26 March 1722; Ezra, b. 16 May 1724. Joseph[3] Geer is said to have married in Preston, 18 Oct. 1713, Susannah Silsby [not identified] and to have had two children: James, b. 17 Jan. 1715 and Susannah, b. 28 March 1717. He died 19 May 1718 and his father administered his estate. However, his will proves that he died unmarried. In it James and Susannah are called his brother and sister (New London County Probates, Book 1, p. 9).

The Vital Records of Preston, Conn. (Barbour Collection (1919)) show the birth of Benajah, son of Joseph and Sarah Geer, born May 31, 1707-19 from the town records, vol. 1, p. 17 and Benajah, son of Joseph and Sarah Geer, born May 31, 1714, from vol. 1, p. 106. There are similar conflicts in the birth dates of some of the other children; Joseph[3] is said to have been born 17 Oct. 1693; Sarah is entered on page 17 as born on 17-16 Feb. 1712 and on page 106 as born 17 Sept. 1712. The record of the marriage of Joseph[2] Geer to Susannah Silsby (vol. 1, p. 17) calls her Susannah Simsby. An exhaustive search of Connecticut and Massachusetts records fails to turn up a Simsby family. This, together with the fact that James[3] Geer, her son, named a son Silsby, would seem to confirm Mr. Walter Geer's conclusion. She was probably the daughter of Jonathan[2] Silsby (Henry[1]) of Ipswich and Lynn, Mass., and Windham, Conn.

Since Joseph Geer and Susannah Silsby were married 18 Oct. 1713, the birth of a son Banajah to the said Joseph and Sarah on 31 May 1714 is manifestly impossible. A further discrepancy comes to light with the discovery of the baptism of Sarah, daughter of Joseph Geer, in the First Congregational Church, Preston, on 1 June 1707, by the Rev. Salmon Treat. It would appear that the child born to Joseph and Sarah Geer on 31 May 1707 was Sarah—not Benajah—and that the dates of birth had been reversed.

A letter to the town of Preston pointing out the discrepancies and questioning whether volume 1 of the Town Records might be a copy of an earlier record and not the original brought the following response from the Assistant Town Clerk: "I have checked the records and they are as you have stated. Though I cannot verify it I believe that the records were probably copied which would account for the fact that the same family was not carried out on the same page."

There is also the possibility that the original records might have been destroyed and, as has happened in other New England towns, been reconstructed from the memories of the inhabitants.

Sarah Geer, the mother of Benajah, Keziah, and Sarah Geer, died after 17 Sept. 1712 and before October 1713. Was she the first wife Sarah Howard, born in Norwich in 1669, daughter of Thomas and Mary (Wellman) Howard, mother of Joseph[3] Geer or did Joseph[2] Geer have two wives named Sarah? The lapse of fourteen years between Joseph and the next child leaves room for question.

Cambridge, Mass.   ANNE BORDEN HARDING.

THE GILBERT FAMILY.

BY J. WINGATE THORNTON, ESQ.*

THERE is a historical propriety in introducing the name of GILBERT into the pages of the New England Register, as none is more honorably or intimately connected with American discoveries, geography, and early history. It stands conspicuous among the illustrious names of Raleigh, Drake, Cavendish, Gosnold, Hawkins, and a host of naval worthies; and, with singular happiness, is joined with the three first named, in lineage, as well as in the less tangible but generous relationship of mind.

The name Gilbert is Saxon. Camden, in his "Remaines concerning Britaine," thus discourses upon its origin and signification. "Gilbert, *German*, I supposed heretofore to signifie Gold-like-bright, as *Aurelius* or *Aurelianus* ; or yellow bright, as *Flavius* with the Romans. For *Geele* is yellow in old Saxon, and still in Dutch, as *Gilvus* according to some in Latine. But, because it is written in Dooms-day booke *Gislebert*, I judge it rather to signifie Bright or brave pledge; for in old Saxon, *Gisle* signifieth a pledge, and in the old English booke of *S. Augustines of Canterbury*, sureties and pledges for keeping the peace are called *Fredgisles*." It is written on the Roll of Battle Abbey, T. Gilbard. Richard Fitz Gilbert, a kinsman of the conqueror, and a principal personage, was, for his services, advanced to great honors and possessions. His son, Earl Pembroke, died 14 King Stephen, 1149, leaving a son, Richard Gilbert, surnamed Strong Bow. The Earls of Clare were of this lineage. Robertus de Gerebert was a *testis* to a deed of William de Vernon, Earl of Devon, to the church of Brumor, in the age of King John, 1199–1216. Gilbert de Thornton was "the King's Serjeant at Law," in 1281, and in 1290, chief justice of the King's Bench.

1060. Gilbert de Gaunt came with William the Conqueror.

1100. Gislebert was Archdeacon of Buckingham.

1115. Gilbert, of Saxon origin, was a citizen of London, joined in the Crusades, and was father of Thomas a Becket.

1148. Gilbert, Lord of Sempringham, Lincolnshire, founded the Order of Gilbertine friars.

1215. Gilbert, treasurer of Lincoln Cathedral.

1240. Gilbert, Archdeacon of Stow.

1414. Robert Gilbert, S. T. P., Precentor of Lincoln — 1418, Prebend of Lincoln, and afterward Bishop of London.

1487. Thomas Gilbert, LL. D., Prebendary of Lincoln.

1492. Thomas Gilbert, Vicar-general of Chelsea College.

The name is eminent in the annals of the Church, State, and Learning of England, through several centuries. Its early and principal home is in Devonshire, and from this stock, distinguished in naval and commercial history and geographical science and discoveries, issued many branches, planted in other portions of the country. They possessed lands in Manaton,

* Special acknowledgement is due to SYLVESTER JUDD, Esq., of Northampton, Hon. SAML. H. PARSONS, Hon. R. R. HINMAN, and J. HAMMOND TRUMBULL, Esq., of Hartford, and Hon. FRANCIS BAYLIES, of Taunton, for their communications.

in or near Dartmoor, in Edward the Confessor's days, 1272–1307.
Westcote, who was born in Shobrook, in Devonshire, in 1567, and wrote
his history of that county in 1630, says that at Marledon, on the River
Darte, is a chapel built by the ancestors of the Gilberts, who have an ancient
monument there; one of them lieth in the church, with his wife, their
proportions cut into stone." He describes Greenway, the ancient seat of
the Gilberts, as "very pleasantly and commodiously placed, with a most
delightsome prospect to behold the barks and boats to pass and repass upon
the river flowing from Dartmouth to Totnes. This hath long continued
in a family of much estimation, the Gilberts alias Jilberts of knightly rank.
It is very anciently written Gislebert, or Gerebert, as in the Conqueror's
Book of Survey among the Tenures in Devon. Of this progeny have been
divers of great desert and sufficiency."

Thomas, son of Jeffrey Gilbert, "married Jane, or Joan, daughter of
William Compton of Compton, in the parish of Marldon, near the Torlay,
who for her partage brought him Compton, in the days of King Edward II.,
1307–1327." Prince, in his "Worthies of Devon," says that the Gilberts
"have matched as they descended into honorable houses, as of Champernoon,
Croker, Hill, Chudleigh, Agar, Molineux, Pomeroy, &c., and have yielded
matches to others, in particular to the noble family of Grenviles. They
have married also divers daughters and heirs, as Compton, Champernon,
Valetort, (whereby they touch the blood royal,) Reynward, Trenoch, Littleton alias Westcott, Kelley and others from whose loins have proceeded
many eminent persons which were of old men of renown. Such was Otho,
called also Otis Gilbert, High Sheriff of Devonshire, 15 Edward IV." 1475–6.

Sir Humphry Gilbert, one of the most accomplished men of his day,
devoted his early years to liberal studies, "computations astronomicall and
cosmographicall, speculations in Alchemy," but especially to mathematics, as
appeared by his subsequent life. He was "a man both valiant and well
experienced in martial affaires." About 1570, he proposed to Queen Elizabeth a plan for a University in the metropolis, which has been edited
recently by Sir H. Ellis, from a MS. in the British Museum. The famous
astrologer, Dr. John Dee, entered in his Diary, November 6, 1577, that "Sir
Umfrey Gilbert came to see me at Mortlake," curiously showing Gilbert's favorite science of numbers, leading his mind to the supposed occult influences of
the stars — but all were believers then, and about four years after, June 17,
1581, Dr. Dee writes, "Young Mr. Hawkins who had byn with Sir Francis
Drake came to me at Mortlake." Drake had returned from his famous
voyage about nine months before, September 26, 1580, and "young Mr.
Hawkins," was without doubt the embryo of Sir Richard Hawkins, whose
history is well known. Queen Elizabeth also consulted Dr. Dee. In 1576,
S. Humphrey published his learned and ingenious "Discourse to prove a
passage by the North West to Cathaia and the East Indies."

The accompanying pedigree is made from the several accounts in Prince,
Westcott, Polwhele, Hakluyt, Purchas, Hollingshed, and Gorges, and the
manuscripts* in the Herald's College, which seem contradictory one to the
other, and inconsistent with themselves; but a cautious collation of the dates
and historical references exhibits the true lineage, stated in the tabular form,
and, it is believed, reconciling the apparent discrepancies, as will appear by
a careful study of the original authorities.

*Copies by Mr. H. G. Somerby, among the papers of the late Dr. Daniel Gilbert, of Boston.

ARMS.—Ar. on a chev. sa. three roses of the first. Crest.—A Dolphin, naivant embowed. Gilberts of Devonshire.—Guillim, London, 1726. Vol. 1, 254.

GILBERT of Compton, Parish of Marldon, Co. of Devon.

Thomas Gilbert = Amy

Jeffrey Gilbert. = Jane or Joan d. and coheir of Wm. Compton of Compton, Esq.

Wm. Gilbert of Compton = Elizth. d. & coh. of Oliver Champernon, Esq. by his wife Egelina d. of Hugh Valetort of Tamerton, Esq.

Wm. Gilbert of Compton = Isabel d. of Wm. Gambon of Moreston, Esq.

Otho or Otes Gilbert, Sheriff of Devon. 15 Edw. IV. 1475. = Elizth. d. to John [or Robert] Hill of Shilston in Modbury, Esq.

Sr. Edm. Baron Carew of Ottery, of the lineage of the noble Courtenays, Denhams, Erchdecons, Talbots, Bigods, &c. = Catharine d. & h. of Sr. Wm. Hudderfield of Shillington.

Elizth. Gilbert = Sr. Tho. Grenvile of Stow in Cornwall, Kn't.

John Gilbert = Elizth. d. of Sr. John Crocker of Axminster of Lynham, Kn't. s. p.

Wm. Gilbert.

Otes Gilbert.

* * * * = Sr. Philip [or Christopher] Champernon.

Thomas Gilbert = Isabel d. & h. to Sr. John Chamond of Compton, Esq. John Reynward of Launcells in Cornwall, Kn't. of Cornwall.

Jane 1st = Sr. John Arundell of Trerice in Cornwall, Kn't.

Richard. John.

Roger Grenvile.

S. John Arundell of Lanihern, Knight.

Katherine, the "Governess" and confidant of Queen Elizabeth = Ashley Otho Gilbert.

Wimond Raleigh sold Axminster = * * * * to John Gilbert.

Katherine Champernon* wido. of Gilbert 1st = 2d Katherine Champernon.

Joan d. of John Drake of Plimoth, bro. of Sr. Francis Drake, the famous Navigator. = Walter Raleigh of Fardell near Plymo.

Sr. John Gilbert, Knt. Cust. Rot. to Sr. Dev. † Knighted by queen E. 1570.

Elizth. d. to Sr. Rob't Hill of Ashton, Knight. s. p.

Elizth. Rich. Chudleigh of Ashton, Knight.

Adrian Gilbert of Sandridge, Devon, Gent. afterward knighted.

Katherine = Geo. s. & to Walter Raleigh of Fardel by a 2d wife.

Lord Lumley = 2d ***1st. = Duke of Norfolk.
Sr. Humphrey Gilbert, Anne, d. to Sr. Anthony Ayer "that high attempting of Agver of Kent. spirit & skilful mathematician and hydrographer, born 1539, Lost in the Squirrel Feb. 6, 1583.

Elizth. = Sr. Walter Raleigh Kn't. Founder of Virginia, born 1552, married Throgmorton Oct. 29. 1618, Knight.

Ann, d. of Sr. Bartho. Fortescue.

1 John Raleigh
2 George.

Walter Raleigh slain in Guiana, Jan. 2, 1618, "a brave and sprightly young man fonder of glory than of safety,"

Raughley Gilbert of Compton, living Anno 1620. = Elizth. d. & heir of Jo. Kelley in Devon.

John Gilbert,‡ = d. of Sr. Richard Molyneux of Sefton.

sons in all.   Humfrey Gilbert, æt. 5, 1620.   Raley, æt. 3, 1620.   Ayer, æt. 3, 1620.   Ferdinand, æt. 2, in 1620.   Amey, æt. 1½ years, in 1620.

* Sr. FERDINANDO GORGES, the FOUNDER OF MAINE, was of this family. His nephew Francis Champernon came over and died here at Kittery, Maine.

† "1608. The Worshipful Knight, Sir John Gilberd, ended his life 5th July and was brought from London to his mansion House at Compton 16th of the same month and buried in Marldon Church 19 July."—Marldon Reg. He practiced arms agreable to the brave spirit of his ancestors : Was held an Expert and ancient soldier even in his younger years wherein he expired : was taken away when he gave not only hope but full assurance of great sufficiency to do his prince and country service. Sir John and his younger brother Capt. Rawley Gilbert were "nephews" of Sir Humphrey and Sir Walter, but by which of their brothers is not certainly ascertained."

‡ From Compton many stems of the old stock branched off — for instance, about 1604, John Gilbert left Compton and settled at Blechington, County of Essex — in 1609 to John Gilbert of Woodford, Essex, were confirmed these Arms. Ar. on a chev. betw. three leopard's faces sa. as many roses or.

4

Queen Elizabeth's governess, Mrs. Kate Ashley, to whom she was fondly attached, exercised the most remarkable influence over the mind of her royal pupil from her earliest years. She was aunt to Sir Humphrey Gilbert, to whom Sir Walter Raleigh was uterine brother, and was married to a relative of Anne Boleyn, the queen's unfortunate mother. Queen Elizabeth placed her chief favor and confidence in her maternal kindred to the end of her life, and Mrs. Ashley's powerful influence was of great advantage to her nephews.

The Rev. Dr. Holmes,* following modern writers, says of Sir Walter Raleigh, " one of the greatest and most accomplished persons of the age in which he lived," that " he was *the first Englishman who projected settlements in America*, and is justly considered the founder of Virginia. To him, and to Sir Humphrey Gilbert, is ascribed the honor of laying the foundation of the trade and naval power of Great Britain;" but a little observation will prove Gilbert's superior title to that distinction, and that Sir Walter was merely his executor. He was thirteen years the senior of Raleigh. The brothers, Sir Humphrey, Sir John, Sir Adrian, and Sir Walter, a goodly company, in youth dwelling under one roof, with congeniality of spirit in their grand and ambitious views, pursued their studies with the enthusiasm of great minds; guided by the genius of Sir Humphrey, in after life, each gave form and action to the thoughts, or rather the thought, which won for them a lasting fame, and has peopled North America with the Anglo-Saxon race. Where can be found a nobler brotherhood? and, with truth, Sir Francis Drake may be added to the family circle at Compton, as their relative.

June 11, 1578, Queen Elizabeth granted letters patent to Sir Humphrey to discover and take possession of all remote and barbarous lands, unoccupied by any Christian prince or people, " for himself and his heirs forever," and soon after, with a fleet of " ten sailes of all sorts of shipping, well and sufficiently furnished for such an enterprise, weighed anchor in the west country and set to sea," upon this first adventure, " having in his companie his two brethren, Walter and Carey Rawley," but returned unsuccessful. Walter, with characteristic ambition, withdrew from the command of the Admiral to accomplish something " worthie of honor," but he too returned, after a disastrous voyage, without success.

Just five years after the date of his patent, June 11, 1583, they again sailed from Plymouth, under the auspices of Sir. Geo. Peckam, the chief adventurer and furtherer of the expedition. Sir Humphrey, the admiral of the fleet, was in the " Delight," of 120 tons, of which William Winter was captain, and part owner, and Richard Clarke, master. Sir Walter, his Vice-Admiral, was obliged to return on account of a contagious sickness on board his bark, which he had built, victualled, and manned at his own expense. On the 5th August, Sir Humphrey took seizen of New Foundland, and the adjacent territories, for the crown of England, by " the ancient ceremony of cutting turf or rod," and his first act was to establish publick worship according to the Church of England. " Edward Haies, gentleman and principal actour" therein, made " A Report of the voyage, and successe thereof, attempted in the yeare of our Lord 1583, by Sir *Humfrey Gilbert*, knight, with other gentlemen assisting him in that action, *intended to discover and to plant Christian inhabitants* in place convenient, upon those large and ample countreys extended northward from the cape of Florida lying under very temperate climes, esteemed fertile and rich in minerals, yet not

* *Annals of America*, Vol. I. p. 155.

in the actual possession of any Christian prince." The admiral selected the "frigat Squirrel,"[*] of ten tons, the better to survey the coast. When last seen, he was seated in the stern of his little "frigat," with an open book, and was heard by the people in the "Hind," to say, "We are as near heaven by sea as by land;" and on that night, the 9th of September, 1583, in a violent storm, "the lights of his ship suddenly disappeared," the vessel foundered, and Sir Humphrey was lost. Thus abruptly was terminated his career, glorious in its inception; he was fortunate in leaving an intimate and thorough knowledge of his designs with his brother, Sir Walter, who, soon after, March 25, 1584, obtained from Queen Elizabeth a virtual renewal of Sir Humphrey's Patent, with all its ample prerogatives, fully developed his plans, and became the founder of Virginia.

Sir Humphrey *projected* and Sir Walter survived to *accomplish* "his noble attempt to possess and people the remote countries of America."

"And now behold the infinite goodness of our God, who even from evil deriveth good; for out of these crosses, turmoils, and afflictions he hath caused to grow the fruit we already see: and much more we are to hope for in New England, Virginia, and the New Foundland."

Meanwhile, Sir Adrian Gilbert, who had at one time "wrought" silver mines at Combemartin, in Devonshire, in 1583, the year of his brother's death, obtained from Queen Elizabeth a Patent for the discovery of a North-west passage to China, to remain in force five years, by the title of "The Colleagues of the Fellowship for the Discovery of the North-west Passage;" but they accomplished nothing worthy of note.

Bartholomew Gilbert sailed from Plymouth May 10, 1603, in the bark Elizabeth, of 50 tons, for further discovery, and to search for the lost colony of Sir Walter Ralegh, which ended in his death, July 29, being "killed by the savages in the wood." He was probably a nephew of Sir Humphrey.

We now approach more immediately to our own time and shores, and in 1607 find Sir John and Capt. Ralegh Gilbert, perseveringly engaged in their hereditary scheme of peopling America with Englishmen. Holmes relates that Sir John Popham and others sent out two ships under the command of George Popham and Raleigh Gilbert, with 100 men, with ordnance and all provisions necessary until they might receive further supplies. They sailed from Plymouth about the last of May, and, falling in with the land of Monhigon on the 11th of August, encamped on an island at the mouth of the Sagadahock, or Kennebeck River, on the coast of Maine. Here, after a sermon was delivered, and their patent and laws were read, they built and fortified a store-house, which they named Fort St. George. On the 5th of December the two ships sailed for England, leaving a colony of 45 persons, Popham being president, and Gilbert, admiral. The death of Ch. J. Popham depressed the colonists; but, says, Gorges "when [July 5, 1608,] they heard of the death of Sir John Gilbert, elder brother of Rawley Gilbert, that was then their president, a man worthy to be beloved of them all, for his industry

---

[*] I have made considerable research to ascertain the size of the early ships, and though there was no definite mode of tonnage, their estimates of size agree substantially with the modern calculation. In Wingate's *Abr.*, 514, 39th Elizabeth, is a statute respecting "Ships with cross-sails," as to "customs," showing a want of any more definite description than could be given by the *tackle* of the ship, though the same statute refers to levying a duty of "50 Soulz per Tun." In Derick's *Memoirs of the Rise and Progress of the Royal Navy*, 1806, 4to. 59–61, he gives a table of 50 ships existing in 1633, and says this is "the earliest List of the Navy I have met with wherein any of the ships' principal dimensions are inserted, and "the first list in which *any nice regard appears to have been paid to the tonnage of the ships.* Previous to 1633, the tonnage of almost "every ship seems to have been rather estimated than calculated, being inserted in even numbers."

and care for their well-being," they unanimously resolved to return to England, and thus ended another fruitless experiment. Says Capt. John Smith, this colony found "nothing but extreme extremities." "During the long winter, and the after time of their abode there, they built a bark, which afforded them some advantage in their return;" probably the first vessel built on these shores.*

To what extent these enterprises, of such "great pith and moment," nurtured chiefly by Devonshire, for more than half a century, influenced that and the West country, can only be conjectured; but the generous contributions of Devonshire, to the New England Colonies, may be safely attributed, in a degree, to their locality, and the spirit of colonization begotten among them by the GILBERTS and their associates; and it is natural, therefore, that we find so many of the good old West of England families among the earliest emigrants to our shores, the Vaughans, Tristrams, Waldron, Bonython, Coffin, Conant, Crocker, Edgecomb, Heale, Goodyear, Ridgway, Cammock, Booth, Jordan, Cary, Gee, Champernoon.† Nor are we disappointed in our search among them for the names most prominent among the early voyagers, as Gilbert, Drake, Hawkins, Winter, etc., so many historical ties between Old and New England. They settled chiefly in Maine, where, as late as 1673, a newly organized county was named DEVONSHIRE, a token of honor and filial affection for the birthplace of their fathers, few of whom could be then living. The GILBERTS, at various dates, came to Massachusetts, Connecticut, and Virginia. Richard Gilbert, "remained one whole year in Virginia," in 1585. Joseph Gilbert, as early as 1645. "Willm. Gylbert was admitted a freeman at Wyndsor, in Connecticut, in 1640. Robert Gilbert was a passenger in the ' Plaine Joan ' for Virginia, in 1635." "A grave honest gentleman," Mr. JOHN GILBERT, was at Dorchester, as early as 1636, and had sons John, Thomas, and Giles, of whom we have a few particulars. About 1640, four brothers, JONATHAN, Thomas, Obadiah, and Josiah GILBERT were living in Connecticut.‡

THOMAS GILBERT, previously at Windsor, had a grant of land in Springfield Jan. 30, 1655, and at Fresh Water Brook, [Enfield,] Feb. 12, 1660. He m. July 31, 1655, *Catharine Bliss*, widow of Nathaniel Bliss, of Springfield, and son of Thomas of Hartford, and March 23, 1656, was admitted a freeman in Springfield. His widow m. Dec. 28, 1664, Samuel Marshfield, by whom she had four children; — her son, *Josiah Marshfield*, m. *Rachel* d.

---

* *Wescott*, in 1630, wrote of Devonshire, " our havens are well replenished with shipping fit for war or peace; and them employed in merchants' affairs, or in fishing voyages, upon our own coasts, and elsewhere in many fair and remote countries, as Canada, Virginia, Newfoundland, and other regions, whence much fish is brought home." "Of our mariners, the whole world brings forth no better; whether you will impress them for valour to adventure or knowledge to perform any action, painfulness to undergo, or patience to endure any extremity, adversity, or want whatsoever." pp. 67–68.

† Francis Champernoon was a nephew of Sir Ferdinando Gorges, the Founder of Maine, and a relative of the mother of the Gilberts and Raleighs. He resided in Kittery, and died there, on his estate, then known as Champernoon's Island, and since as Cutt's Island. He married into the Cutts family, of Essex and Cambridgeshire. His grave, in the family burial-place, on the Island, remains well defined by an oblong pile of stones, carefully replaced within a few years.

‡ In 1685, there was a controversy about a farm on the east side of the river at Weathersfield, (now Glastenbury,) and *Josiah Gilbert's* testimony was obtained in regard to the boundaries of this farm, which once belonged to John Hollister. Josiah Gilbert stated that he lived on this farm, as a tenant, I think, 12 years, and that his brothers, John and Jonathan Gilbert, were concerned with him some of these years. He was on this farm in 1651, but does not state where the 12 years began or ended. The deposition is in a volume labelled " Private Controversies," in the State House at Hartford. Here are 3 brothers, and Obadiah is the fourth.

of *Jonathan and Mary Gilbert;* — her d. *Margaret Marshfield* m. *Ebenezer Parsons,* and was the mother of Rev. Jonathan Parsons, of Newburyport, ancestor of Hon. S. H. Parsons.

Thomas Gilbert, of Springfield, probably son of Thomas and Catharine of the same place, m. Abilene, d. of Samuel Marshfield, Aug. 15, 1680.

Obadiah Gilbert settled in Fairfield, and made his will in Aug. 1674; and mentions sons Obadiah, Benjamin, Joseph, one daughter, and his wife, and makes his *brothers,* Jonathan and Josiah Gilbert, overseers of his will.

Captain JOHN GILBERT, brother of Jonathan, of Hartford, m. Amy, daughter of Thomas and Dorothy Lord of Hartford, May 6, 1647, was admitted freeman May 21, 1657. — The Court sold to him for £10, March 11, 1662-3, land lying between that of Capt. Richard Lord and of C. John Culick, and at "yᵉ landing place on the Rivulet, both parcels being or lying in yᵉ South Meadow at Hartford." May 19, 1663, the "Gener^ll Court" allowed him "eleven pounds out of the Publique Treasury, for and in consideration of his horse that dyed in the country's service." Their children,

John, . born Jan. 16, 164⁷₈

John, . " Feb. 19, 165²₃*

Elizabeth " Feb. 12, 165⁵₆

Thomas, " Sept. 14, 1658, m. Deborah Beaumont, Sept. 27, 1681.

See *Gen. Reg.* IV. 137.

Amy, born April 3, 1663.

Joseph, " April 3, 1666. — Mary Griswold? May 17, 1692—²ᵈElizabeth d. of Joseph Smith? of Hartford, May, 1695.

His will, of Aug. 1, 1690, names his wife Amy, sons Thomas, Joseph, and James, and d. Dorothy Palmer. Estate, £417 19 10. Mrs. Dorothy Lord, in her will, Feb. 8, 1669, leaves land to her "daughter Amy Gilbert and her children," and a legacy to Elizabeth Gilbert.

JONATHAN GILBERT, in 1645,† being about 27 years of age, was a bachelor landholder in Hartford, and soon after married Mary the daughter of John White. They at once entered into the arrangements of life, and the "General Court," with becoming gravity, "recorded" some of the minor details of their social affairs. "Tenth of March, 1646, the names of people as they were seated in the *meeting-house* were read in Court; and it was ordered that they should be recorded, which was as followeth; for the *women's seats* in the middle, 4th seat, Sister Wakeman, Sister Gibbard, Sister *Gilbert,* and Sister Myles."‡ Gilbert had probably arrived in New England at an earlier date, as in April§ of the next year, he was sufficiently familiar with the language of the aborigines to act as interpreter between them and the English government, rendering important service in the subsequent Indian wars and difficulties, by his facility in their language, and his resolute bravery. He was generally selected as the leader in emergencies of danger and importance. He was a man of business, of respectability and enterprise, engaged in the trade and coasting business of the young colonies, possessed of great wealth for that day, and held various civil offices, was collector of the customs at Hartford, marshal of the colony — an office cor-

---

* An English youth, John Gilbert, was captive among the Nipmuck Indians in 1676.— Drake's *Trag. of the Wilderness,* 40.

† The first framed house in Hartford was built in 1635, by Nicholas Clarke for John Tallcott, which proves an extensive settlement there at that date, at least sufficient for protection.—*Ancient MS., quoted in Hon. R. R. Hinman's letter of April* 18, 1850. "If *Connecticut* bee not added to the Government it can be hardly able to support itself. But if it be added, thee revenue will bee sufficient to keep the King wholly out of debt."—Gov. Dongan's *Rep.,* 22 Feb., 1687. "*Doc. Hist. of New York,*" pp. 174, 187.

‡ Bacon's *Hist. Disc.,* 311, 381.   § *Connect. Col. Rec.*

responding to that of High Sheriff — a Representative to the General Court, &c. By grants from the government and by purchase, he acquired large tracts of land in the different settlements, which he subsequently divided among his children. In 1653, he received a grant " at the common landing-place in the little meadow, [at Hartford,] to set up a warehouse," which afterward became a station for considerable traffic, in which Mr. Pynchon, of Springfield, up the river, was largely interested. He imported many goods from abroad, and with him Mr. Gilbert was probably associated in business. Andrew Belcher, of Cambridge and Boston, having business there, married Mary, a daughter of Mr. Gilbert, and their son Jonathan was governor of Massachusetts. To appreciate the position and to picture to the mind the life of Mr. Gilbert, we must turn back two centuries, when the colonists were few, unprotected, and widely separated by dense and unexplored forests and unbridged streams, the chief communication being by water, around the coasts. They were as a handful among the original proprietors, the turbulent, uncivilized savages, then in the meridian of their strength and power, who rather sought the English as allies in their feuds than respected them as equals. For this reason, it is said, they invited the first settlers to Connecticut.

Gookin states that the principal sachem (Uncas) lived at or about Pequot, now called New London, " and held dominion over divers petty Sagamores, as over part of Long Island, over the Mohegans, and over the Sagamores of Quinapeake, yea, even all the people that dwelt upon the Connecticut River and some of the most southerly inhabitants of the Nipmug country, about Quinaboag. They were a very warlike and potent people, and could raise 4000 men fit for war, and held hostility with their neighbors that lived bordering upon them to the east and north, called the Narragansets." Their insolent deportment compelled the English to turn their wars to their own destruction, and, in 1638, many of them were destroyed, and the rest reduced to comparative submission. The increasing power of the white men, and their aggressive policy, excited their jealousy, which was manifested by murders, firings, and all the cruelties of Indian revenge. Such was the state of affairs when the Colony availed itself of Gilbert's services in perilous negotiations with these enraged, crafty, and faithless savages. None but a resolute man, of a cool, penetrating eye, a wary watchfulness, and a fearless temper, could gain respect or safety among them. Uncas, like King Philip, was a patriot, and a settled hatred to his new neighbors fired his heart and mind, and filled the breasts of his people. Thus prefaced, the following relation by Mather,* of incidents in 1646, will be understood : —

" There was *Trouble* and fears raised in the Country, by reason of the *River-Indians*, at *Waranoke*, & *Norwoottuck*, who it seems were secretly contriving the Death of those famous Worthyes, Mr. *Hopkins*, Mr. *Hains*, Mr. *Whiting*, Magistrates in *Connecticut* Colony. For I find upon publick *Record*, that complaints and informations about that matter (in September, 1648) were brought before the Commissioners then assembled at *New-Haven*, where an Indian testified that *Sequasson*, the *Sachim* of *Waranoke* [Westfield?] had given him a sum of money on condition that he would murther the gentlemen mentioned.

---

* " A relation of the Troubles which have happened in New England, by reason of the Indians there. From the year 1614 to the year 1675 ; wherein the frequent conspiracyes of the Indians to cutt off the English, and the wonderfull providence of God, in disappointing their devices is declared." By Increase Mather. Boston : 1677. pp. 60, 63–66

9

"Before the Commissioners convened, Mr. *Haines* had twice sent to *Sequasson:* but he neglected to make his appearance: Wherefore *Jonathan Gilbert* was sent to him again, to signifie from the Commissioners, that they expected Sequassons appearance before them, and to answer what he was accused with, and they promised him free passage both to and from New-haven, withall intimating that his withdrawing himself would greatly augment the suspition of his guilt. The Messenger quickly returned, bringing word, that he could not speak with Sequasson, who he supposed had received notice of his coming by other Indians, and was thereupon fled.

"Whilst the Commissioners were sitting at New Haven, petitions were presented from *Edward Elmere* and some others, complaining that Indians had wilfully and maliciously burned some quantity of pitch, and tarr of theirs, together with some bedding and a cart with its furniture, and tooles, &c., in value about an hundred pounds. And particularly they complained of one *Wasemose*, a *Waranoke* Indian, as guilty therein, as by sufficient evidence they thought they could prove; and that he hath since avoided all the English Plantations; and that he being sent for by a warrant from one of the magistrates of *Connecticut*, fled; but being overtaken and seized by some of the English, he was rescued by the Indians, and the English by them jeered and abused, and particularly *Chickwallop*, Sachim of *Norwootuck:* Whereupon *Jonathan Gilbert* and John Griffin were sent to *Chickwallop* and *Manasanes*. At their return, they informed that they could not meet either with *Chickwallop* or *Manasanes*, but the Sagamores and Indians at *Waranoke* carried it insolently toward the English, vaunting themselves in their Arms, bows and Arrows, hatchets and Swords, some with their Guns ready charged, before and in the presence of the English Messengers, they primed and cockt them ready to give fire, and told them that if they should offer to carry away any man thence, the Indians were re-solved to fight, yet the next morning the *Sachim* with some others offered the English Messengers eight Fathom of *Wampam* towards satisfaction and promised to provide more. The Messengers not having anything to that purpose in their Commission, advised the Sachim to send to the Commission-ers, but he refused. Hereupon *Naymetayhu*, one of the *Sagamores* of *Waranoke*, who, as before came on Sequasson's behalf, was questioned by the Commissioners about these proud Affronts to the English; at first he denied what was charged, and excused some part, but one of the English Messengers being present, and he hearing the rest should be sent for, he fell under most of the charge, professing that he intended no harm to the English."

Mr. Gilbert is frequently referred to in the Colonial Records of Connec-ticut, which, though disconnected, indicate the general current and features of his public life. Thus, in March, 1653, a special warrant was granted to him as marshal, with " power to rayse such considerable forces as hee sees meete " for the arrest of a certain desperado.

*In 1653, and previously, *Stuyvesant*, the Governor of the Dutch Colony of New York, secretly encouraged the Indians to fall upon the English, hoping, by the destruction of the Connecticut Colony, to enjoy more securely their own Territorial title. The Indian Nations having sided with the English or Dutch, were irritated to hostile attacks, which frequently required the attention of the " Commissioners," they supposing Ninigrate, the chief of the powerful Narragansetts, to be in league with the Dutch, while the

---

* Hutchinson's *Hist. of Mass.*, Vol. I. pp. 180–186.

rest of the Indians were with the English. *Jealousy* of the intrigue of Stuyvesant, and the *fear* of the Southern settlements, induced the Commissioners to make an unjust war on the Indians. Only one of the Commissioners, BRADSTREET, to his honor be it recorded, opposed it, and he was sustained by Massachusetts.

During the hostilities between the Narragansett Indians and the Long Island tribe, in 1654, the Commissioners of the English Colonies appointed JONATHAN GILBERT a Messenger to Ninigrate, the chief of the Narragansetts; who returned, 18th Sept., after a short absence, and brought Ninigrate's answer in the words following: "Having acquainted him that the Commissioners were met at Hartford, and that they had perused the letter sent to the Governor of Massachusetts, he answered, he knew nothing of any such letter, and made strange of it."

Concerning his invading the Long-Islanders, he answered: "Wherefore should he acquaint the Commissioners, when as the Long-Islanders had begun with him and had slain a Sachem's son and sixty others of his men, and therefore he will not make peace with the Long Islanders, but doth desire the English will let him alone, and that the Commissioners would not request him to go to Hartford, for he hath done no hurt. What should he do there? If *your* Governor's son was slain, and several other men, would *you* ask counsel of another nation when and how to right yourselves? and added, that he would neither go nor send to Hartford."

Concerning the Upland Indians his answer was, "That they were his friends, and came to help him against the Long-Islanders, which had killed several of his men. Wherefore should he acquaint the Commissioners with it? He did but right his own quarrel, which the Long-Islanders began with him."

A reply worthy of the chief of an independent and patriotic people who understood their national rights.

April 9, 1657, Jonathan Gilbert, with his brother John, to be joined by "an able man," provided by the "Deputies in Windzor," were instructed by the Court "wth all speed to goe to Nortwootuck & Pacumtuck; that they shall acquaint the Sachem and chief there wth the horrible bloody act [of murder] by some Indians that is lately done at Farmington, and tell them that wee expect that they and all or any other Indians whatsoever shall forthw^{th} send Mashupanan or any other that are accessory to that bloody act, either wth these o^{r} messeng^{rs} or so soone as hee or any other accessory thereto bee p^{r}cured by them, & tell them that wee shall looke at them or any other that detaine Mashupanan or any that are accessorie to this act, as our enimyes."

The Commissioners of the United Colonies in September, 1657, again interfering between the hostile tribes, with the authority of superior strength, peremptorily ordered that Uncas, the chief of the Pequots, be required "to p^{r}mit the Podunk Indians to return to theire dwellings & there to ebide in peace & safety, without molestation from him or his, & that the said Indians bee incouraged & invited so to do, by the Government of Connecticott." "And the Gov. of Conn. is desired to signify to the Pocomtick and Norwootick Sachems on charge upon Vnckas in reference to the Podunk Indians, and on desire of their returne to their dwelling and continuance there in Peace; therefore wee desire and expect they will forbeare all hostility against Unckas till the next meeting of the Commissioners." *

* Com^{rs} Rec.

11

THE GILBERT FAMILY.

BY J. WINGATE THORNTON, ESQ.

ACCORDINGLY, the authorities of Connecticut appointed Mr. Allen and Jo. Gilbert " to goe to Pacomtuck to declare to the Indians the mind of the Comissioners concerning them, and that there bee a letter sent to Mr. Pinchon to assist them in it: but if he refuse, and Mr. Holliock, then they shall desist from further proceeding."

In March, 1657-8, " The listed persons for Troopers presented to and allowed by the court [of Connecticut] under the command of Major John Mason were, in Hartford, Mr. Willis, Mr. Lord, Mr. Thomas Wells, Jacob Migatt, *Jonathan Gilbert*, and nine others." This force was probably raised under the authority of the " Commissioners."

Mr. Gilbert, during this period, was actively pursuing his private enterprises. He may have temporarily resided in Westfield, as the Springfield Town Records, under date of Aug. 9, 1656, mention a grant of lands to Jon[n] & John Gilbert at Wornoco, [Westfield,] provided " they build a house within one year." The request was renewed and granted, Dec. 10, 1658.

In November, 1659, Mr. Gilbert was appointed to compel the payment from the Farmington Indians of the annual sum which was due for the two years past, amounting to " the full summe of eighty faddome of wampum, well strungd and merchantable." This was in satisfaction for damages from a fire occasioned by them. In April, 1660, Mr. John Allyn and Jonath: Gilbert were commissioned to bound out to Tantoninus, the Sachem of the Potuncks, the lands which he held, remaining unsold to the English, and about which he and Uncas, the chiefs of their tribes, had quarrelled.

In August, 1661, the court granted " to Jonathan Gilbert a farm to y[e] number of 300 acres of vpland and 50 Acres of meadow, provided it be not preiuditiall " to any other plantation; and Mr. Matthew Allyn, at the same time, received a grant "vpon y[e] same terms."

After this period, Mr. Gilbert was for several years annually elected to the office of " marshall," and was occasionally a representative to the legislature; but his chief attention was given to the improvement of his estate, and the care of his family, many of whom he lived to see happily and honorably settled in life. He was peculiarly fortunate in his wife, who was remarkable for her prudence and energy, which contributed in a great degree to his success, and who was honored in the lives of her children. He died on the 10th of December, 1682, aged 64; and his wife died July 3, 1700, Æ. 74. They lie side by side in the ancient burial-place at Hartford.

The last Will & Testament of Mr Jonathan Gilbert.

In the name of God, Amen. I Jonathan Gilbert of Hartford, in the County of Hartford and Colony of Connecticut, being in perfect health and Good memory at this time & not knowing the time of my dissolution & sensible of mortality and very desirous to leave a settled peace in my family in respect of these Transitory things, I do constitute this my last will and Testament.

Imprimis — I give & bequeath my Immortal soul into the everlasting arms of my Blessed Lord & Saviour Jesus Christ who hath redeemed me with his precious blood, * * * Also I bequeath my body to the earth by comely burial, and also my wish is, that all my lawful debts be paid and discharged out of my moveable estate, which being done, I do dispose of that little estate which God out of his bounty hath betrusted me with, as followeth.

Item. To my dear & loving wife Mary Gilbert, as followeth, the use of my dwelling house, [at Cold Spring] homelotts, orchards, Gardens, Barn, Barnyards, outhouses, warehouse, that part of my Island above that which is commonly known by the name of the Dutch Island all Northward, as also that little land I bought of Mr Callsey, as also that land I did exchange with Mr James Richards, as also that pasture I bought of Andrew Warner, also my Wood-lot on the West side of Rocky Hill, all & every part of the forementioned particulars, during the time of her Widowhood & til my son *Samuel* shall attain to the age of Twenty one years, and then my wish is that [she] shall peaceably surrender unto Samuel his quiet possession at the aforesaid house & land save only what is here excepted viz the seller, great kitchen & all the chambers over it & garret over the said kitchen, & half my warehouse that is to say, the South end seller & room over the seller, and half my home lott, the East end of it & half my Barn & half my barnyard for her use with also full use of water both in the well & pond on the lot without any interruption during her natural life & then immediately after her decease * * * all the aforesaid houseing and land I give to my son Samuel Gilbert & his heirs forever, he paying to his brother Ebenezer Gilbert Thirty pounds in Country pay.

Item: I give to my son Jonathan Gilbert one half of the lands in the bounds of Haddam that I bought of Mr James Bates & Thomas Shaylor * * * or twenty pounds in other estates which he the said Jonathan shall choose which is the completing of his portion to what I have done for him already.

Item: I give to my son THOMAS GILBERT my house & home lot on the South side of the riverlet in Hartford & my meadow land that I did exchange & had of Mr James Richards to possess immediately after his mother's decease, but the house & lott to possess at the age of One & Twenty years; also I give to my son Thomas that Ten acres of land I bought of Lt Robert Webster, also I give to my son Thomas the lower end of my Island, that is to say, from the upper End of that which is called the Dutch Island which I bought of Captain Richard Lord, with a straight line to the great river West & So East on the meadow lotts, I say all my land downward to him & his heirs forever, he paying to his mother Twenty shillings p^r year & Twenty pounds of good hops per year during her natural life.

Item, I give to my son *Nathaniel* Gilbert my farm at *Meriden* with all the house & land thereunto belonging & all priviledges thereunto to him & his heirs forever, & also I give to him Thirty pounds more out of my estate or in Cattle to stock the said farm.

Item: I give to my daughter *Lidia Richelson* Twenty Shillings.

Item: I give to my daughter *Sarah Belcher* Twenty shillings.

Item: I give to my daughter *Mary Holton* Twenty Shillings.

Item: I give to my daughter *Hester Gilbert* one hundred pounds to be paid her within six months after her marriage, or Eighteen years of age, which shall first happen, in Current Country pay or part in household goods, to be prized by indifferent men.

Item: I give to my daughter *Rachel Gilbert* one hundred pounds to be paid her within six months after the day of her marriage or at the age of

13

eighteen years, which shall first happen, in Current Country pay or part in household goods apprized by indifferent men.

Item: I give my son *Ebenezer Gilbert* & his heirs forever all that three hundred acres of land belonging & also that purchase of lands I bought of Captain Daniel Clark lying in *Farmington* bounds, with all the priviledges thereunto belonging, & also that purchase of land I bought of Messecap commonly called & known by the name of Pagan Chaumischaug: also I give to Ebenezer Gilbert Thirty pounds to be paid him by his brother Samuel Gilbert & twenty pounds more to be paid him out of my Estate to stock his farm with; which fifty pounds shall be paid him at the age of twenty one years, & my desire is that my wife do remember Hannah Kelly and give her twenty shillings, and more as her discretion shall guide her, if she proves obedient.

Item. I give to my grand child *John Rosseter* ten pounds to be paid him at the age of Twenty four years in Country pay. Also my will is, that if any of my children prove disobedient & legally convicted so to be, then my wife hath my power to take from such child forty pounds of his or her respective portions and distribute among the others that are obedient.

Also my will is, that if any of my children are taken away by death before they come to receive their respective portions, then that child's portion to be divided equally amongst the surviving.

Also. I give to my grand child *Andrew Belcher* five pounds in Country pay.

Also. I give my grand child *Jonathan Richelson* five pounds in Country pay.

I also make and constitute Captain John Allyn, my brother John Gilbert, & Serjeant Caleb Standly to be helpful to my dear and loving wife, whom I make, constitute & appoint sole Executrix & administratrix to this my last will and Testament & desire that she satisfy them for their paynes, whom I intreat to see this my will attended & performed, revoking all former wills, as witness my hand this 10th day of Septr 1674.

Signed; sealed in the presence of us,   Jonathan Gilbert [*L. S.*]
John Tallcott)
John Gilbert, ∫   " The Inventory was taken 12 feb. 1682–3—Amt.
[£2484. 17*s.* 9*d.*

£   s.   d.
Debts, Cash —— 113 . 0 . 3
Country pay — 68 . 14 . 6
Besides some debts owing from the Estate at *Boston*."
The real estate was valued at £1312.

Hartford Probate Records, Vol. IV.

Note. Jonathan Gilbert, Jr. married Dorothy (d. of Rev. Samuel and Hope) Stow, of Middletown. She was born about 1658. He petitioned the General Court — in consequence " of the smallness of the legacy bequeathed to [him] by his father's will made about 8 or 9 years before his decease " — for some further provision from the estate, pleading that he was the eldest son by a first wife,* and contended that " the law of God in Deut. 21 : 16, 17, seems plainly to hold forth that the first born may not be disinherited on private affection, or deprived of his birthright inheritance." This will was made when his father's " love and affections toward [him] run lowest, and his displeasure at the highest;" but since his " return from the West Indies," his father had been satisfied with his conduct; to gratify whom, "in order to settlement, [he] proposed [his] desire to join in marriage with the daughter of the Reverend Mr. Stow, which, after consideration had, [his] honored father and mother did freely give their consent to and advice in." A complete

* " Jonathan Gilbert was maryed vnto Mara Whight, on Jenuary the twenty ninth, one thousand six hundred forty and five." — *Hartf. Reç.*

Mary, the widow of Jonathan Gilbert, made her will, May 23, 1700, as follows : —

" First, I commit and bequeath my soul & spirit into the hand of Almighty God my Creatour by whome of his meer and only grace I trust to be saved free into eternal Rest through the death and merits of my Saviour & Redeemer Jesus Christ ; and my body (hoping for a joyful & glorious Resurrection) to a Christian Burial."

reconciliation was afterwards obtained, — " with that freedom and expression of love which was beyond my expectation." In this petition he refers to " one of the legatees, Nathaniel," — " deceased since the will was made," — and to *Samuel*, " the youngest brother but one." The widow, Mrs. Mary Gilbert, reminded the court, " that [her] husband's estate came not by descent from his ancestors, but was acquired by himself, and was therefore in a peculiar manner at his dispose," &c.

In 1672, at Boston, Mary, widow and sole executrix of Richard Trusedall, lately deceased, had her will drawn by " Mr. John Hull," and it was approved, Nov. 26, 1674. She mentions her "cousin Richard Emblin," "brother John Hood's two children," "Richard, son of Samuel Truesdale," not of age, "other children of Samuel Truesdale." " William Gilbert, Junr," not of age, son " of my cousin *William Gilbert* sole executor of my will," and " other children by *Rebeckah Gilbert*," his wife [admit^d a mem. of Old So. Chh. May 24, 1678,] left " forty pounds " to buy " a convenient tomb stone " for self and husband. She gave " unto Harvard College at Cambridge £40," " Mr. Thomas Thacher, pastor of the third church in Boston £5, to Mr. Seaborn Cotton, £5, to Mr. John Cotton, Senior, £5, to Mrs. Mariah Mather, £5, to the poor of the Old Church £5, to the town of Boston £10, to the third church of Christ in Boston £5." " Mary Mynate, aged about 45 years," was a witness. This *William Gilbert*, in a letter at " Boston, Novem 10th 1680 " to his "most Kynd and Loveing Grandfather, Mr. Arthur Bridge living in Sherborn in Dorsetshire," says he has rec'd the " sorrowful lines " informing him of the death of his " Grandmother," and " uncle Thomas, his wife, at one time "—mentions the death of " Uncle William in Barbadoes." " Myne and my wife's Kynd love, to y^r self, to Uncle Pond, and Aunt Joan, to Unckle Napper, his sone and daughter and to Margret Emblem and all the rest of my relations " " my Aunt Roe, Robert and Olive Roe, Uncle Phillips children."

—— Gilbert of Mass^{tts} brother of Thomas had a son Samuel of Hebron, Conn^t whose son Samuel born Oct 20, 1755, d. Jan., 1846, leaving son Hon. Ralph Gilbert, Judge of Probate of Hebron, Conn^t.

Suffolk, Oct 31, 1682. Roger Gilbert *vs.* Isaac Waldron.

July 25, 1721. " George Cradock & John Gilbert of Boston, Merchants."

Robert Augur (bro. of " Nicholas, a learned Physician of New Haven," m. Mary Gilbert Nov. 20, 1673.

Mr. John Gilbert, " a brave honest gentleman," (Savage's *Winthrop*, addenda, ii. 346.) probably a Devonshire man, was at Dorchester with his family in the year 163-, then at Taunton after 1636, with sons Thomas, John, and Giles ; was the first Deputy from Taunton to the Gen. Court of New Plimoth in 1639, and died before 1654, survived by his wife Winnifred.

Thomas Gilbert m. Jane, da. of Hugh Rossiter " ancestor of the Connecticut Rossiters.*" This was the first marriage in Taunton. He was a freeman in 1643, Deputy from Taunton in 1651.

Thomas Gilbert went to England in 1653, never returned, and d. there in 1676, his daughter Jane married Samuel Williams and has many descendants.

Thomas Gilbert had children born at Taunton, Hannah, Sept. 28, 1677, and Thomas, July 11, 1781. Of this family were the Gilberts of Rochester, New York, and those wonderful children Lucretia H. and Maria Davidson, of Plattsburg, New York. Of this lineage was Col. Thomas Gilbert, the loyalist, a captain at the siege of Louisburg in 1745, and father of the very respectable and wealthy branch of the family in Nova Scotia. He died in 1796, aged 82 years. †

Bristol County, April 12th, 1703, before Thomas Leonard, Esq., one of her Majesties justices. "*Giles Gilbert* aged seuenty years & upwards " Deposed that he well remembered that his " Brother Thomas Gilbert sometime of Taunton deceased, was in the actual possession of " Rockey Nook" was in controversey betwixt Mr. George Gooding and my cozen [nephew] Thomas Gilbert (as his own p^rticular Lott of Meadow for fifty years agoe last past, and upwards, being long before there was any South purchase of land made. And since my 2^d cousin Thomas Gilbert hath possessed " the same " in his own right from his father Thomas Gilbert."

* The alliances of both the Taunton and Connecticut Gilberts with the Rossiter family, and of the Springfield and Connecticut Gilberts with the Marshfield family, and other intermarriages, furnishes a presumption that they were of one common stock, though documentary evidence of their consanguinity is not preserved.   † Sabine's *American Loyalists*.

"To my son *Thomas Gilbert*, Land in "the North Long Meadow in Hartford."

To son *Samuel Gilbert* Land "called the Pine Field in Hartford."

To son *Ebenezer* " in Hartford, "lot of Thomas Butler dec'd."

Item : "*to my grandson Thomas Dickinson* Twenty pounds of Current Country pay, and also all that is due to me from my Sonne in law Charles Dickinson for the bringing up & keeping of my said grandson Thomas Dickinson; the said sum of Twenty pounds to be paid when he is 21 years of age.

"All the rest of my estate to be divided into 5 equal parts — to sons Thomas and Ebenezer Gilbert — daughters Lydia Chapman, Rachel Marshfield "and the children of my dau^r of Sarah Belcher dec'd to be accounted as one."

"And further the $\frac{1}{7}$th part of the $\frac{1}{5}$th part legacy here given unto Lydia Chapman shall be paid to the sons of my late grandson Jonathan Richelson dec^d when they attayne to twenty one years of age. And my will also is, that if any of the children of my daughter Sarah Belcher dec^d shall happen to dye, before they attayne, the sons to Twenty one, the daughters to Eighteen years of age, the part of such child shall be equally divided to the survivors;

"And my mind and will is, that the rest of the fifth part Legacy given to my daughter Lydia, not otherwise disposed of to the heirs of the late Jonathan Richardson dec^d, shall be equally divided amongst the children of my said daughter Lydia, which she had by her husband Richardson dec^d, minors. Mr. Richard Edwards & my son Ebenezer Gilbert to be joint Executors." "My good friends the Worshipful Caleb Standley Esq & Mr. John Haines to be the Overseers" to advise my Executors and see that this my last will is performed. Witness — Simon Booth. Samuel Parsons, Caleb Stanley Senr."

An inventory of the estate of Mrs. Mary Gilbert, who dyed 3 July, 1700, was taken on the fifth of the same month, and amounted to the sum of £562. 13. 7. Jonathan Bull, and Samuel Isham, Senr. were the appraisers. — *Hartford Probate Records*, Vol. V.

Mrs. Gilbert, born about 1626, was the fourth child of Hugh Welles, one of the founders of Hartford, and niece of the Rev. and Hon. Thomas Welles, governor of Connecticut, who died at Hartford, January 14, 1660, aged 62. Hugh, with his family, removed to Hadley about 1650. His widow, Frances ———, married Thomas Coleman, and died in 1678, bequeathing property to the family of her son Thomas Wells, deceased, to her son John Welles, of Hatfield, and his children, and to her daughter Gilbert; and appointed her son Jonathan Gilbert the executor of her will. Thomas and Hugh were the first and second sons of Thomas Welles,[*] a zealous Puritan and wealthy merchant in London, of the Welles family, in the county of Essex, which was "a branch of the noble family of Wells in Lincolnshire, who were barons of the realm." Incurring the suspicion of the Commissioners, he escaped to this country when about 60 years of age, and was soon followed by a numerous family of sons.

Samuel Welles, the Boston banker of Paris, and John Wells, the eminent advocate, of New York, were of this family.

The following tabular form exhibits a brief statement of the family of Jonathan and Mary (Wells) Gilbert: —

[*] "A Brief General History of the *Welles* or Wells Family, by Albert Welles. 1848." pp. 25. For some of the statements there made authorities should be given. — Morant's *Hist. of Essex County, England.*

2d MARY, sister of Thos. & John Wells and d. of Frances Colman by her 1st husband, HUGH WELLS. She died July 3, 1700, aged 74.—*Gravestone at Hartford.* = JONATHAN GILBERT, landholder in Hartford, in 1645; died Dec. 10, 1682, aged 64. See pp. 229–232. = 1st "Mara Whight," dau. of John White, mar'd Jan. 29th, 1645, at Hartford. She d. about 1650.

Hester or Esther. = Charles Dickinson
Thomas.

Lydia, born Oct. 3, 1654. = 1st Jon'n Richardson, of Stonington.
2d = Chapman.

Rachel = Josiah, son of Samuel Marshfield.*
mar'd 22 Sept. 1686.

Mary = 1st John, eldest son† of Dr. Bray-an Rossiter; he d. in Sept. 1670.
John.
= 2d Samuel Holton, of Northampton.

Nathaniel, of Meriden, died unmar'd.

Ebenezer, of Kensington. = . . .
Hester, born Nov. 13, 1694; d. Feb. 13, 1711–2.
Thomas, b. Sept. 30, 1699.

Samuel, of Colchester, mar'd Oct. 2, 1684.‡ = Mary, d. of Saml. Rogers, of New London.
Jon'n, b. June 29, 1685.
Samuel, b. Feb. 5, 1687.
Nathaniel, b. Sept. 26, 1690.
John, b. April 12, 1692.
Mary, b. Dec. 2, 1696.

Jonathan, of Middletown, born May 11, 1648; died Feb. 1, 1698. = Dorothy, died July 14, 1698.
Mary. 18
John. 15
Jon'n. 12
Nathl. 5
Sarah. 3
Ebenezer. posthumous 5 months.

Mary born Dec. 1649, d. young.

Mrs. Mary Trowbridge. 2d = Captain THOMAS GILBERT, of Boston. = 1st Lydia, d. of Lieut. Samuel Ballatt, of Charlestown; mar'd Nov. 26, 1689. d. March 23, 1708. Her sister Elizabeth, b. Feb. 24, 1673, m. Nov. 25, 1693, Hon. Jonathan Dowse, Esq. of Charlestown, "One of his Majestie's Council," "Justice of the Sup. C. of C. P. for Middlesex," &c.

Thomas, b. 24 Aug. 1697.

Lydia, b. July 9, 1707. = John Pomroy, m. Dec. 13, 1711.
Lydia, b. Aug. 25, 1717.
John, b. Nov. 1712.

Samuel, b. Feb. 21, 1698–9.

Anna, b. July 9, 1692; d. Mch 6, 1707–8.

Mary b. May 20, 1694. = Robert Johnston, m. Jan. 19, 1715.

Elizabeth b. Feb. 7, 1702; m'd "by Dr. Inc. Mather, Prest.," 5 May, 1721; died at Watertown, June 10, 1740.¶ = Ebenezer Thornton, bapt. Jan. 12, 1690; son of Timo. of Boston, who d. 1726, aged 79, and gr. son of Rev. Thomas Thornton, of Yarmouth, who d. at Boston, Feb. 15, 1700, aged about 93.—Sewall's *Ms. Journal.*

Sarah Gilbert b. July 25, 1651; m. July 1, 1670.§ = Andrew Belcher, born at Cambridge, Jan. 1, 1647; was of Boston in 1677; d. Oct. 13, 1717, æ. 70; "the most opulent merchant of his time in Boston."‖

Timothy, born Feb. 2, 1726; removed to = Eunice (d. of James and Sarah Cogswell) Brown,
of New Jersey. | of Ipswich; m. April, 1761.**

THOMAS GILBERT.††

Mary= Geo. Vaughan, Esq., Lt. Gov. of New Hampshire, &c. Son of William by Margarett, d. of Richard Cutts, Esq. of Portsm. N. H.

Sarah = Foye, of Charlestown.

Martha= Hon Anthony Stoddard, Esq. Harv. Col. 1697. d. Feb. 11, 1748, aged 62.

Elizabeth Oliver.

Andrew, born in Hartford, 1671-2.

Anna = Noyes, of Boston.

††Mrs. Teal, 2d.= Hon. JONATHAN BELCHER,= Mary, d. of Wm. Partridge,
of New Jersey. born Jan. 1651. Harv. Col. | Lt. Gov.§§ of New Hamp-
1699; Gov. of Mass. & New shire; b. 19 Oct. 1855, m.
Hampshire, 1730-1741; Gov. of New Jersey at Portsmouth, Jan. 4, 1705
1747-1757; d. Aug., 31, 1757. Founder of | -6; d. 1736, Oct. 6, at Bos-
"Princeton College." There is a portrait of ton.
him in the rooms of the Mass. Hist. Soc.‖‖

¶¶Jonathan, H. C. 1728. Counsellor, Ch. Just. = a sister of Jer'h.
and Lieut. Gov. of Nova Scotia; d. 29 March, | Allen, sheriff of
1776, æ. 65. Suffolk.

Hon. Andrew, of Halifax.

Andrew, Har. Col. 1724. Mem. of the Council;
d. at Milton, Mass. Jan. 24, 1771, aged 65.

* * * | = Lyde, Esq.

* Margaret, sister of Josiah Marshfield, mar'd Ebenezer Parsons, and was the mother of the Rev. Jonathan Parsons, of Newburyport.
† The Rev. John Cotton, of Plymouth, m. a dau. of this family.
‡ July 23, 1705, he was of Hartford, and sold lands to his brother Thomas of Boston. See also page 257 of *Gen. Reg.* 1848.
‖ See Harris' *Cambridge Epitaphs*, 173. *American Quarterly Register*, May, 1841, p. 411, for memoir of him.
§ "Mr. Andrew Belcher was marryed to Mrs. Sarah Gilbert, daughter of Mr. Jonathan Gilbert of Hartford, the 1st July, 1670." — *Hartford Records.*
¶ "Mrs. Elizabeth Thornton, who departed this life June 10, 1740, æt. 37 years." — *Gravestone in Watertown ancient burial-ground.*
** "Here lies what was mortal of Mrs. Eunice Thornton, wife of Mr. Timothy Thornton, who died Sept. 13, 1784, in the 55th year of her age." — *Ipswich burial-ground.*
†† *Genealogical Register,* 1848, pp. 276–8.
‡‡ "We hear from Burlington, in New Jersey, that His Excellency JONATHAN BELCHER, Esq., Governor of the Province, was married there on the 9th day of this month, to Mrs. TEAL, a lady of great merit and a handsome fortune." — *The Independent Advertiser, Boston, October* 3, 1748.
§§ Gov. from Jan. 1697 to July 26, 1703.— Belknap's *History of N. H.,* 152–160, 227.
‖‖ Rev. Mather Byles, D. D. Oct. 13, 1736, styled himself "Your Excellency's affect't nephew," in a poem addressed to Gov. Belcher "on the death of his Lady."
¶¶ "London, January 22. We hear from Cambridge that, Friday last, Jonathan Belcher, Esq., of the Middle-Temple, Son to his Excellency Governor Belcher, was created Master of Arts in a full Senate, by virtue of His Majesty's Mandatory Letter to that University." — *The Boston Weekly News Letter, March* 30, 1733.

18

THOMAS GILBERT, a younger son of Jonathan, of Hartford, by his second wife, Mary Wells, was born about 1655, and, early in life, imbibed a love for business and nautical pursuits, from the scenes at his father's "warehouse,' in Hartford, where a principal part of the foreign and coasting trade of the settlements on the Connecticut was transacted. His brother-in-law, Andrew Belcher, a young merchant, frequently visited that river with his vessels, for purposes of trade, and doubtless favored young Thomas's choice of a maritime life. Mr. Belcher became one of the wealthiest men in New England, was one of the council of safety, in 1689, and a councillor from 1702 to 1717. Gilbert soon commanded one of Belcher's ships, and his history is chiefly connected with naval affairs. His name occurs occasion-» ally in the purchase or sale of lands, mostly derived from his father's estate, and a portion of which was inherited by his children.*

The few facts preserved show him to have been a brave and successful officer, and a leading man in the primitive navy of the colony, during the early French wars, and the universal license of the ocean, when Turks and Algerines, the common enemies to all, skimmed over every sea for prizes. This navy was a fit nursery for the bravery and nautical skill exhibited three-quarters of a century later, by Manly, Whipple, Tucker, Waters, and others, who appeared from the New England shores, rendering signal service in the war of the revolution by their hardihood and skilful seamanship.

By the deposition of Andrew Belcher, August 15, 1690, it appears that "the ship 'Swan,' Capt. Thomas Gilbert, commander,"† had recently arrived from "her late voyage to London." The "Swan," a heavy ship, carrying an armament of twelve guns and a crew of eighteen or twenty men, was under his command for several years. The tonnage of vessels was much smaller at that time, as may be seen by the diminutive size of the ships employed in the long and perilous expeditions of Sir Humphrey Gilbert and Sir Walter Raleigh, and even by the large vessels of a century later, compared with the noble ships engaged in like service in modern times; the number of those competent to take charge of them was comparatively small, and the hazards, at that day, real as well as apparent, gave an importance and dignity to such a command, greatly diminished by the immense progress of maritime science and commerce.

During King William's war, occurred some of the bloodiest passages in the annals of New England. In 1692,‡ the French sent out a squadron to sweep our commerce from the Eastern seas, already covered by hordes of piratical rovers, who were committing fearful depredations. The memory of their atrocities on the ocean was lost in its waters, while the miseries on shore were recorded.

Gilbert was not idle during this period, and he, with his associates,

---

* September 25, 1683, he was at Charlestown, transacting business with Stephen Codman, on account of Edward Johnson. His name is in "A List of the Taxable Inhabitants of Boston, for the year 1695." July 23, 1705, land is conveyed to him by his brother Samuel, of Hartford. John Pomroy, of Boston, husband of Lydia Gilbert, and Ebenezer Thornton of Boston, and his wife, Elizabeth Gilbert, unite in conveying some of their father Thomas Gilbert's land.— *Gen. Reg.* Vol. II. pp. 277, 8.

† "John Coleman, aged 20 years or thereabouts, testifies that, being in the service of *Capt. Thomas Gilburtt*, in the Swan from London, he was Impoured by sᵈ Gilbert to receive what money was due for freight and passengers. Accordingly, I demanded of Richard Weeks, a passenger in said ship from London, aforesaid, being due from him five pounds ten shillings, which sᵈ Weeks sᵈ he had desired Mr. Seth Perry to Pay to Capt. Gilburt's order for him, which Sᵈ Perry accepted to pay & afterwards discounted with Mr. Andrew Belcher upon yᵉ acct of Thomas Gilbert. July 1, 1690."

‡ Waterson's *Cyclopædia of Commerce*, 611, 613.

§ Williamson's *History of Maine*, I. 634, 637.

captured the French ship "Saint Jacob," in the St. Lawrence or "Canady River," at the very entrance of the French possessions, and brought her safely to Boston, where she was condemned as a prize to the captors. This gallant and hazardous exploit was, as usual, a private enterprise, there being technically no government navy; but, having the approbation of the government, it was considered a national undertaking.

The next notice of him is happily preserved in a memoir of the Rev. Dr. Colman,* who in July, in the year 1695, "imbarqued for London (by the will of God)† on board the ship Swan, Capt. Thomas Gilbert, Commander," (then about thirty-nine years of age,) whose fortitude and self-possession in difficulty, manly and generous heart, and desperate and unflinching defence against a superior force, will appear in the following narrative: "On the fourth day the vessel sprang a leak, and the water was heard to pour in on the Starboard tack, which alarmed the sailors. When the winds blew a storm afterward, Mr. Colman governed his fears by looking on the Captain, Mate, and Sailors, to discover what he saw in their faces. When they came into the warm seas a Dolphin, which they had marked with a Scar on his shining back, kept company with the ship for ten or twelve days together, feeding on her bottom.

"At the end of seven weeks a *Seeker* made after them, and soon came up with them. She was a privateer of 20 guns and 100 men, a light and fleet ship; the 'Swan' was heavy laden — 12 guns, and 24 men, sailors and passengers together. The Swan's company bore their broadsides and volies of small arms six or seven times that afternoon, defending themselves and annoying the enemy, but were taken the next morning, having their Boltsprit shot away, and the Mast's rigging so torn and cut, that the masts fell all together, an hour after, by which means the ship became a perfect wreck, and the Company were much looked at by the French when they came into port. On the quarter deck of the Swan four out of seven were wounded, and one mortally. Mr. Colman was much praised for his courage, when the fight was over. He fought like a Philosopher and Christian and prayed 'while the Boatswain and others made Frolick and sport of it.' 'A young *Rake*, a passenger on board, that lisped at Atheism, and spit at Religion every day of the Voyage,' when the great Guns roared, would have crept through the boards to hide himself, and when the firing ceased for a moment, he flew down into the Doctor's room and was seen no more till the ship was taken. The sea was very rough during the engagement. When the 'Swan' struck, the French boat came on board, and the Lieutenant took all the crew's money, and put them into the boat. The crew and some of the passengers were plundered of everything, even their clothing, and then dressed in a few rags of the Sailors. Mr. Colman was put down into the Hold of the Ship, among his

---

* Life of Benjamin Colman, D. D. 5–13.

† Dependence on the Divine Being was recognized in all the common affairs of life, and if the frequency of such reference affords a safe criterion, the sentiment of piety has died with the fathers. In this view, the following "Bill of Lading" presents a contrast with the modern form. It contains the name of GOD four times: "Shipped by the Grace of GOD in good Order and well-conditioned by *Edward Gray of Boston, Ropemaker* in and upon the good Brigantine called the William and Andrew [Pepperell], whereof is Master under GOD for this present voyage William Pepperill, and now riding at anchor, in the Harbor of Boston and by GOD's Grace bound for Rotterdam," &c. . . . "On acco't & Risque of Mr. FFRANCIS GRAY, Upholsterer in Rotterdam," &c. . . . "And so GOD send the good Brigantine to her desired Port in safety, AMEN. Dated in Boston 26th February 1704–5." "yᵉ quantetey Reseued yᵉ qualetey on Known ⅌ mee Wᵐ. *Pepperrell.*"

ragged companions, none of whom knew him till he spoke to them, and they looked at him with astonishment. Mr. Colman bid them divert themselves; "upon which Mr. Grant, the mate of the Swan, (a very grave, prudent, and pious man, fifty years old,) answered with joy: What, Mr. Colman, do you call upon us to be cheerful? What made us sad was to think you would die here, of sorrow; if we do but see you cheerful, we shall all be merry. Madam Allaire, one of the passengers, being brought on board the Captor, about half a day after, entreated that Mr. Colman might be with them in the Great Cabin, or that he might be allowed to see them, — when Madam saw him at the door, half covered with rags and cold, she ran to him and wept upon his neck, & he wept with her. Captain Gilbert burst into tears, and so did Captain Anderson, and his Lieutenant and passengers, moved by the scene. He sat an hour with them, drank, and returned comforted to his hold. Ten days after, they cast anchor before Belle Isle, and proceeded thence up the River Loire, towards the city of Nantz. In the way they were put on board a great hulk, the King's store-ship, and in the morning went to Nantz. The vineyards were very pleasant on the banks of the river, and the fruit delicious to them after so tedious a voyage. After some two months imprisonment within the walls of Dinan, they were freed by an exchange of prisoners with England."

On the 4th of May, 1702, Queen Anne's war with France was declared,[*] and the Massachusetts fishing vessels suffering much from the depredations of the Canadian French cruisers, a fleet was equipped to rid the Eastern seas of their presence, and incidentally to suppress the barbarities committed by the Indians along the shore.

Mr. Belcher was this year chosen to the council for the first time, and under the new administration, just commenced by Gov. Joseph Dudley,[†] doubtless exerted an influence in favor of his brother Gilbert, who, in the following letter, copied from the original manuscript, is virtually represented as the commander-in-chief in this expedition: —

" Cambridge. Juli 11 1702.

S[r]

Yesterday in the afternoon I kist his Excellency's hand and part[d] from him at the Entrance of the Rode to Ipswich from Salem. He comanded me to present his Service to yo[r] Hon[r]. He designed to lodge at Ipswich & to Proceed to the Province of N. Hampshire this day. I hope this day will prove as it promises this morning. His Ex[cy]. also comands me to acquaint yo[r] hon[r] that he hath ordered Capt Thomas Larrimore w[th] his Crew in M[r] Marston Sloop to *ioyn Cap[t]. Gilbert in their Cruise* and that It is his Ex[cy's] Pleasure that it shal be Inserted in the article, w[ch] your Hon[r]. is to project for them, That if their vessels shall happen to be parted by stress of Weather &c. then w[t]ever prizes either of them shal take whilst they are parted and have not recovered one the other shall be at the sole benefit of the Captor, and not lyable to a division amongst the Crews or Companies of both vessels. The Enclosed his Ex[cy] hath Order me to transmitt to yo[r] hon[r.]

My Coz[n] Nath[l] Hubbard hath not had the Small pox and prays that w[n] he hath your Hon[rs]. Order to go to the Castle the Boat may be also order'd to receive him at Charlestown, He fearing it will not be Safe to go over to

---

* Williamson's *History*, Vol. II. p. 33. Graham's *History U. S.*
† Joseph Dudley had arrived only one month before, June 11, 1702, with his Commission as Governor of Massachusetts, Maine, and New Hampshire.

Boston. I thank your hon'. for all yo'. Goodness & friendship to me and pray yo'. Hon'. to be assured that I am and Always will be

Yo'. Hon'ᵉ. most humble Servᵗ

JOHN LEVERETT.*

for The Honᵇˡᵉ
   Isaac Addington Esqʳ.†
    Boston.

What was accomplished in this expedition, and of the remainder of Capt. Gilbert's life, the writer has not learned. His wife Lydia, the mother of his children, whom he married November 25, 1693, was the daughter of Lieut. Samuel Ballat,‡ a respectable citizen of Charlestown, who died November 12, 1708, aged 71. The remains of Captain Gilbert and his wife rest together in the " Granary burial-ground," in Boston, not far from the principal entrance, on the right hand, as shown by their gravestones, from which these inscriptions are taken.

<table>
<tr><td>

Here lyes buried yᵉ
Body of Capᵗ Thomas
Gilburtt departed
This Life Febʸ yᵉ 9ᵗʰ,
17⅜, in yᵉ 64 year
of his age.

</td><td>

Here lies yᵉ body
of Mrs. Lydia, wife of
Capt. Thomas Gilbert
departed this life
March yᵉ 23, 1707–8 in
yᵉ 38 year of her age.

</td></tr>
</table>

---

* Justice of the Superior Court, and President of Harvard College. See in the *Register*, Vol. IV. p. 134, the valuable memoir of the Leverett Family, by Dr. N. B. Shurtleff.

† Chief Justice of the Superior Court. See *Register*, Vol. IV. pp. 117, 118.

‡ " To be Sold the Estate of Samuel Ballet, late of Charlestown, deceased, viz. A dwelling House with a large Garden, Ship building Yard, with a Wharff well accommodated for that or any other Improvement, it being bounded on Charles River; as also three and one half acres of Pasture Land, in Nichol's Field (so called) all lying and being in the town of Charlestown: If any persons are minding to buy the same or any part thereof, they may apply themselves to *Jonathan Dowse of Charlestown Esq.; or Mr. Ebenezer Thornton of Boston*, and know further." — *Boston News Letter*, May 29, 1721.

Lidia d. of Samuel and Lidia Ballatt born 27 Oct. 1670. Lidia wife of Samuel Ballet d. May 1, 1678. Samuel Ballatt admᵈ to Chh. Aug. 15, 1680. And on the " 22ᵈ 6mo. 1680 " John, *Lydia*, and Elizabeth, children of Samuel Ballatt, were bapᵈ." — *Charlestown Rec.*

" Capt. Thomas Gilbert & Mrs. Mary Trowbridge, were marᵈ by yᵉ Revᵈ Increase Mather, Sept. 24, 1708."—*Boston Rec.*

Here lyes buried the
body of Mrs. Mary
Gilbert, Relict of
Capt. Thomas Gilbert
aged 63 years
Died Decemb. yᵉ 30, 1733.

—Copp's Hill Bur. Gro.

Jonathan Dowse and Elizabeth Gilbert m. 25 Nov. 1693. " She died Jan 23, 1700–1, aged 26, leaving 2 sons.

The Gilbert Family: Descendants of Thomas Gilbert, 1582? - 1659 . . . , by Homer W. Brainard, Harold S. Gilbert and Clarence A. Torrey (1953) : Corrections.—In trying to identify Joseph Gilbert of Harwinton, Conn. (born about 1777), the following affidavit was found among the papers accompanying the pension application (W23112) of Miriam (Hopkins) Gilbert, widow of another Joseph Gilbert, a Revolutionary War soldier.

"I Jonathan Marsh, of New Hartford, in County of Litchfield, and State of Connecticut, Now aged 80 years, Testify, and say, that I was born, in the town of New Hartford, on the 1st Day of March 1757, and have always resided in that town, untill the present time. I was intimately acquainted with Joseph Gilbert, of said New Hartford, and with Mirriam Hopkins, whom he married, both before, and after they were married, while they resided in this town. I was not present at their marriage, neither can I recollect the day, or the month, in which they were married, yet I have no doubt of their being legally married, as Early as the year 1773. The said Joseph Gilbert and his wife was [sic] near neighbours to my Father's family, at the time of his marriage, and his family always resided in the neighbourhood with me, while he lived in town, which, was more than twenty five years. One of said Gilberts Brothers, married, my sister. Said Joseph Gilbert, was always a respectable man, in Society, and reared, a large, and respectable family in this town. — I well remember that at the commencement of the Revolutionary War, that the said Joseph Gilbert, Enlisted into a Company Commanded by Captain Griswould, of Torington [sic], for six, or seven months, I think in the month of May 1775, and and [sic] went to lake Champlain, and to St Johns, and Canada. — Aron Austin, was Lieu^t and William Steel, was Ensign, of said Comp^y Both of New Hartford. — In the forepart of the year 1777, in the winter or spring, I was knowing [sic] to the aforsaid Joseph Gilberts, Enlisting into Co^l Webbs Regiment, of Read [sic] Coats, for three years. The officer who Enlisted him, (if mistake not) was Capt James Watson, of Hartford. All the above is true, according to my best Recollection and belief. In testimony whereof I have unto here set my hand, and made oath to same, at New Hartford this 2d day of August 1837, before William Stover, Notary Public

[Signed]   Jonathan Marsh

State of Connecticut, ⎫
County of Litchfield, ⎬ SS
New Hartford ⎭

"Be it Known, that Before me, William Stover, a Notary Public within, and for, the state of Connecticut, on this 2d day of August 1837. Personally appeared, Jonathan Marsh Esq[r] signer of the foregoing Deposition, a Gentleman of unblemished reputation, for truth and viracity, in the Town, County, and state, where he resides, and made oath, to the truth of the same, on the day and year, above written. — In testimony whereof I have Hereunto affixed my official signature, and seal. —

[Signed] William Stover

Notary Public"

This document pertains to Joseph[6] Gilbert (#264, pp. 280-281, *op. cit.*) given as the son of Theodore[5] and Mary (Waters) (#112, pp. 191-192). Note, there is a discrepancy between the birth date of Joseph Gilbert as given on p. 192 ("abt. 1753") and p. 280 ("about 1748-9"). It should be noted that Theodore[5] Gilbert was married 11 June 1850, five months before his 20th birthday.

In this affidavit Jonathan Marsh states that his sister married Joseph Gilbert's brother. John[5] Gilbert (#119, p. 198), son of Benjamin and Elizabeth (Marshfield), married Theodosia Marsh, daughter of Jonathan and Theodosia (Kellogg), of New Hartford, Conn. According to the "Marsh Genealogy" (1895), pp. 190-191, Theodosia, wife of John Gilbert, had a brother Jonathan, born 1 March 1757, the affirmant of this affidavit. If his sister was the wife of Joseph Gilbert's brother, as he stated, then Joseph, too, must have been a son of Benjamin[4] and Elizabeth (Marshfield), and his name should be included in the record on page 126 as another son.

This relationship is born out by the fact that Joseph and Miriam (Hopkins) Gilbert named their second son, Joseph Marshfield. Marshfield occurs as a "middle name" of another grandchild of Benjamin and Elizabeth (Marshfield) Gilbert, Benjamin Marshfield, son of Elnathan Gilbert (#116, pp. 195-196).

According to "The Gilbert Genealogy" (p. 280) Miriam Hopkins, wife of Joseph Gilbert, was "probably daughter of Consider Hopkins, Jr., of Hartford and New Hartford". Note that their first son was named Elias, and the second daughter, Miriam Webster. According to "The History and Genealogy of the Gov. John Webster Family" (1915), p. 87, #4, Miriam Webster married (1), Elias Hopkins and had a daughter Miriam, born in 1755; married (2), William Sedgwick; married (3), in 1777 John Marsh of New Hartford. Miriam (Hopkins) Gilbert, widow of Sgt. Joseph, stated in her application for a pension, 1837, that she was in her 83rd year, hence born about 1754-1755. Moreover, Miriam Webster's third husband, John Marsh, was an uncle of Jonathan Marsh, who made the affidavit.

Joseph and Miriam (Hopkins) Gilbert named another daughter Theodosia, obviously after Theodosia (Marsh) Gilbert, wife of Joseph's brother John. They had also a daughter Clarice, born in New Hartford 30 June 1783 (New Hartford records), who is not named in "The Gilbert Family".

In her own statement in her application for this pension Miriam (Hopkins) Gilbert stated that she married Sgt. Joseph Gilbert 20 March 1773 ("The Gilbert Family" gives the date as 21 March), and that he died 11 Nov. 1812.

Note also on p. 192 of "The Gilbert Family", that Theodore[5] Gilbert is given a son named Jesse who is #266, p. 282, and married Lucy Chapman. Benjamin and Elizabeth (Marshfield) Gilbert, p. 126, are also given a son named Jesse who "m. Lucy Chapman". The eldest daughter of Joseph and Miriam (Hopkins) Gilbert was Lucy, born 28 Aug. 1774. Could she have been named after an aunt Lucy, wife of Jesse Gilbert? Was not Jesse, called a son of Theodore[5] on p. 192, identical with Jesse, son of Benjamin, on p. 126?

Note also, on p. 192, that Theodore[5] Gilbert is given a daughter Mary, who "m. Theodore Cowles?" Compare this statement with that made on p. 197 under #118, the third child of Benjamin[5] Gilbert (brother of John and Joseph and another son of Benjamin and Elizabeth (Marshfield), p. 126): "Mary . . . m. Aug. 1, 1785, Theodore Cowles".

Thus it appears that Theodore[5] and Mary (Waters) Gilbert (#112, pp. 191-192) had only two known children: Theodore, b. 5 Oct. 1751; and Asa, b. 14 Nov. 1755. This is confirmed by a family Bible which Theodore[5] gave to his son Asa,[6]

24

who passed it on to his son Benjamin Franklin[7]. It is still in the possession of a descendant of the last named.

Plymouth, Mass.   ALLEN D. RUSSELL.

DESCENDANTS OF JONATHAN GILLET, OF DOR-CHESTER, MASS., AND WINDSOR, CONN.

By the late SALMON CONE GILLETTE, of Colchester, Conn.

ARRANGED AND ENLARGED

By the Rev. HENRY CLAY ALVORD, A.M., Pastor of the Old South Church, South Weymouth, Mass.

1. JONATHAN[1] GILLET, the progenitor of this branch of the family, belonged, with his brother Nathan, to the company of about one hundred and forty Puritans, which was formed in the counties of Devonshire, Dorsetshire and Somersetshire, England; sailed, with Rev's John Warham and John Maverick as pastors, in the Mary and John, March 20, 1630, and arrived off Nantasket, May 30th following, settlement being made at Dorchester. He was made a freeman there May 6, 1635. There was " graunted to Jonathan Gellet: to fence in halfe an acre of ground about his house leaving a sufficient highway." Further ". . . . the foresayd p'tyes do p'mise to fetch all the Cowes from Jonathan Gillets house to Mr. Woolcotts . . ."; " graunted . . . also to Jonathan Gillet 4 acres" (" over against fox poynt ") ; " the bounds being from Jonathan Gillets pale &c."; and " one [lot] the other side, which was once Jonathan Gilletes."

With the Dorchester Church and Rev. Mr. Warham, he and Nathan removed about 1636 to Windsor, Conn., where he " had a lot granted to him seventeen rods wide " near Mr. Warhams, and across the Poquonnoc road from Alexander Alvord of the same company, whose descendant, Henry of Bolton in the sixth generation, married Mary W. of Colchester in the sixth generation from Jonathan. He and his wife Mary are included in Matthew

25

Grant's church list, made thirty-seven years after the settlement, of twenty-one "members, who were so in Dorchester and came up with Mr. Warham and are still of us." They were also privileged, having paid six shillings, to sit in the long seats in church. He gave 4s. 6d. to the fund in aid of sufferers by the Indian war at Simsbury and Springfield, and was one of the committee of distribution. He died Aug. 23, 1677, and his wife Jan. 5, 1685. Their children were:

i. CORNELIUS,[2] born, as were Jonathan and Mary, before the family removal to Windsor; m. Priscilla Kelsey; d. June 26, 17—, leaving a large family.

ii. JONATHAN, m. 1st, April 23, 1661, Mary Kelsey, who d. April 18, 1676; m. 2d, Dec. 14, 1676, Miriam Dibble, who d. April 18, 1687; had eight children. His descendants include Thomas,[3] Abel,[4] Dea. Abel,[5] Rev. Ashbel,[6] Hon. Francis,[7] U. S. Senator from Connecticut, and William Hooker,[8] the author and actor.

iii. MARY, m. Peter Brown.

iv. ANNA, b. Dec. 29, 1639; m. Oct. 29, 1663, Samuel Filley.

v. JOSEPH, bapt. July 25, 1641; m. 1664, Elizabeth Hawks.

vi. SAMUEL, b. Jan. 22, 1642.

vii. JOHN, b. Oct. 5, 1644; m. July 8, 1669, Mary Barker.

viii. ABIGAIL, bapt. June 28, 1646; d. 1648.

ix. JEREMIAH, b. Feb. 12, 1647; m. Oct. 15, 1685, Deborah Bartlett.

2. x. JOSIAH, bapt. July 14, 1650.

2. JOSIAH[2] GILLET (*Jonathan[1]*) was born in Windsor, Conn., and was baptized July 14, 1650. He married, June 30, 1676, Joanna Taintor, born April, 1657, daughter of Michael Taintor of Branford, Conn. He moved to Colchester in 1702, being one of the first settlers. He died Oct. 29, 1736; and her death was Jan. 23, 1735. They had children:

i. JOSIAH,[3] b. Nov. 24, 1678; d. Oct. 14, 1742; m. Sarah Pellett, March 7, 1711. Children: (1) *Daniel,[4]* b. Feb. 2, 1714, settled in New Haven Co., Conn; (2) *Josiah*, b. Dec. 7, 1715; (3) *Sarah*, b. June 24, 1717; (4) *David*, b. June 13, 1719, d. Oct. 15, 1742; (5) *Elizabeth*, b. April 15, 1721; (6) *Timothy*, b. June 27, 1723; (7) *Charles*, b. April 22, 1728; (8) *Esther*, b. Nov. 24, 1734.

ii. JOANNA, b. Oct. 28, 1680; m. Josiah Strong of Windsor, Jan. 5, 1698, and removed to Colchester in 1703, living near North Pond. Children: (1) *Hannah,[4]* b. Oct. 12, 1699; (2) *John*, b. Jan. (?) 17, 1701; (3) *Damaris(?)*, b. May 8, 1703; (4) *Elizabeth*, b. Oct. 21, 1705; (5) *Mary*, b. Sept. 19, 1707; (6) *Josiah*, b. Sept. 9, 1709; (7) *Eunice*, b. Nov. 19, 1711; (8) *Caleb*, b. Feb. 20, 1714; (9) *Rachel*, b. April 21, 1716; (10) *Dorothy*, b. May 25, 1718; (11) *Joshua*, b. July 20, 1721; (12) *Irene*, b. Oct. 20, 1722; (13) *Asaphel*, b. June 26, 1725.

iii. ELIZABETH, b. Jan. 16, 1682; d. May 10, 1756.

3. iv. JONATHAN, b. June 28, 1685.

v. MARY, b. March 8, 1687; m. Dea. Nathaniel Skinner.

vi. DOROTHY, b. April 15, 1689; m. —— Roberts.

4. vii. SAMUEL, b. Oct. 1, 1690.

viii. JOSEPH, b. March 3, 1695.

ix. MINDWELL, b. Feb. 4, 1696; m. —— Clark; d. May 8, 1784.

x. AARON, b. March 8, 1699; d. Nov. 30, 1730; m. Hannah Clark 1728. Had children. She m. 2d, 1738, Joseph Chamberlain.

xi. NOAH, b. Dec. 5, 1701; was a merchant; m. Abigail ——, who d. Feb. 6, 1739. Children: (1) *Noah,[4]* d. March 2, 1739; (2) *Abigail*, bapt. Oct. 15, 1734.

3. General JONATHAN[3] GILLET (*Josiah,[2] Jonathan[1]*) was born in Windsor, Conn., June 28, 1685, and died in Colchester, Jan. 3, 1755. He

married Jan. 3, 1717, Sarah Ely of Lyme, who died July 4, 1759. They had children:

    i.   SARAH,[4] b. Jan. 1, 1718; m. Joseph Smith, Nov. 30, 1744.
5. ii.   JONATHAN, b. March 22, 1720.
    iii.   MARY, b. Dec. 13, 1723; m. Azariah Storrs of Mansfield.
6. iv.   JOSEPH, b. Dec. 30, 1725.
    v.   NEHEMIAH, b. March 1, 1728; d. Aug. 25, 1814; Lieut. in 8th Conn. in Revolutionary War; m. 1st, Lydia Gillet, Sept. 13, 1757, who d. Aug. 16, 1758; 2d, Martha Storrs, Jan. 22, 1761, who d. July 21, 1827. Children: (1) *Lydia*,[5] b. July 24, 1758; (2) *Olive*, b. March 25, 1762; (3) *Lois*, b. March 21, 1763, d. Oct. 5, 1780; (4) *Azuba*, b. Aug. 20, 1765, d. Oct. 12, 1780; (5) *Martha*, b. April 12, 1767; (6) *Meshullam*, b, Dec. 12, 1769; (7) *Storrs*, b. April 5, 1773, d. Oct. 5, 1828; (8) *Elijah*, b. Jan. 14, 1776, d. March 31, 1860; (9) *Hannah*, b. Jan. 6, 1779; (10) *D*——, b. Aug. 15, 1782, m. —— Dow.
    vi.   JONAH, b. April 10, 1730; d. April 10, 1731.
7. vii. AARON, b. May 23, 1732.
    viii. JOANNA, b. July 8, 1739; d. Jan. 12, 1751.

4.   SAMUEL[3] GILLET (*Josiah*,[2] *Jonathan*[1]) was born Oct. 1, 1690, and died Oct. 8, 1771. He married 1st, Mary Chappell, Jan. 30, 1718, who died Sept. 17, 1732. He married 2d, Abigail ——, in 1733. Children:

    i.   SAMUEL,[4] b. April 20, 1719.
    ii.   ISRAEL, b. Feb. 10, 1722; m. May 14, 1747, Marcy Colman. Children: (1) *Israel*,[5] b. March 30, 1748; (2) *Lydia*, b. Aug. 13, 1750; (3) *Sybil*, b. Oct. 4, 1753; (4) *Ozias*, b. March 4, 1756; (5) *Marcy*, b. Oct. 14, 1758; (6) *Charles*, b. Aug. 8, 1761; (7) *Amasa*, b. Jan. 5, 1764; (8) Capt. *Anson*.
    iii.   ADONIJAH, b. May 30, 1724; killed by Indians on expedition to Crown Point in 1746.
    iv.   ELIPHALET, b. Nov. 1, 1726; d. Aug. 22, 1728.
    v.   MARY, b. April 11, 1729.
    vi.   RUTH, b. Dec. 17, 1731; m. April 4, 1751, John Hinckley.
    vii. ELIPHALET, b. April 29, 1734; d. May 2, 1790; m. March 27, 1760, Lydia Pinneo, dau. of James Pinneo, b. Jan. 30, 1740, and d. Dec. 10, 1804. Children: (1) *Mary*,[5] b. May 17, 1761, d. Sept. 17, 1832; (2) *Caleb*, b. Nov. 12, 1762, d. April 14, 1830, m. Civil Huntington, Oct. 30, 1790, who d. Jan. 20, 1841. Their children: (1) Eliphalet,[6] b. Oct. 11, 1791; (2) Dr. Alfred, b. May 1, 1793, lived and d. in Steuben, N. Y.; (3) Laura, b. June 28, 1795; (4) Henry, b. May 10, 1797; (5) Caleb H., b. March 7, 1800; (6) Dr. Orimel, b. Feb. 28, 1802, d. January, 1884; (7) Dirius Eliza, b. April 30, 1805; (8) Solomon T., b. June 23, 1807, d. Jan. 26, 1868, m. Louise E. Bissell, Oct. 18, 1832; they had two children, one of whom, Abel Bissell, was b. Sept. 7, 1834, and d. Sept. 20, 1860, and the other, Louise, was b. Dec. 28, 1835, and m. P. R. Strong, May 30, 1867; (3) *Joyce*, b. Oct. 9, 1764, m. Nov. 5, 1793, John Lewis of New London; (4) Dea. *Samuel*, b. Nov. 18, 1766, d. June 1, 1855, m. Esther ——, who d. Aug. 2, 1844; (5) Rev. *Eliphalet*, D.D., b. Nov, 19, 1768; (6) *Lydia*, b. Nov. 12, 1770; (7) *Luna*, b. Oct. 5, 1772; (8) *Alvin*, b. June 29, 1774, m. Esther ——, who d. Oct. 9, 1822; (9) *Betsey*, b. June 11, 1780, d. Nov. 30, 1807.
    viii. JERUSHA, b. Oct. 20, 1736; m. Amos Bill, Feb. 3, 1757.
    ix.   CALEB, b. Sept. 3, 1739.

5.   JONATHAN[4] GILLET (*Jonathan*,[3] *Josiah*,[2] *Jonathan*[1]) was born March 22, 1720, and married Phœbe Marvin, granddaughter of " Lyme's Captain," Reinold Marvin. Children:

    i.   SARAH,[5] b. Oct. 24, 1748; m. Ezra Hall of Lyme in 1769. Their dau. *Phœbe*[6] m. Ely[5] Gillett (see 9).
    ii.   REYNOLD, b. April 23, 1750.
    iii.   MARTIN, b. July 19, 1752.

iv. JONATHAN, b. Dec. 15, 1753; m. Zilpha Pratt of Colchester, March 19, 1778.

v. JOSEPH, b. Nov. 5, 1756; m. Mary Miner in Lyme, March 2, 1780. Children: (1) *Daniel*,[6] b. Feb. 20, 1782; (2) *Phœbe*, b. Oct. 16, 1784; (3) *Martin*, b. Dec. 31, 1787; (4) *Mehitable*, b. Nov. 7, 1789; (5) *Joseph*, b. April 5, 1794; (6) *John M.*, b. May 14, 1797, d. December, 1878, m. Phœbe[6] Gillet (see 9, ii.), who d. about 1856; they lived in Liberty Centre, Ohio; (7) *Noah H.*, b. Jan. 29, 1800, d. Jan. 21, 1869; (8) *Benjamin F.*, b. Sept. 24, 1803.

vi. DANIEL, b. Nov. 1, 1758.

vii. ELISHA, b. March 29, 1760.

viii. EZRA, b. June 21, 1762.

ix. JOHN, b. Oct. 16, 1766.

x. SHADRACK, b. Oct. 23, 1769.

6. JOSEPH[4] GILLET (*Jonathan*,[3] *Josiah*,[2] *Jonathan*[1]) was born Dec. 30, 1725, and married Abigail Kellogg, Dec. 8, 1757. Children:

i. JOSEPH,[5] b. Aug. 29, 1758; d. April 29, 1838; m. June 10, 1783, Sarah Root of Hebron, who was b. 1763, and d. Feb. 25, 1850. Their children: (1) *Theodosia*,[6] b. Dec. 5, 1784, m. 1815, Levi Marks; (2) *Patience*, b. Dec. 23, 1786; (3) *Joseph*, b. April 17, 1789, m. July, 1811, Lydia (Belinda?) Berry; (4) *Sarah*, b. April 2, 1792, m. 1822, Moses White; (5) *Asa*, b. Dec. 5, 1793, m. 1815, Lida Berry; (6) *Mary*, b. Aug. 22, 1796, m. 1st, 1853, John Sutphen, 2d, 1870, Ensign Avery; (7) *Aaron*, b. Aug. 8, 1800, m. Betsey Harford; (8) *Harvey*, b. Dec. 27, 1802, d. Oct. 13, 1852, m. March 26, 1839, Eunice Gardner; their children: (1) Sarah,[7] b. April 22, 1840, (2) Adeline, b. Nov. 22, 1841, (3) Jerusha B., b. May 31, 1845, (4) Elizabeth C., b. April 27, 1848; (9) *Ezra S.*, b. Jan. 27, 1808, m. Mandana Smith.

ii. ABIGAIL, b. Dec. 28, 1759.

iii. SARAH, b. Aug. 28, 1762; m. Daniel Gillet of Lyme.

iv. LUCY, b. April 12, 1764.

v. EUNICE, b. Jan. 24, 1766; m. Gurdon Clark.

vi. Capt. JONATHAN, b. March 21, 1768; d. May 22, 1820; m. 1st, April 23, 1800, Betsey Rogers, who d. March 12, 1810; m. 2d, Feb. 12, 1811, Huldah Marvin. Children: (1) *Rogers*,[6] b. Feb 16, 1801; (2) *Mary K.*, b. March 11, 1809; (3) *Abigail R.*, d. Jan. 15, 1809; (4) *Amos*, b. Dec. 18, 1811; (5) *Betsey*, b. April 10, 1813; (6) *Huldah*, b. Aug. 8, 1816.

vii. EZRA, b. Aug. 23, 1769; d. Sept. 15, 1769.

viii. ANNIE, b. Nov. 12, 1770; m. May 17, 1796, —— Root.

ix. EZRA, b. Dec. 11, 1772.

x. ZERUIAH, b. March 18, 1775.

xi. RALPH, b. June 4, 1777; m. Sarah Forsaith. Children: (1) Capt. *Francis*,[6] (2) *John R.*, (3) *Lucy*, (4) *Julia*, (5) *Ezra*.

xii. SAMUEL, b. Aug. 25, 1779; d. Aug. 9, 1842; m. Oct. 9, 1813, Nabby Lord of Lyme. Children: (1) *Elizabeth*;[6] (2) *Samuel S.*, b. Dec. 31, 1815; (3) *Asa E.*, b. Aug. 5, 1817; (4) *Joseph L.*, b. June 27, 1819; (5) *Nancy M.*; (6) *Frances R.*

7. AARON[4] GILLET (*Jonathan*,[3] *Josiah*,[2] *Jonathan*[1]) was born May 23, 1732, and died June 14, 1786. He served in the Revolutionary War. He married, March 31, 1757, Anna Pratt, who died Jan. 22, 1827. Children:

i. AARON,[5] b. Jan. 2, 1758; d. Aug. 17, 1758.

ii. ANNA, b. May 9, 1759; d. April 5, 1779; m. Noah Skinner.

iii. JOANNA, b. May 12, 1761; d. April 24, 1765.

8. iv. MARY, b. March 30, 1763.

v. AARON, b. Feb. 23, 1765; d. 1814; wife d. 1814. One son: *Ely A.*[6] Mack, adopted by his uncle, Josiah Mack, whose name he took; had son: Rev. Josiah A.[7] Mack, who had son, Rev. Charles A.[8] Mack, and other children.

28

9. vi. ELY, b. May 14, 1767.
vii. RUSSELL, b. Aug. 31, 1769; d. Aug. 11, 1811; m. Betsey Dixon, who d. Oct. 2, 1865. Children: (1) *Betsey*,[6] d. Oct. 26, 1871, intestate, and property divided among numerous heirs; (2) *Wealthy*, d. 1835; (3) *Russell*, d. June 18, 1865; no one of the three left children.
viii. HANNAH, b. April 20, 1771; d. March 23, 1773.
10. ix. SOLOMON, b. Aug. 10, 1773.
x. MERCY, b. Feb. 11, 1777; d. Sept. 15, 1840; m. Abner Clapp. Children: (1) *Ralph*,[6] d. Aug. 11, 1865, had 8 children; (2) *Emily*, d. Nov. 9, 1834, m. A. M. Rogers, had 5 children; (3) *Martin G.*, d. 1834 (see 10, ii.); (4) *Ely H.*, had 3 children; (5) *Arnold*, d. September, 1855, had 9 children; (6) *Jennette*, d. June, 1849, had 2 daughters.
xi. ANNA, b. April 5, 1781; d. June 14, 1872; m. 1st, Andrew Carrier; 2d, Elijah Gillett. Children by first husband: (1) *Phebe A.*,[6] b. March 15, 1815, m. L. Holdridge; (2) *Andrew E.*, b. July 2, 1816; (3) *Erastus;* (4) *Electa*, b. May 2, 1818, m. Austin Haling; (5) *Mary*, b. May 20, 1820; (6) *Mercy*, b. June 26, 1822.

8. MARY[5] GILLET (*Aaron*,[4] *Jonathan*,[3] *Josiah*,[2] *Jonathan*[1]) was born March 30, 1763; married 1st, E. Porter, and 2d, Josiah Mack. By first husband there were children:

i. POLLY[6] PORTER, m. P. Buell, and had 6 children.
ii. SALLY[6] PORTER, m. —— Strong, and had 4 children.
11. iii. ANNA[6] PORTER, b. July 13, 1787.

9. ELY[5] GILLET (*Aaron*,[4] *Jonathan*,[3] *Josiah*,[2] *Jonathan*[1]) was born May 14, 1767, and died Dec. 11, 1846. He married, April 8, 1790, Phebe Hall (see 5, i.), born April 24, 1773; died March 24, 1859. Children:

12. i. ELY HALL,[6] b. Oct. 6, 1794.
ii. PHEBE, b. March 17, 1796; d. Aug. 12, 1852; m. John M. Gillett (see 5, v. 6), who d. December, 1878. Children: (1) *Phebe L.*,[7] (2) *Laura A.*, (3) *Lozetta*, (4) *Mary M.*, (5) *Joseph E.*
iii. SARAH ANN, b. July 7, 1809; d. April 18, 1863; m. March 15, 1830, Alfred H. Otis, who was b. Oct. 3, 1812, and d. Sept. 20, 1865. Children: (1) *Albert L.*,[7] b. May 21, 1831, m. 1st, May 21, 1853, Ellen Butler, b. Aug. 10, 1873, 2d, Jan. 10, 1875, Mrs. Josephine Perry; (2) *Sarah Angeline*, b. May 23, 1833, m. July 29, 1858, A. B. Fowler, b. June 15, 1824; (3) *John L.*, b. Jan. 31, 1835, d. Oct. 29, 1837: (4) *John E.*, b. Nov. 11, 1837, d. Sept. 19, 1841; (5) *Frances*, b. Nov. 24, 1839, d. Aug. 14, 1865; (6) Lieut. *George F.* ("Frank G."), b. July 11, 1842, d. Aug. 10, 1878, m. April 16, 1867, Mary E. Hall; children: (1) William H.,[8] b. Oct. 6, 1868, (2) F. Burton, b. Sept. 9, 1870, (3) Ida F., b. Nov. 4, 1874, d. Jan. 8, 1876; (7) *M. Ellen*, b. Dec. 11, 1844, m. July 1, 1863, Sheldon H. Brooks; children: (1) Arthur A.,[8] b. June 10, 1866, m. June 10, 1891, Lettie I. Baker, (2) Charles B., b. Aug. 24, 1868, (3) Amelia F., b. Nov. 13, 1870, d. April 15, 1878, (4) Otis S., b. Oct. 6, 1872, d. April 12, 1873, (5) Inda A., b. June 14, 1874, (6) Alice M., b. Jan. 18, 1877, (7) Esther L., b. March 28, 1880, (8) James G., b. April 29, 1881, (9) Jessie M., b. Sept. 17, 1884, (10) Mary E., b. March 13, 1889.

10. SOLOMON[5] GILLET (*Aaron*,[4] *Jonathan*,[3] *Josiah*,[2] *Jonathan*[1]) was born Aug. 10, 1773, and died March 7, 1856. He married Martha Doolittle, who died May 3, 1871. Children:

i. SOLOMON L.,[6] b. Sept. 20, 1803; m. July 24, 1826, Mary J. Watrous. Children: (1) *Daniel W.*,[7] b. June 20, 1829, m. T. Augusta Brown; (2) *Charles L.*, b. June 28, 1831, d. May 15, 1842.
ii. MARY ANN, b. April 3, 1807; d. July 22, 1834; m. Martin G. Clapp (see 7, x. 3.), who d. Nov. 7, 1834. Children: (1) *Harriet E.*,[7] b.

Aug. 23, 1832, m. P. Ludlow Hyde; children: (1) Francis R.,[8] (2) Mary E., (3) Charles L.; (2) *Charles M.*, b. July 5, 1834, m. and has 2 children.

iii. JOEL D., b. Aug. 27, 1809; m. 1st, Lucy J. Patten; 2d, Catherine Stowe. Children by first wife: (1) *Frances*,[7] m. David B. Winton, and has 6 children; (2) *Emma;* (3) *Charles W.*, m. and has 2 children.

iv. MARTHA M., b. May 26, 1812; m. John Loomis. Children: (1) *Emma*,[7] m. Edward Morgan, d. from burns, and left 1 son; (2) *Frank*, m. and has children.

v. RUSSEL, b. Aug. 13, 1814; d. July 10, 1887; m. 1st, March 18, 1845, Elizabeth Clark, d. Sept. 18, 1859; 2d, May 24, 1860, Martha Storrs. Children: (1) *Solomon L.*,[7] b. Dec. 25, 1849; (2) *Mark D.*, b. Dec. 30, 1852; (3) *Elizabeth S.*, b. April 23, 1861, m. June 12, 1890, Ernest E. Carrier: (4) *Harriet M.*, b. Dec. 13, 1862; (5) *Mary L.*, b. July 21, 1864, m. Sept. 9, 1890, Rev. Curtis M. Geer; 1 child: Dorothy,[8] b. June 17, 1891; (6) *Anna C.*, b. July 30, 1866, m. Sept. 10, 1889, Harris R. Brainard; (7) *Edwin R.*, b. Dec. 14, 1870; (8) *Robert H.*, b. July 24, 1872.

vi. AARON G., b. Jan. 5, 1817; m. Hannah Baldwin. Children: (1) *Mattie M.*,[7] (2) *Mary H.*

vii. CHARLES E., b. Oct. 23, 1823.

11. ANNA[6] PORTER (*Mary[5] Gillett, Aaron,[4] Jonathan,[3] Josiah,[2] Jonathan[1]*) was born July 13, 1787, and died March 19, 1858. She was married Sept. 12, 1806, to Hon. Peyton Randolph Gilbert of Gilead, who was born Sept. 12, 1784, and died Sept. 5, 1857. He represented Hebron in the legislature of 1827, and was a State Senator in 1830 and 1837. Children:

13. i. EDWIN RANDOLPH[7] GILBERT, b. Feb. 10, 1808.
14. ii. JOSIAH CHAMPION[7] GILBERT, b. Feb. 26, 1810.
15. iii. MELISSA ANN[7] GILBERT, b. Aug. 24, 1812.
    iv. ABBY MARIA[7] GILBERT, b. Nov. 21, 1814; d. April 7, 1832.
16. v. CHARLES AUGUSTUS[7] GILBERT, b. March 27, 1817.
17. vi. RALPH PORTER[7] GILBERT, b. Aug. 30, 1819.
18. vii. SAMUEL EPAPHRODITUS[7] GILBERT, b. Dec. 9, 1821.
    viii. SARAH THERESA[7] GILBERT, b. July 21, 1826; d. March 27, 1846.

12. ELY HALL[6] GILLETT (*Ely,[5] Aaron,[4] Jonathan,[3] Josiah,[2] Jonathan[1]*) was born Oct. 6, 1794, and died Dec. 23, 1863. He married, Sept. 30, 1821, Mary Williams (Frederic W.,[5] Ebenezer,[4] Park,[3] Dea. Samuel,[2] Robert,[1] who was the progenitor of the Williams line, and a prominent citizen of Roxbury, Mass., whither he came about 1638, probably from Norwich, Eng.), who was born Dec. 28, 1788, and died Nov. 10, 1864. They resided in Colchester, where their children were born:

19. i. WILLIAM ELY,[7] b. June 21, 1822.
20. ii. EZRA HALL, b. July 15, 1823.
21. iii. MARY WILLIAMS, b. Dec. 24, 1824.
    iv. EMMA LOUISA, b. May 9, 1826; d. April 29, 1856; m. Aug. 10, 1852, Stephen H. Matthews (see 24). One child: *Charles G.*,[8] b. Feb. 2, 1855, d. Sept. 25, 1855.
22. v. JOHN ELBERT, b. Oct. 4, 1828.
23. vi. SALMON CONE, b. June 12, 1830.
24. vii. JANE, b. June 19, 1834.

13. Rev. EDWIN RANDOLPH[7] GILBERT (*Anna[6] Porter, Mary[5] Gillett, Aaron,[4] Jonathan,[3] Josiah,[2] Jonathan[1]*) was born Feb. 10, 1808, and died April 17, 1875. He was pastor of the Congregational Church of Wallingford, Conn., for forty-one years. He married 1st, May 7, 1833, Ann S. Langdon, who was born May 3, 1809, and died Feb.

13, 1841; 2d, July 26, 1842, Dorcas S. Dutton; 3d, Sept. 7, 1852, Ann C. Baldwin, who was born April 1, 1815, and died Aug. 19, 1864; 4th, Nov. 16, 1865, Mary H. Carrington, who was born April 26, 1826. Children:

i. REUBEN R.,[8] b. Nov. 19, 1834; d. June 9, 1836.
ii. CHARLES E., b. Nov. 8, 1836; m. May 16, 1866, Virginia Ewing Crane. Children: (1) *Albert W.*,[9] b. Nov. 3, 1867; (2) *Edwin R.*; (3) *Allan.*
iii. GEORGE L., b. Oct. 9, 1838; d. Feb. 2, 1839.
iv. SAMUEL S., b. Dec. 19, 1844; d. Feb. 17, 1860.
v. SAMUEL D., b. June 15, 1848; m. June 15, 1875, Ellen Peck.

14. JOSIAH CHAMPION[7] GILBERT (*Anna*[6] *Porter, Mary*[5] *Gillett, Aaron,*[4] *Jonathan,*[3] *Josiah,*[2] *Jonathan*[1]) was born Feb. 26, 1810, and died July 26, 1889. He represented Hebron in the legislatures of 1849 and 1855; served as clerk of Gilead Congregational Church from Oct. 7, 1856, till his death, as treasurer of the Society for twenty-six years, and deacon of the Church for twenty-three years. He married, 1st, March 13, 1832, Louisa M. Alvord, daughter of Saul Alvord, Esq., of Bolton, who was born Aug. 31, 1809, and died Nov. 16, 1847; 2d, Sept. 16, 1848. Sarah S. Post, born April 29, 1821, d. Sept. 27, 1886. Children:

i. HENRY CHAMPION,[8] b. June 27, 1839; d. Oct. 4, 1842.
ii. SARAH LOUISA, b. Dec. 14, 1852; d. May 29, 1855.
iii. ARTHUR RANDOLPH, b. Oct. 1, 1857; d. Feb. 3, 1873.

15. MELISSA ANN[7] GILBERT (*Anna*[6] *Porter, Mary*[5] *Gillett, Aaron,*[4] *Jonathan,*[3] *Josiah,*[2] *Jonathan*[1]) was born Aug. 24, 1812, and was married May 21, 1835, to John Meigs Hall; resided in Hartford, Conn. Children:

i. ABBY M.,[8] HALL, b. May 13, 1836; d. Jan. 8, 1879.
ii. MARY E.[8] HALL, b. May 11, 1838; m. July 18, 1861, L. Ward Clark. Children: (1) *Elizabeth*[9] *Clark,* b. April 4, 1864; (2) *Mary G.*[9] *Clark,* b. May 11, 1879.
iii. ELLEN T.[8] HALL, b. May 9, 1840; m. Oct. 12, 1864, Charles D. Tuller. Children: (1) *Edith H.*[9] *Tuller,* b. Aug. 18, 1865, d. June 11, 1878; (2) *Marshall J.*[9] *Tuller,* b. Oct. 1, 1867; (3) *Ralph D.*[9] *Tuller,* b. Aug. 21, 1869; (4) *Mabel C.*[9] *Tuller,* b. April 4, 1873.

16. CHARLES AUGUSTUS[7] GILBERT (*Anna*[6] *Porter, Mary*[5] *Gillett, Aaron,*[4] *Jonathan,*[3] *Josiah,*[2] *Jonathan*[1]) was born March 27, 1817, and died Oct. 20, 1867. He married, June 21, 1842, Mary J. Manson, who was born Jan. 22, 1824, and died Nov. 28, 1868. He resided at Mobile, Ala. Children:

i. CHARLES M.,[8] b. Oct. 10, 1843.
ii. ELLA J., b. Sept. 15, 1846; d. Sept. 26, 1884; m. October, 1883, Julius C. Verhœff.
iii. LOUISA H., b. May 19, 1849; d. May 20, 1868.
iv. ANNA C.. b. Aug. 19, 1851; d. June 13, 1881; m. Jan. 22, 1880, Julius C. Verhœff.
v. WILLIAM A., b. Jan. 19, 1854.

17. Hon. RALPH PORTER[7] GILBERT (*Anna*[6] *Porter, Mary*[5] *Gillett, Aaron,*[4] *Jonathan,*[3] *Josiah,*[2] *Jonathan*[1]) was born Aug. 30, 1819, and died May 16, 1891; was S. S. superintendent for about thirty years; was chosen deacon in 1887; represented Hebron in Connecticut Legislature in 1880; and was a member of the Senate in 1882 and 1883. He married, Sept. 14, 1842, Mary Lauretta Hutchinson, who was born Sept. 23, 1819, and died Dec. 18, 1861. Children:

    i.   ANNA LAURETTA,[8] b. May 11, 1844; m. Jan. 13, 1886, Emerson W. Moore of Talcottville, Conn.

   ii. JOHN RANDOLPH, b. June 13, 1849; m. Aug. 30, 1876, Mary Cordelia Davis, b. June 21, 1852. Children: (1) *Ralph Davis*,[9] b. June 10, 1878; (2) *Albert Champion*, b. Feb. 15, 1881; (3) *Myron Randolph*, b. Sept. 25, 1884.

18. SAMUEL EPAPHRODITUS[7] GILBERT (*Anna[6] Porter, Mary[5] Gillett, Aaron,[4] Jonathan,[3] Josiah,[2] Jonathan[1]*) was born Dec. 9, 1821; married 1st, Cordelia F. Manson, who was born June 3, 1822, and died Nov. 6, 1850; 2d, Dec. 7, 1852, Mary J. Mackey, who was born Feb. 2, 1831. Children:

    i.   FRANK M.,[8] b. July 1, 1847; m. Oct. 20, 1880, Anna Hudspeth. A child: *Frank M.*,[9] b. May 29, 1882.

   ii. DAVID M., b. April 5, 1854; m. Jan. 29, 1878, Emma Healy, b. Aug. 18, 1857. Children: (1) *Samuel H.*,[9] b. Feb. 8, 1879; (2) *Roswell W.*, b. Oct. 11, 1880; (3) *David M.*, b. May 29, 1883; (4) *Mary W.*, b. July 16, 1887.

  iii. IDA A., b. April 17, 1856; m. Feb. 3, 1880, Stephen R. Ward. Children: (1) *Ida*,[9] b. Aug. 1, 1881, d. Jan. 15, 1883; (2) *Ethel M.*, b. April 6, 1883; (3) *George G.*, b. Dec. 1, 1884; (4) *Harold*, b. May 15, 1887.

19. WILLIAM ELY[7] GILLETTE (*Ely H.,[6] Ely,[5] Aaron,[4] Jonathan,[3] Josiah,[2] Jonathan[1]*) was born June 21, 1822. He married in Colchester, May 9, 1848, Bethiah Backus, who was born in Lebanon, April 12, 1829. Children, born in Bolton:

    i.   INFANT dau.,[8] b. July 6, 1849; lived eighteen hours.

   ii. JOSIAH, b. Oct. 16, 1851; d. at New Haven, June 19, 1890; m. at Clinton, May 2, 1888, Irene Manwaring, b. June 23, 1866. One child: *Josiah Augustus*,[9] b. Oct. 16, 1889.

  iii. LIZZIE, b. Oct. 6, 1854; d. at Talcottville, from effect of carriage accident, May 18, 1877.

   iv. MARY, b. Dec. 30, 1858.

20. Prof. EZRA HALL[7] GILLETT (*Ely H.,[6] Ely,[5] Aaron,[4] Jonathan,[3] Josiah,[2] Jonathan[1]*) was born July 15, 1823, and died Sept. 2, 1875. Graduated at Yale College 1841 and Union Seminary 1844; pastor at Harlem, N. Y., 1845–1870; D.D. Hamilton College 1864; Professor of Political Economy and Ethics, University of City of New York, 1870–1875; a voluminous writer and author. He married 1st, Oct. 15, 1851, Maria H. Ripley, who died March 28, 1853; 2d, June 19, 1854, Mary J. Kendall, who died Sept. 10, 1881. Children:

    i.   CHARLES RIPLEY,[8] b. Nov. 29, 1855; University of New York 1874, Union Seminary 1880, of which institution the librarian 1883—; ordained by Presbytery of New York 1886; m. April 26, 1881, Kate Van Kirk. Children: (1) *Carrie Richardson*,[9] b. March 9, 1883, d. Aug. 16, 1883; (2) *Ezra Kendall*, b. Sept. 24, 1884; (3) *Mary Marshall*, b. Nov. 2, 1889; (4) *Charles Robert*, b. June 17, 1891; (5) *William*, b. Dec. 16, 1892.

   ii. WILLIAM KENDALL, b. May 16, 1860; University of City of New York 1880, of which institution Professor of French and Spanish 1890—.

  iii. ALICE WILLIAMS, b. June 7, 1871; d. Nov, 13, 1871.

21. MARY WILLIAMS[7] GILLETT (*Ely H.,[6] Ely,[5] Aaron,[4] Jonathan,[3] Josiah,[2] Jonathan[1]*) was born Dec. 24, 1824, and died in Hartford, Sept. 3, 1888. She was married May 12, 1846, in Colchester, to Hon. Henry Alvord of Bolton, who was born Feb. 8, 1819, and died May 1, 1877; he was a member of the Connecticut Senate in 1861. Children:

i. Louisa[8] ALVORD, b. July 28, 1847; m. Sept. 13, 1870, Arthur B. Carpenter, b. March 12, 1847, and d. Nov. 10, 1888. Children: (1) *Mary L.*[9] *Carpenter*, b. Sept. 9, 1872; (2) *Katherine E.*[9] *Carpenter*, b. Nov. 23, 1874, d. Oct. 28, 1888; (3) *Winifred G.*[9] *Carpenter*, b. Feb. 10, 1876; (4) *Sarah E.*[9] *Carpenter*, b. May 13, 1877, d. Oct. 13, 1888; (5) *Henry T.*[9] *Carpenter*, b. Dec. 17, 1878; (6) *Champion G.*[9] *Carpenter*, b. March 25, 1881, d. Nov. 6, 1888; (7) *Arthur B.*[9] *Carpenter*, b. Jan. 5, 1883; (8) *John A.*[9] *Carpenter*, b. Nov. 16, 1886, d. Nov. 9, 1888.

ii. John Buell[8] ALVORD, b. April 3, 1849; d. July 31, 1857.

iii. Mary Jane[9] ALVORD, b. Dec. 8, 1850; Oberlin College 1875; m. Oct. 31, 1878, Dr. Byron B. Loughead, b. Jan. 29, 1847; Oberlin College 1875; M.D. Western Reserve University 1877. Children: (1) *Charles F.*,[9] b. Oct. 12, 1880; (2) *Mary A.*, b. Dec. 13, 1883.

iv. Phebe Buell[8] ALVORD, b. Oct. 19, 1852; m. Oct. 31, 1878, E. Horatio Talcott, b. Sept. 13, 1847.

v. Henry Clay[3] ALVORD, b. April 30, 1854; University of City of New York 1876; Hartford Theological Seminary 1879; pastor, Montague, Mass., 1879–1886, South Weymouth, Mass., 1886–; m. Oct. 6, 1880, Alice C. Bissell, b. March 18, 1854. Children: (1) *Henry B.*,[9] b. March 24, 1885; (2) *Ruth G.*, b. Jan. 6, 1889; (3) *Robert W.*, b. Feb. 24, 1892.

vi. Emma Gillette[8] ALVORD, b. July 28, 1857; m. Dec. 13, 1882, Clark S. Beardslee, b. Coventry, N. Y., Feb. 1, 1850; Amherst College 1876; Hartford Seminary 1879, and instructor in Hebrew; pastor, Le Mars, Ia., Prescott, Ariz., and West Springfield, Mass.; Associate Professor, Hartford Seminary, 1888–92, and Professor 1892—. Children: (1) *Raymond A.*[9] *Beardslee*, b. Sept. 21, 1883; (2) *Claude G.*[9] *Beardslee*, b. June 25, 1888; (3) *Lyndon S.*[9] *Beardslee*, b. Sept. 30, 1889; (4) *Ruth*[9] *Beardslee*, b. March 5, 1891.

vii. Carrie, b. July 27, 1860; d. Aug. 18, 1868.

viii. Charles Hubbell, b. Nov. 23, 1861; m. Oct. 1, 1891, Clara Alice Hendey.

22. Hon. John Elbert[7] Gillette (*Ely H.*,[6] *Ely*,[5] *Aaron*,[4] *Jonathan*,[3] *Josiah*,[2] *Jonathan*[1]) was born Oct. 4, 1828. He married, June 19, 1854, Sarah Amanda Westfield. He was a member of the New York Assembly 1880–1. Children:

i. Fanny Westfield,[8] b. April 3, 1855; d. Feb. 21, 1856.

ii. John Westfield, b. March 9, 1860; m. Oct. 31, 1888, Grace Fidelia James. Children: (1) *Helen Field*,[9] b. Dec. 19, 1889; (2) *John Westfield*, b. Aug. 26, 1892.

iii. Grace Gatzmer, b. June 21, 1865; d. Sept. 23, 1868.

iv. Ernest Simpson, b. Sept. 18, 1873; d. Aug. 13, 1874.

23. Salmon Cone[7] Gillette (*Ely H.*,[6] *Ely*,[5] *Aaron*,[4] *Jonathan*,[3] *Josiah*,[2] *Jonathan*[1]) was born in Colchester, June 12, 1830, and died there June 5, 1890. He was president of the Colchester Savings Bank. He took great interest in genealogical researches; this collection of family records originating with him. He married 1st, Nov. 14, 1852, Adelaide Huntington, who died Nov. 19, 1868; 2d, March 9, 1870, Mary Willard of Wilton. Children:

i. Walter H..[8] b. Nov. 12, 1855; m. June 1, 1886, Julia E. Williams. Children: (1) *Homer W.*,[9] b. April 4, 1887, d. Aug. 16, 1887; (2 & 3) *Sarah E.* and *Mary A.*, b. Dec. 27, 1887.

ii. Helen C., b. March 7, 1860.

24. Jane[7] Gillette (*Ely H.*,[6] *Ely*,[5] *Aaron*,[4] *Jonathan*,[3] *Josiah*,[2] *Jonathan*[1]) was born June 19, 1834. She married 1st, Stephen H. Matthews, May 9, 1860, who was born Jan. 18, 1822, and died May 14, 1875; 2d, April 13, 1880, Darius M. Linsley, who was born July 21, 1820. Children:

i.   JOHN GILLETTE[8] MATTHEWS, b. Sept. 25, 1862; m. June 28, 1890, Hortense M. Lyon, b. May 4, 1861. One child: *Beatrice Lyon*,[9] b. Dec. 30, 1891.

ii. MARY LOUISA[8] MATTHEWS, b. Aug. 28, 1864; at Mount Holyoke Seminary 1880–83; teacher, Fisk University, 1886–8; missionary, A.B.C.F.M. at Monastir, Bulgaria, 1888.

iii. HOLLEY PORTER[8] MATTHEWS, b. Sept. 6, 1868.

iv. ANNA WILLIAMS[8] MATTHEWS, b. Aug. 20, 1874.

THE BROTHERS JONATHAN AND NATHAN GILLETT
AND SOME OF THEIR DESCENDANTS

Compiled by ALICE LUCINDA PRIEST, B.L., of Brookline, Mass.

The descendants of the Puritan brothers Jonathan and Nathan Gillett of Dorchester, Mass., and Windsor, Conn., were and almost surely are, numerous, yet there is an interesting opportunity for much further investigation of records to identify all the lines through the genealogical reference library at 9 Ashburton Place, Boston.

The April 1893 NEW ENGLAND HISTORICAL AND GENEA-LOGICAL REGISTER published a very able nine-page record of * "Descendants of Jonathan Gillet of Dorchester, Mass., and Windsor, Conn.", compiled by Salmon Cone Gillette and arranged and enlarged by the Rev. Henry Clay Alvord, A.M., both descendants. Their record is altogether concerned with the descendants of Jonathan's youngest child, Josiah. Another very important publication is the April 1939 *American Genealogist* ten-page report of John Insley Coddington, A.M., on "Jonathan Gillett of Dorchester, Mass., and Windsor, Conn., and Mary Dolbere or Dolbiar, his Wife." As the title indicates, its important and convincing mission was to establish the fact of the marriage and the genealogical background of the bride and the believed background of the groom, with no purpose of a record of descendants beyond their children.

This present record concerns principally the early line of Jonathan's third son, Joseph, and, because of later-date opportunities, can correct a few errors in earlier records, make additions, and enlarge on some interesting items.

That Jonathan and Nathan Gillett were brothers is proved by the 8 August 1677 will of Jonathan. To quote: . . . "my wife . . . shall have . . . the Housing & Lands of both my Houselotts, my one and that which was my Brother Nathan Gillett's, . . . "

Henry R. Stiles, A.M., in his 1892 second edition of "Ancient Windsor, Conn." states: "Jonathan Gillett, with his brother Nathan came to Dorchester, Mass., with Rev. Warham, [June 1630] and (both) to Windsor with the first emigration. Both he and his wife were members of the original Dorchester and Windsor churches. . . . There is still extant . . . a copy of the . . . Bible, of 1599 . . . This Bible was brought to New England by this Jonathan Gillett, Senʳ, and afterwards passed into the hands of the present Holcomb family. . . . In this Bible occurs the following manuscript record: 'My father Gille(tt) came into new inglan the secon(d) time in June in the yeare 1634 and Jonathan his sonne was born about half a yeare after he came to land.'" The foregoing record proves that Jonathan Gillett's wife accompanied him on his second trip *from* England to New England; and very strongly suggests that he had married her in England on his return trip to his native land.

Therefore Mr. Coddington's 1939 opening statement is even
*Pages 25-34, this volume.

more than the strongest kind of circumstantial evidence. It is as follows:

"The Parish Register of St. Andrew's Church at Colyton, co. Devon, contains the following marriage record:

"1634   Jonathan Gillett & Mary Dolbiar,   29 March

"This is the answer to the question of the long-sought identity of Mary, wife of Jonathan Gillett, the emigrant from England to Dorchester, Mass., and settler at Windsor, Conn."

Mr. Coddington's next statement is: "There can be very little doubt but that Jonathan Gillett was the son of the Reverend William Gillett or Gyllett, Rector of Chaffcombe, co. Somerset, who was instituted to that benefice 4 Feb. 1609/10, and who died early in 1641", etc.   And there are five valuable pages on the ancestry of Mary Dolbiar (Dolbere) that should all be read.   They include the Colyton baptisms: "1607 Mary, d. of Rockye Dolebeere, 7 June."   "1571 Rawkey, s. of Robarte Dolber of Caddhayn, 17 August."   The marriages: "1563 Robert Dolbere of Cadden & Agnes, d. of one Samson, of Hawkechurche, 26 April."   "1602 Rockye Dolber, s. of Robert Dolber of Cadhaine & Marie, d. of John Michell of Barretshaine, 10 October."

As is amply confirmed by records to follow, Mr. Coddington states also that the child Jonathan Gillett, Jr., was the first son; and that Cornelius Gillett was named for his mother's brother, Cornelius Dolbere, and was the second Gillett son.   (See "Colonial Records of Connecticut", Trumbull, 1850, for lists of Windsor men "made free before the Court."   Vol. I, page 297, date 21 May 1657, gives a list of 65 men, and the 5th name is "Jonath: Gillet, Junir."   Page 315, date 20 May 1658, gives 70 names, with the 62nd, "Cornel: Gillet."   Vol. II, page 100, date 8 Oct. 1668 states "Those presented to stand for freemen" of Windsor, has first of 11 names, "Joseph Gillett."   Page 519, date 11 Oct. 1669, freemen of Windsor alphabetically arranged under initial capital letter, one name below another, under "G" has: "Jonathan Gillet, Senr.—Nathan Gillet—Jonathan Gillet, Jr.—Cornelius Gillet—Josep Gillet.")   Jonathan, Jr., was admitted to the Windsor Church 6 April 1662; Cornelius, 16 Jan. 1665-6.   The order of ages is shown also by the father's 1677 will in listing legacies.   (See "Early Connecticut Probate Records", Manwaring, 1904, vol. I, page 200.)

As was customary in certain regions in old England, Jonathan's youngest son, Josiah, was to continue at home and take care of his mother and own the old home place.   But if Jonathan, Sr., and his wife Mary should both die within four years, his will states, "my son Josiah shall pay some legacies, as to his Brother Jonathan Gillett £4 and a gunn, and to his Brother Cornelius Gillett £4 & to my daughter, Peter Browne's wife, £2, and to my daughter, Samuel ffyllyes wife £2, and to ye two children which I have taken that ware my son Joseph's Dec'd, as ye little son Jonathan £5, and ye garle £5.   My son Jonathan is to have the other 20 acres of Woodland . . . Also Jonathan and Cornelius my sons to have my 11 acres . . . And my son John Gillett to have . . . and Jeremie to have . . ."

There can be no question about Jonathan, Jr., being the oldest son, Cornelius the second, the two married daughters third and fourth, and the deceased son Joseph the fifth child; and that son John was older than son Jeremiah. This is supported by the Windsor records of births and baptisms from 1639, birth of Anna, to 1650, Josiah's baptism.

The fact that the Windsor church record of the birth of Anna or Hannah, 29 Dec. 1639, specifically notes that she was Jonathan Gillett's "first-born in Windsor," seems proof that the entire family was not permanently located in the new town until after the births of the three older children. And the reason might well have been the protective care of the infants. But it is clear that Nathan Gillett went to Windsor in 1636, and remained there, serving in the Pequot War in 1637.

Jonathan Gillett, Sr., died in Windsor 23 Aug. 1677, fifteen days after making his will, and his wife Mary died there 5 Jan. 1685–6, over eight years later, which obviated the payment of legacies by son Josiah. It is important to read the entire will, as well as those of fourteen others of the Gillett family, all to be found in "A Digest of the Early Connecticut Probate Records, Hartford District", 3 volumes, by Charles W. Manwaring, 1904.

What had it meant to Jonathan and Mary Gillett and their seven sons and three daughters to live in New England rather than in Old England? One thing surely, and far the heaviest part of the price, was that not quite two years before Jonathan died they lost their third son, Joseph, aged 34, at the Deerfield, Mass., Bloody Brook Indian massacre: and eight months and a day later, lost their fourth son, Samuel, aged 33, at the Turners Falls, Mass., battle with Indians. Both young men had paid with their lives for going to new settlements along the Connecticut River above the Colony of Connecticut. At a 10 July 1676 meeting of the Connecticut "Councill" (consisting of the Governor, a major, two captains, two "Mr's",), thankfulness was expressed that the people of that Colony have "bountifully" afforded some supply for our brethren in distress in our neighboring "Colonyes", and desire our Windsor brethren to improve what they have gathered of the good people there and that the remainder be distributed to Springfield and those upper towns, "according to the good discretion of Deacon Jnᵒ Moore, John Loomys, Jonath: Gillet, Senʳ and Jacob Drake."

1. JONATHAN ¹ GILLETT (*probably son of Rev. William Gillett*), of England, Dorchester, Mass., and Windsor, Conn., born probably in co. Somerset, England, in 160–, died in Windsor 23 Aug. 1677. He married in Colyton, co. Devon, England, 29 March 1634, MARY DOLBIAR or DOLBERE, bapt. in Colyton 7 June 1607, died in Windsor 5 Jan. 1685–6.

Children:

37

2. i. JONATHAN,[2] b. in Dorchester about 1634–5.
3. ii. CORNELIUS, b. in Dorchester probably about July 1636.
   iii. MARY, b. in Dorchester almost surely in 1638; d. in Windsor 27 Aug. 1719; m. in Windsor, 15 July 1658, PETER BROWNE, b. about 1632, d. in Windsor 9 March 1691–2, aged 60, perhaps son of Peter. 12 children.
   iv. ANNA, b. in Windsor 29 Dec. 1639; d. there 18 Nov. 1711; m. in Windsor, 29 Oct. 1663, SAMUEL FILLEY of Windsor, b. there 24 Sept. 1643, d. 4 Jan. 1711–12, son of William. 10 children.
4. v. JOSEPH, bapt. in Windsor 25 July 1641.
5. vi. SAMUEL, bapt. in Windsor 22 Jan. 1642–3.
6. vii. JOHN, b. in Windsor 5 Oct. 1644.
   viii. ABIGAIL, bapt. in Windsor 28 June 1646; d. in Windsor in 1648.
   ix. JEREMIAH, of Windsor, b. in Windsor 12 Feb. 1647–8; d. in Windsor 1 March 1692–3; m. there, 15 Oct. 1685, DEBORAH BARTLETT of Windsor, b. in Windsor 3 April 1666.
        Children, b. in Windsor:
        1. *Deborah*,[3] b. 6 Aug. 1686; d. in Windsor 22 April 1693.
        2. *Abigail*, b. 21 Feb. 1687–8; d. in Windsor 16 Feb. 1689.
        3. *Jeremiah*, d. in Windsor 21 April 1692.
7. x. JOSIAH, bapt. in Windsor 14 July 1650.

2. JONATHAN[2] GILLETT (*Jonathan*[1]), of Windsor, Conn., according to the family Bible (1599) almost surely born in January 1634–5 or a few days earlier in December 1634, died 27 Feb. 1697–8 (Connecticut Probate Records, Manwaring, vol. 1, p. 557). He married first, in Windsor, 23 April 1661 ANNA KELSEY, born about 1634, died in Windsor 18 April 1676, daughter of William Kelsey of Hartford, Conn.; and secondly, in Windsor, 14 Dec. 1676, MIRIAM DIBBLE of Windsor, born there 19 Feb. 1644–5 and baptized there 7 Dec. 1645, died after May 1703 (according to Connecticut Probate Records, Manwaring, vol. 2, pp. 140, 156 Miriam Gillett was living in May 1700 and later), daughter of Thomas Dibble. In two modern Gillett records there have been errors about the dates of death of Jonathan Gillett and his second wife.

The will of Jonathan[2] Gillett was dated 25 August 1694, and reads in part:

"I Jonathan Gillett of Windsor . . . I give to my son William all my Houseing & Lands lying in the Township of Simsbury, except 5 acres of Marsh lying under the Mountains. I give to my sd son William half my Marsh lying in the Township of Windsor at Wash Brooke which adjoins Simon Drake. I give him 10 acres of Woodland which my Father gave me that abutts south on the land of Thomas Barbour. I give him a Gunn and a Sword. I give to my wife Miriam the benefit of all my Houseing and Lands in Windsor (except what is before given to my son William) until my son Jonathan is 21 years of age, and then ½ of my Houseing and Lands during her natural life. And if she see Cause to marry again I give her £3—10 per annum to be paid her by my son Jonathan, and ⅓ of my Moveable Estate. I give to my son Jonathan all my Houseing and Lands at Windsor (except those given to son William), and also the Land I bought and to have of Father Dibble, he to enter upon ½ of sd houseing and Lands at 21 years of age, and the other half after the decease of my wife. I give to my daughter Mary 10 shillings besides what I have already given her. I give to my daughters Hannah & Miriam, to each of them, ⅓ part of my moveable Estate except 10 shillings to be taken out of their part. Appoint my wife Miriam to be sole Executrix."

38

Witnesses were Henry Wolcott sen. Nathaniel Gillett. Will proven 5 April 1698. Inventory taken by Capt. Timothy Phelps & James Enno. Amount, £360–13–00 Jonathan[1] Gillett, Sr. 1677 inventory, £273–10–00

Probate Records, v. II, p. 140, 17 May 1700: Miriam Gillett, the Relict of Jonathan Gillett request this Court that ½ acre of Land not disposed of by the Will be allotted to her to aid in the Payment of Debts. There being no provision in the Will for the payment of Debts, she, being Executrix, is necessitated to pay them out of her own particular Legacy, (The Court gave her the Land.)

Pobate Records, vol. II, p. 56: Thomas Dibble, Sen., Windsor. Inventory £60–14–01 taken 1 Nov. 1700. Will dated 17 Feb. 1699–1700. "I give to my daughter Miriam Gillett that two acres of meadow she now posseth. Item: To my said daughter Miriam I give, for the use of her son, my best broadcloth coat, hatt and breeches. All the rest of my apparrel to be divided, two parts to my sons Samuel and Thomas, the other part to be to my grandsons Josiah Dibble and Wakefield Dibble. I appoint Mr. John Eliot and son-in-law Samuel Gibbs to be executors."

Children by first wife, born in Windsor:

i. MARY,[3] b. 5 April 1665; d. by 1667.
ii. MARY, b. 21 Oct. 1667; d. in Windsor 19 August 1734; m. (1) by 1689 JACOB BISSELL; m. (2) 30 June 1698 SERGT. PETER BUELL of Simsbury, Conn.
iii. JONATHAN, b. 18 Feb. 1670; d. in Windsor 1 Sept. 1683.
iv. WILLIAM, of Windsor and Simsbury, b. 4 Dec. 1673; d. in Simsbury 27 Jan. 1718–19; m. in Simsbury, 14 Sept. 1699, MARY SAXTON (SEXTON) of Simsbury, b. in Simsbury 4 May 1673. She m. (2) in Simsbury, 22 June 1721, Jonathan Holcomb of Simsbury. Children, b. in Simsbury:
    1. *William*,[4] b. 1 Sept. 1700; d. 16 July 1736 or 1737 (Simsbury record).
    2. *Jonathan*, b. 1 Oct. 1701; d. in Simsbury 7 Jan. 1719.
    3. *Mary*, b. 29 Feb. 1702–3; d. in Simsbury 23 Nov. 1760, aged 58; m. in Simsbury, 20 Oct. 1726, David Eno, b. in 1702, d. in 1745, son of James Eno.
    4. *Richard*, b. in 1705; d. in Simsbury 3 Jan. 1719.
    5. *Eunice*, d. in Simsbury 24 May 1740; m. there, 3 Dec. 1728, David Gaines. 7 children.

Children by second wife, born in Windsor:

v. THOMAS, b. 31 May 1678; d. 11 June 1678.
vi. EBENEZER, b. 28 Oct. 1679; d. 17 Dec. 1680.
vii. SAMUEL, b. 18 Dec. 1680; d. young (not mentioned in his father's will or in the settlement of the estate).
viii. HANNAH, b. 18 Sept. 1682; m. in Hartford, Conn., 23 April 1702, JOHN ANDREWS of Hartford, son of John Andrews.
8. ix. JONATHAN, b. 15 Oct. 1685.
x. MIRIAM, b. 14 March 1688.

3. CORNELIUS [2] GILLETT (*Jonathan* [1]), of Windsor, Conn., born in Dorchester, Mass., probably about July 1636, died in Windsor 26 June 1711. He married, before 1658, PRISCILLA KELSEY, who died in Windsor 7 Jan. 1722–3, sister of Jonathan [2] Gillett's first wife, Mary Kelsey, and daughter of William Kelsey of Hartford, Conn.

In the Connecticut Probate Records, Manwaring, vol. II, page 205: Cornelius Gillett Sen., Windsor. Inventory £44–07–06. Taken 27 July 1711, by Samuel Moore and John Palmer. The children, Priscilla, Abigail, Cornelius, Mary, Hester, Sarah, Joanna and Daniel. Will

dated 2nd June 1711. "I, Cornelius Gillett, Sen., of Windsor, do make
. . . My will is that after my debts and funeral expenses be paid, all my
personal or moveable estate shall be and remain to my wife Priscilla for
her use and to her own dispose as she shall see cause, which I do give
her as her own. Whereas, I have made over my lands by deed of gift,
excepting 4 acres at Wash Brook and 2 acres now in possession of John
Grimes, my will is that whereas my son-in-law Joseph Phelps is become
surety for my son Cornelius for a debt which he owes to Capt. Timothy
Thrall, that the sd 4 acres of marsh at Wash Brook shall be and remain
to my son Joseph Phelps and to his heirs and assigns forever. And I do
hereby give to him, my sd. son Joseph Phelps, also, the 2 acres of land in
John Grimes possession. And I appoint my wife executrix. (Signed)
Cornelius Gillett, Sen. Witnesses: John Moore, Sarah Enno. Will
proven 3 Sept. 1711."

Children, born in Windsor:

i. PRISCILLA,[3] b. 22 Jan. 1659; d. by 1661.
ii. PRISCILLA, b. 30 March 1661; d. after 6 Oct. 1719 (probate record);
   m. by June 1711 JOHN GRIMES (Graham one spelling in 1719).
iii. ABIGAIL, b. 20 Sept. 1663; d. after 17 Jan. 1733, according to the
   will of her second husband; m. (1) in 1687–8, as his second wife,
   DANIEL BIRGE of Windsor, d. 26 Jan. 1697–8, son of Richard
   Birge; m. (2) 11 Feb. 1702–3 JOSEPH LOOMIS of East Windsor,
   son of Joseph Loomis. 3 children by first husband and 2 children
   by second husband.
9. iv. CORNELIUS, b. 15 Dec. 1665.
v. MARY, b. 12 Aug. 1668; d. after June 1711.
vi. HESTER, b. 24 May 1671. (She may have been the Esther Gillett
   who m. in Windsor, 3 Aug. 1705, John Loomis (Loomis Genealogy).)
vii. SARAH, b. in 1673; m. in Windsor, 22 Feb. 1709–10, as his second
   wife, JOSEPH PHELPS, d. in 1716.
viii. JOANNA, b. 22 April 1676; m. (1) by 1703 THOMAS ALLYN of Windsor;
   m. (2) 23 Feb. 1709–10 SAMUEL BANCROFT.
10. ix. DANIEL, b. 30 June 1678.

THE BROTHERS JONATHAN AND NATHAN GILLETT
AND SOME OF THEIR DESCENDANTS

Compiled by ALICE LUCINDA PRIEST, B.L., of Brookline, Mass.

4. JOSEPH[2] GILLETT (*Jonathan*[1]), of Windsor, Conn., and Deerfield,
Mass., baptized in Windsor 25 July 1641, died in Deerfield,
in the tragic warfare at Bloody Brook, 18 Sept. 1675. He
married, probably in Hadley, Mass., in 1663 or 1664, ELIZA-
BETH HAWKES, baptized in Windsor 10 Jan. 1646/7, died
almost surely 1681, daughter of John and Elizabeth Hawkes.
Elizabeth (Hawkes) Gillett married secondly, 16 Dec. 1680,
as his second wife, Nathaniel Dickinson of Hatfield, Mass.

Joseph Gillett was made a freeman in Windwor 8 Oct. 1668 [*] and is again so listed there 11 Oct. 1669. The births of his seven children are recorded there and the deaths of two.

These records indicate the error of statements that Joseph[2] was of Simsbury, Conn., and had nine children; the probable ground for the latter error to be indicated later by a 1686 probate record. While the Windsor birth records of all seven children suggest that the young family did not move to new-town Deerfield until the spring of 1675, Joseph was financially interested in the projective settlement by 1673.

Another erroneous statement is the Joseph Gillett and Elizabeth Hawkes marriage date, and probably the place: "at Windsor 24 Nov. 1664." There is no known Windsor record of the marriage, and Windsor would not have recorded the birth of Joseph's first child, 2 Nov. 1664 [or even 20 Nov. 1664, as one statement has it] if the parents were then not married. Hence the birth record seems to guarantee the marriage by 1664 before 2 Nov.; and it may have been in 1663, but probably not earlier.

Stiles states that John Hawkes' widow sold Windsor lands to their son-in-law Joseph Gillett in 1666, "who probably resided on the Hawkes lands until about 1673 when he removed to Deerfield". Another Windsor record is: "Joseph Gillett, adult, church member 16 (   )".

In 1669 the first house was built in Deerfield; the second house in 1670; and house lots were drawn 14 May 1671. In 1673 at least twenty families were there and at a 7 Nov. 1673 plantation meeting a few over twenty men were present, Joseph Gillet one of them; also Robert Hinsdell (later Hinsdale) and his five sons; and Robert had married (2) Widow Elizabeth Hawkes, and his son had married her daughter Mary Hawkes in 1672 and gone at once to Deerfield with her. Lots No. 31 and 32, drawn 1671 by Robert Hinsdale and Nathaniel Colburne, in 1673 were owned by "Joseph Gillett, son of Jonathan (1), born 1641", and he "built on No. 32 — the Dr. Willard lot; was killed with Capt. Lothrop, Sept. 18, 1675" (Sheldon, "History of Deerfield"). When the lots were sold in 1694 by Joseph Gillett's son, they are described as "Sometime two town lots, 16½ by 72 rods, with a house on it."

In two or three days after Bloody Brook battle, the garrison and inhabitants of Deerfield abandoned the place, and a third village in Hampshire County was given up to desolation. The surviving inhabitants retired to Hatfield and other places.

In 1680 measures were taken for the reoccupation of their lands by the Proprietors of Deerfield, and the spring of 1682 is considered as the date of the permanent settlement. And by the spring of 1682 Joseph Gillett's widow Elizabeth

*Windwor should be Windsor.

41

(Hawkes) was also dead, after having married (2) 16 Dec. 1680, as his second wife, Nathaniel Dickinson of Hatfield, Mass.; and at that date her seven children were all living.

Hampshire County, Mass., Probate Records in Northampton give the following records of the estate of Joseph Gillett: Card Index — Joseph Gillett, Deerfield. Adm., vol. 1, p. 172, year 1676. Inventory, adms., p. 222, year 1682. Ad., Inv., & Dist., p. 257, year 1686.

Page 172, year 1676:

John Hawks presented to this Corte ye Inventory of ye Estate of Joseph Gillit deceased to wch he mad Oath wch Inventory is on ffile with the Recorder of this Corte & Power of administration upon ye Estate of Joseph Gillit Deceased is by this Corte Granted to Elizabeth Gillit the Relict.

Here followeth a copy of ye Inventory of ye Estate of Joseph Gillitt deceased [Inventory difficult to read in the opening part of list of stock, tools, etc. It includes: cow, yearling, young mare: and "due from Eldr Strong 20 due from Caaleb Pomery"]

Above Inventory taken by Quimtan Stockwell
Samll Billing

Sum total 010 — 09 — 00

There is Likewise belonging to this Estate, Land at Deerfield viz two homelotts & Land in ye meadows vallued at 8 Comons.

Debts due from ye Estate 02 — 12 — 00

Page 222, Adms. on Jos. Gillett Estate, April 18, 1682. Nathaniel Dickinson of Hatfield (appearing before magistrates Pynchon & [?] both Assistants of this Jurisdiction & a clerk present — desiring power of administration upon ye Estate of Joseph Gillitt sometyme of deerfield dedeased whose Widdow or Relict sd Dickinson had married & in her Right was administrator to sd Estate, wch ceased at sd Widdow's death, and it being needful to conserve same for his Children sd Dickinson desiring of it. — Granted.

Page 257 — Settlement Estate Joseph Gillett 1686.

Dist. — March 30, 1686 — Additional inventory, of clothes etc. presented by Nathaniel Dickinson, who stated after her marriage to him, the widow of Joseph Gillett "soon after died" . . "the sd Nathaniel Dickinson shewing himself faithful to his trust & also to settled sd children in some comfortable way and there being 4 sons and two daughters" . . eldest son Joseph Gillett, to have a double part, and to have the land for his use till his brothers came of age. Court orders Nathaniel Dickinson, Joseph Barnard & Thomas Wells to make the division.

As Windsor death records show, the youngest child, Hannah,[3] had died 11 Aug. 1683; and Jonathan,[3] second of the four sons referred to in the above probate record, died the following 3rd of June 1686. But there is nowhere suggestion of the deaths of the two older sisters, Elizabeth[3] and Mary,[3] and they were doubtless the "two daughters" of their stepfather's statement; not any imaginary and almost impossible two daughters younger than the Hannah[3] for whom Barbour's Collection gives the birth records of June 30, 1674 and Jan. 30, 1674 (1674-5). There are three records for Joseph's birth, one making it Nov. 2 and two making it Nov. 20; and two different records for sister Mary, one Sept. 1 and the other Sept. 10, 1667.

Children, born in Windsor:

11. i.   Joseph,[3] b. 2 Nov. 1664.
      ii.   Elizabeth, b. 12 June 1666; living 30 March 1686.
     iii.   Mary, b. 10 Sept. 1667; living 30 March 1686.
     iv.   Jonathan, b. 11 Aug. 1669; d. in Windsor 3 June 1686.
12. v.   John, b. 10 June 1671.
13. vi.   Nathaniel, b. 4 May 1673.
     vii. Hannah, b. 30 Jan. 1675; d. in Windsor 11 Aug. 1683.

5. Samuel[2] Gillett (*Jonathan*[1]), of Windsor, Conn., and Hatfield, Mass., baptized in Windsor 22 Jan. 1642/3, slain in the Turners Falls, Mass., fight 19 May 1676. He married in Hadley, Mass., 23 Sept. 1668, Hannah Dickinson of Wethersfield, Conn., and Hadley, Mass., born in Wethersfield 6 Dec. 1648, died after 1687, daughter of Sergt. John Dickinson. She married secondly, in Hatfield, 15 May 1677, Stephen Jennings of Hatfield.

On 19 Sept. 1677 Hannah (Dickinson) Gillett Jennings was captured with two of her Gillett children and fourteen others by Indians. She was taken to Canada, rescued by the heroic work of her husband and others and reached home again about June 1678 with her two Gillett children and her new born daughter of March 1678, Captivity Jennings.

Children, born in Hatfield:

        Hannah,[3] b. 20 Sept. 1669; burned to death in February 1671.
     ii.   Mary, b. 20 Dec. 1671.
14. iii. Samuel, b. 14 May 1673.
     iv.   Hannah, b. 5 Sept. 1674; d. after 1742; m. in Hadley or Hatfield, 9 Feb. 1694, John Taylor of Hatfield and South Hadley, son of John Taylor.

("Genealogies of Hadley Families Embracing the Early Settlers of the Towns of Hatfield, South Hadley, Amherst and Granby", by L. M. Boltwood, 1862. The 1863 Hadley History; 1910 Hatfield History.)

6. John[2] Gillett (*Jonathan*[1]), of Windsor, Conn., born there 5 Oct. 1644, died in 1682, shortly before the Dec. 5th inventory of his estate. He married in Windsor, 8 July 1669, Mercy Barber, baptized there 12 Oct. 1651, died in Suffield, Conn., 29 March 1725. Mercy (Barber) Gillett married secondly, in Windsor, 14 June 1683, Capt. George Norton of Suffield.

Children, born in Windsor:

      i.   Thomas,[3] b. 7 Jan. 1671; d. by 1676.
      ii.   John, b. 6 Aug. 1673; d. unm. in Windsor 4 July 1699.
15. iii. Thomas, b. 18 July 1676.
16. iv. Samuel, b. 16 Feb. 1677/8.
      v.   Nathaniel, b. 3 Oct. 1680 and bapt. in Hartford, Conn., 30 Oct. 1681 (last record of his name).
17. vi. Benjamin, b. in 1680 [?]; named in 5 Dec. 1682 probate as John's son, aged two years.
         No Nathaniel was included among John's children in the 1682 probate. Was there a change or error in names and Benjamin became the permanent name; or twins and Nathaniel died?

vii. MERCY, b. 30 Jan. 1682; m. in Suffield, 24 Dec. 1702, SERGT. JACOB ADAMS of Suffield, son of Jacob Adams.

("Robert Adams Genealogy", by Adams, 1900. "Connecticut Probate Records", Manwaring, vol. 1, p. 307: Gillett, John, Windsor. Inventory £140 — 14 — 06. Taken 5 Dec. 1682 by John Loomis sen. & John Moore. Legatees: The Widow, Mercy Gillett, John age 9 years, Thomas 6, Samuel 5, Benjamin 2, Mercy born 30 January last. Court Record, p. 69: 4 April 1683. Adms. to the Widow, Mercy Gillett, with Jonathan Gillett, Peter Browne, John Barber, & Samuel Barber to be Overseers.)

7. JOSIAH² GILLETT (*Jonathan*¹), of Windsor and Colchester, Conn., born in Windsor and baptized there 14 July 1650, died in Colchester 29 Oct. 1736. He married in Windsor, 30 June 1676, JOANNA TAINTOR, born in April 1657, died in Colchester 23 Jan. 1735, daughter of Michael Taintor of Branford, Conn.

He moved to Colchester in 1702, being one of the first settlers.

Children, born in Windsor:

18. i. JOSIAH,³ b. 24 Nov. 1678.
ii. JOANNA, b. 28 Oct. 1680; m. in Windsor, 5 Jan. 1698, JOSIAH STRONG of Windsor. They moved to Colchester in 1703. 13 children. (Strong Genealogy, 1871.)
iii. ELIZABETH, b. 16 Jan. 1682; d. 10 May 1756.
19. iv. GEN. JONATHAN, b. 28 June 1685.
v. MARY, b. 8 March 1687; m. 13 June 1706 DEA. NATHANIEL SKINNER.
vi. DOROTHY, b. 15 April 1689; m. —— ROBERTS.
20. vii. SAMUEL, b. 1 Oct. 1690.
viii. JOSEPH, b. 8 March 1695.
ix. MINDWELL, b. 4 Feb. 1696/7; d. 8 May 1784; m. —— CLARK.
x. AARON of Colchester, b. 8 March 1699; d. in Boston 30 Nov. 1730; m. in Colchester, 10 July 1728, HANNAH CLARK. Hannah (Clark) Gillett m. (2) in Simsbury, Conn., 15 July 1738, Joseph Chamberlain, Jr.
Child:
1. *Hannah*,⁴ "daughter and only heir of Aaron Gillett" (probate record), b. in 1729; d. in Colchester 29 June 1759, aged 30; m. in Colchester, 11 June 1749, Lemuel Storrs. 5 children, b. in Colchester. (Storrs Genealogy, 1866.)
xi. NOAH, merchant, b. 5 Dec. 1701; m. by 1734 ABIGAIL ——, d. 2 March. 1739.
Children:
1. *Abigail*,⁴ bapt. 15 Oct. 1734.
2. *Noah*, d. 2 March 1739.

8. JONATHAN³ GILLETT (*Jonathan*,² *Jonathan*¹), of Windsor, Conn., born there 15 Oct. 1685, died after 21 Oct. 1735. He married, 18 Nov. 1707 (Windsor record), RUTH SEARLE, of Northampton, Mass., born there 17 Dec. 1681, daughter of John Searle.

Children, born in Windsor:

i. JONATHAN,⁴ b. 26 July 1708; d. 5 Sept. 1708.
ii. DAVID (twin), b. 5 July 1711; d. 14 Aug. 1711.
21. iii. JONATHAN (twin), b. 5 July 1711.

9. CORNELIUS[3] GILLETT (*Cornelius,*[2] *Jonathan*[1]), of Windsor, Conn., except for brief periods in Lebanon and Windham, Conn., born in Windsor 15 Dec. 1665, died there 5 Sept. 1746. He married first, by 1693, perhaps ELIZABETH ————, who died after the birth of her second child 11 March 1695/6; and secondly, probably by 1701/2, DEBORAH ROWELL, born in Simsbury, Conn., 5 Jan. 1683, died in Windsor 29 Sept. 1746, "aged about 74" (Wintonbury Parish record), daughter of Thomas Rowell of Simsbury and Windsor.

He was connected also with the important parish in the town of Windsor established in 1736 and named Wintonbury Parish that ultimately became the town of Bloomfield. The church was organized in February 1738 with 67 members, Cornelius Gillet (fifth name) and wife among them.

Conn. Probate Records, Manwaring, vol. III, p. 554: Cornelius Gillett, Windsor. Invt. £616 — 17 — 05, taken by Robert Barnet, John Loomis, Nathaniel Cole. Will dated 23 August 1746: "I, Cornelius Gillet of Windsor do make this my last will and testament: I give to my son Benjamin Gillet all my real estate. I give to my son Cornelius Gillet 10 shillings old tenor." [Followed by eight duplicate sentences in words and bequest except for the names of the five other living sons and of the three living daughters. The names, in order, are, sons: Daniel, Samuel, Thomas, Jonathan, David. Daughters: Elizabeth Matson, Deborah Talcott, Phebe Gillet.] The will continues: "And the rest of the moveable estate I leave to the disposal of my loving wife and my son Benjamin Gillet. I appoint my son Jonathan Gillet and my son Benjamin Gillet to be executors." (Sgd.) Cornelius Gillet. Witness: Samuel Rowell, Daniel Rowell, Robert Barnet. Court Record. 3 March 1746-7 The last will . . of Cornelius Gillet, late of Windsor . . exhibited by Benjamin Gillet . . proven. Page 125. 3 April 1750: Deborah Gillet, the widow and relict of Cornelius Gillet, now moves . . her right of dower to be set out to her. Court appoints Lt. Solomon Park, Alexander Hoskins and Stephen Goodwin, in Wintonbury Parish, to set out 1 –3 of the land and buildings of the sd decd for her improvement during life.

Children by first wife:

i.   CORNELIUS,[4] b. in Windsor in 1693; d. 23 Oct. 1758, aged about 67 (Wintonbury Parish record).

22. ii.   DANIEL, b. in Windsor 11 March 1695/6.

Children by second wife:

iii.   SAMUEL, b. in Windsor 19 March 1702/3.

iv.   THOMAS, b. in Windsor 1 Aug. 1705.

v.   ELIZABETH, b. in Windsor 31 May 1707; m. ———— MATSON.

vi.   DEBORAH, b. in Windsor 28 Feb. 1708/9; d. in Bolton, Conn., 19 March 1795, in 81st year; m. in Bolton, 1 Dec. 1737, BENJAMIN TALCOTT.

vii.   PHEBE (probably), her father's will the only known record.

viii.   STEPHEN, b. in Windsor 30 June 1713; d. in February 1746, a soldier in the Louisburg expedition; m. 21 Sept. 1738 ANNE LOOMIS (Wintonbury Parish record). Anne (Loomis) Gillett m. (2) in Wintonbury, 11 Sept. 1750, Isaac Fosbury of Sheffield

Children, b. in Windsor (Wintonbury Parish record):

1.   *Stephen,*[5] b. 1 Nov. 1738; d. 23 Oct. 1741.

2.   *Asaph,* bapt. 15 Feb. 1741; d. in October 1741.

3.   *Stephen,* bapt. 24 Oct. 1742; d. 14 July 1745.

4.   *Anne,* bapt. 4 Aug. 1745.

23. ix. JONATHAN, b. in Lebanon 5 July 1716. Town records in Barbour
          Collection.
     x.   DAVID, b. in Lebanon 1 March 1720.
24. xi. BENJAMIN, b. in Windham 25 July 1722.
    xii. MARY, b. in Windham 22 Jan. 1726/7; d. 27 Feb. 1726/7.

10. DANIEL[3] GILLETT (*Cornelius*,[2] *Jonathan*[1]), of Windsor, Conn.,
    born there 30 June 1678, died 16 Aug. 1753, aged 75. He
    married in Windsor, 28 Jan. 1702/3, MARY ENO, born in
    Windsor 12 Oct. 1682, died there 7 Dec. 1773, aged 91
    (Windsor gravestone records), daughter of John Eno.

    Children, born in Windsor:

     i.   DANIEL,[4] b. 17 Nov. 1703; d. 12 Nov. 1769, aged 66 (Windsor
          gravestone); m. 6 Jan. 1726 ANNA FILLEY, born in Windsor 23
          Sept. 1708, d. 11 Dec. 1795, aged 88 (Windsor gravestone), daugh-
          ter of Jonathan Filley.
              Children, b. in Windsor:
              1. *Anna*,[5] b. 13 Dec. 1726; m. in Windsor, 9 Nov. 1744, Gideon
                 Barber, son of John Barber.
              2. *Daniel*, b. 26 Jan. 1728/9; d. 25 April 1743, in 15th year.
              3. *Shuball*, b. in 1731/2; d. 19 July 1744, in 13th year.
     ii. MARY, b. 9 July 1705; m. 23 Dec. 1725 ANTHONY HOSKINS, JR., of
          Windsor.
25. iii. JOHN, b. 11 Sept. 1707.
     iv. ANN, b. 12 March 1710/11; m. SAMUEL BARBER.
     v.   EUNICE, b. 21 Feb. 1716/17; m. in Harwinton, Conn., 7 Feb. 1737/8,
          ISAAC BULL, "ancestor of Dr. Isaac Bull of Hartford" (Torring-
          ton, Conn., History, 1878).
     vi. HANNAH, b. 21 Dec. 1719; m. THOMAS MOORE.
     vii. MARGARET, b. 31 Dec. 1723; m. 24 April 1746 TIMOTHY PHELPS of
          Windsor.
    viii. DOROTHY, b. 15 May 1726; m. 25 Nov. 1747 SAMUEL COOK of
          Windsor.

THE BROTHERS JONATHAN AND NATHAN GILLETT
AND SOME OF THEIR DESCENDANTS

Compiled by ALICE LUCINDA PRIEST, B.L., of Brookline, Mass.

11. LIEUT. JOSEPH[3] GILLETT (*Joseph*,[2] *Jonathan*[1]), of Deerfield,
Mass., and Hartford, Conn., West Division, born in Windsor, Conn., 2 Nov. 1664, died shortly before the Hartford
4th March 1745/6 inventory of his estate. He married first
in Hatfield, Mass., 3 Nov. 1687, the day after he was 23,
ESTHER GULL, born in Hadley, Mass., 21 Nov. 1665, the
third of the four daughters of William and Elizabeth (Smith)
(Foote) Gull of Hatfield (the bride's father was the half
brother of the bridegroom's stepfather, Nathaniel Dickinson,
on their mother's side); and secondly, in Hartford, 17 May
1692, MARY GRISWOLD, born in Windsor, Conn., 16 March
1671, died in Hartford 19 Dec. 1719, daughter of Joseph and
Mary (Gaylord) Griswold and granddaughter of Dea. Edward Griswold. The only known record of Joseph[3] Gillett's
third marriage is in his 9 July 1743 will that begins: "I give
to Elizabeth, my wife, all that estate that she brought with
her when she became my wife, and", etc., which suggests
that she may have been a widow. There is no known reference to her in the settlement of the estate.

Henry R. Stiles in his 1892 Ancient Windsor, Conn., History
and Genealogies (vol. 2, pp. 297–9), gave two compact pages
to an account of a Revolutionary War patriot who suffered
imprisonment in New York City, Jonathan Gillett. But
stated: "Jonathan of West Hartford is one whom we have
failed to connect with the main line; but he evidently belonged to the Windsor Gillettes, and is worthy of commem-
oration in these pages. We therefore reproduce here the
substance of what has been told about him in a little pri-
vately printed volume entitled 'Letters from the Prisons
and Prison-Ships of the Revolution', by Henry R. Stiles,
M.D., issued in 1865, in a limited edition of 80 copies."

The mainspring for this present Gillett record was the
line of the above Lieut. Joseph[3] Gillett, who is now proved
to have been the grandfather (through his second son,
Jonathan[4]) of the Revolutionary War Jonathan Gillett.
And since this is the first printed record of the line, and,
partly, of the descendants of two other sons of Joseph[2] and
Elizabeth (Hawkes) Gillett, the detailed proof of the record
is important.

It is doubtful whether Joseph[3] got back to Deerfield with
the permanent settlement of the spring of 1682, since he was

then only 17½ years old. Notice that it was 30 March 1686, the spring after he reached 21, that the probating of his father's estate was concluded. The court then directed that the "eldest son, Joseph Gillett," should have a double part and have the land for his use till his brothers came of age. In line with new settlement methods, Deerfield Proprietors made the following grants to Joseph, as heir of his father: in 1686, 50 acres at Boggy Meadow: 5 Feb. 1686-7, 19 rods, 4 ft., 6 in. in the Common Field (probably the customary "wanting land" to rectify deficiencies in lot areas): 20 April 1688, wood land, lot No. 30: wood lot on the Mountain, No. 45. 1685 — 90 grants of home lots at a new street at Wapping were made to a harmonious group of young men, Joseph[3] Gillett one of them. (Sheldon's Deerfield History.)

Springfield, Mass., Hall of Records: Deeds, vol. H. page 491: — 20 December 1690, John Stebbins and Benoni Stebbins deed to Joseph Gillet, all three of "Dearfield," the following property there; partly "in exchange for other Land in Dearfield already passed over to sd John and Benoni" and "discharge sd Gillet from any further payment." "One House lot Situate within Township of Dearfield" "A butting on the Town Street Westerly & on an highway Easterly. Bounded by an Houselot formerly Sam[ll] Hinsdells Deceas[d], Northerly and on another Lot of sd Hinsdells Southerly containing by Estimation Four acres and a half." The body of the deed also asserted that John Stebbins' wife Dorothy fully assented, but the signatures were only those of John Stebbins and Benoni Stebbins. Witnesses: Joseph Goddard, Edward Goddard. The two signatures were acknowledged April 1st 169(probably 2). And the Deed was "Rec[d] Jan[y] 15th 1735/6 and Recorded from the Originall."

In England in January 1630, Anna[1], widow of Williama[*] Gull, Sr., married secondly Nathaniel[1] Dickinson, Sr., when her son was probably less than two years old. This Dickinson family came to New England about 1634; were prominently of Wethersfield, Conn., until 1659, by which time there were nine Dickinson sons and two daughters. They moved with a religious group to Hadley, Mass., where prominent Deacon Nathaniel[1] Dickinson died 16 June 1676. He made his will 29 May 1676, and in it states: "To my son William Gull (Son of his wife by her first husband) I give that Three Pounds which he oweth me for a barrell of pork." He gave part of a certain meadow to all his sons and two daughters, to be shared equally; and adds in the will: "The desire of ye testator is yt ye share given unto Frances Dickinson (younger daughter), may, if she see meet, be given to Samuel Gillett's children." The mother of Samuel[2] Gillett's children, Hannah[3] Dickinson, was the oldest child of Frances[2] Dickinson's oldest brother, Sergeant John[2] Dickinson, who also died at the 19 May 1676 Turners Falls battle. (Northampton, Hampshire Co. Probate Records)

William[2] Gull made his will 12 April 1701 (Northampton, vol. 3, pp. 83-4). Bequest: "I give & bequeath to my Loveing Grandchild Eliza-

*Williama should be William.

beth the daughter of my Loving daughter Hesther deceased sometyme wife to Joseph Gillet my Lot in ye Meadow commonly called the great meadows in Hatfield cont by estm. Five [Sixe?] acres." Boundaries on John Wells; Hope Atherton, dec'd; highway east; pond west. Also 3 acres after decease of his wife, Elizabeth. Executors: "my Loveing Kinsman Sam^{ll} Partrigg" Sen (?) or (S ?) & his wife. 18 Dec. 1701(vol. 3, p. 85) concerns the settlement of William Gull's estate. It includes a notice of a 4 July 1690 agreement of William Gull's children "about mother Gulls' est." "July 4, 1690 agree. Gull ch. Sgd." by the following, one name below another, in this order: Robert R Bardwell his Marck, Mary X Bardwell her Marck, Jonathan Root, Anna L Root her Marck, Joseph Gillett, Hester X Gillit her Marcke, Mercy X Gull her marcke. Witness: Daniel White Sam'll Partrigg. There is also a notation: "Nath^{ll} Foote of Weathersfield Exonerates his ffather W Gull of Hatfield 19 Jan. 1686." Inventory lists: "this given to Elizabeth Gillit."

Hampshire Co. Mass. Deeds, Springfield: vol. C, p. 582. Date 25 Aug. 1714. Ebenezer Marsh of Hatfield, Weaver, deeds to Henry Dwight of Hatfield for 25 pounds — "A certain Parcell of land In Hatfield aforesd In the Great Meadow Containing 5 acres (which was formerly William Gull's land)." Boundaries: North, Samuel Dickinson; South, John Well; East on the Great River; West on ye Great Pond. . . . & Elizabeth Marsh, wife, . . . joins. (Sgd.) Ebenezer Marsh Elizabeth X Marsh her mark. 25 Aug. 1714 ackn. by both. Recorded 16 April 1720.

The last known record of Esther[3] (Gull) Gillett is her signature to the probate paper of 4 July 1690. And her father in his will of 10½ years later names only one living child as hers. She died either in the latter part of 1690 or in 1691; almost surely in a home on Town Street, Deerfield, where her husband bought lot 41 in 1690.* Wapping settlement was broken up by "the rough hand of war." Also Joseph[3] Gillett and his brother John[3], and probably young soldier brother Nathaniel[3], became connected with Deerfield garrison. In 1696 Joseph was corporal in that garrison; and was participant in the 16 July 1698 Indian pursuit, usually styled the Promroy Pursuit, as "Corporal gillit" of the 16 Garrison Soldiers at Deerfield, to whom the Mass. General Court granted each an extra £1. (Sheldon, and Mass. Archives). Sept. 16, 1696 brother John[3] Gillett had been captured by the Indians there in Deerfield, and taken to Canada and finally sent to France; and after peace was declared, reached home by 17 June 1698. In 1691, as will be shown in a 17 June 1722 deed, Joseph Gillett sold 20 acres in Deerfield Boggy meadow to John and Benoni Stebbins of Deerfield.

The oldest child of Joseph[3] and Mary (Griswold) Gillett is on the Windsor birth records; but not the next child, and considering the record of Joseph's purchases of land in Hartford it seems probable he was born there. The General Index, Land Records of Hartford, Conn., 1639–1839, pub. 1873, gives the following: Joseph Gillet as Grantee, pages 203–4: From Samuel Sedgwick, 1694 Dec. 10 (vol. 1, p. 134).

---

*Lot 41, Daniel Fisher. John Stebbins bought it about 1688. His sons John and Benoni Stebbins sell to Joseph Gillett in 1690. Timothy Nash held it after 1699.

From S. Hopkins, 1695 April 24. From Samuel Sedgwick, warrantee, 1701 May 9. Also 1705 Feb. 20. Also 1721 Dec. 19. Joseph Gillett, distribution, 1754 Feb. 18 (vol. 8, p. 6).

1892 History Second Church of Hartford, Conn., founded 1670, by Parker: p. 294, Dec. 8, 1700, No. 177, Joseph Gillet rec'd. Baptisms of children of Joseph Gillet: Mary, 1699 Dec. 31, "daughter Goodm. Gillet." Esther, 1701 April 27 "ye daughter Joseph Gillett." Hannah, 1702 Oct. 18. Sarai, 1704 Oct. 4. Abigail, 1705 Sept. 30. Dorothy, 1710 Jan. 21.

Third Church of Hartford founded 1713, in that part of town that in 1854 was incorporated as West Hartford, and Joseph Gillett was one of the original members. In 1717 Joseph Gillet, Jr. and wife joined. In 1735 Jonathan Gillet and his sister "Mrs." Dorotha Gillet. In 1755 Jonathan Gillet: in 1759 Asa Gillet: in 1761 Mrs. Asa Gillet: in 1776 Mrs. Jonah Gillet.

THE REGISTER, vol. xiii., year 1859, p. 239: Hartford, Conn. Records — Births, Marriages, Deaths: From Book lettered "Records of Town of Hartford, 1685–1709, No. 1" Transcribed by Lucius M. Boltwood of Amherst. Cor. Member of the N. E. H. G. Society. The records arranged under A — B — C etc. Evidently condition of old book such that much could not be deciphered with accuracy; and so left blank. Under G at lower part of page 240 was a double column, the one on the right side as follows:

Joseph Gillet
    born May 17
Jona was born
Mary was born
Ester was born Ma(
Hanah was born Nov
Sarah was born Sept 30
Abigail was born Aug. 9
    [top of page 241]
Matthew was born March 4th   Dorothy was born Jan. 1710

Taking the above in connection with the 1743 will of Joseph Gillett of Hartford, and the baptisms of his and Mary's six daughters, it is apparent that here is a record of the order of births of the three sons and six daughters of Joseph and Mary (Griswold) Gillett, entered on a Hartford town book. Why the son Matthew, born between his sisters Abigail and Dorothy, has no baptismal record can only be surmised as perhaps due to infant ill health, or that the baptismal record was overlooked or not clear. The town record must have been together, in one place, and so seemingly reported for record at one time; and if so, after the birth of Dorothy in 1710. This could account for a most probably error in the month of Hannah's birth, "Nov.", since she was bapt. Oct. 18. And if the son Joseph was born May 17 (date of the parents' marriage) then the son Joseph born Feb. 16, 1692 (1692/3) in Windsor to Joseph Gillett (almost surely Joseph[3]) must have died young. A confusion of family dates seems more probable. The son Matthew was doubtless named for his mother's brother, Matthew Griswold. Joseph[2] Griswold made his will 6 Sept. 1716, inventory taken 29 Nov. (Manwaring, vol. II.), and bequeaths to his three sons and " To my daughters, Mary, the wife of Joseph Gillette, and Abigail, the wife of Josiah Phelps, 25 pounds apiece out of moveables. I give to my grandchild Sarah Gillette 5 pounds out of my moveables."

Colonial Records of Connecticut, by Charles J. Hoadley, Librarian State Library, pub. 1870, vol. 5, p. 432; date 1714 May. "This Assembly do establish and confirm Mr. Joseph Gillet of Hartford to be Ensign of the company or trainband at the west division in the town of Hartford, aforesaid, and that he be commissioned accordingly." Vol. 6, p. 184, date 1720 May. "This Assembly do establish and confirm Mr. Joseph Gillet of Hartford to be Lieutenant of the compny or trainband at the West Division in the town of Hartford aforesaid and order he be commissioned accordingly." Vol. 7, p. 381, date 1732 May. "Upon the memorial of Samuel Sedgwick, Joseph Gillett and William Gaylord, of Hartford, committee for the west society in Hartford, praying that a tract of land in Farmington . . . may be annesed to the said society. Resolved by the Assembly, that the inhabitants . . . shall be assessed to the suport of the gospel in the said west parish in Hartford."

In connection with the military services of Joseph,[3] John,[3] and Nathaniel[3] Gillett, note that their mother's oldest brother, who helped about her husband's estate, was Sergeant John[2] Hawks of Deerfield; and a nephew was Colonel John[3] Hawks, "the Hero of Fort Massachusetts".

Hampshire County, Mass., Deeds, Springfield, Court House, vol. D, p. 151, Joseph Gillett grantor. Joseph Gillett of Hartford, Connecticut, yeoman (Did in the year: 1691) for many good causes; Especially in Consideration of a homelott Scituate in Deerfield Sell & Convey unto John & Benoni Stebbins both of Deerfield . . . A certain parcel of land Scituate In the Township of Deerfield — in a Place Commonly Called Boggy meadow, or boggy meadow plaine Containing Twenty acres in Equal halves Between ye sd John & Benoni Stebbins, John Stebbins to have ye North Side & Benoni Stebbins the South, as it is bounded on land of Peter Evans North and land formerly the sd Joseph Gilletts; South butting on ye Common field fence west, on the long hill East, and whereas ye Deed of Conveyance of sd land to sd John & Benoni Stebbins Cannot be found the above Joseph Gillett hath by these presence (Sgd) ye Seaventh Day of June 1722 — Joseph Gillett & Seale [Notice no wife joins]. Wit.: Jonathan Wells, Warham Williams. Hampshire Deerfield June 7, 1722 Joseph Gillett ye Sub. personally appe — & ackn. — before Jonathan Wells J. P. Rec'd 28 Aug. 1722.

Vol. B, page 30. Indexed: Joseph Gillett as Grantee, year 1700 July 16. To all Christian People: - - Samuel Carter of the towne of Deerfield, in the County of West Hampshire - - in consideration of a valuable sum of money, & Estate to me, paid & Delivered by Joseph Jillet of the Towne of Hartford In the County of Hartford within the Colony of Connecticut - - to Joseph Gillet grantor. Joseph Gillet, Have Sold - Two Certain peices, or parcels of land Scituate In the Township of Deerfield. That is to say One parcel of upland which was sometime Two Homelotts, Containing, and being by Estimation — Seven ackers, and One Rood — & is abutting Northward on land of Thomas Allisem Southward on land belonging to Thomas French, Eastward on a hill, on Common land, and Westward on a highway and also one other peice or parcel of land lying In the great Meadow Containing by Estimation ten acres - - & is abutting Northward on land belonging to John Catlin, Southward on land belonging to Mahuma Hinsdell, Eastward on an highway & Westward on the River there, and also all and singular the Messuages houses, buildings — edifices Easements profits, privileges, and appointments whatsoever, with the fruits & advantages - -

Provided: That if the sd Sam^ll Carter pay to said Joseph Jillet his heirs or assynes att the dwelling house of the said Joseph Jillet In Hartford - - twenty pounds of Currant silver money of New England on or before the last day of Sep^t next Ensuing the day of the date hereof without fraud. That then above Conveyance shall be void Sam^ll Carter set my hand in Hartford the Sixteenth day of July 1700

his
Sam^ll X Carter
mark

Wit.: Joseph Allin   John Smith
Francis Whitmore   Caleb Stanley Junr

Personally ackn at Hartford 16 July 1700 — Before me, John Haynes, J. P.
On the 27th day of Novr 1700 This Deed was Received Into the Registers Office, and was here Registered from the Original   P John Pynchon
Conn. Probate Records, Manwaring, vol. III, pp. 554–6: Gillet, Joseph, Gentleman, Hartford.   Inventory £2246 plus.   Taken 4 March 1745/6, by David Ensign, Jonathan Sedgwick, Moses Nash.
Also some real estate at Deerfield, in the county of Hampshire and Province of Massachusetts Bay £100.   Taken 1 April 1746, by Elijah Williams, Benjamin Mun and John Catlin.   Will dated 9 July 1743.
I, Joseph Gillet of Hartford do make this my last will and testament: I give to Elizabeth, my wife, all that estate that she brought with her when she became my wife, and one cow, to be at her dispose forever. Further, I give to my wife, during the time she remains my widow, the free use of ½ of the house I now live in, and also the use of 5 acres of land in my west division lott on the east side of the highway, and the use of half of my land on the west side of the highway, and the use of an iron pott and brass kettle, during the term that she remains my widow. I give to my son Joseph Gillet the dwelling house he now lives in and all that part of my west division lott that lyes on the east side of the highway, and also the one moity or half my sd. lott on the west side of sd. highway, being the north side, to be laid out as not to interfere on my tan houses and fats, which I reserve for the heirs of my son Jonathan dec'd, he doing the duties hereafter enjoyned him to do.   And provided my sd. son should die before me, or survive me and not make a will, then what I have hereby given to him I do hereby give and bequeath to his two sons Stephen Gillet and Asa Gillet, they doing the duties hereafter enjoyned to my son Joseph Gillet to do.   I give to my beloved grandchildren, the children of my son Jonathan Gillet decd, viz: Jonathan Gillet, Mehetabel Gillet and Mary Gillet, the house I now live in, my tan yard and tan houses, and 20 acres of land joining to sd. house and tan yard, to be divided as followeth: my grandson Jonathan to have the ½, and the other half to be divided equally to my sd. granddaughters. I give to my grandson Jonathan Gillet the remaining part of my land in the lot I now live on that is not before disposed of, he paying when he arrives at the age of 22 years, the following legacies, viz. to my daughter Sarah Goodwin £10, and to the heirs of my daughter Abigail Smith deceased £10, and to my daughter Dorothy Bewell £10.   Further my will is that my son Matthew Gillet shall take the whole care to improve what is above given to my grandchildren Jonathan Gillet and Mary and Mehetabell Gillet, for their best advantage until they arrive at lawfull age to receive the same, he being paid out of the income for his care and trouble.   I give to my beloved son Matthew Gillet, over and above what I have done by deed of gift, my lott of land in New Hartford lately purchased of Eliakim Merrell, containing 56¾ acres, and also a yoke of cattle that he has now in his hands or keeping of mine, and also my cane and my long hunting gunn not to be disposed of out of my line of heirs., all which I give to him, he paying to my granddafter Rhoda Andrews £10 old tenor when she arrives at the age of 18 years or marry.   I give to my beloved daughters Elizabeth Marsh, Mary Andrews, Esther Ban-

croft, Hannah Burr, Sarah Goodwin, the heirs of Abigail Smith decd., and Dorothy Bewell, all my moveable estate after my debts are paid, to be equally divided amongst them, the heirs of my daughter Abigail Smith to have but 1/7 part and that to be equally divided amongst them. I give to my 7 daughters, in equal proportion, all my land in Deerfield. I appoint my sons Joseph Gillet and Matthew Gillet to be executors. (Sgd.) Joseph Gillet LS
Witness: John Ensign, Jacob Ensign, Moses Nash

Court Record. Page 6. 4 March 1746: The last will and testament of Joseph Gillet of Hartford decd was exhibited in Court by Joseph and Matthew Gillet, executors. Proven.

Conn. Probate Records, Manwaring, vol. III, p. 271: Gillett, Jonathan, Hartford, Inventory £452 – 06 –01, taken 6 June 1741, and £303 –02 –08 taken 4 May 1741 by Isaac Kellogg, Moses Nash and John Ensign. Court Record p. 79: 6 January 1740/1; Adms. to Joseph Gillett of Hartford. Page 103, 1st December 1741; This Court appoint Moses Dickinson of Hartford to be guardian of Mehetabell Gillett, age 8 years, May age 6, and Jonathan, age 4 years, children of Jonathan Gillett, late deceased. Recog. £300. Vol. XIV. p. 17: 7 February 1742/3, Caleb Andrews and Joseph Gillett, Adms. Adms. exhibited account of their adms. Paid in debts and charges the sum of £160 –02 –09; received £18 –06 –00. Which account is accepted. Vol. XVI. p. 5: 13 Nov. 1750, Mary Gillett, a minor daughter, now 15 years of age, chose Stephen Goodwin of Simsbury to be her guardian. Recog. £500. Page 54. 11 February 1752, Jonathan Gillett, a minor, age 14 years, son of Jonathan Gillett, made choice of his uncle Joseph Gillett to be his guardian. Recog £600. Page 58. 7 April 1752, Joseph Gillett, adms., having made up his account of adms., now moves that distribution be made of the estate, viz., To Jonathan Gillett, only son, a double share; and to Mehetabell and Mary Gillett, to each of them a single share; and also to distribute to the sd. children of Jonathan Gillett what was given to them in and by the last will and testament of their grandfather Joseph Gillett of sd. Hartford deceased, and appoint Capt. Daniel Webster, Moses Nash and Abraham Merrell of Hartford, distributors. Vol. XVIII, p. 6, 1st Nov. 1753 Report of distributors.

Hampshire County, Mass., Springfield. Deeds, vol. 5, p. 531: We Elizabeth Marsh of Sunderland . . . Widow and Caleb Andros and Mary his wife, Nathaniel Bancroft and Esther his wife of Windsor, Noadiah Burr of Farmington and Hannah his wife, Stephen Goodwin of Simsbury and Sarah his wife all in the County of Hartford & Colony of Connecticut, Abiel Smith and Ebenezer Buel and Dorothy his wife all of Litchfield, County Litchfield, Connecticut In consid. of the Sum of Twelve pounds Six Shillings & Six pence — pd by Elijah Williams of Deerfield, Esq. — deed one lot or parcel of Land in Deerfield aforesaid Containing Sixty Seven Acres and thirty four rods and is the lot Number forty five in the Mountain Division so called being Nineteen rods in breadth, bound East on Conn River West on land of Ebenezer Wells in part South on land of Saml Hindsdale, & North on land Recorded to Joshua Carter said lot was drawn by & Recorded to Joseph Gillet. 8th March 1753. Signed Sealed & Delivered by Elizabeth Marsh In Presence of Josiah Burnham Enos Marsh Noah Bissell Wm Woolcott Benjamin Dickinson Solomon Marsh Gideon Thomson David Thomson Abigail Gillett Rebeckah Owen Sarah Rot Elizur Goodrich
[The deed signatures that follow are in one column.]

	his		her	
Elizabeth Marsh	Nathll X Bancraft	Esther X Bancraft	Abiel Smith
	mark	mark	
	her			
Ebenr Buel	Dorothy X Buel	Stephen Goodwin	Sarah Goodwin
	mark		

Hampshire ss. Deerfield March 12 1753: Then Elizabeth Marsh sub-
scriber personally appeared. . . . Before William Williams, J. P. Hart-
ford Co. ss. March 14, 1753, Nath^{el} Bancraft & Esther Bancrof his wife.
. . . Before Wm. Woolcott, J. P. Litchfield Co., March ye 29, 1753
Abiel Smith. . . . Before Ebenr Marsh, J. P. Goshen, Litchfield Co.
. . . March the 30, 1753 Ebenezer Buel & Dorothy Buel. . . . Before
Gideon Thomson, J. P. Hartford Co., Simsbury, April 3rd 1753 Stephen
Goodwin & Sarah his wife — Noadiah Burr & Hannah his wife. Hartford
Co. Wethersfield, April ye 23, 1753 Caleb Andrus and wife Mary. . . .
Before Elizard Goodwin, J. P.

(Deed) Rec'd August 30, 1764 Recorded from original — (Sgd.) Edw.
Pynchon

Child by first wife:

i. ELIZABETH,[4] b. in Deerfield in 1689; d. after 8 March 1753 deed;
    m. in 1707 EBENEZER[3] MARSH (Samuel,[2] John[1]), then of Hatfield,
    later of Sunderland, Mass. 11 children.

Children by second wife, seven youngest born in Hartford:

26. ii.   JOSEPH, b. in Windsor 16 Feb. 1692/3.
27. iii. JONATHAN, born probably in Hartford in 1694 – 1698.
    iv.   MARY, b. 2 Nov. 1699 and bapt. 31 Dec. 1699; d. in Newington, Conn.,
          1 Jan. 1786; m. in Wethersfield, Conn., 15 Feb. 1721/2, CALEB[3]
          ANDREWS (Joseph,[2] John[1]) (Andros, Andrus). 9 children.
    v.   ESTHER, b. in March 1701 and bapt. 27 April 1701; d. after 8 March
          1753 deed; m. NATHANIEL BANCROFT of Windsor.
    vi.   HANNAH, b. in 1702 and bapt. 18 Oct. 1702; d. after 8 March 1753
          deed; m. in the Third Church, Hartford, NOADIAH[4] BURR (John,[3]
          Samuel,[2] Benjamin[1]) of Farmington, Conn. 2 children.
    vii. SARAH, b. 30 Sept. 1704 and bapt. 8 Oct. 1704; d. in Simsbury, Conn.,
          24 Oct. 1792, aged 88; m. in Hartford, 27 June 1727 (also a Sims-
          bury record), STEPHEN[4] GOODWIN (Nathaniel,[3] William,[2] Ozias[1])
          of Simsbury. 5 children.
    viii. ABIGAIL, b. 9 Aug. 1705 and bapt. 30 Sept. 1705; d. in Litchfield,
          Conn., 12 July 1738, "in the 33rd y. of her age"; m. in Litchfield,
          24 Sept. 1729, ABIEL SMITH. 6 children.
28. ix.   MATTHEW, b. 4 March 1707 or 1708.
    x.   DOROTHY, b. in January 1710 and bapt. 21 Jan. 1710; d. in Litch-
          field, Conn., 24 June 1767; m. in the Third Church, Hartford, 19
          Oct. 1736, EBENEZER[4] BUELL (John,[3] Samuel,[2] William[1]). 11
          children.

THE BROTHERS JONATHAN AND NATHAN GILLETT
AND SOME OF THEIR DESCENDANTS
Compiled by Alice Lucinda Priest, B.L., of Brookline, Mass.

12. JOHN[3] GILLETT (*Joseph*,[2] *Jonathan*[1]), of Deerfield, Mass., and
   Lebanon, Conn., born in Windsor, Conn., 10 June 1671,
   died in 1755 (Abridged Compendium of American Genealogy,
   by Virkus, 1925, vol. 1, p. 342). He married in Lebanon, 3
   Jan. 1699/1700, EXPERIENCE[3] DEWEY, born in Westfield,
   Mass., 9 April 1682, daughter of Josiah[2] and Hepzibah
   (Lyman) Dewey.
      His remarkable experience in the last decade of the 17th
   century is of high interest to his descendants; and the
   European part of it was probably duplicated by few New
   England contemporaries.
      As Sheldon's Deerfield History (vol. I. p. 254) states of the year 1696:
   "From beginning to end this proved another troublesome year to the
   town. The Court also provided a garrison; and scouting was continued
   on the frontiers. Although this dangerous service was performed with
   boldness and fidelity, sudden inroads of the enemy could not always be
   averted. Like a whirlwind they came and went, leaving destruction in
   their track." The detailed story of what happened that year to soldier
   John[3] Gillett is told in the Stephen Williams manuscript, beginning:
   "7ber 16, 1696, John Smead & John Gillett being in the woods, looking
   or tracking Bees, were besett by a company of French Mohawks. J. G.
   was taken prisoner & J. S. escaped — the indians fearing a discovery by
   S. 16 of them hastened away toward the town, and three were left with
   J. G. It being lecture day the people were got out of ye meadows, that
   so yr might attend ye lecture, so that ye enemy came as far as Mr. Danl
   Beldings house that was within gun shot of ye fort. . . . [Mr. Belding,
   son Nathaniel, ae. 22, dau. Esther, 13, taken prisoners: wife, 2 sons, 1
   dau. killed: 1 son badly wounded: 2 daus. escaped. Other hostilities at
   fort, in meadow, etc.] . . . the enemy went up Green River & came to
   their companions that they had left wth Gillett. John Smead came into

the Town soon after Mr. Belding's family were well off. Ye 1st night ye enemy lodgd in a round hole near the river, above ye rock, at Nfd st., where ye fires were fresh, thence set away for Canada by ye way of Otter Creek, leaving Connecticut river &c. When they came near Otter creek, they came upon some tracks of Albany indians that were going to Canada, (for in those times ye indians from Albany were wont to go a-scalping, as they call it, to Canada) they sent out their scouts & were upon the lookout, and at length discovered yr smoak; and then they flung down their packs & painted themselves & tyd their English captives to trees & left two men to guard them; & proceeded to yr business, & having dividd themselves into two companies, they sett upon the secure company (wch consistd of six men) & killd two of ym, took two & 2 escapd. Among ye slain was one Uroen an indian known among ye english (& suspectd to be a bloody fellow & sometimes mischievous to ye english). Of their own men one was woundd in ye fleshy part of the thigh (as one had been before at D'f'd). the prisoners were one a Scatacook indian & ye other a young Albany Mohawk. When the skirmish was over, the English were brot up & so they proceedd on their journey. Mr. B. asked the Scatacook Indian, (now his fellow prisoner) what he thought the enemy would do with them, who replyd that they would not kill ye english prisoners, but give some of them to ye french & keep some of them themselves; but he expected to be burnt himself, but when they came to ye lake, one rainy night, they made no fire, and some of them lodgd under ye canoes, from whom this Scatacook made his escape having loosed himself by some means from his cords &c., and altho he was psud the enemy could not recover him &c. As to the young Albany Mohawk, he was kept alive, being of their own nation (the french mohawks went from yr nation over to Canada for ye sak of ye romish religion). Wn Mr. B. & company came to the fort calld Oso, the males were obliged to run the Gauntlet near it. Mr. B being a very nimble or lightfooted man, received but few blows, save at first setting out, but the other men were much abusd by clubs, firebrands, &c;

"They arivd at Canada 8ber 9. Now they found what the Scatacook indian had said, to be true, for the indians kept Mr. B. himself & his daughter with them, & gave J. G. & N. B. to the french. J. G. worked as a servt to ye Nuns at their Farm. N. B. worked for the Holy Sisters. On ye 9th of July following, Mr. B was sold to ye french & lived as a servt with the jesuits at the seminary; his business was to wait upon them & cutt wood, make fires & tend the garden &c. He accounted himself favorably dealt with. In ye winter following Coll Abrm Schyler with some others came to Canada & brought with them a copy of ye Articles of peace between England and France & returnd home wth some Dutch Captives. In Aprill following Coll peter Schyler & Coll A. Schyler & the Dutch Domine, wth some others, came to Canada & the French governor gave liberty to all captives, English & Dutch, to return home, yea alowed them to oblige all under 16 years of age to return wth them, those above yt age were to be at their liberty &c. These Dutch Gentlemen gatherd up wt captives both English & Dutch they could & returned june 8 & took Mr. B and his xdren and Martin Smith with abt 20 more English with them, & arrived at Albany in about 15 days, where ye Dutch showed to him a great deal of kindness, offered to send him home directly to Deerfd Coll Schyler clothd him & his xdren at the desire of his brother Mr. John Belding of Norwalk who paid him for the clothes &c. after about three weeks' stay at Albany, Mr. B and his children went down the River to N. York where his Br had provided a place for his entertainment & from York he went in a vessill to Stamford & from there went to Norwalk to his friends & after some stay there, returnd to D'f'd. J. G. got home a little before him by the way of France & so to England, having received great kindness in England."

Colonel Partridge in a message to the Massachusetts General Court told the story of John Gillett compactly, as follows: "Wheras John Gillet who hath been a very active and willing souldr within the County of Hampshire & Being on the 16th day of Sept 1696 out upon service & together wth some others was that day taken by the Enemy & suffering hardship was carried to Canada Captive & there Remaynd till Septer Last & then was sent from thence Prisonr unto old ffrance & thence (by the later Articles of Peace) the sd Gillet together with other Captives was Released & carried into England: Since his Arrivall there hath Lived & obtained pay for his Passage by the Charitie of some English Marchets there; & now being arrived here Destetute of Money or Cloaths for his P'sent Reliefe Humbly propose it to ye Honoble Genll Corte to allow him something wt this Corte judge meet for his P'sent Reliefe.

Samuel Patrigg —

June 17 1698 — In the House of Representatives — Ordered that there be allowed and paid out of the Publick Treasury the sum of six pounds to the above named John Gillet for the consideration above mentioned (Sgd) Nathl Byfield, Speaker."

Original Simsbury, Conn., joined Windsor on the west. In 1845 citizen Noah A. Phelps published a significant History of Simsbury, Granby and Canton (two towns set off from original Simsbury) in which he stated that in 1675 the New England Colonies became much alarmed by Indian movements and that it was soon manifest that war was inevitable. In October the legislature ordered the evacuation of Simsbury; and again in March 1676, and on the 26th the "settlement was ravaged," "the ruin complete," town deserted for about a year; and the settlement at a stand still, or nearly so, for about ten years. And "For more than thirty years after Philip's war, in 1675, the inhabitants lived in almost daily apprehension of attacks from the Indians." Consideration of this condition may well have decided their location in safer Lebanon, Conn., to such men as Sergeant Josiah Dewey of Westfield and Northampton, Mass., and Deerfield-experienced John[3] Gillett.

The Lebanon tract was sold by Indians in 1692 to four proprietors, and settlement began in 1695. In 1700 the proprietors deeded the land to 51 persons who had taken lots, and formal organization began. Among the 51 named grantees were Josiah Dewey, Sr. and Jr., John and Nathaniel; and John Gillett. An 1810 meeting of grantee descendants included Isaac Gillet. Josiah Dewey, Sr., assisted the four proprietors in distributing the home lots and in making the first division of the common undivided land. That same year he and William Clark of Saybrook bought land adjoining Lebanon on the north and northwest.

The ancestry record of Experience (Dewey) Gillett is pertinent and interesting from the standpoints of provable accuracy; and one unique genealogical sentence rarely duplicated. Sergeant and Deacon Josiah[2] Dewey (Thomas[1]) was born in Windsor, Conn., 1641; as a young man went to Northampton, Mass., where on 6 Nov. 1662 he married Hepsibah[3] Lyman, daughter of Richard[2] and Hepzibah[2] (Ford) Lyman. And according to a 35-page 1928 Ford Genealogy by J. Montgomery Seaver, American Historical-Genealogical Society, Philadelphia (page 23): "Richard Lyman was a descendant (24 generations removed) of Alfred the Great, King of England; also a descendant (21 generations removed) of Henry I., King of France, and a descendant (21 generations removed) of Donal-Bane, King of Scots."

The very able large 1898 "Life of George Dewey, Rear Admiral; and Dewey Family History," published by the Dewey Publishing Company, Westfield, Mass., gives a very detailed valuable account of this Josiah Dewey family, ancestor of Admiral George Dewey. It shows that he moved to Westfield, Mass., 1670, where he was Sergeant of the Guard during Philip's War, and was Deacon of the Church. And its records correct the error of an 1875 Dewey Genealogy that stated that Josiah's wife Hepzibah (Lyman) died about 1670/1; and he married second, Experience. The final conclusive proof of this error was its picture of the Lebanon tombstones of Josiah and his wife, with inscriptions as follows:

"Here lies ye Body of Dn Josiah Dewey He was born in Windsor 1640 Joined ye Church of Christ in Westfield and ordained Deacon Removed to Lebanon In its beginning where he did much Sarvis for God & Man he lived a holy & a Religious & Lived to a great age & he slept in Jesus Septem 7 1732 in ye 92 year of his age.
"Here lies ye Body of ye Worth Mrs Hephzibah ye Wife of Don Josiah Dewey She was the Daughter of Mr Richard Lyman of Hartford She was one that feared ye Lord & Slept in Jesus June ye 4 1732 in ye 89 year of her age."

But this 1898 Dewey Genealogy omitted the record of the youngest known child of Josiah and Hepzibah Dewey, given in later Westfield publications. In 1945 the Westfield, Mass., Athenaeum published family records from the town files at City Hall. And by January 1937 was published the baptismal records of Westfield Church of Christ from 1679 to 1836, which included, page 8: year 1686, 10 mo. 19 d. Mindewell, daughter Josiah & Hephzibah Dewy.

The list of 22 Lebanon homelots laid out on the east side, south to north, of the highway, includes No. 7 to John Dewey, 9 to Dea. Josiah, 10 to Nathaniel, 18 to Josiah Jr.; 19 to John Gilet. The statement is made (p. 390, 1898 Dewey Gen.) that "all had signed in Dec. 1697 except Thomas Root, whose lot went to John Woodward." If "in" means "by" 1697, it demonstrates John Gillett's pre-captivity connection with the settlement. Sheldon's Deerfield History states (p. 173) that after John's Sept. 1696 capture, "Oct. 23, administration was granted on his estate . . . he being killed or captured by the Indians, therefore as to his personal residence in Deerfield is dead." Neither Northampton nor Springfield probate records include this item; perhaps because fire destroyed some in Springfield. 17 Jan. 1728/9 "Josiah Dewey second yeoman" of Lebanon deeded to his son John, two parcels in Lebanon, "one of which is my homelot on which I now live with land adjoining bounded northeastwardly on the main street of Lebanon, northwestwardly on the lot of Dr. Ebenezer Gray and on the southwest by a highway on southeast by land of John Gillett abt 40 acres; the other parcel 18 ac of Timber Hill to the rear of Ebenezer Hunts farm." Recorded Lib. 8 fol 158–9. (p. 393, 1898 Dewey Gen.)

Children, born in Lebanon:

    i.   EXPERIENCE,[4] b. 18 Aug. 1701.
29. ii. JOHN, b. 7 Oct. 1702.
30. iii. EBENEZER, b. in June 1705.
    iv. GERSHOM, b. 26 June 1711.

13. NATHANIEL[3] GILLETT (*Joseph*,[2] *Jonathan*[1]), of Deerfield, Mass., and Lebanon, Conn., born in Windsor, Conn., 4 May 1673, died in Lebanon 10 July 1714, as the vital records of both towns show. He married SARAH ———. The History of Enfield, Conn., by Allen, 1900, vol. 2, gives the following: "Sarah Gillett widow of Nathll Gillett of Lebbanon; died here in this town ye 6th January 1716/17 in ye 37th yeare of her age." She was therefore born in or near 1680.

The Lebanon records give the births of his five children, and the death of one of them, their ages at the time of his death and that his wife's name was Sarah.

Children, born in Lebanon:

31. i.   NATHANIEL,[4] b. 18 Nov. 1702.
32. ii. JOSEPH, b. 11 Oct. 1704.
    iii. ELIJAH, b. 31 July 1706.
         Joseph and Elijah Gillett were soldiers from Enfield, Conn., 2 May 1724, when they were billeted in Hatfield, Mass., at Dr. Thomas Hastings'.
    iv. JONATHAN,b. 5 May 1708; living when his father died.
    v.   JOSHUA, b. 26 Dec. 1710; d. 13 March 1711.

THE BROTHERS JONATHAN AND NATHAN GILLETT
AND SOME OF THEIR DESCENDANTS
Compiled by ALICE LUCINDA PRIEST, B.L., of Brookline, Mass.

14. SAMUEL[3] GILLETT (*Samuel,*[2] *Jonathan*[1]), of Hatfield, Mass., born in Hatfield 14 May 1672 [*sic*], died very shortly before the 6 June 1769 probating of his will. Hence he was aged almost exactly 97 years, oldest among the recorded Gilletts. If there was no younger unrecorded child, he and his just four year old sister Hannah were almost surely the two Samuel[2] Gillett children taken captive with their mother in the Indian attack on Hatfield homes that "began suddenly at 11 A.M. with a blood-curdling yell" 19 Sept. 1677, 17 captives taken; Obadiah[2] Dickinson, uncle of Mrs. (Gillett) Jennings, one of them. 12 left dead, and 4 wounded. In the evening an attack in Deerfield, where one was killed and 4 taken prisoners. After months of negotiations, on 2 May 1678, the living captives set out from Sorel, Canada, with an escort of French soldiers, on their return home and reached Albany 22 May. Captivity Jennings, half sister of the Gillett children, was born 16 (or 14?) March. Historians Sheldon and Boltwood specifically include Samuel[3] as one of the captive children.

By 1697 Samuel[3] married HANNAH[3] HASTINGS, born in Hatfield 19 Jan. 1677, daughter of Dr. Thomas[2] (Thomas[1]) and Anna[2] (Hawkes) Hastings of Hatfield, and niece of Elizabeth[2] (Hawkes) Gillett, wife of Joseph[2] Gillett, uncle of Samuel[3]. Doubtless she died before her husband, since no wife is mentioned in his will. Samuel Gillit of Hatfield and Hannah his wife deeded the following land to Nathaniel Dickinson, 20 Feb. 1703/4, consideration 25 pounds: "a certain part of his house lot in Hatfield ½ of The Breadth Thereof Running from the Town Street to the River Containing Two Acres and a half", "abutting on the Town Street west & on the River East, Bounded by the house lot of Sergt Stephen Belding North and the other Part of ye said Jilletts houselott South." Wit.: Samuel Partridge, Henry Dwight. Sgd., Samuel Gillet, Hannah L Gillet [her mark] (Springfield, Mass., Hall of Records, vol. B, p. 151).

15 Oct. 1719 William Randall of Enfield, Conn., gave a warranty deed to 71 acres to Henry Dwight of Hatfield, Mass., and the witnesses were Samuel Gillett, Joseph Jennings, maternal half brothers almost surely. (History Enfield, Conn., vol. I, p. 2100, Public Documents.)

23 Sept. 1720 will of Stephen Belding of Hatfield, Mass.; witnesses, Thomas Hastings, Scribe, John Belding, Sam'll Gillett, John Hastings. 29 Oct. 1720 all 4, named in order above, personally appeared (1898, Belden Gen., p. 88). "Hatfield men, who were of that troop which rode up the dark valley, on the morning of Feb. 29, 1704" after the previous day Deerfield massacre, included Samuel Gillett. (1910, Wells Hist. Hatfield, Mass.) 1922 "Index, Society of Colonial Wars", lists Samuel[2] Gillett, Sr., and "Samuel Gillett, Jr. 1672–1769, Hatfield, Mass. Soldier at Battle of Deerfield Meadow 1703." (1703/4?) "In 1735 Samuel Hunt petitioned 'ye Court' for a grant of land to the survivors of the Falls fight. In 1736 a grant of six miles square was made. It was located on the north bounds of Deerfield and called Falls Fight Town, finally Bernardston." Mass. Archives, vol. 114: Samuel Jellet, of Hatfield, June 1736, grantee of Bernardston, soldier in the Falls Fight (pp. 598–605). P. 606: Samuel Jellet, jr. of Hatfield, grantee Bernardston, 1736. Vol. 116, p. 190: May 8, 1752 Saml Gillet, propr. Falltown (Bernardston). — When and by whom was this land later deeded away? Wells Hist. Hatfield, p. 126: "In 1708 Samuel Gillett had 1500 trees boxed for tar and turpentine."

15. THOMAS[3] GILLETT (*John*,[2] *Jonathan*[1]), of Windsor, Conn., was born there 18 July 1676 and baptized the 23rd. He was doubtless named for his maternal grandfather, Thomas[1] Barber of Windsor and Simsbury or for that deceased grandparent's energetic namesake son, "Lieutenant Thomas Barber" of Simsbury (1845 Phelps Hist. Simsbury, etc., p. 153). Wintonbury Parish records give the date of his death, 28 Feb. 1761 "in 87th year"; doubtless because his three sons lived in that part of Windsor, and he probably lived with them. Descendants of the family became noteworthy there.

The Parish was the Fifth Society in Windsor, located in the southwest part of the town; the first petition of May 1734 by 27 residents asking only for "local winter church privileges" (November–March), since they were "six miles from Windsor North Society house of worship." In October 1736 the Province Assembly granted a larger petition for "parish privileges" by establishing a parish nearly four miles square, about seven-tenths lay in Windsor, one-tenth in Farmington, two-tenths in Simsbury and so named Win-ton-bury. There were 65 families, 325 persons, and the church organized and located in February 1738 had 67 members; four Gillett families among them. In 45 years over 1147 children were baptized there. In 1845 the parish became the town of Bloomfield.

Thomas[3] married first, in Windsor, and both of Windsor, MARTHA MILLS, who died within a very few years with no record of children born, and and secondly in Windsor, 26 Feb. 1704/5, HANNAH[3] CLARK (*John,*[2] *Hon. Daniel*[1]), born in Simsbury 15 Aug. 1686, died in Windsor 20 Feb. 1708/9, leaving three sons. Stiles in Ancient Windsor states of her grandfather: "Hon. Daniel Clark, an attorney at law, a first settler and man of much influence and position at Windsor; held many public offices; was Secretary of the Colony, 1658–64; & 1665–6." "Married (1) Mary[2] Newberry (Thomas[1])." There is no *known* record of a third marriage, though one seems probable. The following 1726 probate record proves that Thomas[3] was then alive, and might suggest a third marriage about 1716.

Northampton, Mass., Probate Records: Book 4, p. 154. Receipt of Thomas Gillet of Windsor. dated 13 April 1726. I Thomas Gillet of Windsor have Rec'd of my Hon[d] Mother Mercy Norton late of Suffield Dec'd in her life time ye following particulars as part of my portion or share of her estate viz

Thre Pounds ten shillings in Money By ye hands of John Gillet in ye year 1724 And also keeping of my child, providing it with all necessares from ye age of three months until it was seven years old — 6 yr. 9 mo. @ 2s, 6 p per week — as part of his double portion of mother est. this 13 Apr. 1726

Children, born in Windsor:

33. i. ABEL,[4] b. 18 Oct. 1705.
34. ii. JOEL, b. 1 May 1707.
35. iii. JONAH, b. 18 Oct. 1708.

16. SAMUEL[3] GILLETT (*John,*[2] *Jonathan*[1]), of Suffield, Conn., and Granville, Mass., born in Windsor, Conn., 16 Feb. 1677/8. He was five years old when his mother married secondly, Captain George Norton of Suffield, the town that became the boy's home for most of his life. In the later years of his life he lived in Granville, across the line in southwest Mass., and died there "in 1739, aged 60", but was buried in Suffield. (Northampton Probate Records give administration of estate 1934.) He married in Suffield, 22 Jan. 1701/2 (int. 20 Dec. 1701), REBECCA[3] BANCROFT (*Thomas,*[2] *John*[1]), born in Springfield, Mass. (part later Enfield, Conn.), 23 Feb. 1680, a family name that connects with both the Jonathan and Nathan Gillett lines, and the Windsor Stiles family. The immigrant ancestor John[1] Bancroft reached Lynn, Mass., in 1632 and died so soon that to his London poet brother Thomas it seemed no landing, and he wrote the lines:

"You sold your land the lighter hence to go
To foreign coasts, yet (Fate would have it so)
Did ne'er New England reach, but went with them
That journey toward New Jerusalem."

Widow Jane Bancroft received 100 acres in Lynn in 1638. Her daughter Anna[2] married 13 May 1647 Sergt. John Griffin, settled in Simsbury, Conn., had ten children and one of them, Sarah[2] Griffin, married Elias[2] Gillett (Nathan[1]). Son Thomas[2] Bancroft of the Springfield, Mass. region, residence at the "lower wharf," now Enfield, Conn., was a selectman of Westfield; 8 Dec. 1653 married Margaret[2] Wright (Samuel[1]) and their daughter Ruth[3] Bancroft married John Stiles and had many children; and daughter Rebecca[3] married Samuel[3] Gillett; and son Nathaniel[3] had descendants in Granville, Mass. (and Ohio) and it was probably this connection that took Samuel[3] Gillett from Suffield to Granville. Rev. Ezra[5] Stiles, President of Yale from 1772 to 1795, was the son of Rev. Isaac[4] and the grandson of John[3] and Ruth[3] (Bancroft) Stiles, and he wrote of his grandmother's family: "The Family of Bancroft are of a brisk, smart, quick, sensible & lively cast. Grandmother communicated her family spirit to all (her) children", etc. (Stiles Gens. 1892 & 1895).

Children, born in Suffield:

```
36.  i.   SAMUEL,⁴ b. 13 Sept. 1702.
     ii.  JOHN, b. 16 Jan. 1704/5.  Perhaps the 1724 John Gillet of his uncle
          Thomas³ Gillett's 1726 probate record?
     iii. NATHANIEL, b. 10 May 1707; m. Phebe ————.
          Children:
          1.  Rebecca,⁵ b. in Brookfield, Mass. 26 Feb. 1732/3 and bapt. in
              Suffield.
          2.  Phebe, bapt. in Suffield 18 May 1735.
     iv.  HANNAH, b. 19 June 1709; d. in Suffield 2 Nov. 1746, ae. 37; m. there,
          26 Feb. 1728/9 (int. Jan. 10) Joseph⁴ Kent (1898 Kent Gen.).
37.  v.   THOMAS, b. 16 April 1711.
38.  vi.  GARDNER, b. 23 June 1715.
     vii. REBECCA, b. 21 Sept. 1718.
```

17. BENJAMIN[3] GILLETT (*John,*[2] *Jonathan*[1]), of Suffield, Conn., probably a twin and born in Windsor, Conn., 3 Oct. 1680 and brought up in Suffield after his mother's second marriage. He married there, 6 Sept. 1705, ELIZABETH[3] AUSTIN, born there 20 April 1684, dau. of Captain Anthony[2] and Esther Austin. Her gravestone in West Suffield cemetery records her death 7 Oct. 1752, in 68th year.

Children, born in Suffield:

```
     i.    ELIZABETH,⁴ b. 20 Aug. 1706; m. in Suffield, 9 Dec. 1730, JAMES
           ANDROS of Farmington.
39.  ii.   BENJAMIN, b. 2 Nov. 1708.
     iii.  MERCY, b. 16 Dec. 1710; m. in Suffield, 7 Sept. 1736, JOSEPH HALE.
40.  iv.   JOSEPH, b. 15 March 1712/13.
41.  v.    DANIEL, b. 19 Sept. 1715.
42.  vi.   NOAH, b. 22 Jan. 1717/18.
     vii.  JOHN, b. 29 March 1720.
     viii. ISAAC, b. 7 April 1723.
     ix.   CHARLES, b. 19 June 1726.
```

18. JOSIAH[3] GILETT (*Josiah,*[2] *Jonathan*[1]) was born 24 Nov. 1678. [For Josiah[3] and succeeding generations see vol. 47, p. 169, *The Register.*]

Samuel[3]'s probated will is dated March 30, 1769, when he lacked only a month and a half of being 97; and it was signed only by his mark, though formerly he had signed his name. But there is proof that some, perhaps most of it, was written before 1760; half proof, before 1754; and the probability is that it was begun soon after the death of his only son, Samuel,[4] whose estate was in court for administration 14 Aug. 1750. His son Samuel[4]'s record helps the dating of the father's will.

Samuel[4] Gillett had three daughters: Sarah, Martha, who married 16 May 1754 Capt. Perez Graves; Hannah who married 10 Nov. 1757 Oliver Morton. Northampton, Mass., Probate Records for 1750, Book 7, p. 263: Adms. Estate Samuel Gillitt Juner of Hatfield Aug. 14, 1750 to John Billing of Hatfield. Page 276: Invt. by Timothy Cowls, Reuben Wait, John Dickinson Junr. Book 8, p. 18: Feb. 14, 1753 Eleazer Cowl of Hatfield chosen by above 14 year old Hannah Gillit, daughter of Samuel. — This proves that the youngest of the three daughters was born by Feb. 14, 1739, probably a trifle earlier. — Adms., Invt., Settlement Est. Samuel[3] Gillett of Hatfield, 1769: v. 11, p. 77, will, dated 30 March 1769; To my three granddaughters, Sarah Gillet, Martha Gillet & Hannah, daus. of my son Samuel Gillit Dec'd — land in Hatfield — but if any decease before 21, to go to survivors. Remainder to his three daughters, Hannah, Margaret Belding & Mary Evets & to their heirs — to my daughter Elizabeth Bardwell 1 shilling (because of previous gifts) — my son in law Joseph Belding executor. Sgd. Samuel Gillet [his mark]. Wit.: David Wilds, Isr[l] Williams. Probated 1st Tuesday in June 1769 by Israel Williams Esq. Judge of Court.

By Feb. 14, 1760 the youngest granddaughter of Samuel[3] would have been 21; and if the will was written after 16 May 1754 would not granddaughter Martha have been called Martha Graves; and if after 10 Nov. 1757, granddaughter Hannah have been Hannah Morton? The impression is of a grief-absorbed father concentrating impulsively on the three young daughters of his recently deceased only son.

Another important query connected with Samuel[3]'s will concerns his oldest child, Hannah,[4] born 9 Jan. 1697/8. Does the fact that her father's will, written perhaps in 1750, names her only as Hannah, prove that she had never married? No, there are similar proved cases. Her mother's older sister, Margaret[3] Hastings, born in Hatfield in 1674, in 1707 married Nathaniel Evetts. The Guilford, Conn., vital records, Barbour collection, record the marriage in Hatfield, Mass., by Rev. William Williams, May 9, 1722, of Hannah Gillet of Hatfield to Jonathan Evarts of Guilford, Conn. The oldest of their two sons and five daughters, Jonathan, was born 16 Nov. 1723; and the youngest, 7 May 1741. The dates preclude the idea that the bride was Hannah's sister Mary, who was only ten years old at the time of the marriage, though their father's will named her as Mary Evets. The Boltwood genealogies state that Hannah married — Benton of Guilford, Conn., and Mary an Evetts of Killingsworth, Conn.;

and another suggestion is that Mary married a Benton. Proof may come later.

Children, born in Hatfield:

i. HANNAH,[4] b. 9 Jan. 1697/8. No known absolute proof of her further record, but the compiler believes that it was as follows: d. in Guilford or East Guilford 13 Feb. 1774; m. in Hatfield, 9 May 1722, JONATHAN[4] EVARTS (James,[3] James,[2] John[1]) of Guilford, d. there 27 March 1779, in 80th year. 7 children.

ii. MARGARET, b. 1 May 1699; d. in Whately, Mass., in March 1785; m. in Hatfield, 13 July 1727, JOSEPH[4] BELDING (John,[3] Samuel,[2] Richard[1]) of Hatfield, 1696–1778. His mother, Sarah Waite, was the daughter of the noteworthy Sgt. Benjamin Waite. 4 children.

iii. SAMUEL, b. 26 Dec. 1703; d. in Hatfield before the 14 Aug. 1750 administration of his estate; m. in Hatfield, 8 April 1730, SARAH[4] BILLINGS (Richard,[3] Samuel,[2] Richard[1]) of Hatfield, b. 9 Jan. 1704. Her mother was Hannah[3] Marsh (Dea. & Rep. Samuel[2], John[1] whose wife was Anne,[2] daughter of Gov. John[1] Webster).

Children, born in Hatfield:

1. *Sarah*,[5] b. in 173?; d. unm.
2. *Martha*, b. in 173?; d. 28 Oct. 1793; m. in Hatfield, 16 May 1754, Capt. Perez[5] Graves (Elnathan,[4] John,[3] Isaac,[2] Thomas[1]), captain in the Revolution, b. 26 April 1730, d. in Hatfield 17 Dec. 1809. 8 sons and 1 daughter (1896 Graves Gen.).
3. *Hannah*, b. by 14 Feb. 1739; d. after 8 Dec. 1768; m. in Hatfield, 10 Nov. 1757, Oliver[3] Morton (Ebenezer,[2] Richard[1]), d. in Whately, Mass., 16 Sept. 1789, aged 69. The first of eight children was named Samuel Gillett, followed by five other children up to Sarah, b. 7 Dec. 1768; all six children of first wife Hannah. There was a second wife, widow Eleanor (Lyman) Pomeroy, and the sons Oliver and Stephen, born in 1777 and 1779 were hers (1872 Whately Gen.).

iv. ELIZABETH, b. 29 Dec. 1705; m. in 1731 LIEUT. EBENEZER[3] BARDWELL (Ebenezer,[2] Robert[1]), b. in Hatfield 10 Sept. 1707; d. in Whately 14 Nov. 1789. His immigrant ancestor Sgt. Robert[1] Bardwell, from London, married in 1676 Mary[3] Gull, daughter of William[2] and Elizabeth (Smith) (Foote) Gull of Hatfield and their son Ebenezer[2] Bardwell married Mary Field. 5 children.

v. MARY, b. 31 July 1711; m. ———EVETTS

ADDITIONS AND CORRECTIONS
VOLUME 100

Page 43

Hatfield "original old book", page 70, marriage of Joseph Gillit and *
Eliza Hawkes, Nov. 24, 166(3 or 4?). The date is clear except for the last figure in the year, which last figure is a combination of a perhaps underlying 3 and overlying double 4; the 3 fainter than the double 4, which suggests that it was earlier. Mr. Walter E. Corbin writes, "probably should be 1663". And the Hadley-Hatfield and Windsor, Conn., records and situations make that year practically the only possible one, as a detailed long recording could demonstrate.

Mr. Corbin wrote later: "I have found another record entry which will clear up the marriage date 1663 mixed with two 4s. In the old Register Book of William Pynchon of Springfield kept at the Pynchon Building of the Connecticut Valley Historical Society at Springfield, in the Hadley marriages is this, 'Joseph Gillett & Elizabeth Hawkes were marryed Nov. 4 1663.' So the year really is 1663. From the looks of this Pynchon Book

*Page 40, this volume.

I assume that William liked to have copies of records on hand, as he had copied the births, marriages and deaths to about 1693 of Northampton, Hadley, Hatfield and Springfield, and a few other early towns."

Page 105, Hatfield, Dec. 16, 1680, the marriage of Nathaniel Dickensen [his second] and Elizabeth Gillitt. [Later town copy gave the year as 1679, a proved error.] Page 110½, Elizabeth wife of Nathaniel Dickinson died Oct. 11, 1681. On page 111 is the death of Nathaniel Dickinson sen., Oct. 11, 1710.

Page 46 (Page 43, this volume.)

Page 70, marriage of Samll Gillit and Hannah Dickenson, Sept. 23, 1668. Their four recorded children born as follows: daughter Hannah born Sept. 20, 1669: page 96, daughter Mary born Dec. 20, 1670: son Samll born May 24, 1672: daughter Hannah born Sept. 5, 1673. Page 110, Samuel Gillet died May 19, 1676 lost at ye Falls fight. Hannah Dickenson married 2d May 15, 1677 to Stephen Gennings. [Notice the correct birth dates of daughter Mary and son Samuel. Also that the record of the widow's marriage chanced to use her maiden name; but refers to it as a 2nd marriage.]

With page 100 also begins the record of the births of the five children of "Samuel and Hannah Gillit" (Samuel[3] and wife Hannah Hastings): Hannah, Jan. 9, 1697/8: Margaret, May 1 (not 3), 1699: page 100½, Samuel, Dec. 26, 1703: page 101, Elizabeth, Dec. 29, 1705: page 102½, Mary, July 31, 1711.

Northampton, Mass., Probate Index, 1677, vol. 1, page 190: Samuel Gillett, adms., invt., settlement. Hanah Gillett ye Relict of Samll Gillett Deceased Exhibited to this Court An Inventory of her late Husbands Estate who dyed, wch Inventory was ffiled with ye Records of this Corte Power of administration upon ye Estate aforesd is granted unto ye sd Hanah Gillitt Widdow. And for ye settlement of ye sd Estate — this Corte does order yt ye whole Estate be at ye dispose of ye Widdow for her own maintenance & ye maintenance till they come to be of age, and ye sd land to be divided amongst ye Children according to Law Except ye home lott wch is disposed to ye Widdow as her own foe Ever

Here followeth a Coppy of ye Inventory of ye Estate of Samll Gillit of Hatfield who dyed May 18th 1676 —

The inventory was taken by Phillip Smith, Samll Church, Samll Partregg; included 11 items, ("land at Hatfield, Sword, Cowes, hogges, calf" etc.), and the "Sum totall" was 331 –00– 20.

The only date noticed for this probate record was the initial 1677. Mr. Corbin is expert authority for its May 18th date for Samuel[2] Gillett's death. Wells' 1910 Hatfield History states that the soldiers in the early morning May 19, 1676 Falls Fight set out from Hatfield after sunset on Thursday May 18. That is doubtless authority for the date 18 in the probate record. Wells' further states, that when the expedition reached Hatfield again, 45 men were missing, and two were mortally wounded. Two others reached the settlement that night, two on Sunday, two on Monday, and the total loss was 42. "William Allis, John Colefax and Samuel Gillett were killed." (Hatfield men.) Samuel Gillett signed a May 3, 1667 Hadley "west side" petition; and one or more later ones.

Query. Did Samuel[2] and Hannah Gillett have a younger son who became the John Gillett of Wethersfield, Connecticut? An Illinois descendant of said John believes it probable. Proof seems to lie in the chance of discovery of the division of Samuel's land "amongst ye Children."

Page 47 (Page 44, this volume.)

Mindwell[3] Gillett (Josiah,[2] Jonathan[1]) (*Register*, Jan. 1947, p. 47.): Born Windsor, Conn., 4 Feb. 1696/7; died Colchester, Conn., 9 (not 8) May 1784; mar. Lyme, Conn., 3 March 1719/20 (Lyme Land Records, v. 3, p. 338) to John Clark, son of Nathaniel (almost surely John,[2] Thomas[1]) and Sarah (Lay) (De Wolf) Clark of Lyme, Conn. 6 Children. [Data furnished by Mr. John Insley Coddington.]

Page 160 (Page 54, this volume.)

Page 100, Elizabeth, daughter of Joseph[3] and Esther Gillet, born April 12, 1689. (Does this necessarily imply that the home of Joseph and Esther was then in Hatfield or is it possible that the child was born at the Hatfield home of her maternal grandfather, William Gull? But it certainly eliminates the statement that she was born in Deerfield.)

Page 237 (Page 55, this volume.)

12. John[3] Gillett (Joseph,[2] Jonathan[1]) 1671–1755. Sheldon's Deerfield, Mass., Hist., p. 173: After his September 1696 capture by the Indians, on Oct. 23 administration was granted on his estate, "he being killed or captured by the Indians, therefore as to his personal residence in Deerfield is dead."

Page 241 (Page 59, this volume.)

13. Nathaniel[3] Gillett (Joseph,[2] Jonathan[1]) 1673–1714. Sheldon's Deerfield, Mass., Hist., v. 1. p. 261: Year 1698. Two men were sent to Albany. They were guarded by Benj. Wright, William King, Benj. Stebbins, Jona. Taylor and Nath'l Gillet. H. W. Brainard's manuscript Gillett Family, p. 4: Nathaniel Gillett of Lebanon, intestate. Bond signed, Sept. 14, 1714, by Sarah Gillett and Edward Colver. Widow Sarah, Adm. Inventory £142–14 – 04. On inventory is: "the names & ages of ye Children: Nathaniel 12 yrs.; Joseph, 10 yrs.; Elihaj, 8 yrs.; Jonathan, 6 yrs." May this signature of Lebanon's Edward Colver, one of its original proprietors, suggest that he was a possible family connection of the widow? In 1723 his family moved to Litchfield, Conn., and both young Nathaniel[4] and Joseph[4] Gillett lived there also.

Correction: On page 286, data beginning with last paragraph, * "Samuel[3]'s probated will" etc., through pages 287 and 288, to end of genealogy, should precede "15. Thomas[3] Gillett", middle of page 284.

*(Pages 63, 64, 65, 61, this volume.)

JONATHAN AND NATHAN GILLETT DESCENDANTS: CORRECTION:—In October * 1947 REGISTER, page 288, last line, read 24, 1663, *not* 4 1663.

Brookline, Mass.   MISS ALICE LUCINDA PRIEST.

*Page 65, this volume.

Jonathan and Nathan Gillett Descendants: Corrections and Additions: — An apology is due for my too hasty and inefficient examination of the Northampton, Mass., 1769 probate record of the will of Samuel[3] Gillett (Samuel,[2] Jonathan[1]), reported in the October 1947 Register.

Genealogist Walter E. Corbin of Florence, Mass., explains the old method of county probate recording and indexing. "There are two indexes. One for the book or volume the probate papers are entered in; and the other for the files of original papers. Often the book entries are just a brief notice or abstract, or summary of the original papers brought in for probating. The wills are usually copied in the books, entire, although the copyists sometimes have taken liberties with the spelling. Some estates (early) have more in the books than in the files; probably they copied off what they wanted and gave the papers back to the person. And some estates are in the books only; no originals. There are many peculiarities found in the different books. Samuel Gillit's will was from the original.

"In the Samuel Gillit will at the end it says, 'Recorded Lib. G. page 78.' That was the old number, and now it is book 11 and page 78. Those old books are numbered only on the top of the right hand page, and the page on the back, or left side when turned over was not numbered. This was a folio, and the back side really was the same number also. This will was on the back side of page 77, but being the left page in the book and opposite page 78, the one who indexed the book called it 78. One would ordinarily call it page 77a or 77½, to indicate which side of the page it was on. The date on the index card for Samuel Gillit was the probation date; in fact all those dates on the card are the date of probating the estate."

Will of Samuel Gillit   Probate at Northampton, Mass., Box 60 No. 41

"In the name of God Amen, I Samuel Gillit of Hatfield in the County of Hampshire being advanced in Years but of Sound mind and memory, blessed be God — and expecting soon to leave this World do make & ordain this my last Will & Testament —

In the first place I recomend my Soul to God, and my Body to the earth to be buried in decent Christian burial, at ye discretion of my Executors — and as touching such Worldly Estate as I now have, after my Just debts & funeral Expences are paid I give & dispose thereof in the following manner viz —

Impr   I give & bequeath to my Three Grand daughters Sarah Gillit, Martha Gillit & Hannah Gillit daughters of my son Saml Gillit decd. The on half of my Lot in the upper hollow in the Great Meadow, viz that half that lies next to Coles lot, sd moity being about 4¼ acres. ALSO the one half of my Lot in the West farm in Hatfd and the whole of my Lot in ye fourth division of Comons

68

and the whole of my share Interest right & proportion in Hatfield Equivalent so called lying west of Hunstown in this County to be to them & their heirs forever — Nevertheless in case either of them shall decease before they come to be of ye age of twenty one Years, Then I give the whole of ye above bequeathd lands to the Survivors or Survivor of them —

It. — The remainder of my Estate lying & being in the Town Ship of Hatfield I give to my Three daughters Hannah Evets, Margaret Belding & Mary Evets, and to their heirs to be equally divided between them —

It. — I give my Daughter Elizabeth Bardwell One shilling lawful money which with what I have already given her is her full part of my Estate —

It. — I constitute & appoint my Son-in-Law Joseph Belding Executor of this my last will & Testament hereby annulling & making void all other former wills —

In Witness where of I have hereunto set my hand & seal this 30th day of March
his

Anno Domini 1753   (Sgd.)   Samuel   G   Gillet
mark

Witnesses —
Joshua Dickinson
David Wiles
Jos Williams

    Recorded — Lib. G. page 78
    Probated — at a court at Hatfield   June 6   1769"

This will with its important correction of date of making as 1753 instead of 1769, and completion of daughter Hannah's name as Hannah Evets, practically proves her 1722 marriage to Jonathan Evarts of Guilford, Conn., even though it is a Guilford and not an old Hatfield town record: and proves that daughter Mary was then also a Mrs. "Evets."

Mr. Corbin gives also the Northampton, Mass., Probate record, Box 60, No. 40, of the Estate of Samuel Gillit Jr. of Hatfield, Mass. Aug. 14, 1750 John Billing of Hatfield was made administrator and signed a $500 bond; sureties, Samuel Clark of Northampton, Benjamin Pierce of Hadley. And three appraisers appointed: Timothy Cowles, Reuben Wait, John Dickinson; who gave the inventory Nov. 12, 1750. The earliest record was the following:

"We the Subscribers do hereby declare that we decline taking administration on the Estate of our Kinsman Saml Gillet Junr late of Hatfield in the County of Hampshire Decd & desire it may be Granted to John Billing of sd Hatfield Brother in Law to sd. Decd. Signed May 9th 1750, Elesebeth Bardwell (and below)
his
Samuel   S Gillit"
mark

Also October 1947 Register, page 285:

16. Samuel[3] Gillett (John,[2] Jonathan[1]), of Suffield, Conn., and Granville, Mass., in connection with the note "(Northampton Probate Records give administration of estate 1734.)" Mr. Corbin adds the following: Deeds at Springfield, Mass., Vol. H, page 229: Dated, Feb. 25, 1734/5 John Gillett formerly of Suffield, Hampshire Co. Mass. but now of Nowarck in Providence of East Jarsey in America, Dish Turner, conveys to Nathll Copley of Windsor, Hartford Co. Conn. Ship write. land in Suffield & Bedford, Hampshire Co. that came to me from my father Samuel Gillet formerly of Suffield but late of Bedford deceased. Mr. Corbin adds: "Bedford later became Granville, Mass." Northampton, Mass., Probate record, B. 5, page 179, year 1734, gives the following: "Power of adms. on estate of Samuel Gillit Sometime of Suffield who Decd at a Place called Bedford in Co. Hampshire Granted to Samuel Gillit the eldest Son of sd Dec'd & bond taken Nov. 20, 1734." May 2nd 1736 "Widow Rebeckah Gillet" was received by the Suffield, Conn. Church. (Records Cong. Church in Suffield, published 1941 by Conn. Hist. Society, page 11.)

October 1947 Register, page 288, last two lines: *

Pynchon Register Book record: "Joseph Gillett & Elizabeth Hawkes were marryed Nov. 24   1663."

Brookline, Mass.   ALICE LUCINDA PRIEST.

*Page 65, this volume.

SEARCH WARRANT FOR THE APPREHENSION OF MAJOR GENERALS GOFFE AND WHALLEY.*

[Communicated by Mr. HARRY H. EDES, Charlestown, Mass.]

Windsor May 11· 61.

WHEREAS his Maiestie hath sent ouer to the plantation of N: England spetiall Order and Comand. for the App°hending of Collonell Whalley [*Note* 1] and Coll: Goph [*Note* 2] who (are declared to)† stand Convicted for the Execrable murther of the Royall father of oᵘ Gratious Soveraigne and haueing app'hended the said persons to send them ouer to England vnder a strict care to receaue according to their demerits; These are therefore to require you to make diligent search in your plantation (in this Colony)‡ for yᵉ forenamed Gent: Coll: Whalley and Coll: Goffe and to app'hend them being discouered and found out and to secure them in safe Custody and bring them before the Maiestrates or Maiestrate to receaue further order respecting the said psons.

To the Marshall
Jonathan Gilbert [*Note* 3]
or the Constables
of Windsor.

By order from yᵉ Gouernoʳ
and Maiestrates.
Daniell Clark secʳy. [*Note* 4]

Superscribed,
Special order to search for
Col whaley & Goffe
May : 11 : 1661

NOTE 1.

EDWARD WHALLEY—One of the fifty-nine Judges of Charles 1. who affixed their names to the warrant for the King's Execution. January 29, 1648-9.

He was the second son of Richard Whalley, Esq., by his second wife, Frances, daughter of Sir Henry Cromwell, Hinckinbrooke, Knight, the grandfather of the Protector, Oliver, and a grandson of Thomas, Esq. (by his wife Elizabeth), who was the eldest son and heir of Richard Whalley, Esq. of Kirkton, county of Nottingham, a man of great opulence and member of Parliament for Scarboro', 1 Edward VI., who died in 1583, aged 84.

Being a second son, he "was brought up to merchandize," but joined the Parliamentary army at the commencement of the contest between Charles and his Parliament.

He distinguished himself in many battles and sieges, and as a reward for his bravery at the battle of Naseby in 1645, Parliament, Jan. 21, 1645-6, " voted him to be a Colonel of Horse," &c.

Having great confidence in his cousin, the Protector committed the King's person to the charge of Colonel Whalley, and afterwards en-

---

* By the favor of Mr. Edes we have had the privilege of seeing the original of this remarkable document; and we are permitted to announce that a large number of important and original documents never yet published, will soon be furnished by him to the readers of the Register. Some of these documents are of inestimable value.—ED.

† Interlined in the original.

‡ Interlined and crossed out in the original.

trusted him " with the government of the counties of Lincoln, Nottingham, Derby, Warwick and Leicester, by the name of *Major-General,*" and also made him Commissary-General for Scotland.

He was one of the representatives of Nottinghamshire in the Parliament held in 1654 and 1656, and was called up to the Protector's House of Lords.

Gen. Whalley married the sister of Sir George Middleton, Knight, by whom he had several children—-among them John, his eldest son and heir.

Speaking of the characters which Goffe and Whalley sustained in England prior to their flight to the Colonies, President Stiles says, " certainly they were among the personages of the first eminence for great and noble actions in their day."

Gen. Whalley died at Hadley about 1676. Concerning the place of his burial, some have supposed he and Goffe were both buried in New Haven near Judge Dixwell, and the subject is discussed at length in the fourth chapter of Dr. Stiles' History of the Judges ; but since the publication of that work in 1794, wherein it is conceded that Whalley died at Hadley, was there buried, and that if he really was buried in New Haven his remains were taken up and removed from Hadley, the south part of the house wherein Mr. Russell the minister of Hadley resided, and where the two regicides were concealed for upwards of fifteen years, has been taken down (in 1795) ; and in removing the middle part of the front wall next the main street, the workmen discovered the bones of a man, small pieces of wood and some flat stones, which from their position were probably laid on the top of the coffin.

The thigh bone was the only one found to be whole, and was pronounced by Dr. Rogers of Hadley, who examined it, to be that of a large man.

The author of the History of Hadley, page 222, says " these bones must have been those of Gen. Whalley, who was buried near 120 years before."

I am informed that the Rev. Chandler Robbins, D.D., is about publishing some documents relating to the regicides.

NOTE 2.

WILLIAM GOFFE—likewise a member of the " High Court of Justice " which pronounced judgment upon Charles I., and, like Whalley, one of the fifty-nine who signed the King's death warrant.

He was a son of the Rev. Stephen Goffe, a Puritan Divine and Rector of Stanmer, in Sussex. Although he did not receive an academic education, he was possessed of such fine abilities, so well cultivated by his converse with scientific and literary subjects, that the honorary degree of Master of Arts was conferred upon him by the University of Oxford. Living in London with a Mr. Vaughan, a dry salter, and disliking trade, he entered the Parliamentary army on the breaking out of the war. He soon became Quarter Master, then a Colonel of foot, and was afterwards raised by Cromwell to the rank of Major General for Hampshire, Sussex and Berkshire, " a place of great profit."

In 1654 he, with Col. William White and some " Musqueteers," purged the Parliament of the " Anabaptistical Members ; " for which and other services, he was considered " the only fit man " to receive

John Lambert's post of Major General of foot ; and by some " to have the Protectorship settled on him in future time."

Was member of Parliament from Great Yarmouth in 1654, and for the County of Southampton in 1656, and was afterwards, like General Whalley, made one of Oliver's Lords, and signed the order for proclaiming the Protector Richard.

He married a daughter of Gen. Whalley—his companion in exile—and corresponded with her, while at Hadley, over the signature of Walter Goldsmith, and received replies signed Frances Goldsmith. This correspondence was carried on as between a mother and son. Goffe's last letter bears date April 2, 1679.

Goffe and Whalley were devout Congregational Puritans and in perfect accord with the New England fathers. It being dangerous for them to remain longer in England, as the Restoration drew near, they took passage in a ship bound for New England, and while yet in the Channel, received tidings of the proclaiming of Charles II.

They arrived in Boston July 27, 1660, where they were kindly received by Governor Endicott, and visited by the principal inhabitants.

Although they did not attempt to conceal their names or the position they had occupied as Judges of King Charles, they preferred taking up their abode at Cambridge, instead of remaining in Boston, and immediately went thither.

The act of indemnity arrived in November of this year, and upon finding that Generals Goffe and Whalley were not excepted the Government of the Massachusetts was alarmed, on account of the friendly reception which they had given these gentlemen on their arrival.

February 22, 1661, the Governor convened the Court of assistants to consult upon the propriety of securing them, and finding it unsafe to remain longer, they left Cambridge on the 26th and arrived at New Haven on the 7th of March.

Here also they met with kind treatment, especially from the ministers, Rev. John Davenport and Rev. Nicholas Street. Among those most forward in their interest was William Leete, Esq., the Deputy-Governor of the Colony.

The news of the King's Proclamation arriving soon after, they were obliged to flee.

While in New Haven, they were concealed in the house of Rev. John Davenport, from whence they removed to the house of William Jones, Esq., afterwards Deputy Governor of Connecticut, where they remained till the 11th of May, the day on which this warrant was issued, when they removed to a Mill, near the outlet of " Beaver Ponds," in the suburbs of New Haven, and on the 13th were conducted by Mr. Jones, first to a place called Hatchet Harbor, and on the 15th to a cave on the top of a hill about two miles and a half north west of New Haven, which the Regicides named " Providence Hill."

After this they were two years at the house of one Tompkins, near Milford meeting-house, and on the 13th of October, 1664, they started for Hadley, travelling only by night, where the minister of the place, the Rev. John Russell, had consented to receive them. Here they remained for about sixteen years, residing a part of the time at the house of Mr. Peter Tilton, who resided near Mr. Russell.

A drawing of the Judges' Chamber at Mr. Russell's, faces page 202 of Stiles' History of the Judges, and is copied into the History of Hadley, page 220.

General Goffe kept a journal or diary, from the time he left Westminster, May 4, 1660, till the year 1667, in small pocket volumes, written in a kind of short hand, which was quite easily deciphered. This, with other of his papers, was long preserved in the library of the Mathers, in Boston, who obtained them from the family of Mr. Russell, the minister of Hadley.

These papers passed into the hands of Governor Hutchinson, while he was writing his History of Massachusetts, and, unfortunately, were in his house on the night of the 26th of August, 1765, and, with other documents of priceless value to the historian, were destroyed.

I have understood, within a few days, that a portion of Goffe's papers, including letters to his wife, are in existence, and are to be given to the public, in print, at an early day.

Goffe probably died in Hadley, in 1679 or 1680, as he is not heard of at any period *after* 1679 ; April 2d, of which year, as before stated, he wrote the last letter to his wife.

Interesting sketches of both Goffe and Whalley, are given in Hutchinson's History of Massachusetts, Vol. i. p. 213-19, of the London edition, and in the History of Hadley, page 214 *et seq.*

Note 3.

Jona. Gilbert was of Hartford in 1645, and soon after (Mr. Savage says 29 January, 1646) married Mary, daughter of John White, by whom he had several children.

He was possessed of great wealth, and appears to have been engaged in the " coasting business," and a man of considerable note, holding various civil offices—was Representative, Collector of Customs at Hartford; and for many years held the office of Marshall of the Colony, which corresponds to that of High Sheriff at the present day.

He died December 10, 1682, aged 64, and, with his wife who died July 3, 1700, aged 74, is buried at Hartford.

An extended account of this man, and a copy of his will, are contained in the genealogy of the Gilbert Family. *Ante,* Vol. iv., July and October.

Note 4.

Daniel Clark was one of the first settlers of Windsor, Conn., where he was an " attorney at law," and a magistrate.

He was a man of influence, and occupied an honorable position in the affairs of the Colony, of which he was several years Secretary—was Representative 1657-61, an assistant 1662-64, and Captain of the cavalry troop in 1664.

Mr. Clark married in June, 1644, Mary, daughter of Thomas Newberry, of Dorchester, by whom he had a family of ten children. On page 569 of the " History of Ancient Windsor," it is stated that the marriage was solemnized June 15, 1644, while on page 720 I find the date fixed upon to be the 13th of June.

His first wife having died August 29, 1688, he married for his *second* wife, Martha, widow of Simon Wolcott, and sister of Wm. Pitkin, Esq., of Hartford, by whom he had no children.

He was " appointed," by the town of Windsor, to sit in the " great pew " in the Meeting-house, which was " Wainscotted for the sitting of the Magistrates ; " and died August 12, 1710, aged 87.

THE GORHAM FAMILY IN CONNECTICUT AND VERMONT.

By FRANK WILLIAM SPRAGUE, Esq., of Brookline, Mass.

1. CAPTAIN JOHN[1] GORHAM (son of Ralph) married Desire Howland, in 1643. (See REGISTER, *ante*, Vol. 52, page 358.)

2. JABEZ[2] GORHAM (*John*[1]), born in Barnstable, Mass., Aug. 3, 1656, married widow Hannah (Sturgis) Gray.

3. JOSEPH[3] GORHAM (*Jabez,*[2] *John*[1]) was born in Bristol, R. I., Aug. 22, 1692. He gave a receipt, at Fairfield, Conn., June 16, 1725, for a portion of his father's estate. (See REGISTER, *ante*, Vol. 54, page 168.) He married, May 11, 1715, Abigail, daughter of Daniel Lockwood of Fairfield, Conn. " Abigail ye wife of Joseph Gorham, Who died Ianua^ry ye 23^d. 1724-5." (Fairfield Inscriptions, page 16.) He married second, Jan. 13, 1725-6, Deborah Barlow.

Children by first wife, born in Fairfield:

 i. DANIEL,[4] b. Nov. 10, 1717.
 ii. JABEZ, b. Mar. 22, 1718-9; m. Mary Couch, Nov. 27, 1752.
 iii. LOCKWOOD, b. Jan. 1, 1720-1.
4. iv. ICHABOD, b. in 1722, bapt. Jan. 31, 1724-5; m. Sarah Barlow; d. in Roxbury, Conn., Aug. 19, 1799, aged 77.

Children by second wife, born in Fairfield:

 v. SHUBAEL, b. Oct. 28, 1726; m. Rebecca Hurlburt, Jan. 21, 1746-7.
 vi. ABIGAIL, b. Apr. 7, 1728.
 vii. ISAAC, b. Nov. 14, 1730; m. Ann Wakeman, July 26, 1752.
5. viii. JOHN, b. July 4, 1732; m. Abigail Wakeman, Oct. 2, 1754.
 ix. HANNAH, b. May 4, 1737.
 x. MARY, b. Dec. 25, 1739.
 xi. JOSEPH, b. Nov. 20, 1741; m. Mary Gray, Nov. 16, 1763.
 xii. ABIGAIL, b. Apr. 7, 1744.
  " Family Book, Green's Farms" (Fairfield).

4. ICHABOD[4] GORHAM (*Joseph,*[3] *Jabez,*[2] *John*[1]), born in Fairfield, in 1722, baptized Jan. 31, 1724-5, married in Fairfield, Feb. 2, 1748-9, Sarah, born Mar. 28, 1732, daughter of George Barlow. Mar. 22, 1757, he bought a farm of seventy acres in the town of Ridgefield (once a part of Danbury), and sold the same, Apr. 21, 1767. He removed to Roxbury, Conn., where he died Aug. 19, 1799, aged 77. (See Hist. of Woodbury, Vol. 3, page 627.)

 Children:

6. i. DANIEL,[5] b. in Fairfield, Nov., 1749.
7. ii. BENJAMIN, bapt. in Fairfield, Dec. 24, 1752.
 iii. JOSEPH, b. in Fairfield, Dec., 1754.
 iv. PHINEAS, b. in Ridgefield (part of Danbury), Apr., 1757.
8. v. SETH, b. in Danbury, Jan. 18, 1762. (This record is from his family Bible.)

5. JOHN[4] GORHAM (*Joseph,*[3] *Jabez,*[2] *John*[1]), born in Fairfield (Green's Farms), July 4, 1732, married Oct. 2, 1754, Abigail Wakeman. John,[4] of New Fairfield, bought land in Kent, Conn., April 10, 1781. (Land Records, Vol. 7, p. 69.) Joseph[5] Gorham and Timothy St. John were administrators of the estate of John[4] Gorham, of New Milford, Jan. 13, 1806. (Land Records, Vol. 2.) Joseph[5] Gorham, of Kent, gave quit-claim to John[5] and Jared,[5] of Vermont,

of all his right in land on east mountain left him in the will of his mother Abigail Gorham, Sept. 4, 1808. (Land Records, Vol. 2, p. 420.) John,[5] of Bakersfield, Vt., sold to James,[5] of Poultney, Vt., land in Kent, Oct. 25, 1809. (Land Records, Vol. 2, p. 401.) Seth[5] Gorham, of Castleton, Vt., and wife Betsey, sold land in Kent, which came from the estate of her father, Eleazer Thompson. (Land Records, Vol. 12, p. 80.) Seth,[5] of Castleton, Vt., sold one seventh part of undivided land in Kent, Jan. 23, 1810. (Land Records, Vol. 12, p. 84.) The will of Abigail Gorham, of Kent, dated Oct. 2, 1805, and probated Jan. 24, 1811, at New Milford, Conn., gave to her daughters Deborah, Abigail, and Lucy, all her household furniture, and to her sons John, James, Seth, Jeremiah, Wakeman, Hezekiah, and Joseph, all her landed estate of every description lying in Kent, or elsewhere. Mrs. Ella Comstock Peckham, of Utica, N. Y., a descendant of John[4] Gorham and his wife Abigail Wakeman, has sent the writer the following list of the children of John[4] Gorham. The baptisms of the first two, Deborah[5] and John,[5] are at Green's Farms. The will of the mother, Abigail Gorham, mentions the seventh child as *Jeremiah.* The Kent land records, under date of Sept. 4, 1808 (Vol. 2, p. 420), calls the same man *Jared,* of Vermont. Mrs. Peckham's Bible list of children calls him Jared, and the History of Poultney, Vt., calls him Jared. There were but seven sons.

Children :

i. DEBORAH,[5] bapt. Apr. 27, 1755; m. Timothy St. John.
ii. JOHN, bapt. June 20, 1756.
iii. JAMES, bapt. May 28, 1758.
iv. SETH, bapt. June 8, 1760; m. Betsy Thompson.
v. JARED, m. Asenath Morgan.
vi. WAKEMAN, settled in Chittenden, Vt.; m. Polly ———.
vii. ABIGAIL.
viii. ABIGAIL, b. July 19, 1770; m. Solomon Comstock, June 16, 1788.
ix. HEZEKIAH.
x. LUCY.
xi. JOSEPH, b. in 1780; m. Lucy Beecher; removed to Pennsylvania.

6. DANIEL[5] GORHAM (*Ichabod,*[4] *Joseph,*[3] *Jabez,*[2] *John*[1]), born in Fairfield, Nov., 1749, died in Roxbury, Conn., Jan. 25, 1836, in which year his estate was settled. (Woodbury, Conn., Probate Records.) Mary, wife of Daniel Gorham, died in Roxbury, Conn., Jan. 31, 1817, aged 61. Daniel Gorham appears among the Litchfield County pensioners, placed on the pension roll May 15, 1833, age 83. (This agrees with the record of his birth.) There is on record at New Milford, Conn., an agreement between Daniel[5] and his son Daniel,[6] which gives the farm to the son, subject to the life right of the father. It has been claimed that Daniel[5] was the son of Joseph,[4] who died in Norwalk in 1760, and his wife Abigail Lovell, but that Joseph's family returned, immediately after his death, to Barnstable and Nantucket, where four of his children married. He did have a son Daniel,[5] and the last record of him was in the will of his grandfather, at Barnstable, in 1770. The writer has made many researches to find trace in Connecticut of Daniel[5] the son of Joseph[4] and Abigail (Lovell), but without success. None of that family are recorded in Connecticut after 1760.

Children, born in Roxbury, Conn.:

i. AARON,[6]

ii. Lucy, b. Sept. 15, 1782; m. Joseph Treat, Dec. 16, 1806.
iii. Daniel, b. Dec. 16, 1784; d. Dec. 2, 1869; m. Polly Randall.
iv. Eli, b. Jan. 2, 1787; d. Apr. 10, 1867; m. Lætitia Hamilton, July 6, 1811. In 1808, he was a manufacturer of woolen machinery in Oswego, N. Y., and he was the first to introduce carding, or cloth dressing, machinery into western Canada. He established a factory in Newmarket, Canada, in 1809. His son *Charles*,[7] b. Feb. 2, 1818, m. May 20, 1852, Helen Durthie Milne; and their son, Judge Thomas[8] A. Gorham of Milton, Ontario, Canada, b. Nov. 2, 1854, m. Annabella Villiers, Nov. 23, 1893. The writer is indebted to Judge Gorham for some of the Roxbury, Conn., notes.
v. Joseph, b. Dec. 5, 1788; d. Oct. 13, 1839; m. Lydia Haight.
vi. Mary, m. —— Botsford.
vii. Sarah, m. —— Bennett.
viii. Hiram, d. July 31, 1826; m. Hannah Peck.

7. Benjamin[5] Gorham (*Ichabod,*[4] *Joseph,*[3] *Jabez,*[2] *John*[1]), born in Fairfield, Dec. 24, 1752, married Amy Combs, who died in 1829. Benjamin[5] and Amy Gorham deeded land in Danbury, in 1799. Amy Gorham's estate was settled in 1830.

Children :

i. Russell,[6] b. in Danbury, in 1775.
ii. William, b. in Danbury, Jan. 3, 1779; d. in Oneonta, N. Y.; m. at Ridgefield, Mar. 12, 1800, Polly Weed, b. July 1, 1784, d. Aug. 31, 1850. Children, all born in Danbury : 1. *Benton,*[7] b. Dec. 23, 1800. 2. *Sally,* b. Dec. 30, 1804. 3. *George S.,* b. Oct. 4, 1807. 4. *Charles T.,* b. May 29, 1812; m. Apr. 10, 1839, Charlotte E. Hart. He was Ambassador to Holland, during the administration of President Grant, and held many other important offices. For many years he was President of the Marshall, Michigan, Bank. He d. in Marshall, March, 1901. (He employed Miss Louise Tracey, of New Haven, Conn., to trace his line of ancestry, and some of her notes, as well as some Kent, Conn., records, have been used by the writer.) 5. *Rev. Barlow W.,* b. June 24, 1814.
iii. Betsy.
iv. Sally.
v. Mary.
vi. Rebecca.
vii. David.
viii. Laura.
ix. Abigail.
x. Amy.

8. Seth[5] Gorham (*Ichabod,*[4] *Joseph,*[3] *Jabez,*[2] *John*[1]), according to his own family Bible, was born in Danbury, Jan. 18, 1762. The inscription upon his monument at West Rutland, Vt., agrees with the Bible record of his age. He married first, Amelia Dunks, born in Danbury, Mar. 29, 1763, died Oct. 17, 1841 ; and married second, Louisa Everson, in 1842. He died Aug. 29, 1852. Miss Charity[8] Gorham, of West Rutland, Vt., the owner of the family Bible, writes : " My father Chauncey[7] T. Gorham, son of Judson,[6] and grandson of Seth[5] and Amelia (Dunks), remembers both Seth[5] Gorhams, and says they were cousins."

Children :

i. Betsy,[6] b. Feb. 20, 1785; d. July 28, 1866.
ii. Barlow, b. Feb. 21, 1787; d. Feb., 1883.
iii. Deming, b. June 6, 1789; d. Nov. 14, 1861.
iv. Eli, b. Sept. 8, 1791; d. Oct. 7, 1870.
v. Judson, b. Oct. 11, 1794; d. July 30, 1877.
vi. Alonzo, b. Aug. 15, 1801; d. May 11, 1888.
vii. Laura, b. Aug. 9, 1804; d. Feb. 6, 1833.

THE GRANT FAMILY.

[Communicated by John Ward Dean, of Boston.]

The Rev. P. C. Headley, in his *Life and Campaigns of Gen. Grant,*
says " he is of Scotch descent. More than a century ago, his ancestor came to the shores of America, then comparatively a wilderness,
and settled in Pennsylvania, while a brother, who emigrated with him,
went to Canada. By honest industry, our hardy pioneer supported

his growing family upon his forest-girdled clearing, until the Revolutionary war called him to its field of strife. After bravely following the flag of the rising Republic, he returned with the dawn of peace to his home in Westmoreland county, Pennsylvania."

Richard A. Wheeler, Esq., of Stonington, Ct., in a communication to the *Norwich Morning Bulletin*, Nov. 21, 1866, after quoting the above statement of Mr. Headley, shows that it is erroneous; and states that Gen. Grant was a lineal descendant of Matthew Grant, who came to this country in 1630, and settled in Dorchester, Mass., but removed to Windsor, Ct. Mr. Wheeler gives the genealogy from Matthew Grant to the General. A genealogy of this family, with fuller details, is found in the *History and Genealogies of Ancient Windsor, Conn.*, by Henry R. Stiles, M.D., published in 1859, and the supplement published in 1862; but, in this line, they bring the family down only to Noah Grant (grandson of the emigrant), whose birth only is given. I copy the early generations from Dr. Stiles's book, and the later ones from Mr. Wheeler's communication. All of the facts and most of the language are from these two writers.

1. MATTHEW[1] GRANT was one of the original company who came in the Mary and John to Dorchester, in 1630 ; was a freeman there in 1631 ; removed to Windsor among the very earliest ;* was second *town clerk* there, also the first and for many years the principal *surveyor*; was a prominent man in the church ; evidently was just, and exceedingly conscientious in all his public and private transactions and duties. As recorder, he often added *notes*, explanatory or in correction, to the records, which have considerable value to the investigator of the present day. He was the compiler of the *Old Church Record* which Dr. Stiles reprints in his History, and which, in the absence of some of the earliest records of the town of Windsor (1635,–50) assumes a value that can scarcely be overestimated. In short, he was a pious, hardworking, conscientious, Christian man, and a *model town clerk.* He was b. Tuesday, Oct. 27, 1601, and m. Nov. 16, 1625, his 1st wife Priscilla, who d. April 27, 1644, aged 43 years 2 months. He m. 2d, Susannah, widow of William Rockwell, May 29, 1645, in Windsor. She was b. Monday, April 5, 1602, and d. Nov. 14, 1666. Her children by Mr. Rockwell are given in Dr. Stiles's Supplement, p. 69, "Matthew Grant, Recorder," d Dec. 16, 1681, having, for four years preceding, resided with his son John.

His children by his first wife Priscilla were :—(2) *Priscilla,*[2] b. Sept. 14, 1626, m. Oct. 14, 1647, Michael Humphrey ; for their descendants see Stiles's Windsor, art. Humphrey. (3) *Samuel,*[2] + b. in Dorchester, Nov. 12, 1631 ; settled on the little eminence in the rear of East Windsor Theological Institute, which Matthew, the father, speaks of, in 1675–6, in the *Old Church Record,* as being the only place in the meadow which was *not* covered with water in the great

---

* In the State Archives, in vol. of MSS. relating to Private Controversies, p. 138, in a matter concerning lands in dispute between Joseph Loomis, Jr. and Sen., April 21, 1675, Matthew Grant testifies :—

"And if any question my uprightness and legal acting about our town affairs, that I have been employed in, a measuring of land, and getting out of lots of men which has been done by me *from our first beginning here, come next Sept. is* 40 *yere.* I never got out any land to any man, until I knew he had a grant to it from the townsmen, and town's approbation, or about recording after the book was turned to me, which is near 23 years since. I can say with a cleare conscience, I have been careful to do nothing upon one man's desire," &c.

flood of 1638-9 ;* m. May 26, 1658, Mary Porter. (4) *Tahan,*[2] b. in D. Feb. 3, 1633, d. May, 1693 ; m. Jan. 22, 1662, Hannah Palmer ; m. 2d, Hannah Bissel, probably in 1690 ; descendants in Stiles's Windsor. (5) *John,*[2] b. in Windsor, April 30, 1642 ; m. Aug. 2, 1666, Mary Hull ; children in Stiles's Windsor and Supplement.†

3. SAMUEL[2] GRANT, by wife Mary Porter, had :—(7) *Samuel,*[3]+ b. April 20, 1659 ; resided at East Windsor ; d. May 8, 1701. He m. 1st, Hannah Filley, Dec.. 6, 1683, who d. April 18, 1686 ; m. 2d, Grace, dau. of John and Elizabeth (Booth) Miner,‡ April 11, 1688, who was b. Sept. 20, 1670, and d. April 16, 1753. (8) *John,*[3] b. April 24, 1664, d. July, 1695 ; m. June 5, 1690, Elizabeth Skinner, and had, John,[4] b. March 3, 1690-1. (9) *Josiah,*[3] the progenitor of most of the Grant family in Eastern Connecticut, b. March 19, 1668 ; was at E. W. in 1693 ; removed to Stonington 1695 or 6 ; d. March 28, 1732 ; m. at S., July 8, 1696, Rebecca, dau. of Ephraim and Mary (Avery) Miner, and had children—Josiah,[4] John,[4] Oliver,[4] Noah,[4] and Miner ;[4] she d. Jan. 15, 1746-7, aged 75. (10) *Nathaniel,*[3] b. April 14, 1672 ; m. May 16, 1689, Bethiah Warner ; descendants in Stiles's Windsor. (11) *Mary,*[3] b. Jan. 23, 1675. (12) *Sarah,*[3] b. Jan. 19, 1678. (13) *Abigail,*[3] m. April, 1704, Dr. S. Mather.

7. SAMUEL[3] GRANT,. by 1st wife Hannah, had :—(14) *Sarah,*[4]§ b. Sept. 2, 1684.

By his second wife Grace, his children were :—(15) *Hannah,*[4] b. March 28, 1689 ; m. April, 1712, John Gaylord. (16) *Samuel,*[4] b. Sept. 19, 1691. (17) *Noah,*[4]+ b. Dec. 16, 1692, m. June 12, 1717, Martha Huntington, b. Dec. 9, 1696, dau. of John and Abigail (Lathrop) Huntington.‖ (18) *Abigail,*[4] b. Dec. 15, 1695. (19) *Ephraim,*[4] b. Aug. 24, 1698. (20) *Grace,*[4] b. Aug. 17, 1701. (21) *David,*[4] b. Dec. 10, 1703, m. Dec. 21, 1727, Elizabeth Chapman ; descendants in Stiles's Windsor. (22) Capt. *Ebenezer,*[4] b. Oct. 1706, resided at East Windsor ; m. Nov. 10, 1737, Anne Ellsworth, who d. Feb. 1, 1790, in 69th year ; children in Stiles's Windsor.

17. NOAH[4] GRANT, was a resident of Windsor until the town of Tolland was settled when he became an inhabitant of the new town. By wife Martha, had :—(23) *Noah,*[5]+ b. in Windsor, July 12, 1718 ; m. Nov. 5, 1746, Susannah Delano. (24) *Adoniram.*[5] (25) *Solomon.*[5] (26) *Martha.*[5]

23. NOAH[5] GRANT, removed about 1750 to the adjoining town of Coventry. He and his brother Solomon[5] joined the expedition against Crown Point in 1755, and were both killed the same year. By his wife Susannah, he had :—(27) *Noah,*[6]+ b. June 20, 1748 : m. 1st, Mrs. Anna Richardson ; m. 2d, in Pennsylvania, Rachel Kelly. (28) *Peter.*[6]

27. NOAH[6] GRANT, served with distinction in the Army of the Revolution. After the close of the war and the death of his first wife, he

---

* See Stiles's Windsor, p. 46.

† Dr. Stiles in his History gives another son by his first wife, viz., Josiah,[2] who had a son Josiah,[3] b. Nov. 24, 1678 ; but this does not seem to be confirmed by the record printed by him in his Supplement.

‡ John Miner, the father, was a son of Lieut. Thomas and Grace (Palmer) Miner, of Stonington, the first of the name in this country. He was son of William, of Chew Magna co., Somerset. An ancient pedigree of this family is printed in the Register, Vol. xiii. pp. 161-4.

§ Her name and her mother's is *Anna* in the *Old Church Record.*

‖ See E. B. Huntington's Memoir of the Huntington Family, p. 97.

removed from Coventry, Ct. to Pennsylvania. This is doubtless the ancestor of Gen. Grant to whom Mr. Headley alludes as coming to America more than a century ago. By his first wife Anna,· he had : —(29) *Peter.*[7] (30) *Solomon.*[7]

By his second wife Rachel, he had :—(31) *Susan*.[7] (32) *Jesse Root*,[7]+ b. Jan. 1794, still living ; m. June 24, 1821, Miss Hannah Simpson, who was born near Philadelphia, and removed with her father to Ohio, where she was married. (33) *Margaret.*[7] (34) *Noah.*[7] (35) *John.*[7] (36) *Roswell.*[7] (37) *Rachel.*[7]

32. JESSE ROOT[7] Grant, by wife Hannah, had :—(38) Gen. *Ulysses Simpson*,[8] b. April 27, 1822. (39) *Samuel.*[8] (40) *Clara.*[8] (41) *Virginia.*[8] (42) *Ovil L.*[8] (43) *Mary Frances.*[8]

GRANT, WEBB, WARNER, HOLMES.—Seth Grant (Zeth Graunt) emigrated to New England in June 1632. Among his fellow passengers were William Wadsworth, John Talcott, William Goodwin, and John White.* The following year all but Grant had become resident of Newtown, later called Cambridge, Mass. If Grant did not remove to Newtown when his fellow passengers did, he certainly was there in 1634.†

Among the residents of the town was also Richard Webb.

Grant and Webb were among the persons who, in 1636, went through the wilderness and made a settlement on the Connecticut River which they called Newtown and, in February 1636-7, Hartford. On page 359 of the first volume of the Hartford Land Records, which is known as the " Book of Distributions," is a record of the lands of Seth Grant under the date of February 1639.

Thus far no record has been discovered of his marriage or the births of any children, nor is there any record of his death. An inventory of his estate, dated " March the 4th 1646," is printed on pages 481 and 482 of the first volume of the " Colonial Records of Connecticut," but the records do not show any action on the estate.

On pages 313 and 507 of the " Book of Distributions " reference is made to " Seth Grant's children." On page 25 of Vital Records, in volume 1 of Land Records of the Town of Middletown, is entered the marriage, in February 1654, of Robert Warner and Elizabeth Grant, and the births of their children, the second of whom was named Seth, and the youngest Mehetable. March 31, 1687, Robert Warner sold 42 acres of land on the east side of the Connecticut River in Hartford which had been laid out to Seth Grant, and March 1, 1702-3, Robert's son Seth sold land in the same town which had been recorded to Seth Grant³.‡ These facts go to show that Warner's wife was a daughter of Seth Grant.

June 19, 1650, Nathaniel Ely and Richard Olmsted, of Hartford, for themselves and others of that town, one of whom was Richard Webb, entered into an agreement " for the settlinge and plantinge of Norwalke." §

An inventory of the estate of Richard Webb, who " deceased July last," was taken October 5, 1665, and was presented to the court at Fairfield, November 1 following, by the widow, who was appointed administrator.‖ " Elissabeth webb widowe the rellique of Richard webb formerly of norwalke deceased the twentie fowre of January 1680." ¶ The Fairfield Probate Records show that in March 1681 several persons appeared in court and made claim to the estates of both Webb and his wife. Part of the entry read thus :

" Alsoe Richard Holmes Impleads right to a portion out of the estate of the said Elizabeth *by vertu of his wiues realation to her.*" ** The court decreed that " Richard Holmes is to haue Twenty pound part of it in the bed and its furniture as it was prized on the Inuentory which is eight pounds the rest of the

* REGISTER, vol. 14, pp. 300, 301.
† Records of the Town and Selectmen of Cambridge, 1630-1703, pp. 4, 5, 9.
‡ Hartford Land Records, " Book of Distributions," p. 508, and vol. 1, p. 147.
§ Norwalk Land Records, vol. 1, p. 60.
‖ Fairfield Probate Records, vol. 2, p. 8.
¶ Norwalk Land Records, vol. 1, f. 59.
** The italics in this and the following quotations are the contributor's.

Legasy its desired that sum particular things in the Inuentory *that was her owne fathers* Shee may haue at Inuentory price." *

Richard Holmes of Norwalk, " aged 60 years and upwards," made his will October 31, 1704, in which he gave to his wife Sarah the life use of all his real estate " and at her death to *her near kinswoman Mehetable Warner* now living with me." †

The inventory of the estate of Sarah Holmes, widow of Richard, is among the files of the Fairfield Probate court. On the document is an indorsement which shows that *Mehetable Warner*, "now surviving," was nearly related to said Sarah Holmes " *and was her owne sisters child* ", and that soon after the death of the child's mother " *this sarah holmes the childs own aunt went up to Middletown and brought this child home to her husband.*" The court decreed that " Sundry children of Robert Warner dec'd of Middletown are the next of kin in equal degree to said Sarah," and ordered the estate divided among them equally.

The foregoing proves beyond question that Seth Grant had at least two children : Elizabeth wife of Robert Warner of Middletown, and Sarah wife of Richard Holmes of Norwalk.

The settlement of the estate of Webb and his wife shows that they had in their possession property which had belonged to the father of Sarah Holmes (Seth Grant), and that Holmes claimed part of the estate of Elizabeth Webb " by vertu of his wiues realation to her." The inference is that Elizabeth, wife of Richard Webb, was the widow of Seth Grant and, at least, step-mother to Sarah Grant, wife of Richard Holmes of Norwalk. FRANK FARNSWORTH STARR.

Middletown, Conn.

* Fairfield Probate Records, vol. 1675-89, p. 86.
† *Ibid.*, vol. 1702-50, p. 33.

GEORGE GRAVE, OR GRAVES, AND HIS DESCENDANTS.

Compiled by the Hon. R. D. SMYTH, and communicated by Dr. BERNARD C. STEINER.

1. GEORGE[1] GRAVES was one of the earliest settlers of Hartford, Conn., which town he represented in the General Assembly of 1657. He died Sept., 1673. He married twice; Sarah was the Christian name of his second wife.

His children were:

    2. i.   GEORGE,[2] b. 1631; d. Dec. 3, 1692.
    3. ii. JOHN, b. 1633; d. Dec. 31, 1695.
       iii. MARY, m. Dec. 12, 1665, Samuel Dow; d. Sept., 1673.

2. GEORGE[2] GRAVES, JR. (*George*[1]), removed from Hartford to Middletown, where he was representative and marshal. He married Elizabeth Ventress, Apr. 2, 1651.

    Their children were:

       i.   GEORGE,[3] d. single, 1699.
       ii. ELIZABETH, m. Ebenezer Dudley, Oct. 25, 1713; d. Sept. 16, 1751.
           He d. Aug. 29, 1751.
    4. iii. JOHN, d. 1702.
       iv. RUTH, m. Jan. 25, 1699–1700, John Webb.
       v.   MEHITABEL, m. Jan. 1, 1701, James Harrison.
       vi. MERCY.

3. DEACON JOHN[2] GRAVES, OR GRAVE (*George*[1]), of Guilford, married first, Elizabeth Stillwell, Nov. 26, 1657. She died June 3, 1669, and was buried the next day. He married second, Elizabeth Cruttenden, in 1670. After his death, she married successively John Sperry and Benjamin Burwell. Elizabeth Stillwell was the only child of Jasper Stillwell, one of the first settlers of Guilford, Conn., who was the tenth to take the charge to the freemen, on May 22, 1648. His wife was named Elizabeth. His will was made November, 1656, shortly before his death on the 6th of that month. He was buried on the 8th, and the will was proved on the 23d. His estate amounted to £210. 17. 10. His widow survived him. He was a man of means and built a stone house, one of four in the settlement. John Grave, who was a blacksmith by trade, lived in Guilford after his first marriage, on the land allotted to Stillwell. He naturally sided with the Rossiter, or Hartford, party in the troubles connected with the absorption of New Haven Jurisdiction by Connecticut. He seems to have come to Guilford about 1657, and was a freeman there before 1659. He held several town offices, and was town clerk from 1673 to 1685. He was one of the grantees of the town patent in 1685, and frequently served

on commissions to run town boundaries and audit town accounts. He served as a deacon in the church from about 1676 until his death, and represented Guilford twenty-three times in the legislature. In addition to a home lot of 5¼ acres, he owned one parcel of upland in the Great Plaine, 10 acres, and 2½ acres of upland and marsh in the same plain. In 1667, he bought of Robert Kitchel, for £27., the latter's lot in the Little Plain, and six acres of upland on the north side of the country highway.

His children by his first wife were:

5. i. JOHN,[3] b. Feb. 27, 1658; d. Dec. 1, 1726.
    ii. ELIZABETH, b. Apr. 11, 1661; d. young.
    iii. ELIZABETH, b. Sept. 16, 1665; d. May 28, 1687.
    iv. SARAH, b. Mch. 14, 1667-8; m. Thomas Robinson, Jan. 13, 1692.

His children by his second wife were:

    v. ABIGAIL, b. Mch. 6, 1669-70; d. Aug. 13, 1753; m. Ebenezer Benton, June 14, 1694. He d. Jan. 22, 1758.
6. vi. JOSEPH, b. Aug. 17, 1672; d. before 1716.
    vii. DANIEL, b. Sept. 17, 1675; d. Nov. 8, 1675.
7. viii. NATHANIEL, b. Jan. 27, 1677-8; d. Jan. 1727.
    ix. HANNAH, b. Jan. 12, 1679-80; d. Mch. 21, 1757; m. Nathaniel Stone, Jan. 6, 1709. He d. Aug. 6, 1752.

4. JOHN[3] GRAVE (*George[2], George[1]*), of Hartford, married first, May 11, 1681, Susannah, daughter of Robert and Susannah (Treat) Webster. She was born Feb. 26, 1658. He married second, in 1690, Hannah Davies.

His children by his first wife were:

    i. MEHITABLE,[4] m. James Henderson, Jan. 1, 1701.
    ii. ELIZABETH, m. Ebenezer Dudley, of East Guilford, Oct. 26, 1713.

His children by his second wife were:

8. iii. JOHN,[4] b. Mch. 3, 1695; d. Apr. 1759.
    iv. SARAH, b. Sept. 25, 1698.

5. LIEUT. JOHN[3] GRAVE, JR. (*John[2], George[1]*), of Guilford, was tavern-keeper there in 1717. He married Jan. 6, 1684, Elizabeth, daughter of Robert Foote of Branford. She was born March 8, 1664, and died May, 1730.

Their children were:

    i. ELIZABETH,[4] b. July 17, 1686; d. May 25, 1687.
    ii. MEHITABLE, b. Feb. 1, 1687-8; m. Cornelius Hull of Durham, Feb. 1, 1714-15.
9. iii. JOHN, b. Feb. 1, 1689-90; d. July 17, 1763.
    iv. ANN, b. Aug. 29, 1692.
10. v. NOADIAH, b. Dec. 4, 1694; d. July, 1751.
    vi. MINDWELL, b. Nov. 4, 1696; m. Nathaniel Stevens, Nov. 11, 1713.
    vii. SARAH, b. Apr. 14, 1699; m. Thomas French, Dec. 14, 1720.
11. viii. DAVID, b. Jan. 31, 1701; d. Nov. 16, 1726.
    ix. ELIZABETH, b. Jan. 4, 1703; m. Daniel Redfield.
12. x. EBENEZER, b. July 15, 1705; d. Mch. 1, 1785.

6. JOSEPH[3] GRAVES (*John[2], George[1]*) of Guilford, married Margaret ———. Her list in 1716 was £14. 11. 0.

Their children were:

    i. HANNAH,[4] b. Oct. 30, 1699; d. Mch. 24, 1770; m. Samuel Leete of Guilford, Nov. 26, 1723. He d. Feb. 20, 1751.
    ii. ABIGAIL, b. Feb. 22, 1702; m. ——— Way.
13. iii. DANIEL, b. Apr. 9, 1704; d. Sept. 12, 1782.

iv. THANKFUL, b. Feb. 18, 1706; m. Moses Page of Branford, Oct. 20, 1731.
14. v. JOSEPH, b. Feb. 14, 1709.

7. NATHANIEL³ GRAVE (*John²*, *George¹*) married Elizabeth Barnes of Groton, Nov. 25, 1709. His list was £73. 10. 6., in 1716, at Guilford.

Their children were:

i. MARY,⁴ b. Oct. 11, 1712; d. Oct. 31, 1715.
ii. ANN, b. Feb. 8, 1714; m. Stephen Dudley, Nov. 15, 1736.
iii. MARY, b. Apr. 6, 1716; d. Nov. 25, 1776; m. Nehemiah Griswold of Guilford, Jan. 23, 1745. He d. Dec. 31, 1787.
15. iv. NATHANIEL, b. Nov. 26, 1722; d. Nov. 29, 1799.

8. JOHN⁴ GRAVES (*John³*, *George²*, *George¹*), "ye Smith," removed to East Guilford. His list was £43. 16. 0., in 1716. He married first, Phebe Hand, Nov. 19, 1719; and second, Keziah Norton, Aug. 1, 1723.

His children, all by his second wife, were:

i. GEORGE,⁵ b. May 30, 1724.
ii. PHEBE, b. Jan. 20, 1726; m. Enos Hall, Aug. 6, 1750.
iii. SAMUEL, b. Aug. 3, 1728; d. Nov. 5, 1736.
iv. JOANNA, b. Aug. 8, 1730.
v. SARAH, b. Jan. 23, 1733; d. Oct. 8, 1775.
vi. JOHN, b. Oct. 9, 1735; d. Apr. 13, 1791; m. (1) Elizabeth Grave, Dec. 20, 1760; m. (2) Sarah Dudley, who d. Nov. 19. 1799. His children were: 1. *George*, b. Apr. 9, 1760. 2. *John*, b. Oct. 16, 1761. 3. *Titus*, b. Apr. 3, 1765. 4. *Miriam*, m. Joseph Bartlett, May 23, 1787.
vii. SUBMIT, b. Jan. 13, 1738.
viii. KEZIAH, b. June 27, 1743; d. Oct. 8, 1775.
ix. SAMUEL, b. July 11, 1746; lived in Durham and Stonington. His children were: 1. *Joseph*, bap. Apr. 13, 1755. 2. *Benjamin*, bap. Jan. 1, 1758.
x. RUFUS, b. Sept. 27, 1749; lived in Sunderland, Vt.; m. Elizabeth, dau. of Daniel Benton, Nov. 7, 1773; and had children; 1. *Elizabeth*, b. Oct. 2, 1774. 2. *Rufus*.

9. JOHN⁴ GRAVES, JR., ESQ. (*John³*, *John²*, *George¹*), of East Guilford, married first, Elizabeth Stevens, May 10, 1714. She died Feb. 30, 1725. He married second, Abigail Starr, in 1728. She died Aug. 6, 1752. He married third, Naomi, widow of Benjamin Blachley. She died Sept. 22, 1770. His list in 1716 was £120. 7. 0.

His children by his first wife were:

i. ANNE,⁵ b. Apr. 12, 1715; d. May 29, 1801; m. Thomas Griswold of Guilford, Feb. 19, 1735. He d. Jan. 16, 1784.
ii. JOHN, b. Apr. 16, 1717; d. Feb. 17, 1718.
iii. JOHN, b. Apr. 28, 1719; d. Dec. 13, 1759; m. (1) Abigail Pierson, Oct. 15 1744. She d. Dec. 29, 1745; m. (2) Phebe Hart, July 16, 1747. She survived him; m. Jonathan Crampton, in 1761, and d. Feb. 7, 1763. John Graves's only child was *Ruth*, b. Dec. 18, 1745; d. Oct. 1805; m. 1764, Ambrose Evarts.
iv. EZRA, b. July 3, 1722; of East Guilford, Sept. 28, 1747; m. Elizabeth, dau. of Noadiah Grave, and had *Elizabeth*, b. Nov. 15, 1745.

His children by his second wife were:

v. SIMEON, b. Nov. 12, 1729; d. Jan. 2, 1801; m. Naomi Dudley, June 6, 1750. She d. Aug. 28, 1754. Their children were: 1. *Abigail*, b. Nov. 25, 1751; d. Feb. 10, 1822. 2. *Timothy*, b. 1759; d. Jan. 6, 1849. 3. *Rhoda*, b. 1761; d. July 19, 1840; m. 1783, Stephen Conkling.

vi. ELIAS, b. Apr. 10, 1733; of East Guilford; d. May 31, 1802. He
m. (1) Mabel Murray, Feb. 23, 1763, who d. æ. 36, May 10,
1779; m. (2) widow Mary Cleveland Hubbard, from Southold,
Long Island, Mch. 29, 1780, who d. æ. 75, June 21, 1826. His
children were: 1. *Mabel*, b. Oct. 7, 1764; d. Nov. 14, 1764. 2.
John, d. Aug. 20, 1787. 3. *Mabel*, b. Jan. 1, 1781; d. single,
Oct. 5, 1848. 4. *Hubbard*, b. Dec. 19, 1782. 5. *Olive*, b. 1784;
d. young. 6. *Mary*, b. Aug. 26, 1785; m. E. Kimberly.

vii. TIMOTHY, b. Dec. 3, 1740; d. young.

10. NOADIAH⁴ GRAVE (*John³*, *John²*, *George¹*) married Sarah ———.
He lived in Guilford and Durham.

Their children were:

i. SARAH,⁵ b. Mch. 20, 1720-1; m. Aaron Parmelee of Goshen, Apr.
5, 1753.

ii. NOADIAH, b. June 20, 1721; probably d. young, as not mentioned
in his father's will.

iii. ELIZABETH, b. Jan. 21, 1723; m. (1) Ezra Grave; m. (2) Moses
Sheldon of Durham, Apr. 20, 1749.

iv. ABIGAIL, b. Sept. 23, 1725.

v. DAVID, b. Oct. 5, 1728; of East Guilford; d. Nov. 2, 1779; m.
Temperance Dudley, Oct. 15, 1749. She d. æ. 92, June 20,
1822. Their children were: 1. *Temperance*, b. 1750; d. June
5, 1751. 2. *Prudence*, b. Oct. 18, 1751; m. Aaron Blachley,
Oct. 17, 1769. 3. *David*, b. Feb. 1753; d. Mch. 10, 1755. 4.
David, b. Sept. 11, 1756; d. Aug. 10, 1764. 5. *Nancy*, b. Sept.
22, 1758; d. Aug. 24, 1829; m. Stephen Evarts. 6. *Clarissa*,
b. Nov. 4, 1764; d. July 8, 1848; m. (1) Preston Kelsey; m.
(2) James Thomas. 7. *Naomi*, b. Dec. 4, 1768; d. single,
Sept. 11, 1855.

vi. ROSWELL, b. Dec. 5, 1731.

11. DAVID⁴ GRAVE (*John³*, *John²*, *George¹*) married Prudence Willard,
Feb. 17, 1725. She married second, Zachary Field, March 1, 1732,
and died Nov. 27, 1737.

Their only child was:

i. DAVID,⁵ b. Mch. 16, 1726.

12. EBENEZER⁴ GRAVE (*John³*, *John²*, *George¹*) married Mary Isbel,
Feb. 12, 1730. She was born Apr. 19, 1708, and died May 6,
1764.

Their children were:

i. EBENEZER,⁵ b. Nov. 24, 1730; d. Jan. 14, 1814; m. Apr. 14, 1757,
Mary, dau. of Josiah Willard. She d. Mch. 16, 1820, æ. 88.
Their children were: 1. *Anna*, b. Mch. 8, 1758; m. Fiske
Bartlett of Georgia, Vt.; no children. 2. *Luman*, b. Jan. 1,
1760; m. in 1791, Abigail Todd, and removed to Vermont. 3.
Ezra, b. Apr. 28, 1762; d. Aug. 17, 1822; m. Abigail Scranton.
4. *Tamsen*, b. Feb. 21, 1764; m. Rev. William Stone. 5. *Luther*,
b. Feb. 19, 1766; d. single, in Guilford, Ohio. 6. *Mary*, b.
Aug. 30, 1769; m. (1) Samuel Parmelee, Jan. 23, 1793; m. (2)
——— Ward. 7. *Adah*, b. Sept. 24, 1771; m. Abel Blair of
Georgia, Vt. 8. *Justus*, b. Oct. 19, 1773; lived in Guilford,
Ohio; m. (1) Betsey, dau. of William Fowler, Nov. 25, 1801.
She d. Oct, 17, 1822, æ. 44; m. (2) widow Temperance Harris,
Apr. 19, 1824. 9. *Julius*, d. æ. 6 years.

ii. GILBERT, b. Aug. 13, 1732; d. July 10, 1754.

iii. ELI, b. July 20, 1734; of East Guilford; d. Jan. 29, 1795; m. Hannah, dau. of Joseph Wilcox, July 14, 1757. She d. Jan. 1,
1805. Their children were: 1. *Gilbert*, b. Sept. 21, 1758; d.
July 22, 1841; m. Elizabeth Kelsey. 2. *Milton*, b. Oct. 28,
1761; d. May 6, 1816; m. (1) Lucy Buell of Killingworth; m.

85

(2) Sarah Comstock of Essex. 3. *Hannah*, b. May 21, 1764; m. William Parmelee. 4. *Elizabeth*, b. June 22, 1768; m. Eli Tuttle. 5. *Mabel*, b. Mch. 4, 1772; d. Jan. 28, 1837.

iv. ELIZABETH, b. Sept. 24, 1736; d. Apr. 17, 1767; m. John Graves, Jr.

v. AMBROSE, b. Sept. 10, 1738; d. Sept. 22, 1818; m. (1) Jan. 24, 1765, Catharine Field, who d. Nov. 20, 1777; m. (2) 1778, Silence, dau. of Josiah Dudley. She d. Apr. 2, 1822. Children by first wife: 1. *Edmund*, of Sunderland, Vt.; d. June, 1827; m. Beulah Hill. 2. *Ambrose*, b. 1767; d. May 6, 1843; m. Jan. 3, 1789, Nancy Hopson. 3. *Nabby*, b. 1769; d. Apr., 1855; m. Charles Caldwell, Sept. 14, 1788. 4. *Catharine*, b. 1773. 5. *Augustus*, b. 1775. 6. *Mindwell*, b. Nov., 1776; d. single, Mch. 2, 1865. Child by second wife: 7. *Artimesia*, b. Sept. 8, 1779; d. single, Apr. 18, 1874.

vi. ISRAEL, b. Nov. 4, 1740; d. Nov. 10, 1812; m. Rebecca Dudley, who d., æ. 82, Nov. 8, 1828. Their children were: 1. *Chloe*, m. Ashbel Bradley. 2. *Rebecca*, m. Billy Dowd. 3. *Rachel*, b. 1774; m. Orrin Dowd; d. Oct., 1802.

vii. MARY, b. Mch. 15, 1743; d. July 23, 1754.

viii. ANN, b. Feb. 21, 1745; d. July 8, 1776.

13. DANIEL[4] GRAVE (*Joseph[3]*, *John[2]*, *George[1]*), of North Guilford, married first, Elizabeth Stevens, Jan. 20, 1732. She died Aug. 9, 1751. He married second, Elizabeth, widow of John Lee, Dec. 20, 1755. She died July 8, 1798.

His children, all by his first wife, were:

i. ELIZABETH,[5] b. Oct. 14, 1732; d. Aug. 23, 1751.

ii. SARAH, b. Dec. 21, 1733.

iii. DANIEL, b. Feb. 29, 1736; d. Aug. 7, 1751.

iv. ABRAHAM, b. May, 1737: d. July 22, 1794; m. Mch. 14, 1764, Catharine Hall of Wallingford, who d. May 1, 1804. Their children were: 1. *Carine*, b. Nov. 9, 1764; m. Josiah Coan, May 17, 1786. 2. *Daniel*, b. Dec. 25, 1766; went to New York; m. Sept. 10, 1808, Abigail Ransford. 3. *Sarah*, b. Feb. 22, 1770. 4. *Abraham*, b. Dec. 14, 1773; m. ——— Linsley. 5. *Rachel*, b. Feb. 23, 1776; m. Bela Benton. 6. *Nancy*, b. 1789, in her mother's 50th year; d. July 4, 1804.

v. LUCY, b. Nov. 8, 1739; m. John Lee.

vi. THANKFUL, b. 1742; d. Aug. 14, 1751.

vii. BENJAMIN, b. 1747; lived in North Guilford; d. Apr. 16, 1829; m. (1) Freelove Barnes, Dec. 8, 1772, who d., æ. 67, Aug. 27, 1810; m. (2) Abigail Chittenden. His children, all by his first wife, were: 1. *John*, b. Dec. 10, 1775; d. Jan. 4, 1846; m. May 7, 1797, Jerusha Rossiter. 2. *Jerusha*, b. Dec. 10, 1775; d. Sept. 19, 1817; m. Amos Chittenden, Sept. 30, 1794. 3. *Elizabeth*, b. June 27, 1779; m. James Maltby of Northford, in 1829. 4. *Rufus*, b. June 17, 1781; d. young. 5. *Freelove*, b. Dec. 25, 1784; d. Sept. 12, 1848; m. Seth B. Fowler.

viii. EUNICE, b. Mch. 13, 1749; d. June 13, 1751.

14. JOSEPH[4] GRAVE (*Joseph[3]*, *John[2]*, *George[1]*), of Middlefield and Durham, married Elizabeth ———.

Their only child was:

i. THANKFUL,[5] b. July 28, 1742: d. Nov. 18, 1742.

15. NATHANIEL[4] GRAVE (*Nathaniel[3]*, *John[2]*, *George[1]*), of Guilford, married Rebecca Elliott, May 22, 1756. She died July 28, 1820.

Their children were:

i. NATHANIEL,[5] b. Feb. 12, 1757; d. single, Sept. 18, 1782.

ii. SARAH, b. Apr. 8, 1762; d. Jan., 1839; m. 1780, Ebenezer Munger, who d. Apr. 10, 1834.

GRAVES.—It may be of interest to note in connection with George Grave, or Graves, of Hartford, Conn., *ante*, page 260, that besides what is to be found *concerning him in the Memorial History of Hartford County, Conn., Vol. 1, page 241, and the mention of him in the will of Anne Grave, of London, in Waters's Gleanings, Vol. 2, page 1210, there appears in Cussan's History of Hertfordshire (England), Vol. 2, page 262, among the freeholders, in the "Survey off the Burrough off Hartford * * * taken in the yeare one thousand Six hundred twenty one," a "George Graue." MARY K. TALCOTT.
Hartford, Conn.

*Page 82, this volume.

The Grays of Killingworth and Tiverton. Contributed by H. Eugene Bovis, Fairfax, Virginia.

The compilers of the Kelsey genealogy were not able to identify either Daniel Gray, who married Abigail Kelsey at Killingworth, Connecticut, 5 September 1743, or Mary Gray, who married Ensign Gamaliel Kelsey as his first wife at Saybrook, Connecticut, 11 January 1738/9 (Edward A. Claypool, Azalea Clizbee, and Earl Leland Kelsey, *A Genealogy of the Descendants of William Kelsey,* 2 vols. [New Haven, Conn., 1928], 1:142, 252). Who were these Grays?

In looking for a solution to this problem we find, in addition to the marriage of Daniel Gray and Abigail Kelsey, the marriages of Edward Gray to Mary Wellman at Killingworth, 7 March 1744, and Philip Gray to Martha Crane at Killingworth, 23 April 1749 (Killingworth Vital Records, Barbour Index, Connecticut State Library, Hartford, Connecticut). Thus, all four of the Gray marriages took place about the same time. The three Gray men married at Killingworth, and Mary Gray married Gamaliel Kelsey who was born at Killingworth. It would be reasonable, therefore, to assume that Daniel, Mary, Edward, and Philip Gray were somehow related.

The Barbour Index does not show the births of any of these Grays. However, we find in the birth records of Tiverton, Rhode Island, the following births: Daniel, of Edward and Rebecca Gray, 1 April 1718; Mary Gray, 8 October 1719; Edward Gray, 12 June 1721; and Philip Gray, 24 January 1723 (James N. Arnold, *Vital Records of Rhode Island, 1636-1850* [Providence, 1893], *Tiverton,* 4:83). The records of the United Congregational Church of Little Compton, Rhode Island, show that Rebecca Gray of Killingworth was admitted 9 March 1717; that Daniel of Edward Gray, Jr., of Tiverton was baptized 1 June 1718; and that Mary of Edward Gray of Tiverton was baptized 11 September 1720 (Arnold, *Vital Records of Rhode Island, Episcopal and Congregational,* 8:15). Thus, it would seem that Edward Gray of Tiverton married Rebecca ———— of Killingworth about 1717. He and Rebecca had four children: Daniel, Mary, Edward, and Philip.

The question then arises as to when these Grays went to Killingworth. The will of Edward Gray (born 1667) of Tiverton, written 10 December 1722 and proved 7 June 1726, leaves to his sons Philip and Thomas the land "where my son Edward formerly lived" and specified that they were to pay "bonds which testator obliges himself to pay to daughter-in-law Rebecca Gray, to pay to the children of my son Edward, deceased" (Augustus Peck Clarke, *Clarke's Kindred Genealogies* [Cambridge, Mass., 1896], 77, 78; Benjamin Franklin Wilbour, *Little Compton Families* [Little Compton, R.I., 1967], 292, 293). Considering that Edward, Jr., was already deceased when his father's will was drawn 10 December 1722 but that his son Philip was born 24 January 1723, he must have died sometime between April and December 1722, and it would seem that his widow and children were no longer living in his house in December. It therefore appears that after Edward's death Rebecca took the children and returned to Killingworth, where they grew up and married. However, it has not been possible to discover a record of Rebecca Gray's death at Killingworth.

Edward Gray, the father of the four Grays of Killingworth, was born at Tiverton, 10 January 1693, the son of Edward Gray of Plymouth Colony and Tiverton and his first wife Mary Smith, daughter of Philip and Mary Smith of Newport. He was the grandson of Edward Gray of Plymouth Colony and his second wife, Dorothy Lettice (Wilbour, *Little Compton Families,* 292, 293).

GREEN, TIMOTHY.—Information is desired concerning the parentage of Timothy Green, who was in 1714 printer to the colony of Connecticut, and lived in New-London. Savage says (Gen. Dict. ii. 306) he was son of Samuel (son of Samuel of Cambridge), who was born March 6, 1648, married Elizabeth Sill, 1685, and died of small-pox, 1690. This is improbable, for the reason that no record is found in Boston Registry of the births of any children of Samuel (No. 2) and Elizabeth Green, and that Timothy's tomb-stone in New-London gives 1679 as the date of his birth. Moreover Timothy had a child born in 1703 (Records of second church, Boston). Probably Timothy was the youngest son of Samuel of Cambridge, by his second wife Sarah, dau. of Jonas Clark.

My reasons for this belief are: 1st, that the Boston News-Letter, in an obituary notice of Bartholomew Green, son of Samuel of Cambridge, published in 1732, says that Samuel had eight children by his wife Sarah. Savage gives only six, the last of whom was born Sept. 6, 1671. 2dly, in the Middlesex Registry of Deeds there is a conveyance, dated Aug. 2, 1707, by Jonas Green, of New-London, mariner, Bartholomew Green, printer, Joseph Green, tailor, and Timothy Green, printer, all of Boston, and Sarah Green, relict, widow of Capt. Samuel Green, late of Cambridge, to Nathaniel Hancock, of a house and land in Cambridge. Jonas and Bartholomew are the only sons of Samuel's second marriage given in Savage. It seems clear enough that Joseph and Timothy are the two needed to make out the full number of eight children as stated in the News-Letter. It is true that Samuel, of Cambridge, had a son Joseph by his first marriage, but Savage thinks him the Joseph who died in 1672. Jonas is clearly the person of that name who was in New-London in 1694, according to Savage, and of whose family Savage was ignorant, he says. 3rdly, Jonas was a common name among the descendants of Timothy Green. He had a son of the name, and so did his son Thomas. Timothy was, I believe, married three times. His first wife's name (if he had three wives) I cannot learn. The others were Mary Flint, daughter of Capt. John Flint, of Concord; and Abigail Hill, daughter of Capt. Charles Hill, of New-London. I shall be glad of any information concerning the wives and children of Timothy Green, as well as any other fact corroborating my suggestion as to his parentage.

THE GREEN FAMILY
A DYNASTY OF PRINTERS

By WILLIAM C. KIESSEL, of New York University

It was 4 Sept. 1633, that the ship *The Griffin* dropped its anchor off shore from the little settlement called Boston. Among the members of Thomas Hooker's Company was Bartholomew Green with his wife Elizabeth and their four children: Samuel, Nathaniel, Sarah, and Phebe.[1] Modern scholarship has disproved Isaiah Thomas' statement that the Green family came to Massachusetts with Governor Winthrop in 1630.[2] Bartholomew moved his family to Cambridge where he became a freeman on 14 May 1634. He died the following year. His widow Elizabeth died on 28 Oct. 1677, at the age of eighty-eight.[3]

Samuel Green, progenitor of a dynasty of printers, was a promising young man of eighteen when he arrived with his parents in America. The early death of his father threw him upon his own resources. In later years, Samuel was fond of telling his children of the early hardships his family endured; "upon their first coming ashore, he and several others were for some time glad to lodge in empty casks to shelter them from the weather".[4] On 4 March 1635, Samuel was made a freeman and on 30 March 1644, he was appointed Doorkeeper to the House of Deputies.[5]

Cambridge, the home of Samuel Green, was also the location of the first printing press in English America. It had been brought to the colony in the spring of 1638 by the widow of Rev. Josse Glover, a wealthy dissenting clergyman, of Sutton, England, who had died en route.[6] The press came under the control of Harvard College by the marriage on 22 June 1641, of the widow Glover to the college president, Henry Dunster. Managed by Stephen Daye, a locksmith, the press was operated by his son, Matthew, who had received some printing training in England.[7]

Matthew Daye died 10 May 1649. Because Stephen Daye was occupied with land speculations for the Winthrop family, the press

90

was turned over to Samuel Green in his capacity as clerk to the college.[8] He was without any printing experience according to his autobiographical letter to Governor Winthrop dated 6 July 1675: "I was not before used unto it . . . "[9] Despite this apparent handicap, Samuel operated the only printing office in the English colonies until 1665, when the Society for the Propagation of the Gospel sent over a press. For the momentous task of printing John Eliot's Indian Bible, Hezekiah Usher, financial agent for the Society, employed Marmaduke Johnson, a professional printer from England.[9]

Samuel's avocation was the colonial militia, and throughout his life he was known as Sergeant Green. At the age of seventy-five, when he was so old that he had to be carried to the reviewing field, he was commissioned a captain. He also became a large land holder, beginning with his first acquisition in 1658 when the General Assembly granted him 300 acres at Haverhill for his services to the Colony.

It is estimated that 190 imprints were issued from the Cambridge press from 1649 until 1692, the year Samuel retired.[10] The last pamphlet issued was *Ornaments For The Daughters of Zion* by Cotton Mather.[11] The press was subsequently taken to New London where it remained until 1773. It was then moved to Norwich, Conn., five year later to Dresden, now Hanover, N. H., and then to Westminster, Vt., where on 12 Feb. 1781 it was used to print the *Vermont Gazette*. The press is now preserved in the state capital at Montpelier.[12]

Samuel Green had an old-fashioned family — two wives and at least fifteen children. His first marriage to Jane, daughter of Guy Banebridge, produced seven children for which there are records:

Elizabeth,	16 April	1640	Samuel,	6 March 1648
Sarah,	7 Oct.	1642	Joseph	7 March 1649
Lydia,	23 March	1645	Deborah, 19 March 1655	
Lydia,	13 April	1646		

After the death of his first wife, 16 Nov. 1657, Samuel married eighteen year old Sarah Clark, daughter of Elder Jonas Clark, on 22 Feb. 1662. Birth records of the children of this marriage are also incomplete. The six recorded children are:

Jonas,	31 Jan.	1664	Bartholomew, 26 Oct. 1667	
Lydia,	12 Nov.	1665	Mary,	6 Nov. 1669
Elizabeth,	3 Nov.	1666	Dorcas,	6 Sept. 1671

The only plausible explanation for the omission of a second Jonas and Timothy is that they were living in New London, Conn., when Savage was compiling his genealogical data.[13]

Isaiah Thomas often confuses the descendants of Bartholomew Green with those of Percival Green. It is possible the two pioneers were brothers. Each had large families, each lived in Cambridge. Because of duplication of given names, it is often difficult to distinguish between the two branches. However, Samual Abbott Green, former Librarian of the Massachusetts Historical Society, in his family genealogy, has clarified many problems.[14]

Samuel Green died at the age of eighty-seven 1 Jan. 1702. A will, dated 2 Aug. 1707, is the last known record of his widow. In it Sarah Green lists her surviving children: Jonas, mariner, Bartholomew, printer, Joseph, tailor, and Timothy a printer.[15] This is additional proof that Timothy was the son of Samuel Green, Sr., and not of Samuel, Jr., as stated by Isaiah Thomas.[16]

Jonas, the mariner, lived in New London. He married, 29 March 1694, Jane Pygan (born in February 1670), and had six children none of whom entered the printing trade.[17] Three of Samuel's sons, Samuel, Bartholomew, and Timothy, became printers. However, the veritable dynasty of printers, comparable to the Didot family of type founders of France, is descended through Bartholomew and Timothy of the second marriage of their father.

Samuel, Jr., served his apprenticeship with his father, worked briefly in Hartford, and then was called to Boston by Samuel Sewall to succeed printer John Foster, who had died 9 Sept. 1681. Judge Sewall was surety on the town's books for Samuel Green, Jr., and his family, on 16 Dec. 1681.[18] Later, when Sewall was released as public printer, Samuel, Jr., applied for the monopoly of the Boston press, but it was refused by the city council on 7 May 1685.[19] The press was then under the jealous surveillance of the Church-State in Massachusetts, especially after the appointment of Edward Randolph as licenser of the press by Governor Edmund Andros.[20] In the fall of 1689, Samuel, Jr., came under the disapproval of the government when he printed the first newspaper in America, *The Present State of New England Affairs*.[21]

That Samuel Green, Jr., was married and had a family is known definitely from remarks in Sewall's *Diary*. Also, John Dunton, a London bookseller who visited Boston in March 1686, mentioned in his book the particular devotion of Mrs. Green to her children.[22] Isaiah Thomas states that Elizabeth Sill was the wife of Samuel, Jr., but this has been disproved.[23] Elizabeth Alden has also been mentioned as the wife of Samuel, Jr. However, a search through the Alden records does not confirm this assumption.[24] Sewall states that the wife of his employee, Samuel Green, Jr., was Hannah.[25] Students of the Green family agree that Samuel, Jr., married Hannah, daughter of Dea. Richard Butler, of Hartford. The will of Deacon Butler, dated 2 April 1677, bequeathed twenty shillings to his daughter Hannah Green.[26] It is also known that prior to settling in Boston, Samuel, Jr., printed in Hartford.

Equal uncertainty prevailed as to the children of Samuel. One genealogist states that Mary, daughter of Samuel and Hannah Green, married John Kneeland, and that they had eight children, including Samuel Kneeland, a printer.[27] It is more probable, however, that John Kneeland, born in 1668, married Mary, born in 1669, the sister of Samuel, Jr. This same genealogist makes Timothy the son of Samuel, Jr., and calls Bartholomew, brother of Samuel, Jr., by the name of Benjamin, evidently mislead by the signature, "B. Green, printer". Sewall says that Samuel, Jr., had two children, Joseph and Jane, who died in childhood.[28] There are no recorded descendants of Samuel, Jr., in the printing trade. In July 1690, small pox made one of its all too frequent sweeps through Boston. On the 16th of that month, Sewall wrote in his *Diary:* "Mrs. Green, the Printer's wife, dies this day".[29] Samuel Green, Jr., died the following week.

Bartholomew, the second son of Samuel Green and Sarah Clark, was born in Cambridge 26 Oct. 1667. He served his apprenticeship with his father; in 1687 he went to Boston to work for his brother Samuel, Jr., whom we have just discussed. On Samuel, Jr's., death without heirs in July 1690, Bartholomew succeeded to the printing plant.[30] On September 16th the office was completely destroyed in the fire, which swept Boston, and "the best furnished printing press of those few that we know in America was lost; a loss not presently to be repaired".[31]

After this serious disaster, Bartholomew returned to Cambridge and worked with his father until the latter's retirement in 1692.[32] Bartholomew again went to Boston and rented the press of Richard Pierce. The following year he obtained his own press and was licensed to print by the Governor and Council of Massachusetts. For forty years Bartholomew was public printer and considered the leading craftsman of his time. On 24 April 1704, he published, under the direction of Postmaster John Campbell, the *Boston News-Letter*, first regularly issued newspaper in America.[33]

Bartholomew married Mary, daughter of Clement Short.[34] This has been disputed by some who confuse the printer with Capt. Bartholomew Green who married Marie Mather.[35] However, if one reads the papers of Cotton Mather, he will notice frequent references to Marie's widowhood in 1709 and her remarriage in 1711.[36] The Mather genealogy[37] and the records of wills in Charlestown, Mass.,[38] also help clarify the family picture.

Bartholomew Green and Mary had Bartholomew, Mary, Elizabeth, and Deborah. Mary Short died 28 March 1709 at age of forty-two.[39] Bartholomew married secondly, Jane, daughter of Jacob Toppan and Hannah Sewall on 10 June 1710. Judge Sewall officiated at the marriage of his niece. A son, Samuel, was born on 28 July 1712, but died in infancy.[40] Bartholomew Green died 28 Jan. 1732.

Again we run into genealogical problems in marrying off the daughters of Bartholomew and Mary Green. Each is reported to have married an apprentice of her father, a familiar custom in those times. Mary married Bezoan Allen, Elizabeth married Samuel Kneeland, and Deborah married John Draper.[41] However, the Kneeland genealogy, which bounds from one illustrous ancestor to another, finally reaching Scottish nobility in 1225, says that Samuel Kneeland married Elizabeth, a descendant of the famous John and Priscilla Alden.[42]

Deborah Green married John Draper on 24 May 1726.[43] Draper inherited the press of his father-in-law. The first issue of the *Boston News Letter*, published after the death of Bartholomew Green, contained the following notice: "Mr. Bartholomew Green

. . . being dead, . . . it will be carried on . . . by John Draper, son-in-law to the said Mr. Green who has been an assistant with him in the said News-Letter . . . "[44] On 30 Jan. 1734, the house and printing office were destroyed by fire. Neighborly printers lent Draper type until he received new equipment from England, and the Old South Church voted ten pounds to Mrs. Jane Green, widow of its former deacon, Bartholomew Green.[45] Deborah Green died 9 Dec. 1736, at the age of thirty-nine, and John Draper died at the age of sixty on 29 Nov. 1762.[46]

The children of Deborah and John Draper were Richard, born 24 Feb. 1727, and Lydia, born 21 Dec. 1729. Lydia married her cousin, John Green, on 4 Sept. 1755.[47] Richard, who succeeded to the press of his father and to the rôle of printer to the colony, married his cousin, Margaret, daughter of John Green, and grand-daughter of Bartholomew Green, on 22 March 1749. There were no children of this marriage.[47] After the death of Richard Draper on 4 June 1774, the press was continued by his widow Margaret or "Mother Draper" as she was referred to in Trumbull's McFingal.

The Drapers espoused the Tory side in the pre-Revolutionary quarrels, and the *News-Letter* was the medium for conservative Bostonians. During the siege of Boston it was the only paper published in the city.[48] The paper was finally discontinued 22 Feb. 1776, after a continuous existence of seventy-two years. Margaret Green Draper left Boston for Halifax with other royalists on 17 March 1776. The Draper property in Boston was confiscated, and sold on 7 Feb. 1783.[49] The exact date of Margaret Draper's death in London, England, is unknown. Sabine states it was in 1800,[50] but her will dated 1 Dec. 1802, in Pimlico, Middlesex, England, and probated in Boston 12 Feb. 1807, disproves this.[51]

Bartholomew, Jr., born in 1699, was the only surviving son of Bartholomew and Mary Green.[52] He served his apprenticeship with his father, and later worked with John Draper, his brother-in-law. Bartholomew, Jr., then formed a partnership with John Bushell and another brother-in-law, Bezoan Allen. He interrupted his printing business to participate in the Cape Breton campaign in 1744. Upon his return, he petitioned the legislature for the position of Doorkeeper to the General Court. When his request was denied he returned to his printing.

On 19 Nov. 1724, Bartholomew, Jr., married Hannah (born in 1704), daughter of Hannah Harrington and Eleazar Hammond of Newton. They had nine children, all baptised in the Old South Church in Boston:[53]

Mary,	2 Jan. 1726	Nathaniel,	25 April 1735
Bartholomew,	24 Sept. 1727	Elizabeth,	14 May 1738
Hannah,	31 Aug. 1729	Peter,	26 Oct. 1740
John,	15 Aug. 1731	Mary,	27 Feb. 1742
Samuel,	24 Feb. 1733		

In September 1751, Bartholomew, Jr., set up the first printing press in Halifax, Canada.[54] However, before he could begin actual operations, Bartholomew, Jr.'s, career was terminated by his death on 29 Oct. 1751.[55] His widow, Hannah, was still living on 29 Nov. 1760, when she was mentioned in her father's will.[56]

Of the surviving children of Hannah and Bartholomew Green, Jr., Elizabeth married Thomas Hichborn and moved to South Carolina, and Mary married James Dennie, a prominent West Indian merchant. Mary died 6 Sept. 1819.[57] Her claim to fame in the Green dynasty of printers is through her son, Joseph Dennie, born 30 Aug. 1768, who became a famous political pamphleteer.[58] He died 7 Jan. 1812.

Bartholomew, II, never operated an independent press. Although trained to be a printer, he was more interested in the sea. For many years he was a customs officer in Boston. He married Hannah Foster on 7 March 1771.[59a] The will of Bartholomew II, dated 18 March 1778 and probated April 17th the same year, named four daughters, Elizabeth, Hannah, Polly, and Lydia.[59]

The other brother, John, after being apprenticed to his uncle John Draper, formed a partnership with Joseph Russell. On 22 Aug. 1757, they issued the *Boston Weekly Advertiser* "for the purpose of collecting from time to time the newest and best intelligence".[60] This paper continued until 1768 when it merged with Richard Draper's *Boston News-Letter* and several others. This unusual arrangement lasted until April 1773, when the press of John Green's came under governmental disfavor, and it was succeeded as official printer to the British Commissioners by the firm of Mill and Hicks.

On 4 Sept. 1755, John Green married his cousin, Lydia, daughter of John Draper and Deborah Green.[61] He married secondly, Rebecca, daughter of Knight Leveritt. There were no children of either marriage. John Green died in November 1787, and is believed to have been the last of the descendants of Samuel Green of Cambridge to print in Massachusetts.[62] Isaiah Thomas states that John Green died in 1787 at the age of sixty, thus confusing John's birthdate with that of his brother, Bartholomew, II.[63]

We have now discussed Samuel, Jr., and Bartholomew and their descendants, two of the three printer sons of Samuel Green of Cambridge. The third and most prolific son, Timothy, is he whom Isaiah Thomas calls the son of Samuel Green, Jr.[64] This has already been refuted. Further proof is supplied in a letter, dated 12 Feb. 1732, Timothy wrote to Governor Talbott, lamenting the ill health and death of his brother Bartholomew.[64] Born in Cambridge in 1679, Timothy became the progenitor of a line of printers who carried the typographical art to Connecticut, Maryland, and Virginia.

Timothy served his apprenticeship with his father in Cambridge and later worked with his brother, Bartholomew, in Boston. At the age of twenty-one, he opened his own printing shop at Boston; the first book with his imprint is dated 1700. In 1707 he was invited by Governor Saltonstall of Connecticut to become printer to that colony, but he refused to leave a certainty for an uncertainty.[65] Thomas Short, former apprentice and brother-in-law of Bartholomew Green, accepted the position. After Short's death, Timothy was induced to accept the vacancy pursuant to a vote of the General Assembly at its May Session, 1713. For fifty pounds a year, equivalent to the Deputy Governor's salary, Timothy was to print election sermons, proclamations, and laws enacted at the several sessions of the assembly.[66]

In 1713, Timothy began printing in New London, Conn., but his family did not leave Boston until 10 Aug. 1714.[67] Because of his religious zeal, he was known as "Deacon Timothy", and it as such that we shall refer to him to prevent confusion with future Timothy's. Deacon Timothy continued as public printer to Connecticut until his retirement in 1751.

Deacon Timothy Green was married to Mary Flint in Boston by Rev. Cotton Mather 28 Jan. 1702.[68] Five children were born while the family still lived in Boston:

Timothy,   12 Dec. 1703
Samuel,   21 April 1706
John,   25 July 1708
Nathanial, 2 April 1710
Jonas,   28 Dec. 1712[69]

and three children were born after the family moved to New London:

Thomas, 31 Jan. 1715
John,   20 May 1719
Mary,   4 July 1722[70]

Mary Flint Green died 24 May 1748. Deacon Timothy married secondly, Abigail, daughter of Abigail Field and Charles Hill on 26 March 1749. She died 1 March 1779.[71] At the age of eighty-seven, Deacon Timothy Green died.[72]

It becomes increasingly difficult with the mitosis of the Green family to present the succeeding generations in a lucid manner. Of the children of Deacon Timothy, Mary married Robert Hosmer, of New London, 31 Oct. 1745, and died in East Haddam in 1808. Thomas became a pewterer in Boston. John and Nathanial were minor printers. John never operated an independent press. He worked with his father until 1751 and then with his brother Timothy, Jr. In 1757 John died without issue.

Nathanial was more interested in the local militia than in his trade. In 1744 he served as a Lieutenant with General Walcott against Cape Breton.[73] He then returned to New London and helped in the operation of the family press, first, under his father and then with his brothers. Nathanial married Mary, widow of Richard Christopher and daughter of John Pickett, 17 Jan. 1738. They had two daughters: Katharine, born 6 June 1740, and Lydia, born 22 April 1742.[74] Mary died 11 May 1754, and Nathanial in 1758.[75]

Timothy, Jr., the oldest son of Deacon Timothy, worked for his father for a time, and then returned to Boston, where he entered into partnership with his kinsman, Samuel Kneeland, a partnership which lasted from 1726 until 1752.[76] They published the *New Eng-*

land Weekly Journal until 1751, and printed the first English Bible in America.[77] On the retirement of Deacon Timothy in 1751, Timothy, Jr., returned to New London to operate the family press with his brothers, John, Nathanial, and Samuel. Timothy Green, Jr., died on 3 Oct. 1763.[78]

Samuel, II, second oldest son of Deacon Timothy, never operated an independent press. He was trained by his father and remained in the family business at New London. Samuel II married Abigail, daughter of Elizabeth Whitney and the Rev. Thomas Clark of Chelmsford, 12 Nov. 1733. There were nine children of this marriage:[79]

Abigal,	9 Aug. 1734	Anna,	19 Feb. 1741
Thomas,	25 Aug. 1735	Samuel,	23 Nov. 1743
Timothy,	2 April 1737	Mary,	26 July 1746
Elizabeth	23 Nov. 1738	Margaret,	18 Dec. 1749
Lucy,	22 April 1740		

Samuel, II, died in May 1752, and his widow, Abigail, died at the age of seventy-six 17 April 1781.[80]

The three sons, Thomas, Timothy, II, and Samuel, III, all became printers; because of the early death of their father, they served their apprenticeship with their uncle, Timothy, Jr., in New London.

Thomas, after learning his trade, was engaged by Postmaster Benjamin Mecom, who had bought out the printshop of James Parker in New Haven, where he published the *Connecticut Gazette*.[81] Thomas remained in New Haven from 1760 until 1764, when the paper was discontinued. He then moved to Hartford where 29 Oct. 1764, he began the *Connecticut Courant*, oldest existing paper in America.[82] In 1767 he took in Ebenezer Watson as a partner, and on February 8th the following year, Thomas returned permanently to New Haven. Here in addition to being a printer, publisher, editor, bookseller, and stationer, he set up a paper mill.[83] Thomas opposed the Stamp Act, but like other Episcopalians he was a Tory. From 1767 until 1809, his press did most of the printing for Yale College. On 2 Aug. 1781, President Ezra Stiles recorded in his diary: "The press in New Haven (Thomas Green) is a Tory Press and unobliging to the College".[84]

On 30 Sept. 1761, Thomas married Desire Sanford, who died 13 Oct. 1775. There were four children of this marriage:

Thomas, born in Hartford in 1765, baptised 17 Aug. 1766.
Anna, born 21 Sept. 1762, married Amaziah Lucas on 4 May 1794.
Lucy, born 24 March 1764, died of small-pox 13 June 1785.
A son, who died in infancy.[85]

Thomas retired in January 1809, at the age of seventy-four, and died in May (before the 26th) 1812.[86]

Thomas, Jr., was associated with his father in the printing trade. He became a partner in 1799 and on the retirement of his father in January 1809, Thomas, Jr., took full charge of the press. He founded the *Middlesex Gazette* and continued to publish the *Connecticut Gazette* and *New Haven Post Boy*, strong Whig papers.[87]

Thomas, Jr., was married twice. His first wife, Abigail, died 20 Sept. 1781. Their child, Desire, died 11 Aug. 1779. His second marriage was to Abigail Miles 21 March 1782. They had two children: Alfred, born 30 March 1783, and William Samuel, born 16 Dec. 1786. However, there were evidently other unrecorded children, because when Abigail died 24 Feb. 1814, she mentioned Sophia and Lucy in her will. Thomas Green, Jr., continued printing until his death in 1825.[88]

Samuel, III, born in 1743, followed the same pattern as his older brother Thomas. He served his apprenticeship with his uncle Timothy, Jr. Samuel, III, then joined his brother Thomas at New Haven in 1767. He died without issue in February 1799.

The most important of the three sons of Samuel, II, and Abigail Green was Timothy, II, born in 1737. On 1 Nov. 1763, he published the *New London Gazette*, a continuation of the *New London Summary*, which had been printed by the Green family prior to Deacon Timothy's death. In 1773, with his brother-in-law, Judah Paddock Spooner, he branched out and set up a press in Norwich, Conn.[89] In the spring of 1778, President Wheelock of Dartmouth College sent his son John to negotiate with Timothy, II, to set up a press at the college.[90] Timothy, II, declined. Therefore, in October 1778, the Vermont Legislature voted to make Spooner printer for the State.[91] Spooner and Timothy's son, Timothy, III, set up the first press in Westminster, Vt., where they published the *Vermont Gazette* and the *Green Mountain Post Boy*.[92]

Timothy, II, married Rebecca Spooner 2 July 1763. There were eleven children of this marriage:[93]

Timothy, 23 Sept. 1763	A son, died in infancy on 27 Feb. 1775
Thomas Clarke, 14 May 1765	Elizabeth, 12 June 1779
Samuel, 29 Feb. 1768	John, 12 June 1779
Son, 28 July 1770, died in infancy	Henry, 9 Feb. 1782, died
William, 14 Sept. 1771	
Rebecca, 30 April 1773	

Timothy, II, continued in business until May 1793, when ill-health forced him to relinquish the press to his son, Samuel, III. Timothy, II, died 10 March 1796, and his wife, Rebecca, died at the age of sixty-three 8 Feb. 1806.[94]

Elizabeth married Stephen Peck, and Rebecca married Samuel Haynes and died 6 March 1841. William became a minister and died 26 Dec. 1861.[95] John and Thomas followed the trade of booksellers and never operated independent presses. Thomas died 10 Sept. 1844, and John on 25 May 1846. Samuel, III, as previously mentioned, took over the press of his father in May 1793. He continued to publish the *New London Gazette* until his death in September 1860. Timothy, III, helped set up the first press in Westminster, Vt., with his uncle, Judah Paddock Spooner. In 1787, Timothy, III, went to Fredericksburg, Va., where on June 7th he founded the *Virginia Herald*.[96] Timothy Green, III, died 11 Jan. 1851.

We must now retrace our steps to Jonas, youngest son of Dea. Timothy Green and Mary Flint. Jonas served his apprenticeship with his father in New London and then worked for his brother Timothy, Jr., at Kneeland and Green's in Boston. In 1735, he independently issued A Grammar of the Hebrew Tongue by Judah Morris, Professor of Hebrew at Harvard College.[97] Then as a journeyman, Jonas traveled for several years.

Jonas was in Philadelphia in 1738 with either Franklin or Bradford where he learned of a printing opening in Annapolis. In 1740 he was printer to the Maryland colony at £500 a year, which position he held the remainder of his life. In April 1745, he revived the *Maryland Gazette*, which William Parker had first established in September 1727. The paper was continued uninterruptedly by Jonas except for a five months suspension in 1765 in objection to the Stamp Act.[98]

Jonas Green became one of the most active men in Maryland. He was not only an outstanding printer, but was postmaster, deacon, clerk to the General Court, Masonic official, and one of the leading literary figures of Annapolis.[99] From 1756 until 1766, William Rind, former apprentice, was associated with Jonas as a partner in the business. Rind severed relationships to set up a press in Williamsburg, Va.[100] In 1765 appeared Bacon's Laws of Maryland, the greatest project that Jonas undertook and on which his fame rests. After 1765 he was the only printer in the colony, with the exception of Nicholas Hasselback in Baltimore.[101]

On 25 April 1738, at Christ's Church, Philadelphia, Jonas Green married Anne Catherine Hoof, a native of Holland.[102] There were fourteen children of this marriage of whom eight died in infancy.[103]

John,	18 Oct. 1738		Frederick,	20 Jan. 1750
Rebecca,	22 Sept. 1740		Deborah,	19 Jan. 1752
Jonas,	12 Feb. 1743		Elizabeth,	10 Nov. 1753
Catherine,	4 Nov. 1743		Samuel,	27 April 1757
Marie,	7 Jan. 1745		Augusta,	4 April 1760
William,	21 Dec. 1746		? ,	29 Aug. 1755[103]
Anne,	19 Jan. 1748			

Jonas Green died 7 April 1767.[104] After his death, the business was carried on by his widow. In 1768 her oldest son, William, became a partner, serving until his death in August 1770. Anne then continued the printing business solely in her own name until her death 23 March 1775.[105] Isaiah Thomas gives her age at death as forty-two, which would make Anne only five years old at the time of her marriage in 1738.[106]

Frederick assumed control of the family printing business after the death of his mother. He also was appointed printer to the colony and postmaster of Annapolis.[107] In 1777 his young brother Samuel became a partner in the press. For a brief period and for the second time in its history, the *Maryland Gazette* ceased publication, when from 25 Dec. 1777, until 30 April 1779, it was discontinued because of political conditions.[108]

The two brothers continued to operate the press until the death of Frederick on 6 Jan. 1811, and of Samuel less than a week later on January 12th. Frederick had married and had five children: Jonas, a printer, William and James, clerks in the House of Delegates, Louis, employed in the Farmer's Bank of Maryland, and Henry. It is believed that Henry, or possibly his father or uncle, temporarily left Annapolis in 1800 and set up a press in Natchez, Miss., where he published the *Natchez Intelligensia.* "About March or April, 1800 a Mr. Green from Baltimore brought a press to Natchez".[109] The information is so vague that no definite conclusion can be drawn.

Jonas, Jr., the oldest son of Frederick, operated the family press after the death of his father and uncle. He continued to print the *Maryland Gazette* until 12 Dec. 1839, when ill-health caused his retirement. Jonas Green, Jr., died 1 Nov. 1845.[110]

With the death of Jonas, Jr., the Green family dynasty of printers in Maryland came to an end after one hundred years. Since Samuel Green, Sr., issued the *Platform of Church Discipline* from the Cambridge Press in 1649, the family tradition of printing had been followed through six generations, and one hundred and ninety years. The distinguished work of Samuel Green, Sr., of Cambridge, and his descendants in spreading the typographic arts through Massachusetts, Connecticut, Canada, Vermont, New Hampshire, Maryland, and Virginia is unprecedented and unequalled. The Green family is definitely an interesting phenomenon in the history of printing in America.

[1] Savage, James, ed., A Genealogical Dictionary of the First Settlers in New England, 4 vols. (Boston, 1860), II, p. 300.
[2] Littlefield, George E., The Early Massachusetts Press, 1638–1711, 2 vols. (Boston, 1907), I, p. 197.
   Morison, Samuel E., The Founding of Harvard College (Cambridge, 1936), p. 348.
[3] Pope, Charles Henry, The Pioneers of Massachusetts (Boston, 1900), p. 198.
[4] Quoted in Elizabeth C. Cook, Literary Influences in Colonial Newspapers (New York, 1912), p. 34.
[5] Savage, Genealogical Dictionary, II, p. 300.
[6] John Savage (ed.), Governor John Winthrop's History of New England, 1630–1690, 2 vols. (Boston, 1853), I, p. 348.
[7] Nathaniel B. Shurtleff (ed.), Records of the Governor and Company of the Massachusetts Bay in New England, 1628–1686, 5 vols. (Boston, 1853–1854), I, p. 344.
[8] Quoted in Winthrop Papers, Massachusetts Historical Society Collections, 5th Series (Boston), I, p. 422.
[9] Records of the Colony of New Plymouth in New England, 1620–1698, 12 vols. (Boston, 1855–1861), X, p. 447.
[10] Robert F. Roden, The Cambridge Press, 1638–1692 (New York, 1905).
[11] George Parker Winship, The Cambridge Press, 1638–1692 (Philadelphia, 1945), p. 362.
[12] Stephen Daye And His Successors, Published by Harvard University Press (Cambridge, 1921), p. 19.
[13] Savage, Genealogical Dictionary, II, p. 305.
[14] Samuel Abbott Green, An Account of Percival and Ellen Green (Groton, 1876).
[15] THE REGISTER, vol. 28, p. 199.
[16] Isaiah Thomas, The History of Printing in America, 2 vols. American Antiquarian Society Transactions, V–VI (Albany, 1874), I.
[17] The Genealogical Advertiser (Cambridge, 1901), IV, p. 51.
[18] Samuel Sewall, Diary of, Massachusetts Historical Society Collections, 3 vols., 5th series, V–VII (Boston, 1878–1882), V, p. 57.
[19] Clyde A. Duniway, The Development of Freedom of the Press in Massachusetts (Cambridge, 1906), p. 60.
[20] Thomas Hutchinson, The History of Massachusetts, 2 vols. (Salem, 1795), I, p. 318.
[21] Justin Winsor, (ed.), Memorial History of Boston, 4 vols. (Boston, 1885), II, p. 387.
[22] John Dunton, Life and Errors of (London, 1705), p. 129.
[23] Green, Percival and Ellen Green Genealogical Records.
[24] John Alden, The Alden Family (Boston, 1909).
[25] Littlefield, Massachusetts Press, II, p. 27.
   Winship, Cambridge Press, p. 346.

[26] Sewall, *Diary*, V, p. 324.
[27] Stillman Foster Kneeland, Seven Centuries in the Kneeland Family (New York, 1897), p. 51.
[28] Sewall, *Diary*, V, p. 324.
[29] *Ibid.*, V. p. 324.
[30] Littlefield, Massachusetts Press, II, p. 29.
[31] Quoted in Winsor, History of Boston, II, p. 388.
[32] Morison, Samuel E., Harvard College in the Seventeenth Century, 2 vols. (Cambridge, 1936), I, p. 352.
[33] Palfrey, John G., Palfrey's History of New England, 5 vols. (Boston, 1890), IV, p. 304.
[34] William DeLoss Love, Thomas Short, The First Printer of Connecticut (Boston, 1901), p. 24.
[35] Thomas Bridgman (ed.) Copp's Hill Burial Ground, Boston (Boston, 1851), p. 33.
[36] Cotton Mather, Diary of, *Massachusetts Historical Society Collections*, 7th series, vols. VII, VIII (Boston, 1782).
[37] Horace E. Mather, Lineage of Rev. Richard Mather (Hartford, 1890), p. 99.
[38] Thomas B. Wyman, The Genealogies and Estates of Charlestown, Massachusetts, 1629–1818, 2 vols. (Boston, 1879), I, p. 437.
[39] Sewall, *Diary*, VII, p. 252.
[40] *Ibid.*, II, p. 363.
[41] William De Loss Love, Thomas Short, The First Printer of Connecticut (Boston, 1901), p. 25.
[42] Kneeland, Kneeland Genealogy, p. 51.
[43] Thomas Waln Draper, The Drapers in America (New York, 1892), p. 197.
[44] Quoted in Winsor, History of Boston.
[45] Hamilton A. Hill, History of Old South Church, 2 vols. (Boston, 1890), I, p. 467.
[46] Draper, Drapers in America, p. 197.
[47] *Ibid.*
[48] Richard Frothingham, History of the Siege of Boston (Boston, 1849), p. 32.
[49] *Massachusetts Historical Society Collections*, 2nd series (Boston, 1872), X, p. 107.
[50] Lorenzo Sabine, Loyalists of the American Revolution, 2 vols. (Boston, 1864), I, p. 386.
[51] Harold Milton Ellis, Joseph Dennie and His Circle (Austin, 1915), p. 15.
[52] John C. Oswald, A History of Printing (New York, 1928), p. 59.
[53] Frederick S. Hammond, Genealogy of Hammond Families, 2 vols. (Oneida, 1904), II, p. 13.
[54] Thomas G. Wright, Literary Culture in Early New England (New Haven, 1920), p. 80.
[55] Burial Records of St. Paul's Parish, Halifax, Nova Scotia.
[56] Hammond, Hammond Genealogies, II, p. 13.
[57] Laura Green Pedder, The Letters of Joseph Dennie (Orono, 1936), p. 2.
[58] Frank Luther Mott, A History of the American Magazine, 3 vols. (New York, 1930), I, p. 225.
[58a] Early History of Boston Containing Boston Marriages from 1752–1809 (Boston, 1903), p. 430.
[59] Ellis, Joseph Dennie, p. 16.
[60] Quoted in Winsor, History of Boston, II, p. 387.
[61] Draper, Draper Genealogy, p. 197.
[62] Oswald, History of Printing, p. 65.
[63] Thomas, History of Printing, I, p. 147.
[64] Littlefield, Early Printing in Massachusetts, II, p. 73.
[65] Francis Manwaring Caulkins, History of New London, Connecticut, 2 vols. (New London, 1852), I, p. 357.
[66] Benjamin Trumbull, A Complete History of Connecticut, 2 vols. (New London, 1898), I, p. 385.
[67] Sewall, *Diary*, VII, p. 14.
[68] J. Lawrence Bass, Flint Family (Frankford, 1912), p. 5.
[69] Chandler Robbins (ed.) A History of the 2nd Church, or Old North in Boston (Boston, 1852), p. 250.
[70] *The Genealogical Advertiser* (Cambridge, 1901), IV, p. 51.
[71] Thomas Spooner, Records of William Spooner of Plymouth, Massachusetts (Cincinnati, 1883), p. 147.
[72] Caulkins, History of New London, I, p. 471.
[73] *Ibid.*, I, p. 391.
[74] THE REGISTER, vol. 16, p. 15.
[75] *Genealogical Advertiser*, VI, p. 51.
[76] Albert Carlos Bates, "Check List of Connecticut Almanacs", American Antiquarian Society (Albany, 1914), April, 8, 1914, p. 98.
[77] American Antiquarian Society, New Series, vol. 26, p. 32.
[78] THE REGISTER, vol. 16, p. 15.
[79] Caulkins, History of New London, I, p. 471.
[80] Spooner, Records of William Spooner, p. 148.
[81] Charles R. Hildeburn, Sketches of Printers and Printing (New York, 1895), p. 66.
[82] *Papers of the New Haven Historical Society* (New Haven, 1914), VIII, p. 307. Article on Thomas Green, 289–309, by Albert C. Bates.
[83] New Haven Historical Society, VIII, p. 307.
[84] Franklin B. Dexter, The Literary Diary of Ezra Stiles, 4 vols. (New York, 1901), III, p. 549.
[85] William De Loss Love, The Colonial History of Hartford (Hartford, 1935), p. 342.
[86] New Haven Historical Society, VIII, p. 307.
[87] Douglas C. McMurtrie, A History of Printing in the United States, 2 vols. (New York, 1936), I, p. 302.
[88] Oswald, History of Printing, p. 66.
[89] Francis M. Caulkins, History of Norwich, Connecticut (New London, 1866), p. 361.
[90] Douglas C. McMurtrie, The Beginning of Printing in New Hampshire, *The Library*, 4th Ser., Vol. XV (New York, 1935), XV, p. 352.
[91] Abby Maria Hemenway, *Vermont Historical Gazetteer* (Brandon, 1891), V, p. 60.
[92] Henry O. Houghton, Address on Early Printing in America, delivered before the Vermont Historical Society at Montpelier, October 25, 1894.
[93] Spooner, Records of William Spooner, p. 148.

[94] *Ibid.*

[95] John Farmer, Genealogical Register of the First Settlers in New England (Lancaster, 1829), p. 129.

[96] Frederick Hudson, Journalism in the United States from 1690 to 1872 (New York, 1873), p. 122.

[97] Winsor. History of Boston, II, p. 402.

[98] Charles Albrow Barker, The Background of the Revolution in Maryland (New Haven, 1940), p. 63.

[99] Walter Norris, Annapolis, Its Colonial and Naval Story (New York, 1925), p. 74.

[100] McMurtrie, History of Printing, I, p. 115.

[101] Joseph Town Wheeler, The Maryland Press, 1777–1790 (Baltimore, 1938), p. 65.

[102] *Pennsylvania Archives*, 2nd Series (Harrisburgh, 1878), VIII, p. 105. Marriages at Christ's Church, Philadelphia.

[103] Lawrence C. Wroth, A History of Printing in Colonial Maryland, 1686–1776 (Baltimore, 1922), p. 79.

[104] The REGISTER, vol. 16, p. 15.

[105] Wroth, Printing in Colonial Maryland, p. 93.

[106] Thomas, History of Printing, II, p. 157.

[107] Wheeler, The Maryland Press, p. 69.

[108] *Ibid.*, p. 66.

[109] Quoted in Clarence S. Brigham, Bibliography of American Newspapers 1690–1820, American Antiquarian Society, vol. 26, p. 84.

[110] Wheeler. The Maryland Press, p. 70.

THE GRIFFIN FAMILY OF HAMPTON, CONN.

[By George Chandler, M. D., Worcester, Mass.]

Most of the following facts were furnished by Jonathan Clark, Esq., of Hampton, Conn., who has been constantly engaged, for about sixty-eight years, in carefully noting down all facts of the kind that occurred within his extensive and minute observation in that vicinity.

1. Ebenezer[1] Griffin moved from Cambridge to Pomfret—thence to the Canada parish of Windham, now Hampton, Conn. He was a farmer, and bought of William Durkee there one hundred acres of land. He and his wife joined the church there 28 June, 1733, and he was chosen deacon 1 March, 1744. He married Hannah, who was born 20 Jan. 1713, dau. of Dea. Philemon and Hannah (Clary) Chandler of Pomfret. Their children—

1. *Hannah*[2] (ii.), b. 11 Sept. 1732; bp. 28 Jan. 1733; m., 11 April, 1751, James Stedman of Hampton.
2. *Ebenezer*[2] (iii.), b. 20 July, 1734; bp. 28 July, 1734; m., 1 July, 1757, Elizabeth Martin.
3. *Sarah*[2] (iv.), b. 12 Aug., 1736; bp. 15 Aug. 1736; m., 19 Jan. 1757, Thomas Fuller of Hampton.
4. *Lucy*[2] (v.), b. 17 April, 1737; bp. 22 April, 1739; m., 15 Nov. 1758, Hezekiah Hammond.
5. *Mehitable*[2] (vi.), b. 29 Nov. 1741; bp. 6 Dec. 1741; m., 23 Sept. 1760, Thomas Stedman.
6. *Mary*[2] (vii.), b. 16 March, 1744; bp. March, 1744; m., 6 March, 1766, Ephraim Cleveland.
7. *Benjamin*,[2] b. 7 Aug. 1746: bp. 10 Aug. 1746; d. 11 Nov. 1748.
8. *Nathaniel*,[2] b. 23 Aug. 1748; bp. 28 Aug. 1748; d. 7 April, 1754.
9. *Olive*,[2] b. 6 March, 1751; bp. 1751.
10. *Benjamin*[2] (viii.), b. 10 May, 1754; bp. 12 May, 1754; m., 8 Feb. 1776, Chloe Howard; m. 2d, 4 Jan. 1786, Mary Howard.

II. Hannah[2] Griffin [i., 1] m. Capt. James Stedman, by Rev. Samuel Moseley of Hampton, 11 April, 1751. She was then 18 years 7 months old. She joined the church 26 Nov. 1789; d. 30 Aug. 1795, aged 62 years 7 months 21 days. He b. in Brookline, Mass., 1725; made member of the church 15 Nov. 1741; d. 7 Sept. 1788, aged 63. He was a "good farmer, carpenter, joiner, and clock-maker." He was appointed, by the legislature of Connecticut, "captain, in place of Ripley, resigned," 26 June, 1776. Capt. Stedman was, with his company of Hampton militia, in the Revolution, at the battle at "White Plains;" also in Rhode Island; and with his colonel (Thomas Knowlton) when he charged into the very heart of the 42d regiment of Highlanders on Harlem Plains, where he received his mortal wound, from a bullet, in the groin, and was taken off his horse by Captain Stedman's orderly-sergeant Nehemiah Holt, and others, and laid by a fence, out of range of bullets, where he soon bled to death. Capt. S. was with Washington in his retreat before the British through New Jersey. Of that march Sergeant Holt often said, "All night Washington rode at the right of the column, a little in advance, but so near me that I could most of the time put my hand upon the rump of the powerful gray charger upon which he rode, made restive by the cold sleet pouring down upon us, but whose maddened spirit was curbed in and controlled with apparent ease by his more powerful rider, his rein-hand resting upon the pommel of the saddle. Washington spoke scarcely a word during that dreadful march." After the war, Capt. S. was collector of taxes, and held other offices in Hampton. He died of scrofulous disease—beloved, honored, and respected.

Crayon portraits of him and his wife, by Joseph Stewart of Hartford, Conn., are in possession of the writer. His children were—

1. *Thomas,*[3] b. 6 Nov. 1761; bp. 15 Nov. 1761; m. Lucy Warren of Windham. He graduated at Yale College in 1785. He was a lawyer in Hampton, and afterwards a farmer in Massena, N. Y.
2. *Hannah,*[3] b. 23 Nov. 1769; bp. 26 Nov. 1769; d. unm. 14 July, 1795.
3. *Mary,*[3] b. 14 Jan. 1772; bp. 17 Jan. 1773; m., 20 Nov. 1792, Maj. John Wilkes Chandler of Pomfret, Conn., farmer.

III. EBENEZER[2] GRIFFIN [i., 2], when 24 years old, was, by Parson Moseley, m. to Elizabeth, dau. of Ebenezer and Jerusha Martin, when she was 18 years old. She b. 1 Aug. 1738. He was a farmer in Hampton, Conn.

1. *Nathaniel,*[3] b. 13 Oct. 1759; bp. 10 June, 1760; d. 20 Nov. 1760.
2. *Nathaniel,*[3] b. 11 Oct. 1761; bp. 18 Oct. 1761; m. —— Clark, and moved to Whitestown, N. Y.
3. *Hannah,*[3] b. 1 Aug. 1763; bp. 1 Aug. 1763; m., in 1785, Calvin Munn of Greenfield, Mass. He b. in Munson, Mass., 1761. He entered the army, and served until the close of the war of the Revolution. Was at the siege of Yorktown; the taking of Cornwallis; was one of the company that took a gun-boat from the British at Shirley, on James River, and rowed the boat up to head quarters, when LaFayette came on board and conversed with him; was as far north as Stillwater, and west of the Blue ridge; served in Col. Shepherd's and Vose's regiments; was one year under LaFayette's command, in Virginia; witnessed the execution of Andre; under Sullivan when he evacuated Long Island; at the battle of Jamestown; was one of the government troops ordered out for the protection of the U. S. Arsenal at Springfield, Mass., in Shay's insurrection. He was present at the laying of the corner-stone of Bunker Hill Monument, in 1824, and had a pleasant interview with LaFayette, his old commander. He kept tavern in Greenfield where the Mansion House now stands. He d. at Springfield, Vt., 3 May, 1850, and was buried in Greenfield, Mass. She d. at Greenfield, 22 Feb. 1814.
4. *Artemissa,*[3] b. 11 Nov. 1765; bp. 24 Nov. 1765; m. Isaac Burnham.
5. *Elwissa,*[3] b. 23 Feb. 1768; bp. 6 March, 1768; m. Richard Edwards, lawyer in Albany, N. Y.
6. *Olive,*[3] b. 12 April, 1770; bp. 29 April, 1770; m. 1st, Dr. Daniel Lummis; m. 2d, Charles Child of Pomfret, Conn.
7. *Betsey,*[3] b. 24 Aug. 1772; bp. 30 Aug. 1733; m. —— Churchill of Chatham, Conn.
8. *Ebenezer,*[3] b. 6 April, 1775; bp. 9 April, 1775; m. 1st, Mary Fuller of Hampton; m. 2d, Lois Durkee of Hampton; m. 3d, Lydia Hunting. He lives on his grandfather's homestead in Hampton, and was always a farmer. He was one of the judges of the county court many years; represented the town in the legislature in several sessions, and was "Father of the house in 1854." His

1st wife was the only child of Stephen, by his wife Sarah (Bidlack) Fuller, who was burned by the Indians in the battle at Wyoming, 3 July, 1778, in a wheat field—the Indians piling sheaves of wheat about him and other prisoners. She d. 18 June, 1800.

9. *Elisha*,³ b. 6 May, 1777; bp. 18 May, 1777; m. Clarissa Burnett.
10. *Lucy*,³ b. 21 July, 1779; bp. 25 July, 1779; m. William Forbes of Bangor, Me., farmer. He b. in Westboro', Mass.; raised in Brookfield; a merchant in Greenfield, Mass., where he was prosperous until the embargo injured his business, as well as that of others. He moved, in 1799, to Bangor, and purchased a farm, on which he d. in 1843. He was an intelligent and honest gentleman of the old school. She was married just before she was 16 years old, and d. in 1850.

IV. SARAH² GRIFFIN [i., 3], when 20 years old, m., 19 Jan. 1757, Lieut. Thomas Fuller of Hampton. He b. 10 June, 1732, and d. 14 Nov. 1813, in his 82d year. She d. 8 May, 1806, in her 70th year. He was son of Stephen and Hannah (Moulton) Fuller. Children—
1. *Nathaniel*,³ b. 14 May, 1758; m. Mary Durkee, dau. of Andrew and Mary, when she was 16 years 6 months and 4 days old.
2. *Sarah*,³ b. 14 May, 1760; m. 1st, —— Knight; m. 2d, Nathan Jennings. She d. in Chaplin, Conn., 7 June, 1853.
3. *Lucy*,³ b. 8 Aug. 1763; m. Col. Elijah Simons, merchant of Hampton, Conn., son of Jacob S. of Windham, Conn. She d. in Chaplin, 7 April, 1848, in her 85th year.
4. *Thomas*,³ b. 21 July, 1765; m. Polly Fuller, dau. of Joseph of Hampton. He practised medicine in Cooperstown, N. Y. successfully, and was much respected. It was said that he was the original of Cooper's character of " Dr. Elnathan Todd " of the " Spy."
5. *Eleanor*,³ b. 6 Aug. 1768; m., 25 Jan. 1788, Dea. Amasa Clark of Hampton. She d. of fever, 10 Nov. 1833.

V. LUCY² GRIFFIN [i., 4] m., 15 Nov. 1785, Hezekiah Hammond of Hampton, Conn., son of Josiah. She d. 20 Aug. 1824, aged 84 years 4 months 3 days.
1. *Lucy*,³ b. 30 Aug. 1760; m. John Clark, son of Timothy of Coventry.
2. *Olive*,³ b. 8 July, 1764; m. Charles Child of Pomfret, Conn.
3. *Eleanor*,³ b. 19 May, 1769; m. Jacob Holt for his 2d wife.
4. *Asahel*,³ b. 10 May, 1772; m., 9 Dec. 1801, Betsey Robinson. Farmer in Hampton.
5. *Elisha*,³ b. 26 May, 1780; m. Phebe Hitchcock, and lived in West Brookfield, Mass.
6. *Hezekiah*,³ b. 8 Dec. 1782; m. Polly Greenslit.

VI. MEHITABLE² GRIFFIN [i., 5], in her 19th year, m., by Parson Mosely of Hampton, to Thomas Stedman, Jr., son of Dea. Thomas and Anna (Seaver) Stedman of Hampton. He b. in Brookline, Mass., 1732; carpenter and joiner; town clerk of Hampton from its incorporation, 1786, to 1798; representative in legislature in 1787 and 1793. Children—
1. *Mary*,³ b. 14 April, 1762; m. Israel Clark, goldsmith, Newburgh, N.Y.
2. *Anna*,³ b. 7 Aug. 1764; m. Joseph Clark; moved to Alabama.
3. *Elizabeth*,³ b. 5 Aug. 1768; m. Dea. Thomas Williams of Hampton, Conn.

4. *Griffin*,[3] b. 27 Sept. 1770 ; m. Betsey Gordon. Lumber merchant, Hartford, Conn.

5. *Clarissa*,[3] b. 23 Jan. 1772 ; m. Abijah Peck ; moved to Alabama.

6. *Thomas*,[3] b. 19 Aug. 1774 ; unm.

7. *Ebenezer*,[3] b. 23 March, 1777 ; m. Rachel Wattles.

8. *James*,[3] b. 6 Oct. 1779 ; m. Eunice H. Carren. Lawyer, Norwich, Conn.

9. *Patience*,[3] b. 27 July, 1781 ; m. Jonathan Hovey, Jr.

VII. MARY[2] GRIFFIN [i., 6] m., 6 March, 1766, Ephraim Cleveland. Children—

1. *Mary*,[3] b. 30 March, 1768.   2. *Franklin*,[3] b. 13 Aug. 1779.

VIII. BENJAMIN[2] GRIFFIN [i., 10], farmer in Hampton, m., 8 Feb. 1776, Chloe Howard, dau. of John Howard, Jr.   Children—

1. *Clarinda*,[3] b. 16 Nov. 1776.   2. *Molly*,[3] b. 7 March, 1778.

3. *Benjamin*,[3] b. 26 June, 1780.   4. *Sarah*,[3] b. 27 June, 1782.

5. *John*,[3] b. 29 Oct. 1784.

His wife, Chloe, d. 16 Nov. 1784, in her 30th year, and he m. 2d, 4 Jan. 1786, her sister, Mary Howard.   Had—

6. *John*,[3] b. 5 Oct. 1786.

Capt. Benjamin[2] moved, in 1788, to Cooperstown, N. Y.

THE HALE FAMILY OF CONNECTICUT.

By SEYMOUR MORRIS, Esq., of Chicago, Ill.

1.   SAMUEL[1] HAILL, or HALE, was born in 1610.   He was in Wethersfield, Conn., in 1637.   He served in the Pequot war, and received a grant of sixty acres of land from the General Court for his services in that war. In 1639 he was in Hartford, Conn., where he owned a lot on the east side of the river; and in 1642 he settled in Wethersfield, Conn., where he was a selectman in 1647.   He was one of the first proprietors of Norwalk, in 1654, and served as a deputy from that town to the General Court, from 1656 to 1659.   In 1660 he returned to Wethersfield, Conn., where he leased the estate of Governor Welles, on the east side of the Connecticut River. At a town meeting held Feb. 23, 1670, he was chosen as one of a committee of three "to repair the whole meeting house."   He died at Glastonbury, Nov. 9, 1693; and his widow, Mary, died Jan. 19, 1711–12.

Children :

  i.   MARTHA,[2] b. Oct. 2, 1643.

2. ii.   SAMUEL, b. Feb. 12, 1644–5; m. Ruth Edwards.

3. iii.   JOHN, b. Feb. 21, 1646–7; m. Hannah Nott.

  iv.   MARY, b. Apr. 29, 1649; m. Caleb Benjamin.

  v.   REBECCA, b. Oct. 29, 1651.

4. vi.   THOMAS, b. 1653; m. Naomi Kilbourn.

  vii.   BENNEZER, b. July 29, 1661.

  viii.   DOROTHY.

2. LIEUT. SAMUEL² HALE (*Samuel¹*) was born Feb. 12, 1644–5, in Wethersfield, Conn. He married first, June 20, 1670, Ruth, daughter of Thomas Edwards, who died Dec. 26, 1682, aged 30; and married second, in 1695, Mary, daughter of Samuel and Elizabeth (Hollister) Welles, who was born Nov. 23, 1666, and died Feb. 18, 1714–5, aged 48. He resided in Glastonbury, Conn., and was a Justice of the Peace. He died Nov. 18, 1711, aged 67.

Children by first wife:

    i.   RUTH,³ b. Jan. 14, 1670; d. May 7, 1671.
    ii. SAMUEL, b. June 14, 1673–4; d. June 15, 1673–4.
    iii. MARY, b. June 13, 1675; m. John Day.
    iv. SAMUEL, b. July 17, 1677.
    v. RUTH, b. Dec. 1, 1680; m. Thomas Kimberly.

Children by second wife:

5. vi. CAPT. JONATHAN, b. Aug. 21, 1696.
    vii. DAVID, b. Jan. 7, 1700; d. Mar. 31, 1718.
    viii. JOSEPH, b. July 10, 1702; d. Aug. 4, 1702.
6. ix. BENJAMIN, b. July 22, 1707.

3. JOHN² HALE (*Samuel¹*) was born Feb. 21, 1646–7, in Wethersfield. He married, May 8, 1668, Hannah, born June 10, 1649, in Wethersfield, daughter of John and Ann Nott. He died July 19, 1709.

Children:

7. i.   JOHN,³ b. Feb. 7, 1669; m. Mary ———.
    ii. SAMUEL, b. Apr. 3, 1671.
    iii. HANNAH, b. June 1, 1673.
8. iv. THOMAS, b. Sept., 1675; m. Mercy Hurlbut.
    v. REBECCA, b. Nov. 1, 1681; d. Nov. 15, 1681.
9. vi. EBENEZER, b. Dec. 24, 1682; m. Ruth Curtis.

4. THOMAS² HALE (*Samuel¹*) was born in 1653. He married, Oct. 30, 1679, Naomi, daughter of John and Naomi Kilbourn, who was born in 1656, and died May 17, 1735, aged 79. He lived in Glastonbury, Conn., where he died Dec. 23, 1723, aged 70.

Children:

    i.   NAOMI,³ b. Sept. 30, 1680.
    ii. MARY, b. Nov. 20, 1682; m. Oct. 16, 1702, Edward Benton; d. May 3, 1756.
10. iii. THOMAS, b. Sept. 17, 1684; m. Susannah Smith.
11. iv. TIMOTHY, b. 1692; m. Sarah Frary.
12. v. NATHANIEL, b. 1694; m. Abigail Francis.
    vi. RUTH, m. Benj. Hollister, who was b. Feb. 5, 1694. (See Hollister Genealogy, page 57.)
    vii. EUNICE, m. Jan. 4, 1713–4, Ebenezer Kilbourn, who was b. Mar. 27, 1696, and d. Aug. 26, 1759.

5. CAPT. JONATHAN³ HALE (*Samuel,² Samuel¹*) was born Aug. 21, 1696. He married first, Nov. 28, 1717, Sarah, daughter of Dea. Benjamin and Sarah (Hollister) Talcott, who was born Oct. 30, 1699, and died Jan. 15, 1743, aged 44; married second, Hannah ———, who died May 26, 1749, aged 54; and married third, Mrs. Mary Hollister (widow of Josiah Hollister, Jr.), who died Jan. 18, 1780, aged 82. Capt. Hale died July 2, 1772, aged 76.

Children, all by first wife:

    i.   SARAH,⁴ b. Nov. 2, 1718.
13. ii. JONATHAN, b. Feb. 1 (or 7), 1720–1; m. Elizabeth Welles.
    iii. DAVID, b. Jan. 13, 1722–3; d. Jan. 7, 1723–4.

14. iv. ELIZUR, b. Jan. 15, 1724-5; m. Abigail Hollister.
15. v. DAVID, b. Jan. 11, 1727; m. Mary Welles.
    vi. PENLOPE, b. Mch. 13, 1731.
    vii. PRUDENCE, b. Aug. 21, 1733; m. Mar. 30, 1763, Joseph Blague.
16. viii. THEODORE, b. Jan. 26, 1735; m. Rachel Talcott.

6. BENJAMIN³ HALE (Lieut. *Samuel*,² *Samuel*¹) was born July 22, 1707, in Glastonbury, Conn. He married, Jan. 30, 1729, Hannah, daughter of Dea. Benjamin and Sarah (Hollister) Talcott, who was born Oct. 16, 1706, and died Feb. 6, 1796, in her 90th year. He died July 22, 1784, in his 77th year.
Children :
    i. HANNAH,⁴ b. May 9, 1732; m. Timothy⁴ Hale (see 23).
    ii. RUTH, b. July 14, 1734; m. Apr. 6, 1758, Daniel, son of Timothy Hale (lineage untraced). Children: 1. *Ruth*, b. Jan. 14, 1759. 2. *Bathsheba*, b. Feb. 10, 1761. 3. *Rachel*, b. Oct. 28, 1763. 4. *Daniel*, b. Dec. 15, 1765. 5. *Thomas*, b. June 10, 1768. 6. *Mehitable*, b. July 31, 1770. 7. *Happy*, b. Sept. 2, 1772. 8. *Honor*, b. July 2, 1775; d. Jan. 30, 1776.
17. iii. GIDEON, b. Dec. 30, 1736; m. Mary White.
    iv. RACHEL, b. Apr. 25, 1739.
    v. MARY, b. Mch. 1, 1742; d. June 22, 1790.
    vi. BENJAMIN, b. Feb. 1, 1745.
    vii. JOSIAH, b. July 27, 1747; m. May 30, 1771, Ann Welles. Child : *Clarissa*,⁵ b. Sept. 12, 1776; d. Apr. 12, 1854; m. Ephraim Strong, who was b. Dec. 20, 1771, and d. Jan. 20, 1860. (See Strong Genealogy, page 501).

7. JOHN³ HALE (*John*,² *Samuel*¹) was born Feb. 7, 1668, in Wethersfield. He married Mary ———.
Children :
    i. MARY,⁴ b. Nov. 10, 1697.
    ii. JOHN, b. Mar. 10, 1699–1700.
18. iii. SAMUEL, b. Feb. 27, 1701; m. Sarah Smith.
    iv. ANN, b. May 30, 1705.
    v. BENONI, b. Jan. 23, 1706.
    vi. ABIGAIL, b. Dec. 20, 1708.
    vii. THANKFUL, b. Feb. 26, 1710.
    viii. HANNAH, b. Oct. 27, 1712.
    ix. SARAH, Aug. 15, 1714.

8. THOMAS³ HALE (*John*,² *Samuel*¹) was born Sept., 1675, in Wethersfield. He married Mercy, daughter of John and Mary (Deming) Hurlbut, who was born Feb. 17, 1680–1, in Middletown, Conn., and died Aug. 21, 1719, aged 38. About 1721, he removed to Chatham, Conn. He died June 26, 1743, aged 69 years.
Children :
    i. MARY,⁴ m. George Ranney, who d. Mch. 28, 1725.
    ii. THOMAS, b. 1707; m. Abigail ———.
    iii. SARAH, b. 1707; d. Jan. 22, 1797.
    iv. A DAUGHTER, m. Jonathan Smith.

9. EBENEZER³ HALE (*John*,² *Samuel*¹) was born Dec. 24, 1682, in Wethersfield, Conn., and removed to Middletown, Conn. He married first, Ruth, daughter of Samuel and Sarah Curtis, who was born May 17, 1687, in Wethersfield, and died Dec., 1724, at Middletown, Conn.; and married second, Apr. 4, 1725, Abigail, daughter of Thomas Miller of Middletown, Conn.

Children by first wife :

i. HANNAH,[4] bapt. Mar. 26, 1706-7, at Wethersfield.
ii. DOROTHY, bapt. Mar. 21, 1707-8, at Wethersfield.
19. iii. JOSEPH, b. Mar. 17, 1709-10, at Wethersfield; m. Hannah ——.
20. iv. GIDEON, b. July 4, 1712, at Wethersfield.
v. EPHRAIM, b. May 7, 1719, at Middletown.
21. vi. EBENEZER, b. Mar. 15, 1721, at Middletown; m. (1) Sarah Watts; m. (2) Sarah Wood.
22. vii. ELISHA, b. Aug. 23, 1724, at Middletown; m. Sibyl ——.

Children by second wife :

viii. DANIEL, b. Jan. 16, 1725-6; d. Feb. 6, 1725-6.
ix. STEPHEN, b. July 9, 1727.
x. ELIZABETH, b. Jan. 29, 1728-9.
xi. ISAAC, b. Oct. 7, 1730; served in Capt. John Slap's Co., in the pay of New York, May, 1755.

10. THOMAS[3] HALE (*Thomas,[2] Samuel[1]*) was born Sept. 17, 1684. He married, Jan. 11, 1721-2, Susannah, daughter of Nathaniel and Esther Smith of Hartford, Conn. He was killed by lightning, July 4, 1750, aged 66, at Glastonbury.

Children :

i. SUSANNA,[4] b. Mch. 21, 1722-3.
ii. MERCY, b. Nov. 3, 1724.
iii. THOMAS, b. July 25, 1726; d. Nov. 22, 1739.
iv. MOSES, b. June 29, 1729; m. July 29, 1752, Mary Edwards of Cromwell, Conn.
v. JERUSHA, b. Aug. 8, 1730.
vi. MABELL, b. July 17, 1732.
vii. NATHANIEL, b. Aug. 30, 1734.
viii. ASHBELL, b. Apr. 6, 1737.
xi. NAOMY, b. May 13, 1739.

11. TIMOTHY[3] HALE (*Thomas,[2] Samuel[1]*) was born in 1692. He married Sarah, daughter of Lieut. Samuel and Sarah (Boardman) Frary, who was born in 1700, and died Sept. 20, 1770, aged 70, in Glastonbury. He died Aug. 9, 1784, aged 92 years, in Glastonbury, Conn.

Children :

i. SARAH,[4] b. Apr. 7, 1725.
23. ii. TIMOTHY, b. Aug. 3, 1727; m. Hannah[4] Hale (see 6, i).
iii. FRARY, b. Jan. 27, 1728-9.
iv. ISAAC, b. Aug. 11, 1732.

12. NATHANIEL HALE (*Thomas,[2] Samuel[1]*) was born in 1694. He married, Nov. 17, 1717, Abigail, daughter of Sergt. John and Mary (Chittenden?) Francis, who was born Mar. 8, 1695, and survived him. He died Jan. 10, 1738-9.

Children :

i. LUCY,[4] b. Sept. 6, 1718.
24. ii. BENEZER, b. Jan. 26, 1719-20; m. Ann Woodhouse.
25. iii. JUSTUS, b. June 29, 1725; m. Feb. 28, 1749-50, Martha Wright.
26. iv. HEZEKIAH, b. Aug. 29, 1729; m. Jan. 15, 1756, Abigail Hanmer.
v. NATHANIEL, b. Jan. 10, 1738-9.

13. CAPT. JONATHAN[4] HALE (*Capt. Jonathan,[3] Samuel,[2] Samuel[1]*) was born Feb. 1 (or 7), 1720-1. He married, Jan. 18, 1743-4, Elizabeth, daughter of Col. Thomas and Martha (Pitkin) Welles, who

was born Nov. 15, 1722, in Glastonbury, Conn. His will, dated Feb. 8, 1773, was proved Dec. 25, 1776.

Children :

    i. ELIZABETH,[5] b. Dec. 22, 1744; d. Aug. 3, 1746.
    ii. JONATHAN, b. Jan. 15, 1745–6.
    iii. ELIZABETH, b. Aug. 16, 1747; m. —— Huntington.
27. iv. ELISHA, m. Elizabeth Mary Whiting.
    v. GEORGE.
    vi. THOMAS.
    vii. SARAH.
    viii. PENLOPE.
    ix. ANNE.
    x. EUNICE.
    xi. JERUSHA.
    xii. LUCRETIA.

14. DR. ELIZUR[4] HALE (*Capt. Jonathan,*[3] *Samuel,*[2] *Samuel*[1]) was born Jan, 14, 1724–5. He graduated at Yale College in 1742, and studied medicine and surgery, settling at Glastonbury. He married, Mar. 23, 1749, Abigail, daughter of Joseph and Mary (White) Hollister, who was born Apr. 18, 1728, and died Oct. 9, 1807, aged 79. He died at Glastonbury, May 27, 1790, aged 66.

Children :

    i. CAPT. ELIZUR,[5] m. June 8, 1775, Hannah Welles, who was b. Nov. 27, 1749.
    ii. WILLIAM.
    iii. CHARLES.
    iv. JOSEPH.
    v. MATTHEW, m. May 21, 1786, Ruth Stevens.

15. DAVID[4] HALE (*Capt. Jonathan,*[3] *Samuel,*[2] *Samuel*[1]) was born Jan. 11, 1727. He married, Feb. 8, 1753, Mary, daughter of Thomas and Martha (Pitkin) Welles, who was born Mar. 30, 1735, and died June 7, 1814, in her 80th year. He died April 7, 1796.

Children :

    i. MARY,[5] b. Oct. 30, 1753; d. Nov. 4, 1753.
    ii. MARY, b. Dec. 27, 1754; d. Apr. 12, 1815.
    iii. DAVID, b. Nov. 21, 1756; d. June 17, 1800.
    iv. JOHN, b. Nov. 10, 1759.
    v. PRUDENCE, b. Aug. 19, 1761.
    vi. MARTHA, b. Sept. 12, 1763; d. Jan. 11, 1794.
    vii. ASA, b. Mar. 23, 1765; lost at sea, Dec. 3, 1791.
    viii. MABEL, b. June 6, 1768.
    ix. ROGER, b. Mch. 6, 1772.
    x. ELIJAH, b. Mch. 6, 1772.

16. THEODORE[4] HALE (*Capt. Jonathan,*[3] *Samuel,*[2] *Samuel*[1]) was born Jan. 26, 1735, in Glastonbury, Conn. He married, Feb. 23, 1758, Rachel, daughter of Maj. Elizer Talcott. He died May 24, 1807, in his 72d year.

Children :

    i. RACHEL,[5] b. Dec. 12, 1758.
    ii. LUCY, b. Feb. 11, 1761; m. Feb. 6, 1783, James Wright of Wethersfield.
    iii. JEHIEL, b. Mch. 15, 1763; d. Apr. 16, 1763.
    iv. RUTH, b. Mch. 9, 1764.
    v. JEHIEL, b. Aug. 21, 1766; m. July 4, 1798, Olive Smith.
    vi. THEODORE, b. Oct. 23, 1768; d. Jan. 17, 1784.
    vii. SARAH, b. Feb. 16, 1771.

viii. SAMUEL, b. July 24, 1773.
ix. SOLOMON, b. Oct. 7, 1775.
x. JONATHAN, b. Apr. 23, 1777.
xi. ABIGAIL, b. Nov. 17, 1780.

17. GIDEON[4] HALE (*Benjamin,*[3] *Samuel,*[2] *Samuel*[1]) was born Dec. 30, 1736. He married, at Cromwell, Conn., Dec. 23, 1762, Mary White, who was born July 11, 1740.
    Child:
    i. ELIAS WHITE,[5] b. Apr. 18, 1775; d. Feb. 3, 1832; m. Jane Mulhollan, who was b. May 24, 1785, and d. Oct. 5, 1853. Their son, *Reuben Charles,*[6] b. Oct. 13, 1812; d. July 2, 1863; m. Sarah Jane Miller, who was b. Apr. 8,1816, d. Jan. 29, 1884; and had Charles Reuben.[7]

18. SAMUEL[4] HALE (*John,*[3] *John,*[2] *Samuel*[1]) was born Feb. 27, 1701. He married, Feb. 14, 1728-9, Sarah, daughter of Joseph Smith, Sr.
    Children:
    i. MARTHA,[5] b. May 25, 1730.
    ii. JOSEPH, b. Sept. 15, 1732.
    iii. ELISHA, b. Nov. 7, 1734.
    iv. LUCY, b. Sept. 2, 1736.
    v. SAMUEL, b. Mar. 15, 1738-9.
    28. vi. CHILIAB, b. Jan. 20, 1740-1; m. Mary Youngs.

19. JOSEPH[4] HALE (*Ebenezer,*[3] *John,*[2] *Samuel*[1]) was born Mar. 17, 1709-10, at Wethersfield, Conn., and removed with his parents to Middletown, Conn. He married Hannah ———, who died June 22, 1779. He died May 24, 1790.
    Children:
    29. i. HEZEKIAH,[5] b. May 4, 1737; m. Jerusha Parsons.
    ii. JOSEPH, b. May 25, 1740.
    iii. SUBMIT, b. May 12, 1743.
    iv. JOSEPH, b. Oct. 3, 1756.

20. GIDEON[4] HALE (*Ebenezer,*[3] *John,*[2] *Samuel*[1]) was born July 4, and baptized July 6, 1712, at Wethersfield, Conn. He removed with his parents to Middletown, Conn. He married first, Mar. 27, 1746, Sarah Watts, who died Dec. 25, 1763; and married second, Apr. 30 1764, Sarah Wood.
    Children by first wife:
    i. JERUSHA,[5] b. Oct. 5, 1745.
    ii. EPHRAIM, b. Sept. 18, 1747; d. Aug. 26, 1749.
    iii. EPHRAIM, b. Nov. 9, 1749; d. Aug. 23, 1750.
    iv. GIDEON, b. May 4, 1751.
    v. WILLIAM, b. Aug. 14, 1753.
    vi. SARAH, b. Feb. 17, 1755.
    vii. EPHRAIM, b. Feb. 28, 1757.
    viii. LOIS, b. Dec. 10, 1758; d. May 17, 1768.
    ix. JOSEPH, b. Nov. 12, 1760.
    x. ISAAC.
    xi. JACOB.

    Child by second wife:
    xii. ELIZABETH, b. Aug. 22, 1766.

21. EBENEZER[4] HALE (*Ebenezer,*[3] *John,*[2] *Samuel*[1]) was born Mar. 15, 1721, at Middletown, Conn. He married, Mar. 9, 1748-9, at Middletown, Mary Turner. He died May 26, 1760.

111

Children :
i.   MARY,[5] b. Dec. 1, 1750.
ii. RUTH, b. July 19, 1754.
iii. HANNAH, b. June 27, 1756.
iv. EBENEZER, b. Nov. 11, 1758.

22. ELISHA[4] HALE (*Ebenezer,[3] John,[2] Samuel[1]*) was born Aug. 23, 1724,
     in Middletown, Conn. He married Sibyl ———, who owned the
     covenant, July 14, 1751, in Rev. Nathaniel Chauncy's Church at
     Durham. He was a member of Lieut. Abijah Hall's company, in
     Col. John Chester's regiment, on the alarm for the relief of Fort
     William Henry, in Aug., 1757, and served sixteen days. He lived in
     that part of Farmington now Bristol, and died about 1770. Jan. 9,
     1771, administration on his estate was granted to his widow, Sibyl,
     she being appointed guardian of Elisha, Eunice, Phebe and Free-
     love. It is presumed that the widow, Sibyl, married second, as his
     second wife, Eliakim Welton of Wolcott, Conn. " Sibbell Welton,
     consort of Eliakim Welton, of Wolcott, Conn.," died at Paris Hill,
     N. Y., Jan. 20, 1803, in the 85th year of her age.
     Children :
30. i.   CURTIS, bapt. Sept. 22, 1751, at Durham, Conn.
     ii. SAMUEL.
     iii. PHEBE, bapt. June 7, 1754, at Durham, Conn.; m. Charles Ledyard
          of Farmington.
     iv. EUNICE, b. about 1756-7, at Durham, Conn.; m. Aug. 15, 1776, at
          Harwinton, Benjamin, b. Mar. 12, 1754, d. at Perryville, N. Y.,
          Nov. 29, 1836, son of Cornelius and Hannah (Brooks) Graves,
          who served in the Revolution ; removed to Paris Hill, N. Y.,
          where she d. June 6, 1814. Children: 1. *Chauncey*, b. July 10,
          1777. 2. *Freelove*, bapt. Jan. 30, 1780 ; d. at Unionville, Ohio, in
          1858; m. Noah Humiston, who was buried at Harbor Creek,
          Penn. 3. *Clarissa*, bapt. Feb. 22, 1787; d. Jan. 23, 1842, in West-
          moreland, N. Y.; m. at Paris Hill, N. Y., Dec. 22, 1805, Salmon,
          b. Nov. 2, 1779, at Northbury, Conn., d. at Westmoreland, N. Y.,
          Mar. 23, 1843, son of Gideon and Ruth (Prindle) Seymour.
     v.   FREELOVE.
     vi. ELISHA.

23. CAPT. TIMOTHY[4] HALE (*Timothy,[3] Thomas,[2] Samuel[1]*) was born Aug.
     3, 1727. He married Hannah, daughter of Benjamin[3] and Hannah
     (Talcott) Hale (see 6), who was born May 9, 1732.
     Children :
     i.   PHILO,[5] b. Mar. 16, 1785.
     ii.   HANNAH, b. Nov. 14, 1786.
     iii. TIMOTHY, b. Oct. 14, 1788.
     iv.   BENJAMIN, b. Sept. 16, 1790.
     v.   EUNICE, b. Oct. 22, 1792.
     yi.   ANNA, b. Mar. 9, 1795.
     vii. JERUSHA MERRICK, b. Sept. 19, 1797.
     viii. LUCY, b. Mar. 22, 1800.

24. BENEZER[4] HALE (*Nathaniel,[3] Thomas,[2] Samuel[1]*) was born Jan. 26,
     1719-20. He married, Jan. 2, 1744-5, Ann, daughter of Joseph and
     Dorothy (Buck) Woodhouse, who was born Jan. 29, 1718-9.
     Children :
31. i.   JAMES,[5] b. Sept. 27, 1745; m. Sarah ———.
     ii. MARY, b. Sept. 28, 1747.

112

iii. WILLIAM, b. Mar. 24, 1749-50.
iv. ANNA, b. Apr. 5, 1752.
32. v. THEODORE, b. Dec. 1, 1754; m. Sarah Forbes.
vi. ABIGAIL, b. May 1, 1758.
vii. NATHANIEL, b. July 13, 1763.

25. JUSTUS[4] HALE (*Nathaniel,[3] Thomas,[2] Samuel[1]*) was born June 29, 1725, in Wethersfield. He married, Feb. 28, 1749-50, Martha, daughter of Capt. Timothy and Sarah (Walker) Wright, who was born July 5, 1729. He removed to Goshen, Conn., where he died in 1765, aged 40 years, and his widow died in 1812, aged 83.
Children:
i. ADINE,[5] bapt. May 6, 1753.
ii. TIMOTHY, b. Dec. 18, 1755.
iii. SARAH, b. Jan. 9, 1758.
iv. JUSTUS, b. Nov. 11, 1761.
v. PRUDENCE, b. 1764; d. July 13, 1840, unmarried.

26. HEZEKIAH[4] HALE (*Nathaniel,[3] Thomas,[2] Samuel[1]*) was born Aug. 29, 1729, in Wethersfield, Conn. He married, Jan. 15, 1756, Abigail, daughter of Francis and Elizabeth (Curtis) Hanmer, who was born July 13, 1735.
Child:
i. FRANCIS,[5] b. Mar. 14, 1757.

27. ELISHA[5] HALE (*Capt. Jonathan,[4] Capt. Jonathan,[3] Samuel,[2] Samuel[1]*) was born in Glastonbury, Conn. He married, May 18, 1782, Elizabeth Mary, daughter of Col. Nathan Whiting of New Haven.
Children:
i. NATHAN WHITING,[5] b. May 8, 1783.
ii. HORACE, b. May 2, 1786.

28. CHILIAB[5] HALE (*Samuel,[4] John,[3] John,[2] Samuel[1]*) was born Jan. 20, 1740-1. He married, Apr. 22, 1762, Mary Youngs.
Children:
i. AMOS,[5] b. Feb. 20, 1763.
ii. JEMIMA, b. Dec. 31, 17—.

29. HEZEKIAH[5] HALE (*Joseph,[4] Ebenezer,[3] John,[2] Samuel[1]*) was born May 4, 1737, in Middletown, Conn. He married first, Sept. 6, 1764, at Middlefield, Conn., Jerusha Parsons, who died Mar. 30, 1776; married second, Aug. 31, 1777, Rachel Bevins, who died Aug. 29, 1782, at Middletown; and married third, Oct. 29, 1783, Annie Blake of Watertown.
Children by first wife:
i. EUNICE,[6] b. July 8, 1765; d. June 13, 1770.
ii. JOSEPH, b. Apr. 19, 1769; d. Oct. 20, 1770.
iii. HANNAH, b. Dec. 1, 1771.
iv. JERUSHA, b. Mch. 6, 1776.

Children by second wife:
v. HEZEKIAH, b. Oct. 31, 1778.
vi. JOSEPH, b. Aug. 26, 1780.
vii. EUNICE, b. Aug. 22, 1782.

Child by third wife:
viii. SUBMIT, b. July 16, 1784.

30. CURTIS[5] HALE (*Elisha,[4] Ebenezer,[3] John,[2] Samuel[1]*) was baptized
     Sept. 22, 1751, in Durham, Conn. He resided in Harwinton, Conn.,
     and in 1787 bought land in Bristol, Conn. The name of his wife
     is not known.
        Children :
        i.   ELISHA,[6] bapt. Jan. 16, 1785.
        ii.   RHODA, bapt. Jan. 16, 1785.
        iii. THEODORE, bapt. Jan. 16, 1785.
        iv.   EBENEZER, bapt. Aug. 11, 1793.

31. JAMES[5] HALE (*Benezer,[4] Nathaniel,[3] Thomas,[2] Samuel[1]*) was born in
     Wethersfield, Sept. 27, 1745. He married Sarah ———, and re-
     moved to Winchester, Conn., where he lived on the south-west shore
     of Long Lake, west of the mouth of Taylor's Brook, up to 1784.
        Children :
        i.   ABIGAIL,[6] b. May 12, 1778.
        ii.   SARAH, b. Aug. 8, 1780.
        iii. WILLIAM, b. Mch. 16, 1784.

32. THEODORE[5] HALE (*Benezer,[4] Nathaniel,[3] Thomas,[2] Samuel[1]*) was born
     Dec. 1, 1754, at Wethersfield, Conn. He married, Oct. 20, 1779,
     Sarah, daughter of Joseph and Sarah (Treat) Forbes.
        Children :
        i.   RHODA,[6] b. June 21, 1781.
        ii.   PRUDENCE, b. Jan. 4, 1783.
        iii. BETSEY, b. Feb. 14, 1786.
        iv.   SARAH, b. May 20, 1789.

GILBERT HALL'S FAMILY.

[Communicated by ROYAL R. HINMAN of New York.]

GILBERT HALL, of Kent, had a son William and daughter.
The daughter married Mr. Snoath, and died in England.

William Hall, son of Gilbert, signed the covenant in Guilford in 1639; an early settler in Guilford. He d. March 8, 1669. His wife Hester d. in 1683. Had children John and Samuel.

John Hall, son of William, b. 1628, m. Elizabeth Smith of New Haven, Nov. 13, 1669. He d. Jan. 8, 1704. Had children Elizabeth, b. Nov. 1670, d. young; Mary, b. May 13, 1672, m. Daniel Bishop, July 16, 1693; John, b. Feb. 23, 1674, d. 1724; Ebenezer, b. May 3, 1678, m. Deborah Highland, April 11, 1700, he d. 1724, she d. Oct. 27, 1758; Silence, b. Dec. 15, 1679, m. Abraham Morison, Feb. 19, 1710.

Eliphalet, son of John, b. Jan. 13, 1681, m. Abigail Bushnell, May 30, 1705. She d. in 1708, and he m. Mary Grimes in 1710.

Nathaniel, son of John, b. Dec. 1683, m. Rebecca Mallory of New Haven in 1715. He d. in 1748.

Ebenezer, son of John, b. May 3, 1678, m. Deborah Highland, April 11, 1700. She d. Oct. 27, 1758; he d. in 1724. Had children, Ebenezer, Jr., b. Jan. 30, 1701; Daniel, b. April 10, 1702, d. single in 1741; Deborah, b. Oct. 27, 1704, m. Ebenezer Field in 1749; John, b. Aug. 27, 1706; Joseph, b. in 1709; Benjamin, b. May 27, 1712; Esther, b. March 3, 1717, m. Jehial Johnson in 1747; Timothy, b. Nov. 10, 1721.

Eliphalet, son of John, b. in 1681. Had children, Jerusha, b. in 1706, m. Daniel Bowen; Abigail, b. in 1707, m. John Fowler in 1736; Eliphalet, Jr., b. Oct. 22, 1711; Mary, b. in 1714, m. Icabod Wells of Wethersfield.

Nathaniel Hall, b. in 1683, son of John, m. Rebecca Mallory in 1715, d. in 1748. Had children, Justus, b. Oct. 5, 1716; Mathias, b. Jan. 25, 1720, drowned Nov. 9, 1745; Rebecca, b. Nov. 2, 1727, m. Moses Miller of Middletown; Silence, b. in 1730, d. in 1734; Beulah, b. in 1733, m. Billious Ward in 1753.

Samuel, son of Gilbert and brother of John, m. Elizabeth Johnson, Feb. 22, 1674. He d. Feb. 11, 1733. He had children, Elizabeth, b. Feb. 1, 1676, m. Job Paine of Middletown; Ithamar, b. Feb. 10, 1679, m. Judith Leonard of Durham, Nov. 3, 1714, he d. Dec. 20, 1758; William, b. Jan. 15, 1682, m. Lydia Chittenden, Oct. 20, 1715, he d. in 1738; Samuel, Jr., b. Oct. 15, 1687, d. Oct. 21, 1763; Abigail, b. Feb. 1, 1695, d. in 1763.

Ithamar, son of Samuel, b. in 1679. Had children, Judith, b. in 1716, m. Benjamin Hall, Feb. 7, 1740; Elizabeth, b. March 13, 1720, d. Nov. 24, 1736; Anne, b. Nov. 13, 1724.

William, son of Samuel, b. in 1682. Had children, William, b. in 1716, removed to Litchfield in 1750, m. Mercy Barnes of North Haven in 1738; Daniel, b. Feb. 16, 1718; Benjamin, b. March 14, 1724, removed to Litchfield in 1751.

William, Jr., b. in 1716. Had children, William, b. Oct. 28, 1739, m. Mary ——, he d. in 1777; Lydia, b. May 6, 1742; Rachel, b. Nov. 8, 1744.

William, son of William, Jr., b. in 1730, d. in 1777, m. Mary ——. Had children, William, b. Oct. 23, 1758, d. young; Ephraim Smedley,

b. May 19, 1761; Rebecca, b. Feb. 13, 1768, m. Friend Smith; Gideon, b. June 20, 1774, m. Polly Hayden, dau. of Samuel Hayden; David, b. ———.

Gideon, son of William, m. Polly Hayden. Had children, Edom, b. in 1797, d. two years old; Samuel, b. April 9, 1800, d. single, aged about 20; Abigail, b. Oct. 17, 1803; Gideon, b. May 1, 1809, m. L. L. Fosket, Jan. 30, 1844; William S., b. June 24, 1817, d. aged two years. Gideon Hall, the father, married a second wife, and had one child, a daughter, who is living in Winsted, Ct.

Gideon, only surviving son of Gideon, Sen., b. May 1, 1809, m. L. L. Fosket in 1844. Had child, Mary A. Hall, b. Feb. 22, 1846, d. aged six months. This Gideon is a lawyer, and resides in Winsted, Ct.

JOSEPH HAND OF EAST GUILFORD (NOW MADISON), CONN., AND HIS DESCENDANTS.

Compiled by RALPH D. SMYTH and communicated by BERNARD C. STEINER.

1. JOSEPH HAND,[1] son of John of East Hampton, Long Island, settled in the eastern part of the town of Guilford after 1660, and married Jane, daughter of Benjamin Wright, in 1664. She died December, 1724. He died January, 1724. He had four brothers: Shamgar, who settled in Cape May, N. J.; Benjamin and John, Stephen of East Hampton. Joseph Hand seems to have been regarded as one of the substantial men of the town, and served on committees to run boundaries and lay out allotments of land to planters. He headed a petition to the General Court, in 1697, that East Guilford might be made a separate ecclesiastical parish. In 1720, he was sent to the General Court as a representative. On Oct. 27, 1671, Benjamin Wright gave his land at Hammonassett in the east end of Guilford to Joseph Hand and wife for life, and afterwards to their children, and on Dec. 12, 1671, Joseph Hand bought from Richard Hubball all his land in the same quarter.

The children of Joseph and Jane (Wright) Hand were:

   i.   SARAH,[2] b. March 2, 1664–5; d. Aug. 1, 1751.
   ii.   JANE, b. Sept. 19, 1668; d. Dec. 13, 1683.
2. iii. JOSEPH, b. April 2, 1671; d. about 1699.
3. iv. BENJAMIN, b. Feb. 8, 1672–3; d. August, 1744.
4. v.   STEPHEN, b. Feb. 8, 1674–5; d. Aug. 14, 1755.
   vi. ELIZABETH, b. March 12, 1676–7; m. April 5, 1705, Benjamin Wright of Killingworth, her cousin.
   vii. SILENCE. b. March, 1678–9; m. 1st, Ephraim Wilcox of Middletown, Oct. 23, 1698, who d. Jan. 4, 1711; m. 2d, John Warner of Saybrook.
  viii. ANN, b. July 10, 1683; m. Jonathan Wright of Wethersfield.
   ix. JANE, b. April 25, 1686; d. Oct. 27, 1747; m. Cornelius Dowd of Guilford, Feb. 4, 1707. He d. Aug. 14, 1727.

2. JOSEPH HAND,[2] JR. (*Joseph*[1]) of East Guilford, was a seafaring man and on Oct. 19, 1697, while on the sloop Adventure from Fayal was seized and carried to France as a prisoner by a French privateer, commanded by Captain Jean Le Prince, who had boarded and pillaged the sloop. He married Hester Wilcox, daughter of John of Middletown, who died March 15, 1698. After his return

from captivity he married Hannah, daughter of William Seward, in 1699, but died or disappeared shortly after, having no children by her.

His children were:

5. i. JANNA,[3] b. Feb. 17, 1692-3; d. Dec. 9, 1769.
ii. ESTHER, b. 1695; m. William King of Northampton, Mass.
iii. HULDAH, b. Oct. 18, 1697; m. Zachary Smith of Huntingdon, L. I.

3. BENJAMIN[2] HAND (*Joseph[1]*) of East Guilford, was a very prominent citizen of the town, representing it frequently at General Court, and often called on to act as moderator at town meeting. He married Mary Wilcox, daughter of John of Middletown. She died Oct. 24, 1749.

Their children were:

i. NATHANIEL.[3] b. April 12, 1696; d. April 29, 1752; m. Jemima French, dau. of Ebenezer of East Guilford, and had no children. She d. Aug. 8, 1755.
6. ii. JOHN, b. June 12, 1698; d. April, 1739.
iii. MARY, b. June 6, 1700; d. Aug. 20, 1702.
iv. SUBMIT, b. Aug. 5, 1702; d. July 25, 1734; m. Dec. 23, 1727, Ebenezer Bartlett of East Guilford, who d. Nov. 30, 1770.
7. v. EBENEZER, b. Sept. 5, 1705; d.———.
8. vi. BENJAMIN, b. May 7, 1708; d. Dec. 7, 1748.
vii. MARY, b. Aug. 15, 1712.

4. STEPHEN[2] HAND (*Joseph[1]*) of East Guilford, married four times: first, Sarah Wright, Nov. 6, 1700 (she died Sept. 18, 1706); second, Sarah Pierson, Nov. 16, 1708; third, Dorothy, widow of Lieut. John Hopson, March 14, 1734 (she died Oct 6, 1742); fourth, Hannah, daughter of Jeremiah Diggins, and widow of ——— Judd, Sept. 21, 1743 (she died 1766).

By his first wife he had the following children:

i. JOSEPH,[3] b. Nov. 8, 1701; d. June 10, 1702.
9. ii. JOSEPH, b. Jan. 21, 1703.
iii. MARY, b. Oct. 30, 1704; d. Aug. 6, 1780; m. Josiah Meigs, her cousin.
iv. SARAH, b. Sept. 9, 1706; m. ——— Stannard.

The children by his second wife were:

10. v. STEPHEN, b. June 13, 1710; d. 1756.
vi. ABIGAIL, b. Oct. 20, 1712; d. April 15, 1751; m. Daniel Bradley, Nov. 20, 1734.

5. JANNA[8] HAND (*Joseph,[2] Joseph[1]*) of East Guilford, married Feb. 14, 1723, Dorothy, daughter of Deacon John Griswold. She died Feb. 12, 1775.

Their children were:

i. JOSEPH,[4] b, Jan. 24, 1723-4; d. Oct. 29, 1774; m. Lucy, dau. of Jehiel Meigs. She d. June 25, 1778. Their children were: 1. *Lucy,[5]* b. Jan. 18, 1760; d. Feb. 18, 1760. 2. *Janna*, b. Sept. 28, 1761; d. Aug. 2, 1794; m. Joanna, dau. of Col. Return J. Meigs. 3. *Edmund*, b. March 1, 1763; d. June 2, 1812; m. Feb. 20, 1790, Huldah, dau. of John Hopson. 4. *John*, b. June 20, 1768; d. young.
ii. ESTHER, b. Sept. 5, 1725; m. John Huggins of Branford, April 14, 1756.
iii. JANNA, b. Feb. 4, 1728; went to sea and was never heard from.
iv. DANIEL, b. 1732: d. Oct. 16, 1816. Was captain in Col. Tolcott's regiment in 1776. Lived in East Guilford, and m. 1st, Sibbe Smith of Killingworth, Oct. 28, 1759. She d. Sept. 20, 1772. He m. 2d, Lizzie Lynde of Saybrook, May 18, 1774. She d. Aug. 5, 1789. He

117

m. 3d, Chloe Boardman, widow of Walter Price Griswold, of Haddam. She d. aged 84, Nov. 28, 1821. By his first wife, he had: 1. *Esther*, b. Sept. 18, 1760; d. March 12, 1846; m. Wyllys Munger of East Guilford, Jan. 18, 1785. He d. Jan. 31, 1835. 2. *Daniel*, b. April 24, 1762; d. Jan. 15, 1821; m. 1788, Artimesia, dau. of Daniel Meigs of East Guilford. She d. Oct. 11, 1812. They had eleven children, among them Judge George Edward[6] Hand (Y. C. 1829) of Detroit, and Daniel[6] Hand, who gave nearly a million and a half of dollars to the American Missionary Association for negro education. 3. *Sibbe*, b. Sept. 9, 1768; m. Gen. Joseph Buel of Marietta, Ohio. 4. *Mehitable*, b. Aug. 20, 1770; m. Dr. Levi Ward of Rochester, N. Y. The children of his second wife were: 5. *William*, b. Feb. 2, 1776; d. Oct. 3, 1781. 6. *Lizzie*, b. March 7, 1778; d. Oct. 5, 1781. 7. *Anne*, b. 1780; d. Oct. 10, 1781.

v. DOROTHY, b. ——— ; m. Hiel Buel of Killingworth as his fourth wife.

6. JOHN[3] HAND (*Benjamin,[2] Joseph[1]*) of East Guilford, married Deborah ———. After his death, she married June 13, 1745, Nathaniel Porter of Bethlehem, Conn., but died in the same year.

The children of John Hand were:

i. ELIZABETH,[4] b. July 1, 1728; d. 1751.
ii. JOHN, b. Aug. 25, 1730; d. April 6, 1734.
iii. DEBORAH, b. April 2, 1732; m. John Porter, son of Nathaniel, her step-father.
iv. SUBMIT, b. Sept. 7, 1735; d. July 11, 1766; m. James Munger, Jr., June 19, 1754.
v. JOHN, b. Feb. 12, 1738; d. December, 1759.

7. EBENEZER[3] HAND (*Benjamin,[2] Joseph[1]*) of East Guilford, married first, Susannah French, May 31, 1725. She died Feb. 13, 1743. He married second, Mary West, Sept. 13, 1743. She died May 15, 1746. He married third, Anna Crampton, June 10, 1746. She died June 27, 1780.

His children (all by his first wife) were as follows:

i. TEMPERANCE,[4] b. July 17, 1725; m. ——— Kelsey.
ii. ICHABOD, b. April 16, 1728: d. June, 1759; m. April 19, 1748, Hannah Garry of Branford. She d. Sept. 7, 1751. Their children were: 1. *Ichabod*,[5] b. June 16, 1749; d. Jan. 28, 1840; m. Mary Graves. 2. *Anne*, b. June 22, 1751; d. May 21, 1752.
iii. EBENEZER, b. Jan. 9, 1730; m. Mary Evarts, June 20, 1757. Their child was: *Benjamin*,[5] b. March 27, 1759.
iv. JEMIMA, b. May 17, 1732.
v. IRA, b. July 11, 1734.
vi. TIMOTHY, b. June 8, 1739. Was in Capt. Peleg Redfield's company in the French and Indian War. He married, May 18, 1761, Esther Bishop. Their children were: 1. *Anna*,[5] b. Nov. 11, 1762. 2. *Esther*, b. June 13, 1765. 3. *Submit*, b. May 9, 1768.

8. BENJAMIN[3] HAND, JR. (*Benjamin,[2] Joseph[1]*) of East Guilford, married Mary Penfield, Oct. 29, 1730. After his death, she married John Norton, and died July 6, 1785.

Their children were:

i. MARY,[4] b. Nov. 18, 1731.
ii. HULDAH, b. Aug. 21. 1736; m. Peter Penfield.
iii. ABIGAIL, b. Sept. 28, 1743; d. Dec. 20, 1775.

9. JOSEPH[3] HAND (*Stephen,[2] Joseph[1]*) married Hannah Hurlburt, daughter of Nathaniel of Woodbury, Aug. 31, 1731. She died Feb. 9, 1760.

Their children were:

i. SAMUEL,[4] b. June 9, 1733; d. Oct. 28, 1733.

ii. SARAH, b. Sept. 6, 1734; d. Dec. 28, 1746.
iii. SAMUEL, b. Feb. 5, 1738.
iv. SARAH, b. March 31, 1744.
v. JOSEPH, b. April 15, 1749; m. May 8, 1771, Prudence Wright of Say-
    brook. Their child was: *Prudence*, b. June 20, 1773.
vi. HANNAH, b. Dec. 28, 1753.

10. STEPHEN[3] HAND (*Stephen*,[2] *Joseph*[1]) of East Guilford, Litchfield and
     Woodbury, married Jan. 16, 1734, Rachel Walston, daughter of
     Thomas. She died April 24, 1755.
     Their children were:
i. REBECCA,[4] b. Dec. 4, 1734.
ii. RACHEL, b. Sept. 22, 1736.
iii. TIMOTHY, b. Aug. 18, 1738; d. May 20, 1740.
iv. STEPHEN, b. June 6, 1740.
v. TIMOTHY, b. Aug. 28, 1745.
vi. ELIAS, b. Oct. 10, 1747.
vii. NABBY, b. Oct. 15, 1749.

HAND.—Since the publication of the article on the Hand family in the January
REGISTER, I have received several inquiries as to the brothers of Joseph Hand,
viz., Shamgar and Benjamin. My information concerning them, from my
grandfather's notes, is not extensive, but is given herewith in the hope that it
may be of some use.

Shamgar Hand is said to have removed to Cape May, N. J., and to have left
a son, Josiah, who resided in Bridgehampton, L. I.

Benjamin[1] Hand married (1) Feb. 27, 1669, Elizabeth Whittier; married (2)
Jan. 14, 1688, Sarah, daughter of William Ward of Middletown, Conn. His
children by his first wife were: i. Elizabeth[2] Hand, b. Jan. 27, 1672. ii. Sarah,
b. Sept. 22, 1673; died young. iii. Abraham, b. Oct, 2, 1675. iv. Benjamin,
b. July 22, 1677; died young. v. Richard, b. March 2, 1679. vi. Mary, b.
March 24, 1680. vii. Rachel, b. Jan. 23, 1682. viii. Peter, b. Nov. 1, 1683.

His children by his second wife were: ix. Ann, b. Jan. 13, 1689; d. June 23,
1760. x. Sarah, b. July 20, 1697; d. Aug. 16. 1719. xi. Phebe, b. July 14, 1702.
xii. Benjamin. b. Oct. 4, 1706; lived in Middletown, and married Hannah Johnson. Their children were: 1. Benjamin,[3] b. Feb. 8, 1736–7; 2. Sarah, b. Feb.
9, 1738–9; 3. Ann, b. April 8, 1742; 4. Phebe, b. July 15, 1745; 5. Mary, b. Dec.
1, 1747; 6. John, b. Jan. 4, 1750–1; 7. Lois, b. June 13, 1755; 8. Benjamin, b.
Aug. 8, 1756; 9. Hannah, b. Nov. 3, 1765.

Baltimore, Md.   BERNARD C. STEINER.

ESTHER HANFORD (*ante*, vol. 47, page 214).—I have to reply to Dr. Banks,
Haynes Hanford, of Norwalk (son of Capt. Samuel and Jasabell Haynes, and
grandson of Rev. Thomas Hanford) married Elizabeth Ketchum, and had five
children: 1. Jedediah; 2. Joseph, born in 1742; 3. Esther; 4. John, born in
1755; 5. Mary.

403 West 126th St., New York.   ROSELL L. RICHARDSON.

FIVE GENERATIONS OF CONNECTICUT HARRISONS

By Mrs. Frances Harrison Corbin of Orange, Conn.

1. Richard[1] Harrison, from West Kirby, co. Chester, England,[†] came to New England, and took the oath of allegiance at New Haven[‡] 5 Aug. 1644. He removed with his children to Branford, where he died 25 Oct. 1653.

Children, born in England:

    i.   Richard,[2] took the oath of allegiance at New Haven 1 July 1644; lived and owned property at Branford; at the time of the dissatisfaction in the Branford church he sold his holdings, and with his family and with others removed in May 1666 to Newark, N. J., where he died; m. Sarah Hubbard, b. at Wethersfield in 1635, dau. of George and Mary (Bishop) of Wethersfield and Milford, who were later permanent settlers at Guilford; ancestor of the Harrisons of New Jersey.

2. ii. Thomas, b. abt. 1630.

  iii. Mary or Maria, m. at Branford, 27 Nov. 1662, Thomas Pierson, Sr. They removed to Newark, N. J., in 1666.

  iv. Elizabeth, m. (1) Henry Lyne of New Haven, who d. 14 Jan. 1662/3, s. of John of Badby, co. Northampton, Eng.; m. (2) John Lampson of New Haven; m. (3), as his second wife, John Morris of New Haven, with whom she removed to Newark, N. J., where she was living in 1675. Child by first husband: 1. Hopestill, b. abt. 1661.

  v. Samuel (probably s. of Richard), d. at Newark, N. J., in 1705; m. Sarah Johnson.

  vi. Ellen (probably dau. of Richard), m. 25 Feb. 1650/1 John Thompson of New Haven.

---

† The English home of Richard Harrison is revealed by a document in the office of the secretary of state of New Jersey, which is thus described in *New Jersey Archives,* first series, vol. 21, p. 29:

"1668 June 18. Certificate, that Hopestill Lyne, 6 to 7 years old, the daughter of Henry Lyne of New Haven in New England, son of John Lyne of Badby, Northamptonshire, which Henry died January 14, 1662, and had the child Hopestill by his wife Elizabeth, dau. of Richard Harrison of West Kerby, Cheshire, is still alive as sworn to by Richard Harrison, Thomas Johnson, William Meaker and Ellen Johnson."

‡ All places mentioned in this article are situated within the present limits of the State of Connecticut, unless another State or region is indicated in the text or may be easily inferred from the context.

2. ENSIGN THOMAS[2] HARRISON (*Richard*[1]), ancestor of the Connecticut Harrisons, born in England about 1630, died at Branford towards the end of 1704. He married first, in Feb. 1655/6, DOROTHY (———) THOMPSON, widow of John, who was called "farmer;" and secondly, 29 Mar. 1666, ELIZABETH (———) STENT, widow, whose husband had died on the voyage to America. He took the oath of allegiance at New Haven 4 Apr. 1654, but settled at Branford. He was ensign in King Philip's War, and was elected deputy to the General Court 10 May 1677. In a land record dated 14 Nov. 1688 he calls himself 58 years of age.

Children by first wife, born at New Haven:

3. i. THOMAS,[3] b. 1 Mar. 1656/7.
4. ii. NATHANIEL, b. 13 Dec. 1658.

   Children by second wife:

   iii. ELIZABETH, b. at New Haven in Jan. 1667/8; m. WILLIAM BARKER of Branford.
   iv. MARY, b. at Branford 10 Feb. 1668/9; m. 6 June 1699 JOHN LINSLEY, 3D.
5. v. JOHN, b. at Branford 1 Mar. 1670/1.
6. vi. SAMUEL, b. at Branford 11 Aug. 1673.
7. vii. ISAAC, b. at Branford in 1678.

3. LIEUT. THOMAS[3] HARRISON (*Thomas*,[2] *Richard*[1]), born at New Haven 1 Mar. 1656/7, died at Branford 1 Jan. 1725/6. He married, in 1689, MARGARET STENT, daughter of his stepmother; and administration on the estate of Margaret (Stent) Harrison was granted 7 Jan. 1730/1. He served in King Philip's War, was ensign in 1697, was a lieutenant in 1709, in Queen Anne's War, and was also in the expedition to Canada.

Children, born at Branford:

   i. LYDIA,[4] b. 24 Aug. 1690; m. 4 Mar. 1712/13 JOSEPH MORRIS.
   ii. JEMIMA, b. 12 Mar. 1692/3; d. in 1730; m. in Jan. 1727/8, as his second wife, CALEB PARMELEE, who m. (1) Elizabeth Foote and m. (3) Mary Durham.
8. iii. THOMAS, b. 12 Oct. 1694.
   iv. ABIGAIL, b. 17 Mar. 1696/7; m. 9 Dec. 1736 JOSIAH POND.
9. v. BENJAMIN, b. 7 Aug. 1698.
10. vi. JOSEPH, b. 25 May 1700.
11. vii. DAVID, b. 7 Feb. 1702/3.
    viii. AARON, b. 4 Mar. 1704/5; d. 20 Nov. 1708.
    ix. JACOB, b. 6 Oct. 1708; d. *s.p.*; estate administered 20 May 1737; m. 24 Jan. 1734/5 SARAH WARDELL, dau. of Uzal and Phoebe, who m. (2) 22 Oct. 1744 Jonathan Brown.

4. CAPT. NATHANIEL[3] HARRISON (*Thomas*,[2] *Richard*[1]), born at New Haven 13 Dec. 1658, died at Branford 1 Jan. 1727/8. He married HANNAH FRISBIE, born in 1669, died 27 Sept. 1723, daughter of Edward and Hannah. He was deputy in the Assembly and justice of the peace, 1717–1725.

Children, born at Branford:

   i. HANNAH,[4] b. 28 July 1690; d. 5 Oct. 1753; m. JAMES TALMADGE of New Haven.
12. ii. NATHANIEL, b. 26 Jan. 1692/3.
13. iii. DANIEL, b. 12 Sept. 1694.
    iv. MARY, b. 24 Apr. 1696; d. 28 Oct. 1747; m. (1) 7 Jan. 1718/19 WILLIAM HOADLEY; m. (2) 19 Feb. 1742/3 SAMUEL ROSE.

14. v. JOSIAH, b. in Feb. 1698/9.
    vi. ABRAHAM, b. 28 Feb. 1700/1; d. 27 Aug. 1714.
    vii. DOROTHEA, b. 1 Mar. 1702/3; probably d. young.
15. viii. JONATHAN, b. 8 July 1704.
16. ix. AMOS, b. 11 Mar. 1707/8.
    x. SILENCE (twin), b. 30 July 1710; d. 6 Apr. 1713.
    xi. PATIENCE (twin), b. 30 July 1710; d. in July 1711.

5. JOHN[3] HARRISON (*Thomas,[2] Richard[1]*), born at Branford 1 Mar.
   1670/1, died at North Branford 20 Sept. 1746. He married,
   24 Dec. 1702, REBECCA TRUESDALE, born in 1678, died at
   North Branford 3 Oct. 1755, daughter of Samuel and Mary
   (Jackson).
   Children, born at Branford:
   i. ELIZABETH,[4] b. 20 Oct. 1703; d. unm.; will proved 4 Oct. 1768.
   ii. REBECCA, b. 17 June 1705; d. 8 Oct. 1765; m. 25 Nov. 1736, as his
       second wife, CAPT. JOHN BLACKISTON.
   iii. JERUSHA, b. 2 June 1786; m. 3 Jan. 1727/8 ITHIEL
        RUSSELL, s. of Rev. Samuel and Abigail (Whiting).
   iv. MARY, b. 24 July 1710; d. 26 Apr. 1795; m. 20 Feb. 1732/3 TIMO-
       THY HOADLEY.
17. v. JOHN, b. 27 July 1712.
    vi. LYDIA, m. ――― BARKER.
18. vii. EBENEZER, b. in 1717.

6. SERGT. SAMUEL[3] HARRISON (*Thomas,[2] Richard[1]*), b. at Branford
   11 Aug. 1673, died at North Branford 30 June 1731. He
   married, 3 July 1707, ELIZABETH DENNISON, born 24 Nov.
   1684, whose estate was administered 15 Mar. 1757, daughter
   of James and Bethia (Boykim) of East Haven. He was
   confirmed by the Court as sergeant of the Branford trainband
   8 Apr. 1706.
   Children, born at Branford:
   i. LUCY,[4] b. 26 Nov. 1709; will proved 12 Sept. 1786; m. 1 Nov. 1738
      BENJAMIN HOADLEY.
19. ii. SAMUEL, b. 15 Dec. 1712.
20. iii. JARED, b. 31 May 1716.
21. iv. JAMES, b. 23 Mar. 1720/1.

7. ENSIGN ISAAC[3] HARRISON (*Thomas,[2] Richard[1]*), born at Branford in 1678, died at Northford 21 Aug. 1747. He married,
   12 Dec. 1706, PATIENCE TYLER, who died 15 Jan. 1762, daughter
   of Peter and Hannah (Whitehead). He was commissioned
   an ensign in the Second Company of the Branford trainband
   14 May 1719.
   Children, born at Branford:
   i. HANNAH,[4] b. 13 Oct. 1711; d. 2 Sept. 1748; m. 4 Mar. 1733/4
      ICHABOD FOOTE.
   ii. ELIZABETH, b. 26 Jan. 1718/19; m. 6 Feb. 1752 JOHN WILFORD.
22. iii. ISAAC, b. 22 May 1722.
    iv. PATIENCE, b. 16 Aug. 1724; m. 6 Feb. 1746/7 BENJAMIN PALMER.

8. CAPT. THOMAS[4] HARRISON (*Thomas,[3] Thomas,[2] Richard[1]*), born
   at Branford 12 Oct. 1694, died at Litchfield 16 June 1758.
   He married, 21 Apr. 1721, HANNAH SUTLIFF, born at Durham
   in 1696, died at Litchfield 27 Apr. 1790, daughter of John and
   Hannah of Waterbury. In 1739 he removed from Branford
   to Litchfield, and bought 1000 acres of land at South Farms.

He gave 100 acres to each of his nine sons, and retained 100 acres for himself. He was commissioned as captain of the North Company of the Branford trainband 13 May 1731, served in the First Connecticut Regiment in the war against France and Spain in 1739–40, was deputy to the General Court from Litchfield 2 May 1747, and was made justice of the peace for Hartford County 31 May 1750.

Children, all except the last born at Branford:

23. i. THOMAS,[5] b. 14 Dec. 1722.
24. ii. GIDEON, b. 5 Aug. 1724.
25. iii. EPHRAIM, b. 28 Dec. 1726.
26. iv. TITUS, b. 30 Nov. 1728.
27. v. ABEL, b. 2 Feb. 1731/2.
28. vi. JACOB, b. 7 Oct. 1734.
29. vii. LEMUEL, b. 23 Mar. 1737/8.
30. viii. ELIHU, b. 25 Feb. 1739/40.
31. ix. LEVI.

9. BENJAMIN[4] HARRISON (*Thomas,*[3] *Thomas,*[2] *Richard*[1]), born at Branford 7 Aug. 1698, died at Waterbury 6 Mar. 1760. He married at Branford, 19 Oct. 1720, MARY SUTLIFF, born in 1701, daughter of John and Hannah of Waterbury, who married secondly, 30 July 1760, Thomas Clark of Waterbury. Benjamin Harrison settled in Wolcott, with his family, about 1738.

Children, born at Branford:

32. i. BENJAMIN,[5] b. 14 Nov. 1721.
33. ii. AARON, b. 20 Apr. 1726.
iii. ABIGAIL, b. 14 Dec. 1735; m. 11 Dec. 1753 DAVID WARNER, b. 27 Nov. 1731, s. of Dr. Benjamin and Johanna (Strong).

10. JOSEPH[4] HARRISON (*Thomas,*[3] *Thomas,*[2] *Richard*[1]), b. at Branford 25 May 1700, died there 23 July 1748. He married, 8 Jan. 1728/9, SARAH FOOTE, born 4 Oct. 1706, daughter of Stephen, who married secondly, 27 May 1754, as his second wife, Daniel Baldwin.

Children, born at Branford:

i. SARAH,[5] b. 8 Feb. 1729/30.
ii. JOSEPH, b. 14 June 1731; d. 29 June 1750.
34. iii. STEPHEN, b. 14 Nov. 1733.
iv. LEAH, b. 14 Apr. 1736; d. 1 Aug. 1751.
v. RACHEL, b. 13 Jan. 1739/40; m. 8 Feb. 1759 STEPHEN PALMER, JR.

11. DAVID[4] HARRISON (*Thomas,*[3] *Thomas,*[2] *Richard*[1]), born at Branford 7 Feb. 1702/3, died at Northford 21 Mar. 1767. He married, 1 Jan. 1728/9, MARY WOOSTER, born at Stratford 3 Apr. 1707, died at Northford 4 Feb. 1791, daughter of Abraham and Mary (Walker) of Stratford.

Children, born at Branford:

i. RUTH,[5] b. 5 Jan. 1729/30; m. 13 Sept. 1753 DANIEL HEATON.
ii. WOOSTER (twin), b. 21 Feb. 1736/7; d. 10 Mar. 1817; m. SUSANNAH ———.
iii. WESTOVER (twin), b. 21 Feb. 1736/7; d. unm.; will proved 2 Mar. 1768.
iv. ANNA, b. 12 May 1743; d. 30 Sept. 1819; m. (1) 15 Dec. 1762 NATHANIEL COOK; m. (2) 28 Dec. 1764 SAMUEL FOOTE.

12. ENSIGN NATHANIEL[4] HARRISON (*Nathaniel,[3] Thomas,[2] Richard[1]*), born at Branford 26 Jan. 1692/3, died there 4 Feb. 1760. He married at Milford, 18 Apr. 1717, THANKFUL WILKINSON, daughter of Edward and Rebecca, born in 1697, died 20 July 1761. He was ensign in the First Company of the Branford trainband, and was appointed justice of the peace for New Haven County 31 May 1750.

Children, born at Branford:

- i.   MARY,[5] b. 19 Apr. 1718; m. 16 Sept. 1736 DANIEL MALTBY, JR.
- ii. THANKFUL, b. 29 Apr. 1720; d. 28 Feb. 1792; m. 29 Dec. 1743 JOHN ROGERS, JR.
- iii. ABIGAIL, b. 6 Mar. 1721/2; m. 25 Mar. 1745 NATHANIEL FRISBIE.
- iv. HANNAH, b. 8 Nov. 1725; m. 5 Dec. 1751 SAMUEL ROGERS.
- v.   REBECCA, b. 23 May 1731; m. 22 Feb. 1759 JOHN JOHNSON.
- 35. vi. NATHANIEL (twin), b. 3 Aug. 1735.
- vii. SARAH (twin), b. 3 Aug. 1735; m. 13 May 1767 NATHAN FRISBIE.
- viii. MARTHA, b. in 1737; m. 14 Apr. 1761 ELISHA FRISBIE.

13. DANIEL[4] HARRISON (*Nathaniel,[3] Thomas,[2] Richard[1]*), born at Branford 12 Sept. 1694, died there 10 Oct. 1752. He married, 30 June 1720, HANNAH HOADLEY, born 16 Dec. 1694, died 15 Jan. 1747/8, daughter of Samuel and Abigail (Farrington).

Children, born at Branford:

- 36. i.   DANIEL,[5] b. 5 Aug. 1722.
- ii. HANNAH, b. 9 May 1726; d. *s.p.*; m. 13 May 1752 STEPHEN BLACKISTON.
- 37. iii. ABRAHAM, b. 20 Nov. 1728.
- 38. iv. NOAH, b. 19 Mar. 1737/8.
- 39. v.   PETER, b. 11 Nov. 1739.

14. JOSIAH[4] HARRISON (*Nathaniel,[3] Thomas,[2] Richard[1]*), born at Branford in Feb. 1698/9, died at North Branford 13 Dec. 1773. He married, 4 June 1723, LYDIA HOADLEY, born 23 Dec. 1701, died at North Branford 30 Sept. 1780, daughter of Samuel and Abigail (Farrington).

Children, born at Branford:

- 40. i.   JOSIAH,[5] b. 19 July 1724.
- ii. LYDIA, m. 24 Feb. 1762 JOSEPH SMITH.
- iii. ELIZABETH, m. 16 Apr. 1754 JOHN PALMER.
- 41. iv. TIMOTHY, b. 31 Aug. 1729.
- 42. v.   NATHAN, b. 18 Mar. 1730/1.
- 43. vi. MOSES.
- vii. NATHANIEL, b. 16 Sept. 1734; m. ELIZABETH ———.

15. JONATHAN[4] HARRISON (*Nathaniel,[3] Thomas,[2] Richard[1]*) was born at Branford 8 July 1704. He married, 27 July 1726, DESIRE FARRINGTON.

Children, born at Branford:

- 44. i.   JONATHAN,[5] b. 22 May 1727.
- ii. WILLIAM, b. 13 Jan. 1728/9; d. unm.
- iii. BENJAMIN, b. 25 Dec. 1730; d. in 1793.
- iv. DESIRE, b. 16 Apr. 1733; m. 22 Jan. 1756 JAMES BUTLER.
- v.   FARRINGTON, b. in July 1735; d. in Aug. 1735.
- vi. ABIGAIL, b. 11 July 1736; m. 16 Mar. 1760 PHINEAS TYLER.
- 45. vii. FARRINGTON, b. 1 Oct. 1738.
- viii. JACOB, b. 9 Jan. 1744/5.

16. Amos⁴ Harrison (*Nathaniel,³ Thomas,² Richard¹*), born at Branford 11 Mar. 1707/8, died at Northford 26 June 1750. He married, 11 Mar. 1729/30, Esther Maltby, born in 1710, died at Northford 13 Oct. 1765.
    Children:
        i. Esther⁵ (called Lowly), b. 17 May 1731; d. 17 July 1775; m. 12 Nov. 1750 Jonah Todd of Bethany, who m. (2) Abigail Crittenden.
        ii. Mary, b. in 1735; d. (with her infant) 31 May 1760; m. 6 Sept. 1759 Phineas Baldwin, who m. (2) 7 Jan. 1761 Martha Peck of Wallingford.
    46. iii. Amos, b. at Northford in 1736.
        iv. Lois, bapt. 3 Aug. 1740; m. 15 Jan. 1761 Zachariah Ives.
        v. Ann, b. 12 May 1743; d. 30 Sept. 1819; m. 27 Dec. 1765 Samuel Foote.
    47. vi. Edward, b. at Northford in 1746.

17. John⁴ Harrison (*John,³ Thomas,² Richard¹*), born at Branford 27 July 1712, was drowned in Branford River in 1750. He married Lydia Allen, born in 1720, died 6 Apr. 1786, daughter of Capt. Theophilus and Elizabeth (Smith) of East Haven, who married secondly, as his second wife, Josiah⁵ Harrison (40), *q.v.*
    Children, born at Branford:
    48. i. John,⁵ b. 12 Feb. 1742/3.
        ii. Rebecca, b. 16 Nov. 1745; d. 20 Nov. 1845; m. 19 June 1765 Samuel⁵ Harrison (50), *q.v.*
    49. iii. Jarius (posthumous), b. in 1751.

18. Ebenezer⁴ Harrison (*John,³ Thomas,² Richard¹*), born at Branford in 1717, died 27 Jan. 1775. He married, 16 Nov. 1762, Temperance Leete of North Branford.
    Children:
        i. Patience,⁵ m. 19 Sept. 1782 Samuel Rose, 3d.
        ii. Olive, m. 17 Oct. 1784 Francis Hale of East Haven. About 1814 they moved to the West, taking with them the aged mother, Temperance.

19. Capt. Samuel⁴ Harrison (*Samuel,³ Thomas,² Richard¹*), born at Branford 15 Dec. 1712, died at North Branford 28 July 1772. He married Rebecca Rose, born in 1712, died at North Branford 31 Jan. 1795. He was lieutenant of the Second Company of Branford in 1751 and captain of the Branford trainband in 1752.
    Children, born at North Branford:
    50. i. Samuel,⁵ b. in 1737.
    51. ii. Asahel, b. in 1744.
        iii. Eunice, b. in 1747; d. 21 Feb. 1820; m. 20 Nov. 1771 Ithiel Russell, b. in 1744, d. 18 June 1833, s. of Ithiel and Jerusha (Harrison) (5, iii).
    52. iv. Jared, b. in 1753.
    53. v. Jacob.

20. Rev. Jared⁴ Harrison (*Samuel,³ Thomas,² Richard¹*), born at Branford 31 May 1716, died at North Branford 17 May 1770. He married at Chester Hannah Waterhouse, daughter of Capt. Abraham and Hannah (Starkee). He was graduated

at Yale College in 1736, and in 1741 became pastor of the First Congregational Church at Chester.

Children, born at Chester:

54. i. JARED,[5] b. 8 July 1749.
55. ii. STEPHEN, b. 8 Aug. 1752.
56. iii. THEODORE, b. in 1756.

21. JAMES[4] HARRISON (*Samuel,[3] Thomas,[2] Richard[1]*), born at North Branford 23 Mar. 1720/1, died there in Dec. 1794. He married first MARY FOOTE, born 8 Dec. 1724, died at North Branford 12 June 1749, daughter of Daniel and Mary (Barker); and secondly, before 1756, ABIGAIL FOOTE, who died at North Branford 22 Nov. 1769, sister of his first wife.

Child by first wife:

57. i. DANIEL FOOTE,[5] b. at North Branford.

Children by second wife, born at North Branford:

ii. MARY, b. in 1755; d. 26 July 1823; m. 8 Apr. 1777 JARIUS[5] HARRISON (49), *q.v.*
58. iii. PHILEMON, b. in 1761.
59. iv. AUGUSTUS, b. in 1765.
60. v. CALVIN, b. in 1767.

22. ISAAC[4] HARRISON (*Isaac,[3] Thomas,[2] Richard[1]*), born at Branford 22 May 1722, died there 11 Sept. 1770. He married first 21 May 1752, HANNAH JOHNSON, who died 4 Oct. 1753; and secondly, 26 Aug. 1756, REBECCA ROGERS, born 20 Jan. 1729/30, daughter of Noah and Elizabeth (Taintor), who married secondly, in May 1775, Reuben Price.

Only child, by second wife:

i. HANNAH,[5] b. at Branford 20 Nov. 1757; d. 27 Jan. 1804; m. 28 Nov. 1776 CAPT. MASON HOBART, b. 1 Nov. 1752, d. 28 Mar. 1841, s. of Abijah and Mary.

23. THOMAS[5] HARRISON (*Thomas,[4] Thomas,[3] Thomas,[2] Richard[1]*), born at Branford 14 Dec. 1722, died at Litchfield 23 Dec. 1791 and was buried at East Morris. He married, 20 Sept. 1764, SIBYL SHERRY, born in 1738, died 13 Dec. 1835, an Acadian who was left at New Haven by the British ship *Boston*.

Children, born at Litchfield:

i. THOMAS,[6] b. 18 Aug. 1765; m. ELIZABETH TWITCHELL.
ii. MARY ANN, b. 18 June 1769; m. 6 Apr. 1791 JOSEPH MANSFIELD, s. of Joseph of New Haven.
iii. ROSWELL, b. in 1772; d. 25 Dec. 1859; m. (1) in May 1796 ANNA SPERRY, b. in 1770, d. 17 Dec. 1819; m. (2) in 1821 SERVIAH HULL, b. in 1779, d. 26 Feb. 1841; m. (3) 2 Dec. 1841 SARAH MERRIAM, widow, who d. 23 Sept. 1851.
iv. ASAHEL, b. 18 June 1778; d. 30 Mar. 1823; m. 28 Apr. 1808 MIRIAM HARRIS of Canaan, b. 11 June 1786, d. 31 Mar. 1868.

24. ENSIGN GIDEON[5] HARRISON (*Thomas,[4] Thomas,[3] Thomas,[2] Richard[1]*), born at Branford 5 Aug. 1724, died at Litchfield 21 Dec. 1801. He married, 11 Feb. 1746/7, SARAH WOODRUFF, born 27 Dec. 1725, died 17 Jan. 1799, daughter of Capt. Nathaniel and Thankful (Wright) of Litchfield. He was appointed ensign of the Eighth Company 8 Mar. 1759.

Children, born at Litchfield:

i. MARY,[6] b. 29 Nov. 1747; m. 4 Mar. 1767 OBED STODDARD, b. 5 Apr. 1743, d. 3 Dec. 1777, s. of Moses.
ii. SARAH, b. 20 Feb. 1749/50.
iii. JOSEPH, b. 28 Oct. 1752.
iv. ANN, b. 28 July 1754; d. 22 Sept. 1754.

25. LIEUT. EPHRAIM[5] HARRISON (*Thomas,*[4] *Thomas,*[3] *Thomas,*[2] *Richard*[1]), born at Branford 28 Dec. 1726, died at Litchfield 7 Nov. 1791. He married, 15 Feb. 1750/1, HANNAH SANFORD, born at Milford 23 July 1729, died at Litchfield 11 Jan. 1804, daughter of Joseph and Mary (Clark). She was a famous midwife, and assisted at the birth of 2182 children.

Children, born at Litchfield:

i. RACHEL,[6] b. 15 Feb. 1752; d. in 1795; m. LEVI PECK.
ii. DAVID, b. 9 Nov. 1753; d. 13 Apr. 1812; bur. at Morris; m. (1) JERUSHA MARSH; m. (2) MEHITABLE LANDON, b. 5 June 1767, d. 26 Mar. 1827, dau. of Abner and Eunice (Gibbs).
iii. MARY (called POLLY), b. 13 Dec. 1754; d. unm. 10 Apr. 1800.
iv. HANNAH, b. 20 Mar. 1757; d. in 1794; m. (1) ELIJAH PECK, s. of Paul and Sarah (Smith); m. (2) EBENEZER MARSH, s. of Col. Ebenezer and Lucy (Phelps); m. (3) COL. TIMOTHY SKINNER.
v. SOLOMON, b. 17 Apr. 1760; d. 11 Apr. 1834; m. SUSAN GUNN of Milford.
vi. LUCY, b. 29 Mar. 1762; d. in 1812; m. (1) SAMUEL WOODRUFF; m. (2) 14 Oct. 1790 JESSE SPENCER.

26. TITUS[5] HARRISON (*Thomas,*[4] *Thomas,*[3] *Thomas,*[2] *Richard*[1]) was born at Branford 30 Nov. 1728. He married, 18 Feb. 1756, ANNE PECK, daughter of Thomas and Sarah (Smith).

Children:

i. LOIS,[6] b. 6 Nov. 1756.
ii. NOAH, b. 12 July 1759.
iii. ALMON, b. 2 June 1761.
iv. SALMON, physician, b. at Williamstown, Mass., 16 Aug. 1768; d. 14 Nov. 1836; m. 24 Oct. 1797 LYDIA DWIGHT, b. in 1775, d. 15 Feb. 1850, dau. of Joseph and Lydia (Dewey).

27. ABEL[5] HARRISON (*Thomas,*[4] *Thomas,*[3] *Thomas,*[2] *Richard*[1]) was born at Branford 2 Feb. 1731/2. He married first, 26 Mar. 1750, ABIGAIL CHRISSEY; and secondly, 21 Mar. 1759, ANNA GARNSEY.

Child by first wife:

i. ABIGAIL,[6] b. at Litchfield 19 Mar. 1756; m. 11 Oct. 1779 JAMES GOODWIN of Litchfield, s. of Capt. Nathaniel and Elizabeth (Nash).

Children by second wife, born at Litchfield:

ii. A DAUGHTER, b. 9 Jan. 1760.
iii. REUBEN, b. 1 Jan. 1762.

28. JACOB[5] HARRISON (*Thomas,*[4] *Thomas,*[3] *Thomas,*[2] *Richard*[1]), born at Branford 7 Oct. 1734, died at Litchfield 21 Jan. 1776. He married, 13 Feb. 1762, ELIZABETH PLUMB, born 9 May 1742, daughter of Ezra and Elizabeth (Buell).

Children, born at Litchfield:

i. SAMUEL,[6] b. 20 Nov. 1763 [*sic*, see Elizabeth].
ii. ELIZABETH, b. 4 July 1764 [*sic*, see Samuel]; d. 8 Apr. 1808; m. 1 Jan. 1783 NOAH BEACH, b. 27 Aug. 1764, d. 12 Apr. 1851,

s. of Zophar and Elizabeth (Wadhams) of Goshen, who m. (2) 21
Aug. 1808 Sally Spencer.
iii. IRENE, m. ——— MERRILS.
iv. JACOB, b. 8 Aug. 1770; d. 7 Nov. 1841; m. at Great Barrington,
Mass., 26 Sept. 1799, POLLY DWIGHT, b. 30 Jan. 1768, d. 21 Feb.
1846, dau. of Joseph and Lydia (Dewey).

29. ENSIGN LEMUEL[5] HARRISON (*Thomas,[4] Thomas,[3] Thomas,[2] Richard[1]*), born at Branford 23 Mar. 1737/8, died at Litchfield
9 Sept. 1807. He married, 18 Feb. 1762, LOIS BARNES,
daughter of Timothy and Phoebe (Barnes) of Branford. He
was ensign of the Seventeenth Connecticut Regiment.
Children, born at Litchfield:
i. TIMOTHY,[6] b. 31 Oct. 1763.
ii. LEMUEL, b. 17 Nov. 1765; d. at Waterbury 23 Nov. 1857; m. 4
Mar. 1790 SARAH CLARK, b. 5 June 1770, dau. of Thomas and
Mary (Hine) of Waterbury.
iii. JAMES, b. 23 July 1767; d. unm. in New York.
iv. PHOEBE, b. 6 June 1769.
v. WOOSTER, b. 18 June 1772.
vi. OLNEY, b. 24 Nov. 1774; d. 16 Nov. 1776.
vii. LOIS, b. 29 Aug. 1776.
viii. ANDREW, b. in Aug. 1779; d. in 1810.
ix. CAROLINE, b. 18 Sept. 1785.

30. ELIHU[5] HARRISON (*Thomas,[4] Thomas,[3] Thomas,[2] Richard[1]*), born
at Branford 25 Feb. 1739/40, died at Litchfield 3 May 1806.
He married, 19 Jan. 1764, THEDA WOODRUFF, born 8 Oct. 1742,
died 5 Nov. 1815, daughter of Jacob and Anne (Griswold) of
Litchfield.
Children, born at Litchfield:
i. ANNE,[6] b. 11 Dec. 1764; d. 7 July 1802; m., as his second wife,
EZEKIEL TRUMBULL.
ii. LYDIA, b. 8 Jan. 1766; d. 17 Sept. 1806; m. 2 Jan. 1786 DR. JOSEPH
PARKER of Washington.
iii. SIMEON, b. 8 Oct. 1768; d. 3 June 1835; m. 2 June 1796 HANNAH
FARNAM, b. 3 July 1771, d. 3 Mar. 1827, dau. of Gad and Jane
(Bishop).
iv. DAN, b. 4 Sept. 1770; d. 4 June 1811; m. 23 Jan. 1797 ABIGAIL
GOODWIN, b. 15 Nov. 1771, d. 4 Mar. 1839, dau. of Ensign Ozias
and Hannah (Vaille).

31. LEVI[5] HARRISON (*Thomas,[4] Thomas,[3] Thomas,[2] Richard[1]*) died
at Litchfield 14 Nov. 1796. He married, 29 Oct. 1766,
ELECTA WOODRUFF, born 8 Sept. 1747, daughter of Charles
and Prudence (Stoddard).
Children, born at Litchfield:
i. OLIVE,[6] b. 17 June 1767; m. (1) TIMOTHY LINSLEY; m. (2) STEPTOE
WOODRUFF.
ii. ELECTA, b. 12 Apr. 1770; m. 14 Mar. 1791 SAMUEL FROST.
iii. JOHN, b. 25 July 1772; m. 23 June 1800 MAHALA PECK, dau. of
Elijah and Hannah (Harrison) (25, iv).
iv. REBECCA, m. 1 Oct. 1797 LEMAN WOODRUFF, b. 21 Feb. 1773, s. of
Jacob, Jr., and Anne (Orton).
v. SALLY, bapt. 14 Sept. 1788; m. ISAAC CLARK.
vi. BETSEY, bapt. 14 Sept. 1788.
vii. CHARLES, bapt. 15 July 1790.

32. BENJAMIN[5] HARRISON (*Benjamin,[4] Thomas,[3] Thomas,[2] Richard[1]*),
born at Branford 14 Nov. 1721, died at Waterbury 13 Mar.

1760. He married, 24 Dec. 1741, DINAH WARNER, born
11 Feb. 1723/4, died 21 Oct. 1792, daughter of Dr. Benjamin
and Johanna (Strong) of Waterbury, who married secondly,
7 June 1762, Moses Cook of Wallingford.

Children, born at Waterbury:

   i.   JAMES,[6] b. 28 Oct. 1742; d. 23 Oct. 1760.
   ii. JABEZ, b. 11 Oct. 1744; m. 15 Oct. 1772 DEBORAH JOHNSON.
   iii. LYDIA, b. 24 Sept. 1747; d. 6 Aug. 1750.
   iv. SAMUEL, b. and d. in Sept. 1750.
   v. ROZEL, b. 20 Dec. 1751; d. 13 Dec. 1764.
   vi. DANIEL, b. 15 July 1754; m. 13 Jan. 1774 PHOEBE BLAKESLEE, dau.
       of David and Abigail (Howe).
   vii. LYDIA, b. 27 Mar. 1755; m. JOHN HICKOX.

33. CAPT. AARON[5] HARRISON (*Benjamin*,[4] *Thomas*,[3] *Thomas*,[2] *Richard*[1]), born at Branford 20 Apr. 1726, died at Wolcott 5 Sept.
1819. He married at Wolcott, 26 Oct. 1748, JERUSHA WAR-
NER, born 13 Dec. 1727, died 13 Sept. 1819, daughter of
Obadiah and Sarah (Lewis).

Children, born at Wolcott:

   i.   JARED,[6] of Whitestone, N. Y., b. 13 Oct. 1749; d. 21 Jan. 1810;
       m. HANNAH ———.
   ii. MARK, b. 9 Apr. 1751; d. 15 July 1822; m. (1) 30 Mar. 1775 RE-
       BECCA MILES, who d. 2 Aug. 1810; m. (2) 24 Feb. 1811 HANNAH
       BEACH, widow.
   iii. SAMUEL, b. 15 Mar. 1753; m. PHOEBE ———.
   iv. DAVID, b. 3 Dec. 1756; d. 5 Apr. 1820; m. (1) 10 Dec. 1778 HEP-
       ZIBAH ROBERTS, who d. 28 Aug. 1793; m. (2) LYDIA HOTCHKISS,
       who d. 25 July 1838, dau. of Wait.
   v. JOHN, b. 3 Dec. 1758; d. 10 Nov. 1776.
   vi. AARON, d. near New Haven in 1808.
   vii. LUCY, b. 1 Mar. 1762; m. 16 Apr. 1779 NATHAN GILLETTE, s. of
       Zaccheus and Ruth (Phelps).
   viii. LYDIA, b. in 1766; d. 27 Sept. 1796; m. 27 Sept. 1783 DR. JOHN
       POTTER, s. of Joel and Rhoda of Southington.

34. STEPHEN[5] HARRISON (*Joseph*,[4] *Thomas*,[3] *Thomas*,[2] *Richard*[1]),
born at Branford 14 Nov. 1733, died at Westfield, Mass., in
1791. He married, 16 Mar. 1755, SUSANNA BARTHOLOMEW,
born 11 Apr. 1734, daughter of William and Hannah (Williams) of Wallingford.

Children, born at Northford:

   i.   SARAH,[6] b. 24 Feb. 1756; d. 27 Dec. 1772.
   ii. HANNAH, b. 24 July 1758; d. 29 Jan. 1770.
   iii. REUBEN, b. 28 Apr. 1762; m. NANCY BALDWIN, dau. of Jabez and
       Lydia (Barker).
   iv. SIBYL, b. 13 Jan. 1765; m. in 1784 GAD MERICK of West Spring-
       field, Mass.
   v. SUSANNA, b. 3 Nov. 1767; m. ISRAEL STOCKING.
   vi. LOIS, b. 23 Sept. 1769; d. 31 Jan. 1826; m. 20 Dec. 1797 JOHN
       STRONG, JR., of Southampton, Mass., b. 17 Apr. 1769, who m.
       (2) Keziah Shelden.
   vii. STEPHEN, b. 24 Feb. 1772; d. 5 Apr. 1772.

35. NATHANIEL[5] HARRISON (*Nathaniel*,[4] *Nathaniel*,[3] *Thomas*,[2] *Richard*[1]), born at Branford 3 Aug. 1735, died there 22 Apr. 1770.
He married, 19 Dec. 1758, MARY TYLER.

Child:

   i.   MARTHA,[6] b. at Branford 21 June 1760; m. 9 June 1778 NICODEMUS
       BALDWIN, b. 4 Aug. 1755, d. 9 June 1799.

36. **DANIEL⁵ HARRISON** (*Daniel,⁴ Nathaniel,³ Thomas,² Richard¹*), born at Branford 5 Aug. 1722, died at Cornwall in 1806. He married at Branford, 28 Apr. 1748, HANNAH BARKER. About 1765 he removed from Branford to Cornwall.

Children, all except the last born at Branford:

   i. DANIEL,⁶ b. 12 Feb. 1750/1; d. 6 May 1811; m. (1) 10 Dec. 1772 HANNAH PAGE; m. (2) SARAH PARKER.

   ii. JOEL, b. 21 Mar. 1753; m. HANNAH BEARDSLEY; removed to Amenia, N. Y.

   iii. JOSEPH, b. 23 Feb. 1758; d. from exposure in the Revolution, having enlisted as a soldier.

   iv. THANKFUL, b. 12 Aug. 1764; m. REV. JOHN CORNWALL.

   v. ESTHER, b. 15 Oct. 1767; d. 23 Nov. 1767.

   vi. LUTHER, b. 4 July 1769; m. RACHEL JOHNSON.

   vii. ABIGAIL, m. WILLIAM CRANMER; removed to the West.

37. **ABRAHAM⁵ HARRISON** (*Daniel,⁴ Nathaniel,³ Thomas,² Richard¹*), born at Branford 20 Nov. 1728, died on his way to Lebanon Springs, N. Y., 8 Nov. 1790, and was buried at Cornwall. He married, 26 Jan. 1764, HANNAH JOHNSON, who died 12 Dec. 1815 and was buried at Lebanon Springs, N. Y., daughter of Edward and Elizabeth (Barnes) of Branford.

Children, born at Branford:

   i. DEBORAH,⁶ b. 24 Apr. 1765; d. unm. at Lebanon Springs, N. Y., 13 Aug. 1844.

   ii. ABRAHAM, b. 19 Aug. 1767; d. unm. at Lebanon Springs, N. Y., 8 Nov. 1843.

38. **NOAH⁵ HARRISON** (*Daniel,⁴ Nathaniel,³ Thomas,² Richard¹*), born at Branford 19 Mar. 1737/8, died at Cornwall 7 Mar. 1823. He married first, 30 June 1767, HANNAH ROGERS, born at Branford 8 May 1737, died at Cornwall 18 Feb. 1785, daughter of Noah and Elizabeth (Wheeler); and secondly, 21 July 1785, ANNA (HOPKINS) CARTER, born in 1747, died 15 Sept. 1831, daughter of Silvanus and Ruth (Berry) and widow of Thomas of Kent. About 1765 he removed from Branford to Cornwall with his brother Daniel.

Children by first wife, born at Cornwall:

   i. EDMUND,⁶ b. 1 May 1768; d. 4 Jan. 1867; m. 19 Feb. 1795 RUTH HOPKINS, b. at Kent 4 Feb. 1769, d. 24 May 1852, dau. of Elijah and Lois (Fuller) of Warren.

   ii. HEMAN, b. 13 Nov. 1769; d. 23 Mar. 1829; m. REBECCA BRADFORD of Cornwall, b. in 1775, d. 4 Nov. 1843.

   iii. LUMAN, b. 28 May 1776; d. in 1831; m. in 1811 PHOEBE CULVER, dau. of George and Ruth of Long Island, N. Y. They removed to Palmyra, N. Y.

Children by second wife, born at Cornwall:

   iv. HANNAH, b. 10 Dec. 1786; m. in 1807 ELIAS HART, b. 4 Nov. 1784, s. of Elias and Philomena (Burnham) of Cornwall.

   v. AMANDA, b. 20 Mar. 1789; m. in 1807 OLIVER B. HART, s. of Elias and Philomena (Burnham) of Cornwall. They removed to Michigan.

39. **PETER⁵ HARRISON** (*Daniel,⁴ Nathaniel,³ Thomas,² Richard¹*), born at Branford 11 Nov. 1739, died there 22 Oct. 1829. He married, 5 Apr. 1764, MERCY FRISBIE, born 9 Sept. 1744, daughter of Samuel and Rachel (Bartholomew).

Children, born at Branford:

i. CAPT. AMMI,[6] b. in 1765; d. 14 Mar. 1850; m. in Dec. 1783 ELIZA-
BETH BALDWIN, b. 24 Sept. 1758, d. 11 June 1843, dau. of James
and Desire (Parmelee).
ii. LUCRETIA, bapt. 6 July 1766; d. unm. 6 Sept. 1849.
iii. HANNAH, bapt. 14 May 1771; d. young.
iv. CATHERINE, bapt. 6 Sept. 1772; d. unm. 24 Oct. 1829.
v. HANNAH, bapt. 19 Jan. 1777; d. at Bristol in 1849; m. in Nov. 1793
WILLIAM GOULD of Bristol.
vi. ESTHER, bapt. 25 Apr. 1779; m. ASAHEL SMITH; removed to
Whitestone, N. Y.
vii. CHANDLER, bapt. 18 Nov. 1781; killed at sea by a fall from a mast-
head, aged 19.
viii. LYDIA, bapt. 15 Aug. 1784; d. unm. 30 Dec. 1849.
ix. PHILEMON, bapt. 11 Mar. 1787.

40. CAPT. JOSIAH[5] HARRISON (Josiah,[4] Nathaniel,[3] Thomas,[2] Richard[1]), born at Branford 19 July 1724, died there 21 Nov. 1784.
He married first, 16 Feb. 1745/6, PHOEBE BUTLER, daughter
of Jonathan and Lydia; and secondly, 24 Oct. 1754, LYDIA
(ALLEN) HARRISON, born in 1720, died 6 Apr. 1786, daughter
of Capt. Theophilus and Elizabeth (Smith) of East Haven and
widow of John[4] (17).

Children by first wife, born at Branford:

i. JOSIAH,[6] b. 6 Jan. 1746/7; d. 12 Feb. 1774; m. in 1773 TRYPHENA
BALDWIN, b. 25 June 1752, who m. (2) 27 Feb. 1779 Dr. Reuben
Linsley.
ii. PHOEBE, b. 10 Oct. 1748; m. 24 Sept. 1770 BENJAMIN BYINGTON.

Children by second wife, born at Branford:

iii. JUSTUS, b. 13 Oct. 1755; d. 13 Aug. 1826; m. 7 Nov. 1779 SARAH
RUSSELL, b. 10 Mar. 1755, d. 4 Feb. 1846, dau. of Dea. Ebenezer
and Mabel (Dudley).
iv. ISRAEL, b. 15 Feb. 1757; d. unm. 29 July 1790.
v. ITHIEL, b. 27 July 1759; d. 2 Jan. 1818; m. AMY LINSLEY, b. in
1765, d. 27 Oct. 1817, dau. of Israel and Hannah (Moulthrop).
vi. LYDIA, b. 19 July 1762; m. in Apr. 1786 COL. REUBEN PAGE.

41. TIMOTHY[5] HARRISON (Josiah,[4] Nathaniel,[3] Thomas,[2] Richard[1]),
born at Branford 31 Aug. 1729, died at North Branford
14 Feb. 1815. He married, 12 June 1751, LYDIA BUTLER,
born 22 Dec. 1726, d. 29 Mar. 1806, daughter of Jonathan.

Children, born at Branford:

i. TIMOTHY,[6] b. 25 July 1752; d. 3 Apr. 1825; m. 14 Mar. 1776 CLO-
RINDA FOSDICK, b. 19 Mar. 1748/9, d. at North Branford 26 Aug.
1823, dau. of Ezekiel and Abigail (Wright) of Wethersfield.
ii. LYDIA, b. 12 Jan. 1754; m. 9 Aug. 1775 ABIJAH ROGERS. They
removed to Freehold, N. Y., and then to Hudson, N. Y., where
she died.
iii. ELIZABETH, b. 2 Oct. 1755; d. 22 May 1791; m. 11 Mar. 1779
CAPT. ASAHEL[5] HARRISON (51), q. v.
iv. BUTLER, b. 16 Feb. 1757; d. 10 Apr. 1832; m. 14 Feb. 1782 MERCY
LINSLEY, b. 14 Sept. 1754, d. 2 Apr. 1833, dau. of John and
Elizabeth (Barker).
v. RACHEL, b. 13 Mar. 1760; m. JUSTUS BARKER; removed to New
York State.
vi. DOROTHEA, b. 26 Dec. 1762; d. unm. at Suffield.
vii. MOSES, b. 10 Dec. 1764; d. 4 July 1847; m. REBECCA (HARRISON)
MONROE (50, ii), dau. of Samuel[5] and Rebecca (Harrison) and
widow of Frederic.

viii. NATHANIEL, b. 30 July 1767; m. PHOEBE BRADLEY of Hamden,
b. in 1772, d. 30 Jan. 1809.
ix. ESTHER, b. 13 May 1770; d. 9 Apr. 1790; m. in 1789 AUGUSTUS⁵
HARRISON (59), q. v.

42. NATHAN⁵ HARRISON (*Josiah,⁴ Nathaniel,³ Thomas,² Richard¹*),
born at Branford 18 Mar. 1730/1, died at North Branford
17 Aug. 1773. He married, 27 Mar. 1758, MARTHA BALDWIN,
born 5 Aug. 1736, died 22 Nov. 1818, daughter of Israel and
Dinah (Butler).
Children, born at North Branford:
  i. RUFUS,⁶ b. 16 Apr. 1759; d. 12 May 1785.
  ii. NATHAN, b. 25 Mar. 1762; d. 7 Nov. 1839; m. (1) THANKFUL
——, b. in 1762, d. 17 Dec. 1790; m. (2) LOIS BARKER, b. in
1762, d. 6 Feb. 1826.
  iii. JACOB, b. 16 July 1765; removed to Richmond, Va.
  iv. ANNA, b. 30 Aug. 1769; d. 26 Nov. 1842; m. 25 Jan. 1809 AMOS
PAGE, JR., who d. 18 Nov. 1835.
  v. DAVID, b. 22 Sept. 1772.

43. MOSES⁵ HARRISON (*Josiah,⁴ Nathaniel,³ Thomas,² Richard¹*),
born at Branford, died 15 Nov. 1761, a soldier in the French
and Indian War. He married ELIZABETH PALMER, daughter
of John.
Child:
  i. ELIZABETH⁶ (called MOLLE and MARY), b. 4 Oct. 1759; m. 30 Oct.
1778 ELIPHALET BARNES.

44. JONATHAN⁵ HARRISON (*Jonathan,⁴ Nathaniel,³ Thomas,² Richard¹*),
born at Branford 22 May 1727, died in 1790. He married,
26 Aug. 1747, SARAH BALDWIN, born 3 Sept. 1728, daughter of
John and Hannah (Tyler).
Children, born at Branford:
  i. HANNAH,⁶ b. 23 Apr. 1749; m. 23 Mar. 1774, as his second wife,
FELIX NORTON of Guilford.
  ii. SARAH, b. 28 Mar. 1753; d. in 1835; m. 1 Nov. 1785 JOEL IVES.
  iii. DESIRE, b. 29 Jan. 1757; d. 14 July 1846; m. (1) 20 Jan. 1778 JOHN
NEGUS; m. (2) 20 May 1787 CAPT. EDWARD BALDWIN, b. in 1763,
d. 4 Oct. 1823.
  iv. JOHN, b. 29 Nov. 1761; m. 10 May 1787 IRENE WARDELL. They
removed to Freehold, N. Y.
  v. JACOB, b. 19 Apr. 1765; d. before his father.

45. CAPT. FARRINGTON⁵ HARRISON (*Jonathan,⁴ Nathaniel,³ Thomas,²
Richard¹*), born at Branford 1 Oct. 1738, died in 1808. He
married, 29 Sept. 1772, HANNAH WILFORD, born in 1753, died
1 Dec. 1843.
Children, born at Branford:
  i. SAMUEL,⁶ b. 25 Dec. 1774; d. in South Carolina in 1795.
  ii. BETSEY, b. 18 Mar. 1777; m. 18 June 1810 SAMUEL WOODRUFF of
Washington; removed to Michigan.
  iii. SALLY, b. 28 Mar. 1779; m. in 1797 JOHN BEACH of Branford.
  iv. DAVID, b. 20 Aug. 1781; drowned in the West Indies 16 June 1810,
unm.
  v. POLLY, b. 13 Jan. 1784; d. in Jan. 1844; m. CALVIN FRISBIE.
  vi. THOMAS, b. in 1786; d. 15 July 1803.
  vii. JOHN, b. in June 1788; d. in 1864; m. 4 Nov. 1813 BETSEY GRIF-
FING, b. 20 Dec. 1792, dau. of Aaron and Betty (Palmer).

viii. ANN, b. 26 Aug. 1791; m. 16 Aug. 1818 DR. WILLOUGHBY LAY.
ix. JAMES, b. in Apr. 1795; d. in 1820; m. 4 May 1819 SALLY HOADLEY.

46. AMOS⁵ HARRISON (*Amos*,⁴ *Nathaniel*,³ *Thomas*,² *Richard*¹), born at Northford in 1736, died there 25 Oct. 1815. He married, 26 May 1762, ELIZABETH FOWLER, born 27 Feb. 1742/3, died at Northford 13 Mar. 1828, daughter of David and Elizabeth (Hall) of Durham.

Children, born at Northford:

i. AMOS,⁶ b. in 1763; d. in Jan. 1774.
ii. MARY, b. 24 July 1764; d. 30 Dec. 1773.
iii. ABIATHAR, b. in 1767; d. 13 Jan. 1774.
iv. REUBEN, bapt. 1 Jan. 1769; d. *s.p.* 19 Sept. 1845; m. 1 Jan. 1795 SARAH FOOTE, b. 1 Oct. 1767, d. 22 Aug. 1847, dau. of Daniel and Mary (Ingraham).
v. ANNA, b. in 1772; d. 2 Sept. 1775.
vi. AMOS ABIATHAR, b. 6 Feb. 1774; d. 29 Dec. 1846; m. LUCINDA HOUGH, b. in 1780, d. 16 Mar. 1858.
vii. ELIZABETH, b. 22 July 1779; m. 12 Mar. 1799 RUFUS FOOTE, s. of Daniel and Mary (Ingraham).
viii. JACOB, bapt. 5 May 1782; d. 17 Oct. 1855; m. 24 Oct. 1805 HANNAH BARTHOLOMEW, b. in 1786, d. 15 Mar. 1869, dau. of Samuel and Irene (Munson).
ix. ELIZUR, bapt. 8 Aug. 1784; d. 25 May 1850; m. (1) 31 Dec. 1809 REBECCA BARTHOLOMEW; m. (2) 22 Nov. 1837 LYDIA (FOWLER) LINSLEY, widow (second wife) of Richard.

47. EDWARD⁵ HARRISON (*Amos*,⁴ *Nathaniel*,³ *Thomas*,² *Richard*¹), born at Northford in 1746, died there 22 Jan. 1833. He married, 12 Dec. 1771, SARAH DUDLEY, born in 1753, died at Northford 14 Feb. 1837, daughter of Joshua and Elizabeth (Hoadley) of Branford and Woodbury.

Children, born at Northford:

i. ESTHER,⁶ b. 1 Oct. 1772; d. 1 Aug. 1773.
ii. SALLY, b. 9 Mar. 1774; d. 25 Mar. 1784.
iii. BENJAMIN, b. 12 June 1776; d. 3 Sept. 1795.
iv. RACHEL, b. 30 Jan. 1778; m. 17 Feb. 1802 HENRY FOWLER.
v. LEMUEL, b. 6 Oct. 1781; d. 29 Oct. 1781.
vi. POLLY, b. 6 Apr. 1783; d. at New Haven 23 Feb. 1872; m. 7 Oct. 1810 CAPT. SIMEON HOADLEY, b. at Northford 4 July 1780, d. at New Haven 25 Dec. 1867.

48. JOHN⁵ HARRISON (*John*,⁴ *John*,³ *Thomas*,² *Richard*¹), born at Branford 12 Feb. 1742/3, died at North Branford 21 July 1770. He married SILENCE FRISBIE, daughter of Joseph and Sarah, who married secondly, 19 Oct. 1778, Eli Foote of Northford, afterwards of Johnstown and Deerfield, N. Y.

Child:

i. JOHN,⁶ b. at Northford in 1769; d. at North Branford 19 Aug. 1859; m. his first cousin, ABIGAIL⁶ HARRISON (49, i), b. at Branford 27 Nov. 1777, d. at North Branford 5 Dec. 1808, dau. of Jarius and Mary (Harrison).

49. JARIUS⁵ HARRISON (*John*,⁴ *John*,³ *Thomas*,² *Richard*¹), born at Branford in 1751, died there in Nov. 1824. He married, 8 Apr. 1777 MARY⁵ HARRISON (21, ii), born in 1755, died 26 July 1823, daughter of James and Abigail (Foote).

Child:

i. ABIGAIL,[6] b. at Branford 27 Nov. 1777; d. at North Branford 5 Dec.
    1808; m. her first cousin, JOHN[6] HARRISON (48, i), q.v., s. of John
    and Silence (Frisbie).

50. SAMUEL[5] HARRISON (*Samuel,[4] Samuel,[3] Thomas,[2] Richard[1]*), born
    at North Branford in 1737, died there 20 Aug. 1810. He
    married, 19 June 1765, REBECCA[5] HARRISON (17, ii), born at
    Branford 16 Nov. 1745, died 20 Nov. 1845, daughter of John
    and Lydia (Allen).
    Children, born at North Branford:

    i.   GILES,[6] b. 4 Oct. 1765; d. 14 Aug. 1831; m. HARRIET[6] HARRISON
         (57, iii), b. at North Branford in 1782, d. 5 Oct. 1866, dau. of
         Daniel Foote and Lulea (Monroe).
    ii. REBECCA, b. 26 Feb. 1767; d. 15 June 1862; m. (1) in Mar. 1790
         FREDERIC MONROE; m. (2) MOSES[6] HARRISON (41, vii), q.v., s.
         of Timothy and Lydia (Butler).
    iii. REV. ROGER, B. A. (Yale, 1791), b. 12 Feb. 1769; d. s.p. in 1853;
         m. LOIS ROSE, who d. at Tolland, Mass., 14 June 1820, aged 46,
         and was bur. at North Branford, dau. of Capt. Jonathan; pastor
         of the church at Tolland, Mass.
    iv. EUNICE, b. 16 May 1772; m. 16 Oct. 1796 ELISHA ROSE.
    v.   BETSEY, b. 19 Aug. 1779; d. 14 Sept. 1872; m. COL. THADDEUS[7]
         HARRISON, b. in 1783, d. 10 Dec. 1857, s. of Butler (41, iv) and
         Mercy (Linsley).

51. CAPT. ASAHEL[5] HARRISON (*Samuel,[4] Samuel,[3] Thomas,[2] Rich-
    ard[1]*), born at North Branford in 1744, died there 30 Dec.
    1820. He married, 11 Mar. 1779, ELIZABETH[6] HARRISON
    (41, iii), born at Branford 2 Oct. 1755, died 22 May 1791,
    daughter of Timothy and Lydia (Butler).
    Children, born at North Branford:

    i.   SAMUEL.[6]
    ii. ELIZABETH, bapt. 28 Aug. 1785.
    iii. ASAHEL, b. 1 Apr. 1791; d. 12 Apr. 1791.

52. JARED[5] HARRISON (*Samuel,[4] Samuel,[3] Thomas,[2] Richard[1]*), born
    at North Branford in 1753, died in Apr. 1800. He married,
    25 July 1776, MARY McCLEAVE of New Haven.
    Children, born at North Branford:

    i.   SARAH HALL,[6] b. 19 July 1778.
    ii. MARY (called POLLY), b. 6 Sept. 1780.
    iii. LAVINIA, b. 8 July 1783; m. 3 Jan. 1812 JOSIAH HARRISON.
    iv. LYDIA, b. 13 June 1785.
    v.   HORACE, b. 15 Apr. 1788.

53. JACOB[5] HARRISON (*Samuel,[4] Samuel,[3] Thomas,[2] Richard[1]*), born
    at North Branford, died at Guilford in 1826. He married,
    13 Dec. 1781, LOIS RUSSELL.
    Children:

    i.   OFFANA,[6] b. 9 Dec. 1783.
    ii. LOIS, b. and d. 28 Mar. 1791.
    iii. TRUMAN, of Guilford.

54. CAPT. JARED[5] HARRISON (*Jared,[4] Samuel,[3] Thomas,[2] Richard[1]*),
    born at Chester 8 July 1749, died at Salisbury 22 Sept. 1842.
    He married, in 1772, ASENATH STEVENS, born at Saybrook

10 Sept. 1750, died at Salisbury 16 June 1816, daughter of Ebenezer and Lucy (Griswold).

Children:

i. ROSWELL,[6] b. 2 May 1773; d. 29 Dec. 1860; m. (1) ELIZABETH GUERNSEY; m. (2) 3 Jan. 1808 CATHERINE STEELE, b. 5 Nov. 1776, d. in 1841, dau. of Rev. Eliphalet and Elizabeth (Stevens).
ii. OLIVE, b. 9 Aug. 1774; d. at Colebrook 5 Jan. 1818; m. (1) ALEXANDER SPENCER of Northeast Precinct, N.Y.; m. (2) REV. CHAUNCEY LEE, D.D.
iii. BENJAMIN, b. 15 May 1776; d. at Bloomingdale, Ohio, 20 Apr. 1828; m. in 1806 PARMELIA STEELE, b. in Sept. 1786, d. at Fredonia, N. Y., 10 Nov. 1868.
iv. SALLY, b. 28 July 1780; d. at Honesdale, Pa., 26 Feb. 1841; m. 2 Oct. 1799 JUDGE MARTIN STRONG, b. 7 Dec. 1778, d. 28 Feb. 1838, s. of Col. Adonijah and Abigail (Bates).
v. BEULAH, m. SAMUEL LEE, b. in 1784, d. at Columbia, Tenn., 12 Oct. 1830, s. of Jonathan and Mabel (Little).
vi. JARED STEVENS, b. 9 July 1786; d. at Salisbury 27 Apr. 1864; m. (1) 27 Oct. 1808 HANNAH LEE, b. 26 Jan. 1788, d. 10 June 1824, dau. of Dr. Jonathan of Pittsfield, Mass.; m. (2) HARRIET ———, b. in 1807, d. 31 July 1880.
vii. ASENATH, m. ——— SCOVILLE.

55. STEPHEN[5] HARRISON (*Jared*,[4] *Samuel*,[3] *Thomas*,[2] *Richard*[1]), born at Chester 8 Aug. 1752, died at Huntingdon Valley, Pa., 5 June 1834. He married first, 29 July 1773, SUSANNA FRANKLIN, born at North Canaan 6 Dec. 1751, died 4 Jan. 1805, daughter of John and Kezia (Pierce); and secondly, HULDAH CUNNINGHAM.

Children by first wife:

i. WILLIAM,[6] m. LYDIA CHAPIN.
ii. LUCY, b. 7 June 1775; m. DANIEL FULLER.
iii. STEPHEN, b. 16 May 1777; d. 5 Mar. 1865; m. MARY DODSON.
iv. JARIUS, b. 3 Apr. 1779; d. 1 Mar. 1853; m. HULDAH FULLER.
v. LYDIA, b. 1 Mar. 1781; m. JACOB STEELE.
vi. CLARISSA, b. 27 Mar. 1783; d. 22 Dec. 1820; m. JOHN DODSON.
vii. MERRITT, b. 12 May 1785; d. 2 Nov. 1799.
viii. SUSANNA, b. 8 Dec. 1789; m. ISAAC HOPKINS.

Children by second wife:

ix. EZEKIEL CUNNINGHAM, b. 3 Sept. 1806; d. 12 June 1876; m. REBECCA KOONS.
x. MERRITT FRANKLIN, b. 29 July 1808; m. SARAH EDWARDS.
xi. JULIA REBECCA, b. 5 June 1813; m. ROSS HOYT.
xii. EDNA DAVALL, b. 29 Mar. 1815; m. DARWIN STILES.

56. THEODORE[5] HARRISON (*Jared*,[4] *Samuel*,[3] *Thomas*,[2] *Richard*[1]), born at Chester in 1756, died at Wethersfield 20 May 1836. He married, 17 Apr. 1780, CLOTILDA WRIGHT, born in 1753, died at Wethersfield 20 July 1829, daughter of Nathaniel and Martha (Goodrich).

Children, born at Wethersfield:

i. SAMUEL,[6] b. in 1795; d. 2 Sept. 1830.
ii. JARED, b. in 1796; d. 11 Feb. 1846; m. 30 Apr. 1829 CAROLINE LOVELAND, bapt. 11 Aug. 1799, d. 16 Mar. 1862, dau. of John and Esther (Buck).
iii. OSMUND, b. 9 Oct. 1798; d. 30 Mar. 1895; m. (1) DIANTHA GRISWOLD, b. 16 Oct. 1807, d. 24 Feb. 1837, dau. of Simeon and Joanna (Riley); m. (2) PRUDENCE GRISWOLD.

57. DANIEL FOOTE[5] HARRISON (*James,[4] Samuel,[3] Thomas,[2] Richard[1]*)
was born at North Branford. He married first, 7 Mar. 1780,
LULEA MONROE, born in 1759, died 1 July 1791; and secondly
LYDIA ———, born in 1764.
Children by first wife, born at North Branford:

   i. LEAVERITT,[6] b. 17 Sept. 1781.
   ii. HARRIET, b. in 1782; d. 5 Oct. 1866; m. GILES[6] HARRISON (50, i),
      q.v., s. of Samuel and Rebecca (Harrison).
   iii. FREDERICK, bapt. 25 Aug. 1785.
   iv. DIODESIA.

Child by second wife:

   v. SALLY, b. at North Branford in 1795; m. WALTER RODNEY, b.
      10 Feb. 1793.

58. PHILEMON[5] HARRISON (*James,[4] Samuel,[3] Thomas,[2] Richard[1]*),
born at North Branford in 1761, died 6 Aug. 1825. He
married, in 1784, SARAH WOLCOTT, born 7 May 1767, daughter
of Dr. Jeremiah and Sarah (Goodsell).
Children:

   i. JAMES,[6] b. 28 Dec. 1786; d. at New Haven 18 Feb. 1861; m.
      27 Oct. 18— CHARLOTTE LYNDE, dau. of John Hart of New Haven.
   ii. RANSOM, lost at sea.
   iii. JEREMIAH, m. at Baltimore, Md., ———; removed to New Orleans,
      La.
   iv. JOHN, d. at Macon, Ga.
   v. HENRY, m. HENRIETTA HOODS.

59. AUGUSTUS[5] HARRISON (*James,[4] Samuel,[3] Thomas,[2] Richard[1]*),
born at North Branford in 1765, died at Harwinton 7 May
1811. He married first, in 1789, ESTHER[6] HARRISON (41, ix),
born at Branford 13 May 1770, died 9 Apr. 1790, daughter of
Timothy and Lydia (Butler); and secondly EUNICE BUNNELL,
who died at Harwinton 16 Aug. 1858.
Child by first wife:

   i. BENJAMIN A.,[6] d. at Suffield.

Children by second wife:

   ii. MARIA.
   iii. DELIA, bapt. in Nov. 1798; d. at Harwinton 13 Mar. 1872.
   iv. EUNICE, b. 19 June 1801; m. 25 Aug. 1821 JOHN BROOKS BARTHOL-
      OMEW of Harwinton, b. 19 Oct. 1795, d. 10 Feb. 1859.
   v. PHILA AMELIA.
   vi. AUGUSTUS.

60. CALVIN[5] HARRISON (*James,[4] Samuel,[3] Thomas,[2] Richard[1]*), born
at North Branford in 1767, died there 12 Feb. 1831. He
married, 25 Mar. 1788, ABIGAIL LINSLEY, born in 1770, died
at North Branford 4 Apr. 1820, daughter of Israel and Hannah
(Moulthrop).
Children, born at North Branford:

   i. JEREMIAH,[6] b. 28 May 1789; d. *s.p.* 28 Apr. 1853; m. (1) 13 Oct.
      1824 HARRIET LINSLEY, who d. 8 Sept. 1836; m. (2) 17 Apr.
      1842 JULIA ANN FRISBIE, who d. 18 Aug. 1845; m. (3) 14 Mar.
      1847 MINNIE MIX.
   ii. MARY, b. 20 Oct. 1791; m. MARCUS BRONSON of Waterbury.
   iii. JAMES, b. 21 Nov. 1794; d. at Madison 18 Feb. 1867; m. in Sept.
      1817 CLARISSA DUDLEY.

iv. CALVIN, b. 18 Feb. 1797; d. at Wallingford 6 Apr. 1870; m. ANN BARTHOLOMEW, b. 4 June 1797, d. at Wallingford 13 Nov. 1873, dau. of Jonathan.

v. ISRAEL, b. 15 Apr. 1798; d. at Wallingford 5 July 1868; m. (1) 4 Dec. 1825 NANCY GAYLORD; m. (2) 21 Oct. 1841 SARAH G. HULL.

vi. MINOR, b. 16 Oct. 1801; d. at Wallingford 27 May 1840; m. 1 Nov. 1821 EMELINE HALL, b. 14 Apr. 1801, d. 29 Oct. 1842, dau. of Benjamin and Lydia (Cook).

vii. ABIGAIL, b. 5 Jan. 1805; m. STEPHEN CAMP of Waterbury.

THE HAUGHTON FAMILY OF NEW LONDON, CONN.—The following records were copied from old family papers now in the possession of the contributor, who also constructed from these data the short genealogy which closes the article.

Mr. Sampson Haughton died February the 26th 1756 in the 64th Year of his Age.

Mrs Sarah the Wife of Mr. Sampson Haughton died December 14, 1749 Aged 49 years.

Mr. Lebbeus Haughton died Feb. ye 12 1753 in his 29th

Mrs Sarah Haughton died Nov. 24 1760 in the 96th year of her Age.

Mr. Samson Haughton Died Feb. ye 24 1761 in the 27th year of his Age.

Mr. William W. Haughton departed this life Nov. 3rd 1819 in the 46th year of his age.

George Haughton died March 31st 1822 aged 66 years.

Catharine Haughton wife of Richard Haughton deceased 9th of Aug. 1670.

Wm. Young and Margaret Horton were married Dec. 7, 1715.

Children of Samson and Sarah Haughton

Christopher, born 23. Feb. 1702/3.

Abigail, born Aprl. 16. 1687	Marey, born July 23. 1704
Samson, born May 29. 1692	Jerusha, born Jan. 25. 1706/7
Ebenezer, born July 28. 1699	Katharine, born March 19 1711

Samson Haughton Sen. died Jan 12. 1718

Samson Haughton & Sarah Pemberton were married July 23 1718.

James, their son, born Ap. 29. 1719
Sarah, born July 19. 1721
Libbeus, born March 11 1724

Libbeus Horton of New London & Rhodilla Griswold were married May 7. 1778 by Rev. Andrew Lee.

Mr. Samson Haughton died Feb. 26 1756.

Samson son of the above died Feb. 24. 1761.

James Haughton of New London son of Mr. Sampson Haughton of New London and Deborah Baley of Groton daughter of Mr. John Baley were joyned in marriage covenant Jan. 4. 1748/9.

Their children

Sarah, born Ap. 14 1750	George, born June 7. 1758
Lebeus, born Aug 14. 1752	Elizabeth, born Feb 12. 1761
James, born Ap. 9 1756	

Deborah died Aug 15. 1767 & James married Philenah Whiting daughter of Col. John Whiting of New London April 28. 1768.

Wm. Whiting, born Jan 28. 1769 died Jan. 28 1774
Charles, born April 6 1770 Died Nov. 26. 1773
Wm. Whiting, born Jan 12. 1774
Charles, born Aug 18. 1775
Philena, born Dec 19 1776

Philena died Ap. 12 1781 and James and Ruth Adgate were married June 6th 1782.

Sampson Haughton son of Sampson & Sarah born Oct. 8. 1731

From these records the contributor has prepared the following genealogy of the early Haughtons of New London, Conn. In the "History of Montville, Conn.," the records of the two Sampson Haughtons, father and son, with their wives and children, are not correctly given.

1. RICHARD HAUGHTON died at Wethersfield, Conn., 23 May 1682. He married first, CATHERINE ——— (said to have been the widow of Nicholas Charlet of Boston), who died 9 Aug. 1670; and secondly, MARY ———.

In his will, dated 12 May 1682, he calls himself "Richard Haughton of Beverly . . . detained at Wethersfield by sickness." He requests "My beloved friends Mr. Nathaniel Standly and Mr. William Pitkin both of Hartford . . . to take care of the vessel building at Middletown . . . Mr. John Ffoster of Boston to assist them." He appoints executors but mentions no heirs. (Hartford Probate Records, vol. 1, p. 317.) The county court records, p. 56, 21 June 1682, show that "Mr. John Harris appeared in Court and presented letter of Adms. granted by the Hon. Simon Bradstreet Esq. Gov. of Mass. to Capt John Hull Esq. Assistant to Mary Haughton the Relict, widow of Richard Haughton deceased . . ." From this it appears that the name of the widow was Mary and not Alice, as is sometimes given.

Child by first wife:

2. i. SAMPSON.

2. SAMPSON[2] HAUGHTON (*Richard[1]*) died 12 Jan. 1718. He married SARAH ——, who died 24 Nov. 1760, in her 96th year.

Children:

i. ABIGAIL,[3] b. 16 Apr. 1687 and bapt. at New London, Conn., 9 Feb. 1693/4; m. at New London, 27 Dec. 1705, JOHN WICKWIRE.

ii. SARAH, bapt. at New London, Conn., 9 Feb. 1693/4; m. at New London, 30 July 1713, CLEMENT STRATFORD, sailor.

3. iii. SAMPSON, b. 29 May 1692 and bapt. at New London, Conn., 9 Feb. 1693/4.

iv. MARGARET, bapt. at New London, Conn., 10 Nov. 1694; m. 7 Dec. 1715 WILLIAM YOUNG.

v. ELIZABETH, bapt. 7 Mar. 1696.

vi. A CHILD, bapt. 25 June 1699.

vii. EBENEZER, b. 28 July 1699 and bapt. 5 Nov. 1699. Several children.

viii. CHRISTOPHER, b. 23 Feb. 1702/3.

ix. MAREY, b. 23 July 1704; probably the Mercy Haughton who m. at New London, Conn., 13 Jan. 1726, Richard Downer of Norwich.

x. JERUSHA, b. 25 Jan. 1706/7.

xi. KATHARINE, b. 19 Mar. 1711.

3. SAMPSON[3] HAUGHTON (*Sampson,[2] Richard[1]*), born 29 May 1692, died 26 Feb. 1756, in his 64th year. He married, 23 July 1718, SARAH PEMBERTON, who died 14 Dec. 1749, aged 49 years. (Sarah, daughter of Joseph Pemberton, was baptized at New London, Conn., 30 Mar. 1701. See W. K. Watkins's Pemberton Family, 1892, p. 5.)

Children:

4. i. JAMES,[4] b. 29 Apr. 1719.

ii. SARAH, b. 19 July 1721.

iii. LIBBEUS, b. 11 Mar. 1724; d. 12 Feb. 1753, in his 29th year.

iv. SAMPSON, b. 8 Oct. 1731; d. 24 Feb. 1761, in his 27th [? 29th] year. Perhaps others.

4. JAMES[4] HAUGHTON (*Sampson,[3] Sampson,[2] Richard[1]*) was born 29 Apr. 1719. He married first, 4 Jan. 1748, DEBORAH BALEY, who died 15 Aug. 1767, daughter of John Baley of Groton; secondly, 28 Apr. 1768, PHILENA WHITING of Montville, Conn., baptized at the Second Congregational Church of Newport, R. I., 22 May 1743 (Arnold's Vital Records of Rhode Island, vol. 8, p. 456), died 12 Apr. 1781, daughter of Col. John Whiting, who moved from Newport to New London; and thirdly, 6 June 1782, RUTH ADGATE.

Children by first wife:

i. SARAH,[5] b. 14 Apr. 1750.

ii. LEBEUS, b. 14 Aug. 1752; m. 7 May 1778 RHODILLA GRISWOLD.

iii. JAMES, b. 9 Apr. 1756.

iv. GEORGE, b. 7 June 1758; d. 31 Mar. 1822, aged 66.

v. ELIZABETH, b. 12 Feb. 1761.

Children by second wife:

vi. WILLIAM WHITING, b. 28 Jan. 1769; d. 28 Jan. 1774.

vii. CHARLES, b. 6 Apr. 1770; d. 26 Nov. 1773.

viii. WILLIAM WHITING, b. 12 Jan. 1774; m. 23 Nov. 1796 OLIVE CHESTER, b. 12 Mar. 1777, d. 3 Nov. 1819, daughter of Dea. Joseph and Elizabeth (Otis) Chester of Bozrah, Conn.

Children:

1. *John W.,*[6] b. 1 Jan. 1797; m. Clarissa Fitch.

2. *Richard,* b. 13 Oct. 1799; d. in Boston 27 Apr. 1841.

   3. *Frederick William Augustus,* b. 28 Jan. 1801; d. at Charleston, S. C., in July 1839.

   4. *Mary H.*

   5. *Julia Ann,* b. 28 May 1805; d. 25 Aug. 1853; m. at New London, Conn., 3 Aug. 1824, Henry Augustus Richards, b. in 1801, d. in 1855.

   6. *James,* b. 4 June 1807; d. 2 Jan. 1888; m. Eliza Richards.

   7. *Susan Decater* of Uncasville, Conn.

 ix. CHARLES, b. 18 Aug. 1775.

 x. PHILENA, b. 19 Dec. 1776; m. WILLIAM P. WHALEY (History of Montville).

Norfolk, Conn.   ANNETTE RICHARD FALLOWS.

THE HAYES FAMILY OF CONNECTICUT AND NEW-JERSEY.

Communicated by A. C. M. PENNINGTON, Brev. Col. U. S. A., Capt. 2d Artillery, Brev. Brig. Gen. U. S. Vols.

1. SERGEANT THOMAS[1] HAYES married Elizabeth Peck, daughter of Joseph Peck, in Milford, Conn., Oct. 29, 1677, by Major Treat, the magistrate, as was the custom at that date, ministers not having the right. They had:

    2. i.   ROBERT, b. Sept. 30, 1679, at Milford, Conn.; d. Oct. 28, 1759, at Newark, N. J.

    3. ii. JOSEPH, ⎱ by second wife, dau. of Robert Denison, one of the origi-
    4. iii. THOMAS, ⎰   nal settlers of Newark.

       iv. ELIZABETH, m. —— Freeman.

       v.   HANNAH.

2. ROBERT[2] (*Thomas[1]*) m. Hannah ——; no issue. He was a man of property, and some time before his death he provided that the Presbyterian Church in Newark should have his home lot of four acres, including his residence, at the corner of Broad and Hill streets, where now stands a hotel. His brother Joseph owned property and lived a short distance above on the opposite side of the street. In a will made 1749, he (Robert) mentions his wife Hannah and sisters Elizabeth Freeman and Hannah Hayes. He gave the equal half of all his lands to his brother Joseph; the other half he gave to the sons of his deceased brother Thomas, viz.: Thomas and Daniel.

3. JOSEPH[2] (*Thomas[1]*) m. Elizabeth Day. They had:

    i. DAVID, who m. and had: 1. *Robert*, who had John and Joseph. 2. *David*, who had David A., Esther, m. Tichenor, and Anna, m. King. 3. *Joseph*. 4. *Mary Combs*. 5. *Abigail Pike*. 6. *Lydia Drake*. 7. *Elizabeth Congar*. 8. *Rachel*. 9. *Isaac*, who had John and Oliver. 10. *Moses*, who had Jabez W. and George.

    ii. SAMUEL, who m. Sarah Bruen, and had: 1. *Bruen*, d. unmarried. 2. *Phœbe*, m. Jabez Pierson. 3. *Hannah*, m. Samuel Congar (second wife), and had Samuel H., the librarian of the New-Jersey His. Soc. (office in Newark), and Bruen H. 4. *Sarah*, m. Samuel Pennington (second wife), and had: Jabez P., Samuel H., and Alex. C. M. The latter had (second child) Alexander C. M. Pennington [the compiler], who m. Clara Miller French, dau. of Prof. John French, D.D., U. S. Military Academy, *ante*, vol. xxv. pp. 290 and 336. 5. *Samuel*, who had: Samuel, Sarah, Elizabeth and James.

    iii. JOSEPH, no issue.

    iv. MARTHA, no issue.

4. THOMAS[2] (*Thomas[1]*) m. and had children:

    i. THOMAS, who had: 1. *John*. 2. *Hannah*, m. Elias Osborn. 3. *Elizabeth*, m. Henry Osborn. 4. *Thomas*, d. 1814.

    ii. DANIEL, d. 1775, no issue.

Sergeant Thomas Hayes in 1696 was chosen by the town "to order the prudential affairs of the neck," i. e. the lands then lying in common, without division fences, east of the present line of the New-Jersey Railroad, constituting three (3) wards of the city. Jan. 1st, 1696-7, "The men chosen to make the town rate and to make assessments on those persons that don't give in a list of their estates are Joseph Harrison, Nathaniel Ward, Seth Tompkins, Zopher Beach, and Thomas Hayes." Seth Tompkins was the son of Deacon Michael Tompkins, who, before the settlement of Newark, secreted in his house at Milford the regicides Goffe and Whalley. In 1698 Thomas Hayes was "with Joseph Harrison, Jasper Crane, and Matthew Canfield to view whether Azariah Crane may have land for a tan-yard out of the common and in case the men above mentioned agree that he shall have the land, he, the said Azariah Crane shall enjoy it so long as he doth follow the trade of tanning."

In 1702 Sergeant Thomas Hayes and Ensign Eliphalet Johnson are chosen assessors for the south end of the town. It is a reasonable conclusion that Thomas Hayes was an intelligent, respectable and influential member of the community. The date of his death is uncertain. Thomas Hayes witnessed a legal instrument in 1712,—perhaps that Thomas Hayes who died in 1749, aged 56. The elder Thomas was living in 1705, when he took a share of land formerly of his brother-in-law John Dennison. There was a Thomas Hayes at Milford in 1645 who came from Wethersfield. Milford was settled in 1639 by people from Wethersfield and New-Haven. This was that Thomas Hayes who with Major Treat, Elder Buckingham and Lieut. Fowler proposed to the town to build a fulling and saw-mill for the town of Milford. Perhaps this Thomas was the father of *Sergeant* Thomas. There seems to be some foundation for the tradition that three persons of the name of Hayes came to Connecticut, as among the inhabitants of Norwalk in 1651 were a Nathaniel Haies and Samuel Haies. In 1694, Nathaniel, James and Samuel Hayes. The name of Hayes appears in Rev. J. Pruden's list of scholars. It is probable that his children had only a common school education. Joseph Hayes m. Elizabeth Day. He was living in July, 1777. By his will of that date he gives his sons David and Samuel all his lands and meadows, and to his daughter Martha all his personal estate, and directs that the estate left by his son Joseph be divided equally among the three. The following is from Alden's *American Epitaphs, Inscriptions,* &c.: "Major Samuel Hayes, descendant from one of the original settlers of Newark, died on the 1st of June, 1811, in the 83d year of his age. He sustained the character of an honest and well-informed man. At an early period he took an active part in the revolutionary struggle, and was a distinguished officer in the militia during the war which secured to his beloved country the blessings of freedom and independence. In 1759 he was commissioned as a deputy surveyor for East Jersey, and, until disabled by paralysis, for half a century he traversed more or less, Bergen, Essex and Morris, with his compass and chain. In 1766 he was the master of a vessel on a voyage to Nova Scotia, and subsequently sailed for other ports. He was one of three commissioners for forfeited estates during the revolution, and in the faithful discharge of his duty incurred the displeasure of the royalists. In July, 1780, the refugees surprised and took him from his house at night and lodged him in the Sugar House in New-York, and detained him some months, together with his fellow commissioners," all atrocious rebels. He served the county and town in various offices until 73 years of age; a self-made man, stern, decided and energetic, His wife died June, 1803, aged 71. Thomas Hayes of 1645 possibly was Sergeant Thomas Hayes, but it is doubtful, indeed improbable.

THE HAYES FAMILY OF WINDSOR AND GRANBY, CT.

Communicated by the Rev. CHARLES W. HAYES, A.M., of Westfield, N. Y.

GEORGE HAYES, born in Scotland, 1655, went as a young man to Derbyshire, Eng., where, it is said, he had an uncle, with whom he lived for a time; thence to London, and there, hearing of the new "land of promise in the Western World," embarked for New England, and is first known at Windsor, Ct., 1682.[*]

Two years earlier, 1680, came John Hayes from Scotland to Dover, N. H., to become the founder of another wide-spread New England family, many of whom still cling around their old homes of Dover, Berwick and North Yarmouth.[†] The Dover and Windsor Hayeses are certainly of a common Scottish stock; but the degree of relationship between their founders has not yet been traced.

George Hayes married first, Sarah —— (surname illegible in Windsor records), who died at Windsor, March 27, 1683, leaving one child, George, born March 26, died April 3, 1683. He married second, Windsor, August 29, 1683, Abigail Dibble (as now written, but on early records and gravestones, Dibol), daughter of Samuel (fourth son of Thomas of Simsbury, son probably of Robert of Dorchester, 1634), born Windsor, January 19, 1666. The births of three sons and four daughters of this marriage are recorded at Windsor, the last in June, 1697; and in 1698 he is found at Simsbury, in that town now the town of Granby, and in the little hamlet of "Salmon Brook," so called from a little stream, famous in old time for salmon, crossing its one street. A deed of December 30, 1698, from Thomas Griffin to "George Haize formerly of Windsor," consideration £28, is recorded at Simsbury. His name appears in the "Minister's Rate," 1700, "George Hayes, £00-8-11;" in "Wood Rate," Jan. 31, 1700-1, "George Hayz, £00-1-5;" in "Centry Rate," 1701, "Georg Hayse £00-7-6, being 3½d. on yᵉ pound;" in list of freemen same year, "George Hayse;" and in the "Lyst of Simsbury lands taken by yᵉ Sizers," "Georg Haiz Mead 4 ac. 1 r. 8 s. upland £01-16-0." By deed of March 6, 1708, John Matson conveys to "Georg hayse of yᵉ town of Simsbury Husbandman," land "lying between the lowᵉ meadow lotts and the uper Meadow Lotts upon a little brook by reason of the windingness of said brooke is called Crooked brooke —being ten acres more or less." Jan. 2, 1723, the town granted to "yᵉ severall persons hereafter named the quantaties of land hereafter expressᵈ:" to "George Hays Sener 138 acres;" "Daniel Hays 120;" "George Hays Juner 99;" "William Hays 75;" "Samuel Hays 60." (To complete the list of variations in the orthography of the name, it is spelled "Haze" in the before-mentioned deed of 1698, and "Hais" in a deed of 1713 to Daniel, the eldest son.)

George Hayes died at Simsbury, Sept. 2, 1725. By will dated April 30, proved Oct. 5, 1725, he bequeaths to his wife Abigail during her widowhood, his "dwelling house, barn, orchard, home lot and pasture," with household goods as far as needful, and one cow; to the four elder sons,

---

[*] Ezekiel Hayes, of New Haven, great-grandson of George.

[†] Savage, Gen. Dict. ii. 437. Thomas Hayes, of Milford, Ct., 1645 (perhaps founder of the New Jersey family, see REG. xxvii. 79), and Nathaniel, of Norwalk, 1652, have no apparent connection with the Dover and Windsor families.

"Daniell, George, William and Samuell," two-thirds of his residuary estate, and to his six daughters, " Abigail, Sarah, Mary, Johanna, Thankfull and Doritha," the remaining third, with the addition of £10 to Daniel and £5 to Abigail ; and to his youngest son Benjamin, who with Abigail was then living with him, the " Bever Marsh " of ten acres, and his share in " oure Saw Mill at Salmon Brook," the said Benjamin to " dwell and live with me and support me in all my wants and necessities," and " to behave himself towards me as a dutyfull Child ought to do towards a dutyfull parent, during my natural life."* The date of his wife's death, and their burial place, are as yet unknown; the latter is probably in the older cemetery at " Hop Meadow," which dates from 1683.†

In his will he calls himself " yeoman," and "about seventy years of age; " and its expression of entire and humble Christian faith we may hope is his own, and more real than formal.

His five sons and six daughters by his second marriage all survived him, married and left descendants.

    i. ABIGAIL, b. Windsor, Aug. 31, 1684; received by her father's will £5 more than the other daughters " by reason of her Lameness ;" m. Paul Tompkins ; joined in deeds of release to Daniel and George, March 22, 1734.

2. ii. DANIEL, b. W., April 26, 1686.

    iii. SARAH. b. W., Jan. 22, 1687[-8] ; m. John Gosard (or Gozzard), son of Nicholas and Elizabeth, of Windsor, b. 1682.

    iv. MARY, b. W., Jan 6, 1689[-90] ; m. William Rice, probably of Norwich or New London.

    v. JOANNA, b. W., Oct. 2, 1692; d. after 1760 ; m. James Hillyer, of Simsbury (eldest son of James Hillyer and Mary, dau. of John and Ann Wakefield, of Watertown, and widow of Ebenezer Dibble), b. S., Jan. 28, 1679. Their dau. Joanna[3] m. Nov. 6, 1725 (?), Amos Wilcox (or Wilcoxson) of S., and d. a. about 100. Her second dau. Joanna Wilcox,[4] b. May 26, 1740, d. Dec. 17, 1812, m. Job Case, of Simsbury, and had 6 sons and 5 daus., of whom the eldest daughter, Joanna[5] Case, was b. Aug. 1760, and baptized the same year, in presence of her mother, grandmother and great-grandmother, in the female line, all Joannas ; and three of the four surviving forty years more into the present century. The great-granddaughter m. Israel Case, of Simsbury.

3. vi. GEORGE, b. W., March 9, 1695.

4. vii. WILLIAM, b. W., June 13, 1697.

5. viii. SAMUEL, b. Simsbury, c. 1699.

    ix. THANKFUL, b. S., c. 1701; on earliest church covenant at Salmon Brook, c. 1739 ; m. S., Oct. 9, 1717, Nathaniel Holcombe, son of Nathaniel and Martha (dau. Peter) Buell, of Windsor, and had 12 children : 1. Hannah,[3] probably m. John Reuel ; 2. Nathaniel ;[3] 3. Thankful,[3] m. Adonijah Burr ; 4. Elizabeth,[3] m. Moses Dibble ; 5. Mercy,[3] m. 1, Obed Holcombe, 2, Moses Dibble ; 6. Elijah,[3] m. Violet Cornish ; 7. Joseph,[3] m. Elizabeth Wilcox ; 8. Ephraim,[3] b. Dec. 22, 1721, m. Dorcas, 4th daughter Samuel Hayes ; 9. Amos ;[3] 10 and 11 unknown ; 12. Roger,[3] m. Mary or Mercy Gillett.

    x. DOROTHY, b. S., c. 1703-4 ; on church covenant 1739 with husband ; m. her first cousin Abraham Dibble, son of Thomas Dibble and Mary Tucker, probably his second wife, as he m. 1709 (according to Stiles, Hist. Windsor) Hannah Hosford.

6. xi. BENJAMIN, b. S., probably c. 1706.

2. DANIEL[2] HAYES (George[1]), born Windsor, April 26, 1686, was in 1707-8 taken prisoner by the Indians, carried to Canada, and kept in captiv-

* He had already given Benjamin by deed £50 of his portion.
† Simsbury, at first called " Massacoe," was settled as early as 1664; made a town (21st in the colony) 1669-70; first grants at Salmon Brook in 1679. Granby was set off in 1786.

144

ity at least five years; finally released (by earning his own ransom, for which he was afterwards reimbursed by order of the General Court of Connecticut) and returned to live to a good old age in Salmon Brook village. The romantic story of his sufferings and heroism in his long captivity is given quite fully in Phelps's History of Simsbury, Hartford, 1845, and in "A Long Journey," by the present writer, Portland, Me., 1876. He built in 1720 the house occupied by him and his descendants for four generations (and the oldest in the town when taken down in 1871) on the east side of "Salmon Brook Street," in the lower or southern part of the village. In this house the first Congregational Society (of which he and his wife became members at its organization, c. 1739) met for worship until 1743, when the first meeting-house was built. "He was," says Phelps, "a prominent citizen, often employed in public affairs, and during many years a pillar in the church at Salmon Brook." He became a freeman October, 1717; received grant of 120 acres from the town, January 2, 1723 ; deed of release from brothers and sisters, March 22, 1734 ; died at Salmon Brook, Sept. 23, 1756. His grave in the old Salmon Brook Cemetery is still marked by a substantial stone (the oldest in the ground) with a quaint inscription, copied from the stone by me in 1875, as follows :

> Here lies ye Body
> of m^r Daniel Hays
> who Served his Gene
> ration in a Steady
> Course of Probity &
> Piety & was a Lover
> of Peace & God's
> Public Worship &
> being satisfied with
> Long Life left this
> World with a Comfo
> rtable Hope of Life
> Eternal Sept 23 1756
> In ye 71 year of his Age

By his will of Feb. 21, 1750, proved Nov. 30, 1756, he bequeaths to his wife Mary one-half his real estate for life, and one-third of his personal property ; to his (second) son Ezekiel £200, his daughter Martha £150, daughter Zilpah £250 ; the rest of his estate to sons Daniel and Joel, his executors, in equal shares.

He married first, Simsbury, March 1, 1716, Martha Holcombe, who died Simsbury, Jan. 9, 1717 ; married second, Simsbury, May 4, 1721, Sarah Lee, of Westfield, Mass. (probably, I should say almost certainly, daughter of John Lee, son of Walter, and Elizabeth Crampton of W.), born April 24, 1692, died Simsbury, July 14, 1738; married third, c. 1739, Mary ——, named in his will, and on earliest church covenant at Salmon Brook with him, probably that year. Children by first marriage, 1 son ; by second marriage, 5 sons and 5 daughters, all born Simsbury.

  i. Daniel, b. Dec. 20, 1716 ; m. Abigail Hayes, dau. of Samuel[2]; had Daniel,[3] Obadiah,[3] and 5 daughters; Daniel[3] had Daniel,[4] and he Daniel[5] ; Obadiah[3] had Dea. Chester[4] ; descendants at Granby.
  ii. Sarah, b. March 22, 1722.
  iii. Ezekiel, b. June 21, 1723 ; d. May 6, 1724.

iv. EZEKIEL, b. Nov. 21, 1724 ; rem. to New Haven, m. 1749, Rebecca Russell, dau. Judge John Russell and Sarah Trowbridge ; had *Rebecca*[4] (m. Capt. Abel Frisbie), *Ezekiel*,[4] *Rutherford*[4] (whose son Rutherford[5] married Sophia Burchard, and was the father of the Hon. Rutherford B.[6] Hayes, LL.D., ex-president of the United States), *Sarah*,[4] *Mary*[4] and *Abigail*.[4] He m. 1774, Mrs Abigail Brown, of New Haven, and had by her four children ; d. New Haven, Oct. 17, 1807.*

v. BENONI, b. Jan. 8 ; d. Jan. 16, 1726.
vi. MARTHA, b. Nov. 8, 1726.
vii. JOEL, b. Oct. 2, 1728 ; d. Granby, May 27, 1800 ; Lieut. in Revolutionary army ; m. 1751, Rebecca Post, of Norwich ; had *Joel*[4] (born 1753, d. 1827, minister of South Hadley, Mass., 45 years, father of the late Oliver Bliss[5] Hayes, of Nashville, Tenn., Joel[5] Hayes, of S. Hadley, and Dr. Roswell P.[5] Hayes, of Cincinnati), *Rebecca*,[4] *Rufus*,[4] *Zilpah*,[4] *Rufus*,[4] *Roswell*,[4] *Calvin*[4] (father of the late Horace[5] and Curtiss[5] Hayes, of New York), *Luther*,[4] *Roswell*,[4] and *Newton*[4] (many years proprietor of Franklin House, Broadway, N. Y., died 1868).

viii. ELIZABETH, b. March 5, 1730 ; d. March 4, 1737.
ix. SILENCE, b. Nov. 11, 1731 ; d. March 2, 1737.
x. AARON, b. Sept. 6, 1733 ; d. Feb. 27, 1737.
xi. ZILPAH, b. Aug. 25, 1735 ; d. April 1, 1737. (But see her father's will of 1750, above.)

3. GEORGE[2] HAYES (*George*[1]), born Windsor, March 9, 1695 ; received grant of 99 acres, 1723 ; on church covenant at Salmon Brook, with wife Sarah, 1739 ; by will of Oct. 31, 1765, devises his estate to Sarah his wife, sons Jonathan, George, Elisha, David, Benjamin, Jacob, Elijah and Amos, only daughter Mary (or Mercy), and heirs of daughters Zeruiah Lamson and Jane Lamson. Inventory of real estate, 107 acres; whole appraisal, £185 11s. He married first, ——, who died c. 1735, and second, 1735–6, Sarah ——, named in will. By first marriage, 3 sons and 3 daughters ; by second marriage, 5 sons and 2 daughters.

i. JONATHAN, b. June 15, 1722 ; m. 1743, Mary Loomis, dau. of Philip, of Simsbury. (Loomis Geneal. 30.) Had *Jonathan*[4] (of Rupert, Vt.), *Mary*,[4] *Philip*[4] and *Moses*.[4]
ii. ZERUIAH. b. Dec. 15, 1724 ; m. Lamson.
iii. GEORGE, b. Dec. 12, 1727.
iv. ELISHA, b. Sept. 6, 1730 ; m. 1754, Mercy Lamson ; had *Zilpah*,[4] *Elisha*,[4] *Mary*,[4] *Jemima*,[4] *Temzen*,[4] *Amasa*[4] and *Rhoda*.[4]
v. JANE, b. Nov. 15, 1733 ; m. Lamson.
vi. MARY, or MERCY, b. c. 1735 ; m. Phelps, of E. Granby.
vii. DAVID, b. Dec. 6, 1744 ; on church covenant, 1772, with wife ; had *Zophar*[4] (d. in U. S. service, 1812), and *Theodore*,[4] m. Martha, dau. Ozias Higby, of Granby ; deed to him 1784 ; house at Bushy Hill, Granby.
viii. BENJAMIN, b. April 13, 1747 ; d. Granby, 1810 ; m. 1st, his cousin Rosanna, eldest dau. of Samuel[2] Hayes (q. v. inf.) ; m. 2d, Mrs. Martha (Hecock) Bishop ; m. 3d, Hannah Fuller ; had *Thaddeus*,[4] *Alpheus*[4] who left numerous descendants at Washington, Pa., *Alice*,[4] m. Dimock Fuller of New York, *Zaccheus*,[4] *Patty*,[4] m. Charles Cadwell of New York, *Elizur*,[4] father of Anson E.,[5] the father of Everett A.,[6] of Madison, Wis., *Rosanna*,[4] *Flora*,[4] m. Elam Kendall, of Granby, *Sheldon*,[4] and *Benjamin Sheldon*[4] of Washington, Pa.
ix. JACOB, b. Dec. 10, 1749.
x. ELIJAH, b. March 22, 1752 ; on church covenant with wife, 1774.
xi. AMOS, b. Sept. 6, 1755 ; " Tythingman " and " Packer," 1791.
xii. JANE, b. Nov. 15, 1756 ; ⎫ d. before 1765.
xiii. SARAH, b. Jan. 18, 1759 ; ⎭

* For descendants of Rebecca (Hayes) Frisbie, see *Whitney Family*, i. 183, 498; and of Ezekiel[2] and Rutherford,[3] see *Trowbridge Family*, pp. 42-4.

4. WILLIAM[2] HAYES (*George*[1]), born Windsor, June 13, 1697; tythingman 1742, grand juror 1748 and 1754; received grant of 75 acres, 1723; m. first, Sept. 4, 1723, Joanna Lee (undoubtedly sister of Sarah, wife of Daniel, above), born Westfield, Mass., 1702 (she or daughter Joanna on church covenant 1743) died Simsbury, Dec. 27, 1748 ; married second, ———— (Mary, w. of William Hayes, died March 27, 1760, and William Hayes, probably son of this William, married Rachel Lewis, Jan. 15, 1761). By first marriage are recorded four sons and five daughters; by second marriage, one daughter.

    i.   WILLIAM, b. April 5, 1725 ; on church covenant as " Jr.," c. 1739 ; probably m. 1761, Rachel Lewis.
    ii. JOANNA, b. Aug. 12, 1727.
    iii. JUDAH, b. Jan. 3, 1730; m. 1760, Honora Lamson ; had *Chloe*,[4] *Lydia*,[4] *Honora*,[4] *Mary Ann*[4] and *Rosetta*.[4]
    iv. RHODA, b. March 31, 1732.
    v.   DUDLEY, b. March 24, 1735 ; one of the two survivors from Granby of the disastrous expedition of 1762 against Havana ; m. 1756, his cousin Anne Hayes, dau. of Benjamin, q. v. inf. ; had *Anne*[4] and *Zenas*[4] ; was ancestor of Willis G. Hayes, of Granby.
    vi. SILENCE, b. March 9, 1737.
    vii. AARON, b. Aug. 18, 1739.
    viii. ————, daughter, d. 1748.
    ix. ROSANNA, b. April 15, 1748.
    x.   JENNY, b. Oct. 15, 1754.

5. SAMUEL[2] HAYES (*George*[1]), born Simsbury, c. 1699; received grant of 60 acres, 1723 ; on church covenant at Salmon Brook, 1739, with wife; tythingman 1751 ; deed to son Andrew, 1759 ; will of Nov. 8, 1759, gives to wife Elizabeth and sons Samuel, Asahel and Andrew, five shillings each, " having given them the whole of what I intend for their portion;" to son Silas his house, barn and homestead; and other bequests to his five daughters Lydia, Elizabeth, Abigail, Dorcas and Susanna. At Granby is recorded a deed of March 7, 1787, from Samuel his father to Silas, " in consideration of a valuable sum, Divers good causes, love and good will which I have received from my son Silas Hayes." From this it would appear that he lived to a great age. He married, Simsbury, July 16, 1719, Elizabeth Willcockson (Willcokson in Sims. Rec.; also Wilcoxson, finally Wilcox), daughter probably of Samuel, of Meadow Plain, Simsbury, son of " Serg[t] Samuel," a well-known early settler of Simsbury, and third son of William, from St. Albans, Hertfordshire, Eng., to Massachusetts, 1635, and later to Hartford and Stratford. They had four sons and five daughters, all named in will above.*

    i.   LYDIA, b. Feb. 18, 1720.
    ii. ELIZABETH, b. Oct. 17, 1721 ; m. 1740, Joseph Gillett, of Simsbury.
    iii. ABIGAIL, b. Nov. 3, 1723 ; m. 1742, Daniel Hayes, above.
    iv. DORCAS, b. March 15, 1727 ; m. Ephraim Holcombe, son of Nathaniel and Thankful, fifth dau. George Hayes, above.
    v.   SAMUEL, b. March 26, 1730 ; d. Dec. 25, 1801 ; res. " Bushy Hill," Sims. ; large farm-house built by him in 1753 still occupied and in good condition; on church covenant 1753, " Deacon," " Captain," Representative, &c. ; m. 1750, Rosanna Holcombe, dau. Judah (3d son of Nath. ii.) and Hannah (Buttolph) H. of Sims., b. 1732, d. 1814. They had seven sons and three daughters :
          1. *Rosanna*,[4] b. 1751, m. her cousin Benjamin Hayes, son of George.
          2. *Seth*,[4] b. 1753 ; d. 1839; m. Mehetabel, dau. Dr. Josiah Topping ; had Hilpah, Melissa, Mehetabel, Seth, Cullen and Ansel.

    * See REGISTER, xiv. 304, xxvii. 192; Savage, iv. 546.

3. *Theodosia*,[4] b. 1757; m. Gen. Chauncey Pettibone, of Granby.
4. *Samuel*,[4] b. 1759; d. 1831; large landholder at Prattsburgh,
   N. Y., from 1806; m. Anna Pettibone, dau. of Ozias, of
   Granby; had Sarah,[5] Nancy,[5] Cephas[5] (g. f of Warren H.,[7]
   architect, of Minneapolis, Minn.), Samuel,[5] now of Platts-
   burgh, N. Y., Casson,[5] Chauncey[5] and Drayton.[5]
5. *Temperance*,[4] b. 1761; m. Luther Foote; had Calvin,[5] of Erie,
   Pa. (Judge), and Temperance.[5]
6. *Levi*,[4] b. 1763; removed to Granville, O.; m. 1786, Ruhama
   Parsons; had Levi L.,[5] Rev. Orlin P.,[5] Ruhama,[5] m. Kilborn,
   Rosanna,[5] Anson B.,[5] of Granville.
7. *Pliny*,[4] b. 1766; d. Bristol, N. Y., 1831; rem. to Western
   N. Y., in 1798; m. 1787, Lucretia Jewett, dau. Capt. Joseph
   Jewett of Revolutionary army, and Lucretia, dau. Dr. The-
   ophilus Rogers. of Lyme, Ct.; had Pliny,[5] 1788–1831, M.D.,
   Harv. 1815, of Canandaigua, N.Y., father of the Rev. Charles
   W.[6] and Robert P.[6] Hayes, of Buffalo; Henry,[5] of Quincy,
   Ill.; Emma L.,[5] m. Theodore Brown, E. Bloomfield, N. Y.;
   Harold,[5] father of Dr. P. H.,[6] of Binghamton, N. Y., and
   Dr. R. S.,[6] of E. Bloomfield; Gunilda,[5] m. D. Howland,
   Brooklyn, Mich.; Mumford;[5] Hector,[5] now of Muir, Mich.;
   Guy,[5] and Elizabeth A.,[5] m. 1st, Hervey Blackmer, 2d, Jo-
   seph Plumb.
8. *Simeon*,[4] b. 1768; d. Prattsburgh, 1841; m. 1st, Elizabeth
   Holley, dau. Rev Israel, of Granby; had Betsey M.,[5] m.
   Israel Skinner; Emily,[5] m. Orlando P. Fay; Simeon,[5] and
   three others; m. 2d, Elizabeth Gilbert; had George,[5] George
   Edward,[5] of Buffalo, N. Y., D.D.S., founder of the " Hayes
   School of Natural Sciences," of Buffalo; Willis G.,[5] Joseph
   B.[5] and Henry O.[5]
9. *Joseph*,[4] b. 1771; d. Granby, 1857; m. Clarissa Gillett, of
   Granby; had Mary,[5] m. Hector Miller, William R.,[5] Pris-
   cilla D. F.,[5] m. J. G Hurlburt, New Britain, Ct., and Mary.[5]
10. *Martin*,[4] b. 1776; d. Greene, Pa., 1847; m. 1798, Mary Camp,
    dau. Rev. Samuel, of Ridgebury, Ct.; had Lester,[5] Alson,[5]
    Mary M.,[5] m. Thomas J. West; Joseph M.,[5] Rev. of Salem,
    Wis., and Roxy A.,[5] m..Samuel Hilborn; descendants at
    Greene, Erie Co, Pa.

vi. ASAHEL, b. June 3, 1732; m. Martha Holcombe, dau. David; had
    Asahel,[4] b. 1750. m. Anne Clauson, of Fredericksburgh, N.Y.; *Mich-
    ael*,[4] *Martha*,[4] *Oliver*,[4] *Apphia*,[4] *Asenath*,[4] *Benajah*,[4] *Lewry*[4] (or
    Lura), and *Anne*.[4]

vii. SUSANNA, b. Nov. 26, 1735; m. Reuben (son of David) Holcombe; had
     Phineas,[4] Rev. *Reuben*,[4] of Sterling, Mass., *Increase*,[4] *Nahum*[4]
     (g. f. of Dr. William Fred.[6] Holcombe, of N. Y.); *Seth*,[4] of Canan-
     daigua, N. Y., *Orator*[4] and *Sylvanus*.[4]

viii. ANDREW, b. May 29, 1737; deed by him, Granby, 1784.
ix. SILAS, b. Feb. 28, 1740; " Capt.": m. Sims. 1757, Hannah Holcombe,
    dau. Judah, above; had *Oliver*,[4] *Silas*,[4] *Hannah*,[4] and probably
    others.

6. BENJAMIN[2] HAYES (*George*[1]), living with his father in 1725; died
Simsbury, Oct. 19, 1744 ; married and had three sons and two daughters,
perhaps others.

i. ZEDEKIAH, b. Oct. 31, 1730: m. 1753, Elizabeth Graham, of Windsor;
   had *Ann G.*,[4] *Elizabeth*,[4] *Benjamin*,[4] *Asa*,[4] *Zadock*,[4] *Sarah*,[4]
   Dianthy.[4]
ii. ZADOCK, b. Oct. 26, 1732.
iii. HANNAH, b. Nov. 24. 1735.
iv. ANNE, b. May 9, 1738; m. Dudley Hayes, son of William,[2] above.
v. ENOS, b. July 11, 1740.

DESCENDANTS OF ROBERT HEBERT OF SALEM AND BEVERLY, MASS.

Compiled by HARVEY HEBARD and RALPH D. SMYTH (son of Lovine Hebert) ; and communicated by BERNARD C. STEINER, Ph.D. (grandson of Ralph D. Smyth).

DURING the latter years of Mr. Smyth's life,* he paid much attention to tracing out his mother's family, and together with Mr. Hebard prepared a complete genealogy of the Heberts. This is still in manuscript, and from it the following facts are taken. The spelling of the family name is extremely varied, and that of each branch is followed.

* Hon. Ralph Dunning Smith of Guilford, Conn., whose collections and those of Harvey Hebard, Esq., have been used in preparing this article, died September 11, 1874, in his seventieth year. See Necrology, REGISTER, vol. 29, pp. 326–28.—J. W. D.

We hear of Robert Hebart and his wife Joan first at Salem, Mass., where he was an early settler. His name appeared in the list of settlers for 1646: "Robert Hibberd and wife Joan." Felt (*Annals of Salem*, ii., 175, 176) states that he was in Salem in 1639, and refers to him as "Robert Hebard, salt-maker." He may have been one of those who came over for the purpose of assisting John Winthrop, Jr., at his salt works. The records of the First Church of Salem state that "Rob't Hebbert and Joanna his wife" were admitted to communion May 3, 1646. In 1659, he ¡bought thirteen acres of land in Salem from William Hascoll, and is descr bed as "Robert Hibbird, bricklayer." (*Essex Deeds*, Book i., p. 63.) He later removed to Beverly, and in 1670-1 conveys land there to a married daughter. (*Essex Deeds*, Book iv., p. 87.) He is then described as "Robert Hibbert, bricklayer." His will is dated April 9, 1684 (*Essex Probate Records*, Book No. 2, Old Series, p. 35), and to it he makes his mark, which, as he could write, shows him to have been very feeble. In the will, he states that he has already made some provision for his children during his life time, and confirms these grants. A life estate in most of the property is given to his wife, and she is made executrix. The inventory of the estate was £281. 6. 6.

1. ROBERT[1] HEBERT was born in England in 1612, and died in Beverly, May 7, 1684. His wife's maiden name and the date of her birth are unknown. She died at Beverly in 1696. Their children, born in Salem, were:

    i. MARIE,[2] b. Nov. 27, 1641; m. Nicholas Snelling of Gloucester, Nov. 8, 1664.

2. ii. JOHN, b. Jan. 24, 1642-3; m. (1) Abigail Graves, Oct. 20, 1670; (2) Ruth Walden, Sept. 16, 1679; (3) Lydia ———, 16—.

    iii. SARAH, b. Sept. 26, 1644; d. Nov. 8, 1644.

3. iv. JOSEPH, bap. May 7, 1648; m. Elizabeth ———.

4. v. ROBERT, bap. May 7, 1648; m. Mary Walden, 1673.

    vi. JOHANNA, b. Feb. 23, 1651; m. John Swanton of Beverly.

    vii. ELIZABETH, b. May 6, 1653.

    viii. ABIGAIL, b. May 6, 1655; m. Thomas Blachford of Beverly.

5. ix. SAMUEL, b. June 20, 1658; m. Mary Bond.

2. JOHN[2] HEBARD or HIBBERT (*Robert*[1]) was a carpenter, and lived at Beverly. He died March 27, 1718. In November, 1713, he made over all his property to his son Zaccheus. Thus there was no administration upon his estate. In a deed of property sold by him in 1707, he is described as "husbandman." By his first wife, Abigail Graves, his children were:

    i. ZACCHEUS,[3] b. 1671; m. (1) Susannah ———, 1721; (2) Jane ———, 1722.

    ii. WILLIAM, b. 1673. He lived at Salem, was a clothier, and m. Ruth Rose, dau. of Richard of Salem.

    iii. MARY, b. 1675; m. Joshua Jewett, probably son of Joseph of Rowley.

    iv. GEORGE, b. 1678; settled at Rowley; m. Sarah ———.

By his second wife, Ruth Walden, his children were:

6. v. JOHN, bap. June 4, 1682; m. Dorothy Graves, June 6, 1708.

    vi. RUTH, b. Aug. 12, 1683.

    vii. ELIZABETH, b, June 19, 1686.

    viii. MARTHA, b. June 2, 1689.

    ix. SARAH, b. April 19, 1691; d. May 11, 1700.

    x. ROBERT, b, 1695; d. young.

    xi. DANIEL, b. 1701; d. at Amenia, 1777.

3. Joseph[2] Hibbert (*Robert*[1]) of Beverly, died May 10, 1701. By his will, dated April 19, 1701, he leaves an estate in most of his property to his wife, to continue till her death or remarriage. The eldest son, Jeremiah, shall assist his mother in the management of the estate, until he is of age, and then shall receive half the income of the estate "to his own particular disposing," if he has proved a "loving and obedient son to his mother." The children of Joseph and his wife Elizabeth were:

    i. Mary,[3] b. ———; m. Daniel Collins, May 12, 1692.
    ii. Joanna, b. 1676; d. Oct. 14, 1678.
    iii. Dorcas, bap. 1692; m. Nathaniel Abbott, youngest son of George of Andover, Oct. 22, 1695. He d. Dec. 1, 1749, and she d. Feb. 7, 1743.
    iv. Elizabeth, b. 1692; m. Benjamin Hascall of Gloucester.
    v. Abigail, b. 1692; d. young.
    vi. Sarah, bap. 1692; d. 1700.
    vii. Bridget, b. May 11, 1687; m. Matthew Corey (son of Giles Corey?).
    viii. Rebecca, b. July 13, 1692; m. Joshua Clark.
7. ix. Jeremiah, b. Aug. 9, 1693; m. (1) Mary Derby of Salem, Mass., March 2, 1704; (2) Hannah Leach.
8. x. Joseph, b. 1695; m. Mary Stone.

4. Robert[2] Hibbird (*Robert*[1]) of Beverly and Wenham, Mass., removed from the latter place to Windham, Conn., in 1700, whither his sons Robert and Joseph had removed in 1698. The sons were made townsmen at Windham in August, 1698, and the father brought a letter to the Congregational Church there on October 29, 1700. It is said that many curious incidents occurred in the life of this man, making it quite romantic. He was a person of great activity and energy. His estate was settled in the Probate Court at Hartford, October 2, 1710. He died at Windham, April 29, 1710. His wife, Mary Walden, daughter of Edward of Wenham, died March 7, 1736, aged 81. Their children were all born at Wenham, and were:

    i. Mary,[3] b. Aug. 18, 1674; m. Jonathan Crane (probably son of Jonathan of Norwich), July 31, 1705.
9. ii. Robert, b. June, 1676; m. Mary Reed, Dec. 3, 1702.
10. iii. Joseph, b. May 15, 1677; m. Abigail Kendall, April 20, 1698.
11. iv. Nathaniel, b. 1680; m. Sarah Crane, dau. of Jonathan.
12. v. Ebenezer, b. May, 1682; m. Margaret Morgan, March 16, 1709.
    vi. Martha, b. February, 1684; m. Ephraim Culver, son of Edward of Norwich.
    vii. Josiah, b. 1686.
    viii. Hannah, b. 1691; m. Joseph Talcott.
    ix. Sarah, b. 1694; d. *s.p.* Oct. 9, 1762.
    x. Abigail, b. 1694; d. *s.p.* 1760.
    xi. Lydia, b. 1699; d. young, 1706.

5. Samuel[2] Hebert (*Robert*[1]) of Beverly, died intestate April 17, 1702, leaving an estate valued at £128. 2. 2. His wife, Mary Bond, daughter of John of Newbury and Haverhill, administered upon the estate. Their children were:

    i. Samuel,[3] b. March 10, 1681; d. young.
    ii. Abigail, b. Feb. 24, 1682; m. Daniel Eaton, Jr., probably of Reading.
    iii. Deborah, b. July 19, 1685; m. Ebenezer Russell, 1710.
    iv. Mary, b. 1686; m. Stephen Danforth of Ipswich.
    v. Joanna, b. 1688.
13. vi. Jonathan, b. May 24, 1691; m. Annah ———.

6. JOHN[3] HEBBERT, Jr. (*John*,[2] *Robert*[1]) of Lynn, Beverly, Andover, Haverhill and Methuen, was alive in 1750, when he gave land to his son. The date of his death is not known. The children of John[3] and his wife Dorothy Graves were:

i. ELIZABETH,[4] b. at Lynn, Feb. 12, 1709.
ii. EBENEZER, b. at Lynn, March 15, 1710; m. Abigail Whittier, dau. of Richard; lived at Methuen, and d. July, 1789.
iii. JOHN, b. at Beverly, Nov. 24, 1716; m. Hannah Pattie of Methuen, December, 1742; lived at Methuen, and was a farmer.
iv. DOROTHY, b. at Andover, April 20, 1720.
v. MARTHA, b. at Andover, May 17, 1724.
vi. JOSEPH, b. at Andover, July 5, 1726; m. Rebecca Sawyer, 1750; lived at Newbury, Vt., and d. 1806. His wife d. 1807.
vii. DANIEL, b. at Methuen, 1728; m. Ruth Hughes, 1750; lived at Haverhill, Mass., and Middletown, Conn.
viii. RUTH, b. at Methuen, 1730; d. Feb. 9, 1736.

7. JEREMIAH[3] HEBERT (*Joseph*,[2] *Robert*[1]) of Manchester, Mass., "husbandman" and "seaman," died May, 1743. He probably removed from Beverly after the death of his first wife. He died intestate leaving an estate of £289. 6. 0., of which his widow was made administratrix. His children, by his first wife, Mary Derby, were:

i. JEREMIAH,[4] b. at Beverly, June 6, 1705; d. young.
ii. MARY, b. Nov. 7, 1706; m. —— Lee.
iii. SARAH, b. Aug. 27, 1708; m. —— Leeman.
iv. JEREMIAH, b. July 4, 1712; m. Elizabeth ——, and d. 1784.

By his second wife, Hannah Leach, his children were:

v. JOSEPH, b. Dec. 22, 1723; m. Louisa Ingals (b. June 27, 1725), Oct. 31, 1744, and was a sea captain. On Dec. 15, 1755, he brought the first news to New England of the great earthquake at Lisbon.
vi. HANNAH, b. May 9, 1725; m. —— Lee.
vii. JEMIMA, b. Oct. 18, 1726; m. —— Bishop.
viii. BENJAMIN, b. May 15, 1728; imbecile; d. *s.p.*

8. JOSEPH[3] HEBBERT (*Joseph*[2] *Robert*[1]), a weaver and rope maker, of Beverly, Mass., Preston, Conn., and Salem, Mass., died at the last place, 1746, leaving an estate of £136. 3. 1. The children of Joseph[3] and his wife Mary Stone were:

i. HENRY,[4] b. at Beverly, July 21, 1717.
ii. SAMUEL, b. at Beverly, April 20, 1719.
iii. ESTHER, b. at Beverly, Nov. 15, 1720.
iv. JACOB, b. at Preston, 1723; m. Rachel Bennett of Gloucester, Mass., Oct. 9, 1747; lived at Gloucester and Watertown, Mass., and d. at the latter place in 1809.

9. ROBERT[3] HEBARD (*Robert*,[2] *Robert*[1]) of Wenham, Mass., and Windham, Conn., died June 26, 1742. By his wife, Mary Reed (died March 7, 1763, aged 76), he had the following children:

i. JOHN,[4] b. Oct. 30, 1704; m. Martha Durkee of Windham, Sept. 22, 1725; lived at Canterbury, Conn., and d. 1762.
ii. ROBERT, b. April 30, 1706; m. (1) Ruth Wheelock (dau. of Dea. Ralph and sister of Pres. Eleazer Wheelock) Nov. 6, 1730; (2) Joanna Cleveland, May 12, 1760; lived at Windham, and d. April 12, 1771.
iii. JOSIAH, b. Sept. 30, 1708; d. Dec. 19, 1733.
iv. SAMUEL, b. May 2, 1710; lived at Windham; d. Nov. 29, 1792; m. (1) Lydia Kingsley, Jan. 17, 1738. She d. April 16, 1747. He m. (2) Mary Burnett, Sept. 27, 1748. She d. April 8. 1809, aged 83.
v. MARY, b. Dec. 14, 1711; m. Samuel Lawrence, Nov. 6, 1733.
vi. JOSHUA, b. Oct. 19, 1713; m. Ruth Boss. He lived at Windham, Conn., and Hampton, Vt., and d. Dec. 19, 1788.

vii. DAVID, b. March 19, 1716; m. (1) Elizabeth Swan, Sept. 8, 1743. She d. Feb. 15, 1762. He m. (2) Dorcas Thorpe, Jan. 26, 1763. She d. July 31, 1801, aged 77. He was a farmer, and lived at Killingly, Conn.
viii. MARTHA, b. Sept 9, 1718; d. Sept. 23, 1718.
ix. HANNAH, b. April 22, 1721.
x. SETH, b. April 19, 1724.

10. JOSEPH[3] HEBARD (*Robert*,[2] *Robert*[1]) of Wenham, Mass., and Windham, Conn., died February 28, 1755. He was one of the fifteen who formed the church at Windham, December 10, 1700. By his wife, Abigail Kendall (died December 6, 1756), he had the following children :

i. ABIGAIL,[4] b. March 15, 1699; m. ——— Thacher.
ii. JOSIAH, b. Feb. 9, 1701; d. Jan. 26, 1703.
iii. JOSEPH, b. Jan. 15, 1703: d. May 15, 1751. He was a physician, and lived at Windham. He m. (1) Anna Strickland, 1726. She d. Jan. 31, 1741. He m. (2) widow Martha (Smith) Gould, Feb. 1, 1742. She d. 1801. He was a man of extraordinary perseverance and of great moral worth. A physician of great learning and skill, his practice at his death was very extensive. He d. of a protracted fever caused by over exertion, in the manhood of his life.
iv. MARY, b. 1705; m. Seth Carey, 1721.
v. JOANNA, b. June 25, 1707.
vi. JEMIMA, b. Aug. 16, 1711; m. ——— Martin.
vii. MEHITABEL, b. Sept. 29, 1713; m. ——— Terrill.
viii. RUTH, b. Sept. 30, 1717; m. ——— Shalock.
ix. MOSES, b. April 10, 1719; d. March, 1813; m. Hannah Murdock, March 31, 1744. He lived at Windham, Conn., and Sturbridge, Mass.

11. NATHANIEL[3] HEBARD (*Robert*,[2] *Robert*[1]) of Windham, Conn., died April 26, 1725. His children, by his wife Sarah Crane, were :

i. NATHANIEL,[4] b. Jan. 3, 1703; d. May 16, 1704.
ii. SAMUEL, b. July 21, 1704; d. July 21, 1704.
iii. ANNA, b. May 30, 1705; m. John Gray.
iv. DEBORAH, b. May 28, 1707; m, Isaac Robinson.
v. NATHANIEL, b. Oct. 23, 1709; m. Abigail Couch.
vi. JONATHAN, b. Oct. 23, 1709; of Greenwich, Conn.; m. Sarah ———.
vii. PAUL, b. March 4, 1712; d. Jan. 12, 1791; lived at Norwich, Conn. He m. (1) Deborah Lawrence, Jan. 6, 1735; (2) Martha Dodge, dau. of Amos, April 30, 1741. She d. Oct. 22, 1801, aged 89. He was for many years sheriff's deputy for Windham Co., and held several responsible offices and trusts.
viii. ZEBULON, b. Feb. 20, 1714; d. July, 1788, leaving an estate inventoried at £1,961. 2. 10. He was captain in the militia, and lived at Windham. He m. Hannah Bass, dau. of John, March 3, 1737.
ix. SARAH, b. June 27, 1717; m. Ebenezer Spencer.
x. ELISHA, b. Dec. 11, 1719. He lived at Windham, and m. Mary Palmer, Aug. 6, 1744.
xi. GIDEON, b. May 2, 1721; lived at Windham, and d. May 2, 1804. He m. Elizabeth Kingley, Dec. 14, 1748. She d. Feb. 4, 1814. His inventory was £2,255. 54.

12. EBENEZER[3] HEBERT (*Robert*,[2] *Robert*[1]) of Windham and Scotland, Conn., died October, 1752. By his wife, Margaret Morgan, he had the following children :

i. PRUDENCE,[4] b. Feb. 3, 1711, at Windham; m. ——— Dolan.
ii. MARGARET, b. May 10, 1713, at Windham; m. ——— Welch.
iii. NATHAN, b. Nov. 16, 1715, at Windham; lived at Scotland, and d. 1797. He m. (1) Zippora Bushnell, Dec. 14, 1738. She d. January, 1763; (2) widow Irena Warner.

iv. REUBEN, b. May 21, 1718, at Scotland (Preston).
14. v. EBENEZER, b. March 16, 1720, at Scotland (Preston).
vi. KEZIAH, b. May 19, 1722.
vii. ABIGAIL, b. June 11, 1724; m. Joseph Carey, Dec. 10, 1741.
viii. SHUBAEL, b. Aug. 2, 1726, of Middletown, Conn.; m. Margaret
Southmayd of Middletown, July 23, 1752, and d. June 28, 1755.

13. JONATHAN³ HIBBERT (*Samuel,² Robert¹*) was a tailor, living at Portsmouth, N. H., Coventry, Conn., and Dudley, Mass. He married
Annah ———, and died 1751. Their children were:

i. ANNAH,⁴ bap. April 7, 1718, at Coventry.
ii. JONATHAN, bap. 1720; of Dudley, Mass.; m. Experience Wafleld, 1740.
iii. SAMUEL, bap. 1721; of Dudley; m. Mary ———.
iv. SOUTHWICK, bap. 1722; of Dudley; m. Abigail Collier of Shrewsbury, Mass., Feb. 11, 1757.
v. SETH, bap. 1724; of Woodstock, Conn.; d. Oct. 25, 1761; m. Eunice
———.
vi. MARY, bap. 1726; m. Mark Ellwell of Thompson, Conn., April 15,
1754.

14. Lieut. EBENEZER⁴ HEBERT, Jr. (*Ebenezer,³ Robert,² Robert¹*) married
Hannah Downer, daughter of Dr. Andrew (she died 1779), and was
a saddle and harness maker in Lebanon Crank, now Columbia,
Conn. He traded in London, and was lost on a passage from England about 1759. Children:

15. i. EBENEZER,⁵ b. Sept. 26, 1743; d. April 16, 1802.
ii. WILLIAM, b. 1750; d. 1834; m. (1) Bathsheba Strong, Aug. 27, 1769.
She d. 1779. He m. (2) Ann Bishop of Bolton, Dec. 24, 1781.
She d. 1816. He m. (3) Mrs. ——— Phelps of Bolton.
iii. CYPRIAN, b. 1755; m. Sarah Burritt of Stratford, Conn. His name
is also spelt Zipperae or Ziphron. He went to Wyoming, Penn.,
with his mother and stepfather, Caleb Spencer, and was killed in
the massacre there, July 3, 1778. Stone's "Poetry and History
of Wyoming" and Miner's "History of Wyoming" contain
notices of him.

15. Lieut. EBENEZER⁵ HEBERT (*Ebenezer,⁴ Ebenezer,³ Robert,² Robert¹*)
married Ann Spencer, daughter of Edward, November 9, 1769 (she
died October 25, 1838). He was ensign of a picked company called
the Roxbury Rangers at the battle of Bunker Hill, June 17, 1775.
The next day, he was promoted for bravery for a lieutenancy. He
remained with the army until December, when he returned to Bolton, Conn., where he had formerly resided. In February, 1776, he
removed with the family of his wife to Wyoming, Penn. He was
with Sullivan when he made his inroad upon the Indians in New
York. He was out at various times during the war, and was in the
field at the time of the famous massacre. After the war, he was
one of the pioneers of Kentucky, where he spent some seven years.
He returned sick and disabled to Wilkesbarre, where he died, aged
59. His widow died at Loudonville, Ohio. Their children were:

i. OLADINA,⁶ b. December, 1770; m. Josiah Pell.
ii. CALVIN, b. Nov. 26, 1774; m. (1) Mary Tilbury of Wyoming, Penn.,
1801. She d. March 8, 1802. He m. (2) Elizabeth Turner of
Kingston, Penn., 1806. He d. November, 1852.
iii. CLARA, b. April, 1776; m. (1) Ebenezer Halstead; (2) ———
Baldwin.
iv. LOVINE, b. Dec. 24, 1780; m. Richard Smith, Jr., of Southbury,
Conn., Dec. 24, 1800. He d. Aug. 8, 1826. She d. Feb. 24, 1844.
Ralph⁷ Dunning Smyth was her second son.
v. ANNA, b. 1783; d. July 25, 1846.

HIGHLAND, HILAND.—The following record is from a MS. compiled by the late Hon. Ralph D. Smyth:

1. GEORGE[1] HIGHLAND, or HILAND, was at Guilford on Sept. 4, 1651, when he took the oath of fidelity. He may have come from Wethersfield. He had a home lot with an orchard, containing 1½ acres, and a parcel of upland of 10 acres. Later in his life he sold these lands, and bought a new home lot containing 2 acres, adjoining a parcel of pasture land containing 13 acres and a piece of land in the plain. He married Mary, daughter of Abraham Cruttenden, about 1665, and died Jan. 21, 1692-3. He left no sons, but his daughters all married in Guilford, and left descendants who were among the most prominent families claiming a Guilford origin. Hon. Hiland Hall of Bennington, Vt., member of Congress and afterwards Governor of that State, was a descendant.

Children:

i. *Elizabeth*, b. June 18, 1666; d. in 1749; m. Dec. 13, 1689, Isaac, son of John Parmelee of Guilford, who d. Jan. 23, 1749.

ii. *Hannah*, b. Jan. 29, 1669; d. May 19, 1752; m. in 1694, John Hill, Jr., of Guilford, who d. Feb. 10, 1740.

iii. *Mary*, b. May 12, 1672; d. Apr., 1738; m. Feb. 1, 1692, Thomas, son of Samuel Hall of Middletown and Guilford, who d. Feb. 1, 1753.

iv. *Deborah*, b. in 1674; d. Oct. 27, 1758; m. Apr. 11, 1700, Ebenezer, son of John Hall of Guilford, who d. Dec., 1723.

Baltimore, Md.   BERNARD C. STEINER.

LUKE HILL OF WINDSOR, CONN., AND JOHN HILL OF GUILFORD, CONN., AND THEIR DESCENDANTS.

Compiled by Hon. RALPH D. SMYTH, and communicated by Dr. BERNARD C. STEINER.

Two families of Hills are connected with the early history of Guilford, but no relationship between them has been traced.

1. LUKE[1] HILL, of Windsor, later removed to Simsbury, where he was living in 1694. He married Mary Hart, May 6, 1651.
Their children were:

    i. LYDIA,[2] b. Feb. 18, 1651–2.
    ii. MARY, b. Sept. 20, 1654; m. July 30, 1677, John Saxton.
    iii. EBENEZER, b. at Farmington, March, 1656–7.
2. iv. TAHAN, b. Nov. 23, 1659; d. Dec. 16 or 18, 1692.
3. v. LUKE, b. March 6, 1661.
    vi. ABIGAIL, b. April 16, 1664.
    vii. ELIZABETH, b. Oct. 18, 1666.
4. viii. JOHN, b. Nov. 28, 1668.

2. TAHAN[2] HILL (Luke[1]), born Nov. 23, 1659, married Nov. 29, 1688, Hannah Parmelee. He died Dec. 16 or 18, 1692; and she married second, Thomas Merrill of Saybrook. Tahan was listed at Guilford in 1690.
Their children were:

    i. HANNAH,[3] b. Nov. 17, 1689; m. March 31, 1710, Samuel Bushnell.
    ii. TAHAN, b. 1691.

3. LUKE[2] HILL, JR. (Luke[1]), born March 6, 1661, married Hannah ——, or Anna ——, and lived for a time at Guilford. He seems to have been of roving disposition.
His children were:

    i. EBENEZER,[3] b. Nov. 23, 1687, at Guilford.
    ii. ANNA, b. Dec. 3, 1692.
    iii. KEZIAH, b. Feb. 24, 1695, at Wethersfield.
    iv. LUKE, b. at Simsbury, Sept. 16, 1698.
    v. LYDIA, b. at Simsbury, Feb. 25, 1700.
    vi. ISAAC, b. at Branford, May 27, 1703.

4. JOHN[2] HIL (Luke[1]), of Saybrook, born Nov. 28, 1668, married April 14, 167(Jane Bushnell.
Thei child was:

    i. SAMUEL,[3] b. May 29, 1671.

---

1. JOHN[1] HILL, SR., the head of the other and more important family, became freeman at Guilford before 1657, having been at Branford in 1646. He died June 8, 1689. During the troubles between Connecticut and New Haven, he was of the Rossiter faction. Suits against him for slander are discussed in Steiner's History of Guilford, page 95. He was one of the lesser planters, being known as Goodman Hill. His home lot was on the south side of the Green,

and contained about an acre and three-fourths. In addition to this, he had other lands. He married first, Frances ———, who was the mother of his children, and who died May, 1673; and married second, Catharine, widow of Alexander Chalker, Sept. 22, 1673. His children were:

2. i. JOHN,[2] b. Jan. 10, 1650; d. May 9, 1690.
3. ii. JAMES, d. October, 1707.
   iii. HANNAH, b. Jan. 18, 1652-3.
   iv. ELIZABETH.
   v. SARAH.

2. JOHN[2] HILL, JR. (*John*[1]), born Jan. 10, 1650, cordwainer, of Guilford, married Thankful, daughter of Thomas Stow of Braintree and Middletown. She was born in 1638, and died November 18, 1711. He inherited the home lot. He died May 9, 1690.
His children were:

   i. MARY,[3] b. May 8, 1671; d. Aug. 23, 1671.
4. ii. JOHN, b. July 18, 1672; d. Feb. 10, 1740.
   iii. ELIZABETH, b. Feb. 20, 1673-4; m. James Lord of Saybrook, Dec. 13, 1693.
   iv. MARY, b. Feb. 1, 1675-6; d. Jan. 2, 1730; m. Josiah Rosseter of Killingworth, May 9, 1710. He d. Sept. 23, 1751.
5. v. SAMUEL, b. Feb. 21, 1677-8; d. May 24 or 28, 1752.
   vi. NATHANIEL, b. April 27, 1680; d. single, Oct. 10, 1764. He lived in Guilford, where his list was £1. 19. 0., in 1716.
6. vii. JAMES, b. April 25, 1682; d. March 25, 1715.

3. JAMES[2] HILL (*John*[1]), cordwainer, of Guilford, married in 1682, Sarah ———, who died May 8, 1729. He had a " parcel of upland lying at East End given him by his father," was one of the early settlers of East Guilford, and prominent in the movement to have it made a separate society. He died in October, 1707.
His children were:

   i. SARAH,[3] b. Aug. 24, 1683; d. Dec. 4, 1711; m. Samuel Darwin of Guilford, Jan. 5, 1710.
7. ii. ISAAC, b. Sept. 5, 1685.
   iii. JAMES, b. Feb. 11, 1688; lived in Killingworth; m. ——— Bowen.
   iv. ANN, b. March 4, 1689-90; m. Ephraim Bushnell of Saybrook, Oct. 16, 1712.
8. v. DANIEL, b. June 8, 1692; d. Jan. 30, 1745.
9. vi. JOHN, b. Dec. 18, 1694; d. Feb. 16, 1746.
   vii. CHARITY, b. March 4, 1696; m. John Johnson, at New Haven, June 20, 1722.
10. viii. MICHAEL, b. Oct. 22, 1698; d. June 23, 1752.
   ix. MARY, b. March 2, 1701; d. young.

4. JOHN[3] HILL, 3d (*John*,[2] *John*[1]), born July 18, 1672, married Hannah, daughter of George Hiland, or Highland. She died May 19, 1752. He inherited the home lot, and owned an acre and a quarter of land in plain, and received from his mother-in-law a parcel of land on Jan. 27, 1701-2. His list in 1716 was £48. 5. 0. He died Feb. 10, 1740.
His children were:

   i. JOHN,[4] b. June 13, 1695; d. Sept. 6, 1756; m. Hannah Dibble of Saybrook, Sept. 10, 1716. She d. April 12, 1739. He lived at Saybrook and Hartford after his wife's death. Their children, all born at Saybrook, were: 1. *Hannah*,[5] b. Oct. 12, 1717; d. single at Guilford, Dec. 6, 1736. 2. *John*, b. Oct. 20, 1719; d. Feb. 16, 1746;

m. (1) Ruth ——; (2) —— Doolittle. 3. *Elijah*, b. Feb. 18, 1723. 4. *Elizabeth*, b. Dec. 20, 1725. 5. *Susannah*, b. March 29, 1729. 6. *Mary*, b. March 1, 1731.

ii. HANNAH, b. May 3, 1699; lived single, at Guilford, and d. March 13, 1768.

iii. ELIZABETH, b. Oct. 1, 1705; d. April 14, 1781; m. John Stone, Nov. 7, 1738, who d. Feb. 16, 1751.

iv. THOMAS, b. Sept. 27, 1708; d. Feb. 23, 1792; m. May 23, 1734, Hannah Pierson, who d. May 6, 1791. He lived in Guilford. Their children were: 1. *Lucy*,[5] b. July 29, 1735; d. Dec. 13, 1745. 2. *Hannah*, b. July 27, 1737; d. Dec. 27, 1808; m. Nathaniel Johnson of Guilford, Dec. 10, 1761, who d. March 10, 1798. 3. *Elizabeth*, b. Sept. 9, 1739; d. July 28, 1748. 4. *Thomas*, b. May 20, 1743; d. April 4, 1820; m. Elizabeth Fairchild, Oct. 13, 1751, who d. Feb. 28, 1812.

v. GEORGE, b. April 5, 1710; d. Feb. 9, 1787. He lived in Guilford, and m. Ruth, dau. of Thomas Robinson, Oct. 23, 1738. She d. Nov. 21, 1792. Their children were: 1. *Rachel*,[5] b. Dec. 29, 1739; d. Dec. 25, 1773. 2. *Benjamin*, b. Dec. 17, 1741; d. Dec. 20, 1815. 3. *Ruth*, b. Aug. 7, 1744; d. Nov. 11, 1820; m. Zimra Bradley of East Guilford, 1769, who d. æ. 81, Sept. 26, 1821. 4. *Leah*, b. June 19, 1748; m. (1) Giles Truby, who d. April, 1780; m. (2) Elijah Leete, in 1786, who d. April 19, 1825.

vi. BENJAMIN, b. Jan. 19, 1712; d. young.

vii. REUBEN, b. Nov. 2, 1715; went to Canada.

viii. ABIGAIL, b. May 10, 1720; d. Oct. 11, 1774.

5. COL. SAMUEL[3] HILL (*John*,[2] *John*[1]), born Feb. 21, 1677–8, hatter, of Guilford, married Huldah, daughter of Samuel Ruggles of Roxbury, Mass., June 9, 1709. She was born July 4, 1684, and died Aug. 29, 1762. His "faculty" was rated at £12. in 1716, and his list was £89. 16. 6. He was so often elected to the General Assembly that the story is told that, at town meeting, the moderator would rise and say: "We are assembled to elect Col. Sam Hill and some one to go with him to the next General Court." His name is still used in Guilford to express superiority, *e.g.* "He runs like Sam Hill." He was quite a large land holder, and was town clerk from 1717, and also clerk of the proprietors of the common and undivided lands. He was clerk of the Probate Court from 1720 to 1725, when he was chosen judge, which position he held until his death, in May, 1752. He was also justice of the New Haven County Court, and easily the prominent man of his time.

His children were:

i. SAMUEL,[4] b. March 5, 1711; d. single, Feb. 12, 1783. He was somewhat an imbecile, yet did much copying of town and probate records of Guilford.

ii. HULDAH, b. Dec. 30, 1712; d. Jan. 9, 1773; m. Roswell Woodward, March 26, 1747. He d. Sept. 10, 1773. They had no children.

iii. HENRY, b. Aug. 2, 1714; d. July 17, 1751; m. Sarah, dau. of Rev. John Hart of East Guilford. She d. June 20, 1789. His estate amounted to £1737. 12. 3. His widow later married successively Dr. Thomas Adams and Rev. Amos Fowler. Henry Hill had one child: *Hon. Henry*,[5] b. Oct. 15, 1750; A.B. Yale, 1772; d. Dec. 21, 1827; m. Leah, dau. of Daniel Stone, Nov. 21, 1774, and was the father of George,[6] the poet, A.B. Yale, 1816. (See Dexter's Yale Biographies, I., p. 577.)

iv. NATHANIEL, b. March 10, 1716; A.B. Yale, 1737; d. Nov. 16, 1771; m. Nov. 30, 1748, Anna, dau. of Charles Caldwell. She d. April 25, 1800. Their children were: 1. *Nathaniel*,[5] b. Nov. 16, 1749; d. Dec. 7, 1831; m. Sarah Butler of New London, April 5, 1781. 2. *Anna*, b. Sept. 24, 1752; m. in 1790, Darius Stone of Patterson, N. Y. 3. *Huldah*, b. Feb. 21, 1755; d. Feb. 3, 1838; m. Samuel Johnson of Guilford, May 24, 1780, who d. June 20, 1836. 4. *Sarah*, b. Feb. 3, 1765; d. single, Oct. 31, 1795.

v. MARY, b. Nov. 5, 1717.
vi. THANKFUL, b. March 8, 1719; d. April 5, 1719.
vii. JOSEPH, b. April 14, 1721; d. April 25, 1722.

6. JAMES[3] HILL (*John*,[2] *John*[1]), born April 25, 1682, of Guilford, married Mary Fry, Jan. 15, 1710. He died March 25, 1715. In 1716, her list was £18. 7. 6.

Their children were :

i. MERCY,[4] b. December, 1710; d. May 27, 1762; m. Eliphalet Hall, June 2, 1743. He d. March 16, 1782.
ii. JAMES, b. Feb. 28, 1712; d. October, 1798; lived in Killingworth; m. Hannah Nettleton, who d. in 1822. Their children were : 1. *Hannah*,[5] b. April 14, 1744; m. June 11, 1767, Abner Hull. 2. *Sibyl*, b. Oct. 10, 1746; m. Ezra Parmelee of Newport, Vt. 3. *Marcy*, b. Feb. 26, 1747; m. Absalom Kelsey of Newport, Vt. 4. *James*, of Killingworth, b. Nov. 30, 1749; d. in 1802; m. Eleanor Hull, who d. 1804. 5. *Noah*, of North Madison, b. Oct. 22, 1751; d. April 29, 1826; m. in 1777, Caroline, dau. of Eliab Parmelee. She d. March 7, 1827. 6. *John*, b. Feb. 4, 1754; d. single, Aug. 5, 1777. 7. *Thankful*, b. Feb. 9, 1756; d. 1799; m. Elias Parmelee. 8. *Selah*, b. Feb. 8, 1758; m. Sally Turner; d. in New Hampshire. 9. *Henry*, b. July 21, 1761; d. March 28, 1834; lived at Killingworth; m. Lucy Doolittle. 10. *Joseph*, b. April 15, 1765; d. Sept. 29, 1840; lived in North Madison; m. Hester, dau. of Samuel Butler of Essex. 11. *Dr. Benjamin*, b. April 15, 1765; d. in 1849; lived at Le Roy, N. Y.; m. in 1796, Jemima Stannard. 12. *Molly*, b. Feb. 20, 1767; d. single; had an illegitimate dau., Alpha Baldwin.

7. ISAAC[3] HILL (*James*,[2] *John*[1]), born Sept. 5, 1685, lived in Woodbury in 1738. His list in East Guilford, in 1716, was £53. 6. 6. He married Ann, daughter of Joshua Parmelee, July 5, 1711. She died March 27, 1752.

Their children were :

i. ISAAC,[4] b. Sept. 9, 1712; d. Sept. 22, 1712.
ii. ISAAC, b. July 20, 1714; d. Feb. 21, 1716.
iii. JAMES, b. February, 1716; d. single, March 10, 1734.
iv. ISAAC, b. Dec. 18, 1717; lived in Goshen in 1738, and Woodbury in 1741; m. (1) Caroline Perry, Nov. 16, 1741; m. (2) Esther, dau. of Benajah Stone. He probably d. in Wallingford. His children were : 1. *Rousel*,[5] bapt. Aug. 26, 1744; d. in 1802. 2. *Abiga'l*, b. Sept. 25, 1749. 3. *Ann*, b. 1755.
v. SARAH, b. Dec. 11, 1719.
vi. SUBMIT, b. Dec. 12, 1721; d. March, 1756; m. Nov. 10, 1748, David Hotchkiss of Woodbury.
vii. SILAS, b. March 23, 1724; d. young.
viii. AHIRA, b. Jan. 27, 1726; d. in Woodbury in 1777; m. (1) Jan. 29, 1754, Mehitabel Lewis, who had no children; m. (2) Hannah ———, by whom he had : 1. *Josiah*,[5] b. May 8, 1774. 2. *Rhoda*, bapt. June 18, 1775.
ix. ANN, b. April 10, 1728; d. young.
x. CHARITY, b. May 2, 1730.
xi. SUSANNAH, b. Nov. 3, 1732.
xii. DANIEL, b. Jan. 30, 1734; of East Guilford; d. Sept. 21, 1756; m. Feb. 6, 1751, Lucy Parmelee. She d. April, 1798. Their children were : 1. *John*,[5] b. July 8, 1751; lived in East Guilford; m. Rhoda ———. 2. *Moses*, b. July 26, 1754. 3. *Sarah*, b. Aug. 28, 1756; m. Isaac Winstone, March 22, 1779. 4. *Lucy*, b. June 30, 1759.
xiii. JONATHAN, b. Jan. 30, 1734; of Woodbury; d. Feb. 10, 1793; m. Elizabeth Perry, April 19, 1758. Their children were : 1. *Anne*,

b. April 19, 1759. 2. *Reuben*, b. Feb. 26, 1761. 3. *David*, b. Feb. 10, 1765; d. in 1845; m. and lived at Bethlehem. 4. *Jonathan*, b. March 25, 1769. 5. *Daniel*, b. March 22, 1767; d. March 2, 1849; m. Electa Minor, who d. Feb. 7, 1840; lived in Woodbury.

xiv. HULDAH, b. Sept. 12, 1735.

xv. ZENAS, bapt. June 4, 1738, at Woodbury; m. Keziah ———, and had children: 1. *Sarah,*[5] b. March 20, 1762. 2. *Zenas*, b. Dec. 26, 1764. 3. *Jesse*, b. Dec. 10, 1766.

8. DANIEL[3] HILL (*James,*[2] *John*[1]), born June 8, 1692, weaver, of East Guilford, left an estate valued at £2295. 2. 8. In 1716 his list was £59. 9. 6, and the value of his weaver's trade £3. He married Mindwell, daughter of Obadiah Wilcox, April 20, 1714. He died Jan. 30, 1745; and she died Feb. 3, 1770.

Their children were:

i. REUBEN,[4] b. in 1715; d. Nov. 17, 1804; m. (1) Mary Jacobs, who d. Feb. 6, 1776, by whom were all his children; m. (2) Dorcas, widow of Jonathan Murray, who d. aged 78, Nov. 24, 1794. His children were: 1. *Mercy,*[5] b. Jan. 31, 1744; d. Jan. 5, 1831; m. Hull Crampton, who d. Nov. 21, 1796. 2. *Reuben*, b. Feb. 25, 1746; lived in East Guilford; d. Sept. 23, 1835; m. February, 1775, Hannah, dau. of Noah Scranton. She d. March 20, 1833, aged 82. 3. *James*, b. Feb. 11, 1749; of East Guilford; d. Sept. 16, 1825; m. in 1776, Mabel, dau. of Moses Blackley. She d. Jan. 16, 1811. 4. *Lydia*, b. Nov. 27, 1752; m. Ishi Norton of East Guilford, who d. July 21, 1801. 5. *Anna*, b. Oct. 22, 1755; d. Feb. 6, 1797; m. Jan. 15, 1789, Daniel Evarts. 6. *Ezra*, b. April 19, 1759; removed to Sunderland, Vt.; m. Olive, dau. of Noah Scranton.

ii. JAMES, b. in 1717; d. February 26, 1740, single.

iii. DANIEL, b. Oct. 29, 1719; d. at Crown Point, Nov. 25, 1761; m. May 25, 1748, Mary Hoyt, who d. July, 1801, aged 87. Their children were: 1. *Mary,*[5] b. March 28, 1750; d. single, September, 1816. 2. *Hannah*, b. Nov. 3, 1752; d. single, November, 1818. 3. *Daniel*, b. Oct. 22, 1755; d. single, June 12, 1823.

iv. DEA. TIMOTHY, b. May 22, 1722; by his father's will he was to be educated at Yale, but he did not graduate there. He d. Feb. 6, 1781, in East Guilford, and the funeral sermon, preached by Rev. Jonathan Todd, was published. He m. Oct. 27, 1748, Elizabeth Stevens, who d. April, 1801. Their children were: 1. *Timothy,*[5] b. July 27, 1749; m. Elizabeth, dau. of Benjamin Norton. He lived at Turin, N. Y., in 1808. 2. *Elizabeth*, b. March 25, 1756; d. May 26, 1833; m. Jonathan Dudley, Feb. 4, 1778, who d. April 5, 1796. 3. *Mindwell*, b. Sept. 10, 1759; m. Jonathan Lee, who d. Nov. 4, 1844.

v. ABNER, b. June 6, 1726; lived in East Guilford; m. Dec. 27, 1770, Sarah Bibbins. Their children were: 1. *Abner,*[5] b. Oct. 11, 1771; d. young. 2. *Beulah*, b. Sept. 18, 1773; m. Edmund Graves of Sunderland, Vt. 3. *Abner*, b. March, 1776.

vi. MINDWELL, b. Feb. 15, 1729; d. single.

vii. IRENA, b. June 12, 1732; d. Oct. 8, 1809; m. Jedidiah Stone, Jr., of Killingworth, July 9, 1755, who d. February, 1816.

9. JOHN[3] HILL (*James,*[2] *John*[1]), born Dec. 18, 1694, of East Guilford, married first, Elizabeth Dibble, Oct. 8, 1716, who died February, 1721. He married second, Marah Shalor, Dec. 7, 1721, who died May 8, 1729; and he married third, Ruth Richardson, Jan. 6, 1730. She survived him, and married ——— Doolittle of Waterbury. John Hill's list in 1716 was £32. 8. 6, and his trade as shoemaker and tanner was rated at £3. He died Feb. 16, 1746.

The children by his first wife were:

i. ABRAHAM,[4] b. Jan. 22, 1720; d. April 26, 1720.

ii. ELIZABETH, b. Feb. 23, 1721; d. Aug. 23, 1721.
iii. JOHN, b. Feb. 23, 1721; of East Guilford; d. July 23, 1786; m. in 1757, Rebecca, widow of David Hoyt, and dau. of John Scranton. She d. aged 76, May 5, 1798. Their children were: 1. *John*,[5] b. July 13, 1758; tailor; of East Guilford; d. Dec. 1, 1830; m. (1) Abigail Gray of Clinton, who d. aged 44, April 3, 1800; m. (2) Cate Fyler of North Guilford, who d. Nov. 13, 1806, aged 46; m. (3) Mary Hayden of Haddam, who d. Oct. 9, 1847, aged 79. 2. *Ichabod*, b. Dec. 19, 1760; went to New York State. 3. *Abram* or *Abraham*, b. May 16, 1763; d. September, 1840; lived in Madison; m. Lydia, dau. of Selah Murray, Sept. 29, 1784. 4. *Rebecca*, b. in 1767; m. June 15, 1780, Samuel Ackersley.
iv. JONAS, b. March 18, 1718; d. Oct. 23, 1736.

The child by his second wife was:

v. ABRAHAM, b. Dec. 26, 1722; d. Oct. 18, 1759; lived in East Guilford; m. Hannah Nott, Feb. 27, 1745. She d. June 14, 1786, having m. (2) Eliphalet Hall, March 7, 1762, who d. March 16, 1782. Abraham Hill had no children.

The children by his third wife were:

vi. NATHANIEL, b. Oct. 26, 1730; of Cheshire, Conn.; m. Jan. 1, 1756, Esther Field. They had: 1. *Betty*,[5] b. Oct. 15, 1756. 2. *Beulah*, b. Sept. 21, 1757. 3. *Esther*, b. Aug. 1, 1759.
vii. BETTSY, b. Nov. 22, 1731.
viii. RUTH, b. May 15, 1735.
ix. JONAS, b. July 18, 1742; of Wallingford.

10. MICHAEL[3] HILL (*James*,[2] *John*[1]), born Oct. 22, 1698, of Guilford and Saybrook, married first, Sarah, daughter of Isaac Parmalee, Oct. 17, 1720. She died May 4, 1730; and he married second, Anna Spenser of Saybrook, Dec. 15, 1730. After his death, June 23, 1752, she married Dea. Samuel Bushnell. She died Feb. 10, 1786.
His children by his first wife were:

i. WILLIAM,[4] b. Jan. 28, 1722; d. April 30, 1741; had an illegitimate daughter, *Sarah*.
ii. MICHAEL, b. March 1, 1724; lived in Sharon; m. (1) Flora Ward, Sept. 12, 1751, who d. March 27, 1752; and m. (2) widow Anna ———, by whom he had: 1. *Henry*,[5] of Westbrook, b. in 1753, who d. childless, Oct. 7, 1799. 2. *Michael*, of Westbrook. 3. *Flora*. 4. *Sarah*. 5 and 6. *Two other daughters*.
iii. SARAH, b. March 11, 1727; d. at Salisbury, Conn.; m. Asher Grinnell.
iv. PELEG, b. April 20, 1730; d. Feb. 29, 1812, at Catskill, N. Y.; m. Dorcas Tucker, Dec. 15, 1754. They had: 1. *Sarah*,[5] b. Nov. 26, 1755. 2. *Peleg*, b. Dec. 5, 1757; of Greensboro', Vt. 3. *Hiland*, b. Nov. 8, 1759; of Catskill, N. Y. 4. *James*, b. Sept. 12, 1761; of Greensboro', Vt. 5. *Richard*, b. Nov. 27, 1763; lived near Boston. 6. *Dorcas*. 7. *A daughter*.

His children by his second wife were:

v. ANNA, b. at Guilford, May 30, 1733; school teacher; d. May 3, 1766, single.
vi. AARON, b. May 30, 1733; d. at New London, Oct. 5, 1743.
vii. MARY, b. Jan. 1, 1736; d. at New London, Oct. 23, 1743.
viii. BEULAH, b. Aug. 1, 1741; d. at New London, July 14, 1743.
ix. REV. WILLIAM, b. July 13, 1743; d. Dec. 9, 1823; lived at Lyme and Essex; m. (1) Hannah Platt of Essex, April 15, 1765; m. (2) Martha, widow of Josiah Baldwin, by whom he had no children. His children were: 1. *Col. Joseph*,[5] b. Jan. 23, 1766; d. single. 2. *William Asa*, b. Jan. 29, 1768; d. Dec. 4, 1826; of Westbrook; m. Betsey, dau. of Ephraim Kelsey. She d. Aug. 21, 1854, aged 78. 3. *Hannah*, b. Sept. 25, 1771. 4. *Jerusha*, m. Gideon Hayden of Essex. 5. *Aaron*.

161

x. SAMUEL, b. Aug. 17, 1745; of Lyme; d. December, 1818; m. Jan. 2, 1769, Edith Bayley, who was b. 1745. Their children were: 1. *Christopher*,[5] b. Jan. 28, 1771; d. single, Sept. 5, 1800. 2. *Edward*, b. Oct. 4, 1772; d. Oct. 4, 1773. 3. *Edward*, b. Sept. 7, 1774; m. Elizabeth, dau. of Ezra Lee, who was b. Aug. 31, 1774. 4. *Mary Ann*, b. March 24, 1777; d. in 1843; m. Rev. Seth Lee of Grassy Hill, Lyme, who d. in 1826. 5. *Mehitabel*, b. March 26, 1779; d. Sept. 5, 1843. 6. *Roxanna*, b. Jan. 9, 1782; m. (1) Isaac McCray of Ellington, Conn.; m. (2) —— Holbrook of Medway, Mass. 7. *Sarah*, b. Jan. 28, 1784; d. March 7, 1849; m. (1) —— Rogers; m. (2) —— McCray of Ellington.

xi. AARON, b. April 1, 1752, at Saybrook; d. Feb. 7, 1779, single, on home passage from West Indies.

NOTES ON THE FAMILY OF JOHN HILL OF GUILFORD, CONN.

By Edwin A. Hill, Esq., of Washington, D. C.

These notes are prompted by, and intended as a supplement to, Dr. Steiner's articles on Luke and John Hill, in the Register, *ante*, page 87. [1]

The late Benjamin S. Hill and the writer, his son, were some years engaged in preparing a genealogy of the descendants of John[1] Hill, and the MS.* comprises several hundred pages, bringing the male lines down to a late period.

Those interested in this family might like to know that Dr. Alvan Talcott's manuscript genealogies of Guilford families contain quite an extended account of the descendants of John[1] of Guilford. The original is in the library of the New Haven Colony Historical Society at New Haven, Conn., and a copy is filed in the office of the town clerk of Guilford.

Smith's History of Guilford, page 20, states that "John Hill, by trade a carpenter, came from Northamptonshire, in England, as early as 1654, and settled upon the *north* side of the green, on the place now [1877] occupied by E. C. Bishop and Tabor Smith." Dr. Steiner, Register, *ante*, page 87, says *south* side. In the Talcott MS. it is stated that he was by trade a carpenter, and came early to Guilford, but not in the first company; that he was at Branford in 1646, but came with his family soon after to Guilford, the tradition being that the Hill family were "North Britons." There is a tradition in the family of Michael[3] (James,[2] John[1]), that he was of Welsh descent. That the John Hill of Branford, in 1646, was John of Guilford seems questionable, in view of the fact that in Vol. 1, Part 2, page 71, of New Haven Probate Records will be found an "Inventory of the estate of John Hill late of Branford deceased taken by Moses Craft and John Frisbye," in 1678, while John of Guilford died there some years later. The latter does not appear in the list of Guilford freemen of 1650, though Dr. Steiner states he was a freeman there before 1657. On the 14th of May, 1655, however, John Hill and Goodwife Hill testified in court at Guilford. Of his English ancestry and date of birth nothing is known. The inventory of his estate, dated June 13, 1689, and taken by Thomas Macoke and Stephen Bradlye, is headed "The inventory of the estate of John Hill the aged, deceased," and amounted to £123. 00. 09.

As his son John was born in 1644, and his daughters Sarah and Elizabeth may have been older than John, he presumably must have been born before 1624, especially to have been called "the aged" at the time of his death.

He was twice married: First to Frances ———, prior to his arrival at Guilford, and, according to Dr. Talcott, before his emigration; and second to Katharine Chalker. "John Hill of Guilford m. Katern Chalker 23 September, 1673." (Records of Saybrook, Ct., in Register, IV., 138.) Savage (II., 417) says she was "probably the widow of Alexander Chalker," concerning whom Hinman, in his "Early Puritan Settlers," page 517, remarks: "Alexander Chalker was an early settler in Saybrook; on page 96, vol. 1, at Saybrook, he m. Kathrine Post, Sept. 29, 1649,

---

* The MS. concerning the descendants of John[1] Hill may at some future time be published, if there should be sufficient interest to warrant it. In the meantime, the writer will be glad to receive and to give any information.

[1] Page 156, this volume

163

and had issue," among others, " 4. Catern, b. Sept. 8, 1657 ; m. John Hill, of Greenfield [Guilford], 1673." If we follow Hinman, she was only sixteen years old when she became John Hill's second wife, at which time his eldest son was nearly thirty-three years old; but Savage is most likely correct. In 1670, John Hill is first styled " Sr." He died June 8, 1689. According to Savage, his will was made in September preceding his death, but my copy gives the date Sept. 28, 1680. It was proved June 17, 1689, and names his wife Katharine, his sons John and James, his daughter Tapping, and the children of his deceased daughters Sarah and Elizabeth, of whom Frances Allen was to receive a double portion. On the second Monday of June, 1695, the following record was made (New Haven County Court Records, I., 232) : " The legacies yet due out of y⁰ estate of John Hill of Guilford deceased is 9lb 20s which is to be distributed to 13 grand-children of the deceased the eldest of them viz. Frances Allen to have 1lb 5s 5d as a double portion, and each of the rest to have 12s 20d as a single portion to every of them."

The writer has a short manuscript genealogy, written Dec. 26, 1847, by his grandfather, Julius⁶ (Reuben,⁵ Reuben,⁴ Daniel,³ James,² John¹), of Madison, Conn., who was much interested in genealogy, in which he gives the children of the first John as : 1. John, born 1644. 2. James, born 1646. 3. Ann, born 1648; died 1706. This Ann is perhaps the Hannah whom Dr. Steiner says was born Jan. 18, 1652–3, though it may be that there was both an Ann and a Hannah. Dr. Talcott, also, gives the dates 1644 for John, and May 15, 1646, for James. The writer has the death date of John, Jr., as May 8, 1690, and of James as Oct. 8, 1707.

Ann,² or Hannah, Hill (*John¹*) evidently married a Tapping. Savage, (IV., 254) mentions a James Tapping, of Milford, whose wife's name was Ann. She died in 1732. This James Tapping may have been the son, born Feb. 12, 1643, of Capt. Thomas Tapping (or Topping) of Wethersfield, Milford, and Branford, by his wife, Emma (Savage, IV., 255).

Sarah² and Elizabeth² Hill (*John¹*) seem to have married and died before their father's will was made in 1680. One of them had married —— Allen, and had had a daughter Frances, who in 1695 was older than the other living children of these daughters. Henry Allen, of Milford, Conn., according to Savage (I., 31), had wife Sarah, who died in 1680, and a daughter Frances, born in 1676. Orcutt (History of Stratford, II., 1115) gives only John (not mentioned by Savage) and Frances—who married, in 1704, John Hall of Middletown, whose heirs in 1742 were Joseph Cornell and wife Elizabeth, Joseph Sage, Jr., and wife Mary, James Ward and wife Abigail, and Samuel Stow and wife Mary, all of Middletown—as the children of Henry Allen, so it would appear that the four children named by Savage as born before Frances, 1676, died before John¹ Hill's will was made.

James² Hill (*John¹*) had wife Sarah ——, whose surname is not given by Dr. Steiner. Dr. Talcott's MS. on the Griswold family states that Sarah, daughter of Michael Griswold of Wethersfield, born Sept. 30, 1662, married —— Hill. There seems to be no other male member of the Guilford family of Hill having a wife Sarah, at a sufficiently early date, except him. The will, dated in 1678, of Michael Griswold, of Wethersfield, who died in 1684, refers to his daughter Sarah Hill. James² and Sarah Hill had children named Isaac and Michael ; and Michael Griswold, of Wethersfield, and wife Ann had sons Michael and Isaac.

With reference to the various lines of descendants traced by Smyth and Steiner, they agree in general quite closely with the writer's MS., except with an occasional difference in dates, and a child of James³ (John,² John¹), not given by them, viz., Lydia, born Sept. 9, 1713; also their Zenas,⁴ son of Isaac³ (James,² John¹), is Jonas in the writer's account. The baptism June 4, 1738, was of Jonas, not Zenas (see Cothren's Woodbury, III., 146). The births of the children of Zenas and Keziah are correctly given (Cothren's Woodbury, III., 55, 57, 59), but there is no known evidence to connect Zenas with Isaac,³ and Zenas may prove to be a descendant of Luke Hill, for Ebenezer³ Hill (Luke,² Luke¹) had a son Zenas, born in Goshen, Conn., Jan. 4, 1730. It may be that Jonas⁴ never married. Cothren (Woodbury, III., 565) gives his death as June 12, 1802, aged 63.

Luke Hill of Windsor, Conn., and John Hill of Guilford, Conn., and Their Descendants: Additions and Corrections: — These additions and corrections are to the article which appeared in The Register, vol. 57, p. 87 et * seq., and are taken from the notes of Donald Lines Jacobus.

Luke¹ Hill married 6 May 1651 Mary Hout (Windsor Records, The Register, 5:228). Her name is shown as Hoyt in Stiles' "History of Windsor", 2:292, and in Savage's "Genealogical Dictionary", 2:418. The spelling Hart, appearing in The Register, 57:87, may be a mis-reading of the original text. The possibility exists that Mary may have been an unrecorded daughter of Reverend Ephraim Huit or of Simon Hoyt, both among the earliest settlers of Windsor. Note that the eldest daughters of both Rev. Ephraim and Luke were named Lydia.

Isaac³ Hill (*Luke,² Luke¹*), born 27 May 1703 in Branford, Conn., married 16 Jan. 1733, Esther Stone, daughter of Benajah and Hannah of Guilford (Wallingford V.R., 5:509). He died 25 Oct. 1741 (Wallingford V.R., 5:549). Esther married secondly, 9 May 1745, Ebenezer Shelley of Guilford (Guilford V.R., 2:59).

The above vital records had been previously erroneously assigned to Isaac⁴ Hill of the family of John Hill of Guilford.

Children of Isaac³ and Esther Hill:

Cloe, born 20 Nov. 1733 (Wallingford V.R., 5:506)
Bille) New Haven Probate File No. 4963, 6 Nov. 1741
Phineas) " " " "
Isaac) " " " "
Abraham) " " " "

Child of Ebenezer and Esther (Hill) Shelley:
Ebenezer, born 18 April 1746 (Guilford V.R. 2:79)

Isaac³ and his brothers, Ebenezer³ and Luke,³ were first settlers of Goshen, Conn. ("History of Goshen", by Hibbard, page 42).

*Pages 156-162, this volume.

Isaac⁴ Hill (*Isaac,³ Luke,² Luke¹*), Revolutionary soldier. Data from National Archives File S31-747 states he was born 16 April 1740 in Guilford, but records of that town do not show his birth. More likely he was born in Goshen or Wallingford shortly before his father's death and lived in Guilford after his mother's second marriage to Ebenezer Shelley in 1745. He was pensioned on Certificate 28920 under the Act of 7 June 1832. He married, 29 Sept. 1762, Eunice Mallory (Stratford L.R., 5:72).

Children:
Abraham Enoch, born 9 Oct. 1763 (Stratford L.R.:72)
Benajah, born 1774 (National Archives S31-747); bapt. 18 Sept. 1774 by
   Mr. Lewis of the Plains (Shelton, Huntington Cong. Ch., vol. 3, p. 105).
Sally, born 10 Dec. 1781 (National Archives S31-747)
Seth, born 1776 (D.A.R. Lineage Book, Vol. 160)
           Seth married Polly Stinson.
Isaac (probably). He is mentioned with Benajah in Southbury land records,
   vol. 8:305.

New York, N. Y.   H. A. Thomas.

EXCERPTS FROM THE HITCHCOCK GENEALOGY.

Compiled for the Register by H. G. Cleveland, Esq., of Cleveland, Ohio.

Luke¹ Hitchcock (brother probably to *Matthias Hitchcock*, New Haven, 1639), place and time of birth unknown, took freeman's oath in New Haven, Ct., 1644, and soon after removed to Wethersfield, Ct.; in 1659 signed an agreement to remove to Hadley, Mass. He died Nov. 1, 1659, leaving a wife Elizabeth, probably sister of William Gibbons, of Hartford, Ct., and three children, as follows:

   i.   John,² b. ——; m. Sept. 27, 1666, Hannah Chapin (daughter of Dea.
        Samuel Chapin), and d. Feb. 9, 1712.
  ii. Hannah, b. 1645; m. Oct. 2, 1661, Chiliab Smith, of Hadley, Mass.
 iii. Luke, b. June 5, 1655; m. Feb. 14, 1676-7, Mrs. Sarah Dorchester, widow of Benjamin Dorchester and daughter of Jonathan Burt, and d.
        Jan. 24, 1727.

John² Hitchcock, by wife Hannah Chapin, had:

   i.   Hannah,³ b. Sept. 10, 1668; m. Samuel Parsons.
  ii. John, b. April 13, 1670; m. Mary Ball.
 iii. Samuel, b. Aug. 21, 1672; m. Sarah Weller.
 iv. Luke, b. March 23, 1674-5; m. Elizabeth Walker.
  v. Nathaniel, b. Aug. 28, 1677; m. Abigail Lombard.
 vi. David, b. Feb. 7, 1678-9; m. Elizabeth Ball.
vii. Jonathan, b. Nov. 26, 1682; d. Feb. 26, 1683.
viii. Sarah, b. Jan. 11, 1686-7; d. April 17, 1690.

Ensign John³ Hitchcock, by wife Mary Ball, daughter of Samuel and Mary Ball, of Springfield, Mass., had:

i. John,[4] b. Dec. 14, 1692 ; m. Abigail Stebbins.
ii. Mary, b. March 20, 1694–5 ; d. young.
iii. Sarah, b. Dec. 20, 1697 ; m. Samuel Gunn, Jr.
iv. Mary, b. March 20, 1699 ; m. —— Ames.
v. Abigail, b. May 4, 1703 ; m. Samuel King.
vi. Nathaniel, b. Sept. 23, 1705 ; m. Hannah Taylor.
vii. Thankful, b. Oct. 1, 1707 ; m. Jonathan Scott.
viii. Jerusha, b. Feb. 23, 1709; m. Daniel Warner.
ix. Margaret, b. Oct. 25, 1712 ; m. —— Cooley.
x. Samuel, b. June 9, 1717 ; m. Ruth Stebbins.
xi. Mercy, b. June 9, 1717 ; m. —— Sikes.

Samuel[4] Hitchcock, by wife Ruth Stebbins, had:

i. Ruth,[5] b. Oct. 5, 1739 ; m. —— Bush.
ii. Margaret, b. May 25, 1741; m. Richard Falley, of Westfield, Mass., Dec. 24, 1761. She d. Feb. 18, 1820.
iii. Lois, b. March 1, 1742–3; m. Oliver Chapin.
iv. Samuel, b. Dec. 16, 1744 ; m. Thankful Hawks.
v. Eunice, b. Dec. 8, 1746 ; m. —— Alexander.
vi. Naomi, b. Oct. 29, 1749 ; m. —— Parsons.
vii. Arthur, b. Sept. 15, 1751 ; m. Lucy Cooley.
viii. Edithha, b. Sept. 27, 1754 ; m. —— Flagg.
ix. Elias, b. April 19, 1757 ; m. —— Ferry.
x. Oliver, b. Feb. 18, 1760 ; m. Elizabeth Hitchcock.
xi. Heman, b. Feb. 17, 1762 ; m. —— Tolman.
xii. Gaius, b. April 30, 1765 ; m. Sarah Wells.

Margaret[5] Hitchcock (Samuel,[4] John,[3] John,[2] Luke[1]), b. Westfield, Mass., May 25, 1741; died in Volney (now Fulton), N. Y., Feb. 11 or 18, 1820. She married in Westfield, Mass., Dec. 24, 1761 or 1762, *Richard Falley*, Jr., who was born in the District of Maine, at George's River, Jan. 31, 1740, and died in Westfield, Mass., Sept. 3, 1808, a son of Richard and Anna (Lamb) Falley. He commanded a company at the battle of Bunker Hill, and his eldest son Frederick[6] (afterward a Major), then fourteen years old, was his drummer, and drummed all through the fight. Previously, at the age of sixteen, he became a soldier in the French and Indian war, and at the capture of Fort Edward, on the Hudson, was made prisoner by the Indians, adopted by an Indian chief, taken to Montreal, and was finally bought by a lady for sixteen gallons of rum, and by her was sent home to Westfield, Mass. He was for many years superintendent of the Armory at Springfield, Mass., and noted as a man of powerful physique and great strength. Children, all born in Westfield and Springfield, Mass., were:

i. Lovisa[6] Falley, b. Dec. 3, 1763; m. Medad Fowler ; d. May 20, 1807.
ii. Frederick[6] Falley, b. Jan. 2, 1765 ; d. unm. July 5, 1828, in Ohio.
iii. Margaret[6] Falley, b. Nov. 15, 1766 ; m. William Cleveland ; d. Aug. 10, 1850, at Black Rock, near Buffalo, N. Y.
iv. Richard[6] Falley, b. Sept. 15, 1768 ; m. Amanda Stanley ; d. Feb. 28, 1835, in Ohio.
v. Russell[6] Falley, b. Oct. 5, 1770 ; m. Pamelia Chapman, of Blandford, Mass. ; d. March 29, 1842, in Perrysburg, Wood Co., Ohio.
vi. Daniel[6] Falley, b. Dec. 3, 1772 ; d. young.
vii. Daniel[6] Falley (again), b. Nov. 15, 1773 ; m. Elizabeth Holland, of Chester, Mass. ; d. Fulton, N. Y., at 80.
viii. Ruth[6] Falley, b. Dec. 7, 1775 ; m. Samuel Allen ; d. 1827, in New York city.
ix. Lewis[6] Falley, b. Jan. 15, 1778 ; d. unm. 1810, Charleston, S. C.
x. Samuel[6] Falley, b. Oct. 9, 1780 ; m. Ruth Root of Montgomery, Mass. ; d. 1873, Granville, O.

xi. ALEXANDER[6] FALLEY, b. April 4, 1783. Lost—not heard from after age of 35 years.

Dea. WILLIAM[6] CLEVELAND (*Aaron*,[5] *Aaron*,[4] *Aaron*,[3] *Aaron*,[2] *Moses*[1]) was born in Norwich, Conn., Dec. 20, 1770, and died at Black Rock, near Buffalo, N. Y., August 18, 1837, at the residence of his son-in-law, Hon. Lewis Falley Allen. He learned the trade of silversmith and watchmaker, and lived some time in Salem, Mass., but finally settled in Norwich, his native place. He married in ——, Mass., 1795–6, Miss *Margaret Falley*, a granddaughter of Richard Falley, who was a native of the Isle of Guernsey, France, but kidnapped when a lad at school and brought to Nova Scotia. She was born in Westfield, Mass., Nov. 15, 1776, and died at Black Rock, near Buffalo, August 10, 1850. Children were as follows:

i. FRANCIS,[7] b. Dec. 28, 1796, in Worthington, Mass.; m. Harriet Stuart, a native of Winchester, Va.
ii. WILLIAM FALLEY, b. Sept. 10, 1798, in Salem, Mass.; d. Feb. 13, 1801.
iii. MARGARET, b. Jan. 19, 1801, in Salem; m. her cousin, Hon. Lewis Falley Allen, now of Buffalo.
iv. SUSAN, b. Jan. 6, 1803, in Salem; d. in Norwich, Conn., Feb. 6, 1805.
v. RICHARD FALLEY (Rev.), b. June 19, 1804, in Norwich, Conn.; m. Anne Neale, of Baltimore, Md.
vi. SUSAN SOPHIA, b. May 7, 1809, in Norwich, Conn.; m. George D. Fuller. She d. May 30, 1838, leaving a son and a daughter.

Rev. RICHARD FALLEY[7] CLEVELAND (*William*,[6] *Aaron*,[5] *Aaron*,[4] *Aaron*,[3] *Aaron*,[2] *Moses*[1]), and in the HITCHCOCK line (*Margaret*[6] *Falley*, *Margaret*,[5] *Samuel*,[4] *John*,[3] *John*,[2] *Luke*[1]), was born in Norwich, Conn., June 19, 1804; graduated at Yale and at Princeton, N. J. He married at Baltimore, Md., Sept. 10, 1829, Miss Anne Neale, daughter of Abner and Barbara (Real) Neale, and became the pastor of a church in Windham, Conn., subsequently in Caldwell, Essex Co., N. Y., Fayetteville, Onondaga Co., N. Y., and Holland Patent, Oneida Co., N. Y., in which latter place he died, Oct. 1, 1853. She survived her husband many years, and passed away July 19, 1882, aged 78, at the old home there. Children were nine, as follows:

i. ANNE NEALE,[8] b. Baltimore, Md., July 9, 1830; m. Rev. Eurotas P. Hastings.
ii. WILLIAM NEALE (Rev.), b. Windham, Conn., April 7, 1832; m. Mrs. Anne Thomas.
iii. MARY ALLEN, b. Portsmouth, Va., Nov. 16, 1833; m. William E. Hoyt.
iv. RICHARD CECIL, b. Caldwell, N. J., July 31, 1835; lost at sea Oct. 22, 1872.
v. STEPHEN GROVER (Hon.), b. Caldwell, N. J., March 18, 1837; elected governor of New York, 1882, and president of the United States, 1884; m. at the Executive mansion in Washington, D. C., June 2, 1886, Frances, dau. of the late Oscar Folsom, Esq.,* of Buffalo, N. Y.
vi. MARGARET LOUISA, b. Caldwell, N. J., Oct. 28, 1838; m. Norval B. Bacon.
vii. LEWIS FREDERICK, b. Fayetteville, N. Y., May 2, 1841; lost at sea, Oct. 22, 1872.
viii. SUSAN SOPHIA, b. Fayetteville, N. Y., Sept. 2, 1843; m. Hon. Lucien T. Yeomans.
ix. ROSE ELIZABETH, b. Fayetteville, N. Y., June 13, 1846.

* Oscar Folsom, Esq., was a descendant in the eighth generation from John[1] Folsom (a native of Hingham, in Norfolk, England, who came to New England and settled at Hingham and afterwards removed to Exeter); through John,[2] Abraham,[3] Daniel,[4] Abraham,[5] Asa,[6] and John B.[7] his father.—See *Folsom Genealogy*, REGISTER, XXX. 207–31.

JOHN HOBSON, OR HOPSON, OF GUILFORD, CONN., AND HIS DESCENDANTS.

Compiled by Hon. RALPH D. SMYTH, and communicated by Dr. BERNARD C. STEINER.

1. JOHN[1] HOBSON came to Guilford probably about 1660. He may have been a son of John Hobson of Rowley, Mass. On June 1, 1665, he was made constable, and on Sept. 20, 1667, he was chairman of a committee of six to search and report what lands in the town were suitable for a third division. On Feb. 19, 1667-8, he was made townsman, and reelected until 1671. He appears to have rented the Whitfield or Major Thompson farm, and Nov. 22, 1706, sold 84¼ acres of land for rent of the farm. No home lot is recorded to him until about 1690, when he bought one of Aaron Blachley, containing nine acres and seven rods of upland and swamp, between the land of the Wrights, Hughes, Thompson, and Abraham Cruttenden. On Aug. 12, 1685, he was appointed ordinary keeper. In 1671 he was on the committee to run the boundary between Guilford and Branford; and was made planter, Dec. 11, 1672. He married first, Sarah ———, who died Sept. 8, 1669; married second, Dec. 9, 1672, Elizabeth, daughter of Edward Shipman of Saybrook, who died in 1683; and married third, Elizabeth, daughter of John Allin of New Haven. He died July 3, 1701.

Children by first wife:

2. i. JOHN,[2] b. Mch. 16, 1665-6; d. Jan. 12, 1730-1.
   ii. FRANCES, d. Mch., 1673.

   Children by second wife:

   iii. ELIZABETH, b. June 22, 1674; d, Jan. 28, 1752; m. in 1694, Comfort Starr, who d. May 1, 1743.
   iv. ABIGAIL, b. Dec. 16, 1679; d. young.

   Child by third wife:

3. v. SAMUEL, b. Jan. 10, 1683-4.

2. LIEUT. JOHN[2] HOPSON, JR. (*John*[1]), of Guilford, married first, Feb. 28, 1700, Dorothy, daughter of William Lord of Saybrook, who died Oct. 12, 1705; and married second, Feb. 5, 1707, Dorothy, daughter of Andrew Leete. He was a glazier and tavern keeper. In 1716, his list was £90.

   Children, by first wife:

4. i. JOHN,[3] b. Mch. 22, 1703; d. Dec. 27, 1771.
   ii. SARAH, b. Aug. 14, 1705; m. June 28, 1731, Hezekiah Parmelee of New Haven.

3. LIEUT. SAMUEL[2] HOPSON (*John*[1]), of Guilford, married first, Jan. 20, 1710, Mary Fowler, who died Oct. 17, 1717; married second, Jan. 25, 1726, Anne, daughter of William Leete; and married third, Mercy, daughter of John Collins, Jr. His list in 1716 was £48.

   Child by first wife:

   i. SAMUEL,[3] b. Oct. 21, 1710; of Woodbury, 1750, and Wallingford, 1760.

Children by second wife:

ii. ANN, b. Dec. 23, 1727.
iii. WILLIAM, b. May 3, 1729.
iv. SARAH, b. June 29, 1731.
v. MARY, b. Aug. 4, 1737.
vi. HANNAH, b. Apr. 2, 1740.
vii. JOHN, b. Sept. 29, 1741.
viii. JORDAN, b. Sept. 21, 1745.

4. JOHN[3] HOPSON (*John,[2] John[1]*), of Guilford, married, Feb. 15, 1726, Deborah, daughter of Daniel Bartlett, who died May 12, 1783.

Children :

5. i. JOHN,[4] b. Apr. 6, 1727; d. Aug. 2, 1786.
   ii. NATHANIEL, b. Oct. 12, 1729; d. Oct. 20, 1729.
   iii. NATHANIEL, b. Mch. 7, 1731; d. Oct. 7, 1736.
6. iv. EBENEZER, b. Feb. 18, 1734; d. Aug. 8, 1808.
   v. DEBORAH, b. Oct. 22, 1736; d. Apr. 5, 1765; m. Apr. 13, 1759, Daniel Hubbard, who d. Mch. 19, 1819.
   vi. TIMOTHY, b. Jan. 25, 1739; d. while at Yale College, Oct. 4, 1756.

5. CAPT. JOHN[4] HOPSON (*John,[3] John,[2] John[1]*), of Guilford, served in the Revolutionary war, and lived in that part of the town then called North Bristol, now North Madison. He married, Apr. 6, 1749, Millicent, daughter of Gideon Chittenden, who died Dec. 6, 1814.

Children :

i. JOHN,[5] b. July 16, 1750; d. Nov. 8, 1751.
ii. SARAH, b. Sept. 4, 1752; m. in 1771, Noadiah Norton of North Bristol, who d. May 15, 1805.
iii. JOHN, b. Feb. 14, 1755; d. Apr. 15, 1820; lived in North Bristol, where he was deacon; m. Eunice, dau. of Nathan Wilcox of Killingworth, who was b. June 14, 1749, and d. Apr. 11, 1792. Children: 1. *Theodore,[6]* b. Aug. 4, 1788; m. Apr. 6, 1814, Matilda, dau. of Abner Bishop, and had five children. 2. *Nathan Wilcox,* b. Feb. 16, 1792; d. Sept. 7, 1847; m. May 2, 1815, Lucy M., dau. of Edmund Hand, who d. Oct. 6, 1841. They had two daus.
iv. MILLICENT, b. Aug. 4, 1756; d. Apr. 12, 1828; m. Daniel Meigs of East Guilford, who d. May 12, 1822.
v. DEBORAH, b. Dec. 31, 1759; d. May 9, 1779; m. Feb. 4, 1778, Capt. Heman Brainard of Higganum, who d. July 8, 1808; had one child, *Deborah Hopson,* b. Jan. 5, 1779
vi. HULDAH, b. Dec. 18, 1761; d. Jan. 18, 1842.

6. EBENEZER[4] HOPSON (*John,[3] John,[2] John[1]*), of Guilford, married first, Mch. 8, 1764, Mercy Davis, who died Sept. 5, 1772 ; and married second, Nov. 24, 1776, Eunice Parmele, who died Mch. 29, 1817.

Children by first wife :

i. MARY,[5] b. June 30, 1765; d. in 1841; m. Oct. 28, 1784, Gen. Eli Fowler, who resided in Branford, and d. Sept. 30. 1850.
ii. TIMOTHY, b. July 19, 1767; d. Aug. 28, 1769.
iii. NANCY, b. Sept. 29, 1770; d. Nov. 6, 1856; m. Jan. 3, 1789, Ambrose Graves of Guilford, who d. May 6, 1848.

Children by second wife :

iv. WILLIAM, b. Sept. 19, 1777; d. June 19, 1786.
v. EUNICE, b. Nov. 21, 1780; d. Apr. 27, 1788.
vi. TIMOTHY, b. July 9, 1785; d. single, Mch. 14, 1817.
vii. WILLIAM, b. Jan. 27, 1788; d. Jan. 25, 1798.
viii. EBENEZER, b. Jan. 11, 1792; d. Sept. 30, 1828; m. Feb., 1828, Olivia Pratt, dau. of William Stone; no children.

JOHN HODGKIN OF GUILFORD, CONN., AND HIS DESCENDANTS.

Compiled by Hon. RALPH D. SMYTH, and communicated by Dr. BERNARD C. STEINER.

1. JOHN[1] HODGKIN came from County Essex, England, and arrived at Guilford as Gov. Leete's man, about 1648. He was admitted to the oath of fidelity, May 11, 1654. He married, Apr. 4, 1670, Mary, daughter of John Bishop, and died in Jan., 1681/2. On Sept. 7, 1654, he was made one of the "two cow keepers appointed to keep the young cattle beyond East River." After his death, his widow married twice; first, Isaac Johnson, July 16, 1682, and second, after his death, which occurred Oct. 28, 1687, ——— Field. On Nov. 3, 1696, the East Creek land of John Hodgkin, which amounted to 10 acres 3 roods and 3 rods, and was inventoried at £25, was delivered to his eldest son John,[2] and, as his double portion amounted to £13 only, he contracted to pay " when orderly demanded " his sister Mary her full portion, viz : £6. 10. 0 in current pay, and to give his brother Thomas the remainder of the estate, viz.: £5. 10. in land when the latter " shall come of age to receive his portion & orderly demand it."

Children :

i. JOHN,[2] b. Apr. 12, 1671; d. Jan. 18, 1727; m. Mch. 10, 1697, Mary Hull, who d. "an antientwoman," Nov. 12, 1750; no children. His list was £74. 3. 9. in 1716.

ii. MARY, b. Dec. 9, 1672; m. Barnabas Beers of Stratford.

iii. ELIZABETH, b. 1674; m. Christopher West, Mar. 17, 1709, and had a dau. *Mary.*

2. iv. JOSEPH, b. July 1, 1675; d. May 28, 1756.

v. THOMAS, b. 1677; d. Apr. 25, 1754; m. in 1708, Abigail, dau. of John Parmelee, who d. Oct. 22, 1766; no children. He lived in East Guilford, and was listed at £79. 13. 6 in 1716, and his weaving trade was assessed at £3. He owned 3 acres of land near Fence Creek, bought July 9, 1708.

2. JOSEPH[2] HODGKIN (*John*[1]), of Guilford, married first, Mch. 1, 1704, Elizabeth Hill ; and married second, Hannah ———, who died June 15, 1759. His list in 1716 was £54. 15. 6.

Children :

3. i. ABRAHAM,[3] b. Feb. 4, 1705; d. Mch. 6, 1770.

ii. MARY, b. May 11, 1706; m. ——— Curtiss.

4. iii. JANNA, b. Apr. 7, 1709; d. June 5, 1757.

5. iv. JOSEPH, b. Mch. 2, 1711; d. Aug. 9, 1752.

v. JOHN, b. Nov. 30, 1714; lived in Wallingford; m. Nov. 13, 1745, wid. Sarah Chub; no children.

6. vi. NOAH, b. Oct. 14, 1716; d. May 4, 1783.

vii. ELIZABETH, b. Jan. 14, 1720; d. Sept. 21, 1802; m. (1) Benjamin Chittenham, who d. in 1760; m. (2) Mar. 9, 1761, Daniel Norton, who d. Dec. 4, 1789.

7. viii. EBENEZER, b. June 20, 1722; d. Nov. 23, 1794.

3. ABRAHAM[3] HODGKIN (*Joseph,*[2] *John*[1]) married Jan. 17, 1730, Hannah, daughter of John Maltbie of Saybrook, who died Dec. 1, 1779. Their children were :

i. ABRAHAM,[4] b. Apr. 9, 1731; m. Sarah Stone, Mch. 20, 1755. Children : 1. *Sarah,*[5] b. Apr. 28, 1756. 2. *Joseph,* b. Nov. 27, 1758. 3. *Nabby,* b. Jan. 3, 1762. 4. *Roswell,* b. May 25, 1765. 5. *Abraham,* b. Dec. 18, 1766. 6. *Abner,* b. Aug. 7, 1772. 7. *Oliver,* b. Oct. 16, 1774.

ii. HANNAH, b. Feb. 16, 1733; m. Nov. 1, 1753, John Bishop.
iii. JOHN, b. 1736; d. Feb. 23, 1737.
iv. JANE, b. May 9, 1738; m. Edward Lewis, Sept. 7, 1757.
v.   SAMUEL, b. Apr. 21, 1743; of Cornwall, N. Y.; m. Mary ――――
     Children: 1. *Mary.*⁵ 2. *Sarah.* 3. *Hannah.* 4. *Samuel.*
vi. LYDIA, b. Nov. 7, 1745; m. Jan. 14, 1768, John Hall.

4. JANNA³ HODGKINS (*Joseph,*² *John*¹), of Killingworth, married in 1729, Sarah Edwards of East Hampton, who died July 3, 1753. Children:

i.   MARY,⁴ b. Aug. 6, 1730; m. Jan. 3, 1753, Daniel Rutty of Killingworth.
ii. LUCY, b. Feb. 21, 1732.
iii. THOMAS, b. Oct. 9, 1733; d. July 5, 1753.
iv. SARAH, b. Aug. 27, 1735; d. Aug. 9, 1753.
v.   ELIZABETH, b. Jan. 2, 1737-8.
vi. ANNE, b. Apr. 8, 1741.

5. JOSEPH³ HODGKIN, JR. (*Joseph*², *John*¹) married Feb. 21, 1737, Lydia, daughter of Theophilus Redfield, and died Dec. 16, 1784, aged 68. She married second, Nov. 15, 1753, Levi Leete. Children:

i.   ABIGAIL,⁴ b. Sept. 28, 1738; m. (1) Edmund Ward, Jr., who was lost at sea in 1765; m. (2) William Johnson, who was killed in the Revolutionary War.
ii. THOMAS, b. July 26, 1740; d. May 27, 1825; m. June 1, 1758, Elizabeth Parmelee, who died Dec. 14, 1787. Children: 1. *Joseph,*⁵ b. Oct. 3, 1759; d. in camp in 1776. 2. *John,* bapt. Sept. 4, 1761. 3. *Ambrose,* b. 1763; lived in Simsbury. 4. *Eunice,* bapt. July 14, 1765. 5. *Thomas,* b. 1767; d. Jan. 1802.

6. NOAH³ HODGKIN (*Joseph,*² *John*¹) married, Mch. 2, 1741, Hannah, daughter of Dea. Seth Morse, who died July 10, 1794. Children:

i.   NOAH,⁴ b. Sept. 22, 1742; m. Mch 27, 1762, Elizabeth Kimberly. Children: 1. *Noah,*⁵ b. Nov. 5, 1763; m. Mereb Turner, and had a dau. *Sally,*⁶ bapt. Nov. 13, 1796. 2. *Elizabeth,* b. Dec. 16, 1765; m. Oct. 23, 1787, Phinehas Meigs of Durham. 3. *Hannah,* b. Sept. 25, 1768; d. Oct. 27, 1769. 4. *George,* b. Sept. 4, 1772. 5. *Seth,* b. May 1, 1776; m. Stella Hale. 6. *Harvey,* b. Feb. 18, 1779.
ii. SETH, b. Sept. 18, 1743; d. Sept. 14, 1751.
iii. ELIZABETH, b. Oct. 19, 1745; d. Sept. 5, 1751.
iv. HANNAH, b. July 30, 1750; d. Aug. 28, 1751.
v.   LOIS, b. July 30, 1750; d. Aug. 27, 1751.
vi. Rev. BERIAH, b. Mch. 27, 1752; m. Thankful Dickinson of Haddon, Sept. 4, 1774; pastor of the Fourth Guilford Church, 1784 to 1789, and then at Greenville, N. Y., from 1783 to 1824 or '25; d. Feb. 1829, aged 77. Children: 1. *Beriah,*⁵ of Prattsburg, N. Y. 2. *Joseph,* b. Feb. 20, 1778; of Pultney, N. Y. 3. *Rev. James Harvey,* author of "Congregational and Presbyterian Ministers of Western New York."
vii. JOSEPH, b. Mch. 30, 1754; d. Jan. 2, 1755.
viii. JOSEPH, b. Jan. 2, 1755.

7. EBENEZER³ HODGKIN (*Joseph,*² *John*¹) married first, Nov. 15, 1744, Jerusha, widow of John Hall, who died May 29, 1790; and married second, Sarah ――――. Children, all by first wife:

i.   REUBEN,⁴ b. Mch. 5, 1750; d. Oct. 8, 1825; m. Prudence Seward, who d. Dec. 7, 1815. Children: 1. *Wealthy,*⁵ b. 1779; m. Edmund Frisbie. 2. *Ruth,* b. Jan., 1781; d. Mch. 22, 1835; m. Cal-

172

vin Crampton, Feb. 22, 1808. 3. *Amanda*, b. Nov. 5, 1784; d. Oct. 21, 1835; m. Sept. 10, 1804, Jedidiah Parker of Guilford, who d. Feb. 12, 1853. 4. *Harvey*, b. 1795; m. (1) Mariah Hunt, who d. July 27, 1817, aged 25; m. (2) May, 1819, Almira Hunt, who d. Oct. 23, 1828, aged 27. He d. Mch. 25, 1830. Children by second wife: i. David Alonzo.[6] ii. Ruth M., b. Oct. 10, 1822; d. Aug. 31, 1849; m. Herman M. Painter, June 15, 1845.

    ii.   Dea. EBENEZER, b. Oct. 2, 1758; lived in Richmond, Mass.; m. Jan. 16, 1791, Ruth Hubbard. Children: 1. *Jerusha*,[5] b. July 7, 1792. 2. *Rev. John*, b. 1795; lived in Lenox, Mass.; d. Feb. 19, 1862; had six or seven children. 3. *Maria*. 4. *Rev. Ebenezer*, b. 1803; many years missionary to the Choctaws; d. at Lenox, Mass., Oct. 28, 1867. 5. *Frederic*.

SAMUEL HODGKINS, OR HOTCHKISS, OF NEW HAVEN, CONN., AND HIS DESCENDANTS.

Compiled by Hon. RALPH D. SMYTH, and communicated by Dr. BERNARD C. STEINER.

1. SAMUEL[1] HODGKINS was living at New Haven, Mch. 2, 1648, and died there, Dec. 28, 1663. He married, Sept. 7, 1642, Elizabeth Caverly.
    Children:

  2. i.   JOHN,[2] b. 1643; d. 1689; will proved Sept. 23, 1689.
  3. ii.   SAMUEL, b. 1645; d. 1705; at Guilford Town Meeting, Feb. 22, 1668, it was voted to accept him as a planter, but it does not appear that he came.
    iii.   JAMES, b. 1647.
    iv.   Ens. JOSHUA, b. Sept. 16, 1651, of New Haven; d. 1722; m. (1) Mary Pardee, Nov. 29, 1699; m. (2) Hannah Tuttle, May 3, 1709.
    v.   THOMAS, b. Nov. 31, 1654, of Sperry's Farms; d. Dec. 21, 1711; m. Nov. 27, 1677, Sarah Wilmott.
    vi.   DANIEL, b. Mch. 9, 1657; of New Haven; d. Mch. 10, 1712; m. June 6, 1683, Esther Sperry.

2. JOHN[2] HOTCHKISS (*Samuel*[1]), of New Haven, married, Dec. 5, 1672, Elizabeth Peck.
    Children:

  4. i.   JOHN,[3] b. Oct. 11, 1673.
  5. ii.   JOSHUA, b. 1675; d. 1741.
  6. iii.   JOSEPH, b. June 3, 1678; d. Jan. 31, 1740.
    iv.   JOSIAH, b. July 24, 1680; lived in Cheshire in 1704; d. 1733; m. ———, who d. 1732.
  7. v.   CALEB, b. Oct. 18, 1684.
    vi.   ELIZABETH, b. July 18, 1686.

3. SAMUEL[2] HOTCHKISS, of East Haven, married, in 1676, Sarah Talmage.
    Children:

    i.   MARY,[3] b. Jan. 1, 1679.
    ii.   SARAH, b. Apr. 7, 1681.
    iii.   SAMUEL, b. Mch. 6, 1683.
    iv.   JAMES, b. Dec. 8, 1684.
    v.   ABIGAIL, b. Feb. 12, 1686.

4. CAPT. JOHN[3] HOTCHKISS (*John*,[2] *Samuel*[1]), of Cheshire, married Mary Chatterton, in 1694.

Children :

i. JOHN,[4] b. 1694; of Cheshire; m. Miriam Wood.
ii. HENRY, of Cheshire.
iii. JOSIAH, of Cheshire; d. 1732.

5. JOSHUA[3] HOTCHKISS (*John*,[2] *Samuel*[1]), of New Haven, married Susanna Chatterton.

Children :

i. JOSHUA,[4] b. 1773; of New Haven; d. June 17, 1795.
ii. CALEB, m. Phebe ———, who d. at New Haven, Feb. 19, 1795, aged 80.

6. JOSEPH[3] HOTCHKISS (*John*,[2] *Samuel*[1]), of Guilford, weaver, married, in April, 1699, Hannah, daughter of Isaac Cruttenden, who died Mch. 28, 1756. In 1716 his list was £50. 11s., and his weaver's faculty was assessed at £2. He removed to Guilford about the time of his marriage, and owned several tracts of land there.

Children :

i. JOSEPH,[4] b. Sept. 3, 1700; d. Sept. 5, 1740; m. in 1725, Thankful Stone, who d. Sept. 14, 1751. Children : 1. *Ezekiel*,[5] b. Mch. 14, 1726; of New Haven. 2. *Daniel*, b. July 2, 1728; of Wallingford. 3. *Rachel*, b. Mch. 18, 1730; d. Aug. 15, 1802; m. Miles[5] Hotchkiss, her cousin, Dec. 1, 1748. 4. *John*, b. 1732; lived in Guilford; d. Oct. 30, 1799; m. Apr. 20, 1756, Obedience, dau. of Joseph Stone, who d. May 28, 1797. 5. *Mary*, b. 1735; d. Mch. 18, 1743. 6. *Thankful*, b. Oct. 22, 1736 (?); m. Sept. 3, 1755, Elihu Stone of Branford and Litchfield. 7. *Joseph*, b. Oct. 22, 1736; of Wallingford. 8. *Amos*, b. Jan. 2, 1739; removed to Vermont; m. (1) Mch. 19, 1760, Desire Dowd, who d. Feb. 1, 1797; m. (2) ———, who d. Aug. 26, 1805. 9. *Ebenezer*, b. Jan. 5, 1741; d. Nov. 23, 1760.
ii. ISAAC, b. Dec. 25, 1702; d. Sept. 17, 1752; m. July 8, 1724, Elizabeth, dau. of Josiah Avered; lived in Woodbury in 1740. Children : 1. *Isaac*,[5] b. July 1, 1725; d. Oct. 26, 1755. 2. *Miles*, b. Feb. 11, 1728; d. May 13, 1810; m. his cousin, Rachel[5] Hotchkiss; his house was burnt Sept. 7, 1796; no children. 3. *Elizabeth*, b. Oct. 7, 1731; d. Mch. 29, 1818; m. Elon Lee, of Meriden, May 16, 1750, who. d. May 10, 1806. 4. *Lucy*, b. Dec. 1, 1736; m. ——— Norton, of Winchester.
iii. WAIT, b. Jan. 18, 1704; m. Nov. 2, 1731, Sarah Bishop, who d. Apr. 24, 1761; removed to Wolcott after the death of his wife. Children : 1. *Wait*,[5] b. Nov. 18, 1733; removed to Waterbury and Wolcott, before 1770; m. Oct. 16, 1759, Lydia Webster of Bolton. 2. *Lois*, b. Oct. 5, 1735; d. Mch. 9, 1818; m. Phinehas Johnson, Dec. 11, 1760. 3. *Sarah*, b. June 5, 1738; d. Feb. 5, 1746. 4. *Selah*, b. Dec. 24, 1742; m. Rebecca ———.
iv. HANNAH, b. Sept. 13, 1707; d. July 20, 1793; m. Jan. 7, 1730, Joseph Stone, Jr., of Guilford, who d. Sept. 18, 1774.
v. DEBORAH, b. Jan. 18, 1710; d. young.
vi. MILES, b. July 28, 1712; d. young.
vii. MARK, b. July 1, 1714; of Guilford; d. Nov. 19, 1775; m. (1) Dec. 25, 1739, Margaret Crawford, who d. Jan. 7, 1750; m. (2) Jan. 8, 1751, Miriam Lee, who d. Mch. 31, 1788. Children by first wife : 1. *Deborah*,[5] b. Feb. 23, 1743; m. ——— Sanford, of New Milford. 2. *Mary*, b. Oct. 13, 1746; d. young. Children by second wife : 3. *Timothy*, b. Jan. 11, 1752; d. in the Revolutionary war in a prison ship. 4. *Eunice*, b. 1754; d. Feb. 27, 1827; m. May 23, 1770, William Lee of Guilford, who d. Apr. 29, 1795. 5. *Isaac*, b. Oct. 7, 1756; lived in Guilford; d. Aug. 28, 1835; m. Jan. 5, 1783, Ann Spinning, who. d. Aug. 17, 1844. 6. *Ira*, b. May 10, 1758; of Branford; d. 1826; m. Mch. 30, 1782, Abigail Frisbie, who d. Feb.

18, 1836. 7. *Eber*, b. May 26, 1762; of Guilford; d. Sept. 2, 1832; m. (1) Leah Page, who d. Sept. 11, 1794; m. (2) Sarah Whiting, who d. Jan. 29, 1830, aged 65.

7. CALEB³ HOTCHKISS (*John*,² *Samuel*¹), of New Haven, married, Feb. 14, 1706, Mehitable, daughter of Isaac Cruttenden.
Children :

 i. MEHITABLE,⁴ b. Nov. 24, 1706; d. Nov. 2, 1725.
 ii. RACHEL, b. Oct. 26, 1709.
 iii. CALEB, b. June 6, 1712; d. July, 1779, killed by British soldiers, at New Haven; m. Jan. 6, 1736, Mehitable Atwater, who d. Mch. 18, 1804. Children: 1. *Stephen*,⁵ b. Nov. 4, 1737. 2. *Mehitable*, b. Mch. 31, 1742. 3. *Jonah*, b. June 12, 1745; m. Elizabeth Atwater, Mch. 18, 1772. 4. *Amos*.
 iv. ELIPHALET, b. June 28, 1714.
 v. JOEL, b. Mch. 18, 1716; m. Sarah ———; d. 1777; eight or more children.
 vi. NEHEMIAH, b. Apr. 20, 1719.

HODGKIN GENEALOGY: ADDITIONS.—The following genealogy extends the line of Beniah⁵ Hotchkin (Hodgkin) (6, vi, 1) as given in "John Hodgkin of Guilford, Conn., and His Descendants," by Hon. Ralph D. Smyth, in the REG- * ISTER, vol. 58, p. 282.
As stated by Hon. Ralph D. Smyth, in his "History of Guilford, Conn.," 1877, p. 29, "John Hodgkin's descendants gradually modified the name in Hotchkin." Rev. James Hervey⁵ Hotchkin, grandson of Noah⁴ Hotchkin, in a letter (now in possession of the contributor) written 19 March 1849 to his grandson, Dr. Gurdon Beriah⁷ Hotchkin, stated "Our name was originally spelled 'Hodgkin.' My grandfather, Noah, spelt it 'Hochkin.' My father, Rev. Beriah, inserted the 't', and this is the present spelling in our different branches of the family." This spelling is confirmed by an original letter (also in the possession of the contributor) of Rev. Beriah⁶ Hotchkin written to his son, Rev. James H.⁶ Hotchkin, in November 1813, in which the names, both in address and signature, are spelled "Hotchkin."

Thus, while Hon. Ralph D. Smyth, to be consistent in his tabuation in the REGISTER, spelled all the names "Hodgkin," the above quoted letters show the names of Beriah⁴ and James Hervey,⁵ as written by those men themselves, to have already been changed to the present form.

REV. JAMES HERVEY¹ HOTCHKIN (*Rev. Beriah*,⁴ *Noah*³ *Hochkin*, *Joseph*² *Hodgkin*, *John*¹ *Hodgkin*), B.A. (Williams, 1800), pastor of the Presbyterian Church at West Bloomfield, N. Y., and at Prattsburg, N. Y., 1809–1830; first president of the Board of Commissioners of Auburn Theolog-

*Page 172, this volume.

ical Seminary; author of "History of the Purchase and Settlement of Western New York," born at Cornwall, Conn., 23 Feb. 1781, died at Prattsburg 21 Sept. 1851. He married 16 Sept. 1804 Rebecca Hall, who died at Prattsburg 12 Mar. 1856.

Children:
2. i.   BERIAH BISHOP,[6] b. at West Bloomfield 18 Dec. 1805.
    ii.   JAMES HERVEY, b. at West Bloomfield 16 May 1808.
    iii. AUGUSTINE HALL, b. at Prattsburg 1 Nov. 1810.
    iv. JOHN NILES, b. at Prattsburg 2 Oct. 1813.
    v.   SAMUEL, b. at Prattsburg 4 May 1817.
    vi. WILLIAM HENRY, b. at Prattsburg 25 Oct. 1820. His son, Samuel, married a niece of Hon. William H. Seward, and settled in Kansas.

2. REV. BERIAH BISHOP[6] HOTCHKIN (*Rev. James Henry,[5] Rev. Beriah,[4] Noah[3] Hochkin, Joseph[2] Hodgkin, John[1] Hodgkin*), editor of a newspaper at LeRoy, N. Y., pastor of the Presbyterian Church at Sequoit, N. Y., Potsdam, N. Y., and for many years previous to his death a writer of religious books and a contributor of articles to religious journals, born at West Bloomfield, N. Y., 18 Dec. 1805, died, as a result of being struck by a vehicle in Philadelphia, 13 Oct. 1878. He married Elizabeth Alice Fitch, born at Burlington, Vt., 23 July 1807, daughter of Samuel Fitch.

Children:
    i.   ALICE REBECCA,[7] b. at LeRoy 26 May 1828; d. in Philadelphia, Pa., 29 Apr. 1914.
3. ii.   GURDON BERIAH, b. at Clinton, N. Y., 12 Nov. 1830.
    iii. REV. SAMUEL FITCH, Protestant Episcopal minister for many years at Bustleton, Pa., writer of many volumes of local history of the suburbs of Philadelphia, b. at Sequoit, N. Y., 2 Apr. 1833; d. at Bustleton in 1913.
    iv. HELEN, b. at Sequoit, N. Y., 2 Nov. 1834; d. in Philadelphia, Pa., 22 Jan. 1898. With her sister she conducted for many years a private school for girls at Marple, Pa.

3. DR. GURDON BERIAH[7] HOTCHKIN (*Rev. Beriah Bishop,[6] Rev. James Hervey,[5] Rev. Beriah,[4] Noah[3] Hochkin, Joseph[2] Hodgkin, John[1] Hodgkin*), M.D. (University of Pensylvania, 1855), physician, surgeon in the First Pennsylvania Volunteer Cavalry at the outbreak of the Civil War, later chief surgeon of that regiment until the close of the War, active participant in religious and temperance work, organizer and teacher of a Sabbath School for negroes, born at Clinton, N. Y., 12 Nov. 1830, died at Altoona, Pa., 12 Mar. 1915. He married at Media, Pa., 15 Nov. 1855, SARAH JANE COCHRAN, born at Radnor, Pa., 15 Sept. 1833, died at Duncansville, Pa., 25 Oct. 1891, daughter of Isaac and Ann (Hawkins) Cochran.

Children:
    i.   ELIZABETH ALICE,[8] b. at Media, Pa., 11 Sept. 1863; unmarried.
    ii. WILLIAM ROWLAND, of Montclair, N. J., advertising and merchandising executive for John Wanamaker and Gimbel Brothers in Philadelphia and New York City, general merchandising counsel for retailers, former president of The Sphinx Club, New York City, author of various books and of many articles on merchandising and advertising in trade papers, b. at Huntingdon, Pa., 6 June 1868; m. at Altoona, Pa., 19 June 1895, EMMA JANE BLACK, b. at Altoona 27 Aug. 1870, daughter of James A. and Tamar (VanAlman) Black.
       Child:
       1. *James Rowland,* of Montclair, S.B. (Massachusetts Institute of Technology, 1921), manufacturer of mechanical accessories at Irvington, N. J., b. in Philadelphia 8 Feb. 1899; m. 10 Oct. 1931 Betty Beggs, b. at Glen Ridge, N. J., 6 Oct. 1908, daughter of John and Cora (Paige) Beggs.
       Three children died in infancy.

Montclair, N. J.   WILLIAM ROWLAND HOTCHKIN.

HOISINGTON.—John Hossenton (or Hoisington) was residing at Farmington, Conn., in 1713, where children were born, viz. : i. John, b. Nov. 5, 1713. ii. Sarah, b. April 6, 1715. iii. Elizabeth, b. June 20, 1717. iv. Elisha, b. Nov. 8, 1719. v. James, b. Dec. 10, 1721. vi. Thankfull, b. Sept. 1, 1724. vii. Nathaniel, b. Feb. 18, 1726-7. viii. Joab. ix. Ebenezer, b. about 1730.

The name is found in Farmington records as Hossenton, Horsington and Hoisington, and appears to relate to the same family ; the last is the recent spelling. What is known of the ancestry and previous residence of this family ? What are the dates of births of sons Joab and Ebenezer ? These last emigrated to Windsor, Vt., about 1765.

John Hassenton, described as of Hadley, Mass., took freeman's oath, Feb. 8, 1678-9. See REG., vol. iv. p. 25 (1850). What is known of his ancestry, family and descendants ? Was *John* of Farmington of his descendents ? Address,
Monmouth, Ill. ALMON KIDDER.

A LETTER OF DIRECTIONS TO HIS FATHER'S BIRTH-PLACE, BY JOHN HOLMES, OF HADDAM, CONN.—1725.

This Letter of Directions—from John Holmes—in Haddam—in New England—for to find—the place where his Father—was Born and—Brought vp In London : He was Son to Thomas Holmes—Councler of Grase—in* Who Liued in Saint-Tandrs†—parrich in Holborn—in the Roson Crown Cort‡—in Grasen Lain§ upper site—a Gainst Grasin walks—His Mother's Maden Name was Mary Thetford. Grandfather was Slain in the Time of the Seuel warrs—att Oxford Sege—Our : Cort : of : arms are the 3 Spord Coks fighting in a Golden feild—My father Came out of England in the Time of the Grat plage —and he thought to haue gon Down into Norfolk—to a place caled Lyn whare—we had a Small pece of Land—one Edmond Beel—was Tennant and had been for many years before but all places being garded he Culd Not pass—whear upon he Came for uirjaney‖—thenking to have Returned—in a fue years—But it was other ways ordered —for the Contry proued unhelthy to : him and he was poor and Low in the World—after a while he Recruted—and as It was ordred—Marred —in New york To one Lucrese Dodly—Dafter to—Mr.—Thomas Dodley—of London, who keep the tanes Cort¶—in—Clare Streat** in Common Gardin†† in London. She had Two—Brothers—But She Died—a bout 6—and thirty year a Go—my father Died—in Dec^m 12th—1724— Being a uery aged man—my father so long as he Liued he Liued in hopes of seeing England a Gain—But he is Dead an Gon and Left but only me his Son. being thirty—8—years—of age— — . These Directions Taken by John Holmes on his father's Death bead.

[A copy of the foregoing Letter was inserted in the *Register*, vol. x. p. 242. This appears to have been in many particulars incorrect. D. Williams Patterson, formerly of West Winsted, Conn., but now of Newark Valley, N. Y., a well known antiquary and genealogist, has prepared an exact transcript of the original Letter of Directions, which he has had published in New York, in a tasty manner, with notes, being No. 1 of the publications of the " U. Q. Club." (See Book Notices in this number.)

Instead of making corrections and placing them in the errata, as is usual, it was thought better to reprint the Letter entire, as given by Mr. Patterson. A few explanations, taken from the notes made by the above named gentleman, are appended as foot-notes.

We learn from the genealogy annexed, in the pamphlet by Mr. Patterson, that Thomas[2] Holmes, who was the father of John,[3] the writer of the letter, died at the age of 98. John,[3] b. in New London, Conn.,

---

* Gray's Inn.
† St. Andrew's Parish.
‡ Rose and Crown Court.
§ Gray's Inn Lane.
‖ Virginia.
¶ Probably the tennis court.
** " Clare street, in London, lies nearly midway between Covent Garden Market, and Lincoln's Inn Fields."
†† Supposed to be " Covent Garden."

March 11, 1686–7, m. Feb. 11, 1706–7, Mary Willey, dau. of John
and Miriam (Moore) Willey, and died in East Haddam May 29, 1734.
Children : *Thomas,*[4] b. Dec. 4, 1707, m. Jan. 9, 1732, Lucy Knowlton,
dau. of Lieut. Thomas and Susannah Knowlton ; *John,*[4] b. Feb. 24,
1708–9, m. Lucretia Willey, dau. of John and Elizabeth (Harvey)
Willey, and had two sons and one daughter ; *Lucretia,*[4] b. July 14,
1711 ; tradition says that she m. a man named Willey, who died soon
after marriage, and that then she m. Joseph Willey, son of John and
Elizabeth (Harvey) Willey, and it is verified by the record, which
shows that Joseph Willey m. May 22, 1727, Lucretia Willey. She
had a daughter Elizabeth. He had a second wife, Rebecca, by whom
he had nine children ; *Mary,*[4] b. Feb. 7, 1712–13, m. Abel Willey, son
of Abel and Hannah (Bray) Willey, and had four children who are
mentioned ; *Christopher,*[4] b. June 4, 1715, m. March 2, 1736, Sarah
Andrews, dau. of Samuel and Eleanor (Lee) Andrews ; *Grace,*[4] b.
Aug. 4, 1717, m. March 2, 1736, Robert Hungerford, son of John and
Deborah (Spencer) Hungerford, and had ten children ; *Eliphalet,*[4] b.
July 12, 1722, m. Jan. 25, 1742, Damaris Waterhouse. He d. Nov.
30, 1743, and his widow m. (2d) Joseph Comstock, of East Haddam,
by whom she had five children ; *Sarah,*[4] b. June 14, 1726, m. Na-
thaniel Niles ; *Abigail,*[4] b. Aug. 1, 1729, d. Aug. 26, 1811, unmarried.
EDITOR.]

ANCESTORS OF REV. SAMUEL HOPKINS, D.D., OF NEWPORT, AND THEIR CHILDREN.

[Communicated by SYLVESTER JUDD, Esq., of Northampton.]

JOHN HOPKINS settled at Cambridge in 1634, was admitted freeman in 1635, and removed to Hartford in 1636. He died in 1654, leaving a widow, Jane, and two children, Stephen and Bethia. The widow married Nathaniel Ward, of Hadley, and the daughter married in 1652, Samuel Stocking, of Middletown, and, after his decease, James Steele, of Hartford. John Hopkins may have been related to Edward Hopkins, Esq., of Hartford.

STEPHEN HOPKINS, only son of John, married Dorcas Bronson, daughter of John Bronson, of Farmington, and resided at Hartford. He died in 1689, and his widow in 1697. He names, in his will, six children, viz.: John, Stephen, Ebenezer, Joseph, Dorcas, Webster, and Mary Hopkins.

JOHN HOPKINS, son of Stephen, settled in Waterbury, where he died, Nov. 4, 1732. His wife died May 30, 1730. Their children were : — John, b. March 29, 1686 ; Consider, b. March 29, 1687 ; Stephen, b. Nov. 19, 1689 ; Timothy, b. Nov. 16, 1691 ; Samuel, b. Dec. 27, 1693, graduat :d at Yale College 1718 — Minister of West Springfield ; Mary, b. Jan. 27, 1696–7 ; Hannah, b. April, 25, 1699 ; Dorcas, b. Feb. 12, 1706.

TIMOTHY HOPKINS, son of John, of Waterbury, married Mary Judd, daughter of Dea. Thomas Judd, of Waterbury, June 25, 1719. He died in W., Feb. 5, 1748–9, aged 57. Their children were : — SAMUEL, b. Sept. 17, 1721, Y. C. 1741 — Minister at Great Barrington and Newport ; Timothy, b. Sept. 8, 1723 ; Huldah, b. Dec. 22, 1725 ; Hannah, b. April 11, 1728 ; Sarah, b. May 25, 1730 : James, b. June 26, 1732 ; Daniel, b. Oct, 16, 1734, Y. C. 1758 — Minister at Salem ; Mary, b. June 27, 1737 ; Mark, b. Sept. 18, 1739, Y. C., 1758 — was a lawyer, as I am informed.

[The following very interesting Letter from Dr. Hopkins, of Newport, to Rev. Jonathan Judd, of South Hampton, never before published, accompanied the above brief Genealogy.]

Newport, Nov. 5, 1798.

DEAR SIR — It is near thirty years since I have had anything direct from you, and I do not remember that I have written you since ; which I am *now* disposed to consider as my fault. The import of your line to me then was, that you considered me as a great and wicked heretic, highly deserving rebuke.* I believe I have published nothing since that would lead you to have a better opinion of me, had you read my writings, which to me is improbable.

However, considering our consanguinity ;† that we originated in the same town, were classmates at college, and the intimacy which took place between us when we were young, and entering on the stage of life, there is, perhaps, no reason for our living strangers to each other. I therefore now sit down to write you by post, as I know of no other way of conveyance, presuming you are yet in this world, though I have heard nothing of you for a considerable time.

* Mr. Judd was strongly opposed to some of the opinions of Dr. Hopkins.
† The mother of Dr. Hopkins was a sister of Mr. Judd's father.

You are about a year older or younger than I am, I think; but I do not remember which. I was 77 years old on the 17th day of last September. But very few of our cotemporaries are now living, and we shall soon be called off the stage of life. I think I have heard of the death of the wife of your youth; and that you have since married another wife, but who, or from whence, or whether she be yet alive, I know not. You have children, I conclude, some or all of them grown up and settled in the world; but how many you have had, whether they be all alive, and what proportion of males and females, I have not been informed.

I have had eight children — five sons and three daughters — which were all born in Great Barrington. Four of them are deceased, viz.: my youngest son, Daniel, who died in Maryland in the year 1788, in the 25th year of his age; my three daughters, Betsy, Joanna, and Rhoda, all lived to marry, and left issue. My oldest daughter left two sons who are now with their father in North Carolina. Joanna married a Fisher, in Medway, and has left but one child, a daughter, now in her 17th year, who lives with me. Rhoda married to John Anthony, and died in this town, soon after her first child was born, in 1792. Her child, a son, is now living, and is with his father's parents at Killington, in Vermont. My first wife died at Great Barrington, in August, 1793, having gone there on a visit to her children, and hoping that it might be for her health, having been in a decline many years. Since that, I have married a second wife, a maiden lady, who originated from Boston, with the entire approbation of all my congregation and friends, who is a very great help and comfort to me in my advanced years.

My church and congregation were large and flourished, before the war with Britain, but in that war were greatly diminished and impoverished; from which state they have not risen. However, I have my daily food and live comfortably and in peace, having neither poverty nor riches, as a temptation to lead me astray. My family consists only of myself, Mrs. Hopkins, and my grand-daughter above mentioned.

I have only one brother and one sister living. The latter lives with a married daughter of hers, whose husband has lately moved from Waterbury to the north-west part of Connecticut, or in the bounds of New York State. The former is at Salem I suppose you know. He is minister of a large and flourishing congregation, who are very kind to him, and they attend his ministry better than congregations commonly do at this day. They give him many valuable presents, and 600 dollars per annum. He preaches three sermons every Sabbath.

My oldest son, David, lives in Maryland, near Baltimore. He has a large plantation; has had two wives, both of which are dead. He is left a widower, with three daughters. Is now chosen General of the Militia of the County in which he lives. My third son, Levi, lives in the north-west part of Virginia, near the Apalachian mountains. Has a wife and six children living. He lost his eldest daughter lately, who was a promising young woman. My second and fourth sons, Moses and Samuel, live at Great Barrington. Moses is a man of business. He is a farmer and a merchant. He is Register of that part of the County in which he lives, and Justice of the Peace. Owns a grist-mill and a saw-mill on the river, which can go the whole year. He has nine children, all likely. None of them have yet left him. Samuel lives in my house and occupies the farm. He has a wife and three children. He is an honest, industrious man; lives much within himself, by the produce of the farm; owes nobody, and has money in his pocket.

I enjoy a comfortable measure of health, through the distinguishing mercy of God, and have fewer complaints than men of my years commonly have. Am able to attend the public services of the Sabbath constantly, and we have a weekly conference at my house every Thursday evening. But religion is very low with us, and in these parts.

I have printed seven sermons. Five of them have been reprinted in America, and three of the five have been printed in Scotland. I have also printed two other pamphlets — a Dialogue concerning the slavery of the Africans, and another small pamphlet. The former has had a second edition in New York. I have also published an answer to Dr. Mayhew's two sermons, to prove there are promises to the unregenerate, of 145 pages. A reply to Mr. Mill's exceptions to some passages in the 10th section of the foregoing, containing 184 pages. In the year 1773, I published a book of 220 pages, containing " An Inquiry concerning the nature of true holiness," of 78 pages, which has since been reprinted at New York. It also contained answers to Messrs. Moses Mather, William Hart, of Saybroook, and M. Hemmenway, who had written in opposition to something which I had published, and to some writings of Mr. Edwards and Dr. Bellamy. In the year 1783, I published a book of 194 pages, entitled, " An Inquiry concerning the future state of those who die in their sins."

In 1793, I published " A System of Doctrines contained in Divine Revelation, with a treatise on the Millenium," in two volumes, octavo, containing 1244 pages. The Treatise on the Millenium, of 158 pages, has been reprinted in Europe.

In 1796, I published The Life of Miss Susanna Anthony, of 193 pages; of which a second edition is agreed upon with the printers, Hudson and Goodwin, at Hartford.

I have written " Memoirs of the Life of Mrs. Osborn," which is now at the press at Worcester, which is to contain about 400 pages, and is expected to be published before next spring.

We are going into a world of light, where it will be known what truth and what errors we have imbibed and contended for in this dark world; and then all matters will be set right; to which I feel no reluctance — hoping I sincerely love the truth, and that I am building on the sure foundation laid in Zion, whatever hay and stubble may be found with me. And as to others, who are the professed friends of Christ, I desire not to judge any of them before the time.

If this should find you alive and in health, and you should find it in your heart to write me by the same conveyance in which this goes, you would much oblige

Your kinsman and old friend,

Rev. Jonathan Judd.   S. HOPKINS.

P. S. Mrs. Hopkins wishes you to think of her as your respectful friend.

THE HOTCHKISS FAMILY

By DONALD LINES JACOBUS, M.A., of New Haven, Conn.

1. SAMUEL[1] HOTCHKISS, who appeared very early in New Haven, Conn., is traditionally supposed to have been a native of County Essex, England, but no proof of this has been found. He married, 7 Sept. 1642, ELIZA-BETH CLEVERLY, and died 28 Dec. 1663.

Children :
- 2. i. JOHN,[2] b. abt. 1643.
- 8. ii. SAMUEL, b. abt. 1645.
- iii. SARAH, m. JEREMIAH JOHNSON of Derby. He and Joshua Hotchkiss are called brothers in Court records.
- 4. iv. JOSHUA, b. 16 Sept. 1651.
- 5. v. THOMAS, b. 31 Aug. 1654.
- 6. vi. DANIEL, b. 8 June 1657.

2. JOHN[2] HOTCHKISS (*Samuel[1]*), born about 1643, died at New Haven in 1689. He married, 4 Dec. 1672, ELIZABETH PECK, born 16 Mar. 1649, died before 1732, daughter of Henry and Joan.

Children :
- 7. i. JOHN,[3] b. 11 Oct. 1673.
- 8. ii. JOSHUA, b. abt. 1675.
- 9. iii. JOSEPH, b. 8 June 1678.
- 10. iv. JOSIAH, b. 24 Jan. 1680.
- v. A DAUGHTER. I have been unable to locate her.
- 11. vi. CALEB, b. 18 Oct. 1684.
- vii. ELIZABETH, b. 18 Jan. 1686; d. unm. 13 Sept. 1723.
- viii. RUTH, b. abt. 1688; d. 24 Mar. 1773; m. (1) 12 Mar. 1718, JONATHAN SACKETT, b. 6 June 1655, d. 4 Feb. 1727; m. (2) 11 Dec. 1728, BENJAMIN DORMAN, b. 15 Oct. 1673, d. 1748.

3. SAMUEL[2] HOTCHKISS (*Samuel[1]*), born about 1645, died 29 Dec. 1705. He resided at East Haven, founding that branch of the family. He married first, in 1678, SARAH TALMADGE, daughter of Robert and Sarah (Nash) ; and secondly HANNAH ———, who died 19 Jan. 1712.

Children by first wife :
- i. MARY,[3] b. 1 Jan. 1679; d. 12 Nov. 1723; m. 1 Mar. 1699, CALEB TUTTLE, b. 29 Aug. 1674, d. 1751.
- ii. SARAH, b. 7 Apr. 1681; m. ——— ———.
- 12. iii. SAMUEL, b. 6 Mar. 1683.
- iv. JAMES, b. 8 Dec. 1684.
- v. ABIGAIL, b. 12 Feb. 1686.
- 13. vi. EBENEZER, bapt. 16 Dec. 1688.

4. JOSHUA[2] HOTCHKISS (*Samuel[1]*), born 16 Sept. 1651, died 22 Dec. 1722. He was Ensign, Sheriff, and a man of prominence in New Haven. He married first, 29 Nov. 1677, MARY PARDEE, who died about 1684; secondly, about 1685, HANNAH TUTTLE, born 24 Feb. 1662, died 17 Feb. 1719 ; and thirdly, about 1719, MARY ASHBUN of Milford.

Children by first wife :
- i. MARY,[3] b. 30 Apr. 1679; d. after 1730.
- 14. ii. STEPHEN, b. 25 Aug. 1681.
- iii. MARTHA, b. 14 Dec. 1683; m. 25 Mar. 1702, THOMAS BROOKS of Wallingford.

Children by second wife:

iv. HANNAH, b. abt. 1686; d. 3 Aug. 1723; m. 10 May 1709, EBENEZER PECK.

v. PRISCILLA, b. 30 Dec. 1688; m. JOHN SPERRY of Woodbridge, b. 3 Mar. 1684, d. 1754.

15. vi. ABRAHAM, b. abt. 1691.

vii. ABIGAIL, b. 12 Oct. 1695; d. 30 Aug. 1735; m. 7 Jan. 1722, DANIEL WINSTON, b. 18 Aug. 1690, d. 17 Jan. 1780.

viii. DESIRE, b. abt. 1698; d. Oct. 1702.

16. ix. ISAAC, b. June 1701.

17. x. JACOB, b. Feb. 1704.

5. THOMAS² HOTCHKISS (*Samuel¹*), called Sergeant, appears to have owned lands in Hamden and Woodbridge. He was born 31 Aug. 1654, and died 27 Dec. 1711. He married, 27 Nov. 1677, SARAH WILMOT, who was born 8 Mar. 1663, and died in 1731, having married secondly, about 1713, Lieut. Daniel Sperry.
Children:

18. i. SAMUEL,³ b. 7 Sept. 1680.

ii. SARAH, b. 13 Feb. 1683; m. 3 Feb. 1709, JOSEPH TURNER, b. 13 Nov. 1672, d. 11 Oct. 1759.

iii. ANNA, b. 12 Dec. 1684; m. 13 Dec. 1705, SAMUEL JOHNSON (see New Haven County Court Records, vol. ii, p. 245), b. 3 Sept. 1678, d. 1755.

iv. WILLIAM, d. unm. 1731.

19. v. ABRAHAM.

vi. DORCAS, d. 17 Mar. 1744; m. JOHN YOUNGS of Southold.

vii. LYDIA, m. (1) EBENEZER JOHNSON of Wallingford, b. 15 Apr. 1688, d. 18 Apr. 1732; m. (2) 15 Sept. 1736, NATHANIEL HALL.

6. DANIEL² HOTCHKISS (*Samuel¹*), called Sergeant, born 8 June 1657, died 10 Mar. 1712. He married, 21 June 1683, ESTHER SPERRY, born Sept. 1654. She married secondly Stephen Pierson.
Children:

i. ELIZABETH,³ b. 30 Aug. 1684; m. 13 Jan. 1702, CALEB MATTHEWS.

20. ii. DANIEL, b. Aug. 1687.

21. iii. OBADIAH, b. 20 Mar. 1690.

iv. ESTHER, b. 25 Nov. 1693.

v. REBECEA, b. 14 Feb. 1697; m. (1) 15 Nov. 1720, THOMAS IVES of Wallingford; m. (2) 1 Dec. 1748, Ens. EDWARD PARKER.

vi. JEMIMA, b. 26 Nov. 1702; m. 11 Apr. 1727, JONATHAN ANDREWS of Wallingford.

7. JOHN³ HOTCHKISS (*John,² Samuel¹*), born 11 Oct. 1673, died 17 Apr. 1732. He was called Captain, and founded the first Cheshire branch of the family. He married MARY CHATTERTON, born 29 Nov. 1673, died 26 July 1744, daughter of William and Mary (Clark).
Children:

22. i. JOHN,⁴ b. 27 June 1694.

ii. LYDIA, b. 31 Aug. 1697; m. 12 Sept. 1716, STEPHEN CLARK.

iii. MARY, b. 1 Apr. 1701; d. 13 Nov. 1787; m. 26 Aug. 1732, JOSHUA HOTCHKISS.

23. iv. AMOS, b. 27 June 1704.

24. v. JAMES, b. 24 Nov. 1706.

vi. ROBERT, b. 12 May 1709; d. 23 Apr. 1732.

vii. MIRIAM, b. 20 Feb. 1712; m. 4 June 1730, ABEL SPERRY.

25. viii. HENRY, b. 1 Apr. 1715.

ix. BENJAMIN, b. 10 May 1718; d. young.

8. JOSHUA³ HOTCHKISS (*John,² Samuel¹*), born about 1675, resided at New Haven, and died 14 Aug. 1741. He married SUSANNAH CHAT-

TERTON, born 17 Sept. 1678, daughter of William and Mary (Clark). She married secondly Abraham Dickerman.

Children:

 i. THANKFUL,[4] b. 15 June 1701; m. (1) 10 June 1725 JAMES GILBERT, b. 18 Sept. 1700, d. 1728; m. (2) 30 Dec. 1731, CALEB BRADLEY.
26. ii. CALEB, b. 27 July 1703.
27. iii. JOSHUA, b. 22 Dec. 1707.
 iv. RUTH, b. 16 Mar. 1712; d. 30 Mar. 1773; m. THOMAS GILBERT, b. 14 Feb. 1709, d. 19 Oct. 1775.

9. JOSEPH[3] HOTCHKISS (*John,*[2] *Samuel*[1]), founder of the Guilford branch of the family, was born 8 June 1678. He married, Apr. 1699, HANNAH CRUTTENDEN.

Children:

28. i. JOSEPH,[4] b. 3 Sept. 1700.
 ii. ISAAC, b. 25 Dec. 1702; d. 17 Sept. 1752; m. 8 July 1724, ELIZABETH AVERED. The male line became extinct in the next generation (see REGISTER, vol. 58, p. 284).
 iii. WAIT, b. 18 Jan. 1704; m. 2 Nov. 1731, SARAH BISHOP. He was founder of the Wolcott branch of the family (see REGISTER, vol. 58, p. 284).
 iv. HANNAH, b. 13 Sept. 1707; d. 20 July 1793; m. 7 Jan. 1730, JOSEPH STONE.
 v. DEBORAH, b. 18 Jan. 1710; d. young.
 vi. MILES, b. 28 July 1712; d. young.
 vii. MARK, b. 1 July 1714; d. 19 Nov. 1775; m. (1) 25 Dec. 1739, MARGARET CRAWFORD; m. (2) 8 Jan. 1751, MIRIAM LEE (see REGISTER, vol. 58, p. 284).

10. JOSIAH[3] HOTCHKISS (*John,*[2] *Samuel*[1]), founder of the second Cheshire branch of the family, born 24 Jan. 1680, died May 1732. He married, 8 Dec. 1715, ABIGAIL PARKER, who, with her husband and child, died in the Wallingford epidemic of May 1732.

Children:

 i. JOSIAH,[4] b. 13 Oct. 1716; d. young.
 ii. ELIZABETH, b. 25 Jan. 1718. Probably she m. 11 Aug. 1742, EBENEZER BISHOP of Woodbridge, b. 29 July 1710, d. 1778.
29. iii. JOSIAH, b. 3 Apr. 1720.
 iv. LUDWICK, b. 13 Jan. 1723; d. 1803; m. three times. He founded the New Britain branch of the family (see *History of New Britain*, p. 413).
30. v. LENT, b. 2 June 1726.
 vi. TRYAL, b. 20 Mar. 1728; d. 1732.

11. CALEB[3] HOTCHKISS (*John,*[2] *Samuel*[1]), born 18 Oct. 1684, resided at New Haven, and died 4 Apr. 1763. He married first, 14 Feb. 1706, MEHITABEL CRUTTENDEN, who died 30 Nov. 1750, aged 68; and secondly ———— ————, who died 23 Aug. 1759.

Children by first wife:

 i. MEHITABEL,[4] b. 20 Nov. 1706; d. 2 Nov. 1725.
 ii. RACHEL, b. 26 Oct. 1709; m. (1) EBENEZER WOLCOTT, who d. 1729; m. (2) 28 Oct. 1731, THOMAS HUMPHREVILLE, b. 8 Feb. 1705, d. 16 Sept. 1738; m. (3) 7 Nov. 1745, SAMUEL PARDEE.
31. iii. CALEB, b. 6 June 1712.
 iv. ELIPHALET, b. 28 June 1714; d. 31 Mar. 1726.
32. v. JOEL, b. 18 Mar. 1716.
33. vi. NEHEMIAH, b. 20 Apr. 1719.

12. SAMUEL[3] HOTCHKISS (*Samuel,*[2] *Samuel*[1]), born 6 Mar. 1683, resided at East Haven, and died 22 Dec. 1740. He did not, as most pub-

lished accounts assert, marry Sarah Bradley, who was wife of his
cousin Samuel (no. 18), but married MARY ———. She married
secondly Henry Tolles.
Children:

 i. JAMES,[4] b. 11 Feb. 1707; d. young.
 ii. JAMES, b. 17 Mar. 1711; d. 10 May 17—.
 iii. SARAH, b. 12 Mar. 1713; d. 17 Sept. 1773; m. (1) THOMAS SHEPARD;
   m. (2) 26 May 1757, CALEB HITCHCOCK.
34. iv. SAMUEL, b. 5 Jan. 1715.
 v. MARY, b. 5 Mar. 1718; m. SAMUEL GOODSELL.
 vi. ABIGAIL, b. 27 Feb. 1721; d. 3 Sept. 1743; m. NATHANIEL BARNES,
   b. 11 Jan. 1707, d. 10 Dec. 1798.
 vii. JOSEPH, b. 15 Feb. 1725; d. 27 Apr. 1776; m. ESTHER RUSSELL, b.
   1729, d. 14 Sept. 1788 (for descendants, see *Tuttle Genealogy*, p.
   174).
 viii. JAMES, b. 13 Jan. 1728.
 ix. ENOS, b. 13 May 1731; m. 5 Feb. 1756, ELIZABETH SHEPARD. Children: 1. *Enos*,[5] b. 1757; d. young. 2. *Enos.* 3. *Stephen.* 4.
   Hannah, m. Jonathan Finch. 5. *Samuel*, b. 1778.

13. EBENEZER[3] HOTCHKISS (*Samuel*,[2] *Samuel*[1]), baptized 16 Dec. 1688,
  removed to New Milford. In 1743, Ebenezer Hotchkiss of New
  Milford deeded to Samuel Hotchkiss and the rest of the heirs of
  Samuel Hotchkiss, Jr., deceased, all his right to the estate of Lieut.
  Samuel, deceased, and of Samuel, Jr., deceased (New Haven Deeds,
  vol. 12, p. 24). He was probably father of the Dea. Ebenezer
  of New Milford who died in 1796, and whose descendants are given
  in Orcutt's *History of New Milford*. He married ——— ———.
  Child:

 i. DEA. EBENEZER[4] (probably).

14. STEPHEN[3] HOTCHKISS (*Joshua*,[2] *Samuel*[1]), born 25 Aug. 1681, removed to Wallingford, probably to that part of the town which is
  now Cheshire, founding the third Cheshire branch of the family.
  He married, 12 Dec. 1704, ELIZABETH SPERRY, born 17 Jan. 1683,
  died 17 May 1760, daughter of John and Elizabeth (Post). He
  died 5 Mar. 1755.
  Children:

35. i. JOSHUA,[4] b. 26 Aug. 1705.
 ii. MARY, b. 1 Jan. 1708; d. 15 Aug. 1764; m. (1) 27 Feb. 1735, ABRA-
   HAM BARNES, b. 1710, d. 1742; m. (2) 30 May 1745, JOSEPH IVES,
   b. 10 Dec. 1709, d. 29 Mar. 1766.
 iii. HANNAH, b. 10 Jan. 1710; d. young.
 iv. ESTHER, b. 18 Feb. 1712; d. 22 July 1732, without issue; m. 11 June
   1731, EPHRAIM TUTTLE, b. 10 Apr. 1710, d. 2 Feb. 1773.
 v. ELIZABETH, b. 25 Aug. 1714; d. 19 Apr. 1733.
36. vi. GIDEON, b. 5 Dec. 1716.
37. vii. STEPHEN, b. 1 Dec. 1718.
38. viii. SILAS, b. 20 Dec. 1719.
 ix. HANNAH, b. 23 Feb. 1722; m. 23 Feb. 1744, STEPHEN ATWATER.
 x. BATHSHEBA, b. 1 Sept. 1726; m. RALPH LINES of Cheshire, b. 23 May
   1716, d. 27 Feb. 1781.
39. xi. BENJAMIN, b. 1 Feb. 1728.
 xii. NOAH, b. 24 Mar. 1730; d. 13 Jan. 1760.

15. ABRAHAM[3] HOTCHKISS (*Joshua*,[2] *Samuel*[1]), born about 1691, resided
  at Bethany, and owned lands at Farmington, afterwards deeded
  away by his children and their heirs. He married DEBORAH
  THOMAS, baptized 27 May 1694, died after 1762, daughter of Joseph

and Abigail (Preston). He died in 1725, and his widow married secondly Dr. John Carrington.

Children:

    i. MABEL,[4] b. abt. 1719; d. 19 Feb. 1798; m. 6 Apr. 1738, ISAAC BEECHER, b. abt. 1716, d. 28 Oct. 1801.

    ii. HANNAH, b. abt. 1721; d. before 1748; m. 1 Sept. 1743, JAMES SHERMAN, b. 24 Jan. 1716.

    iii. DEBORAH, b. abt. 1723; m. 29 Mar. 1743, Capt. JOHN LINES, b. 13 Mar. 1720.

    iv. DORCAS, b. 1725; d. unm. 1790.

16. ISAAC[3] HOTCHKISS (*Joshua,*[2] *Samuel*[1]), born June 1701, resided in Bethany, where he died in Sept. or Oct. 1750. He married, 22 Apr. 1725, RACHEL CARNES, daughter of Thomas and Anna.

Children:

    i. ABRAHAM,[4] d. young.

40. ii. ISAAC.

    iii. MARTHA, m. 26 Oct. 1749, JOSIAH LOUNSBURY.

    iv. RACHEL.

41. v. JACOB, b. abt. 1736.

    vi. JOSEPH, m. at Woodbridge, 10 June 1760, ELIZABETH BROOKS of Glastonbury. The birth of their daughter *Lois*[5] is recorded at Milford 8 June 1761.

    vii. ABIGAIL, bapt. 11 Mar. 1744.

    viii. ABIGAIL, bapt. at Cheshire Apr. 1746.

    ix. REUBEN (twin), bapt. at Cheshire May 1749.

    x. LOIS (twin), bapt. at Cheshire May 1749.

17. JACOB[3] HOTCHKISS (*Joshua,*[2] *Samuel*[1]), born Feb. 1704, married, 30 Apr. 1729, ELIZABETH DICKERMAN, born 12 June 1706. This family lived at Bethany.

Children:

42. i. JABEZ,[4] b. 4 Aug. 1729.

    ii. TIMOTHY, b. 11 Apr. 1731; d. 1776, without issue.

43. iii. ELIJAH, b. 13 May 1733.

    iv. MARTHA, b. 26 June 1735; m. 18 Oct. 1758, TIMOTHY LEEK, who d. 1820.

    v. ELIZABETH, b. 9 Apr. 1738.

    vi. HANNAH, b. 18 Apr. 1740.

44. vii. ABRAHAM, b. 9 Feb. 1743.

    viii. MARY, b. 30 Mar. 1745.

    ix. JACOB, b. 2 June 1747.

    x. ABIGAIL, b. 7 May 1750.

18. SAMUEL[3] HOTCHKISS (*Thomas,*[2] *Samuel*[1]), born 7 Sept. 1680, married, 10 Jan. 1705, SARAH BRADLEY, born 7 Jan. 1680, daughter of Benjamin and Elizabeth (Thompson). He lived presumably at Hamden, and died in 1730.

Children:

    i. THOMAS,[4] m. 3 Dec. 1730, LYDIA DORMAN, b. 2 Aug. 1706, dau. of Benjamin and Ruth (Johnson). They had a son *Samuel,*[5] b. 7 July 1732, but shortly after they removed to parts unknown.

    ii. DESIRE, m. DANIEL REXFORD, b. 27 May 1711. They removed to Berkhamsted.

    iii. WILLIAM, d. unm. 1745. His uncle Caleb Bradley was his guardian.

45. iv. JOSEPH.

    v. SARAH, d. 26 Jan. 1759; m. 16 Mar. 1732, NATHANIEL TURNER, b. 4 Aug. 1708.

19. ABRAHAM[3] HOTCHKISS (*Thomas,*[2] *Samuel*[1]) married ELIZABETH JOHNSON, born 10 May 1685, daughter of William and Sarah (Hall).

This family evidently lived at Hamden, but the identity of Abraham's children can only be established by late Hamden deeds.

Children:

    i.   ABIGAIL,[4] d. 1792; m. 50 Sept. 1737, EBENEZER MUNSON, b. 16 June 1717.

46. ii. DAVID, b. 19 Aug. 1724.

    iii. ELIZABETH, d. 7 Feb. 1802; m. 8 Feb. 1745, GEORGE PRICHARD of Waterbury, b. 5 Oct. 1724, d. 21 Oct. 1820.

20. DANIEL[3] HOTCHKISS (*Daniel,*[2] *Samuel*[1]), born Aug. 1687, married SUSANNAH BRADLEY, born 10 July 1684, died 25 July 1751, daughter of Benjamin and Elizabeth (Thompson). He died in 1733, and she married secondly John Blakslee.

Children:

47. i. DANIEL.[4]

48. ii. SOLOMON.

49. iii. ELIPHALET, b. 1 Nov. 1727.

50. iv. OBADIAH, b. 9 Apr. 1731.

21. OBADIAH[3] HOTCHKISS (*Daniel,*[2] *Samuel*[1]), born 20 Mar. 1690, removed to Cheshire, where he married, Jan. 1716, EUNICE BEACH.

Child:

    i. LOIS,[4] b. 11 Jan. 1717; m. 20 July 1735, ABNER MATTHEWS.

THE HOTCHKISS FAMILY

By DONALD LINES JACOBUS, M.A., of New Haven, Conn.

22. JOHN[4] HOTCHKISS (*John,*[3] *John,*[2] *Samuel*[1]), born 27 June 1694, died 3 Feb. 1777. He was a captain, and lived at Cheshire. He married, 10 Mar. 1719, MIRIAM WOOD, who was born about 1700 and died 10 Jan. 1765.

Children:

51. i.   JASON,[5] b. 12 May 1719.
    ii.   SARAH, b. 13 July 1721; m. 14 June 1738 AUGUSTUS BRISTOL, b. 26 Nov. 1711, d. 4 Feb. 1742.
    iii. DOROTHY, b. 28 Dec. 1723; d. bef. 1753; m. 27 Dec. 1742 SAMUEL BENHAM, b. 5 Jan. 1720, d. abt. 1754.
    iv. HANNAH, b. 3 July 1726; m. 28 Feb. 1745 JOSEPH BUNNELL, b. 17 Jan. 1723.
    v.   MIRIAM, b. 10 Sept. 1728; m. 16 June 1747 GIDEON CURTIS.
    vi. NAOMI, b. 23 Feb. 1731; m. 6 Nov. 1749 SAMUEL ADAMS.
    vii. LYDIA, bapt. Feb. 1733.
52. viii. JOHN, b. 16 Sept. 1735.
53. ix. ELIJAH, b. 6 Mar. 1738.
    x.   MARY, b. 5 Dec. 1740; m. 12 May 1757 THOMAS BROOKS.

23. CAPT. AMOS[4] HOTCHKISS (*John,*[3] *John,*[2] *Samuel*[1]), born 27 June 1704, lived at Cheshire, and died 17 Jan. 1773. He married first, 25 Feb. 1731, ELIZABETH MATTHEWS, who died 17 Sept. 1731; and secondly OBEDIENCE MUNSON, daughter of Samuel and Martha (Ferns), who was born 13 Oct. 1702.
    Children by second wife:

    i.   ELIZABETH,[5] bapt. 23 Dec. 1733; m. (1) 6 May 1752 JONATHAN BRISTOL, b..27 July 1725, d. 1762; m. (2) 1 Mar. 1769 ABNER BLAKESLEE.
    ii. ROBERT, bapt. June 1736; d. Apr. 1750.
54. iii. AMOS, b. 27 Mar. 1738.
    iv. OBEDIENCE, b. 7 Jan. 1740; had son *Roswell,*[6] b. 4 July 1765; m. 23 Feb. 1769 ABNER AUSTIN.
    v.   LOIS, b. 2 July 1743; had daughter *Tryal Hitchcock,*[6] b. July 1759, who m. in 1778 Samuel Anthony; m. 14 Nov. 1765 WILLIAM JONES.
    vi. MARLOW, b. 20 June 1745; m. 13 Nov. 1764 TITUS LINES, b. 19 Mar. 1741, d. 1770.

24. JAMES[4] HOTCHKISS (*John,*[3] *John,*[2] *Samuel*[1]), born 24 Nov. 1706, lived at Cheshire, and died 6 Mar. 1781. He married, 23 July 1728, TAMAR MUNSON, daughter of Samuel and Mary (Preston), who was born 5 Dec. 1707 and died 2 Oct. 1788.
    Children:

    i.   JAMES.[5]
55. ii. BENJAMIN, b. 3 Mar. 1730.
56. iii. ASA, b. 24 Nov. 1731.
    iv. ROBERT, b. 17 June 1733.
    v.   EUNICE, b. 28 Mar. 1735; d. 16 Jan. 1737.
    vi. TAMAR, b. 24 Aug. 1736.
    vii. EUNICE, bapt. 29 Jan. 1738; m. 15 Feb. 1758 ANDREW DURAND.
    viii. WAITSTILL, bapt. Oct. 1740; m. EUNICE BRADLEY. Children: 1. *Asa,*[6] b. 23 Nov. 1764. 2. *Eunice,* b. 25 Mar. 1768. 3. *Waitstill,* b. 18 May 1771; m. 25 May 1800 Phebe Cowell. 4. *Lydia,* b. 30 June 1775. Probably others.
    ix. REUBEN, b. 5 Feb. 1743.
    x.   LYDIA, b. 11 Aug. 1745.
    xi. LOIS, m. 3 Jan. 1770 JOHN IVES.

25. HENRY[4] HOTCHKISS (*John,*[3] *John,*[2] *Samuel*[1]), born 1 Apr. 1715, was a captain, lived at Cheshire, and died 9 June 1799. He married first, 23 Nov. 1736, SARAH BENHAM, daughter of Nathan and Sarah (Beecher), who was born at West Haven about 1712 and died 19 Nov. 1751; and secondly LYDIA BROOKS, widow, who was born about 1719 and died 7 Mar. 1793.
    Children:

57. i.   JOSEPH,[5] b. 18 Dec. 1738.

ii. HENRY, b. 2 Sept. 1739; m. 4 Jan. 1759 ESTHER SMITH. Children:
1. *Mary*, b. 29 Sept. 1760. 2. *Esther*, d. 20 Dec. 1778. 3. *Chauncey*,
b. 10 Feb. 1765. 4. *Lyman*, b. 20 Feb. 1768; m. 20 Oct. 1790 Olive
Brown. 5. *Amasa*, b. 26 Nov. 1769. Probably others.
iii. JONAH, b. 26 Jan. 1741; d. Sept. 1742.
iv. SARAH, b. 5 Feb. 1743; d. 19 Sept. 1812; m. 2 Dec. 1762 VALENTINE
HITCHCOCK, b. 15 Apr. 1741, d. 28 Apr. 1809.
58. v. JONAH, b. 28 Oct. 1745.
vi. MARY, b. 1 Feb. 1747; d. 1747.

26. CALEB[4] HOTCHKISS (*Joshua,[3] John,[2] Samuel[1]*), born 27 July 1703, died
27 Oct. 1785. He lived at Hamden. He married, 19 Dec. 1728,
RUTH MUNSON, daughter of John and Sarah (Cooper), who was
born 30 Jan. 1708 and died 21 May 1785.
Children:

59. i. HEZEKIAH,[5] b. 27 Sept. 1729.
60. ii. JOHN (twin), b. 12 Nov. 1731.
iii. SARAH (twin), b. 12 Nov. 1731.
61. iv. JOSHUA (twin), b. 12 Feb. 1734.
v. SUSANNAH (twin), b. 12 Feb. 1734; m. 17 July 1754 EZRA DAGGETT.
62. vi. LEMUEL.
vii. RUTH, m. 15 Nov. 1763 ICHABOD PAGE.
viii. ESTHER.

27. JOSHUA[4] HOTCHKISS (*Joshua,[3] John,[2] Samuel[1]*), born 22 Dec. 1707,
married, 18 Dec. 1732, OBEDIENCE COOPER, daughter of Samuel
and Elizabeth (Smith), who was born 25 July 1712.
Children:

i. HANNAH,[5] b. 14 Jan. 1734.
ii. CHARLES, b. 8 July 1736; m. 11 Feb. 1762 ELIZABETH HARRIS.
iii. TIMOTHY, b. 16 Mar. 1742.
iv. EUNICE, b. 11 July 1745; m. 5 Aug. 1762 JOHN DAVIES of Litchfield.
v. LOIS, b. 16 Aug. 1749; prob. m. 29 Dec. 1772 AARON SMITH of New
Fairfield.

28. JOSEPH[4] HOTCHKISS (*Joseph,[3] John,[2] Samuel[1]*), born 3 Sept. 1700,
died 5 Sept. 1740. He lived at Guilford. He married, 1725,
THANKFUL STONE, who died 14 Sept. 1751.
Children:

63. i. EZEKIEL,[5] b. 14 Mar. 1726.
64. ii. DANIEL, b. 2 July 1728.
iii. RACHEL, b. 18 Mar. 1730; d. 15 Aug. 1802; m. 1 Dec. 1748 MILES[5]
HOTCHKISS (*Isaac,[4] Joseph,[3] John,[2] Samuel[1]*), b. 11 Feb. 1728, d.
13 May 1810.
iv. JOHN, b. abt. 1732; d. 30 Oct. 1799; m. 20 Apr. 1756 OBEDIENCE
STONE, who d. 28 May 1797.
v. MARY, b. abt. 1734; d. 18 Mar. 1743.
vi THANKFUL, m. 3 Sept. 1755 ELIHU STONE of Litchfield.
65. vii. JOSEPH, b. 22 Oct. 1736.
viii. AMOS, b. 2 Jan. 1739; removed to Vermont.
ix. EBENEZER, b. 5 Jan. 1741; d. 23 Nov. 1760.

29. JOSIAH[4] HOTCHKISS (*Josiah,[3] John,[2] Samuel[1]*), born 3 Apr. 1720, lived
at Cheshire, and married, 8 Dec. 1741, ABIGAIL BARTHOLOMEW.
Children:

66. i. JOSIAH,[5] b. 26 Dec. 1742.
67. ii. BENONI, b. 4 Aug. 1752.
Probably others.

190

30. LENT[4] HOTCHKISS (*Josiah,*[3] *John,*[2] *Samuel*[1]), born 2 June 1726, died 8 Apr. 1760. He married, 20 Dec. 1750, ABIGAIL CHAUNCEY, who married secondly Isaac Tyler.

Children:

    i. RUTH,[5] b. 29 Oct. 1751; m. 20 Dec. 1775 WILLIAM PERKINS, b. 6 Jan. 1755. They removed to Pomfret, Vt.
    ii. ABIGAIL (twin), b. 2 Sept. 1753.
    iii. LENT (twin), b. 2 Sept. 1753; d. 2 Dec. 1805; m. SARAH BALL, b. 19 Oct. 1765, d. 22 May 1803. They removed to New Haven. Besides several children who died young, they had: *John B.,*[6] b. abt. 1793, d. 24 Aug. 1839, a shipmaster of New Haven.
    iv. MARTHA, b. 2 Aug. 1757; m. 16 Nov. 1773 ELISHA JONES.

31. CALEB[4] HOTCHKISS (*Caleb,*[3] *John,*[2] *Samuel*[1]), born 6 June 1712, died 5 July 1779. He lived at Hamden. He married, 6 Jan. 1737, PHEBE ATWATER, who was born 20 Oct. 1714 and died 19 Feb. 1795.

Children:

68. i. STEPHEN,[5] b. 4 Feb. 1738.
    ii. PHEBE, b. 12 Oct. 1739; d. young.
    iii. MEHITABEL, b. 20 Mar. 1742; d. 18 Mar. 1804; m. 11 Nov. 1761 ELIJAH[4] HOTCHKISS of Derby (43), b. 13 May 1733, d. 2 Sept. 1806.
69. iv. JONAH, b. 12 June 1745.
    v. AMOS, b. 22 May 1750; m. 12 Sept. 1773 REBECCA GILBERT.
    vi. ASA, d. 1800.

32. JOEL[4] HOTCHKISS (*Caleb,*[3] *John,*[2] *Samuel*[1]), born 18 Mar. 1716, died in 1777. He married first, 5 Nov. 1741, MARY SHERMAN, born 19 Mar. 1719; and secondly SARAH ———.

Children:

70. i. ELIHU,[5] b. 16 Aug. 1742.
    ii. JOEL, b. 9 Nov. 1745; d. in 1819; m. MARTHA PECK. Administration on his estate was granted to Peninah and Mehitabel Hotchkiss, with Medad Hotchkiss as surety.
    iii. MARY, b. 25 Jan. 1748; d. young.
    iv. ELIPHALET, b. 14 Apr. 1750; removed to Litchfield; m. ESTHER BEECHER, bapt. 26 Aug. 1752.
    v. ELIAS (twin), b. 18 Mar. 1752; d. 1822; m. EUNICE ATWATER, b. 1753.
    vi. MARY (twin), b. 18 Mar. 1752.
    vii. RACHEL, b. 21 Feb. 1754.
    viii. ELDAD, b. 21 Apr. 1756; m. ABIGAIL ATWATER, b. 1759.
    ix. MEDAD, b. 21 Apr. 1758; d. young.
    x. MEDAD, b. 7 Oct. 1760; d. 1828.
    xi. MEHITABEL, b. 14 July 1764.

33. NEHEMIAH[4] HOTCHKISS (*Caleb,*[3] *John,*[2] *Samuel*[1]), born 20 Apr. 1719, died in 1769. He married, 8 Nov. 1739, MARY REXFORD, daughter of Arthur and Elizabeth (Stevens), who was born about 1720 and died 2 Aug. 1770.

Children:

    i. NAOMI,[5] b. 15 Mar. 1741; m. 13 Dec. 1764 JAMES BRADLEY, JR.
    ii. AMY.
    iii. NEHEMIAH, b. 11 Jan. 1745; m. 25 Jan. 1768 REBECCA OSBORN.
    iv. MARY, b. 2 Jan. 1747; m. 17 Mar. 1768 ENOCH MOULTHROP.
    v. MARTHA, m. JONATHAN SPERRY of Southbury.
    vi. ARTHUR, d. June 1760.

34. SAMUEL⁴ HOTCHKISS (*Samuel,*³ *Samuel,*² *Samuel*¹), born at East
     Haven 5 Jan. 1715, died at Northford in 1774. He married MARY
     GOODSELL.
     Children:
     i.   MARY,⁵ b. abt. 1745; d. 1779.
     ii. SARAH.
     iii. SAMUEL.
     iv. EBENEZER, b. abt. 1758; d. 1774.
     v.   HANNAH, m. 28 Mar. 1786 JACOB BUNNELL of Branford, b. 12 Dec.
          1761.

35. JOSHUA⁴ HOTCHKISS (*Stephen,*³ *Joshua,*² *Samuel*¹), born 26 Aug.
     1705, died 29 Dec. 1788. He lived at Cheshire. He married,
     2 Feb. 1732, MARY⁴ HOTCHKISS, born 1 Apr. 1701, died 13 Nov.
     1787.
     Children:
71. i.   JOHN,⁵ b. 27 Feb. 1733.
     ii. ELIZABETH, b. 30 Mar. 1735; m. (1) 23 Nov. 1752 EBENEZER BEN-
          HAM, b. 31 Oct. 1726, d. 25 Dec. 1755; m. (2) 25 Mar. 1758 AMOS
          OSBORNE of Waterbury.
     iii. MARY, b. 11 Aug. 1737; d. 19 June 1738.
     iv. MARY, b. 5 June 1739; m. 10 Jan. 1760 WILLIAM WHEELER, JR.

36. DEA. GIDEON⁴ HOTCHKISS (*Stephen,*³ *Joshua,*² *Samuel*¹), born at
     Cheshire 5 Dec. 1716, died 3 Sept. 1807. He married first, 18 June
     1737, ANNA BROCKETT, who died 1 Aug. 1762; and secondly, 22
     Feb. 1763, MABEL STILES. He settled at Waterbury, and his de-
     scendants are given in Anderson's *History of Waterbury.*
     Children by first wife:
     i.   JESSE,⁵ b. 9 Oct. 1738; d. 29 Sept. 1776; m. 2 Oct. 1759 CHARITY
          MALLORY, and left issue.
     ii. DAVID, b. 5 Apr. 1740; m. (1) 21 Nov. 1763 ABIGAIL DOUGLAS, who
          d. 5 Apr. 1775; m. (2) 5 July 1775 PENINAH TODD; left issue.
     iii. ABRAHAM, b. and d. 3 May 1742.
     iv. ABRAHAM, b. 25 Mar. 1743; d. 29 Oct. 1806; m. 30 Dec. 1767 HAN-
          NAH WEED.
     v.   GIDEON, b. 31 Dec. 1744; d. 6 Jan. 1819; m. MARY SCOTT; left issue.
     vi. HULDAH, b. 27 June 1747; d. 28 Mar. 1774; m. 8 Apr. 1773 JOSEPH
          PAYNE.
     vii. ANNA, b. 22 Oct. 1749; m. 16 Mar. 1775 REUBEN WILLIAMS.
     viii. AMOS, b. 24 Nov. 1751; m. 24 Dec. 1772 ABIGAIL SCOTT; left issue.
     ix. SUBMIT, b. 2 June 1753; m. 15 June 1775 DAVID PAYNE.
     x.   TITUS, b. 26 June 1755; m. RACHEL GUERNSEY.
     xi. EBEN, b. 13 Dec. 1757; m. 15 Feb. 1781 MARY SANFORD; left issue.
     xii. ASAHEL, b. 15 Feb. 1760; m. (1) 22 Mar. 1781 SARAH WILLIAMS, who
          d. 28 Mar. 1794; m. (2) 7 June 1794 PHEBE MERRIAM; left issue.
     xiii. BENONI, b. and d. 27 July 1762.

     Children by second wife:
     xiv. MABEL, b. 23 May 1764; d. 5 May 1797; m. CHAUNCEY JUDD.
     xv.   PHEBE, b. 29 Aug. 1765; d. 1789; m. REUBEN WILLIAMS.
     xvi. HANNAH, b. 14 Oct. 1766; d. 26 Nov. 1766.
     xvii. STILES, b. 30 Jan. 1768; m. POLLY HORTON; had issue.
     xviii. OLIVE, b. 21 Nov. 1769; m. ———— JONES.
     xix. MELLICENT, b. 6 May 1771; m. DAVID SANFORD.
     xx.   AMZI, b. 3 July 1774; removed to Meriden.

37. DEA. STEPHEN⁴ HOTCHKISS (*Stephen,*³ *Joshua,*² *Samuel*¹), born 1 Dec.
     1718, lived at Cheshire. He married first THANKFUL COOK, who

was born about 1718 and died 14 Sept. 1760; secondly, 2 Mar. 1762, ANNE (ROYCE) JOHNSON, widow of Daniel; and thirdly, 13 Sept. 1782, THANKFUL BROOKS.

Children by first wife:

i. ESTHER,[5] b. 23 Oct. 1742; d. 15 Oct. 1749.
ii. THANKFUL, b. 14 Mar. 1745; m. (1) 5 May 1767 TITUS PRESTON, b. 29 Jan. 1744, d. 7 June 1770; m. (2) 21 Mar. 1771 STEPHEN COOK.
iii. SUSANNAH, bapt. Aug. 1747; d. 15 Oct. 1749.
iv. ESTHER, b. 9 June 1750.
v. SUSANNAH, b. 20 July 1752.
vi. STEPHEN, b. 15 July 1754.
vii. SAMUEL, b. 22 Oct. 1755.

38. SILAS[4] HOTCHKISS (*Stephen,[3] Joshua,[2] Samuel[1]*), born 20 Dec. 1719, died in Jan. 1783. He removed to Waterbury. He married first, 12 May 1748, LOIS (RICHARDS) BRONSON, widow of Benjamin, who died 7 Feb. 1776; and secondly ABIGAIL ———, who died 31 Aug. 1794.

Children by first wife:

i. CHLOE,[5] b. 19 Jan. 1749.
ii. HESTER, b. 2 Jan. 1751; d. 23 Feb. 1787; m. 21 Nov. 1774 JOSEPH PAYNE.
iii. STEPHEN, b. 24 Aug. 1753; d. 9 Sept. 1826; m. 31 Dec. 1778 TAMAR RICHASON; left issue.
iv. TRUMAN, b. 18 June 1760; d. May 1838.
v. LOIS, b. 21 Mar. 1763; d. 23 Aug. 1763.

39. BENJAMIN[4] HOTCHKISS (*Stephen,[3] Joshua,[2] Samuel[1]*), born 1 Feb. 1728, lived at Cheshire, and married, 16 Apr. 1751, ELIZABETH ROBERTS.

Children:

i. ABRAHAM BARNES,[5] b. 21 Jan. 1752; d. 3 Feb. 1752.
ii. ELIZABETH, b. 15 Feb. 1753.
iii. HANNAH, b. 14 June 1755.

40. ISAAC[4] HOTCHKISS (*Isaac,[3] Joshua,[2] Samuel[1]*), born about 1729, died in 1777. He lived at Woodbridge, and married ANNA ———.

Children:

i. LORANIA,[5] bapt. 30 Aug. 1752.
72. ii. ABRAHAM.
iii. PETER.
73. iv. ISAAC, b. abt. 1758.
v. ICHABOD.
Perhaps other children.

41. DEA. JACOB[4] HOTCHKISS (*Isaac,[3] Joshua,[2] Samuel[1]*), born about 1736, died 26 June 1825. He lived at Woodbridge, and married, 25 Jan. 1763, MARY PERKINS, daughter of Thomas and Rachel (Peck), who was born 20 Aug. 1744.

Children (order uncertain):

i. ZEDEKIAH.[5]
ii. ZACCHEUS.
iii. MARY, m. ——— THOMAS.
iv. HULDAH, m. ——— HULL.
v. RHODA, m. ——— WARNER.
vi. LUCY, m. ——— WARNER.
vii. HANNAH, m. ——— THOMAS.

42. JABEZ⁴ HOTCHKISS (*Jacob,³ Joshua,² Samuel¹*), born 4 Aug. 1729, lived at Bethany, and married LYDIA SPERRY, daughter of Stephen and Lydia (Holt).
Children:
- 74. i. STEPHEN,⁵ b. 31 Oct. 1761.
- ii. MARY, b. 3 June 1762.
- iii. TIMOTHY, b. 22 Jan. 1766.
- iv. LYDIA, b. 1 Apr. 1768; d. 1773.
- v. ELEAZER, b. 4 June 1770.
- vi. LYDIA, b. 7 June 1774.

43. ELIJAH⁴ HOTCHKISS (*Jacob,³ Joshua,² Samuel¹*), born 13 May 1733, founded the second Derby branch of the family, and died 2 Sept. 1806. He married, 11 Nov. 1761, MEHITABEL⁵ HOTCHKISS, daughter of Caleb (31), who was born 20 Mar. 1742 and died 18 Mar. 1804.
Children:
- 75. i. LEVERETT,⁵ b. 6 Oct. 1762.
- ii. PHEBE, b. 2 Aug. 1764.
- iii. ELIJAH, b. 16 Nov. 1766.
- iv. ELIZABETH, b. 17 June 1769; d. 29 Aug. 1794.
- v. MEHITABEL, b. 22 July 1772; d. 4 Nov. 1833.
- vi. CYRUS, b. 16 July 1774; d. 27 Jan. 1846; m. CATHARINE ———, who d. 24 Feb. 1832; had issue.
- vii. NABBY, b. 30 Aug. 1777; m. EZRA LEWIS.
- viii. BURR, m. MARY TOMLINSON.
- ʼix. REBECCA.

44. ABRAHAM⁴ HOTCHKISS (*Jacob,³ Joshua,² Samuel¹*), born 9 Feb. 1742, lived at Hamden, and died 8 June 1778. He married, 7 Feb. 1769, PHEBE AUGUR, who was born about 1739 and died 29 Mar. 1813.
Children:
- i. POLLY,⁵ b. 13 Nov. 1770; m. REV. TILLOTSON BROWNSON.
- ii. ELIAS, b. 13 Aug. 1772; d. 7 July 1830; m. (1) CHLOE TODD, b. abt. 1778, d. 27 July 1797; m. (2) ESTHER DICKERMAN, b. abt. 1779, d. 2 Nov. 1826. For descendants see *Dickerman Genealogy*, p. 383.
- iii. HULDAH, b. 22 July 1774; d. without issue.

45. JOSEPH⁴ HOTCHKISS (*Samuel,³ Thomas,² Samuel¹*) lived at Bethany, and married first, about 1737, LYDIA THOMAS, who was born 28 Sept. 1709 and died shortly after Feb. 1738. He married secondly, 15 Oct. 1738, PATIENCE COLLINS, daughter of Joseph, who was born 8 Oct. 1719 and died 8 Jan. 1754.
Children by second wife:
- 76. i. JOSEPH,⁵ b. 21 May 1739.
- 77. ii. SAMUEL, b. 19 June 1741.
- iii. PATIENCE, b. 22 Apr. 1743; m. SAMUEL HINE of Milford.
- 78. iv. WILLIAM, b. 9 Oct. 1744.
- v. JONAS, b. 20 Aug. 1746; m. MABEL ———.
- 79. vi. BENJAMIN, b. 2 June 1748.
- vii. JOEL, b. 19 Mar. 1752; d. 29 Jan. 1816; m. 16 Jan. 1777 ABIGAIL SPERRY, b. 16 May 1753, d. 15 Aug. 1837, daughter of David and Abigail (Perkins). They lived near Litchfield, and were buried at Northfield. They left issue.
- viii. EZEKIEL, b. 5 Jan. 1754; m. REBECCA THOMAS, daughter of Gershom.

46. DAVID⁴ HOTCHKISS (*Abraham,³ Thomas,² Samuel¹*), born 19 Aug. 1724, removed to Woodbury, and died 24 June 1777. He married,

10 Nov. 1748, Submit Hill, who died Mar. 1756.
Children :
   i. Sibyl,[5] b. 29 May 1749 ; m. 1773 Simeon Taylor of Woodbury.
   ii. David, bapt. 20 Jan. 1751.
   iii. Huldah, b. 16 Apr. 1752 ; m. ——— Yale.
   iv. Eliza, b. 3 Feb. 1754 ; m. (1) Jesse Munger of Guilford; m. (2) ——— Hine.
80. v. Reuben, b. 8 Mar. 1756.

47. Daniel[4] Hotchkiss (*Daniel,*[3] *Daniel,*[2] *Samuel*[1]), born at New Haven, founded the fourth Cheshire branch of the family. He married Mamre Cook, daughter of Capt. Ephraim.
Children :
   i. Daniel,[5] b. 19 Aug. 1744 ; d. 28 July 1827 ; m. 24 Aug. 1769 Sarah Smith.
   ii. Susanna, b. 2 Mar. 1746 ; m. 27 Sept. 1769 Ephraim Smith.
   iii. Ephraim, b. 16 Aug. 1747 ; d. 1817 ; m. Elizabeth ———.
   iv. Lydia, b. 9 Mar. 1749.
   v. Esther, b. 23 Sept. 1750 ; m. Jan. 1773 Jotham Gaylord.
   vi. Mamre, b. 15 July 1752 ; d. Sept. 1804 ; m. 14 Mar. 1776 Dea. Lemuel Hitchcock of Cheshire, Durham, N. Y., and Windham, N. Y., b. 20 Dec. 1749, d. 27 June 1829.
   vii. Robert, b. 4 Apr. 1754 ; lived at Cheshire ; m. Lucy Brooks (?).
   viii. Solomon, b. 20 June 1756 ; removed to Bethany ; d. 20 Apr. 1849.
   ix. Elizabeth, b. 4 Dec. 1757 ; d. 29 June 1808 ; m. 20 Nov. 1777 Ezra Bristol, b. 9 Jan. 1753, d. 9 May 1819.
   x. Tirzah, b. 14 Aug. 1759 ; d. 6 Sept. 1786 ; m. Elijah Wooding of Bethany, b. abt. 1761, d. 7 Nov. 1825.
   xi. Salmon, b. 14 Nov. 1761.
   xii. Candace, b. 14 Apr. 1763 ; m. 1 May 1783 Enos Tuttle, Jr., of New Haven.
   xiii. Rebecca, b. 5 Jan. 1765 ; m. Joel Wilmot of Bristol.
   xiv. John Cook, b. 8 Sept. 1767 ; m. Sarah[6] Hotchkiss, daughter of John (71).

48. Solomon[4] Hotchkiss (*Daniel,*[3] *Daniel,*[2] *Samuel*[1]), of Woodbridge, died Apr. 1763. He married, 16 Dec. 1748, Eleanor Perkins, daughter of Seth and Elizabeth (Munson), who was born 3 Sept. 1726 and died 9 May 1816.
Children :
   i. Elizabeth,[5] b. 5 Dec. 1749 ; m. 16 Mar. 1777 Daniel Johnson of Oxford.
81. ii. Solomon, b. 20 Mar. 1752.
82. iii. David, b. 26 Oct. 1754.

49. Dea. Eliphalet[4] Hotchkiss (*Daniel,*[3] *Daniel,*[2] *Samuel*[1]), born 1 Nov. 1727, died 5 July 1803. He founded the first Derby branch of the family. He married, 26 Dec. 1751, Comfort Harger, daughter of Jabez, who was born 10 Sept. 1720 and died 11 Mar. 1802.
Children :
   i. Susannah,[5] b. 6 Jan. 1753 ; m. 13 June 1774 Daniel Tomlinson.
83. ii. Levi, b. 2 May 1754.
   iii. Eliphalet, b. 1 Apr. 1756 ; d. 25 Feb. 1775.
   iv. Moses, b. 28 Dec. 1757 ; d. 9 May 1799 ; m. 25 Jan. 1787 Sarah Bryan of Milford, who d. after 1828. Child : 1. *Sally M.,*[6] b. abt. 1790 ; d. 29 Apr. 1828.
   v. David, b. 30 Dec. 1759 ; d. 30 Aug. 1776.
   vi. Philo, b. 26 Nov. 1761 ; d. 22 June 1787. Children : 1. *Philo.*[6] 2. *Nancy.*

50. OBADIAH[4] HOTCHKISS (*Daniel,*[3] *Daniel,*[2] *Samuel*[1]), born 9 Apr. 1731, lived at New Haven, and died 23 Mar. 1805. He married, 16 Nov. 1758, MERCY PERKINS, daughter of Daniel and Martha (Elcock), who was born 30 Jan. 1730 and died 14 Jan. 1797.

    Children:

84. i. ELI,[5] b. 18 Sept. 1758.
    ii. LYDIA, b. 26 Jan. 1761; d. 2 Mar. 1793; m. 26 Sept. 1782 JARED THOMPSON.
85. iii. OBADIAH, b. 4 Sept. 1762.
    iv. SILAS, b. 16 Mar. 1765; d. 24 Sept. 1776.
86. v. JUSTUS, b. abt. 1772.

THE HOTCHKISS FAMILY

By DONALD LINES JACOBUS, M.A., of New Haven, Conn.

51. JASON[5] HOTCHKISS (*John,*[4] *John,*[3] *John,*[2] *Samuel*[1]), born 12 May 1719, lived at Cheshire, and died 19 May 1776. He married first, 27 Dec. 1744, ABIGAIL ATWATER, daughter of Moses and Sarah

(Merriman), who was born 13 Sept. 1725 and died 23 Feb. 1773; and secondly, 17 Feb. 1774, MRS. THANKFUL TUTTLE.
Children by first wife:

i. ABIGAIL,[6] b. 12 July 1746; d. young.
ii. SARAH, b. 1 May 1750; m. 10 July 1771 WILLIAM LAW.
iii. DAVID, b. 28 Mar. 1752; m. 26 Dec. 1771 ABIGAIL MERRIAM.
iv. JONATHAN, b. 7 May 1754.
v. ABIGAIL, b. 19 Sept. 1756; m. ——— BENNETT.
vi. JASON, b. 13 May 1759.
vii. MERRIMAN, b. abt. 1762; d. 16 June 1812; m. (1) 30 Dec. 1785 ESTHER HULL, d. 19 Feb. 1789; m. (2) KETURAH HOUGH, daughter of John, d. 2 Mar. 1795; m. (3) 27 May 1796 BETSEY DURAND, b. abt. 1773, d. 9 Apr. 1848.
viii. LYDIA, b. 22 July 1764.
ix. RUFUS, b. 29 Mar. 1769; m. 27 Dec. 1792 LOWLY DOOLITTLE.
x. ANNA, b. 23 Feb. 1773.

52. JOHN[5] HOTCHKISS (*John,*[4] *John,*[3] *John,*[2] *Samuel*[1]), born 16 Sept. 1735, lived at Cheshire, and married, 14 Feb. 1756, PHEBE GILLAM.
Children:

i. ———,[6] b. 4 Jan. 1758.
ii. ———, b. 31 Mar. 1760.
iii. ———, b. 9 Apr. 176-.
iv. MIRIAM WOOD, b. 1 Mar. 1767.
v. CORNELIUS, b. 29 Oct. 1769.
vi. SOCRATES, b. 11 May 1774.

53. ELIJAH[5] HOTCHKISS (*John,*[4] *John,*[3] *John,*[2] *Samuel*[1]), born 6 Mar. 1738, lived at Cheshire, and died 11 June 1797. He married, 8 June 1758, ELIZABETH KELLOGG, who was born 31 May 1738.
Children:

i. DOROTHY,[6] b. 22 May 1759; m. LYMAN ATWATER.
ii. ADA, m. MUNSON DURAND.
iii. SAMUEL, b. 22 May 1765; m. and had issue.

54. AMOS[5] HOTCHKISS (*Amos,*[4] *John,*[3] *John,*[2] *Samuel*[1]), born 27 Mar. 1738, lived at Cheshire, and died 24 July 1784. He married, 6 Apr. 1758, MRS. ELIZABETH (BEADLES or BEADEL) MERRIAM, daughter of Capt. Nathaniel.
Children:

i. ROBERT,[6] b. 11 June 1760.
ii. SAMUEL SHARP BEADLES, b. 24 Mar. 1762.
iii. MIRIAM, b. 10 Jan. 1764; m. 12 Feb. 1784 SAMUEL HOTCHKISS (see Addenda).
iv. LOUISA, b. 10 Jan. 1766; m. 16 June 1784 CORNELIUS B. COOK.
v. AMOS, b. 13 Apr. 1768.
vi. MARLOW, b. 22 Feb. 1770.
vii. GEORGE, b. 4 June 1772.

55. BENJAMIN[5] HOTCHKISS (*James,*[4] *John,*[3] *John,*[2] *Samuel*[1]), born 3 Mar. 1730, lived at Cheshire and Mt. Carmel, and married, 12 Dec. 1751, MARTHA BROOKS.
Children:

i. MARTHA,[6] b. 27 Dec. 1752.
ii. SIMEON, b. 26 Nov. 1754.
iii. JERUSHA, b. 10 Mar. 1756.
iv. DESIRE, b. 10 June 1758.
v. STATIRA, b. 16 Nov. 1765.

vi. BENJAMIN, b. 17 Dec. 1767.
vii. DAVID BROOKS, b. 7 Aug. 1769.
   Perhaps other children.

56. ASA[5] HOTCHKISS (*James,*[4] *John,*[3] *John,*[2] *Samuel*[1]), born 24 Nov.
    1731, lived at Cheshire, and died 1 July 1763. He married, 2 May
    1752, MARY ANDREWS.
       Children :
    i. SARAH,[6] b. 6 Mar. 1753.
    ii. ROBERT, b. 14 June 1755, " of Collumbier."
    iii. GILES.
    iv. LOWLY.
    v. JARED, b. 12 Sept. 1761.
    vi. CHLOE, b. 2 Mar. 1763.

57. JOSEPH[5] HOTCHKISS (*Henry,*[4] *John,*[3] *John,*[2] *Samuel*[1]), born 18 Dec.
    1738, lived at Cheshire, and died 28 Mar. 1783. He married first,
    9 Mar. 1761, MARY HALL, who died 14 Feb. 1776 ; and secondly,
    1 Jan. 1778, MRS. RUTH DOOLITTLE, who survived him and died
    before 1807.
       Children by first wife :
    i. ZURAH,[6] d. 19 Oct. 1777.
    ii. SARAH, b. 27 Aug. 1764.
    iii. MILES, b. 27 Dec. 1766 ; d. 12 Oct. 1777.
    iv. MARY, b. 12 Mar. 1769 ; d. 4 Dec. 1777.
    v. CHLOE, b. 30 July 1771 ; d. 31 Aug. 1837 ; m. LEVI BRISTOL, as his
         second wife.
    vi. MARTHA, b. 1 July 1773 ; d. 24 Jan. 1805 ; m. 21 Nov. 1791 LEVI
         BRISTOL, b. 16 Sept. 1767, d. 19 Dec. 1841. They removed to
         Plymouth.
    vii. JOSEPH, b. 13 Feb. 1776 ; m. 10 May 1797 NABBY BUNNELL.

58. JONAH[5] HOTCHKISS (*Henry,*[4] *John,*[3] *John,*[2] *Samuel*[1]), born 28 Oct.
    1745, lived at Cheshire, and died 19 Sept. 1812. He married, 14
    Aug. 1764, EUNICE TYLER, who died 12 Feb. 1835.
       Children :
    i. AZUBAH,[6] b. 2 June 1765 ; d. 17 Nov. 1803 ; m. 30 June 1785 JOB
         SPERRY, bapt. 14 Oct. 1762, d. 7 Feb. 1825.
    ii. ADONIJAH, b. 19 Jan. 1767 ; m. 28 May 1788 SYLVIA SEYMOUR.
    iii. EUNICE, b. 21 Oct. 1768 ; d. 17 June 1771.
    iv. JONAH, b. 13 Apr. 1771 ; d. 7 Jan. 1850 ; m. 6 Oct. 1794 CHLOE
         BRADLEY, d. 20 Oct. 1862. Children : 1. *Hannah,*[7] b. 28 Oct.
         1795. 2. *Sarah,* b. 15 Mar. 1798. 3. *Hiram,* b. 18 Feb. 1801. 4.
         Caroline, b. 10 Feb. 1806. 5. *Azubah,* b. 15 May 1811. 6. *Hiram
         Alvestus,* b. 14 Sept. 1815.
    v. ABNER, b. 30 Apr. 1774 ; d. 10 May 1774.
    vi. HENRY, b. 13 Sept. 1775 ; d. 1794.
 87. vii. MILES, b. 28 Aug. 1778.

59. HEZEKIAH[5] HOTCHKISS (*Caleb,*[4] *Joshua,*[3] *John,*[2] *Samuel*[1]), born 27
    Sept. 1729, lived at Hamden, and died 8 May 1761. He married
    first, 12 Dec. 1751, SARAH BRADLEY, who died 3 Sept. 1753 ; and
    secondly, 19 June 1754, MARY WOODING, daughter of John and
    Desire (Cooper), who was born 20 Nov. 1731, and married sec-
    ondly Enos Johnson.
       Child by first wife :
    i. HEZEKIAH,[6] b. 25 Dec. 1752 ; d. 1 Apr. 1827 ; m. 6 May 1781 GRACE
         WILCOX of Clinton, d. 9 June 1829, aged 71.

198

Children by second wife:

ii. DANIEL, b. 1 Apr. 1755; d. at North Haven 9 Nov. 1800; m. 20 Aug. 1782 ACHSAH ANDRUS, bapt. 1757.
iii. JARED, b. 15 Mar. 1757; d. 20 Feb. 1758.
iv. JARED, b. 6 Mar. 1761.

60. JOHN⁵ HOTCHKISS (*Caleb,*⁴ *Joshua,*³ *John,*² *Samuel*¹), born 12 Nov. 1731, died July 1779. He married, 28 Aug. 1755, SUSANNAH JONES, daughter of Timothy and Jane (Harris), who was born 1732 and died 1813.

Children:

i. LOUISA,⁶ b. 3 Mar. 1756; d. 1822; m. DANIEL BISHOP.
ii. GABRIEL, b. 15 Sept. 1757.
iii. SUSANNAH AUGUSTA, b. 6 Aug. 1759.
iv. SOPHIA CHARLOTTE, b. 3 Mar. 1761.
v. FREDERICK WILLIAM, bapt. 31 Oct. 1762.
vi. SUSANNAH CAROLINE, bapt. 15 Apr. 1764.
vii. LEWIS GEORGE, bapt. 1 Dec. 1765.
viii. GEORGE LEWIS, bapt. 12 Apr. 1767; m. 6 Feb. 1785 EUNICE COOK of Wallingford.
ix. SUSANNAH JANE, bapt. 28 May 1769.
x. TIMOTHY JOHN, bapt. 2 June 1771.
xi. MARIA JANE, bapt. 13 June 1773.

61. JOSHUA⁵ HOTCHKISS (*Caleb,*⁴ *Joshua,*³ *John,*² *Samuel*¹), born 12 Feb. 1734, died 3 June 1795. He married MARY PUNDERSON, daughter of Thomas and Mary (Miles), who was born 28 Jan. 1738 and died 4 Mar. 1821. They lived at Westville.

Children:

i. SILAS,⁶ bapt. 7 May 1758; d. 22 May 1848; m. 17 Dec. 1777 ESTHER GILBERT. James G. Hotchkiss was administrator of his estate.
88. ii. ELEAZER, bapt. 7 May 1758.
iii. LUCINDA, bapt. 6 Jan. 1760; m. 19 Apr. 1780 JAMES THOMPSON.
89. iv. ELIJAH (twin), bapt. 4 Apr. 1762.
v. ELISHA (twin), bapt. 4 Apr. 1762; d. young.
90. vi. JOSEPH PUNDERSON, bapt. 27 May 1764.
vii. ELISHA, bapt. 26 Sept. 1767; d. 9 July 1839; lived at Bethany.
viii. CALEB, bapt. 4 Mar. 1770; m. HANNAH ——, bur. 3 Oct. 1809, aged 39 (Episcopal Church records).
91. ix. MILES, bapt. 28 June 1772.

62. LEMUEL⁵ HOTCHKISS (*Caleb,*⁴ *Joshua,*³ *John,*² *Samuel*¹), married first, 2 Jan. 1757, MARY MALLORY of Stratford, who died 19 Apr. 1762; and secondly, 6 Mar. 1765, PARTHENA MURRAY of New Milford. He lived at New Haven.

Children by first wife:

i. THADDEUS,⁶ b. 24 Sept. 1757; d. 1787; m. ——. Children: 1. *Parthena.*⁷ 2. *Thaddeus.*
ii. HEPHZIBAH, b. 14 Mar. 1760; m. (1) 1 Jan. 1777 DAVID MOULTHROP; m. (2) 14 Nov. 1780 PHINEHAS ANDRUS.
iii. MARY (twin), b. 3 Apr. 1762.
iv. AURELIUS (twin), b. 3 Apr. 1762; bapt. as PARMELIA.

Children by second wife:

v. LYMAN, b. 9 Jan. 1766.
vi. HANNAH, bapt. 2 Apr. 1775.
vii. LEMUEL, bapt. 21 Mar. 1779.

63. EZEKIEL⁵ HOTCHKISS (*Joseph,*⁴ *Joseph,*³ *John,*² *Samuel*¹), born at Guilford 14 Mar. 1726, removed to New Haven, and died 1779. He married, 25 Jan. 1750, HANNAH ALLING.

Children:

92. i. Enos,[6] b. 6 June 1751.
    ii. Mary, b. 14 May 1753; m. Israel Bradley.
    iii. Hannah, b. 9 Jan. 1755; m. 1778 Glover Ball.
    iv. Rachel, b. 1 Jan. 1757; m. James Brannen.
    v. Rhoda, b. 10 Feb. 1759; m. (1) Samuel Chatterton, b. 13 Mar. 1755, d. 16 Oct. 1789; m. (2) 20 Oct. 1792 Benjamin Brown.
    vi. Lois, b. 17 July 1761; d. 26 Nov. 1828; m. Samuel Hibbart.
    vii. Eber, b. 26 Nov. 1764.
    viii. Phebe, b. 6 Nov. 1766; m. William Hitchcock.
    ix. Ezekiel, b. 6 Nov. 1768; d. unm. after 1779.

64. Daniel[5] Hotchkiss (*Joseph,[4] Joseph,[3] John,[2] Samuel[1]*), born at Guilford 2 July 1728, removed to Cheshire, and died 13 Sept. 1807. He married Eunice ———, who died 5 July 1811, aged 77.
    Children :
    i. Thankful,[6] b. 15 Feb. 1753.
    ii. Eunice, b. 8 Jan. 1755; m. ———.
    iii. Isaac, b. 4 Mar. 1757.
    iv. Lucy, b. 7 Mar. 1759; m. May 1785 Laban Hall.
    v. Thomas, b. 25 Nov. 1763.
    vi. Lydia, b. 30 Mar. 1766.
    vii. Hannah.
    viii. Daniel.
    ix. Damaris.
    x. Moses, b. 27 Feb. 1776.

65. Joseph[5] Hotchkiss (*Joseph,[4] Joseph,[3] John,[2] Samuel[1]*), born at Guilford 22 Oct. 1736, removed to Cheshire. He married, 30 July 1761, Hannah Atwater.
    Children:
    i. Ebenezer,[6] b. 3 Sept. 1766.
    ii. Salina, b. 7 Nov. 1768.
    iii. Hannah, b. 17 Jan. 1771.
    iv. Joseph, b. 12 Mar. 1773.
    Probably other children.

66. Josiah[5] Hotchkiss (*Josiah,[4] Josiah,[3] John,[2] Samuel[1]*), born 26 Dec. 1742, lived at Cheshire, and married Sarah Perkins, daughter of Elisha and Eunice (Perkins), who was born 28 Aug. 1741.
    Children:
    i. Abigail,[6] b. 12 Dec. 1765; d. 19 Dec. 1847; m. 4 Dec. 1788 Joel Moss, b. 7 July 1766, d. 6 Mar. 1847.
    ii. Israel, b. 30 May 1767; d. 21 Feb. 1840; m. 20 Sept. 1792 Martha Royce, b. 7 Mar. 1765, d. 15 Mar. 1840. Children: 1. *Nathaniel Royce,[7]* b. 6 Sept. 1793. 2. *Josiah,* b. 24 Jan. 1795; d. 30 Aug. 1832. 3. *Elizur,* b. 8 Oct. 1797; d. 8 Oct. 1834. 4. *Maria,* b. 26 Jan. 1800; m. ——— Andrews. 5. *Israel,* b. 28 Apr. 1802. 6. *Caroline,* b. 1 Mar. 1804; m. Aaron Brooks. 7. *Sybil,* b. 21 June 1806; d. 7 Mar. 1808. 8. *Seth,* b. 18 Sept. 1808; d. 1888. 9. *Charles Lester,* b. 16 Mar. 1813.
    iii. Josephus, b. 2 Aug. 1768; d. 23 Mar. 1821; m. 11 Nov. 1790 Sarah Benham. Children: 1. *Benoni,[7]* b. 8 May 1794; removed to Campbellsville, Ky. 2. *Lois,* b. 27 Oct. 1795. 3. *Sarah,* b. 13 Dec. 1797. 4. *Delos,* b. 25 Oct. 1802. 5. *Mary,* b. 6 July 1807. 6. *Eunice,* b. 16 Nov. 1809.
    iv. Eunice, b. 28 Aug. 1770.
    v. Salma, b. 17 May 1772; m. 27 Nov. 1794 Rebecca Hall.
    vi. Sarah, b. 13 Dec. 1777.

67. Benoni[5] Hotchkiss (*Josiah,[4] Josiah,[3] John,[2] Samuel[1]*), born 4 Aug. 1752, lived at Cheshire, and died 27 Feb. 1835. He married first,

200

5 Sept. 1771, HANNAH NORTON, who was born about 1748 and died 16 May 1788; and secondly LUCY ———, who was born about 1764 and died 23 Nov. 1821. The record of this family is incomplete.

Children by first wife:

i. HULDA ANN,[6] b. 1772.
ii. WILLIAM, b. abt. 1780; d. 4 Sept. 1785.
iii. ALBERT, b. abt. 1783; d. 12 Nov. 1786.
iv. MARY, b. 6 Dec. 1786.

Children by second wife:

v. ELIZA, b. abt. 1793; d. 20 Aug. 1795.
vi. ALBERT, d. 15 Sept. 1795.
vii. FREDERICK H., b. 12 Aug. 1803.

68. CAPT. STEPHEN[5] HOTCHKISS (*Caleb*,[4] *Caleb*,[3] *John*,[2] *Samuel*[1]), born 4 Feb. 1738, lived at New Haven, and died 19 Dec. 1800. He married first, 10 Dec. 1767, ABIGAIL SCOTT, who was baptized 16 Nov. 1746 and died 4 May 1789; and secondly MRS. ELIZABETH (OSBORN) MILES, widow of James, who was born 29 Apr. 1750.

Children by first wife:

i. LUCY,[6] b. 4 Sept. 1769.
ii. WILLIAM SCOTT, b. 29 Jan. 1772; d. 28 July 1835; m. 12 Dec. 1795 MARY THOMPSON, b. 8 May 1773. The family of his son, *William Scott, Jr.*, appears in the *Tomlinson Genealogy*, p. 77, and the family of his son, *Isaac Thompson*, in the same volume, p. 79.
iii. PHEBE, b. 11 July 1773.
iv. STEPHEN, b. 22 Sept. 1777.
93. v. GEORGE, b. 6 Mar. 1780.
vi. WYLLYS, b. 20 Dec. 1782; d. 1852, leaving his estate to his wife LUCRETIA.

69. JONAH[5] HOTCHKISS (*Caleb*,[4] *Caleb*,[3] *John*,[2] *Samuel*[1]), born 12 June 1745, lived at New Haven, and died 15 Nov. 1811. He married, 18 Mar. 1772, ELIZABETH ATWATER, who was born 30 Jan. 1748 and died 16 Apr. 1827.

Children:

i. ELIZABETH,[6] b. 10 June 1773; d. 15 Apr. 1796; m. JUSTUS[5] HOTCHKISS (86), b. abt. 1772, d. 6 May 1812.
ii. SUSANNAH, b. 24 June 1775; d. 1 Mar. 1825; m. 27 Apr. 1800 JUSTUS[5] HOTCHKISS (86), widower of her sister.
94. iii. EZRA.
95. iv. RUSSELL.
96. v. ELIAS.

70. ELIHU[5] HOTCHKISS (*Joel*,[4] *Caleb*,[3] *John*,[2] *Samuel*[1]), born at New Haven 16 Aug. 1742, removed to Litchfield, and died 12 May 1835. He married, 1769, LYDIA ROBINSON, who died 2 June 1836, aged 93. (Gravestone inscriptions, Morris, Conn.)

Children:

i. SALLY,[6] m. BENJAMIN WEBSTER.
ii. LYDIA, b. abt. 1774; d. 4 Jan. 1860.
iii. MARY, b. 26 Dec. 1776; d. 9 Sept. 1851.
iv. RACHEL, b. 28 Feb. 1779.
v. LYMAN, b. 26 May 1781; d. 15 Mar. 1861; m. CLARISSA ———, d. 7 Mar. 1855, aged 70.
vi. ELIHU.
vii. BETSEY.

71. JOHN[5] HOTCHKISS (*Joshua*,[4] *Stephen*,[3] *Joshua*,[2] *Samuel*[1]), born 27 Feb. 1733, lived at Cheshire, and died 9 Nov. 1794. He married first,

25 Oct. 1756, ABIGAIL SMITH, daughter of Ebenezer and Hannah (Smith) of West Haven, who was born 31 Aug. 1725 and died 19 Apr. 1760; and secondly, 26 Jan. 1761, SARAH GILLAM.

Child by first wife:

i. MARY,[6] b. 23 June 1758; m. JOSEPH JOHNSON of Woodbridge.

Children by second wife:

ii. NOAH, m. 17 Apr. 1782 ABIGAIL HITCHCOCK.
iii. JOSHUA GILLAM, b. 6 Oct. 1764; d. young.
iv. BENJAMIN.
v. EBENEZER, b. 18 Jan. 1768.
vi. ABIGAIL SMITH, b. 8 July 1769.
vii. SARAH, m. JOHN COOK[5] HOTCHKISS (47, xiv).
viii. SUSANNAH, b. 18 July 1773.

72. ABRAHAM[5] HOTCHKISS (*Isaac,*[4] *Isaac,*[3] *Joshua,*[2] *Samuel*[1]), born at Bethany, lived there, and died at Waterbury 24 Nov. 1802. He married ROSETTA SPERRY, daughter of Ezra and Ruth (Sperry).

Children (order unknown):

i. IRA,[6] removed to Sheffield, Mass.
ii. MARK, b. abt. 1770; d. at New Haven 26 Feb. 1826.
iii. ABRAHAM.
iv. CALVIN.
v. BELA, m. ———. Child: 1. *Rachel.*[7]
vi. ANN, m. ——— HALY.
vii. RACHEL, m. ——— UPSON.

73. ISAAC[5] HOTCHKISS (*Isaac,*[4] *Isaac,*[3] *Joshua,*[2] *Samuel*[1]), born about 1758, lived at Bethany, and died 11 May 1828. He married ELIZABETH CLARK, who was born about 1762 and died 6 Jan. 1859.

Children (order unknown):

i. PHILO,[6] b. abt. 1778; d. 18 July 1858; m. PATTY LINES, b. abt. 1783, d. 12 Mar. 1864; left issue.
ii. ISAAC.
iii. CLARK, m. ——— LINES. His only son, *Isaac,*[7] removed to Michigan.
iv. PATTY, m. JOHN WHITE.
v. FANNY, m. ABEL PRINCE.
vi. REBECCA, m. HIRAM[7] HOTCHKISS (109).
vii. ELIZABETH, m. MILES FRENCH.

74. STEPHEN[5] HOTCHKISS (*Jabez,*[4] *Jacob,*[3] *Joshua,*[2] *Samuel*[1]), born 31 Oct. 1761, lived at Bethany, and died 5 Nov. 1847. He married HANNAH BROWN, who was buried 28 Feb. 1847.

Children:

i. HARRIET.[6]
97. ii. HARLEY, b. 12 Sept. 1791.
iii. REBECCA, m. MINOTT COLLINS.
iv. WEALTHY, d. young.
98. v. EBER, b. abt. 1796.
vi. STEPHEN, m. 10 Sept. 1837 ABIGAIL HOTCHKISS, who was bur. 29 May 1842, aged 42.
vii. HANNAH, m. JOHN RUSSELL.
99. viii. JARED, b. abt. 1804.
ix. JESSE, m. CAROLINE SPERRY.
100. x. GEORGE.

75. LEVERETT[5] HOTCHKISS (*Elijah,*[4] *Jacob,*[3] *Joshua,*[2] *Samuel*[1]), born 6 Oct. 1762, lived at Derby, and died 3 Oct. 1826. He married, 14 Aug. 1785, SARAH BURRITT, who was born about 1763 and died 8 Jan. 1842.

Child:

i. WYLLYS,[6] b. 25 Apr. 1788; d. 24 Nov. 1872.

76. JOSEPH[5] HOTCHKISS (*Joseph,*[4] *Samuel,*[3] *Thomas,*[2] *Samuel*[1]), born 21 May 1739, lived at Bethany, and died 26 Apr. 1800. He married, 10 June 1762, HANNAH THOMAS, daughter of Joseph and Dorcas (Richardson), who died about 1821.

Children:

     i. TEMPERANCE,[6] m. STRONG SANFORD.
101. ii. SILAS, b. 1766.
     iii. DAVID ELISHA.
     iv. HANNAH, m. ELIHU HITCHCOCK.
     v. JOSEPH or JOSEPHUS, d. 1842; m. ELIZABETH BEERS.
     vi. LYMAN, perhaps the one who m. MOLLY BRADLEY, b. 28 Apr. 1767.

77. SAMUEL[5] HOTCHKISS (*Joseph,*[4] *Samuel,*[3] *Thomas,*[2] *Samuel*[1]), born 19 June 1741, lived at Bethany, and died 1804. He married, 23 Dec. 1762, LYDIA PECK, who died about 1804.

Children:

     i. LYDIA,[6] b. abt. 1765; d. 13 July 1815; m. JOHN THOMAS.
     ii. MOSES.
     iii. JAMES, of Homer, N. Y.
     iv. ABNER.
     v. AARON.
     vi. BILDAD.
     vii. MARY.
     viii. HEPHZIBAH.
     ix. SAMUEL.
     x. ZIBA.

78. WILLIAM[5] HOTCHKISS (*Joseph,*[4] *Samuel,*[3] *Thomas,*[2] *Samuel*[1]), born 9 Oct. 1744, lived at Westville, and died before 1793. He married ELIPHAL HINE.

Children:

     i. JANE,[6] b. 1765; d. 1849; m. DAVID HINE of Woodbridge, b. 1762, d. 22 Dec. 1851.
102. ii. JOHN.
103. iii. DAVID, b. abt. 1769.
     iv. ELIPHAL, m. 3 Apr. 1782 FRANCIS MOORE of New Haven.
     v. ANNA, m. 2 Oct. 1788 ISAAC FENN of Milford.
     vi. GEORGE, d. 31 Jan. 1775.
     vii. SARAH.

79. BENJAMIN[5] HOTCHKISS (*Joseph,*[4] *Samuel,*[3] *Thomas,*[2] *Samuel*[1]), born 2 June 1748, lived at Bethany, and died 20 Mar. 1809. He married SARAH DOWNS, who was born 29 Nov. 1747, and married secondly Ephraim Buckingham.

Children:

     i. AMOS,[6] b. 6 Feb. 1777.
     ii. SALLY, b. 16 Aug. 1778.

80. REUBEN[5] HOTCHKISS (*David,*[4] *Abraham,*[3] *Thomas,*[2] *Samuel*[1]), born 8 Mar. 1756, lived at Woodbury, and died 27 June 1834. He married in 1783 THANKFUL MINOR, who died 4 May 1842.

Children:

     i. JERUSHA,[6] b. 25 Apr. 1784; d. 1 June 1784.
     ii. JERUSHA, b. 20 June 1785; m. 1813 JUDSON MORRIS.
     iii. JOSIAH, b. 4 Nov. 1787; m. 19 Oct. 1809 BETSEY BROTHWELL, and had issue.
     iv. HERVEY, b. 13 Feb. 1790; d. 15 Sept. 1793.

v. BETSEY, b. 16 July 1792; d. 8 Nov. 1822.
vi. REUBEN HARVEY, b. 11 June 1794; m. (1) 13 Dec. 1820 SALLY ROOT,
d. 19 July 1835; m. (2) 26 Oct. 1836 ELIZABETH M. COMSTOCK;
had issue.
vii. DAVID, b. 5 Nov. 1796; m. (1) 12 Feb. 1824 RACHEL NORTON, d.
17 Jan. 1851; m. (2) 25 Mar. 1852 JULIA M. HOWARD; had issue.
viii. GERVASE, b. 2 July 1801; m. 25 Apr. 1848 SARAH COGSWELL, and
had issue.
ix. RUTH, b. 16 Dec. 1803; d. 24 Oct. 1820.

81. SOLOMON⁵ HOTCHKISS (*Solomon,⁴ Daniel,³ Daniel,² Samuel¹*), born
20 Mar. 1752, lived at Woodbridge, and died 6 Apr. 1793. He
married ———.
Children:
i. LEVINA,⁶ d. unm. 1795.
ii. JOHN.
iii. ANNA.
iv. LUCIUS.

82. DEA. DAVID⁵ HOTCHKISS (*Solomon,⁴ Daniel,³ Daniel,² Samuel¹*), born
26 Oct. 1754, lived at Woodbridge, and died 5 June 1823. He
married first, 15 May 1777, LYDIA BEECHER, who was born about
1756 and died 28 June 1785; and secondly ABIGAIL ———, who
was born about 1754 and died 17 Oct. 1845.
Children by first wife:
104. i. DAVID,⁶ b. abt. 1779.
105. ii. HARVEY, b. abt. 1781.
iii. LYDIA.
iv. ELEANOR, m. 1805 ABNER BALDWIN.
Children by second wife:
v. ELIZABETH, bapt. 8 May 1788.
vi. HENRY.
vii. KETURAH.
viii. A DAUGHTER.
ix. HARRIET, bapt. 27 May 1798; m. 1 May 1816 GARRETT JOHNSON of
Derby.

83. LEVI⁵ HOTCHKISS (*Eliphalet,⁴ Daniel,³ Daniel,² Samuel¹*), born 2
May 1754, lived at Derby, and died about 1832. He married first
PHEBE ———, who died 3 Apr. 1789; secondly BETSEY ———,
who died 8 Apr. 1791; thirdly SARAH ———, who died 1 Dec.
1801; and fourthly Susannah ———, who died in 1839.
Children by first wife:
106. i. ELIPHALET,⁶ b. abt. 1777.
ii. LEVI.
iii. BETSEY, b. abt. 1782; d. 21 Aug. 1819.
iv. PHEBE, b. abt. 1784; d. 19 Aug. 1873.
v. ABIGAIL, m. ISAAC THOMPSON.
vi. DAVID.
vii. A DAUGHTER, m. CHAUNCEY BALDWIN.

84. ELI⁵ HOTCHKISS (*Obadiah,⁴ Daniel,³ Daniel,² Samuel¹*), born 18 Sept.
1758, lived at New Haven, and died 13 May 1813. He married
EUNICE ATWATER, who was born 2 June 1762 and died 13 Feb.
1817.
Children:
i. LYDIA,⁶ b. abt. 1794; d. 12 Sept. 1826; m. JAMES BRADLEY.
ii. CLARISSA, m. (1) MINER HOTCHKISS of Middletown; m. (2) REUBEN
SKINNER of New York.
iii. HARRIET, m. JUSTUS HARRISON.

85. OBADIAH[5] HOTCHKISS (*Obadiah*,[4] *Daniel*,[3] *Daniel*,[2] *Samuel*[1]), born 4 Sept. 1762, lived at New Haven, and died 28 Jan. 1832. He married, 12 Feb. 1782, HANNAH LEWIS, who was born about 1757 and died 22 Nov. 1831.

Children :

   i.   SILAS,[6] b. 11 Oct. 1784; d. 2 Oct. 1795.
  ii. DEA. LEWIS, b. 25 Dec. 1786; d. 14 Oct. 1859; m. HANNAH TROW-
        BRIDGE, b. 24 Mar. 1792, d. 24 Aug. 1873.
 iii. HANNAH F., b. 7 Apr. 1796; d. 4 May 1815.

86. JUSTUS[5] HOTCHKISS (*Obadiah*,[4] *Daniel*,[3] *Daniel*,[2] *Samuel*[1]), born about 1772, lived at New Haven, and died 6 May 1812. He married first ELIZABETH[6] HOTCHKISS, daughter of Jonah (69), who was born 10 June 1773 and died 15 Apr. 1796 ; and secondly, 27 Apr. 1800, SUSANNAH[6] HOTCHKISS, sister of his first wife, who was born 24 June 1775 and died 1 Mar. 1825.

Children by second wife :

107. i.   HENRY,[6] b. 29 Apr. 1801.
108. ii. LUCIUS, b. 1 Mar. 1803.

THE HOTCHKISS FAMILY

By Donald Lines Jacobus, M.A., of New Haven, Conn.

87. Miles[6] Hotchkiss (*Jonah,[5] Henry,[4] John,[8] John,[2] Samuel[1]*), born 28 Aug. 1778, lived at Cheshire, and died 23 Nov. 1839. He married first, 4 Dec. 1800, Polly Ives, who died 22 Nov. 1815; and secondly Joanna ————, who died 4 Nov. 1830.

Children by first wife:

 i. Richard,[7] b. 9 Dec. 1801.
 ii. Lent, b. 26 Nov. 1803.
 iii. William, b. 18 Apr. 1806.
 iv. Abigail, b. 26 May 1808.
 v. Mary, b. 26 Dec. 1810.
 vi. Sally Rosilla, b. 23 Jan. 1813.
 vii. Miles, b. 15 Nov. 1815.

Child by second wife:

 viii. A son, b. 13 Oct. 1819.

88. Eleazer[6] Hotchkiss (*Joshua,[5] Caleb,[4] Joshua,[8] John,[2] Samuel[1]*), baptized 7 May 1758, lived at Westville, and died between 12 Oct. and 11 Nov. 1822. He married, 14 Dec. 1779, Naomi Gilbert, daughter of Michael and Betha, who died 29 Mar. 1836, aged 75.

Children:

 i. Betsey,[7] bapt. 20 Aug. 1780; m. ———— Tyler.
 ii. Michael Gilbert, bapt. 12 Oct. 1783; d. 9 Dec. 1848; m. Asenath ————, d. 20 Dec. 1861, aged 78.
 iii. Parmelia, b. 19 Apr. 1785; d. 1 Jan. 1866; m. 12 Oct. 1806 Leverett Dickerman, b. 11 Dec. 1779, d. 31 Jan. 1861.
 iv. Eleazer, bapt. 6 Aug. 1792; d. 13 Apr. 1841; m. Fanny L. ————.

89. Elijah[6] Hotchkiss (*Joshua,[5] Caleb,[4] Joshua,[8] John,[2] Samuel[1]*), baptized 4 Apr. 1762, lived at Westville, and died in Sept. 1849. He married, 3 Mar. 1782, Rebecca Osborne, daughter of Jehiel and Rebecca (Sperry), who was baptized 23 Sept. 1764 and died in Dec. 1842. The record of this family is incomplete.

Child:

 i. Rufus,[7] b. abt. 1790; d. 6 Mar. 1863; m. Priscilla ————, b. abt. 1800; d. 15 June 1847.

90. Joseph Punderson[6] Hotchkiss (*Joshua,[5] Caleb,[4] Joshua,[8] John,[2] Samuel[1]*), baptized 27 May 1764, lived at Cedar Hill, New Haven, and died 14 Mar. 1838. He married first Rhoda Wooding, daughter of John and Hannah (Holbrook), who was born about 1765 and died 1 Feb. 1823; and secondly, 11 May 1823, Mrs. Sarah Tuttle, who died in 1841.

Children by first wife:

 i. Clarissa,[7] b. 18 Dec. 1786; d. 17 Sept. 1846; m. 10 Jan. 1808 Lyman Atwater of Cedar Hill, b. 3 Mar. 1783, d. Mar. 1862.
 ii. Henry, b. abt. 1791; d. 9 Apr. 1826; m. Polly ————.
 iii. Anna, b. 5 Nov. 1795; d. 26 Feb. 1836; m. 12 Dec. 1813 Medad Atwater of Cedar Hill, b. 18 Oct. 1788.

91. Miles[6] Hotchkiss (*Joshua,[5] Caleb,[4] Joshua,[8] John,[2] Samuel[1]*), baptized 28 June 1772, lived at Westville, and died between 8 Feb.

and 13 Mar. 1837. He married at Milford, 18 Nov. 1792, ANER HEPBURN, who died 12 Mar. 1836, aged 65.

Children:

i. SALLY,[7] b. abt. 1795; d. 17 Oct. 1874; m. GEORGE MORSE, b. abt. 1778, d. 11 Oct. 1856.
ii. CAROLINE, m. 1 Nov. 1820 CLARK SMITH DUNNING.
iii. EUNICE, b. abt. 1799; d. 23 May 1884; m. JOHN B. LEWIS, b. abt. 1804, d. 3 Aug. 1847.
iv. EMMA M.
v. MILES, b. abt. 1805; d. 27 May 1848; m. 31 Dec. 1826 ELIZA D. CADWELL, who m. (2) ——— Bodge and d. 31 Mar. 1869, aged 61.

92. ENOS[6] HOTCHKISS (*Ezekiel,[5] Joseph,[4] Joseph,[3] John,[2] Samuel[1]*) born 6 June 1751, lived at New Haven, and died in 1792. He married ——— BRADLEY, daughter of Isaac and Lois of East Haven.

Children:

i. ESTHER.[7]
ii. SARAH·
iii. REBECCA, m. WHITING IVES.
iv. EZEKIEL, b. abt. 1785; d. 12 June 1849; m. SARAH LARRABEE, d. 1852.

93. GEORGE[6] HOTCHKISS (*Stephen,[5] Caleb,[4] Caleb,[3] John,[2] Samuel[1]*), born 6 Mar. 1780, lived at New Haven, and died in 1821. He married, 26 Sept. 1802, PEGGY COLLIS.

Children:

i. DANIEL COLLIS,[7] b. abt. 1804; m. 19 Sept. 1827 ELIZABETH[7] HOTCHKISS, daughter of Russell (95). They removed to New York City.
ii. GEORGE WYLLYS, b. abt. 1806.
iii. HENRY SCOTT, b. abt. 1808.
iv. ELIZABETH DAVIS, b. abt. 1810.
v. WILLIAM DUMMER, b. abt. 1812.

94. EZRA[6] HOTCHKISS (*Jonah,[5] Caleb,[4] Caleb,[3] John,[2] Samuel[1]*), of New Haven, died in 1868. He married first NANCY AUGUR, who was born 14 Nov. 1785 and died 20 Apr. 1836, aged 50; and secondly CATHARINE ———.

Children by first wife:

i. CHARLES F.,[7] removed to Rochester, N. Y., and Vineland, N. J.; m. 30 Oct. 1827 OLIVIA EUNICE TROWBRIDGE, b. 31 May 1806.
ii. LEONARD S., m. 27 June 1833 LOUISA HUBBARD.

95. RUSSELL[6] HOTCHKISS (*Jonah,[5] Caleb,[4] Caleb,[3] John,[2] Samuel[1]*), born about 1780, lived at New Haven, and died 1 Jan. 1843. He married first ———, who was born about 1786 and died 22 May 1834; and secondly, 9 June 1835, ELIZABETH ANN HUBBARD.

Children by first wife:

i. RUSSELL,[7] m. 25 Dec. 1833 CATHARINE E. WADSWORTH.
ii. ELIZABETH, m. 19 Sept. 1827 DANIEL COLLIS[7] HOTCHKISS (93, i.).
iii. MARY, m. 23 Dec. 1829 DAVID HOADLEY, JR., of New York.
iv. HENRY O.
v. EDWARD.

96. ELIAS[6] HOTCHKISS (*Jonah,[5] Caleb,[4] Caleb,[3] John,[2] Samuel[1]*), of New Haven, died in 1865. He married JULIA ———.

Children:

i. THOMAS W.[7]
ii. ELIAS.
iii. GEORGE W., m. JULIA GILBERT.
iv. JAMES F.

v. CAROLINE, m. 1 Aug. 1838 GUSTAVUS BRADLEY.
vi. FRANCES ELIZABETH, m. ALLEN B. HITCHCOCK.
vii. NANCY, m. HENRY WHEELER.

97. HARLEY[6] HOTCHKISS (*Stephen*,[5] *Jabez*,[4] *Jacob*,[3] *Joshua*,[2] *Samuel*[1]), born
12 Sept. 1791, lived at Bethany, and died 26 Mar. 1860. He mar-
ried HARRIET COLLINS.
Children :
  i. WEALTHY ANN,[7] m. THOMAS GILYARD.
  ii. ANDREW T., d. in 1877 ; m. BELINDA BUCKINGHAM.
  iii. HARRIS, d. young.
  iv. CHARLES T., b. 9 July 1834 ; removed to Cheshire ; m. EMMA V.
      WATSON.

98. EBER[6] HOTCHKISS (*Stephen*,[5] *Jabez*,[4] *Jacob*,[3] *Joshua*,[2] *Samuel*[1]), born
about 1796, lived at Bethany, and died 28 Nov. 1851. He married
THIRZA DRIVER.
Children :
  i. DILAZON.[7]
  ii. GRACIA.
  iii. SAMANTHA.
  iv. JANE.
  v. SAMUEL.
  vi. HOOKER.

99. JARED[6] HOTCHKISS (*Stephen*,[5] *Jabez*,[4] *Jacob*,[3] *Joshua*,[2] *Samuel*[1]), born
about 1804, lived at Bethany, and died 24 Aug. 1854. He mar-
ried, 13 Sept. 1840, AMY FRENCH of Prospect.
Children :
  i. HENRY HOOKER,[7] bapt. 24 Mar. 1842 ; d. young.
  ii. CAROLINE LUCINA, bapt. Dec. 1844.

100. GEORGE[6] HOTCHKISS (*Stephen*,[5] *Jabez*,[4] *Jacob*,[3] *Joshua*,[2] *Samuel*[1]),
lived at Bethany, and married, 4 Apr. 1841, LAURA SPERRY.
Children :
  i. ERBAN EVANDER,[7] bapt. 13 Aug. 1843 ; m. ELIZABETH CRABTREE.
  ii. A DAUGHTER.
  iii. A DAUGHTER.

101. SILAS[6] HOTCHKISS (*Joseph*,[5] *Joseph*,[4] *Samuel*,[3] *Thomas*,[2] *Samuel*[1]),
born about 1766, lived at Bethany, and died before 28 Feb. 1848.
He married SUSANNAH PECK.
Children :
109. i. HIRAM.[7]
110. ii. WOOSTER, b. abt. 1793.
     iii. TEMPERANCE, m. WILLIAM ANDREW.
     iv. DEBORAH.
     v. MARTHA.

102. JOHN[6] HOTCHKISS (*William*,[5] *Joseph*,[4] *Samuel*,[3] *Thomas*,[2] *Samuel*[1]),
lived at Westville, and married, 2 May 1785, HULDAH SPERRY.
Children :
  i. IRA,[7] b. abt. 1790.
  ii. OBEDIENCE, b. abt. 1791.
  iii. SALLY ALMIRA.
  iv. JOHN MILES.

103. DAVID[6] HOTCHKISS (*William*,[5] *Joseph*,[4] *Samuel*,[3] *Thomas*,[2] *Samuel*[1]),
born about 1769, died 12 Jan. 1846. He married MERCY BRADLEY,
who was born about 1766 and died 30 Jan. 1854.

Children :

i. LUCY,[7] b. abt. 1792 ; m. ISAAC BLAKE.
ii. LEWIS, b. abt. 1797 ; d. 17 Aug. 1803.
iii. HANNAH, b. abt. 1799.
iv. WILLIS, b. 29 Mar. 1803 ; d. 18 Sept. 1884 ; m. MARY A. KIMBERLY, b. 3 July 1812, d. 9 Feb. 1900. He lived at Derby and had issue.
v. LEWIS, b. 14 Oct. 1806 ; d. 19 Feb. 1887 ; m. ELIZA HULL. He lived at Derby and had issue.
vi. EUNICE, m. SHELDON MOULTHROP.
vii. SARAH M., b. 17 Feb. 1814 ; d. 14 Apr. 1895 ; m. WILLIAM BALDWIN of Derby, b. 18 Sept. 1811 ; d. 2 June 1887.

104. DAVID[6] HOTCHKISS (*David,[5] Solomon,[4] Daniel,[3] Daniel,[2] Samuel[1]*), born about 1779, lived at Woodbridge, and died 24 June 1842. He married HULDAH ———, who was born about 1782 and died 21 July 1836.
Children :

i. HUBBARD,[7] b. abt. 1798 ; d. 26 Oct. 1849 ; m. 9 Aug. 1820 HANNAH ALLEN. Child : 1. *Hannah E.*,[8] bapt. 3 Aug. 1828 ; m. William A. Warner.
ii. MARIA, bapt. Oct. 1803.
iii. SALLY CAROLINE, bapt. 31 Aug. 1806.
iv. HENRIETTA, bapt. 26 June 1808.
v. HENRY LUCIUS, b. 10 May 1810 ; lived at New Haven ; d. 26 May 1861 ; m. LUCY COWELL, b. 28 Apr. 1815, d. 21 Nov. 1896, who m. (2) ——— Webster. Children : 1. *Sarah,[8]* d. young. 2. *George Henry,* b. 6 Mar. 1840 ; d. 28 June 1904 ; m. Caroline Austin ; left issue.

105. HARVEY[6] HOTCHKISS (*David,[5] Solomon,[4] Daniel,[3] Daniel,[2] Samuel[1]*), born about 1781, lived at Bethany, and died 9 Dec. 1855. He married, in 1805, SARAH ALLING, who died 21 Sept. 1862.
Children :

i. SHELDON ALLING,[7] b. 22 Apr. 1808.
ii. ELIZA SAMANTHA, b. 18 Sept. 1810 ; d. 14 Feb. 1876.
iii. SOLOMON, b. 18 June 1813 ; d. 7 Jan. 1886 ; m. CHARLOTTE HEMINGWAY, b. abt. 1821, d. 28 May 1893.
iv. BEECHER DELOS, b. 11 Feb. 1815 ; d. 30 Oct. 1866 ; m. BETSEY PERKINS, b. abt. 1821, d. 3 Oct. 1863.
v. JULIUS LEONARD, b. 17 June 1817 ; d. 17 Feb. 1879 ; m. SOPHRONIA ———.
vi. THEODORE NELSON, b. 20 Dec. 1819 ; d. 27 Feb. 1888 ; m. LUCIA SPERRY.
vii. SARAH FINETTE, b. 29 Oct. 1822 ; d. 15 Jan. 1878 ; m. 5 Mar. 1848 DEWITT CLINTON CASTLE of Seymour.
viii. ORLANDO THOMAS, b. 8 Aug. 1825 ; d. 11 Dec. 1828.
ix. HARVEY HARPIN, b. 16 Feb. 1828 ; lived at Prospect ; m. 15 Feb. 1852 CHARLOTTE ELIZA ALLING.
x. MARGARET DIANTHE, b. 16 June 1830 ; d. 14 Feb. 1872 ; m. MATTHEW TREWHELLA of Cheshire.

106. ELIPHALET[6] HOTCHKISS (*Levi,[5] Eliphalet,[4] Daniel,[3] Daniel,[2] Samuel[1]*), born about 1777, lived at Derby, and died 21 Sept. 1858. He married NANCY ———, who died 15 Nov. 1865.
Children :

i. WILLIAM.[7]
ii. ALBERT.
iii. MARY ANN.
iv. BURR.
v. HARRIET.
vi. ELI.
vii. JOHN.

viii. PHEBE.
ix. JANE.
x. HANNAH.
xi. AMELIA.
xii. HARVEY.

107. HENRY[6] HOTCHKISS (*Justus,[5] Obadiah,[4] Daniel,[3] Daniel,[2] Samuel[1]*),
born 29 Apr. 1801, lived at New Haven, and died 15 Dec. 1871.
He was president of the New Haven Bank. He married, 22 May
1823, ELIZABETH DAGGETT.
   Children:
   i. ELIZABETH SUSAN.[7]
   ii. MARY ANN FORBES.
   iii. MARTHA PRESCOTT, m. DR. JOHN O. BRONSON.
   iv. SUSAN VIRTUE.
   v. MARY ANN, m. CAPT. CHARLES HERVEY TOWNSHEND.
   vi. HENRY LUCIUS, b. 12 Dec. 1842; m. 25 Feb. 1875 JANE LOUISA
       FITCH TROWBRIDGE. Children: 1. *Henry Stewart,[8]* b. 1 Oct.
       1876. 2. *Helen Southgate,* b. 24 Nov. 1880. 3. *Elizabeth Trow-
       bridge,* b. 26 Mar. 1885.

108. LUCIUS[6] HOTCHKISS (*Justus,[5] Obadiah,[4] Daniel,[3] Daniel,[2] Samuel[1]*),
born 1 Mar. 1803, lived at New Haven, and died 29 May 1880.
He married first, 18 Oct. 1827, MARIA MELCHER STREET, who was
born 1 Jan. 1807 and died 2 Sept. 1833; and secondly, Oct. 1834,
CATHERINE LADD STREET, who died 29 May 1880.
   Children by first wife:
   i. MARIA LOUISE FORBES,[7] b. 2 Aug. 1828; d. 15 June 1889; m. 15 Sept.
      1847 CHARLES MULOCK of New York.
   ii. JUSTUS STREET, b. 4 Feb. 1831; m. 9 May 1866 FANNY WINCHESTER,
       b. in Boston 9 Oct. 1838, d. 24 Jan. 1912. He is a director of the
       Second National Bank, New Haven. Child: 1. *Fanny Winchester,[8]*
       b. 26 July 1879; d. 31 July 1879.
   iii. ANNA MARIA, b. 10 Aug. 1833; d. 31 Aug. 1833.

109. HIRAM[7] HOTCHKISS (*Silas,[6] Joseph,[5] Joseph,[4] Samuel,[3] Thomas,[2]
Samuel[1]*), died in 1849. He married REBECCA[6] HOTCHKISS, daughter of Isaac (73).
   Children:
   i. WALES,[8] b. 1825; m. FRANCES AUGUSTA COLLINS. Children: 1.
      Charles,[9] b. Mar. 1853; m. Lily Bell. 2. *Dr. Lucius Wales,* b. 31
      Dec. 1859; m. 3 June 1891 Alice H. Greene.
   ii. ANDREW, d. unm.
   iii. ELIZA A., m. ——— SANFORD.
   iv. HART, b. 2 July 1833; d. 16 Feb. 1867; m. REBECCA TEMPLE. Child:
       1. *Edith,[9]* m. Dr. Clarence E. Skinner.

110. WOOSTER[7] HOTCHKISS (*Silas,[6] Joseph,[5] Joseph,[4] Samuel,[3] Thomas,[2]
Samuel[1]*), born about 1793, lived at New Haven, and died 8 Oct.
1849. He married first ———, who died 22 Dec. 1831, aged 36;
secondly, 25 Nov. 1832, JENNETTE TYLER, who died 15 Jan. 1847,
aged 45; and thirdly MARY ATWATER.
   Children by first wife:
   i. MARY,[8] m. ——— GIDDINGS.
   ii. GEORGE.
   iii. EMILY.
   iv. SUSAN.
   v. CHARLES.
   Children by second wife:
   vi. A DAUGHTER, b. abt. 1833; d. 1 Mar. 1847.
   vii. A DAUGHTER, b. abt. 1835; d. 24 July 1845.

ADDENDA

Of the many unplaced Hotchkisses whose records come to hand only the following need be considered here:

(1) TIMOTHY HOTCHKISS of Cheshire (perhaps identical with 27, iii, who was born at New Haven 16 Mar. 1742) married, 4 Mar. 1762, LUCY ANDRUS, who died 27 Apr. 1772.

Children:

    i.   SAMUEL, b. 14 Dec. 1762; m. 12 Feb. 1784 MIRIAM⁶ HOTCHKISS, daughter of Amos (54), b. 10 Jan. 1764.
    ii.   AMBROSE, b. 14 Jan. 1765; m. 25 Dec. 1791 LUCRETIA BALDWIN.
    iii. ANER, b. 24 Dec. 1766.
    iv. BRIANT, b. 31 May 1769.
    v.   LUCY, b. 23 Apr. 1772; d. 6 May 1772.

(2) The descendants of John Hotchkin of Guilford, sometimes supposed (despite the spelling of the name) to be brother of Samuel¹ Hotchkiss, are given in REGISTER, vol. 58, p. 281. One branch, which settled in New Haven, is not carried out there, and is given here in order to prevent any confusion between this family and the New Haven Hotchkisses.

JOSEPH⁵ HOTCHKIN (*Abraham,⁴ Abraham,³ Joseph,² John¹*), born at Guilford 17 Nov. 1758, married ABIGAIL HORTON, daughter of Samuel and Sarah of Wolcott, who was baptized at Woodbridge 30 Sept. 1759. He removed to Richmond, Mass., and later, together with his brother Oliver, to New Haven., Conn., where he died 29 Apr. 1827. His widow died 4 Dec. 1829.

    Children:

    i.   ELIAS,⁶ b. abt. 1783; d. at New Haven 17 Aug. 1824, leaving children: 1. *Charles,*⁷ b. abt. 1810. 2. *Mary Ann*, b. abt. 1812. 3. *Amanda Charlotte*.
    ii.   TABITHA, m. ——— GASTON.
    iii. LOVINIA, m. ——— KINGSLEY.
    iv. ABIGAIL, m. ——— DUDLEY.

(3) A Hotchkiss family settled in Norfolk, Conn., about 1763, but it was not connected with the line of Samuel¹ in time to be inserted in its proper place. It is now nearly certain that James, Enos, and Samuel, the heads of the Norfolk branch, were two sons and a grandson of Samuel³ (12) of East Haven.

12, viii. JAMES⁴ HOTCHKISS (*Samuel,³ Samuel,² Samuel¹*), born at East Haven 13 Jan. 1728, married DOROTHY ASPINWALL of Norfolk.

    Children:

    i.   LEVI,⁵ ⎫
    ii.   MARY, ⎬ bapt. 2 Oct. 1763.
    iii. SARAH, ⎭
    iv. REBECCA, bapt. 6 May 1764.
    v.   DAVID, bapt. 29 June 1766.
    vi. ASENATH, bapt. 30 Oct. 1768.
    vii. CYRUS, bapt. 29 July 1770.
    viii. JAMES, bapt. 16 Aug. 1772.
    ix. PHEBE, bapt. 19 June 1774.
    x.   IRA, bapt. 14 June 1778.
    xi. CHARLOTTE, bapt. 16 Apr. 1780.

12, ix. ENOS⁴ HOTCHKISS (*Samuel,³ Samuel,² Samuel¹*), born at East Haven 13 May 1731, married, 5 Feb. 1756, ELIZABETH

SHEPARD. The birth of their child Elihu is recorded at East Haven, but unfortunately the name was given as Enos in Dodd's East Haven Register, and this error was followed in the account given above (REGISTER, vol. 66, p. 330). Elihu, Elizabeth, and Ruth, children of Enos and Elizabeth, were baptized at Norfolk 2 Oct. 1763, together with three children of James and Dorothy, a fact which serves to identify Enos and James as the East Haven brothers.

Children:

  i.   ELIHU,[5] b. at East Haven 1757; bapt. at Norfolk 2 Oct. 1763.
  ii.   ELIZABETH, } bapt. 2 Oct. 1763.
  iii. RUTH, }
  iv. A CHILD, d. 17 Jan. 1763.
  v.   JOHN, bapt. at Norfolk 17 June 1764.
  vi. ENOS.
  vii. STEPHEN.
  viii. HANNAH, m. JONATHAN FINCH.
  ix. SAMUEL, b. at East Haven 1778.

34, iii. SAMUEL[5] HOTCHKISS (*Samuel,*[4] *Samuel,*[3] *Samuel,*[2] *Samuel*[1]), removed from Northford to Norfolk, and died Jan. 1799. He married ELIZABETH ———.

Children:

  i.   CHLOE,[6] bapt. 12 Apr. 1778.
  ii.   BETSEY, bapt. 26 Nov. 1780.
  iii. DAMARIS, bapt. 27 Apr. 1783.
  iv. SAMUEL, bapt. 5 June 1785.
  v.   LUMEN PHELPS, bapt. 8 June 1788; m. HANNAH ———.
  vi. JAMES, bapt. 22 Jan. 1791.
  vii. ABIGAIL, bapt. 12 July 1798; perhaps the child who d. July 1798.
  viii. ELIZA AURELIA, bapt. 13 June 1802.

JOSIAH HOTCHKISS, perhaps the oldest child of James (12, viii), married ASENATH ———.

Children:

  i.   OLIVER, ⎫
  ii.   JOSIAH, ⎪
  iii. ASAHEL, ⎬ bapt. 15 Oct. 1799.
  iv. ASENATH, ⎪
  v.   DANIEL, ⎪
  vi. CYRUS, ⎭
  vii. A CHILD, d. Apr. 1790.
  viii. CHARLOTTE, bapt. 27 Aug. 1801.

(4) THOMAS[4] HOTCHKISS (18, i) was probably the man reported dead or captured in the French War, 7 Sept. 1756. If so, his family may not have removed from Hamden as supposed. It will be noted that he had a son Samuel, born 7 July 1732. In 1816 the estate of Samuel Hotchkiss, Jr., of Hamden was distributed to his children Samuel, Amasa, and Sarah, and the children of his daughter Mary, deceased.

(5) Thanks to the courtesy of Mrs. F. A. Sanford of Westfield, Mass., it is possible to make additions and corrections in the line of DEA. GIDEON[4] HOTCHKISS (36). Descendants are certain that the twelfth child attributed to him, Asahel,[5] was in reality the child of Gideon's eldest son, Jesse.[5] Gideon's daughter Olive (36, xviii) married William Jones.

36, i. JESSE[5] HOTCHKISS (*Gideon,*[4] *Stephen,*[3] *Joshua,*[2] *Samuel*[1]), born 9 Oct. 1738, died 29 Sept. 1776. He married, 2 Oct. 1759, CHARITY MALLORY of Stratford.

Children :

A. i. ASAHEL,[6] b. 15 Feb. 1760.
  ii. CHARITY, b. 24 Mar. 1761; m. RIVERUS RUSSELL of Homer, N. Y., and of York, Livingston Co., N. Y.
  iii. BEULAH, b. 13 Mar. 1762; d. 24 Oct. 1776.
  iv. GABRIEL, b. 13 Aug. 1763; d. 22 Jan. 1765.
  v. REBECCA, b. 7 Jan. 1765.
  vi. TEMPERANCE, b. 3 Dec. 1767.
  vii. APALINA, b. 3 Jan. 1769; m. AMRAPHEL HOTCHKISS, her first cousin.
  viii. CHLOE, b. 5 Jan. 1771.
  ix. ANNA, b. 19 May 1772; m. ABIJAH GUERNSEY. Their daughter *Althea* m. 3 Oct. 1821 Asahel Augustus Hotchkiss, her first cousin.
  x. HULDAH, b. 9 Mar. 1774.
  xi. JESSE, b. 3 Aug. 1776.

36, ii. DAVID[5] HOTCHKISS (*Gideon,*[4] *Stephen,*[3] *Joshua,*[2] *Samuel*[1]), born at Waterbury 5 Apr. 1740, died at Windsor, N. Y., 8 May 1826. He married first, 21 Nov. 1763, ABIGAIL DOUGLAS, daughter of Alexander and Sarah (Ballard), who died 5 Apr. 1775; and secondly, 5 July 1775, PENINAH (PECK) TODD, daughter of Timothy and Lydia (Lines), and widow of Charles. He removed, with all his family except Lavinia and Frederick, to Windsor, Broome Co., N. Y.

Children by first wife :

  i. ASENATH,[6] b. 11 July 1764; m. ELMORE RUSSELL.
  ii. SARAH, b. 20 Mar. 1766; m. JUSTIS BEECHER of Homer and Windsor, N. Y.
B. iii. FREDERICK, b. 6 Mar. 1768.
  iv. LAVINIA, b. 9 Jan. 1770; m. STEVEN WILLIAMS of Cheshire, Conn.
C. v. AMRAPHEL, b. 25 June 1772.
  vi. CYRUS, b. 15 Apr. 1774; m. SALLIE ANDRUS. Children: 1. *Carver.*[7] 2. *Clarissa,* m. Jeffrey Sage. 3. *Giles.* 4. *Parthenia,* m. Julius Edwards. 5. *Sophronia,* m. ——— Orton of Brooklyn, N. Y.

Children by second wife :

  vii. CHARLES TODD, b. 24 June 1776; m. RHODA BARRETT.
  viii. ABIGAIL, b. 25 Apr. 1778; m. WILLIAM COBURN.
  ix. GILEAD, b. 12 Oct. 1780; m. SARAH HOADLEY.
  x. PENINAH, b. 21 Feb. 1782; m. SYLVESTER HULSE.

A. ASAHEL[6] HOTCHKISS (*Jesse,*[5] *Gideon,*[4] *Stephen,*[3] *Joshua,*[2] *Samuel*[1]), born at Waterbury 15 Feb. 1760, died at Sharon, Conn. He served in the Revolution, and received a pension at the age of 80. He married first, 22 Mar. 1781, SARAH WILLIAMS, who died 28 Mar. 1794; secondly, 7 June 1794, PHEBE MERRIAM; thirdly MRS. COWLES; and fourthly MRS. WAKEMAN.

Children by first wife :

  i. SALLY,[7] b. 27 Oct. 1781.
  ii. CURTISS, b. 4 May 1783; had children born at Waterbury.
  iii. DYER, b. 24 June 1785.
  iv. ESTHER, b. 21 May 1788.

Children by second wife :

  v. TEMPY, b. 27 Feb. 1797; m. ——— ANDREWS.
D. vi. ASAHEL AUGUSTUS, b. 30 June 1799.
  vii. MARCUS, b. 1 Sept. 1801.
  viii. PHEBE MARIA, b. 5 Aug. 1805.

B. FREDERICK[6] HOTCHKISS (*David,*[5] *Gideon,*[4] *Stephen,*[3] *Joshua,*[2] *Samuel*[1]), born at Waterbury 6 Mar. 1768, died 25 Mar. 1846. He married,

9 Mar. 1790, RHODA HOPKINS, daughter of John, who died 12 Mar. 1814. After the death of his father in 1826 he removed to Windsor, N. Y.

Children:

i. MARILLA,[7] b. 11 Mar. 1791; d. 7 Apr. 1873; m. LEBBEUS SANFORD.
ii. CHLOE, b. 16 Apr. 1794; d. 22 Apr. 1812.
iii. JULIA, b. 7 Feb. 1796; d. 10 Nov. 1883; m. JONAH WOODRUFF.
iv. DAVID MILES, b. 27 Nov. 1797; d. 15 Apr. 1878; m. (1) ZERVIAH STEVENS; m. (2) HANNAH (DOOLITTLE) BRISTOL. Ten children.
v. LAURA, b. 4 Sept. 1800; d. 1813.
vi. CLARISSA, b. 6 Jan. 1806; d. 16 Jan. 1873; m. ELISHA HALL.
vii. FREDERICK HOPKINS, b. 5 Nov. 1808; d. 1808.

C. AMRAPHEL[6] HOTCHKISS (*David,*[5] *Gideon,*[4] *Stephen,*[3] *Joshua,*[2] *Samuel*[1]), born 25 June 1772, lived at Windsor, N. Y. He married his first cousin, APALINA[6] HOTCHKISS, daughter of Jesse.

Children:

i. STILES,[7] m. LYDIA BEECHER, daughter of Justis and Sarah (Hotchkiss).
ii. FREDERICK, m. JEMIMA COMSTOCK.
iii. GIDEON, m. ANN EVARTS.
iv. OLIVE, m. JEDEDIAH SMITH.
v. HARRY, m. AMANDA HEMPSTEAD.
vi. AMRAPHEL.
vii. JESSE, m. BETSEY HEMPSTEAD; lived at Cornwall, N. Y.

D. ASAHEL AUGUSTUS[7] HOTCHKISS (*Asahel,*[6] *Jesse,*[5] *Gideon,*[4] *Stephen,*[3] *Joshua,*[2] *Samuel*[1]), born 30 June 1799, lived at Sharon, Conn., and died 21 Apr. 1885. He married, 3 Oct. 1821, his cousin, ALTHEA GUERNSEY.

Children:

i. ANDREW,[8] inventor of the first projectile for rifled cannon.
ii. ABIJAH, d. young.
iii. BENJAMIN BERKLEY, inventor of revolving cannon and rapid-fire guns. His widow endowed the Hotchkiss School at Lakeville, Conn.
iv. FRANKLIN AUGUSTUS.
v. FREDERICK ABIJAH.
vi. DOTHEA ANNA, m. —— MCKELVEY.
vii. SARAH MINERVA.
viii. CHARLES.
ix. DWIGHT.
x. WILLIAM.

Hotchkiss-Johnson-Thompson: Additions.—The following items relate to genealogies that have recently appeared in the Register.

Elias Hotchkiss (96. Register, vol. 67, p. 224) married first Almira Wood-[1] ward and secondly Julia ———. I am indebted to Mrs. Natalie R. Fernald of Washington, D. C., for the name of his first wife. Probably all of his children were by his first wife. [2]

In Register, vol. 66, pp. 15–17, evidence was presented to prove that Walter Johnson of Wallingford was son of Jan Wouters of Branford, Conn., Flatbush, L. I., and New York. The following record from Branford, contributed by Miss Ethel Lord Scofield of East Haven, confirms this conjecture: On 31 Jan. 1703/4 John Wooters, "some time since a resident of Branford, now a Sojourner in the town of Wallingford," conveys land in Branford. Witnesses: John Hall and Walter Janson. (Branford Deeds, vol. 2, p. 203.)

Eleanor Johnson, who married 14 Oct. 1714 Joseph Cook of Wallingford and Goshen, and whose parentage has not hitherto been determined, was probably a daughter of Walter Johnson by his second wife. The names Walter and Lambert appear among her children.

John Thompson (4. Register, vol. 66, p. 200) married Anne Vicaris at Bos-[3] ton 4th of the 6th month 1656. Mary Thompson (17, x. *ib.*, p. 208) did not [4] marry William Hotchkiss, whose wife Mary was daughter of Isaac Thompson (9, iii, 3. *ib.*, p. 204).

New Haven, Conn.   Donald Lines Jacobus.

[1] Page 207, this volume.
[2] Pages 307-309, this volume.
[3] Page 474, Vol. III of this work.
[4] Page 482, Vol. III of this work.

215

—(Communicated by W. J. P., of Camden, N. J.)

" To Mr Jhon [*sic*] Coit
att
N— London

Honoured Sir & Madm J blush & tremble on my knees while J study how to approach your Presence, to ask of you a Blessing for which J have long address'd ye Skies. From my first Acquaintance at your House I have wish'd my Happiness thence; nor have I yet found it in my Power to seek it from an Other. My careful Thoughts with ceasless Ardors commend ye Affair to that Being, who alone inspires a pure & refined Love. The Eye-Lids of ye Morning discover me in my secret Places, with my first Devotions solliciting ye dear important Cause; and ye Evening-Shades are conscious to ye Vows J make for ye fr Creature, who next to Heaven holds the Empire of my Heart. And now while I write J pray ye great Master of Souls to incline yours to favour my Address. By ye Love of God J beseech you—Ye happy Parents of my Partner Soul—but J forbare till J may be honoured with ye Oppertunity of a personal Application. In ye mean time J consecrate my best Wishes To ye Jnterest of yr Family—& with ye higest Respect subscribe my Self, Sir and Madam, yr most devoted most humble Servant   D. Hubbard "

Stonington Decmber, 1730

Note.—Daniel Hubbard, the writer of the above letter, was the son of Rev. John Hubbard, Jr. (H. C. 1695), and was born April 3, 1706, probably in New Haven. He was graduated at Yale College in 1727. A sketch of his life will be found in "Yale Biographies and Annals," by Prof. F. B. Dexter, page 354. His proposal was accepted, and he was married August 13 (or 18), 1731, to Martha, daughter of John Coit of New London, to whom the letter is addressed. He settled at New London in the practice of the law. He was appointed sheriff in 1735, and held the office till his death March 24, 1741-2. He left three sons and two daughters. His widow married, Sept. 6, 1744, Thomas Greene of Boston (see Coit Genealogy, page 32). There used to be twin portraits of Mr. Greene and his wife, a little above miniature size in ovals in one frame on copper painted by Copley, which was in the possession of Miss Mary G. Chapman of Boston. I used to see the picture often when a child. Augustus T. Perkins describes it in his Sketch of Copley and some of his Works, page 66. I am not quite sure that the lady was the adorable Miss Coit, though the probability is that she was. Thomas Greene had two wives. His first wife was Eliza daughter of John Gardiner of Gardiner's Island, and his second the above Mrs. Martha (Coit) Hubbard. There are portraits of Thomas Greene and his wife Martha, painted by Copley, in the possession of their great-grandson, Rev. David Greene Haskins D.D., of Cambridge. They are described by Mr. Perkins, pp. 65-6. Mr. Greene's portrait is dated Sept. 25, 1758. It was therefore painted when Copley was only 21 years old.

                                        W. J. P.

RICHARD HUGHES OF GUILFORD, CONN., AND HIS DESCENDANTS.

Compiled by Hon. Ralph D. Smyth, and communicated by Dr. Bernard C. Steiner.

1. Richard[1] Hughes, the name also spelled Hewes, Hues, and Huse, was one of the earliest settlers of Guilford, as he drew one of the early lots of land. His name appears in the first list of planters for 1650, where it is spelt "Hues." He may have come from Dorchester, Mass., as one of his name was there in 1639. At Guilford he was a member of the church, and appears to have been an esteemed and worthy citizen. At a particular Court held at Guilford, May 5, 1659, "The inventory of the estate of

Richard Hughes, late of Guilford deceased, was presented by William Stone who had married the widow of the deceased, which was proved by said William Stone and his wife for the quantity, and by Robert Kitchel and Abraham Cruttenden, Sr., for the value—amount £96 . 4s . 7d."

Administration of the estate was granted, May 23, 1659, to William Stone, upon promise and engagement to perform the payment of all debts and portions according to the court's appointment.

At a particular court (Guilford), Aug. 21, 1659, William Stone appeared bringing in a parcel of goods sent as a token from friends in England to be distributed betwixt Widow Hughes and her eight children but not specifying how. The Court, with consent of William Stone, who married said widow, divided what part of them as was sent with such general order only, one third to said William Stone for the widow and the two children that are yet remaining with her—viz., Martha and Rebecca—and the other six parts between the other six children in equal proportions, appointing Mr. Kitchel and Abraham Cruttenden, Sr., to see the distribution made accordingly.

Richard[1] Hughes died July 3, 1658, and his widow, Mary, married second, May, 1659, William Stone, who died Nov., 1683.

Children:

    i. RICHARD,[2] b. 1638, in England; was in England in Feb., 1661, in the settlement of his father's estate.
2. ii. SAMUEL, b. Feb., 1640-1; d. May 11, 1693.
    iii. MARY.
    iv. DEBORAH, m. Oct. 10, 1665, Thomas Buck of Wethersfield.
3. v. NICHOLAS, of Guilford and Stratford, Conn.; d. 1691.
    vi. SARAH, b. Aug. 1, 1651; the Guilford School Dame; d. unmarried, Apr. 17, 1714.
    vii. ELIZABETH, b. Apr. 14, 1653.
    viii. MARTHA, b. 1655; d. May 30, 1729; m. July 2, 1677, Nathaniel Brown of Middletown, who d. May 9, 1712.
    ix. REBECCA, b. 1657; m. (1) Sept. 10, 1674, Alexander Bow of Middletown, who d. Nov. 6, 1678; m. (2) Aug. 8, 1679, Thomas Forman.

2. SAMUEL[2] HUGHES (*Richard[1]*), of Guilford, a freeman there Mar. 13, 1669, inherited his father's home-lot of 5 acres, and a parcel of marsh land adjoining, which contained 1¾ acres, and bought 8 acres more in 1670. He married, Apr. 26, 1665, Mary, daughter of Henry Dowd.

    Children:

    i. MARY,[3] b. Feb. 14, 1666; d. June 26, 1676.
    ii. ABIGAIL, b. July 22, 1668; d. young.
    iii. SAMUEL (twin), b. Dec. 29, 1670; d. Dec. 30, 1670.
    iv. ELIZABETH (twin), b. Dec. 29, 1670; d. Jan. 13, 1674-5.
    v. MARY, b. May 20, 1676; d. May 16, 1767; m. Feb. 9, 1693, Nathaniel Bishop of Guilford, who d. May 1, 1714.
    vi. ABIGAIL, b. Jan. 22, 1678; m. Dec. 29, 1703, Nathaniel Parks of Guilford, who d. Dec. 18, 1764.

3. NICHOLAS[2] HUGHES (*Richard[1]*) was a blacksmith, and lived in Guilford, with the encouragement of the town, in 1669 and 1670. He inherited from his father a parcel of land containing 6 acres in the little plain. In 1684, he lived in Stratford, and married, about 1692, Abigail, daughter of John Thompson and widow of Jonathan Curtiss, who married third, Aug., 1695, Samuel Sherman, Jr., and died Feb., 1719.

He probably had no children.

NOTICE OF THE HUNTINGTON FAMILY.

Albany, N. Y., July 10, 1847.
Rev. William Cogswell, D. D.,
Editor of the N. E. Historical and Genealogical Register:

Sir, — Being related to the Huntington family on the maternal side, and having found a manuscript letter from Joseph Huntington to Roger Huntington, dated Coventry, Ct., March 25, 1793, giving an account of the early ancestors of the family, I send you the following *extract* from it in order to furnish some of the facts which may be wanted in making out a sketch for publication.

As this family has been considerably prominent, and highly respectable in this country, I have taken it for granted, that you will give it a place in your Register.

" Near the close of the reign of Charles the first, (1648,) the original stock of our family in America, who was a citizen of Norwich in England, and a Religious Puritan under persecution, with his wife and three sons, embarked for America. His name was Simon. He was nearly fifty years of age; his wife was some years younger. Their three sons who were in the bloom of youth, were named Christopher, Simon, and Samuel.

They made their course for the mouth of Connecticut river, but our progenitor being seized with a violent fever and dysentary, died within sight of the shore, whither he was brought, and now lies buried in Saybrook or Lyme, as both towns were but one at first. I have in vain enquired for his grave when I have been there, as no monument has been erected to his memory.

His widow who was a lady of a good family, piety and virtue, and had a valuable fortune left her in money; not long after his death, was married to a gentleman in Windsor, named Stoughton, and there she finished her life in affluence and comfort.

The three sons settled first at Saybrook: but soon after, the youngest, namely, Samuel, removed to New Jersey and settled in Newark.

About the time that Samuel removed to New Jersey, the other two brothers, namely, Christopher and Simon, came to Norwich, and there lived in honor and piety to a good old age.

The sons of Christopher, were Christopher, Thomas and John; the sons of Christopher last mentioned, were Christopher, Isaac, Jabez, Matthew, Hezekiah, John and Jeremiah; the sons of Thomas, were Thomas, Jedediah, Christopher, Eleazer, William and Simon; John left but one son, bearing his own name.

The branch of Simon, the son of Simon: — His sons were Simon, Joseph, Samuel, Daniel and James; the sons of the last mentioned Simon, were Simon, Eleazer and Joshua; the sons of Joseph were Nathaniel, Jonathan, David and Solomon; the sons of Samuel were Samuel, Caleb, John and Simon; the sons of Daniel were Daniel, Jonathan and Benjamin; the sons of James were James, Peter and Nathaniel.

Samuel who removed to New Jersey, left one son, Samuel, who had three sons, Thomas, Simon and Samuel.

At the time of the emigration of Simon, a brother of his, whose name was Samuel, was Captain of the king's life guard, and much in his favor." Yours,

Fred. S. Pease.

FAMILY OF HUNTINGTON.

North Hadley, 1 mo., 22, 1849.

Esteemed Friend, the Publisher of the N. E. Hist. and Gen. Register:

I inclose a copy of a letter written by Dr. Joseph Huntington, minister a long time in Coventry, Ct. I have nothing to show the date of the letter. I take some interest in this account, being a descendant of the Huntington family — my mother being of that name. — I am of the seventh generation from the original Simon, in the line of his son Christopher.

Very Respectfully thy Friend,

DEXTER M. LEONARD.

Copy of a letter from Dr. Joseph Huntington, of Coventry, Ct., to his brother, Mr. Eliphalet Huntington, of Windham, Ct., who remained on the homestead.

Near the close of the reign and tragical death of Charles the first, who was then the king of Great Britain, (ie.) near the year 1640, (for in 1648 the king was beheaded) the original stock [progenitor] of our family in America, who was a citizen of Norwich in England, and a religious Puritan under persecution, (with many others in those days) with his wife and three sons embarked for America.

His name was Simon Huntington. This good man was grandfather to your grandfather and mine. He was nearly fifty years of age, and his wife some years younger. Their three sons were in the bloom of youth. Their names were Christopher, Simon, and Samuel. They made their course for the mouth of Connecticut river. But our progenitor being seized with a violent fever and dysentery, died within sight of the shore; whither he was brought, and now lies buried, either in Saybrook or Lyme, as both towns were but one at first. His widow, our grandfather's grandmother, was a lady of good family, piety, and virtue, and had a valuable fortune left her in money; and not long after, she married to a gentleman in Windsor, which town was settled almost as early as any in Connecticut. His name was Stoughton. There the good lady finished her life in affluence and comfort. The three sons settled first at Saybrook; but soon after, the younger, viz., Samuel, removed into New Jersey and settled at Newark, where there is a respectable family of our name and kindred, though not very numerous in the branches of it. Not long after the settlement of our ancestors at Saybrook, the venerable Mr. Fitch came over, to take the pastoral charge of them. Soon after this, they made a discovery of the township that we call Norwich, and which they so named in regard to the city of Norwich in England, from whence the most respectable part of them came. The people began to emigrate from Saybrook to Norwich in considerable numbers, and all dearly loved their minister. A warm contention arose between the emigrants and those that remained at Saybrook, with regard to their minister, which Mr. Fitch decided very wisely. He told them that he had a dear love for them all; but that he could do no other than cleave to the major part, wheresoever their residence might be. Accordingly, as the greater part of his charge soon removed to Norwich, he also settled there; was the first minister of that town, a faithful and worthy servant of Christ, and a friend to the souls of men. Laboring many years in the sacred work there, until old age deprived him of farther usefulness; he then removed to Lebanon and there died. This good man was the progenitor of all who bear the name in Norwich, and the towns adjacent.

219

But to return to our family; about the time that Samuel, before mentioned, removed to Newark, the other two brethren came to Norwich, viz., Christopher and Simon, and there lived in honor, piety and prosperity, to a good old age. The sons of Christopher were, Christopher, Thomas, and John. The sons of this last mentioned Christopher, were Christopher, Isaac, Jabez, Mathew, Hezekiah, John, and Jeremiah. The sons of Thomas were, Thomas, Jeddidiah, Christopher, Eliezer, William, and Simon. John left but one son, bearing his own name. This you will note, brings the pedigree of our family down in one branch of it, to a collateral line with your father and mine, i. e., in the branch of Christopher the son of Simon, who was the original stock of all who bear the name in this country. I [will] next acquaint you with another branch, i. e., the branch [of] Simon, son of the original Simon, from whence you and I have our descent direct. His sons were Simon, Joseph, Samuel, Daniel, and James. The sons of the last mentioned Simon, were Simon, Ebenezer, and Joshua. The sons of Joseph, were, Joseph, Nathaniel, Jonathan, David, and Solomon. The sons [of] Samuel, were, Samuel, Caleb, John, and Simon The sons of Daniel, were Daniel, Jonathan, and Benjamin. The sons of James, were James, Peter, and Nathaniel. With regard to that branch in New Jersey, descended from Samuel, son of the original Simon, he left one son, Samuel by name, on a collateral line with our grandfather Joseph. This Samuel had three sons, Thomas, Simon, and Samuel, which were on a collateral line with your father and mine. This is an account of all the male issue of our family, from the original Simon, down to our immediate parents, and contains a series of about a century and a half.

We have kindred of the same name now in England, and among them some very respectable, as the family was at the time of the emigration of our progenitors.

A brother of the orignal Simon, whose name was Samuel, was captain of the king's life guard, and much in his favor. With regard to the succeeding branches of our family in this country, they are somewhat numerous, though not so much dispersed as some other families.

ERRATA.—In vol. v. p. 163, for " Samuel " read " *Thomas*," which[*] was the name of the Huntington who went to Newark, N. J. He m. Hannah, da. of Jasper Crane. " Samuel " was son of Thomas. S. H. C.

[*]Page 219, this volume.

HUNTINGTON.

Thomas was the name of that son of Simon Huntington who removed to New Jersey, not Samuel, as is stated in the January number of the Register, * p. 46. It appears from the printed colonial records of Connecticut, that Thomas Huntington was made a freeman of Con. in May, 1657, Cris. Huntington, in May, 1658, and Simon Huntington in Oct. 1663. Thomas Huntington married Hannah, daugh. of Jasper Crane, and, with Robert Treat, Sam. Swaine, and their associates, the first settlers of Newark, N. J., signed the agreements, " none shall be admitted freemen or free Burgesses within our Town upon Passaic river, in the province of New Jersey, but such Planters as are members of some or other of the Congregational churches," and " we will with care and diligence provide for the maintenance of the purity of Religion professed in the Congregational churches." Thomas Huntington was of the Brandford company, which consisted of the Rev. Abraham Pierson and a very large part of his church. His name is found often on the records of the town. In 1675, the General Assembly " being invited hereunto by the Insolence and outrages of the Heathens in our neighboring colonies, not knowing how soon we may be surprised," enacted " that there shall be a place of Fortification or Fortifications made in every Town of the province, and a House therein for the securing of women and children, provision and ammunition, in case of eminent danger by the Indians." Capt. Swain, Sarg. Johnson, and Sarg. Huntington were " chosen by vote to join with the commissioned Military officers to consider about and contrive for the fortifications belonging to our Town," it having been previously agreed " that two Flanckers shall be made at two corners of the meeting house with Palisadoes or Stockades." In 1675 Thomas Huntington was one of seven " Townsmen " chosen " to carry all Town business according to the best of their judgment for the good of the Town, except disposing of land, admitting Inhabitants, and the way of levying rates." He appears as one of the Townsmen until Jan. 1, 1684–5, when he was chosen a Deputy to the General Assembly. We have no record of his death, or notice of him after that year. In 1702, " Samuel Huntington, (son and heir in law of Thomas Huntington, dec.,) inhabitant of Newark, planter," sold lands " formerly belonging to Thomas Huntington aforesaid," and " for fifteen pound current silver money," six acres, &c. The will of this Samuel is dated Nov. 11, 1704, and it was proved Nov. 19, 1712. His children were Thomas, Simon, and a dau. Hannah. The two sons, in 1724, were inhabitants of the district west of Newark mountains, now called Morris County. There Simon died in 1770, aged 74. A Samuel Huntington died in Newark in 1784, aged 74, who, though not mentioned in his father's will, seems to have been the brother of Simon the son of Samuel, to whom he bequeathed " my sermon book the Ten Virgins."

The above facts may be of some interest to the numerous descendants of Simon Huntington. The error, with respect to the name of the brother who settled in Newark, though trivial, is important enough to demand a short notice from one having access to documentary evidence sufficient for its correction.

*Page 220, this volume.   S. H. C.

HUNTINGTON.

A reverential and an historical regard for this family, and particularly for the family of my maternal grandfather, has led me to collect some of the facts relative thereto for publication in the Register.

Doct. Thomas Huntington was the youngest son of John Huntington* and his wife Civil Tracy, born at Norwich, Ct., 13 January, 1745. He removed to Ashford, Ct., about 1770, where, on the 7th January, 1773, he married Molly, daughter of Ichabod Ward and his wife Phebe Tyler, who was born at Attleborough, Mass., 8 March, 1753. He was a graduate of Yale College, Class of 1768. While at Ashford he followed the practice of medicine as a profession, and was also engaged in mercantile pursuits, in which he accumulated considerable property. In the spring of 1799, he removed to Longmeadow, Mass.; thence, in December, 1800, he removed to Hartford, Ct.; and thence, in June, 1801, to Canaan, Litchfield Co., Ct., where he purchased a farm under cultivation, with dwelling-house and other buildings, of Gideon Lawrence, son of Daniel Lawrence of the same place.

This westward movement to a point very much short of what we are now familiar with as the far West, was then thought to be a very considerable reach into the land, which lie beneath the setting sun. Here he resumed the practice of medicine, and was variously engaged in farming, manufacturing and mercantile pursuits. Somewhat eccentric in his habits and manners, he was a pattern of persevering industry, temperance, frugality, and other virtues. He died at Canaan, 22 Feb. 1835. His wife d. 31 Mar. 1828. Their children were all born in Ashford.

Thomas, the eldest, was born 29 September, 1773, and was married to Mary Burbidge, of New York, about 1808. He was liberally educated, and opened a law office in Hartford, Ct., where he continued until his decease, which occurred 9 Nov., 1833. His wife died at New York, about 1839. They had a son named Erastus.

Molly (or Mary as she was generally called,) was born 17 Oct., 1776. She married Alban Rose, of Canaan, in 1821, and is now living with her husband at Geneva, N. Y.

Erastus was born 8 January, 1779. He was engaged in mercantile pursuits, in Albany, in 1804–5–6, in company with a person named Pratt. They kept a dry goods store. He died at Havana, Cuba, 17 Sept., 1807, where his monument still remains.

Matilda was born 29 December, 1780. She married Salmon Pease, of Canaan, 14 June, 1803, and is now living with her husband at Charlotte, Vermont.

Clarissa was born 17 June, 1784, and is now living at Charlotte, Vt.

Horace was born 18 July, 1786, and died at Canaan, 13 March, 1846. He married Chloe Franklin, daughter of Silas Franklin, of Canaan, in 1813, who died 23 Feb. 1843, aged 50. Their children were Horace F., Mary, Miles H., John and Martha.

Miles was born 29 April, 1789, and died 1 May, 1790.

Owen was born 15 May, 1792. He married Eunice Day, daughter of Thomas Day, in 1815. Their children are Clarissa and Anne. He died lamentably in the wilds of California, in the fall of 1850, whither he went in the spring of the same year, where his remains are laid, without a stone to mark the spot. He had the melancholy satisfaction of stopping at Havana, on his way out, and seeing the stone which commemorated the death of his brother Erastus. Frederick S. Pease.

Albany, March, 1856.

*Youngest should be fifth.

JOHN HUNTLEY AND SOME OF HIS DESCENDANTS

Contributed by Mrs. Alice P. Huntley of Hanover, Mass.

The ancestry of John[1] Huntley who was in Boston as early as 1640, and settled in Lyme, Conn., about 1660, is still in question. Some authorities presume that he was of the Huntley Sept of the Clan Gordon, whose estates are located in the Town of Huntley, Aberdeenshire, Scotland. Sir George Gordon, Earl of Huntley, was associated with the founding of the Virginia Company in 1613, and there are various families of Huntleys who settled in Northumberland and Westmorland Counties in Virginia. Other authorities say that the family descends from the Gloucestershire family, who traces its descent from one Baderon who went with his brother Wythenoec from Brittany to England with William the Conqueror in 1066. In an ancient charter of Virginia, 23 May 1606, there appears the name of John Huntley, who states that he was from the City of London. In either case the name is very old, and the descendants in America have reason to be proud of their lineage.

The Aspinwall records of Boston have the first record of John Huntley in 1647 when he signs as witness for power of attorney for Thomas Bayes (Asp. 323) and again in 1648 when he signs for Thomas Foster (Asp. 233). On page 140 of these same records there appears an account between John Huntley and John Pease in regard to a load of fish which Huntley sold in the Barbadoes, shipped in the "Welcome, Mr. John Allen, Mr."

The deposition of John Prace ae 65 yrs. dated 1 July 1679, states: "29 or 30 years ago, Mr. Hanniford, Mariner, lived in Boston in the house next adjoining the house and grounds of Hope Allison, standing on land on which William Griggs lately built a house, and this house and land was accounted to be Hanniford's own property, and John Huntley lived on and thereof and paid the said Hanniford rent for the same, and said Huntley's wife died there of small pox. They were Mr. Hanniford's tenants." This statement gives the proof of Mr. Huntley's first marriage.

An Elizabeth Huntley married in Beverly, Mass., Samuel Corning and had children, Samuel, Elizabeth and Remember. She died 18 Aug. 1688, aged about 85 years. Could this be John Huntley's sister? He was in Salem, Mass., about 1650, as the Ipswich Quarterly Court Records contain a deposition by Richard Smith who states: "Jno Huntley being at the Iron Works." Many citizens of Salem migrated to Lyme, Conn., about the same time that John Huntley went, and it may be that his second wife Jane was from this town. William Bennet of Manchester, Mass., had children Moses, Aaron, Jane and Elizabeth, which correspond to the names of John Huntley's children. Also Henry Bennet settled next to the farm of John Huntley in Lyme.

On the other hand the surname "Curtis" persists throughout the generations of Huntleys until about 1750. John Huntley had a mortgage of Philip Curtis of Roxbury. There being no proof of either of these suppositions, we only await further research, concerning the name of John Huntley's second wife.

Probably about 1650 John Huntley married for the second time, and we find recorded in the Boston records:

Moses sonne of John and Jane Huntley bourne 1 July 1652
Aaron sonne of John and Jane Huntley bourne 15 Apr. 1654

The next record of the family is in Roxbury, where they attended the church there, and where the baptisms of the family are recorded;

Oct. 20, 1657 ———— Huntley, wife of John Huntley adm.
    to the Church
Oct. 27, 1657 baptized Moses Huntley
                    Aaron Huntley
                    Elizabeth Huntley
Dec. 3, 1660 baptized Mary Huntley.

This is the record of John Eliot, pastor of the church.

In Suffolk Deeds, vol. 3, p. 334 is a deed dated Roxbury 27 Feb. 1659, as follows:

John Huntley, cooper, in company with John Chandler both of Roxbury, deed to Philip Curtis 27 Feb. 1659, for £23 worth of cattle, the house and shop of John Huntley with an orchard of 1 acre in Roxbury, and also four acres of pasture land of John Chandler. (mortgage)

Shortly after this deed, Mr. Huntley must have migrated to Lyme, Conn., for on the town records of Lyme, 12 July 1665, John Huntley shared in the fourth division of land as follows:

John Huntley hath laid out for his portion of land granted by the town (Saybrooke) on the East side of Saybrooke (Lyme) for an hundred pound estate, from . . . . 71 acres, for his lott and twenty acres for his calf pasture land. The meadow within it is bounded south by the land of William Measurer; on the North by the common, on the west by the highway; on the east by the common.

From the Lyme Land Records, 20 July 1674:

John Huntley hath laid out to him one the midell of Wolfe Oyland, tow ackers of
meadow more or less bounded every way with the water. He hath also laid out to
him a home lott containing forty three ackers and half of upland more or less,
bounded west one the highway; north one Balishazzer DeWolfes land; South upon
Wm. Waller's land; East upon the commons. Lying one both sides of Duck River
with one dwelling house. Also three ackers and halfe of meadow at the head of
Duck River bounded one the meadow of Wm. Measurer, North one the swamp of
Balishazzer DeWolfe; East and West with his own land. Att. Mathew Griswold,
Renold Marvin.
John Huntleys' ear mark is one halfe pene out one the under side of each ear, and a
slitte one the of ear. 11 Mar. 1674.

Sometime before 1669 Jane, the wife of John Huntley, died and
in the diary of Thomas Minor of Stonington appears the following:
"The fouerth moneth is June, and hath 30 day. tusday the first,
the day the court began, that court I maried huntley and marie
barons" 1669.

Marie barons, or Mary Barnes, appears to be the daughter of
John Barnes of Gloucester, Mass., and his divorced wife Sarah who
married John Tinker. After the death of Sarah, Mary Barnes was
brought up by John Tinker's second wife, Alice Smith, who afterwards married William Measurer and came to live in the next farm to
John Huntley. She named her first child Sarah for her mother
and her second child Alice for the woman who brought her up.
(Gen. John Tinker of Lancaster)

The only mention of John Huntley in public life was his partici-
pation in the New London-Lyme riot, when he with many of his
neighbors protested the boundary line between Lyme and New
London 12 Mar. 1671/2.

John Huntley died in Lyme 16 Nov. 1676 (Lyme Land Records,
vol. 1, p. 30), leaving his widow Mary and his six children whom he
mentions in his will, proved in court 1677.

The last will & testament of John Huntley being very sick & weak of body, but
of perfect memory 16 Nov. 1676
Imprimus, I give & bequethe my Soule to god that gave & my body to the earth
from whence it came to be decently buried at the discretion of my executors hereafter mentioned.
2. I give and bequethe to my dear & beloved wife the one thurd part of all my
estate & my dwelling house to live in peaceable during her natural life.
3. I give to my sonne Aaron haffe an acre of land in the new lott joyning to the
orchard fence on one side & the front fence on the other side to set him a house
upon & part of the frute of the orchard as my wife & he shall agree & one thurd of
all the increase of all my land unto him and his heirs forever, he improving his time
upon it; & after the decease of my wife all the lands & meadow of mine in the Towne
of Lyme paying unto each of my children on his possessing of the lands, tenn
pounds apeece viz; to my sonne Moses tenn pounds, to my Daughter Elizabeth
tenn pounds, to my Daughter Mary tenn pounds, to my Daughter Sarah tenn
pounds, to my Daughter Alice tenn pounds.
And of this my last will and testament I doe Appoynt and make my dear and
loving wife & my Sonne Aaron ye joynt executors;
Signed and sealed in prescence of us
    Bathazathar DeWolfe
    Wm. Measurer
                              John Huntley (X)

The inventory of the estate was given in the Town Book of Lyme, a total of £218.00.04 and his children's ages as follows:

Moses	ae 24
Aaron	ae 22
Elizabeth	ae 19
Marah	ae 16
Sarah	ae 7
Alice	ae 3

After the death of John Huntley several parcels of land were laid out to his estate by the town of Lyme, as recorded in the Lyme Land Records:

14 Mar. 1676: Layed out to the estate of John Huntley one both sides of four mile River, twenty acres of upland and meadow, be it more or less, and is bounded West with the commons; South with the land layed out for Henry Benet; East with the commons; North with the lands of John Larabe; East and West 55 Rods, north and south forty nine rods, the aforesaid twenty acres being the second division.

15 Mch. 1687/8: Laid out to the estate of John Huntley and Aaron Huntley at the cove commonly called Sunkapogosuts, thirty acres of upland be it more or less with allowance for surveyors land. Land is bounded north by Thomas Champean; East with the common at an ashe tree marked at the north east corner and a black oak tree marked at the southeast corner. Southerly by R. Smith's land. Westerly by the highway, being upon the account of the fourth division.

25 Sep. 1702: Laid out to the estate of John Huntley dec'd and taken up by his son Aaron Huntley, executor to estate, ninety-five acres of land; be it more or less, at Walnut Tree Hill, the most westward hill, beginning at the northward end, being in length two hundred and 10 rods, in width at the northward end 14 chains, at the southward end 22 chains, at the northwest corner with a black oak tree marked on all four sides; and a chestnut stadell standing by it marked; at the northeast corner with a stadell marked on four sides; at the southeast corner with a chestnut tree marked on four sides; at the southwest corner with a white oak tree marked on four sides, being upon the account of the last part of the fourth division, it being full satisfaction for the same.

Children:

2. i. MOSES, b. in Boston 1 July 1652.
3. ii. AARON, b. in Boston 15 April 1654.
   iii. ELIZABETH, bapt. in Roxbury, Mass., 27 Oct. 1657; d. in Groton, Conn., 26 Dec. 1741, at the home of her daughter, Mrs. William Latham (*New York Genealogical & Biographical Record*); m. in 1677 JOHN LEWIS of New London, d. in 1717, son of John Lewis.
     Children (surname *Lewis*):
     1. *Elizabeth*, b. 27 Sept. 1678.
     2. *Mary*, b. 12 April 1679.
     3. *Sarah*, b. 18 Aug. 1683.
     4. *John*, b. 16 Aug. 1685.
     5. *Samuel*, b. 3 June 1687.
     6. *William*, b. 22 Oct. 1690; m. 23 Feb. 1715 Elizabeth Borden. Children: (1) Hannah, b. 26 Nov. 1716. (2) Joseph, b. "1 day of" 1718. (3) Jane, b. 10 Feb. 1720. (4) Elizabeth, b. 12 Feb. 1722. (5) Borden, b. 14 Jan. 1725. (6) William, b. 11 June 1727. (7) Ely, b. 9 March 1729/30.
     7. *Hannah*, b. 24 Oct. 1692.
     8. *Moses*.
     (Parkhurst manuscript, Hartford.)
   iv. MARY, bapt. in Roxbury, Mass., 3 Dec. 1660.
   v. SARAH, b. about 1669.
   vi. ALICE, b. about 1673.

2. MOSES² HUNTLEY (*John¹*), of Lyme, Conn., born in Boston 1

July 1652 and baptized in the First Church of Roxbury 27
Oct. 1657. He married in Lyme, 18 Jan. 1680, ABIGAIL
(CHAPELL) COMSTOCK, widow of John Comstock.
Children, born in Lyme (Lyme Land Records, vol. 1, p. 49):

4. i.   MOSES,³ b. 31 May 1681.
   ii. MARY, b. 26 Dec. 1683; m. 2 Jan. 1706/7 JOHN BENET, d. 15 Dec.
        1730, son of Henry Benet (Lyme Land Records, vol. 2, p. 81).
        Children (surname *Benet*):
        1. *Samuel*, b. 14 Dec. 1707.
        2. *Abbegale*, b. 6 April 1709.
        3. *John*, b. 18 Aug. 1710.
        4. *Jane*, b. 25 May 1714.
        5. *Mary*, b. 30 May 1716; d. 21 April 1731 (Lyme Land Records,
           vol. 2, p. 51).
        6. *Sarah*, b. 29 Jan. 1719.
        7. *Elijah*, b. 20 May 1722.
        8. *Jedidiah*, b. 24 Jan. 1724.
5. iii. JOHN, b. 9 Sept. 1686.

3. AARON² HUNTLEY (*John¹*), of Lyme, Conn., born in Boston 15
April 1654 and baptized in the First Church of Roxbury 27
Oct. 1657, died in Lyme 24 May 1741/2, aged 91. He married, 22 Feb. 1676, MARY CHAMPION, died 10 Dec. 1732,
aged 84, daughter of Henry Champion. (Lyme Town Records, Book 2, p. 6.)
    Aaron Huntley lived with his parents in Lyme in the sec-
tion now called East Lyme or Huntley Hollow, until his
father's death when he built himself a house upon the lot his
father gave him and managed his father's estate for the widow.
    In the Lyme Town Records, Book 2, p. 6, is the following:

"We the heirs of Henry Champion dec'd . . . do mutually agree to
divide the estate of our honored father above sd. into 4 equal shares; one
to the children of Henry Champion dec'd, son of Henry aforesd. one to
children of Thomas dec'd; and one to Sarah Benet, and one to Mary
Huntley, daus. of sd. Henry Champion.
        Aaron Huntley in behalf of wife
        Henry Benet   "   "   "   "
        John Waide   "   "   "   " and children"

    On the town records the maiden name of Mary was left
blank and at some later date the name Chamberlain was inserted. The above record corrects this misstatement.
    Aaron Huntley was a soldier in King Philip's War and on
the enrollment list at Voluntown having drawn Lot No. 148.
He drew Cedar Swamp Lot No. 50 in lists compiled 1 July
1701.
    Lyme Land Records, p. 265: 2 Oct. 1702:

Laid out to Aaron Huntley fifty one acres of Upland, swamps and bogge,
be it more or less, the west side of Four Mile River above the Tilestons
twenty acre lott, bounded Ely with the sd. River, Nly and Wly with the
commons, Sly partly with the commons and partly with the Tileston's
boundary . . . upon the account of the last grant of the fourth division
for him and his wife, and son John's right, which is in full satisfaction for
the same.
    1 Jan. 1702/3: Aaron Huntley renewed the bounds of his land at Four

Mile River before giving grants of land to his sons. Under the tax list for Gov. Andros 1688 Aaron or Iron Huntley is listed as follows:

1 person	20	£	00s	00d
house and land	02	£	00s	00d
2 oxen & 4 cows	22	£	00s	00d
2; 3 yearlings				
3 yearlings	08	£	00s	00d
1 mare 1 coult				
11 sheep	12	£	00s	00d
	64	£	00s	00d

His will dated 1745, bequeaths to his son Daniel dec'd gifts of lands, to his daus. Elizabeth, wife of Mathew Beckwith and Ruth, wife of Sollomon, to the dau. of Solomon, Mary Lattimore, and to David's children, Simon who Lived with him, and Lidy who cared for him so tenderly in his sickness.

Wit; Lewis DeWolfe, Elisha Huntley, Josiah DeWolf.

Children, born in Lyme:

6. i.   JOHN,[3] b. 24 Nov. 1677.
   ii. ELIZABETH, b. 16 March 1679; m. (1) as his second wife WESTHALL COGSWELL, who d. 21 April 1709; m. (2) MATHEW BECKWITH, sadler, of Lyme.
        Child by first husband (surname *Cogswell*):
        1. *Martha.*
7. iii. AARON, b. 1 Dec. 1680.
8. iv. DANIELL, b. 25 May 1682.
   v.   MARAH, b. 14 Feb. 1685; probably d. young.
   vi. JANE, b. 10 Sept. 1686; d. young.
9. vii. DAVID, b. 17 March 1687/8.
   viii. SOLLMON, b. 31 May 1691; d. 9 Aug. 1712; m. 13 Feb. 1710 RUTH———.
        The estate of Sollmon Huntley was administered by Aaron Huntley and widow Ruth was made guardian of the child Mary on 14 Oct. 1712.
        Child:
        1. *Mary,*[4] b. in 1712 (Lyme Land Records, vol. 14, p. 119); m. 14 Feb. 1733 Robert Lattimore of New London, Conn., son of Capt. Robert and Elizabeth Lattimore (First Church of Christ, New London).

4. MOSES[3] HUNTLEY (*Moses,*[2] *John*[1]), of Lyme, Conn., born there 31 May 1681, died in East Haddam, Conn., before 1746. He married, 21 Jan. 1706/7 RACHEL HARRIS who may have been a sister of Richard Harris who was mentioned in the will of Richard Smith as the son of his wife Elizabeth, widow of John Harris. The name Richard Harris persists through all the descendants of this family.

Moses Huntley lived in Lyme on land deeded to him from his father Moses, selling 14 Oct. 1726 to Nathaniel Clark, Jr., land at Walnut Hill and on 28 Aug. 1728 50 acres at Sunkepogset to William Borden. A deed in East Haddam, dated 2 March 1750, records that he bought of Daniel Driggs for £110 currency money of N. E., land on the West side of 8 Mile River, adjoining land of Samuel Griffin, and on the highway, containing 65 acres more or less with dwelling.

Administration of the estate of Moses Huntley was granted in East Haddam in 1746, William Huntley of Lyme, executor. Children:

 i. ABIGAIL,⁴ b. in Lyme 22 Aug. 1708; m. in East Haddam, 11 April 1728, NATHANIEL BECKWITH, b. in East Haddam 6 Jan. 1707, d. 13 March 1793.
   Children (surname *Beckwith*), b. in East Haddam:
   1. *Nathaniel.*
   2. *Abigail*, b. 12 Nov. 1730.
   3. *Lucy*, b. 5 May 1732.
   4. *Rachel*, b. 24 May 1734.
   5. *Elisha.*
   6. *Martin*, b. 10 Feb. 1737/8.
   7. *Eunice*, b. 9 Feb. 1739/40.
   8. *Bethuel*, b. 22 Dec. 1741.
   9. *Jabez.*
   10. *Niles.*
   11. *Rachel.*
10. ii. WILLIAM, b. in Lyme 24 June 1712.
 iii. JABEZ, b. in Lyme 21 Sept. 1721; m. (1) 27 March 1746 PATIENCE VAUGHAN, b. 1 Dec. 1722; m. (2) SARAH (————) BECKWITH.
   Jabez Huntley enlisted as a private in the French and Indian War, campaign of 1758 in the Third Regiment, Col. Eleazer Fitch under Capt. Timothy Mather of the Eleventh Company, and was discharged 18 November. He was also in the Ninth Company, Capt. Zebulon Butler of Lyme Fourth Regiment, Col. Eleazer Fitch, 1759.
   A Jabez Huntley appears on the pension list in New London company 12 Oct. 1818, aged 94.
   In the Lyme Records, vol. 14, p. 12, 8 Nov. 1776, Jabez Huntley, his wife Sarah (wid. Beckwith) and Silas Beckwith, sell to Amos Huntley of Lyme land adj. sd. Amos on w. and from the highway 2½ acres.
11. iv. BENEJAH.
12. v. MOSES.
   Perhaps George and others.

5. JOHN³ HUNTLEY (*Moses*,² *John*¹) was born in Lyme, Conn., 9 Sept. 1686. He married first SUSANNA (DEWOLFE) CHAMPION, daughter of Balthazar and Alice DeWolfe and widow of Henry Champion, Jr.; and secondly, 22 July 1741, HANNAH PERSON of Guilford, Conn.

Children by first wife, born in Lyme:

 i. JOHN,⁴ b. 3 June 1709.
13. ii. JABEZ, possibly b. in 1718.

Children by second wife, b. in Lyme:

 iii. HANNAH, b. 21 June 1742; probably m. 5 Oct. 1762 EDWARD DE-WOLFE.
   Children (surname *DeWolfe*):
   1. *Daniel*, b. 14 Oct. 1763.
   2. *Edward*, b. 14 Feb. 1765.
   3. *Benjamin*, b. 24 Aug. 1766.
   4. *Sylvannus*, b. 2 March 1768; d. 14 March 1768.
   5. *Ephraim* (twin), b. 11 Feb. 1772.
   6. *Manaseh* (twin), b. 11 Feb. 1772.
 iv. ZELOTUS, b. 22 March 1744.
 v. ZEPHANIAH, b. in February 1745/6; m. in East Haddam, 22 March 1806, ESTHER FOX. No children.

Zephaniah Huntley appears in the Census of 1709 and 1810 in Lyme, Conn.

vi. JEHIEL, b. 7 Feb. 1748/9; d. 7 May 1833. He was of the Connecticut Militia and was pensioned in Chenango County, N. Y., 25 April 1833, aged 89. Jehiel Huntley of Concord in the State of New York sold land in Lyme to William Angell (Lyme Records, vol. 14, p. 508). He was of Hillsdale, Columbia Co., N. Y., in the Census of 1790.

6. JOHN³ HUNTLEY (*Aaron*,² *John*¹), born in Lyme, Conn., 24 Nov. 1677, died there before 1750. He married in Lyme, 2 Feb. 1699, ELIZABETH ———.

His will was probated in 1750 and he mentions his wife Elizabeth, his two sons Peter and Joseph to whom he gives five shillings, having given them deeds of gift before; Mary, wife of Joseph Alger, to whom he gives his Bible; and son Samuel who has two-thirds of his personal property.

On 22 Feb. 1702–3 Aaron Huntley to his son John Huntley a parcel of land in Lyme both Upland and meadow at Four Mile River, on both sides of the River; 44 acres Adj. Town commons and Henry Champion's land.

Children, born in Lyme:

14. i. JOHN,⁴ b. 19 Oct. 1699.
ii. ELIZABETH, b. 2 Jan. 1701/2; d. young.
iii. MARY, b. 20 June 1703; m. 28 April 1731/2 (Church Record 27 April 1732/3) JOSEPH ALGER.
    Children (surname *Alger*):
    1. *Joseph*, b. 21 April 1733.
    2. *Mary*, bapt. 16 March 1740.
    3. *Keturah*, bapt. 7 Oct. 1744.
15. iv. PETER, b. 4 March 1705.
16. v. JOSEPH, b. 27 Jan. 1707.
17. vi. BENJAMIN, b. 5 Feb. 1709.
vii. LUCY, b. 15 Dec. 1711; d. young.
18. viii. SAMUEL, b. 23 Dec. 1713.
ix. LUCY, b. 22 April 1716; d. 31 Jan. 1738/9 (First Ecclesiastical Society Records).
x. SARAH, b. 17 June 1718; d. 25 May 1761 (Lyme Land Records, vol. v, p. 307); m. TIMOTHY MATHER, JR.
xi. ELIZABETH, b. 30 Sept. 1721; d. 19 June 1737 (First Ecclesiastical Society Records).

7. AARON³ HUNTLEY (*Aaron*,² *John*¹), of Lyme, Conn., born in Lyme 1 Dec. 1680, died 26 Sept. 1748, leaving his widow. He married in Lyme, 27 July 1707, DEBORAH DEWOLFE, born in 1690, daughter of Stephen and Hannah DeWolfe.

He lived in Lyme all his life on land bequeathed him by his father. He acted as Deputy to the General Assembly with Thomas Lee, for the Town of Lyme 13 Oct. 1720 (Conn. Col. Public Rec., Hoadley). The northern boundary of Aaron Huntley's farm, and a list of his neighbors is contained by a record in Trumbell's Col. Rec. which reads as follows:

The rights of a distinct society were granted to the northern inhabitants of Lyme, and the dividing line given as follows; . . . beginning by the cove at the N.W. Cor. of Lt. Lord's farm, thence by sd. farm, and Thomas

Lord's farm, easterly, then more southerly taking into the sd. society Joseph Ransom's farm, then easterly to the middle of the pond called Roger's Pond, including the farm of Peter Pierson and John Mack, from thence easterly to the line of the East Society in Lyme, at the North End of Aaron Huntley's farm. . . . 20 Jan. 1702/3 he received a gift of land from his father, "a parcel of upland, marsh, bogs, meadow, 28 acres and halfe more or less in Lyme. On west side of 4 mile river a little above the Tillotsons, twenty acres, and was granted by the towne as 4th division. Nly and Wly with the Commons, Sly by Daniel Huntley, Ely by 4 Mile River."

On 24 Jan. 1723 he received a gift of land from his father at 4 Mile River, 12½ acres at the West end of Lyme and 2½ acres south of the highway that goes over the river.

In his will dated 1748, he bequeaths to his wife, to his son Aaron and daughter Hannah, wife of Ebenezer Mack, five shillings apiece. He also mentions his daughters Deborah, Ruth, Phebe, Ester and Jemima, whose receipts of bequest were signed by Solomon Gee, Samuel Huntley, Nicodemus Miller and William Robins Jr. respectively, husbands of the daughters. He divides his remaining house and lands equally between his sons Nathan and Timothy as follows:

"My son Nathan Huntley should have ye North End of my house and ye Southern End of my land, and my son Timothy ye other part of ye house and ye North End of my land and my little feald ye North side of ye Highway, and my land adjoining to Daniel Beckwith and Moses Noyes land."

Children, born in Lyme:

i. HANA,[4] b. 22 July 1708; d. in 1796; m. 30 April 1728 EBENEZER MACK, d. in 1777, "while bringing in the back log", son of John and Sarah (Bagley) Mack of Lyme. Hana (Huntley) Mack was the ancestress of Joseph Smith, the originator of the Mormon faith. (Smith-Hale Genealogy.)
   Children (surname *Mack*):
   1. *Phebe*, b. 20 Jan. 1728/9.
   2. *Deborah*, b. 16 Sept. 1730.
   3. *Solomon*, b. 15 Sept. 1732.
   4. *Hannah*, b. 15 Oct. 1734.
   5. *Samuel*, b. 15 Nov. 1736.
   6. *Hepsibah*, b. 7 May 1740.
   7. *Stephen*, b. 15 June 1742.
   8. *Elisha*, b. 16 July 1745.
   9. *Azuba*, b. 28 Nov. 1748.
19. ii. AARON, b. 14 Sept. 1710.
   iii. SOLMON, b. 1 Sept. 1712; d. before 1724 (church records).
   iv. DEBORAH, b. 20 Aug. 1714; d. in Lyme 26 March 1807, aged 96; m. 29 May 1731 SOLOMON GEE of Lyme, d. 13 April 1796, aged 71.
   Children (surname *Gee*):
   1. *Stephen*.
   2. *Deborah*.
   3. *Solomon*, b. in 1736.
   4. *William*, b. in 1739.
   5. *Ruth*, b. in 1741.
   6. *Sarah*.
   v. RUTH, b. 1 March 1716/17; m. in Lyme SAMUEL[4] HUNTLEY.
   vi. STEPHEN, b. 28 Feb. 1718/19; not mentioned in his father's will.
   vii. PHEBE, b. 1 March 1721/2; d. in 1797, aged 77 years; m. as his second

wife, 13 March 1740, CAPT. NICODEMUS MILLER, d. in Marlow, N. H., 14 June 1781, aged 67.
    Children (surname *Miller*):
    1. *Lemuel*, b. 21 June 1742; m. Mary Beckwith.
    2. *Esther*, b. 1 July 1744; m. James Munsell.
    3. *Pathama*, b. 16 July 1746.
    4. *Phebe*, b. 10 Jan. 1748/9; m. Zopher Mack.
    5. *Bethuel*, b. 19 Sept. 1751; m. Jemima Huntley.
    6. *Eunice*, b. in Marlow.
    7. *Ama* or *Amma*, b. in Marlow; m. Russell Huntley.
  viii. EASTER, b. 21 May 1724; m. in Lyme, 20 May 1741, WILLIAM ROB-INS, JR. (Lyme Births, Marriages & Deaths, vol. 1, p. 14).
    Children (surname *Robins*):
    1. *Pheby*, b. 27 May 1742.
    2. *Esther*, b. 5 March 1743/4.
    3. *William*, b. 10 Sept. 1745.
    4. *Jemima*, b. 3 April 1752.
    5. *Dmihal*, b. 20 April 1754.
    6. *Lydia*, b. 18 Oct. 1756.
    7. *Ruben*, b. 10 March 1759.
20. ix. NATHAN, b. 2 June 1726.
    x. JEMIMA, b. 30 Aug. 1728; m. 26 May 1754 EBER LEWIS and went with him to Marlow, N. H.
   xi. TIMOTHY, b. 22 Oct. 1731; d. 26 Sept. 1748. He was placed under the guardianship of his brother Nathan 11 Oct. 1748 (New London Probate Records, vol. J. 5, p. 74). The guardianship was discharged 3 Nov. 1752. His share in the house and land was deeded to his brother Nathan.

8. DANIEL[3] HUNTLEY (*Aaron*,[2] *John*[1]), born in Lyme, Conn., 25 May 1682, died there 14 Jan. 1732/3, aged 42 (First Ecclesiastical Society Records). He married, 27 July 1720, HANNAH BROWN of Colchester, Conn. Hannah (Brown) Huntley married secondly, 6 March 1735, Thomas Baker.
    On 20 Jan. 1702/3 Aaron Huntley gives a deed of gift to his son Daniel; Parcel of land in the Town of Lyme, on the West side of 4 Mile River adj. the Tillotson's 20 acre lot, 22 acres and halfe, more or less. Sly with the Tillotson's and common; Ely with 4 Mile R. Nly with Aaron Huntley Jr. and Wly with Commons. 24 Jan. 1723 Aaron Huntley deeds to his son Daniel a gift of land west of Aaron Huntley's land at 4 Mile R.
    The will of Daniel Huntley, dated 1733, bequeaths to his wife Hannah; to his 1st son Daniel the dwelling and farm; to his 3d. son James; his 4th son Amos; and to his 2d. son Jacob, the land in Colchester which came to him from his wife Hannah.
    Children, born in Lyme (Lyme Births, Marriages & Deaths, vol. 2, p. 291):
21. i. DANIEL, b. 17 Aug. 1721.
22. ii. JACOB, b. 5 June 1723.
23. iii. JAMES, b. 16 Aug. 1725.
24. iv. AMOS, b. 31 Oct. 1727.

9. DAVID[3] HUNTLEY (*Aaron*,[2] *John*[1]), born in Lyme, Conn., 17 March 1687/8, died 27 July 1738. He married first in New London, Conn., 11 July 1711, MARY MUNSELL (church

records), died 26 May 1737 (First Ecclesiastical Society Records), undoubtedly the daughter of Thomas and Lydia Munsell; and secondly JOANNA ———

Joshua Hempstead in his diary speaks of this Munsell family, records the marriages of the children, including Mary's and tells of the tragic death of the mother. There is reason to believe that David Huntley lived for a time in Scotland precinct near the town of Norwich, Conn. All civil and church records of this town are destroyed, and therefore there is no record of the births of children.

On 11 Feb. 1724 Aaron Huntley deeds to his "son David and to his two eldest sons that shall survive him, land of 48 acres with dwelling bounded on the highway, the common land, land of Josiah DeWolfe and land and meadow of Moses Noyes."

Administration of the estate of David Huntley, 12 Sept. 1738, shows widow Joanna (New London Probate, vol. J. 4, p. 56, also D., pp. 335, 344).

Children by first wife, born probably in Scotland, Conn.

25. i.   DAVID, b. about 1717.
26. ii. ELIJAH, b. about 1723.
27. iii. ELISHA, b. about 1724.
    iv. LYDIA, b. about 1727; mentioned in the will of Aaron Huntley in 1745; m. 1 Nov. 1747 JAMES BACHUS of Norwich, Conn., son of Joseph and Elizabeth (Huntington) Bachus.
        Children (surname *Bachus*):
        1. *Joseph*, b. 14 Sept. 1748; d. young.
        2. *Mary*, b. 28 Nov. 1749; d. 25 Oct. 1753.
        3. *Ezekiel*, b. 14 Feb. 1751; d. young.
        4. *Lois*, b. 9 Aug. 1752. In the Norwich Probate Records for 16 Nov. 1764: Lois Bachus, a minor of more than 12 yrs., dau. James Bachus, late of Norwich, made choice of her uncle Elijah Huntley as guardian.
        5. *Mary*, b. 1 Jan. 1754; m. James Camp.
28. v.   JONATHAN, b. 9 March 1728.
29. vi. EZEKIEL, bapt. 4 April 1731.
    vii. MARY, bapt. 23 Sept. 1733 (First Ecclesiastical Society Records, Lyme); possibly the Mary who m. in Lyme, 10 Aug. 1757 (Lyme Records, vol. 1, p. 125), CYRUS LEE.
    viii. SIMON, bapt. 25 Dec. 1736; d. 1 Oct. 1743, aged 6 years (First Ecclesiastical Society Records, Lyme).

JOHN HUNTLEY AND SOME OF HIS DESCENDANTS

Contributed by Mrs. ALICE P. HUNTLEY of Hanover, Mass.

10. WILLIAM[4] HUNTLEY (*Moses,[3] Moses,[2] John[1]*), born in Lyme, Conn., 24 June 1712, died 24 June 1759. He married MARTHA SAWYER, daughter of Jacob Sawyer. (Lyme Book of Deeds, vol. 11, p. 264: William Huntley and Martha, Zephaniah Fox and Elizabeth, to Jonathan Haynes, land of their honored father Jacob Sawyer.)

William Huntley served in the French and Indian Wars in 1759 in the 9th Company, Capt. Zebulon Butler, of the 4th Regiment, Col. Eleazer Fitch; also in the campaign of 1758, he enlisted 4 April and was discharged 19 November in the 11th Company, Capt. Timothy Mather of Lyme, the 3d Regiment. William Huntley of Col. Fitch's regiment to the hospital at Ft. Edwards 15 June to 31 Oct. 1759.

Administration of his estate in Hartford, Conn., 8 July 1777, in which is mentioned his wife Martha, sons Abner and Curtais, and daughters Jerusha Perkins, Dorcas Congdale and Keturah.

Children:

30. i. ABNER.[5]
    ii. CURTAIS.
    iii. JERUSHA, m. ——— PERKINS.
    iv. KETURAH, m. as his second wife, 8 Jan. 1786, JOHN AMES.
        Child (surname *Ames*):
        1. *John Noyes*, b. 15 May 1787.
    v. DORCAS, m. ——— CONGDALE.

11. BENEJAH[4] or BENEGAR HUNTLEY (*Moses,[3] Moses,[2] John[1]*), born probably in East Haddam, Conn., died in Lyme, Conn., in 1776, and his probate bond was signed by Lydia Huntly and Benejar, Jr. He married in Southold, Long Island, N. Y., in 1740, ESTHER HOWELL.

He returned to Lyme from Southold about 1743 and sold his land in East Haddam to George and Lemuel Griffing. He lived in the northern section of Lyme where he had land adjacent to Seth Lord and his brother William.

Children, order of births uncertain, born in Lyme:

   i. NEHEMIAH,[5] bapt. in Southold 12 Oct. 1743; d. *s.p.* before 1791; m. MARCY ———.

       He was active in the church in East Lyme, where he was called an evangelist.

31. ii. RICHARD HARRIS, b. 3 Dec. 1745.

  iii. RACHEL, b. about 1746; d. in Antrim, N. H., 17 March 1830, ae. 84; m. AARON[5] HUNTLEY and lived in Marlow, N. H.

  iv. BENEJAR, b. 6 Jan. 1747 (Lyme Births, Marriages and Deaths, vol. 1, p. 48); recorded as living in New London County, Conn., during the Census of 1790, ae. 43; m. LYDIA ———. No children.

32. v. MOSES, b. about 1748.

33. vi. HOWELL (HOEL), b. about 1750.

34. vii. RUFUS.

  viii. ADRIEL, b. 5 April 1752; d. 26 Feb. 1778; m. 18 March 1777 LYDIA MINER, d. in East Haddam, Conn., 15 Sept. 1838, who m. (2) Jonathan Miner of Lyme, m. (3) Champlin Harris, m. (4) Benjamin Stedman.

       Adriel Huntley was on the Lexington Alarm list from the town of Lyme in 1775. He was promised a sergeant's commission if he would go home and in the space of eight days enlist ten men to return with him. He enlisted twelve men the day after he came home and they returned to the army in Roxbury.

       Children:

       1. *Lucretia.*[6]

       2. *A son*, b. and d. 19 Jan. 1777.

35. ix. JONATHAN, b. about 1757.

  x. HANNAH, b. about 1759; d. in Lempster, N. H., 15 Jan. 1847, ae. 88; m. HEZEKIAH[5] HUNTLEY and went to live in Marlow, N. H.

It seems reasonable that two more sons may be added to this list, Noah of East Haddam and Warren of Colchester, who were Revolutionary soldiers.

The relationship of the other sons is proved by affidavits filed by Hoel Huntley and wife of Adriel, Moses Huntley of Waterford, Vt., and Jonathan of Dummerston, Vt. These are on file in Washington, D. C.

  xi. NOAH, b. about 1757.

       He enlisted in the Revolutionary War 20 July to 10 Dec. 1775, 8th Company, Joseph Jewett, 8th Regiment, Col. Huntington, Boston Camps in Roxbury. Corporal in Capt. Cooke's company, Col. John Crane's artillery regiment. Continental Army, 1 Jan. 1780 to 31 Dec. 1780, 4 months as corporal and 8 months as sergeant. Bombardier, Capt. Jotham Drury's company, September to December 1777. On command at Ft. Mifflin, October 1777 in Jersey November 1777.

       The estate of Noah Huntley was administered in East Haddam 13 Aug. 1792.

  xii. WARREN, a Revolutionary soldier from Colchester, Conn., in 2d Regiment, Gen. Spencer's in Roxbury and at Bunker Hill. Quartermaster, commissioned 13 May app. 29 July. Ensign, commissioned 26 Sept. 1775. 1776. 22d Continental, at New York battle of Long Island, White Plains, Peekskill. Warren Huntley a second lieutenant.

12. MOSES⁴ HUNTLEY (*Moses,³ Moses,² John¹*), born probably in East Haddam, Conn., died at Ft. Edwards 19 Aug. 1760. He married MARY SAWYER, sister of Martha Sawyer who married William Huntley. (Lyme Records, vol. VII, pp. 262, 264.)

30 Aug. 1762: Mary Huntley to Jonathan Haynes her share in the estate of Jacob Sawyer of Lyme. (Book of Deeds II.)

Administration of the estate of Moses Huntley in 1763 names his wife Mary as administratrix.

Moses Huntley enlisted with his brothers Jabez and William 4 April, campaign of 1758, in the 3d Regiment under Capt. Timothy Mather of Lyme of the 11th Company and was discharged 18 November. He enlisted in the 9th Company, Capt. Zebulon Butler of Lyme, 4th Regiment, Col. Eleazer Fitch 1759. Reported from the 4th Regiment in the hospital in Ft. Edwards 30 July to 24 Oct. 1760.

Child:

36. i.   MOSES,⁵ b. about 1739.

13. JABEZ⁴ HUNTLEY (*John,³ Moses,² John¹*), possibly born in 1718, died at the home of his son Jabez in East Machias, Maine, in 1810, ae. 93.

The ancestry of this man, the founder of the Machias branch of the family, has long been debated. The names of the men in the family would lead one to suppose that they originated from the Moses branch, but the only space that he fits in is as the son of John. He migrated to Nova Scotia in 1760 at the same time that a number of the DeWolfe family went, and it may be that he was put in charge of his mother's family. He settled around Kingsport and Canard, but after about ten years sold out his holdings of 250 acres, including 150 acres dyked marsh which stretched across the Canard and Habitant R. for ten pounds, a suit of clothes and a beaver hat. The reason he gave for selling was "The upland is no good, it has no stones in it". He went to what is now the state of Maine, where his descendants still live among the stones he found growing there. He went with David Gardner to what is now Machias, and settled around Gardner's Lake.

The tradition at Machias states that his wife was a Caldwell, but another writer claims that she was a Longfellow. The son Frederick without doubt married a Caldwell, and many confuse the father with the son as a first settler.

Jabez Huntley served in the Revolutionary War from 14 Sep. 1775 to 13 Dec. 1775 as Sergeant in Capt. Smith's company. Was reduced to private 1 Nov. 1775. Company stationed at Machias, Lincoln Co., for the defence of the seacoast. Also priv. in Capt. Jos. Seavey's co., Col. Benj.

Foster, from 5 Dec. to 25 Dec. 1778. He was among the men who were paid a bounty of one pound each at Machias 18 Oct. 1777 for enlistment in service of U. S. by Col. John Allen. Mrs. Elizabeth Sanborn in her writing states that the tradition exists that General Warren died in his arms at the Battle of Bunker Hill.

Children:

   i.   TAPHENAS,[5] b. in 1749; d. 30 April 1841, ae. 92; m. NATHAN LONG-FELLOW and came from Cornwallis, N. S., with Mrs. Jonathan Longfellow to Machias in 1767.

          Children (surname *Longfellow*):
          1. *Taphenas*, b. 22 Feb. 1770.
          2. *William*, b. 17 Feb. 1773; d. young.
          3. *Jonathan*, b. 27 Dec. 1775.
          4. *Ana*, b. 18 July 1778.
          5. *Abigail*, b. 31 Aug. 1781; d. young.
          6. *David*, b. 20 April 1791; d. young.

37. ii.   FREDERICK, b. in 1750.

   iii. RUFUS, b. in Nova Scotia. He went to sea. He was taken prisoner by the British and was found by his brother Jabez when the latter went west. Perhaps he was the Rufus Huntley on the list of prisoners delivered by Col. Gabriel Johannot by Charles Waller, commissary of prisoners, at Rhode Island, 17 March 1778, reported a seaman. There was a Rufus Huntley a seaman on State Sloop *Winthrop*, commanded by Capt. George Little, engaged 30 May 1782, discharged 1 Oct. 1782. Roll sworn to at Boston.

   iv. WARREN, b. in Nova Scotia in 1755; m. in Boston, 13 Feb. 1777, MERCY or MARCY GODFREY.

          (Could this Marcy (Godfrey) Huntley be the Mary Huntley buried in Copp's Hill Burial Ground in Boston, who died 28 Sept. 1798, in the 64th year of her age? Her daughter, Mary Armstrong, is also buried there, having died 28 Sept. 1798, in the 36th year of her life.)

          This was possibly the Warren Huntley, seaman on board the Frigate *Boston*, commissioned by Capt. Samuel Tucker, engaged 30 Dec. 1778. Reported sick in Boston 20 Feb. 1779. Roll made up for advance pay 1 month.

38. v.   JABEZ, b. in 1760.

   vi. SALLIE, of Machias and Jacksonville, Maine, m. 17 July 1787 ACHBEL BARNES.

   vii. DELANA, m. ———— DEMON.

   viii. ADRIEL.

14. JOHN[4] HUNTLEY (*John*,[3] *Aaron*,[2] *John*[1]), born in Lyme, Conn., 19 Oct. 1699, died 25 May 1728. He married in Lyme LYDIA ROBBINS, died 22 April 1728, daughter of Joseph Robbins.

    25 April 1727: Deed of sale from John and Lydia Huntley of Lyme, in which he calls himself the son of John Huntley and refers to his honored father Joseph Robins. He had a deed of gift from his father.

    9 July 1728; Lyme Adm. bond of John Huntley with Aaron Huntley as surety upon estate of John Huntley, Jr. Estate of £163, consists of house, well and lot of land, 42 acres with

small orchard. This property after quitclaimed by brothers of John, Jr. and sold to Joseph.

Child:

i.   HEZEKIAH,[5] b. 13 Feb. 1725.
> New London Probate Records, vol. J. 3, p. 90: 22 July 1729 Court appoints John Huntley of Lyme to be guardian of Hezekiah Huntley, the only child of John Huntley, Jr.

15. PETER[4] HUNTLEY (*John,*[3] *Aaron,*[2] *John*[1]) was born in Lyme, Conn., 4 March 1705. He married first, 20 March 1729, MARY RANSOM, born 13 May 1709, d. 5 July 1732 (First Ecclesiastical Society Records), daughter of Joseph and Jane Ransom; and secondly, 14 Feb. 1732/3, SARAH ROBBINS (First Church of Christ, New London).

He had a gift of deed from his father 28 Dec. 1727, when he received 24 acres below the falls at 4 Mile River (Book of Deeds, Lyme, vol. 4, p. 24).

New London Prob., vol. J. 6a, pp. 26, 30, 32: 14 Oct. 1783 Court appoints Jasper Huntley of Lyme administrator of estate of Peter Huntley of Lyme, deceased.

14 Oct. 1783: Jasper Huntley appointed administrator for the estate of Sarah Huntley, with Elisha Boge.

Children by first wife:

i.   PATIENCE,[5] b. 18 March 1730/1.
ii. PETER, b. and d. in 1732.

Children by second wife:

iii. LOIS, b. 26 Feb. 1733 and bapt. 5 May 1733; d. in August 1793.
iv.   SARAH, b. 1 May 1736 and bapt. 11 July 1736.
39. v.   EZRA, b. 4 Aug. 1738.
vi.   HANNAH, b. 4 Aug. 174–.
40. vii. JASPER, b. 4 Sept. 1749.

16. JOSEPH[4] HUNTLEY (*John,*[3] *Aaron,*[2] *John*[1]), born in Lyme, Conn., 27 Jan. 1707, died in 1758. He married first, 7 Jan. 1729, RUTH WILLIAMS, born about 1713 (First Church of Christ, New London), daughter of Thomas and Sarah (Rogers) Williams; and secondly, 24 Oct. 1741, EUNICE WELCH, sister of John Welch of Windham, Conn.

At the time of Joseph's first marriage he was living in New London on land laid out to him on the "west side of Fergoes." (Joshua Hempstead's Diary 22 Nov. 1733). Soon after the death of his wife, he sold this land, 48 acres to his brother Samuel 6 Oct. 1742, and returned to Lyme. He had land by deed of gift from his father, and by purchase of his brother Samuel on 4 Mile River adjacent to his brothers Benjamin and John.

New London Prob., vol. G., p. 234, the will of Joseph Huntley mentions his wife Eunice; his four older children, John, Mary and Lucy and Elizabeth, and his other children by Eunice. In the adm. of his est. (Lyme Record Book, vol. 10, p. 99) Joseph Huntley gives to his four older children, one half the farm; his son John to have 2 shares, on the N. E. part where he can place his house, and each daughter 1 share ea. Mary and Lucy on the northerly side, and Elizabeth on the westerly part adj. her husband Ebenezer Chapman.

The final administration of the estate, 20 March 1768, mentions his daughter Martha; Hannah, wife of Lemuel Beckwith; Susannah, wife of Stephen Ransom, and Abigail.

Children by first wife:

41. i. JOHN,[5] b. about 1730.
    ii. MARY.
    iii. LUCY.
    iv. ELIZABETH, m. 17 June 1755 EBENEZER CHAPMAN of Lyme.

        Children (surname *Chapman*):
        1. *Eunice*, b. 1 Jan. 1756.
        2. *Edward*, b. 1 July 1760.
        3. *John*, b. 15 July 1762.
        4. *Bersheba*, b. 16 July 1764.
        5. *Robert*, b. 1 May 1766.
        6. *Ezekiel*, b. 12 March 1768.
        7. *Phebe*, b. and d. 9 Aug. 1770.
        8. *Rachel*, b. 15 Aug. 1772.
        9. *Elizabeth*, b. 2 April 1774.
        10. *Asael*, b. 26 Feb. 1776.
        11. *Moses*, b. 10 Jan. 1778.
        12. *Susa*, b. 28 Feb. 1782.
        13. *John*, b. 27 Sept. 1783.
        14. *Ebenezer*, b. 12 Sept. 1785.

Children by second wife:

    v. SUSANNAH, b. 18 Dec. 1742; m. STEPHEN RANSOM.
    vi. HANNAH, b. 23 Feb. 1744/5; m. LEMUEL BECKWITH.
42. vii. JOSEPH, b. 13 Jan. 1746/7.
    viii. EUNICE, b. 14 Feb. 1749/50; d. young.
    ix. MARTHA, b. 10 March 1752; m. perhaps 3 March 1772 ICHOBOD YOUNGS of Sharon, Conn.
    x. ABIGAIL, b. 8 Dec, 1753.
    xi. DAVID, b. 8 May 1756; d. young.

17. BENJAMIN[4] HUNTLEY (*John*,[3] *Aaron*,[2] *John*[1]), born in Lyme, Conn., 5 Feb. 1709, died 20 May 1737/8 (First Ecclesiastical Society Records). He married, 27 April 1732, LYDIA BECKWITH, daughter of Joseph and Marah (Lee) Beckwith. Lydia (Beckwith) Huntley married secondly, 30 Dec. 1739/40, John Crossman of New London (Joshua Hempstead Diary).

Benjamin Huntley had land deeded to him from his father on 13 Jan. 1736, adjoining his brother Samuel (Book of Deeds, vol. 5, p. 475).

His will, dated 10 April 1739, mentions his wife Lydia and prays that she will quitclaim the deed to house, barn and land, which he leaves to his father and mother for life. After their death he divides the property between his brothers

Peter, Samuel and Joseph. Mary Alger and Lucia his sisters have already quitclaimed.

Child:

   i.   Curtais,[5] b. 5 May 1735 and bapt. 14 Dec. 1735; d. 4 March 1736/7 (First Ecclesiastical Society Records).

18. Samuel[4] Huntley (*John*,[3] *Aaron*,[2] *John*[1]), born in Lyme, Conn., 23 Dec. 1713, died before 1770. He married, 5 May 1736, Ruth[4] Huntley, died 15 June 1805, aged 88 years and buried in the old Fox Farm Cemetery in Lyme, daughter of Aaron Huntley.

Samuel Huntley had a gift of land from his father 13 Jan. 1736, adjoining the land of his brother Benjamin. (Book of Deeds 5, p. 476) and inherited under his father's will two-thirds of his personal effects. He bought land from his brother Joseph in New London and three of his children were born there, but he returned to Lyme after 1745.

The estate of Joseph Huntley was administered by Elijah Smith and Isaac Tubbs, and the receipts of bequest were signed by his sons, Benjamin, Samuel, Aaron, Solomon and Hezekiah and daughters Molley Chapman, Ruth and Hepsibah.

Children:

     i.   Solomon,[5] b. in Lyme 19 June 1737; d. in action 2 Oct. 1759.
           He enlisted in the French and Indian War, campaign of 1758, 11th Company, Capt. Timothy Mather, 3d Regiment, Col. Eleazer Fitch, 28 May to 31 October. He enlisted also in the campaign of 1759, in the 9th Company, Capt. Zebulon Butler, 4th Regiment, Col. Elezer Fitch of Windham.
     ii.   Hepsebeth, b. 9 Oct. 1738; m. as his second wife Zopher Mack.
43. iii. Benjamin, b. in New London 3 March 1741.
     iv. Molley, b. in New London 12 Aug. 1743; m. 26 May 1765 Edward Chapman.
     v.   Ruth, b. in New London 6 March 1745; d. before 1777.
44. vi. Samuel, b. 11 March 1747.
   vii. Lemuel, b. 7 Nov. 1748; d. young.
  viii. Esther, b. 2 Feb. 1750; d. young.
45. ix. Aaron, b. 4 Nov. 1752.
46. x.   Hezekiah, b. 20 May 1754.
    xi. Mehepzebeth, b. 2 June 1756; d. young.
   xii. Solomon, b. in Lyme 7 Jan. 1761. According to the Census of 1790 he lived in Bennington, Vt., where he had four sons and four daughters. He probably moved to New York State.
           (Lyme Land Records, vol. 5, p. 307; Lyme Records, vol. II, p. 307.)

19. Aaron[4] Huntley (*Aaron*,[3] *Aaron*,[2] *John*[1]), born in Lyme, Conn., called Aaron Huntley 3d, 14 Sept. 1710, died 18 Nov. 1763. He married, in June 1738, Mary Leach.

His estate was administered by Stephen and Nathan Huntley in 1764. The widow Mary went with her son Sylvanus to Marlow, N. H.

Children, born in Lyme:

i. STEPHEN,[5] b. in Lyme 25 March 1740; m. (1) in Lyme, 2 April **1764**, PHEBE TUBBS, d. 14 March 1775; m. (2) in Lyme, 27 Nov. **1777**, MRS. LYDIA BROCKWAY.
    In the Census of 1790 for New York State he was living in Canaan Town, Columbia, Conn.

    Children by first wife:
    1. *Catherine*,[6] b. 10 Feb. 1765; d. 24 Dec. 1770.
    2. *Lucinda*, b. 2 May 1767; d. 4 Dec. 1774.
    3. *Catherine*, b. 24 Dec. 1770.
    4. *A son*, b. and d. 9 March 1775.
    Child by second wife:
    5. *Stephen*, b. 27 Jan. 1779.
    (Lyme Births Marriages and Deaths, vol. I, p. 127.)

ii. NAOMY, b. 14 Feb. 1742/3.

47. iii. SYLVANNUS, b. the last of August 1749.

48. iv. RUBEN, b. 25 Sept. 1752.

v. BETHANIEL or BETHUEL, b. in Lyme 15 Oct. 1755; according to the Church Genealogy m. EUNICE CHURCH, daughter of Titus Church.
    He was in Marlow, N. H., in the Census of 1790, with two children, a boy and a girl; and in 1800 in Leicester, Addison County, Vt. He was in West Gillinbury, Canada, later and had children Theodore and Harvey.

49. vi. ZENUS, b. 16 Jan. 1759 (Lyme Births, Marriages and Deaths, vol. 7, p. 162).

241

JOHN HUNTLEY AND SOME OF HIS DESCENDANTS
Contributed by Mrs. Alice P. Huntley of Hanover, Mass.

20. Nathan⁴ Huntley (*Aaron,³ Aaron,² John¹*), born in Lyme, Conn., 2 June 1726, died in Marlow, N. H., 31 April 1798, aged 72. He married, 6 Oct. 1746, Luce Smith, died 25 March 1802, daughter of Quarles and Mary Smith.

In 1761 Nathan Huntley sold his property in Lyme and with his brothers and sisters and their families migrated to Marlow. Nathan Huntley and Eber Lewis were chosen first selectmen and Nathan served again in that capacity in 1770 and 1771. He was also surveyor of highways.

His house was on top of Marlow Hill where nothing now remains but a few cellar holes. The entire village was moved from the Hill into the valley when the business changed from farming to the tanning of hides and the once fertile fields still surrounded by their stonewalls are grown up to woodland.

Nathan Huntley served in the Revolutionary War in Capt. Jeremiah Stile's company, Col. Paul Dudley's regiment and was present at the Siege of Boston.

Children, born in Lyme:
- i. Azuba,⁵ b. 28 June 1747; d. 31 Oct. 1748.
- 50. ii. Rufus, b. 4 June 1749.
- 51. iii. Isaiah, b. 24 Nov. 1751.
- 52. iv. Nathan, b. 9 Aug. 1754.
- 53. v. Russell, b. 26 June 1758.
- 54. vi. Elisha, b. 15 Dec. 1760.
- vii. Luman, of Marlow and Charlestown, N. H., b. 15 May ——; m. Lurena Beckwith, daughter of Eleazer and Hannah (Lewis) Beckwith. Sevens sons.

   On 16 Aug. 1838 Lurena Huntley, widow of Luman, claimed dower rights in the estate of Luman, her husband.

(Lyme Births, Marriages and Deaths, vol. I, p. 46.)

21. Daniel⁴ Huntley (*Daniel,³ Aaron,² John¹*) born in Lyme, Conn., 17 Aug. 1721. He married in New London, Conn., 16 May 1745, Susannah Beckwith, died in Horton, N. S., 18 March 1799.

Daniel Huntley sold his property in Lyme in 1760 and migrated to Nova Scotia to take up lands vacated by the Arcadians. He was among the passengers of the schooner "Hope" who settled around Scott's Bay, Cornwallis Township.

He is listed in Horton among the town officers for King's County in 1792 as fence viewer and member of the board of health. His name appears also on the "Old Roll Book."

Children, born in Lyme:

   i.   SUSANNAH,⁵ b. 16 April 1746; m. SAMUEL⁵ HUNTLEY..
55. ii. DANIEL, b. 13 Oct. 1748.
   iii. ISAAC, b. 24 Dec. 1753; d. 19 Sept. 1754.
   iv. ISAAC, b. 14 June 1756; d. 22 March 1760.
   v. HANNAH, b. 8 Aug. 1758.
   vi. JASON, b. 4 May 1761; m. in Horton, 15 Jan. 1801, NANCY GROGAN.
   (Lyme Births, Marriages and Deaths, vol. I, p. 23.)

22. JACOB⁴ HUNTLEY (*Daniel*,³ *Aaron*,² *John*¹), born in Lyme, Conn., 5 June 1723, reported dead 14 Oct. 1762. He married in Worcester, Mass., 22 April 1744, LYDIA ALLEN (Early Massachusetts Marriages), born 25 Sept. 1714, daughter of Joseph and Miriam (Wight) Allen. Lydia (Allen) Huntley married secondly in Sturbridge, Mass., 12 May 1779, Dea. Joseph Benson and perhaps went with him to the town of Washington, Mass.

Jacob Huntley enlisted in the French and Indian Wars 14 April 1762 in Capt. Robt. Durkee's company, First Connecticut Regiment.

The administration of his estate was recorded in Ellington Parish in Windsor, Conn., in 1763.

Colchester, Conn., Records, vol. 6, part 1, p. 13: 8 Oct. 1755. Daniel, Amos and James Huntley of Lime state that Jacob Huntley has acquitted to them all his rights and title in lands in the township of Lime, and they acquit all rights in the township of Colchester.

Colchester Records, vol. 5, p. 311: 25 Dec. 1745. Jacob Huntley of Sturbridge, in Co. of Worcester, sells to John Tozer a lot of land which was apportioned to John Brown of Col. dec'd in the 1st division of common lands, and described on the proprietor's records. £28. 10s. old tenor.

Children:

56. i. JACUB,⁵ b. 12 March 1745.
   ii. DEBORAH, b. 18 April 1746; d. in 1746.
57. iii. AMOS, b. 23 Sept. 1747.
   (Vital Records of Sturbridge, Mass.)
   iv. LYDIA, bapt. in 1754.
   v. ANN, bapt. in Bolton, Conn., 14 Dec. 1755.
   vi. MIRIAM, b. about 1756; m. in Brimfield, Mass., 3 June 1779, BENJAMIN STEBBINS.
      Children (surname *Stebbins*):
      1. *Benjamin.*   2. *Jacob.*
             3. *Iddo.*

23. JAMES⁴ HUNTLEY (*Daniel*,³ *Aaron*,² *John*¹), born in Lyme, Conn., 16 Aug. 1725, died at the home of his son Marvin in East Lyme, aged 94 years and is buried in the "Old Stone Yard" in Lyme. He married in Lyme, 21 Aug. 1750, LUCRETIA SMITH, daughter of Samuel and Mary (Marvin) Smith.

James Huntley received a gift of land from his father and lived there most of his life. In his later years he lived with his son in West Exeter, Otsego Co., N. Y.

He commanded a company of Militia in 1776 in Experience Storr's regiment.

Children, born in Lyme:

58. i. PHINEAS,⁵ b. 14 Jan. 1754.
59. ii. RENOLD, b. 30 March 1756.
   iii. ENOCH, b. 1 Oct. 1758; d. 1 June 1786.
   iv. IRENE (RENY), b. 9 March 1761; m. (1) 21 Dec. 1780 JAMES RYAN of New London, Conn.; m. (2) in 1796 WILLIAM MOOR of Waterford, Conn.

   Children by first husband (surname *Ryan*).

   1. *Polly*, b. 13 Nov. 1781: d. 20 Aug. 1787.
   2. *Joseph*, b. 29 Oct. 1784.
   3. *Lucretia*, b. 9 May 1787.
   (Parkhurst Manuscript, Hartford, vol. 3, p. 106.)

60. v. IRA, b. 3 June 1764.
61. vi. MARVIN, b. 11 Nov. 1766.
   vii. ANNA, b. 2 Jan. 1769; m. ——— LEWIS and lived in Pennsylvania.
   They had a son Charles.
62. viii. JAMES, b. 17 May 1771.
   ix. SETH, b. 8 July 1773; d. 9 Sept. 1787.
63. x. ELKANAH, b. 19 Sept. 1775.
64. xi. SILAS, b. 3 Aug. 1777.
   xii. LUCRETIA, b. 18 Aug. 1781; m. SILAS BEEBE.
   (Lyme Births, Marriages and Deaths, vol. 1, p. 69.)

24. AMOS⁴ HUNTLEY (*Daniel,³ Aaron,² John¹*), born in Lyme, Conn., 31 Oct. 1727, died 1 Sept. 1804, aged 77 and is buried in the Layville Yard in Lyme. He married, 21 May 1749, PHEBE MACK.

Amos Huntley received a gift of land from his father Daniel ' and lived in Lyme all of his life.

In his will, probated in 1804, Amos Huntley names his wife Phebe; sons Martin, Dan, Amos, Reu; children of Reu, Sarah, Spicer and Lodovick; his daughters Phebe, Lovicy, Lucy and Zubee.

Phebe Huntley's will, probated in 1816, bequeaths to her sons Martin and Dan; her daus. Lucy Watrous and Azuba Munsell; the heirs of her dau. Phebe Rowland; the heirs of Lovicy Huntley; heirs of Amos Huntley; heirs of Reu Huntley.

Children, born in Lyme:

65. i. MARTIN.⁵
   ii. HULDAH (twin), b. 1 Aug. 1752; d. young.
   iii. ELIZABETH (twin), b. 1. Aug. 1752; d. young.
   iv. PHEBE, b. 10 Sept. 1754; m. 28 May 1772 HENRY ROWLAND.
   The will of Henry Rowland of Warren, Herkimer Co., N. Y., names his second wife Martha; son Palmer and dau. Catherine Hall; also Amos Rowland, Oliver Rowland, Phebe Huntley.and Cyrena Sherber.

   Children (surname *Rowland*):

   1. *Palmer*, b. 16 July 1773.
   2. *Amos*, b. 16 July 1775.
   (Lyme Births, Marriages and Deaths, vol. 1, p. 160.)

244

v.   DAN, b. 20 Nov. 1756; d. in New Lyme in 1835; m. in Lyme, 15
     Feb 1780, LOVICE PECK, d. 6 Aug. 1828, daughter of Silas and
     Elizabeth (Caulkins) Peck.
        In the fall of 1810 Dan Huntley, in company with others from
     Lyme, exchanged their Connecticut farms for lands in Ohio. In
     June 1811 Dan Huntley with Joseph Miller, Peter Chapman and
     Perry Beckwith set out from Connecticut in wagons, and settled
     on the road leading from Dodgeville to Morgan. When the town
     of Lebanon was organized in 1813 Dan Huntley was one of the
     trustees. In 1825 the name of the town was changed to New
     Lyme.
        Child, b. in Lyme:
        1. *Elizabeth*,⁶ b. 25 Feb. 1794; d. in 1846; m. in New Lyme,
            Ohio, Joseph Miller.
vi. LOVICE, b. 11 Feb. 1759; m. 14 March 1776 REUBEN⁴ HUNTLEY.
vii. AZUBAH, b. 22 May 1761; m. 25 Dec. 1783 JOHN MUNSELL.
        Children (surname *Munsell*):
        1. *Azubah*, b. 25 Sept. 1784.
        2. *Mehitable*, b. 5 May 1789.
        3. *Betsy*, b. 10 March 1791.
        4. *John*, b. 10 Feb. 1793.
        5. *Joseph*, b. 17 Dec. 1796.
        6. *Luman*, b. 20 Sept. 1799.
66. viii. AMOS, b. 17 March 1764.
67. ix.   REU, b. 28 Oct. 1766.
x.   LUCY, b. 7 July 1769; m. 1 Nov. 1787 GUERDON WATROUS.
        Children (surname *Watrous*):
        1. *Richard*, b. 27 Oct. 1788.
        2. *Daniel*, b. 27 Oct. 1791; d. 30 Oct. 1791.
        3. *Amos*, b. 11 Oct. 1792.
        4. *Allen*, b. 3 April 1795.
        5. *Dan*, b. 25 April 1797.
        6. *Oliver*, b. 30 March 1800.
        7. *Erastus*, b. 27 April 1802.
        (Lyme Births, Marriages and Deaths, vol. 2, p. 11.)
xi. MOLLEY, b. 6 Dec. 1775; d. in 1792, aged 17.

25. DAVID⁴ HUNTLEY (*David*,³ *Aaron*,² *John*¹), born perhaps in
     Scotland, Conn., about 1717, died at Cause Island 31 Aug.
     1745. He married, 27 Oct. 1742, MARY TINKER of Lyme,
     daughter of Samuel and Jemima (Smith) Tinker. Mary
     (Tinker) Huntley married secondly, 16 Oct. 1750, Elijah
     Hill of Lyme.
        David Huntley was a soldier and seaman in the merchant
     marine of that time in the Colony's sloop "Defence," Capt.
     John Prentice, 1745. After David's death his widow Mary
     sued the estate of John Prentice for wages amounting to
     £45. 16s. in 1749. A commission was appointed to settle the
     account.

        Children, born in Lyme:
68. i.   ELIHU,⁵ b. 30 Aug. 1743 and bapt. 27 Nov. 1743.
ii. MEHITABLE, b. 22 Sept. 1745; m. 14 Oct. 1770 JAMES ROBINSON of
     New London, Conn.
        Children (surname *Robinson*):
        1. *Polly*, b. 21 Jan. 1771; d. 24 Dec. 1773.
        2. *Four children* (two sons and two daughters), b. in December
            1775; d. soon.
        3. *Bettey*, b. 25 July 1777.
        (Parkhurst Manuscript, Hartford.)

245

26. ELIJAH[4] HUNTLEY (*David*,[3] *Aaron*,[2] *John*[1]), born perhaps in Scotland, Conn., about 1723, died in Franklin, Conn., 20 Nov. 1815, aged 92. He married first, in Norwich, Conn., 15 April 1752, ANNE DOWNER, died 24 April 1782, in her 59th year, widow of Edmund Downer; and secondly in Franklin ZERVIAH ABBE, died 19 Nov. 1806, aged 45, daughter of Isaac and Eunice Abbe. (Franklin town records, vol. 1, pp. 54, 61, 84.)

Elijah Huntley was placed under the guardianship of Renold Marvin. He bought a lot of land in Norwich in 1752.

He served one day in the Revolutionary War in Capt. Huntington's company of 4th Batt., Wadsworth regiment.

Children by first wife, born in Norwich:

    i.   EZEKIEL,[5] b. 12 April 1752; d. 16 Feb. 1753.
69. ii.   SOLOMON, b. 29 March 1754.
70. iii.   EDMUND, b. 1 March 17—.
71. iv.   ANDREW, b. 16 Jan. 1757.
72. v.   CALVIN, b. 9 Dec. 1759.
    vi.   LOIS, b. 6 Jan. 1762; d. young.
    vii.   LUTHER, of Windham, Conn., b. 1 April 1765; d. in Windsor 17 Aug. 1846, ae. 86 [?]; m. 19 Aug. 1833 EUNICE LINCOLN. In the Census of 1810 he was listed with three children.

(Norwich Records, vol. 2, p. 147.)

Children by second wife, born in Franklin:

    viii.   ANNA, b. 4 April 1786.
    ix.   ZERVIAH, b. 4 June 1788.
    x.   EUNICE, b. 3 March 1789; d. 9 July 1811.
    xi.   LOIS, b. 6 June 1790; d. in February 1791.
    xii.   SARAH, b. 29 May 1792.

27. ELISHA[4] HUNTLEY (*David*,[3] *Aaron*,[2] *John*[1]), born perhaps in Scotland, Conn., about 1724, died of the smallpox in 1760. He married in Norwich, Conn., 10 April 1749, MARY WALBRIDGE (Norwich Records, vol. 2, p. 120), died at the home of her son Ezekiel 12 Dec. 1800. Mary (Walbridge) Huntley was a widow for over 40 years.

Elisha Huntley served in the French and Indian Wars in the Campaign of 1756 under Lieutenant Colonel and Capt. William Whiting of Norwich, in the Second Company of the Second Regiment. He was reported sick in Albany.

Norwich Registry of Deeds, Book 12, p. 102: 6 July 1751. Elisha Huntley buys of Andrew Durkee piece of land in the section of Norwich called Pottapauge, of abt. 2 acres and 35 rds. with dwelling, adj. lands of Ebenezer Wallbridge, Ephraim Story and the highway. The cooper's shop and tools excepted.

Child:

    i.   EZEKIEL,[5] b. in Norwich 1 April 1750; died in Hartford, Conn., in 1837; m. (1) in Norwich, 17 Dec. 1786, LYDIA HOWARD, d. 3 Oct. 1787; m. (2) in Norwich, 28 Nov. 1790, ZERVIAH (SOPHIA) WENTWORTH, b. in 1767, d. in Hartford 28 Aug. 1833, daughter of Jared and Abigail (Wilson) Wentworth.

Ezekiel Huntley served from 11 July to 16 Dec. 1775 in the Revolutionary War in the First Company of the Eighth Regiment under Capt. Jedidiah Huntington, which was stationed on the Sound until ordered to Boston Camp at Roxbury. He was reported sick at the hospital in Stamford, Conn., and was a pensioner in Hartford in 1832, at which time he was 82 years old. He lived the latter part of his life with his daughter in Hartford.

Child:

1. *Lydia*,[6] b. in Norwich 1 Sept. 1791; d. in Hartford 10 June 1865, aged 73; m. in Hartford, Charles Sigourney. She became one of the leading female poets of her day.

28. JONATHAN[4] HUNTLEY (*David*,[3] *Aaron*,[2] *John*[1]) was born perhaps in Lyme, Conn., 9 March 1728. He married in Lyme, Conn., 22 Aug. 1754, SARAH STEPHENS SMITH, born 19 Sept. 1733, daughter of Nathaniel and Sarah (Rogers) Smith.

Jonathan Huntley served in the French and Indian Wars in the Campaign of 1755, Sept. 9 to Nov. 4 in the Sixth Company of the Third Regiment, under Capt. Joshua Abel of Norwich, Capt. Eliphalet Dyer of Windham.

Children:

i. MARTIN,[5] b. May 1755; d. 13 Jan. 1756.
ii. MARCY, b. 17 Dec. 1756.
iii. JONATHAN, a Revolutionary soldier, b. 4 Dec. 1758; killed in operations around New York 29 Sept. 1776.
iv. ZADOCK, b. in Lyme, Conn., 8 Feb. 1761; d. 8 Aug. 1846; m. in Stephentown, N. Y., ELIZABETH (BALIS) CLAYTON.

In the Census of 1790 he is given at Ballston, N. Y., and at the Palatinate, Montgomery Co., N. Y., in 1800, five girls and one boy.
Zadock Huntley was a Revolutionary soldier in the Militia Regiment in 1778, Col. McClellan's regiment. In Tyler's Brigade under Sullivan in Rhode Island, August to September 1778.

v. ABEL, b. in Lyme, Conn., 9 June 1763; lived in Stephentown, N. Y.
73. vi. ELIJAH, b. 11 Aug. 1765.
vii. NAOMY, b. 30 Aug. 1767.
viii. LYDIA, b. 4 Sept. 1769.
ix. ELIPHALET, b. 7 Sept. 1771.
x. MATHEW, b. 13 Dec. 1773.

(Lyme Births, Marriages and Deaths, vol. 1, p. 57.)

29. EZEKIEL[4] HUNTLEY (*David*,[3] *Aaron*,[2] *John*[1]), baptised in Lyme, Conn., 4 April 1731, died in Lyme. He married first MARY AVERY of Lyme, Conn., died in 1757 (Church Records), daughter of Nathaniel and Abigail Avery; and secondly in Lyme, 8 Nov. 1759, NAOMY TIFFANY. The will of Nathaniel Avery of Lyme mentions his granddaughters Abigail and Hannah Huntley, daughters of his daughter Mary.

Ezekiel Huntley lived in Lyme on land deeded to him by his grandfather, Aaron Huntley.

His name appears as at station 48 on the Brigantine "General Green", Commander Gideon Olmstead of Hartford, 17 Apr. 1782. This ship was taken by the British on the first trip, with about 83 men and 16 guns, May 1782, by the

Ship of War Virginia, and sent into New York. The American seamen taken in this ship by the British died in prison ships in New York. Some came home in the flag of truce, *Jersey*, and some died on the way home. ("Maritime Connecticut During the American Revolution", by Louis F. Middlebrook.) Ezekiel Huntley died a few days after he reached his home in Lyme.

Children by first wife, born in Lyme:

    i.   ABIGAIL,[5] bapt. 20 July 1757; m. in Norwich, Conn., 10 Dec. 1779, MARTIN ABEL, son of Ens. Simon and Parnel (Wills) Abel.

        Children (surname *Abel*):
        1. *Polly*, b. 27 July 1781.
        2. *Henry*, b. 19 Sept. 1783.
        3. *Martin*, b. 21 Jan. 1792.

    ii. HANNAH, bapt. 4 Arpil 1758; m. in Lyme, 28 May 1775, DAN CHADWICK.

        Children (surname *Chadwick*):
        1. *Molley*, b. 18 April 1776.
        2. *Dan*, b. 22 Dec. 1777.
        3. *Elias*, b. 15 May 1780; d. 3 July 1780.
        4. *Lois*, b. 18 Sept. 1781.
        5. *Eleas*, b. 7 Jan. 1784.
        6. *Elizabeth*, b. 14 June 1786.
        7. *Abigail*, b. 17 April 1790.
        8. *Anna*, b. 4 Feb. 1792.
        9. *Dan*, b. 27 Aug. 1798.

Children by second wife, born in Lyme:

    iii. RUFUS, bapt. 18 Sept. 1764; d. young.
    iv. LOES, bapt. 18 Sept. 1764; m. URIAH SANFORD.
    v. ELIAS, bapt. 28 July 1765.
74. vi. ASHER, b. 1 March 1767.
75. vii. EZRA, bapt. 2 June 1771.
76. viii. RUFUS, bapt. 2 Sept. 1778.
77. ix. EZEKIEL, bapt. 21 May 1780.

    (Lyme Book of Deeds, vol. 22, p. 327: 17 Sept. 1803. Quitclaim deed by the children of Ezekiel Huntley, late of Lyme dec'd. Ezra Huntley of Stonington, Martin Abel and wife Abigail, Hannah Chadwick, Rufus Huntley, Naomy Huntley, Lois Sanford and Asher Huntley.)

30. ABNER[5] HUNTLEY (*William*,[4] *Moses*,[3] *Moses*,[2] *John*[1]), born in Lyme, Conn., 24 Jan. 1746, died probably in Earnest Town, Upper Canada, almost 90 years of age. He married, 26 June 1768, LUCRETIA ROWLAND.

Abner Huntley was on the roll of Revolutionary soldiers from the Town of Lyme 8 May to 18 Dec. 1775 in the Eighth Company of the Sixth Regiment, Col. Parsons, Samuel Gale. He was one of Col. Parsons' soldiers sick in Stamford and discharged November 1776.

Immediately after the war he went to Kinderhook, N. Y., living there for nine years, but having a daughter who had moved to Canada, he went to Earnest Town, Upper Canada.

Children, born in Lyme:

i. MARCY,[6] b. 29 April 1769.
ii. ABNER, b. 4 Aug. 1773.
iii. WILLIAM, b. 22 Jan. 1778.
iv. SETH, b. 29 June 1780.
(Lyme Births, Marriages and Deaths, vol. 1, pp. 84, 85.)

31. RICHARD HARRIS[5] HUNTLEY (*Benegar*,[4] *Moses*,[3] *Moses*,[2] *John*[1]), born in Lyme, Conn., 2 Dec. 1745, died in Vernon, Conn., 2 April 1824, aged 78 years. He married in Colchester, Conn., 17 March 1768, RACHEL LITTLE, born about 1748, probably the daughter of Rev. Ephraim and Elizabeth (Woodbridge) Little.

Children, born in Colchester:

i. RICHARD HARRIS,[6] b. 7 Dec. 1768.
ii. ERASTUS, b. 8 Dec. 1770.
iii. WILLIAM F., b. 1 March 1773.
iv. CAROLINE MATILDA, b. 20 March 1775; m. 13 Oct. 1796 ELIJAH WILLIAMS of Willington, Conn.
v. AURELIA, b. 13 Jan. 1777.
vi. AUGUSTUS, b. 5 Jan. 1779.
vii. PHILON or PHILO, b. 8 Sept. 1781.
viii. NABBY (ABIGAIL), b. 21 Feb. 1784; m. in Putney, Vt., 31 July 1803, NAHUM TOWNSEND.
ix. DEMARUS, b. 30 April 1785; m. AMOS OTIS.
x. CHARLES, b. 12 March 1787.
xi. IRENA, m. 20 Nov. 1826 JUSTIN RATHBUN.

32. MOSES[5] HUNTLEY (*Benegar*,[4] *Moses*,[3] *Moses*,[2] *John*[1]), born in Lyme, Conn., about 1748, died in Waterford, Vt., 1 March 1846, aged 88 years 7 months. He married HANNAH ———, who died in Waterford 27 May 1841, aged 83 years.

On 14 Aug. 1832 Moses Huntley gave an affidavit as being 72 years old. He lived in Lyme until 1787 or 1788, when he moved to Marlow, N. H., and lived in that place and in the adjoining town of Lempster for about thirteen years. He then moved to Putney, Vt., where he lived for two years, and thence to Waterford where he was a deacon of the church.

He was a Revolutionary soldier, serving in the Connecticut Militia in 1778 in Col. McClellan's regiment of Connecticut men and served in Tyler's brigade under Sullivan in Rhode Island, August to September 1778. Caledonia list of pensioners, 1840, Moses Huntley of Waterford, Vt., ae. 80, living with Dennis Huntley.

Children, first four born in New Hampshire:

i. ANSEL,[6] b. in Lempster 28 Jan. 1793.
ii. MOSES.
iii. HULDAH, b. about 1790; m. in Waterford, 1 June 1808, SAMUEL GASKILL, JR.
iv. MARIA, m. in Waterford, 16 April 1834, THOMAS PERSONS.
v. DENNIS, b. in Waterford about 1798.

33. HOWELL (HOEL)[5] HUNTLEY (*Benegar*,[4] *Moses*,[3] *Moses*,[2] *John*[1]), born in Lyme, Conn., about 1750, died 17 Aug. 1842, aged 93. He married HANNAH HOLMES.

Howell Huntley lived in the North Society of Lyme, near the Colchester line.

He enlisted in Capt. Lord's company, Col. John Ely's regiment, in the Revolutionary War, 1775. During the war he was wounded and was in feeble health from its effects until his death. He was 84 years old when on the list of pensioners for Lyme, 24 Sept. 1833.

Children, born in Lyme:
i. LYDIA,[6] m. JOHN BOGUE.
ii. HANNAH, m. ——— BEEBE.
iii. HOEL.

34. RUFUS[5] HUNTLEY (*Benegar*,[4] *Moses*,[3] *Moses*,[2] *John*[1]), born in Lyme, Conn., about 1752, died 14 July 1826. He married in Lyme, 22 Feb. 1797, HANNAH FREEMAN.

Rufus Huntley went to Putney, Vt., where his son Jabez was born and then to Madison County, N. Y., settled in DeRuyter.

He was on the Revolutionary War Pension list for Madison County in 1840. Conn. Line enl. at Lyme and went to Roxbury.

His will was filed at Madison County, 11 Sept. 1826, and mentions his wife Hannah and his son Rufus.

Children:
i. JABEZ,[6] b. 24 Feb. 1800.
ii. RUFUS, b. in 1808.

35. JONATHAN[5] HUNTLEY (*Benegar*,[4] *Moses*,[3] *Moses*,[2] *John*[1]), born in Lyme, Conn., about 1757, died in Dummerston, Vt., 27 May 1834. He married in Dummerston BETSY ———, who died 12 Nov. 1835, aged 85 years.

In 1775 he gave an affidavit for his brother Moses of Waterford that they both resided in Lyme with their father. In the Census of 1790 he was given as of Marlow, N. H., and from there he went to Dummerston, where he was residing 28 Aug. 1832, aged 76 years.

He was called Elder Huntley and preached in the Hague School house for many years. He was pastor of the Baptist Church in 1827.

Jonathan Huntley was a private in the Connecticut Militia and was placed on the pension list 23 Sept. 1833 when he was 78 years old.

Child, born in Dummerston.
i. LYMAN,[6] b. in 1797.

36. MOSES[5] HUNTLEY (*Moses*,[4] *Moses*,[3] *Moses*,[2] *John*[1]) was born in Lyme, Conn., about 1739. He married PHEBE ———.

He may have been the Moses Huntley, mariner, who enlisted in the New York regiment of men raised in Connecticut, 29 June 1762, Capt. Nordham.

Moses Huntley was living in Gilsum, N. H., about 1768, with his wife Phebe.

Child:

i. MOSES,[6] b. in Gilsum 29 June 1768.

37. FREDERICK[5] HUNTLEY (*Jabez*,[4] *John*,[3] *Moses*,[2] *John*[1]) was born in Connecticut in 1750. He married LIZZIE or MARY CALDWELL.

He moved with his family from King's County, N. S., to Cutler, Maine, about 1800.

Children, born in Nova Scotia:

i. JABEZ,[6] b. about 1773.
ii. FRED, b. about 1775.
iii. DANIEL, b. about 1778.
iv. JACOB, b. about 1780.
v. JAMES, b. about 1782.
vi. MERRITT, b. about 1785.
vii. ABIGAIL, m. in January 1816 SAMUEL SEAVEY.
viii. WILLIAM.
ix. REUBEN, b. about 1797.
x. RUFUS, b. about 1798.
(Maine Census of 1850.)

38. JABEZ[5] HUNTLEY (*Jabez*,[4] *John*,[3] *Moses*,[2] *John*[1]), born in Nova Scotia in 1760, died in Ontario, Canada, in 1816. He married in Machias, Maine, 23 Dec. 1782, BETTEY or BETSY SMITH, died in Ontario in 1816, daughter of Isaac and Sarah (Wiswell) Smith.

He served as a private in Capt. Joseph Seavey's company, Col. Benjamin Foster's regiment, during the Revolutionary War, enlisted 25 June 1777 and discharged 16 July 1777, service 23 days. Also same regiment 17 days on alarm. Also Lieut. John Scott's detachment from 6th Regiment, service between 31 Aug. 1779 and 20 Nov. 1779, 8 days at Penobscot.

Jabez Huntley moved to Plattsburg, N. Y., where two of his sons, Adriel and Enoch were living. When they reached there it was winter and they remained until spring. They then started on their western trip and on the shores of Lake Ontario Jabez found his brother Rufus. Liking the country they decided to stay there, but were taken sick and died in less than two months. The children returned to Plattsburg.

Children, born in Machias:

i. ISAAC SMITH,[6] b. 26 March 1785.
ii. TAPHENAS, of Machias, b. 6 Feb. 1787; d. in Machias; m. her cousin, JAMES[6] HUNTLEY.
iii. ENOCH HILL, b. 1 Dec. 1793.
iv. MOSES, b. 24 May 1796.
v. ELETHERE S., b. 24 Aug. 1798.
vi. ADRIEL, b. 12 Feb. 1799.

vii. JOSEPH WARREN, b. 8 July 1800.
viii. CHRISTOPHER COLUMBUS, b. 18 Aug. 1802; drowned in Plattsburg when 18 years of age.
ix. HIRAM, b. 17 Aug. 1805.
x. BENIAH, b. 12 Jan. 1808.
xi. BETTEY, b. 24 April 1811; d. 28 Nov. 1816.

39. EZRA[5] HUNTLEY (*Peter,*[4] *John,*[3] *Aaron,*[2] *John*[1]) was born in Lyme, Conn., 4 Aug. 1738.

He migrated to Charlotte, precinct of Duchess County, N. Y., from which place he relinquished to Jasper Huntley of Lyme, his brother, his rights in Peter Huntley's estate and deeded him land near 4 Mile R., 23 May 1767. (Lyme Book of Deeds, vol. 12, p. 77.)

Children, born in Duchess County:
i. JASPER,[6]
ii. TIMOTHY.
iii. EZRA.
iv. PHEBE, m. JACOB MEAD and had a son, Jasper Huntley Mead.
v. MARY, m. PETER DUMAS and had a son, Jasper Dumas.
vi. JOHN.
(Will of Jasper[6] Huntley of Manlius, N. Y.)

40. JASPER[5] HUNTLEY (*Peter,*[4] *John,*[3] *Aaron,*[2] *John*[1]) was born in Lyme, Conn., 4 Sept. 1749. He married in Lyme, 31 Dec. 1768, AZUBAH MACK, daughter of Stephen Mack.

In the Census of 1790 he was given as living in New London County and was in Lyme in 1783, when he administered his father's estate with Elisha Boge.

Children, born in Lyme:
i. SARAH,[6] b. 26 July 1771; m. 31 Aug. 1788 WILLIAM[6] HUNTLEY.
ii. HANNAH, b. 20 Nov. 1773; d. in November 1790.
iii. EZRA, b. 1 Jan. 1777.
iv. AZUBAH, b. 23 Nov. 1782; d. in June 1784.
v. JASPER, b. 13 Nov. 1790; d. 6 Dec. 1790.

41. JOHN[5] HUNTLEY (*Joseph,*[4] *John,*[3] *Aaron,*[2] *John*[1]), born in Lyme, Conn., about 1730, died in Columbus County, N. Y., in 1768. He married in Lyme, 13 Dec. 1747, LOIS BECKWITH, daughter of Mathew and Elisheba (Reiner) Beckwith.

His will, filed in July 1767, bequeaths to his wife Lois, his daughter Elisheby and his sons Williams, Raner and John.

Children, born in Lyme:
i. JOHN.[6]
ii. VASHTY, b. 13 Sept. 1748; d. young.
iii. ELISHEBA, b. 24 Aug. 1751.
iv. WILLIAMS, b. 15 Feb. 1756.
v. CURTAIS, b. 20 Sept. 1758; d. young.
vi. SABRA, b. 1 Sept. 1761; d. young.
(Lyme Births, Marriages and Deaths, vol. 1, p. 68.)
vii. RAYNOR, b. in Columbia County about 1763.

42. JOSEPH[5] HUNTLEY (*Joseph,*[4] *John,*[3] *Aaron,*[2] *John*[1]), born in Lyme, Conn., 13 Jan. 1746/7, died in Groton, Conn., 16 Jan. 1826, aged 80 years. He married in Lyme, 4 May 1768, LYDIA SAWYER.

He shared with the children of his mother Eunice in the second half of his father's estate:

His name appears on the roll of Revolutionary War soldiers serving 8 May to 18 Dec. 1775 in the First Company, Sixth Regiment, with Col. and Capt. Parsons.

Children, born in Lyme:

i.   ABRAHAM,[6] b. 30 March 1769.
ii. OLIVE, b. 6 Oct. 1771; m. 15 Oct. 1795 ELY SPENCER of East Haddam, Conn.
iii. JOSEPH, b. 19 July 1775.
iv. HOPE, b. 15 Jan. 1778.

(Lyme Births, Marriages and Deaths, vol. 1, p. 127.)

43. BENJAMIN[5] HUNTLEY (*Samuel,*[4] *John,*[3] *Aaron,*[2] *John*[1]) was born in New London, Conn., 3 March 1740. He married in New London BETHIAH DORAN.

Lyme Book of Deeds, vol. 15, p. 6: 8 Dec. 1774. Manchester in Co. of Charlotte, N. Y. Benjamin Huntley quitclaims right in ests. of his mother Ruth, widow of Samuel and dau. of Aaron.

Benjamin Huntley served in the Revolutionary War in detachment under Capt. Nathan Smith, Apr. 1778, 3 days, 23 Apr. to 25 Apr. Enlisted 21 Jan. 1778 in Capt. Gideon Bornson's company, at Montreal, Gen. Arnold's regiment.

Children, born in Lyme:

i. DURAN,[6] b. 4 Aug. 1764.
ii. LOVINA, b. 5 June 1766; m. in Lyme, 19 April 1789, DAN PECK, son of Silas and Elizabeth Peck. They migrated to New Lyme, Ohio.
    Children (surname *Peck*):
    1. *Lemuel*, b. 29 Oct. 1787; d. 17 Jan. 1788.
    2. *Silas*, b. 8 May 1789.
    3. *Edward C.*, b. 20 Oct. 1790.
    4. *Ansel*, b. 23 Sept. 1792.
    5. *Polly*, b. 15 June 1801.
    6. *Lyman*, b. 18 June 1803.

44. SAMUEL[5] HUNTLEY (*Samuel,*[4] *John,*[3] *Aaron,*[2] *John*[1]) was born in Lyme, Conn., 11 March 1747. He married in Lyme, 7 Oct. 1767, SUSANNAH HUNTLEY, perhaps the daughter of Danuel and Susannah (Beckwith) Huntley.

He was in Lempster, N. H., before 1778 and in Leicester, Vt., in 1790.

Samuel Huntley served in the Revolutionary War 9 May to 7 July 1775, in the Seventh Company, Capt. Edward Mott of Preston, Sixth Regiment, Col. Parsons. He served also in the Northern Department under Gen. Schuyler.

Children:

i.   LEMUEL,[6] b. in Lyme 8 Aug. 1768.
     Probably
ii. LUCINDA.
iii. STERLING.
iv. DAVIS.
v.   JOHN.
vi. SAMUEL.

JOHN HUNTLEY AND SOME OF HIS DESCENDANTS

Contributed by MRS. ALICE P. HUNTLEY of Hanover, Mass.

45. AARON[5] HUNTLEY (*Samuel*,[4] *John*,[3] *Aaron*,[2] *John*[1]), born in Lyme, Conn., 4 Nov. 1752, died in Antrim, N. H., 18 Feb. 1819. He married RACHEL[5] HUNTLEY (Benegar,[4] Moses,[3] Moses,[2] John [1]), died 17 March 1830, aged 84 years.

He moved to Marlow, N. H., about 1773, where the earmark of his kine is registered: a swallow-tail in each ear and a halfpenny in the under side of each ear.

Aaron Huntley enlisted as a private in Capt. Samuel Canfield's company, Col. Benj. Bellow's regiment, 28 June 1777, to re-enforce the garrison at Ticonderoga. 8 days service, discharged 5 July.

Children, born in Marlow:

i. NEHEMIAH,[6] b. 6 July 1776.
ii. ROSWELL, b. 21 May 1784.
iii. WILLIAM, b. 14 Dec. 1786; d. young.
iv. WILLIAM, b. 9 April 1789.
v. JONATHAN, b. 5 May 1791.
vi. AARON, b. 16 Jan. 1794.
vii. FANNY, b. 20 Aug. 1796.

(Marlow Record Book, vol. 3, p. 44.)

46. HEZEKIAH[5] HUNTLEY (*Samuel*,[4] *John*,[3] *Aaron*,[2] *John*[1]), born in Marlow, N. H., 20 May 1754, died there 4 May 1853, aged 99 years. He married HANNAH[5] HUNTLEY (Benegar,[4] Moses,[3] Moses,[2] John[1]), d. in Lempster, N. H., 15 Jan. 1847, aged 88 years, sister of Harris and Rachel.

His home in Marlow was near Huntley Mountain on one of the finest farms of the district:

Children, born in Lempster:

i. CHARLES,[6] b. 13 May 1780.
ii. LYDIA LEWIS, b. 10 Sept. 1784.
iii. BENEJAH FRANCIS, b. 29 Aug. 1786 or 7.
iv. RICHARD HARRIS, b. 30 Oct. 1790.

47. SYLVANNUS[5] HUNTLEY (*Aaron*,[4] *Aaron*,[3] *Aaron*,[2] *John*[1]) was born in Lyme, Conn., the last of August 1749. He married there MEHITABLE TUBBS.

He went to Marlow, N. H., with his mother, "the widow Mary Huntley," where his child was born.

Mehitable (Tubbs) Huntley was active in the Baptist

Church in Marlow, where she was listed as a member 26 July 1783.

Child:

i. SYLVANNUS,[6] b. in Marlow 28 July 1795.

48. RUBEN OR REUBEN[5] HUNTLEY (*Aaron*,[4] *Aaron*,[3] *Aaron*,[2] *John*[1]), born in Lyme, Conn., 25 Sept. 1752, died in Elmira, N. Y., in 1836. He married in Lyme, 14 March 1776, LOVICE HUNTLEY, daughter of Amos and Phebe (Mack) Huntley. (Lyme) Births, Marriages & Deaths: Ruben, son of the widow Mary Huntley married Lovice Huntley.)

Ruben Huntley was a Revolutionary War soldier, serving in the First Company, Capt. Parsons, Sixth Regiment, Col. Parsons, and the Connecticut Continental. He was placed on the pension list 10 Apr. 1833, ae. 84.

He lived in his later life with his daughter in Chenango County, N. Y.

Children, born in Lyme:

i. MICAIL,[6] b. 27 Oct. 1777.
ii. RICHARD, b. 18 March 1780.
iii. GILES, b. 19 Nov. 1781.
iv. TABER, b. 27 Nov. 1787.
v. POLLY, b. 14 Nov. 1791; m. probably as his first wife EZRA[6] HUNTLEY, son of Ezra Huntley.
vi. URSULA, b. 19 Nov. 1797; m. probably 26 March 1819 SHERMAN MUNSEL (church record).
vii. JULY ANN, b. 9 Oct. 1806; m. as his second wife EZRA[6] HUNTLEY.

49. ZENUS[5] HUNTLEY (*Aaron*,[4] *Aaron*,[3] *Aaron*,[2] *John*[1]) was born in Lyme, Conn., 16 Jan. 1759. He married there, 14 Feb. 1784, ELIZABETH PECK, daughter of Silas and Elizabeth (Caulkins) Peck.

Zenus Huntley went to Otsego County, N. Y., and in the Census of 1790 he was in Canaan Town, Columbia County, N. Y., with his brother Stephen.

Children, born in Lyme:

i. CALKINS,[6] b. 15 Feb. 1785.
ii. DAN (ZENUS), b. 27 Feb. 1787.
(Lyme Births, Marriages and Deaths, vol. 1, p. 92.)

50. RUFUS[5] HUNTLEY (*Nathan*,[4] *Aaron*,[3] *Aaron*,[2] *John*[1]), born in Lyme, Conn., 4 June 1749, died in Marlow, N. H., 27 April 1802, aged 52 years. He married ESTHER MOOR, died 22 March 1817, aged 69 years, daughter of Asa Moor of Lyme.

Rufus Huntley lived most of his life in Marlow.

He served 8 days in the Revolutionary War in Capt. Canfield's company, Col. Benj. Bellow's regiment as corporal, from 28 June 1777 to 5 July 1777.

Keene Prob. Docket 112: Will of Rufus Huntley, dated 7 Apr. 1802, wills to his wife Esther, his son Martin, and to his daus. Lucy, wife of Asa Way, and Clarenda.

Children, born in Marlow:

i. MARTIN,[6] b. 24 July 1779.
ii. LUCY, b. 5 March 1782; m. in Marlow, 29 Sept. 1801, ASA WAY.

iii. CLARENDA, b. 18 Sept. 1784; m. in Marlow, 20 Dec. 1804, NATHANIEL BROWN of Bolton, N. H.

51. ISAIAH[5] HUNTLEY (*Nathan,*[4] *Aaron,*[3] *Aaron,*[2] *John*[1]), born in Lyme, Conn., 24 Nov. 1751, died in Duxbury, Vt., 21 Dec. 1820, aged 69 years. He married in Lyme, 5 Sept. 1779, ELIZABETH CHURCH, died 13 Feb. 1841, aged 87 years, daughter of Simeon Church of Lyme.

Isaiah Huntley served as a Revolutionary soldier for 6 days from 28 June to 3 July in Capt. Canfield's company, Col. Benj. Bellow's regiment, to re-enforce the garrison at Ticonderoga.

All of his sons became ministers of the gospel except one.

Children, born in Marlow, N. H.:

i. CALVIN,[6] b. 11 Aug. 1780.
ii. NATHAN, b. 7 Jan. 1782.
iii. ISAIAH, b. 20 Nov. 1787.
iv. LELAND, b. 3 Dec. 1790.
v. ALLEN, b. 13 Dec. 1792.
vi. WEALTHY, b. 16 March 1795; d. in Duxbury 7 Aug. 1869 (Church genealogy); m. 17 April 1816 DAVIS MARSHALL of Waterbury, Vt. Children (surname *Marshall*):
   1. *Julia Mathilde,* b. 17 Nov. 1816; d. 16 May 1852.
   2. *Henry G.,* b. 11 June 1819; d. 1 April 1879.
   3. *Langdon,* b. 30 Nov. 1822; d. 8 April 1890.
vii. SELDIN, b. 20 Oct. 1797.
(Marlow Record Book, vol. 3, p. 42.)

52. NATHAN[5] HUNTLEY (*Nathan,*[4] *Aaron,*[3] *Aaron,*[2] *John*[1]), born in Lyme, Conn., 9 Aug. 1754, died in Marlow, N. H., 29 Sept. 1798. He was called Nathan, Jr. He married first, in Lyme, MARY PERSONS (PEARSON), daughter of Richard and Mary Ann (Ely) Persons; and secondly, in Marlow, 16 Nov. 1791, EUNICE ROYCE. Eunice (Royce) Huntley married secondly James McCally of Hillsboro, N. H. (Marlow Record Book, vol. 3, p. 9.)

Nathan Huntley served in Capt. Wetherbee's company, Col. Isaac Wyman's regiment, at Mt. Independance, 5 Nov. 1778.

Children by first wife:

i. GUERDON,[6] b. 22 Dec. 1776; d. four weeks old.
ii. ENOCH, b. 12 April 1778.
iii. LOYNES or LOINS, b. 15 Nov. 1780.

Children by second wife:

iv. ELISHA, b. 4 May 1795.
v. MARY, m. NATHANIEL RICHARDSON.

53. RUSSELL[5] HUNTLEY (*Nathan,*[4] *Aaron,*[3] *Aaron,*[2] *John*[1]), born in Lyme, Conn., 26 June 1758, died in Marlow, N. H., 9 March 1808, aged 49 years. He married in Alstead, N. H., 17 Feb. 1779, AMA or AMMA MILLER, died 1 June 1829, aged 67 years, daughter of Nicodemus and Phebe (Huntley) Miller.

Russell Huntley moved to Marlow with his father.

Lyme Book of Deeds, vol. 16, p. 318: 8 Oct. 1782. Deed quit-claiming heirs of Nicodemus Miller in estate of their uncle Elisha Miller of Lyme. Lemuel Miller and Bethuel Miller for ourselves and in behalf of our sisters, Eunice and Bethena Miller. Also James Munsell and Esther, his wife, and Russell Huntley and Ama, his wife.

He served 1.7 day in Col. Bellow's regiment at Ticonderoga, 7 May 1777.

Children, born in Marlow:

i.   ELIJAH,⁶ b. 29 March 1779.
ii. PHEBE, b. 14 Dec. 1782; m. MARTIN⁶ HUNTLEY, son of Rufus and Esther (Moor) Huntley.
iii. LUTHER, b. 27 Aug. 1786.
iv. HUBBARD, b. 4 March 1793.
v.   ETHELINDA, b. 4 Jan. 1798; m. in Marlow, 27 Jan. 1814, LELAND LEWIS of Lempster, N. H.
     Children (surname *Lewis*):
     1. *Hubbard R.*
     2. *Henry A.*
     3. *George R.*
     4. *Melissa*, m. David Reynolds.

54. ELISHA⁵ HUNTLEY (*Nathan,*⁴ *Aaron,*³ *Aaron,*² *John*¹), born in Lyme, Conn., 15 Dec. 1760, died in Marlow, N. H., 17 Jan. 1835, aged 75 years. He married CLARRY or CLARRISSY GUSTIN, died 28 Sept. 1850, aged 86 years, daughter of John and Lydia (Mack) Gustin.

Elisha Huntley went with his father to Marlow. He became very prominent in the affairs of the town, kept a hotel, was postmaster and justice of the peace. He was not only commanding officer of the old militia, but judge of the Court of Common Pleas in 1809, was appointed judge of the Circuit Court in 1816 and judge of the Court of Sessions in 1821.

He was among the recruits mustered by Maj. Scott to reenforce the garrison at Ticonderoga, June 1777. He served 6 days in Capt. Samuel Canfield's company, Col. Benj. Bellow's regiment.

Children, born in Marlow:

i.   ELISHA,⁶ b. 19 April 1782; d. 2 March 1784.
ii.   RHODA, b. 28 Sept. 1786; m. in Marlow, 9 Jan. 1806, JAMES MATHER.
iii. LUCINDA, b. 2 Feb. 1789; d. 2 Feb. 1790.
iv.   CURTIS, b. 21 Nov. 1790.
v.   POLLY, b. 28 April 1793; d. 22 Feb. 1795.
vi.   POLLY, b. 10 Sept. 1795.
vii. OLDEN (ALDEN), b. 5 Jan. 1798.
viii. LUCINDA, b. 24 April 1800; m. in Marlow, 30 April 1818, JONATHAN RICHARDSON.
ix.   RUFUS, b. 14 Jan. 1803.
x.   AMANDA, b. 21 Oct. 1808; m. ——— BAKER.
(Marlow Record Book, vol. 3, p. 161.)

55. DANIEL⁵ HUNTLEY (*Daniel,*⁴ *Daniel,*³ *Aaron,*² *John*¹), born in Lyme, Conn., 13 Oct. 1748, died in Horton, N. S., prior to 7 June 1803. He married first, in Horton, 3 Dec. 1772,

SARAH ELLS, died 27 March 1779, daughter of Joshua and Mary Ells; and secondly, 9 Aug. 1780, BETSY WICKWIRE, born 7 June 1760, daughter of Peter and Rhoda (Scofield) Wickwire.

Peter Huntley deeded to Daniel Huntley "the lands which my Father Daniel Huntley Junior deceased owned in Cornwallis, that is to say, a lot of land lying the north side of Pero River containing upland and marsh about three hundred acres which my Father bought from William Allen Chipman. Also a lot of land lying on Cornwallis Mountain containing about Four Hundred and Seventy acres and was laid out to Daniel Huntley Senior."

Children by first wife, born in Horton:

i. ANN,⁶ b. 25 Feb. 1773; m. DAVID SAMPSON PINEO of Pugwash, N. S.
ii. ELIZABETH, b. 6 March 1775; m. LEONARD WOODWORTH of Woodstock, N. B.
iii. ABIGAIL, b. 18 Oct. 1776; m. BRANCH WOODWORTH of Shepody, N. B.

Children by second wife:

iv. DANIEL, b. 20 Dec. 1781.
v. PETER, b. 26 Nov. 1783.
vi. CHARLOTTE, m. 2 Jan. 1808 GEORGE JESS, son of George Jess.
    Child (surname *Jess*):
    1. *William*, b. 2 Jan. 1822.
    Probably others.
vii. SARAH (twin), b. 22 Oct. 1786; m. 11 Aug. 1808 PATRICK COFFILL of Newport, N. S.
viii. BETSY (twin), b. 22 Oct. 1786; d. young.
ix. ENOCH, b. 22 Aug. 1788.
x. JAMES, b. 15 April 1790.
xi. SUSANNAH, m. THOMAS PRITCHARD of Pictou, N. S.
xii. REBECCA, m. DAVID JACKSON of Woodstock, N. B.
xiii. ASA, b. in 1802.

56. JACUB or JACOB⁵ HUNTLEY (*Jacob,⁴ Daniel,³ Aaron,² John¹*) was born in Sturbridge, Mass., 12 March 1745. He married ABIGAIL ———, who died in Bakersfield, Vt., in 1829. He may have been the Jacob Huntley who was living in Bakersfield in 1795 with his wife Abigail.

Children:

i. SETH P.,⁶ b. 12 March 1796.
ii. JACOB, b. 14 Feb. 1798.
iii. JOSEPH STODDARD, b. 2 June 1800.
iv. PATTEY WEBSTER, b. 7 May 1802.
v. ALVIN, b. 26 Sept. 1803.
vi. ABIGAIL, b. 4 April 1805.
vii. RANDALL, b. 9 Nov. 1806.
viii. RHODA HAMILTON, b. 12 Feb. 1809.
ix. HORATIO, b. 5 March 1811.
x. POLLY, d. 3 Jan. 1813.

57. AMOS⁵ HUNTLEY (*Jacob,⁴ Daniel,³ Aaron,² John¹*), born in Sturbridge, Mass., 23 Sept. 1747, died in Pierpont, Ohio, 16 May 1828. He married LOIS (perhaps COOK).

He lived in the town of Washington, Mass., where he engaged in farming until 1811 when he went to Pierpont,

Ashtabula County, Ohio. He arrived in Pierpont in 1811 and made a beginning on his farm at Lot 42, which was then a part of Denmark. In the fall of that same year he returned to Washington for his family.

The first school house was erected in 1813 or 1814 and the first term therein was taught by Lucy Huntley, the youngest daughter of Amos Huntley.

When the Presbyterian Society was organized on 8 Nov. 1823 Amos Huntley and wife, James Huntley and wife, were listed among the members.

The first election of the town of Pierpont, after its separation from Denmark, took place at the home of Amos Huntley on 18 June 1818.

Amos Huntley answered the Lexington Alarm from East Windsor, Conn., and served under Capt. Amasa Loomis in 1775.

Children, born in Washington:

i. LYDIA,[6] b. 27 Dec. 1777.
ii. AMOS, b. 12 Nov. 1779.
iii. ELISHA, b. 6 May 1781.
iv. WILLIAM, b. 25 Sept. 1783.
v. EZEKIEL, b. 3 Jan. 1785.
vi. LOIS, b. 2 June 1786; m. in Washington, 27 April 1806, ROGER CAMPBELL.
vii. SILVIA, b. 3 June 1789.
viii. JAMES (twin), b. 4 July 1793.
ix. ANNE (twin), b. 4 July 1793; m. in Denmark ELIHU KNAPP.
x. ORANGE (twin), b. 19 May 1796.
xi. ORIN (twin), b. 19 May 1796.
xii. LUCY, b. 11 May 1799.
xiii. HIRAM, b. 18 Dec. 1803.
(Vital Records of Washington.)

58. PHINEAS[5] HUNTLEY (*James*,[4] *Daniel*,[3] *Aaron*,[2] *John*[1]), born in Lyme, Conn., 14 Jan. 1754, died in West Exeter, N. Y., 30 Aug. 1820, in his 66th year. He married RHUMAH TIFFANY. He lived in Lyme until after 1790, when he moved to West Exeter.

His will, filed in Otsego County, names his wife Rhumah, his son Calvin, daus. Betsy Marsh, Rhumah Peck, Lucretia Matheson, and his grandsons Elisha Ely, Jacob and Ira Marsh, Calvin Peck and Abner Matheson.

Children, born in New York:

i. ELISHA,[6] b. in 1780; d. in 1803, aged 23 years.
ii. RHUMAH, b. in 1786; m. 21 Feb. 1809 WILLIAM E. PECK of East Haddam, Conn., son of Elisha and Olive Peck. They lived in Spring Prairie, Wis.
Children (surname *Peck*):
1. *Rhumah H.*, b. 6 Jan. 1811.
2. *Betsy Ann*, b. 31 Aug. 1813.
3. *Calvin H.*, b. 15 April 1814.
4. *Lucretia*, b. 29 April 1816.
5. *Deborah T.*, b. 20 June 1819.
6. *Jedidiah W.*, b. 25 July 1821.
7. *Caroline H.*, b. 26 July 1823.

8. *Charaldine*, b. 11 May 1826.
9. *Albert E.*, b. 10 July 1834.
(Peck genealogy.)
iii. ALBERT PHINEAS, b. 20 Nov. 1810.
iv. CALVIN, b. 15 Jan. 1818.
v. BETSY, m. ELY T. MARSH of West Winfield, N. Y.
vi. LUCRETIA, m. ——— MATHESON of West Winfield, N. Y. They lived in Sergeant's Bluff, Iowa.

59. RENOLD or REYNOLD[5] HUNTLEY (*James*,[4] *Daniel*,[3] *Aaron*,[2] *John*[1]), born in Lyme, Conn., 30 March 1756, died in Manlius Center, N. Y., 9 Sept. 1839, aged 83 years. He married first, in Lyme, in 1780, JERUSHA MACK, died 10 Feb. 1787; and secondly, 26 Aug. 1787, MRS. ESTHER McKNIGHT.

He lived in New London, Conn., until after 1792, when he moved to Manlius Center.

Children by first wife, born in Lyme:
i. WILLIAM,[6] b. 22 May 1781.
ii. LYDIA, b. 9 Sept. 1782; m. in Lyme, 9 Sept. 1802, JOHN MUNSELL.
iii. REYNOLD, b. 30 April 1784.
iv. STANTON (ADAM S.), b. 12 Nov. 1786.

Children by second wife:
v. FANNY, b. 19 June 1788.
vi. DANIEL, b. 15 Aug. 1792.
(Lyme Births, Marriages and Deaths, vol. 2, p. 2.)

60. IRA[5] HUNTLEY (*James*,[4] *Daniel*,[3] *Aaron*,[2] *John*[1]), born in Lyme, Conn., 3 June 1764, died in Manlius, N. Y., in October 1814. He married in 1786 POLLY LEE, born in 1763, died 9 July 1839, daughter of Jason and Abiah (Brown) Lee.

His will, dated 18 Aug. 1814, wills to his son Ira Jr., Enock, Lee and James, to his dau-in-law Nancy, wife of son Lee, to her dau. Sabrina; to his gr-son James Lasher, younger son of Frederick Lasher, and to Lucretia Lasher, his dau.

Children, born in Manlius:
i. IRA,[6] b. in 1788.
ii. LEE.
iii. ENOCK.
iv. JAMES.
v. LUCRETIA, m. FREDERICK LASHER.
Child (surname *Lasher*):
1. *James*.

61. MARVIN[5] HUNTLEY (*James*,[4] *Daniel*,[3] *Aaron*,[2] *John*[1]), born in Lyme, Conn., 11 Nov. 1766, died there when nearly 88 years old. He married first, 9 April 1789, CAROLINE LORD, died 25 Aug. 1807, aged 37 years; and secondly, 3 March 1808, MARY DOUGLAS, born in New London, Conn., 30 Sept. 1778, died 6 Oct. 1844, aged 66 years, daughter of Joseph and Mary (Thompson) Douglas.

Marvin Huntley lived all his life in Lyme and held a large tract of land there.

In his will, dated 1854, he bequeaths to his sons Marvin Jr., Abel Lord, and Joseph D., and to his daus. Sally Caulkins, Hariot Rogers, Caroline Daniels, Mary, and Asenathe Peck dec'd.

Children by first wife, born in Lyme:

i. SALLY,[6] b. in May 1790; m. 26 March 1807 DANIEL CALKINGS of Waterford, Conn. (Waterford V. R., 1–7)

ii. MARVIN LORD, b. 25 Oct. 1792; d. 8 June 1794.

iii. HARRIOT, b. 13 July 1795; m. in Lyme, 4 Sept. 1821, JOHN ROGERS, JR.

iv. A SON, b. and d. 14 June 1797.

v. ASENATH, b. 8 Aug. 1798; m. 27 May 1818 JESSE PECK.

Children (surname *Peck*):

1. *Jesse Marvin*, b. in 1820.
2. *Peter Lord*, b. in February 1823.
3. *David M.*, b. 25 May 1833 (?).
4. *Caroline*, b. 23 March 1834.
5. *Lydia A.*, b. 4 July 1836.
6. *John Smith*, b. in June 1837.
7. *Joseph*, b. in July 1838; d. young.

vi. MARVIN, b. 10 Aug. 1800.

vii. CAROLINE, b. 15 Jan. 1803; m. ——— DANIELS.

viii. ABEL LORD, b. 12 June 1805.

ix. LYDIA, b. 17 Aug. 1807; d. 19 Dec. 1827.

Children by second wife:

x. JOSEPH DOUGLAS, b. 23 Sept. 1809.

xi. MARY, b. 12 July 1813; m. perhaps in East Lyme, 16 June 1853, ELIJAH LOOMIS of Salem, Conn.

62. JAMES[5] HUNTLEY (*James,*[4] *Daniel,*[3] *Aaron,*[2] *John*[1]), born in Lyme, Conn., 17 May 1771, died in West Winfield, N. Y., 26 Aug. 1849, aged 78 years. He married, in 1795, LYDIA CAULKINS, died 14 Aug. 1865, in her 89th year.

James Huntley moved to West Exeter, N. Y., and then to West Winfield, where he was known as Deacon Jim Huntley.

He enlisted in the War of 1812, but never saw service.

Children, born in West Exeter:

i. EUNICE,[6] b. in 1796; d. 11 April 1796.

ii. JAMES CALKINS, b. 10 April 1797.

iii. EXPERIENCE, b. 19 Jan. 1799; d. 31 March 1883; m. 16 March 1819 BENJAMIN PRESCOTT, d. 28 July 1847.

iv. ELIZA, b. 1 April 1800; d. 16 July 1856; m. 4 Nov. 1817 DANIEL JOSSLYN, d. 14 June 1873.

v. ISAAC, b. 22 Jan. 1802.

vi. LYDIA, b. 12 Aug. 1803; d. 10 July 1865; m. 14 Feb. 1827 PHINEAS HALL.

vii. EUNICE, b. 19 March 1805; d. 24 Aug. 1841; m. 6 Feb. 1828 CHARLES BARSTOW, d. in November 1887, aged 89 years.

viii. CHARLES, b. 5 July 1807.

ix. LYMAN, b. 3 Feb. 1809.

x. LESTER, b. 17 Dec. 1810.

xi. ROXY ANN, b. 27 June 1812; d. 12 June 1911, aged 99 years; m. 24 June 1840 MYRON ELDRED.

xii. ELISHA, b. 13 Nov. 1813.

xiii. LORING, b. 26 July 1815.

xiv. PORTER CALKINS, b. 26 March 1818.

xv. WASHINGTON, b. 28 Dec. 1819; d. aged 1 day.

xvi. FLORUS, b. 19 May 1822; d. aged 2 years 1 month.

(Bible record of Maud Cutler in the Albany State Library.)

63. ELKANAH[5] HUNTLEY (*James*,[4] *Daniel*,[3] *Aaron*,[2] *John*[1]), born in Lyme, Conn., 19 Sept. 1775, died 29 March 1855. He married in Waterford, Conn., 14 Nov. 1799, NANCY (ANNA) BISHOP, born 2 June 1780.

Elkanah Huntley lived in that section of Lyme called East Lyme.

Children, born in East Lyme:

i. NANCY,[6] b. 1 Oct. 1800.
ii. JAMES, b. 18 Feb. 1802.
iii. JONATHAN BISHOP, b. 23 Jan. 1804.
iv. EMILIE, b. 4 June 1806; m. 8 Oct. 1831 WILLIAM HUMES of Sterling, Conn.
v. SALLY, b. 4 Aug. 1808; m. in East Lyme, 13 Jan. 1839, JOHN MC-CRARY.
vi. DELIA B., b. 16 Sept. 1810; m. ——— LUSH.
vii. GILES B., b. 24 Sept. 1812; d. 3 Feb. 1815.
viii. MARYETTE, b. 16 Aug. 1814; m. ——— SNELL.
ix. MERCY GILBERT, b. 12 July 1816; m. 27 April 1834 FRANCIS B. LEE. They lived in Norwich, Conn.
x. NICHOLAS A., b. 3 Feb. 1817; d. 1 April 1819.
xi. LUCY ANN, b. 10 March 1820; m. ——— FITCH.
xii. ELKANAH ALLEN, b. 11 May 1822.

64. SILAS[5] HUNTLEY (*James*,[4] *Daniel*,[3] *Aaron*,[2] *John*[1]), born in Lyme. Conn., 3 Aug. 1777, died there 6 Oct. 1832, aged 55 years. He married, 25 Nov. 1804, BETSY BEEBE, born 11 Oct. 1780, died 9 Nov. 1858, aged 78 years, probably daughter of Azariah and Diademy (Marvin) Beebe.

He served in the War of 1812 as sergeant from 15 Aug. 1814 to 25 Aug. 1814 under Commander Lynde Reed.

Children, born in Lyme:

i. BETSY,[6] b. in 1805; d. in Lyme 10 March 1892, aged 87 years; m. 28 Sept. 1823 SELDEN ROGERS.
ii. MIRANDA, b. in 1806; m. 13 Nov. 1825 ABIJAH PEARSON of East Lyme, b. 14 Aug. 1795.
    Children (surname *Pearson*):
    1. *Phebe Elizabeth*, b. in 1826.
    2. *John Percival*, b. in 1828.
    3. *Mary Ann*, b. in 1830.
    4. *Reuben Rogers*, b. in 1832.
    5. *Nancy Miranda*, b. in 1834.
    6. *Frances Caroline*, b. in 1836.
iii. ALMIRA, b. in 1807; m. PETER PEARSON, son of Peter Pearson.
    Children (surname *Pearson*):
    1. *Henry Clay*, b. 16 Jan. 1829.
    2. *Sarah Elizabeth*, b. 4 Feb. 1839.
iv. ERASTUS S. S. S., b. in 1814.
v. DIADEMA, b. in May 1818; d. aged 14 months.
vi. CAROLINE MATHILDE, b. in 1822; d. unm. in Lyme 24 Dec. 1905, aged 85 years 7 months 19 days.

65. MARTIN[5] HUNTLEY (*Amos*,[4] *Daniel*,[3] *Aaron*,[2] *John*[1]), born in Lyme, Conn., 22 Sept. 1750, died 16 April 1834, aged 83 years. He married first, 26 Aug. 1773, MEHITABLE SILL, died 12 Jan. 1786, daughter of Thomas and Jemima (Dudley) Sill; and secondly, 3 Sept. 1787, PHEBE MACK, died 2 Feb. 1847, aged 81 years, daughter of Zopher Mack.

Children by first wife, born in Lyme:

i. CHARLOTTE,[6] b. 9 Jan. 1775; m. PETER JAYNE. Three children born in Ohio.
ii. JEMIMA, b. 1 Jan. 1777; d. 12 July 1777.
iii. SILL, b. 17 Dec. 1779.
iv. GURDEN, b. 6 June 1782.
v. ERASTUS, b. 5 Aug. 1785; d. in the West Indies in the winter of 1801.

Children by second wife:

vi. MARTIN, b. 27 Jan. 1789.
vii. SELDEN, b. 13 March 1791.
viii. MEHITABLE, b. 17 Feb. 1793.
ix. CLARRY, b. 5 Sept. 1795; m. ———— WILEY of Ohio. Had child Rhuhamy.
x. ELISHA, b. 27 June 1797.
xi. POLLY, b. 4 April 1798.
xii. PHEBE, b. 2 Nov. 1802.
xiii. ERASTUS CALVIN, b. 19 April 1805.

(Lyme Births, Marriages and Deaths, vol. 1, pp. 53, 54.)

66. AMOS[5] HUNTLEY (*Amos*,[4] *Daniel*,[3] *Aaron*,[2] *John*[1]) was born in Lyme, Conn., 17 March 1764. He married DELIGHT TINKER.

Amos Huntley lived in Lyme until about 1800, when he moved to Amsterdam, Montgomery Co., N. Y.

Lyme Book of Deeds, vol. 24, p. 81: 22 Nov. 1808. Amos Huntley of Amsterdam, Mont. Co., N. Y., gives power of attorney to Nathan Tinker, to sell land in No. Soc. of Lyme adj. Martin Huntley, which was land from the home tract of his late father Amos Huntley,

Children, born in Amsterdam:

i. NATHAN,[6] b. 8 April 1785.
ii. AMOS, b. 16 Nov. 1790.
iii. MARTIN, b. 25 Sept. 1794.
iv. SILAS.
v. RUSSELL.
vi. DELIGHT, m. in Amsterdam, in 1806, JAMES BILLINGTON.

67. REU[5] HUNTLEY (*Amos*,[4] *Daniel*,[3] *Aaron*,[2] *John*[1]) was born in Lyme, Conn., 28 Oct. 1766. He married first, 18 Sept. 1788, ABIGAIL MACK; and secondly, 26 Feb. 1793 or 4, ELIZABETH BOOGE (BODGE).

The inventory of his estate was registered in New London, Conn., in 1815. (New London, vol. J, pp. 236, 266.)

Children by first wife, born in East Lyme:

i. SARAH (SALLY),[6] b. 8 June 1789; m. PETER DAVENPORT.
ii. SPICER MACK, b. 1 April 1792.

Children by second wife:

iii. PHEBE, b. 7 July 1793.
iv. LODOVICK MACK, b. 7 March 1794 or 7.
v. CHARLES, b. 19 Oct. 1795.

(Lyme Births, Marriages and Deaths, vol. 1, pp. 9, 151; vol. 2, p. 9.)

68. ELIHU[5] HUNTLEY (*David*,[4] *David*,[3] *Aaron*,[2] *John*[1]), born in Lyme, Conn., 30 Aug. 1743 and baptized 27 Nov. 1743, at the First Ecclesiastical Society, died in Lyme 13 Sept. 1836, aged 93 years. He married first ————; and secondly,

NAOMI BROCKWAY, born 5 May 1753, daughter of Jedidiah and Sarah (Fox) Brockway.

Elihu Huntley served in the Revolutionary War from 10 May to 19 Dec. 1775 in the Sixth Regiment, Col. Samuel H. Parsons, Eighth Company, Capt. Samuel Gale, and was present at the siege of Boston and then remained at Roxbury. He was pensioner residing in New London, Conn., in 1832. He enlisted as a private in Capt. Lord's company, Col. John Ely's regiment, was in the Battle of White Plains, and discharged after serving 3 months. He enlisted in 1778 and served one month in Capt. Carew's company, Col. Worthington's Connecticut regiment, and was in Gen. Sullivan's retreat from Rhode Island. He enlisted in 1779 and served 8 months as a private in Capt. David Dorrance's company, Col. Fithian Sill's Connecticut regiment, stationed at New Jersey. He enlisted 15 July 1780 from Lyme as a private in the Fifth Company, under command of Lieut. Thomas Anderson's First Regiment, Col. Josiah Starr. Discharged 5 Dec. 1780.

Naomy (Brockway) Huntley applied for a pension 17 Nov. 1836, at which time she was 83 years old. Barnabas B. and Lucy Huntley were made administrators for her estate 4 Dec. 1878.

Children by first wife:

i. ELIHU.[6]
ii. WILLIAM.
iii. ANN.

Children by second wife:

iv. GIDEON, b. 15 Aug. 1777.
v. SETH, b. 1 May 1779.
vi. JEDIDIAH BROCKWAY, b. 1 May 1783.
vii. SARAH, b. 28 May 1785.
viii. DEBORAH, b. 8 March 1787; d. 11 Dec. 1897, aged 91 years; m. WILLIAM TILLOTSON.
ix. MEHITABLE, b. 14 Jan. 1789.
x. BARUCK, b. 29 Jan. 1792.
xi. BARNABAS, b. 23 May 1794.
xii. ALANSON, b. 1 July 1796.
(Lyme Births, Marriage and Deaths, vol. 2, p. 20.)

69. SOLOMON[5] HUNTLEY (*Elijah*,[4] *David*,[3] *Aaron*,[2] *John*[1]), born in Norwich, Conn., 29 March 1754, died in Manlius, Onandaga County, N. Y., 4 March 1847, aged 93 years. He married first RUTH ———; and secondly, 12 Feb. 1835, ABIGAIL PLATTS, born in Chatham, Conn., 1 May 1782, died in Syracuse, N. Y., 10 Dec. 1867.

He enlisted in Capt. Throop's company, of Norwich, 7 June 1777, and was discharged 7 June 1780. Service 3 years. He was on the roll of Capt. Jotham Brewster's company, Col. Huntington's regiment, in 1776 and was reported missing after the Battle of Long Island. He was a prisoner on board a British ship.

After his service he went to what is now Syracuse and his house was on Onandaga Hill.
Children by first wife:
i.   HEMAN,[6] b. in 1800.
ii.   ACEL or ASAHEL, b. 25 July 1802.
iii. LEUTALUS, b. 3 Aug. 1804.
iv.   SOLOMON.

70. EDMUND[5] HUNTLEY (*Elijah*,[4] *David*,[3] *Aaron*,[2] *John*[1]) was born in Norwich, Conn., 1 March 175–.   He married ———.
He was on the list of Capt. Jotham Brewster's company, Col. Huntington's regiment, for the Revolutionary War, in 1776, which was engaged in the Battle of Long Island.
Child:
i.   EDMUND,[6] b. about 1818.
      Probably others.

71. ANDREW[5] HUNTLEY (*Elijah*,[4] *David*,[3] *Aaron*,[2] *John*[1]), born in Norwich, Conn., 16 Jan. 1757, died in Moors, N. Y., 6 April 1836.   He married in Lebanon, Conn., in 1794, ZELINDA BOSWORTH, born in 1773, daughter of Ichobod and Abigail (Chappel) Bosworth.
He served in the Revolutionary War from 3 Aug. to 12 Sept. in Capt. Wheeler's company, Col. Chapman's regiment, in 1778, which was present at the Battle of Rhode Island.
Children, first three born in Lebanon and the rest in Moors:
i.   LOIS,[6] b. 11 Sept. 1794.
ii.   CLARISSA, b. 9 Dec. 1796.
iii. ANNA, b. 5 Feb. 1799; d. 14 Aug. 1800.
(Lebenon, V. R., vol. 1, p. 154.) *
iv.   ANDREW M., b. in 1801.
v.   EDMUND B., b. in 1803.
vi.   LORINDA (twin), b. in 1808; m. BENJAMIN F. LOVEY.
          Children (surname *Lovey*):
          1. *William P.*, b. in 1833.
          2. *Benjamin F.*, b. in 1835.
          3. *Charles C.*, b. in 1839.
          4. *Alson H.*, b. in 1844; d. in the Civil War.
          5. *Harriet M.*, b. in 1847.
vii. ZELINDA (twin), b. in 1808; m. AARON B. MANNING.
          Children (surname *Manning*):
          1. *Maria*, b. in 1840.
          2. *William F.*, b. in 1842.
viii. HARRIET, b. in 1811.
ix.   ALSON, b. in 1814.
x.   THEODA, b. in 1822; m. ALSON BLODGETT.
          Children (surname *Blodgett*):
          1. *Elizabeth*, b. in 1851.
          2. *Edmund C.*, b. in 1853.

72. CALVIN[5] HUNTLEY (*Elijah*,[4] *David*,[3] *Aaron*,[2] *John*[1]), born in Norwich, Conn., 9 Dec. 1759, died in Ellington, Conn., 11 Aug. 1825.   He married in Franklin, Conn., 2 Dec. 1784, EUNICE GUILE, died in Ellington.
Children, born in Franklin:
i.   JOEL,[6] b. 3 March 1787.
ii.   POLLY, b. 18 Jan. 1789.

*Lebenon should be Lebanon.

iii. SALLY, b. 29 Oct. 1790; m. perhaps ASA SMITH of Ashford, Conn.
iv. LOUISA, b. 16 April 1795.
v. SUSAN, b. 19 Sept. 1797.
vi. LYDIA, b. 4 March 1800; d. young.
(Franklin V. R., vol. 1, p. 72.)

73. ELIJAH[5] HUNTLEY (*Jonathan,*[4] *David,*[3] *Aaron,*[2] *John*[1]), born in
Lyme, Conn., 11 Aug. 1765, perhaps the Elijah Huntley
who died in Averill Park, N. Y., 30 July 1822, aged 60 years.
He married ———.
    Child:
i. ELIJAH,[6] b. in 1798.
    Probably others.

74. ASHER[5] HUNTLEY (*Ezekiel,*[4] *David,*[3] *Aaron,*[2] *John*[1]), born in
Lyme, Conn., 1 March 1767, died in Granger, Ohio, 1 March
1849. He married in Colebrook, Conn., 14 Nov. 1792,
BETSY WILDER TIFFANY (Colebrook V. R., vol. 1, p. 40),
died in Bath, Summit Co., Ohio, 16 Feb. 1837.
    Asher Huntley was with his father on board the Brigan-
tine "General Green" 17 April 1782 in the Revolutionary
War ("Maritime Connecticut During the American Revolution", by Louis F. Middlebrook).
    He was in Bristol, N. Y., about 1804, in Canandaigua
where he bought land in 1804, 1809, 1816 and 1823, selling
there in 1812, 1814, 1815, and 1836. He went to Granger
about 1835.
    Children, born in Hartland, Conn.:
i. ASHER,[6] b. 25 Aug. 1793.
ii. EZRA, b. 29 Sept. 1795; d. in 1826.
iii. BETSY, b. 27 July 1799.
iv. LEVI, b. 12 Aug. 1801.
v. LEONARD, b. 5 March 1804.

75. EZRA[5] HUNTLEY (*Ezekiel,*[4] *David,*[3] *Aaron,*[2] *John*[1]), born in
Lyme, Conn., and bapt. 2 June 1771, died in 1817. He
married in Stonington, Conn., 29 Dec. 1796, EUNICE HOLMES.
Eunice (Holmes) Huntley married secondly, 6 Jan. 1825
(Bozrah V. R., vol. 1, p. 23), ABEL GATES of Salem, Conn.
    Ezra Huntley lived in North Stonington near the home
of his wife's parents. His estate was administered with
mention of his wife Eunice.
    Children, born in Stonington:
i. EZRA,[6] b. 25 July 1798.
ii. OLIVER DENNISON, b. 3 July 1803.
iii. POLLY, b. 14 May 1804; m. in Bozrah, Conn., 17 March 1825,
    GEORGE M. CROCKER.
iv. HENRY HOLMES, b. 6 July 1808.
v. LUCY BAGLEY, b. 23 March 1810.
vi. JULIA ANN, b. 10 Jan. 1815; m. in Preston, Conn., 29 Dec. 1833,
    DANIEL W. CROCKER.
(Stonington V. R., vol. 4, p. 91, North Stonington V. R., vol. 1, p. 17.)

76. RUFUS[5] HUNTLEY (*Ezekiel,*[4] *David,*[3] *Aaron,*[2] *John*[1]), born in
Lyme, Conn., and bapt. 2 Sept. 1778 at the First Ecclesias-
tical Society, died in Medina, Ohio, 4 April 1860 (Bible

record of Mrs. Ward). He married, 22 Dec. 1799, POLLY LAY (Early Connecticut Marriages).

Rufus Huntley lived in Lyme until about 1811, then went to Massachusetts and thence to Canandaigua, N. Y. (History of Ontario Co.). From there he went to Medina about 1836.

Children:

i. ALEXANDER.[6]
ii. ELIAS.
iii. CHARLES, b. in 1813.
iv. CALVIN WHEELER.
v. LEVIRRA, m. DELNO RANDALL. They lived in Coddingville, Ohio.
vi. ELSIE, m. —— CODDING.
vii. SEYMOUR.

77. EZEKIEL[5] HUNTLEY (*Ezekiel*,[4] *David*,[3] *Aaron*,[2] *John*[1]), born in Lyme, Conn., and baptized 21 May 1780, died in Granger, Ohio, 6 March 1853. He married, 8 Sept. 1803, RUTH MINER, died in Granger 25 Dec. 1851, daughter of Elisha Miner (Lyme Vital Records, vol. 2, p. 73).

Ezekiel Huntley went to Canandaigua, N. Y., when he was about 39 years old, where he lived until about 51 years old. He then went to Granger.

Children, born in Bozrah, Conn.:

i. WILLIAM ASHER,[6] b. 19 July 1804.
ii. ELIAS SANFORD, b. 9 Oct. 1806.
iii. MARY MINER, b. 6 Aug. 1808; d. 23 Feb. 1853; m. in Granger HENRY INGRAHAM.
iv. ELIZA ANN, b. 23 June 1810; d. in Royalton, N. Y., 4 Aug. 1891; m. in Richmond, N. Y., 3 Nov. 1831, ORRIN SIBLEY.
v. EMMA WAY, b. 4 Feb. 1813; d. in Ohio 29 Nov. 1864; m. 7 Aug. 1831 GEORGE HAZEN.
vi. NANCY, b. about 1814; m. WASHINGTON BIGELOW, b. in Broome County, N. Y.
    Children (surname *Bigelow*):
    1. *Elbridge.*   3. *Elnora.*
    2. *Sherman.*   4. *Emma.*
vii. EZRA, b. 28 April 1815/16.
viii. LEANDER.

HUNTLEY GENEALOGY: CORRECTION. — In regard to the Chapman family, mentioned in the Huntley Genealogy, page 61, of *The Register* of January 1947, * may I submit that recent investigation indicates that Ebenezer and Elizabeth (Huntley) Chapman had only twelve children, not fourteen, and that the last two named in Mrs. Alice P. Huntley's fine article were actually grandchildren, sons of her son Edward, born 1 July 1760.

The Barbour Index of Connecticut Vital Statistics record the marriage of Ebenezer Chapman and Elizabeth Huntley on 17 June, 1755; give Ebenezer's death as 12 Sept. 1785, and the births of twelve children between 1756 and 1782 — Eunice, Edward, John, Bersheba, Robert, Ezekiel, Phebe, Rachel, Elizabeth, Asahel, Moses, and Susan, the same as Mrs. Huntley's first twelve. The same twelve are assigned to Ebenezer and Elizabeth in the Chapman genealogy by Rev. Edward M. Chapman, in the William Chapman of the New London line.

*Page 239, this volume.

The will of Capt. Edward Chapman, brother of Ebenezer who married Eliza-beth Huntley, is number 1038 in the probate department at the Connecticut State Library, made 31 Oct. 1793. He gives land to Asel Chapman, his nephew and to his nephew Moses Chapman, son of brother Ebenezer. Distribution of his estate was made 20 Feb. 1795 to his brothers and sisters. Ebenezer was already dead so his children are all named among the heirs, "to nephew Edward Chapman, Elizabeth Chapman, heirs of Eunice Harris and niece Susanna Chapman. Asahel and Moses to have no part in this" — as they were given land in the will. No Ebenezer or John is mentioned.

Again in the Lyme Records, vol. I, p. 171 (Barbour Index): "Edward Chapman 2nd married Barsheba Chapman July 3, 1781. Children: Caleb, son of Edw. & Basheba b. 1782; John, son of Edw. & Barsheba, b. 1785; Ebenezer, son of Edw. & Barsheba, b. 1788.

"John, the son of Ebenezer and Elizabeth (Huntley) Chapman, died in 1783 and his sister Phebe d. y."

Norwich, Conn. MISS ELIZA W. AVERY.

JOHN HUNTLEY AND SOME OF HIS DESCENDANTS: ADDITIONS AND CORRECTIONS.

Vol. 100

Page 267, line 55. *For* 22 *substitute* 28. (Page 229, this volume.)
Page 270, line 55. *For* 1711 *substitute* 1716. (Page 232, this volume.)
Page 271, line 29. *Omit* d. young. (Page 233, this volume.)

Vol. 101 (Page 243, this volume.)

Page 142, line 43. *For* Aug. *substitute* April.
Page 143, line 41. *Add* b. 22 Sept. 1750. (Page 244, this volume.)
Page 148, line 29. *For* 88 years 7 months *substitute* 85 years.

Hanover, Mass. (Page 249, this volume.) MRS. ALICE P. HUNTLEY.

HUNTLEY GENEALOGY: ADDITIONS: — Recent study into the ancestry of Jabez Huntley (13), THE REGISTER, January 1947, page 58, has brought to light cer- * tain interesting new facts. In this issue Jabez Huntley is claimed to be the son of John,[3] Moses,[2] John.[1] I believe in the light of new facts found that he is the son of Moses,[3] Moses,[2] John.[1]

In the Lyme, Conn., Land Records three separate entries lead one to suppose they were recorded for immigration purposes: "Jabez Huntley b. in Lyme 21 Sept. 1721; Patience Huntley b. 1 Dec. 1722; Jabez m. at Lyme, 27 Mar. 1746 Patience Vaughan."

This Jabez Huntley was the son of Moses Huntley (4) and Rachel Harris and was a brother of Abigail, William and Benejah. No further records appear in Lyme in respect to this Jabez, although there was another Jabez living in Lyme with his wife Sarah in 1776. This may have been the Jabez Huntley who lived in Westfield, Mass., in 1790.

Jabez Huntley (13), as previously reported, removed to Horton, N.S., where a deed concluded 10 Jan. 1768 names his wife *Patience*.

A deed recorded at Horton Twp., King's Co., N. S., concerns Jabez Huntley of Machias in the County of Lincoln, and Commonwealth of Massachusetts, and Jonathan Crane of Horton 1808.

In all these deeds at King's County, Jabez Huntley calls himself proprietor of the township of Horton, and one states that the grant or patent was issued 29 May 1761. The deed conveys a lot of 450 acres, being all the share not yet divided or set off, except the marsh on Grand Pré and along the River Cornwallis.

It would seem by these records that if Jabez Huntley did not get to Nova Scotia until 1760 and was married in Lyme 1746 that the majority of his chil-dren were born in Lyme, Conn.

Hanover, Mass. MRS. R. E. HUNTLEY.

*Page 236, this volume.

NEHEMIAH[4] JACKSON OF WOODSTOCK, CONN., AND SOME OF HIS DESCENDANTS

Contributed by Russell Leigh Jackson, of Salem, Mass.

1. Nehemiah[4] Jackson (*Joseph,*[3] *Jonathan,*[2] *Nicholas*[1]), born at Cumberland, R. I., 11 Sept. 1744, died at Woodstock, Conn., 18 Apr. 1825. He married 2 Feb. 1767 Esther Abbot, born at Ashford, Conn., in 1748, died at Woodstock 15 Sept. 1833, daughter of Nathaniel and Esther (Lyon) Abbot.

Early in life Nehemiah Jackson moved from Cumberland to Woodstock, where he was a successful farmer, owning a large tract of land in the northern part of the town (now known as North Woodstock) near the Massachusetts line. The house which he built still stands, although it is not now owned by any member of the family. Like the majority of the townspeople, he espoused the cause of the colonists and enlisted for service in the Revolution as a corporal in Capt. Peter Perritt's company, serving from 10 July to 10 Dec. 1776.

Although he was the first of Joseph Jackson's children to take up residence in Connecticut, he was not the only member of the family to do so.   His brother Jeremiah[4] Jackson, born 2 Aug. 1739, lived at Woodstock, where he married Phoebe Murray and was the father of Matthew Murray[5] Jackson and John[5] Jackson, both soldiers of the Revolution.   Sometime before 1721 Caleb Jackson, son of Caleb and grandson of Nicholas, married Mary Averill and moved to Enfield and Ashford, Conn., where his four children were born, among them Dr. James Jackson who settled at Rochester and Madison, N. H.   Three of Nehemiah Jackson's brothers, Lieut. Eleazer Jackson, Michael Jackson, and Benjamin Jackson, took up lands in Cornish, N. H., and left numerous progeny in that State.

Both Nehemiah Jackson and his wife are buried in the Bradford-Marcy burying ground at Woodstock, and in 1933, at a reunion of the family, a Revolutionary War marker was placed on his grave and unveiled by his great-great-great-grandson, Edward Lawrence Jackson.

Children, born at Woodstock:

 i. SALLY,[5] b. 10 Sept. 1767; d. unm., 16 Feb. 1849.
 ii. CHARLES, b. 3 Nov. 1770.
 iii. LEVINA, b. 1 Oct. 1771; d. *s.p.* 26 Dec. 1852; m. 21 Feb. 1798 SETH SMITH of Amherst, Mass., b. at Wilbraham, Mass., 12 July 1775, d. at Amherst 15 Dec. 1856, son of Eleazer and Abigail (White) Smith.
2. iv. WILLARD, b. 2 Oct. 1776.
 v. JOHN, b. 12 May 1778.
 vi. NEHEMIAH, a student at Woodstock Academy, 1802–3, and a lieutenant in Capt. Samuel Dresser's (New London) company 21–27 June 1813, in the War of 1812, b. 29 July 1780; d. unm.
 vii. CHLOE, b. 2 Sept. 1782; d. 18 Feb. 1869; m. 1 Dec. 1808 ADOLPHUS CHILD, a sergeant in Capt. Hadlock Perrin's (New London) company 21–28 June 1813, and later an ensign in another company, b. 25 Mar. 1785; d. in March 1867, son of Lemuel and Dorcas (Perry) Child.

    Children (surname *Child*):
    1. *Justus*, b. 21 Sept. 1809; d. 24 May 1868; m. 21 Sept. 1834 Betsy Budlong of Bridgewater, N. Y.
    2. *Nancy*, b. 27 Aug. 1813; m. A. H. Palmer of Sandwich, Ill.
    3. *Lemuel Morris*, b. 7 Feb. 1816; d. in Kansas 9 Aug. 1878; m. Amy Colgrove.
    4. *Rev. Thomas Perry*, b. 8 June 1817; m. Atezera Eaton.
    5. *Rowena*, b. 16 Aug. 1822; m. 10 Mar. 1844 William Bennett.
    6. *Mary*, b. 16 July 1824; m. 1 Nov. 1859 Samuel I. Cooley.
 viii. ESTHER, b. 20 Jan. 1785; m. DANA LYON, a private in Capt. Comfort S. Hyde's company from 1 Sept. to 30 Oct. 1813, son of Moses and Matilda (Bradford) Lyon.
3. ix. NATHAN, b. 21 June 1787.
4. x. CHESTER, b. 13 Sept. 1789.
 xi. MARY, b. 15 Dec. 1791; d. before 1840; m. 29 Aug. 1816 OLCOTT FISHER of Woodstock, a soldier in Capt. Hadlock Perrin's company (Eleventh Regiment) in the War of 1812, b. 29 Dec. 1786, d. 24 Feb. 1875, son of Olcott and Mary (Allen) Fisher of Woodstock.

    Child (surname *Fisher*):
    1. *Lucien Bonaparte*, b. 4 May 1817; d. 12 Sept. 1850; m. at Eastford, Conn., 31 Oct. 1838, Emily Howard, b. 23 Feb. 1817, d. 1 Mar. 1898, daughter of Jonathan and Sarah (Smith) Howard.   One son.

2. WILLARD[5] JACKSON (*Nehemiah*[4]), of Woodstock, Conn., farmer,

born at Woodstock 2 Oct. 1776, died there 13 June 1840. He married 8 July 1798 ORINDA GOODELL, born at Woodstock 2 Oct. 1776, died 2 Apr. 1869, daughter of Asa and Alice (Corbin) Goodell.
Children:

i. PEREGRINE,⁶ b. 3 Oct. 1799; d. 15 Feb. 1863; m. JULINA ELLIS.
ii. LYDIA, b. 25 Oct. 1800; m. 1 July 1821 CALVIN HARDING, son of Ralph and Azabah (Goodell) Harding of Sturbridge, Mass.
5. iii. WALTER, b. 8 Feb. 1805.
iv. OTIS, b. 8 Nov. 1808; m. (1) 11 Nov. 1837 HANNAH FRISSELL, b. in 1809, daughter of Samuel and Sally Frissell; m. (2) 3 Jan. 1854 RUTH JAMERSON, b. 26 Dec. 1821, daughter of Seth and Lydia (Hastings) Jamerson of Hardwick, Mass.
   Children by second wife:
   1. *Mary Jane*,⁷ b. 15 Nov. 1854; m. 25 Dec. 1880 Henry W. Ayers, b. 1 Mar. 1844, son of James Converse and Lauretta (Ruggles) Ayers of Hardwick.
   2. *William Otis*, of Bridgewater, Vt., b. 6 Oct. 1861.
v. MARY, b. 22 Aug. 1810; d. in 1813.
vi. CHARLES, b. 21 Sept. 1813; m. at Southbridge, Mass., 23 Dec. 1838, ANNIS BUGBEE, b. 13 Sept. 1816, d. 11 Aug. 1877, daughter of Marcus and Sylvia (Corbin) Bugbee of Union, Conn.
   Children:
   1. *George Washington*,⁷ b. 23 Oct. 1838; d. 6 Apr. 1844.
   2. *Charles Addison*, b. 2 Nov. 1843.
   3. *Monroe*, b. 14 Sept. 1845; d. 28 Dec. 1845.
   4. *Annis Maria*, b. 18 June 1847.
vii. LUCRETIA, b. 9 Jan.1816; d. 10 Mar. 1851; m. 30 Sept. 1844 CLINTON HOWARD of Union, Conn., son of Manassah and Dorothy (Corbin) Howard.
6. viii. JOHN, b. 4 Sept. 1818.
ix. BENJAMIN, b. 5 Aug. 1822; d. 28 June 1899; m. MARTHA AUSTIN, b. 7 June 1825, d. in 1905, daughter of Dea. Nathan and Sally Austin.
   Child:
   1. *Herbert*,⁷ of Worcester, Mass., b. 3 May 1852.

3. NATHAN⁵ JACKSON (*Nehemiah⁴*), of Woodstock, Conn., farmer, a musician in Col. Jonathan Lyon's (New London) regiment from 30 June to 27 July 1813 in the War of 1812, born at Woodstock 21 June 1787, died there 22 June 1828. He married in 1817 PRISCILLA MARCY, born in 1795, died 29 Oct. 1850, daughter of Lemuel and Nancy (Carpenter) Marcy of Sturbridge, Mass.
Children:

7. i. ELIJAH MARCY,⁶ b. 22 Apr. 1818.
ii. NANCY, b. 2 Dec. 1820; d. 20 Apr. 1910; m. (1) JOHN A. MASON of North Woodstock, son of Noah and Huldah (Perry) Mason; m. (2) CHARLES HENRY ALLEN, b. in 1818, d. 22 Aug. 1897, son of Charles Henry and Mehitable (Parker) Allen and widower of her sister Sarah Jackson.
   Child by first husband (surname *Mason*):
   1. *Lucy E.*, m. Sidney E. Morse of Easthampton, Mass.
iii. SARAH, b. 28 Oct. 1822; d. 22 Aug. 1878; m. 26 Apr. 1841 CHARLES HENRY ALLEN, b. in 1818, d. 22 Aug. 1897, son of Charles Henry and Mehitable (Parker) Allen of Springfield, Mass. He m. (2) NANCY JACKSON, his sister-in-law.

Child (surname *Allen*):
1. *Ellen Maria*, b. 29 Dec. 1842; d. 11 Oct. 1911; m. Rev. Benjamin Warren Atwell, D.D., b. at Wakefield, Mass., 2 Aug. 1838, d. 28 Mar. 1912, son of Joseph Warren and Abigail (Melbourne) Atwell.

   Rev. Benjamin Warren Atwell was a member of the first class of the Theological School at St. Lawrence University. He was pastor of the Universalist Church at Newburyport, Mass., in 1862. In 1864 he entered the communion of the Protestant Episcopal Church and in 1866 was ordained deacon and priest by Bishop Thomas March Clarke of Rhode Island. He then became assistant to the bishop at Grace Church in Providence, R. I., and was subsequently rector of the Church of the Messiah in that place and later of St. Stephen's Church at Lynn, Mass. For a time he lived in Maine, whither he went to be rector of St. Thomas's Church at Camden and to organize a school for boys. In 1885 he was rector of Immanuel Church, Manton, R. I., and he served at one time as assistant at Trinity Church at Pottsville, Pa. At the invitation of Bishop Bissell he became general missionary in Vermont, and was afterward rector of Trinity Church at Shelburne, Vt. In 1904 he moved to Burlington, Vt., and in 1906 to Newton, Mass. Children (surname *Allen*): (1) ———. (2) Albert Henry, b. 2 Nov. 1844; d. 17 Oct. 1860.
iv. NEHEMIAH, b. 29 Aug. 1826; m. 19 May 1849 Hepsibeth Dodge of Woodstock.

4. CHESTER⁵ JACKSON (*Nehemiah⁴*), born at Woodstock, Conn., 13 Sept. 1789, died there 25 Dec. 1861. He married at Woodstock, 4 July 1816, HANNAH LYON, born at Woodstock 4 Sept. 1797, died there 22 Jan. 1890, daughter of Moses and Matilda (Bradford) Lyon, and a descendant of Gov. William Bradford of the *Mayflower*.

Chester Jackson served from 21 June to 15 July 1813 in Capt. Samuel Dresser's (Loudon) Company in the War of 1812. He was a successful farmer at Woodstock, interested in town affairs, and a staunch Democrat.

Children:
i. ADELINE,⁶ b. 11 Sept. 1816; d. at Medfield, Mass., 9 Feb. 1910; m. 7 July 1839 LARNED CADY CORBIN, b. 20 Apr. 1819, d. at Abington, Mass., 1 June 1889, son of Samuel and Betsy (Barber) Corbin.
   Children (surname *Corbin*):
   1. *Charles Clinton*, b. 19 June 1843; d. 16 Nov. 1927; m. at Holland, Mass., 1 Oct. 1871, Gertrude M. Harvey, b. 28 Sept. 1852, daughter of John Harvey of Woodstock. Eleven children.
   2. *Emily H.*, b. 11 May 1845; d. in 1918; m. 5 Mar. 1862 Joseph Mills. Ten children.
   3. *George Arnold*, of Woodstock, Burrillville, R. I. (1877), and Pascoag, R. I., b. 17 Sept. 1849; m. 19 Dec. 1872 Caroline B. Jeffers, b. 16 July 1853, daughter of John Rufus and Caroline A. (Brown) Jeffers.
   4. *Albert Herman*, of Medfield, Mass., b. 19 June 1852; d. at Medfield 1 June 1926; m. 30 June 1878 Ella M. Bowers, b. 4 Mar. 1857. Two children.
   5. *Harriett M.*, b. 16 May 1856; d. 30 Jan. 1890; m. 20 June 1875 Albert E. Lippitt of Woodstock, Conn., son of Nathaniel and Persis (Phipps) Lippitt. Two children.
   6. *Cora*, b. 1 May 1858; d. *s.p.*; m. (1) 1 June 1893 Albert S. Perrin of Brooklyn, Conn.; m. (2) Thomas O. Talbot of Brooklyn, son of William and Nancy (Ketch) Talbot.

7. *Benjamin,* b. 29 Sept. 1860; d. unm. 13 June 1884.

8. ii.   CAPT. GEORGE JEREMIAH, b. 26 Mar. 1819.

iii.   WILLIAM CHESTER, b. 24 July 1821; d. 30 Jan. 1904; m. 3 Apr. 1842 NANCY BURDICK, daughter of Rowland and Lydia (Geer) Burdick of Westerly, R. I.
   Children:
   1. *Charles Ambray,*[7] b. 11 Apr. 1851; m. Emma Arnold. Child: (1) William.[8]
   2. *Ellen,* m. Henry Newton.

iv.   JOSEPH BRADFORD, b. at Woodstock 22 Oct. 1824; d. 22 Feb. 1907; m. 5 Feb. 1850 FRANCES EMMA BURDICK, daughter of Joel and Sally (Kenyon) Burdick of Hopkinton, R. I.
   Children:
   1. *Nellie Jane,*[7] b. 8 Nov. 1854; d. 7 Apr. 1936; m. Almon Maro Butler of Brooklyn, Conn., b. 11 Feb. 1854, son of Thomas Harvey and Rosetta (Eastman) Butler. Children (surname *Butler*): (1) Vivian Lenore, b. 10 Feb. 1877. (2) Lulu Alma, b. 6 Aug. 1884; m. Leon Kilpatrick of Brooklyn, Conn.
   2. *Effie Adella,* b. 1 July 1860; d. 7 Jan. 1931; m. Albert Copeland of Pomfret, son of David and Lucy (Lyon) Copeland. Children (surname *Copeland*): (1) Royal, m. Edith Harvey. (2) Harold, m. Marie LeDuc. (3) Vera E., m. Michael Harrington.
   3. *Harriett Elizabeth,* b. 20 Jan. 1863; d. 19 Aug. 1892; m. Willard G. Wells. Children (surname *Wells*): (1) Frances M., m. (1) Roland L. Corbin, son of Charles and Gertrude M. (Harvey) Corbin; m. (2) William Darling. (2) John, m. Eliza ———. (3) Mary, m. George Darling.
   4. *Almeda German,* b. 4 May 1865; b. 6 May 1884; m. Joseph Newell.

v.   EDWARD LEFEVRE, b. at Woodstock 27 Oct. 1827; d. 22 Mar. 1909; m. 1 Sept. 1849 MARY PACKARD
   He with his brother, William Chester Jackson, conducted a dancing school at Woodstock.
   Child:
   1. *Frederick,*[7] m. Elizabeth Schesler. Child: (1) Edward,[8] b. in 1901; m. Rachel Kenyon. Child: (a) *Edward Lawrence,*[9] b. in 1925; killed in an accident in 1936.

vi.   HARRIETT SUSAN, b. 6 Dec. 1832; m. CHARLES A. NICHOLS.
   Child (surname *Nichols*):
   1. *Florence,* b. in 1854; d. in 1938; m. Richard Wiggins, of Willimantic, Conn.

vii.   MARCIA ANN, b. 23 Mar. 1835; m. NATHANIEL ESTABROOK, son of Calvin and Mary (Estabrook) Estabrook.
   Children (surname *Estabrook*):
   1. *John.*
   2. *Calvin Lewis,* d. in 1910; m. Abigail Burden. Eight children.

5. WALTER[6] JACKSON (*Willard,*[5] *Nehemiah*[4]), was born at Woodstock, Conn., 8 Feb. 1805. He married SALLY SABIN, who was born in 1803 and died 7 Feb. 1878.
   Children:

i.   SARAH,[7] b. 30 Nov. 1827; d. 21 Mar. 1899; m. (1) 14 Mar. 1847 WILLIAM S. HOPKINS, d. 27 Jan. 1859; m. (2) 2 Mar. 1862 JOHN A. PECKHAM, d. at Milford, Mass., 29 Mar. 1887.
   Child by first husband (surname *Hopkins*):
   1. *George Nelson,* undertaker and business man for many years at Pittsfield, Mass., b. 22 Nov. 1851; m. 18 May 1881 Mary A. Westcott, daughter of A. A. Westcott of Hopedale, R. I.
   Child by second husband (surname *Peckham*):
   2. *John Walter,* b. 6 July 1863; b. 16 Aug. 1864.

ii.   MARY, b. 2 Feb. 1830; m. EMERY DEXTER.
      Children (surname *Dexter*):
      1. *Henrietta*, b. 1 Jan. 1851; m. 1 Jan. 1872 Benjamin H. Lister,
          b. 6 June 1852, d. 12 Sept. 1914.
      2. *Mary F.*, b. 22 Mar. 1853; d. 24 Dec. 1854.
      3. *Ida M.*, b. 7 Sept. 1856; d. 8 Feb. 1924; m. 25 May 1879
          Benjamin F. Hopkins, b. 13 Aug. 1857.
      4. *Emery Frank*, b. 16 Aug. 1859; moved to Idaho and died there.
      5. *William L.*, b. 28 May 1862; m. Annie F. Kenyon.
      6. *Frederic*, b. 22 Mar. 1865; m. (1) 7 Sept. 1886 Minnie F. Salis-
          bury, b. 4 Dec. 1870, d. 20 Aug. 1888, daughter of Henry A.
          and Alzada (Brown) Salisbury; m. (2) Alice B. Salisbury, b.
          1 Feb. 1874, daughter of Henry A. and Alzada (Brown)
          Salisbury.
iii. MERRILL WALTER, b. 22 Jan. 1833; d. 22 Mar. 1893; m. (1) RUTH
      PAGE, daughter of Nathan Page; m. (2) PRISCILLA H. DAVIS, of
      Plainfield, Conn., b. 17 Dec. 1836, d. 12 Aug. 1906, daughter of
      Obed and Rhoda (Brown) Davis.
      Children by first wife:
      1. *Elixie*,[8] m. Alpha Hill. Child (surname *Hill*): (1) Walter, of
          Cranston, R. I.
      2. *Earl P.*, m. Florence Wilder.
      3. *Leila*, b. 27 Jan. 1858; d. 27 Feb. 1861.
iv.   FRANK P., b. 4 Jan. 1835; d. at Milford, Mass., 20 Jan. 1884; m.
      4 Oct. 1858 ANNE TUCKER, b. in 1839, daughter of William Tucker
      of Woodstock.
v.   JEROME, b. 16 Aug. 1837; d. at Noroton Heights, Conn., 13 Feb.
      1910; m. (1) 12 Sept. 1866 ELLEN J. ROUNDS, b. 25 Apr. 1843, d.
      23 May 1871, daughter of George and Mary Ann (Warren) Rounds
      of Burrillville, R. I.; m. (2) EMMA S. MORSE, b. 22 June 1845, d.
      at Thompson, Conn., 15 Dec. 1881.
      Jerome Jackson enlisted 1 Aug. 1862 at Danielson, Conn., in
      Company K, Eighteenth Connecticut Infantry, and was honorably
      discharged 27 June 1865 at Harper's Ferry, Va.
      Children:
      1. *Minnie Adele*,[8] b. 15 June 1867; d. at Peru, Mass., 18 Apr.
          1896; m. 16 Sept. 1886 Charles I. Stowell. Children (sur-
          name *Stowell*): (1) Leo Merrill, b. 16 June 1887; m. at De-
          troit, Mich., 27 June 1917, Helen May Outley, daughter of
          Jonathan Stickney and Mary (McDermott) Outley. No
          children. (2) Charles Irving, b. 17 Feb. 1891; d. 8 Sept.
          1913. (3) Olive Priscilla, b. 21 Jan. 1890; m. 4 Oct. 1913
          Frank J. Cartier, son of Robert and Eliza (McKay) Cartier.
          No children.
      2. *Mabel*, b. 22 July 1868; d. 23 Aug. 1868.
      3. *Frank Warren*, b. 26 May 1870; d. *s.p.* 10 Feb. 1902; m.
          31 Dec. 1895 Claire B. Spinney.
      4. *Gertrude*, b. 3 May 1871; m. at Tie Siding, Wyo., 6 June 1891
          George H. Carroll. Children (surname *Carroll*): (1) Frank
          Jackson. (2) Elvin Knight.
vi.   MARTHA CHENEY, m. DENNISON PALMER JORDAN.
      Children (surname *Jordan*):
      1. *Dayton DeForest*, b. 23 Nov. 1861.
      2. *Bertha Hessie*, b. 18 Jan. 1872; m. 22 Dec. 1892 Ernest Ells-
          worth Torrey, b. 15 May 1867, son of Charles Davis and
          Martha Westcott (Warren) Torrey. Eight children.
vii. ELLEN, b. in 1845; m. 7 Jan. 1868 JOHN KEACH, of Northampton,
      Mass., business man, a soldier in Company K, Eighteenth Massa-
      chusetts Regiment, from 1862 until his honorable discharge in
      1865, b. at Brooklyn, Conn., in 1840, son of John and Harriett
      (Young) Keach.
      Children (surname *Keach*):
      1. *Merrill H.*, b. 22 Jan. 1869; d. 21 Feb. 1924.

2. *John Everett,* b. 4 July 1874; d. at Missoula, Mont., in 1926; m. in 1907 Alice Belle Ricker of Maine, B.A. (Smith, 1898), teacher. Children: (1) John R., b. in 1909. (2) Dorcas E., b. in 1914.
3. *Walter Edmund,* b. 26 June 1878; d. in Wisconsin in February 1924; m. 25 Mar. 1911 Dora Stacy, b. 14 Feb. 1877.
4. *Robert Nelson,* b. 16 Nov. 1881; d. 11 May 1885.

6. JOHN[6] JACKSON (*Willard,[5] Nehemiah[4]*) was born at Woodstock, Conn., 4 Sept. 1818. He married, 4 Mar. 1849, ROSETTA D. HOWARD, daughter of John and Lydia (Bugbee) Howard. Children:

    i.   HON. FRANK R.,[7] b. 17 Oct. 1853; m. 23 Dec. 1876 JULIA PUTNAM, b. 14 Oct. 1859, daughter of Freeman and Huldah (Morse) Putnam.
        Frank R. Jackson was a prominent member of the Woodstock Theft Detecting Society, serving as clerk (1891–2), vice president (1895–6) and president (1897–8). He was messenger in the House of the Connecticut Legislature in 1886, 1891, and 1893, and was a representative in 1895 and a Senator in 1899. He engaged in the lumber business at Willimantic for many years.
        Child:
        1. *Eva Miriam,[8]* b. 28 Mar. 1878; m. 3 Oct. 1899 Edwin O. Sumner, of Woodstock, a graduate of Woodstock Academy, selectman for three years, postmaster for six years, member of the firm of Jackson & Sumner of Willimantic, superintendent of streets and sewers of Willimantic, representative (1899) to the Connecticut Legislature, b. 15 Feb. 1869, son of Azel C. and Sarah J. (Hanks) Sumner. Children (surname *Sumner*): (1) Stanley Jackson, B.A. (Yale, 1924), insurance agent, b. 6 Mar. 1902; m. Helen Peale of Norwich, Conn., b. 16 Feb. 1900, daughter of Arthur L. and Mary (Plummer) Peale. (2) Homer Hanks, a graduate of Worcester Academy in 1928, insurance agent, b. 4 Aug. 1907.
    ii.   MERRILL S., d. *s.p.* at Hartford, Conn., about 1917; m. BERTHA MAY BURDICK, of Hampton, Conn.

7. ELIJAH MARCY[6] JACKSON (*Nathan,[5] Nehemiah[4]*), a member in 1842 of the Woodstock Theft Detecting Society, born at Woodstock, Conn., 22 Apr. 1818, died at Newton, Mass., in 1887. He married, 22 May 1844, MELETIAH CURTIS SESSIONS, born 16 Apr. 1823, died at Melrose, Mass., in 1905, daughter of Judge Abijah and Elizabeth (Childs) Sessions, of Union, Conn.
    Children:

9. i.   HENRY CLINTON,[7] b. 15 Jan. 1848.
    ii.   WILLIAM E., of New Jersey, b. 6 Nov. 1865; m. at Everett, Mass., 23 Aug. 1906, FLORENCE ABBIE DAVIS, b. in 1886.
        Children:
        1. *Roger Sessions,[8]* b. 2 Nov. 1907.
        2. *Dorothy Edna,* b. 21 July 1910.
        3. *Clinton.*

8. CAPT. GEORGE JEREMIAH[6] JACKSON (*Chester,[5] Nehemiah[4]*), born at Woodstock, Conn., 26 Mar 1819, died at Warwick, R. I., 13 Nov. 1861. He married, 5 Mar. 1843, LUCY TRACY BURDICK, born at Canterbury, Conn., 22 Aug. 1817, died at Providence, R. I., 18 Oct. 1897, daughter of Rowland and Lydia (Geer) Burdick. She married secondly Horatio Nelson

Angell of Providence and thirdly Daniel Dyer of Davisville, North Kingstown, R. I.

Capt. George Jeremiah Jackson early in life worked on his father's farm and later, in 1849, joined the gold rush to California, making the trip *via* Cape Horn. On his return he became engaged in commerce, acting as master mariner and merchant, and extending his voyages to the West Indies. He was a member of the Woodstock Theft Detecting Society.

Children:

10. i. ALFRED ANDREW,[7] b. at Voluntown, Conn., 27 Feb. 1846.
    ii. HELEN LUCY, b. 15 Apr. 1848; d. 3 Feb. 1852.
    iii. GEORGE WINFIELD, b. 25 Jan. 1853; d. 25 June 1899; m. (1) 27 Jan. 1877 MARY ELLEN O'DONNELL, b. in 1858, d. 13 Jan. 1883, daughter of John and Ellen O'Donnell; m. (2) 22 Nov. 1883 CORINNE EVELYN RIENDEAU, daughter of Joseph and Alvina Riendeau.
        Children by first wife:
        1. *William Henry,*[8] vice president of Sperry & Hutchinson in Los Angeles, Calif., and also president of The Legal Discount System, Inc., b. 17 Jan. 1878; d. in 1935; m. 21 Nov. 1904 Grace M. Shaw, daughter of Walter A. and Florence (Franklin) Shaw. Child: (1) Doris,[9] m. Daniel Warnberg. Children (surname *Warnberg*): (a) *Marion Louise*, (b) *Donald Eugene.*
        2. *John F.*, b. 26 May 1882; d. young.
        3. *George Winfield.*
        Children by second wife:
        4. *Alfred Joseph*, b. 19 Oct. 1884.
        5. *Edmund Francis*, b. 15 Mar. 1887.
        6. *Winfield Scott*, b. 11 Nov. 1889.
        7. *Philip Andrew.*
        8. *Corinne Lucy*, b. 1 Oct. 1895; m. Capt. Guy Gooding Allen, U. S. Army, d. in 1917.
        9. *Joseph Anthony*, b. 8 Aug. 1899.
    iv. FRANCIS BRADFORD, b. 11 June 1854; d. 3 May 1855.
    v. OTIS EUGENE, b. 14 Jan. 1856; d. young.

9. HENRY CLINTON[7] JACKSON (*Elijah Marcy,*[6] *Nathan,*[5] *Nehemiah*[4]), born at Woodstock, Conn., 15 Jan. 1848, died at Medford, Mass., 3 Mar. 1919. He married 11 Nov. 1870 ELIZA LEWIS WAITT, born at Malden, Mass., 13 Jan. 1851, died at Medford 25 Nov. 1925, daughter of Joseph and Elizabeth (Abbott) Waitt.

Children:

i. FRANCES ELIZABETH,[8] b. 25 Jan. 1872; d. at Arlington 7 Feb. 1934.
ii. HENRY CLINTON, b. at Malden 10 Sept. 1873; d. 30 Dec. 1922; m. 3 Oct. 1900 CLARA WILD GOODWIN, b. 14 Sept. 1875, daughter of James Otis and Emma Warren (Wild) Goodwin of Medford.
    Children:
    1. REV. OTIS GOODWIN,[9] A.B. (Dartmouth, 1925), B.D. (Cambridge Episcopal Theological School, 1928), rector of St. Mark's Protestant Episcopal Church at Oakley, a suburb of Cincinnati, Ohio, and of St. Paul's Church at Flint, Mich., b. at Medford 1 Sept. 1902; m. 25 Nov. 1928 Arline Moseley Hayden, B.A. (Smith, 1919), b. at Hartford, Conn., 6 Jan. 1899, daughter of Howard C. and Caroline (Moseley) Hayden. Children: (1) Mary Waitt,[10] b. in September

1929. (2) Andrew Hayden, b. 18 Nov. 1930. (3) Sarah
Frances, b. 18 Apr. 1933. (4) Eleanor, b. 25 Sept. 1936.

2. *Clinton Waitt*, b. at Medford 5 Aug. 1909; m. at Brookline,
Mass., 11 Aug. 1935, Alice Gunn, b. 26 Aug. 1916, daughter of
Capt. William Ellis and Gertrude (Fontham) Gunn of
Brooklyn, N. Y. Child: (1) Clinton Ellis,[10] b. 13 Mar. 1937.

3. *Richard*, of New York City, A.B. (Dartmouth, 1933), LL.B.
(Columbia, 1938), lawyer, captain of the Varsity hockey
team at Dartmouth, instructor of Latin, 1933–1935, at
Phillips Andover Academy, a member of Phi Beta Kappa,
b. 28 Dec. 1910.

4. *Thomas Waitt*, b. 20 Nov. 1915.

iii. LILLIAN, b. in 1875; d. young.

iv. ANNE, b. in 1878; d. young.

v. MARY WAITT, b. 28 Mar. 1880; d. *s.p.* at Medford 27 Jan. 1936; m.
10 Apr. 1927 FRANK GIBBS of Medford.

vi. FREDERICK ELIJAH, vice president of the National Shawmut Bank
of Boston, a former director of the Merchants National Bank of
Salem, a member of the Winchester Country Club, and the Bank
Officers Association of Boston, b. at Needham, Mass., 3 Feb.
1882; m. 18 Oct. 1919 GLADYS CAROLYN DAY, b. at Swanzey, N. H.,
22 Feb. 1895, daughter of Auburn Jacob and Abby Adams (Underwood) Day.
Children:

1. *Nancy Carolyn*,[10] b. at Medford 4 Apr. 1921.

2. *Elizabeth*, b. at Medford 27 June 1923.

vii. GRACE ISABELLE, b. 16 Jan. 1889; m. at Woburn, Mass., 14 Nov.
1911, GEORGE NASON BARDEN of Woburn.
Child (surname *Barden*):

1. *Frances Eleanor*, b. 10 Mar. 1913; d. 6 Dec. 1932.

10. ALFRED ANDREW[7] JACKSON (*Capt. George Jeremiah*,[6] *Chester*,[5]
Nehemiah[4]), born at Voluntown, Conn., 27 Feb. 1846, died
at Gardiner, Maine, 8 Mar. 1919. He married first, in 1868,
ELIZABETH CROWELL HALLETT; and secondly, at Providence,
R. I., 3 Mar. 1894, NETTIE SNOW LEIGH, born 8 Nov. 1871,
daughter of Amos Little and Mercy Higgins (Snow) Leigh of
"Leigh's Hill," Newbury, Mass.

Alfred Andrew Jackson was educated in village schools and
for a time attended the University of Pennsylvania. On
26 May 1862 he enlisted in Company F, Ninth Rhode Island
Infantry, and was mustered out 2 Sept. 1862. After teaching
school at Pomfret, Conn., he was appointed by President
Hayes in 1878 an inspector in the Counterfeit Money Bureau
of the Department of Justice and was stationed for some time
in Winnipeg, Canada, and Niagara Falls, N. Y. He was intensely interested in the subject of immigration and devoted
many years trying to persuade Congress to pass an immigration restriction bill. A bill was finally enacted during the
administration of President Harding, several years after the
death of Mr. Jackson. Interested in journalism, he at one
time published a magazine in which he expressed his views on
the subject of immigration, which incidentally furnished the
subject for many addresses delivered by him in various parts
of the country. He was president and one of the founders of
the Stephen Hopkins Literary Society of Providence, R. I.
He was also an expert mechanic.

Child:

i. RUSSELL LEIGH,[8] the compiler of this article, was b. at Providence, R. I., 17 Feb. 1896.

After attending public schools and a business college, he was engaged in newspaper work on the *Newburyport Herald*, and later the *Haverhill Gazette* and the *Salem Evening News*. He was assistant special agent of War Trade Board, 1917–1919, in Washington, D. C., and Boston, Mass. In 1930 at the time of the tercentenary celebration of the Massachusetts Bay Colony, he was appointed a special emissary by Newbury, Mass., to carry greetings from that town to the corporation of Newbury, co. Berks, England.

He is a member of the Sons and Daughters of First Settlers of Newbury, Mass., the New England Historic Genealogical Society, the Descendants of Colonial Clergy, the Essex Institute, and the Salem Fraternity. He served also as president of the Society for the Prevention of Cruelty to Children at Salem.

He was the author of "The Pearsons and Their Mills," "The Davenport Family of Newburyport," "Old Essex as a Factor in the Settlement of the Great Northwest," "Dr. Benjamin Tompson," "Dr. Hall Jackson," and he contributed biographies of Dr. Hall Jackson and Nathaniel Tracy to the Dictionary of American Biography.

JAGGER FAMILY OF SOUTHAMPTON, LONG ISLAND, N. Y.: CORRECTION.—It has been the impression of the descendants of the early Jagger family of Southampton, Long Island, N. Y., that they are descended from John, son of the first

Jeremiah Jagger (also known as Gager) of Stamford, Conn., proprietor 1641, formerly of Wethersfield, Conn., 1637, and Watertown, Mass., 1630, who is said to have come to America in 1630 in the ship *Arbella*, one of Gov. John Winthrop's fleet (THE REGISTER, vol. 78, p. 288) and settled in Watertown (Ancient Wethersfield by Henry R. Stiles, vol. 2, p. 459; History of Stamford, Conn., by E. B. Huntington).

This theory probably originated in the History of Southampton, L. I., by George R. Howell, 1887, p. 327, but it is an error. They are descended from John Jagger of Southampton, 1641, said to have probably been a brother (not a son of Jeremiah Jagger (Gager) of Stamford (Genealogical Dictionary of the First Settlers of New England by James Savage, vol. 2, p. 534).

A comparison of the two family records which follow, viz., John Jagger of Southampton and John Jagger of Stamford will show that they were two different persons.

1. JOHN¹ JAGGER, of Southampton, Long Island, N. Y., will made 18 Aug. 1698 and proved 29 Oct. 1699. He married HANNAH ———.

Children:

    i.   JOHN,² d. *s.p.*
    ii.   JEREMIAH, d. in 1744; m. HANNAH ———, who d. before 1740.
    iii. BENJAMIN.
    iv. SAMUEL, d. before 1726.
    v.   JONATHAN, b. in 1678; d. 1 March 1761.
    vi. ELIZABETH, b. 21 July 1699.
    vii. SUSANNAH.
   viii. LYDIA.

Authorities: History of Southampton, L. I., by George R. Howell, p. 327; Census Records, Southampton, 1698; Suffolk County, N. Y., Wills, 1691–1703, by William S. Pelletreau, p. 190.

2. JOHN² JAGGER (also known as *Gager*) (*Jeremiah¹*), of Stamford, Conn., born in Wethersfield or Stamford, Conn., in 1640/45, will dated 20 Oct. 1682 and probated in Stamford 16 Feb. 1684. He married HANNAH³ CROSS, daughter of John² Cross (William¹) of Windsor, Conn. John² Jagger was in Stamford in 1641.

Children:

    i.   ELIZABETH,³ b. in 1665/66; d. before May 1686.
    ii.   HANNAH, b. in 1666/67; m. SAMUEL WEBB.
    iii. SARAH, b. in 1669/70; m. ——— KETCHUM.
    iv. MARY, b. in 1672/73; m. (1) EPHRAM PHELPS; m. (2) JOHN COPP.
    v.   JONATHAN, b. in 1674/75; d. 8 May 1752; m. REBECCA HOLMES.

Authorities: Probate Records, Stamford, Conn., by E. B. Huntington; Will of John Cross of Windsor, Conn.; Early Connecticut Probate Records by Charles W. Manwaring, vol. 2, pp. 53, 375; Will of John Jagger of Stamford, Conn.; Probate Records, Stamford, Fairfield Co., Conn.; Miner and Allied Families by Lillian L. (Miner) Selleck; History and Genealogy of the Families of Old Fairfield, Conn., by Donald L. Jacobus; American Genealogist, vol. ix, p. 56; History of Stamford, Conn., by E. B. Huntington.

I determine the date of birth (1640/45) of John² Jagger (Gager) of Stamford from the following records of the age of his next younger brother Jeremiah:

"Jeremiah Gager, 1666, in Court of Records is said to be 25 years of age" (b. 1641). (History of Stamford, Conn., by E. B. Huntington.)

The same record is chronicled in the Stamford Town Records, pp. 50–51, gives his age as about 20 (b. 1646). Therefore, I state the date of birth of his older brother John as 1640 to 1645.

All three sons of the first Jeremiah, that is, John, Jeremiah and Jonathan were also known as Gager.

"John Jagger propounded for Freeman in Stamford, Conn. 1670" (Author, James Savage). He was a large land holder in Stamford, probably land granted him in 1667 in Stamford in recognition of his father's service in the Pequot Indian War. He dealt extensively in real estate and records of his sales and purchases of land in Stamford appear several times a year from 1667 to 1684. The time of his death will be found in the Stamford Land Records.

He was also known as Gager to wit: "John Gager has land assigned him in

1667 in Court of Records" (History of Stamford, Conn., by E. B. Huntington, p. 183).

All this proves that John Jagger (Gager), oldest son of the first Jeremiah, lived all his life or from infancy in Stamford, and did not go to Southampton, Long Island, as stated by Howell. He states that the first mention of John Jagger on the town records of Southampton was in 1651 when he was granted a house lot, but he appears to have overlooked mention in this same book, p. 30, of "John Jagger on a list of persons who came to Southampton within a few years after the settlement of the town" (in 1639).

It is not certain in the mind of the writer whether the John Jagger of Southampton 1641 and the John Jagger of 1651 were one and the same persons or whether the John of 1641 was the father of John 1651. I have not found any mention in records of this John between 1641 and 1651. Therefore, it would seem that they were one and the same person.

According to the History of Southampton, L. I., page 31A., a reconstruction of the town and transfer of the site took place about 1648. It is possible that John Jagger was allotted a house lot shortly after that and moved from the old town to the new site in 1651.

John Jagger (Gager), son of the first Jeremiah of Stamford, could not have been granted a house lot in Southampton "on condition that he continue to work at his trade as a carpenter" in 1651 as he was only a boy of 11 to 16 years old at that time.

John Jagger of Southampton had three daughters born in 1699 and after. These could not have been the children of John Jagger (Gager) of Stamford as he died in *1684*. And they could not have been his grandchildren (children of a son John) because he had only one son and he was named Jonathan, born in 1674.

The Southampton family were much younger than the Stamford family.

Historians state that most of the people who settled Southampton came from Lynn, Dorchester and Watertown, Mass. It is possible that John Jagger 1641 of Southampton went from Watertown, where his supposed to be brother Jeremiah settled.

The tradition in our family is that we are descended from two brothers who came to this country at an early date and they were seafaring people.

Jeremiah Jagger (Gager) of Stamford was captain of a trading vessel plying between New England and the British West Indies.

My ancestors changed their name definitely and permanently from Jagger to Gager in the fifth generation.

The same misconception occurs between the family of Jonathan[2] Jagger, son of the first John of Long Island, and the family of Jonathan,[3] son of the first John of Stamford. They have been interchanged by historians. The Jagger family genealogy as contained in Howell's History of Southampton, L. I., is very much confused and contains many errors.

San Francisco, Calif.   HARRY G. GAGER.

JAGGER-GAGER GENEALOGY

By HARRY G. GAGER, of San Francisco, Calif.

Jeremiah Jagger was born probably about 1600–10 in England or Holland. The surname Jagger or its equivalent dates back in England to about 1272–1300 (William Jaggard, a census of England, 1272). Prior to that time the family probably resided in Holland where the name Jager is found at an early date. Surnames came into use on the continent of Europe as early as the year 1000 before they did in England.

The name is an occupational name probably derived from the personal name "Jack" and related to "Jockey"; also one who works draught horses for hire; teamster, and has its origin in Holland. The family tradition is that the name had its origin in Holland.

Jager is found in the 14th century in the parish of Kirkburton and West Riding District of Yorkshire Co., England, and in the 16th century is found in the same places as Jagger, and in 1602 in Elland, also in Yorkshire Co. (Dictionary of English and Welsh surnames by Charles W. Bardsley. 1901) and others.

Jeremiah Jagger married Elizabeth and is said to have come to America in 1630 in the ship *Arbella* one of Gov. Winthrop's fleet (New England Historical and Genealogical Register, 1924, vol. 78, p. 288) and settled in Watertown, Mass.; from there he went in 1636 to Wethersfield, Conn. He fought in the Pequot Indian War of 1637 and he and his three sons were granted tracts of land in recognition of this service.

In 1641 he went to Stamford, Conn., as one of the original proprietors. Was master of a trading vessel plying between New England ports and the British West Indies. He died Aug. 14, 1658 in the West Indies where he went four years before his death. He probably died in the Island of Barbados where we find a Francis Jagger (presumably a relation) was a land owner in 1638 (New England Historical and Genealogical Register, vol. 39, p. 134). His widow married Robert Usher.

After he came to this country he became known as Gager as well as Jagger. He and his three sons are all recorded in various histories under both names. In the fifth generation the name Gager was definitely and permanently adopted. This family are not related to Dr. William Gager who also was a passenger on the *Arbella* in 1630, nor to John Gage another passenger on the same ship.

Because Jeremiah Jagger-Gager came to America with Gov. Winthrop's fleet which sailed from England does not necessarily prove whether he was born in England or Holland, or which country he started from on his voyage to America. He may have gone from England to Holland in 1608 as many Englishmen did to escape religious persecution. Most of them went to Leyden. Later becoming dissatisfied with conditions in Holland many of them emigrated to America. Gov. Winthrop states in his "Journal" that there were passengers on board the *Arbella* from Holland.

Children:

2. i. JOHN,² b. in Wethersfield or Stamford, Conn., 1636–1640.
3. ii. JEREMIAH, b. in Stamford, Conn., 1640–41.
   iii. JONATHAN, b. in Stamford, Conn., 1651–54; living in Stamford in 1673, not in 1687.
   iv. ELIZABETH, b. in Stamford, Conn., 18 Sept. 1657; d. 17 Dec. 1657.

2. JOHN² JAGGER (*Jeremiah¹*), of Stamford, Conn., born in Wethersfield or Stamford, Conn., 1636–40. Will probated 16 Feb. 1684, Stamford. He married HANNAH CROSS who died 1675–82, daughter of William Cross (born about 1580, of Gent, Belgium, and London, England).

Children:

   i. ELIZABETH,³ b. 1665–66; d. before May 1686.
   ii. HANNAH, b. 1667/68; m. SAMUEL WEBB.
   iii. SARAH, b. 1669/70; m. —— KETCHUM.
   iv. MARY, b. 1672/73; m. (1) 21 May 1691 EPHRAM PHELPS, b. Nov. 1663, d. 30 Oct. 1697; m. (2) JOHN COPP.
       Child by first husband (surname *Phelps*):
       1. *Ephram*, b. Nov. 1663; d. 28 Sept. 1692.
4. v. JONATHAN, b. Stamford, Conn., 1674/75.

3. JEREMIAH² JAGGER (*Jeremiah¹*), of Stamford, Conn., born in Stamford Conn., about 1640/41, died in 1690. He married —— FERRIS, daughter of Peter Ferris, Jr.

Children:

   i. SARAH,³ b. in 1676/77; m. (1) 9 Apr. 1702 JOHN WEBSTER, who d. 8 Mar. 1717, son of Nicholas Webster and Sarah Waterbury. She m. (2) JAMES SLAWSON as his second wife.
       Children (surname *Webster*):
       1. *John*, b. 24 June 1704; d. 8 March 1717.
       2. *Sarah*, b. 10 Aug. 1706.
       3. *Rachel*, b. 23 July 1708; d. April 1710.
       4. *Nicholas*, b. 18 Dec. 1710; d. 15 Oct. 1734.
   ii. ELIZABETH, b. 1678/79; m. 10 June 1697 BENJAMIN HOYT, JR., b. 7 Dec. 1671, d. in 1747, son of Benjamin Hoyt and Hannah Weed.
       Children (surname *Hoyt*):
       1. *Deborah*, b. 9 Aug. 1698; m. 14 Dec. 1721 Deacon Stephen Ambler, b. 22 June 1698.
       2. *Benjamin*, b. 24 Aug. 1700.
       3. *David*, b. 23 Jan. 1702.
       4. *Abraham*, b. 16 June 1704.
       5. *Samuel*, d. 29 Aug. 1706.
       6. *Ebenezer*, b. in October 1712; m. Mercy Hoyt.
       7. *Jagger*, b. 21 Dec. 1714; m. (1) Sarah Weed; m. (2) Jemima Clason.
       8. *Hannah*, b. 8 Dec. 1716.
       9. *Benjamin*, b. 13 June 1718.
       10. *Jonas*, b. 8 May 1720.

iii. MARY, b. in 1682/83; m. 29 March 1704 CAPTAIN AND DEACON SAMUEL[3] HOYT, b. in 1679/84, d. in 1766/67, son of Benjamin[2] Hoyt (Simon[1]).

Children (surname *Hoyt*):
1. *A child*, d. 29 Aug. 1706.
2. *Mary*, b. 20 Feb. 1711/12.
3. *Elizabeth*, b. 29 Nov. 1713; d. same day.
4. *Samuel*, b. 8 Feb. ———; m. (1) 8 Mar. 1738 Abigail Hoyt; m. (2) 6 Apr. 1756 Martha Blackley, dau. of Samuel Blackley.
5. *Joanna*, b. 14 Jan. 1716/17; d. 12 March 1717.
6. *Ebenezer*, b. about 1720; d. in 1783.
7. *Elizabeth*, b. 17 Feb. 1721.
8. *Hannah*, b. probably 20 July ———; d. 1 Aug. 1724.
9. *Sarah*.

iv. JEREMIAH, b. in 1684/85; d. unm. 6 Oct. 1706.

4. JONATHAN[3] JAGGER (*John*,[2] *Jeremiah*[1]), of Stamford, Conn., born in Stamford in 1674/75, died there 8 May 1752. He married, 22 Aug. 1700, REBECCA HOLMES, daughter of Francis Holmes.

Children:
i. HANNAH,[4] b. Aug. 1701; m. 20 June 1723 THOMAS NEWMAN, b. about 1698, d. 15 Sept. 1743.

Children (surname *Newman*):
1. *Thomas*, b. 24 July 1724; d. 15 Sept. 1743.
2. *Jeremiah*, b. 29 May 1726.
3. *Daniel*, b. 3 May 1728.
4. *Hannah*, b. 20 June 1730.
5. *Rebecca*, b. 2 June 1735.
6. *Stephen*, b. 10 Jan. 1738/9; d. in April 1799; m. 11 Nov. 1766 Sarah Maltby, b. 1 May 1750, d. 12 Sept. 1826, daughter of David[3] Maltby (Jonathan,[2] William[1]).

5. ii. JOHN, b. 7 Dec. 1702; d. 31 March 1743.
iii. JEREMIAH, b. probably 14 Dec. 1704; d. 12 Feb. 1710/11.
iv. JONATHAN, b. probably 14 Dec. 1704; d. 24 Feb. 1705/06.
v. MARY, b. 6 Dec. 1705; d. in February 1705/06.
vi. JEREMIAH, d. 18 Feb. 1712/13.
vii. JONATHAN, b. 15 Dec. 1715; d. 8 Sept. 1755.
viii. MARY, b. 20 June 1719; d. 17 Sept. 1745; m. 9 Nov. 1737 SAMUEL[3] DART, as his 2nd wife, b. in New London, Conn., 12 Dec. 1705, d. 5 April 1769 at Bolton, Conn., son of Daniel[2] Dart (Richard[1]).

Children (surname *Dart*):
1. *Sarah*, b. 30 July 1738; m. 27 March 1755 William Dart.
2. *Mary*, bapt. 23 March 1740; m. 17 April 1760 Solomon Loomis.
3. *Elizabeth*, b. 19 Nov. 1741; d. infant.
4. *Samuel*, b. 31 July 1743; m. 30 April 1767 Abigail Brown.
5. *Nath*, b. 18 Feb. 1744/45; m. 19 March 1767 Dorothy Gains.
6. *Rebecca*, d. Nov. 1732.

Authorities:

Ancient Wethersfield, Conn., by Henry R. Stiles.
History of Stamford, Conn., by Rev. E. B. Huntington.
Stamford Reg. births, marriages & deaths, by Rev. E. B. Huntington.
Gen. First Settlers in America, by James Savage.
Probate Records of Stamford, Conn.
Probate Records of Fairfield, Conn.
Miner & Allied Families of Conn., by Lillian L. (Miner) Selleck.
History and Gen. of the families of Old Fairfield, Conn., by Donald L. Jacobus.
American Genealogist, vol. 9–etc., by Donald L. Jacobus.

Wills of John Cross and Samuel Cross.
Wills of 3. Jeremiah² Jagger.
Hoyt Family Genealogy, by David W. Hoyt.
Woodhull Genealogy, by Mary G. Woodhull.
New York Gen. & Biog. Record, vol. 64, p. 180.
Personal letters of descendants.
Probate Records, Hartford, Conn.
Vital Records, Bolton and Vernon, Conn.
New England Hist. & Gen. Register, vols. 52–56.

5. JOHN⁴ JAGGER (*Jonathan,*³ *John,*² *Jeremiah*¹), of Stamford, Conn., and Bedford, Westchester Co., N. Y., born in Stamford 7 Dec. 1702, died in March 1743. He married in Greenwich, Conn., 9 Nov. 1732, by Samuel Peck, Justice of the Peace, REBECCA INGERSOLL.

Children (surnames of sons were changed to Gager after reaching adult age):

  6. i.   JOHN⁵ (Gager), b. 24 Jan. 1732/33; d. in 1800–10.
     ii. REBECCA, b. in July 1734; m. at Congregational Church, Stamford, Conn., 4 July 1758, WILLIAM GALE.

        Children (surname *Gale*):
        1. *William,* b. 10 Feb. 1759.
        2. *Isaac,* b. 17 Nov. 1760.
        3. *Reuben,* b. 30 Jan. 1763.
        4. *Joseph,* b. 14 Dec. 1764.
        5. *Nat,* b. 20 Oct. 1766.
        6. *Isaac,* b. 17 Sept. 1768.
        7. *Betsy,* b. 19 Dec. 1770.
        8. *Rufus,* b. 14 July 1774.
        9. *Jeremiah,* b. 21 Jan. 1780.

  7. iii. JEREMIAH (Gager), b. 17 June 1736; d. in 1805.
     iv. REUBEN (Gager), b. 28 Feb. 1738/39; m. 5 May 1780 at St. John's P. E. church, Stamford, Conn., JOANNA HOLLY. He served in the Rev. War.
  8. v. NATHANIEL (Gager), b. 19 Dec. 1739; d. after 1800.
     vi. HANNAH, b. 30 May 1741.
     vii. NEMIAH, b. 2 May 1743; d. 10 Feb. 1744/45.

6. JOHN⁵ GAGER (Jagger) (*John,*⁴ *Jonathan,*³ *John,*² *Jeremiah*¹), born 24 Jan. 1732/33, died 1800–10. He married, 6 Jan. 1763, at Presbyterian church, Brinkerhoff, Fishkill Twp., Dutchess Co., N.Y., by Rev. Chauncey Graham, MERCY BROWN (N.Y. Gen. & Biog. Rec., vol. 69, p. 291). She probably was the daughter of Tristram Brown, born 1702/03, died 16 Feb. 1763, and Abigail Parke, born 1703/04, died 20 Oct. 1754.

Children, all born in Dutchess Co., N. Y.:

     i.   NATHANIEL,⁶ b. 1763/64; d. prior to 1849; m. 27 May 1798 MARY GRIFFIN.
     ii.   HANNAH, b. 1764/65; d. 23 Aug. 1857; m. before 1784 TIMOTHY GILBERT.
     iii. JOHN, b. 1 Aug. 1767; d. 4 May 1850; m. 6 Jan. 1791 ANNA WARD.
     iv. PHOEBE, b. 17 July 1771; d. 28 Jan. 1851; m. ANTHONY WHEELER as his second wife.
     v.   THOMAS, b. 13 Nov. 1774; d. 8 Nov. 1846; m. 5 July 1787 HANNAH UNDERHILL.
     vi. SARAH, b. about 1776; m. 26 Jan. 1796 JOSEPH MEAD.
     vii. JOSHUA REUBEN, b. 2 Sept. 1781; d. 24 Oct. 1855; m. MARTHA WHEELER.

viii. NATHAN, b. 4 Mar. 1787; d. 5 May 1872; m. (1) 17 Dec. 1809 PHOEBE
WOOD; m. (2) 10 April 1859 ANNA M. HOLDEN.
ix. NOAH, b. 9 Sept. 1789; d. 7 May 1864; m. about 1815 WELTHA
HUNTLY.
x. ROBERT, d. 18 Nov. 1852.

7. JEREMIAH⁵ GAGER (Jagger) (*John,*⁴ *Jonathan,*³ *John,*² *Jeremiah*¹),
of Westminster, Mass., born 17 June 1736, died in 1805. He
married 29 May 1771 at Westminster, Mass., RUTH WALKER,
born in 1750, died 3 Oct. 1805, daughter of Daniel Walker
and Hannah Wood.

Children:

i. HANNAH, b. 21 Oct. 1779; d. 5 Nov. 1853; m. 7 May 1801 ASHEL
REED SEAVER.
ii. REBECCA, b. 9 Sept. 1781; m. JEREMIAH WOOD.

8. NATHANIEL⁵ GAGER (Jagger) (*John,*⁴ *Jonathan,*³ *John,*² *Jere-
miah*¹), of Westchester Co. and Phillipstown, Putnam Co.,
N. Y., born 19 Dec. 1739, died after 1800, probably in Troy,
N. Y. He married ELIZABETH ———.

Children:

i. WILLIAM DUSENBURY⁶, b. in 1787; d. in 1871; m. LOUISA EVANS.
ii. BEVERLY ROBINSON, b. in 1788; d. in June 1868; m. 16 April 1810
ELIZABETH ROY (or RAY).
iii. JOHN, d. about 1816; m. PHOEBE ———.
iv. ANNA M., m. ——— McCULLOUGH.
v. POLLY, m. JOHN ELLIS.

Authorities

American Genealogist, vol. 10, pp. 179; vol. 11, pp. 88, 95, 159, 162, 225.
Stamford Town records, pp. 104, 113, 125, 131, 135, 137, 146.
Bates-Selleck Genealogy, by H. S. Gorham.
Barbour collec. vital records. Connecticut State Library.
Ancient Windsor, vol. 2, p. 182, by Henry R. Stiles.
Various family Bible records and personal letters from descendants, also tombstone, census
and War Dept., Pension office and County Clerks office records.

THE REVEREND SAMUEL JOHNSON, D.D., OF CONNECTICUT.[1]

Communicated by the Rev. GEORGE D. JOHNSON, A.M., Rector of St. Paul's Church, Newburyport.

THE subject of this sketch, Samuel Johnson, was born in the year 1696, Oct. 14, in Guilford, Conn. His great-grandfather, Robert, was one of the early settlers of New-Haven, having emigrated from Kingston-upon-Hull, in Yorkshire, about 1637. The family seems to have been distinguished by no professional or civil eminence, till at the beginning of the eighteenth century, when, from the peculiar state of the religious world, Samuel Johnson was forced into a position of prominence, which made his name widely known, both in England and America. In the century and a half which has elapsed since Johnson was on the stage of the world, such wonderful progress has been made in every department of knowledge and thought, that his name is now in danger of being ranked among the "forgotten worthies" of New-England: but no more pure and noble life was ever lived among men, whose sole aim it was to serve God, and do good, as far as in them lay, in their day and generation. The era in which he lived, was one on which we are beginning to look back with somewhat the feelings with which we regard the age of romance, — when mailed knights, by the might of a single arm, and the valor of one dauntless heart, overthrew hosts of infidel enemies, and joined battle, with the most serene confidence in their own invincible prowess, with giants and monsters whose very description made our childhood shiver with fright. In this age, when faith sits so lightly on the best of us, and the form of religion is changed with so little concern and interest, I am afraid it is almost impossible to understand the intense earnestness of the men of a hundred years ago, — with whom the *form* of faith was as vital as the faith itself, and quite as nearly concerned their temporal, as their eternal salvation. When Johnson was born, England was yet engaged, as Buckle expresses it, in the last struggle between barbarism and civilization, though "good" King William and Queen Mary sat on the throne,—Spain was bound hand and foot under the awful tyranny of the holy office of the inquisition, and men dared not breathe a word against its power. France was slowly awaking to something resembling spiritual freedom, though the expulsion of the Jesuits was only just thought of, and Voltaire was not yet in long clothes. In this country, New-England was illustrating the grand principle for which our venerated Puritan forefathers are popularly supposed to have left the shores of their mother country,— religious toleration,— by cutting off the ears of Quakers, and hanging witches in Salem. The name of a bishop was considered a synonym for the fines of a star chamber, the tortures of rack and thumb-screw, or the flames of Smithfield. The Church of England was looked upon by those who had come to this country, as a shade worse, if possible, than the scarlet-robed woman who sat on her seven hills: and the determination to resist her encroachments, and keep her prelates from these shores, was as fierce and unbending, as was the resolution of the so-called

---

[1] This valuable paper was read before the NEW-ENGLAND HISTORIC, GENEALOGICAL SOCIETY, Sept. 4, 1872, and is now printed at their request.—[EDITOR.]

pioneers of religious liberty to abolish every form of religion but their own. The prominent point of interest to churchmen, in Dr. Johnson's long and varied career, is the mental conflict through which he came out of congregationalism into the Church of England, — and the untiring zeal with which he labored to promote her interests in this country: but he was a man of so large an understanding, so prominently connected with the progress of education and knowledge generally, during his life, that even to those who have no sympathy with him in his views of church government, his life cannot but be interesting. The quiet beauty of his autobiography and diary, — the inimitable quaintness and modesty of his own account of the great events, *quorum magna pars fuit*, — make it a strong temptation to the writer of this article to let him speak entirely for himself: but the propriety of condensing for such a sketch as this, entails the necessity of diluting with comment what would be infinitely stronger in its unadorned simplicity.

His education must have begun at an exceedingly tender age, as we find him, before he had arrived at the mature period of six years, suddenly and overwhelmingly impressed with the necessity of acquiring the Hebrew language, from the fact of his coming upon certain words in that tongue, in one of his grandfather's books, and learning that the scriptures were written originally in Hebrew and not in English. After a fruitless effort to embark him in a business life, his father gave him the opportunity to "be bred to learning in that college [Yale] which was about that time founding." At the age of ten, we find him complaining that his tutor, whose name is not mentioned, was "such a wretched poor scholar, though a minister, that he could teach him little or nothing, so that he in a manner lost half a year." At fourteen he entered Yale College, then at Saybrook, graduating in 1714, with hardly as much progress as boys are now required to have made for entrance into college. In his own words: "But this lad considered these as only the beginning of things on which he was to go on and make a much greater proficiency in the course of his studies, — and for the rest of his time he was under the tuition of one Mr. Fiske, for Logic, Physics, Metaphysics and Ethics, — for Mathematics, further than the golden rule in Arithmetic, or a little surveying, was not yet tho't of." They heard, indeed, in 1714, when he took his bachelor's degree, of a new philosophy, that of late was all in vogue, — and of such names as DesCartes, Boyle, Locke and Newton: but they were cautioned against thinking anything of them, because the new philosophy, it was said, would soon bring in a new divinity and corrupt the pure religion of the country: and they were not allowed to vary an ace in their thoughts from Dr. Ames's *Medulla Theologiæ* and *Cases of Conscience*, and Wollebius, which were the only systems of divinity that were thumbed in those days, and considered with equal, if not greater, veneration than the bible itself: for the contrivance of those and the like scholastical authors was to make curious systems in a scientific way out of their own heads, and under each head to pick up a few texts of scripture, which seemed to sound favorably, and accommodate them to their preconceived schemes.

It was a work of no great difficulty for a young man of this period, to acquire all the learning then within reach in this country, and Johnson having become master of all that was ordinarily accessible, was regarded as an adept, an opinion in which he confesses to have himself shared: but the accidental discovery of Bacon's *Instauratio Magna*, and a most thorough and repeated study of it, as he says, "soon brought down his towering imaginations. He soon saw his own littleness in comparison with Lord Bacon's greatness, whom he considered over and over again, so that he found himself like one at once emerging out of the glimmer of twilight into the full sunshine of open day."

Yale College might be described, at this time, as in a state of schism. Complaints of the inefficiency of the instructors at Saybrook were so frequent, that some of the students had withdrawn to Hartford, to pursue their studies under the direction of the ministers settled there; while others came to Guilford, to study with Mr. Johnson. There was a strong movement to change the place of the college from Saybrook to Wethersfield, near Hartford; and the matter assumed such importance that it was brought before the general court, which decided unanimously that the college should be removed to New-Haven. This, of course, failed to give satisfaction to the Wethersfield faction, and for some time longer the feud was kept up, till by a peremptory act of the government, all the scholars "were ordered to repair to the established college." Dr. Johnson's own account of the obedience rendered to this order, written half a century after, shows that time had not much softened his wrath at these obstinate collegiate schismatics. "They made," he says, "an appearance of submission, and came all at once, in a caravan; but it soon appeared, they had no good intention. They found fault with everything, and made all the mischief they could, as they were doubtless instructed to do: and after six weeks, went all off, two and two at once, and continued in their former faction till the next general assembly, when the difference was compromised by this agreement, that they should return to their duty, and abide; and that in case they did so, the degrees that had been given them, should be allowed good, and a state-house should be built at the public expense at Hartford. In consequence of this they put an end to the faction, and the scholars came and abode at New-Haven, but proved a very vicious and turbulent sett of fellows." As yet the college had had no president; and about this time, Mr. Timothy Cutler, who graduated at Harvard in 1701, was chosen to the office. For a year, Johnson continued to act under him as a tutor, when he accepted the position of minister in West Haven, in 1720, at the age of twenty-four. There is a document existing which shows that he had already entertained strong doubts of the validity of presbyterian orders; and I give an extract from this, as showing his deep conscientiousness, as well as his remarkable modesty. The title is: "My present thoughts of Episcopacy, with what I conceive may justifie me in accepting Presbyterian ordination. Written at West Haven, Dec. 20, An. Dom. 1719." The argument is lengthy, showing that he believes Episcopacy to be of divine right, but of a "positive," not a "moral" nature. Therefore, as Providence had placed him in the circumstances in which he stood, the obligation on him was "dissolved" for the "observance of this institution:" and then, in his own words: "Having thus stated the case, I leave it to impartial advice whether this be good divinity or not, that any circumstances will justifie me in what I propose to do: and if so, I submit it also to be considered whether my circumstances are such, which are these.

1. The passionate intreaties of a tender mother.

2. That my breaking forth upon an attempt of that nature, would be of vastly more disservice to the best interest of the Church itself, than my going over to it could be of service to it.

3. That it can't be without most fatal jealousies to this Colledg, and the effects of it must be mischievous.

4. That I must thereby be exposed to great dangers and difficulties, to which I am a great stranger.

5. My want of that politeness and those qualifications which would be requisite in making such an appearance.

6. That in order to taking Episcopal orders, there are many things to be complied with, which I do not sufficiently understand.

7. That the times, 'tis to be feared, are very difficult at home, and it's likely not so good encouragement to such designs as might be wished for.

8. That although I seem tolerably well satisfied in these my thoughts of the right of Episcopacy, yet considering the meanness of my advantages, and the scantiness of my time hitherto, I have reason to be very jealous whether I have not too much precipitated into these opinions.

And then, finally, perhaps I may in the meantime be doing some service to promote the main interest of religion, tho' it be not in a method so desirable."

A note, added two years afterwards, gives the result: "Upon these principles I continued easy about two years, and then upon a more careful examination of the matter, I found I could not, with a good conscience, continue to administer in the name of Christ, when I was under persuasion I had never had a regular commission from him. And therefore, I thought it my bounden duty to come over to the Episcopal side, that I might live and die in the unity of the Church. Accordingly I, with Dr. Cutler, Mr. Hart, Mr. Whittlesey, Mr. Elliott, Mr. Wetmore, and Mr. Browne, made our public declaration for the Church, Sept. 13, 1722, at Yale College, New Haven."

These facts are so well known in Connecticut ecclesiastical history, and so well described by Dr. Beardslee in his most excellent work on that subject, that no apology is necessary for omitting the various steps by which these gentlemen were brought to this conclusion. But there is something wonderfully striking in the picture suggested by the thought of these men standing calmly before the assembled dignitaries of the college, as champions of an ecclesiastical body whose name was as hateful to our worthy New-England fathers, as ever it was to the most bitter Scotch covenanter. An argument followed, of course, before Gov. Saltonstall, in which a vigorous effort was made to "reclame" these erring brethren. The discussion was begun "with calmness and decency," but the steadiness of the men who declined to be reclaimed, and the unpleasant strength of their position, based as it was entirely on the words of scripture, and unquestioned history, seem to have had anything but a soothing effect on the minds of the theological champions, whose aim was always to be *first* pure, *then* gentle. Dr. Johnson describes the result, — "A harangue against them by an old minister in a declamatory way" was delivered with an amount of energy and directness that convinced the governor of the uselessness of the debate, so that he "genteelly" put an end to the conference. It is impossible, at this day, to imagine the horror and dismay which spread over the land at this awful defection on the part of men of such prominence as the president and professors of Yale College. It was too much to believe that men could deliberately come out of the glorious sunlight of congregational freedom, into the dismal twilight, if not the infernal gloom, of prelatic superstition. President Woolsey, as Dr. Beardslee quotes, speaking of the event, says: "that greater alarm would scarcely be awakened now, if the theological faculty of the College were to declare for the Church of Rome, avow their belief in transubstantiation, and pray to the Virgin Mary."

The year following, Cutler, Johnson and Browne sailed for England, followed by Wetmore, where they received orders in the Established Church, and, with the exception of Browne, who died of small-pox, returned the following year, 1723, to enter on their labors as missionaries under the venerable society for the propagation of the gospel in foreign parts. Dr. Cutler was chosen rector of Christ Church, Boston, which was erected that year. Johnson was appointed missionary in Stratford, Conn., where the church had been established for some years, but was struggling against many and painful difficulties.

The diary of Dr. Johnson, during his year's stay in England, is, in itself, a most delightful piece of reading, but its spirit can hardly be shown by extracts. The fervent piety and earnest devotion of these pilgrims from the new to the old world, — their unfeigned awe and veneration, as they came in contact with the grand old monuments of England's past and present glory, — the glimpses of social life, whose freedom is somewhat startling to our more rigid modern ideas, — all make the temptation to quote almost too strong for the duty suggested by a sense of propriety, in abbreviating as much as possible, in a sketch of this kind.

Thirty years were spent by Dr. Johnson in the work of the ministry, his field being a large part of the colony of Connecticut, west of the river. During this period, Bishop Berkeley visited America; and for two years there was a most intimate communion between the two, on which, in his autobiography, Dr. Johnson dwells with extraordinary pleasure. In 1754, he was chosen president of King's College, New-York, which was founded at this time. In this capacity he served for nine years, resigning the office, at last, in terror of the small-pox. This scourge had been particularly fatal to him, in his family and friends, as it had taken away his wife, his eldest son, and his friend the Rev. Mr. Browne, — and his fear of the disease seemed to amount to an absolute horror. His resignation of the presidency was in 1763; and Mr. Myles Cooper succeeded him in the office. The church in Stratford received him again as rector, and here the remainder of his days were spent, in the faithful discharge of the duties of his office, in correspondence with many of the bishops and clergy of the mother church in England, and in an active share in the literary and religious controversies of the day.[1]

His son, William Samuel Johnson,[2] LL.D., had been sent abroad to England, as agent for the colonies in a law-suit with regard to the claims of

[1] Mr. Johnson received the degree of Master of Arts from both Oxford and Cambridge, while he was in England. His publications were chiefly controversial. In 1746 he published a work on ethics, entitled "A System of Morality;" and in 1752, a compend of logic and metaphysics, and another of ethics, originally prepared for the use of his sons. The two latter were printed in Philadelphia, by Franklin, as text books for use in the university of Pennsylvania. He was also the author of an *English* and a *Hebrew Grammar*, 1767. His *Memoir* by Dr. Chandler was published in 1805. (See Drake's *Dictionary*.)—[EDITOR.]

[2] William Samuel Johnson. LL.D. (Y. C. 1788), D.C.L. (Oxon. 1766), was born in Stratford, Conn., Oct. 7, 1727, and died there Nov. 14, 1819. He was graduated at Yale in 1746. He inherited the intellectual and moral traits of his distinguished father, and, as will be seen below, left his mark upon the political fabric under which we live. He was a delegate to the Congress in New-York, in 1765; member of the council (Colonial); from October, 1766, to 1771, agent of Connecticut in England; from 1772 to 1774, a judge of the superior court of Connecticut; a commissioner for adjusting the boundary between the proprietors of the Philadelphia and Susquehanna Co.; delegate to the Congress in 1784-7; one of the framers of the federal constitution, and his great influence there is evident from the published and unpublished debates of that memorable convention. He first proposed the Senate as a branch of the legislative department. He was United States senator in 1789-91, and aided in drawing up the federal judiciary act. He succeeded Dr. Myles Cooper in the presidency of Columbia College, and held the office from 1787 to 1800. (See sketch of his life by John T. Irving, 1830; Drake's *Dictionary*.)—[EDITOR.]

the eastern states on the newly settled lands at the west. In October, 1771, the year following the Boston Massacre, he returned, in time to close the eyes of his venerable father, who died on the festival of the Epiphany, Jan. 6, 1772. His remains lie in the church-yard in Stratford; but the frosts of a hundred winters have shivered the marble on which was inscribed the epitaph written by his devoted friend, Myles Cooper. As a worthy tribute to a noble life, I give it here, though it would seem as if so honored a tomb should not have been suffered to have been left without name or inscription, to mark the spot where Dr. Johnson lies:—

> " If decent dignity and modest mien,
>   The cheerful heart and countenance serene;
>   If pure religion and unsullied truth,
>   His age's solace, and his search in youth;
>   If piety, in all the paths he trod,
>   Still rising vig'rous to the Lord his God;
>   If charity, through all the race he ran,
>   Still wishing well, and doing good to man;
>   If learning, free from pedantry and pride;
>   If faith and virtue walking side by side;
>   If well to mark his being's aim and end,
>   To shine thro' life, a husband, father, friend;
>   If *these* ambition in thy soul can raise,
>   Excite thy reverence, or demand thy praise,
>   Reader — ere yet thou quit this earthly scene
>   Revere his name, and be what he has been."

In conclusion, it may be mentioned that his son, Dr. Johnson the second, served after the revolution as president of King's College, when the name was changed to the more patriotic title which it now bears, Columbia. By one of those singular "revenges of time," the son of William Samuel, and grandson of the father of Episcopacy in Connecticut, married the grand-daughter of Jonathan Edwards, the great New-England apostle of Calvinism, — and thus the blood of the two grand, opposing phases of New-England theology, flowed on in one stream, in the veins of their descendants. Calvinism and Arminianism, Prelacy and Congregationalism, — Cavalier and Roundhead, — were blended in the bewildering mixture; and as the swords of Prescott and Linzee will hang peacefully, side by side, as long as this country lasts, in the city for whose possession they were brandished by hostile hands, — so let discord end between the two theologies. May they go on, working their own work, in their own way, under the same Almighty Guide, — respecting each other's merits, forgetting each other's faults, till the great day comes, which shall decide the vexed questions between them, forever, when we render our final account to our Maker.

WALLINGFORD (CONN.) JOHNSONS.

By Frederick C. Johnson, M.D., of Wilkes-Barre, Penn.

1. William[1] Johnson of Wallingford, Connecticut, emigrated to America presumably about 1660, and settled at New Haven. In Dec., 1664, he married Sarah, daughter of John and Jane (Wollen or Woolin) Hall. He was one of the founders or original proprietors of Wallingford, in 1670; and one of the signers of the compact.

In the town records of New Haven he is sometimes mentioned as "Wingle" Johnson, and is recorded as "husbandman" and "planter." He died in 1716, and his will is recorded at New Haven.

Children:

   i.   Lieut. William,[2] b. September 5, 1665; d. in 1742.
   ii. John, b. July 20, 1667; d. 1744.
   iii. Isaac, of Woodbridge, Conn.; called Deacon and Captain; b. Oct. 27, 1672; d. Oct. 27, 1750; m. in 1699, Abigail, daughter of John Cooper, whose epitaph is given in New Haven Historical papers, Vol. 3, p. 544.
   iv. Abraham, b. 1669.
   v. Abigail, b. December 6, 1670; m. Joseph Lines.
2. vi. Jacob, of Wallingford, b. September 25, 1674; d. July 17, 1749.
   vii. Sarah, b. November 6, 1676; m. Samuel Horton.
   viii. Samuel, b. September 3, 1678; m. Anna Hotchkiss.
   ix. Mary, b. April 1, 1680; m. Samuel Bishop, Jr.
   x. Lydia, b. July 7, 1681; m.——Andrews.
   xi. Hope, twin, b. May 10, 1685.
   xii. Elizabeth, twin, b. May 10, 1685; m. Abraham Hotchkiss.
   xiii. Ebenezer, b. April 15, 1688; m. Lydia Hotchkiss.

2. Jacob[2] Johnson, (*William*[1]), of Wallingford, born in New Haven, Sept. 25, 1674; died July 17, 1749; married Dec. 14, 1693, Abigail, daughter of John and Abigail (Merriman) Hitchcock. [See Hitchcock family.] Abigail was a granddaughter of Capt. Nathaniel Merriman, an original proprietor of Wallingford. Jacob was sergeant of the Wallingford train band, and is referred to in the records as "Sergeant" Jacob. He was deputy to the general court. His will is recorded at New Haven.

Children:

   i.   Reuben,[3] b. August 27, 1694; m. March 11, 1718, Mary Dayton. [Tuttle Family, p. 214, gives names of children.]
3. ii. Dea. Isaac, b. Feb. 21, 1696; d. April 23, 1779; m. Sarah Osborne, Nov. 23, 1723.
   iii. Enos, b. 1698; d. 1786; had a son Shuborn.
   iv. Abigail, b. 1699; m. Capt. Benjamin Holt. [Tuttle Family, p. 214.]
   v. Lieut. Caleb, b. 1703; d. Oct. 13, 1777; m. Rachel Brockett.
   vi. Israel, b. 1705; d. 1747; m. Jan. 26, 1732, Sarah Miles. Children, according to Davis's "Wallingford": 1. *Eunice*, b. 1734. 2. *Anna*, b. 1736; 3. *Prudence*, b. 1738; 4. *Caleb*, b. 1739; 5. *Miles*, b. 1741; 6. *Jacob*, b. 1742; 7. *Rebecca*, b. 1744; 8. *Warren*, b. 1747; 9. *Silas*, b. 1749.
4. vii. Daniel, b. 1709; d. Oct. 14, 1780: m. Dec. 24, 1732, Joanna Preston.
   viii. Sarah, b. 1710; m. Daniel Bartholomew. [Bartholomew Family, p. 86.]
5. ix. Capt. Abner, b. Aug. 2, 1702; d. Dec. 28, 1757; m. Dec. 14, 1726, Charity, daughter of Isaac and Rebecca (Tuttle) Dayton, of New Haven. [Tuttle Family.]

6. x. Rev. Jacob, b. at Wallingford, April 7, 1713; d. at Wilkes-Barre, Pa., March 15, 1797. This line is being traced by Dr. F. C. Johnson, Wilkes-Barre, Pa.

3. Deacon Isaac³ Johnson (*Jacob²*, *William¹*), born February 21, 1696; died April 23, 1779 ; married November 23, 1723, Sarah Osborne.

Children, from town records:

- i. Abigail,⁴ b. 1727.
- ii. Sarah, b. 1729.
- 7. iii. Isaac, b. 1731.
- iv. Esther, b. 1735.
- v. Rachel, b. 1740; m. Stephen Todd, b. March 3, 1735, son of Stephen and Lydia (Ives) Todd. They removed to Salisbury, Herkimer Co., N. Y., in 1792. Issue: Isaac; Jehiel, who m. Hannah Steel; Stephen; and Bertha. This family is being traced by Mrs. William H. Faust, of Ann Arbor, Michigan.
- vi. Rebecca, b. 1744.

Davis's " Walingford " names all of above except Rebecca, and gives in addition, Joseph, born 1725, and Lois, born 1738.

4. Daniel Johnson³ (*Jacob²*, *William¹*), born 1709 ; died 1780 ; married in 1732, Joanna Preston, who was born 1714, and died 1781. He was a trial justice under the King.

Children:

- i. Charles,⁴ b. 1735.
- 8. ii. Capt. Solomon, b. 1740. Descendants of this line are being traced by Edward H. Johnson, of Philadelphia, Pa.
- iii. Joanna, b. 1743.
- 9. iv. Lieut. Daniel, b. 1746. Descendants of this line have been traced by George Ransom Johnson, of Cheshire, Conn.
- v. Israel, b. 1748.
- vi. Justin, b. 1752.
- vii. Abigail, b. 1753.
- viii. Joshua, b. 1757.
- ix. Mindwell, b. 1758.
- x. Rebecca, b. 1759.

5. Captain Abner³ Johnson (*Jacob,²* *William¹*) of Wallingford, born Aug. 2, 1702 ; died December 28, 1757 ; married December 14, 1726, Charity, daughter of Isaac and Rebecca (Tuttle) Dayton, the great grand-daughter of Ralph Dayton, the colonist. [Tuttle Family, p. 214.] He was Captain of the train band at Wallingford. His will is at New Haven.

Children:

- i. Dayton,⁴ b. Feb. 8, 1728.
- ii. Lydia, b. 1730; d. 1812; m. May 16, 1749, Ebenezer Fitch; great grand-mother of Elliott Fitch Shepard.
- 10. iii. Hezekiah, b. March 12, 1732; d. Feb. 21, 1810. This line is being traced by Capt. S. Albert Johnson, of Boonville, N. Y.
- iv. Abner, b. Aug. 6, 1738; graduated at Yale, 1759.
- 11. v. Jacob, b. 1742; d. 1816; m. Esther Hotchkiss; was a soldier in the Revolution. He removed to Johnstown, N. Y.
- vi. Charity, b. May 19, 1744; m. (first) John Dinon; m. (second) Samuel Hickox.

6. Rev. Jacob³ Johnson (*Jacob,²* *William¹*), born at Wallingford, April 7, 1713; died March 15, 1797. While pastor at North Groton, he married Mary, daughter of Capt. Nathaniel and Mary (Williams) Giddings, of Preston, Conn. She was born in 1730, and

died in Wilkes-Barre, Pa., about 1791. His biography is given in Dexter's Graduates of Yale.

Rev. Jacob Johnson's monument at Wilkes-Barre, Pa., has the following epitaph :

Rev. Jacob Johnson, A.M. | Born at Wallingford, Conn., April 7, 1713. | Died at Wilkes-Barre, Pa., March 15, 1797. | Graduated at Yale College, 1740. | Pastor of Congregational Church, | Groton, Conn., 1749–1772. | First pastor of Wilkes-Barre Congregational | (subsequently First Presbyterian) | 1772–1797. | He made missionary journeys to the | Six Nations. | Preaching in the Indian language. | He was an early and outspoken advocate | of American liberty and a commanding | figure in the early history | of Wyoming. | He wrote the articles of capitulation | following the destruction of the | infant settlement | by the British and Indians | in 1778 | and was a firm and self-sacrificing | defender of the Connecticut title | throughout the prolonged land contest. |

Children, all born in Connecticut :

i.   JEHOIADA PITT,[5] b. 1767; d. at Wilkes-Barre, Pa., in 1830. Left a large family.
ii. JACOB; had daughter Mary, who m. P. N. Foster of Wilkes-Barre, Pa.
iii. LYDIA, m. Col. Zebulon Butler, commander of the patriot forces in the battle of Wyoming. Left numerous descendants.
iv. CHRISTIANA O., m. William Russell of Wilkes-Barre, Pa.; no issue.

7. ISAAC JOHNSON[4] (*Deacon Isaac,[3] Jacob,[2] William[1]*) was born June 23, 1731. Davis's " Wallingford " says he married Abigail——. The manuscript records at Wallingford name the following children :

i.   DAVID,[5] b. 1758.
ii. MARY, b. 1759.
iii. LOIS, b. 1761.
iv. STEPHEN, b. 1763.
v.   ISAAC, b. 1766.
vi. WARREN, b. 1768.

8. CAPT. SOLOMON[4] JOHNSON (*Daniel,[3] Jacob,[2] William[1]*), of Wallingford, born May 4, 1740 ; died April 4, 1700. He was a Revolutionary soldier, and sea captain. He left a son, Charles, who was born 1767, in Wallingford, Conn. ; died 1848, in Durham, N. Y.; married at New Haven, Conn., Elizabeth Rice. His son, Solomon Rice Johnson, born 1797, at Durham, N. Y. ; married Mary Whittlesey of Saybrook, Conn. ; d. at Durham in 1833. His son, Solomon Whittlesey Johnson, of New York City and Warwick, New York, President of the American News Company, married Sept. 12, 1853, Adelaide Hine of Cairo, N. Y. His son Edward Hine Johnson is now a resident of Philadelphia, Pa.

9. LIEUT. DANIEL[4] JOHNSON (*Daniel,[3] Jacob,[2] William[1]*), born March 24, 1746 ; died 1830; married Rebecca Hitchcock.
Children :

i.   CEPHAS,[5] b. 1782.
ii. AUGUSTUS, b. 1783.
iii. WILLETT, b. 1785.
iv. DAN, b. 1787.
v.   RANSOM, b. 1788.
vi. LOUISA, b. 1791.

10. CAPT. HEZEKIAH[4] JOHNSON (*Abner,[3] Jacob,[2] William[1]*) of Wallingford and Hamden, Conn., born March 12, 1732 ; died Feb. 21,

1810; married Nov. 1758, Ruth, daughter of Lieut. Caleb and Ruth (Sedgwick) Merriman, great grand-daughter of Capt. Nathaniel Merriman, who was one of the founders of Wallingford, and of Maj.-Gen. Robert Sedgwick, charter member and second captain of the "Ancient and Honorable Artillery Company" of Boston. He was a soldier of the Revolution.

Children :

i. CALEB[5], b. July 18, 1759; graduated at Yale, 1785.
ii. GEORGE, b. Nov. 7, 1760.
iii. CHARLES, b. Nov. 2, 1762.
iv. LUCINDA, b. 1763.
v. RUTH, b. MAy 31, 1765; m. Asahel Hall of Salisbury, N. Y.
vi. BELCHER, b. Dec. 25, 1767; d. June 20, 1837; m. Hannah, daughter of Reynolds and Mary (Rathbun) Cahoon. He removed to Salisbury, N. Y., about 1790.
vii. HEZEKIAH, b. Dec. 25, 1779; m. Elizabeth Tuttle, and inherited the homestead at Hamden, Conn.
viii. DIANTHA, b. July 22, 1770; m. Joseph Shepherd.
ix. SOPHIA, b. Oct. 31, 1774; m. —— Dayton, of New Haven, Conn.
x. CHARITY BETSEY, b. March 23, 1777; m. —— Kneelon.
xi. LUCINDA, b. May 3, 1783; m. Nathan Burr, of Kingsboro, N. Y.

11. JACOB[4] JOHNSON (*Abner*,[3] *Jacob*[2], *William*[1]), born 1742; died 1816; removed to Johnstown, N. Y., about 1800; was a Revolutionary soldier; married Esther Hotchkiss, and had eight children. One son, Jacob,[5] married Sarah Jewett, and is the fourth Jacob in the family. [Tuttle confuses the four Jacobs mentioned in this article.] Jacob[4] had a son Caleb, among whose sons was Judge Stephen Hotchkiss Johnson, father of the Rt. Rev. Joseph H. Johnson, D.D. (born 1847), present Protestant Episcopal Bishop of Los Angeles, California.

THE NEW HAVEN AND WALLINGFORD (CONN.) JOHNSONS.

By James Shepard, Esq., of New Britain, Conn.

There were three brothers by the name of Johnson quite early at New Haven, Conn., viz.: 1. John. 2. Robert. 3. Thomas.

1. John[1] Johnson consented to the covenant at New Haven in 1639. At a court held the third of Nov., 1641, Robert Johnson made claim to the house and lot that was his brother's, John Johnson's deceased. The said Johnson had, before his death, removed to "the Bay" (Massachusetts), and settled at Rowley.

2. Robert[1] Johnson is said to have come from Yorkshire, England (see Salisbury's "Family Histories," Vol. 2, p. 288), as early as 1641, with his four sons, viz.:

4. i. John,[2]
5. ii. Robert.
6. iii. Thomas.
7. iv. William.

They are generally named in the order here given, but the order of their birth is uncertain. The only clew we have to the date of birth of Robert's children is that Dr. Steiner says William was "born about 1630," that Robert's son Robert graduated from Harvard in the class of 1645, and that Thomas, the son of Thomas, is called "Thomas Senr." in the record of his second marriage at New Haven, in 1663, thereby showing that he was older than Thomas the son of Robert. The death record at Newark, N. J., of Thomas Senr., makes the date of his birth 1630. Thomas the son of Robert was probably born soon after 1630, and judging from the college record, his brother

296

Robert was a number of years older. The first we find of Robert Johnson in New Haven is when he made claim to his brother's house, in 1641, upon which he had a verbal claim to secure a loan made in England to his brother John. Robert appears to have been undecided as to whether he would remain in New Haven or go with his brother to "the Bay." In 1644 he was appointed by the General Court a viewer of damage done by "cattell and hoggs" in the Yorkshire quarter; in 1648 he was on a committee entrusted by the General Court to devise means for effectually protecting from such damage; and in 1649 he was made a committee to ascertain "what quantity of corne every man hath sowen or planted this yere that he is to be paid for." In 1649 he "desired that he might haue libertie to make a well in ye streete neere his house." In 1646 he bought six and a half acres of land " in the Necke," and in that year it was recorded that "Thomas yale hath sold unto Robert Johnson 62 acres of upland." (Hoadly's New Haven Colony Records, Vol. 1.) He lived in that part of New Haven then called Yorkshire quarter, now represented by York Street. The name of this quarter may have been derived from Johnson's former residence in England. He died in 1661. The inventory of his estate is dated Nov. 26, 1661, and amounts to £404, 04, 03. His will is recorded at New Haven, in Vol. 1, first part, page 101, and is as follows—

"A writing exhibited as the last Will and Testament of Robert Johnson of New Haven, Deceased."

"Imp. I bequeath my soul to Jesus Christ and my body to the Dust. Also I give to my son Thomas twentie pound as ye other two John and William have had and then my sonne Thomas after my wife has had her thirds to make an equall division among ye sd. three brothers and the land in ye sd. yorkshire quarter I would have my sonn Thomas to have that is ye nine acres belongs to ye housse in part of his portion and I give Jeremiah Johnson a little red cow.

The witnesses,   ROBERT JOHNSON
WILLIAM BRADLY.   his p mark.
CHRISTOPHER TOD, his C T mark."

Jeremiah Johnson, to whom Robert Johnson gave "a little red cow" in his will, was probably Robert's nephew, the son of his deceased brother Thomas.

The name of Robert Johnson's first wife is unknown. He left a widow Adeline, who became the second wife of Robert Hill of New Haven, Jan. 7, 1662. He died in Aug., 1663. On May 22, 1666, she became the second wife of John Scranton of Guilford, Ct., who died Aug. 27, 1671. She deeds land, on Oct. 21, 1781, to "her two sons-in-law, sons to * * * Robert Johnson, of New Haven deceased, to wit, Thomas Johnson and John Johnson husbandman," thereby showing that she was not the mother of the said sons. In this deed she is described as "Adelin Scranton Widow & Relict of John Scranton." She was therefore the step mother of Thomas and John, and after successively marrying three widowers, we find her a widow in 1681. She died in April, 1685.

3.   THOMAS[1] JOHNSON was early in New Haven, and was drowned, with Thomas Ashley, in the harbor, in 1640. It is said that he came with his brother Robert, and he left four sons: i. Thomas,[2] of New Haven and Newark, N. J., 1666, the progenitor of the New Jersey Johnsons. He died Nov. 5, 1694, aged 64. ii. Daniel, of New

Haven. iii. William, of New Haven and Wallingford, Ct., married Sarah Hall, and had 14 children. iv. Jeremiah, of New Haven. Another account omits Jeremiah, and places John of Guilford as the first son; and still another says that William was an independent emigrant from Co. Essex, England, and no relation to these Johnsons from Hull. I have been unable to find any original record of the children of Thomas who, according to Hoadly's New Haven Colony Records, Vol. 1, died in 1640. The children of William, and his descendants in the line of Jacob, are given in the REGISTER, Vol. 55, page 369; and the family of William's son John is given in the Street Genealogy, of 1895, page 15.

4. JOHN[2] JOHNSON (*Robert*[1]) doubtless was born in England. He married Hannah, daughter of John and Hannah Parmlee of Guilford, Ct., Sept., 30, 1651. According to the General Index No. 1, of the New Haven Probate Records, his estate was probated in 1687. His name is in the Index of Vol. 2, with references to pages 5 and 20, but page 5 is missing. The original page 20 is now the first remaining page of records in the said volume, and refers to a petition of John Hodkins, Thomas Tuttle and John Penderson, upon which the Court orders the administrators of the estate of John Johnson deceased, namely, Samuel Johnson and John Johnson, to give an account of their administration within 21 days. This is the only matter concerning his estate that now remains in the Probate Records. No date is given, but the New Haven County Court Records show that his estate was probated as early as 1689. On June 17, 1689, " Samll Johnson and John Johnson Adm. to the estate of their late father John Johnson late of New Haven deceased, intestate, appearing in court was enquired of why they had not put an issue to their paymt. of Debts & dividing of lands according to court order. * * * After much debate about the matter Samll. Johnson propounded that they might choose two men to divide the land & he should be satisfied therein. Whereupon Samll. Johnson chose Ensgn. Samll. Munson & John Johnson chose Lieut. Abraham Dickinson, which the Court approved." (County Court Records, Vol. 1, p. 171.) What interest, if any, John Hodkins, Thomas Tuttle and John Penderson had in the estate is still unknown.

There was some difficulty about the estate, and Samuel left for parts unknown before June 11, 1690, when he was summoned to appear before the court "for his breach of the peace, but it was sd he had withdrawn himself out of towne. * * * John appearing but his brother Samll. being gone it was referred to another time." (County Court Records, Vol. 1, p. 179.) This is the last record found appertaining to the estate. Their mother, the widow Hannah Johnson, was also present at this hearing. Several deeds in the land records by Samuel and John Johnson administrators, show that they were the sons of the deceased John, and their mother Hannah was living as late as March 15, 1693.

The children of John and Hannah Johnson were:

i. DAVID,[3] b. Feb. —, bapt. Mar. 1, 1652.
ii. SAMUEL, b. Feb. 25, 1653, bapt. Mar. following; left New Haven before June 11, 1690.
iii. HANNAH, b. Feb. 4, 1656.
iv. HANNAH, m. Samuel Hummason, June 21, 1677.

8. v. JOHN, b. Aug. 27, 1661; m. Mabel Grannis, Mar. 2, 1684–5.
  vi. SARAH, b. Aug. 26, 1664, baptized the next day; m. John Wolcott of New Haven, Feb. 8, 1683.
 vii. RUTH, b. April 3, 1667; m. Benjamin Dorman, Oct. 10, 1698.
viii. ABIGAIL, b. Apr. 9, 1670; m. Joseph Foot of Branford, before March 15, 1693.
  ix. DANIEL, b. Feb. 21, 1671; m. Mary, dau. of Andrew Sanford of Milford, Dec. 23, 1707. She was the widow of Thomas Tuttle. (Tuttle Family, page 141.)

5. ROBERT² JOHNSON (*Robert¹*), says Dr. Samuel Johnson, "was bred at Cambridge whose name you see near the beginning of their catalogue. He went to his unkle at Rowley and was said to be a very promising candidate for the ministry and was to be settled there but died young." He graduated in the class of 1645. His will was made 13 Sept., 1649, and probated March, 1650. This explains why he is not mentioned in his father's will.

6. THOMAS² JOHNSON (*Robert¹*) died Jan. 4, 1694–5. The "Tuttle Family" gives him several children, but he gave his homestead, that was his father's, and other lands, to his nephew John Johnson, son of John, before his death; and after his decease his nephew John, with wife Mabel, appeared before the Probate Court and swore that it was the will of their uncle Thomas Johnson that all his cattle should be given to his brother William, of Guilford. This disposition of his property indicates that he had no children living at the time of his death; and this inference is corroborated by Dr. Samuel Johnson, who said, in 1757, that this Thomas died a batchelor. The children given in the "Tuttle Family" belong to Thomas the son of Thomas, and the three sons recorded to Thomas Johnson in New Haven, between 1651 and 1664, are, according to Mrs. Salisbury, named in the will of Thomas of Newark.

7. WILLIAM² JOHNSON (*Robert¹*), born about 1630, settled at Guilford, Conn., as early as 1653. He was deacon, town clerk, and many times deputy, from 1665 to 1694. He married Elizabeth, daughter of Francis Bushnell, and died Oct. 27, 1702. (Steiner's History of Guilford, Conn., page 128). He had eleven children, of whom Samuel³ was the father of the celebrated divine, and first President of Columbia College, Dr. Samuel⁴ Johnson of Stratford, Conn. For his family, and other Guilford Johnsons, see Dr. Alvin Talcott's mss. genealogies of Guilford, Conn., families, at the rooms of the New Haven Colony Historical Society, at New Haven, or the copy of the same at the Town Clerk's office at Guilford.

8. JOHN JOHNSON³ (*John,² Robert¹*) was born Aug. 27, 1661, and married, March 2, 1684–5, Mabel, daughter of Edward Granniss and (according to Savage) his second wife Hannah, daughter of John Wakefield of New Haven, Conn. Although sometimes called "Mabel," her name was Mehitable, as appears by numerous deeds, &c. These names are sometimes used interchangeably, and that they belong to the same person in this case is shown by the fact that her brothers John and Joseph Granniss, on Feb. 17, 1721, deed her a piece of land under the name of Mabel Johnson, and on May 14, 1725, she sells the same land under the name of Mehitable Johnson.

John and Mabel Johnson at one time lived in what is now West-field, New Haven, and he had also his grandfather Robert's home-stead in Yorkshire quarter, which was given him by his uncle Thomas. He made his will Dec. 10, 1712. His widow Mehitable was appointed administratrix, the first Monday of Feb., 1712–13. His will is recorded at New Haven, Vol. 4, page 117, and is as fol-lows:

" In the name of God Amen. I John Johnson Senior of New Haven being at this time Sick and weak in my Body Yet of perfect mind and memory thanks be to God for it I Do make and ordain this my Last will and Testament. In manner and form following— firstly and principally I Give my Soul to God hoping for Acceptence and mercy through the merits and righteousness of Christ Jesus my Lord and my body I com-mit to the Earth to be burried Decently at ye discrestion of my Exrt hereafter named and as Concerning ye disposing of all such Temporal Estate as it hath pleased God to bestow upon me I give and dispose there-of as followith— firstly that all my just debts and funeral Expenses shall be paid and Dyscharged.

item, I give and bequeath all my Estate both personall and Real that I shall Dye in my possession of to my persent Dear and Loving Wife Mahitabell Johnson to be wholly and Intirely at her Dispose and Use for her own Comfort or for ye bringing up my children or otherwise to dispose of as they may need and as She Can spare, ytt my will is that the whole of my Estate be Intirely at my wife's Dispose So Long as Shee shall Live a widdow and at her decease or marriage my will is that shee shall have Intirely at her Dispose one third part of what Shall then be Remaining of my Estate and the rest Divided Equally amongst my children Excepting twenty pounds which I do hereby Give of my Es-tate to my Daughter Sarah Johnson more than her Equall Share with the Rest of my children and also my will further is that my Son John John-son Shall have his Equall Share with the Rest of my Children besides What he hath already Had of me and I do Nominate and appoint and hereby Constitute my Present Dear and Loving Wife Sole Executrix of this my last Will and Testament and I do hereby Revoke all former Wills By me at any time made before this. In Witness whereof I have hereunto Set my hand and Affixed my seal this 10th. Day of December 1712.

his
JOHN X JOHNSON.
mark

Signed Sealed and published
   to be the Last will and Testament of the above said John Johnson

Before ye witness	Witnesses Sworn In Court in the
JOHN PUNDERSON	Usual form
JOHN LATHROP	Test Jos' WHITING, Clerk."

" Children names,
John, Thomas, Ann, Sarah, Joseph 14, Benjamin 11, Robert 8, James 6, Mahitabell 5, Hannah 3, year old."

Various deeds show that widow Mehitable resided in New Haven until 1729 or later, but in 1732 was living in Middletown, Conn., and in 1738 at Branford, Conn. In a deed dated Dec. 31, 1751, Thomas of Middletown, Joseph of Hartford, Benjamin of Durham, Robert of Middletown, Timothy Rose of Woodbury and Mehitable his wife, give to " our brother in law Benjamin Hands of Middle-town " land that was " our Honrd. Father's Mr. John Johnson of New Haven, decd.," and also land sold by Moses Blackslee to " our Honrd. Mother Mrs. Mehitable Johnson decd.," thus showing that she died between 1738 and 1751. Her tombstone at Durham, Conn., says she died Dec. 9, 1745, aged 79.

The children of John and Mabel Johnson were :

9. i.   JOHN,[4] b. March 3, 1686-7. He is John of Wallingford.
  ii.   THOMAS, b. Jan. 12, 1689-90; removed to Middletown, Conn., in or before 1722. He was called Capt.
  iii.   ANNE, b. Feb., 1691; m. Willet Ranney of Middletown, Conn., April 20, 1720.
  iv.   SARAH, b. April 9, 1694.
  v.   DANIEL, b. April 22, 1696; not named in the list of children appended to his father's will.
  vi.   JOSEPH, b. Dec. 2, 1698; was living in Durham, Conn., in 1732, Middletown, Conn., 1738, and Hartford, Conn., in 1751.
  vii.   BENJAMIN, b. March 9, 1701; removed to Durham, Conn.
  viii.   ROBERT, b. June 5, 1703; lived at Middletown, Conn., 1732.
  ix.   JAMES, b. Sept. 3, 1705.
  x.   MEHITABLE, b. Feb. 29, 1707-8; Timothy Rose of Branford, Conn., Sept. 22, 1730. She was living there in 1738, but lived at Woodbury, Conn., in 1751.
  xi.   HANNAH, b. May 23, 1710; m. Benjamin Hands of Middletown, Conn., between 1732 and 1738. (New Haven Land Records, Vol. 9, p. 277, and Vol. 10, p. 460.) He was son of Benjamin and Sarah (Ward) Hands, b. Oct. 4, 1706. (Steiner.)

9.   JOHN[4] JOHNSON (*John,*[3] *John,*[2] *Robert*[1]) was born March 3, 1687-8. He removed to Wallingford, and there married, Jan. 12, 1711, Sarah Jennings, the widow of Nathaniel Hitchcock who died May 12, 1710. She at that time had three Hitchcock children, viz.: i. Sarah, born March 31, 1705; married Aaron Cook, June 14, 1722. ii. Elizabeth, born Jan. 11, 1707. iii. Hannah, born Jan. 11, 1709; married Caleb Mathews, March 7, 1727; died Dec. 5, 1731. The John Johnson of Wallingford (see John,[2] son of Walter,[1] *post*), who married Mary Chatterton in 1710, should not be confounded with this (No. 9) John, who lived in the south western part of the town, by "Fresh medows," near the Cheshire line; while the former lived at what is now Meriden. I find no record after 1722 of more than one John Johnson in Wallingford. He is identified by two deeds in New Haven Land Records, Vol. 6, pages 644-5, in the first of which Mehitable Johnson, of New Haven, gives her "loving son John Johnson of the town of Wallingford" 9 acres of land, being part of land laid out to "my Honoured ffather-in-law John Johnson late of New Haven deceased," dated April 30, 1725. The same day, John Johnson of Wallingford deeds this land to Benjamin Todd, and describes it as part of the land of "my Honoured grand ffather John Johnson Decd."

In Mrs. Evelyn MacCurdy Salisbury's "Family Histories and Genealogies" (Vol. 2, page 288), containing much valuable information, but some mistakes, is a letter from a great-grandson of Robert[1] Johnson, Dr. Samuel[4] Johnson of Stratford, written to his son Hon. William Samuel[5] Johnson, and dated Jan. 6, 1757, a part of which (with generation numbers added to indicate the line of John of Wallingford) is as follows:

"* * And now I proceed to set down to you all I know of our progenitors. The Father of our Family in this country was John [Robert] Johnson, one of the first founders of New Haven, and lived on the northwest Corner of the Square of Lots Mr. Mix and the Colleges are on, over against Darling's. He came from the noted town of Hull (*al*

Kingston-upon-Hull) near York in Yorkshire, and it was said he had two Brothers, one the Father of the Johnsons at Newark in the Jersies, the other the Father of those in Boston Government, who settled at Rowley about 20 miles eastward of Boston.   John [Robert] our ancestor had John[2], Robert[2], Thomas,[2] and William.[2]   John[2] had John,[3] Samuel,[3] and Daniel,[3] the two last * * died * * leaving no male issue. * * * [John[3]] was Father to John[4] (who settled at Wallingford * * *) and Thomas[4], who is Capt. Johnson of Middletown * * * "

It is interesting to note that the male line as given by Dr. Johnson, largely from his personal knowledge, is identical with the lineage as here worked out from the records, in 1897, one hundred and forty years later, and without any knowledge of that letter. This is especially important, as all published Johnson genealogy of this branch omits one generation, leaving out the middle John. This was probably caused by his living at New Haven, cotemporaneously with John the son of William, or Wingle.*

While John[3] (John,[2] Robert[1]) may have been obscure in a sense, as stated, he was by no means an unworthy man.   The large amount of property received by deeds of gift from his uncle Thomas shows him to have been a favorite with that uncle, and he must have been in some respects the superior of his cousins and brothers, in order to have merited these favors.   The numerous deeds given by his widow after his decease shows that he was a large land owner. His son John,[4] of Wallingford, left an unusually large estate for those times, over three thousand pounds, and although there was another John Johnson in Wallingford with him, for more than ten years, he was considered of such importance that any reference to John Johnson of Wallingford was always understood as referring to John the son of John, Jr.   One deed in the Wallingford records describes John Johnson as a weaver, and, judging from the inventory, this John was the one who died in 1744. John Johnson, of Wallingford, died Oct. 17, 1744. His widow died July 14, 1748. His will, dated Feb., 1743–4, is recorded in New Haven, Vol. 6, page 573. It names wife Sarah, son Daniel, son Jennings, son Amos, daughter Barbary, wife of Abraham Ives, daughter Ester, wife of Merriman Munson, daughter Phebe, wife of Dydimos Parker, daughter Ruth, wife of Abel Hall, daughter Patience, " who is unmarried." The land given to his three sons was to " be entailed unto my said sons and to their heirs for ye space of one hundred years from ye date of this present will," but notwithstanding this provision, most of it passed out of the family in a few years. The inventory of his estate amounted to the unusually large sum of £3017. 7. 1.

The children of John and Sarah Johnson were:

i.   ESTHER,[5] b. May 4, 1712; m. Merriam Munson, Jan. 24, 1733.
ii. RARBARA, b. Feb. 5, 1714; m. Abraham Ives, May 11, 1736.
iii. DAMARIS, b. Jan. 31, 1716; m. Wait Ebernantha, Dec. 29, 1737.
iv. DANIEL, b. Dec. 14, 1717; m. Ruth Todd, Dec. 26, 1744. He d. in 1761.
v.   PHEBE, b. April 28, 1720; m. Dydimus Parker.
vi. JENNINGS, b. Jan. 7, 1722; m. Sarah Johnson, Oct. 20, 1748. He removed to Southington, Conn., where the land he left is still owned by his descendants. His family is given in Timlow's History of that town, page cxxxvii.
vii. RUTH, b. Oct. 1, 1723; m. Abel Hall.
10. viii. AMOS, b. Mar. 4, 1726; m. Abigail Holt, Apr. 24, 1746.
ix. PATIENCE, b. July 28, 1728; m. Daniel Culver, Dec. 17, 1746.

* See REGISTER, *ante*, Vol. 55, page 369.—EDITOR. (Page 292, this volume.)

We thus find that Sarah (Jennings) Johnson was the mother of twelve children, three by her first and nine by her second husband.

10. AMOS[5] JOHNSON (*John*,[4] *John*,[3] *John*,[2] *Robert*[1]), born March 4, 1726 ; married April 24, 1746, Abigail, daughter of Joseph and Abigail (Curtis) Holt. This parentage is shown by a deed from William Johnson and Tamer (Holt) Johnson of Durham, and Amos Johnson and Abigail (Holt) Johnson of Wallingford, conveying "Two Rights of land which formerly belonged to Ensign Thomas Curtiss late of Wallingford Deceased," Jan. 16, 1748–9. (Wallingford Land Records, Vol. 11, p. 521.) He resided in the parish of Northford, in the town of Wallingford, near the Branford town line. He served in the French and Indian war, 1758–9. Davis's History of Wallingford says that he died in the Revolutionary War, at White Plains, N. Y., 1776, but this is an error, because he was living at Northford, Dec. 9, 1783, when he and his wife Abigail leased their house, &c., at Northford, to Moses and Esther Peck. (Wallingford Land Records, Vol. 23, page 423.) It is certain, however, that one Amos Johnson of Wallingford, Conn., was in Capt. James Peck's Co., Sept. 17, 1777, but I do not know whether it was this Amos or his son. Amos Johnson who died at White Plains was probably from Branford, Conn., and son of Edward and Elizabeth (Barnes) Johnson. (Woodruff's Litchfield, Conn., Register, page 113.) Amos of Wallingford gave numerous deeds of land, between 1747 and 1785, the last of which bears date April 27, 1785. Family tradition says that he removed west, about 1785, where he died, and that his widow returned and married Jonah Todd. Jonah Todd of Woodbridge, Conn., died between 1802 and 1804, leaving a widow Abigail.

The children of Amos and Abigail Johnson were :

i. LUCY,[6] b. Sept. 11, 1747; m. Samuel Preston, Sept. 7, 1769.
ii. ESTHER, b. Nov. 16, 1749 ; m. Moses Peck.
iii. SIBYL, b, Sept. 16, 1751.
iv. AMOS, m. at Wallingford, Eunice Daly, Sept. 15, 1777; bought land at Farmington, Conn., Oct. 14, 1780.
v. SIMEON, m. Merriam Johnson, March 4, 1773. His father deeds him land in 1772.
vi. ELIHU, b. June 7, 1773.

1. WALTER[1] JOHNSON. Savage says he was at Middletown, Conn., 1684, but no record of him is now found there, neither has his parentage or previous history been learned. He was at Wallingford, Conn., as early as Feb. 23, 1691–2, when he agrees "with Roger Tyler for a certain piece of land that was granted to him in lieu of a home lott at the north end of said town." (Wallingford Land Records, Vol. 1, page 151.) Several other pieces "laid out to Walter Johnson" are referred to on page 175, the same book, under date May 4, 1692. Several deeds to and from his sons Lambert and John are also of record, on various dates up to 1718. Two deeds in 1714 give each of his sons their portion of his estate, and refer to land they had already received that was their "own mother's." His wife was a daughter of Nehemiah Roys of Wallingford, as is shown by the will of the said Roys, which gives 5 shillings to his grandson John Johnson, and a cross cut saw to John's father, Walter Johnson. (Wallingford Land Records, Vol. 2, page 75.) In a deed dated April 11, 1721,

John Johnson refers to land "that has, may or should come unto me * * * in the right of my Honored grandfather Mr. Nehemiah Roys." (*Ibid*, Vol. 3, page 401.) Walter Johnson died Feb. 6, 1731.

His children were :

2. i. JOHN,[2] m. Mary Chatterton, Nov. 2, 1710.
3. ii. LAMBERT, m. Rebecca Curtis, Mar. 1, 1716.

2. JOHN[2] JOHNSON (*Walter*[1]). No birth record. He married Mary, daughter of John and Mary (Clements) Chatterton of New Haven, Conn., who was born April 28, 1692. Davis's History of Wallingford says "she died within that year," the year of her marriage, but she was living March 19, 1719, when "John Johnson and Mary his wife, formerly Mary Chatterton," deed a portion of the estate of John Chatterton her father, and Lydia Chatterton her sister, to Barnabas Baldwin. (New Haven Land Records, Vol. 5, page 270.) The genealogies in Davis's History were compiled by Elihu Yale, and he appears to have repeatedly overcome seemingly conflicting records by putting some one out of the way and creating for them a death record. Thus, when he supposed that he had found one John Johnson with two wives, he disposed of the matter by saying the first wife "died," and so Mr. Yale got out of trouble by making trouble for all who consult these premature death records in his work. But this did not kill Mary Johnson, for in fact she lived until Sept. 21, 1774, when she died a widow in New Jersey. Instead of one John with two wives, there were two Johns each with his own wife, living at Wallingford at the same time for over ten years; just as there had been in the prior generation two John Johnsons living at the same time in New Haven.

John,[2] the son of Walter,[1] lived in the north part of Wallingford, which is now Meriden. He removed to Whippenny, N. J., before June 9, 1722, as is shown by a deed of that date. (New Haven Land Records, Vol. 4, page 115.) This is the second branch of Connecticut Johnsons in New Jersey.

His children, recorded at Wallingford, Conn., were :

i. JOHN,[3] b. Aug. 12, 1711; d. in N. J., May 4, 1776.
ii. HANNAH, b. Dec. 31, 1712.
iii. ELISHA, b. Sept. 8, 1714.
iv. MOSES, b. July 26, 1716.
v. CAZIAH, b. April 22, 1718.
vi. ESTHER, b. April 20, 172-.

3. LAMBERT[2] JOHNSON (*Walter*[1]). No birth record. He married Rebecca, daughter of Thomas and Mary (Merriman) Curtis, March 1, 1716, who was born Aug. 21, 1697. He died at Wallingford, Conn., Nov. 27, 1726. His widow "Ribeckah" was appointed to administer on his estate, April 3, 1726. (New Haven Probate Records, Vol. 5, page 360.) His will is recorded in the same Vol., page 426, and names Benjamin, eldest son, son Cornelius, and daughters Mary, Anna and Rebekah.

His children were :

i. BENJAMIN,[3] b. Dec. 10, 1716.
ii. CORNELIUS, b. Feb. 13, 1719.
iii. MARY, b. June 3, 1720.
iv. ANNA, no birth record.
v. REBECCA, no birth record.

SUPPLEMENTARY NOTES ON THE JOHNSON FAMILY.

Communicated from the MSS. of Hon. RALPH D. SMYTH, by DR. BERNARD C. STEINER.

In addition to the account given by Mr. James Shepard in the REGISTER, [1] *ante*, page 132, I am able to add the following data:

1. JOHN[1] JOHNSON, of Rowley, married Susan ——, and had children:
    i. JOHN[2], who lived at Rowley, and was captain in King Philip's war; m. Dec. 1, 1655, Hannah, dau. of Anthony Crosby, and had: 1. *John*[3], b. 1668; 2. *Samuel*, b. 1671; 3. *Hannah*, and perhaps others.
    ii. ELIZABETH.
    iii. THOMAS.

3. THOMAS[1] JOHNSON (*ante*, page 133) had children:
    i. THOMAS[2], m. Ellena——, and had: 1. *Joseph*[3], b. Nov. 30, 1651; 2. *John*, b. Apr. 27, 1654; 3. *Abigail*, b. Jan. 16, 1656–7; 4. *Loving* (dau.), b. Nov. 5, 1659. 5. *Thomas*, b. July 11, 1664; 6. *Eliphalet*, b.1668; d. Apr. 20, 1718; had ch.: i. Eliphalet. ii. Nathaniel, b. Feb. 6, 1698; d. æ. 67, Apr. 26, 1766; lived in Newark, N. J.; m. Sarah, dau. of Capt.David Ogden, who d. Apr. 20, 1777, ae. 78. (Their ch. were: 1. Thomas[5]. 2. David, b. 1720; d. Oct. 22, 1776. 3. Stephen, b. May 17, 1724; A. B. Yale, 1743; lived in Lyme, Conn., d. Nov. 8, 1786. 4. Martha, m.——Ward. 5. Catharine, m.——Banks.) iii. John. iv. Samuel. v. Timothy.
    ii. DANIEL, of New Haven, m. Martha——; and had: *Daniel*[3], b. May 26, 1656.
    iii. WILLIAM is given a second wife, Abigail, by Mr. Smyth. His dau. *Abigail*,[3] b. Dec. 6, 1670; m. Joseph Lines, May 30, 1692.
    iv. JEREMIAH,* of Derby, had the following ch.: 1. *Jeremiah*[3], b. Apr. 25, 1664. 2. *Samuel*, b. Mch. 8, 1670. 3. *Tamar*, m.——Wooster. 4. *Benajah*. 5. *A son*.

7. DEA. WILLIAM[2] JOHNSON (Robert[1]) of Guilford (*ante*, page 135), married Elizabeth Bushnell, July 2, 1651.
    Their children were:

---

* See account of his descendants in " Seymour, Past and Present," pp. 495–502; published by William C. Sharp, Seymour, Conn., 1902. Also, see references in " Town Records of Derby, Conn., 1655–1710 "; published by the Sarah Riggs Humphreys Chapter, D. A. R., Derby, 1901.—JAMES SHEPARD.

[1] Page 296, this volume.

i. ANNA,³ b. 1652; d. 1702; m. John Fowler of Guilford, in 1682. He d. Dec., 1735.
ii. HANNAH, b. Mch. 24, 1654; d. young.
iii. ELIZABETH, b. 1655; m. Dec. 11, 1674, Samuel Hall of Guilford. He d. Feb. 11, 1733.
iv. MARY, b. Feb. 1, 1656–7; d. July 6, 1732; m. Dec. 23, 1676, Thomas Stone. He died Dec. 1, 1683.
v. SARAH, b. Nov. 22, 1658; d. 1666.
vi. MARTHA, b. Dec. 27, 1659; d. May 8, 1660.
vii. DANIEL, d. young.
viii. ABIGAIL, b. Oct. 24, 1661; d. 1664.
ix. MERCY, b. Jan. 11, 1665; d. 1688; m. John Scranton of Guilford, who d. Sept. 2, 1703.
x. SARAH, Aug. 13, 1667; d. Oct. 10, 1669.
A. xi. SAMUEL, b. June 5, 1670; d. May 8, 1727.
xii. NATHANIEL, b. Apr. 12, 1672; d. June 24, 1672.

A. DEA. SAMUEL³ JOHNSON (*William²*, *Robert¹*) of Guilford, married Nov. 7, 1694, Mary, daughter of David Sage of Middletown. She died Mch. 13, 1726. His list in 1716 was £87.14. 9; and his fulling mill was rated at £3.

Their children were:

i. WILLIAM,⁴ b. Sept. 4, 1695; d. Oct. 18, 1695.
ii. SAMUEL, b. Oct. 14, 1696; A. B. Yale, 1714; d. Jan. 6, 1772; first president of King's College, now Columbia University; m. (1) Charity, dau. of Col. Richard Floyd, and widow of Benjamin Nicoll, Sept. 26, 1725. She d. June 1, 1758; and he m. (2) Sarah, widow of William Beach, June 18, 1761. She d. Feb. 9, 1763. By his first wife he had: 1. *William Samuel⁵*, b. Oct. 7, 1727; A. B. Yale, 1744; d. Nov. 14, 1819. Signer of the Federal Constitution, and president of Columbia College. 2. *William*, b. Mch. 9, 1730–1; A. B. Yale, 1748; d. June 20, 1756, at London.
iii. MARY, b. May 8, 1699; d. Aug. 31, 1779; m. Mch. 21, 1723, Ebenezer Chittenden, father of Gov. Thomas Chittenden, of Vt.
iv. DAVID, b. June 5, 1701; lived in Durham and in New York State; m. Ruth———. Their ch. were: 1. *Mercy*,⁵ b. Mch. 6, bap. Mch. 13, 1727–8. 2. *David*, bap. June 14, 1730; m. Jerusha Thomas, Mch. 14, 1751. 3. *Mary*, bap. Mch. 3, 1733–4.
v. ELIZABETH, b. Oct. 19, 1703; d. Sept. 28, 1712.
vi. CAPT. NATHANIEL, b. Apr. 17, 1705; d. June 24, 1793; lived in Guilford; m. (1) Aug. 2, 1727, Margery, dau. of John Morgan of Groton. She d. Oct. 2, 1752; and he m. (2) in 1755, Diana, dau. of Capt. Andrew Ward, and widow of Daniel Hubbard. She d. Mch. 27, 1797. His ch., all by the first wife, were: 1. *Margery⁵*, b. Feb. 24, 1728. 2. *Samuel*, b. Mch. 18, 1729; d. May 1, 1808; lived in Guilford; m. (1) June 20, 1756, Margery Collins. She d. Aug 13, 1806: and he m. (2) Oct. 7, 1807, Ruth, widow of George Bartlett. She d. Oct. 11, 1829. 3. *Timothy*, b. Aug. 17, 1732; of Branford; d. Aug. 12, 1758; m. Feb. 10, 1757, Mary, dau. of Dr. Orchard Guy. She d. Sept. 15, 1816, having m. (2) Dr. Wm. Gould, May 5, 1763. 4. *Nathaniel*, b. Oct. 4, 1735; of Guildford; d. Mch. 16, 1798; 'm. Hannah, dau. of Thomas Hill, Dec. 10, 1761. She d. Dec. 27, 1808. 5. *William*, b. Dec. 17, 1737;was killed in the Revolutionary war; m. Abigail, dau. of Joseph Hotchkin, and widow of Edmund Ward, in 1760. 6. *Rachel*, b. May 12, 1742; d. Nov. 23, 180–.
vii. ABIGAIL, b. Apr. 19, 1707; d. Aug. 6, 1781; m. George Bartlett of North Guilford, Apr. 24, 1728. He d. Feb. 13, 1766.
viii. WILLIAM, b. Apr. 19, 1709; d. single, in Middletown; with his brothers, Samuel and Daniel, sold his estate in Guilford to brother Nathaniel, Apr. 20, 1730.
ix. MERCY, b. Dec. 19, 1710; d. June 23, 1725.
x. ELIZABETH, b. Feb. 20, 1713; d. Aug. 13, 1718.
xi. TIMOTHY, b. Oct. 19, 1715; d. May 29, 1732.

DUTCH JOHNSONS IN CONNECTICUT

By Donald Lines Jacobus, M.A., of New Haven, Conn.

Among the numerous Johnson families of old Connecticut we have reason to suppose that two, at least, were of Dutch origin. There has been much speculation concerning the antecedents of William Johnson of New Haven and Wallingford, Conn., whose family is given in the Register, vol. 55, p. 369. Mr. James Shepard surmises that he might have [1] been a son of Thomas Johnson, one of the three brothers from Yorkshire, Eng., who was drowned in New Haven harbor in 1640 (Register, vol. 56, [2] p. 133). This poor Thomas has been of inestimable value to the genealogists, who have bestowed on him as offspring a large number of stray Johnsons. In strict fact, he left two sons, Thomas of Newark, N. J., and Jeremiah of Derby, Conn. (New Haven Proprietors' Records, vol. 2, pp. 329–330) ; and there is not a shadow of evidence to prove that William was his son.

Then, who was William Johnson? Perhaps the following facts will throw some light on the question. The death of a certain "Old Richard" Johnson is recorded in New Haven on 25 March 1679. His estate was administered 1 April 1679, when we find him called, not Richard, but "Dericke" Johnson (Probate Records, vol. 1, p. 182), and after the payment of debts, the court granted the remainder of his estate to William Johnson (County Court Records, vol. 1, p. 115 ; and Deeds, vol. 1, p. 73). No mention is made of the relationship between them, but it is evident that they were not father and son. If, however, we remember that Richard is called Derrick, and that William himself frequently appears on record as Wingle, it is pretty safe to assume that they were of Dutch descent, and very likely stood in the relation of uncle and nephew to each other.

Much more perplexing is the origin of Walter Johnson of Wallingford, Conn., whose immediate family has been carefully compiled by Mr. James Shepard and published in the Register, vol. 56, p. 139. Up to the [3] present time nothing has been known concerning him, except that he appeared in Wallingford before 1692, married a nameless daughter of Nehemiah and Hannah (Morgan) Royce, and died in 1731, leaving two sons, John and Lambert. The following record from the Dutch church of Flatbush, L. I., adds considerably to our meagre information : "1689, July 5. Wouter Jansen widv. of Johana Rys of N. Eng. at Wallinford, to Tryntie Henerig, wid. of Wm. Edwards, liv. Pennu (?)." Two facts are made clear by this record of our Walter Johnson's second marriage. In the first place it discloses the full name of his first wife, Joanna Royce. In the second place, taken in connection with his signing his name Janson in Wallingford deeds, it indicates Dutch blood. Moreover, it leads to the surmise that John was Walter's only child by the Royce alliance, and that Lambert was the offspring of this second marriage. At any rate, John is named in his grandfather Royce's will, while Lambert is not ; and John deeds away Royce land, while Lambert does not. Moreover, late in life, Walter Johnson deeds a piece of land to his son Lambert, in consideration of which the latter is to maintain his father and mother for the rest of their lives. It looks very much as if this widow Tryntie was Lambert's mother.

Yet, interesting as these discoveries are, they do not go very far toward lifting the veil that obscures the early life of Walter Johnson. The prob-

[1] Page 292, this volume.
[2] Page 297, this volume.
[3] Page 303, this volume.

lem is made more complex by a power of attorney (Wallingford Deeds, vol. 5, p. 454), granted in 1728 by John Benham of Kings Co., N. Y., Lambert Johnson and wife Anna of Richmond, N.Y., Jacob Johnson and wife Sara of Richmond, and Evert Van Namen and wife Winefrut. John, Anna, Sarah, and Winifred were four of the children of Joseph Benham of Wallingford by his wife Winifred King of Boston. Lambert and Jacob Johnson and Evert Van Namen, husbands of the three Benham girls, lived on Staten Island, where they belonged to the Dutch Reformed Church. This document is surprising, as it proves that two Dutch Johnsons, of the same generation as Walter, married Wallingford girls; and one of them bore the name of Lambert, which was also the name of one of Walter's sons. A natural supposition is that they were brothers of his, and met the Benham girls while visiting his home.

As is well known, the Dutch rarely bore a permanent surname, but went by a patronymic derived from the father's Christian name. Thus, Lambert Johnson and Jacob Johnson were simply Lambert and Jacob, sons of John or Jan; but before 1700 the Dutch in America had begun to retain the father's patronymic after the English fashion, so it need not surprise us to find in the Staten Island records that Lambert and Jacob Johnson were sometimes known as Lambert and Jacob Wouters. This implies that they were sons of a certain Jan Wouters (John son of Walter), and that they sometimes retained the Wouters and sometimes called themselves Jansen after their father's Christian name. This makes it all the more likely that Walter Johnson was their brother, for, as the son of Jan Wouters, he would be named after his grandfather Walter or Wouter.

Consequently, it is necessary to locate a Jan Wouters who could have been father of Walter, Lambert, and Jacob. And what is our amazement to learn that Jacob Johnson, son of John Wouters, was born in Branford, Conn., 31 December 1672 (Branford Records, vol. 1, p. 174). Here is a Dutch Jacob Johnson who, learning the English tongue in his infancy, would be most eligible to marry an English girl. That he is identical with the Jacob of Staten Island is proved by the father's name; and his wife, Sarah Benham, was born four years later, 6 September 1676. According to Savage, Jan Wouters lived at Branford from 1667 to 1673; and, when we come to search for his antecedents we find that in 1667 he owned salt meadows in Flatbush, L. I., the very place where Walter Johnson, undoubtedly his son, married his second wife. From Branford he returned to Flatbush, where in 1678 he hired out his son Ruth (Rutgert) to his brother-in-law Laurens Jurianse. He was living in 1695, when he calls himself of New York.

Jan Wouters is by no means an uncommon name, and it will therefore require some evidence to prove that our man of that name, who was a master-shoemaker by trade, was identical with Jan Wouters Van der Bosch, whose name appears in the Flatbush Church Records of this period. On 12 May 1678 were baptized Jacobus, aged $5\frac{1}{2}$, Judith, aged $2\frac{5}{8}$, and Jan, aged $1\frac{1}{4}$, children of Jan Wouters Van der Bosch and Weintie Peters, who came from Stanford, New England. It is probable that the original record reads "Branford," and that "Stanford" is an error of the copyist who prepared these records for the press; for a limited search in Stamford, Conn., has failed to reveal the presence there of any Jan Wouters or Van der Bosches. Moreover, the age of Jacobus (the Latinized form of Jacob or James) exactly corresponds with the age of Jacob Johnson, son of Jan Wouters, who was born at Branford in December 1672. On the whole, it is extremely improbable that two Jan Wouters, one at Branford and the other at Stamford, each had a son Jacob born in the same month of the same year. Another proof of identity is the fact that Jan Wouters Van der Bosch married Weintie Peters, while Laurens Jurianse Haf married Kenira Peters; and we have already mentioned that Laurens Jurianse was brother-in-law of our Jan Wouters.

With these facts established, it is possible to sketch the earlier generations of Walter Johnson's family.

1. JAN[1] WOUTERS VAN DER BOSCH, son of Wouter Van der Bosch, born about 1638, resided at Flatbush, L. I., and Branford, Conn., and died after 1695. He married first ARENTJE ARENTS; and secondly WEINTIE PETERS, whose sister Kenira Peters married, 5 July 1676, Laurens Jurianse Haf. The Peters family came from Amersfoort.

Children by first wife:

   2. i. LAMBERT[2] JANSEN, bapt. at New York 17 Nov. 1660.
     ii. HENDRICK JANSEN, bapt. at New York 30 Mar. 1663.
   3. iii. WOUTER JANSEN, b. probably at Flatbush abt. 1666.

Children by second wife:

     iv. RUTGERT JANSEN, bapt. at New York 16 Nov. 1669; m. there ANNETJE GERRETS.
     v. BENJAMIN JANSEN, bapt. at New York 9 Apr. 1671.
   4. vi. JACOB JANSEN, b. at Branford 31 Dec. 1672.
     vii. JUDITH JANSEN, b. abt. Dec. 1675; m. JOHN ANDERSON of New York.
     viii. JAN JANSEN, b. abt. Feb. 1677.
     ix. SARA JANSEN, bapt. at Flatbush 5 Dec. 1680.
     x. CORNELIS JANSEN, bapt. at Flatbush 20 Jan. 1682.
     xi. STINTIE JANSEN, bapt. at Flatbush 28 Sept. 1684.
   5. xii. ANTJE JANSEN (?), b. abt. 1688.

2. LAMBERT[2] JANSEN or WOUTERS (*Jan*[1]), baptized at New York 17 Nov. 1660, settled on Staten Island. He married ANNA BENHAM of Wallingford, who was born in 1669.

   Children:

     i. WINNIFRET[3] JANSEN, bapt. at Staten Island 5 May 1696. The witnesses of the christening were Jan Wauterzen (perhaps her uncle Jan Jansen) and Tryntie Hendricksen (perhaps Walter Johnson's wife Tryntie Henerig).
     ii. AAFYE, bapt. 7 Sept. 1698. The witness was Jacob Jansen.
     iii. LAMBERT, bapt. 22 Apr. 1707. The witness was Evert Van Namen.
     iv. SARA, dau. of Lambert "Wouters," bapt. 19 Apr. 1709. The witnesses were Evert Van Namen and Sarah Jans.

3. WOUTER[2] JANSEN (*Jan*[1]), born, probably at Flatbush, about 1666, settled at Wallingford, Conn., where he was known as Walter Johnson, and died 6 Feb. 1731. He married first JOANNA ROYCE, who was born about 1670 and died about 1688; and secondly at Flatbush, 5 July 1689, TRYNTIE HENERIG, widow of William Edwards.

   Child by first wife:

     i. JOHN,[3] b. abt. 1688; m. 2 Nov. 1710, MARY CHATTERTON of New Haven; removed to Whippenny, N. J. (REGISTER, vol. 56, p. 140) *

   Child by second wife:

   6. ii. LAMBERT, b. abt. 1691.

4. JACOB[2] JANSEN or WOUTERS (*Jan*[1]), born at Branford 31 Dec. 1672, married SARAH BENHAM of Wallingford, who was born 6 Sept. 1676, and settled on Staten Island.

*Page 304, this volume.

Children:
  i. JACOB,[3] bapt. 25 Mar. 1701. The witnesses were Lambert and
     Reyne Jansen.
7. ii. CORNELIS, son of Jacob "Wouters," bapt. 20 Apr. 1703. The wit-
     nesses were Thomas Sutton and Susanna Du Secoy.
  iii. WYNTIE, bapt. 3 July 170-. The witnesses were Lambert Jansen
     and his wife.
  iv. JOHANNA, bapt. 22 Apr. 1707.
  v. BENJAMIN, son of Jacob "Wouters," bapt. 23 Oct. 1711. The wit-
     nesses were Hendrick Maarlin and Antie Wouters.

5. ANTJE[2] JANSEN or ANNA JOHNSON (*Jan*[1]), born about 1688, died
   after 1752, seems to belong to this family. As Antie Wouters she
   witnessed the christening of Benjamin Jansen. She married JOHN
   JENNER or JENNES of Staten Island, and in accordance with Dutch
   custom appears on record under her maiden name of Wouters at
   the christening of her daughter Sara, and of Johnson at the christening of her daughter Elsje.
   Children:
  i. SARAH JENNER, bapt. 5 June 1720. The witnesses were Evert Van
     Namen and Jenneken Van Naman.
  ii. JOHN JENNER, m. AELTYE MARLIN, and had issue: *Aentje, Jan,
     Willem*, and *Elsye*.
  iii. LAMBERT JENNER, m. ANNA MARLIN, and had issue: *Sara, Antie,*
     and *Maria*.
  iv. ANTJE JENNER, m. JOACHIM STILLWELL, and had issue: *Richard*
     and *Jan*.
  v. WILLEM JENNER, m. JANNETYE GARRETSE, and had issue: *Antje*.
  vi. ELSJE JENNER, bapt. 1 Sept. 1734. The witnesses were Lambert
     Jenner and Wyntje Johnson.

6. LAMBERT[3] JOHNSON (*Walter*,[2] *Jan*[1]), born about 1691, died 27 Nov.
   1726, lived at Wallingford. He married, 1 Mar. 1716, REBECCA
   CURTIS.
   Children:
  i. BENJAMIN,[4] b. 10 Dec. 1716; m. 11 Apr. 1751, MARY DOOLITTLE.
     His family lived at Bantam, Conn., where his sons *Benjamin*[5] and
     Lambert are buried.
8. ii. CORNELIUS, b. 13 Feb. 1719.
  iii. MARY, b. 3 June 1720.
  iv. ANNA, m. 12 Oct. 1743, AZARIAH PERKINS of Bethany, Conn.
  v. REBECCA, m. (1) 3 Apr. 1745, BENJAMIN PERKINS; m. (2) 13 Mar.
     1752, JOHN WILMOT; m. (3) 3 Aug. 1756, SAMUEL THOMAS. She
     lived at Woodbridge, Conn.

7. CORNELIS[2] JANSEN (*Jacob*,[2] *Jan*[1]), baptized in the Dutch Church on
   Staten Island 20 Apr. 1703. He married SARAH MAMBRUT, evidently of French stock.
   Children:
  i. SARAH,[4] bapt. 6 Apr. 1724. The witnesses were Antony Van Pelt
     and Lady Mambrut.
  ii. MARIA, bapt. 20 Feb. 1726. The witnesses were Jaques Seguin and
     Lady Mambrut.
  iii. RACHEL, bapt. 25 Dec. 1728. The witnesses were Estienne and
     Marie Mersereux.

8. CORNELIUS[4] JOHNSON (*Lambert*,[3] *Walter*,[2] *Jan*[1]), born at Wallingford
   13 Feb. 1719, removed to Waterbury, Conn., where he died about
   1802. Administration was granted on his estate 3 May 1802

(Waterbury Probate Records, vol. 3, p. 317). He married ELIZA-
BETH LEWIS.

Children:

i.   ELIZABETH,[5] b. 2 Jan. 1750; d. 12 Sept. 1766.
ii. ASA, b. abt. 1751; d. 13 Dec. 1751.
iii. ASA, b. 24 June 1754; d. 8 Feb. 1758.
iv. JESSE, b. 27 July 1756; m. 23 Aug. 1780, HANNAH BEACH, widow of
     John.
v.   CORNELIUS, b. 13 Nov. 1758; d. June, 1762.
vi. LYMAN, b. 21 Jan. 1761; m. 6 Mar. 1780, MARY HOADLEY.
vii. CORNELIUS.

ONE LINE OF DESCENT
FROM
CAPT. EDWARD JOHNSON OF WOBURN, MASS.

By ALFRED JOHNSON, Litt.D., of Boston, Mass.

1. CAPT. EDWARD[1] JOHNSON † (*William, John, William*), joiner,
baptized at Canterbury, co. Kent, England, 16 Sept. 1598, emigrated
to New England in 1637, and died at Woburn, Mass., 23 Apr. 1672.
He was one of the founders of the town of Woburn, where, as well as
in the Colony at large, he held many important public offices.   He is
famous as the author of the "Wonderworking Providence of Sion's
Savior in New England."   He married, about 1620, SUSAN MUNNTER,
who was born about 1597 and died at Woburn 7 Mar. 1689/90.

　　　Children, all except the second baptized at Canterbury,
　　　England:

i.   EDWARD,[2] bapt. 18 Feb. 1620/1.
ii.   WILLIAM, b. probably in 1622; bur. 26 Jan. 1622/3.
iii. GEORGE, bapt. 3 Apr. 1625.
iv.   SUSAN, bapt. 1 Apr. 1627.
v.   WILLIAM, bapt. 22 Mar. 1628/9.
vi.   MARTHA, bapt. 1 May 1631.
vii. MATTHEW, bapt. 30 Mar. 1633.
2. viii. JOHN, bapt. 10 May 1635.

2. JOHN[2] JOHNSON (*Capt. Edward[1]*), baptized at Canterbury, England, 10 May 1635, died at Canterbury, Conn., about 1720.
He married, 28 Apr. 1657, BETHIA REED, who died at Canterbury, Conn., 2 Dec. 1717, probably daughter of Esdras of
Salem, Wenham, Chelmsford, Woburn, and Boston, Mass.
He was by occupation a housewright or carpenter, and owned
a sawmill in Woburn.   In 1712 he and his wife Bethia were
taken to the home of their son Obadiah in Canterbury, Conn.,
where they passed the remainder of their days.

　　　Children, born at Woburn:

i.   JOHN,[3] b. 24 Jan. 1657/8; m. MARY CARLEY.
ii. BETHIA, b. 20 Jan. 1659/60; m. (1) JONATHAN KNIGHT of Cambridge,
     Mass.; m. (2) JOSEPH WOOLCOTT of Cambridge.

*Cf. records of the birth and baptism of Isaac K. Newton, pp. 40, 90, of the original
records.

† For further information about Capt. Edward Johnson, his wife, and children, and
for his paternal and maternal ancestry, see REGISTER, vol. 67, pp. 169–180.

311

iii. WILLIAM, b. 29 Sept. 1662; d. at Canterbury, Conn., 23 Sept. 1713; m. at Cambridge, Mass., 18 Feb. 1690/1, MARY COOK. He removed to Plainfield, Conn., being one of the original settlers and prominent men of that town, and later of Canterbury.

3. iv. OBADIAH, b. 15 June 1664.

v. JOSEPH, b. abt. 1666; lived in that part of Plainfield, Conn., which was after Oct. 1703 Canterbury, and probably d. there 16 Mar. 1755; m. ELIZABETH ———, who d. at Canterbury 11 Dec. 1724.

vi. SAMUEL, b. 29 Oct. 1670.

vii. NATHANIEL, b. 15 May 1673.

3. OBADIAH³ JOHNSON (*John,*² *Capt. Edward*¹), born at Woburn, Mass., 15 June 1664, died at Canterbury, Conn., before 17 July 1740, when his will was proved. He married, 7 Sept. 1696, REBECCA BROOKS,* who died 1 Dec. 1752, daughter of Thomas of Canterbury. He removed when a young man to Plainfield and Canterbury, Conn., where he purchased a tract of land on the Quinebaug River, and was one of the first settlers and a prominent man. He was town clerk, and town meetings and religious services were held at his house. For upwards of forty years there seems to have been scarcely any progressive public movement in the community, either political, patriotic, or religious, which did not receive his support, and scarcely a petition or agreement which does not bear his signature.

Children:

i. MARY,⁴ b. at Plainfield 10 Oct. 1697; d. a widow after 1772; m. 19 Oct. 1717 MOSES CLEAVELAND.

ii. JACOB, b. at Plainfield 16 Mar. 1699; d. 29 Jan. 1738/9; m. (1) at Canterbury, 14 June 1722, MARY SHEPARD, who d. 5 Mar. 1731/2; m. (2) 8 May 1734 JUDITH HAYNES.

4. iii. OBADIAH, b. at Plainfield (later Canterbury) 23 June 1702.

iv. ESTHER, b. at Canterbury 1 Sept. 1704; d. 1793; m. 19 July 1726 JOHN FISH of Canterbury.

v. JOHN, b. at Canterbury 6 Oct. 1707; d. 13 June 1726.

vi. ABIGAIL, b. at Canterbury 29 Sept. 1710; m. 19 June 1729 PHINEAS BROWN.

4. OBADIAH⁴ JOHNSON (*Obadiah,*³ *John,*² *Capt. Edward*¹), born at Plainfield (later Canterbury), Conn., 23 June 1702, died there 10 Apr. 1765. He married, 6 Nov. 1723, LYDIA CLEAVELAND, born 7 Dec. 1704, died 5 June 1775, daughter of Josiah and Mary (Bates). Like his father, Obadiah was a leading man in church and town affairs, and his will shows that he was possessed of considerable wealth in notes and lands. He was lieutenant and later captain, and served in the French and Indian War; and he was a deacon in the Separatist Church.

Children, born at Canterbury:

i. WILLIAM,⁵ b. 13 Aug. 1724; d. at Canterbury 2 Oct. 1810; m. (1) 29 Nov. 1750 BETTY FASSET, b. at Canterbury 13 Jan. 1727, d. there 1 Apr. 1779; m. (2) 23 Feb. 1780 LODEMA FULLER, who d. 14 Sept. 1797; m. (3) 7 Oct. 1798 ELIZABETH DYAR.

ii. OLIVE, b. 23 Aug. 1726; d. at North Bridgewater, Mass., 25 Feb.

* Much search had failed to discover the maiden name of this Rebecca, until the will of her father Thomas Brooks, which mentions "daughter Rebecca, and son-in-law Obadiah Johnson," was found in Feb. 1914 in the New London, Conn., Probate Records.

1748/9; m. Rev. John Porter, first minister at North Bridgewater (now Brockton).

iii. Jedidiah, bapt. June 1729; d. 27 Oct. 1732.

iv. John, b. 23 Mar. 1730/1; d. 13 Mar. 1804; m. at Canterbury, 11 Mar. 1756, Phyllis Pellet, who d. in New York State in 1807.

v. Lydia, b. 4 Oct. 1733; m. (1) 10 Apr. 1752 Amos Fasset; m. (2) 5 Apr. 1759 David Paine.

vi. Obadiah, b. 18 Feb. 1735/6; d. at Canterbury 27 Oct. 1801; m. (1) 29 Apr. 1762 Mary Howard of Windham, Conn., who d. 10 Dec. 1763; m. (2) 6 July 1765 Lucy (Cady) Spaulding of Plainfield, Conn., b. at Plainfield 11 Apr. 1742, d. 6 July 1814. In 1775 Obadiah Johnson was major of the Third Connecticut Regiment, of which Israel Putnam was colonel. He saw service during the siege of Boston and at Bunker Hill. He later became a lieutenant-colonel and colonel.

5. vii. Jacob, b. 24 Mar. 1739/40.

viii. Abigail, b. 7 Nov. 1742; m. 23 Apr. 1761 Joseph Clark.

ix. Ebenezer, b. 16 July 1745; d. 8 Oct. 1774; m. at Preston, Conn., 5 Dec. 1765, Lydia Brewster.

5. Jacob[5] Johnson (*Obadiah,[4] Obadiah,[3] John,[2] Capt. Edward[1]*), born at Canterbury, Conn., 24 Mar. 1739/40, died at Plainfield, Conn., 9 Aug. 1819. He married, 7 Apr. 1763, Abigail Waldo, born at Windham, Conn., 15 July 1744, died at Plainfield 7 Mar. 1822, daughter of Edward and Abigail (Elderkin). He inherited the farm on Black Hill in Plainfield where he lived. In 1788 he and his family left the declining Separatist Society, and returned to the Orthodox Church.

Children, born at Plainfield:

i. Louisa Abigail,[6] b. 14 June 1764; d. 25 Apr. 1838; m. Stephen Bennett.

6. ii. Alfred, b. 27 July 1766.

iii. Anson, b. 13 Oct. 1768; d. 27 July 1769.

iv. Jacob, b. abt. 1775; d. at Brunswick, Me., 29 Apr. 1862; m. at Freeport, Me., 16 Sept. 1805, Isabella Nichols, b. at Cohasset, Mass., 10 May 1778.

v. Waldo, b. abt. 1778; d. at Plainfield 1 Oct. 1828, aged 50 years; m. before 1822 Ruth ———.

vi. Anson, b. 25 Aug. 1780; d. at New Carlisle, Ohio, 20 June 1859; m. 1808 Huldah Huntington of Windham.

vii. Obadiah Elderkin, b. 15 Jan. 1783; d. 22 Sept. 1811; m. 10 Sept. 1809 Lucy Morse.

viii. Ebenezer Murray, b. 19 Nov. 1786; d. at Terre Haute, Ind., 6 May 1858; m. 22 Nov. 1815 Elizabeth Huntington of Windham.

6. Alfred[6] Johnson (*Jacob,[5] Obadiah,[4] Obadiah,[3] John,[2] Capt. Edward[1]*), born at Plainfield, Conn., 27 July 1766, died at Belfast, Me., 12 Jan. 1837. He married at Newburyport, Mass., 26 May 1788, Sarah Cross, born at Newburyport 17 June 1764, died at Belfast 6 Apr. 1838, daughter of Gen. Ralph and Miriam (Atkinson). He was graduated at Dartmouth College in 1785, studied divinity with the Rev. John Murray of Newburyport and with the Rev. Levi Hart of Preston, Conn., and was ordained a clergyman of the Orthodox Congregational Church at Freeport, Me., 29 Dec. 1789, being the first minister of that town. In 1805 he was called to Belfast, where he remained as minister until he resigned in 1813. He is spoken of by Governor Crosby in

his Annals as a man of commanding presence, a bold, strong thinker, and learned in his profession. He represented Freeport in the General Court of Massachusetts in 1791, and served as chaplain during the War of 1812. He was one of the founders of Bowdoin College, and was for seventeen years a member of its Board of Government, a position which has since been filled by his son and grandson, bearing the same name. The finances of Belfast being embarrassed during the War of 1812, Mr. Johnson voluntarily relinquished his salary to the town. Children, born at Freeport:

7. i. ALFRED,[7] b. 13 Aug. 1789.
   ii. RALPH CROSS, b. 25 Sept. 1790; d. at Belfast 14 Nov. 1874; m. (1) at Camden, Me., 25 Nov. 1839, SARAH WINSLOW CUSHING; m. (2) at Warren, Me., 16 Nov. 1847, FRANCES DECKER MCLELLAN.

7. ALFRED[7] JOHNSON (*Alfred*,[6] *Jacob*,[5] *Obadiah*,[4] *Obadiah*,[3] *John*,[2] *Capt. Edward*[1]), of Belfast, Me., born at Freeport, Me., 13 Aug. 1789, died at Belfast 22 Mar. 1852. He married at Newbury, Mass., 5 Oct. 1817, NANCY ATKINSON, born at Newbury 22 July 1797, died in Boston 10 May 1864, daughter of Lieut. Amos and Anna (Knowlton). He was graduated at Bowdoin College in the Class of 1808, and was admitted to the Maine bar in 1811. For a period of twenty years he was judge of probate for Hancock (later Waldo) County, and during that time no appeal was ever taken from any of his decisions. He served as captain during the War of 1812, and for several years as judge advocate in the militia. In 1819 he was elected representative to the General Court of Massachusetts. In the same year he was a member of the convention which formed the constitution of the State of Maine, and was immediately chosen a representative to the Legislature of the new State. From 1838 until his decease, fourteen years later, he was one of the trustees of Bowdoin College, having been elected to this position to fill the vacancy caused by the death of his father. Judge Williamson, in his History of Belfast, vol. 1, says: "As a lawyer and as a literary man, the opinion of Judge Johnson was often sought, and as often cited for its weight and authority; but in matters of business, or on questions of expediency, it was proved to be no less valuable." Children, born at Belfast:

i. ALFRED,[8] b. and d. 18 Aug. 1818.
ii. RALPH CROSS, b. 8 Dec. 1819; d. in New York City 24 Apr. 1902; m. at Augusta, Me., 24 Dec. 1853, JULIA EMERSON LAMBARD.
iii. ANN SARAH, b. 21 Dec. 1821; d. in New York City 6 July 1890; m. at Belfast, 29 Oct. 1843, DR. NAHUM PARKER MONROE.
iv. ALFRED WALDO, b. 20 Dec. 1824; d. in Boston 14 Nov. 1869; m. in Boston, 25 Dec. 1861, ANNA MARIA CROSBY.
v. GEORGE ATKINSON, b. 5 June 1827; d. 4 July 1827.
vi. FRANCES EMILY, b. 26 Aug. 1828; d. at Augusta, Me., 8 Mar. 1854; m. at Belfast, 29 Oct. 1850, CHARLES ALLEN LAMBARD.
vii. MARY LOUISA, b. 9 Aug. 1832; d. at Narragansett Pier, R. I., 11 Aug. 1912; m. in Boston, 22 May 1860, JEAN ANTONIN GABRIEL, VICOMTE DE SIBOUR.
viii. EDWARD, b. 30 June 1840; d. in Boston 18 Jan. 1906; m. in Boston, 15 Sept. 1870, GEORGIANA PARKER MILLER.

ON THE SAYBROOK BRANCH OF THE FAMILY OF DEPUTY GOVERNOR WILLIAM JONES OF NEW HAVEN, CONN.

By Edwin A. Hill, Esq., of New Haven, Ct.

When the Strong Genealogy was published some years since, the statement was made on page 161 that Isaac Jones of New Haven (son of Deputy Governor William), by wife Deborah Clark, had a son Isaac born 1698 at New Haven, who resided at North Bolton, Conn., and died in 1782, and who was the father of Joel, born 1721, and, through him, the ancestor of the Hon. Anson Jones, ex-president of the Republic of Texas, etc., etc.

This statement is incorrect. Isaac, the grandson of the Deputy Governor, was born Dec. 23, 1702, lived in Saybrook, and died there Aug. 3, 1759, and was one of the ancestors of the Saybrook family; the other being his brother James Jones, born May 16, 1709, who died in Saybrook in May, 1768.

There was another Jones family in Saybrook, descended from Thomas Jones of Guilford, 1639, who returned to England about 1654. Of his four children, (1) Sarah married John Pratt of Saybrook, June 8, 1665; (2) Samuel moved to Saybrook and married Mary Bushnell (who was undoubtedly one of the daughters of Deacon Francis Bushnell), where he had issue and perpetuated the name; (3) Nathaniel died at Branford in 1668, and (4) Thomas died January, 1651. I have never found proof of any relationship between Thomas of Guilford and Deputy Gov. William of New Haven, though such relationship is not impossible. Mrs. Amelia D. Stearns, of West Newton St., Boston, has for some time been collecting information concerning the descendants of Thomas Jones of Guilford, and has a fine collection of records pertaining to that family.

The statement in the Strong Genealogy was criticized in The New York Biographical and Genealogical Record (vol. iv., page 40) in the following language : —

" Mr. Allyn S. Kellogg of Vernon, Conn., has called my attention lately to the fact, which we discussed in 1861, that Isaac Jones of North Bolton, Ct., was not a descendant of Depty. Gov. William Jones. Mr. Savage shows (Gen. Dict. 11, 561) that Isaac Jones, son of Isaac of New Haven, was born Dec. 23, 1702, and the Rev. Isaac Jones of Litchfield, Conn., himself a member of the New Haven family, when writing some years before 1850 to Miss Sophia Jones, a sister of Hon. Anson Jones, M.D., ex-president of the Republic of Texas, referred to this Isaac Jones, giving for his birth the same date given by Savage, and saying that he lived and died in Saybrook, and assuming that he was the grandfather of Miss Sophia Jones' father. Here begin the kinks in this pedigree, and the Hon. Anson Jones, M.D., though he saw the discrepancy, and tried to explain it, seems never to have found the true solution of the difficulty. He died Jan. 9, 1858, and from his papers his son Cromwell Anson Jones, when not more than 20 years old, took the defective pedigree, which he furnished to Rev. Mr. Dwight for the Strong Genealogy."

When the late Alvan Talcott, M.D., compiled his manuscript Genealogies of Guilford Families (the original of which is now deposited in the library of the New Haven Colony Historical Society, and a copy of same with the town clerk of Guilford), he fell into this same error and incorporated into his record of the descendants of Dept. Gov. William all of the known descendants of Isaac of North Bolton. At a later date, however, either himself or some other person has made entries on the MSS. in the N.H. Col. Hist. Society, to the effect that Isaac of North Bolton was not a descendant of Dep. Governor William, but of Lewis Jones of Watertown, Mass., and that Isaac of North Bolton was No. 25 of the descendants of Lewis in Goodwin's Genealogical Notes of Connecticut Families (see page 129). My own descent is through the Saybrook family ; and in 1874 I spent several days visiting my great aunts — the Misses Harriet and Temperance Jones — in the old Jones homestead, near the railroad station in Old Saybrook, for the purpose of gathering up for future use all that could be derived from their records, documents and memories pertaining to the genealogy and history of the Saybrook branch of the family ; and I then made abstracts of documents which fully settle the question of the connection of the Saybrook with the New Haven family. Quite recently a case came to my notice where a family of the name, misled either by the Strong Genealogy or the Talcott MSS., before they were corrected, traced back to Isaac of North Bolton, and confidently claimed descent from Dep. Governor William. I have thought, therefore, that the present was a proper time to settle this question for all time.

The following are abstracts made by me in Saybrook, in 1874,

from the original documents then in the possession of the Misses
Harriet and Temperance Jones : —

N° 1. Quit Claim Deed dated Feb. 10 1742-3 from Timothy Jones of
New Haven and Samuel Jones of Wallingford, Conn. " to their bretheren "
Isaac Jones and James Jones of Saybrook and Jacob Jones of Ridge-
field, Ct.

N° 2. Receipt dated Feb. 11 1742-3 — John Tallmadge of New
Haven and Samuel Elwell of Fairfield Ct acknowledge receipt from their
brethren Isaac Jones, Jacob Jones, and James Jones, their share of the
estate of their honored father Mr Isaac Jones late of New Haven deceased.

Other documents could be given, but the two abstracted above
settle the question fully, and enough is enough. It is not my intention now to give more than a very brief sketch of the descendants
of Isaac and James of Saybrook. Mr. Timothy Jones of Danbury, Conn., (who is a descendant through Jacob of Ridgefield), is
co-operating with me in preparing for publication a genealogy of
the descendants of Deputy Governor William Jones of New
Haven, which we desire to make as complete as possible, and I
wish to call attention to the fact and request all who claim descent
from the Deputy Governor, whether of the name Jones or not, to
forward their family records to either Mr. Timothy Jones or myself. I am also investigating the ancestry of the Deputy Governor
and would be very glad to hear from any one who can throw any
light, however small, upon this question, which we shall discuss in
the genealogy. We have very little on the descendants of James
Jones of Saybrook, and I trust this article will meet the eye of
some one of his descendants who will communicate with me at once.

Among the lines of the family not well traced out at the present
time, and concerning which I would be very glad to receive information, are the following : —

1. Descendants of *James Jones* of Saybrook, born May 16, 1709 (as
already noted).

2. Of Theophilus Eaton Jones of Norwalk, Conn., born March 20, 1706,
who married Sarah Cornell, daughter of Paul and Susanna Cornell.

3. Isaac Jones, son of John Jones and Hannah Bassett, born at Milford ?
May 6, 1748, who married Mary Pond.

4. Phineas Jones, brother of Isaac, born Dec. 4, 1751, married Mary
Brooks.

5. James Jones, brother of Isaac, born Oct. 16, 1758, said to have served
in Revolution.

6. William Jones, born May 31, 1722, Eaton born Aug. 26, 1730, John
born May 25, 1747, and Daniel born Mch. 18, 1745-6, all children of Samuel
and Sarah Jones of Wallingford, Ct.

7. Basil Jones, son of William of Marblehead, residing in New Haven
in 1739-40.

8. Harris Jones, born Sept. 9, 1734, son of Timothy of New Haven.

9. Isaac Jones, born July 7, 1740, son of Ensign Isaac of Saybrook by
wife Deborah Parker.

10. Zachariah Jones, born Sept. 3, 1744; Caleb born Sept. 3, 1748, and Samuel born May 15, 1754, sons of Caleb Jones and Mary How of Wallingford, Conn.

11. Nathaniel Jones, of Wallingford, born Mch. 20, 1717, who married Sarah Merriman (except his sons Reuben and Nathaniel).

This list could be extended, but I will go no further with it, but, instead, will request all descended from Deputy Governor William to send in their family records at once to either Mr. Timothy Jones of Danbury or to the writer, Edwin A. Hill, care of A. F. Wood's Sons, 2 Church St., New Haven, Ct.

MEMORANDUM OF THE SAYBROOK FAMILY.

1. Ensign ISAAC JONES of Saybrook, son of Isaac and Deborah (Clark) Jones of New Haven and guardian of Depty Govr William, born in New Haven Dec. 23, 1702, married prior to Nov. 9, 1726, Deborah, daughter of John and Mary (Buckingham) Parker, of Saybrook, born May 12, 1704. Mr Jones died Aug. 3, 1759. Children:

   i. HESTER, b. Oct., 1726; d. June 27, 1811, æ 77.
   ii. PARKER, b. about 1734.
   iii. ISAAC, ⎱ b. July 7, 1740; d. Dec. 25, 1822.
   iv. Son, ⎰ d. in two days.
   v. MABEL (some say Temperance), married Ezekiel Butler.
   vi. MOLLY.
   vii. SYBIL.

Mrs. Amelia D. Stearns has lately written me as follows: " My record of the family of Isaac and Deborah (Parker) Jones is not just like yours. My record begins with Hester, b. Oct. 11, 1726; then Isaac, b. July 7, 1730, d. May 2, 1739 ; a son, twin to Isaac, died the same month; then Temperance, without date ; then Parker ; then Mabel; then Molly, who died Feb. 24, 1866, æt. 70; then Sybil; lastly Isaac, who is called a minor in the will. I do not assert that this is a correct list of the children. It is made up of such names and dates as were in my collection, and placed as nearly in correct order as I could determine. I did not suppose that Temperance was the same as Mabel. Probably the daughter, Hannah, who was baptized March 17, 1742, died before the will was made."

The descendants of Parker Jones are the only ones that have been traced as yet. We are desirous of hearing from descendants of the other children, particularly of Isaac.

2. JAMES JONES of Saybrook, brother of the preceding and son of Isaac and Deborah (Clark) Jones, of New Haven, born May 16, 1709 (or 1708 according to Savage), married Sarah Willard.
   Of his children I have record of:—

   i. SARAH, b. May 27, 1741.
   ii. JAMES, b. Jan. 19, 1743-4.
   iii. TIMOTHY, b. June 5, 1755.
   iv. GEORGE, b. Feb. 14, 1759.

The probate records name in addition (will dated Mch. 2, 1768) sons *William, Elisha, Joseph,* and daughters *Deborah Stevens* and *Hannah Gladding.*

There are also probate proceedings on the estate of one Joseph Jones of Saybrook (whom I presume to be the son of Isaac). His

Joseph's will is dated Mch. 29, 1773, and mentions wife *Mary*, sons *Morris* and *Samuel*, and daughters *Temperance, Ruth, Margaret, Mary* and *Elizabeth;* also a brother *Benjamin*, who is made executor.

This is about all that we know at present about the descendants of James of Saybrook, and we would be very glad to know more. The Saybrook records are very incomplete, and it is quite difficult to make much headway in genealogical researches in Saybrook without the use of private family records. Hence this article, in the hopes that those interested in the family and having access to original records, will kindly copy, and forward the same for use in our work in hand.

THOMAS JONES OF GUILFORD, CONN., AND HIS DESCENDANTS.

Compiled by Hon. RALPH D. SMYTH, and communicated by Dr. BERNARD C. STEINER.

1. THOMAS[1] JONES was one of the pioneer settlers of Guilford, and came with Mr. Whitfield. His name is the sixth on the plantation Covenant signed June 1, 1639, on the passage of Mr. Whitfield's company to Guilford. He was evidently a young man, and probably was a relation of William Jones of New Haven. He appears to have been the first Marshal at Guilford, and to have held that office without a dissenting vote. Perhaps he was not married when he came to Guilford, though this is not certain. He married a Mrs. Mary Carter, probably a widow, with a daughter Mary Carter who subsequently married Samuel Ward of Branford, Jan. 1, 1658.

He was a witness in the first court, Aug. 14, 1645, and was chosen or rather reappointed Marshal at a court held Oct. 7, 1646. To this office he was annually rechosen until June 17, 1650, when George Bartlett was chosen " to succeed in his room in that office when he removes," Thomas Jones to retain office until then. On June 9th, 1651, " George Bartlett was chosen to succeed brother Jones in the Marshal's place, when Providence shall remove him." Before June 10th, 1652, he had removed, and John Fowler was chosen Marshal. He left his property and family in Guilford, and may have intended to return. His wife died Sept. 16, 1650, and probably soon afterward his place was sold and transferred to John Meigs. The deed was given many years later, however, on Mar. 4, 1667-8, by Lieut. William Chittenden, " the said Thomas Jones's Agent." Thomas Jones had died many years before that date. Mr. Davenport, in a letter to Gov. John Winthrop, Jr., dated about Mar. 10, 1655, wrote as follows : " Mr. Disborough and Goodman Jones died lately of the small pox in England or Scotland."

Thomas Jones evidently came to Guilford for a more free exercise of his religious and perhaps political opinions, and returned to England when his friends came in power. When Mr. Whitfield tendered his reasons to the Church of Guilford, Feb. 20, 1649-50, for his removal, and enquiry was made of every man concerning his particular ability in paying to the ministers for the present, and in probability to continue according to ordinary providence, " Thomas Jones professed his willingness and hoped to be able to continue his present payments."

His home lot lay next that of John Bishop, on the east side of the Green, and he held in addition 6 acres of upland and swamp near by, 4½ acres of upland in the East Creek Quarter, and 5½ acres of marsh land there. In the Neck he held 9¾ acres of upland, and also owned 8 acres of marsh at " Salt-holes."

On June 12, 1656, Mary Carter demanded £40 sterling from Thomas Jones's estate, which the court ordered to be paid her. This sum consumed all the inventory but £1.3.8., which was ordered to be kept for the children.

Children :

2. i. SAMUEL,[2] b. in Guilford; d. Nov. 1704.
   ii. NATHANIEL, d. single, in Branford, May, 1668, leaving an estate of £52.6.0., of which £45.15.0 was due him as a portion of his father's will in England.

iii. Sarah, m. June 8, 1668, Ens. John Pratt of Saybrook, a blacksmith, b. Feb. 20, 1644; d. July, 1726.
iv. Thomas, b. Aug., 1650, at Guilford; d. Jan. 5, 1650–1.

2. Capt. Samuel[2] Jones (*Thomas[1]*), of Saybrook, married, Jan. 1, 1666, Mary, daughter of Dea. Francis Bushnell. She died in 1727.

He was made an elector Oct. 16, 1667, a constable in 1669, was confirmed by the General Assembly as lieutenant of the Saybrook trainband on May 8, 1684, and was made its captain on May 11, 1699.

Children :

3. i. Samuel,[3] b. middle of Nov., 1667.
ii. Mary, b. Dec. 3, 1670; m. Dec. 11, 1690, John Parker.
iii. Martha, b. Jan. 18, 1672–3; m. ——— Whittlesey.
iv. Thomas.
v. John.
vi. Caleb, m. May 23, 1725, Rachel Clark of Farmington.
vii. Sarah.

3. Samuel[3] Jones, Jr. (*Samuel,[2] Thomas[1]*), of Saybrook, married, June 12, 1690, Deborah, daughter of Zachary Sanford, who was born Jan., 1666.

Children :

i. Deborah,[4] b. Aug. 17, 1691; d. Dec. 19, 1695.
ii. Samuel, b. Nov. 29, 1694.
iii. Daniel, b. May 18, 1697.
iv. Gideon, b. Sept. 21, 1699; d. May 5, 1701.
v. Cornelius, b. Sept. 11, 1701.
vi. Nathaniel, b. Mch. 8, 1704.

LIEUTENANT GOVERNOR WILLIAM JONES, OF NEW HAVEN JURISDICTION, AND HIS DESCENDANTS.

Compiled by Hon. Ralph D. Smyth, and communicated by Dr. Bernard C. Steiner.

1. Lieut. Gov. William[1] Jones, emigrant to New Haven, styles himself, in a deed dated March 3, 1689/90, "sometime of Martins in the fields, Westminster, Esquire, now of New Haven in the County of New Haven in New England, Planter." He may have been a son of Col. John Jones the Regicide, executed Oct. 16, 1660, who married, as a second or third wife, Jane, the widow of Roger Whetstone and sister of Oliver Cromwell the Protector.

William[1] Jones is said to have been born in 1624, at London, where he was an attorney. He arrived at Boston, July 27, 1660, in the same ship with Whaley and Goffe, and brought his sons William and Nathaniel with him, born by a first wife. He married second, at London, Hannah, born in London in 1633, daughter of Gov. Theophilus Eaton of New Haven, July 7, 1659. By a deed of indenture, dated Mar. 20, 1658/9, Theophilus

321

Eaton of Dublin in Ireland, Esquire, son and heir to Theophilus Eaton, Governor, late of New Haven in New England, of one part, and Hannah Eaton of London, spinster, daughter of Theophilus Eaton, and Thomas Yale of New Haven in New England, Gentleman, of the other part, conveyed the estate of Gov. Eaton.

An agreement made by some of his heirs is on the New Haven County records. Among them are Andrew Morrison, in right of his wife Sarah, and John Morgan, in right of his wife Elizabeth. These women are spoken of as children of the whole blood of William Jones, Esq. "Jones's Bridge" in Guilford took its name from him. Lieut. Gov. Jones died Oct. 17, 1706, and Mrs. Hannah (Eaton) Jones died May 4, 1707.

Children :

- 2. i. WILLIAM,[2] lived at Guilford; d. May 23, 1700.
- ii. CALEB, d. unmarried, in 1677.
- 3. iii. NATHANIEL, d. Aug. 21, 1691.
- iv. HANNAH, b. in 1659 in England; m. (1) Oct. 2, 1689, Patrick Falconer of Newark, N. J., who died Jan. 27, 1692; and m. (2) in 1710, James Clàrk of Stratford.
- v. THEOPHILUS, b. in New Haven, Oct. 2, d. Oct. 5, 1661.
- vi. SARAH, b. in New Haven, Aug. 16, 1662; m. Oct. 21, 1687, Andrew Morrison.
- vii. ELIZABETH, b. in New Haven, Aug. 28, 1664; m. John Morgan of Groton. Did she marry ——— Williams?
- viii. SAMUEL, b. in New Haven, June 20, d. Dec. 16, 1666.
- 4. ix. JOHN, b. in New Haven, Oct. 6, 1667; A.B., Harvard College 1690; d. Jan. 28, 1718–19.
- x. DIODATE, b. in New Haven, Mar. 15, 1669; d. Apr. 5, 1670.
- 5. xi. ISAAC, b. in New Haven, June 20, 1671.
- xii. ABIGAIL, b. in New Haven, Nov. 10, d. Nov. 15, 1673.
- xiii. REBECCA, b. in New Haven, Nov. 10, d. Nov. 15, 1673.
- xiv. SUSANNAH, b. in New Haven, Aug. 18, 1675; d. in 1705; m. Apr., 1700, Nathaniel, son of Phinehas Wilson. He was a scapegrace, for account of whom see Savage's Gen. Dict., vols. 2, p. 568, and 4, p. 587, also 4 Conn. Col. Rec., 354.

2. WILLIAM[2] JONES (*William[1]*) was of Guilford, where he was listed in 1690 at £22.5.0, and had a quarter acre home lot and a cow. His inventory Mar. 19, 1701, was £141. He married, in 1687/88, Abigail, daughter of John Morse of Dedham or Boston. She died Sept. 23, 1737.

Child :

- 6. i. CALEB,[3] b. in 1688; d. May 24, 1754.

3. NATHANIEL[2] JONES (*William[1]*), of New Haven, married, Oct. 7, 1684, Abigail, daughter of David Atwater. His inventory was £308.8.6.

Children :

- i. HANNAH,[3] b. May 6, 1687.
- 7. ii. THEOPHILUS, b. Mar. 18, 1690.
- iii. ABIGAIL, b. Mar. 26, 1692, posthumous.

4. JOHN[2] JONES (*William[1]*) lived in New Haven. He married first, Hannah ———; and married second, Mindwell ———. About 1709, he preached a year and a half at Greenwich. He was drowned by breaking through the ice in New Haven harbor. His inventory was £242.12.9.

Children :

- 8. i. THEOPHILUS EATON,[3] b. Mar. 20, 1706.
- ii. HANNAH, b. Jan. 15, 1708; d. Feb. 16, 1709.

iii. HANNAH, b. July 28, 1710; d. Mar., 1730.
iv. JOHN, b. Feb. 7, 1712.
v. MINDWELL, b. Sept. 14, 1715.
vi. ABIGAIL, b. Jan. 25, 1718.

5. ISAAC[2] JONES (William[1]), of New Haven, married first, Nov. 21, 1692, Deborah Clark of Stratford, who died May 28, 1733; and married second, Oct. 1, 1735, Mrs. Abigail Chatterton, who died Sept., 1757.
   Children, all by first wife:
   9. i. SAMUEL,[3] b. Sept. 26, 1693; d. Aug., 1773.
   10. ii. WILLIAM, b. July 20, 1694.
   11. iii. TIMOTHY, b. Oct. 30, 1696.
       iv. MARY, b. Oct. 6, 1698.
       v. DEBORAH, b. Sept. 25, 1700.
       vi. ISAAC, b. Dec. 23, 1702.
       vii. HANNAH, b. Feb. 15, 1704; d. Jan. 3, 1709.
       viii. JACOB, b. Mar. 20, 1706–07; living in Ridgefield in 1743.
   12. ix. JAMES, b. May 16, 1709.
       x. EBENEZER, b. Feb. 25, 1712; d. Sept. 23, 1713.

6. CALEB[3] JONES (William Jr.,[2] William[1]), of Guilford, died May 24, 1754. He married first, July 5, 1723, Mary, daughter of John Bishop, who died Jan. 23, 1724/25; and married second, Jan. 19, 1726, Elizabeth Lucas, who died Oct. 22, 1782. His list in 1716 was £49.16.0, and his faculty (carpenter trade and making wheels) was rated at £2.
   Child by first wife:
   i. MARY,[4] b. Oct. 26, 1724; m. Jan. 26, 1768, Nathaniel Foote of Bramford, and had four children, all daughters, who were unmarried. He d. Feb. 6, 1785.
   Children by second wife:
   ii. AARON, b. Oct. 4, 1727; d. Nov. 30, 1803; lived in Milford; m. Nov. 7, 1771, Anna, dau. of John Forsdick, who was b. Jan. 23, 1736, and d. Oct. 30, 1808; no children.
   iii. SIBYL, b. Jan. 13, 1728; m. Sept. 11, 1756, Samuel Hoadley of Bramford, who d. June 6, 1804.
   iv. TRYPHENA, b. Nov. 2, 1730; m. Joseph Roberts.
   v. HANNAH, b. Jan. 3, 1735; d. Feb. 1, 1740.
   vi. WILLIAM, b. Aug. 20, 1737; d. Nov. 24, 1739.

7. THEOPHILUS[3] JONES (Nathaniel,[2] William[1]) was a joiner, and lived in Wallingford. He married first, Dec. 26, 1711, Hannah Mix, who died Nov. 26, 1754; and married second, Sept. 22, 1755, Sarah Moss.
   Children, all by first wife:
   i. CALEB, b. Nov. 4, 1712; m. Mary, dau. of Zachariah Hard. Children: 1. Anna,[5] b. Aug. 19, 1742. 2. Zachariah Hard, b. Sept. 3, 1744. 3. Hannah, b. Jan. 8, 1746. 4. Caleb, b. Sept. 3, 1748. 5. Samuel, b. May 15, 1754.
   ii. LYDIA, b. Nov. 4, 1714; m. Feb. 4, 1735, Joseph Moss.
   iii. NATHANIEL,[4] b. Mar. 30, 1717; lived in Wallingford; m. June 8, 1743, Sarah Merriman, and had: 1. Abigail,[5] b. Sept. 26, 1744. 2. Daniel, b. Oct. 17, 1748. 3. Sarah, b. Aug. 16, 1750. 4. Eunice, b. Jan. 27, 1752. 5. Benjamin, b. Feb. 5, 1757. 6. Amos, b. Aug. 3, 1758. 7. Reuben, b. Oct. 11, 1759. 8. Hannah, b. Feb. 24, 1761.
   iv. HANNAH, b. Oct. 4, 1720; m. Aug. 5, 1740, Jehiel Merriman.
   v. THEOPHILUS, b. Nov. 1, 1723; d. Oct. 8, 1815; lived in Wallingford; m. May 24, 1757, Anna Street, who d. Aug. 10, 1811, aged 76.

Children: 1. *Sarah*,[5] b. Mar. 30, 1758. 2. *Nicholas*, b. Nov. 25, 1760; d. Aug. 25, 1848. 3. *Anna*, b. 1772; d. Oct. 1, 1776.
vi. ABIGAIL, b. Dec. 28, 1726; m. Mar. 16, 1747, Benjamin Dutton.
vii. NICHOLAS, b. Dec. 17, 1729; d. Apr. 24, 1760; m. (1) Mary ———;
m. (2) Eunice ———. Children by first wife: 1. *Charles*,[5] b. May 19, 1752. 2. *Patience*, b. Mar. 27, 1754. Children by second wife: 3. *Mary*, b. Apr. 30, 1756; d. May 6, 1760. 4. *Eunice*, b. Feb. 26, 1758; d. Mar. 31, 1758. 5. *Mary*, b. Feb. 26, 1760.
viii. DANIEL, b. Oct. 28, 1731; d. May 1, 1737.

8. THEOPHILUS EATON[3] JONES (*John*,[2] *William*[1]) lived in Norwalk, and married, Oct. 17, 1728, Sarah, daughter of Paul Cornel.
   Children:
   i. HEZEKIAH,[4] b. Oct. 22, 1729; d. young.
   ii. ABIGAIL, d. Sept. 14, 1737.
   iii. HANNAH, b. Feb. 29, 1735–6.
   iv. HEZEKIAH, b. Jan. 28, 1737–8.

9. SAMUEL[3] JONES (*Isaac*,[2] *William*[1]) lived in Wallingford. He married first, Sarah ———, who died Nov. 9, 1760; and married second, April 12, 1762, Esther Pratt.
   Children, all by first wife:
   1. MARY,[4] b. Dec. 5, 1720.
   ii. WILLIAM, b. May 31, 1722.
   iii. DIODATE, b. Mar. 5, 1724.
   iv. HESTER, b. Mar. 9, 1727.
   v. EATON, b. Aug. 26, 1730.
   vi. DANIEL, b. Mar. 18, 1745–6.
   vii. JOHN, b. May 24, 1747.

10. WILLIAM[3] JONES (*Isaac*,[2] *William*[1]) lived in Marblehead, Mass. He married Isabella (? Burrington), and died Oct. 17, 1730. She married second, July 22, 1735, John Jaggar.
    Children:
    i. BURRINGTON,[4] b. Apr. 16, 1721.
    ii. WILLIAM, b. Sept. 5, 1723.
    iii. BASIL, b. Apr. 29, 1725. He chose his grandfather, Isaac Jones, as his guardian, Apr. 26, 1739–40.
    iv. DEBORAH, b. Oct. 29, 1727.

11. TIMOTHY[3] JONES (*Isaac*,[2] *William*[1]) lived at New Haven. His will was dated Aug. 20, 1781. He married first, Nov. 16, 1726, Jane Harris of Middletown: and married second, Anna ———.
    Children:
    i. ELIZABETH,[4] b. Nov. 29, 1729; m. ——— Roberts.
    ii. DEBORAH, b. Sept. 4, 1730; m. Isaac Gridley, and had a son *Isaac*, who graduated at Yale, 1773.
    iii. ISAAC, b. Dec. 3, 1731; A. B. Yale, 1757; d. in 1812; lived in New Haven; m. (1) June 5, 1768, Elizabeth Trowbridge, who d. Apr. 4, 1769; m. (2) Sibyl ———. Child by first wife: 1. *William Trowbridge*,[5] b. Feb. 25, 1769. Children by second wife: 2. *Isaac*, Yale, 1792. 3. *Mary*. 4. *William*. 5. *Henry*, Yale, 1796. 6. *Timothy*, Yale, 1804. 7. *Algenon Sydney*, Yale, 1807. 8. *Frances*. 9. *Harriet*.
    iv. SUSANNAH, b. Aug. 10, 1733; m. Aug. 28, 1755, John Hotchkiss of New Haven, A. B. Yale, 1748, who d. July 5, 1779.
    v. HARRIS, b. Sept. 9, 1734.
    vi. TIMOTHY, b. Oct. 1, 1737; A. B. Yale, 1757; d. May 14, 1800; lived in New Haven; m. (1) June 20, 1765, Mary Trowbridge; m. (2) Mrs. Rebecca (Hart) Lynde, dau. of Rev. William Hart, who d. Oct. 26, 1819. 1. A *son*,[5] b. Apr. 5, 1767; d. young. 2. *Elizabeth*,

324

m. Joseph Lynde. 3. *William Rosewell*, b. a deaf mute; never married; lived with his sister Elizabeth.

vii. JANE, b. Oct. 31, 1740.

viii. MARY, b. Dec. 12, 1743; m. Oct. 31, 1764, John Lothrop, who d. 1789; lived at New Haven.

ix. WILLIAM, b. Jan. 26, 1745–46; A. B. Yale, 1762; d. in 1783; lived in New Haven; m. ——, and had one dau., *Anna*,[5] who m. Solomon Huntington of Windham.

JORDAN.—In the article on Thomas Clark, *ante*, page 132, it implies that his * wife Ann (Bishop), widow of John Jordan of Guilford, Conn., had by her first husband (Jordan) but two children, *John* and *Mary.* She also had *Joanna*, who married Thomas[2] Chittenden (William[1]), as will be seen by reference to Dr. Talcott's "Chittenden Family," page 13.   (Mrs.) NELLIE F. CARY.

Westfield, Mass.

*Page 417, Vol. I of this work.

JOHN AND THOMAS JORDAN OF GUILFORD, CONN., AND THEIR DESCENDANTS.

Communicated by Bernard C. Steiner from notes compiled by Hon. Ralph D. Smyth and Matt B. Jones, Esq., of Boston.

1. John[1] and Thomas[1] Jordan, probably brothers, were among the first planters of Guilford. John Jordan signed the plantation Covenant of June 1, 1639. Thomas may have been too young at that time. They were both persons of distinction among the early Colonists. John Jordan's name appears as one of the trustees in the Deed of Uncas to the settlers of Guilford, Dec. 17, 1641, and again with Mr. Disborow's and his brother Thomas Jordan's in the deed of Weekwash to Mr. Whitfield, Sept. 20, 1641. He died, probably, early in Jan., 1649–50, as his inventory is dated Feb. 1, 1649–50. In 1654 Thomas Clarke of Milford had married Ann, widow of John Jordan.

Thomas[1] Jordan, one of the most prominent of the settlers of Guilford, was young, perhaps not quite of age, when the colony was planted. He was one of the associate Judges of the Particular Court chosen Oct. 7, 1646, and Treasurer from an early period. He was Representative in the Plantation Court, 1651–1654, at all the sessions, and was appointed by the Plantation Court to go to Boston with an answer to the General Court of Massachusetts, 1653. At a court at Guilford, Sept. 1, 1654, he took down the evidence in "short hand." About 1655 he returned to England, as he no longer appears on the Town and Colony Records. In a letter written by him to Mr. Leete, from England, he gives his house to Andrew Leete, who had married his daughter, Elizabeth Jordan, June 1, 1669. In 1706, William Leete and Caleb Leete were administrators of their grandfather " Mr. Thomas Jordan dec'd late of old England," part of whose land had been laid out first to Mr. William Leete and Mr. Thomas Jordan in common and never divided. His grandchildren were, besides William and Caleb, Samuel, Dorothy, Abigail, and Mercy Leete.

On Sept. 12, 1666, William Leete wrote to Gov. John Winthrop asking him (4 Mass. Hist. Soc. Coll., vii., p. 558) to try to gain Mr. Jordan's consent to the intermarriage of Jordan's daughter Elizabeth to Leete's son Andrew. On Mch. 25, 1674, a letter was shown the townsmen of Guilford, from Thomas Jordan to Gov. Leete, authorizing the recording. of Jordan's land to Andrew Leete, with the condition that " should he bury her and take another wife," after his death the land " shall go to the children of my daughter, or for want of heirs of her body to my lawful heirs."

1. John[1] Jordan married Ann, daughter of John Bishop, and had the following children:

    i.   Hannah,[2] m. June 28, 1666, Esbon Wakeman.
    ii. Elizabeth, d. 1720; m. Nov. 17, 1664, Daniel Hubbard, who d. 1720.
    iii. Mary, m. Abraham Post (wrongly called *Abner* in Register, vol. 59, p. 132).
2. iv. John, b. Mar., 1646–7.

2. John[2] Jordan (*John[1]*) was a cooper, and married Deborah ———, who died in 1677. He removed to Middletown, and sold his home-lot in Guilford to William Leete, Jr., on June 24, 1679. Before

1689 he was in Saybrook. He died, presumably, about 1713, as on June 26 of that year, Abraham Chalker, executor of the last will and testament of " Mr. John Jordan, late of Saybrook," sets off to the deceased's daughter Mary her part of the lands of her father at Ironmine plain. (Saybrook Records, vol. 2, p. 372.) From Saybrook Records, vol. 2, pp. 372 and 386, and vol. 3, p. 386, it appears that John Jordan had a son James, and a daughter Mary who married John Ingham, Mar. 2, 1716. (Saybrook Records, vol. 2, p. 401.) He also had a daughter Hannah, as appears from Saybrook Records, vol. 3, p. 310, where James Jordan conveys land, Apr. 4, 1716, to " my loving sister Hannah Bate, of Saybrook aforesaid, widow and Relique of Samuel Bate, late of Saybrook." Hannah married first, Samuel Bates of Haddam, who died before 1716; and married second, in 1717, John Stannard. It is also reasonably certain that John[2] Jordan had a daughter Catherine, who married William Bushnell, Apr. 10, 1701. This view is strengthened by the fact that Mary Jordan, on the same day upon which Abraham Chalker set off to her a portion of the land of her father, as above described, deeds to William Bushnell (husband of Catherine) two parcels of land, " being the whole of that land given to me by my Honored father, Mr. John Jordan, late of Saybrook, deceased," and " one-third part of that meadow commonly called Pond Meadow that was my Honored Father's Mr. John Jordan's aforesaid."

————

Thomas[1] Jordan married Dorothy ————, and had the following children :

    i.   Elizabeth,[2] b. 1650; d. Mar. 4, 1704; m. June 1, 1669, Andrew Leete, who d. Oct. 31, 1702.

    ii.   Mary, b. May 27, 1652.

JORDAN OF GUILFORD, CONN.—Supplementary to the notes of Dr. Bernard C. Steiner on John and Thomas Jordan of Guilford, Conn., and their descendants, printed in the REGISTER vol. 62, page 333, it may be said that John[2] Jordan * (John[1]) married a second time, and the evidence seems reasonably satisfactory that his second wife was Katharine, daughter of Alexander and Katharine (Post) Chalker, and that she was the mother of James[3] (John,[2] John[1]) Jordan, and probably of Catherine Jordan who married William Bushnell.

A return of arbitrators to settle a difficulty between Thomas Avery *et al.* and James Jordan and Stephen Post, in behalf of his brethren, concerning a piece of land in Saybrook (Saybrook Records, vol. 2, p. 137), dated Oct. 25, 1705, recites that " the meadow descended from Mr. Stephen Post, now in possession of his grand-children Abram and James Post and his great-grand-child James Jurdan."

Abraham, son of Stephen Post of Saybrook, married Mary, the sister of John[2] Jordan, as noted by Dr. Steiner. Katharine, daughter of Stephen Post, married Alexander Chalker, and was the mother of four daughters: Mary, b. 1653, who married Richard Cozzens; Katharine, b. 1657; Sarah, b. 1659; Jane, b. 1662.

It has been stated that Katharine, daughter of Alexander Chalker, married John Hills, but Saybrook Records (vol. 1, p. 123) afford ample proof that John Hills married the widow, and not the daughter, of Alexander Chalker. The process of elimination shows that in this Chalker family must be found the granddaughter of Stephen Post, who married John[2] Jordan, and further proof appears from the fact that Abraham, son of Alexander Chalker, executor of John[2] Jordan's will (will not found), recites himself as the " cousin " (uncle) of Mary[3] Jordan (John,[2] John[1]). Of the three younger Chalker girls, Katherine, by reason of age and the passing down of the name in the next generation, seems probably to have been the wife of John[2] Jordan (John[1]). MATT B. JONES. *101 Milk Street, Boston.*

*Page 326, this volume.

GENEALOGICAL ITEMS OF THE KELLOGG FAMILY.

[By D. O. KELLOGG, a member of the N. E. Hist. Gen. Soc.]

There seems a propriety in introducing the name of KELLOGG into this "Register," as the earliest history of the family locates them in New England, and connects them with its annals. For several generations they are believed to have remained there, though now the name is found in many parts of the United States, and their descendants have become numerous. The name is found in the early records of the first settlements on the Connecticut River, but no connected history of the family of those days has been discovered.

It is not pretended that these fragments embrace more than a brief record of a portion of the family, and it is admitted that they are entirely deficient in relation to the immigration of its progenitors from Europe, as well as to the history of their early descendants. Much remains to be known before a complete genealogy can be written. It is, however, hoped that this beginning may stimulate some one having leisure, and feeling sufficient interest in the research, to continue the subject, until a full record shall be published.

The present writer has been unable, in the limited investigations his pursuits have permitted, to trace back the progenitors to their first settlement in America, or to their European home immediately prior to their immigration. An existing similarity of name, now in Scotland, gives a probable clue to their early history. Tradition relates that they were originally Scotch, and that, being partizans of James VI., of Scotland, they came with that prince to England when he ascended the throne of Great Britain as James I.—where they remained until their settlement in New England. They came here soon after the landing of the Pilgrims at Plymouth, and settled somewhere in Massachusetts.

The Herald's College, London, records two ancient families in Scotland, bearing the name of KELLOCK. One was of the nobility,—the head of which was a duke. No trace of such rank now remains. The other were commoners, having a heraldic claim to the distinction of *a coat of arms*, the description of which is, for the present, omitted. The simplicity of American institutions suggests that the claim of descent should be based on the latter.

Late inquiries in Scotland, by the writer, led to the discovery of two families, now residing there,—one in Fifeshire, the other in Dumfriesshire,—there may be others, of the same name as that in heraldry. The Gaelic idiom justifies the belief that, originally, the name was written KILLOCH. The guttural sound given by the Scotch to the letter *h*, at the termination of words, is very nearly the American sound of *g*, and accounts for the change of spelling in this country. When surnames were first introduced into Britain, the names of cities, towns, manors, estates, and local objects were often adopted by families. This suggests a probable explanation of the origin and meaning of the name. In the Gaelic language, KIL is a burial place, and LOCH a lake. Thus KILLOCH indicates *Lake Cemetery*, or the family of the *Lake Burial Ground*. In process of time the name has become KELLOCK, in Scotland, and KELLOGG in the United States.

Materials now at hand serve only to give an imperfect account of that branch of the family settled in western Massachusetts, a century and a half ago, and of such of their descents as were among the early emigrants to the State of New York.

(1) STEPHEN KELLOGG,[1] resided in Westfield, Mass., on the river of that name, in the early part of the eighteenth century, and is believed to have been a farmer. Particulars of his birth, marriage and family have not been ascertained.

(2) SILAS,[2] son of Stephen, was born in Westfield, in 1714, married Ruth Root, daughter of Josiah Root, of the same place, b. March, 1722. They settled in Sheffield, Mass., in early life, and were among the first settlers of that then frontier town. He was clerk of the land office established there by the proprietors of Sheffield, embracing the present town of that name, and the town now known as Great Barrington. He was a man of high social and religious character, and died about 1790. His widow survived him many years, and d. there in 1818, at the advanced age of 96. They had four sons and five daughters, all of whom married, and most of them lived to old age, viz. :

(3)   I. EPHRAIM,[3] b. in 1740 ; resided in Sheffield ; a farmer.

(4)   II. ENOS,[3] b. in 1742 ; resided in Sheffield ; a farmer.

($\frac{5}{11}$)   III. ASA,[3] b. Feb. 19, 1745 ; m. Lucy Powell of S., who was b. Feb. 27, 1746 ; d. Nov. 9, 1816 ; settled in Galway, Saratoga Co., N. Y., during the revolution ; was a farmer ; held the offices of justice of the peace and captain of the militia,—then important stations ; was a deacon in the presbyterian church, and universally respected. He d. June 4, 1820, aged 75.

(6)   IV. ELEANOR,[3] b. 1747 ; m. Joab Austin ; set. in Sheffield ; d. in Homer, N. Y., Aug. 20, 1835.

(7)   V. RUTH,[3] b. 1749 ; m. Solomon Kellogg ; set. in New Hartford, Ct. ; removed to Paris, Oneida Co., N. Y. ; d. at an advanced age ; had 12 sons.

(8)   VI. RHODA,[3] b. 1753 ; m. Moses Kellogg ; set. in New Hartford.

(9)   VII. MIRIAM,[3] b. 1755 ; m. Dr. Lewis Beebe ; set. in Pawlet, Vt.

(10)   VIII. SILAS,[3] b. 1757 ; m. Rhoda Root of Sheffield ; resided in that town through life, and represented it for several years in the Legislature ; was a member of the Convention of 1821, for amending the Constitution of Massachusetts ; served much in public life, and was highly respected. He d. at an advanced age, leaving sons and daughters.

(11)   IX. ANNA,[3] b. in 1760 ; m. James Hickok ; set. in Lansinburgh, N. Y., and d. in old age.

Asa,[3] (5) who m. Lucy Powell, had 7 sons and 2 daughters, who lived to mature age.

($\frac{12}{26}$)   I. FREDERICK,[4] b. in Sheffield, Sept. 27, 1766 ; m. 1, Polly Phelps ; 2, Tryphena White ; 3, Mrs. Brown. Left Galway in 1803 ; set. in Brutus, Cayuga Co., N. Y. ; a farmer ; d. in Auburn, Oct. 16, 1832, leaving the example of a well spent life. Had a large family of sons and daughters.

($\frac{13}{32}$)   II. EZRA,[4] b. in S., June 26, 1769 ; m. Abigail Olmstead ; set. in Galway ; d. Oct. 13, 1836. Had sons and daughters.

(14)   III. MARTIN,[4] b. in S., June 22, 1771 ; m. Rhoda Smith ; set. in Mexico, Oswego Co., N. Y. ; d. Jan. 27, 1854. Had 3 sons and 1 daughter.

($\frac{15}{41}$) IV. CHARLES,[4] b. in S., Oct. 3, 1773 ; m. Mary Ann Otis, daughter of David Otis of Galway, Oct. 21, 1794,—a direct descendant of John Otis, one of the English colony who settled Hingham, Mass., in 1635. She was b. Nov. 3, 1774. They set. in that part of Sempronius, Cayuga Co., N. Y., now known as Kelloggsville; resided there about forty years, then removed to Ann Arbor, Mich. He d. there May 11, 1842, aged 68 ; and she, Oct. 14, 1844, aged 70. He was a farmer, and for many years a merchant also ; was much in public life, having been a member of the New York Legislature, four years; a representative in Congress two years, and for several years a judge of the county courts, besides serving many years in minor offices. In his public employments he secured the confidence and esteem of the people. Through life he maintained a consistent religious character, and left an unsullied name and many excellent examples, a precious legacy to his descendants. Had six sons and five daughters.

($\frac{16}{52}$) V. ASA,[4] b. in S., Nov. 12, 1777 ; m. 1, Margaret Stewart, b. April 18, 1786; d. June 11, 1819 ; 2, Ann Stewart, b. May 15, 1794 ; d. April 17, 1843. He d. Aug. 23, 1836 ; was an estimable and successful merchant, first in Milton, N. Y., then for many years in Troy, N. Y. Had sons and daughters.

(17) VI. LUCY,[4] b. Nov. 11, 1779 ; m. 1, David Westcott ; 2, Reuben Hewett ; d. in western New York, April 13, 1851.

($\frac{18}{65}$) VII. WARREN,[4] b. in Galway, June 2, 1783 ; m. Abigail Paine of Troy, b. Nov. 6, 1790, who survives. He d. Feb. 23, 1835 ; was an honorable and successful merchant in Troy. Had sons and daughters.

(19) VIII. ALEXANDER CYRUS,[4] b. in G., June 22, 1785 ; m. 1, Ann Sayles ; 2, Ann Hinman Davis, now living. He was many years a merchant in Troy ; removed to Connecticut, and d. in Bridgeport, June 13, 1846. Left two sons and two daughters.

(20) ELECTA,[4] b. in G., May 6, 1788 ; m. Alanson Kennedy. They settled in western New York. She d. Sept. 1839.

Frederick,[4] (12) *who m.* 1, *Polly Phelps ;* 2, *Tryphena White, had*

(21) I. SILAS,[5] b. in G., June 6, 1789 ; m. Martha Simpson of Brutus; farmer; resides in Ira, N. Y.; has sons and daughters.

(22) II. POLLY,[5] b. in G., June 6, 1790 ; m. William G. Beach, res. in Dexter, Mich.

(23) III. LUCINDA,[5] b. in G., Aug. 10, 1791 ; m. David Dixon. She is a widow ; res. in Lima, Mich.

(24) IV. ALVAN,[5] b. in G., Jan. 12, 1793 ; m. Sylvia Stow, formerly a cloth dresser, of whom Ex-President Fillmore learned that trade ; is now a farmer; res. in Scott, N. Y. ; has been many years a justice of the peace, supervisor, &c., and has served in the legislature. Has sons and daughters.

(25) V. WEALTHY,[5] b. in G., Oct. 24, 1794 ; m. Milo Phelps. Is a widow ; set. in Painesville, O. : now res. in Ladoga, Wis.

(26) VI. AMANDA,[5] b. in G., Aug. 24, 1796; m. Henry Perine ; res. in Ira.

331

(27) VII. FREDERICK,[5] b. in G., Nov. 26, 1797; m. 1, Sally Everet; 2,
———; set. in Scott; cloth dresser; d. in Alleghany Co.,
N. Y., Dec. 28, 1857. Had sons and daughters.

(28) VIII. ASA,[5] b. in G., April 26, 1800; m. Sarah St. John; resided
in Calhoun Co., Mich.; farmer; d. May 7, 1854.

(29) IX. LUCY,[5] b. in Brutus, June 1, 1803; m. Amos Carter; r. in Ira.

(30) X. ISRAEL PHELPS,[5] b. in B., Oct. 24, 1808; m. 1, Eliza Whiting; 2, ———; farmer; r. in Wyocena, Columbia Co.,
Wisconsin.

(31) XI. HARRIET,[5] b. in B., Dec. 10, 1810; m. Hicks P. Phelps; res.
in Wyocena, Wis.

(32) XII. CHARLES WHITE,[5] b. in B., May 21, 1815; m. Demmis D.
Comstock of Fort Ann, merchant, New York; r. in Brook-
lyn; has one son, *Peter Comstock*,[6] and two daughters,
Gertrude,[6] and *Fanny*.[6]

Ezra,[4] *who m. Abigail Olmsted, had, all b. in Galway—*

(33) I. EZRA POWELL,[5] b. March 18, 1795; m. Margaret Anderson;
res. in Galway; has one son.

(34) II. MERCY CROSBY,[5] b. May 12, 1797; d. Aug. 13, 1805.

(35) III. CLARISSA H.[5] b. June 12, 1799; m. Samuel Dauchy; r. in
Troy.

(36) IV. JONATHAN CROSBY,[5] b. Dec. 18, 1801; d. Oct. 12, 1810.

(37) V. ABIGAIL ANN,[5] b. Jan. 9, 1804; m. Sears E. Smith; res. in
Cleveland, O.

(38) VI. SYLVESTER TRUMAN,[5] b. March 22, 1806; m. Lucy Ann
Lindsley, merchant in New York; res. in Yonkers; has
sons and daughters.

(39) VII. RUTH ANN,[5] b. June 11, 1808; m. Lewis Goodrich; d. Feb.
5, 1833.

(40) VIII. LUCY,[5] b. May 2, 1811; m. R. E. Gillet; r. in Cleveland.

(41) IX. MARY,[5] b. July 10, 1813; m. Rev. Charles S. Renshaw; d.
Sept. 26, 1839.

Charles,[4] (15) *who m. Mary Ann Otis, had—*

(4 2/7 6) I. Day Otis,[5] b. in Galway, Aug. 7, 1796; m. 1, Ann Eliza
Smith of Lansinburgh, b. Feb. 26, 1797, d. Aug. 3, 1829;
2, Mary Ann Dimon of Fairfield, Ct., b. Dec. 31, 1804, d.
May 17, 1840; 3, Harriet Walter Odin of Boston, b. Oct.
27, 1804. A merchant, first in Owasco, N. Y., then 23
years in Troy, now in New York, resides in Brooklyn, N.
Y. Has occasionally served in public life, having been a
member of the New York Legislature, Mayor of Troy, and
U. S. Consul at Glasgow, Scotland. Has five sons.

(43) II. DWIGHT,[5] b. in Marcellus, N. Y., Oct. 4, 1797; m. Minerva
Annable, who d. ———; settled in Ann Arbor, Mich.;
res. now in New York. Has five sons, *Charles Annable*,[6]
Calvin Whitwood,[6] *Dan W.*,[6] *William Henry*,[6] and *George
Dwight*,[6] and one daughter, *Julia*.[6]

(44) III. DOR,[5] b. in Aurelius, N. Y., Feb. 8, 1799; m. Lucretia Annable; res. in Ann Arbor. Has served as a justice of the
peace, and in other offices.

(45) IV. DELIA,[5] b. in Kelloggsville, April 7, 1803; m. Calvin Whitwood; res. in Auburn, N. Y.

332

(46) V. Abigail Ann,[5] b. in K., June 10, 1804 ; m. Ethan A. Warden ; res. in Auburn.

(47) VI. Charles Harvey,[5] b. in K., Sept. 19, 1808 ; m. Frances Amelia Parmelee of Lansingburgh, where they now reside ; merchant and manufacturer in Troy ; has four sons,— *William P.,*[6] *Warren T.,*[6] *Francis Pelatiah,*[6] and *Henry Parmelee;*[6] and three daughters, *Mary Frances,*[6] *Amelia L.,*[6] and *Harriet Odin.*[6]

(48) VII. Electa Semanthy,[5] b. in K., July 28, 1810 ; m. Col. William A. Abell of Ann Arbor ; res. in Peekskill, N. Y.

(49) VIII. Dan W.,[5] b. in Galway, March 26, 1812 ; m. 1, Esther A. Bull of Troy ; 2, Kate Fake of Lansingburgh ; 3, Emma S. Congdon of Syracuse. Was two years secretary of the Michigan Senate under Gov. Woodbridge's administration ; merchant in New York ; res. in Brooklyn.

(50) IX. Dorliska,[5] b. in K., Jan. 17, 1816 ; m. Dr. Cyrus Backus ; res. in Peekskill.

(51) X. Frances Louisa,[5] b. in K., March 6, 1818 ; m. Seth T. Otis of Chicago, Ill., who has been U. S. Consul to Basle, Switzerland ; res. at Almond, Allegany Co., N. Y.

(52) XI. John Quincy,[5] b. in K., March 24, 1823 ; m. Helen Mary Dauchy of Troy ; merchant in New York ; res. in Yonkers. Has one son, *George Abel,*[6] and two daughters, *Fanny Louisa,*[6] and *Clara Dauchy.*[6]

Asa,[4] (16) *who m.* 1, *Margaret Stewart ;* 2, *Ann Stewart ; had, all b. in Troy :—*

(53) I. Eliza,[5] b. July 27, 1805 ; d. Sept. 8, 1806.

(54) II. Warren Stewart,[5] b. March 1, 1807 ; m. Lucy Ann Rawdon of New York ; res. in Hempsted, L. I. ; has sons and daughters. *Ralph Rawdon,*[6] d. at two years old ; *Edward H.,*[6] *Lucy Ann,*[6] *Margaret Anne,*[6] *Leavitt Rawdon,*[6] *Warren S.,*[6] *Isaac Merritt,*[6] *Susan A.,*[6] *I. Newton Phelps.*[6]

(55) III. Edward Asa,[5] b. June 15, 1808 ; d. Oct. 20, 1809.

(56) IV. Edward,[5] b. Jan. 20, 1810 ; m. Sarah Hastings, who d. ——; res. in Independence, Mo. Has sons and daughters.

(57) V. Asa,[5] b. July 2, 1811 ; never married ; d. 1848.

(58) VI. Eliza,[5] b. Aug. 5, 1813 ; d. Sept. 15, 1815.

(59) VII. Margaret Ann,[5] b. March 1, 1821 ; m. Francis Newlands ; resided at West Point, N. Y. ; d. Feb. 20, 1858.

(60) VIII. Jane Eliza,[5] b. April 27, 1822 ; d. July 15, 1823.

(61) IX. Jane Eliza,[5] 2d, b. Sept. 26, 1823 ; m. James S. Knowlson; resides in Troy.

(62) X. Mary,[5] b. Aug. 12, 1826 ; m. George Redfield of Troy ; d. 1847.

(63) XI. William,[5] b. Aug. 25, 1829 ; d. Nov. 15, 1830.

(64) XII. Henry,[5] b. Aug. 25, 1829 ; m. Sarah May ; resides in Westminster, Vt. ; has children.

(65) XIII. Caroline,[5] b. May 6, 1833 ; d. Sept. 15, 1835.

Warren,[4] (18) *who m. Abigail Paine, had, all b. in Troy :—*

(66) I. George William,[5] b. Feb. 27, 1812 ; m. Charlotte Elizabeth Cobb of Albany ; was a merchant in Troy ; d. April 15, 1849 ; left one son, *Sanford Cobb,*[6] and one daughter, *Frances Southwick.*[6]

(67) II. John Paine,[5] b. Oct. 11, 1814; unmarried; merchant in New York.

(68) III. Henry Lyman,[5] b. April 28, 1817; graduate of Washington College, Ct.; m. Frances A. Wilson of Troy; merchant in Cleveland, O.; has two sons, *Lewis Southwick*,[6] and *William Cooper*,[6] and 3 daus., *Elizabeth Homer*,[6] *Mary Lyman*,[6] and *Ellen Wheeler*.[6]

(69) IV. Mary Elizabeth,[5] b. Oct. 11, 1818; d. March 8, 1820.

(70) V. Frances Lucretia,[5] b. Jan. 25, 1821; m. Maj. George H. Thomas, U. S. A.; res. at Fort Mason, Texas.

(71) VI. Julia Augusta,[5] b. Dec. 6, 1822; unmarried; res. in Troy.

(72) VII. Charles Augustus,[5] b. March 26, 1825; graduate of Harvard University, 1845; studied law in Montgomery, Ala.; practised in New Orleans; removed to New York in 1851; now a merchant there.

(73) VIII. Samuel Cobb,[5] b. April 23, 1828; d. Sept. 24, 1828.

(74) IX. Caroline Louisa,[5] b. Oct. 25, 1830; d. Dec. 3, 1830.

(75) X. Ellen Maria,[5] b. Sept. 17, 1831; d. Aug. 27, 1832.

(76) XI. Homer Hall,[5] b. Dec. 9, 1833; d. May 23, 1837.

Day Otis,[5] *now of Brooklyn, has five sons.*

(77) I. Burr Smith,[6] b. in Owasco, Aug. 8, 1826; m. Kate Curtis of N. White Creek, N. Y.; merchant in New York.

(78) II. Charles Day,[6] b. in Troy, June 4, 1828; m. Mary Elizabeth Cobb of Boston; merchant in B.; resides in Brookline, Ms.

(79) III. George Dimon,[6] b. in Troy, July 13, 1833; graduated at the University of Vermont, 1853; m. Harriet A. Sanborn of Peru, N. Y.; counsellor at law; office and residence, N. Y.

(80) IV. Theodore Dwight,[6] b. in Troy, April 17, 1835; settled in Ida County, Iowa.

(81) V. Day Otis, 2d,[6] b. in Troy, March 31, 1837; graduated at Hobart College, Geneva, 1857; resides in Boston.

GENEALOGICAL ITEMS OF THE KELLOGG FAMILY.

[By D. O. KELLOGG, member of N. E. Hist. Gen. Society.]

The hope expressed in the article, to which this is a continuation, that it might be the means of eliciting earlier, more correct, and more comprehensive genealogical items of the Kellogg family, has happily not been disappointed. Though the information gathered to this time, does not carry us back to the immigration of its progenitors from Europe, nor to its previous history, yet the progress made in that direction is highly satisfactory, and encourages the further hope that some more persevering hand, interested in the inquiry, will, with the materials now at command, pursue it to that result.

It will be seen, by this article, that the former supposition, that the first of the name, in this country, settled originally in Massachusetts, is probably erroneous. The earliest knowledge of the family now obtained, locates it in Connecticut. As early as 1639—only 19 years from the arrival of the Plymouth colony—the name is found on the records of Hartford in that State.

The writer is chiefly indebted for these additional items to Lucius M. Boltwood, Esq., of Amherst, Mass., and to the Hon. Ensign H. Kellogg, of Pittsfield, in the same State, to both of whom he returns his acknowledgmeets, with thanks. The latter remarks, in his correspondence, " he has little doubt that a vigorous inquirer might go up and down the Connecticut River, the home of the early emigrants and their immediate descendants, and put the American part of our family genealogy in a perfectly satisfactory light." Entirely concurring in this belief, the question arises, *who* will make the investigation? The sooner it is done, the easier it will be accomplished.

The former article began with STEPHEN KELLOGG, of Westfield, Mass., and indicated him as of the *first* generation, noting the successive generations from him, by the corresponding numerals. As we are now carried back one generation, the same numbers will be continued to the same generations, to avoid confusion, designating the generation of the father of Stephen by the superior letter ᴬ. In some instances the individuals then referred to will be re-introduced, for the purpose of adding such additional items as have since been gathered. With these preliminary remarks I proceed.

82. Lieut. JOSEPHᴬ KELLOGG, makes his first cis-Atlantic appearance in Farmington, Ct., at an early period of the settlement of that town. Whence he came, and the date of his settlement there, has not been ascertained. He joined the church, in that town, Oct. 9, 1653. Removed to Boston in 1659, and there purchased a homestead. The Boston records show the registry of a deed, from Peter Oliver, merchant, to him, spelling his name *Kelog*, dated Oct. 9, 1659, describing him as " formerly of Farmington, but now of Boston, weaver," conveying a house and lot " fronting on the street leading to Roxbury,"—now Washington street. The place is so indefinitely described that it cannot, at this distance of time, be located. The records also show a mortgage from him, of a subsequent date, to Sergeant Thomas Clark of Boston, merchant, on the same place, for £100, payable within 5 years, with £10 annual rent till paid, but do not disclose how he alienated it. Thence he removed to Hadley, Mass., about 1662, where he died about 1707. His will was dated 1707, and the inventory of his estate, in probate, bears date Feb. 4, 1708. His residence there was the place where the Rev. John Brown, D.D., subsequently lived and died, and on which Dea. Hitchcock now resides.

These further investigations have served to confirm the opinion, before expressed, that the family originally came from Scotland.

There was a Nathaniel Kellogg in Hartford, Ct., as early as 1639, who afterwards removed to Farmington. Whether he was father or brother of Joseph, or neither, does not appear. There was also a Samuel Kellogg, supposed to have been a brother, who settled in Hatfield. Daniel Kellogg, whose previous history is unknown, was settled in Norwalk, Ct., in 1655. He died there in 1688, leaving a large family of sons and daughters. Nothing has come to the writer's knowledge connecting him with the family of Lieut. Joseph; and yet it seems highly probable they had a common origin. The coincidence of family names, particularly that of Martin, which is found in almost every stock of Kelloggs in this country, is sufficient to make us suspect a relationship. For whatever items may be given of this latter family, I am indebted to A. S. Kellogg, Esq., of Vernon, Ct., who is, no doubt, able to fill up the record of this branch to a more satisfactory extent.

Lieut. *Joseph*[A] married 1st, Joannah ——, who died in Hadley, Sept. 14, 1666; 2d, May 9, 1667, Abigail Terry, b. in Simsbury, Ct., Sept. 21, 1646, daughter of Dea. Stephen Terry of Dorchester, Windsor and Simsbury. She was living in 1715.

His children by his first marriage were:—(83) *Elizabeth*,[1] b. Mar. 5, 1651, d. young;—(84) *Joseph*,[1] b. Aug. 11, 1653, d. young;—(85) *Nathaniel*,[1] baptized Oct. 29, 1654, d. young;—(86) *John*,[1] bap. Dec. 29, 1656, m. Dec. 23, 1680, Sarah Moody, who d. 1689, in Farmington; 2d, Ruth ——;—(87) *Martin*,[1] m., 1st, Dec. 10, 1684, Anna Hinsdill; 2d, Feb. 1690, Mrs. Sarah Lane;—(88) *Edward*,[1] b. Oct. 1, 1660, m. Dorothy ——, and removed to Brookfield;—(89) *Samuel*,[1] b. in Hadley, Sept. 28, 1662, m. Sept. 22, 1687, Sarah Merrill, of Boston, lived in Hartford, Ct., d. about 1717;—(90) *Joannah*,[1] b. Dec. 8, 1664, m. Nov. 29, 1683, John Smith of Hadley;—(91) *Sarah*,[1] b. in H. Aug. 27, 1666, m. April 27, 1686, Samuel Ashley, of Westfield.

By second marriage: (92, previously numbered 1,) *Stephen*,[1][†] b. Apr. 9, 1668; m. May 8, 1695, Lydia Belding; removed to and lived in Westfield, and d. there June 5, 1722, æt. 54, as appears from his monument now, or lately, in Westfield grave-yard. With him began the genealogy of the family, as will be perceived in the former article;—(93) *Nathaniel*,[1] b. Oct. 8, 1669, m. June 28, 1692, Sarah Boltwood, resided many years in Hadley, 3d precinct, now Amherst, where he was one of the original members of the Congregational Church Nov. 7, 1739. He d. there Oct. 30, 1750, a. 81;—(94) *Abigail*,[1] b. Oct. 9, 1671;— (95) *Elizabeth*,[1] b. Oct. 9, 1673, m. Nov. 27, 1691, John Nash;—(96) *Prudence*,[1] b. Oct 14, 1675, m. April 18, 1699, Dea. Abraham Merrill of Hartford, and d. Sept. 21, 1747, æt. 72;—(97) *Ebenezer*,[1] b. Nov. 22, 1677, is said to have removed to Colchester, Ct.;—(98) *Jonathan*,[1] b. Dec. 25, 1679, removed to Colchester, where he d. Aug. 8, 1771, æ. 92; —(99) *Daniel*,[1] b. March 22, 1681-2, d, July 5, 1684;—(100) *Joseph*,[1] b. May 12, 1684, m. July 5, 1710, Elizabeth Colton of Springfield, lived in Hatfield, and d. Sept. 9, 1724;—(101) *Daniel*,[1] b. June 10, 1686, did not live to adult age ;—(102) *Ephraim*,[1] b. —— 2, 1687, probably d. young.

92. STEPHEN [1] KELLOGG, by wife Lydia Belding, had : (103) *Stephen*,[2] b. Feb. 3, 1695, m. June 18, 1734, Mary Cook, and d. Dec. 1738 ;—(104) *Lydia*,[2] b. Jan. 24, 1697, perhaps m. Jan. 17, 1733–4, Benjamin Lewis of Colchester, Ct.;—(105) *Moses*,[2] b. Oct. 26, 1700, d. Sept. 15, 1704 ;—(106) *Abigail*,[2] b. Dec. 27, 1702, probably m. Benj. Sheldon, to whom she was published Aug. 13, 1726 ;—(107) *Daniel*,[2][†] b. Dec. 16, 1704, m. May 13, 1731, Hannah Noble of Sheffield, who was b. in Westfield, Oct. 11, 1707 ; he d. at Westfield Jan. 11, 1756 ;—(108) *Ephraim*,[2] b. July 2, 1707 ;—(109) *Mercy*,[2] b. Oct. 30, 1709 ;—(110) *Noah*,[2] b. Feb. 13, 1711, s. in Sheffield, had sons, one of whom, *Pliny*,[3] resided in the Black River country, N. Y., and d. there about 1830 ;—(111) *Silas*,[2] b. April 7, 1714, m. May 10, 1739, Ruth Root. He d. Jan. 24, 1792, aged 78. She d. Jan. 18, 1817, æ. 95 ;—(112) *Amos*.[2][†] b. Sept. 30, 1716, m. May 27, 1747, Prudence Sedgwick, resided in Sheffield, and d. there Nov. 26, 1770, a. 54.

107. DEA. DANIEL [2] KELLOGG resided in Sheffield, and is said to have gone on the expedition of Montgomery to Quebec. This must be an error, that service having occurred in 1775. He probably went on Wolfe's expedition, and d. at Westfield on his return. He and Philip Callender were the first deacons in the church first established in Sheffield, under Rev. Jonathan Hubbard. By wife, Hannah Noble, he had : (113) *Hannah*,[3] b. May 15, 1732, d. May 26, 1732 ;---(114) *Hannah*,[3] b. June 25, 1734, d. Sept. 10, 1738 ;---(115) *Abigail*,[3] b. Oct. 29, 1736, d. Nov. 8, 1736 ;---(116) *Daniel*,[3] b. Nov. 11, 1737, d. Oct. 15, 1738 ;---(117) *Marcy*,[3] b. April 22, 1740, probably m. June 21, 1759, Joseph Callender of Sheffield ;---(118) *Stephen*,[3] b. June 26, 1742, probably m. Jan. 23, 1768, Mary Austin ;---(119) *Hannah*,[3] b. Aug. 10, 1744 ;---(120) *Daniel*,[3] b. Nov. 5, 1746, probably m. Rhoda ——, and settled in Vermont. After his death she m. Jan. 8, 1778, Jesse Kellogg, and d. Sept. 14, 1813, a. 62 ;---(121) *Gideon*,[3] b. July 6, 1751, resided and d. in Sheffield, was deaf and mute.

112. AMOS [2] KELLOGG, by wife Prudence Sedgwick, had : (122) *Ebenezer*,[3][†] b. Feb. 29, 1748, m. Dec. 3, 1772, Sarah Austin, who d. Mar. 1819, æt. 69. He d. May 10, 1827, æt. 80 ; lived and died in Sheffield ; ---(123) *Josiah*,[3] b. April 15, 1750, d. Dec. 12, 1750 ;---(124) *Jesse*,[3] b. Aug. 28, 1751, m. Jan. 7, 1778, wid. Rhoda Kellogg ; l. and d. at Sheffield ;---(125) *Abigail*,[3] * b. Nov. 23, 1752 ;---(126) *Prudence*,[3] * b. Sept. 23, 1754 ;---(127) *Mary*,[3] * b. Oct. 5, 1758 ;---(128) *Amos*,[3] b. Sept. 27, 1760, set. at Paris, Oneida Co., N. Y.;---(129) *Aaron*,[3] b. July 19, 1762, set. at Paris, Oneida Co., N. Y.;---(130) *Josiah*,[3] b. Aug. 12, 1764 ;---(131) *Joanna*,[3] * b. July 4, 1766.

3. EPHRAIM[3] KELLOGG, (see vol. xii. p. 202), eldest son of Silas,[2] m. Ruth Hosmer about 1765, and d. in 1818, æt. 78. He s. on the farm in Sheffield occupied since his death by his son Elisha. He was in the Revolutionary army at the time of Burgoyne's defeat, having left home in harvest

---

* One of these daughters m. Noah Hubbard, son of Jonathan. Another, who m. a Mr. Winslow and settled in Vermont, had sons, cf whom are Rev. Hubbard Winslow of Geneva and Rev Gordon Winslow of Staten Island, N. Y.

time on the expedition. His wife used to relate, that farm labor was so scarce, that from a large crop, she hardly harvested grain enough to live on for the year. He left four sons and five daughters. (133) *Hosmer*,[4] m. and s. in Sheffield, d. Feb. 12, 1836; a deacon in the Congregational Church; (had thirteen children, nine of whom were living in 1844---six sons and three daughters---viz.: Albert,[5] Edwin,[5] Hosmer,[5] George,[5] and Charles,[5] all merchants s. in White Pigeon, Mich., and Norman,[5] a Presbyterian clergyman, s. in Mishawaka, Ind.; Harriet[5] m. Frederick Brown, lived in Sheffield; Ruth,[5] in White Pigeon; and Maria[5] m. —— Chapin, and settled in Uxbridge, Mass. Charles was drowned in St. Joseph's river);---(134) *Ephraim*,[4] m. and s. in Sheffield, d. in 1844. (Had three sons and three daughters, viz.: Nelson[5] s. in Sheffield; Edburgh,[5] in Newburgh, Ill.; Ephraim,[5] a clergyman, in Avon, N. Y.; Adelia,[5] m. —— Stevens, in Richmond, N. Y.; Jane,[5] m. —— Richards, Lenox, Ms.; and Eleanor,[5] m. —— Callender, Sheffield); —(135) *Elisha*,[4] m. Jane Saxton, d. in Sheffield, 1857. (Had three sons and two daughters, viz.: Frederick,[5] s. in Newburgh, N. Y.; Hon. Ensign H.[5] in Pittsfield, Ms., counsellor at law, has been much in Public life, having been Speaker of the House of Representatives, and Senator in the Massachusetts Legislature, besides serving in various other responsible offices; James E.[5] in Sheffield; Mary,[5] m. —— Ward, in Bergen, N. Y.; and Ruth,[5] m. —— Arnold, in Sheffield);—(136) *Donny*,[4] m. and s. in Sennett, N. Y., then in Phelps, N. Y., and when he removed from thence is not known. Had two sons and two daughters—Augustus,[5] s. in Sheffield; Milton,[5] in White Pigeon; Catherine,[5] in Sheffield; and Caroline[5] d. in 1833 ;—(136) *Vienna*,[4] m. —— Dibble, s. in Bergen, N. Y., d. in 1838 ;—(137) *Esther*,[4] m. Oliver Porter, d. in Paris, N. Y., in 1827 ;—(138) *Sarah*,[4] m. Hosea Bills, s. in Sheffield ;—(139) *Mary*,[4] m. Edmund Fellows,s. in Weedsport, N.Y.;—(140) *Urania*,[4] m. Amos Bacon, s. in Dundee, Mich.

4. Enos[3] Kellogg, 2d son of Silas,[2] m. Abigail Seymour, s. in Sheffield, removed to Hubbardston, Vt., and thence to Batavia, N. Y., where he d. in 1803. Had children : (142) *Lucyne*,[4] b. Aug. 21, 1766, m. Jonathan Burrall, s. in Sheffield, thence in Salisbury, N. Y., and d. there in 1839 ;—(143) *Orsamus*,[4] b. May 12, 1768, s. in Illinois ;—(144) *Eleanor*,[4] b. Feb. 4, 1770 ;—(145) *Abigail*[4] and (146) *Ruth*[4] b. June 12, 1774 ;—(147) *Enos*,[4] b. April 24, 1776, prob. d. in Mobile, Ala.;—(149) *Seymour*,[4] b. March 21, 1779, s. in Illinois ;—(150) *Elisha*,[4] s. in Ohio, d. about 1820 ;—(151) *Ira*,[4] s. in Michigan.

10. Silas[3] Kellogg, youngest son of Silas,[2] who m. Rhoda Root, and resided in Sheffield, d. in 1836, æt. 79, had : (152) *Chauncey*,[4] lived and d. in Sheffield ;—(153) *Norman*,[4] s. in Sheffield ;—(154) *George*,[4] resides in Erie, Pa., merchant ;---(155) *Silas R.*,[4] resides in Sheffield, physician ;---(156) *John*,[4] d. at the south ;---(157) *Rhoda*,[4] m. Consider Morgan, s. in Sheffield ;---(158) *Frances*,[4] m. Jonathan Church, s. in Sheffield ;---(159) *Maria*,[4] m. Jay Shears, s. in Sheffield ;---(160) *Nancy*,[4] m. —— Flint, s. in Reading, Mass.

122. Ebenezer[3] Kellogg, son of Amos,[2] who m. Sarah Austin, had, (161) *Amasa*,[4] b. April 2, 1774, d. Nov. 4, 1775 ;—(162) *Wealthy*,[4] b. Dec. 13, 1775 ;—(163) *Amasa*,[4] b. Feb. 5, 1777 ;—(164) *Amos*,[4] b. Nov. 18, 1778 ;—(165) *Ebenezer*,[4] b. Nov. 5, 1780 ;—(166) *Sarah*,[4] b. May 21, 1783 ;—(167) *Henry*,[4] b. June 6, 1786, d. in Sheffield March 19, 1813.

5. Asa[3] Kellogg, son of Silas,[2] m. Lucy Powell, Feb. 27, 1766.

14. Martin[4] Kellogg, son of Asa,[3] had three sons : *Cassius,*[5] of Mexico, N. Y.; Rev. *Martin Powell,*[5] residing in Ohio ; and Rev. *Lewis,*[5] a clergyman lately s. in. Whitehall, N. Y.

19. Alexander Cyrus[4] Kellogg, son of Asa,[3] had daughters, *Maria*[5] who m. 1st, Charles Mills, 2d, Dr. Graves, resides in Corning, N. Y.; *Margaret,*[5] m. Charles E. Osborne, resides in Corning, N. Y.; and sons, *Alexander*[5] and *Cyrus.*[5]

43. Dwight[5] Kellogg, son of Charles,[4] (15) d. at Yonkers, N. Y., Aug. 19, 1859, æ. 62.

49. Dan W.[5] Kellogg, son of Charles,[4] (15) has one son, *Charles Dor,*[6] b. July 3, 1842, member of Princeton College, N. J.; and one dau. *Emma Louise,*[6] b. July 12, 1858. Had two sons who d. early, *George Dwight,*[6] b. Feb. 28, 1836, d. May 3, 1837, and *Augustus Fake,*[6] b. June June 17, 1852, d. April 12, 1858.

The records of Sheffield show several families of the name that the writer has been unable to trace, who, no doubt, descended from the same stock. Will not some of their descendents show *where* they belong ? With the publication of this, the further investigation of the subject will be resigned to other hands. *William Kellogg* m. Nov. 11, 1747, *Keziah Dewey; Nathan Loomis K.* m. Aug. 1752, Diadama Austin. *Timothy* m. Keziah ———— ; *Jason* m. Miriam ———— ; *Joel* m. Susanna ———— ; *Jacob* m. April, 1758, Mary Harmon ; and *Stephen* m. Mindwell ————. All these had children from 1747 to 1790.

Many of the name are now residing in Hadley, Amherst, New Salem, &c., Mass., descendants, probably, of Nathaniel,[1] (85), son of Lieut. Joseph,[4] (82). From this branch it is believed descended Rev. David, D.D., of Framingham ; Hon. Daniel, LL.D., of Brattleboro', Vt., many years Judge of the Supreme Court of that State ; and Henry, Counsellor-at-law, of Bennington, Vt., brother of the latter.

For what follows the writer hopes he may not be regarded, in any quarter, as trespassing on the prerogatives or sensibilities of the other branch, to which he claims kindred. His chief object is to make such a beginning as shall stimulate others, more directly concerned, to pursue the investigation, until the genealogy of the entire family shall have been recovered and traced to its European origin.

THE CONNECTICUT BRANCH OF KELLOGGS.

174. Daniel[1] Kellogg of Norwalk, Ct., to whom reference has al-ready been made, was there in 1655 ; was selectman in 1670 ; d. in 1688. Inventory dated Dec. 5, 1688, £400. Nothing is ascertained of his origin, or connecting him, certainly, with other families of the name in Ct. or Mass. He m., 1st ———— ————, who d. 1664 or 1665 ; 2d, in 1665, Bridget Bouton, dau. of John, a French protestant, who d. in 1689.

Children by first marriage : (175) *Mary,*[2] b. ———— 1662-3, m. 1680, Joseph Platt of Milford ; (176) *Rachel,*[2] b. Feb. 1663-4, m. Abraham Nichols.

Children by second marriage : (177) *Sarah,*[2] b. Feb. 1665-6, m. Daniel Brinsmade ;—(178) *Elizabeth,*[2] b. Aug. 1668, d. 1690. Part of

her estate was at Wallingford ;—(179) *Daniel*,²[†] b. May 7, 1671, m.
——, name unknown ;—(180) *Samuel*,²[†] b. Feb. 1674, m. Sep. 6, 1707,
Sarah Platt, dau. of Dea. John ;—(181) *Lydia*,² b. April, 1676, m. John
Clerke ;—(182) *Benjamin*,² b. Mar. 1678, d. 1702, æ. 24. Inventory
Nov. 2, £166 ;—(183) *Joseph*,²[†] b. Mar. 1678, m. 1st, Sarah Plum ; 2d,
Mary Lyon.

179. DANIEL² KELLOGG lived in Norwalk, and d. about 1709, æ. 38.
Inventory, July, 28, 1709, £500, gives names and ages of five children :
(184) *Daniel*,³[†] b. March 7, 1699, m. Eunice Jarvis ;—(185) *John*,³ b.
1701, m. Jan. I, 1729-30, Ann Coley of Fairfield ; resided in Norwalk, and d. April 17, 1740, æ. 39 ; inventory, £1,500 ; widow m. ——
Hayes ; (had Ezra,⁴ b. 1731 ; Mary,⁴ b. 1732-3 ; Ann,⁴ b. 173⁴⁄₅ ; John,⁴
b. 1737 ; Seth,⁴ b. 1739-40. Ezra and Seth were probably of Danbury,
Ct., Feb. 12, 1755) ;—(186) *Benjamin*,³ b. 1704, had sons Samuel⁴ and
Justus.⁴ He r. in Wallingford, Ct., May 13, 1725 ;—(187) *Johannah*,³ b.
1706 ;—(188) *Eliasaph*,³ b. July, 1709, m. 1734, Rachel Benedick,
dau. of Ensign Thomas, had nine children, b. 1735–1749, viz.: Joannah,⁴
Rachel,⁴ Rachel 2d,⁴ Lydia,⁴ Esther,⁴ Thomas,⁴ Eliasaph,⁴ Milisan,⁴ and
Deborah.⁴

180 SAMUEL² KELLOGG, who m. Sarah Platt, had (189) *Sarah*,³ b.
Sept. 26, 1705 ;—(190) *Samuel*,³ b. Dec. 23, 1706, m. Ann ——. He
d. 1754, æ. 48. The distribution of his estate names seven daughters :
Lois,⁴ m. Benjamin Whitna, Ann,⁴ m. Nathan Jarvis, Ruth,⁴ Elizabeth ⁴
m. Matthew Reid, Mary,⁴ Esther,⁴ Sarah.⁴ Perhaps there were sons,
Stephen⁴ and others ;—(191) *Mary*,³ b. June 29, 1708 ;—(192) *Martin*,³
b. March 23, 1711, d. July, 1756, a. 45. His will names Mercy his wife,
and five children ; Eliphalet,⁴ Mercy,⁴ Martin,⁴ Samuel,⁴ and Nathan.⁴ The
latter m. Rachel Carter ;—(193) *Abigail*,³ b. Jan. 19, 1712-13 ;—(194)
Lydia,³ b. Oct. 30, 1715 ;—(195) *Gideon*,³ b. Dec. 5, 1717, d. Sept.
1771, æ. 54. Had Israel,⁴ Gideon,⁴ Samuel,⁴ and perhaps others ;—(196)
Epenetus,³ b. June 26, 1719, d. June 19, 1774, æ. 55. He m. Jemima
——, who d. June 9, 1789, æ. 70—see grave stones in Norwalk—had
Epenetus,⁴ Lydia,⁴ b. 1763, d. May 7, 1779, æ. 16, and probably others.

183. JOSEPH² KELLOGG m. 1st, Nov. 25, 1702, Sarah Plum of Milford,
dau. of Dea. John, who d. Aug. 17, 1712 ; 2d, Oct. 10, 1712, Mrs. Mary Lyon
of Norwalk, widow of Andrew. He resided in Norwalk, and d. about 1721.
Children named in the distribution of his estate, June •21, 1721 :—(197)
Elizabeth,³ b Oct. 5, 1703 ;—(198) *Sarah*,³ b. April 5, 1706 ;—(199)
Joseph,³ b. Sept. 26, 1707, d. 1731, æ. 24 ;—(200) *Rachel*,³ b. July 15,
1710, m. 1729, William Reed, had Joseph⁴ and William⁴ ;—(201)
Hannah,³ b. Aug. 1, 1712 ;—(202) *David*,³[†] b. Sept. 28, 1715, m. Feb.
28, 1733-4, Judith Raymond of N., dau. of Daniel : (Had Mary,⁴ b. ——
1734 ; Rachel,⁴ b. 1737 ; Judith,⁴ b. 1739 ; Joseph,⁴ b. 1741-2) ;—(203)
Benjamin,³ b. Sept. 26, 1717.

184. DANIEL³ KELLOGG lived in Norwalk, d. Dec. 2, 1762, a. 63.
He m. 172–, Eunice Jarvis of Huntington, L. I., who d. Nov. 19, 1767,
æ. 63. They had : (204) *Daniel*,⁴ (had Ebenezer,⁵ Daniel,⁵ Elijah,⁵
Nathan Fairchild,⁵ Mabel⁵ m. —— Nash and d. 1833, perhaps others) ;
—(205) *Elizabeth*,⁴ unm. in 1762 ;—(206) *Jarvis*,⁴ b. 1731, m. Hannah
——. He d. March 22, 1815, æ. 84. She d. June 19, 1832, æ. 89. (Had
a son Jarvis,⁵ deacon at N., d. July 18, 1831, æ. 64 ; m. 1792, Mercy

Sellick, who d. April 23, 1850, æ. 80. Another son Charles,[5] b. June 17, 1800, r. in N.) ;—(207) *Millicent*,[4] m. before 1762 ;—(208) *Ebenezer*,[4] [†] b. April 5, 1737, m. Hannah Wright ;—(209) *Eunice*,[4] m. and d. before her father, leaving children ;—(210) *Sarah*,[4] m. before 1762 ;— (211) *Abigail*,[4] unm. in 1762.

These eight children are named in the will of their father, dated Jan. 15, 1762. If there are others, they d. before him, probably unmarried.

208. Rev. EBENEZER KELLOGG, who m. Oct. 20, 1763, Hannah Wright of N., dau. of Rev. Ebenezer Wright of Stamford, and Hannah Allyn, graduated at Yale College 1757, and was ordained Pastor at North Bolton, now Vernon, Ct., Nov. 24, 1762, d. at that place Sept. 3, 1817, a. 80, in the 55th year of his ministry. She d. June 7, 1807, æ. 67.

They had six children : (212) *Ebenezer*,[5][†] b. Oct. 21, 1764, m. Abigail Olmsted, and others ;—(213) *Daniel*,[5] b. June 25, 1766, m. Susannah Griggs of Tolland, Ct., d. Feb. 20, 1855, a. 88. (Had a large family, of whom are Edmund B.[6] b. May 27, 1809, and Elijah C.[6], both Lithographers in Hartford) ;—(214) *Hannah*,[5] b. May 24, 1768, m. Dea. Phineas Tallcott, d. 1836 ;—(215) *Thomas Wright*,[5] b. June 24, 1770, m. Mary Hubbard. He d. 1836 : was prominent in town affairs : left a large family ;—(216) *Eunice*,[5] b. Nov. 15, 1773, m. Scottoway Hinkley, M. D., d. 1824 ;—(217) *Elizabeth*,[5] b. Nov. 9, 1781, d. July 15, 1784.

212. EBENEZER[5] KELLOGG, Esq., lived in Vernon ; held various town offices, and was rep. to the Legislature. He d. May 10, 1812, a. 47. Was thrice m.: 1st, Abigail Olmsted of E. Hartford, dau. Nathaniel Olmsted and Sarah Pitkin, she d. Jan. 29, 1797, æ. 38; m. 2d, Hannah Olmsted, dau. of Ashbel and Hannah ; 3d, Elizabeth Sheldon, who still survives.

Had twelve children : (218) *Ebenezer*,[6] b. Oct. 25, 1789, graduate of Yale College 1810, Professsor in Williams College for 29 years, d. Oct. 2, 1846, æ. 57 ;—(219) *Martin*,[6] b. Nov. 6, 1791, d. in the army at New London, Oct. 1, 1814, æ. 23 ;—(220) *George*,[6] b. March 3, 1793, manufacturer at Rockville, Ct. Has had five children : Ebenezer Noble,[7] wool-dealer, Hartford : names of others unknown ;—(221) *Allyn*,[6] b. Aug. 17, 1794, farmer in Vernon : (has two sons, Allyn Stanley,[7] grad. Williams College 1846 ; Martin,[7] grad. Yale College 1850, now a clergyman at Grass Valley, Cal.) ;—(222) *Nathaniel Olmsted*,[6] b. Feb. 26, 1796, manufacturer in Vernon, has been rep. and senator in the Ct. legislature, d. May 13, 1854, a. 58. Left no children

202. Capt. JOSEPH[4] KELLOGG, b. in Connecticut 1742, d. at Somers, in that State, 1795, whose family genealogy has been communicated, appears to have descended directly from Daniel[1] (174) of Norwalk. Information from one of his descendants gives the name of *Joseph* as his grandfather, and states that the latter was carried away by the Indians and lived with them, a captive in the wilderness, six years. The name thus given places him in this descent as the son of *David*[3] (202), the son of *Joseph*[2] (183), the son of *Daniel*.[1] Capt. Joseph[4] is said to have served in the revolutionary army under Gen. Washington.

He m. Nov. 2, 1772, Lucy Warner, and had ten children : (223) *Joseph*,[4] b. Aug. 26, 1773, d. young ;—(224) *Lucy*,[4] b. Feb. 8, 1775, d. young ;—(225) *Lucy 2*,[4] b. Jan. 21, 1777 ;—(226) *Joseph 2*,[4] b. April 3, 1779 ;—(227) *Martin*,[4] b. Nov. 21, 1780 ;—(228) *Horace*,[4] b. Aug. 31,

1783 ;—(229) *Jonathan Dwight,*[4] b. Sept. 11, 1785 ;—(230) *Daniel W.*[4] b. Oct. 31, 1787 ;—(231) *William,*[4] b. Nov. —, 1790 ;—(232) *Samuel,*[4] b. Dec. —, 1795.

THE KELLOGG FAMILIES OF COLCHESTER, CONN.

By JAMES H. PERRIN, Esq., of Lafayette, Indiana.

THE chief sources from which the following is taken are the town records of Hebron, Colchester, Hadley and Hatfield; Judd's History of Hadley; Randall's Colchester Epitaphs, in the REGISTER for 1889; and the Kellogg articles in the REGISTER, xii., 201–6, xiv., xv., 125–32. The last articles [1] mention four early Kelloggs, antecedents unknown :

    i.   LIEUT. JOSEPH, of Farmington, Boston, and Hadley, descendants given.

    ii.   NATHANIEL, Hartford 1639, removed to Farmington.

    iii. SAMUEL, supposedly brother of the above Nathaniel, settled at Hatfield.

    iv. DANIEL, settled at Norwalk 1655, descendants given.

The present article gives some account of the Samuel falsely supposed to be a "brother of the above Nathaniel." As Nathaniel was adult in 1639, while Samuel was not married until 1664, they seem unlikely to have been brothers, especially as Samuel is not mentioned in the will of Nathaniel.* An account is also given of the descendants of Ebenezer and Jonathan Kellogg, sons of Lieut. Joseph, referred to in the REGISTER for April, 1860, as having removed to Colchester. Pedigrees of allied families have been traced back, whenever possible, to the first person of the name in Colchester.

The writer will be grateful for any information concerning the ancestry of the Samuel Kellogg whose descendants are here given.

---

* Records of the Particular Court, Hartford, ii. 118, will of Nathan[ll] Kelog, June 4 1657 : Being weak in body * * * gives whole estate to dear and loving wife Elizabeth Kelog during her life, after her death all his houses and lands in Farmington to his brother John Kelog and to sister Jane Aallisun and sister Rachel Cane, all dwelling in old England, they to pay to cousin Joseph Kelog's three children six pounds sterling to be divided equally betwixt them * * *. Inventory Dec 21 1657, £366:5.

[1] Pages 329-342, this volume.

1. SAMUEL[1] KELLOGG was probably born prior to 1642; died at Hatfield, Mass., Jan. 17, 1711. Married 1st, Nov. 24, 1664, Sarah, widow of Nathaniel Gunn of Hartford, and daughter of Robert Day,* of Hartford. She was killed by the Indians, 19th Sep. 1677. Married 2d, March 20, 1679, Sarah, daughter of Thomas Root† of Westfield.‡ She died Jan. 5, 1719.

Children :
- 2. i. SAMUEL,[2] b. Hadley, April 11, 1669.
  At Hatfield :
- 3. ii. NATHANIEL, b. June 4, 1671.
  - iii. EBENEZER, b. June 2, 1674.
  - iv. JOSEPH, b. Sept. 9, 1676; killed by the Indians Sept. 19, 1677.
  - v. JOHN, b. April 25, 1680; resided at Hatfield; d. probably unm. Will 1755.
  - vi. THOMAS, b. Oct. 21, 1681; d. unm. Hatfield prior to 1758.
  - vii. SARAH, b. April 13, 1683; m. May 8, 1701, "by Rev. Isaac Chauncy," to Abraham Morton of Hatfield.

2. SAMUEL[2] KELLOGG (*Samuel[1]*) was born at Hadley, April 11, 1669; removed after 1701 to Colchester, Conn., where he died August 24, 1708. Married 1690 Hannah[3] Dickinson,§ who was born 1666, died August 3, 1745. Will of Mrs. Hannah, dated Colchester, April 18, 1745, mentions following children. Proved Jan. 7, 1745-6.

Children, all born at Hatfield :
- 4. i. SAMUEL,[3] b. May 18, 1694.
- 5. ii. JOSEPH, b. June 18, 1696.
  - iii. HANNAH, b. Sept. 11, 1699.
  - iv. EUNICE, b. August 3, 1701; m. July 11, 1728, Benj. Quiterfield.

3. SERGT. NATHANIEL[2] KELLOGG (*Samuel[1]*) was born at Hatfield 1671; died at Colchester August 22, 1757. Married 1st, Margaret ——— who died Dec. 13, 1747, æ. 71; married 2d, May 29, 1748, widow Priscilla Williams of Colchester. Will dated 1756; proved 1757; mentions numbers of his children and grandchildren. (*Vide* Randall's Colch. Epitaphs.)

The following curious extract is from the old Colonial Records of Connecticut :‖

" At a meeting of the Governour and Council May 24, 1712. *Present,* The Honourable Gurdon Saltonstall, Esq[r] Governour . . . . . etc . . . . .

Whereas Jonathan Bigelo went from Hartford post to New London, in a deep snow last winter, being agreed by Major Talcot and M[r] Lord, deceased, to find a horse and subsistence at his own cost, and allowed double post wages, the said Bigelo nevertheless applied to M[r] Tainter, justice of peace at Colchester, to have a horse impressed for him from Colchester to New London, and the said justice having impressed for him a good horse of Nath[ll] Kellogge of the same town, which horse

---

* Robert Day came in "Elizabeth," from Ipswich, Co. Suffolk, England, to Boston, Apr. 1634, æ. 30, with wife Mary, æ. 28. *Vide* Hist. Hartford.

† Thomas Root was at Salem 1637; Hartford 1639; removed about 1659 to Northampton, where he was one of the seven founders of a church 1661; died there July 17, 1694.

‡ Judd.

§ Nathaniel[1] Dickinson came to Wethersfield from England 1637. Rep. 1646-56. (Removed to Hadley 1659. Died June 16, 1676.)

Nathaniel[2] Dickinson, son of above, born August 1643, or perhaps four years earlier; m. 1st, 1662, Hannah ———, who died Feb. 23, 1679; m. 2d, 1680, widow Elizabeth Gillett; m. 3d, 1684, Elizabeth, widow Samuel Wright. He died Oct. 11, 1710.

Hannah[3] Dickinson, daughter of above, born 1666.

‖ Transcribed and published by Charles J. Hoadly, State Librarian.

the said Bigelo rode so extream hard in that bad season that he was extreamly wrong'd as appear'd by evidence produced to this board; ordered, that the treasurer pay to the said Kellog 20s. for the said damage, and that said Bigelo, if he can't shew any reason to the contrary, be made to allow it."

Children at Hadley :

i.   MARGARET,³ b. Feb. 15, 1697; m. —— Campfield.
ii. EDITHA, b. Nov. 13, 1699; m. March 21, 1727, Joseph Pratt, b. June 30, 1698, son of Serg' Joseph Pratt and Sarah Colyer, who were married July 22, 1697. Sarah Pratt d. Nov. 20, 1730.

At Colchester :

6. iii. NATHANIEL, b. May 8, 1703.
iv. SARAH, b. Dec. 27, 1707; m. Feb. 19, 1728–29, Mr. Judah Lewis, first pastor of Colchester church; d. April 17, 1732.
v.   LYDIA, b. May 29, 1710; m. 1st, May 28, 1730, Capt. John Hopson, b. Nov. 12, 1707, son of John Hopson from R. I., who m. Jan., 1704, Sarah Northam. Capt. John d. August 6, 1751. His widow m. 2d, Henry Bliss of Lebanon, and d. March 31, 1761.
7. vi. JOHN,* b. probably 1713.
8. vii. ABNER, b. probably 1716.
9. viii. EZRA, b. Sept. 6, 1724.

4. SAMUEL³ KELLOGG (*Samuel,² Samuel¹*) was born at Hatfield May 18, 1694; married Jan. 8, 1735–6, Abigail Sterling. He died July 31, 1738. She died August 23, 1802, æ. 93. Children, born at Colchester :

i.   ABIGAIL,⁴ b. Oct. 29, 1736; m. Dec. 8, 1757, Joseph Gillett. He d. Dec. 4, 1814, æ. 90; she d. May 14, 1822. He was son of Jonathan Gillett who m. Sarah Eley Jan. 3, 1717. Jonathan d. Jan. 3, 1755. Sarah Eley d. July 4, 1759, æ. 65.
ii. SAMUEL, b. Dec. 20, 1738; d. Nov. 24, 1827. Married Mary —— who d. Feb. 23, 1813, æ. 70.
iii. HANNAH, b. Sept. 30, 1740.
iv. ANN, b. Nov. 30, 1742; d. young.
v.   MARY, b. April 27, 1745.
vi. EUNICE, b. Feb. 26, 1747; m. Jan. 16, 1777 —— Carter.
vii. DANIEL, b. Jun. 1, 1749; d. May 28, 1829. Married Elizabeth—— who d. May 23, 1815, æ. 70.

5. JOSEPH³ KELLOGG (*Samuel,² Samuel¹*) was born at Hatfield June 18, 1696; married Abigail Miller Oct. 23, 1717. At Colchester :

i.   JOSEPH,⁴ b. August 8, 1718; m. Nov. 15, 1739, Susanna Keny.
10. ii. DANIEL, b. May 6, 1720.
iii. MERCY, b. May 20, 1723.
iv. MOSES, b. —— 10, 1725; m. Sept. 3, 1755, Dinah Sears of Middletown.
v.   ELIJAH, b. Jan. 15, 1728; m. June 3, 1754, Hannah Arms of Colchester.
At Hebron :
vi. EZEKIEL, b. Nov. 24, 1732; m. July 2, 1759, Ann Owen.
vii. ABIGAIL, b. Nov. 27, 1734.

6. NATHANIEL³ KELLOGG (*Nathaniel,² Samuel¹*) was born May 8, 1703, at Colchester; died April 1, 1762. Married July 1, 1725, Elizabeth Williams, daughter Charles, born Feb. 13, 1702. Children:

i.   CHARLES,⁴ b. Sept. 17, 1726; m. April 24, 1748, Sarah, dau. John Hitchcock. Perhaps lived at Bolton.

—————
* The writer is convinced that this John is the same with the one who married Mary Newton (see p. 62), although same doubt is expressed by Randall, 310, REG. xliii., 44–5.

ii.   ELIZABETH, b. July 8, 1729; m. May 9, 1750, Elihu Clark. He was
      born Nov. 8, 1727, son of Noah Clark and Sarah Taintor, who
      were married June 10, 1719.
iii. SARAH, b. Feb. 22, 1731-2; m. ———— Bingham.
iv.   DELIGHT, b. Oct. 5, 1734; m. ———— Andrus.
v.   MARGARET, b. Jan. 7, 1736-7; m. ———— Webb.
vi.   NATHANIEL, b. July 10, 1739.
vii. ANN, b. Jan. 28, 1741-2.
viii. ASA, b. May 14, 1746; d. young.

7. JOHN³ KELLOGG* (*Nathaniel,² Samuel¹*) was born probably 1713;
   died Jan. 22, 1762. Married April 2, 1738, Mary³ Newton, born
   March 1, 1719, died July 2, 1844. She was the daughter of Major
   Israel² Newton (son of James¹ of Kingston, R. I.) and Hannah
   ————. Major Israel was born March 5, 1694; died May 24,
   1745, at siege of Cape Breton. Mrs. Hannah died May 28, 1780,
   æ. 88. Children at Colchester:

i.   JUDAH,⁴ b. March 8, 1739.
ii.   MERCY, b. June 11, 1741; m. March 2, 1786, Asa³ Graves. He was
      b. May 8, 1747; son of Peter² Graves and Sarah Wedge, who were
      m. July 1, 1742. Benjamin¹ Graves d. Dec. 30, 1752, æ. 76.
iii. JOHN, b. Dec. 20, 1743.
iv.   ISRAEL, b. May 31, 1746; m. 1775, Hannah Ingham.
v.   MARY, b. Dec. 17, 1749; m. May 31, 1768, Isaac³ Foote.†
vi.   HANNAH, b. Dec. 8, 1751.
vii. ELISHA, b. Nov. 15, 1755; m. June 9, 1776, Susanna⁴ Day.‡

8. ABNER,³ KELLOGG (*Nathaniel,² Samuel¹*) was born probably 1716;
   died Nov. 18, 1754, æ. 38. Married June 26, 1740, Lydia Otis.
   (For full account of Lydia Otis' ancestry see Stiles' Hist. Windsor,
   1893). Children at Colchester:

i.   DELIGHT,⁴ b. April 6, 1741; possibly, if not probably, died young.
ii.   LYDIA, b. Jan. 15, 1742-3.
iii. CAPT. ABNER, d. July 24, 1821, æ. 76.
iv.   DAVID, m. 1766, Elinor Williams.
v.   RACHEL.
vi.   EZEKIEL, b. Sept. 17, 1748.
vii. MARGARET, b. Jan. 16, 1751-2.
viii. SARAH.
ix.   EZRA, b. Sept. 5, 1754.

9. EZRA³ KELLOGG (*Nathaniel,² Samuel,¹*) was born Sept. 6, 1724; died
   at Colchester Jan. 5, 1754. Married Ruth ————, who married,
   2d, Nov. 4, 1757, Henry Stiles, and died 1812, æ. 86. Children:

i.   SARAH,⁴ m. ———— Crocker (?)
ii.   RUSSELL, b. July 16, 1750.
iii. OLIVER.

10. DANIEL⁴ KELLOGG (*Joseph,³ Samuel,² Samuel¹*) was born at Col-

* See former footnote on this John.
† Nathᵘ¹ Foote and Ann Clark married July 4, 1711.
Daniel² Foote b. Feb. 6, 1716-7; married June 9, 1743, Margaret Parsons.
Isaac³ Foote b. Jan. 4, 1744-5.
‡ John¹ Day, perhaps of Hartford, died Oct. 17, 1754, æ. 77. Wife Mary, perhaps sister
of Thomas Wells, died May 12, 1714.
Jos.² Day, born Sept. 27, 1702, at Colchester; married April 1, 1729, Esther Hungerford;
died Oct. 26, 1793.
Jos.³ Day, born Colchester May 6, 1731; married Nov. 13, 1754, Susanna Brainard, born
Sept. 24, 1731. She was daughter Stephen Brainard and Susanna Gates, who were married
Dec. 24, 1730.
Susanna⁴ Day, born Jan. 27, 1755.

chester May 6, 1720; married May 27, 1745, Anna Dewey of Hebron. Children at Hebron:

i. ANNA,[5] b. April 18, 1746; m. June 17, 1773, Solomon, son of Thomas Perrin, Jr., and Jerusha Porter (see Porter Gen., 1893). Resided at Vernon, where she d. Sept. 8, 1826. Children: 1. *Anna*, m. Reuben Sumner. 2. *Jerusha*, m. Henry P. Sumner. 3. *Solomon*, m. Salem, Va., Sarah Neal, dau. Joel Bott and Lucy May; d. 1833, New Orleans, leaving son James Joel, who m. Margaret, dau. Judge Samuel Cason of Indiana. 4. *Aaron*, m. Lois Lee. 5. *Asahel*, post. ext.

ii. DANIEL, b. Sept. 10, 1747; m. May 31, 1770, Rachel Taylor of Chatham. Revolutionary soldier.

iii. MARY, b. Sept. 3, 1749.

iv. HANNAH, b. June 16, 1752; d. inft.

v. HANNAH, b. May 7, 1756.

vi. CHARLES, b Aug. 8, 1763; d. inft.

vii. ABIGAIL, b. June 19, 1765.

viii. CHARLES, b. July 18, 1772.

SOME DESCENDANTS OF LIEUT. JOSEPH KELLOGG.

1. **EBENEZER**[2] **KELLOGG** (*Joseph*[1]) was born at Hadley Nov. 13, 1677; married July 6, 1706, Colchester, Mabel Butler, who died Sept. 3, 1742, æ. 60. He died August 22, 1746. Children:

i. ABIGAIL,[3] b. June 25, 1707; m. Samuel Gillett.

ii. EBENEZER, b. Jan. 30, 1709-10; m. May 10, 1752, Abigail[2] "Rowlee"; d. Feb. 9, 1788. (Elnathan[1] Rowley and Abigail Cone m. Dec. 26, 1723. Abigail[2] dau. b. Oct. 2, 1730.)
   1. *Abigail*, b. Jan. 27, 1754; d. young.
   2. *Ebenezer*, b. March 16, 1756.
   3. *Abigail*, b. Dec. 29, 1758.
   4. *Mabel*, b. August 3, 1763.
   5. *Butler*, b. July 21, 1766; m. Jan. 9, 1788, Sarah Treadway. She d. Jan. 9, 1845, æ. 78.

iii. ELIZABETH, b. Sept. 25, 1712.

iv. MARY, b. Jun. 3, 1715; m. —— Merrils.

v. PRUDENCE, b. Dec. 24, 1717; m. May 6, 1736, Wm. Roberts, son of Wm. Roberts and Elizabeth Northam, who were m. July 20, 1705.

2. **JONATHAN**[2] **KELLOGG** (*Joseph*[1]) was born at Hadley Dec. 25, 1679; married Jan. 3, 1710-11, Ann, daughter of James Newton of Kingston, R. I. She was born April 13, 1692; died August 14, 1769. Jonathan died August 8, 1771. Children:

i. JONATHAN,[3] b. at Colchester Sept. 18, 1712; m. Jan. 5, 1735, Mary Niles.
   1. *Margery*, b. Sept. 6, 1738.
   2. *Martin*, b. "last Sabbath in January, 1740-1;" m. Feb. 4, 1762, Sarah Treadway (?) See p, 64.

ii. JOSEPH, b. June 6, 1714; d. probably June 16, 1762. Married Jan. 15, 1740-1, Sarah Clark, dau. John Clark and Mindwell ——, b. August 13, 1723.
   1. *Silas*, b. August 25, 1742.
   2. *Esther*, b. May 21, 1745.
   3. *Sarah*, b. August 11, 1749.
   4. *Anna*, b. Sept. 28, 1752.

iii. MARGARET, b. August 10, 1716.

iv. STEPHEN, b. March 15, 1724.

v. SILAS, b. Jan. 11, 1732-3; m. June 21, 1768, Sarah Kook.
   1. *Molly*, b. April 26, 1769.

2. *Joseph*, b. Dec. 2, 1770; d. young.
3. *Sarah*, b. July 11, 1772.
vi. MARTIN, b. Feb. 15, 1734–5; m. Feb. 4, 1762, Sarah Treadway (?).
See p. 63.
See p. 63.
1. *Bethiah*, b. Oct. 24, 1762.
2. *Martin*, b. Dec. 16, 1764.
3. *Jonathan*, b. May 4, 1767.
4. *Eve*, b. Feb. 4, 1770.

DISCONNECTED.

WILLIAM, son of Moses Kellogg, born at Colchester, Jan. 28, 1756.

ISRAEL KELLOGG and Abigail Northam married at Colchester, Jan. 31, 1752. He died Feb. 12, 1784, æ. 63. She died June 9, 1780, æ. 50. Children:

i. JONATHAN, b. Oct. 10, 1754.
ii. ISRAEL, b. May 18, 1756.
iii. AMOS, b. Aug. 5, 1758.
iv. ABIGAIL, b. Nov. 15, 1760.

AARON KELLOGG married at Colchester, July 10, 1740, Mary, dau. Benjamin Lewis. Children:

i. LUCY, b. Mar. 21, 1741; d. inft.
ii. LUCY, b. Feb. 19, 1742; m. May 26, 1768, Eliphalet Chamberlin.
iii. SOLOMON, b. July 14, 1744.
iv. AARON, b, Aug. 9, 1746; m. July 3, 1766, Rhoda Jones.
v. LYDIA, b. Feb. 23, 1749.
vi. MARY, b. Aug. 23, 1751; m. May 31, 1763, Isaac Foote.
vii. HANNAH, b. Mar. 17, 1754.
viii. DANIEL, b. Sept. 3, 1756.
ix. LOVINA, b. Mar. 10, 1760.

KELLOGG—FOOTE.—In the article on the Kelloggs of Colchester which appears in this number, pp. 59-64, under the head of " Disconnected Items." it is stated * that Mary, daughter of Aaron Kellogg, married May 31, 1763, Isaac Foote. This is incorrect; the Mary who married Isaac Foote may have been the daughter of Abner[3] Kellogg. J. H. PERRIN.
*Pages 342-347, this volume.

DOROTHY, UNIDENTIFIED WIFE OF EDWARD KELLOGG

By RUTH LINCOLN KAYE, of Alexandria, Va.

Was Dorothy, wife of Edward Kellogg (1660-1729?) of Hadley and Brookfield, Mass., and Lebanon, Conn., identical with Dorothy, daughter of John and Isabel (Mason) Bissell, born in 1665 in Windsor, Conn.?

The identity of this colonial wife, long sought by the Kellogg family, has never been established. The writer, after years of research among colonial families up and down the Connecticut River and following many will-o'-the-wisps named Dorothy, has come up with a circumstantial case which is submitted herewith for critical appraisal.

The search for Dorothy Kellogg's own surname started in Hadley where she was married, but no family of the time had a reported daughter by name of Dorothy. Next followed Hatfield, Northampton, Westfield, Springfield, Longmeadow, Simsbury, Windsor, Hartford, Wethersfield, Farmington, and other towns on the river. Family books and genealogical sections of town histories were gone over minutely. Next, the families of girls whom the brothers of Edward Kellogg married and the families of boys whom the Kellogg girls married were researched. Finally, even the families that intermarried with Dorothy's children were studied. There was only one Dorothy of the right period unaccounted for; only one who hadn't died unmarried or been reported as marrying someone other than Edward Kellogg. This was Dorothy Bissell. Naturally, this does not prove she is the one looked for, but the writer has discovered circumstantial evidence which suggests the identification.

First consider the facts:

Dorothy, wife of Edward Kellogg

The known facts about Dorothy Kellogg are these. Before 1692 she was married to Edward Kellogg, born in 1660, living in 1729, fourth son of the emigrant, Joseph Kellogg (1626-1708) and his first wife, Joanna (d. 1666), of Hadley, Mass. Joseph operated the ferry across the Connecticut at Hadley and ran an inn or hostel; hence his sons had plenty of opportunity to become acquainted with many families who lived some distance away and stopped at the inn.

Edward and Dorothy Kellogg had nine children: Joseph (b. 1692), Joanna (b. 1694), Thomas (b. 1696), Dorothy (b. 1700), Catherine (b. 1702), Mary (b. 1703), Ephraim (b. 1707), Eleanor (b. 1710), and Edward (b. 1713). The first four children were born in Hadley, and the last five in Brookfield, whence the family had moved by 1701.

Their home in Brookfield was near the intersection of the Bay Path from Hadley and the road from Springfield to Boston. They lived here until 1729, at which time the family that remained (Edward, his wife Dorothy and their son Edward) removed to Lebanon, Conn. Possibly the main reason for the move was that their second son Thomas (the eldest, Joseph, was killed by the Indians in Brookfield in 1710) had removed to Lebanon where he mar-

348

ried in 1720 and prospered, buying and selling land. Thomas joined the Goshen Parish Church there and, significantly, was baptized as an adult in 1722, as his mother and brother Edward were later baptized. He seems to have persuaded his parents and youngest brother to join him in Lebanon, though he himself did not live there after 1731. There is no mention of his father Edward, Sr., after 1729, and until now there has been no published record of his mother, Dorothy, after that date.

In perusing the original records of the Goshen Church of Lebanon, the writer recently discovered that Dorothy Kellogg agreed to the church covenant 25 September 1737, and was baptized "at Mr. Loomas's" 29 September four days later. (This could not have been her daughter Dorothy, who had married Thomas Ainsworth and may even have died by that date.) The fact of her adult baptism at a friend's or relative's home instead of at church, as was customary, indicates that Dorothy was too ill or infirm to go to the church, indeed, may have been on her deathbed. There is no further mention of Dorothy in the church records after that date. The circumstance of her baptism is significant, both because it points to the possible time of her last illness and because it gives a clue to the home in which she lived, possibly with relatives. Her children known from records to be living in 1737 were Ephraim, who was serving at Fort Dummer, and Edward as yet unmarried, else he and his wife might have provided a home for their mother.

Who then was "Mr. Loomis", in whose home presumably Dorothy was living? His identification might point to Dorothy's own family. Perhaps he was a nephew, cousin, brother or an "in-law."

Examination of church records, Loomis genealogies and Connecticut local histories disclosed that there were the brothers, John and Thomas Loomis, who lived in Lebanon at the time, having removed there in 1707/8 with their uncle, Deacon John Loomis who died there in 1715, and their mother and stepfather, Sarah and John Bissell. Sarah (b. 1662) was the daughter of Daniel and Sarah (Crow) White of Hatfield, Mass., and had married (1) Thomas Loomis (1653-1688) of Hatfield, by whom she had John (1681-1755) and Thomas (1684-1765). After her first husband's death she married (2) in 1689 John Bissell (1661-1740), and had four more children in Windsor: Benjamin, Sarah, John and Daniel Bissell. The whole family, Sarah, John Bissell, their four children and her two children by Thomas Loomis, Sr., removed to Lebanon 1707/8.

John Loomis, called in colonial records "Ensign Loomis", married (1) Martha Osborn of Lebanon and (2) Ann Lyman. His brother Thomas was an original member of the Goshen Parish Church of Lebanon, organized 1729, and married (1) Elizabeth Fowler and (2) Hannah Hunt of Lebanon. The writer concludes that Dorothy Kellogg was baptized at Thomas's house rather than at Ensign John's because of the appellation "Mr.", rather than "Ensign": "Dorothy Kellogg was baptized at Mr. Loomis's."

Exhaustive search of the families of the four wives of John and Thomas Loomis disclosed no Dorothys, the thought being that Dorothy Kellogg might have been a relative of one of them. Finally, with the clue that "Mr. Loomis" was probably Thomas Loomis whose stepfather John Bissell of Windsor, had removed with children and stepchildren to Lebanon in 1707/8, the writer studied the Bissell family of Windsor.

Dorothy Bissell

The emigrant John Bissell (1591-1677) was keeper of the ferry at Windsor, Conn. By his wife, Mary Drake, he had six children, the oldest named John also (d. 1693), who kept the ferry from 1658 on. John, Jr., had eight children, the first four by his first wife, Isabel Mason (d. 1663): Mary (b. 1659), John (1661-1740), hereinafter, Daniel (b. 1663) and Dorothy (b. 1665).

This is the sole record of Dorothy Bissell which has been found. There is no record of her baptism, marriage or death. If she lived to maturity, she was, however, certainly the aunt by marriage to John and Thomas Loomis, aforementioned.

Her brother John Bissell (1661-1740) married in 1689 as her second husband the widow Sarah (White) Loomis, who had two small sons aged 4 and 8, John and Thomas, surnamed Loomis. John and Sarah had four children and the whole family removed to Lebanon 1707/8, as has been said above.

The circumstantial evidence

Evidence identifying Dorothy Kellogg as identical with Dorothy Bissell centers around baptism, the location of the families, their occupation and family names.

Baptism: Mrs. Dorothy Kellogg was baptized as an adult in 1737 in Lebanon, Conn., therefore she had not been baptized as a child. Dorothy Bissell was born in 1665 in Windsor; there is no record of her baptism there, either as child or adult. By this circumstance it is possible Dorothy Bissell may have been Dorothy, wife of Edward Kellogg.

Location: John Bissell the 3rd removed to Lebanon in 1707/8 with his family including the stepsons, John and Thomas Loomis. Edward and Dorothy Kellogg removed from Brookfield to Lebanon 1729. Edward presumably died not long after, since there is no further mention of him. His wife (or widow) Dorothy Kellogg is mentioned twice more in official records, namely when she took the church covenant and when she was baptized "at Mr. Loomas's" in 1737. If Dorothy Kellogg was born Dorothy Bissell, she could have been baptized at the home of her step-nephew Thomas Loomis, her brother John Bissell's stepson.

Occupation: Dorothy Kellogg's husband was the son of the ferry-man at Hadley, Mass., just upstream from Windsor where Dorothy Bissell's father John operated the ferry. Possibility: Dorothy Bissell, daughter of the Windsor ferryman could have easily met and married Edward Kellogg, son of the Hadley ferryman.

Family names: Dorothy Kellogg gave three of her children Kellogg family names: Joseph, Joanna, Edward; the other six were named

Thomas, Dorothy, Catherine, Mary, Ephraim, and Eleanor. Dorothy Bissell has a sister Mary, an aunt Mary, an uncle Thomas, and these first cousins, all children of her Uncle Thomas: Thomas, Joseph, Ephraim and Ephraim again.

Lost wives have been identified on less evidence than this. In this instance has a case been made? Has anyone corroborating evidence from other unpublished records?

DOROTHY, UNIDENTIFIED WIFE OF EDWARD KELLOGG

By DONALD LINES JACOBUS, M.A., of New Haven, Conn.

Under the above title, an attempt was made (THE REGISTER, vol. 123, p. 114-117, April 1969) to identify Dorothy, wife of Edward [1] Kellogg, with Dorothy Bissell, the daughter of John[2] Bissell by his wife Israel (wrongly called Isabel) Mason. The Bissell-Mason connections were considered and set forth at considerable length in two articles in *The American Genealogist*, 26:84-94 and 27:100-101. Most of the mistakes in the recent article were caused by trusting the most unreliable account of the Bissell family in Henry R. Stiles' *The History of Ancient Windsor* (1859).[*]

May I try to set the record straight once again? John[1] Bissell did indeed die in 1677; there is no authority that I know of for calling his wife Mary Drake. A nameless wife, perhaps mother of his children, died in 1641; he thereafter had another nameless wife whose death, as wife of John "Sr.", was recorded in 1665. Stiles made the mistake of applying the last record to John Jr., thus killing off his one and only wife and making it necessary to postulate a second wife for him.

John[2] Bissell did not die in 1693 as stated in the recent article, but died as Cornet of the Troop at "Yorke" prior to 15 Oct. 1688 (*Colonial Records of Connecticut*, 3:91, 450). An inventory of the estate of Lt. John Bissell who "died at New York, 1688," was exhibited 7 Mar. 1688/9 and a later one on 15 Mar. 1693/4 which, however, was dated 7 Nov. 1688; the distribution in 1693/4 names the surviving children and calls the daughter Dorothy, Dorothy *Stoughton* (C. W. Manwaring's *A Digest of Early Connecticut Probate Records*, 1:406-407, which is inaccurate in omitting the name of the son Hezekiah from the distribution, though it appears in the original paper on file).

The recent article states that John Bissell, Jr., "had eight children, the first four by his first wife, Isabel Mason (d. 1663)." He had nine children, the birth of the youngest, Samuel, not being recorded, but Samuel was named in the distribution of his father's estate and had later probate of his own. All the children were by Israel (not Isabel) Mason, the one and only wife, and she did not die in 1663 (evidently meant for 1665 when John's stepmother died) but survived her husband. Her administration bond, dated 7 Mar. 1688/9, completely omitted in Manwaring, *op. cit.*, is in File No. 586 of the Hartford Probate District; in it her name is twice written Izraell and once Israell. At marriage, the recorder Matthew Grant spelled her name "Izrell." She was admitted to the Windsor Church in 1686 as Israel Bissell. So it cannot be doubted that her name was actually Israel, not Isabel. The name Israel means "warrior of God" and if her birth was expected when Capt. John Mason left to fight the Pequots in

---

[*] Dr. Claude W. Barlow, of Worcester, Mass., also called our attention to some of the errors in the original article in the April issue.—Editor.

[1] Pages 348-351, this volume.

1637 (quite likely since she married in 1658), the name may have been chosen before he left and was bestowed even though the child turned out to be a girl.

The recent article states that it was Dorothy Bissell's brother John³ Bissell who married Sarah (White) Loomis and moved to Lebanon. Not so. John³ Bissell (*John*,² *John*¹), born 4 May 1661, died without issue prior to 30 May 1690 when the Court ordered distribution of the estates of John Bissell sen. of Windsor and John Bissell Junr. In 1694 the Court approved a distribution of "the Estate of Lt. John Bissell, sen., of Windsor, and John Bissell, son" (Manwaring, *op. cit.*, 1:407-408). A complaint was made and the following month the distribution was rectified; in this later record, the two decedents are called John Bissell, sen. and John Bissell, Jr., and it is clear that the widow and mother (Israel) was then still living. This distribution also calls one of the heirs Dorothy *Stoughton*. The John who settled in Lebanon was John³ (*Thomas*,² *John*¹).

The circumstantial evidence on which the theory was built that Dorothy³ Bissell married Edward Kellogg therefore evaporates completely. Not only was she called Stoughton in two probates of the family, but the New London deed of Peter Mason which mentions several quitclaims he had received from other Mason heirs refers to a quitclaim dated 23 June 1710 from Samuel Stoughton and Dorothy Stoughton (New London Deeds, 7:70).

Since my two articles above mentioned were published in 1950 and 1951, I have learned that Dorothy³ Bissell was a widow when she married Samuel Stoughton. To complete her record, the following is offered.

Dorothy Bissell, born at Windsor 10 Aug. 1665, married first, at Windsor, 21 Jan. 1685, Nathaniel² Watson, b. 28 Jan. 1663/4, son of Robert and Mary (Rockwell) Watson; he died 19 Aug. 1690 and she married second, no record found, Samuel Stoughton, b. 8 Sept. 1665, d. in 1711/12, son of Ens. Thomas and Mary (Wadsworth) Stoughton. Dorothy survived her second husband. She had two Watson children: i. *Anna*, b. 1686, mar. (1) 18 Dec. 1707, Benjamin Allen, b. 14 Oct. 1686, d. 14 Dec. 1712, and (2) 27 March 1718, Nathaniel Loomis, b. 7 March 1694/5, d. 2 Aug. 1758; ii. *Nathaniel*, b. 1690, d. 10 Sept. 1733, administration on whose estate was granted to his brother-in-law Nathaniel Loomis. Dorothy had two known children by her Stoughton husband: iii. [*Capt.*] *Samuel*, b. 10 Sept. 1702, d. in 1789, mar. Abial ——; and iv. *Israel*, d. 14 Dec. 1712.

THE KIMBERLY GENEALOGY

Compiled by Mrs. Arthur J. Trethewey of Roslindale, Mass., for
James C. Kimberly of Neenah, Wis.

The name Kimmerley or Kimmerly is derived from the parish of
Kimberley or Kimberly in county Norfolk, England. Various
spellings of the name appear in the early English records, thus:
Eustace de Kimberle, co. Norfolk, A.D. 1308 ("History of Norfolk
County", p. 442); Hugh de Kymberly, Burgess of Great Yarmouth
(*ibid.*); 1571, Robert Kymberlie and Ross Ives, marriage license in
London; 1611, Baptized John, son of William Kemberley, St.
James, Clarkenwell. Other spellings found are Kimersley, Kimerly,
Kommerly and even Cimerly.

1. Thomas Kimberly was baptized in Wotten-sub-Edge,
Gloucestershire, on 24 June 1604. He was the son of Abraham and
Katherine (Howe) Kimberly, who were married 4 Oct. 1602. He
was a tailor by trade and served his time in London.

Thomas Kimberly and his wife, Alice, came with the Non-
Conformists to Dorchester in New England in 1636*. In 1638 the
family removed to the new settlement of New Haven, Conn., where
Thomas Kimberly was admitted a freeman in November 1639. He
was a member of the train band in 1640 and marshal of the New
Haven Colony from 1643 to 1661 and was one of the seventy proprietors.

Alice Kimberly died 10 Oct. 1659 in New Haven and Thomas
Kimberly married as his second wife, Mary, daughter of Robert
Seabrook of Stratford, Conn., and widow of William Preston of
New Haven. She died in 1673.

In 1659 Thomas Kimberly was in Stratford and bought land
there of Joseph Hawley "18–10–1663". In 1667 he was admitted
a "sojourner" of Stratford and died there in 1673. His will, dated
11 January 1671–2, names his wife Mary, sons Nathaniel, Thomas,
Eleazer and Abraham, daughter Abiah Boardman and her three
children, Hachaliah and Joseph Preston and grandchildren: Nathaniel, Elizabeth and Mary Hayes. The inventory value of the
estate was £160 16s.

Children by first wife:

 i. Thomas,[2] b. in 1632, probably in London; d. *s.p.* in February 1705
  in New Haven, Conn.; m. Hannah Russell, daughter of James
  and Mary (Hall) Russell, who died 28 Nov. 1714 in New Haven.
2. ii. Abraham, b. in 1635.
3. iii. Nathaniel, b. in 1636.
 iv. Mary, b. in 1637; m. Nathaniel Hayes of Norwalk, Conn.
4. v. Eleazer, bapt. 17 Nov. 1639 in New Haven.
 vi. Abiah, bapt. 19 Dec. 1641 in New Haven; m. Israel Boardman.

2. Abraham[2] Kimberly (*Thomas[1]*) was born in 1635 in Stratford,
  Conn. He married Hannah, surname unknown, before 1655,
  and they lived for a time in New Haven. They were, how-

---

*Anthony R. Wagner, College of Arms, London, E.C.4.

ever, in "the County of Albemarle in the Province of Charolina", when their four younger children were born. The family returned to Connecticut and resided in Stratford, where Abraham Kimberly, Senior, died before 1680 and his widow married John Curtis. She died before 21 October 1701, as the following proves:

"John Blakeman, Senr. of Stratford, and Benjamin Hurd of Woodbury, legatees of our late mother Hannah Curtis, deceased, by virtue of marriage with our present wives, the daughters of said Hannah, conveyed 21 Oct. 1701, to brother Abraham Kimberly of Stratford, all right to dwelling house which belonged to our mother."

Children:

i. HANNAH,[3] b. 11 Jan. 1655 in New Haven.
ii. MARY, bapt. 25 July 1659 in New Haven.
iii. MARY, b. 4 May 1668 in "Albemarle, Charolina"; m. JOHN BLAKEMAN.
iv. ABIGAIL, b. in 1670 in "Albemarle, Charolina"; m. EBENEZER BLAKEMAN.
v. SARAH, b. 1 Aug. 1672 in "Albemarle, Charolina"; m. BENJ. HURD.
5. vi. ABRAHAM, b. 4 March 1674–5 in "Albemarle, Charolina".

3. NATHANIEL[2] KIMBERLY (*Thomas*[1]), of Stratford and West Haven, Conn., was born in 1636, died in West Haven in 1705. His wife's surname is unknown, but her Christian name was MIRIAM, for in 1668 Winthrop mentioned Miriam, wife of Nathaniel Kimberly.

In his will, which is dated 26 Oct. 1705 and proved the following November, Nathaniel Kimberly calls himself "tailor". The will names his wife, daughters Elizabeth Mallory, Sarah Blakeslee and Mary Chittenden, only son Nathaniel and granddaughter Abiah Kirby.

Children, born in New Haven:

i. SARAH,[3] m. 20 Nov. 1684 SAMUEL BLAKESLEE.
ii. ELIZABETH, m. (1) 30 Dec. 1686, in New Haven, THOMAS OR JOHN MALLORY; m. (2) BENJAMIN BARNES of Waterbury, Conn.
6. iii. NATHANIEL.
iv. ABIAH, b. 19 Jan. 1670; d. 28 April 1704 in New Haven; m. JOSEPH KIRBY.
v. MARY m. JOSEPH CHITTENDEN of Guilford.

4. ELEAZER[2] KIMBERLY (*Thomas*[1]), baptized 17 Nov. 1639 in New Haven, died in Glastonbury, Conn., 5 Feb. 1708–9, "about the 70th y. of his age". The inscription on his gravestone at Glastonbury, Conn., states that he was the first male child born in New Haven. He married first, about 1662, MARY ROBBINS, born 20 Jan. 1641–2, died before 1680, daughter of "Gentleman John Robbins" and his wife, Mary Wells. Her identity is established by a document filed in the distribution of the estate of John Robbins (1660), one clause reading, "Granted to Mr. Kimberly that is to match with Mary Robbins. . . ." Eleazer Kimberly married secondly, about 1680, RUTH CURTIS, died 29 Dec. 1683 in Wethersfield, two

months after the birth of her daughter Mary, daughter of Thomas Curtis; and thirdly ———.

He was schoolmaster in Wethersfield in 1661 with a salary of £25 a year; this was increased in 1677 to £32 and from 1682 to 1689 he received £42.

Admitted a freeman of Wethersfield in 1677, he recorded that year "132 acres of land on east side of river". This was Lot No. 28, Naubec Farms, and was his "wife's portion", being part of the estate of John Robbins, Gentleman. Cattle ear-marks were registered to him in 1674 and he was chosen rate-maker in 1675.

Eleazer Kimberly represented Glastonbury in the General Assembly from 1696 to 1698, and he was Town Clerk from 1692 to 1708.

In 1693 he was elected Commissioner of Glastonbury and in May 1696 he was chosen to succeed John Allyn, the veteran secretary. He held the office of secretary until his death. In October 1696 he was appointed with John Allyn and Maj. James Fitch as a committee to revise the laws of the Colony. In May 1698 he received the appointment of Justice of Hartford County.

Eleazer Kimberly was one of the best penman of his time, as is attested by the town and colony records. On 20 May 1708 he recorded in the Connecticut Records (vol. III, fol. 397–9) "A list of the names of the proprietors of New Haven," containing 251 names, among them those of his brothers Thomas and Nathaniel. The record is all in his handwriting and in its mechanical execution is one of the finest original documents extant.

His will was dated 30 Jan. 1708–9 and devised his property to his son Thomas and daughters Elizabeth and Ruth. Thomas and Elizabeth were named executors with Samuel Hale and John Curtis as overseers. The inventory of his estate, dated 11 Feb. 1708–9, was made by John Kilborn and William Wickham and the inventory value was £356–04–11.

Children by first wife, born in Weathersfield:

7. i. THOMAS,[3] b. 27 or 29 Sept. 1681.
   ii. MARY, b. 29 Oct. 1683.

Children by third wife:

   iii. ELIZABETH.
   iv. RUTH, d. 4 Nov. 1711 in Glastonbury.
   v. A DAUGHTER living in 1708–9.

5. ABRAHAM[3] KIMBERLY (*Abraham,*[2] *Thomas*[1]), born "in the County of Albemarle in The Province of Charolina", 4 March 1674–5, died in Newtown, Conn., in 1727 or 1728. He married in Stratford, 11 May 1696, ABIGAIL FITCH, daughter of Thomas and Abigail (Goodrich) Fitch of Wethersfield.

In 1701 Abraham Kimberly bought the interest of his sisters in their mother's homestead; in 1706 he bought rights

in Stratford from his Uncle Eleazer Kimberly of Glastonbury, and in 1706 he sold the latter property as well as land
laid out to Thomas Kimberly. In 1726, when he was of Newtown, he sold land in Stratford. (See Stratford Deeds.)

Administration of the estate of Abraham Kimberly, Sr.,
was granted 26 July 1727 to his son Abraham and on 17
May 1742, an agreement for the division of this estate was
entered into by Abraham Kimberly, Jr., John and Abigail
Lake, Joseph and Sarah Prindle, Thomas and Mary Leaven-
worth, all of Newtown, Gideon Kimberly of Wilton, Conn.,
Thomas Kimberly of Woodbury, Conn., Josiah and Prudence
Smith of Stratford, and John and Abiah Curtis of Woodbury.

Children, first three born in Stratford, the others in Newtown:

 i. HANNAH,[4] b. 19 Jan. 1698; m. JAMES HURD.
 ii. ABIGAIL, b. 25 April 1699; m. JOHN LAKE, b. in 1688, son of Thomas
   and Sarah (Peet) Lake.
8. iii. ABRAHAM, b. 29 April 1702.
 iv. GIDEON, m. MARY OSBORNE and resided in Wilton.
 v. SARAH, m. JOSEPH PRINDLE, son of Ebenezer and Elizabeth (Hubby)
   Prindle and grandson of William and Mary Desborough.
 vi. MARY, m. 10 Jan. 1731–32, THOMAS LEAVENWORTH of Newtown.
 vii. ABIAH, m. (1) 4 Jan. 1715–16 JOHN LAKE; m. (2) JOHN CURTIS of
   Woodbury.
 viii. PRUDENCE, m. JOSEPH SMITH of Stratford.
 ix. THOMAS, m. 28 Jan. 1742 LOIS TUTTLE and lived in Roxbury and
   South Britain, Conn.

6. NATHANIEL[3] KIMBERLY (*Nathaniel,*[2] *Thomas*[1]), of West Haven,
  Conn., died there in 1720. He married, 22 Sept. 1692, in
  New Haven, Conn., HANNAH DOWNS, born 19 January
  1670–1 at New Haven, daughter of John Downs.

He was called "Lieutenant," but no record of his appointment has been found.

Administration on his estate was granted 5 December
1720 to his widow Hannah. His seven children are named in
the settlement.

On 29 Aug. 1721 John Lyon and Hannah, his wife, of
"Colony of Connecticut" conveyed land "which our father
Nathaniel Kimberly of New Haven, bought of John Mal-
lory."

On 3 June 1747 Zuriel Kimberly of New Haven, Abraham
Kimberly, Joseph Parmalee and Abigail his wife, all of Guilford, Thomas Pike and Hannah his wife, and Benjamin
Treadwell and Mary his wife, all of Fairfield, conveyed to
brother Nathaniel Kimberly of New Haven, rights from
father Nathaniel Kimberly deceased.

Children, born in New Haven:

 i. HANNAH,[4] b. 13 April 1694; m. (1) JOHN LYON of Fairfield; m. (2)
   THOMAS PIKE of Fairfield.
 ii. ABIGAIL, b. 28 July 1696; d. 28 Nov. 1763; m. 19 Sept. 1716, in
   Guilford, JOSEPH PARMELEE.
 iii. MARY, b. 24 July 1698; m. BENJAMIN TREADWELL of Fairfield.

9. iv.   NATHANIEL, b. 11 March 1700/1.
   v.   BATHSHEBA (BARSHUA), b. 28 Feb. 1703; m. in New Haven SAMUEL
         WILSON.
10. vi. ZURIEL, b. 25 Nov. 1706.
11. vii. ABRAHAM, b. 21 March 1709.

7. THOMAS³ KIMBERLY (*Eleazer,² Thomas¹*), born 27 or 29 Sept.
1681, died 29 Jan. 1729–30 in Glastonbury. He married, 24 February 1703–4, RUTH HALE, died 14 May
1737, daughter of Samuel Hale of Glastonbury. At the
time of their marriage they were both of Glastonbury and
Thomas is buried there.

Thomas Kimberly was admitted an attorney in April 1712
and served as representative from Glastonbury to the General Court in 1708, 1711, 1714 and 1725.

His epitaph in the Glastonbury cemetery reads: "Here lies
interred the body of Thomas Kimberly, Esq., one of his
Majesty's Justices of the Peace and Quorum, Speaker of
the House of Representatives, etc. In all of which trusts his
eminent abilitys distinguished him. He was the son of
Eleazer Kimberly, Esq., ae. 48 y. 4 m. born Septr. 6 A.D.
1681."

Children, born in Glastonbury:
   i.   ELEAZER,⁴ b. 10 Nov. 1704; d. young.
   ii.   THOMAS, b. 28 Jan. 1706; d. 7 June 1733.
12. iii. SAMUEL, b. 7 Feb. 1707–8.
   iv.   RUTH, b. 20 Feb. 1709/10; m. JEREMIAH GOODRICH.
   v.   MARY, b. 6 June 1712; m. JADUTHAN SMITH.
   vi.   SON, b. 1 Aug. 1714; d. young.
   vii. ELIZABETH, b. 30 June 1715; d. 6 Jan. 1798; m. ISRAEL FOOTE.
   viii. ELEAZER, b. 26 Oct. 1717; d. young.
13. ix. JOHN, b. 2 May 1719.
   x.   SARAH, b. 2 Oct. 1721; m. DANIEL HOUSE, b. 26 Oct. 1720.
   xi.   ANNE, b. 18 May 1725; d. 8 Feb. 1747–8.

8. ABRAHAM⁴ KIMBERLY (*Abraham,³ Abraham,² Thomas¹*), of Newtown, Conn., was born 29 April 1702. He married, 21 Oct.
1725, in Newtown, ABIGAIL ADAMS, born in Stratford, daughter of Freeman and Mary (Griffin) Adams.

Abraham Kimberly was one of the original proprietors of
Newtown.

Children, recorded in Newtown:
   i.   JEDEDIAH,⁵ b. 8 Feb. 1725–6.
   ii.   ANNA ("ANAH"), b. 8 Aug. 1727; m. JOHN DUNNING.
   iii. SARAH, b. 31 Aug. 1729; m. EBENEZER FAIRCHILD.
   iv.   ABIAH, b. 13 Aug. 1731; m. MICHAEL DUNNING.
   v.   MARY, b. 3 March 1733.
   vi.   FITCH, b. in Newtown 22 Dec. 1736; d. there in 1813; m. ABIGAIL
         WOODRUFF, b. in 1738, d. in 1837.
         He was a private in the War of the Revolution and was in the
         battles of Brandywine, Germantown and Monmouth.
         Child:
            1. *Susanna,⁶* b. in 1759; d. in 1850; m. in Watertown, Conn., 6
               Feb. 1783, Joseph S. Merriam, b. in 1761, d. in 1839.
14. vii. ABRAHAM, b. 6 Jan. 1739.

9. NATHANIEL⁴ KIMBERLY (*Nathaniel,³ Nathaniel,² Thomas¹*), born 11 March 1700/1 in New Haven, Conn., died 15 Aug. 1780 or 1781, aged 80 or 81, in West Haven, Conn. He married, 22 April 1724, in New Haven, HANNAH CANDEE, born in New Haven in 1703, died there 13 Jan. 1781, aged 77, daughter of Samuel and Abigail (Pinion) Candee.

Children:

15. i. ISRAEL,⁵ b. about 1725.
    ii. ABIGAIL, b. about 1726; d. 12 Sept. 1789, aged 63, in West Haven; m. 11 March 1757 LAMBERTON SMITH.
16. iii. SILAS, b. about 1743.

10. ZURIEL⁴ KIMBERLY (*Nathaniel,³ Nathaniel,² Thomas¹*) was born 25 Nov. 1706 in New Haven, Conn. He married first, in New Haven, 26 Nov. 1730, HANNAH HILL, born in New Haven in December 1702, died there 8 June 1768, aged 65, daughter of John and Hannah Hill; and secondly, 17 Dec. 1766, MARTHA HITCHCOCK, widow of John Hitchcock.

Children by first wife:

i. SARAH,⁵ bapt. 15 Aug. 1731; d. 8 Nov. 1780, aged 49, in New Haven.
ii. NATHANIEL, b. 21 Jan. and bapt. 25 Jan. 1734; d. 26 Oct. 1739, aged 4 years.
17. iii. JOHN, b. 6 Sept. and bapt. 10 Sept. 1738.
iv. HANNAH, b. 8 May 1741.
18. v. NATHANIEL, b. 12 May 1743.
vi. SUSANNA, b. 9 Sept. and bapt. 14 Sept. 1746; d. 28 Oct. 1798, aged 51; m. in New Haven, 15 May 1771, ELI BEECHER.

11. ABRAHAM⁴ KIMBERLY (*Nathaniel,³ Nathaniel,² Thomas¹*) was born 21 March 1709 in New Haven, Conn. He married first, in Guilford, Conn., 7 March 1730, by Rev. James Honeyman, MARY SHEARMAN of Newport, died 18 Nov. 1766; and secondly MISS WINSCOTT.

About 1740 he moved from West Haven to Guilford and was the first of the name to settle in that town.

Children, recorded in Guilford:

i. ISAAC SHERMAN,⁵ b. in Guilford 23 Jan. 1733/4; m. in 1759 SARAH WHEATON.
      He served as a lieutenant in the Connecticut Militia under Capt. Augustus Collins, Col. Thaddeus Cook's second battalion. Child:
      1. *Sarah,*⁶ m. Ebenezer Allen.
ii. MARY, b. 14 Aug. 1735; m. JACOB BUSWELL.
iii. KATHERINE, b. 14 Oct. 1736; m. PINNOCK DOWD.
19. iv. ABRAHAM, b. 5 Sept. 1738.
v. ELIZABETH, b. 10 Oct. 1740; m. NOAH HOTCHKISS.
vi. HANNAH, b. 8 Jan. 1743; m. ABRAHAM PARMALEE.
vii. SARAH, m. NATHAN FOWLER.
20. viii. GEORGE, b. in 1746.
ix. JACOB, m. MARY COAN.
x. BENJAMIN.
xi. ABIGAIL, b. 7 March 1758; m. EBEN HALL.
21. xii. SHERMAN.
22. xiii. ROBERT.
xiv. RUTH.

12. SAMUEL[4] KIMBERLY (*Thomas,[3] Eleazer,[2] Thomas[1]*), born in Glastonbury, Conn., 7 Feb. 1707–8, died at the General Assembly in New Haven, Conn., in 1750. He married ———.

Children:
i. RUTH,[5]
ii. THOMAS, b. 1747.

13. JOHN[4] KIMBERLY (*Thomas,[3] Eleazer,[2] Thomas[1]*), born 2 May 1719 in Gilead, Conn., died 26 April 1773. He married, 29 Oct. 1741, MARY HUBBARD, who died 26 April 1812, aged 88. He served in the French and Indian Wars.

Children, recorded in Glastonbury, Conn.:
i.   MARY,[5] b. 7 Nov. 1743; m. 20 March 1766, SAMUEL GIBBONS.
ii. SARAH, b. 28 Feb. 1745–6.
iii. ELIZABETH, b. 9 Oct. 1747.
iv. ANN, b. 13 Oct. 1749; d. young.
v.   ANN, b. 25 Feb. 1752; d. 22 Jan. 1773, "in her 20th yr."
vi. ABIGAIL, b. 21 Feb. 1754.

14. ABRAHAM[5] KIMBERLY (*Abraham,[4] Abraham,[3] Abraham,[2] Thomas[1]*), born 6 Jan. 1739 in Newtown, Conn., died in 1808. He married first, 14 Feb. 1760, TAMAR BENNETT (BURRITT?), died 1 Oct. 1768, aged 30, in giving birth to a son, Abel Burritt; and secondly, ISABEL ———, and removed to Sandgate, Vt., and later to Salem, N. Y.

His will is dated 21 Jan. 1808 and was probated 14 June 1809. It mentions his wife Isabel, eldest son Abel Burritt, sons Abraham and Ichabod, daughters Jerusha Busby and Sally Ann, two grandchildren, Jonathan Northrop and Ann Pack, children of his daughter Mary.

It is said that both Abraham and his brother Fitch served in the French and Indian wars in 1756.

On 7 Jan. 1777 the General Assembly appointed Abraham Kimberly lieutenant of the Western Alarm List, 16th Regiment, Connecticut Line. (D.A.R. Lineage Book, 92:30.)

Children by first wife:
i.   MARY,[6] bapt. 31 Aug. 1760; m. GEORGE NORTHROP.
ii. ABEL, d. young.
iii. JERUSHA, b. 18 May 1766; m. ——— BUDBY.
iv. ABEL BURRITT, bapt. 16 Oct. 1768; m. CURRENCE PRINDLE, b. 7 Oct. 1773 in Newtown and removed in 1784 with her parents to Sandgate, Vt.

Children by second wife:
v.   ABRAHAM.
vi. ICHABOD, b. in 1780; d. in 1845; m. about 1802 CLARRY HURD. It is stated that they had a son Clark, b. in 1811, d. in 1873, m. in 1834 Polly Green, b. in 1815, d. in 1891. (D.A.R. Lineage Book, 92:30.)
vii. SALLY ANN.

15. ISRAEL[5] KIMBERLY (*Nathaniel,[4] Nathaniel,[3] Nathaniel,[2] Thomas[1]*), born about 1725, died in 1768. He married first, in September 1744, in New Haven, Conn., ESTHER SMITH, born 8

July 1729 in New Haven, daughter of Joseph and Esther (Morris) Smith; and secondly, 7 Dec. 1749, in New Haven, MARY TOLLES, born 29 Oct. 1729 in New Haven, died 28 Aug. 1807, age 78, in West Haven, daughter of Henry and Mary (Goodsell) Tolles.

Child by first wife:

    i. ESTHER,[6] b. 24 Nov. 1744 in New Haven; d. 26 May 1764, aged 20, in West Haven.

Children by second wife.

23. ii. AZEL, b. about 1752.
    iii. MARY, b. about 1753; d. 13 Sept. 1833, aged 80, in West Haven; m. (1) SETH THOMAS; m. (2) JAMES B. REYNOLDS.
24. iv. GILEAD, b. about 1755.
    v. SARAH, b. about 1758; d. 7 June 1830, aged 71; m. (1) BENJAMIN SMITH; m. (2) LEWIS HUBBELL of Newton; m. (3) ANDREW BARTHOLOMEW of Wallingford, Conn.
25. vi. NATHANIEL, b. about 1759–60.
    vii. HANNAH, b. about 1761; d. 3 Sept. 1854, aged 93, in West Haven.
26. viii. EZRA, b. about 1763.
    ix. GIDEON, b. about 1765; d. *s.p.* 13 Jan. 1815, aged 50, in West Haven.
27. x. LIBERTY, b. about 1767.
28. xi. ISRAEL.
    xii. HULDAH, d. 19 June 1819; m. LEMUEL NICHOLS of Waterbury, Conn.

16. SILAS[5] KIMBERLY (*Nathaniel,[4] Nathaniel,[3] Nathaniel,[2] Thomas[1]*), born about 1743, died 17 Jan. 1803, aged 60, in West Haven, Conn. He married first, in West Haven, SARAH SMITH, born 24 Oct. 1750 in New Haven, died 3 April 1793, aged 42, in West Haven, daughter of Jonathan and Mary (Catlin) Smith; and secondly MARTHA (MERWIN) TOLLES, born 26 May 1754 in New Haven, daughter of Joseph and Martha Merwin and widow of Abraham Tolles.

When Tryon invaded Connecticut, Capt. Silas Kimberly commanded a company and was captured on 1 Sept. 1781, when the enemy landed at West Haven.

Children by first wife:

    i. HETTY,[6] b. about 1771; d. 21 May 1825, in West Haven; m. SAMUEL CLARK.
29. ii. ELIAKIM, b. about 1772.
    iii. ABIGAIL, m. ——— BARDWELL.
    iv. LOUISA, b. about 1777; d. 5 Oct. 1794, aged 17, in West Haven.
    v. SILAS, m. CLARA SMITH, dau. Justus and Rebecca (Humphreyville) Smith; living in Conway, Mass., in 1829.
    vi. HULDAH, m. HORACE KIMBERLY.
    vii. SARAH, b. about 1784; d. 19 June 1794, aged 10 yrs., in West Haven.
    viii. LESTER, b. 20 Jan. 1787 in New Haven; d. 13 Oct. 1811 in New Haven.
    ix. DENNIS, b. 23 Oct. 1790, in New Haven; d. *s.p.* 14 Dec. 1862 in New Haven, aged 73. He was an eminent lawyer.
    x. FRANCIS, sea captain, b. about 1792; d. Aug. 1827, aged 37, at sea; m. ADAH WARD, b. about 1794, d. 8 Feb. 1876, aged 82, in West Haven, dau. John and Eunice (Richards) Ward.

17. JOHN[5] KIMBERLY (*Zuriel,[4] Nathaniel,[3] Nathaniel,[2] Thomas[1]*), born 6 Sept. and baptized 10 Sept. 1738, in New Haven, Conn., died before 1767. He married, 21 May 1761, in New

Haven, LYDIA WISE, born about 1746, died 13 May 1797, aged 51, in New Haven. She married secondly, 26 Nov. 1780, in New Haven, Isaac Bishop.

Children, born in New Haven:

i. JOHN,[6] b. 24 Aug. 1762 and bapt. 25 Oct. 1767.
ii. SARAH, b. 10 Sept. 1765 and bapt. 25 Oct. 1767; d. 6 Sept. 1807, aged 41, in New Haven; m. 23 April 1791, in New Haven, SOLOMON MUDGE.

18. NATHANIEL[5] KIMBERLY (*Zuriel,*[4] *Nathaniel,*[3] *Nathaniel,*[2] *Thomas*[1]) was born 12 May and baptized 22 May 1743 in New Haven, Conn. He married MABEL THOMPSON, born 5 Nov. 1745 in New Haven, died in April 1808, aged 63, daughter of John and Elizabeth (Bradley) Thompson.

Nathaniel Kimberly served in the War of the Revolution with the rank of captain.

Children, born in New Haven (the first 3 baptized 6 March 1774 in the Second Congregational Church in New Haven):

i. WILLIAM H.,[6] d. in 1820; m. in 1812 ELIZABETH WEBB, b. in 1783, d. in 1866.
ii. ESTHER, m. 11 Nov. 1796, in Troy, N. Y., ORSAMUS KELLOGG.
iii. SAMUEL.
iv. NATHANIEL, b. 23 Jan. 1775; d. 19 Feb. 1846; m. ANN TITTLE, b. 3 Nov. 1787, d. 26 Feb. 1872.
v. HENRY, bapt. 19 July 1778; d. *s.p.*
vi. SARAH, bapt. 4 March 1781.
vii. JOHN, bapt. 1 Oct. 1784.
viii. THOMPSON.

19. ABRAHAM[5] KIMBERLY (*Abraham,*[4] *Nathaniel,*[3] *Nathaniel,*[2] *Thomas*[1]), born in Guilford, Conn., 5 Sept. 1738, died 16 April 1808, aged 70. He married, 1 July 1764, in Guilford, THANKFUL CHITTENDEN, born 1 July 1740, died 28 July 1834, daughter of Daniel and Abigail (Downs) Chittenden of North Guilford.

Children, recorded in Guilford:

i. IRA,[6] b. 16 Dec. 1764 in Guilford; d. 6 March 1843; m. in Guilford, 29 Dec. 1824, ABIGAIL SCRANTON, b. 12 Aug. 1785 in Guilford, d. 18 June 1877.
   Child:
   1. *Mary,*[7] b. 26 May 1827; m. George Hill.
ii. MARY, b. 25 Feb. 1767; d. 13 Feb. 1850; m. NATHAN CHIDSEY.
iii. PITMAN, b. 23 March 1769; d. unm. 16 Feb. 1853.
iv. EDMUND, b. in May 1771; d. 15 March 1772.
30. v. JOHN, of Troy, N. Y., b. 19 June 1773.
31. vi. HAZARD, of Troy, b. 8 Dec. 1776.
vii. ISRAEL, "of Canada," b. 9 May 1778.
viii. ABIGAIL, b. 21 May 1781; m. AMMI PALMER.
ix. AMANDA, b. 2 June 1783; m. ELIAS GOULD.

20. GEORGE[5] KIMBERLY (*Abraham,*[4] *Nathaniel,*[3] *Nathaniel,*[2] *Thomas*[1]), of Saybrook and Guilford, Conn., born in 1746 in Guilford, died 25 July 1817. He married in Guilford, 1 Nov. 1774, BEULAH MORSE, born 10 Aug. 1746 in Guilford, died there 1 Nov. 1809.

Children, recorded in Guilford:

- i. ABRAHAM,[6] b. 2 July 1775; killed by a load of wood on 11 Sept. 1778.
- ii. JOHN, b. 20 Aug. 1777.
- iii. DAVID, b. 25 Nov. 1779.
- iv. BEULAH, b. 10 Dec. 1781; d. 20 Oct. 1847; m. MARTIN MORSE.
- v. GEORGE, b. 1 Feb. 1784; d. 22 June 1824.
- vi. ANNE, b. 18 March 1787; d. 26 Aug. 1849.
- 31½. vii. ELI, b. 2 Nov. 1792.

21 SHERMAN[5] KIMBERLY (*Abraham,[4] Nathaniel,[3] Nathaniel,[2] Thomas[1]*) married ———.

Child:

- i. JUSTUL,[6] b. 22 July 1803; m. MABEL ———.

22. ROBERT[5] KIMBERLY (*Abraham,[4] Nathaniel,[3] Nathaniel,[2] Thomas[1]*) died 17 April 1803. He married, in 1781, HANNAH COAN, born in 1758, died 14 Oct. 1841. Hannah (Coan) Kimberly married secondly, 20 May 1817, Dr. Jared Foote, who died 11 Oct. 1820.

He was the "only one from Guilford" at the surrender of Burgoyne. "He was in Captain Shipman's Company, Colonel Thaddeus Cook's regiment, both actions, Saratoga; wounded in latter engagement".

Children:

- i. PAMEL,[6] b. 1 Sept. 1782; d. 2 June 1866; m. JEREMIAH HUBBARD.
- 32. ii. JOSIAH, b. Oct. 1784.
- 33. iii. ABRAHAM, b. 13 Nov. 1786.
- 34. iv. ABEL, b. 21 Dec. 1788.
- v. HANNAH E., b. 6 July 1791; d. 26 June 1856; m. ISAAC MEIGS.
- 35. vi. ERASTUS COAN, b. 10 Sept. 1794.
- 36. vii. DAVID ROBERT, b. in 1797.
- viii. LUCRETIA, b. in 1799; d. 29 June 1879; m. in Guilford, 25 June 1827, MARVIN HENDERSON.

23. AZEL[6] KIMBERLY (*Israel,[5] Nathaniel,[4] Nathaniel,[3] Nathaniel,[2] Thomas[1]*), born about 1752, died 25 May 1802, aged 50, in New Haven. He married AMY SMITH, born about 1752, died 17 Aug. 1831, aged 79, in New Haven, daughter of George and Abigail (Mallory) Smith.

Children:

- 37. i. LEVERETT,[7] b. about 1772.
- ii. LINUS, d. 21 Sept. 1775 in West Haven.
- 38. iii. LINUS, b. about 1777.
- 39. iv. DAVID, b. 4 Oct. 1778, in Farmington.
- v. POLLY, m. AMOS WHITE.
- vi. GRATIA, m. WM. F. SIMPSON of Bethlehem.
- vii. GEORGE, probably d. *s. p.*
- viii. JERRE, probably d. *s. p.*

24. GILEAD[6] KIMBERLY (*Israel,[5] Nathaniel,[4] Nathaniel,[3] Nathaniel,[2] Thomas[1]*), born about 1755, died 12 Feb. 1831, aged 76, in West Haven, Conn. He married first, MARY BROCKETT, born 7 Aug. 1765, died 22 Feb. 1804, aged 38, in West Haven, daughter of Hezekiah and Mary (Beecher) Brockett; and secondly MARY GILL, born 12 Oct. 1760, died 5 Sept. 1830, aged 69, in West Haven, daughter of Barnabas and Ellis

(Bangs) Merrick, and widow of ———— Bradley and of Ebenezer Gill.

Children:

40. i. WILLIAM[7].
    ii. MARIA, b. about 1787; d. 25 Nov. 1865, aged 78 in West Haven; m. ELIAKIM KIMBERLY.
    iii. ELIZABETH, m. FRANCIS B. DAVIS.
    iv. HANNAH, b. about 1791; d. 24 Sept. 1806, aged 15 (also recorded as October 1806?)
    v. A CHILD, d. 21 Oct. 1795.
    vi. LYDIA, b. in September 1796; d. 21 May 1887, aged 90; m. JOHN NEAGLE.

25. NATHANIEL[6] KIMBERLY (*Israel,[5] Nathaniel,[4] Nathaniel,[3] Nathaniel,[2] Thomas[1]*), born about 1759, died 5 Sept. 1804 in West Haven, Conn. He married ELIZABETH SMITH, born about 1757, died 24 Sept. 1812, aged 55, in West Haven, daughter of Nehemiah and Eunice (Smith) Smith.

Children:

    i. HORACE,[7] b. about 1780; d. 20 Jan. 1825, aged 45, in West Haven; m. HULDAH KIMBERLY, daughter of Silas and Sarah (Smith) Kimberly.
        Children:
        1. *Abigail,*[8] m. Elisha Benham.
        2. *Sally.*
        3. *Sophia,* m. Newton Platt.
    ii. JOHN, d. in November 1782 in West Haven.
    iii. JOHN, d. 5 Sept. 1784 in West Haven.
    iv. NEHEMIAH, b. 27 May 1786 in West Haven; d. *s.p.* 20 Oct. 1856; m. MARY GRAVES.
    v. BETSEY, m. ———— HITCHCOCK.
    vi. LUCRETIA, m. ———— WRIGHT.
    vii. LOVISA, m. SIMEON SMITH.
    viii. EUNICE, m. EDWIN NIMUS.

KIMBERLY GENEALOGY CORRECTIONS: — Anent, THE REGISTER, vol. CII* pp. 102–112: — Page 102, line 9 from bottom. For *Hall,* read *Ball.*
Page 102, line 3 from bottom. Abraham[2] Kimberly was not born in Stratford that town not being settled until 1639, and his father not coming to New England until 1636. He was born in England, and probably earlier than 1635, the date given in the text.
Page 103, remove Abigail, fourth child of Abraham[2] Kimberly. The error originated in Orcutt's History of Stratford. The births of Mary, Sarah and Abraham, in Carolina, are entered in Stratford records, but no Abigail. These three were evidently the only surviving children of their mother Hannah, as witness the deed cited in the text. Ebenezer Blakeman married Abigail Curtis, not Kimberly.
Page 103. Elizabeth, second child of Nathaniel[2] Kimberly, m. John (not Thomas) Mallory. Delete date of birth of the fourth child, Abiah; the date given is actually the birth date of her brother Nathaniel's wife.
Pages 103–4. The only two known wives of Eleazer[2] Kimberly are correctly stated, and no proof has been found that he had a third wife. By the first wife there was probably a son Eleazer who died in youth. The five surviving children

*Pages 354-364, this volume.

were probably all by the second wife, Ruth, the two recorded children, Thomas and Mary, probably being younger than the other three. The daughter Mary m. at Glastonbury, 17 June 1708, John Hubbard. The unnamed daughter was Sarah, and she m. at Wethersfield, 25 Jan. 1699/1700, John Kilborn. These two daughters and their husbands are named in records of Eleazer's estate, to be seen in print in Manwaring's Digest. The daughter Elizabeth died at Glastonbury, unmarried, in Nov. 1746, leaving a will; the abstract of this, in Manwaring's Digest, contains very serious errors, and the original should be consulted.

Page 105, children of Abraham³ Kimberly. The daughter Sarah was bapt. at Stratford, 23 July 1704 (Stratfield Church records), and was therefore older than Gideon. An omitted child, Jedidiah, was bapt. at Stratfield, 4 July 1708, but d. young. The Newtown deed mentioned in line 3 was dated *1724*, not *1726* (see Jacobus, Families of Old Fairfield, vol. 1, p. 362, from which the deed items were quoted). The husband of the eighth child, Prudence, was *Josiah* Smith as given in the agreement of heirs, and the name *Joseph* Smith in the list of children is erroneous.

Page 106, line 5. Abraham, b. *22*, not *21*, March 1709.

Page 106. Thomas Kimberly (No. 7) served as representative from Glastonbury to the General Court at 41 sessions between 1708 and 1729, and at times held the offices of Clerk of the House and Speaker; he was also chosen Ensign of the Glastonbury company.

Page 106. Abraham Kimberly (No. 8) was hardly one of the original proprietors of Newtown, as stated, as the town was incorporated in 1711, and this Abraham was born in 1702. Transfer this statement to the account of his father. His sixth child, Fitch, did not die "there" (Newtown), but at Watertown, Conn., 31 May 1813; the wife of Fitch, Abigail Woodruff, was bapt. at Milford, Conn., 20 Aug. 1738, and died at Watertown, 12 Feb. *1827*, not *1837*, her age being stated as 90.

Page 107. Nathaniel Kimberly (No. 9) died *1780*, not *1781*.

Page 107. The first wife of Zuriel Kimberly (No. 10) died 8 June *1766*, not *1768*; his second marriage occurred, as correctly stated, 17 Dec. 1766. The first child, Sarah, was born 16 Aug. 1731. The second child, Nathaniel, was born and bapt. 1734/5.

Page 107. Abraham Kimberly (No. 11) founded the Guilford branch of the family, and the account given of his children and grandchildren is apparently drawn to some extent from Dr. Alvan Talcott's manuscript genealogies of Guilford families, the original of which is owned by the New Haven Colony Historical Society; a photostatic copy is at the State Library, Hartford, Conn. Discrepancies of both dates and names are noted, but since Dr. Talcott's manuscript is not an original source, it is thought best to refer readers who are interested in this branch to the Talcott manuscript and to the original vital, church, probate and land records of Guilford.

Page 108. Samuel Kimberly (No. 12) did not die in *1750*; he served as representative of Glastonbury at thirty sessions of the General Assembly between 1751 and 1760. He was confirmed lieutenant in 1752. His last legislative service was in October 1760; his will was dated 28 Oct. 1760 and probated 13 May 1761. His wife was Mary Talcott, and he had four children.

Page 108. John Kimberly (No. 13) was elected to twenty-one sessions of the General Assembly between 1761 and 1773, but his death occurred slightly before the Assembly met at the last session to which he had been elected. His will and other original sources show that he had thirteen children. They were mostly girls, and the only sons died young. The husband of the first child, Mary, was Samuel *Gibson*, not *Gibbons*, of Middletown and Eastbury, Conn.

Page 108, next to bottom line. The recorded date of the first marriage of Israel Kimberly was 10 Sept. 1744, and this wife, Esther Smith, died 30 Nov. 1744 aged under 16.

Page 109, line 15. For *Newton*, read *Newtown*. The date of the third marriage, in same line, was 2 Apr. 1803.

Page 111. It is doubted that David (No. 39), fourth child of Azel (No. 23), was born in Farmington.

New Haven, Conn.   DONALD LINES JACOBUS.

THE KING FAMILY OF SUFFIELD, CONNECTICUT.

Communicated by EDMUND JANES CLEVELAND, Esq., of Hartford, Conn.

FROM the year 1634, or an earlier date, immigrants by the name of King have continued to arrive in America; a large number, evidently, in addition to the considerable list given by Savage, and those mentioned in the foregoing volumes of the REGISTER, and also in other publications.

1. WILLIAM[1] KING lived in Uxborough, Devonshire,* England; a fisherman. While on his last voyage, upon his business, he was cast away and drowned upon the banks of Newfoundland. This statement (made in 1796 by Alexander King, from whose genealogical notes much of the following is taken) may have been tradition, for Savage mentions: William King of the Isle of Shoals [New Hampshire and Maine, inhabited chiefly by fishermen], died May 28, 1664, leaving William.

William[1] King, according to the above narrative, had two sons, who both came to America:

2. i. JAMES,[2] of Ipswich, Mass., and Suffield, Conn., m. 1st, Elizabeth Emerson; 2d, widow Hannah Loomis.
   ii. WILLIAM, settled in one of the southern States; of him there is no further account.

2. JAMES[2] KING (*William[1]*) was born probably in England (is inferred from the above account); settled in Ipswich prior to 1672; about 1678 he came with his family to Suffield, of which town he was one of the original proprietors, his name being the 58th in the list of one hundred of the first grantees, in the order of their grants. The first grant of land made to him was in October, 1678, which lot was laid out south of the School lot, and upon which he built and lived. He dug a well that was still used 1803. Suffield (previously called Stoney River, and Southfield) was a part of Hampshire Co., Mass., until 1749. Among the names of the localities in Suffield found upon the early records is King's Hill. He was by trade a cooper. He died at Suffield, May 13, 1722, leaving a large landed estate. He married 1st, Elizabeth Emerson, who descended from a respectable family in England. She reared her daughters in habits of industry, and in making lace. Her mother was by Queen Elizabeth presented a piece of linen, afterwards a carefully preserved heirloom, and given to her daughter Agnes. She died January 30, 1715. He married 2d, February 27, 1716, widow Hannah Loomis. By his 1st marriage he had children:

3. i. JAMES,[3] b. at Ipswich, March 14, 1675; m. Elizabeth Huxley.
   ii. WILLIAM, b. at Suffield, Jan. 4, 1679; d. Sept. 30, 1680.

---

* Devonshire was apparently the seat of a large King family. Burke's General Armory blazons 38 King and 15 Kinge arms. KING (Devonshire, and Towcaster co. Northampton). Sable, a lion rampant between three crosses crosslet or, ducally crowned argent.

    iii. AGNES, b. at Suffield, July 15, 1681 [*Savage* mentions " Annis b. 1681 "*]; d. at Suffield, Jan. 7, 1732–3; m. at Suffield, Oct. 5, 1699, as first wife, John Austin, b. at Rowley, Mass., Oct. 22, 1672, d. at Suffield, May 18, 1737, a son of Captain Anthony and Esther. Town clerk, etc. (For descendants, see *Hinman's Conn. Settlers*, 1852, p. 82.)

    iv. BENONI, b. at Suffield, Dec. 5, 1685; d. June 27, 1686.

    v. JOSEPH, b. at Suffield, June 15, 1687; d. Jan. 23, 1688.

4. vi. JOSEPH (again), b. at Suffield, May 10, 1689; m. Mrs. Mary (Wilson) Jesse.

    vii. BENJAMIN, b. at Suffield, Nov. 21, 1690; m. April 24, 1712, Remem-berance Hall or Hitt, had a numerous family; one married descendant living, 1803, in First Society of Suffield.

    viii. MARY, b. at Suffield, April 20, 1692; m. 1st, Nov. 8, 1711, Victory Sykes; 2d, in old age, John Harman. A son was father of Deacon *Henry A.[5] Sykes*, b. at Suffield, Sept. 22, 1810, d. Dec. 15, 1860; biographical sketch of him in *Bi-Centennial Anniversary of Suffield*, Oct. 12, 1870, p. 109.

5. ix. WILLIAM (again), b. at Suffield, Sept. 29, 1695; m. 1st, Bethia Bed-lake; 2d, Mrs. Anne Adams.

3. JAMES[3] KING (*James,[2] William[1]*) was born at Ipswich, Mass., March 14, 1675, and died at Suffield, Conn., July 15, 1757. During his lifetime Suffield was changed from a wilderness into an attractive town. He amassed a considerable landed estate, which is still enjoyed by descendants. He married, June 23, 1698, Elizabeth Huxley, who died August 20, 1745, daughter of Thomas Huxley of Hartford, Conn., and Suffield, by his first wife, Sarah Spencer, daughter of Sergt. Thomas Spencer (brother of Jared and John) of Cambridge and Hartford, by his second wife, Sarah[2] (Nathaniel[1]) Bearding. Their children were:

    i. ELIZABETH,[4] b. Aug. 6, 1699; m. July 22, 1725, Anthony Austin, Jr., and settled at Sheffield. (For descendants, see *Hinman's Conn. Settlers*, p. 83.)

    ii. JAMES, b. Feb. 18, 1701; m. Miriam Hamlin. Several children.

    iii. THOMAS, b. March 20, 1703; d. Jan. 7, 1759; m. June 1, 1727, Susanna Jesse; had several children, of whom only one, a daughter, survived him.

    iv. JOHN, b. May 17, 1705; lived to old age; m. May 24, 1727, Persis Holcomb; had only one son, b. June 4, 1728 (who was drowned in Agawam river, Feb. 15, 1751), and several daughters, one of whom, *Alice,[5]* m. Thaddeus[4] (*Joseph,[3] James,[2] William[1]*) King.

6. v. EBENEZER, b. at Suffield, Dec. 8, 1706; m. Abigail Seymour.

7. vi. JOSEPH, b. Aug. 13, 1709; m. Eunice Seymour.

    vii. NATHANIEL, b. Feb. 2, 1712; d. January, 1802; m. April 20, 1731, Anne Trumbull; had several children.

    viii. Dr. AMOS, b. May 6, 1715; d. 1745; was educated to the practice of physic; was considered a champion wrestler, and, in a contest with a competitor, received an injury; from its results he languished two years, and died without any family.

    ix. SARAH, b. Aug. 20, 1720; m. Nov. 15, 1737, Elijah Sheldon, and was living in 1803.

4. Capt. JOSEPH[3] KING (*James,[2] William[1]*) was born at Suffield, May 10, 1689; died March 6, 1756; was captain of a military company, and much occupied in public business. He married 1st, at Hartford, May 2, 1717, Mrs. Mary (Wilson) Jesse of Hartford, who died September 11, 1737, widow of David Jesse, and evidently sister of Nathaniel Wilson[†] and daughter of Phineas Wilson from Dublin,

---

* Agnes and Annis are the same christian name.—EDITOR.
† See REGISTER, xlii. 143, and *Hoadly's Conn. Colonial Rec.*, vi. 59.

a wealthy merchant of Hartford, by his 1st wife, Mary Sandford, only daughter of Nathaniel and Susanna Sandford. He married 2d, June 2, 1740, Hannah Devotion, daughter of Rev. Ebenezer[3] (John,[2] Edward[1] of Roxbury) Devotion, minister of the town. Children by 1st marriage:

    i.   ABIGAIL,[4] b. Jan. 9, 1719; d. Aug. 5, 1797; m. 1st, Oct. 2, 1746, Dr. Pelatiah Bliss, b. March 23, 1723, d. at Green Bush, near Albany, N. Y., Dec. 26, 1756, son of Peletiah[5] (Peletiah,[4] Lawrence,[3] Thomas[2] of Hartford, Thomas[1] of Belstone, Eng.) Bliss and Ann Stoughton, daughter of John Stoughton of Windsor, Conn. Physician of Suffield, surgeon of a regiment under Gen. Phineas Lyman in the old French war; he died on return from Lake George camp. She m. 2d, April, 1765, David Poxley of Stockbridge; they separated a few years later. (For descendants, see *Bliss Genealogy*, by John Homer Bliss, p. 74.)

    ii. JOSEPH, b. Oct. 1, 1722; d. Jan. 27, 1724.

By 2d marriage:

8. iii. JOSEPH (again), b. April 15, 1741; m. Mrs. Tryphena (Kendall) Bowker.

9. iv. ELIPHALET, b. Feb. 6, 1743; m. 1st, Mary Remington; 2d, Silence Rumrill.

    v.   HANNAH, b. Aug. 23, 1744; m. Jan. 17, 1765, Beldad Granger. Seven children.

    vi. EPAPHRAS, b. May 11, 1746; d. Feb. 17, 1767.

    vii. Capt. ASHBEL, b. Jan. 26, 1748; m. Dec. 19, 1782, widow Jemima Smith; captain of a military company. Five children.

    viii. Capt. THADDEUS, b. June 25, 1749; d. January, 1792; captain of a military company, 1787; m. 1st, December, 1774, Alice[5] (John,[4] James,[3] James,[2] William[1]) King; were divorced May, 1787, by General Assembly. He m. 2d, Sept. 20, 1787, Lucy Johnson. By 1st marriage he had two sons and one daughter; one child d. January, 1792, in infancy.

    ix. THEODORE, b. Dec. 21, 1750; m. 1st Jan. 8, 1778, Anne Mather, who d. May 7, 1791; 2d, May 28, 1792, Sibbel Hanchet. By 1st marriage five children.

    x.   MARY, b. July 22, 1752; m. Dec. 17, 1772, Elijah Granger. Ten children.

    xi. ICHABOD, b. May 14, 1756; m. late in 1778 Louisa Adams.

5. Lieut. WILLIAM[3] KING (*James,[2] William[1]*), born at Suffield, September 29, 1695; died January 8, 1774. Was a selectman; several years Deputy (contemporary with Capt. Samuel Kent, May, 1762, both representing Suffield) in General Assembly; inherited much of his father's estate, and left the best landed interest in Suffield; farmer and weaver. He married 1st, June 29, 1717, Bethia Bedlake of Westfield, Mass.; she died May 21, 1768. He married 2d, February, 1770-2, widow Anne Adams. By 1st marriage twelve children, of whom eleven died before his death, ten of them without families. His eldest son:

10. i. WILLIAM,[4] b. Aug. 10, 1721; m. 1st, Sarah Fuller; 2d, Lucy Hathaway.

6. EBENEZER[4] KING (*James,[3] James,[2] Wiliam[1]*), born at Suffield, December 8, 1706; died at Suffield, June 17, 1781; married March 30, 1724 or 1727, Abigail Seymour, who died June, 1796. An Ebenezer King, of Suffield, kept many years King's or lower ferry across Connecticut River. At her decease his widow left one hundred and eighty descendants. His eldest son:

i. EBENEZER,[5] b. at Suffield, Feb. 22, 1728, of Suffield; d. at Suffield, April 10, 1810; m. 1st, Dec. 11, 1751, Chloe Kent, b. Feb. 7, 1732, d. at Suffield, Oct. 11, 1772; a daughter of Joseph[3] (John[2] of Suffield, John[1]) Kent, and first wife Hannah[2] (Samuel[1] of Suffield) Gillet. He m. 2d, Aug. 10, 1773, Eunice Hale. He had eighteen children, all except one living 1803. By 1st marriage: 1. *David*,[6] b. at Suffield, April 16, 1758; d. at Suffield, May 4, 1832; m. Hannah Holly, daughter of Isaac Holly, and had a son.

7. JOSEPH[4] KING (*James*,[3] *James*,[2] *William*[1]), born August 13, 1709; died at Suffield, June 4, 1772; married Eunice Seymour, daughter of Jonathan Seymour. Lived with his father until his father's death, and in the same house until his own death. Children:

i. Dr. ALEXANDER,[5] b. Oct. 26, 1737; d. at Suffield, October 12, 1802, of Suffield; physician; selectman thirty years; was deputy in the General Assembly from June, 1768, for many years (in October, 1772, he and Gideon Granger represented Suffield), town clerk from December, 1774, to decease; m. Jan. 31, 1765, Experience Hitchcock. Children: 1. *Orestes*,[6] b. Oct. 31, 1765; 2. *Charles*,[6] b. Oct. 29, 1769; 3. *Alexander*[6]; 4. *Joseph*,[6] b. August, 1774; 5. *Orestes*[6] (again), b, June 21, 1779.
ii. JONATHAN, b. Feb. 28, 1742.
iii. GIDEON, b. March 4, 1747.
iv. EUNICE, b. April 20, 1750.

8. JOSEPH[4] KING (*Joseph*,[3] *James*,[2] *William*[1]), born April 15, 1741; married September 12, 1769, Mrs. Tryphena (Kendall) Bowker, daughter of Joshua Kendall, Jr. [By her 1st marriage she had: Hannah Bowker.] Children:

i. JOSHUA KENDALL,[5] b. Oct. 16, 1770; m. Granger ——; his son, *Oren Kendall*,[6] had a daughter.
ii. IRENA, b. Nov. 6, 1772.
iii. EPIPHRAS, b. Jan. 16, 1775.
iv. SON, b. and d. April 11, 1777.
v. JOHN BOWKER, b. Dec. 9, 1779; his son, *John Newton*,[6] had a son and daughter.

9. ELIPHALET[4] KING (*Joseph*,[3] *James*,[2] *William*[1]), born February 6, 1743; died 1821; married 1st, November, 1768, Mary Remington, who died June, 1798. He married 2d, October or November, 1798, Silence Rumrill. By his 1st marriage, eight sons and one daughter. His children were:

i. EPAPHRAS.[5]
ii. ROGER, b. at Suffield, Jan. 16, 1771; d. Aug. 15, 1855; came to Troy, N. Y., 1794. Had children: 1. *Cornelia*[6]; 2. *Louis*[6]; 3. *Myron*[6]; 4. *Cornelia*[6] (again); 5. *Henry A.*[6]; 6. *George*[6]; 7. *Mary E.*[6]; 8. *George A.*[6]; 9. *Harriet C.*[6]; 10. *Eliphalet R.*[6]; 11. *Cornelia A.*[6]; 12. *Harvey J.*,[6] lawyer, Troy; 13. *Lydia M.*[6]
iii. JONATHAN.   iv. SETH.
v. SETH (again), b. 1778; d. in New Ipswich, Hillsborough Co., N. H., in old age; he lived there forty years.
vi. EPIPHALET.   vii. HENRY.   viii. AUGUSTINE.   ix. MARY.
x. ELIJAH.   xi. MATILDA.   xii. LUCY.
xiii. AURRELIA.   xiv. HARRIET.   xv. SHERLOCK.

10. Ensign WILLIAM[4] KING (*William*,[3] *James*,[2] *William*[1]), b. August 10, 1721; died March 8, 1691. Inherited his father's estate, still owned by descendants; was by General Assembly appointed, June, 1768, ensign of the 2d trainband of Suffield. He married 1st, December 28, 1743, Sarah Fuller, who died July 13, 1744; 2d, June 26, 1747, Lucy Hathaway, born August 21, 1725, died

February 18, 1817, daughter of Samuel Hathaway. Children by 2d marriage:

i. SARAH,[5] b. June 13, 1748; d. prior to 1803.
ii. ELIZABETH, b. June 22, 1751; m. either Leavitt or Pickett.
iii. LUCY, b. April 4, 1753; m. Norton, and left descendants.
iv. WILLIAM, b. Dec. 23, 1755. Had children: 1. *James*,[6] of Lansing, Mich.; 2. *Elizabeth*[6]; 3. *Willis*[6]; 4. *George*,[6] of Hartford.
v. SETH, b. at Suffield, Sept. 20, 1758; d. at Suffield, Feb. 10, 1846; of Suffield; a soldier in the Revolution; m. 1st, at Westfield, Mass., Feb. 12, 1784, Lydia Ballantine, b. at Westfield, March 15, 1759; d. at Suffield, Feb. 14, 1817, a daughter of Rev. John Ballantine* and Mary[4] (Lusher,[3] Nathaniel,[2] John[1] of Dedham) Gay. He m. 2d, Mrs. —— (Reynolds) Bascom, granddaughter of Rev. Peter Reynolds of Enfield, Conn. Children, all b. at Suffield, by 1st marriage:

1. *Sarah*,[6] b. June 16, 1785; m. Col. Horace Smith of Amherst, an early abolitionist; s. p.
2. *Seth*,[6] b. June 26, 1788, of South Windsor, Conn.; an officer in the American Revolution; m. Anne Moore, a daughter of Col. Eli[5] (Samuel Goffe,[4] Samuel,[3] John,[2] John[1] of Dorchester, 1630) Moore and Anne Wells.† Nine children.
3. *John A.*,[6] b. Nov. 1, 1790, of Suffield; m. 1st, Sally Stocking, daughter of Ansel Stocking and Prudence Crosby or Cresby; 2d, Prudence Baker, daughter of Enos Baker, and had by 1st marriage two children, by 2d marriage four children.
4. *Lydia*,[6] b. Feb. 4, 1793; m. Epaphras Mather, a son of Elijah[9] (Elijah,[8] Nathaniel,[7] Dr. Samuel,[6] Rev. Samuel,[5] Timothy[4] b. 1628, of Dorchester, Mass., Rev. Richard,[3] Thomas,[2] John[1]) Mather and Jerusha Roberts. (For descendants, see *Mather Genealogy*, by Horace E. Mather, p. 202.)
5. *Mary B.*,[6] b. March 21, 1795; m. Henry Loomis, son of Nathaniel[6] (Graves,[5] Nathaniel,[4] Nathaniel,[3] John,[2] Joseph[1] of Windsor) Loomis and Bethena Bronson. (For descendants, see *Loomis Genealogy*, by Prof. Elias Loomis, p. 153.)
6. *Lucy*,[6] b. Aug. 18, 1797.   7. *Ebenezer*.[6]

vi. BETHIA, b. May 23, 1760; m. either Pickett or Leavitt.
vii. ROXANNA, b. Aug. 13, 1762; m. Hitchcock of Suffield. Children:
1. *Alexander*[6] *Hitchcock*, unm., of Cheektowaga, Erie Co., N. Y.;
2. *Apollos*[6] *Hitchcock*, m., of Cheektowaga; 3. *James*[6] *Hitchcock*, m., of Cheektowaga; *Daughter*,[6] m. Vaughn.
viii. MARY, b. June 23, 1764; m. Capt. Joseph Fuller, and were parents of *Joseph*[6] *Fuller*.
ix. Dr. APOLLOS, b. Nov. 29, 1766; d. Jan. 27, 1810; was educated for the practice of medicine.

* Son of John[3] (John,[2] William[1] of Boston, 1651) Ballantine and Mary[5] (Adam,[4] Adam,[3] Gov. John[2] of Mass., Adam[1]) Winthrop. See *Hinman's Conn. Settlers*, p. 121.
† See *Stiles's Ancient Windsor*, p. 705.

KINGSLEY (*ante*, p. 215).—It is probable that the John Kingsley who married in Windham, Conn., Feb. 19, 1755, Mary Burnap, was the son of Amos and Ruth (Adams) Kingsley, of Windham, who were married Jan. 12, 1723, and had ten children as follows: 1, Amos; 2, Isaiah, b. June 11, 1725; 3, Nathaniel, b. 1726; 4, JOHN; 5, Samuel; 6, Joseph; 7, Eliza; 8, Alice; 9, Abiah; 10, Ruth.

The Kingsley line is as follows:—

John,[1] of Dorchester, Mass. and Taunton, Mass. He was in Dorchester in 1635, and he died in Rehoboth, Mass. His wife's name is not known. He was NOT John Kingsley of Milton, whose wife was a Daniels, though often confused with said John of Milton.

Eldad,[2] of Rehoboth, Mass.; b. in Dorchester, 1638; m. in Rehoboth, 1662, Mehitable Morey. He d. in Swansea, Mass., Aug. 30, 1679.

John,[3] of Rehoboth; b. there May 6, 1665; m. 1st, July 1, 1686, Sarah Sabin. He moved in 1703 to the place that was afterwards Windham, Conn. He had by his first wife ten children.

Amos,[4] of Windham; b. in Rehoboth, Jan. 18, 1696; d. April 23, 1787; m. Ruth Adams.   HENRY S. RUGGLES.

Wakefield, Mass.

THOMAS KIRKHAM OF WETHERSFIELD, CONN., AND HIS DESCENDANTS.

Compiled by Hon. RALPH D. SMYTH, and communicated by Dr. BERNARD C. STEINER.

1. THOMAS[1] KIRKHAM emigrated from England and settled at Wethersfield, Conn., where he married, March 24, 1683/4, Jane ———.

Children:

  i. RUTH,[2] b. Jan. 28, 1684-5.
2. ii. SAMUEL, d. Jan. 11, 1744.
3. iii. HENRY.

2. SAMUEL² KIRKHAM (*Thomas¹*), of Branford, married, May 28, 1707, Mary Goodrich of Branford, who died Jan. 15, 1772.

Children :

   i. ELIZABETH,³ b. June 16, 1708.
   ii. PATIENCE, b. Jan. 13, 1710-11; m. Nov. 28, 1733, David Parmelee of Guilford.
   iii. JOANNA, b. Feb. 23, 1712-13.
   iv. REBECCA, b. Mch. 1715-16; m. Nov. 20, 1734, Admire Parks.
4. v. SAMUEL, b. Feb. 1, 1717-18; d. Oct. 20, 1768.
   vi. LYDIA, b. July 10, 1720.
5. vii. JOHN, b. Sept. 11, 1722; d. May 17, 1770.
   viii. MARY, b. June 20, 1725.
   ix. SARAH, b. Jan. 27, 1731-2.

3. HENRY² KIRKHAM, or KIRCUM (*Thomas¹*), lived in Wethersfield, and married, Dec. 21, 1719, Martha, daughter of Samuel Burr of Hartford.

Children :

   i. SAMUEL,³ b. Jan. 1, 1721.
   ii. ELIJAH, b. Nov. 24, 1722.
   iii. SARAH, b. Feb. 21, 1726.
   iv. HENRY, b. Aug. 30, 1728.
   v. NATHANIEL, b. Dec. 11, 1730.

4. SAMUEL³ KIRKHAM, JR. (*Samuel,² Thomas¹*), of Guilford, married Jane, daughter of John Fosdick, who died Apr. 16, 1794.

Children :

   i. MERCY,⁴ b. Apr. 30, 1753.
6. ii. BENJAMIN, b. Apr. 13, 1755; d. Oct. 20, 1808.
7. iii. WILLIAM, b. 1756; killed Feb. 18, 1804.
   iv. SAMUEL, drowned Aug. 3, 1757.
   v. EBER, d. May 28, 1775.
   vi. ANNA, d. Mch. 16, 1774.
   vii. WEALTHY.
   viii. MARTHA.
   ix. DAVID, d. young.

5. JOHN³ KIRKHAM (*Samuel,² Thomas¹*), of Stoney Creek, married Esther, daughter of David Maltby of Northford.

Children :

   i. LEVI.⁴
8. ii. PHILEMON, b. Oct. 8, 1763.
9. iii. DANIEL, d. Apr. 17, 1832.
   iv. ELIHU, d. July 23, 1820.
   v. SOLOMON.
10. vi. SAMUEL, b. Apr. 1770; d. Sept. 14, 1827.
   vii. ESTHER.
   viii. ANNA, b. 1773; m. Stephen Frisbie; d. Dec. 18, 1857.
   ix. ZERVIAH.
11. x. ELI, b. 1780; d. May 10, 1845.

6. BENJAMIN⁴ KIRKHAM (*Samuel,³ Samuel,² Thomas¹*) married, May 21, 1786, Ruth, daughter of Ebenezer Evarts, who died July 3, 1828.

Children :

   i. ANNA FORSDICK,⁵ b. Feb. 28, 1787; m. Truman Jacobs, Jr., of North Haven.

   ii.   BELA STONE, b. 1789; d. at sea, on a privateer.

   iii. CALEB EVARTS, b. 1790; d. of small pox, Feb. 3, 1795.

   iv. BENJAMIN MORTIMER, b. Jan. 1794; d. of whooping cough, Feb. 25, 1795.

   v.   CALEB EVARTS, b. 1798; d. single, at sea.

7. WILLIAM[4] KIRKHAM (*Samuel*,[3] *Samuel*,[2] *Thomas*[1]) married Deborah Whitney of Branford, probably in 1786, when she was dismissed from the Cranford Church to the Fourth Church in Guilford. After his death, she married second, Bela Buel, and died at Guilford, May 15, 1841.

   Children:

   i.   SAMUEL,[5] b. Sept. 2, 1787; m. Catharine O'Reardon, in Ireland; removed to the banks of the Delaware River; had a large family.

   ii. NANCY, b. Oct. 25, 1790; m. (1) Sept. 6, 1818, George Foster, from whom she was divorced; m. (2) William Tryon of Clinton.

   iii. DAVID, b. May 25, 1793; lived in Madison; d. single, in 1836.

   iv. WILLIAM, b. Nov. 23, 1795; removed to Ohio; d. single.

8. PHILEMON[4] KIRKHAM (*John*,[3] *Samuel*,[2] *Thomas*[1]) married twice. He removed to Norton, Ohio.

   Children:

   i.   GEORGE,[5] m. Feb. 12, 1828, Caroline A., only daughter of Stephen Baldwin; practiced law at Akron, Ohio; had children: *Susan*,[6] m. William A. Hall of New York; and *Augustus*.

   ii. BETSEY.

9. DANIEL[4] KIRKHAM (*John*,[3] *Samuel*,[2] *Thomas*[1]) married, June 9, 1799, Sarah, daughter of Isaac Johnson.

   Children:

   i.   BEDAD,[5] b. May 18, 1800; d. Aug. 16, 1828; m. Apr. 21, 1819, Ruth, daughter of Constans Redfield, who d. Nov. 14, 1856, having m. (2) Sept. 13, 1829, George, son of Thomas Hill of Guilford, from whom she was divorced in Oct., 1855. Bedad[5] had one child, *Sarah*,[6] who m. Horace, son of James Leete.

   ii. ERASTUS RODNEY, b. Sept. 2, 1801; d. at sea, May 3, 1826.

   iii. ISAAC JOHNSON, b. May 23, 1809; lived at Derby, Conn.; d. there Mch. 7, 1872; m. Delany Frisbie, and had: *Richard Monson*,[6] *Ellen Roselia, Calvin Crampton, Daniel Erastus, Austin Parker, Guilford Montgomery, Benjamin Franklin, Jane Eliza*, and *George Albert*.

   iv. DANIEL MALTBY, b. Jan. 31, 1818; d. single, in Ohio, in 1839.

10. SAMUEL[4] KIRKHAM (*John*,[3] *Samuel*,[2] *Thomas*[1]) married, June 1, 1799, Chloe Field, who died in Ohio, in 1856.

   Children:

   i.   GEORGE ANSON,[5] b. Mch. 24, 1800; d. Apr. 7, 1852; lived in Guilford; m. (i) Aug. 27, 1820, Patty Isbell, who d. Mch. 8, 1828, aged 28; m. (2) Julia Towner, who m. (2) Benjamin C. Leete. Children: *William L.*,[6] lived in Branford; *Mary*, m. Simon W. Shaler of Deep River; *Laura B.*, m. (1) George Jewel, from whom she was divorced, and m. (2) Justin O. Leete; *George Harrison*; and *George*.

   ii. LAURA B., b. Sept. 7, 1802; d. Oct. 6, 1834; m. Oct. 16, 1822, Russel Benton of Guilford.

   iii. JOHN BATES, b. Dec. 27, 1804; drowned June 3, 1816.

   iv. ELIZA ANN, b. Sept. 14, 1806; m. Frederic W. Williams of Guilford.

v.   HARRIETT MALTBY, b. Feb. 2, 1808; m. Charles Beeman of Deep River.

vi.   MARIETTA, b. July 14, 1811; m. July 16, 1834, William Mundine of Georgetown, S. C.

vii.   SUSANNAH COLLINS, b. June 3, 1814.

viii.   JOHN HARRISON, b. Mch. 20, 1816; d. at sea, Sept., 1836.

ix.   CLARISSA GRISWOLD, b. Feb. 2, 1818; m. Levi Farnsworth of Ohio.

x.   JANE AMORETT, b. Dec. 21, 1820; d, Aug. 19, 1856; m. Niles P. Starkie of Deep River.

11.   ELI[4] KIRKHAM (*John,*[3] *Samuel,*[2] *Thomas*[1]), of Guilford, married, Nov. 10, 1801, Sarah Ward, who died at New Haven, July 5, 1854.

Children:

i.   MARY ANN,[5] b. Sept. 30, 1802; m. Dec. 25, 1823, Samuel A. Barker.

ii.   CATHERINE WARD, b. Mch. 8, 1806; m. Nov. 5, 1828, John Kennedy of New Haven.

iii.   REV. ELI MALTBY, b. Dec. 13, 1813; d. May 14, 1841; m. Henrietta Tuttle of Fair Haven; no children.

GENEALOGICAL NOTES OF THE KIRTLAND FAMILY IN THE UNITED STATES.

[Communicated by Rev. F. W. CHAPMAN of Ellington, Conn.]

THE Kirtlands of this country are supposed to have descended from NATHANAEL[1] KIRTLAND of Lynn, Mass., who is reputed to have resided previous to his emigration to this country, in Silver Street, London.

He had one son, *John*, who removed to Saybrook, during his minority, and was adopted by Mr. John and Mrs. Susannah Wastall. They having no children made him their sole heir, as appears by a will, dated in 1672. Said John Wastall died Feb. 12, 1682, and his wife Susannah, March 18, 1684.

2. JOHN[2] KIRTLAND, son of Nathanael[1] K., the first settler, m. at Saybrook, Lydia Pratt, the dau. of Lieut. William Pratt, one of the early settlers of that town, Nov. 18, 1679, and had by her ten ch. Said Lydia Pratt was b. Jan. 1, 1659. The respective dates of the decease of Mr. and Mrs. Kirtland have not been found.

Ch.: (3) *John*,[3][†] b. Jan. 11, 1681;---(4) *Priscilla*,[3] b. Feb. 1, 1682, m. Thomas Jones;---(5) *Lydia*,[3] b. Oct. 11, 1685, m. 1st, Mr. Griffin; m. 2d, in 1740, Mr. Conklin; d. *s. p.*;---(6) *Elisabeth*,[3][†] b. June 27, 1688, m. John Shipman;---(7) *Nathanael*,[3][†] b. Oct. 24, 1690;---(8) *Philip*,[3][†] b. May 28, 1693;---(9) *Martha*,[3][†] b. Aug. 11, 1695, m. Rev. Henry Wills;---(10) *Samuel*,[3][†] b. Jan. 19, 1699;---(11) Rev. *Daniel*,[3][†] b. June 17, 1701;---(12) *Parnell*,[3][†] b. Oct. 16, 1704, m. John Tully.

3. JOHN[3] KIRTLAND was twice married. First, to Temperance Buckingham, the daughter of Rev. Thomas Buckingham of Saybrook, as is supposed, about the year 1702. By her he had three children. Second, to Lydia Belden, March 29, 1716, by whom he had nine children. Mrs. Lydia Kirtland d. Nov. 7, 1749. The date of Mr. John Kirtland's decease is not known.

Ch. by the first marriage: (13) *Hester*,[4] b. March 19, 1704, m. 1st, Dea. Jedediah Chapman; m. 2d, Robert Chapman;—(14) *John*,[4][†] b. July 5, 1708;—(15) *Temperance*,[4][†] b. Nov. 10, 1710, m. Andrew Southworth.

Ch. by the second marriage: (16) *Elias*,[4] b. Jan. 21, 1718, d. at 3 months;—(17) *Elisha*,[4][†] b. Aug. 11, 1719;—(18) *Lydia*,[4][†] b. Oct. 28, 1721, m. Elisha De Wolf;—(19) *Parnell*,[4] b. Jan. 29, 1724;—(20) *Constant*,[4] b. Jan. 24, 1726, d. Feb. 1727;—(21) *Constant*,[4][†] b. Dec. 24, 1727;—(22) *Ezra*,[4][†] b. Oct. 11, 1728;—(23) *Elisabeth*,[4] b. Sept. 1, 1732, d. Sept. 1739;—(24) *Dorotha*,[4] b. April 21, 1735, d. 1739.

6. JOHN SHIPMAN m. Elizabeth[3] Kirtland, Jan. 11, 1715, by whom he had one child:---(25) *Elizabeth*,[4] b. June 27, 1688.

7. NATHANAEL[3] KIRTLAND was twice married. First, to Sarah Chapman, by whom he had two children. Mrs. Sarah Kirtland d. Feb. 6, 1716. Second, to Phebe De Wolf, by whom he had ten children. He was, as appears from Saybrook Records, a prominent man in the town of Saybrook. The time of his decease is not known.

Ch. by the first marriage: (26) *Sarah*,[4] b. Sept. 1, 1714;—(27) An infant,[4] b. Feb. 5, 1716, d. Feb. 9, 1716.

Ch. by the second marriage : (28) *Mary*,⁴ b. March 11, 1718 ;—
(29) *Nathanael*,⁴ b. Dec. 11, 1718 ;—(30) *Daniel*,⁴ b. Dec. 24, 1721 ;—
(31) *Jedediah*,⁴ b. March 25, 1724 ;—(32) *Phebe*,⁴ b. April 13, 1726 ;—
(33) *Reynold*,⁴ b. Jan. 20, 1728 ;—(34) *Stephen*,⁴ b. May 28, 1732 ;—
(35) *Priscilla*,⁴ b. Feb. 12, 1740.

8. PHILIP³ KIRTLAND m. Lydia Marvin of Lyme, June 16, 1726, by
whom he had ten children, The dates of Mr. and Mrs. Kirtland's decease
have not been found.

Ch.: (36) *Philip*,⁴[†] b. Dec. 17, 1727 ;—(37) *Nathan*,⁴ b. June 21,
1729, d. Sept. 30, 1744 ;—(38) *Gideon*,⁴[†] b. May 17, 1731 ;—(39)
Lydia,⁴ b. Jan. 12, 1733 ;—(40) *Esther*,⁴ b. March 3, 1735 ;—(41) *Hannah*,⁴ b. Feb. 13, 1737 ;—(42) *Elizabeth*,⁴[†] b. May 23, 1740, m. Eleazer Warner ;—(43) *Sarah*,⁴ b. Oct. 27, 1742 ;—(44) *Abner*,⁴[†] b. Dec.
6, 1745 ;—(45) *Mary*,⁴ b. Dec. 12, 1748.

9. Rev. HENRY WILLS m. Oct. 27, 1718, Martha³ Kirtland, by whom
he had nine children.   Mr. Wills was ordained the pastor of the Second
Church in Norwich, Oct. 8, 1718, and was dismissed in 1750, having
retained his office 32 years.   Rev. Henry Wills d. Sept. 30, 1758.
When Mrs. Martha Wills d. is unknown to us.

Ch.: (46) *John*,⁴ b. Sept. 14, 1719 ;—(47) *Martha*,⁴ b. April 20,
1721 ;—(48) *Parnell*,⁴ b. March 14, 1723 ;—(49) *Lydia*,⁴ b. Nov. 25,
1725 ;—(50) *Henry*,⁴ b. Jan. 20, 1728 ;—(51) *Hannah*,⁴ b. July 13,
1730 ;—(52) *Ruth*,⁴ b. Jan. 21, 1733 ;—(53) *Joshua*,⁴ b. Aug. 28,
1735 ;—(54) *Temperance*,⁴ b. May 19, 1738.

10. SAMUEL³ KIRTLAND m. Martha Whittlesey of Saybrook, March
31, 1731, and had by her six children.   Mr. Samuel Kirtland d. in February, 1760, in the 63d year of his age.   Mrs. Martha Kirtland d. in
August, 1759, in her 59th year.

Ch.: (55) *Samuel*,⁴[†] b. Jan. 10, 1732 ;—(56) *Martha*,⁴ b. Nov. 26,
1733 ;—(57) *Martin*,⁴[†] b. March 31, 1735 ;—(58) *Ambrose*,⁴ b. Jan.
27, 1737, d. May, 1737 ;—(59) *Ambrose*,⁴[†] b. March 28, 1738 ;—
(60) *Charles*,⁴ b. July 24, 1740.

11. Rev. DANIEL³ KIRTLAND m. Mary Perkins, July 15, 1723.   He
graduated at Yale College in the class of 1720 ; studied Theology, and
was ordained Pastor of the Third Church in Norwich (Newent) Dec. 10,
1723, being their first minister.   After preaching to that people nearly 30
years he became deranged, and his connection with the church was dissolved, on account of that calamity.   He lived to the age of 72 ; d. very
poor, in 1773, and, not having had any monumental stone, the spot which
his remains occupy in the burial ground is forgotten and unknown.   He was
the father of Rev. Samuel Kirtland, the well-known and faithful missionary to the Oneida Indians, for forty years and upwards, and the grandfather of the former President Kirkland of Harvard University.   He had
ten children.

Ch.: (61) *Mary*,⁴ b. July 16, 1724, d. May, 1725 ;—(62) *Daniel*,⁴ b.
Oct. 1, 1725 ;—(63) *Mary*,⁴ 2d, b. April 15, 1727, d. Sept. 9, 1739 ;—
(64) *Hannah*,⁴ b. July 6, 1729 ;—(65) *Anne*,⁴ b. July 24, 1731 ;—(66)
Elizabeth,⁴ b. Sept. 5, 1733 ;—(67) *John*,⁴ b. Nov. 15, 1735 ;—(68)
Jabez,⁴ b. Jan. 5, 1738 ;—(69) *Lydia*,⁴ b. Dec. 14, 1739 ;—(70) Rev.
Samuel,⁴[†] b. Nov. 20, 1741.

12. JOHN TULLY of Saybrook m. Feb. 17, 1731, Parnell³ Kirtland. Mr. Tully was for many years one of the leading men of the town. Several volumes of the Records of Saybrook are in his handwriting, as Clerk.

Ch.: (71) *Parnell*,⁴ b. June 28, 1732 ;—(72) *John*,⁴ b. March 12, 1734, d. March 13, 1762 ;—(73) *Ann*,⁴ (74) *Daniel*,⁴ twins, b. Nov. 24, 1736 ; Ann d. Sept. 1, 1739 ; Daniel d. Sept. 23, 1739 ;—(75) *Charlotte*,⁴ b. April 23, 1739 ;—(76) *Mary*,⁴ b. July 21, 1742 ;—(77) *Sarah*,⁴ b. June 26, 1745.

13. JEDEDIAH CHAPMAN of West Brook, Ct., m. June 6, 1723, Hester⁴ Kirtland, by whom he had eight children. Mr. Chapman was for many years the most prominent man in the society of West Brook, where he resided, in civil, military, and religious affairs. He was a Major of Infantry ; a lawyer by profession, and chosen deacon of the church in 1732, in which capacity he served until his death. He was distinguished as a Christian gentleman, exhibiting a rare combination of talents in connection with fervent piety and ardent zeal in the cause of Christ. He d. at West Brook, Feb. 10, 1764, in the 61st year of his age. His widow, Mrs. Hester Chapman, after his decease, m. Robert Chapman of East Haddam, April 22, 1766.

Ch.: (78) *Hester*,⁵ b. April 30, 1724 ;—(79) *Jedediah*,⁵ b. Dec. 15, 1726 ;—(80) *Temperance*,⁵ b. Feb. 1, 1729 ;—(81) *Ann*,⁵ b. March 22, 1731 ;—(82) *Reuben*,⁵ b. Oct. 29, 1733 ;—(83) *Charity*,⁵ b. March 2, 1736 ;—(84) *Chloe*,⁵ b. 1742 ;—(85) *Tabitha*.⁵

14. JOHN⁴ KIRTLAND m. Lydia Gilbert, at what time is not known. The names of their children have been furnished by one of their descendants, with no dates except the birth of the youngest child. They had seven children.

Ch.: (86) *Lydia*⁵;—(87) *Temperance*⁵;—(89) *John*,⁵ d. at sea, unmarried ;—(90) *William*⁵;—(91) *Joseph*⁵;—(92) *Hester*⁵;—(93) *Asa*,⁵ b. Dec. 7, 1746.

15. ANDREW SOUTHWORTH m. Jan. 27, 1732, Temperance⁴ Kirtland, and had by him eight children. The dates of Mr. and Mrs. Southworth's decease have not been found.

Ch.: (94) *Andrew*,⁵ b. Sept. 22, 1733 ;—(95) *Nathan*,⁵ b. Dec. 1, 1735 ;—(96) *Temperance*,⁵ b. Nov. 7, 1737 ;—(97) *Otis*,⁵ b. March 10, 1741 ;—(98) *Ann*,⁵ b. July 1, 1743 ;—(99) *Prudence*,⁵ b. Jan. 1745 ;— (100) *Martin*,⁵ b. Dec. 1747 ;—(101) *Gideon*,⁵ b. May, 1750.

17. ELISHA⁴ KIRTLAND m. Deborah Lay, and had two children, and perhaps others. Nothing very definite in regard to this family has been ascertained.

Ch.: (102) *James*⁵;—(103) *Elias*.⁵

18. ELISHA DE WOLF, who m. Lydia⁴ Kirtland, resided at Horton, Nova Scotia, and is said to have had a large family. The name of but one of the children has been received.

Ch.: (104) *James R.*⁵

21. CONSTANT⁴ KIRTLAND m. Rachel Brackett of Wallingford, Ct., April 20, 1753, by whom he had ten children. They resided at Wallingford. Mr. Kirtland d. Feb. 3, 1792, aged 65. Mrs. Kirtland died Feb. 17, 1812, aged 80.

Ch.: (105) *Isaac,*[5] b. March 30, 1754 ;—(106) *Turhand,*[5] b. Nov. 16, 1755, died in Ohio in 1844 ;—(107) *Mary,*[5] b. Dec. 23, 1757 ;—(108) *John,*[5] b. Dec. 20, 1759, died at Whitestown, N. Y.;—(109) *Billious,*[5] b. June 29, 1762 ; *d.* Oct. 25, 1805 ; was an eminent physician, to which profession he was born, if one may judge from his singular christian name ;—(110) *Rachel,*[5] b. July 9, 1764 ;—(111) *Jared,*[5] b. Aug. 8, 1766, d. in Ohio in 1832 ;—(112) *George,*[5] b. July 2, 1769, d. April 20, 1793 ;—(113) *Lydia,*[5] b. Feb. 27, 1772 ;—(114) *Sarah,*[5] b. March 19, 1778.

22. EZRA[4] KIRTLAND m. Olive Wakeley in the year 1752, by whom he had two sons, and perhaps other children. He removed from Saybrook to Bridgeport, Conn., in 1748, where he resided until his death, which occurred in 1799, when in his 71st year.
Ch.: (115) *Ezra,*[5] b. 1753 ;—(116) *Zebulon,*[5] b. 1755.

36. PHILIP[4] KIRTLAND m. Sybil Pratt, Nov. 29, 1757, by whom he had three children. The dates of Mr. and Mrs. Kirtland's decease are not known.
Ch.: (117) *Sybil,*[5] b. Oct. 1, 1758 ;—(118) *Philip,*[5] b. Jan. 3, 1761, d. Jan. 1, 1765 ;—(119) *Nathan,*[5] b. Jan. 14, 1763.

38. GIDEON[5] KIRTLAND m. Lydia Wilcox, Dec. 17, 1761, and had by her five children. Nothing farther has been found.
Ch.: (120) *Gideon,*[5] b. April 14, 1763 ;—(121) *Lydia,*[5] b. Oct. 13, 1764 ;—(122) *Sarah,*[5] b. Feb. 13, 1766 ;—(123) *Ruth,*[5] b. April 3, 1768 ;—(124) *Philip,*[5] b. June 17, 1770.

42. ELEAZER WARNER m. Jan. 14, 1762, Elizabeth[4] Kirtland, and had by her eight children. Nothing farther has been ascertained.
Ch.: (125) *Andrew,*[5] b. Nov. 15, 1762 ;—(126) *Eleazer,*[5] b. April 2, 1764 ;—(127) *Philip,*[5] b. Feb. 16, 1766 ;—(128) *Sylvester,*[5] b. Feb. 21, 1768 ;—(129) *Kirtland,*[5] b. Feb. 8, 1770 ;—(130) *Nathan,*[5] b. March 23, 1772 ;—(131) *Betty,*[5] b. April 4, 1775 ;—(132) *Lydia,*[5] b. Feb. 14, 1779.

44. ABNER[4] KIRTLAND m. Mercy Pratt, dau. of Daniel Pratt, about the year 1770, and had by her eight children. The dates of Mr. and Mrs. Kirtland's decease are not known.
Ch.: (133) *Mercy,*[5] b. July 13, 1771, never married ;—(134) *Mary,*[5] b. Nov. 1773, never married ;—(135) *Abner,*[5] b. April 13, 1776 ;—(136) *Elisha,*[5] b. Jan. 30, 1779 ;—(137) *Daniel,*[5] b. April 1, 1781 ;—(138) *Philip,*[5] b. Jan. 8, 1784 ;—(139) *Lydia,*[5] b. March, 1786 ;—(140) *Deborah M.*[5]

55. Dea. SAMUEL[4] KIRTLAND was thrice married. First, to Thankful Bushnell, May 7, 1755. By her he had four children. Second, to Mehetable Lord, Nov. 1, 1786. Third, to Hepsibah Bushnell, May 1, 1804. The dates of their respective deaths are not known to the compiler.
Ch.: (141) *Azubah,*[5] b. Dec. 19, 1756, at Saybrook ;—(142) *Samuel,*[5] b. Aug. 31, 1760, at Saybrook ;—(143) *Lydia,*[5] b. March 23, 1763, at Saybrook ;—(144) *Benjamin,*[5] b. Dec. 18, 1769, at Saybrook.

57. MARTIN[4] KIRTLAND m. Sarah Meigs, March 16, 1758, and had by her six children.
Ch.: (145) *Martin,*[5] b. March 29, 1759 ;—(146) *Sarah,*[5] b. Feb. 19, 1761 ;—(147) *Charles,*[5] b. Oct. 27, 1762 ;—(148) *Mary,*[5] b. Aug. 19, 1765 ;—(149) *Eleazer,*[5] b. Oct. 22, 1767 ;—(150) *Clarinda,*[5] b. Sept. 10, 1773.

59. AMBROSE[4] KIRTLAND m. and had one child, and perhaps others. The name of his wife has not been ascertained.

Ch.: (151) *Ambrose,*[5] b. 1760, d. Jan. 7, 1784, aged 23.

70. Rev. SAMUEL[4] KIRKLAND (or KIRTLAND) m. Jerusha, dau. of Jabez Bingham of Salisbury, Conn., in Sept. 1769. He became, previous to his marriage, a pupil in the Indian school, under the care of the Rev. Dr. Wheelock. He afterward went as a Missionary to the Oneida Indians, among whom he labored for more than 40 years. He had six children. He d. March 28, 1808, aged 66. His grandson, Rev. Samuel K. Lothrop, D. D., of Boston, wrote a Biography of him, which was published in Sparks's American Biography.

Ch.: (152) *John Thornton,*[5]* (153) *George Whitfield,*[5] twins, b. Aug. 17, 1770 ;—(154) *Jerusha,*[5] m. John H. Lothrop, Esq.;—(155) *Sarah,*[5] m. Francis Amory, Esq.;—(156) *Samuel,*[5] grad. at Harv. Col. 1803 ;— (157) *Eliza,*[5] who m. Professor Edward Robinson of the New York University.

THE KIRTLAND OR KIRKLAND FAMILY.

By V. C. SANBORN, of La Grange, Ill.

ALTHOUGH from time to time many facts have come to light as to the origin of the Kirkland family, no published collection of these facts exists. The four principal sources of information about this family are:

1. Dr. Lothrop's Memoir of Rev. Samuel Kirkland, in Sparks's "Library of American Biography."

2. Savage's "Genealogical Dictionary."

3. Mr. F. W. Chapman's "Kirtland Family" (REGISTER, Vol. xiv.), * and his published "Pratt Genealogy."

4. Lewis and Newhall's "History of Lynn."

Dr. Lothrop's account was the earliest, forming a basis for future researches; and as his account has been very generally accepted, it seems advisable to quote it here, in order, by the genealogy given later, to emphasize the corrections which have been made by discoveries subsequent to 1845, when Dr. Lothrop published his memoir. He says:

"The Kirkland family, as the name shows, is of Scotch descent. In this country it may be traced back to Saybrook, Ct., in 1635. Among the 36 heads of families who were the early settlers of that place, the name of John Kirkland appears, who is said to have come from Silver St., London. He had a son John, who was the father of ten children, of whom Rev. Daniel Kirkland was the youngest but one, and born in 1701."

In fact, John Kirtland was not one of the early settlers of Saybrook, for he did not move there till 1672, nor have I been able to find any authority for the statement that he came from Silver St., London. Mr. Chapman, I believe, discovered in the Saybrook records the connection between John Kirtland of Saybrook and Nathaniel of Lynn; and Mr. S. G. Drake published in his "Founders of New England" (REGISTER, Vol. xiv.) the sailing list of the *Hopewell* in 1635, with names of the brothers Philip and *Pages 375-379, this volume.

Nathaniel Kirtland as passengers. Lewis and Newhall's "History of Lynn" gives much fragmentary information about Philip and Nathaniel; and Savage supplements this with many dates and facts. But an essential link in the Lynn records seems to have been overlooked by these authors, namely, that in 1638, when Philip and Nathaniel were but 24 and 22 years of age respectively, there were *two* Philip Kirtlands in Lynn. This point establishes a connection between the American settlers and a certain John Kirtland of Buckinghamshire, whose will I quote hereafter.

Before tabulating the early generations, let me say a word as to the family name. All the records show that the name of our family was spelled "Kirtland," "Kyrtland" or "Kertland" from 1616 to 1773, both in this country and in England. On what authority rests the present spelling, I cannot say; Dr. Lothrop thought that the family was of Scotch descent; and probably the change from Kirtland to Kirkland, as a supposed original spelling, was made about 1780 by Rev. Samuel Kirkland, and soon after was adopted by his connections. His brother Joseph, writing in 1773 to another brother, John, announcing the death of their father, Rev. Daniel Kirtland, signs his name and directs his letter "Kirtland." This letter is now in the possession of Major Kirkland of Chicago.

The name "*Kirtland*" is not to be found in English records or pedigrees, so far as I have been able to ascertain. In Essex, in the 13th century, Peter de Kirteling appears as the witness to a grant of land; but no further mention of the name occurs. No family of that name registered its pedigree at the Herald's Visitations of Buckinghamshire or elsewhere. "*Kirtland*" may be derived from "*Curtland*" (meaning lack-land), and Burke's "General Amory" describes the arms of *Curtland* (no location given) as, *Or, three cinquefoils pierced gules*. The name "*Kirkland*," however, is an old English name; the family being situated principally in Cumberland, and the "General Armory" gives the coat of—"KIRKLAND": (Kirkland, County Lancaster, Brampton, County Derby; founded by Gamel, Lord of Kirkland, County Derby, and Eastbourne, County Sussex, *temp.* William I.) *Sable, three mullets argent within a bordure engrailed or, quartering* KIRKLAND (ancient) *Sable, three mullets argent*."

A clue to the origin of the American family is furnished by the will of John Kirtland of Newport-Pagnell, Bucks., England, dated 1616. Mr. H. F. Waters printed this will in the REGISTER, Vol. xli., page 60, and I quote his abstract:

"John Kirtland of Tickford in the parish of Newport-Pagnell, County Bucks., Gentleman, 12 Dec, 1616, proved 1 Aug. 1617. To son Nathaniel all that part of my dwelling house in Tickford wherein I now inhabit, sometime called by the name of Emberton's,* adjoining to the tenement in tenure of William Coningham and to the house and ground of me the said John Kirtland, sometime Thomas Horton's. Legacies to Mary Kirtland my now wife, sons Francis and Joseph Kirtland and daughters Abigail, Susanna and Mary Kirtland. To my eldest son John Kirtland the house or tenement sometime Thomas Horton's (next the above) and adjoining a tenement of heirs of William Barton deceased. Wife Mary and her five children as above. To godson John Kirtland, son of my brother Philip Kirtland, 14s 4d, and to the rest of the children of the said Philip 2s 6d each to be paid unto the said Philip for their use. To the children of my brother Fras. Kirtland 2s 6d apiece. To Francis Foster clerk 10s. Wife Mary to be executrix, friends Geo. Hull and Jno. Horley of Newport-Pagnell to be overseers.

"*Phylip Kyrtland* one of the witnesses. Weldon, 82."

* "Paganus de Emberton, of Tykford Priory, Bucks., 1187," Dugdale's "Monasticon."

From the above it will be seen that the American Kirtland family starts with:—

1. (JOHN[1]?) KIRTLAND,—of whom we know only (from his son John's will) that he had,—

  2. i.   JOHN,[2] born about 1580.
  3. ii.   PHILIP, born about 1585.
     iii.   FRANCIS, born about 1590, married and had children.

2. JOHN[2] KIRTLAND (*John?*[1]) of Tickford in the parish of Newport-Pagnell, Bucks., "Gentleman"; his will quoted above, names the following children:

i.	JOHN.[3]	iv.	JOSEPH.[3]
ii.	NATHANIEL.[3]	v.	ABIGAIL.[3]
iii.	FRANCIS.[3]	vi.	SUSANNA.[3]
	vii.	MARY.[3]	

3. PHILIP[2] KYRTLAND or KERTLAND (*John?*[1]) probably of Sherrington, Bucks., witness to his brother John's will in 1616, mentioned in that will as having son John and other children. No record of his taking passage for New England. Lewis says Philip Kertland, first shoemaker of Lynn, Mass., came there in 1635. This may have been Philip[2] the father or Philip[3] his son; the latter we know came over in 1635. Probably Lewis confused the two, as have others. The first definite record of Philip Kertland Senior is in 1638, when 10 acres in Lynn were granted to "Philip Kertland *Senior*" and 10 acres to "Philip Kertland *Junior*." (Lewis & Newhall). In 1643 the father's signature appears on Goody Armitage's petition, a facsimile of the signatures being given in the REGISTER for January 1879, page 61. (This may have been the signature of son Philip, but I think he was then on Long Island.) Children of Philip[2] by wife unknown,—

  1.   JOHN[3], born 1607, mentioned by name in his godfather and uncle John's will, 1616. In 1659 he made deposition as to his brother Philip's estate. Residence unknown; perhaps at Saybrook, where lived his sister Susanna Wastall, who in 1683 gave to her "childless brother John" a small house and lot in Saybrook. Perhaps also this is the John who was supposed by Dr. Lothrop to have been the father of John[4]. No record is found of his death.
  4. ii.   PHILIP[3], born 1614.
  5. iii.   NATHANIEL,[3] born 1616.
     iv.   SUSANNA,[3] birth unknown, married John Wastall or Westall of Wethersfield. He was a Deputy there in 1643, Goodwin says, and moved to Saybrook in 1653, says Savage; selectman in Saybrook, a prominent man there, and allowed to keep an Inn in 1663. He died in 1683, and left a good estate to adopted son John[4] Kertland. Susanna Wastall died 1684.

4. PHILIP[3] KYRTLAND or KERTLAND (*Philip,*[2] *John?*[1]), born in 1614, was too young to be mentioned by name in his uncle John's will in 1616; he was one of the other "children of brother Philip" there mentioned. His earliest definite record is on the sailing list of the ship *Hopewell* from London April 1, 1635,—"Philip Kyrtland, from Sherrington in Bucks., aged 21; Nathaniel Kyrtland from Sherrington in Bucks, aged 19." (See under Philip[2] for possible items about him in Lynn records.) In 1638 was granted 10 acres by town of

Lynn. In 1640, he and his brother Nathaniel,[3] with many other Lynn people, settled on Long Island, but Philip[3] must soon have returned to Lynn, from the dates of his children's births on the Lynn records. In 1652 he bought from Nathaniel Tyler his house and lands in Lynn. Philip[3] died before 1659, for we find in Salem Court Files July 17th, 1659, the following:

"Deposition of John Kirtland, aged about 52. I often heard my brother Phylip say oft times that his wife should have all hee had to dispose of so long as she live; and to my best rememberance hee gave £15 to his dafter Mary and £10 to his dafter Sara, £10 to his dafter Susanna and £10 to his dafter Hanna, this to be giuen to them at ye day of marriag, the land not to be sould so long as she liues."

William Harcher of Lynn, aged about 65, stated that when Philip Kertland was going to sea he told him substantially as above. On October 14th, 1659, Evan Thomas (a vintner who came to Boston from Wales, with wife Jane and four children, in 1640), announces his intention of marrying the widow Alice Kertland of Lynn; and he made conveyance of estate in trust for her children April 24, 1661. By wife Alice, Philip Kertland had the following children, all born in Lynn:

i. MARY[4], born June 3, 1640.
ii. SARAH[4], born September 27, 1646, married John Davis, October 5, 1664.
iii. SUSANNA[4], born March 8, 1652.
iv. HANNAH[4], } twins, born June 12, 1654.
v. EBENEZER[4], }

5. NATHANIEL[3] KYRTLAND or KERTLAND (*Philip,[2] John?[1]*), born in 1616. He was an infant (or perhaps unborn) at the date of his uncle John's will. Came over with his brother Philip[3] on the *Hopewell* and settled in Lynn. Not named in the division of land in Lynn, 1638; in that year was defendant in law suit brought by Isaack Disberowe (REGISTER, 1887, page 361). Went to Long Island with his brother Philip, and, Savage says, staid there some years, marrying Parnell —— and settling in Southold, L. I. Returned to Lynn before 1658, was selectman there 1678, and died there in 1686 (*Lewis & Newhall*). Savage gives the following children:

6. i. NATHANIEL,[4] born at Southold, L. I.
ii. PHILIP[4] (perhaps a son of Philip[3]), probably born on Long Island. Married Ruth Pierce (Query: daughter of Capt. Michael Pierce?) October 14, 1677. Was a soldier in King Philip's war, at Hadley, credited from Lynn, April 6, 1676 (REGISTER, 1887, page 79). In 1685 with other Lynn ex-soldiers, petitioned for a tract of land in the Nipmugg Country, on account of services in the late wars.
iii. ANN[4], born in Lynn April 16, 1658.
7. iv. JOHN[4], born in Lynn, August, 1659.
v. HANNAH[4], born in Lynn, April 15, 1662.
vi. ELIZABETH[4], born in Lynn, March 20, 1664, married William[2] Pratt of Saybrook, son of Lieut. William Pratt.
vii. MARY[4], } twins, born in Lynn, May 15, 1667.
viii. MARTHA[4], }

6. NATHANIEL[4] KERTLAND or KYRTLAND (*Nathaniel,[3] Philip,[2] John ?[1]*). Fined at Lynn in 1667, with two others for "Prophaining ye Lord's Day by going to William Crafts' house and drinkeing of his Sider and Rosteing of his aples without his or his wife's consent" (*Lewis & Newhall*). Was a soldier in King Philip's War, credited to Capt.

Manning in 1676 (REGISTER, 1888, page 95). Married Mary
Rand (probably daughter of Robert of Lynn), who survived him, and
in 1690 married Dr. John Henry Burchsted of Lynn (*Lewis & Newhall*). Children were:

i. NATHANIEL⁵ born May 3, 1677.
ii. MARY⁵, born Feb'y 1, 1680.
iii. PRISCILLA⁵, born April 9, 1683.
iv. ELIZABETH⁵, born June 22, 1685.

7. LIEUT. JOHN⁴ KERTLAND or KIRTLAND (*Nathaniel,³ Philip,² John?¹*),
   adopted in minority by his aunt Susanna³ (Kertland) Wastall. Mr.
   Chapman in his Pratt Genealogy quotes Saybrook Records, Vol. 1,
   page 78, year 1672:

"This agreement, between Mr. John Wastall of Saybrook and Mr. Nathaniel Cortland (*sic*) of Linne in Mattachewsetts. . . Ye said Cortland
doth resign up his sonne John to ye disposal of ye said Wastall and his
wife Susanna. . . . The said Wastall both promise that ye said John
Cortland shall succeed in ye estate of ye said Wastall."

John Kertland married Nov. 18th, 1679, Lydia, daughter of Lieut.
Wm. Pratt, an early and influential settler of Saybrook, and upon
the death of Mr. and Mrs. Wastall succeeded to a good estate left
by them. John Kirtland was somewhat prominent in local affairs,
and was appointed Lieutenant of the fort at Saybrook in 1702 and
again in 1708. (Colonial Records of Ct., Vols. 4 & 5). He died
January 20, 1716, having had the following children:

i. JOHN,⁵ born July 11, 1681, married 1st, Temperance Buckingham; 2d,
   Lydia Belden.
ii. PRISCILLA, born February 1, 1683, married Thos. Jones.
iii. LYDIA, born October 11, 1685, married 1st, Mr. Griffin; 2d, ———
   Conklin.
iv. ELIZABETH, born Jan'y 27, 1688, married John Chapman.
v. NATHANIEL, born Oct. 24, 1690, married 1st, Sara Chapman; 2d,
   Phœbe De Wolf.
vi. PHILIP, born May 28, 1693.
vii. MARTHA, born August 11, 1695, married Rev. H. Wills.
viii. SAMUEL, born Jan'y 19, 1699, married Martha Whittlesey.
ix. REV. DANIEL, born June 17, 1701 (Yale 1720), ordained first pastor
   of Newent church at Norwich, Ct., 1721, married July 15, 1723,
   Mary Perkins, probably daughter of Jabez Perkins and Hannah
   (Lothrop), and had five sons and seven daughters, among them
   Rev. Sam'l Kirkland, Missionary to the Oneidas, and father of
   President John Thornton Kirkland of Harvard University.
x. PARNELL, born October 16, 1704, married John Tully.

Mr. F. W. Chapman's "Kirtland Family" (REGISTER. Vol. xiv.), *
to which I have alluded, gives the family record of John⁴ Kirtland,
from the point reached above, for several generations; and so this
article is merely intended to present a record of the first three
generations in this country, and to call attention to their English
connection.

The will of John Kirtland, which Mr. Waters discovered and printed
(REGISTER, Vol. 41, p. 60) is valuable in the proof it furnishes as
to the location of the family in England; and it is to be hoped that
further research will be made to trace the pedigree of the English
Kirtlands or Kirklands.

Both Sherrington and Newport Pagnell are towns in the northern
part of Buckinghamshire, within a few miles of each other.

*Pages 375-379, this volume.

MEMOIR OF COL. THOMAS KNOWLTON, WITH A GENEAL-
OGY OF THE KNOWLTON FAMILY.

[By Ashbel Woodward, M. D., of Franklin, Conn.]

Were you to make inquiries among the people of New England generally concerning their ancestry, in nine cases out of ten they would tell
you that they were descended from one of three brothers who came over
from Old England *about* the year 16—; and in nine times out of ten
they would be wrong. But it so happens in the Knowlton family that
three brothers did actually come to New England and settle in Ipswich;
John[1], William[1], and Dea. Thomas;[1] for both John[1] and Thomas[1] call
William[1] their brother; evidence of the most satisfactory character.

The second brother, William[1] Knowlton, was a bricklayer. He married
Elizabeth ———. He died in 1654 or 5. The inventory of his estate,
taken July 17, 1655, was £37 2s. 1d. His debts were £27 14s. 1. We
have his descendants for several generations, but it is not our present purpose to include his branch of the family in this brief sketch.

The third brother, Dea. Thomas[1] Knowlton, was born in 1622. He m.
first, Susanna ———. His second wife was Mary Kimball, to whom he
was m. May 17, 1682. It does not appear that he had children.

On the 19th of Nov. 1678, Dea. Thomas[1] thus writes: " I gave a coat
to brother William, and his two boys I keept to scool from the age of 5 to

8 years, and a girl from the age of one & a half years till she was married." He died April 3, 1692, aged 70 years.

(1) JOHN,[1] though the last to be noticed, was the eldest of the three brothers. He took the freeman's oath in 1641, was in Ipswich in 1641 perhaps, or earlier. He made his will Nov. 29, 1653. He m. Margery ———, and had John,[2] Abraham,[2] and Elizabeth.[2]

(2) JOHN,[2] m. Sarah ———. He took the freeman's oath in 1680, and died Oct. 8, 1684. His children were—

    (3)   I. WILLIAM,[3] b.———. Lived in Wenham, and had wife Lydia.
    (4)   II. JOSEPH,[3] b. 1651 ; married, Aug. 14, 1677, Mary Wilson.
    (5)   III. SAMUEL,[3] b. ——— ; m. April, 1669, Mary Wilt or Witt.
    (6)   IV. NATHANIEL,[3] Dea. b. June 29, 1658. He m. May 3, 1682, Deborah Jewett.

Dea. NATHANIEL[3] (6) and DEBORAH had—

    (7)   I. NATHANIEL,[4] b. May 3, 1683 ; m. Feb. 1702–1703, Mary Bennett.
    (8)   II. JOHN,[4] b. Dec. 1685.
    (9)   III. JOSEPH,[4] b. April, 168-.
    (10)   IV. ABRAHAM,[4] b. Feb. 27, 1688–9.
    (11)   V. ELIZABETH,[4] b. Sept. 18, 1692.
    (12)   VI. THOMAS,[4] b. Nov. 8, 1702.
    (13)   VII. DAVID,[4] b. May, 1707 ; m. Feb. 1731–2, Esther Howard. David,[5] son of David,[4] died Dec. 10, 1732.

NATHANIEL[4] (7) and MARY had—

    (14)   I. MARY,[5] b. June 3, 1704.
    (15)   II. WILLIAM,[5] b. Feb. 8, 1705–6 ; married Martha of Boxford, to whom he was published, Feb. 13, 1728. He removed to Ashford, Conn., about 1740. His estate was distributed in March, 1757.
    (16)   III. NATHANIEL,[5] b. June 30, 1708.
    (17)   IV. JEREMIAH,[5] b. July 13, 1712, and died young.
    (18)   V. 2d JEREMIAH,[5] b. Aug. 2, 1713.

WILLIAM[5] (15) and MARTHA had—

    (19)   I. LUCY[6]; baptized Feb. 20, 1736.
    (20)   II. WILLIAM[6]; baptized.
    (21)   III. DANIEL[6]; baptized Dec. 31, 1738; m. 1st, Nov. 3, 1763, Elizabeth Farnham of Ashford, Conn.; m. 2d, April 24, 1788, Rebecca Fenton of Willington. He served through the French war and that of the Revolution. During the last, he was commissioned as Lieut. He died March 30, 1835.
    (22)   IV. THOMAS[6]; baptized Nov. 30, 1740; m. April 5, 1759, Anna Keyes of Ashford. An extended memoir of *Col. Thomas Knowlton* has already been published in the Jan. No. of the Reg. for the present year.
    (23)   V. NATHANIEL;[6] baptized March 9, 1745.
    (24)   VI. MARY,[6] bapt. ; m. March 9, 1748–9, Ezekiel Tiffany of Ashford.
    (25)   VII. SARAH;[6] bapt.; m. ——— Kendall of Ashford.
    (26)   VIII. LUCY;[6] bapt. ; m. Abijah Brooks of Ashford.
    (27)   IX. PRISCILLA;[6] baptized.

Lieut. DANIEL[6] (21) and ELIZABETH had—

(28)   I. DANIEL,[7] b. Dec. 7, 1765 ; m. Betsey Burchard. He died Feb. 1834. He had 7 children, the fourth of whom, son Phineas, died a soldier in the army.

(29)   II. ELIZABETH,[7] b. March 24, 1768; m. Frederick Chaffee of Ashford.

(30)   III. NATHANIEL,[7] b. Dec. 24, 1770, m. Hannah Farnham.

(31)   IV. EPHRAIM,[7] b. Oct. 3, 1773.

(32)   V. MARTHA[7], b. Feb. 24, 1777 ; m. Charles Brandon of Ashford.

(33)   VI. KEZIA,[7] b. Feb. 9, 1781 ; m. Jan. 3, 1805, Amasa Lyon, Esq. of Ashford. Their 4th son and 7th child was the late *Gen. Nathaniel Lyon*,[8] who was born in Ashford, July 14, 1818. Was educated at West Point, &c., &c.*

(34)   VII. HANNAH,[7] b. April 19, 1783 ; m. Daniel Knowlton, Esq. Their eldest son, Miner,[8] was educated at West Point. Was subsequently a Professor in that Institution, and now holds a commission in the army of the U. S.

By wife Rebecca had—

(35)   VIII. ERASTUS FENTON,[7] b. Jan. 29, 1790 ; m. Waite Windsor of Gloucester, R. I.

(36)   IX. MARVIN,[7] b. Sept. 3, 1794 ; m. Calista Leonard of Stafford, Conn.

Col. THOMAS (22)' and ANNA had—

(37)   I. FREDERICK,[7] b. Dec. 4, 1760, d. Oct. 9, 1841. He served in the campaign of 1776, and was with his father in the battle at Harlem Heights.

(38)   II. SALLY,[7] b. Nov. 23, 1763.

(39)   III. THOMAS,[7] b. July 13, 1765.

(40)   IV. POLLY,[7] b. Jan. 11, 1767.

(41)   V. ABIGAIL,[7] b. June 20, 1768.

(42)   VI. SAMSON,[7] b. Feb. 8, 1770 ; d. Sept. 10, 1777.

(43)   VII. ANNA,[7] b. March 19, 1773.

(44)   VIII. LUCINDA,[7] b. Nov. 10, 1776, died Feb. 16, 1805. Col. Thomas Knowlton was slain in battle at Harlem Heights, Sept. 16, 1776. Anna, wife of Col. Knowlton, died May 22, 1808.

---

* The memorable battle in which Gen. Lyon lost his life was fought near Springfield, Missouri, August 10th, last. He engaged the enemy at immense odds, having but 5500 men, while the rebels Price and McCullough had 21,000 ; yet, with his few brave men, he so cut the enemy to pieces that they were forced to retreat. He was shot dead at the head of his column, early in the day, but Gen. Siegel and Maj. Sturgis conducted the battle, and secured a retreat, capturing many prisoners. Gen. Lyon knew he attacked at great risk, but he knew the enemy were immediately to be reinforced, and he decided to fight him before he was stronger. The slaughter of the rebels was very great, but the extent is not known. We lost some 200 of our men. As yet, it is the hardest battle of the war, unless that of Lexington be greater, the facts of which have not yet reached us.

KNOWLTON.—On pages 344-346 of this magazine for October, 1861, Volume [*] 15, there is given a Genealogical Table of the Knowlton Family by Ashbel Woodward, M.D., in which several omissions and errors appear. The list of descendants of Lieutenant Daniel and Col. Thomas Knowlton given on page 346, should read as follows:

Lieut. Daniel[6] (21) and Elisabeth had:
(28) i. Daniel,[7] born Dec. 7, 1765: married Betsey Burchard. He died February, 1834. He had seven children, the fourth of whom, son Phineas,[8] died a soldier in the army.
(29) ii. Elisabeth,[7] b. March 24, 1768; m. Frederick Chaffee, of Ashford.
(30) iii. Nathaniel,[7] b. Dec. 24, 1770; m. Sarah Leaeh, and had children: Farnham,[8] Emily A.,[8] Hosea,[8] Myron,[8] William[8] and Nathaniel.[8]
(31) iv. Manassah,[7] twin brother of Nathaniel,[7] b. Dec. 24, 1770; m. 1st, Lydia Burton and had children: Oren,[8] Ephraim,[8] Isaac,[8] Orendia,[8] Almira,[8] Maria,[8] George W.,[8] and Permelia[8]; m. 2d, Elisabeth Card; m. 3d, Clarissa Cogswell.
(32) v. Ephraim,[7] b. Oct. 3, 1773.
(33) vi. Martha,[7] b. Feb. 24, 1777, m. Charles Brandon, of Ashford.
(34) vii. Keziah,[7] b. Feb. 9, 1781; m. Jan. 3, 1805, Amasa Lyon, Esq., of Ashford. Lineage of husband and children already given; see page 351.
(35) viii. Hannah,[7] b. April 19, 1783; m. Daniel Knowlton, Esq., and had sons: Miner,[8] Danford,[8] Edwin,[8] and daughters: Amanda,[8] Miriam,[8] and Elvira[8]. Their eldest son, Miner, was educated at West Point; was subsequently assistant professor in that institution, and now holds a commission in the Army of the United States. See page 225.

By wife Rebecca, had:
(36) ix. Erastus Fenton,[7] b. Jan. 29, 1790; m. Waite Windsor, of Gloucester, R. I.
(37) x. Marvin,[7] b. Sept. 3, 1794; m. Calista Leonard, of Stafford, Conn.

Col. Thomas[6] (22) and Anna, had:
(38) i. Frederick,[7] b. Dec. 4, 1760; d. Oct. 9, 1841. He served in the campaign of 1776, and was with his father at the battle at Harlem Heights.
(39) ii. Sally,[7] b. Nov. 23, 1763.
(40) iii. Thomas,[7] b. July 13, 1765.
(41) iv. Dolly,[7] b. Jan. 11, 1767.
(42) v. Abigail,[7] b. June 20, 1768.
(43) vi. Samson,[7] b. Feb. 8, 1770; d. Sept. 10, 1777.
(44) vii. Anna,[7] b. June 8, 1771; d. June 4, 1772.
(45) viii. Anna,[7] b. March 19, 1773.
(46) ix. Lucinda,[7] b. Nov. 10, 1776; d. Feb. 16, 1805.

[*]Pages 384-386, this volume.

THE ANCESTRY OF ANNA KNOWLTON

Contributed by Arnold Perkins Danz, E.E., P.E., of Larchmont, N. Y.

Anna Knowlton of Preston, Conn., married Jabez[3] Fitch (*Samuel,[2] Rev. James[1]*) of Norwich, Conn., 1 April 1719.

The "Brewster Genealogy" says Anna was the daughter of Joseph Knowlton. Miss Mary Perkins, in "Old Houses of ye Ancient Town of Norwich", says Anna was probably a daughter of Thomas Knowlton. There were several Joseph and Thomas Knowltons of the right age to be the father of Anna and at least one of each was living in or near Norwich, shortly before Anna's marriage.

But no vital record or Bible record has been found giving Anna's place or date of birth. The "Brewster Genealogy" says Anna died 25 Aug. 1778, "in ye 81st year of her age"; so she was born in 1698.

Despite this lack of a positive record of birth, it has been possible, through the suggestion of Mrs. B. L. Benn, and largely through careful, persistent research through countless probate and land records, through deeds and wills in Salem and Boston, Mass.; in Providence, Scituate, and Glocester, R. I.; in Hartford, Norwich, Preston, and Ashford, Conn., to assemble seven separate pieces of circumstantial evidence (or lack of evidence) which together make such a strong case that there can no longer be any reasonable doubt as to the identity of Anna's ancestors. They are Joseph[2] Knowlton (*William[1]*) who married in Ipswich, Mass., 14 Aug. 1677, Mary[3] Wilson (*Thomas,[2] Theophilus[1]*).

The evidence follows:

(1) Anna (Knowlton) Fitch named her first child, Elisha. There had been only one Elisha in either the Fitch or Knowlton family prior to this, namely, Justice Elisha Knowlton, of Providence, son of Joseph,[2] and now seen to be Anna's brother, as will appear.

(2) Anna's son, Jabez[4] Fitch, Jr., named one of his children Theophilus Wilson Fitch. Note that Mary[3] Wilson, wife of Joseph[2] Knowlton above, was a grand-daughter of Theophilus Wilson.

(1) and (2) indicate clearly that Anna must have been closely related to Mary Wilson. This eliminates the possibility of any Thomas Knowlton being Anna's father and narrows the search to Joseph[2] or his son, Joseph[3].

(3) Joseph,[3] born in 1681, would have been only seventeen when Anna was born in 1698.

(4) The only record of any wife of Joseph[3] Knowlton appears in Rhode Island Law Cases, vol. 10, pp. 6–10, where "Deborah Knolton of Newport, widow and admin. of Joseph Knolton, house carpenter", sued John Coddington, 21 March 1739, re a bond, dated in 1736, which he had given to Joseph Knolton and on which Joseph had signed for receipt of sums of money in 1737. This shows that Joseph[3] died between September 1737 and March 1739.

Joseph[3] Knowlton was in Newport, R. I., as early as 1709, and was "of Newport" in 1729, when he was employed by Capt. Godfrey Malbone and made a deposition (Rhode Island Law Cases, vol. 2, p. 2). He was employed by a committee to build Block Island pier in 1735, and when the construction was discontinued he petitioned the General Assembly (*ibid.*, vol. 3, p. 52) for a refund of 200 pounds which was granted on 17 Aug. 1735. He was known to have also resided in Providence and Glocester, R. I., and several of his deeds in Newport were dated from June 1713 to August 1728.

"Deborah Knowlton, wife of Joseph, died Sept. 20, 1744, aged 67". Her tombstone was found, inscribed as above, in the Common Ground Cemetery, in Newport.

Joseph's daughter, Mary, was married in 1734 to William Hagan (or Haggen).

Joseph[2] had died prior to 16 March 1722/3 as evidenced by the following:

Essex Deeds, 50:8—Claim dated 16 March 1723 of Joseph Knowlton of Newport, R. I., son and heir of Joseph Knowlton, deceased, formerly of Ipswich, Essex Co., N.E.———I, Joseph Knowlton, house carpenter, by right which was my great grand fathers, Theophilus Wilson, late of Ipswich . . . etc Witnessed 18 March 1722/3; received for record 15 Dec. 1727.

(5) The search for Lucy Whipple, suggested by the Rev. Mr. Stocking as a possible wife of Joseph,[3] was fruitless. Although a careful search was made in Salem, Mass., and in Rhode Island, no one of that name and of the proper age was found in either the Ipswich or the Providence Whipple family.

So 3, 4, and 5 leave Joseph[3] as a possible very young father of Anna, but a very doubtful one.

(6) Anna's presence in Norwich and Preston before her marriage made it seem doubtful that she was a daughter of Joseph and Mary, largely because it was believed that they had removed from Ipswich to Wenham, Mass., and died there. But this was found in Salem records. . . .

Essex Bk 58:77 I, Mary Knowlton of Providence, R. I., relict of Joseph Knowlton, deceased————[concerning money] "which came from my grand father, Theophilus Wilson." This was signed 11 Oct. *1730*, by Mary Knowlton, Colony of R. I.

It was found that Joseph[2] had sold some of his property in 1684 and 1696, prior to the birth of Anna, and the two deeds which follow apparently ended any further ownership in Ipswich.

Essex Deeds, 15:184: On 9 June 1703, a deed was signed by Joseph Knowlton, Sr., of Ipswich and Mary W(ilson) Knowlton and witnessed by "Jane Wil*l*son, relict, widow of Thomas Wilson *late deceased*". Thomas and Jane were the parents of Mary Wilson.

Essex Deeds, 21:53: On 22 March 1708/9, Joseph and Mary Knowlton signed a deed and Jane Willson also signed and was mentioned as "honored mother".

It will be seen from Essex Deed, 50:8, quoted above, that Joseph[2] had died before 18 March 1722/3. From Mary Knowlton's deposition above, we see that she was residing in 1730 in Providence, perhaps with or near her son, Elisha; and it is reasonable to assume that Anna had come to Connecticut or Rhode Island with her father and mother.

We know there were Knowlton cousins in Norwich, and Providence would not be too far away for cousins to visit.

Further investigation may, however, place all three, Joseph,[2] his wife Mary, and daughter Anna, as residents of Preston, Conn., for a few years prior to Anna's marriage in 1719.

A Joseph Knowlton was accidentally killed in Norwich in 1718. He may have been Anna's father.

The Rev. Mr. Stocking wrote that the Joseph so killed was the son of Benjamin Knowlton of Springfield. But there were many land records signed or witnessed by a Joseph Knowlton of Springfield from 1715/16 to 1734 (Springfield Deeds, Books C 179, D 172, D 563 .... G 394, *et al.*). As yet the writer has found no other Joseph "of Springfield" at that time; so there is little doubt that the man who was killed was some other Joseph Knowlton.

The "Brewster Genealogy" records the marriage of Jabez Fitch to "Anna, daughter of Joseph Knowlton *of Preston, Conn*": and Preston and Norwich were so near that it would not be at all strange for a man from Preston to have an accident in Norwich.

(7) Jabez[4] Fitch kept a diary for forty years. It is printed in *Mayflower Descendant.* See particularly, volume 1, page 39, for Sept. 4th to 9th, 1755.

Jabez had travelled from Norwich to Stonington, thence to Scituate, R. I. On the fourth he "went to Uncle Knowlton's. Ye fifth I went to Squire Brown's—Sunday, ye 7th, I came back to my uncle's—Ye 8th went to hunt bairs with Cozen Thos. Ye 9th. I set out to come home".

This could mean only that Anna must have had a brother who had a son, Thomas, or that someone other than a real uncle, was so called.

The Rev. Mr. Stocking gives us a list, seemingly complete, of eight children of Elisha Knowlton, but no Thomas is included. Elisha had a brother, Daniel, but he is supposed to have died childless. If the remaining brother, Joseph[3], had a son Thomas, no record of him has been found.

So all the towns mentioned above were searched for probate and land records and it was found that Elisha removed from Providence to Glocester, had many land transactions there, and finally, in 1745, sold his homestead and removed to Scituate. He was living there in 1755 when Jabez Fitch, Jr., came avisiting. Elisha had a grown son, Thomas, there with whom to go hunting bears, and there were two more previously unrecorded daughters, Keziah and Lydia.

See the following for authority:

Scituate, R. I.—Probate Book 1, page 401: Will of Thomas Knowlton, late of Scituate, yeoman; presented 13 Feb. 1759, — mentions "honored father, Elisha Knowlton, who in his lifetime had not given so much to my two sisters, Keziah Knowlton and Lydia Wheaton — other sisters (another copy of the will on page 414 reads 'sister') and my beloved wife, Lydia (now pregnant), my daughters, Susanna, Mary, and Lydia, and that child" to be.

In Providence Land Records, Elisha appears in nineteen transactions, beginning as Grantee, 13 March 1713/14, and appearing lastly as Grantor 25 May 1734. About 1728, he begins to be called Elisha Knowlton of Glocester (see Book 71:9), where he appears in seven land transactions.

He signed a deed as Town Clerk in Glocester, 4 March 1731/2; see Book 1:36.

As early as 1738, he and Ruth Place were witnesses together; see Book 67:163. In 1740, Elisha and son, Thomas, were jointly witnessing deeds; see Book 71:24/25.

Elisha's wife Lydia appears to have died between 1737 and 1741; and on 16 Feb. 1742, Elisha and Ruth Place were married by Richard Steere, Justice.

In Book 69:11 Glocester Land Evidence, 2:p 52, we find that on 4 Dec. 1743, the signatures are now Elisha and Ruth Knowlton.

The Annals of Providence—649 lists Thomas, Keziah, and Lydia as children of Elisha and Lydia Knowlton, and says Thomas married Lydia Tourtellotte.

Keziah was a witness to the signing of one of Elisha's deeds in 1734/5 (Glocester Deeds Book 1: p 181). Note in her brother's will above that Keziah had not married, but that Lydia had apparently married ———— Wheaton.

Book 2:124—On 20 Nov. 1745, Elisha and Ruth Knowlton of Glocester sell "my homestead farm on which I now dwell—Township of Glocester, R. I.", and there is mention of "Ruth, wife of said Elisha".

Book 4, page 61, Scituate Deeds — Elisha Knowlton mentions "my son Thomas Knowlton of Scituate".

Book 6, page 25 — Glocester Deeds — Thomas Knowlton of Scituate refers to "my honored father, Elisha", and signs a receipt on the 12 April 1756.

Book 1, page 215 — Scituate R. I., Probates — Thomas Knowlton who had been appointed guardian of the estate of his father Elisha, became "not capable of taking care of himself — nor yet of his father's" so on 7 Dec. 1752, a guardian was appointed; but from Book 1:219 we find Thomas recovered and again appointed 7 July 1753, but Elisha is still unable to care for his estate.

Book 1: page 399 — Elisha Knowlton died intestate, 20 Oct. 1757, and Ruth Knowlton, widow of said Elisha, was appointed Adminx 5 March 1759.

Scituate V.R., Vol. 3, Thomas Knowlton was called "Elder" and performed several marriages, 1756 to 1764.

These records leave no doubt that Anna had a brother, Elisha, living, not far from Norwich, Conn., in Glocester and later in Scituate, R. I., and they therefore establish her identity as the daughter of Joseph[2] and Mary (Wilson) Knowlton.

LARKHAM. — BRUEN. — PERCIVAL.—Thomas Larkham, Pastor of the church of Northam, in Piscataquake—have an adventure or stocke in the Patents or Plantation at Pascataquake sold by one Obadiah Brewen, of Cape Anne, Alias Glocester in New England, to the proper vse of me, my executors, &c.—which was sold said Bruen by Richard Percivall, now or heretofore of Shrewsbury, in Old England, as appears by a writting of sale drawn by Richard Percivall, bearing date 22 Oct., 1635.

[The above is an abstract of a document, dated Sept. 13, 1642, to be found in the Massachusetts Archives. Northam is now Dover, in New Hampshire. Thomas Larkham, the successor of Hanserd Knollys, and the fourth minister there, born in Lyme, Eng., May 2, 1601, was a grad. of Jesus' College, Cambridge, and had been settled at Northam, Eng., prior to coming to this country. His ministry at Dover ended in 1642, and he returned to England, where he died in 1669. He was succeeded at Dover by Rev. Daniel Maud, a former schoolmaster in Boston.

Obadiah Bruen, youngest son of John Bruen of Bruen Stapleford, county of Chester, Eng., bap. Dec. 22, 1606, came to Plymouth with Rev. Richard Blynman—went afterward to Gloucester—was made freeman in 1642 ; clerk of the writs, and commissioner to end small causes, in 1643 ; was selectman and representative—went to New London, 1650, and was there recorder many years, and one of the patentees of the Colony of Connecticut. He emigrated to Newark, N. J., in company with about fifty families, and bought the place of the Indians in 1667. He had a wife, Sarah, and two children born in Gloucester; Hannah, in 1643, and John, in 1646. Rev. Matthias Bruen born in Newark, April 11, 1793, who was a noted minister in New York City, and died there Sept. 6, 1829, was of this family. A memoir of Rev. Mr. Bruen was published, anonymously, in 1831. There is a notice of him in Sprague's *Annals of the American Pulpit*, Vol. iv. pp. 543—548. See Babson's *History of Gloucester*, pages 65 and 66. A notice of Obadiah Bruen, the ancestor, with a fac-simile of his autograph, may be found in Caulkins's *History of New London*, pages 155, 156, 141. His " Life " was originally published in 1641, again in 1799, and reprinted in New York in 1857, with a portrait. To the last edition is added a preface of 4 pages and a folding tabular pedigree of Bruen of Stapleford. See Whitmore's *Handbook of American Genealogy.*]

THE DESCENDANTS OF ROBERT LAY OF SAYBROOK, CONN.

By Edwin A. Hill, Ph.D., of Washington, D. C.

The account of the Lay family given in the Salisbury Family Histories and Genealogies, relates almost wholly to the descendants of the first John Lay of Saybrook, and the authors, in their text, Vol. I., page 333, as also in the Lay Pedigree Chart, No. VII., given in the Supplement to Vol. III, place Robert[3] Lay, the Westbrook tavern keeper, husband of Mary Grinnell, as the son of John[2] and Sarah (Marvin) Lay, and grandson of John[1] Lay by his second wife Abigail; but the matter is presented in such a way as to plainly indicate a doubt as to the accuracy of the line. In fact, John[2] Lay, husband of Sarah Marvin, was born in 1670, and would have been only eleven years old at the birth, in 1681, of his reputed son Robert,[3] and the line is unquestionably wrong, as has been often noted. In 1895, I obtained from Miss E. E. Lay of Guilford, Conn. (No. 22-vii of this genealogy), a manuscript upon the descendants of Robert[1] Lay, the joint compilation of herself and her nephew the Rev. E. C. Starr of Cornwall, Conn. (No. 44-i of this genealogy), which was based upon family records, and various conversations had by herself (born 1828) with her great uncle James Lay (No. 13), a brother of her grandfather Col. Asa Lay (No. 14), of the Revolutionary army, one of the individuals referred to in Prof. Murdock's account as quoted in the Salisbury genealogies, her father Steuben Lay (No. 22), and her own brothers and sisters. This document I then copied in part, and upon it this genealogy is to some extent based. This partial copy, with notations made by myself, I shall file in manuscript in the library of this Society, and it will contain considerable biographical matter which cannot here be published for lack of space.

1. Robert[1] Lay was the first of a line of at least eight successive individuals of the name, in lineal descent. The surmise of Savage, that he was a brother of Edward of Hartford, Saybrook, and Portsmouth, R. I., and of John of Saybrook and Lyme, is confirmed by many family traditions. He was born about 1617, and died July 9, 1689, aged 72, the gravestone being still extant in Essex, Conn., cemetery.

He married, Dec., 1647 (Lay MSS. and Saybrook Records, I-143), Sarah Fenner, widow of John Tully, who died in England in 1644-5. She came to America in 1646-7, with son John, who was baptized in 1638, and a younger daughter, and in the company of her brothers Arthur and William, and died May 25, 1676, aged 59. Her son, the ancestor of the Tully family of Saybrook, was a noted teacher of mathematics and navigation, and a compiler of almanacs. The will of William Fenner, proved at Newport, R. I., Sept. 6, 1680, names his brothers Arthur and John, his "late sister Lay" and her two surviving children, and his sister Phebe Ward.

Robert[1] Lay was of Lynn, Mass., in 1638, and came to Saybrook in 1649. He lived in the present town of Essex (formerly a part of Old Saybrook), on the north side of what is now the street on Essex Point, leading to the steamboat dock. He was a freeman, May 21, 1657 (Col. Rec., I-297), and "desired," May 17, 1660, "to take care of any of the estate of Mr. Fenwick, y^t is subject to loss and damage " (Col. Rec., I–535) ; a deputy to the General Court, 1666 and 1678, and a large land owner, being one of the patentees of Saybrook, and owning land both near Essex Point and in the " Oyster River Quarter " (now Westbrook).

There is recorded in Saybrook Records an agreement between Capt. George Denison and wife Ann, of the one part, and Mr. Robert Lay of Saybrook, of the other part, providing for the marriage of their children John Denison and Phebe Lay.

Children :

    i.   PHEBE,[2] b. 5 Jan., 1651; d. 1699; m. 26 Nov., 1667, John, son of Capt. George and Ann (Borodell) Denison of Stonington. (See Denison Genealogy, and Hist. of Stonington, Conn., page 389 *et seq.*) Children: 1. *Phebe*, b. 1667; d. young. 2. *John*, b. 1 Jan., 1669. 3. *George*, b. 28 Mch., 1671. 4. *Robert*, b. 17 Sept., 1673. 5. *William*, b. 7 Apr., 1677. 6. *Daniel*, b. 28 Mch., 1680. 7. *Samuel*, b. 23 Feb., 1683; d. young. 8. *Ann*, b. 3 Oct., 1684. 9. *Sarah*, b. 29 July, 1692. 10. *Phebe*, b. probably between 1684 and 1692.

2. ii. ROBERT, b. 6 Mch., 1654.

2. ROBERT[2] LAY (*Robert[1]*), called " Jr." on the Town Records (Vol. I, page 143), where his marriage and the births of his children are recorded, born 6 Mch., 1654, died in 1742, married 22 Jan., 1679–80, Mary, born in 1660, daughter of Thomas Stanton by wife Sarah, daughter of Capt. George Denison. He lived in Essex, at the Lay homestead.

His will was dated Apl. 22, 1731, and the estate was appraised at £6,712. 19s. 7d. The widow, Mary, was executrix, Oct. 11, 1743. The will names all the children except Phebe, who probably died single before her father. (For baptisms of the first three children, see History of the First Church of Stonington, pages 196–197.)

Children :

3. i.   ROBERT,[3] b. 27 Jan., 1681.
    ii. SARAH, b. 19 Feb., 1682–3.
4. iii. MARY, b. 3 Oct., 1685; probably m. (1) Christopher Miner, 9 Mch., 1704; m. (2) Samuel Denison (see Wheeler's Stonington, 343, 468).
    iv. THOMAS, b. 10 May, 1688; mention of his lands occurs in 1711, on Saybrook Records (see Vol. II., p. 474).
    v. SAMUEL, b. 25 July, 1691; d. 5 Aug., 1691.
    vi. TEMPERANCE, b. 25 July, 1691; d. 1755.
5. vii. SAMUEL, b. 13 Feb., 1694–5.
    viii. PHEBE, b. 14 Aug., 1698.
    ix. DOROTHY, b. 3 June, 1701.

3. ROBERT[3] (*Robert,[2] Robert[1]*), " son of Robert Lay Jr. and Mary Stanton, born Jan. 27th 1680." (See Savage, Stanton Genealogy, and Saybrook Records, I., 143).

" Robert Lay jr. and Mary Grenell were married each to the other the 12th day of December in the year 1703 " (Saybrook Records, II, 168), following which entry are the birth records of all the children, as given below, except Jonathan and John.

Two adjoining tombstones in Westbrook cemetery read as follows :

" Here lies the body of Robert Lay died July 1st 1738 aged 57 years."

" Here lies the body of Mrs Mary ye wife of Mr Robert Lay, who died June ye 9th, A. D. 1755, in ye 71st year of her age."

The will of Robert Lay, " secundus," dated June 27, 1738, proved July 26 following, in Guilford Probate Court, mentions wife Mary, and all of the eight children except John; Peabody Grinnell, a brother-in-law, being appraiser of the estate.

Robert[3] Lay lived at Westbrook, was the first of the name to settle there, and was the well known " tavern keeper " who kept the tavern near the so-called Dr. Cone house. Mary his wife was the daughter of Daniel and Lydia (Peabody) Grinnell, granddaughter of Daniel Grinnell, of Little Compton, R. I., by wife Mary, daughter of William and Mary Wodell of Boston, Mass., and Portsmouth and Tiverton, R. I., and great-granddaughter of Matthew and Rose Grinnell, of Newport, R. I. (See Austin's Gen. Dict. of R. I. Settlers.) Daniel Grinnell in his will mentions his daughter " Mary Lay," although Austin makes no mention of her. Lydia Peabody, her mother, was the daughter of William and Elizabeth (Alden) Peabody, of Little Compton, R. I., and granddaughter of John Alden of the *Mayflower*. The Grinnell family were of Huguenot extraction. Mary (Grinnell) Lay was one of the original members of the church at Westbrook.

Children :

6. i. ROBERT,[4] b. 20 Dec., 1705.
7. ii. CHRISTOPHER, b. 27 Feb., 1707-8.
    iii. LYDIA, b. 26 June, 1710; m. 3 Feb., 1730-1, John Waterhouse (Bailey II, 113).
8. iv. DANIEL, b. 3 Oct., 1712.
9. v. JEREMIAH, b. 13 Jan., 1715.
    vi. PHEBE, b. 27 May, 1717; m. 1 June, 1740, Benjamin Merrill (Bailey, II, 114). (See Hyde Gen., No. 6052.)
10. vii. JONATHAN, b. 1721.
    viii. JOHN, m. Deborah ———; evidently died without issue, as his will, dated Sept. 17, 1756 (Guilford Probate Rec., VII, 104), names no children, and at death of his wife, Deborah, leaves all his lands to his brothers Christopher, Daniel, Jeremiah and Jonathan, and names his sisters Lydia Watrous and Phebe Merrill, who receive bequests of money.

4. MARY[3] LAY (*Robert,[2] Robert[1]*), born in Saybrook (now Essex), 3 Oct., 1685, is, I think, the one referred to in Wheeler's Stonington, pages 343, 468, because, while the descendants of John Lay are quite fully traced by Prof. Salisbury, there seems to be no Mary Lay among them who could have been the one mentioned by Wheeler, who states that Christopher, son of Dr. Joseph and Mary (Avery) Miner, of Stonington, baptized July 13, 1684, married Mary Lay, Mch. 9, 1704. The death of her first husband, Christopher,* is not given, but her marriage to Samuel[4] Denison (George,[3] Capt. George,[2] John[1] of Stortford, Eng.), occurred probably in 1709. They lived in Stonington till July 4, 1716, when they removed to Westbrook. The wife of George Denison was Mercy, daughter of John and Desire (Howland) Gorham, and granddaughter of John Howland of the *Mayflower*. The children are as given below (see Denison Genealogy, page 208), but the descendants can be more fully traced in Wheeler's Stonington, page 343 et seq.

* In Wheeler's History of the First Church of Stonington, Conn., is the admission, 28 April, 1708, of widow Mary Miner (page 192), and the baptisms, 6 June, 1708, of Mary and Joanna, daughters of Christopher Miner (page 207). These entries doubtless are of Mary[3] Lay and her children by her first husband.

Children by second husband:

i. SARAH DENISON, b. 6 Jan., 1710; m. William Babcock.
ii. SAMUEL DENISON, b. 23 Oct., 1711.
iii. MERCY DENISON, b. 1713; m. Nathaniel Chapman. (See Chapman's Chapman Family.)
iv. ELIZABETH DENISON, bapt. 6 June, 1714.
v. JOANNA DENISON, b. 13 Dec., 1716; m. Moses Tyler.
vi. MARY DENISON, b. 6 Jan., 1718.
vii. GEORGE DENISON, b. 6 Jan., 1718.
viii. CHRISTOPHER DENISON, b. 1720.
ix. GIDEON DENISON, b. 1724.
x. STEPHEN DENISON, b. 6 Feb., 1725.

5. SAMUEL[3] LAY (*Robert*,[2] *Robert*[1]) was born in Saybrook (now Essex), 13 Feb., 1694-5. The following from Vol. II of Saybrook Records refers, I presume, to him, since no Samuel of this generation is given in the Salisbury Genealogies among the descendants of John Lay:
"Samuel Lay and Hannah Hayden married 1st June, 1726."
Children, from Saybrook records:

i. MARY,[4] b. 29 Dec., 1728.
ii. SARAH, b. 7 Feb., 1731-2. The marriage of Reuben Chapman and Sarah Lay (Bailey, II, 115) may refer to her; and if so, their descendants can be traced at page 79 *et seq.* of Chapman's Chapman Family.
iii. HANNAH, b. 17 Mch., 1734-5.
iv. PHEBE, b. 26 Feb., 1737-8. Bailey (II, 115) gives the marriage of John Hull and Phebe Lay, Sept. 27, 1764, which may refer to her.
v. TEMPERANCE, b. 30 Sept., 1740.
vi. SAMUEL, b. 1 Mch., 1743-4.
vii. ROBERT, b. 4 Jany., 1746-7.

6. Dea. ROBERT[4] LAY (*Robert*,[3] *Robert*,[2] *Robert*[1]), born in Saybrook West Parish (Westbrook), 20 Dec., 1705 (or 1706, as stated in the Lay MSS.), married, 3 Nov., 1729, Jemima Pratt (not mentioned in Chapman's Pratt Family), and had seven children, as recorded on page 234, Vol. IV, of Saybrook records.

He was for forty years Deacon of the Westbrook Congregational Church. By the terms of his father's will he received "my grandfather's silver cup." He lived in the old Lay homestead in Westbrook, situated on the principal street leading to the shore, and directly opposite the cemetery.

The following inscriptions are from adjoining stones in Westbrook Cemetery:

"In memory of Dea. Robert Lay who departed this life Jany. 1, 1790 in the 84th year of his age."

"In memory of Jemima Lay wife of Robert Lay, who departed this life Mch. 9, 1766, in the 56th year of her age."

That there was a second marriage is indicated by the following from Vol. II, page 116, of Bailey's Early Conn. Marriages: "Deacon Robert Lay and Elizabeth Denison married June 24, 1768."

Children, from town records:

i. JEMIMA,[5] b. 3 Jan., 1733.
ii. LYDIA, b. 5 Jan., 1735.
iii. SARAH, b. 14 Jan., 1737.
11. iv. ROBERT, "Son of Dea. Robert and Mrs. Jemima Lay died Oct. 10, 1740 æ 1 year" (Westbrook Cemetery).

v. ANNA, b. 30 Apl., 1741. The marriage of George Wright and Anna
   Lay, 1 Oct., 1760 (Bailey, II, 115) probably refers to her.
vi. PHEBE, b. 15 Feb., 1743.
vii. ROBERT, b. 8 June, 1745.
viii. ARIGAIL, b. 25 June, 1747. She became the wife of Dea. Jonathan
   Lay (No. 15), according to Salisbury Genealogies; but in the Lay
   MSS. the *first* wife of Dea. Jonathan is given as *Mary* Lay, daughter of Robert and Jemima, who died in 1831.

7. LIEUT. CHRISTOPHER⁴ LAY (*Robert,*³ *Robert,*² *Robert*¹) was born 27
   Feb., 1708–9, in Saybrook West Parish. My account of this
   family is based almost wholly upon the stones extant in Westbrook
   Cemetery. Whether there were any children other than those
   mentioned below I am not advised. The widow's name was Mary,
   and the marriage (see Bailey) 5 Dec., 1765,. of " Capt. Samuel
   Crane and Widow Mary Lay," undoubtedly refers to her. " Lieut.
   Christopher Lay died Oct. 3, 1759 in his 52ᵈ year " (Westbrook
   Cemetery).
   Children :
   i. LUCRETIA,⁵ b. 1749 ; d. " 25 Nov., 1754, æ. 5 years."
   ii. DENEY, b. 1754 ; d. " 6 Nov., 1759, æ. 5 years."
   iii. JOHN, b. 1755–6 ; d. " 7 Nov., 1759, in 3d year."

8. DANIEL⁴ LAY (*Robert,*³ *Robert,*⁹ *Robert*¹), born 3 Oct., 1712, in West-
   brook, married Anna, daughter of Edward and Mary (Post) Bull,
   who was born 15 Mar., 1712. The gravestones in the Westbrook
   Cemetery read :
   " In memory of Mr. Daniel Lay who died Dec. 28, 1782, in the
   70ᵗʰ year of his age."
   " In memory of Mrs. Anne wife of Mr. Daniel Lay, who died
   March 5, 1790, in the 76ᵗʰ year of her age."
   He settled on land deeded to him 22 Feb., 1734–5, by his father,
   at Chestnut Hill, so called, in Saybrook West Parish. His will
   (Saybrook records, at Deep River, Vol. I, p. 37) mentions his son
   Daniel, who received various tracts of land.
   Children :
   12. i. DANIEL,⁵ bapt. Feb., 1738–9.
   13. ii. JAMES.
   14. iii. ASA, b. 1749.
   iv. ANNA BULL, probably m. Joseph Denison, 5 May, 1771 (Bailey, II,
      117).

8. JEREMIAH⁴ LAY (*Robert,*³ *Robert,*² *Robert*¹), born 13 Jan., 1715–6,
   in Westbrook, married, 20 Mch., 1739–40, Prudence Belden, at Westbrook (Bailey, II, 114). He died probably after 24 Feb., 1792.
   Saybrook records (II, 415) give : " Jeremiah, son of Jeremiah and
   Prudence Lay, born Oct. 5, 1745 " ; and in Westbrook Cemetery
   is the gravestone inscription : " Mrs Deborah wife of Mr Jeremiah
   Lay, died Feby 24 1792 æ 72," perhaps a second wife. The Lay
   MSS. credits Jeremiah⁴ with the six children named below, but
   gives no dates.
   Children :
   i. PRUDENCE,⁵ probably m. Ezra Crane, 27 Nov., 1760 (Bailey, II, 115).
   ii. SYBIL, probably m. Job Kelsey, 1 Dec., 1763 (Bailey, II, 115).
   iii. JEREMIAH, b. 5 Oct., 1745 ; probably d. in New York, in 1778,

on the prison ship *Blazmon Castle*; and probably m. Statia Bushnell, 8 Mch., 1773 (Bailey, II, 118).
  iv. AARON.
  v. LOIS.
  vi. HULDAH.

10. JONATHAN[4] LAY (*Robert*,[3] *Robert*,[2] *Robert*[1]), whose birth is not found
on the town records, is named in his father's will, and also in the
will of his brother John, so there can be no question as to the relationship. He is evidently the innkeeper referred to by Prof.
Murdock, and in the Salisbury Genealogies, where it is stated that
he was born in 1721, died of the smallpox in 1779, and that he
married Mary Spencer, who was born in 1721, and died in 1793.
The gravestones in Westbrook Cemetery, however, give as follows:
  " In memory of Mr Jonathan Lay who died Feby 12 1777, in
the 69th year of his age."
  " In memory of Jonathan Lay, who died Oct 7 1793, in the 8th
(or 80th, stone rather illegible) year of his age."
Neither of which agree well with the Salisbury date of birth, but
it is not absolutely certain that they refer to this family.
  Children:
    i. JONATHAN,[5] "son of Jonathan Lay, bapt Apr. 11, 1742-3 " (Church
      records quoted by Rev. E. C. Starr); probably d. young.
15. ii. JONATHAN, b. 10 Apl., 1748; d. 13 Apr., 1831.
16. iii. MARY, b. 21 Oct., 1749.
17. iv. EZRA, b. 26 Apl., 1752; d. 31 Jan., 1793.
18. v. HANNAH, b. 27 Apl., 1754; d. 16 May, 1824.
    vi. PHEBE, b. 20 Mch., 1758; d. 1789 or '90; m. Dr. William Gayle, and
      had several children.
19. vii. JOHN, b. 28 Aug., 1760; d. 5 Feb., 1844.
    viii. LYDIA, b. 7 Sept., 1763; d. 7 Dec., 1764.

11. ROBERT[5] LAY (*Robert*,[4] *Robert*,[3] *Robert*,[2] *Robert*[1]), born 8 June, 1745,
in Westbrook, married 5 Mch., 1772 (Bailey, II, 117), Desire, born
15 Jan., 1751, daughter of Josiah Wolcott of Hebron and Saybrook.
The following inscriptions, from Westbrook Cemetery, refer to
this family:
  " In memory of Mr Robert Lay who died June 4 1813 aged 68
years "
  " Lucy, dau. of Robt and Desier Lay, died Aug 31 1794 in 10th
year "
His son Robert[6] Lay, who married Chloe Chapman (see Chapman
Family No. 813 and 937, pp. 106, 126), sold the estate, and removed to Springfield, New York; his son Robert[7] Lay lived and
died in Montreal; and his son Robert[8] Lay at one time lived in Scranton, Penn.
  No records of the children of Robert[5] Lay, except as above, have
been obtained by me, but are probably in Saybrook town records
(at Deep River, Conn.), and the Westbrook Congregational Church
Records (at Westbrook).

12. DANIEL[5] LAY (*Daniel*,[4] *Robert*,[3] *Robert*,[2] *Robert*[1]), born in 1734 or '7,
bapt. Feb., 1738-9, died in 1807, married first, 15 May, 1763
(Bailey, II, 45), Mercy, born 27 Dec., 1742, died 29 Dec., 1775
(No. 2583 of Chapman's Chapman Family), daughter of Nathaniel

Chapman, and a descendant of John Howland of the *Mayflower* (see No. 4–iii of this genealogy); and married second, 14 Jan., 1779 (Bailey, II, 118), Hannah (Stannard), widow of Francis Kelsey.

Daniel[5] Lay subsequently removed, with his family, to western New York.

Children by first wife:

    i.   CHRISTOPHER.[6]
    ii. NATHANIEL, bapt. 1 Apl., 1764.
20. iii. JERUSHA, born 9 Oct., bapt. 13 Dec., 1767.
    iv. ANN.   ⎫ These three died, respectively, 26 Nov., 1769, 15
    v. NANCY.   ⎬ Mch., 1771, and 22 Feb., 1773, but the name of the last,
    vi. An INFANT. ⎭ and the order of death and birth, is unknown.

Children by second wife:

    vii. ANNA, bapt. 2 June, 1780.
    viii. DANIEL, bapt. 30 Jan., 1785.
    ix. LOUIS, bapt. 24 Sept., 1786.
    x.   ABNER, bapt. 21 Sept., 1788; moved to Canada.
    xi. LOVINA, bapt. 21 Jan., 1790.
    xii. BENJAMIN, bapt. 9 Dec., 1792 ; moved to N. Y. State.
    xiii. JOHN, bapt. 14 Dec., 1794.
    xiv. HANNAH.
    xv. MATILDA.
    xvi. A DAUGHTER.
    xvii. A DAUGHTER.

13. JAMES[5] LAY (*Daniel,*[4] *Robert,*[3] *Robert,*[2] *Robert*[1]), styled " Lieut.," lived to an old age in Westbrook, and is said to have had some musical ability. He married, Nov., 1767, Abigail Bushnell. No record of any children has been obtained, but " Our New England Ancestors," page 93, states that Capt. Jedediah Post married Abigail, daughter of James and Abigail (Bushnell) Lay, and granddaughter of Daniel and Ann (Bull) Lay.

Child:

21. i. ABIGAIL.[6]
    Perhaps others.

14. COL. ASA[5] LAY (*Daniel,*[4] *Robert,*[3] *Robert,*[2] *Robert*[1]), born in 1749, died 23 Feb., 1814, married, 18 Apr., 1770, Sarah, daughter of Josiah and Lucy (White) Wolcott, of Hebron and Saybrook, Conn. (Bailey, II, 117). He served with distinction in the war of the Revolution, and lived and died in Westbrook.

Children :

    i.   ASA WOLCOTT,[6] b. 1 Nov., 1770; d. 20 Aug., 1799.
    ii. SARAH, b. 13 Jan., 1773; d. 17 July, 1852; m. Eber Bushnell, 4 June, 1794 (Bailey, II, 119).
    iii. RICHARD, b. 1 Jan., 1775; m. Anna Woodward.
    iv. PHEBE, b. 15 May, 1777; m. John Hart Fowler, 1 July, 1897 (Bailey, II, 120).
    v. CATHARINE, b. 13 July, 1779; d. 28 Apr., 1863; m. Peter Farnham.
    vi. URU, b. 4 Nov., 1785; d. 16 Dec., 1868; m. Hiel Hull.
    vii. THEODORA, b. 9 Apr., 1785–6; d. 3 Jan., 1787.
22. viii. STEUBEN, b. 4 Mch., 1787; d. 25 Feb., 1869.
    ix. THEODORA, b. 3 June, 1789; d. 12 Feb., 1851.
    x.   EDWARD BLISS, b. 14 Aug., 1792; d. 4 Feb., 1863.
    xi. ALFRED FRENCH, b. 23 Jan., 1794; d. 11 Aug., 1810.
    xii. LUCY WHITE, b. 9 May, 1797; d. 11 Aug., 1884.

THE DESCENDANTS OF ROBERT LAY OF SAYBROOK, CONN.

By EDWIN A. HILL, Ph.D., of Washington, D. C.

15. HON. and DEA. JONATHAN[5] LAY (*Jonathan,[4] Robert,[3] Robert,[2] Robert[1]*), born 10 Apr., 1748, died 13 Apr., 1831, married first, 5 Apr., 1769, Abigail,[5] daughter of Robert[4] and Jemima (Pratt) Lay (No. 6), as stated in the Salisbury Genealogies (see also Bailey II, 116), whose gravestone in Westbrook Cemetery reads : "In memory of Mrs. Abigail wife of Mr. Jonathan Lay, who died May the 31, 1771 in the 24th year of her age." He married second, Anna Murdock, Jan. 9, 1772 (Bailey II, 117), whose gravestone, also in Westbrook Cemetery, reads : "Mrs Anne, Consort of Mr Jonathan Lay died Sept 9 1803 in her 67th year." His third wife was Nancy, daughter of Jared and Elizabeth (Walker) Elliot, of Killingworth, Conn. (see Elliot Genealogy). He had no issue by any of his wives.

He often represented the town in the legislature, was Judge of Probate and of the Court of Common Pleas of the County, County Treasurer, and Deacon of the Congregational Church of Westbrook from 1797 until his death in 1831. For other details see Salisbury Genealogies.

16. MARY[5] LAY (*Jonathan,[4] Robert,[3] Robert,[2] Robert[1]*), born 21 Oct., 1749, in Westbrook, Conn., married first, 9 Nov., 1768, Enoch Murdock ; married second, 27 July, 1780, Jesse Wood (Bailey, II, 118; Prof. Murdock calls the name of her second husband *James*, not Jesse, but see Hyde Genealogy, 911, agreeing with Bailey) ; and married third, Maj. Richard White of Lyme, whom she survived several years.

Children by first husband :

i. A DAUGHTER, m. —— Hale of Catskill, N. Y.
ii. A DAUGHTER, m. —— Elliott of Catskill, N. Y.

Children by second husband :

iii. EZRA WOOD, d. in 1794.
iv. ANNE WOOD (twin), m. Dr. —— Cone of East Haddam, Conn. ; resided in Westbrook; had several children.
v. PHEBE WOOD (twin), m. —— Hayden of Westbrook; had three children.
vi. RICHARD WOOD, a merchant of Saybrook, Conn.; d. in 1831.
vii. SOPHIA WOOD, m. David Waite of East Lyme, Conn. ; moved to Clinton, N. Y.; had two children.
viii. MARIA WOOD, m. Robert Chadwick; lived in Lyme, Conn., and St. Louis, Mo.; had two daughters, one m. to Edward Hutchins of New York and had several children, one of whom, Robert Chadwick Hutchins, was Surrogate of the City of New York, the other daughter m. to —— Barnum, proprietor of the Barnum Hotel, St. Louis, Mo.

17. EZRA[5] LAY (*Jonathan,[4] Robert,[3] Robert,[2] Robert[1]*), born 26 Apr., 1752, in Westbrook, Conn., died there, 31 Jan., 1793, married, 31 Mch.,

1785, Mehitabel Kelsey of Westbrook (Bailey, II, 118). Prof. Murdock says that Ezra was a joiner, and was taken prisoner by the British during the Revolution. His gravestone in Westbrook Cemetery reads: "In memory of Ezra Lay who died Feby 1 1793 in the 40th year of his age."

Children:

i. JONATHAN,⁶ b. 1786; d. 7 Oct., 1793, in 8th yr.
ii. ANNA, m. John Kirtland of Saybrook Point, who was b. 29 May, 1776; had a son *John L.* (see Chapman's Pratt Genealogy, p. 277).
iii. HANNAH.

18. HANNAH⁵ LAY (*Jonathan,*⁴ *Robert,*³ *Robert,*² *Robert*¹), born 27 Apr., 1754, in Westbrook, died 16 May, 1824, married first, Feb. 5 or 6, 1772, Abraham, son of John and Frances (Conckling) Murdock, who was born about 1751, and died aged 26; and married second, 17 May, 1780, Seth Smith of East Lyme, Conn.

Children by first husband:

i. ABRAHAM MURDOCK, d. in infancy.
ii. ANNA MURDOCK, b. 29 Mch., 1773; d. 16 Aug., 1819; m. about 1794, John J. Avery, b. 17 Mch., 1776; had numerous descendants, traced in Sweet's Avery Genealogy, page 100 *et seq.*
iii. REV. DR. JAMES MURDOCK, b. 16 Feb., 1776; d. 10 Aug., 1856; m. Lydia Atwater (see Salisbury Genealogies).

Children by second husband*:

iv. WILLIAM SMITH.
v. JOHN SMITH.
vi. ELIZA SMITH.

19. JOHN⁵ LAY (*Jonathan,*⁴ *Robert,*³ *Robert,*² *Robert*¹), born 26 Aug., 1760, in Westbrook, died 5 Feb., 1844, in Buffalo, N. Y., married, in 1784, Phebe Lee of East Lyme, Conn., who was born May, 1762, died 3 Feb., 1835. He was of the class of 1780, Yale; lived for a few years on the farm left him by his father, at Horse Hill, Westbrook; then removed to Catskill, N. Y.; became a merchant; moved later to Clinton, N. Y., and was a farmer there; for two years a member of the General Assembly of New York; and died at the residence of his son Charles, in Buffalo.

Children:

i. MARY,⁶ b. 1785; m. Eli Hart of Clinton, N. Y., b. 1785, a merchant of New York City; had a dau., *Helen,* who m. Ernest Fielder of that city, and had children Mary, Helen, Louisa, Edward, and Ernestine.
ii. CHARLES, b. 1788; d. 1793.
iii. PHEBE (twin), b. 1789; m. William Comstock; d. childless, in Batavia, N. Y., in 1856.
23. iv. JOHN (twin), b. 1789; d. 1853.
v. HARRIET, b. 10 July, 1792; m. 1 Mch., 1815, at Clinton, N. Y., Hon. Phineas Lyman Tracy; d. childless, at Batavia, N. Y., 18 May, 1872; he d. 22 Dec., 1876.
24. vi. JONATHAN, b. 1794; d. 1874.
vii. CHARLES, b. 1796; d. 1865; m. Emily, dau. of David Waite of Lyme, Conn.; had two children, *Emily S.* and *Harriet Tracy.*
25. viii. GEORGE WASHINGTON, b. 1798; d. 1860.
ix. JULIETTE, b. 1800; d. Oct., 1872; m. Rev. Henry Axtell; left three children, *Harriet, Juliette,* and *Minnie.*

* The Lay MS. states that there was a large Smith posterity, and that a grandson, William Nathan Hannell Smith, of Raleigh, N. C., was a member of Congress prior to the war, and was also Chief Justice of the State of North Carolina.

x. GUSTAVUS, b. 1803; m. Pauline Helden; had five sons and two daughters.

20. JERUSHA[6] LAY (*Daniel,[5] Daniel,[4] Robert,[3] Robert,[2] Robert[1]*), born 9 Oct., bapt. 13 Dec., 1767, in Westbrook, Conn., died 14 Apr., 1862, in Westbrook, married Capt. Richard, son of Jonathan and Hannah (Goodrich) Stokes, who was born 20 Jan., 1762, in Branford, Conn., and died 7 Nov., 1848, in Westbrook.

Although a Revolutionary War pensioner, his title of Captain came to him as a sailor, for his Revolutionary services were as a private. His pension was granted for 17 months' service in New Jersey troops. He enlisted at Lyme, Conn., and served under Capt. Chapman and Col. Ledyard. On this family, see Chapman Genealogy, page 199, and Our New England Ancestors, page 71, also Conn. Men in the Revolution, page 654.

His gravestone in Westbrook Cemetery reads: "Capt. Richard Stokes died Nov, 7 1848 æ 85 yrs a Revolutionary pensioner. Jerusha Stokes his wife died April 14 1862 æ 94 yrs 6 mos."*

Children:

i. RICHARD STOKES, b. 25 Jan., 1787.
ii. HENRY STOKES, b. 4 July, 1789.
iii. JOHN STOKES, b. 25 Oct., 1791.
iv. FANNY STOKES, b. 21 Oct., 1793.
v. WILLIAM STOKES, b. 20 May, 1796.
vi. ELIZA STOKES, b. 8 May, 1798.
vii. CHARLES STOKES, b. 7 Nov., 1801.
viii. NANCY STOKES, b. 10 Sept., 1804.
ix. EDWARD STOKES, b. 20 Feb., 1806.

21. ABIGAIL[6] LAY (*James,[5] Daniel,[4] Robert,[3] Robert,[2] Robert[1]*) married, 1 Apr., 1790 (Bailey, II, 119), Capt. Jedediah, son of John and Chloe (Chapman) Post (see Chapman Genealogy, p. 79), who was baptized at Westbrook, 29 Dec., 1771, and died 16 Apr., 1863.

He was largely interested in building vessels, which he sailed to West Indian ports, and was a man of great force of character, well read in the law, holding important town offices, and for several years Justice of the Peace, etc. (see Our New England Ancestors, p. 93; and pp. 93-95 for descendants).

Children:

i. WOOLCOTT POST, b. 19 Apr., 1789; d. soon.
ii. LYDIA POST, b. 1790.
iii. DENCY POST.
iv. ABIGAIL POST.
v. CATHARINE POST.
vi. RICHARD POST, b. 1799; d. 22 May, 1823, at sea.
vii. HENRY LAY POST, b. 17 Mch., 1803.
viii. CHLOE POST, b. 1804.
ix. JEDEDIAH POST, b. 7 Apr., 1807.
x. TEMPERANCE POST, b. 1 Mch., 1809.
xi. CORNELIA POST, b. 9 Jan., 1813.
xii. SAMUEL POST, b. 11 Oct., 1819.

22. STEUBEN[6] LAY (*Asa,[5] Daniel,[4] Robert,[3] Robert,[2] Robert[1]*), born 4 Mch., 1787, in Westbrook, died 25 Feb., 1869, married, 8 Sept., 1813, Martha Wright of Norwich, Conn., and resided in Westbrook.

* Their descendants are numerous, and an account of them will be found in the writer's article on The Descendants of Capt. Jonathan Stokes of Branford, to appear in the next issue of the REGISTER. (Pages 457-461, Vol. III of this work.)

Children :
    i. MARY[7] HELEN, b. 22 Aug., 1815; d. 13 Aug., 1872; m. 16 Sept.,
       1850, Alfred Gladwin of Saybrook; had one child, *Linnie Cathar-*
       ine, m. Merrit B. Bradt.
   ii. SARAH ANN, b. 7 Oct., 1817; d. 2 Feb., 1891; m. 1839, Ralph Tyler
       of New Haven, Conn.; had five children.
26. iii. LYDIA AUSTIN, b. 6 Sept., 1819.
   iv. MARTHA HUBBARD, b. 6 Oct., 1821; m. 14 Mch., 1845, Charles F.
       Leete of Guilford, Conn.; no issue.
    v. ASA STEUBEN, b. 21 Oct., 1823; d. Sept., 1824.
   vi. JONATHAN, b. 23 Sept., 1825; d. 15 Mch., 1893; m. 5 Nov., 1848,
       Ann Jeannette Bulkley of Winthrop; had one child.
  vii. EMMIE ELIZABETH, b. 28 Apr., 1828; lived in Guilford, Conn.; com-
       piler of the Lay MS. quoted in this paper; d. unmarried, in Guil-
       ford, 14 June, 1903.
 viii. LUCY REBECCA, b. 8 Oct., 1831; d. 15 Mch., 1891; m. Nov., 1853,
       Edward D. Ransom of Woodstock, Conn.; had one child.

23. JOHN[6] LAY (*John,[5] Jonathan,[4] Robert,[3] Robert,[2] Robert[1]*), born in
    Westbrook in 1789, died in 1853, in Buffalo, N. Y., married Fanny
    Atkins.
    Children :
      i. JOHN,[7] inventor of the Lay dirigible torpedo.
     ii. HENRY.
    iii. HARRIET.
     iv. MARY.

24. JONATHAN[6] LAY (*John,[5] Jonathan,[4] Robert,[3] Robert,[2] Robert[1]*), born in
    Westbrook, in 1794, died in 1874, in Milwaukee, Wis.
    Children :
      i. CHARLES HENRY.[7]
     ii. EDWARD TRACY.
    iii. JARED COCHRAN, a New York physician.

25. GEORGE[6] WASHINGTON LAY (*John,[5] Jonathan,[4] Robert,[3] Robert,[2]*
    Robert[1]), born Dec., 1798, in Westbrook, graduated at Hamilton
    College, N. Y., in 1817, studied law at Batavia, N. Y., and was in
    law practice there. He was elected in 1832 to the U. S. House of
    Representatives, 23d and 24th Congress, where he was on intimate
    terms with Adams, Webster, and other public men, and was Repre-
    sentative in 1842, from Genesee Co., to the New York Assembly.
    He served as U. S. minister to Sweden and Norway, and received
    the honorary degree of A.M. from Yale in 1860.
    Children :
      i. JOHN[7] FOOTE, A.B., Yale, 1841.
     ii. GEORGE WASHINGTON, A.B., Yale, 1841.
    iii. ALBERT TRACY, a lumber merchant and contractor, in Chicago, Ill.

26. LYDIA[7] AUSTIN LAY (*Steuben,[6] Asa,[5] Daniel,[4] Robert,[3] Robert,[2]*
    Robert[1]), born in Westbrook, Sept. 6, 1819, married, 7 Apr., 1842,
    John, son of Comfort and Sally (Post) Starr (see Starr Genealogy,
    pp. 130, 131), who was born in Guilford, Conn., 23 July, 1820.
    Children :
      i. REV. EDWARD COMFORT STARR, b. 12 Jan., 1844, of Cornwall, Conn.
     ii. SARAH ELIZABETH STARR, b. 9 July, 1845.
    iii. JOHN WOLCOTT STARR, b. 9 Mch., 1848; Yale, B.A. 1871, M.A. and
         B.D. 1874; d. unmarried, 22 June, 1875.
     iv. CATIE, b. 30 June, d. 7 Sept., 1858.

LEAVENS (*ante*, page 224).—I made a similar inquiry for the maiden name of Elizabeth, second wife of John Leavens, who died at Woodstock, Conn., Oct. 26, 1696, in the REGISTER, Vol. 51, p. 361, and at last am able to give the answer. At my request, Miss Louise Tracy, of New Haven, has examined records in that city and has perfectly determined the identity of the person in question. She was the daughter of Edward Preston and granddaughter of William Preston, and born 29 Sept., 1655.

The records show that Elizabeth Preston, daughter of Edward, married John Levins, Nov. 23, 1674; and the home of this new family was at Stratford. Then the family was called back to Roxbury, the birthplace of John Leavens; and again removed, in the migration that went out from Roxbury, to found Woodstock, Conn., in 1686. It is a singular fact that the widow, notwithstanding her large incumbrance of children, attracted the attention of Peter Aspinwall, a bachelor some years younger than herself. He, too, had come out in the migration from Roxbury, and had been in full acquaintance and church fellowship with the family many years. He married Elizabeth Leavens in the second year of her widowhood, and she bore to him one daughter. The Aspinwall records do not speak kindly of this alliance, but she seems to have been a faithful wife, and he was a man of versatile power and eminent usefulness. He was a pioneer of Killingly, and a great benefactor to the incipient town and its primitive church. It is a pitiful fact that there is no monument to him, or even record of his death. The wife Elizabeth, too, "fell on sleep" unnoticed, and her grave cannot be found.

We are glad to have rescued her identity from utter forgetfulness. She sprang from an excellent family, her career was eminently diversified with adventure, and it becomes her Leavens posterity to honor her memory.

15 Grove Terrace, Passaic, N. J. (Rev.) PHILO F. LEAVENS.

LEAVENWORTH. — A private graveyard was once in existence on Good Hill in Roxbury, Conn., near the Woodbury town line, on the road leading to "Tophet." It was established in 1805 (Roxbury Deeds, vol. 2, p. 538) by Elihu Leavenworth, who for this purpose conveyed a corner of his farm to Capt. David Leavenworth, Gideon Leavenworth, Morse Leavenworth, Thomas Beardslee, Ephraim Beardslee, and Samuel Thompson, reserving one seventh of the lot to himself. About forty years ago the Elihu Leavenworth farm, adjoining the graveyard, came into possession of a man who resided there until recently, when it was again transferred. The present owner found the graveyard under cultivation, the only indication that it had been used as a burial ground being gravestones which had been thrown alongside the wall. Other stones and fragments were found in the cellar, where they were used as table tops and as props for a stove.

The Beardslee stones were removed several years ago to the modern cemetery in Roxbury, so that all but one of those still remaining on Good Hill are Leavenworth stones. The facts derived from the records still decipherable are given below, the words in brackets having been supplied by the contributor.

Capt. David Leavenworth, died 23 Mar. 1820, ae. 82.
    Olive his wife, died 8 Oct. 1804, ae. 67.
Olive, wife of Capt. David Leavenworth, died 8 Oct. 1804, ae. 63.
E. L. [*footstone of Elihu Leavenworth.*]
Martin Leavenworth, died 16 Feb. 1813, ae. 28.
Shelden, son of Gideon Levenworth, died 14 Apr. 1800, ae. 14.

Morse Leavenworth, died 12 Nov. 1822, ae. 58.
Loi[s, wife of] Gideon L[eavenworth,] [*illegible*] Sep[*illegible*].
[*illegible*] Leavenworth [*illegible*].
Abigail, wife of Ephraim Beardslee, died 15 Mar. 1812, ae. 43.

The Leavenworth Genealogy (followed therein by later publications) states that Thomas[2] Leavenworth, son of Thomas[1] and Grace, married Mary Jenkins, daughter of David, basing the assertion on the fact that Thomas[2] called David Jenkins his father-in-law. This is erroneous. Grace, widow of Thomas[1] Leavenworth, married secondly David Jenkins, as surmised by Cothren (History of Woodbury). Thomas[2] Leavenworth married Mary Dorman, born 12 May 1680, daughter of Edmund and Hannah (Hull) of New Haven, Conn. In the settlement of the estate of Edmund Dorman in 1711 his daughter Mary is called wife of Thomas Levensworth of Stratford. It is likely that Mary Dorman was mother of all the children of Thomas, since the youngest was named Edmund, and the son Thomas[3] named a son Dorman.

John[3] Leavenworth, son of Thomas[2] and Mary (Dorman), married first Deborah Moss, born 10 Feb. 1714/15. They were parents of the Capt. David and grandparents of the Morse Leavenworth whose gravestone inscriptions are given above. The Leavenworth Genealogy gives Deborah's maiden name as Hurd instead of Moss.

The same publication assumes that John[2] Leavenworth, the only other son (besides Thomas[2]) of Thomas[1] and Grace, left no issue. John removed from Stratford, Conn., to Newtown, Conn., married Phebe Wooster of Derby, Conn., (see New Haven Probate Records and Derby Deeds), and died in Feb. 1762. In his will he mentioned wife Phebe, son Thomas, and daughters Alice Camp, Sarah Botsford, and Abigail Turner; also son Lemuel Camp and grandsons Jabez Botsford and Jeremiah Turner, Jr. (Danbury Probate Records, vol. 1, p. 229.)

New Haven, Conn.   DONALD LINES JACOBUS.

GENEALOGY OF THE DESCENDANTS OF JOHN LEE.

By the Rev. Samuel Lee, A.M., of New-Ipswich, N. H.

AMONG the early emigrants to New-England there are several,— six or seven at least,—of the name of Lee. John Lee, of Farmington, Connecticut, came to this country in 1634. I find the following notices of him:

In the "Book of Rolls," so called, in London, there is a list[1] of a company who sailed from Ipswich in the ship Francis, John Cutting, master, bound for New-England "the last of April, 1634", (in an official paper containing the above list, the date is "the Tenth daye of April"), in which we find the name of "John Lea," aged 13, in the care of William Westwood. Westwood was 28 and his wife, Bridget, 32 years of age.

In the "Records of the Colony of the Massachusetts Bay" we find the following notices of Westwood: He took the freeman's oath March 4, 1635; is "sworn Constable" of the plantation at Connecticut, Sept. 5, 1635. On the 3rd of March following he is made a member of a "Commission" "to govern the people att Connecticut." He was among the original proprietors of Hartford. May 22, 1661, he is called "Mr." and made a member of a commission for Hadley, and with authority, not given to other members, "to join persons in marriage at Hadley."

In Stuart's "Hartford in the Olden Time" we find the following: William Westwood was a native of Essex County, in England; he settled in Newtown, now Cambridge, and moved to Connecticut in 1635; was present at the first court held in Connecticut, April 26, 1636, and at every subsequent court during the continuance of the commission. He was a deputy from Hartford for several years,— the last time in 1656. In or about the year 1658 he removed to Hadley, Mass., where he spent the remainder of his life.

John Lee, of course, was under the care of Westwood, and went with him from Boston to Hartford. In 1641 a colony from Hartford settled the town of Farmington. John Lee was one of them. His house was where is now Miss Porter's school for young ladies. It is a common tradition among his descendants that he came from Colchester,—whose nearest port was Ipswich,—and the name, Lee, is a very common one in the records of that town. Among the first proprietors of Farmington was Deacon Stephen Hart, and young Lee may have had special reasons for emigrating with Deacon H. He afterward married his daughter Mary.

---

[1] This list is printed in the Register (for October, 1860), xiv. 331.

The following are such facts as the writer has been able to obtain in relation to our family :

JOHN[1] LEE, the emigrant, born in England, about 1620; came to New-England, 1634; removed to Hartford, Ct., 1635; one of the original settlers of Farmington, 1641; married Mary Hart, 1658; himself and wife joined the church, Aug. 15, 1660; his inventory, £359, dated Oct. 30, 1690. In the old cemetery in Farmington is his tombstone, with the following inscription. It is a coarse unhewn slab, some two feet in height and eighteen inches wide, that must have been broken out of the stone by a dull tool driven lengthwise and leaving the letters jagged :

I : L : A G' 70	[John Lee: Aged 70
D E ' S E D	deceased
8 : 8 : 1690	8th month, 8th day, 1690.]

His children were :

  2. i.   JOHN,[2] b. June 11, 1659; bap. July 22, 1660.

     ii.   MARY,[2] b. Aug. 14, 1664; m. Dec. 28, 1682, Stephen Upson, son of Thomas Upson, of Waterbury, Conn. Children: 1. *Mary*,[3] b. Nov. 5, 1683; m. Richard Walton, son of John. 2. *Stephen*,[3] b. Sept. 30, 1686; m. Sarah, dau. of Isaac Bronson; d. Sept. 10, 1777. He represented the town in the colonial assembly in Oct., 1743, at which time he bore the title of Captain. 3. *Elizabeth*,[3] b. Feb. 14, 16$\frac{90}{91}$; m. Thomas Bronson. 4. *Thomas*,[3] b. March 1, 1692; m. 1732, Rachel, dau. of Deacon Thomas Judd. He moved to Farmington, then to Southington, now the eastern part of Wolcott. 5. *Hannah*,[3] b. March 16, 1695; m., first, Thomas Richards,—second, John Bronson. 6. *Tabitha*,[3] b. March 11, 1698; m. John Scovill, 2nd. 7. *John*,[3] b. Dec. 13, 1702; m. Elizabeth, dau. of Deacon Thomas Judd. 8. *Thankful*,[3] b. March 14, 1706; m. James Blakeslee.

  3. iii.   STEPHEN,[2] b. April, 1669.

  4. iv.   THOMAS,[2] b. 1671.

  5. v.   DAVID,[2] b. 1674.

     vi.   TABITHA,[2] b. 1677; m. Oct. 23, 1701, Preserved Strong, son of her step-father, Jedidiah Strong and Freedom Woodward. They removed to Coventry, Conn., where she died, June 23, 1750, aged 73. He died Sept. 26, 1765, aged 85. Their children were: *Noah*,[3] *Elizabeth*,[3] *Moses*[3] and *Aaron*[3] (twins), *Tabitha*,[3] *Mary*,[3] *Enoch*.[3]

Mary, the widow of John[1] Lee, married for her second husband Jedidiah Strong, of Northampton, Mass., Jan. 5, 1692, to which place she removed, taking with her the two youngest children. She died Oct. 10, 1710. The cause of her death was the falling of the horse on which she was riding, while on her way with her husband to visit their children in Coventry, Conn. She was over 70 years of age. Her husband went to reside with his children in Coventry, and died there May 22, 1753, aged 96.

2. JOHN[2] LEE (*John*[1]) resided in Farmington, and was annually appointed to offices of honor and trust in the town. He was street and land surveyor, and was one of the committee appointed by the proprietors to treat with the Sachem Marsakepe, and to obtain his signature to a deed conveying to them the tract of land named Farmington. He joined the church Nov. 24, 1686; his wife, Jan. 3, 1687. He married, Dec. 27, 1682, Elizabeth (b. in 1664), daughter of Thomas Loomis, of Windsor, Conn. Her mother was Mary, daughter of Deacon Thomas Judd, of Farmington. John[2] Lee died April 24, 1773. Their children were:

    i.   JOHN,[3] b. Dec. 7, 1683; bap. Nov. 27, 1686. Died young.

6. ii. JONATHAN,[3] b. March 20, 1686; bap. Nov. 27, 1686.

    iii. MARY,[3] b. March 15, 16$\frac{89}{90}$; bap. May 4, 1690.

    iv. ELIZABETH,[3] b. 1692; bap. Feb. 6, 1692. Died in infancy.

7. v.   SAMUEL,[3] b. March 23, 1694; bap. April 1, 1694.

8. vi. HEZEKIAH,[3] b. June 6, 1697; bap. July 6, 1697.

    vii. ELIZABETH,[3] b. March 6, 1700; m. Dec. 28, 1721, Samuel Langton. She died Oct. 11, 1750. Their children were: *Samuel*,[4] b. Oct. 23, 1723; minister at Old York. *Sarah*,[4] b. 1730. *Elizabeth*,[4] b. 1732.

    viii. RUTH,[3] b. June 14, 1703; m. March 14, 1722–3, William Judd, of Farmington. Their children were: 1. *Lois*,[4] b. Jan. 2, 1724; m. 1744, Hezekiah Wadsworth. 2. *John*,[4] b. Jan. 1, 1726, a lawyer at Canaan, Conn. 3. *Ruth*,[4] m. John Gridley. 4. *Eunice*,[4] m. Daniel Webster, of Hartford, Conn. 5. *Jesse*.[4] 6. *William*,[4] a lawyer at Farmington. 7. *Elizabeth*,[4] m. Joseph Skinner, of Hartford, Conn.

3. STEPHEN[2] LEE (*John*[1]) was a physician, and one of the first settlers in that portion of the original tract of land which is now called New Britain. He received a grant of five roods of land from the town in January, 1689, on the westerly side of the highway (provided it doth not hinder former grants) and the watering place, he building on it within four years, or else it is to return to the town again; and in March following "the Court" was applied to, to lay out Stephen Lee's lot as near as they can according to grant. Kensington was made an independent society about 1708, the church was organized in 1710, and the Rev. Mr. Burnham settled over the society in 1712. At the time of his settlement there were but fourteen families in the place, and the church consisted of ten members, seven males and three females. Stephen Lee and wife stand at the head of the list of the original members of this church, having united with the church in Farmington, Oct. 5, 1709.

Stephen[2] married, Oct. 1, 1690, Elizabeth Royce, of Wallingford; died June 7, 1753. Children:

9. i.   ISAAC,[3] b. Sept. 5, 1691.

    ii. ELIZABETH,[3] b. April 8, 1693. Died in infancy.

    iii. ELIZABETH,[3] b. July 12, 1694.

    iv. SARAH,[3] b. Nov. 8, 1696; m. Jan. 18, 1722, John Langton; owned the covenant May 12, 1710.

v. STEPHEN,[3] b. April 18, 1700. Killed Sept. 13, 1718, by the discharge of a gun.

vi. MARTHA,[3] b. Feb. 17, 170½; m. May, 1727, Noah Hart, of Wallingford ; m., second, Joseph Francis.

vii. MARY,[3] b. Sept. 7, 1704; m. Benjamin Beckley; d. Aug. 18, 1725.

viii. EBENEZER,[3] b. Sept. 14, 1706.

ix. HANNAH,[3] b. Oct. 15, 1708 ; bap. May 8, 1709 ; m. Nathaniel North.

10. x. JOSIAH,[3] b. Aug. 13, 1710.

4. THOMAS[2] LEE (*John[1]*), married, first, Sept. 11, 1707, Mary Camp, of Hartford, Conn. ; owned the covenant July 11, 1708 ; second, married, in 1725, Elizabeth Hubbard. He was a mason by trade ; died Sept. 26, 1740. Their children were :

i. LYDIA,[3] b. June 22, 1708 ; bap. July 11, 1708; m. Feb. 2, 1738, Samuel Norton.

ii. MARY,[3] b. Oct. 2, 1710 ; bap. Oct. 16, 1710.

11. iii. JARED,[3] b. Nov. 12, 1712 ; bap. 1712.

12. iv. JOSEPH,[3] b. Sept. 9, 1714.

v. MARY,[3] b. Jan. 7, 1716.

13. vi. JOHN,[3] ⎫
14. vii. THOMAS,[3] ⎬ twins, b. Dec. 17, 1717.

viii. JAMES,[3] b. 1720 ; died at Hartford, 1742 ; gave by will his estate to his five brothers, excepting £10 in money to his sister Lydia.

15. ix. EBENEZER,[3] b. 1727.

5. DAVID[2] LEE (*John[1]*) was by trade a weaver. He married, first, Sept. 5, 1695, Lydia, daughter of his step-father, Jedidiah Strong. He removed to Coventry, Conn., where she died, July 16, 1718. He married, second, May 27, 1719, Elizabeth ———. He lived in Lebanon in 1729, and there died in 1759. His children were :

16. i. JEDIDIAH,[3] b. Feb. 1, 1697.

ii. LYDIA,[3] b. April 20, 1699; d. May 5, 1699.

iii. LYDIA,[3] b. Jan. 23, 1702.

17. iv. DAVID,[3] b. June 26, 1705.

v. JOSIAH,[3] b. Oct. 6, 1707.

vi. ABIGAIL,[3] b. 1713.

18. vii. JONATHAN,[3] b. July 14, 1718.

6. JONATHAN[3] LEE (*John,[2] John[1]*) was a resident of Kensington and a Deacon of the Congregational Church. His house is now standing in a street called " Christian Lane," from the character of its first inhabitants, emigrants from Farmington. He married, June 4, 1713, Mary Root. He died Jan. 16, 1756. She died Sept. 14, 1764. Their children were :

i. MARY,[4] b. Oct. 4, 1714; m. May 22, 1735, Andrew Hooker.

ii. ELIZABETH,[4] b. July 15, 1716; m. ——— Hubbard.

iii. LUCY,[4] b. Jan. 10, 1720 ; d. Nov. 13, 1776.

iv. RUTH,[4] b. Aug. 3, 1722 ; m. John Gridley.

409

19. v.   JOHN,[4] b. April 22, 1725 ; m. May 7, 1752, Sarah Cole ; d. in
    New Britain, 1795.
    vi.   EUNICE,[4] b. May 24, 1732 ; m. 1760, Caleb Galpin.

7.   SAMUEL[3] LEE (*John,*[2] *John*[1]) m. Dec. 4, 1713, Eunice
Goodwin ; died Sept. 14, 1760.   He had one daughter :

    i.   HANNAH,[4] m. ——— Andrus.

8.   Captain HEZEKIAH[3] LEE (*John,*[2] *John*[1]), married, Dec. 28,
1728, Sarah, daughter of Dr. Samuel Porter, of Farmington, Conn.
He owned the covenant and had his children baptized before 1734.
He removed, first, to Litchfield, and afterward to Goshen, between
July 6 and Oct. 22, 1750.   He was considered a substantial and
valuable man.   He owned lands in Goshen.   He died in Harwinton
in 1763 or 4.   His children were :

    i.   SARAH,[4] b. Oct. 27, 1729 ; m. Alexander McKinstry ; d. in
        Ellington, Ct., Jan. 28, 1758.
    ii.   DANIEL,[4] a commissioned officer and a very brave man ; killed
        by the Indians in the French War.
    iii.   HEZEKIAH,[4] m. Lydia Thompson, of Middletown, Ct.
    iv.   MARY,[4] m. Jan. 10, 1754, Jacob Williams, of Castleton, Vt.
    v.   SAMUEL,[4] b. 1744 ; physician ; m. March 23, 1769, Sarah, dau.
        of Dr. J. Marsh, of Norwich, Ct.   Distinguished in his
        profession, and of great muscular strength and agility.   Sur-
        geon in the war of the revolution.

9.   ISAAC[3] LEE (*Stephen,*[2] *John*[1]) was a physician and resided in
Middletown, 1755, and in Kensington, 1768 ; was a member of the
church.   He married, Dec. 8, 1713, Mary Hubbard, of Middletown ; died Aug. 6, 1780.   Their children were :

    i.   TIMOTHY,[4] b. Nov. 8, 1714 ; d. Sept. 14, 1731.
    ii.   ISAAC,[4] b. Jan. 17, 171$\frac{6}{7}$; m., first, Tabitha Norton ; second,
        Elizabeth Grant ; third, Mary Hall ; died in 1802.
    iii.   MARY,[4] b. Aug. 6, 17$\frac{17}{18}$ [?] ; d. Sept. 29, 1731.
    iv.   STEPHEN,[4] b. March 6, 17$\frac{22}{23}$; m. Feb. 6, 1746, Catharine Forbs.
    v.   JERUSHA,[4] b. March 18, 17$\frac{24}{25}$.
    vi.   THANKFUL,[4] b. Nov. 9, 1726 ; m. Solomon Atkins, Feb. 25,
        1748.
    vii.   JERUSHA,[4] b. Feb. 15, 1731 ; m. Elisha Burnham, Nov. 9, 1748.

Mary, wife of Isaac, died, and he married, second, Susannah
Walcott of Middletown.   Their children were :

    viii.   *Susannah,*[4] b. June 10, 1742 ; d. Feb. 1, 1759.
    ix.   *Josiah,*[4] was a sea captain.   During the revolutionary war was
        captured with his vessel, and imprisoned several years in
        England.
    x.   *Mary,*[4] m. Samuel Wainwright ; d. in 1832.

10.   JOSIAH[3] LEE (*Stephen*[2] *John*[1]), married Nov. 12, 1732,
Hannah Warren, of Glastenbury, Conn.   He was Deacon of the
church in New Britain, and Captain of the Militia in New Britain ;

also Captain in the French War. He moved to Lenox, Mass., about the commencement of the revolution. Their only child:

     i.   ELIZABETH,[4] married John Patterson, attorney, and afterward Brigadier General in the Continental Army, by whom she had one son: 1. *Josiah Lee,*[5] bap. Feb. 1, 1767.

In 1791, Deacon Lee and General Patterson moved to Chenango county, N. Y., where Deacon Lee died in 1797.

11. Deacon JARED[3] LEE (*Thomas,*[2] *John*[1]), married, first, June 5, 1735, Rhoda Judd, daughter of John Judd, of Farmington. He lived in Southington, Conn., was a Deacon in the Congregational church; was also a justice of the peace, an office of some note at that time, and some of his dockets are still in existence, in his own hand-writing. An ancient law-book, published in London, England, which he used over one hundred years ago, is in the possession of the family. His first wife was burned to death by her clothes taking fire, Feb. 12, 1771, aged 62. Sept. 4, 1771, he married Elizabeth Hall. He died in 1780. His children were:

     i.   SETH,[4] b. March 31, 1736; m. Sept. 3, 1761, Sarah Ingersoll; second, Joanna Johnson. Graduate (1759) and tutor at Yale; physician.
     ii. AMOS,[4] b. July 19, 1738; m. May 28, 1765, Anna Camp.
     iii. TIMOTHY,[4] b. Nov. 26, 1740; m. April 23, 1772, Lucy Camp.
     iv. NOAH,[4] b. March 26, 1743.
     v. RHODA,[4] b. March 11, 1744; m. April 27, 1769, Ashbel Cowles; d. 1812.
     vi. LOIS,[4] b. April 24, 1747; m., first, Asahel Lewis; second, 1796, Samuel Lewis; d. 1823.

12. JOSEPH[3] LEE (*Thomas,*[2] *John*[1]), married, first, Jan. 1, 1743, Elizabeth Rolla, daughter of Nathaniel Stanley. She was born in Farmington, Conn., Jan. 16, 1718; died May 30, 1749; m., second, Jan. 8, 1750, Prudence Curtis. He was a captain in the French war, resided for a time in Goshen, moved from there to Suffolk, Long Island; died in 1792. His children were:

     i.   THOMAS.[4]
     ii. MATTHEW.[4]
     iii. SARAH,[4] d. Jan. 15, 1749.
     iv. JOHN,[4] b. May 20, 1749; d. May 31, 1749.
     v. JOHN,[4] b. Dec. 16, 1751.
     vi. SARAH,[4] b. Aug. 24, 1753.
     vii. PRUDENCE,[4] b. Aug. 11, 1754.

13. JOHN[3] LEE (*Thomas,*[2] *John*[1]), married, Jan. 6, 1742, Lydia Porter. He died Dec. 1, 1746. His estate was inventoried £802, debts £393, distributed Aug. 23, 1764. His widow married Dr. Daniel North, March 15, 1750, and died Jan. 23, 1780, aged 64. His children were:

     i.   JAMES,[4] b. Sept. 30, 1742; m. June 13, 1764, Lucy Boras. He died in 1823.

ii. EUNICE,[4] b. June 6, 1744.
iii. LYDIA,[4] b. 1745; d. in infancy.
iv. WILLIAM,[4] b. 1747; m. 1770, Elizabeth ———; d. 1829.
v. BENJAMIN,[4] b. 1749, bap. 1749.
vi. SYBIL,[4] b. 1751, bap. 1751.

14. THOMAS[3] LEE (*Thomas,*[2] *John*[1]), twin brother of John, married, first, Isabel Sedgwick, April 27, 1739; second, widow Martha Forward, of Simsbury, Conn. He died in 1807. His children were:

i. THOMAS,[4] resided in Simsbury (now Canton); d. in New Hartford.
ii. MILES,[4] went to Sheffield, has descendants there.
iii. DAVID.[4]
iv. ISABELLA.[4]

15. EBENEZER[3] LEE (*Thomas,*[2] *John*[1]), married, June 20, 1750, Abigail Bull. He was a physician in Farmington, Conn. Their children were:

i. MOSES,[4] b. Feb. 4, 1751.
ii. LIVERIUS,[4] b. April 9, 1754.
iii. ELIZABETH,[4] b. Nov. 28, 1755.
iv. EBENEZER,[4] b. Jan. 7, 1757.
v. Son b. in Northington, July 11, 1767; d. 1767.
vi. NATHANIEL,[4] m. Abigail Warner, of Westfield, Mass., and d. there.

16. JEDIDIAH[3] LEE (*David,*[2] *John*[1]), married, Sept. 6, 1722, Lucy ———. He resided in Willington, Conn. Their children were:

i. ELIAS,[4] b. July 26, 1723.
ii. LYDIA,[4] b. Nov. 10, 1726; m. a Penton or Benton.
iii. JERUSHA,[4] b. 1728; m. ——— Brown.
iv. ZEBULON,[4] b. Dec. 7, 1730; d. in infancy.
v. JOSIAH,[4] b. 1735.
vi. JEDIDIAH,[4] b. 1736; m. 1773, Hannah Fay.
vii. OLIVER,[4] b. 1738.
viii. ZEBULON,[4] b. 1740.
ix. SIMON,[4] b. 1741.

Jedidiah died at Willington in 1749. His will is dated April 11, 1748. Elias, his eldest son, and Lucy Lee his wife, were appointed administrators of the estate. His property inventoried £925 13s. Elias was appointed guardian to the younger children, July 3, 1750.

17. DAVID[3] LEE (*David,*[2] *John*[1]), married Mary ——— in Coventry, Ct., where he for a time resided. He removed from there to "Plantation No. 4, in Barkshire Co. Province of Marsitusits Bay" before 1762. His son was ·

i. DAVID,[4] b. Jan. 11, 1739; m. Tabitha ———, and resided in Becket, Mass., where he held offices of honor and trust.

18. Rev. JONATHAN[3] LEE (*David,*[2] *John*[1]), graduated at Yale College, 1742; married, first, Sept. 3, 1744, Elizabeth, daughter of the Rev. Joseph Metcalf, of Falmouth, Mass.; and second,

widow Love Graham Brinckerhoff. He died in Salisbury, Ct., after a pastorate of 44 years, Oct. 8, 1788. His children were:

   i. JONATHAN,⁴ b. Oct. 26, 1745; d. 1812.
   ii. ELIZABETH,⁴ b. Sept. 4, 1747; d. March 31, 1830; m. the Rev. Thomas Allen, of Pittsfield, Mass. REG., ix. 128; xxiii. 216.
   iii. SAMUEL,⁴ b. 1749; d. 1830; m., first, Hannah Morse; second, Eliza Brown.
   iv. CHLOE,⁴ b. 1751; d. 1753.
   v. RHODA,⁴ b. 1752; d. 1804; m., first, John Ensign; second, Deacon Alpha Rockwell.
   vi. SALOME,⁴ b. 1754; d. 1817; m., first, Samuel Robbins; second, Judge Nathan Hale, of Goshen, Ct.
   vii. ELISHA,⁴ b. 1757; m. Elizabeth Odingwell Allen; lawyer in Sheffield, Mass.
   viii. MILO,⁴ b. 1760; d. 1830; m. Ruth Camp; deacon.
   ix. CHAUNCEY,⁴ b. Nov. 9, 1763; d. Dec., 1842; m., first, Abigail Stanley; second, Olive Harrison Spencer; third, Rebecca Green Haynes. Was a minister in Sunderland, Vt., then in Colebrook, Ct., from 1800 to 1830. He d. in Hartwick, N.Y.
   x. ROBERT WALKER,⁴ b. April 4, 1765; m. Jerusha Bushnell.
   xi. LOVE,⁴ b. Dec. 5, 1767.

19. Deacon JOHN⁴ LEE (*Jonathan,*³ *John,*² *John*¹), married May 7, 1752, Sarah Cole. He resided in New Britain and died there in 1795. His wife died in 1800, aged 70. Their children were:

   i. JONATHAN,⁵ b. Oct. 19, 1753; d. Nov. 6, 1754.
   ii. JONATHAN,⁵ b. Oct. 13, 1755.
20. iii. SAMUEL,⁵ b. Oct. 2, 1757.
   iv. ORRIN,⁵ b. Oct. 9, 1760; m. 1784, Charlotte Hart; d. in Granby.
   v. JOHN,⁵ b. April 25, 1763; m. Polly Hart; d. 1830.
   vi. SARAH,⁵ b. Aug. 13, 1767; m. Ozias Hart; d. Oct. 19, 1827.

20. SAMUEL⁵ LEE (*John,*⁴ *Jonathan,*³ *John,*² *John*¹), married, first, 1784, Sibyl Stanley; and second, 1794, Sarah Burnett; d. March 31, 1803. His children were:

   i. LAURA,⁶ b. Jan. 19, 1796; m., first, Erastus Wilcox; second, Elisha Galpin; d. in Flint, Michigan, Aug. 15, 1856.
   ii. SAMUEL⁶ (the writer of this article), b. in Kensington, Ct., March 18, 1803; graduated at Yale Coll. 1827; at the Theological Seminary, New-Haven, 1830. [Ord. in Sherborn, Mass., Nov. 4, 1830; res. April 27, 1836; inst. pastor of the church in New-Ipswich, N. H., May 5, 1836. Author of A Historic Discourse at the Centennial Celebration of the First Congregational Church in New Ipswich, N. H., 1860; and other works.—EDITOR.]

DESCENDANTS OF EDWARD AND JOHN LEE OF GUILFORD, CONN.

Compiled by Hon. RALPH D. SMYTH, and communicated by
Dr. BERNARD C. STEINER, of Baltimore.

EDWARD[1] LEE, or Leigh, or Lees, came to Guilford about 1675, and married Elizabeth Wright, daughter of Benjamin, a resident of that place, in 1676. She died about 1685, and he married again, Abigail Stevens, daughter of Thomas of Guilford. She died August, 1727. He died in the preceding April. Wright gave by will, land to his daughter, in October, 1685. This land consisted of a home lot of one acre in the present borough of Guilford, a parcel of marsh land at Sandy Point and forty-four acres of upland. This land, Edward Lee conveyed to his son Samuel[2], the only surviving child of his first wife. He owned land in the vicinity of the West River in 1706, and removed there about 1710, after he had transferred his other property to Samuel[2] Lee. He also owned two lots in the Cohabitation land (now North Guilford). His list in 1716 was £95.12.6. He is supposed to have been a brother of George[1] Lee of Saybrook, who married Martha —— and died 1728, and of (2) JOHN[1] LEE of East Guilford. He was one of the smaller planters of Guilford. Savage's Genealogical Dictionary, iii. 75, calls him Lees and says he was perhaps son of Hugh of Saybrook.

The children of Edward Lee and Elizabeth Wright were:

      i. JOSEPH[2], b. 1678; d. Dec. 5, 1692.
3.   ii. SAMUEL, b. June 25, 1681; d. Aug. 26, 1727.

The children of Edward Lee and Abigail Stevens were:

      iii. MARY, b. July 4, 1689; d. s. June 9, 1752.
      iv. SARAH, b. Feb. 27, 1690–1; m. Nicholas Bond, of Hebron, Conn.
4.   v. LEMUEL, b. Dec. 1, 1693.
5.   vi. THOMAS, b. Aug. 15, 1696.
6.   vii. EBENEZER, b. Feb. 25, 1698–9; d. Sept. 24, 1751.
      viii. ABIGAIL, b. May 9, 1699; d. Jan. 27, 1767; m. David Chapman, son of Robert of East Haddam, on Feb. 5, 1724.

2. JOHN[1] LEE was a cooper, and lived in Killingworth in 1688, but later removed to East Guilford, where he resided in 1696, when he was given liberty to build a Sabbath-Day house on the Guilford Green. His list in 1716 was £95.3.0, and his cooper's trade was rated at £5. He married Elizabeth, daughter of Dennis Crampton of Guilford, in 1686, and died Feb. 14, 1718. She died June 23, 1746.

Their children were:

7.   i. JOHN[2] Jr., b. May 5, 1688, at Killingworth; d. at Guilford, March, 1717.
8.   ii. JOSEPH, b. Aug. 26, 1690; d. Dec. 31, 1753.
      iii. ELIZABETH, b. Nov. 30, 1692; d. s. Jan., 1725.
9.   iv. JONATHAN, b. May 26, 1695; d. Feb. 10, 1750.
      v. MARY, b. July 25, 1697; m. Samuel Allis, of Stratford.
      vi. DANIEL, b. July 6, 1699; d. s.
      vii. DEBORAH, b. Oct. 12, 1702; d. s. Oct. 20, 1765.
10. viii. NATHANIEL, b. Dec. 22, 1704; d. Dec. 20, 1753.
      ix. RACHEL, b. 1708.

3. SAMUEL[2] LEE (*Edward[1]*), of Guilford, married Abigail Bishop, daughter of John Jr., Sept. 18, 1700. She died June 5, 1751. His list in 1716 was £39.

Their children were:

      i. SUSANNAH[3], b. June 23, 1707; d. Oct. 20, 1707.
      ii. ABIGAIL, b. June 22, 1710; m. John Benton, of Guilford, Dec. 15, 1730; d. July 8, 1733.
11. iii. SAMUEL, b. April 22, 1713; d. March 3, 1787.

4. LEMUEL[2] LEE (*Edward[1]*) of Berlin, Conn., lived in 1716 at Guilford, where his list was £21 and one horse. He resided on the West river, near his father, until he removed from Guilford. He married 1st, Mary Burnett, on Feb. 25, 1716. She died March 2, 1719, and he married 2d, Mary West.

By his first wife he had one child:

      i. SAMUEL[3], b. March 26, 1717.

The children of Lemuel and Mary (West) Lee were:

      ii. ANNA,[3] b. March 1, 1722–3; d. Dec. 15, 1746.
      iii. MARY, b. Oct. 8, 1724.
      iv. MINDWELL, b. May 13, 1726; d. June 16, 1743.
      v. LEMUEL, b. May 11, 1729; d. Dec., 1746.
      vi. ABIGAIL, b. April 8, 1733; d. Dec. 16, 1749.
      vii. LEWIS, b. July 23, 1734; d. Dec. 14, 1746.

5. THOMAS[2] LEE (*Edward[1]*) had a home lot at Bluff Head in North Guilford, and removed thence with his brother Lemuel, to Berlin. He married Nov. 15, 1721, Elizabeth Sanford of Fairfield, who died March 9, 1746.

Their children were:

    i. STEPHEN[3], b. Oct. 10, 1722.
    ii. EDWARD, b. Jan. 17, 1725.
    iii. THOMAS, b. Oct. 13, 1730.

6. EBENEZER[2] LEE (*Edward[1]*) bought his brother Lemuel's land on Nov. 27, 1722, and always resided in Guilford. He married May 16, 1721, Sarah Chidsey, daughter of Joseph. She died March 7, 1778.

Their children were:

    i. MARY[3], b. May 2, 1722.
12.   ii. ELON, b. May 16, 1724; d. May 10, 1806.
    iii. RACHEL, b. Feb. 23, 1727; m. Jasper Griffing, of Guilford, 1761, and d. March 4, 1811. He d. Nov. 1, 1800.
    iv. RHODA, b. Nov. 29, 1728; d. June 20, 1741.
    v. SARAH, b. June 2, 1732.
    vi. LUCY, b. 1739; m. John Norton of Guilford, Dec. 7, 1758.
13.   vii. WILLIAM, b. 1741; d. April 29, 1795.

7. JOHN[2] LEE (*John[1]*), of East Guilford, married Rachel, daughter of Stephen Bishop. His list in 1716 was £30.6.0. He had land at the Neck in East Guilford, given him by his father in 1712.

Their only child was:

14.   i. JOHN[3], b. 1714; d. Aug. 8, 1752.

8. JOSEPH[2] LEE (*John[1]*), of East Guilford, married 1st, Lois Pond on June 24, 1730; 2d, Rebecca Lewis. Probably all his children were by his first wife.

They were (the order of their birth is uncertain):

15.   i. JOSEPH[3].
    ii. JOSIAH, b. July 11, 1733; d. May 7, 1751.
    iii. MIRIAM, m. Mark Hodgkiss, Jan. 8, 1751.
    iv. ELIZABETH, m. Nathaniel Spencer, of Haddam.
    v. LUCY, b. June 10, 1734; m. John Cruttenden; d. Feb. 10, 1786.
    vi. PHINEHAS, b. Nov. 5, 1736; d. Aug. 13, 1747.

9. JONATHAN[2] LEE (*John[1]*), of East Guilford, married Hope, daughter of Jonathan Murray, of Guilford, on August 15, 1719. After his death she married, about 1755, William Judd, Esq., of Waterbury, who died January 29, 1772. She died February 27, 1787.

Their children were:

    i. ANN[3], b. Oct. 1, 1720; m. Ebenezer Munger, of East Guilford, May 3, 1742, and d. Aug. 22, 1788. He d. June 20, 1793.
    ii. MARY, b. May 2, 1722; d. y.
    iii. MARY, b. Feb. 10, 1723; m. ——— Perry.
16.   iv. JONATHAN, b. May 22, 1726; d. Feb. 17, 1803.
    v. HOPE, b. May 1, 1728; m. Timothy Terrell, of Woodbury, Feb. 26, 1754. He d. Aug. 29, 1785.
    vi. SELAH, b. June 23, 1737; d. Jan. 5, 1757.

10. NATHANIEL[2] LEE (*John[1]*), of East Guilford, married 1st, Temperance Bishop, daughter of Nathaniel, April 3, 1728. She died March 29, 1751. He married 2d, Mary Turner, April 6, 1752. She died in 1764.

The children of Nathaniel and Temperance (Bishop) Lee were:

    i. TEMPERANCE[3], b. Jan. 29, 1729; d. y.
    ii. JAMES, b. Sept. 2, 1730; d. March 19, 1751.
17. iii. NATHANIEL, b. April 11, 1735.
    iv. EXPERIENCE, b. Sept. 10, 1737.
    v. TIMOTHY, b. Feb. 22, 1740; d. Oct. 7, 1753.
    vi. SIMEON, b. July 16, 1745; d. Dec. 25, 1771.
    vii. PHINEHAS, b. Oct. 17, 1747; d. Aug. 2, 1770.
    viii. JENNIE, b. May 11, 1750; d. May 17, 1770.

The child of Nathaniel and Mary (Turner) Lee was:

    ix. SARAH, b. Aug. 6, 1753; m. Aaron Foster, of East Guilford, Dec. 10, 1769. He d. March 12, 1773.

11. SAMUEL[3] LEE, JR. (*Samuel,[2] Ebenezer[1]*), of Guilford, married Ruth, daughter of Deacon Seth Morse, January 6, 1742. She died March 3, 1804.

Their children were:

    i. SAMUEL[4], b. Oct. 1, 1742; d. May 31, 1819. He was a man of much prominence in the town, representing it several times in the legislature. During the Revolutionary war he was most zealous in his patriotism, and served on several important town committees. In 1778, he was appointed lieutenant in the 7th Connecticut regiment. In 1780, he enlisted a company of coast guards in Guilford and was on duty with them for 165 days. His course of action against the Tories was a determined one (see Steiner's History of Guilford, p. 443). His wife was a remarkable woman, of great force of character. She was Agnes Dickinson (b. Mar. 21, 1745; d. July 2, 1830), dau. of Azariah and Hepzibah of Haddam. She mar. Capt. Lee on Nov. 7, 1764. Their children were: 1. *Rebecca[5]*, b. Mar. 17, 1766; d. Dec. 6, 1859; m. Timothy Seward of Guilford Dec. 3, 1783 (see Seward Genealogy in N. E. Hist. Gen. REGISTER for July, 1898). Among their grand-children was Rachel Stone Seward, who m. Ralph D. Smyth. 2. *Lucy*, b. July 8, 1770; m. Joel Griswold (d. July 19, 1835) of Guilford in 1790, and d. Mar. 24, 1854. 3. *Ruth*, b. Aug. 13, 1778; m. Abner Benton (d. Mar. 14, 1804) of Guilford in 1800, and d. Mar. 9, 1854.
    ii. TIMOTHY, b. Feb. 22, 1745; m. Freelove Crampton, Sept. 13, 1775 (d. July 6, 1836). She died Sept., 1822. They had one daughter, *Freelove[5]*, b. 1789; d. s. May 26, 1833. He was a revolutionary soldier and lived in Guilford.
    iii. LEVI, b. 1747; removed to Horner, N. Y.

12. ELON[3] LEE (*Ebenezer,[2] Edward[1]*), of Guilford, married Elizabeth, daughter of Isaac Hotchkiss, May 16, 1750. She died March 29, 1818.

Their children were:

    i. SARAH[4], b. Mar. 23, 1752; m. Miles Johnson of Guilford, Mar. 25, 1774; d. Mar. 14, 1775.
    ii. ELON, b. June 17, 1757; m. Deborah Johnson, Dec. 30, 1778; d. Jan. 31, 1783. She d. Dec. 9, 1843. After his death she married Amos Dudley of Guilford (d. Sept. 8, 1823), July 15, 1794. Their children were: 1. *Sarah[5]*, b. Dec. 30, 1780; m. John Dudley of Guilford, 1805; d. Dec. 27, 1849 (he d. Jan. 9, 1816). 2. *Deborah*, b. Mar. 31, 1783; m. William Dudley (d. July 16, 1845) of Guilford, Feb. 8, 1808; d. Oct. 25, 1827.
    iii. EBER, b. Dec. 23, 1760; d. May 31, 1855. He lived in Guilford and Meriden, and mar. Huldah, dau. of David Bishop, Nov. 20, 1789. She d. Oct. 19, 1836. Their children were: 1. *Elon[5]*, b. Dec. 15, 1790; m. (1) Lydia Palmer, Dec. 5, 1810; (2) Eunice Howard, Oct., 1822; lived at Clarkestown, N. Y. 2. *David*, b. May 9, 1792; lived at Philadelphia, Penn.; m. (1) Sarah, dau. of Capt. James Castle; (2) Rachel, sister of first wife. 3. *Orrit*, b. Nov. 7, 1793;

417

m. Elah Camp of Durham, Dec., 1819. 4. *Erastus*, b. Sept. 28,
1795; lived at Canton, Ohio, and d. s. Sept. 24, 1843. 5. *Eli*, b.
June 7, 1800; m. (1) Lydia Evarts; (2) Betsey Taylor; (3)
widow Mary (Rhodes) Ellis.

  iv. ELIZABETH, b. Feb. 20, 1763; m. John Arden, 1790; d. Dec. 3, 1795.
  v. JOEL, b. Apr. 9, 1767, of Guilford; d. Nov. 19, 1836; m. Mary, dau.
of James Davis, Feb. 1, 1798. She m. (2) Amos Fowler, Jan.
17, 1848, and died Sept. 7, 1863, æ. 94. Their children were:
1. *Polly*, b. Sept. 22, 1792; d. Sept. 25, 1794. 2. *Joel Alvah*, b.
July 5, 1794; died in the west about 1877; m. Amanda Shelly,
Mar., 1817. 3. *Maria*, b. Aug. 27, 1796; d. Jan. 19, 1826; m.
Joel Parmelee of Guilford, 1818. 4. *Davis*, of Guilford, b. Oct.
11, 1798; d. Nov. 2, 1867; m. Harriett Elliott, Jan. 1, 1838. 5.
James Edward, b. Oct. 11, 1798; d. Nov. 19, 1889; m. Ruth Merwin, Sept. 28, 1825. 6. *Gilbert Miner*, b. Sept. 14, 1802; d. Feb.
12, 1894; m. Phebe Ricks; lived in Wisconsin. 7. *Henry Salem*,
b. Sept. 15, 1807; d. June 6, 1842; of Manhanset, L. I.; m. Ann
Brooks. 8. *Justin*, b. Apr. 11, 1810; m. Matilda Hotchkiss, Sept.
20, 1866. He is still living.

  vi. VENE, b. Nov. 27, 1770, of Pennsylvania; d. 1849; m. (1) Rebecca Palmer, Nov. 16, 1793. She died June 14, 1794, leaving
one son, *Horace*. He mar. (2) Polly Johnson, who had one son,
John Fletcher.

13. WILLIAM³ LEE (*Ebenezer*², *Edward*¹), of Guilford, married Eunice
Hotchkiss, daughter of Mark, May 23, 1770; she died February
27, 1827. Their children were:

  i. WILLIAM⁴, b. July 16, 1771; d. June 1, 1840.
  ii. REUBEN, b. Sept. 28, 1773; m. Lois, dau. of Philemon Hall. Their
children were: 1. *Eunice*. 2. *Sarah*. 3. *Eliza Ann*. 4. *Alvan*.
  iii. TIM; b. Nov. 1, 1775; d. Nov. 1846; m. Lois Barnes, June 10, 1797.
Their children were: 1. *Frederic William*, of Guilford; m. (1)
Nancy Stannard, (2) wid. Rebecca Stannard. 2. *George Augustus*.
3. *Lyman*, of Little Valley, N. Y.; m. Harriett Rathbone.
  iv. CHARLES, b. Sept 7, 1777; d. Sept. 12, 1787.
  v. SARAH, b. July 6, 1782; m. ———— Eggleston, of Rochester, N. Y.
  vi. ELON, b. Mar. 12, 1786; d. Dec. 22, 1856; m. Grace Stone, May 17,
1808. Their children were: 1. *Eunice*, b. Jan. 22, 1812; m. Henry
Benton, April 8, 1832. 2. *Myrta Ann*, b. May 6, 1815; m. Jason
Field, April 15, 1835. 3. *Edward William*, b. Aug. 6, 1819; d. Jan.
25, 1840. 4. *Hubbard Stone*, b. July 6, 1822, of Ann Arbor, Mich.;
m. Sarah Eliza Willett. 5. *Eliza Polly*, b. July 25, 1825; m. Walter
Hinckley, Oct. 4, 1846.
  vii. CHARLES, b. Nov. 29, 1788, of Guilford; d. Sept. 5, 1845; m. Achsa
Parmelee of Guilford, July 8, 1812. (She died Nov. 9, 1866.) They
had one child, *Harriett Clarissa*, b. Mar. 10, 1818.
  viii. JONATHAN, b. April 12, 1791; m. Ruth ————; lived at Rochester,
N. Y., and d. Nov. 3, 1838.

14. JOHN³ LEE, Jr. (*John*², *John*¹), married Elizabeth ————. After his
death she married Daniel Grove of North Guilford, who died September 12, 1782. She died July 8, 1798. Their children were:

  i. JOHN⁴, b. May 20, 1739; m. Lucy Graves. Their children were:
1. *Linus*, bap. May 26, 1771, and 2. *Daniel*, b. Mar. 13, 1774.
  ii. AZARIAH, b. Dec. 21, 1740; d. Aug. 12, 1762.
  iii. STEPHEN, b. ————, 1742.

15. JOSEPH³ LEE (*Joseph*², *John*¹), married March 23, 1736, Mary, daughter of Nathaniel Bayley of Guilford. Their children were:

  i. DAVID⁴, b. July 3, 1740; d. July 2, 1742.
  ii. MARTHA, b. Mar. 21, 1743; m. Nathan Field.
  iii. RUTH, b. April 29, 1747.
  iv. NATHAN, b. Sept. 13, 1750.

16. JONATHAN[3] LEE (*Jonathan[2], John[1]*), of East Guilford, married Mary, daughter of Ebenezer Bartlett, June 27, 1751. She died September 23, 1825. Their children were:

   i. SUBMIT[4], b. June 14, 1753; m. David Hatch of Norfolk.
   ii. ABIGAIL, b. July 11, 1754; m. 1772, Theophilus Scranton (d. Dec. 1?, 1827), of Guilford; d. Dec. 23, 1840.
   iii. ANNA, b. Nov. 10, 1756; m. Josiah Munger, Mar. 22, 1780. He d. Dec. 27, 1822.
   iv. MARY, bap. July 8, 1759; m. Jacob Conkling, a tailor, who came to Guilford from Long Island.
   v. JONATHAN, b. April 9, 1762; d. Nov. 4, 1844; m. 1789, Mindwell, dau. Dea. Timothy Hill of East Guilford. He lived in East Guilford, afterwards Madison. Their children were: 1. *Lydia[5]*, b. April 7, 1790; d. Jan. 24, 1796. 2. *Anna*, b. Dec. 29, 1791; m. Jonathan Judd and removed to Orange, Conn. She was living at New Haven in 1850. 3. *Selah*, b. Sept. 21, 1794; m. Electa Ann Bushnell, and lived in Madison. 4. *Julia*, b. Sept. 2, 1796. 5. *Mary*, b. Nov. 6, 1798; d. Sept. 24, 1800. 6. *Chloe*, b. April 6, 1801; m. Wm. H. Bishop. 7. *Jonathan Trumbull*, b. Mar. 5, 1803; m. Betsy B. Judd, Nov. 22, 1827, and lived in Madison. 8. *Timothy H.*, b. Dec. 8, 1805; d. of cholera Sept. 8, 1832. 9. *Charlotte*, b. 1808; m. Orlando Wilcox of New Haven. 10. *Henry*, b. Aug. 2, 1810; m. (1) Rosalind Smith (d. July 22, 1848, æ. 32), May 6, 1840; (2) Abigail Dudley, Nov. 6, 1840, and lived in Madison. 11. *Alexander Hamilton*, b. May 27, 1813; d. July 5, 1835.
   vi. SELAH, b. Sept. 5, 1765; d. Aug. 23, 1791; m. Sarah Dudley, dau. of Gilbert. She d. Mar. 9, 1854. Their children were: 1. *Horace[5]*, b. ———; d. æ. 5 mos., 15 days. 2. *Polly*, b. Sept. 18, 1789; d. s. Nov., 1826.

17. NATHANIEL[3] LEE (*Nathaniel[2], John[1]*), of East Guilford and Whitestown, N. Y.; married Mabel, dau. of Deacon Timothy Meigs of East Guilford, Dec. 7, 1757. She d. October 20, 1800. Their children were:

   i. TIMOTHY[4], b. Aug. 14, 1760; d. at Whitestown, July, 1803.
   ii. CLEMANIA, b. Dec. 18, 1763.
   iii. FREDERIC, b. April 3, 1766, of East Guilford, captain in the U. S. revenue service; gave the name Madison to East Guilford when it was set off as a separate town; founded Lee's Academy there; was one of the earliest Jeffersonian Republicans of the town; m. Anna, dau. of Asher Fowler; had no children; d. May 27, 1831. She d. Nov. 13, 1855.
   iv. STATIRA, b. May 24, 1768.
   v. SIMEON, b. May 26, 1771.
   vi. ALEXANDER, b. Mar. 5, 1774.
   vii. HARRIET, b. Nov. 7, 1776.
   viii. URIAH, b. Mar. 29, 1780.

LELLOCK—KELLOGG.—On page 77, vol. iii. of his Genealogical Dictionary of New-England, Mr. Savage devotes quite a paragraph to what he styles the "almost impossible name" of *Lellock*, *Joseph*, Boston, who by wife Joanna, had born to him son Martin, 22 Nov., 1658, as appears by the second copy of the Records, the original of which is lost. This name, which Mr. Savage afterward thinks should be *Sellock* (iv. 51), should doubtless read *Kellogg*. Joseph Kellogg, whose first wife was *Joanna*, removed, between 1656 and 1658, from Farmington to Boston, and thence as early as 1662 to Hadley. Between 1656 and 1660, Savage gives him son *Martin*, but does not mention the date of his birth, which undoubtedly should be 22 Nov., 1658.

Hartford, Conn. L. M. B.

Lineage of Lydia Lincoln, Second Wife of William Chapman of New London, Connecticut. Contributed by Grace Louise Knox, West Hartford, Connecticut.

For some time, researchers of the William Chapman line have sought further information about his second wife, Lydia Lincoln. I believe she was the daughter of Samuel[3] Lincoln (*Thomas[2]*, *Thomas[1]*) and Sarah[3] Royce (*Jonathan[2]*, *Robert[1]*). Sarah, one of ten children, was born October 1665 to Jonathan and Deborah (Calkins) Royce (Norwich, Connecticut, Vital Records, 1:33). Samuel Lincoln was born at Taunton, Massachusetts, 16 March 1658 (*Vital Records of Taunton, Massachusetts. . .* 2 vols. [Boston, 1929], 1:269). The County Court Records of New London, Connecticut, for September 1682 states "Samuel Linkhorns of Taunton and Sarah Roice of Norwich being legally convicted of fornication before marriage, the court has adjudged them to pay a fine to the County Treasury, the sum of five pounds. Capt. James Fitch of the County in behalf of the above named, for the payment of their fine" (6:34). The Norwich Land Records (1:132) record eighteen acres of pasture land belonging to Samuel Lincoln of Windham, Connecticut, more or less at Yantick butting south on land of Hugh Calkin, west on Thomas Post and Hugh Calkin, north and east on commons. Part of it was his father-in-law Royce's pasture lot and part a grant from the town, this parcel delivered to him as part of his mother-in-law Royce as appears upon the record entered 21 January 1694/5.

As further evidence of the parentage of Lydia: in the distribution of the estate of Jonathan Royce, 22 September 1690, "Samuel Linkon" received five pounds. Again the Norwich Deeds (3B:443) show that William Chapman was one of those mentioned in David Royce's estate as one of the heirs. He joins others in a deed dated 5 March 1712/3 to Samuel Gager of Norwich.

Lydia is mentioned in the distribution of her grandfather Thomas Lincoln of Taunton, 1694, in which he distributes his property to his surviving children: to Thomas, his son, he gave "5 parcels of land which he may sell if needed for his maintenance provided that Thomas cause to be payable to Lidiah, daughter of Thomas Senior's son, Samuel, 50 shillings when she shall arrive at the age of 18 years" (Bristol County Deeds, 2:260). The same provision is requested for "Lidiah" in the deed of land to Jonah Lincoln, son of Thomas, Sr.

Sarah (Royce) Lincoln must have died soon after the birth of Lydia and before 2 June 1692, when Samuel Lincoln married Elizabeth Jacobs (Windham Vital Records, A-24). Seven children were born to them: Samuel, Thomas, Marcy, Elizabeth, Jonah, Jacob, and Nathaniel. When Elizabeth (Jacobs) died around 1727, Samuel married in 1729 Experience (————) Lanphere, widow of Shadrack Lanphere who died 29 January 1728 (*Register,* 14[1860]: 167). Experience and her son Joseph were administers of his estate. On 23 February 1732 Samuel Lincoln and Experience his wife, "for love to our children, Oliver, Ann, Prudence, Experience, and Mary Lanphere of Westerly and Solomon and John of Norwich, and Hezekiah of Lebanon, Connecticut, deeded to said eight children, 48 acres in Westerly which former husband, Shadrach Lanphere, had possessed" (John O. Austin, *Genealogical Dictionary of Rhode Island* [Albany, 1887], 119).

On 9 May 1732 Samuel Lincoln made his will which was exhibited at the Court of Probate held at Windham, 3 March 1737/8. Portions of it read:

Imprimas: I having already given to my daughter Lydia Chapman sundry things out of my estate, I now give her five shillings in or as money out of my estate as her portion.

Item: I having formerly given to my son Samuel Linkon and Jacob Linkon and Jonah Linkon sundry tracts of land as may appear by their deeds of gift from me, I now give and bequeath to them, two shillings as their portion in full.

Item: I having formerly given to my son Thomas Linkon three parcels of land, I now make and ordain him my executor of this my will and I now give to him one half of all my goods and chatles as his portion.

Item: I give to my daughter Mary Martin and Elizabeth Linkon all the rest and residue of my goods and chatles after my debts, and ten pounds to Experience my beloved wife by an agreement before marriage.

Samuel Linkon

Witnesses:
Samuel Webb Jr.
Richard Abbe
Mary (her mark) Abbe

William Chapman's first wife, Hannah Lester, whom he had married 27 March 1690, died in 1701. He married second, 11 August 1702, Lydia Lincoln. His will was dated 21 August 1734 and Lydia is named executrix.

IDENTITY OF ELLEN (——) LINDLEY

By Retta Bostwick Perry, of Lawrenceville, Pennsylvania

The identity of Ellen, wife of John Lindley of New Haven, Guilford, and Branford, Connecticut, has long been an enigma to researchers in her husband's family. She was his first wife. It is known that they were married and had two children, Sarah and John, Jr., when they moved from New Haven to Guilford in 1648. Town records of the latter place list the births of two more children: Mary, born 22 Feb. 1651 (vol. A, p. 122) and Hanna, born 1 April 1654 (*ibid.*). On 6 April 1654 Ellen was buried and thus passes from the stage of history.

An excellent clue to her origin is given by Donald Lines Jacobus in his "Barnes Families of Long Island and Branford, Conn.," The Register, vol. 123, pp. 88-90. He suggests that the two younger children, namely Mary and Hannah, were brought up by relatives in East Hampton, Long Island. Whose relatives? They could not have been John's as he is supposed to have had only a younger brother, Francis, then unmarried, in this country at the time. Therefore, they must have been Ellen's.

Before we turn to East Hampton we should list some other probabilities as guidelines: (1) Ellen must have been born between 1620 and 1630; nearer the middle of the decade seem most likely. (2) While from those dates she could have been born in this country, the likelihood of her being part of an immigrant family is much greater. (3) Her family should have been in the New Haven area at the time of her marriage in 1644 or 1645 and in East Hampton, Long Island, at the time of her death in 1654.

A search of East Hampton families reveals the following: Ellen, daughter of Ralph and Alice (Goldhatch) Dayton, was baptized in Ashford, co. Kent, England, on 3 Dec. 1626. References consulted say that while it is not definitely known that she came to America with her family "it is likely". The father lived in New Haven from 1639 to 1649. From thence he went to East Hampton where he lived until his death in 1658 (Rattray, p. 268). Thus, all the right times and places are satisfied.

The clincher, though, is the will of Ralph[1] Dayton. Among other bequests he leaves "to my sonn Linly's children . . . .". Unfortunately, some early reader of this will called the name "Brinley". Later writers copied and re-copied it without verification. In the original the *L* is very plain. One wonders how it could have been mistaken for *Br*.

Therefore, it would seem that Ellen Dayton, born in England in 1626, came to America with her family by 1639, lived with them in New Haven until her marriage to John Lindley in 1644 or 1645, moved with him to Guilford, Conn., in 1648 and died there in 1654. Her two younger children, Mary and Hannah, could have been brought up in East Hampton either by her father's family or that of her sister Alice, wife of Thomas Baker, a prominent citizen of that

*Pages 92-94, Vol. I of this work.

place. We offer this solution of the three hundred year old mystery of Ellen's identity.

Sources consulted were: Ray Keyes Lindsley, *Connecticut Lindsleys: The Six Johns*, Bristol Conn., 1948; THE REGISTER, vol. 123, pp. 88-90; Jeannette Edwards Rattray, *East Hampton History*, Garden City, New York, 1953; H. P. Hedges, *History of East Hampton*, N. Y., 1897; original will of Ralph Dayton.

LOCKWOOD GENEALOGY.—For some reason, the descendants of David[5] Lockwood (182 in the Lockwood Genealogy) were not obtained and do not appear in the exhaustive book compiled by Frederic A. Holden and E. Dunbar Lockwood. That they may be preserved, they are here given :

The line to David[5] Lockwood from Robert,[1] who came from England about 1630, runs : (1) Jonathan,[2] (12) Robert,[3] (49) Samuel,[4] (182) David.[5]

David[5] Lockwood was born in Greenwich, Conn., June 21, 1760, and died in New Milford, Conn., Dec. 24, 1841. He resided in Greenwich during the Revolutionary War, and married Sarah Closson, or Clason, who was born Jan. 25, 1762. They had :

    i.   Polly,[6] b. Feb. 4, 1781; m. Nov., 1802, James Somers; d. June 15, 1813.

A. ii. Roswell, b. Jan. 21, 1783.

   iii. Lyman, b. Feb. 10, 1786; m. (1) Laura Mead; m. (2) Ruth Smith. Had, by first wife, *Emily*,[7] *Mary Ann*, and *Charles*, and by second wife, *Henry*.

   iv. Jerusha, b. Aug. 14, 1790; m. in 1815, John Wooster. Had: *Mary*, *Peter*, *David*, and *Susan* who m. ———— Sandford.

   v. Ithamar, b. Dec. 15, 1792; d. June 10, 1844.

   vi. Closson, b. Aug. 20, 1794; d. May 8, 1796.

   vii. Stanley C., b. Mch. 4, 1800; m. Sarah Starr. Had : *Jerusha*,[7] *Sarah*, and *Henry*.

  viii. Charles, b. Feb. 10, 1803; m. Eliza Ives of Bristol, Vt. Had : *Lucy Jane*,[7] *Ann Maria*, *Elizabeth*, and *Henry*.

A. Roswell[6] Lockwood (David,[5] Samuel,[4] Robert,[3] Jonathan,[2] Robert[1]) born Jan. 21, 1783, married, Oct. 11, 1805, Thalia, daughter of John and Esther (Smith) Oviatt, and died Dec. 13, 1863. They had :

    i.   Henry,[7] b. Aug. 3, 1807; m. (1) Feb. 17, 1836, Sarah Sophia Midhurst, on the Island of Java, where he was a missionary; m. (2) Cathalina Lansing Dox, Aug. 11, 1840, at Geneva, N. Y.; d. Nov. 21, 1883. Had, by second wife: *James R.*[8]; *Henry Roswell*, b. Apl. 3, 1843, d. Sept. 20, 1905, a clergyman at Syracuse, N. Y.; *Elizabeth R.*, b. May, 1845, d. Jan. 18, 1860; and *Mary*, m. Charles Armstrong.

   ii. Eliza Ann, b. Dec. 29, 1810; m. Nov. 11, 1834, James O. Bloss; d. Apl. 3, 1880. Had : *Sarah Louise*, b. Aug. 4, 1835, d. Nov. 22, 1853; *Henry Lockwood*, b. Nov. 23, 1836; *Charlotte Sophia*, b. Sept. 16, 1838, m. Mch. 25, 1868, James A. Daly, d. Oct. 2, 1892; *James Orville*, b. June 19, 1840, d. Nov. 23, 1847; *Charles Finney*, b. Jan. 9, 1842, d. young; *John Jay*, b. Oct. 11, 1843, d. Sept. 19, 1864; *Celestia Angenette*, b. Sept. 1, 1845; *James Orville*, b. Sept. 30, 1847; and *Harriet Eliza*, b. Dec. 28, 1849.

   iii. Sarah Jerusha, b. Feb. 10, 1813; m. Jan. 13, 1859, Henry Hanford; d. May 6, 1897.

   iv. Susan, b. Oct. 17, 1817; m. July 25, 1843, David Bush; d. Nov. 17, 1897. Had : *Charles*, *David*, and *Susan Thalia*.

   v. Charlotte, b. Mch. 21, 1819; m. Apl. 10, 1845, John Fairbanks; d. Mch. 22, 1871. Had : *Caroline A.*, and *Charlotte*.

vi. Caroline, b. May 24, 1821; d. Dec. 6, 1902.
vii. Charles C., b. July 4, 1823; m. May 28, 1849, Arna S. Lyman; d. Oct. 25, 1856.
viii. John David, b. Apr. 30, 1828; d. Sept. 18, 1828.

44 Wall St., New York City. JAMES ORVILLE BLOSS.

———

THE SECOND WIFE OF JOSEPH LOOMIS OF WINDSOR, CONN.—It has been stated many times that Joseph[2] Loomis, son of Joseph[1] and Mary (White) Loomis, married as his second wife Mary Chauncey. However, the contributor of this article has never found documentary proof for this statement.

On page 39 of "Some Early Records and Documents of and relative to the Town of Windsor, Conn., 1639–1703," being a true copy of the private vital records kept by Matthew Grant of Windsor and published by the Hartford Historical Society in 1930, is this record "Josep lomis mared Mary Sharwod June 28, 1659."

A Mary Sherwood, born about 1639, the daughter of Thomas[1] Sherwood by his second wife, Mary Fitch, had brothers Stephen, Matthew, and Isaac. The Mary Sherwood who married Joseph Loomis named three of her sons Stephen, Matthew, and Isaac.

Mr. A. C. Bates, Librarian of the Connecticut Historical Society, copied the signature found in the Windsor records as Mary Harwod. Due to the use of the old form of the letter "s," the name was doubtless Mary Sharwod."

Cleveland, Ohio. ELISHA S. LOOMIS.

———

THE SECOND WIFE OF JOSEPH LOOMIS OF WINDSOR, CONN.—For many years it has been stated that the second wife of Joseph Loomis (son of Joseph and Mary (White) Loomis) was Mary Chauncey, but the contributor never found any documentary proof of this statement.

Careful search, however, shows that Joseph Loomis married 28 June 1659 Mary Sherwood, daughter of Thomas and Mary (Fitch) Sherwood. ("Some Early Records and Documents of and Relative to the Town of Windsor, Conn., 1639–1703," 1903, p. 39.)

Thomas[1] Sherwood married secondly, about 1638, Mary Fitch, daughter of Thomas and Ann (Reeve) Fitch, by whom he had six children, Mary, Ruth, Stephen, Matthew, Abigail, and Isaac. ("Daniel L. Sherwood and His Paternal Ancestors," 1929; also "History of the Fitch Family," 1930, vol. 1.)

Mary Sherwood, the oldest of this group of six children, was born about 1639 and so was twenty years of age at the time of her marriage to Joseph Loomis. The names of her three brothers, Stephen, Matthew, and Isaac were given to three of her sons.

Mary (Fitch) Sherwood married secondly, in 1658, John Banks. In her will she mentions her children, Matthew, Mary, Ruth, and Isaac Sherwood, and "daughter" Hannah Lumis.

As Mary (Fitch) (Sherwood) Banks had no daughter Hannah Loomis through marriage, it is safe to say that "granddaughter" was meant for "daughter," thereby proving the identity of the second wife of Joseph Loomis.

Cleveland, Ohio. ELISHA S. LOOMIS.

424

THE SECOND WIFE OF JOSEPH LOOMIS OF WINDSOR, CONN.—The conclusion of Mr. Elisha S. Loomis (*ante*, p. 203) that the second wife of Joseph Loomis, Jr., was * Mary Sherwood, daughter of Thomas and Mary, is amply justified. But in quoting the will of her mother, Mrs. Mary Sherwood-Banks, he states that it mentions her "daughter" Hannah Lumis.

In April 1938 the contributor of this note examined the will and made the following abstract of that portion under discussion: "I giue to my son steuen sharwods daughtour Ruth sharwod . . . to my son mathew sharwods daughtour mary sharwod . . . I giue to hanah Lomis my Red Pluch peticot and y° best of my two gren aporons and my Cearsy peticot and one pair of sheats . . . to my daughtour Ruth . . . to my sone steuen . . . to my sone Jsack . . . to my son mathew . . ."

From this abstract it is noted that Mrs. Banks gave legacies to her son Stephen Sherwood's daughter Ruth, to her son Matthew Sherwood's daughter Mary, and then to "Hannah Lumis" without specifying relationship. Hannah Loomis was the eldest surviving child of Joseph Loomis by his second wife, Mary Sherwood, and Mary (Sherwood) Loomis had been dead over a decade before Mrs. Banks wrote her will. The granddaughter was undoubtedly intended in this legacy, as Mr. Loomis concluded, but there is no reason to correct a supposed error in the will.

What, may one inquire, is the record evidence for the statement that Mary, second wife of Thomas Sherwood, and mother of the above Mary (Sherwood) Loomis, was born a Fitch? In 1886 an account of the Sherwood family appeared in Orcutt's "History of Stratford," which carefully distinguishes between the Fairfield and Stratford Sherwoods, and states the name of the second wife of Thomas Sherwood of Fairfield as Mary, without any indication as to her name at birth. Three years later, Mrs. Elizabeth Hubbell Schenck published the first volume of her "History of Fairfield," and in the account of the Sherwood family, on page 408, states the second marriage of Thomas Sherwood to Mary (without any mention of the name Fitch) and also the second marriage of this Mary to John Banks; yet on page 351, in her account of the Banks family, she states of Mr. John Banks: "His second wife was Mary Fitch wid. of Thomas Sherwood 1 of Fairfield."

This seems to be the origin of all subsequent statements that this Mary was born a Fitch. It cannot fail to strike the careful genealogist as odd that Mary was identified as a Fitch in the account of her second husband's family, but was not identified at all in the account of the family of her Sherwood husband, who was the father of all her children. It is also to be noted that Mrs. Schenck's account of the Sherwood family was supplied by W. L. Sherwood of Newark, N. J., who was engaged in compiling a Sherwood Genealogy (never published), who had worked on the family many years, and who had a knowledge of the family never equalled by any subsequent historian.

The account of the Banks family, on the other hand, appears to have been the work of the late Mrs. Schenck herself; and with all due respect to the memory of this estimable historian, her work as a genealogist was at times very erratic. It will be seen (page 351) that she presents a detailed abstract of the will of John Banks, including a legacy to his step-son Matthew Sherwood; and on turning to the Sherwood family, it will be seen that this Matthew Sherwood, the son of Thomas and Mary, did marry a Mary Fitch. In view of the many demonstrable lapses of this character which may be found in the genealogical section of Mrs. Schenck's book, it is perhaps fair to suggest that her eye was caught by this marriage of Matthew Sherwood to Mary Fitch and that in a moment of abstraction she wrote the name Fitch after the name of Matthew's mother, Mrs. Mary Sherwood-Banks.

However that may be, neither the present writer, in research in the original records covering several years while he was engaged in compiling "Families of Old Fairfield," nor the late Orrando Perry Dexter, who worked on the Fairfield records for seventeen years, and whose manuscripts are accessible at the Fairfield Historical Society, found the slightest evidence for identifying Mrs. Mary Sherwood-Banks as a Fitch. The two books referred to by Mr. Elisha S. Loomis are both based, so far as early American records are concerned, very largely on previous publications, hence the statements in them can hardly be accepted in lieu of contemporary record evidence except where the record evidence is directly cited.

New Haven, Conn.   DONALD LINES JACOBUS.

*Page 424, this volume.

THE LUCAS FAMILY.

[Communicated by J. R. LUCAS, Esq., of St. Paul, Minnesota.]

1. WILLIAM[1] LUCAS came from England; was one of the first settlers of Middletown, Connecticut, where he married, July 12, 1666, Hester Clark, who died April 15, 1690. He died in Middletown, April 29, 1690. They had:—

 2. i. WILLIAM, b. April 26, 1667; d. 1759.
 ii. JOHN, b. Oct. 14, 1669.
 iii. MARY, b. Dec. 5, 1672 ; m. Jno. Scovel; had issue.
 iv. SAMUEL, b. April 15, 1682.

2. WILLIAM[2] (William[1]), lived and died in Middletown; married, July, 1695, Elizabeth Rowley, of Windsor. He died in 1759. They had:—

 3. i. WILLIAM, b. 1703.—ii. EBENEZER.—iii. GIDEON.—iv. SAMUEL.—v. ELIZA-BETH.—vi. MARTHA.—vii. DEBORAH.—viii. HANNAH.

3. WILLIAM[3] (William,[2] William[1]), lived in Middletown, South Farms; married Mary Spellman, who died about 1735, aged 25 years. He then married (about 1707) Jerusha Bow, who died about 1750, aged 47 or 48 years. He then married widow Sarah Ward. He died in 1768, aged 65 years. He had, by his first wife, three children ; by his second, five ; and by his third, two, viz. :—

 4. i. WILLIAM, b. about 1729 ; d. in Simsbury, Conn.
 5. ii. RICHARD, b. Nov. 16, 1731 ; d. Oct. 1806.
 iii. MARY, b. about 1732 or 1733 ; m. Mr. Norton ; had issue.
 iv. GIDEON 1st, d. young.—v. GIDEON 2d.—vi. JERUSHA.—vii. ELIZABETH.—viii. RHODA 1st, d. young.—ix. RHODA 2d, m. Mr. Swain.
 6. x. SETH, m. Isabell.

4. WILLIAM[4] (William,[3] William,[2] William[1]), lived in Branford, Durham, and Simsbury, Conn.; married (about 1750 or 1760), his cousin Triphena Jones (her mother being a Lucas), who was born in 1729, and died in Lansing, co. Tompkins, N. Y., in 1826, aged 96 years. He died in Simsbury, Conn., aged about 55 years. Their children were all born in Branford. They had :—

 i. SAMUEL, b. 1754; m. Lucy Starr ; no issue; lived in Berkshire, N. Y. ; d. March 13, 1819.
 ii. TIMOTHY, d. in Revolutionary service on board privateer "Royally."
 7. iii. WILLIAM, b. April 11, 1760 ; d. Aug. 9, 1842.
 iv. JOEL, m. Betsey Wicks ; d. in Union, N. Y.
 v. OLIVER, m. Jonathan Chapin ; had issue ; d. Lansing, N. Y., a. 80.
 vi. POLLY, d. unmarried in Lansing, N. Y., a. over 80.

5. RICHARD[4] (William,[3] William,[2] William[1]), married, Dec. 26, 1758, Sarah Darrow, of Branford, who died Dec. 24, 1778, aged 39 years. He then married, Jan. 10, 1780, widow Boardman, of Middletown. He died October, 1806. He had by first wife eight children, and one by second wife, viz. :—

 i. EDMOND, b. Oct. 31, 1760.—ii. ASEHENT, (?) b. Sept. 22, 1762.—iii. AMA-ZIAH, b. July 20, 1764.—iv. SALLY, b. Feb. 29, 1767.—v. STEPHEN, b. April 9, 1770.—vi. LINDAY, b. March 10, 1772.—vii. LUCY, b. July 22, 1774 ; d. Nov. 15, 1792.—viii. RUFUS, b. Dec. 3, 1776.—ix. HULDAY, b. June 22, 1781.

6. SETH[4] (William,[3] William,[2] William[1]), married Isabell ———. They had :—

 i. SAMUEL.—ii. SETH.—iii. HARRY.—iv. WILLIAM.—v. ALUSA.—vi. RHODA.

7. WILLIAM⁵ (*William*,⁴ *William*,³ *William*,² *William¹*), was four years in the Revolutionary army; was wounded and a prisoner in the "Old Sugar House," in New-York, in the winter of 1780. He lived in Simsbury, Conn., also in Sandisfield, Mass., from whence he removed to Berkshire, co. Tioga, N. Y., thence to Madison county. He married, in 1794, Jane Brown, of Blandford, Mass., who was born Dec. 20, 1765, and died April 16, 1836, aged 70 years. He died Aug. 9, 1842, aged 82 years, and was buried beside his wife in New-Woodstock, co. Madison, N. Y. Their children were all born in Sandisfield, Mass. They had :—

    i.   CORINTHA, b. May 20, 1795 ; m. 1834, Duncan Lapham, of Painesville, Ohio ; had William and Samuel.
8. ii. WILLIAM,   b. Jan. 7, 1797; d. July 31, 1860.
    iii. SAMUEL 1st, b. May 8, 1799 ; d. March 12, 1803.
9. iv. ROBERT,   b. Oct. 25, 1800 ; d. July 23, 1847.
    v.   LUCY,   b. May 25, 1802 ; unmarried.
10. vi. SAMUEL 2d, b. May 11, 1804 : d. March 18, 1847.
    vii. ROXANA,   b. Aug. 28, 1806 ; m. Leverett Hamilton, of Madison Co., N. Y.; had Leverett L., Henry Homer, and Lorenzo L.
11. viii. LOVADER, b. Nov. 6, 1808 ; d. Jan. 28, 1867.
    ix. JANE, b. July 31, 1810 ; d. Jan. 7, 1811.

8. WILLIAM⁶ (*William*,⁵ *William*,⁴ *William*,³ *William*,² *William¹*), married, Jan. 6, 1830, in Saybrook, O., Nancy M. Baird, who was born in July, 1810, and died Aug. 29, 1843, in Saybrook, O. He died, same place, July 31, 1860, aged 64 years. They had :—

    i.   NANCY, b. June 19, 1831 ; d. March 8, 1837.
    ii. WILLIAM, b. Aug. 27, 1833.

9. ROBERT⁶ (*William*,⁵ *William*,⁴ *William*,³ *William*,² *William¹*), married, Oct. 3, 1830, in Ashtabula, O., Ann Crandall, who died in Palos, co. Cook, Ill., June 16, 1835. He then married, Feb. 3, 1837, widow Hannah F. Mott. He died in Palos, Ill., July 23, 1847. He had by first wife three children, and by second wife three, viz. :—

    i.   GEORGE HOMER, b. March 13, 1832.
    ii. CHARLES HENRY, b. Aug. 20, 1833 ; d. July 9, 1836.
    iii. JAMES ROBERT, b. Nov. 17, 1834.
    iv. ANN ELIZABETH, b. 24, 1838.
    v. LUCY SELINA,   b. Feb. 28, 1842.
    vi. HANNAH LOUISA, b. April 4, 1846.

10. SAMUEL⁶ (*William*,⁵ *William*,⁴ *William*,³ *William*,² *William¹*), lived in Smithfield, N. Y.; married in September, 1841, Julia A. Laird. He died March 18, 1847. They had :—

    i.   WARREN, b. Oct. 3, 1842.

11. LOVADER⁶ (*William*,⁵ *William*,⁴ *William*,³ *William*,² *William¹*), lived in Cazenovia, N. Y.; married, Jan. 29, 1840, Sarah L. Hamilton, who was born in Nelson, N. Y., in 1816, and died March 6, 1841. He married again, March 20, 1842, widow Eliza Ann Warner. He died Jan. 28, 1867, aged 58 years. He had, by his second wife :—

    i.   FRANK ELIEZER, b. Jan. 21, 1843 ; d. July 10, 1847.
    ii. HENRY LOVADER, b. Oct. 12, 1845.
    iii. SARAH LOUISA, b. Oct. 14, 1847 ; d. March 28, 1862.
    iv. EMMA ROXANA, b. Nov. 28, 1849.
    v. WILLIAM FRANK, b. Aug. 22, 1853.

Information relating to any persons bearing the name of Lucas will be thankfully received by the compiler of this article.

WILLIAM LUDDINGTON OF MALDEN, MASS., AND EAST HAVEN, CONN., AND HIS DESCENDANTS.

By James Shepard, Esq., of New Britain, Conn.

1. William[1] Luddington, born about 1607, of Malden, Mass., 1640 to 1660, by wife Ellen, born in 1619, was the first progenitor of the name in this country. Before him came, in 1635, Christian Luddington, a girl of eighteen.

Much of interest concerning William[1] Luddington is to be found in Lewis S. Patrick's leaflet, entitled " The Luddington Family, the First of the Name in America," Marinette, Wis., 1886.

He is supposed to have come to this country about 1640, settling in that part of Charlestown which afterwards became Malden, and later removing to New Haven.

He died in 1661, and, according to Pope's " Pioneers of Massachusetts," John Wayte (Waite) petitioned for administration in Middlesex Co., Oct. 1, 1661; and the inventory was filed by James Barrat, as administrator, Apr. 1, 1662. What interest, if any, either of these parties had in the estate is not known. His estate was also probated at New Haven, the inventory of Mar. 3, 1662-3, relating thereto, being found in Hoadly's New Haven Colony Records, vol. 2, p. 485.

In addition to the Colony record, we find the following:

" At a court held at New Haven, March 3, 1662-3." — " An inventory of ye estate of Willm. Luddington deceased was presented amounting to . . . . . . taken ye . . . the widow upon oath attested to ye fulness of it to the best of her knowledge. John Cooper & Mathew Moulthrop upon oath attested that the aprizamt was just to the best of their light. The widow being asked if her husband made noe will answered yt she knew of none for she was not home when he died. Mathew Moulthrop testified that he made none. The matter respecting ye childrens portions was deferred till next court & the . . . widow with him yt shee was to marry & all her children above fourteen years of age was ordered then to appear & the court would order the estate & consider how the childrens portion shall be " [provided]. (Proprietors' Records, vol. 3, p. 15.)

The one " yt she was to marry " was John Rose, as is shown by the New Haven records of births, etc., vol. 1, p. 29, which records the marriage of John Rose and Widow Luddington, in 1663. That this marriage took place between March 3 and May 5, 1663, is shown by the following:

March 3, 1662-3, " John Tuttle doth alineate for ever to Widdow Luddington all his part of top land meadow about Stony river," etc.

May 5, 1663, " John Rose who married widdow Luddington was called to know wt security he would give for ye childrens portions yt was not yet of age to receive ym. But most of ye children that should have appeared at Court being not well & soe not fit to come the matter was respited till another time & he told yt he must give bond when called thereto." (Proprietors' Records, vol. 3, pp. 15, 19.)

Savage, in his " Dictionary," vol. 3, says that William Luddington's " widow m. George Rose," but in the corrections at the end of vol. 4, changes the name to John. Dodd's "East-Haven Register," and Dr. Haven's MS. history of East Haven, contain the error "George" instead of John.

Dodd's "Register" makes no mention of the first William Luddington until 1662, when it speaks of his death; and we have been unable to find any record of him at New Haven of an earlier date than 1662. The inventory, however, shows that he owned a house and land there at the time of his decease; and at some time, one hundred acres of land was set out to him, as appears by a deed from his son William to Thomas Robinson, July 25, 1723, of a " part of that tract of land set out to my father William Luddington which tract contains one hundred acres." (New Haven Land Records, vol. 6, p. 305.) The name of William Luddington's wife is given as Ellen, by Savage and Wyman; but in Corey's "History of Malden, Mass.," p. 146, in a petition of Malden women for the retension of the Rev. Mr. Matthews, dated Oct. 28, 1651, it appears as Hellen.

William Luddington, age 50, his son Thomas, age 20, and John, age 17, deposed Oct. 29, 1657. William, age 51, deposed again Feb. 5, 1659; and his wife Ellen, age 40, deposed the next day. James Barret and William Luddington brought suit for slander, Mar. 27, 1660; and Ellen Luddington, relict of William, and Thomas his heir, gave a release to James Barret, administrator of William's estate, May 25, 1662. (Mr. Patrick's notes, from Middlesex County files.)

The iron works, where William Luddington died, were on the river that divides East Haven from Branford, and the records show that his real estate was in that vicinity, on that side of the river, which was then a part of New Haven. These iron works, established in 1655, were the first in Connecticut, and were continued for about twenty-five years. The furnace was supplied with bog ore from North Haven. (Barber's "Hist. Coll. of Conn.," p. 204.) All servants, workmen and others employed there were under the jurisdiction of New Haven. (Proprietors' Records, vol. 2, p. 243.) Shepard's Geological Survey of Connecticut, p. 28, in speaking of beds of bog ore formerly worked until exhausted, says: "This was the case in North Haven and Branford and some other towns bordering the sound." That their supply of ore was cut off, was the probable cause of stopping the works, about 1680.

The only records found of Ellen (Luddington) Rose after 1663 are as follows:

New Haven, Dec. 14, 1665, "An inventory of the Estate of Wm. Shepheard deceased taken the 7th of December . . . and upon oath attested by the wife of John Rose."

New Haven, Feb. 5, 1666, "Edward Preston Attornie on the behalfe of John Hathaway of Trenton, as administrator to ye estate of Wm. Shepheard deceased . . . Patrick Moran and John Rose called to give account of ye sd estate according to Inventory (onely yt which was payd to John Rose for his wives attendance on ye sd Shepheard wⁿ he was sick) and engaged to give bond," etc. (Proprietors' Records, vol. 3, pp. 77, 98.)

What interest, if any, Patrick Moran and John Rose, or their wives, had in the estate of William Shepard, and why they took possession of the said estate, is not known; but the facts indicate relationship of some kind, as yet not proved. This John Rose we suppose to have been the son (born in 1619) of Robert Rose, who came in the *Francis* in 1634; and if so, Widow Luddington was his second wife; and she must have died before

1670, when this John Rose married his third wife, widow Phebe Potter. Children :

 2. i. THOMAS,[2] b. 1637; removed to Newark, N. J.
  ii. JOHN, b. 1640; supposed to have been one of the brothers referred to in the settlement of his brother Henry's estate as living in 1676. It is thought that all the early references to John Luddington in Dodd's "East-Haven Register" relate to his nephew John,[3] the son of Thomas.[2] The only record of John[2] in New Haven, aside from that of his brother Henry's estate, is Dec. 12, 1664, when John and Thomas Luddington testified in Town Court and Thomas called John "his brother." (Proprietors' Records, vol. 3, p. 4.) Mr. Patrick thinks John removed to Vermont.
  iii. MARY, b. Feb. 6, 1642–3; supposed to have been one of the sisters referred to as living in 1676.
  iv. HENRY, d. 1676. Inventory of the estate of "Henry Luddington late of N. haven slayne in ye warre taken & apprised by Mathew Moulthrop & John Potter Janry. 3, 1676." "Upon exhibiting of ye above sd inventory & acco[t] for settlement & distribution this court settles ye administration upon Wm. Luddington onely brother p[e] sent to ye deceased & for the distribution (there being two brothers & sisters besides the sd William). This court doe order four pounds thirteen shillings four pence a piece to ye sd four & the rest of the estate to W[m] Luddington for his part & trouble & paynes about it. As attests James Bishop Clerk." (New Haven Probate Records, vol. 1, part 1, p. 174.)
  v. HANNAH; supposed to have been one of the sisters referred to as living in 1676.
 3. vi. WILLIAM, b. about 1655; d. Feb. 1737; m. (1) Martha Rose; m. (2) June, 1690, Mercy Whitehead.
  vii. MATTHEW, b. Dec. 16, 1657; d. Jan. 12, 1657–8.

2. THOMAS[2] LUDDINGTON (*William*[1]) born in 1637, removed to Newark, N. J., in 1666. On Apr. 16, 1689, he sold ten and a half acres of land, with old house and barn thereon, at the New Haven Iron Works, to John Thompson, at which time he described himself as of "Newark, New Jersey, Husbandman." (New Haven Land Records, vol. 1, p. 452.) The following, concerning his life at Newark, is from a Luddington MS., compiled by Mr. Patrick.

 At a town meeting May 13, 1672, Martin Tichenor and Thos. Luddington each had allowed them one and a half acres of land for staying on their place the first summer, when most of the settlers returned to Connecticut for the winter. In 1667, he was one of the persons appointed to make a rate of every man's estate. Thomas Luddington's estate at that time was put down at £122, and £81 after the deduction had been made. On Feb. 6, 1667, he was granted lot No. 60, probably three acres ; and more land was granted to him in 1669, '70 and '73. He was the surveyor of the "land and swamp" in 1680 ; surveyor of highways in 1681 ; and also committee in laying out the third division of land, and other lands in 1682, '83 and '84. On May 1, 1692, he sold three and a half acres of his home lot to Thomas Brown. After the town meeting in Aug., 1672, all trace of him is lost.

 One Thomas Luddington was at Hanover, N. J., in 1721. In 1731, a Thomas Luddington and his wife Sarah sold salt meadow, but it is not probable that this was the Thomas who was born in 1637.

 Children :

 4. i. JOHN,[3] m. Rebecca Clark.
  ii., etc. [Perhaps Thomas of Hanover, N. J., and others.]

3. WILLIAM[2] LUDDINGTON (*William*[1]), born about 1655, died Feb., 1737. He married first, Martha, daughter of John[2] Rose (Robert[1]), and second, by the Rev. Samuel Russell, June, 1690, Mercy, daughter of John and Martha (Bradfield) Whitehead. (Branford Church Records.) The parentage of his first wife is proven by the will of John Rose of New Haven, which mentions "wife phebe" and "daughter Martha Luddington," dated April 18, 1683. (New Haven Probate Records, vol. 1, part 1, p. 190.) For the parentage of his second wife, see REGISTER, *ante*, vol. 55, page 184. On Mar. 26, 1683, William Luddington had three persons in his family, estate £52, and land 24½ acres. In 1702, he had eleven persons in his family, estate £54, and land 27 acres. In the land division of 1709 he was rated at 8 persons, estate £70, and land 11½ acres. (Dodd's East-Haven Register, pp. 34, 38, 46.)

Records show that he must have been a man of intelligence and ability, and that he had the confidence of the parish in which he lived.

Dodd's "Register" puts the age of William[2] Luddington as 51, at the time of his death in 1737, which is evidently a mistake, perhaps a misprint for 81. William Luddington was appointed administrator of his brother Henry's estate in 1676, and must have been 21 at that time, therefore born as early as 1655.

His estate was probated Feb. 7, 1736-7, and the distribution to the several parties named in the will was made July 4, 1737, and is recorded in New Haven Probate Records, vol. 6, p. 222. The widow's thirds appear to have been insufficient for her support, as is shown by a deed from her to Gideon Potter of New Haven, dated Oct. 19, 1739, in which she tells that "having by the providence of God been brought unto needy circumstances yt by many witnesses doth and may approve." (New Haven Land Records, vol. 11, p. 86.) Widow Mercy Luddington died Nov. 23, 1743, aged 75. (Dodd's East-Haven Register, p. 169.) Her will, made Jan. 7, 1742-3, was presented Dec. 5, 1743, when James Way, her son-in-law, was appointed executor. The will names son Eliphalet; grandchildren, viz.: John Dawson's children, Benjamin Mallory's children; granddaughter Elizabeth Goodsell; grandchildren, viz.: John Luddington's children, Jude Luddington and Elizabeth Rose; granddaughter Mary Mallory; and daughter Dorcas Way. (New Haven Probate Records, vol. 6, p. 528.) An agreement was made Feb. 6, 1743-4, between James Way, executor, and Eliphalet Luddington whereby he took certain lands and paid all debts and legacies (New Haven Probate Records, vol. 6, p. 543); after which there was land to the amount of £20. 14. 2. set to each child or their heirs, with the exception of the heirs of John, the division being made Sept. 3, 1744 (*ibid*, vol. 6, p. 565). Whether John's heirs were in fact omitted, or whether it was only an omission in copying, does not appear. The Elizabeth Goodsell named in connection with the estate of Mercy Luddington is the Elizabeth Penfield named in the will and distribution of William Luddington's estate.

Children by first wife:

5. i.   HENRY,[3] b. 1679; d. 1727; m. Sarah Collins.
6. ii. ELEANOR, m. May 13, 1714, Nathaniel Baley of Guilford, Conn.

7. iii. WILLIAM, b. Sept. 25, 1686; m. Feb. 28, 1710–11, Anna Hodge.
   Children by second wife:
8. iv. MERCY, b. May 31, 1691; m. Ebenezer Deans of Norwich, Conn.
9. v. MARY, b. May 31, 1691; d. Oct. 11, 1742, aged 52; m. in 1715, John Dawson.
10. vi. HANNAH, b. Mar. 13, 1693; d. June 4, 1719, aged 27; m. Isaac Penfield.
11. vii. JOHN, b. Jan. 31, 1694; d. Oct. 30, 1726; m. Elizabeth Potter.
12. viii. ELIPHALET, b. Apr. 28, 1697; d. Jan. 26, 1761; m. Abigail Collins.
    ix. ELIZABETH, b. 1699; d. July 28, 1707, aged 8.
13. x. DOROTHY, b. July 16, 1702; d. Sept. 19, 1742; m. Benjamin Mallory.
14. xi. DORCAS, b. July 16, 1704; m. in 1722, James Way.

4. JOHN[3] LUDDINGTON (*Thomas,*[2] *William*[1]) who died before July 8, 1731, married, in 1703, Rebecca Clark. (New Haven County Court Records, vol. 2, p. 125.) He remained in New Haven after his father removed to Newark, N. J., and was located in East Haven at "Bridge swamp," where his son James succeeded him. In 1683, he had only one person in his family, and four acres of land; and in 1702, he was listed as one person, with two acres. (Dodd's East-Haven Register, pp. 18, 60, 34, 38.) On July 8, 1731, "Rebecca Luddington Relict and Widow of John Luddington, late of East Haven decd.," and James Luddington, each of East Haven, deeded land to Gideon Potter "that descends to us the said Luddingtons by the Decd John Luddington." (New Haven Land Records, vol. 9, p. 68.) On Apr. 6, 1737, the widow deeded land to her "son in law Edward Canodise." (New Haven Land Records, vol. 10, p. 353.)
   Children:
   i. JAMES,[4] b. Aug. 8, 1703; d. in the French and Indian War, Sept. 3, 1756; m. Jan. 2, 1735, Eleanor, dau. of Ebenezer Deanes. [See No. 8.] His name appears in Waterbury tax lists for 1743 and 1744, and the birth of one child is recorded there. He was a soldier in the French and Indian War, from Apr. 23, 1755, until his death Sept. 3, 1756. (Conn. Hist. Society Collections, vol. ix., pp. 27 and 127.) Administration on his estate was granted to his widow Eleanor, the first Monday in Mar., 1757. The distribution was made Mar. 30, 1757, to widow Eleanor, to only son Lemuel, Elizabeth, second daughter Hannah, and Eunice. (New Haven Probate Records, vol. ix., pp. 40 and 48.) Children: 1. *Elizabeth,*[5] b. Apr. 23, 1737; m. June 18, 1760, Zachariah Deanes, b. Sept. 28, 1737, according to Prof. F. B. Dains of Chicago, Ill., and had six children whose names and baptisms are given in Windham Church Records. 2. *David,* b. Mar. 19, 1739; was not living when his father's estate was probated in 1757. 3. *Hannah,* b. Mar. 19, 1744; called *Anna* in Hist. of Waterbury, Appendix, p. 86. 4. *Eunice,* b. May 11, 1751. 5. *Lemuel,* b. 1748; m. Hopestill ——, and had four sons and two daughters (Patrick's MS.).
   ii. REBECKAH.
   iii. ABIGAIL, b. Aug. 28, 1707; d. Oct. 9, 1742; m. July 19, 1736, Edward Canodise.
   iv. ELIZABETH, b. Sept. 1710; d. Dec. 13, 1713.

5. HENRY[3] LUDDINGTON (*William,*[2] *William*[1]) married, Aug. 20, 1700, Sarah, daughter of William Collins. According to Dodd, he was a carpenter. On Feb. 25, 1755, William Luddington of Branford (son of Henry[3]), cordwainer, deeds "right that falls to me by my Hon[rd] Mother Sarah Collins Ludinton of New Haven decd, Daughter of William Collins decd." (New Haven Land Records,

432

vol. 18, p. 562.) In the land division of Sept. 18, 1705, he was rated at £25 estate, with 4 persons in family, and received 10 acres of land. (New Haven Proprietors' Records, copy vol. 4, p. 158.) Administration on his estate was granted July 3, 1727, to " Sarah Luddington Relict and Widow of the Decd." Nathaniel, Moses, and Aaron Luddington, his three minor sons, " made choice of their ――――― for their guardian." (New Haven Probate Records, vol. 5, p. 379.) The inventory, taken Aug. 7, 1727, with an addition thereto Apr. 10, 1728, amounted to £201. 18s. Sarah Luddington chose her mother as guardian, June 27, 1728 ; Henry did the same, May 4, 1730; and Thomas the same, July 5, 1731. (New Haven Probate Records, vol. 5, pp. 392, 432, 450 ; vol. 6, pp. 5, 6.)

Children, the names and births of the first two from New Haven records, the rest from Dodd:

i. DANIEL,[4] b. June 21, 1701; m. (1) Hannah, dau. of John Payne, Sr., of New Haven by wife Mary (New Haven Land Records, vol. 8, p. 269; vol. 18, p. 487; and vol. 21, p. 372), who was born Nov. 3, 1708, and d. May 17, 1740; and m. (2) Oct. 14, 1741, Susanna Clark of Wallingford, Conn., to which place he afterwards removed. She was probably dau. of Ebenezer and Elizabeth (Lothrop) Clark, b. Sept. 3, 1717 (Wallingford Records). Children by first wife : 1. Daniel,[5] b. Feb. 22, 1726-7; d. Feb. 8, 1737, aged 9. 2. Ezra, b. Dec. 21, 1728; served in the French and Indian War, from Apr. 23 to Aug. 31, 1755. (Conn. Hist. Society Collections, vol. ix., p. 27.) 3. Solomon, b. Nov. 3, 1732; was living at South Hampton, Pa., in 1768. (New Haven Land Records, vol. 30, p. 491.) 4. Hannah, b. Nov. 4, 1734. Children by second wife : 5. Phebe, b. Nov. 19, 1742. 6. Daniel, b. May 9, 1744; m. Apr. 16, 1773, Mabel Lee. (Farmington Records.) 7. Titus, b. Sept. 13, 1747. 8. Collins, d. young. 9. Collins, b. about 1749; admitted to church in New Britain, Conn., Dec. 31, 1780; m. Feb. 9, 1775, Sarah, dau. of Elijah Smith, Sr., and his wife Sarah (Grimes) ; removed to Oswego, N. Y.; was in the war of the Revolution; d. in 1821, at Candor, N. Y.; five children. (Andrews's Ecclesiastical Hist., First Church of New Britain, Conn., p. 185.) 10. John, d. young. 11. John.

ii. WILLIAM, b. Sept. 6, 1702; m. (1) Nov. 5, 1730, Mary Knowles of Branford, Conn., where he resided. She d. Apr. 16, 1759; and he m. (2) Apr. 17, 1760, Mary Wilkinson of Branford. His family record is found at Branford. Children : 1. Submit,[5] b. Feb. 10, 1732-3; m. June 28, 1754, Stephen Johnson of Branford. 2. Mary, b. May 20, 1736. 3. Henry, b. May 25, 1739; m. May 12, 1760, Abigail Luddington, according to Mr. Patrick's MS., but Dodd calls her " Sarah "; had twelve children; was in the French and Indian War, from April 10, 1756, to Aug. 23, 1757, when he deserted. (Conn. Hist. Society Collections, vol. ix., pp. 144, 225.) 4. Lydia, b. July 25, 1741; m. Aug. 28, 1761, William Buckley of Branford (Branford Records), but Dodd says " Aaron." 5. Samuel, b. Apr. 30, 1744. 6. Rebeckah, b. May 10, 1747. 7. Anne, b. June 20, 1750. 8. Stephen, b. Oct. 18, 1753. " On Monday night after ye 20th of May Last [1754] part of dwelling house of William Luddington of Branford . . . was burnt with two of his children and all his household goods, viz, Rebecca age 7 years Anne Aged 4 years." (Branford Records.)

iii. SARAH, b. Feb. 1703 ; d. Mar. 27, 1709.

iv. DINAH, b. Jan. 16, 1704; m. Oct. 5, 1725, Isaac Thorpe.

v. LYDIA, b. Feb. 9, 1707; m. Dec. 5, 1732, Moses Thorpe. Isaac Thorpe and Dinah his wife, and Moses Thorpe and Lydia his wife, all of New Haven, deeded, Apr. 28, 1755, to Nathaniel Ludinton of East Haven, land that " fell to us being heirs to the Estate of Aaron Luddington of sd East Haven decd." (New Haven Land Records, vol. 19, p. 313.)

vi. NATHANIEL, b. Apr. 2, 1708; m. (1) Mary Chidsey, who d. May 7, 1758, in her 67th year (gravestone at East Haven); and m. (2) widow Eunice Smith, dau. of Samuel and Mary (Heminway) Russell. (Dodd's East-Haven Register, p. 133; New Haven Land Records, vol. 30, p. 13; and Tuttle Family, p. 173.) Child by first wife: 1. *Lucy,*[5] m. Russell Grannis. Children by second wife: 2. *Eunice*, m. Matthew Rowe. 3. *Nathaniel*. 4. *Mary*.

vii. MOSES, b. Oct. 8, 1709; m. Eunice, dau. of John and Mary (Foot) Chidsey. (Dodd's East-Haven Register, p. 118.) His brother Daniel, on Mar. 29, 1731-2, deeded him all right "in certain land which was the home lott and Dwelling of my Honoured ffather Henry Luddington, dec." (New Haven Land Records, vol. 9, p. 150.)

viii. AARON, b. June 6, 1710; d. at sea, before Apr. 28, 1755. (New Haven Land Records, vol. 19, p. 313.)

ix. ELISHA, b. Aug. 1712; d. Mar. 12, 1715.

x. ELISHA, b. Jan. 7, 1716; living at Phillepse Precinct, in Dutchess County, N. Y., Feb. 24, 1755. (New Haven Land Records, vol. 19, p. 71.) His name appears in the tax list of that county, 1748. His dau. *Abigail*[6] m. Henry[5] Luddington. (Patrick's MS.)

xi. SARAH, b. Mar. 6, 1714; living at New Haven, unmarried, Nov. 17, 1745. (New Haven Land Records, vol. 11, p. 220.) Dodd says she m. Daniel Mead.

xii. THOMAS, b. 1718; drowned May 30, 1743.

6. ELEANOR[3] LUDDINGTON (*William,*[2] *William*[1]) married, May 13, 1714, Nathaniel, son of John and Mary (Goodrich) Bailey of Guilford. He was born in 1682, and died Dec. 17, 1741, age 59. She died May 31, 1748. His family record is found at Guilford, where he and his wife were living Aug. 29, 1738, when they deeded land to their son-in-law Jonathan Blakeslee of Guilford, which was "our Honoured ffarthers William Luddington Deceased." (New Haven Land Records, vol. 11, p. 2.) Jan. 18, 1743-4, she was "Relict widdow of Nathaniel Baly late of Guilford," when she deeded land from her father's estate to her "son-in-law Cornelius Dowde of sd Guilford." (New Haven Land Records, vol. 12, p. 277.) The estate of Nathaniel Bayley was distributed Dec. 29, 1741, to Dorothy Blakesley, wife of Jonathan Blakesley, Mary Lee, wife of Joseph Lee, Jr., Hitty Dowde, wife of Cornelius Dowde, Hannah Bayley, and Zerviah Bayley. (Guilford Probate Records, vol. 4, p. 116.)

Children:

i. MARY BAILEY, b. 1715; m. Joseph Lee, Jr.

ii. DOROTHY BAILEY, b. Mar. 5, 1717; m. Mar. 21, 1733-4, Jonathan, son of Ebenezer Blakesley, Jr., of New Haven. (See REGISTER, *ante*, vol. 56, p. 285.)

iii. MEHITABLE BAILEY, b. Feb. 10, 1720; m. Cornelius Dowde.

iv. HANNAH BAILEY, b. May 4, 1722.

v. ZERVIAH BAILEY, b. Aug. 18, 1725.

7. WILLIAM[3] LUDDINGTON (*William,*[2] *William*[1]), born Sept. 25, 1686, married, Feb. 28, 1710-11, Anna Hodge. He removed to Waterbury, Conn., before Nov. 28, 1744, when he sold land from his father's estate. (New Haven Land Records, vol. 12, pp. 307, 393.) On Dec. 11, 1723, he subscribed to an agreement to live in Waterbury four years and build a house there; and in 1729 he was among the new inhabitants, with a wife and four children. He bought land in the north part of the town in 1738, and Oct. 8, 1740, was one of the signers, of Northbury (now Plymouth), of a petition

to the General Assembly against building a new meeting house " at present," and offering to give a building for public worship. (New Hist. of Waterbury, vol. 1, pp. 295, 300, 363, 663.) His name, according to Miss K. A. Prichard, appears in the Waterbury tax lists for 1739-41-42-44-46, and 48 to 54, inclusive.

Children :

    i. MATTHEW⁴, b. Apr. 23, 1712; d. about 1752; m. Lydia Smith, who d. Feb. 6, 1798, aged 82. His name was in the Waterbury tax list for 1739, and 1751. Children: 1. *Joseph*,⁵ m. Mercy, widow of Jeremiah Peck, Jr. (History of Waterbury, Appendix, p. 86.) 2. *Mabel*, m. Isaac Mallory. 3. *Timothy*. His mother was appointed his guardian the first Monday in Oct., 1752. (New Haven Probate Records, vol. 8, p. 184.) He was in the French and Indian War from Mar. 31 to Nov. 24, 1757, when he deserted. (Conn. Hist. Society Collections, vol. ix, p. 172. He was killed in battle at East Haven Heights, during the Revolutionary war. (Patrick's MS.) 4. *Samuel*, m. in 1777, Desire Barnes. (Tuttle Family, p. 633.) His mother was appointed his guardian, the first Monday in June, 1755. (New Haven Probate Records, vol. 8, p. 448.)

   ii. RUTH, b. June 7, 1713 : m. in 1735, Jonathan, b. Jan. 7, 1712, son of Henry and Mary (Frost) Cook. (Branford, Conn., Records.)

  iii. NAOMI, b. Dec. 15, 1716; m. (1) in 1740, Josiah Tuttle; and m. (2) in 1751, Gideon Allin. (Hist. of Waterbury, Appendix, p. 86.)

  iv. ELIZABETH, b. Feb. 9, 1720; m. Apr. 5, 1755, William Francher. (Hist. of Waterbury, Appendix, p. 49.)

   v. ABRAHAM, b. Nov. 30, 1721; d. Oct. 20, 1758; m. July 23, 1747, Catharine, dau. of Ebenezer Elwell; five children. (Hist. of Waterbury, Appendix, p. 86.)

  vi. SAMUEL, b. Aug. 10, 1723; served in the French and Indian War, in 1756. (Conn. Hist. Society Collections, vol. ix, p. 212.)

  vii. JOSEPH, b. Apr. 3, 1726.

8. MERCY³ LUDDINGTON *(William,² William¹)*, born May 31, 1691, married, Mar. 17, 1706-7, Ebenezer Deanes of Norwich, Conn. He was son of Abraham Dains, the name being variously spelled. Ebenezer and his wife Mercy were living at New Haven, May 2, 1739, when they sold land from their father's estate ; and at Scotland, Windham Co., Conn., when they sold more land, Oct. 11, 1744. (New Haven Land Records, vol. 11, p. 59 ; vol. 12, p. 297.) He was a member of the church at Hampton, Conn., Dec. 28, 1729; and Ebenezer and Mercy Dean were among the original members of the church at Scotland, at its organization in 1735. The parentage of Ebenezer, the date of his marriage, and the date of birth of their first child, is from a private letter of Prof. F. B. Dains to Mr. Patrick. The other children are according to Weaver's MS.

Children :

    i. ELINOR DEANES, b. Feb. 4, 1709-10; m. Jan. 2, 1734-5, James Luddington, son of John, No. 4.

   ii. ZURVIAH DEANES, b. Mar. 31, 1721.

  iii. HANNAH DEANES, b. Aug. 9, 1722; d. Feb. 18, 1746-7.

  iv. JOHN DEANES, b. June 29, 1724; m. Jan. 22, 1745-6, Rachel Bond; six children.

9. MARY³ LUDDINGTON *(William,² William¹)*, born May 31, 1691, married, in 1715, John, born in 1677, son of Robert Dawson, a farmer of Foxen, East Haven, Conn. He died Aug. 28, 1732; and she died Oct. 11, 1742, aged 52. She was his second wife, his first wife having been Sarah Chedsey, born Dec. 8, 1689, died May 22, 1709. (Descendants of Robert Dawson, p. 14.) John and Mary Dawson were living at East Haven, Conn., June 25, 1737. (New Haven Land Records, vol. 10, p. 366.) Dodd's East-Haven Register erroneously gives Mrs. Dawson's name as Mercy, although he calls it Mary in her death record.

Children (from Dawson Family) :

i. TIMOTHY DAWSON, b. Apr. 27, 1716; d. May 15, 1740. Margaret Dawson, who m. Nov. 6, 1759, Richard Darrow, is supposed to have been his widow.
ii. ROBERT DAWSON, b. Mar. 2, 1718, d. Jan. 26, 1799; m. (1) Thankful, widow of William Grannis, who d. June 29, 1787; and m. (2) Dec. 6, 1787, Mary Russell; six children.
iii. ANNA DAWSON, b. 1720; d. young.
iv. TITUS DAWSON, b. 1722; d. Sept. 28, 1742.
v. JOHN DAWSON, m. Mary Moulthrop; removed to Southington, Conn., about 1762; d. at New Hartford, Conn., May 19, 1787; six children.

10. HANNAH³ LUDDINGTON (*William,² William¹*), born Mar. 13, 1693, died June 4, 1719, age 37, married Isaac, son of Samuel and Mary (Frisbie) Penfield. He was living at New Haven, Feb. 22, 1721–2, when William Luddington deeded land to his "son Isaac Penfield." (New Haven Land Records, vol. 8, p. 418.) He died Oct. 22, 1754, age 70. Their daughter Elizabeth received a full share of William Luddington's estate, in 1737 ; and a share of the widow's thirds, in 1744, as Elizabeth Gudsel.

Child :

i. ELIZABETH PENFIELD, b, 1715; m. (1) Aug. 31, 1737, Isaac Godsell; m. (2) Caleb Chedsey, Jr.; d. Jan. 8, 1767, aged 52; eleven children, on record at New Haven.

11. JOHN³ LUDDINGTON (*William,² William¹*), born Jan. 31, 1694, died Oct. 30, 1726, married, before Apr. 10, 1722, Elizabeth, born Sept. 24, 1697 (Patrick's MS.), daughter of John and Elizabeth (Holt) Potter of East Haven. (New Haven Land Records, vol. 6, p. 47.) After his death, she married second, Oct. 2, 1734, Thomas Wheadon of Branford (New Haven Marriages; and Probate Records, vol. 6, p. 354), and died Sept. 3, 1746. Administration on the estate of "John Luddington Late of New Haven Decd.," was granted to "Elizabeth Luddington Widdow & Relict of said decd.," Jan. 2, 1726-7. The inventory, Aug. 7, 1727, amounted to £202. 3. 6. Divison was made Nov. 6, 1727, to the widow, to John, Elizabeth, and Jude. (New Haven Probate Records, vol. 5, pp. 336, 386, 397.) John chose Samuel Potter, Jr., May 5, 1735, for his guardian; Elizabeth chose Thomas Robinson, Mar. 10, 1735-6; and Jude chose Gideon Potter, Sept. 1, 1740. (New Haven Probate Records, vol. 6, pp. 166, 181, 313).

Children :

i. ELIZABETH⁴, m. Mar. 15, 1739, John Rose of Branford, where she was living in 1759. (Branford Land Records, vol. 8, p. 66.)
ii. JOHN, b. June 26, 1723. Dodd says he d. May 30, 1743, aged 20. His will, dated Oct. 4, 1743, probated the first Monday in Dec., 1757, named his brother Jude, and sisters Mary Wheadon and Elizabeth Rose. His uncle Gideon Potter was executor. (New

Haven Probate Records, vol. 8, p. 314.) The "sister Mary Wheadon" does not appear in the probate of his father's estate. She may have been dau. of his step-father, Thomas Wheadon.

iii. JUDE, b. July 23, 1725; m. (1) Martha Page; m. (2) widow Mary (Wade) Frisbie. (Patrick's MS.) He was living at Southington, Conn., Nov. 12, 1748. (New Haven Land Records, vol. 13, p. 479.) In deeds, he was called of Branford, in 1757 and 1761. (Branford Land Records, vol. 8, pp. 243, 151.) He served in the French and Indian War, in 1757. (Conn. Hist. Society Collections, vol. ix, p. 225. Children (from Patrick's MS.) by first wife: 1. *John*[5], b. 1749; d. Sept. 10, 1841, aged 92; m. (1) Sarah Palmer; m. (2) May 7, 1795, Jane Ely. 2. *Daniel*, m. Naomi Searl of Southampton, Mass. 3. *Martha*, m. Noah Stone. Children by second wife: 4. *Jude*, m. Huldah Carrier, of Colchester, Conn. 5. *Elizabeth*, b. Mar. 1763; m. Elijah Williams. 6. *Aseneath*, b. 1765; m. Asa Miller of West Springfield, Mass.; d. Nov. 6, 1845. 7. *Lucinda*, b. 1770; d. Dec. 31, 1840; m. in 1799, Nathan Stevens of Wilbraham, Mass.

12. ELIPHALET[8] LUDDINGTON (*William*,[2] *William*[1]), born Apr. 28, 1697, died Jan. 26, 1761, according to gravestone at East Haven (Dodd says, born June 1, 1697), married Aug. 20, 1720, Abigail, daughter of David and Abigail (Thompson) Collins, who was born Sept. 14, 1700. (Patrick's MS.) She died Dec. 12, 1790, aged 90. His will was probated the first Monday of Feb., 1761, by Abigail Luddington and Nathaniel Luddington, executors. The inventory, dated the first Monday in Mar., 1761, amounted to £45. 1. 8. It included his "cutlas Sword and belt." Joseph Grannis of New Haven, in right of his wife Olive, appealed from the decision approving the will. Amos Frisbie and Mary his wife, of Woodbury, Litchfield County, also appealed. Division of the estate, the first Monday in Apr., 1762, was to the widow Abigail Luddington, to Jesse, Isaac, Amos, and Hannah Luddington, to Abigail Barnes, Alline (Olive) Grannis, Mary Frisbie, and granddaughter Anne Luddington. (New Haven Probate Records, vol. 9, pp. 465, 467, 557, 653, 678).

Children:

i. JESSE[4], b. 1722; d. Feb. 8, 1799; m. in 1749, Mehitable, b. Apr. 17, 1726, dau. of John and Martha (Tuttle) Smith; seven children. (Tuttle Family, p. 36.)

ii. ISAAC, m. Mary, dau. of Samuel and Lydia Goodsell. Children: 1. *Appeline*[5]. 2. *Mary*, m. (1) Isaac Grannis, Jr.; m. (2) Seth Barnes. 3. *Martha*, m. Jared Grannis. 4. *Isaac*. 5. *Asa*. 6. *Sarah*, m. Joseph Howd. 7. *Anna*, m. Jacob Hitchcock. 8. *Jared*, m. in 1798, Sarah Goodsell. 9. *Ame*.

iii. AMOS, m. June 7, 1757, Mercy Thomson. Adm. on his estate granted to his widow Mercy, the first Monday of Sept., 1766. Inventory £163. 2. 0. Distribution to the widow and two daughters, whose names are not given. (New Haven Probate Records, vol. 10, pp. 353, 355, 418.) Served in the French and Indian War, from Sept. 11 to Dec. 9, 1755. (Conn. Hist. Society Collections, vol. ix, p. 31.) Children: 1. *Sibyl*,[5] m. Joel Dawson. 2. *Ame*.

iv. ASA, d. in the French and Indian War, in which he served from Aug. 8 to 24, 1757. (Conn. Hist. Society Collections, vol. ix, p. 231.)

v. MARY, m. Amos Frisbie.

vi. OLIVE, m. Joseph, son of Thomas and Mehitable (Thompson) Grannis; d. of small pox, Mar. 30, 1788.

vii. AME, d. young.

viii. HANNAH, d. young.

ix. ABIGAIL, m. Enos Barnes; removed to Litchfield, Conn., where she d. June 8, 1768; five children. He d. Mar. 2, 1799, age 75. (Woodruff's Litchfield Register, p. 15.)

x. ELAM, d. before Jan. 20, 1761, the date of his father's will; m. May 5, 1748, Anna Finch. Child: 1. *Anna*⁵, b. Oct. 6, 1751; m. John Chidsey, 3d. This Anna is thought to be the grandaughter "Anne Luddington" named in the will and distribution of Eliphalet Luddington.

13. DOROTHY³ LUDDINGTON (*William,² William¹*), born July 16, 1702, died Sept. 19, 1742, married Benjamin Mallory, who was born Nov. 5, 1701. After her death, he married second, Mary O'Neal, by whom he had seven children. He died about 1762. Benjamin Mallory and Dorothy his wife joined her mother Mercy, and some of the children of William Luddington, in a deed of the "new lott," to John Howel, June 25, 1737. (New Haven Land Records, vol. 10, p. 366.)

Children:

i. DAVID MALLORY, b. 1734; d. 1736, age 2 years.
ii. MERCY MALLORY, b. 1736; d. Sept. 19, 1742, aged 6.
iii. JOSEPH MALLORY, m. (1) Thankful, dau. of Jonathan and Bridget (Hunnewell) Roberts, of East Haven, Conn., who was b. Mar. 24, 1729, and d. July 30, 1773; m. (2) in 1774, Eunice, dau. of Benjamin and Hannah (Abbott) Barnes; d. at Wolcott, Conn., June 9, 1791; ten children. (REGISTER, *ante*, vol. 54, p. 324.)
iv. ISAAC MALLORY, m. Mabel⁵ Luddington (Mathew⁴, William³, No. 7). Children: 1. *Asa.* 2. *Jared.* 3. *Lorana*, m. Lemuel Shepard of Southington. 4. *Ame.*
v. MARY MALLORY, d. young.

14. DORCAS³ LUDDINGTON (*William,² William¹*), born July 16, 1704, married, in 1722, James Way. (New Haven Land Records, vol. 10, p. 366).

Children:

i. MERCY WAY, b. Aug. 30, 1728.
ii. HANNAH WAY, b. 1735; d. Feb. 9, 1737.
iii. MARY WAY.
iv. JAMES WAY, b. Jan. 5, 1741.
v. TIMOTHY WAY, b. Mar. 16, 1745; m. (1) Oct. 4, 1765, Abigal Dawson, who d. Dec. 15, 1766; m. (2) Rhoda Rose; m. (3) Hannah Shepard; twenty children.

PRE-REVOLUTIONARY McLOUDS IN CONNECTICUT

By ROBERT M. and HELEN C. SEARCH, of New Harbor, Maine

This article is presented not as proven fact, but, rather, in the hope that others may be interested in studying the problem and have some of the answers to the many questions. It is the accumulation of several years work collecting items relating to "McLoud" in the hope of proving the identity of Angus McCloud who married in the First Ecclesiastical Society, Hartland, Conn., 18 Feb. 1784, Sarah[5] Giddings (Joshua,[4] Thomas,[3] John,[2] George[1]). This couple were the grandparents of the Rev. Anson McLoud, Minister of the Congregational Church, Topsfield, Mass., 1841-1869. Besides consulting many genealogies and histories, research was carried on in the Connecticut State Library and in various towns in Connecticut. Invaluable help was rendered by Miss Frances Davenport, Head of the Reading Room in the Connecticut State Library in Hartford, and special credit must go to Mrs. Gloria M. Meurant of Tolland, Conn., whose patient and friendly help made this article possible.

1. DANIEL McCLOUD, of Norwalk, Conn., parentage, place and date of birth not known, died probably in Norwalk between 1745 and 1750. He married, probably about 1736, ELIZABETH ———,

whose identity has not been definitely proved.* Elizabeth married, secondly, about January 1752, as his second wife, Samuel[3] Buck (Samuel,[2] Henry[1]) of Wethersfield, Conn., by whom she had one son, William, born 21 Nov. 1752. (Heman R. Timlow,*Ecclesiastical and other Sketches of Southington, Conn.*, 1875, part 2, p. xxxvi; Henry R. Stiles, *History of Ancient Wethersfield, Conn.*, 2:144, in which by error her name is given as Elizabeth M. Lead).

Only one direct reference to Daniel McCloud of Norwalk has been found, that of the birth of what is presumed to be his fifth child, Sarah, born in Stamford, Conn., 28 Sept. 1745. He is referred to in the probate records when his widow is appointed guardian of his son Daniel in 1750 (see footnote), again in 1755 when his daughter Anne, age 14, chose "her father" Samuel Buck to be her guardian (Manwaring, *op. cit.*, 3:594). Charles Thornton Libby in his genealogy of the Knowles family (THE REGISTER, 80:130) refers to Mary McCloud, who married Samuel[4] Knowles, as "daughter of Daniel and Elizabeth of Norwalk." Thus it seems definitely established that there was a Daniel McCloud of Norwalk, that his wife's name was Elizabeth and that they had several children. Of those listed below all but Elizabeth and Michael are referred to in one or more of the records as children of Daniel of Norwalk. In this connection it may be significant that Mary (McCloud) Knowles named her only daughter Elizabeth after her sister.

Children:

i. MARY, b. about 1737; d. in Hartford 1 Oct. 1769; m. in Wethersfield, 6 Oct. 1757, SAMUEL[4] KNOWLES (John,[3] Samuel,[2] Richard[1]). Children (surname *Knowles*): 1. *Elizabeth.* 2. *John* (THE REGISTER, 80:130; Stiles, *op. cit.*, 2:476; F. W. Bailey, Early Connecticut Marriages, Book 3, p. 10).

ii. ELIZABETH, b. about 1738; d. in Wethersfield 28 Oct. 1771, "In her 34th year" (gravestone) ; m. there, by Rev. James Lockwood, formerly of Norwalk, 18 Oct. 1759, WILLIAM[4] GRISWOLD (Caleb,[3] William,[2] Michael[1]). Children (surname *Griswold*): 1. *Elizabeth.* 2. *Caleb.* 3. *William.* 4. *James* (Gene E. Griswold, *Griswold Family*, 1935, 2:243; Stiles, *op. cit.*, 2:400; Bailey, *op. cit.*, Book 3, p. 10, where she is referred to as a "London Lady;" and records in the Town Clerk's office, Wethersfield).

iii. ANNE, born about 1741; d. in West Hartford, Conn., 10 March 1805; m. in West Hartford or Wethersfield, 9 May 1765 (intention West Hartford 28 April 1765), STEPHAN[6] WEBSTER (Isaac,[5] Stephan,[4] Jonathan,[3] Robert,[2] John[1]). Children (surname *Webster*): 1. *Mary.* 2. *Theodore.* 3. *Stephan.* 4. *Norman.* 5. *William.* 6. *William.* 7. *Allen.* 8. *Anna.* 9. *McCloud.* (W. H. and M. R. Webster, *History and Genealogy of the Gov. John Webster Family of Connecticut*, 1915, p. 216; Stiles, *op. cit.*, 2:494; Bailey, *op. cit.*, Book 3, p. 12).

*Charles William Manwaring, *Early Connecticut Probates*, 3:594: "Court Record, p. 135: - 3 July 1750. Daniel McCleod, 7 years of age, son of Daniel McCleod, late of Norwalk decd.: Elizabeth McCleod, late of Norwalk, now of Wethersfield, appointed to be his guardian. Recog. £400 money, with John Welles of Wethersfield." This shows that Elizabeth removed to Wethersfield after the death of her husband. It is reasonable to assume that she returned to her native town. Since it was customary for close relatives to be co-signers of bonds of this type, the fact that John Welles signed with her may indicate that her maiden name was Welles, or at least a relationship with him.

2. iv. DANIEL, b. about 1743.
   v. SARAH "McClough," b. in Stamford, Conn., 28 Sept. 1745 (Stamford vital records, 1:67) ; presumed to have d. young.
   vi. ? MICHAEL. Fairfield County (Conn.) Probate Record 4000, 2 Aug. 1748, shows a Micael MacCloud, a minor in the Town of Norwalk, became a ward of Nathaniel Benedict. Nathaniel Benedict is frequently mentioned in the records, but no further reference to Michael was found.

2. DANIEL McCLOUD (MacCloud, Cloud) , of Pomfret, Conn., born perhaps in Norwalk about 1743, died in Pomfret 19 Nov. 1771, AET. 28 (Pomfret vital records, 2:9; gravestone) . "Daniel McCloud, Carpenter, fell from a staging and survived but a few hours at Pomfret" (*Providence Gazette*, 30 Nov. 1771; James Arnold, *Vital Records of Rhode Island*, 14:96) . He married in the Congregational Church in Brooklyn, Conn., 13 May 1764, MARY[4] CLEVELAND (Samuel,[3] Edward,[2] Moses[1]) , born in Pomfret 4 Dec. 1740, died perhaps in Brooklyn before 3 April 1787, when her youngest son was made ward of William Smith (E. G. and H. G. Cleveland, *Cleveland-Cleaveland Genealogy*, 1:156; Bailey, *op. cit.*, Book 1, p. 389) . Mary married, secondly, in Brooklyn, 24 Oct. 1779, Samuel Whittaker, by whom she had at least two children, Lemuel and Polly (Bailey, *op. cit.*, Book 1, p. 41; will of Eli Cloud, 27 June 1811) .*

There is no proof that Daniel McCloud of Pomfret was the son of Daniel of Norwalk. However, he would have been the right age and there were very few McClouds in Connecticut at this time. A thorough search of the records in the Connecticut State Library failed to reveal any other Daniel McCloud who could have married Mary Cleveland in 1764. In the record of their marriage in the Brooklyn Church he is called Daniel Cloud (Bailey, *op. cit.*, Book 1, p. 38) . All of the Pomfret records call him MacCloud and this spelling and MaCloud are used in the Cleveland genealogy. Mary is called McCloud when she gives bonds with her brother, Joseph Cleveland, as guardian for her four sons 22 July 1772. On 27 Feb. 1772 Josiah Fasset and Joseph Holland, "apprisers," returned the inventory of the estate of Daniel Cloud (Records in the Connecticut State Library) .

H. R. Stiles in his *History of Ancient Wethersfield*, 1:408, shows a Daniel McCloud in the Canadian Campaign in 1759. The *Connecticut Historical Collections*, 10:108, 191, 244, show him in this campaign and others in 1760 and 1761. Ellen D. Larned in her *History of Windham County, Connecticut*, 2:12, lists Daniel McCloud as one of twenty-one voters in Brooklyn signing a petition against building a new meeting house. These were the supporters of the "Malbone Church" (i.e. the Episcopal Church) , and Richard M. Bayles in his *History of Windham County, Connecticut*, 1889, p. 593, shows that in April 1770 Daniel McCloud was one of those who petitioned to be relieved of his Church Taxes for this reason.

---

*The Inscriptions Index in the Connecticut State Library lists a Mary Cloud of Brooklyn, Conn., who died 13 Aug. 1783, aged 41. It is not known to whom this record refers.

Daniel and Mary (Cleveland) McCloud had four sons, all of whom used the name Cloud and removed to Vermont. The records of their deaths are on file in the office of the Secretary of State in Montpelier. The will of the youngest son, Eli, who died in Waterford, Vt., 13 Jan. 1812, proves that the Mary Cloud who married Samuel Whittaker was his mother for he mentions his "brother" and "sister" Lemuel and Polly Whittaker. It would also seem from his will, a copy of which is on file in the Connecticut State Library, that he was at one time a resident in that part of Pennsylvania the jurisdiction of which was so hotly contested between Pennsylvania and Connecticut, since he leaves "unto Nabby Fasset of Brantrim in the State of Pennsylvania, all of the property that Josiah Fasset Esq. of sd. Brantrim has of mine in his hands."* The inventory of Eli Cloud, also on file in the Connecticut State Library, includes a note against Eddie Winslow given in Pennsylvania in 1808.

Children, recorded in Pomfret vital records:

i. FOREST, b. 25 Nov. 1764; d. in Norwich, Vt., 22 Dec. 1834, aet. 70 (according to his death record) or 22 Dec. 1835 (according to his gravestone), buried in Fairview Cemetery, Norwich. Made a ward of his mother 22 July 1772; mentioned in the will of his brother Eli 27 June 1811.

ii. NORMAN, b. 16 Oct. 1766; d. in Norwich, Vt., 26 May 1845, aet. 81 [?], buried in Fairview Cemetery, Norwich; m. RUBY[5] WRIGHT (John,[4] Aaron,[3] Samuel,[2] Abel[1]) (Emma E. (Neal) Brigham, *Neal Family*, 1938, p. 120). Made ward of his mother 22 July 1772. On tax list, Brooklyn, Conn., 20 Aug. 1788 (Larned, *op. cit.*, 2:250). Joint land owner with Jeptha Cleveland in Norwich in 1797 (Cleveland, *op. cit.*, 3:2281). Mentioned in will of his brother Eli 27 June 1811. Called father of Rufus Bailey Cloud (E. M. Lovejoy, *History of Royalton, Vermont*, 1911, p. 728). Ten children (L. C. Aldrich and F. W. Holmes, *History of Windsor County, Vermont*, p. 596).

iii. DANIEL, b. 25 July 1769; d. in Charleston, Vt., 18 Sept. 1847, aet. 78, buried in Bly Cemetery, Charleston. No record of his marriage has been found, but the will of Eli mentions him and his son Harvey "of Waterford." Made ward of his mother 22 July 1772.

iv. ELI, born 2 Sept. 1771; d. in Waterford, Vt., 13 Jan. 1812, apparently unmarried or a widower without direct heirs since he leaves his real estate to Zenas Goss, son of Abel Goss of Waterford, with instructions to pay his debts and funeral charges, erect a pair of gravetones at his grave ($40.00), give to the Congregational Society of Waterford $200.00 toward a new meeting house to be erected within two years of his death, and buy a burying cloth ($20.00) for those buried in the graveyard on his farm. Made ward of his mother 22 July 1772, when he is called Eli McCloud; and later, 3 April 1787, ward of Capt. William Smith of Brooklyn, when he is called Eli Cloud; Joseph Cleveland, again, signing the bond with William Smith. Will and inventory on file in the Connecticut State Library.

The only other person of this name found in the Pre-Revolutionary records of Connecticut is Norman McLeod who died at the home of Elisha (or Elijah) Hurlburt in Chatham, Conn., 1 Jan. 1769.

*"Brantrim" is Braintrim, Westmoreland Co., Conn. See William Brewster, *History of the Certified Township of Kingston* [Pa.], p. 186, for a list of towns in Westmoreland County which now lie in the Counties of Luzerne, Wyoming and Bradford, Pa.

Norman McLeod was a sea faring man who was apparently taken sick on board ship in Chatham and went to the home of Elisha Hurlburt "for to be taken care of." The account of the expenses of Elisha Hurlburt (Middletown Probate District file 2269) show various charges: "to going for the docktor, to two quarts rum, to boarding him and tending him a fortnet and a day, and to sending to danbury for to try and get that note settled that is against John mcclane." The last item is "to one winding sheet, etc." From the inventory of his estate (Middletown Probate, 2:146) it would seem that Norman was master or mate of a vessel since he had a compass and quadrant, and that he was a man of some learning. In the list of his books were a "small old bible of French dialogues, homens Illiad, Ollids Art of Love, New Journale Cook, Hudebrats," and the note against John McLean (John McLean was selectman of Danbury at this time (cf. Susan H. Hill, *History of Danbury*, 1896, p. 91) . No further reference to Norman McLeod has been found. Anne (McCloud) Webster and Daniel McCloud of Pomfret each named a son Norman and the name is found frequently among the descendants of Angus McCloud of Hartland.

PRE-REVOLUTIONARY MCLOUDS IN CONNECTICUT: CORRECTION.—In THE REGISTER for April 1962, p. 98, will be found Sarah "McClough," b. in Stamford, Conn., 28 * Sept. 1745 (Stamford vital records, 1:67) ; presumed to have d. young.

I submit the following in reference to Sarah, fifth child of Daniel McCloud of Norwalk, Conn.: "Joshua Risley, b. ca. 1742; d. at East Hartford, 12 Oct. 1822; . . . m. (1) at Wethersfield, 17 Feb. 1765, Sarah MacLeod (McCloud) , b. ca. 1745, d. at East Hartford, 6 Sept. 1800, aet. 55" (*American Genealogist*, 25:242) . H. R. Stiles, *The History of Ancient Wethersfield, Conn.*, 1904, 2:548, shows this marriage but gives the bride's maiden name as "[Maitland ?]." Undoubtedly this is the Sarah referred to in the April issue of THE REGISTER as "presumed to have d. young."

Joshua and Sarah (McCloud) Risley had a daughter Esther who married Reuben Roberts of Hartford, Conn. Mrs. Beatty is a descendant of this marriage.

Baltimore, Md.   JOSEPH M. BEATTY.

*Page 441, this volume.

McKEAN OF GUILFORD, CONN., AND DURHAM, N. Y.

By Lewis D. Cook, F.A.S.G., of Philadelphia, Pa.

Patrick[1] McKean, born probably in North Ireland of Scots ancestry in 1705; died testate in Guilford, Conn., 8 May 1775. He married Mary ——— who died 5 Jan. 1766 (Talcott, Guilford Families, an unpublished manuscript in the New Haven Colony Historical Society).

Their sons James, Patrick and Barnabas had military service in the Revolution (Bernard Christian Steiner, *A History of . . . The Present Towns of Guilford and Madison*, 1897, p. 447, 454; Henry P. Johnston, ed., *The Record of Connecticut Men in the Military and Naval Service During the War of the Revolution*, 1889, p. 585).

Children:

    i.   James,[2] b. 12 May 1742; d. 10 Jan. 1784; m. 24 Feb. 1763 Prudence Brownson (Register of Congregational Church, New Milford, Conn.).

    ii.   Keturah, b. 6 Feb. 1744.

    iii. Laughton, b. 9 Oct. 1746; d. 16 May 1749.

    iv. Patrick, b. in May 1749; d. 2 March 1825; m. Rachel Bradley, bapt. 20 April 1751, daughter of Daniel[3] and Abigail (Howd) Bradley (The Register, vol. 57, p. 141, April 1903).

    v.   Honor, b. 4 March 1751; d. 3 Dec. 1814; m. 24 June 1773 James Hall, b. 30 Dec. 1752, d. on a British Prison Ship in New York 16 Jan. 1780 (David Brainard Hall, *The Halls of New England*, 1883, p. 44).

2. vi. Barnabas, b. 27 July 1754.

2. Barnabas[2] McKean born in Guilford, Conn., 27 July 1754, died after 1810. He married about 1775 Mabel Hall, born 18 March 1755, daughter of Justus and Lucy (Munger) Hall of that town (D. B. Hall, *op. cit.*, p. 39). "Mabel McKean, wife of Barnabas, died September 26, 1819. United with the Church May 3, 1806" (Register of the First Presbyterian Church, Durham, Greene Co., N. Y.; copy in the New York Genealogical and Biographical Society).

The 1790 Census of Guilford Town, New Haven Co., Conn., lists Barnabas McKean as head of a family of 1 male over 16 [himself], 4 males under 16, and 6 females. He removed thence, with other Connecticut families, to Durham where in the 1810 Census he appears as head of a family of 6 (*History of Greene County, New York*, 1884, p. 41). But he does not appear in the 1820 Census and the settlement of his estate is not found in the surrogate's records in Greene County. Inquiries have been made of the surrogates of several adjacent counties without success.

Children (incomplete; the births of the children are not found in the Connecticut vital records):

    i.   "POLLY"³ (MARY), b. in Guilford 11 Aug. 1777 or 1779; d. in Burwick, Woodbridge Co., Ontario, Canada, in 1854 (*The American Genealogist*, vol. 17, p. 154, January 1941; *Abridged Compendium of American Genealogy*, vol. 7, p. 522 (1942)); m. (1), in Bethlehem, Conn., 10 Aug. 1800, LYMAN WESTOVER, b. in Sheffield, Mass., 14 March 1779. They moved to Durham, where she was admitted an adult member of the church on 8 July 1810. She m. (2), PETER MITCHELL.

3. ii.   BARNABAS HENRY.

    iii.   HOSEA, "son of Barnabas McKean, and Hannah Rose, daughter of Henry Rose;" m. 15 July 1810 ――――― (Register of the Reformed Church, Oak Hill, Greene Co., N. Y.).

    iv.   PIERCE URBAN, bapt. at the First Presbyterian Church, Durham, 3 May 1806; d. in Medina, Orleans Co., N. Y., in 1854; m. in 1828 LUCY ANN BULLOCK. b. in Dutchess County, N. Y., in 1799 (*Landmarks of Orleans County, New York*, ed. by Isaac S. Signor, 1894, p. 328). He was appointed an Ensign in the 49th Regiment of Infantry, Greene County, in 1821 (*Military Minutes of Council of Appointment of the State of New York, 1783-1821*, compiled and edited by Hugh Hastings, 1901, vol. 3, p. 2262).

        Their son, *Andrew Jackson*, b. in Ridgway, Orleans Co., N. Y., 22 June 1835; m. in Paris, Kent Co., Mich., 22 May 1859, Jane Amelia Cardinal (Edmund James Cleveland, *The Genealogy of the Cleveland and Cleaveland Families*, 1899, p. 1898). Their youngest daughter, *Mary*, m. in 1855 John W. Card, b. in Berkshire County, Mass., 27 Feb. 1829 and went to Medina in 1844 (*ibid.*, p. 144).

    v.   ELIZABETH, bapt. 3 May 1806, with her brother Pierce, above.

3. BARNABAS HENRY³ McKEAN was born in Guilford, Conn. (according to the death certificate of his daughter Sarah Ann, although there is no entry in the Connecticut vital records). As "Harry M'Kean of Durham" he married 21 Sept. 1806 SUSAN TOWNSEND of Greenfield, N. Y. (Register of Presbyterian Church of Greenfield (now Greenville), Greene Co., N. Y.).

Barnabas McKean was listed as head of a family of 5 in the 1810 Census of that County, but was not listed in that of 1820; and the probate of his estate has not been found in the surrogate's records of that or any adjacent counties in New York. Although his daughter Sarah Ann was married evidently in New York City or Brooklyn in 1836, Barnabas H. McKean is not found listed in the city directories there. His wife Susan was born in Fishkill, Dutchess Co., N. Y., 10 Oct. 1788, daughter of John and Sarah (Tappen) Townsend, formerly of Poughkeepsie and later of Greenfield, N. Y. (*New York Genealogical and Biographical Record*, vol. 89, p. 151 *et seq.*, July 1958). Susan

McKean, wife of Barnabas, died at 715 North 20th Street, Philadelphia, Pa., 29 Nov. 1864, apparently visiting there and was buried in or near Catskill, Greene Co., N. Y., according to her death certificate. No gravestone has been found in the village cemetery there with the name of McKean.

Children (others):

i.   SARAH ANN,[4] b. in Durham 16 Jan. 1814; d. at her home in New Hamburg-on-Hudson, Dutchess Co., N. Y., 26 March 1900, aged 86 years 2 months (death certificate) and buried in Greenwood Cemetery, Brooklyn; m. in New York, 10 April 1836, according to a family memorandum, JOHN WEBSTER COCHRAN, listed as "Machinist," in the city directory for that year, b. in Enfield, N. H., 16 May 1811, d. testate in Brooklyn, N. Y., 2 Jan. 1873, aged 61 years 8 months (death certificate) and buried in Greenwood Cemetery (*American Artisan*, N. Y., 8 March 1871; Appleton's Cyclopedia of American Biography, 1887, vol. i, p. 671), son of Jacob[4] Cochran of that place (b. 9 July 1782, d. in Stratham, N. H., 9 March 1836, founder of the "Cochranites" religious sect) and wife Abigail Stephenson Colcord (THE REGISTER, vol. 110, p. 233, July 1956). John Webster Cochran was an internationally famed inventor of fire-arms. The family resided in Paris, France, from 1846, when the eldest daughter, *Helen*, was placed in a boarding school there, and at the outbreak of the French Revolution in 1848 took refuge in England and soon returned to New York City.

ii.   CAROLINE, m. WILLIAM CHOLLET, son of Frederick Chollet (1764-1848) and Rebecca (Bogardus) Chollet (1779-1832) of Catskill, Greene Co., N. Y. Evidently they moved to New York City, where their daughter was married in 1857, but they are not found in the surrogate's records or city directories. Their only child, *Louise Evelyn*, b. about 1839; d. in New York City 25 Dec. 1904; m. in St. Thomas's Church, 13 May 1857, William Furniss, who d. in 1882.

PETER MALLORY, NEW HAVEN, CONN., 1644, AND SOME OF HIS DESCENDANTS.

By James Shepard, New Britain, Conn.

1. Peter Mallory signed the planters' covenant at New Haven, Conn., 1644. The name is variously spelled in the early records there as Mallery, Malery, Mallary, Malary, Mallorye, Malorie, Mallory and Malory, but in later years it most frequently appears as "Mallory." The wife of Peter Malary united with the first church of New Haven in 1663. On Jan. 2, 1687, Peter Mallery of New Haven, planter, gives land to his son Peter, "whereof I the said Peter Mallary with Mary my wife have hereunto put our hands and seal," both signing by mark, his mark consisting of his initials, P. M., a step higher than signing with a simple cross. [New Haven land records, vol. 1, p. 370.] This Mary was probably the only wife he ever had. His home lot and most of his land was near the Milford town line at a place commonly called West Side Farms, now West Haven, in the town of Orange. The deed to his son John, dated March 25, 1687, was of "land lieing within New Haven township on the west river at the West farms, containing one acre and half, bounded by the highway that runneth from the Oyster point on the north, on the East by land of John Clark, on the south by land belonging to my son Thomas Mallery, on the west by a path that runneth between it and my other land whereon I dwell." [New Haven land records, vol. 1, p. 339.] That he was a large land owner is evidenced by numerous deeds on record in vol. 1. He repeatedly gave land to his sons John, Peter and Thomas. He also gave land "by way of portion in part with my loving daughter Rebecca Bunnell, to my loving son-in-law Benjamin Bunnell," dated July 2, 1684, and to his "daughter-in-law Mary Mallery widow, relict of Thomas Mallery my son lately deceased, * * * during the nonage of her son Thomas" with the proviso that if he die before he is twenty-one, then it shall go to her son Daniel at lawful age, and if he die then to her son Aaron, and if they three all die then "it be and remain unto my said daughter, * * * Signed with consent of my son Peter Jr." April 28, 1691.

On Aug. 30, 1697, he deeded all his "estate undisposed of * * * moveable, real or personal, to his son Peter Husbandman and son John Cordwainer" in consideration of life support. [Vol. 1, p. 729.] This deed and one or two others about the same date are signed by a simple P instead of P. M., his usual mark. He was undoubtedly in feeble health and perhaps had been feeble for many years. In the County Court Records, vol. 1, p. 45, Nov. 8, 1671, we find "This Court upon yᵉ allegations pʳsented on behalf of Peter Mallory Senʳ for freedom from training doth free him from yᵉ sd service." He died after Aug. 30, 1697, when he disposed of the balance of his property, and before Nov. 24, 1701, when John Malary conveys to John Smith "land belonging to yᵉ heirs of Thomas Malary * * * leading down to yᵉ dwelling house formerly belonging to peter malary my deceased father." [New Haven land records, vol. 2, p. 53.]

Mary Mallory's death is recorded in New Haven as "Dec., 1690."

Eleven children are recorded to Peter Mallory on the New Haven records, born on the dates here given.

Children:

    i.   REBEKAH,[2] b. May 18, 1649. The Strong family says she m. Benjamin Bunnell, son of William Bunnell and his wife Ann, dau. of Benjamin Wilmot. This is confirmed by the deed before referred to of Rebecca's portion to Benjamin Bunnell. The will of her brother, Samuel Mallory, mentions "sister Rebecca Bunnell's son Benjamin."

2. ii.   PETER, b. July 27, 1653.

   iii. MARY, b. Oct. 28, 1655; d. young.

   iv. MARY, b. Sept. 28, 1656.

3. v.   THOMAS, b. April 15, 1659.

   vi. DANIEL, b. Nov. 25, 1661.

4. vii. JOHN, b. May 10, 1663.

5. viii. JOSEPH, b. ———, 1666.

6. ix.   BENJAMIN, b. Jan. 4, 1668.

7. x.   SAMUEL, b. March 10, 1672-3.

   xi. WILLIAM, b. Sept. 2, 1675.

2. PETER[2] MALLORY (*Peter*[1]), born July 26, 1653 ; m. Elizabeth Trowbridge, May 28, 1678, dau. of William and Elizabeth Trowbridge of New Haven, as shown by a deed of gift Jan. 4, 1684. [New Haven land records, vol. 1, p. 329.] He was "discharged from the service of training" by the New Haven County Court April 26, 1706.

    Children, from the New Haven records :

    i.   PETER,[3] b. April 22, 1679.

8. ii.   CALEB, b. Nov. 3, 1681.

   iii. PETER, b. Aug. 2, 1684.

   iv. ELIZABETH, b. April 27, 1687.

   v.   JUDITH, b. Sept. 2, 1689.

   vi. BENJAMIN, b. April 3, 1692; m. Eunice Butler of Wethersfield, Dec. 22, 1715, and settled in Stratford. [Orcut's History of Stratford.]

   vii. STEEVEN, b. Oct. 12, 1694.

   viii. EBENEZER, Nov. 29, 1696.

   ix. ZACHEUS, b. May 22, 1699.

   x.   ABIGAIL, b. Aug. 5, 1701.

   xi. ZIPPORAH, b. Dec. 15, 1705.

9. xii. PETER, b. March 1, 1708.

       Also see Orcutt's Stratford for further records of Benjamin, Stephen, Zacheus, Zipporah and Peter.

3. THOMAS[2] MALLORY (*Peter*[1]), was born April 15, 1659 ; m. Mary Umberfield, March 26, 1684 ; d. Feb. 15, 1690. On Jan. 15, 1691, "An Inventory of yᵉ estate of Thomas Mallary late of New Haven Decd, Intestate was Exhibited in Court attested by yᵉ widow & appraisers Sworn in Court according to Law and Approved. And Administration of yᵉ estate of yᵉ Decd was granted to Mary Mallary, wid, Relict of yᵉ Deceased. *** The Children, Thomas 5 yʳ old, Daniel 2, and Aaron 1. *** John Smith appointed by yᵉ Court to assist yᵉ minor children." [New Haven County Court records, vol. 1, page 192, now with the Clerk of the Superior Court.] Amt of Inventor £220 19. 00. John Smith and John Clark Appraisers. [New Haven Probate records, vol. 1, p. 114.]

    Children, from New Haven Records :

    i.   THOMAS,[3] b. Jan. 1, 1685. Cothren's History of Woodbury, Conn., p. 165, says this Thomas "was first of the name" Mallory in "Ancient Woodbury" where he died, July 21, 1783.

10. ii. DANIELL, b. Jan. 2, 1687.

   iii. AARON, b. March 10, 1689-10.

4. John[2] Mallory (*Peter*[1]), born May 10, 1644; m. Elizabeth, dau. of Nathaniel Kimberly of New Haven, "Taylour," Dec. 30, 1686, as shown by New Haven Records and by deed of gift dated Feb. 16, 1703. [New Haven land records, vol. 2, p. 258.] Administration on the estate of John Mallory was granted to his widow Elizabeth May 6, 1712. Inventory sworn to by Elizabeth Mallory. Amt. £163 07. 6. Children's names, Elizabeth, Rebeckah of full age, Mehitable 17, Silence 14, Obedience 4. On Oct. 12, 1714, " Eliza Mallary, adm. es[t] of John Mallary late of New Haven Decd. exhibits a Nuncupative will of the said John Mallery authorizing the said Elizabeth to make sale of one half of the orchard for paying the Debts," &c. Approved on the testimony of Elizabeth Mallery aged about 23, and Silence Mallery aged about sixteen, saying that their father desired the sale made " to pay his debts and particularly the debt Due the Colledge and have her [his wife] use the rest of it for her Comfort and not break the farme by selling any part of it." [New Haven Probate records, vol. 4, p. 289.]

On the first Monday of August, 1715, the Probate records call the administratrix " Elizabeth Mallory alias Barnes " [vol. 4, p. 355], showing that she had married ———— Barnes.

Children, from New Haven records:

i. John,[3] b. Sept. 6, 1687.
ii. Elizabeth, b. May 1, 1691.
iii. Rebeckah, b. Sept. 15, 1693.
iv. Mehitable, Dec. 19, 1695; m. Jonathan Griffin, May 16, 1717.
v. Silence, b. Oct. 13, 1698.
vi. John, b. March 1, 1709–10.
vii. Obedience, b. April 11, 1704.

5. Joseph[2] Mallory (*Peter*[1]), born 1666; m. in 1693, Mercy, dau. of Thomas and Mercy Pinion and granddaughter of Nicholas and Elizabeth Pinion. Haven's manuscript history of East Haven (with the New Haven Colony Historical Society) says this Joseph was the first of the name Mallory to reside in East Haven, probably about 1693. From deeds in the New Haven land records his mark was " I M." On Nov. 13, 1727, he quit claimed his right in land " which belonged to my father pinion."

Children, all except Hannah, from New Haven records:

i. Mercy,[3] b. 1690.
ii. Thankful, b. Aug., 1694.
iii. Abigail, b. Aug., 1696.
iv. Joseph, b. Nov. 5, 1698.
11. v. Benjamin, Nov. 5, 1701.
vi. Hannah, Sept. 1, 1709.

6. Benjamin[2] Mallory (*Peter*[1]), born Jan. 4, 1668. The two wives and children assigned to this Benjamin on page 162 of Baldwin's Candee family belong to his nephew, Benjamin, the son of (*Joseph*,[2] *Peter*[1]). On Jan. 6, 1700–1, " Peter Malorie, John Malorie and Samuel Malorie presented an account to y[e] court of an estate appertaining to their brother Benjamin Malorie who went to sea about ten years since from whom they have no certain intelligence since his departure, whereupon y[e] court orders sd account to be entered upon record and appoints the sd Peter Malorie * * * conservator of y[e] same in case he returns." The estate included land

given him " by his father Peter Malorie," and in the " hands of his sister-in-law Thomas Malorie's widow." [New Haven County Court records, vol. 2, p. 53.] On March 6, 1702, " John Malary of New Haven entereth his caveatt against any Record to be made of y^t Land y^t was formerly his Brother Benjamin Malary Lying at ye west side near a cove called Malborn's cove." [New Haven land records, vol. 2, p. 152.] Peter and Samuel Malary give a warrantee deed of "land formerly Belonging to our Brother Benjamin " to Ebenezer Down, March 4, 1702–3. [Same vol. p. 158.]

7. SAMUEL² MALLORY (*Peter¹*), born March 10, 1672–3. His will dated Dec. 20, 1709, was presented by his relict Mary on the first Monday in Jan., 1711–12, and is recorded in New Haven Probate Court records, vol. 3, p. 313. It begins with "The Lord having Visited me his poor servant wth Sickness and not Knowing how ye Lord may deal wth me," &c. It mentions his wife, "each of his brothers and sisters," but does not give their names, also his "sister Rebecca Bunnell's son Benjamin " and the eldest son of his "deceased brother Thomas." He appointed his wife and his "brother-in-law John Sanford " executors. Inventory sworn to by Mary Mallary and John Sanford. Amt. £85 6. 0.

8. CALEB³ MALLORY (*Peter,² Peter¹*), born Nov. 3, 1681; m. Miriam Blakesley, Feb. 13, 1706–7. Administration on the estate of Caleb Mallery late of New Milford Decd. granted unto Miriam, widow and Relict of said deceased, Sept. 3, 1716. [New Haven Probate, vol. 4, p. 417.] Inventory filed Nov. 15, 1716. John Bostwick Senr. and Stephen Noble appras. Amt. £113 13. 8. [Same vol. p. 438.]

Children, from New Haven records :

i. MIRIAM,⁴ b. May 23, 1708.
ii. DEBORAH, b. May 11, 1710.
iii. CALEB, b. Aug. 3, 1712.
iv. JOHN, b. April 7, 1715.

9. PETER³ MALLORY (*Peter,² Peter¹*), born April 22, 1679; m. Mary ————. He died at New Haven. Administration on his estate granted to Mary Mallery, widow and relict, first Monday in April, 1769. [New Haven Probate, vol. 10, p. 597.]

Children :

i. DAVID.⁴ Eliakim Mallery, of New Haven, appointed his guardian Aug. 6, 1772. [Vol. 2, p. 277.]
ii. CALVIN. Elias Beach, of New Haven, appointed his guardian Nov. 2, 1777. [Vol. 12, p. 217.]
iii. JAMES. Eliakim Mallery appointed his guardian first Monday in April, 1781. [Vol. 13, p. 11.]

10. DANIEL³ MALLORY (*Thomas,² Peter¹*), born Jan. 2, 1687; d. at New Haven, 1760. Will made Feb. 12, 1760; proved third Monday in May, 1760. Abigail, Daniel and Thomas Mallery executors. Will names wife Abigail, sons Daniel of Woodbury and Thomas of Waterbury, daughters Abigail Smith, Esther Osborne, Eunice Clark, Hannah Smith and heirs of dau. Sarah Bunnell. Amt. of Inventory £590 19. 7. [New Haven Probate, vol. 9, p. 350.]

Children, from New Haven records :

i. ABIGAIL,[4] b. May 29, 1716; m. ——— Smith.
ii. ESTHER, b. June 18, 1718; m. ———- Osborne.
iii. DANIEL, b. Feb. 4, 1719–20; removed to Woodbury, Conn.
iv. LOIS, b. Nov. 30, 1721.
v. THOMAS, b. Aug. 12, 1723; removed to Waterbury, Conn.
vi. EUNIS, b. Aug. 8, 1725; m. ——— Clark.
vii. HANNAH, identified only by her father's will; m. ——— Smith.
viii. SARAH, identified only by her father's will; m. ——— Bunnell.

11. BENJAMIN[3] MALLORY (*Joseph,[2] Peter[1]*), born Nov. 5, 1701; m.
Dorothy Luddington, dau. of William and Mercy (Whitehead)
Luddington of East Haven, Conn., granddaughter of William and
Ellen Luddington. She d. Sept. 19, 1742, age 40 [Dodd's History
of East Haven], and he married 2d, Mary O'Neal.

His will dated Dec. 10, 1762 [New Haven Probate, vol. 10, p.
79], appoints his wife Mary executrix and names children Joseph,
Isaac, David and Mary ; but he left children not named in his will,
as the widow Mary was appointed guardian to Simeon when the
will was proved, and Levi, a minor son of Benjamin Mallory, made
choice of Daniel Wheadon as his guardian in Dec., 1764. On the
third Monday in June, 1763, Timothy Luddington of New Haven,
was appointed guardian to David, a minor son of Benjamin
Mallory. Deeds in the New Haven records describe this Benjamin
as "Benjamin the son of Joseph."

Children, according to Dodd's History, by first wife :
i. DAVID,[4] b. 1734; d. 1736, age 2 years.
ii. MERCY, b. 1736; d. Sept. 19, 1742, age 6 years.
12. iii. JOSEPH.
iv. ISAAC; m. Mabel Luddington. Children: Asa, Jared, Lorana and
Ame.
v. MARY; d. young.

By second wife :
vi. DAVID; m. Mary Wardell, 1769.
vii. MERCY.
viii. LEVI.
ix. DOROTHY.
x. JOHN.
xi. MARY.
xii. SIMEON.

12. JOSEPH[4] MALLORY (*Benjamin,[3] Joseph,[2] Peter[1]*), m. Thankful, dau.
of Jonathan and Bridget (Hunnewell) Roberts, then of East
Haven, Conn. She d. July 30, 1773, aged 43 years. Was born at
Wallingford, Conn. (Meriden Parish), March 24, 1729. He m.
2d in 1774, Eunice, dau. of Benjamin and Hannah (Abbott)
Barnes. He and his wife Eunice were admitted to special ordi-
nances at the church in East Haven, March 5, 1775, and the same
day his son Joseph and their son, Noah Woodruff, were baptized.
He probably lived in East Haven until about 1780. On May 2 of
that year he bought sixty-seven acres of land in Waterbury (the
part which is now Wolcott, Conn.), and she bought the same day
forty-eight acres in her own name. In both deeds they are
described as of New Haven. On Aug. 15, 1780, he and wife
Eunice quit claim their right in the estate of her father and described themselves as of Waterbury. [Southington, Conn., land
records.]

He and his wife united with the Congregational Church in Wolcott, 1781. He d. June 9, 1791. She made will Nov. 16, 1793; d. Nov. 22, 1793; will proved Dec. 31, 1793; both estates probated at Waterbury, Conn. The distribution of his estate, July 2, 1792, was to the widow; sons Benjamin, Amos, Ezra, Joseph and Woodruff; and daughters Abigail Cook, Thankful Shepard, Eunice and Elizabeth. In her will she calls Noah Woodruff Mallory her "only son," and names daughters Eunice and Elizabeth Mallory.

Children, by first wife:

i. BENJAMIN,⁵ b. 1751; bapt. March 23, 1756; m. Eunice Talmadge, Dec. 19, 1774.
ii. ELIZABETH, b. 1754.
iii. AMOS, b. 1756.
iv. ABIGAIL, b. 1760; m. Samuel Cook of Wallingford, Conn.
v. THANKFUL, b. July 4, 1762; m. 1st, Samuel Shepard of Southington, Conn., Jan. 1, 1787. He died Feb. 15, 1803, and she m. 2d, Clark Royce, Jan. 17, 1813, who died Feb. 16, 1826. She died March 27, 1832.
vi. EZRA, b. 1767.
vii. JOSEPH, b. before July 31, 1773; bapt. March 5, 1775.

By second wife:

viii. NOAH WOODRUFF, bapt. March 5, 1775.
ix. EUNICE, no record except distribution and will.
x. ELIZABETH, no record except distribution and will.

There is no birth, death or marriage on record in vol. 1 at the Registrar's Office in New Haven, by the name of Mallory, other than those herein given.

MALTBY-MALTBIE-MOLBY

By the late DOROTHY (MALTBY) VERRILL, of North Vancouver, B. C.

The first two generations of Maltby in New England were given at length in the "Maltby-Maltbie Family History", published in 1916, by Birdsey L. Maltbie and compiled and edited by Dorothy Maltby Verrill. Consequently the present article begins only with records of the third generation.

7. JOHN³ MALTBY (*John*,² *William*¹), born in Saybrook, Conn., 10 Sept. 1698, probably died at Guilford, Conn., 17 Sept. 1778. He married in Saybrook, 12 Nov. 1724, MEHITABEL CLARKE. John Maltby was of Wallingford in 1753, 1763.
It is believed he had a son, John, born about 1730-1, who is the following: (Ref. New York Hist. Society, 1891) "[John?] Maltby of Wallingford, Conn., enlisted April 19, 1759 in the New York Provincial Troops, aged 28." If he is John⁴ (John,³ John,² William¹), his brother, William, born in 1727, was, in 1757, in Col. Lyman's Regt., 13th Company, Capt. Preston (Conn. Hist. Soc., vol. 9, 193). His sister, Mehitable, is called "of Wallingford" in 1755.

The compiler believes that John,[3] born in 1698, and a son, John, born about 1730-1, have been confused, and that the latter is the John who married in 1761, Jane Smith, widow of David Smith. John is called "of Wallingford". David Smith was of Saybrook and his will was probated at Guilford in 1760; Jane was living in 1790. A note received states: "John Maltby's estate was settled by his *brother-in-law*, Jonathan Osborne. While in 1763, Wallingford deed of John Maltby, names his son-in-law Jonathan Osborn".

Children:

i. Esther,[4] b. in Middletown 28 Dec. 1725; m. 17 April 1744 Daniel Hurd, Jr., b. 16 Sept. 1722. Res. Killingworth, Conn.
   Child (surname *Hurd*):
   1. *Seth*, m. Thankful Ray.
ii. William, b. in Saybrook 29 April 1727; probably d. unm.
iii. Mehitabel, b. in Saybrook. "Mehitabel Malbe of Wallingford m. John Osborn of New Haven, 30 Jan. 1755".
   Children (surname *Osborn*):
   1. *Jonathan.*   3. *Nancy.*
   2. *Abigail.*   4. *Mehitable.*
                5. *Lois* [?]
iv. Abigail, b. in 1731; m. in New Haven, 27 May 1765, John Cornwall, b. in Branford in August 1738.
   Children (surname *Cornwall*), b. in New Haven:
   1. *Eden Burroughs*, b. 20 March 1766.
   2. *Lydia*, b. 27 Nov. 1770.

8. Nathaniel[3] Maltby (*John*,[2] *William*[1]) was born in Saybrook, Conn., 29 Dec. 1700. His will probated in Guilford, 24 May 1733. He married in New Haven, Conn., 4 Dec. 1723, Deborah Jones, said to be daughter of Isaac, and granddaughter of Dept. Gov. William Jones of New Haven.

Child:

i. Elizabeth,[4] b. in Saybrook 4 Sept. 1724; d. in New Haven 16 Oct. 1810; m. William Lyon, b. in Boston, Mass., 10 April 1716, d. in New Haven 31 Jan. 1767.
   Children (surname *Lyon*):
   1. *William.*   5. *John Howard.*
   2. *Nancy*, d. young.   6. *Anne.*
   3. *Mary.*   7. *Nathaniel.*
   4. *Elizabeth.*   8. *Sarah.*

9. William[3] Maltby (*John*,[2] *William*[1]), born in Saybrook, Conn., 6 July 1703, supposed to have died unmarried.
10. Capt. William[3] Maltby (*William*,[2] *William*[1]), sea captain, born in New Haven, Conn., 26 May 1700, died before 1735. He married in New Haven, 12 Feb. 1723-4, Sarah Davenport of Stamford, Conn., daughter of Rev. John Davenport and first wife, Martha (Gould) Selleck, granddaughter of John Davenport and Abigail Pierson. In 1735 Captain Maltby's widow married Rev. Eleazer Wheelock, of Lebanon, N. H., founder of Dartmouth College.
   That William Maltby was a Captain is proved by the death of his widow, as follows, "Mrs. Sarah Maltby relict of Capt.

William Maltby of New Haven and daughter of Rev. John
Davenport, of Stamford, she died in Lebanon, Nov. 13, 1746,
age 43". (Ref. New Haven Rec., vol. I, p. 131; "Davenport
Genealogy").

William's son, William, baptised 20 June 1731, is conceded by
Donald Lines Jacobus to be he of Muster Roll of Men "raised
and passed Muster in the Co. of Suffolk, 1759, Gilbert Potter,
Captain, Jesse Platt, Joseph Brewster, Lieuts. William Maltby,
April 19, aged 28, Seabrook (Saybrook) Conn., Capt. Strong's
Company of Militia".

Probably he is the "William Maltby who served in the 13th
Company, Capt. Preston's, Wallingford, Dec. 15, 1757".

Children, baptised in New Haven:

    i.   ELIZABETH,[4] bapt. 27 March 1726; m. 15 May 1754 DR. THADDEUS BETTS,
        M.D. (Yale College, 1745), descendant of Thomas Betts of Guilford.
        Children (surname *Betts*):
        1. *Sarah.*   2. *William.*   3. *Mary.*

18. ii.   JOHN, b. 3 Aug. 1727.
    iii. WILLIAM, bapt. 6 April 1729.
    iv. SARAH, bapt. 26 July 1730.
    v.   WILLIAM, bapt. 20 June 1731. French-Indian Wars, 1755-1759.
    vi. MARY, "died in youth".

11. CAPT. JOSEPH[3] MALTBY (*Daniel,*[2] *William*[1]), sea captain, was
born in Branford, Conn., 31 May 1712. He married about 1735
ELIZABETH PRATT, daughter of Jonathan and wife Elizabeth
————————Pratt, of Hartford, Conn. Administration of estate
17 Aug. 1749.

Children, baptised in Branford:

    i.   ELIZABETH,[4] bapt. 25 July 1736; m. (1),————————MATSON, of Vershire,
        Vt.; m. (2), DAVID RITTER, of New Haven, Conn.

19. ii.   JOSEPH, bapt. 21 May 1738.
    iii. HANNAH, bapt. 5 June 1740.
20. iv. WILLIAM, bapt. 13 June 1742.
21. v.   NOAH, b. 23 Sept. 1744.
22. vi. JONATHAN, bapt. 24 Aug. 1746.
    vii. MARTHA, b. 2 Aug. 1748.

12. CAPT. DANIEL[3] MALTBY (*Daniel,*[2] *William*[1]) was born in Branford, Conn., 30 Oct. 1715. Lieut., 1757, 2nd. Regiment, French
and Indian War; Captain, 1761. He married in Branford, 16
Sept. 1736, MARY HARRISON, daughter of Nathaniel and
Thankful (Wilkinson) Harrison. (French and Indian War Rolls,
vol. I). Campaign of 1757. Lieut. Maltbie's Company. Daniel
Maltbie (of Northford in Branford) Lieut.

"The Colony of New Haven to Lieut. Daniel Maltbie, Lieut.
of the Company under his command in ye 2nd Regiment under
Col. Newton for their service all ye time of the Alarm for the
Relief of Fort William Henry and parts adjacent".

Gen. Assembly holden at New Haven 8 Oct. 1761 (Col.
Rec. of Connecticut, 1757-1761, vol. XXI, p. 578). "This
Assembly do establish Mr. Daniel Maltbie to be Captain of
the 14th Company in the 2nd Regiment of this Colony".

Children:

   i.   ESTHER,⁴ b. 30 Aug. 1739; m. about 1760 JOHN KIRKHAM of Stony Creek.
            Children (surname *Kirkham*):

1. *Levi.*		6. *Eli.*	
2. *Philemon.*		7. *Elihu.*	
3. *Samuel.*		8. *Solomon.*	
4. *Anne.*		9. *Esther.*	
5. *Daniel.*		10. *Zerviah.*	

23. ii.   DANIEL, b. 7 Jan. 1742.
   iii. MARY, b. 5 June 1744; d. about 1797; m. (1), 20 Feb. 1765, SAMUEL
           BROWN of Goshen; m. (2),————JUDD. Lived in Pompey, N. Y.
           "Several children; one was Rebecca".
   iv. HANNAH, b. 25 Sept. 1746; m. 11 Feb. 1768 SIMEON FRISBIE of Branford.
   v.   LUCRETIA, b. 22 May 1749; d. 7 Jan. 1778; m. in Guilford, 6 Feb. 1772,
           JOSIAH FOWLER.
           Child (surname *Fowler*):
             1. *Maltby*, b. 7 Jan. 1777; d. in January 1778.
24. vi. BENJAMIN, b. in Northford 11 May 1750.
25. vii. ZACCHEUS, b. in June 1754.
   viii. SABRA, b. 10 May 1756; d. unm.
   ix. THANKFUL, b. 5 Feb. 1758; m. 10 July 1775 ISAAC BARTHOLOMEW of
           Branford. Soldier in Rev. War, was of Goshen; after 1801, Tompkins
           Co., N. Y.; 1818, Evans, Erie Co., N. Y.
           Children (surname *Bartholomew*):

1. *Phebe.*		3. *Sabra.*	
2. *Jehiel.*		4. *Isaac.*	

   x.   LYDIA, bapt. 12 Oct. (or 18 Dec.?) 1760.
   xi. SARAH, bapt. 23 June 1765.

13. CAPT. BENJAMIN³ MALTBY (*Daniel,² William¹*), baptised in
Branford, Conn., 23 June 1717, died in Northford 9 July 1796.
Ensign, 1755; Lieut., 1757; Captain, 1768, Committee of Inspection, Branford, 5 Feb. 1776; Committee for supplying
families of Officer and Soldiers belonging to Branford, 11 Oct.
1777. He married first, in Branford, 16 Sept. 1736, SARAH
HARRINGTON, daughter of Deacon Samuel Harrington; and
secondly, in Durham, 26 Oct. 1752, ELIZABETH FOWLER,
daughter of Josiah and Hannah (Baldwin) Fowler.

His military record follows (Col. Rec., vol. 10. 1751-1757;
p. 415): "Gen. Assembly held at New Haven, Nov. 5, 1755.
This assembly do establish Mr. Benjamin Maltbie, Ensign".
("Gen. Assembly holden at New Haven, 8 Oct. 1761", p. 578,
Col. Rec. Conn., 1757-1767, XI): "This assembly do establish
Mr. Benjamin Maltbie, Lieut. 14th Co., 2nd Reg. of this
Colony". (Col. Rec. Conn., 1768-1772, vol. 13, p. 13): "Gen.
Ass. holden at Hartford June 10, 1768. This ass. do establish
Mr. Benjamin Malbie to be Captain of the 14th Comp. or
train band, in the 2nd Regiment in this Colony".

Children by second wife, born in Northford:

   i.   ELIHU,⁴ b. in 1753; d. 19 Dec. 1753, ae. 2 weeks.
26. ii. BENJAMIN, b. 20 Jan. 1755.
   iii. THADDEUS, b. 19 Dec. 1756-7. "Enlisted at outbreak of Rev. War; for
           gallant conduct was soon made corporal of his company; from hard-
           ship and privation he fell fatally ill from exposure at Ticonderoga. A
           young cousin was sent for him and from the Northern Army to North-
           ford the long journey was performed slowly and painstakingly, both

boys riding the same horse; Thaddeus leaning forward on his cousin's shoulder; dying shortly after his return". A Chapter of Children of American Revolution in St. Paul, Minn., was named for him, March 1896.

27. iv. JONATHAN, b. 21 April 1759.
    v. ELIZABETH, b. 16 April (or May?) 1761; d. 22 March 1781; m. 16 March 1780 ELNATHAN TYLER. A daughter, d. 13 Feb. 1781, aged 5 weeks.
    vi. SARAH, b. 5 May 1763 (or 11 May, see Linsley Gen.); d. 16 March 1848; m. in Northford, 28 Sept. 1786, JAMES LINSLEY (see Linsley Genealogy).

        Children (surname *Linsley*):

1. *James Harvey*	6. *Dan Evelyn.*
2. *Olive.*	7. *Sarah Melvina.*
3. *Esther.*	8. *Delight Urania.*
4. *Emily.*	9. *John Stephen.*
5. *Elizabeth Maltby.*	10. *Jeremiah.*

28. vii. ISAAC, b. 11 Nov. 1767.
29. viii. STEPHEN, b. in July, bapt. 20 Aug. 1769.

15. SAMUEL[3] MALTBY (*Samuel,*[2] *William*[1]), born in Branford, Conn., 21 Oct. 1718, died 1 Dec. 1771. He married first, in Branford, 13 Oct. 1743, ABIGAIL WILFORD; secondly, in Branford, 22 Jan. 1745-6, REBECCA FOOTE, daughter of Stephen and Elizabeth (Nash) Foote; and thirdly, 1 May 1755, MARY FOWLER, daughter of David Fowler.

Child by first wife:

    i. ABIGAIL,[4] b. 22 April 1744; m. BILLE TYLER of Branford.

Children by second wife:

30. ii. SAMUEL, b. 15 Nov. 1746.
31. iii. JAMES, b. 30 May 1749.
32. iv. JONATHAN, b. 21 Oct. 1751.
    v. REBECCA, b. 25 May 1754; d. 15 May 1755.

16. CAPT. JONATHAN[3] MALTBIE (*Jonathan,*[2] *William*[1]), born in Stamford, Conn., 29 June 1720, died 13 Aug. 1745. He married in Stamford, 27 Feb. 1743-4, ABIGAIL HOLMES, "of Greenwich".

Child:

33. i. JONATHAN,[4] b. 17 Dec. 1744.

17. DAVID[3] MALTBIE (*Jonathan,*[2] *William*[1]) was born at Stamford, Conn., 7 Feb. 1727-8. He married there, 28 Sept. 1749, SARAH HOLLY, daughter of Ensign John and Hannah (Slauson) Holly. The widow of David Maltbie, married 6 Nov. 1768 David Webb of Stamford.

Children:

    i. SARAH,[4] b. 1 May 1750; m. STEPHEN NEWMAN.
        Children (surname *Newman*):

1. *Rufus.*	4. *Maltbie.*	7. *William.*
2. *Rebecca.*	5. *Stephen.*	8. *Cate.*
3. *Ralph.*	6. *Sally.*	9. *Andrew.*
	10. *Rebecca.*	

ii. HANNAH, b. 10 Oct. 1751; d. young.
iii. DAVID, b. 22 Aug. 1753; d. 1 Jan. 1758.
iv. ABIGAIL, b. 21 July 1756; m. 6 June 1782 SAMUEL WEBB, son of David
and Ruth (Waterbury) Webb.
Children (surname *Webb*):

1. *Cate.*	5. *Sarah.*
2. *David Maltbie.*	6. *Abigail.*
3. *John.*	7. *Elizabeth.*
4. *James.*	8. *Mary Ann.*

34. v. DAVID, b. 4 April 1759.
vi. HANNAH, b. 29 April 1762; m. 16 Oct. 1781 SAMUEL HOYT.
Children (surname *Hoyt*):

1. *James Maltbie.*	4. *Sally.*	7. *Elihu.*
2. *Harriet.*	5. *Maria.*	8. *Emily.*
3. *James Maltbie.*	6. *Samuel Blachley.*	9. *Emily.*

18. REV. JOHN[4] MALTBY (*William,*[3] *William,*[2] *William*[1]), born in
New Haven, Conn., 3 Aug. 1727, died 30 Sept. 1771. He
married 7 Nov. 1754 SUSANNA HUTCHINGS.

Yale College, 1747; 2nd Presbyterian Minister at Bermuda,
1750. Rev. Jonathan Maltby, born in 1759, wrote a genealogy
of the Maltby family (owned by the compiler) in which he
states that the above (his second cousin) "came to New Haven
in 1771, from South Carolina to my Father's in Northford,
on his way to Dartmouth College to succeed President Wheelock. In two weeks he was a corpse" . . . . . "President
Stiles" (of Yale) "said of him, 'he was the best Hebrewisher
of the age' ". From Bermuda he went as minister to the
Presbyterian Church at Wilton, S. C.

Children (possibly list is incomplete), order of birth unknown:

i. ELIZABETH,[5] m. DR. W. SMITH STEVENS, Charlestown, S. C.; had a
daughter, *Susan Eliza,* living in 1809.
ii. WILLIAM, supposed to be he of Papers of First Council of Safety, Rev.
War Party in South Carolina. "June-November, 1775, William Maltby,
8 (St. Helena, 26 October)".
iii. JOHN DAVENPORT. A deed, 16 Sept. 1787, gives him of Warwick (Bermuda), Mariner, and Hester his wife, to Dr. Richard Bell of Southampton, 1st Party sells to 2nd, one undivided 3rd part in several tracts of
land.
John Davenport Maltby's father was ordained by the New York
Presbytery. Possibly he is the following. 1st and 2nd Presbyterian
Churches, New York. "John Maltby and Esther Johnson his wife had a
son, Daniel, b. Aug. 5, 1786, bapt. 15 Aug. 1786". (Query as to whether
Hester of Bermuda record was Esther of New York.)
iv. MARGARET, m. STOW WOOD, merchant of Bermuda.

19. JOSEPH[4] MALTBY (*Joseph,*[3] *Daniel,*[2] *William*[1]), born in Branford,
Conn., 21 May 1738, living in 1799, in the vicinity of Whites-
boro, N. Y. The name of his wife is not known, although deeds
record them as "Joseph Maltby and wife". Eldest child was
born in 1768. In 1766, of Goshen, also 1770, 1773, 1774; of
Lenox, Mass., 1776; son, Chandler, born in 1779, in Goshen;
of Harwinton, 1780; of Caanan church, 1782; Litchfield, 1790;
of Goshen church, 1795.

It is thought that the wife of Joseph Maltby might have
been a Crittenden. His brother, William Maltby, of Lenox, in a

deed, 1779, to James Richardson, was signed in the presence of Aaron *Adams* and *Huldah* Crittenden, while a deed of Joseph Maltby, Lenox, executed 1776, is to Stephen Crittenden of Lenox. This is evidently Stephen, born in 1752, in Guilford, Conn. He and his brothers, Timothy and Seymour, were of Lenox, and Timothy Crittenden married *Huldah* Adams, Canterbury, Conn.

Children:

35. i.   JOSEPH,⁵ b. in 1768.
    ii. MARY, b. 4 Feb. 1769.
36. iii. CHANDLER, b. in Goshen 28 April 1779.
37. iv. GROVE, b. 3 May 1782, bapt. in Caanan 15 Aug. 1782.
    v.   ELIZABETH, bapt. in Caanan in March 1785.
    vi. ERASTUS.
    vii. HANNAH.
    viii. GRACE.

20. WILLIAM⁴ MALTBY (*Joseph,*³ *Daniel,*² *William*¹) was born in Branford, Conn., 13 June 1742. He married first, about 1763, LYDIA RITTER, died between 1770-1775, daughter of Thomas and Mary (Everdeen) Ritter, of Hartford; secondly in Lenox, Mass., about 1774-5, CATHERINE LEE, died in Vershire, Vt., 3 Dec. 1798, daughter of Stephen and Catherine (Forbes) Lee; and thirdly, SUBBMITTA GIBBS.

William Maltby was of Hartford, 1764; of Caanan, 1770-71; of Lenox, 1772-79; of Vershire, 1780-82, 1796.

He was a soldier in the Rev. War. (Mass. Soldiers and Sailors in Rev. War, vol. 16.) "William Maltby, residence not given, served in a company commanded by Captain Oliver Belding of Lenox, Colonel John Brown's regiment, in 1777." Also (*ibid.*) "William Maltby, private, Capt. Charles Dibble's Co., Col. Rossiter's Regiment, Berkshire Co. Enlisted 18 Oct. 1780; discharge, 22 Oct. 1780, service 4 days on the alarm at the Northward".

Rev. Jonathan⁴ Maltby, first cousin of William, in his manuscript, wrote of him: "William said to me, 'I have nineteen sons and daughters and it may be twenty' ". Only sixteen have been found.

Children by first wife, born in Lenox and Vershire:

    i.   MARY,⁵ b. 22 Nov. 1764; living in 1849 in Wisconsin; m. CHARLES AVERY, d. in Cattaraugus, N. Y.
    ii. ELIZABETH, b. 13 July 1766; m. AARON POST.
         Four children living 1849.
38. iii. WILLIAM, b. 3 July 1768.
    iv. LYDIA, b. 17 Jan. 1770; d. 17 Nov. 1792.

Children by second wife:

    v.   CATHERINE, b. 19 Nov. 1775; in Oberlin, Ohio, in 1839; m. ISRAEL MATHISON.
         Three children living in 1849; two were ministers.
39. vi. STEPHEN LEE, b. 22 Jan. 1777.
40. vii. JOHN, b. 22 Oct. 1778.

viii. IRA, b. 18 March 1780; d. aged 17 years.
41. ix. ISAAC.
   x. ANNA, b. in 1781.
42. xi. BENJAMIN.
   xii. HULDA.
   xiii. PERCY, b. in 1789; d. in 1792.
   xiv. ALVA, b. in 1796; d. aged 9.
   xv. SALLY, living in 1849; m. JOHN B. WATKINS.
   xvi. PERCY, d. aged 30; m. FREDERIC BROWN. One son living in 1849.

21. NOAH[4] MALTBY (*Joseph*,[3] *Daniel*,[2] *William*[1]) was born in Branford, Conn., 23 Sept. 1744. He married HULDAH————.
He enlisted in the Revolutionary War from Goshen. 17th Regiment, Col. Sheldon, for the defence of coast and forest until 1 March 1780.
He was of Springfield, Mass., going to Salisbury in 1764. Here, about five miles east of Salisbury, an old Atlas lists "Maltby's Siding". Went to Goshen, 1776; Woodbury, 1785. His will is dated 1 November 1785.
There were eight children. Of the three daughters given below we do not feel certain that they are correct.

Children:

   i. HULDAH,[5] bapt. 22 Sept. 1771.
   ii. EDIN (or ADIN), bapt. 22 March 1773.
43. iii. NOAH, b. 24 Nov. 1774.
44. iv. FREDERICK, b. in Litchfield 4 Dec. 1776. (Possibly father of Sophia Maltby who m. 14 March 1819 James Kimball. Resided in Bradford, Vt.)
   v. POLLY (?). A Polly Maltby m. in Branford, 12 April 1797, Calvin Mansfield.
   vi. SALOME (?). A John Lyman of New Hartford, b. in 1778; m. Salome Maltby of the same place.
   vii. SOPHIA (?).
   viii. JOHN, b. 13 Feb. 1786 (Woodbury, Conn., record); m. in 1812 DEBORAH SCOVALL, daughter of Reuben Scovall. Think he is the John of Winchester, Conn. Will 1827, "Youngest dau. Deborah, my dau. Huldah, my son Ephraim".

22. JONATHAN[4] MALTBY (*Joseph*,[3] *Daniel*,[2] *William*[1]), born in Branford, Conn., 10 July 1746, died 3 Oct. 1801. He married LYDIA BARTHOLOMEW.
He was of Goshen, 1770, when his brother, Joseph Maltbie, sold him "three acres, Dwelling House and Shop . . . "
Revolutionary War Rolls record him as "Jonathan Malby, residence not given, served as a private in Company commanded by Capt. Josiah Yale, of Lee or Lenox, in 1781, on an alarm at Stillwater. Enlisted Oct. 10, 1781. Discharged Oct. 20, 1781. Service 12 days".
In 1782 there was a Jonathan Maltby in Lenox, Mass. He may have been Jonathan[4] (Joseph,[3] Daniel,[2] William[1]), or he may have been Jonathan[4] (Samuel,[3] Samuel,[2] William[1]). The records of Vershire, Vt., cited by the present town clerk of Vershire (1955), assure us that Jonathan[4] (Joseph,[3] Daniel,[2] William[1]) and his brother, William, were among the first settlers of Vershire, and that this Jonathan was the I[st] Clerk

of the Proprietors of Vershire, 28 Aug. 1783, and that he continued in that office for a number of years.

Children:

45. i.   JONATHAN,[5] b. 9 Jan. 1772.
46. ii. JOSIAH, b. 5 June 1774.
    iii. ALICE, b. 13 July 1775.
    iv. LYDIA, b. 2 June 1777; m. as his second wife, JUDGE JOHN LARABEE, b. in Plainfield, Conn. Removed to Pownal, Vt.
47. v.   JESSE, b. 28 March 1782.
    vi. ELIZABETH, b. 1 April 1788.
48. vii. GEORGE W., b. 5 April 1790.
    viii. PATTY B. (or MARTHA), m.————RICHARDSON of West Fairlee, Vt.

MALTBY-MALTBIE-MOLBY

By the late DOROTHY (MALTBY) VERRILL, of North Vancouver, B. C.

23. DANIEL[4] MALTBY (*Daniel,*[3] *Daniel,*[2] *William*[1]), born in Branford, Conn., 7 Jan. 1742, died at Norfolk 19 Jan. 1779. He married, 22 Dec. 1763, MARGARET MUNSON, born in Wallingford 14 April 1744, daughter of Moses and Phebe (Merriman) Munson.

Children:

    i. ANNE,[5] b. in Goshen 13 Aug. 1765; m. in Norfolk, in June 1800, SAMUEL STEVENS.
49. ii. JEHIEL MERRIMAN, b. in Goshen 20 Sept. 1767.
    iii. DANIEL MUNSON, b. in Norfolk 28 Aug. 1770; d. unm.
    iv. SALLY, b. in Norfolk 14 July 1772.

50. v. ZACHEUS, b. in Norfolk 19 Aug. 1774.
vi. HANNAH, bapt. 3 Nov. 1776; d. aged 1 year.

24. BENJAMIN[4] MALTBY (*Daniel,*[3] *Daniel,*[2] *William*[1]), born in Northford 11 May 1750, died 1 Jan. 1847. He married in Norfolk, 5 July 1771, ABIGAIL MUNGER, daughter of Rueben and Elizabeth (Dudley) Munger.

He was of Branford in 1776, removing for a short time to Stony Creek. Of Norfolk, 1781; to Groton, Tompkins Co., N. Y.; to Southington, Ohio, in 1820, where Deacon Benjamin died aged 96. In an obituary notice, the "New York Observer" wrote of him: "He was a true patriot. He warmly espoused the cause of the country. He possessed the spirit of '76 and cheerfully devoted his property and his personal efforts to obtain freedom and Independence. The good of his country he earnestly sought till his death".

Children:

51. i. SIMEON,[5] b. 20 Nov. 1772.
52. ii. BENJAMIN, b. 7 May (June ?) 1773.
iii. ABIGAIL, b. 19 Feb. 1775; d. 4 Jan. 1823; m. 6 Oct. 1794 ASA PRESTON.
Children (surname *Preston*):

1. *Harris.*	4. *Candace.*	7. *Abigail E.*
2. *Laura.*	5. *Benham.*	8. *Sabra L.*
3. *Buel.*	6. *Rosa Clemen.*	9. *Julia E.*

53. iv. JACOB, b. 11 Nov. 1776.
54. v. AMMI, b. 26 June 1779.
vi. HANNAH, b. 16 April 1781; d. in Southington, Ohio, 15 July 1823; m. 10 May 1803 ALEXANDER KNAPP.
Children (surname *Knapp*):

1. *Alexander Horace.*	3. *Benjamin S.*
2. *Jesse Maltby.*	4. *Henry E.*
5. *Samuel Isaac.*	

55. vii. ELON, b. in Norfolk 8 March 1783.
viii. LOIS, bapt. 18 May 1786; d. in January 1794.
56. ix. NATHANIEL HARRISON, b. in Norfolk 1 March 1786.
x. JULIA, b. in Norfolk 17 Oct. 1790; m. 8 Jan. 1812 IRA ROSE.
Children (surname *Rose*):

1. *Lucy.*	3. *Hannah.*
2. *Samuel.*	4. *Laura.*
5. *Julia*	

57. xi. DANIEL, b. in Norfolk 3 April 1793.
58. xii. JESSE, b. in Norfolk 9 March 1797.

25. ZACHEUS[4] MALTBY (*Daniel,*[3] *Daniel,*[2] *William*[1]), born in Northford (?) in June 1754, died in Eden, N. Y., about 1835. He married JERUSHA ROSE.

Revolutionary War record: (vol. viii, Conn. Rev. Rolls) "Maltbie, Zacheus. Continental Regiment, 1775; 1st Regiment. General Wooster. 6th Company—Capt. Douglas. Time of Service—6 months, 26 days". "Regiment recruited in New Haven. Raised on first call for troops by Gen. in April-May 1775. Marched to New York latter part of June and encamped at Harlem. Took part in operations above Lake George and Champlain. Assisted in the reduction of St. John's in October. Stationed at Montreal. Adopted as Continental 6th Company

1st Regiment. Capt. William Douglas of Northford. Zacheus Maltbie discharged in Northern Department Nov. 28, 1775". He was of Branford until 1781; Norfolk, 1783; bought land in Lee., Mass., 1797; recorded as of New Marlborough, Mass.; and, 1800, as of Lee, "Hatter".

Children, probably all born at Norfolk:

i.   JERUSHA,[5] bapt. 7 Dec. 1783; m. in Branford, 22 Sept. 1800, JEHIEL BARTHOLOMEW. 1801 to Dryden, Tompkins Co., N. Y.; 1818 to Erie Co.; about 1836 to Coldwater, Mich.
      Children (surname *Bartholomew*):
      1. *Watson Hines.*   3. *Phebe.*   5. *Isaac.*
      2. *Amos Adams.*   4. *Noah Willis.*   6. *Jehiel.*
      7. *Clarinda.*

ii.   LUCRETIA, bapt. in 1783; m. 5 May 1798 NATHANIEL HOLT. (Conn. Marriages give this as "Holt". It is an error.)

iii.   MOLLY ROSE, bapt. 7 Dec. 1783; m. JEDIDAH TUCKER of Eden, N. Y Removed to Locke, N. Y.
      Child (surname *Tucker*):
      1. *Charlotte.*

iv.   ZACHEUS, bapt. 29 Aug. 1784; d. in December 1785.

v.   SABRA, bapt. 5 May 1787; m. in Dryden, N. Y., 12 Feb. 1812, JESSE BRADLEY BARTHOLOMEW. Removed to Ionia County, Mich.
      Children (surname *Bartholomew*):
      1. *Juliana.*   3. *Sophrina.*   5. *Adonijah.*
      1. *Minerva.*   4. *Artemus.*   6. *Juliana.*
      7. *Lemi.*

vi.   PATIENCE, bapt. 6 Aug. 1791; d. same month.

59. vii.   ZACHEUS, bapt. 25 May 1793/4.

60. viii.   SAMUEL, bapt. 16 April (Aug. ?) 1797.

61. ix.   JONATHAN, bapt. 12 April 1801.

x.   SARAH MATILDA, bapt. 9 Aug. 1807.

26. BENJAMIN[4] MALTBY (*Benajmin,*[3] *Daniel,*[2] *William*[1]), born 20 Jan. 1755, died 10 May 1823. He married in North Branford, 22 Jan. 1778, REBECCA TAINTOR, daughter of Nathaniel and Submit (Tyler) Taintor, of Branford, Census 1790.

Children:

62. i.   THADDEUS,[5] b. 15 Jan. 1779.

ii.   BENJAMIN, b. 11 Nov. 1780; d. *s.p.* in 1834; m. in 1811 WEALTHY W. CHITTENDEN.

63. iii.   DE GRASSE, b. 14 Sept. 1782.

iv.   ELIZABETH, b. 20 June 1784; d. 12 June 1840; m. 6 May 1820 JUDGE BENNETT BRONSON of Waterbury.
      Children (surname *Bronson*):
      1. *Rebecca Taintor.*
      2. *Susan.*

v.   REBECCA, b. 19 April 1786; d. in May 1786.

vi.   JULIUS, b. 5 Jan. 1788.

65. vii.   SAMUEL, b. 27 Jan. 1790.

66. viii.   ELBRIDGE, b. 23 Jan. 1792.

67. ix.   ERASTUS, b. 2 Dec. 1796.

x.   ELIZA REBECCA, b. 13 April 1800; d. 18 Aug. 1882 (?); m. 27 April 1820. CAPT. JONATHAN CLARK FOWLER. "Went to White Hollow".
      Children (surname *Fowler*):
      1. *Benjamin Maltby.*
      2. *Levi.*
      3. *Oscar Alonzo.*

27. Rev. Jonathan[4] Maltby (*Benjamin,*[3] *Daniel,*[2] *William*[1]), born in Branford, Conn., 21 April 1759, died in Fair Haven 14 Sept. 1850. He married in North Branford, 17 June 1787, Submit Taintor, died 18 Dec. 1848, daughter of Nathaniel and Submit (Tyler) Taintor.

Graduated Yale College, 1779. Studied Theology with Rev. Benjamin Trumbull of North Haven. Went to Savannah, Ga.; to New Haven; and later taught in an Academy in Killingworth. Then he spent three years in Vernon, N. Y., and returned to Fair Haven. He was a student at Yale in 1775, and wrote a lengthy article "In Time of the Revolution". He wrote: "Some of the first young men, the flower of Northford, fell in the contest". Names mentioned include: "Capt. William Douglas, Sergt. Levi Munson, Corporal Josiah Fowler, Jun., Benjamin Henshaw, privates Nathaniel Bunnel, Caleb Cooke, John Elwell, Samuel Cook, Joseph Hawkins, Abner Tharp" (Thorp)"from Northford". "News of the capture of St. John's, Canada, was brought to New Haven by a brother of Gen. Ethan Allen. Col. Fitch ordered out the cannon . . . The gallant Allen, soldier like, leaped on the cannon at the last fire, swung his hat and cried 'God save the Continental Congress'. 'Three Cheers', O, it was done to the life. It was my first term in Yale College. January 17, 1776. Another detachment under Major Douglas of three months men was ordered to New York. Ensign Titus Monson (died on Long Island March 1776), Joseph Bunel, Solomon Linly and my brother Thaddeus Maltby were a part. Again in May 1776, Lieut. Ambrose Baldwin, Sergeant Benjamin Norton, Corporal Thaddeus Maltby and Dan Bartholomew, Peter Farnham, Factor Monroe and Dick Negro, seven men from that little village marched to the Northern army. Four of these fell victims to the cause of their country. Thaddeus Maltby, Dan Bartholomew, Factor Monroe and Dick Negro and two of the militia to New York, Edwin Foot and Dan Page . . . After decease of Col. Douglas, May 1777, the Reg. was commanded by Col. Meigs . . . Sergt. Levi Munson and Ser. Benjamin Norton early entered the army and retired 1783. Lieut. Serg. Munson was captured with Gen. Allen and was with him in prison two years in England. . . . . . (Munson was appointed Lieutenant and served during the war. Capt. Isaac Foote was a warm and active officer, commanded a detachment of the troops to New York, 1776. Jonathan Maltby* and Solomon Talmage of the same troop, with others, were dispatched under Capt. Treat of Milford to the capture of Burgoyne . . . . Mr. Josiah Fowler and others were with Major Meigs in the expedition to Long Island, when ninty of the enemy were captured. They were guarded one night in the Episcopal Church in Northford on their way to Hartford.

---

*Jonathan[4] (Samuel,[3] Samuel,[2] William[1]).

Mr. Elihu Fowler was in the battle of White Plains (was a marksman) . . . . Jonathan Fitch served during and Peter Lyon were at the taking of Cornwallis . . . Capt. Jonathan Munson, Capt. Solomon Talmage, Mr. Elihu Foot, Squire John Potter and Mr. James Linly were pensioners . . . "

Another article is headed "Maltby Place, April 21, 1848. Birthday of my 90th Year," which deals largely of July 1779, when "Tryon and Traitor Arnold with three or four thousand British troops entered New Haven. After one night in town they cross next morning to East Haven . . . on Tuesday I was one of a————" [*illegible*] "party on East Haven hights, where balls were whistling constantly. A cannon ball took off all upper part of a Mr. Pardee's head, several men were wounded . . . While in New Haven three of my class went out with Capt. Hillhouse, David Austin, Elizur Goodrich are wounded. Austin bringing in a prisoner".

Rev. Jonathan Maltby was the first to write a genealogy of the Maltby family. The original MS. is owned by the compiler. It is particularly important due to the fact that some of the Revolutionary War Rolls are missing.

In this MS. he writes, "Squire Samuel Maltby, Yale College, Class 1712; was father to Samuel of Northford. He and my father were first cousins. He had three sons, Samuel, James, and Jonathan* . . . . Jonathan married a Culver. He and Sol. Talmage were detached from the troop under Capt. Treat of Milford and were with him at the Capture of Burgoyne; went to Lenox, Mass."

It will be evident that Jonathan's memory was excellent, and as he lived at Northford in early life, and must have known well this second cousin, Jonathan, it seems certain that he did know the war record of Jonathan, son of Samuel.

The 2nd Regt. of Militia was composed of companies from New Haven, Milford, Branford and Derby. Not all the Company rolls have survived; hence the importance of the written statements of Rev. Jonathan Maltby.

Children:

    i. Isaac Taintor,[5] b. 29 Aug. 1788; d. in Fairhaven, Mich., 6 March 1841; m. Clarissa Pardee of East Haven. A child died in infancy.
68. ii. Jonathan, b. 19 April 1790.
    iii. Abial Holmes, bookseller and publisher, b. 12 May 1792; d. *s.p.* in New Haven in 1853; m. Sarah Booth Lyon, daughter of Nathaniel Lyon of New Haven.
69. iv. Oliver Ellsworth, b. 12 May 1794.
    v. George, b. 16 Oct. 1796; d. in New Haven in 1861; m. Jane Betsey Dixon.
        Child:
        1. *Elizabeth*,[6] b. in 1848.
70. vi. Lucius, b. 25 Jan. 1798.
    vii. Amoret Submit, b. 11 Jan. 1801; d. unm.
    viii. Harriet Grace, b. 14 Aug. 1804, Vernon St., N. Y.; d. unm.

---

*Jonathan[4] (Samuel,[3] Samuel,[2] William[1]).

28. Brig. Gen. Isaac[4] Maltby (*Benjamin,*[3] *Daniel,*[2] *William*[1]), born in Northford 10 Nov. 1767, died in Waterloo, N. Y., 20 Oct. 1819. He married in Hatfield, Mass., 10 Nov. 1790, Lucinda Murray, only child of General Seth and Elizabeth (White) Murray, of Hatfield.

Yale College, 1786. Recorded, 1789, at the First Church, New Britain, when he was licensed to preach. Representative from Hatfield in Massachusetts Legislature, 1809-10. Author of three books on Military Science, viz: "Elements of War", "Military Tactics" and "Court Martial". Twice chosen Presidential Elector. Served through the War of 1812, and made Brigadier-General in 1813, with headquarters at Boston. He was an "eminent teacher of music".

Children, born in Hatfield:

71. i. Seth Murray,[5] b. 31 July 1791.
   ii. Elizabeth White, b. 27 Feb. 1794; m. 11 June 1817 Rev. Ephraim Chapin.
      Children (surname *Chapin*):

1. *Ephraim.*	3. *Maria M.*	5. *Charles.*
2. *Eliza L.*	4. *Louise.*	6. *Henry.*
	7. *Edward Payson.*	

72. iii. Benjamin, b. 30 June 1796.
   iv. Maria, b. 15 March 1799; d. in Buffalo, N. Y., 29 Sept. 1864; m. 17 Nov. 1824 Thomas C. Love.
      Children (surname *Love*):

1. *Julia.*	4. *Elizabeth Murray.*
2. *George Maltby.*	5. *Albert Haller.*
3. *Maria.*	6. *Marie.*

   v. Aurelia, b. 4 July 1801; d. 12 Oct. 1898; m. 5 Sept. 1821 Caleb Fairchild of Waterloo, N. Y.
      Children (surname *Fairchild*):

1. *Isaac Maltby.*	3. *Joseph Lewis.*
2. *Mary Elizabeth.*	4. *Julia Ann Norton.*
	5. *Frances Aurelia.*

   vi. Julia Ann, b. 22 May 1804; d. in San Francisco, Calif., 12 Dec. 1873; m. 3 Jan. 1829 Charles Norton of Buffalo, N. Y.
      Children (surname *Norton*):

1. *Lucinda.*	3. *Edward.*
2. *Henry.*	4. *Julia.*

73. vii. Isaac Fowler, b. 10 Feb. 1807.
   viii. Lucinda, b. 28 April 1810; d. in 1890; m. 5 May 1834 Joseph Salter of Buffalo, N. Y. Six children, all d. young.
   ix. Martha Church, b. 6 June 1813; d. aged 4 months.
   x. Martha Church, b. 16 Dec. 1815; d. 27 July 1889; m. 16 June 1838 Harlow Swaine Love, of Waterloo, N. Y.
      Children (surname *Love*):
      1. *Charlotte Cutler,* d. aged 10 months.
      2. *John Lord* (Attorney General).
      3. *Lelia.*
      4. *Jeannie.*
      5. *Martha Maltby.*

29. Col. Stephen[4] Maltby (*Benjamin,*[3] *Daniel,*[2] *William*[1]), baptized in Northford 20 Aug. 1769, died 22 Jan. 1812. He married there, 27 Sept. 1788, Abigail Williams, daughter of the Rev. Warham and Anne (Hall) Williams, of Northford.

Abigail's grandson (grandfather of the compiler) was
seventeen when his grandmother died. He said "She was a
very beautiful woman . . . When she married Stephen, the
folks all said they were the handsomest couple ever stood up
in Northford". Rev. Jonathan Maltby, his elder brother,
wrote of him: "Stephen was an eminent teacher of music and
was much employed at home and abroad". He was appointed
Deacon, 31 May 1804; he was one of the Grand Jurors for
Branford, or Northford, in 1794. Grandsons of Stephen Maltby
always referred to him as "Colonel". Apparently he belonged
to some local regiment.

Children, born in Northford:

74. i.   AUGUSTUS WILLIAMS,⁵ b. 22 Oct. 1789.
    ii. ELIJA (BELIGUR), bapt. 1 May 1791; d. unm. "He was in the Epirer des-
         patched ship U. S., from the Mediteranian".
75. iii. STEPHEN ELUTHEROUS, bapt. 17 July 1796.
    iv. JULIA ANN, bapt. 23 Dec. 1810; d. in New Haven about 1885; m. in
         1835-6 HENRY BIDWELL.
              Child (surname *Bidwell*):
              1. *Henry Stuart*, b. in 1838.

30. SAMUEL⁴ MALTBY (*Samuel,³ Samuel,² William¹*), born in Northford 15 Nov. 1746, died there 18 Aug. 1774. He married 11
Feb. 1768 ROSANNA COE of Wallingford, daughter of Simeon
and Anna (Morris) Coe of Durham. His widow married
secondly, 30 Nov. 1786, John Page.

Children, born in Northford:

76. i.   JOHN,⁵ b. 8 Dec. 1768.
77. ii. TIMOTHY, b. 9 April 1770.
78. iii. MORRIS, b. about 1772.
    iv. ANNE, b. 23 Feb. 1773; d. 10 Sept. 1775.

31. JAMES⁴ MALTBY (*Samuel,³ Samuel,² William¹*), born in Northford
30 May 1749, died 11 Feb. 1820. He married SARAH COE,
daughter of Simeon and Anna (Morris) Coe, of Durham.

Children:

    i.   SARAH,⁵ b. in Northford 15 May 1787; m. AUGUSTUS TYLER, son of
         Elnathan and Phebe (Atwater) Tyler.
              Children (surname *Tyler*):
              1. *Martha*.   2. *David Atwater*.
    ii. EUNICE, b. 18 April 1788; d. unm.
79. iii. JAMES, b. 18 July 1789.
    iv. WILLIAM, b. 4 Oct. 1796; d. unm. 24 Oct. 1820.
80. v.   HENRY, b. 29 March 1799.

32. JONATHAN⁴ MALTBY (*Samuel,³ Samuel,² William¹*), born in
Branford, Conn., 21 Oct. 1751, died in New York State after
1804. His second cousin, Rev. Jonathan Maltby, wrote of
him, "he married a Culver. Went to Lenox, Mass."
     (Land records of County of Berkshire, Middle District
Registry, Pittsfield, Mass.) 23 March 1786, a Jonathan Maltby
of Lenox purchased land in the town of Pittsfield. Deed

recorded 4 April 1787. On 3 April 1787 Jonathan Maltby of Pittsfield sold land of the identical description. Deed recorded 4 April 1787.

William Maltby acknowledged a Deed of Sale of land located in Lenox, before a Notary and witnessed in Orange County, Vt., 8 Nov. 1784. Had the above Jonathan been Jonathan of Vershire, he would have acknowledged the Deed of Sale before a Notary in Orange County. We assume that the 1786-87 transactions were executed by Jonathan[4] (Samuel,[3] Samuel,[2] William[1]), and that he later went to Hebron Town, Washington Co., N. Y. Land records of Washington County, and of Onondaga County, N. Y. (including mortgages), leave no doubt that the Jonathan of Camillus, Onondaga Co., N. Y., was the Jonathan of Hebron Town (P. O. Salem), Washington County.

In 1774, the distribution of estate of his father, Samuel Maltbie, late of Branford, mentions "land bounded West by Caleb Calver's land". Calver is evidently Culver, and we find: "Caleb Culver, b. 1754, Wallingford, went to Lenox, Mass." In 1782 a Lenox deed from Jonathan Maltbie to Jonathan Hinsdale, mentions: "land bounded South by Rev. Samuel Munson and Dan Culver". Dan Culver, born in 1756, was brother of above Caleb. He removed to Aurelius, N. Y. It would seem probable that Jonathan's wife was a near relative of these Culvers. Unfortunately, there was another Jonathan Maltby, a contemporary, who was also in Lenox, a second cousin, born 10 July 1746 (Joseph,[3] Daniel,[2] William[1]), and it has been impossible to determine in some Lenox records which Jonathan is intended. Jonathan, born in 1751, may have had a second wife, as a descendant states, "he married Polly Foote". A deed recorded in Branford, 1 Jan. 1781, is by Jonathan Maltbie of Branford to his brother James. He appeared personally and signed this deed, 26 Dec. 1780. By 2 Aug. 1790 a Jonathan Maltby* was in Salem, N. Y. In 1792 Jonathan Molby of Salem bought land from George Guthrie in Hebron Town, N. Y. In 1804, in Camillus, Richard Rosa and Nancy Rosa his wife, deed land there to Jonathan Molbey. In 1810 he and his family are recorded in the Census (Town of Camillus, Onondaga Co., N. Y.), as Maltby. Of his four sons, two retained the spelling "Maltby" and two took the spelling "Molby".

Proof that he took part in the Revolutionary War is furnished from manuscripts written by his second cousin. Rev. Jonathan Maltby, who also resided at Northford. (This MS. is owned by the compiler.)

---

*Williams Papers, Albany, New York, State Library, vol. 3, p. 28 "Salem, August 2, 1790   Mr. John Williams Sir: Please to let the bearer thereof Mr. Jonathan Maltby have one Sickle and charge the same to me and you will oblige your humble Sarvt   Thomas Collins".

In the MS. "In Time of the Revolution", he wrote: "Jonathan Maltby" (son of Samuel) "and Solomon Talmage of the same troop, with others were dispatched under Capt. Treat of Milford to the Capture of Burgoyne".

This follows: "Capt. Isac Foote . . . commanded a detachment of troops to New York, 1776". "Capt. Treat" was Samuel Treat, later Major in this same Regiment, the Second, part of second Brigade. They fought in the battles of 19 Sept. and 9 Oct. 1777. Upon General Burgoyne's surrender, General Gates referred to them as "two excellent militia regiments from Connecticut". (Ref. from Assist. Ref. Librarian, Dorothy W. Bridgwater, Yale University.)

In his manuscript genealogy of the Maltby family, Rev. Jonathan Maltby records: "Squire Samuel Maltby, Yale College, class 1712, was father to Samuel of Northford. He and my father were first cousins. He had three sons, Samuel, James and Jonathan . . . Jonathan married a Culver. He and Sol Talmage were detached from the troop under Capt. Treat of Milford and were with him at the Capture of Burgoyne, went to Lenox, Mass."

Children of Jonathan Maltby (or Molby), of Camillus, N. Y.:

 i. Lucy,[5] said to have died aged about 16 to 18.
81. ii. Jacob Maltby, "born in Connecticut" probably 28 Feb. or 1 March 1782.
82. iii. Chester Molby, b. 8 Dec. 1788.
83. iv. William Maltby, b. 4 July 1800.
84. v. Isaac Molby, probably b. about 1805-6.

33. Capt. Jonathan[4] Maltbie (*Jonathan,*[3] *Jonathan,*[2] *William*[1]), born in Stamford, Conn., 17 Dec. 1744, died in Fairfield 11 Feb. 1798. He married there, 23 Oct. 1768, Elizabeth Allen, daughter of Lieut. David and Sarah (Gold) Allen. He is recorded in "Sketches of Bunker Hill and Monument" as "Capt. Jonathan Maltbe".

In 1775 (Civil and Military List of Rhode Island), is recorded: "Capt. Dudley Saltonstall, 1st Lieut. John Paul Jones", and among three other lieutenants, "Lieut. Jonathan Maltbie".

In 1776 a letter from Col. Gurdeon Saltonstall, NewLondon, 23 Jan. 1776, to Silas Dean, delegate to the 1st and 2nd Congress at Philadelphia, mentions: "Second Lieut. Maltbie's crew". His commission as Lieut. is dated 12 Oct. 1776. Signed by John Hancock. In 1777, he was 1st Lieut. of Connecticut Continental Frigate "Trumbull". His commission as Captain is in possession of a descendant. It is dated 21 March 1791. Signed "G. Washington. By the President Thos. Jefferson". At this time he became Captain of the "Trumbull". Later he was appointed Master of the *Argus*, a cutter in the service of the United States for the protection of the revenue.

Children:

85. i. JOHN,[5] bapt. 30 (20?) April 1769.
    ii. SARAH, bapt. 19 (17?) April 1772; m. SAMUEL ROWLAND.

Children (surname *Rowland*):

1. *William Maltbie.*	5. *Elizabeth.*	9. *Andrew.*
2. *George.*	6. *Jonathan Maltbie.*	10. *Edward Sherman.*
3. *Samuel.*	7. *Henry.*	11. *Julia Burr.*
4. *Charles.*	8. *James.*	

34. DAVID[4] MALTBIE, "ESQ." (*David,*[3] *Jonathan,*[2] *William*[1]), born 4 April 1759, died in New York City 24 Nov. 1807; buried in Stamford, Conn. He married 19 Nov. 1786 NANCY DAVENPORT, daughter of Silas and Mary (Webb) Davenport, descended from Rev. John Davenport of New Haven.

"He was Sherriff of Fairfield County and was a member of the Rutgers Street Church".

He was a soldier in the Revolutionary War. "Capt. Jonathan Whitney's Company, David Maltbie discharged 8 Jany. 1777. Served 1 month 21 days. Ninth Regiment Militia under General Wooster. In 1776-77 marched to Westchester border. The 9th Regt. had but lately returned from New York. After the battle of White Plains, Oct. 28, 1776, the Assembly ordered the 9th, 10th, 13th and 16th Militia Regiments to march to Westchester border and place themselves under General Wooster's command". "Capt. Jonathan Whitney's Company. Canaan, Fairfield County. David Maltbie, private, discharged 23 Jan. 1777; 1 month, 5 days service".

The 1790 Census records him as of Norwalk and Stamford.

Children:

86. i.   WILLIAM DAVENPORT,[5] b. 4 Jan. 1789.
    ii. MARY CATHARINE, b. 11 Jan. 1791; d. in Syracuse, N. Y., 8 May 1848; m. JOHN TURNIER.
87. iii. JAMES RUFUS, b. 12 (15?) May 1793.
88. iv. JOHN ROBERT, b. 11 April 1795; d. in Huntsville (Vicksburg) in 1824. (Another record states he d. in Pittsburgh, Pa.)
    v.   CHARLES DAVID, v. 30 Dec. 1797; d. unm. of yellow fever in Rio de Janeiro. (Another record states he d. at the West Indies.)
    vi. EBENEZER DAVENPORT, b. 20 Jan. 1799.
    vii. ALBERT SYLVESTER, b. 4 Jan. 1802; d. 25 Dec. 1862. Graduate Yale Medical School with high honors. He was Editor of the Utica, N. Y *Opal.*

NOTES ON NEW HAVEN FAMILIES

By DONALD LINES JACOBUS, M.A., of New Haven, Conn.

MANSFIELD

1. RICHARD[1] MANSFIELD, of New Haven, married at St. Mary Archer, Exeter, England, 10 Aug. 1636, GILLIAN DRAKE, and died at New Haven 10 Jan. 1665. His widow married secondly Alexander Field, and died in 1669.

2. JOSEPH[2] MANSFIELD (*Richard*[1]), the elder of his two sons, was born about 1638, and died 15 Nov. 1692. He married MARY POTTER, daughter of William and Frances (REGISTER, vol. 54, p. 24). In * Mansfield's "Descendants of Richard and Gillian Mansfield," published in 1885, is a very incomplete account of Joseph's family, and it says of his daughters Mary and Elizabeth that they "probably died unmarried." An entry in the New Haven County Court Records (vol. 1, p. 210), dated 14 June, 1693, mentions Joseph's widow Mary and his children, Mary Tirhan, Martha Sperry, Marcy Bristow, Silence Wilcocks, Elizabeth Johnson, Comfort Benham, Joseph Mansfield, Ebenezer Mansfield, and Japhet Mansfield.
    Children:
- 3. i. MARY,[3] b. 6 Apr. 1658.
    - ii. MARTHA, b. 18 Apr. 1660; m. RICHARD SPERRY, b. 20 Jan. 1652, d. 1734.
    - iii. MERCY, b. 26 July 1662; d. after 1734; m. JOHN BRISTOL, b. 4 Sept. 1659, d. at Newtown, Conn., abt. 1735.
- 4. iv. SILENCE, b. 24 Oct. 1664.
    - v. ELIZABETH, b. 20 Sept. 1666; m. Lieut. WILLIAM JOHNSON, son of William and Sarah (Hall), b. 5 Sept. 1665, d. 1742. William and Elizabeth Johnson of New Haven, she being daughter of Joseph Mansfield, dec., acknowledged receipt of their portion from their uncle, Nathaniel Potter, Sr., he being brother to their mother, Mary Mansfield, dec. (New Haven Deeds, vol. 5, p. 131, recorded 1718).
    - vi. COMFORT, b. 6 Dec. 1668; m. JOHN BENHAM, b. 15 Sept. 1664, d. 1744.
    - vii. JOHN, b. 8 Apr. 1671; d. 22 Dec. 1690.
    - viii. JOSEPH, b. 27 Dec. 1673; d. 8 Oct. 1739; m. ELIZABETH THOMAS, b. abt. 1677, d. 4 Mar. 1763.
    - ix. EBENEZER, b. 6 Feb. 1677; d. 3 Aug. 1745; m. 20 Apr. 1710, HANNAH BASSETT, who d. 22 Jan. 1766.
    - x. JAPHET, b. 8 July 1681; d. 1745; m. 16 Jan. 1703, HANNAH BRADLEY, who d. 27 Oct. 1768.

3. MARY[3] MANSFIELD (*Joseph*,[2] *Richard*[1]) was born 6 Apr. 1658. In the County Court record referred to above, her married name is given as Tirhan, a variant for Turhand. The only man in the vicinity bearing this uncommon name, who could be her husband, was Thomas Tirhan of Guilford, Conn., who died in 1696, leaving

*Page 154, Vol. III of this work.

a widow Mary and children Henry, Samuel, and Abigail (New Haven County Court Records, vol. 1, p. 241). But Mary had been married before, as administration on the estate of Henry Wise of Guilford, deceased, was granted, 11 June 1684, to his widow Mary (County Court Records, vol. 1, p. 147), and in June 1686, there is further record of this estate, mentioning the widow Mary, Thomas Terhan present husband to the relict, and two children, unnamed (County Court Records, vol. 1, p. 160). John Hill of New Haven, who was born 10 Jan. 1650, and died 1710, married for his second wife, Aug. 1703, Mary Turhan. Consequently Mary married first HENRY WISE of Guilford; secondly THOMAS TURHAND of Guilford; and thirdly JOHN HILL of New Haven. In 1712, administration on the estate of Mary Hill of New Haven, deceased, was granted to Henry Turhand of Wallingford; and the estate was distributed to her son Henry, daughter Mary wife of Israel Barnes, and the heirs of her daughter Sarah Wright, deceased (New Haven Probate Records, vol. 4, pp. 55, 89).

Children by first husband:

i. SARAH[4] WISE, m. ——— WRIGHT.
ii. MARY WISE, d. after 1756; m. 31 Dec. 1707, ISRAEL BARNES of New Haven, b. 22 Apr. 1680, d. 1751.

Children by second husband:

iii. HENRY TURHAND, of Wallingford; m. 7 Nov. 1712, ELIZABETH MERRIMAN, b. 4 May 1693.
iv. SAMUEL TURHAND, not named in the distribution of his mother's estate.
v. ABIGAIL TURHAND, not named in the distribution of her mother's estate.

4. SILENCE[3] MANSFIELD (*Joseph,*[2] *Richard*[1]) was born 24 Oct. 1664. The Mansfield Genealogy says she married a Chatfield, and there is plenty of evidence to prove that her second husband was a CHATFIELD; but the County Court record previously mentioned gives her name, in 1693, as Wilcocks. The Wilcox and Wilcoxson families of Connecticut descend from William Wilcoxson of Stratford, one of whose sons, Obadiah, settled in East Guilford, and died in 1714, leaving widow Silence. The comparative infrequency of the name Silence, together with the fact that Silence Mansfield's sister Mary married two Guilford men, make it probable that OBADIAH WILCOXSON was her husband; and furthermore, Obadiah's daughter Jemima married Rev. John Merriman of Southington, and had a grandson Norman Mansfield Merriman, whose name helps to substantiate the theory; but the following would seem absolute proof. In 1750, Samuel[4] Mansfield (Ebenezer,[3] Joseph,[2] Richard[1]) died without issue, and his estate, excepting the widow's dower, reverted to his uncles and aunts (of whom Silence was one) or their representatives. On 22 May 1753, John Merriman and his wife Jemima of Farmington, and Mindwell Hill and Thankful Norton, widows, of Guilford, deeded to Joel Bradley of New Haven one-fifth part of land that was Samuel Mansfield's, deceased (New Haven Deeds, vol. 17, p. 358). As Jemima, Thankful, and Mindwell were daughters of Obadiah Wilcoxson by his wife Silence, and as this deed proves them to be heirs of Samuel Mansfield, their mother must have been this Silence Mansfield

whose name in 1693 is given as Wilcocks. She was Obadiah's third wife, and considerably younger than he. By his first wife, Mary ———, he probably had Ephraim and Janna (cf. Savage's " Genealogical Dictionary," and Wilcox's " The Descendants of William Wilcoxson," published in 1893) ; and according to Savage, his second wife was Lydia ———. She was Lydia Alling of New Haven, daughter of John and Ellen (Bradley), born 2 Aug. 1656, an identification which is proved by the fact that John Alling, in his will of 6 May 1689, names his grandchildren Ebenezer and Mary Wilcocks (New Haven Probate Records, vol. 2, p. 80). By Lydia, Obadiah had : Mary, born 1676, married Thomas Munson of New Haven ; Lydia, born 1678, died young ; Obadiah, born 1679, died young ; Ebenezer, born 1682. By Silence, Obadiah had Children :

i. TIMOTHY⁴ WILCOXSON, b. 15 Nov. 1690; d. before his father, without issue (New Haven Probate Records, vol. 4, p. 295).
ii. JOHN WILCOXSON, b. 9 Nov. 1692: d. 1 May 1753; m. 11 Jan. 1719, DEBORAH PARMELEE.
iii. JOSEPH WILCOXSON, b. abt. 1694; d. 15 July 1770; m. 1722, HANNAH GOODALE.
iv. MINDWELL WILCOXSON, m. 20 Apr. 1714, DANIEL HILL of Guilford.
v. JEMIMA WILCOXSON, b. 30 Oct. 1699; m. at Wallingford, 24 Feb. 1726, Rev. JOHN MERRIMAN of Southington, b. 16 Oct. 1691, d. 17 Feb. 1784.
vi. THANKFUL WILCOXSON, b. 4 Apr. 1702; m. 6 Sept. 1722, SAMUEL NORTON of Guilford.
vii. SILENCE (?) WILCOXSON, for whose existence Savage is authority.

MUNSON-FERNS

SAMUEL³ MUNSON, son of Samuel² and Martha (Bradley), and grandson of Capt. Thomas¹ and Joanna, was born 28 Feb. 1669, resided in Wallingford, Conn., and died 23 Nov. 1741. According to Munson's " The Munson Record " (p. 90), his first wife was MARTHA ———, who died 7 Jan. 1707, leaving eight children. The following facts shed some light on this lady's identity, which has hitherto remained a mystery. In May 1704, administration on the estate of Samuel Ferns, Sr., of New Haven, deceased, was granted to Thomas Sperry. Later in the same year, an agreement was made by Thomas Sperie and Samˡˡ Munson, sons-in-law to Samuel Ferns of New Haven, deceased, providing for the disposal of his estate and for the maintenance of Samuel Ferns [Jr.] (New Haven County Court Records, vol. 2, pp. 152, 173). Since Samuel Munson's first wife, Martha, was living at this time, it seems certain that she was a daughter of Samuel Ferns. Her birth and marriage are not recorded in the vital records, where we find the births of three of his children : Samuel, Elizabeth, and John. As Samuel, Jr., had to be maintained by his brother-in-law, it is likely that he was an invalid or an imbecile. Although he was heir to some property, he executed no deeds, and there is no probate of his estate. Probably it went to Thomas Sperry in return for maintenance. As for the son John, he seems to have died in his father's lifetime. In 1705, Widow Sackett and her son John were appointed guardians to John, son of John Ferns, deceased (New Haven County Court Records, vol. 2, p. 202). On 26 June 1712, James Ferns, minor child of John Ferns, late resident at Woodbury, deceased, chose Serjᵗ Samuel Mundson of Wallingford to be his guardian (New Haven Probate Records, vol. 4, p. 54). In 1724, on the death of James Ferns of Milford, some dispute arose as to whether his

472

estate should go to his uncle, Samuel Ferns of New Haven, or to John Olmstead of Norwalk, whose wife was sister of the half blood to the deceased (New Haven Probate Records, vol. 5, pp. 200, 216). As the court decided in favor of the uncle, it is assumed that the estate came from the father's side, and that Olmstead's wife was half-sister on the mother's side; and this is substantiated by the Norwalk records, which show that John Olmstead's wife was Mary, daughter of Robert Small, " transient, sometime of Norwalk." From these facts and conjectures it is possible to construct this pedigree of the family:

1. SAMUEL[1] FERNS, of New Haven, died in 1704.
     Children :
     i.   SAMUEL,[2] b. 2 July 1663; living in 1724; probably d. unm.
     ii. ELIZABETH, b. 7 Dec. 1665; d. 22 Apr. 1718; m. 18 Nov. 1684, THOMAS SPERRY, b. 13 July 1658, d. 1722.
  2. iii. JOHN, b. 3 Mar. 1668.
     iv. MARTHA, b. abt. 1670; d. 7 Jan. 1707; m. abt. 1688, SAMUEL MUNSON of Wallingford, b. 28 Feb. 1669, d. 23 Nov. 1741.

2. JOHN[2] FERNS (*Samuel*[1]), born 3 Mar. 1668, died before 1705, and probably before his father. He lived at Woodbury, Conn., and married the widow of Robert Small, who, by her former husband, had a daughter Mary Small, who married, 29 Feb. 1718, John Olmstead of Norwalk, Conn.
     Children :
     i.   JOHN,[3] must have d. unm. before his brother, unless his name, which appears only in the modern copy of the court records, be a clerical error for James.
     ii. JAMES, of Milford, Conn., d. unm. 1724.

RECORD OF THE MARCY FAMILY.

Com. by Prof. OLIVER MARCY, LL.D., of the Northwestern University, Evanston, Ill.

THERE are two families by the name of Marcy in the United States. One family is descended from John Marcy, of whom the first written notice appears in Elliot's Church Record in Roxbury, Mass., as follows : " John Marcy took the Covenant March 7, 1685." Among his descendants are the late Secretary of State, William Larned Marcy, General Randolph B. Marcy, and Erastus E. Marcy, M.D., now well known to our history and literature.

The other family is represented by the Hon. Daniel Marcy, of Portsmouth, New-Hampshire, and Peter Marcy and descendants, of New Orleans. The father of Daniel and Peter Marcy came to this country about eighty years ago from the island of Marie Galante, W. I. His father went to that island from France.

De Marcy, or, simply *Marcy*, is now a name quite common in France and its colonies. The name appears to have come into Normandy with Rollo (A.D. 912), thence it went to England with William the Conqueror (A.D. 1068), and became very common in Cheshire, where the orthography is now universally Massey or Massie. In this form (Massey) it is common in the English and Irish Peerage.

In evidence that the present French form of the name obtained somewhat in England, I find in " The Patents of King John " (A.D. 1208) mention made of one " Radus de Marcy."

We propose to trace only the family of John Marcy, whom we find at Roxbury.

1. JOHN MARCY was the son of the high sheriff of Limerick, Ireland.* He was born about the year 1662 ; joined Elliot's church in Roxbury, Mass., March 7, 1685. In April, 1686, he with Benjamin Sabin, Jonathan Snithers, Henry Bowen, John Frizzel, Mathew Davis, Nathaniel Gary, Thomas Bacon, Peter Aspinwall, George Griggs, Benjamin Griggs, Ebenezer Morris and John Lord, took possession of Quatosett (Woodstock, Conn.), granted (1663) by the colony of Massachusetts to the town of Roxbury. He married Sarah Hadlock, daughter of James and Sarah (Draper) Hadlock, of Roxbury. She was born Dec. 16, 1670. They lived and died in Woodstock. He died Dec. 23, 1724, aged 62 years. She died May 9, 1743, aged 73. Their children were:

    i.   ANNA, b. in Roxbury, Oct. 11, 1687 ; m. Ebenezer Grosvenor, of Pomfret.
2. ii.   JOHN, b. Nov. 17, 1689 ; m. Colburn.
3. iii. JAMES, b. Feb. 26, 1691 ; m. Ainsworth.
4. iv. EDWARD, b. June 28, 1695 ; m. Haskins.
5. v.   JOSEPH, b. Sept. 18, 1697 ; m. Throop.
6. vi. BENJAMIN, b. March 11, 1699 ; m. Corbin.
7. vii. MOSES, b. April 18, 1702 ; m. Morris.
8. viii. SAMUEL, b. July 28, 1704 ; m. Russell.
   ix. SARAH, b. Feb. 8, 1707 ; m. Johnson, 1728.
9. x.   EBENEZER, b. June 6, 1709 ; m. Martha Nicholson.
   xi. ELIZABETH, b. Nov. 8, 1711.

---

* The authority for this statement is a memorandum made by the Rev. Laban Ainsworth, of Jaffrey, N. H., about the year 1785. The memoranda were given him by his mother, the daughter-in-law of John Marcy. The date of his birth is computed from data on his tombstone now seen at Woodstock, Conn.

2. JOHN[2] (*John[1]*), was born in Woodstock, Conn., Nov. 17, 1689. He was married to Experience* Colburn, January 14, 1712, by the Rev. Josiah Dwight. He was the executor of his father's will, which is still extant. He was a farmer in Woodstock. Children:

- 10. i. ISRAEL, m. Abigail Fuller.
- ii. DEBORA, m. Harris.
- iii. —— m. Saunders.
- iv. JOHN, bap. 1727; d. April 11, 1801, at Windsor, Vt., aged 77.
- v. SARAH, bap. July 23, 1728.
- vi. SARAH, bap. April 19, 1730.
- vii. GRACE, bap. Feb. 4, 1733.
- viii. JAMES, bap. May 12, 1734.

3. JAMES[2] (*John[1]*), was born in Woodstock, Conn., February 26, 1691. He married Judith Ainsworth, daughter of Edward and Joanna (Hemmingway) Ainsworth, who was born January 25, 1722. He died January 29, 1765. They had:

- 11. i. JAMES, bap. Feb. 2, 1729; m. Sarah Robins.
- ii. URIAH, bap. May 9, 1731.
- 12. iii. REUBEN, b. 1732; m. Rachel Watson.
- iv. ELISHA, bap. Jan. 2, 1735.
- v. JUDAH, m. Lord.
- vi. ANNA, m. Underwood.
- vii. LOVIA, m. Lyon.
- viii. JERUIAH, bap. 1739.

4. EDWARD[2] (*John[1]*), was born at Woodstock, Conn., June 28, 1695. He married —— Haskins. Children:

- i. DOLLY, m. Dresser.
- ii. MARY, m. (1) Remington, (2) Babbitt.
- iii. MARTHA, m. Plympton.
- iv. MIRIAM, m. Thomas Newell.
- v. MEHITABEL, m. John Newell.

5. JOSEPH[2] (*John[1]*) (" Capt."), was born in Woodstock, September 18, 1697, where he died October 18, 1795, aged 88 years. He married Mary Throop, sister of the Rev. Amos Throop, pastor of the church in Woodstock. She died February 12, 1790, aged 85 years. They had:

- i. JOSEPH, b. May 9, 1729; killed by Indians in Vermont, May 24, 1746.
- 13. ii. STEPHEN (" Capt."), b. Sept. 4, 1730; d. Dec. 4, 1776.
- iii. ESTHER, b. Jan. 26, 1732; m. Perrin; d. May 16, 1807.
- 14. iv. NATHANIEL, b. Feb. 25, 1733; m. Grosvenor; d. Nov. 29, 1798.
- v. REBECKA, b. Nov. 10, 1735.
- 15. vi. ICHABOD, b. Dec. 27, 1737.
- 16. vii. HADLOCK, b. Jan. 30, 1739; d. 1821.
- 17. viii. SMITH, b. Oct. 28, 1742; d. Aug. 1829.
- ix. LYDIA, b. Sept. 23, 1744; m. Dr. Morse, of W. Woodstock.
- x. THOMAS, b. April 9, 1746; d. July 4, 1769; killed by frightened horses.

6. BENJAMIN[2] (*John[1]*), was born March 11, 1699. He married Mary, daughter of James and Hannah (Eastman) Corbin. They had:

- i. LOIS, m. Jabesh Hendrick, of Wilbraham.
- ii. HANNAH, m. (1) Isaac Skinner, (2) Samuel Warner.
- 18. iii. BENJAMIN, m. Loisa Gilbert.
- iv. ELIZABETH, m. Thomas Tiffany, of Ashford, Ct.
- v. MARY, b. 1733; m. Capt. Wm. Ainsworth; d. Nov. 23, 1815.
- vi. EUNICE, m. Dodge.
- 19. vii. ASAHEL, m. Priscilla Dunham.
- viii. DOLLY, m. Samuel Munger, of Brimfield.

7. MOSES[2] (*John[1]*), " Col.," was born April 18, 1702. In 1723 he

---

* " Experience, wife of John Marcy, owned the covenant, April 6, 1727."—*Ch. Rec.*

married Prudence Morris. He moved to Sturbridge, Mass., in 1732, where he became "the principal man in the colony."* He was the first justice of the peace; the first representative to the general court from the town; was moderator at 70 town meetings. During the French war he fitted out soldiers for the army at his own expense, but was afterward remunerated by the town. At a meeting of the church, held March 18, 1752, to compromise with the "separatists," Moses Marcy was moderator, and the historian speaks of the "excellent spirit displayed by the excellent and venerable moderator." He died Oct. 9, 1779, "leaving an honorable name, a large estate, and a numerous family." A list of persons married by himself includes 55 marriages; the list beginning in 1755 and ending in 1776, a period of 21 years. In this list we have the following, probably his children:

> "MARY MARCY, m. Westbrook Remington, July 4, 1755."
> "MARTHA MARCY, m. Gershom Plympton, March 2, 1758."
> "MIRRIAM MARCY, m. Timothy Newell, Jan. 1767."
> "DANIEL MARCY, m. Hannah Morris, March 3, 1763."
> "MAHITABEL MARCY, m. Jonathan Newell, May 12, 1771."
> "MARTHA MARCY, m. Jared Freeman, Dec. 22, 1774."

They had also:

20. i.   JEDEDIAH, m. Mary Healy; d. in Dudley.
    ii. MOSES, unm.
21. iii. ELIJAH, m. Stacy.
22. iv. DANIEL, m. Hannah Morris.

8. SAMUEL^2 (*John^1*), born in Woodstock, Conn., July 28, 1704; married Mary Russell, of Ashford, February 13, 1724. They had:

23.   WILLIAM, bap. May 24, 1730.
24.   ZEBEDIAH, bap. Aug. 27, 1732; m. Priscilla Morris.
        TABITHA, bap. Sept. 19, 1734.
25.   SAMUEL (?), b. Oct. 19, 1739; m. Esther Peak; d. Feb. 1820.
        ZAVIAH, m. Paul.
        SYBELL, bap. March 24, 1745.

9. EBENEZER^2 (*John^1*), born at Woodstock, Conn., June 6, 1709; married Martha Nicholson, July 25, 1738; lived in Dover, Duchess co., N. Y.; died December 10, 1808. Farmer. They had:

    i.   MAHITABEL, m. Ward.
    ii. DOLLY, m. Hodgkis.
    iii. JERUSHA, m. Conitt.
26. iv. GRIFFIN.
    v.   JOSEPH, unm.
27. vi. EBENEZER, m. Martha Spencer.
28. vii. ZEBULON, m. Jerusha Conet.
    viii. SARAH, m. Marcy.
    ix. AMBROSE L. Lived in Greene, Chenango co., N. Y.
    x.   BENJAMIN.

10. ISRAEL^3 (*John,^{2} John^1*), married Abigail Fuller. They had:

29. i.   JONATHAN, m. Hannah Stone.
    ii. BETHIA, m. Levi Utley.
30. iii. ISRAEL, m. Jerusha White.
    iv. FANNY, unm.
    v.   EXPERIENCE, d. Nov. 23, 1818, aged 53, at W. Woodstock.
31. vi. ABRAHAM, m. Ursula Stone; d. June 23, 1837, aged 77.

---

* History of Sturbridge, Mass., by the Rev. Joseph S. Clark.

11. JAMES³ (*James*,² *John*¹), married Sarah Robins, of Eastford, Conn. They had:

  32. i. JAMES.   ii. URIAH.   iii. SARAH.
  33. iv. ELISHA.
  34. v. DAVID.
      vi. BETSEY.
      vii. JOB.

12. REUBEN³ (*James*,² *John*¹), born 1732; married Rachel Watson, of Barrington, R. I. Farmer in Ashford, Conn. They had:

      i. MATTHEW.   ii. EDWARD.
  35. iii. REUBEN.
  36. iv. SIMEON (M.D.), b. Aug. 19, 1770; d. Dec. 6, 1853, at Canajoharie, N.Y.

13. STEPHEN³ (*Joseph*,² *John*¹), "Captain," was born in Woodstock, Conn., September 4, 1730. He married Mary Howard, Dec. 21, 1752; died Dec. 4, 1776. She died December 7, 1779. They had:

      i. ESTHER, b. Nov. 5, 1753; d. Jan. 31, 1756.
  37. ii. JOSEPH, b. Nov. 22, 1758; d. Oct. 13, 1838.
  38. iii. STEPHEN (M.D.), b. Jan. 1, 1760. Practised medicine in Plymouth, Mass.; d. March 24, 1804.
      iv. SYLVESTER, lost at sea.
      v. REBECCA, b. June 13, 1765; d. March 17, 1844.
      vi. MARY, b. April 3, 1768.
      vii. HANNAH, b. Dec. 10, 1770; d. Jan. 26, 1836, at Brighton, Ohio.
      viii. DOROTHY, b. 1772.

14. NATHANIEL³ (*Joseph*,² *John*¹), was born in Woodstock, February 25, 1733. He married Hannah Grosvenor. He lived and died in West Woodstock, Conn. He died November 29, 1798. She died September 15, 1790, aged 53 years. They had:

      i. CLARISSA, m. Wilkinson.
  39. ii. ALFRED, } twins, { m. Rebecca Perin; d. Jan. 31, 1855.
      iii. LYDIA, } { m. David Perin; d. April 7, 1848.
      iv. PRUDENCE, d. Jan. 6, 1851, aged 84; unm.
  40. v. NATHANIEL, m. Amy Bradway; d. May 12, 1854.

15. ICHABOD³ (*Joseph*,² *John*¹) ("Captain"), was born in Woodstock, December 27, 1737. He married (1) Elizabeth Grosvenor, daughter of Ebenezer and Lucy (Cheeney) Grosvenor, of Pomfret. She was sister of General Lemuel Grosvenor, who was with General Putnam at the battle of Bunker-Hill, and afterward married his daughter. Elizabeth Grosvenor was born June 19, 1740, died December 28, 1792. She was the mother of nine children. He married (2) Miss Williams, of Brooklyn, Conn. No children. He died September 12, 1803, aged 66. They had:

      i. LUCY, b. July   ; m. Drake, Wilksbarre, Pa.
      ii. ELIZABETH, m. (1) Marcy; (2) Drake.
      iii. CHLOE, b. Oct. 3, 1769; m. Noah Perrin, of Pomfret.
  41. iv. GROSVENOR, b. Oct. 10, 1771; m. Bartholemew.
      v. EBENEZER, b. Oct. 3, 1774; d. at Dover, N. Y., unm.
      vi. MARY, b. Aug. 17, 1776; m. John Mowry.
  42. vii. THOMAS, b. Aug. 27, 1778; m. Anna Henry.
  43. viii. ICHABOD, b. July, 1780; m. Watrous.
      ix. JOSEPH, d. young.

16. HADLOCK³ (*Joseph*,² *John*¹), was born in Woodstock, Jan. 30, 1739. He graduated at Yale College 1861, ranking eighth in a class of 29. Studied law. He married Althea, daughter of the Rev. Abel Stiles (1762). He died at Hartland, Vt., December 29, 1821. She died January 26, 1784, aged 39. He was a man of talent and learning, but eccentric. He frequently preached as well as practised at the bar. He was extensively known in Connecticut, New-Hampshire and Vermont. They had:

    i.   Sophia, b. Dec. 2, 1764; m. Major Fox.

17. Smith³ (*Joseph,² John¹*), was born October 28, 1742. He married Patience Lawton, who was born February 15, 1744. He lived in Otis, Mass., where he died August 1, 1829. She died in Freedom, Ohio, 1841, aged 97. They had:

44. i.   Howland, b. April 11, 1767.
45. ii. Lawton, b. Sept. 27, 1768.
46. iii. Thomas, b. Feb. 19, 1770.
    iv. Bradford (Rev.), b. March 9, 1772.
    v.   Michael B., b. Aug. 8, 1775.
    vi. Patia, b. July 8, 1777; m. Steven Babcock.
    vii. Mary T., b. Sept. 17, 1779; m. Lyon.
    ix. Sarah, b. April 25, 1785; m. Steadman.

18. Benjamin³ (*Benjamin,² John¹*), married Loisa Gilbert, of Mansfield. She was 21 years of age and he 52. They had:

47. i.   Calvin, m. Abigail Vinton, June 28, 1804.
    ii. Olive.   iii. Clara.
    iv. Alpheus, } twins.
    v.   Lebeus, }

19. Asahel³ (*Benjamin,² John¹*), was born March 25, 1738. He married Priscilla Dunham, of Woodstock. He died March 2, 1819, aged 81. She died March, 1829, aged 89. They had:

48. i.   Benjamin, m. Hannah Starks.
49. ii. Asahel, b. Oct. 1778; m. Persis Burley.
50. iii. Laban, b. March 7, 1780; m. Fanny Howe.
    iv. Elizabeth, b. May 16, 1786; m. Elam Russell.

20. Jedediah³ (*Moses,² John¹*), married Mary Healy, of Dudley, Mass. They lived and died in Dudley. They had:

    i.   Joseph, b. Oct. 21, 1749; d. Oct. 25, 1779.
    ii. Jedediah, b. July 23, 1751; d. Jan. 20, 1756.
51. iii. Jedediah, b. July 26, 1756; m. Ruth Larned.
    iv. Mary, b. Jan. 19, 1760.
    v.   Rhoda, b. May 4, 1762; m. Healy.
52. vi. Daniel, b. April 27, 1765; m. Betsey Larned.

21. Elijah³ (*Moses,² John¹*), married Stacy. They had:

    i.   Prudence, unm.
    ii. Sarah, m. Russell Smith, Sturbridge.
53. iii. Elijah, m. Mary Hobbs; d. aged 42.
    iv. Lemuel, m. Nancy Carpenter.

22. Daniel³ (*Moses,² John¹*), was married by his father (a justice of the peace) to Hannah Morris, of Dudley, March 3, 1763. They had:

54. i.   Morris, m. Sally Morse.
55. ii. Marvin, m. Richards, of Boston.
    iii. Daniel, lost at sea.
    iv. Mahitabel, m. Dr. Charles Negus, Dudley, Mass.
    v.   Dorothea.
    vi. Abigail, m. Jacob Mason, Craftsbury, Vt.
    vii. Betsey.

23. William³ (*Samuel,² John¹*), was born in Woodstock. He was married (1) to Lucy Bugbee, of Stafford (1758). Moved to Belchertown, Mass.,

1776. Was drafted into the army, but his son Gardner went in his stead. Moved to Hartland, Vt., 1778. Wife Lucy died 1792. Married (2) Rosanna Tucker, 1793. Died April, 1813, aged 81. They had (1 m.):

 56. i. CHESTER, b. 1760.
 57. ii. GARDNER, b. June 12, 1762 ; m. Elizabeth Danforth.
 58. iii. WILLARD, b. Oct. 3, 1764.
  iv. OLIVE, m. Willard.
 59. v. WINTHROP, b. June 17, 1769 ; m. Abigail Sargeant.
  vi. SALOME, m. Ebenezer Pike.
 60. vii. LEVI, b. Sept. 3, 1774 ; m. Ruth Sargeant ; d. 1838.
  viii. (2 m.) POLLY, b. Nov. 21, 1797 ; m. Perkins.
  ix. SALLY, b. Oct. 22, 1799 ; m. Daniel Gilbert.

24. ZEBEDIAH[3] (*Samuel,*[2] *John*[1]), was baptized Aug. 27, 1732. He was married to Priscilla Morris, of Woodstock. Moved to Stafford 1779, thence to Willington 1782. He was a farmer, and died in Willington in 1806. They had:

  i. MOLLY, d. 1776, aged 19 (at Woodstock).
  ii. PRISCILLA, m. Jedediah Converse, Woodstock.
 61. iii. ZEBEDIAH, b. 1760 ; d. 1851.
  iv. ADEN, d. young.
  v. LAURA, m. Danton, of Willington.
  vi. HANNAH, m. Daniel Dimmock.
  vii. DORCAS, m. Joseph Lamb, of Vermont.
  viii. MARTHA, m. Thomas Knowlton, Ashford.
  ix. THOMAS, d. aged 2 years.
  x. ADEN, d. in the prison ship in New-York harbor.
  xi. POLLY, m. James Curtis, Marcellus, N. Y.

25. SAMUEL[3] (*Samuel,*[2] *John*[1]), born in Woodstock, Conn., Oct. 19, 1739 ; married Esther Peak ; lived in Woodstock, Vt. ; died at Windsor, Vt., Feb. 1820, aged 80. They had:

  i. ESTHER, b. Aug. 28, 1763 ; m. Isaac Packer.
 62. ii. ALVAN, m. Polly Bunce.
  iii. PROSPER, m. Jane Dutton ; d. May 15, 1855, aged 82.
 63. iv. OREN, b. April, 1774 ; m. (1) Polly Work, (2) Lucy Work.
  v. AVIS, m. Prouty.
  vi. JOHN S., d. in Georgia.
  vii. DORCAS, m. (1) Proctor, (2) Seymour Burnham.
  viii. SAMUEL, m. Ruth Hatch ; d. Dec. 10, 1846.
  ix. LOIS, m. David Brown.
  x. STEVEN, b. Oct. 13, 1785 ; d. at Wethersfield, Vt., July 21, 1806.
  xi. REBECCA, m. Otis Prim.

26. GRIFFIN[3] (*Ebenezer,*[2] *John*[1]), was born in Dover, Duchess county, N. Y., where he lived and died. He married Temperance Kelsey. They had:

  i. MOSES, m. Susan Cutler ; d. May, 1809.
  ii. GRIFFIN.   vii. ANNA.
  iii. BENJAMIN.   viii. DOROTHEA.
  iv. SARAH.   ix. ABBY.
  v. MAHITABEL.   x. RUTH.
  vi. RACHEL.   xi. SOPHIA.

27. EBENEZER[3] (*Ebenezer,*[2] *John*[1]), was born at Dover, Duchess county, N. Y., 1741. He married Martha Spencer, daughter of Jonathan and Content Spencer, of Saybroook, Conn., afterward of Fishkill, N. Y., Feb. 11, 1768. He was proprietor and mill owner in Wyoming Valley, Pa.; was at the fort on the east side of the river when the massacre occurred on the

west side. The boats being removed he was unable to be present at the fight. (See Peck's History of Wyoming.) They had:

      i. JONATHAN, b. May 22, 1770 ; m. Elizabeth Marcy.
      ii. ELIZABETH, b. Dec. 7, 1771.
      iii. MARTHA, b. Jan. 23, 1774 ; d. July 26, 1818.
      iv. CONTENT, b. April 8, 1776.
      v. THANKFUL, b. on Pocono Mt. during the flight from the massacre.
64. vi. EBENEZER, b. Feb. 10, 1780.
65. vii. JARED, b. June 6, 1782 ; d. Dec. 18, 1816.
66. viii. JOSEPH, b. Feb. 19, 1787.

28. ZEBULON³ (*Ebenezer,² John¹*), was born in Dover, Duchess co., N. Y., May 28, 1744 ; died in the Wyoming Valley, Penn., Sept. 21, 1826. He married Jerusha Conet, who was born March 14, 1743, and died March 29, 1819. He was a proprietor in the Wyoming Valley. They had:

      i. ZEBULON, b. Oct. 9, 1767 ; d. Jan. 19, 1770.
      ii. JOHN, b. June 9, 1769 ; d. May 5, 1840.
      iii. LYDIA, b. Jan. 3, 1772 ; d. June 18, 1817.
67. iv. NICHOLSON, b. Nov. 3, 1773 ; d. Jan. 30, 1827.
      v. SARAH, b. Aug. 9, 1776 ; d. on Pocono Mt. in the flight from the massacre, July 20, 1778.
      vi. SARAH, b. June 24, 1778 ; d. Oct. 14, 1854.
      vii. ZEBULON, b. July 10, 1780 ; d. Nov. 9, 1834. Surveyor. Lived at Scranton, Penn.
      viii. ABEL, b. April 24, 1782 ; m. Eunice Spencer.
      ix. JERUSHA, b. Nov. 8, 1783.

29. JONATHAN⁴ (*Israel,³ John,² John¹*), married Hannah Stone. They had :

      i. JONATHAN, m. Polly Harrington.
      ii. POLLY, m. Laban Harrington.
      iii. HANNAH, m. Adams.
      iv. RHODA, m. Elijah Bugbee.
      v. AZUBA, m. Simeon Harrington.
      vi. WELTHY, unm.
      vii. LYDIA, m. Lloyd Burt.

30. ISRAEL⁴ (*Israel,³ John,² John¹*), married Jerusha White. Died at Deerfield, Mass. (tombstone inscription), Nov. 9, 1823, aged 64. They had:

      i. JERUSHA, m. Wm. Heridon, of Sturbridge.
      ii. NABBY, m. Spear, of Deerfield.
      iii. ALICE, unm., d. Aug. 27, 1842, aged 53, at Deerfield.
      iv. SALLY.   v. FANNY.

31. ABRAHAM⁴ (*Israel,³ John,² John¹*), married Ursula Stone. He died June 23, 1827, aged 77. She died April 26, 1850, aged 90. They had:

      i. ISAAC, unm. Lived in Woodstock, Ct.
      ii. JOHN A., m. Sabra Hayward ; d. Oct. 13, 1864, aged 79.
      iii. JOSHUA, b. Nov. 10, 1787 ; m. Patty Smith ; d. Sept. 2, 1848. Lived at Hillsboro' Bridge, N. H.
      iv. PRUDENCE, m. Ebenezer Hamblin, Coventry, Ct.
      v. CHARLES, unm.
      vi. ABRAHAM, m. Sally Wilbur, Burlington Falls, N. Y.
      vii. CHESTER, m. Damoras Clark, W. Woodstock, Ct.
      viii. LEONARD, m. Sally Lillie.

32. JAMES⁴ (*James,³ James,² John¹*), was born Sept. 1, 1772. Married

(1) Polly Shaw, 1798; (2) Sally Flint, 1803. He died Feb. 22, 1845, aged 72. They had:

    i.   James, b. Aug. 24, 1800; m. Betsey Lyon.
    ii. Polly, b. Sept. 15, 1804; m. Erastus Fletcher.
    iii. Loren, b. Nov. 5, 1805; m. Eliza Adams.
    iv. Sally, b. April 22, 1809; d. Sept. 11, 1809.

33. Elisha[4] (*James,[3] James,[2] John[1]*), was born Jan. 24, 1784. He married Lucy Chandler. They had:

    i.   Samantha, b. May 15, 1809; d. Dec. 25, 1823.
    ii. Emily, b. Oct. 8, 1810; m. Charles Church.
    iii. Diantha, b. July 19, 1812; d. Aug. 16, 1812.
    iv. Lucy, b. May 1, 1814; m. Leonard B. Wright.
    v.   Elisha W., b. May 13, 1816; m. Mary Prince.
    vi. Albert, b. May 16, 1820; m. Mary Hait.
    vii. Sarah, b. July 2, 1822; d. March 2, 1824.

34. David[4] (*James,[3] James,[2] John[1]*), married Sybell Perrin. They had:

    i.   Mary Ann, b. Feb. 7, 1813; m. Elisha Kinney.
    ii. Uriah P., b. Nov. 25, 1814; m. Ann Fisk.
    iii. Mellissa B., b. May 24, 1818; m. Horace Kinney.
    iv. Job.

35. Reuben[4] (*James,[3] James,[2] John[1]*), was born in 1768. He married Hannah Sumner, of Roxbury, Mass. She was born in 1770, and died in Berlin, Ct., in 1843. His life was spent as a farmer in Willington, Ct., where he died in 1824. They had:

    i.   Edward, d. in Will co., Ill.
    ii. Samuel Sumner (M.D.). Living in Cape May co., N. J.
    iii. Matthew, judge in Cape May co., N. J.
    iv. William W., b. Nov., 1805; m. Martha Knowlton.
        There were sisters.

36. Simeon[4] (*Reuben,[3] James,[2] John[1]*), was born August 19, 1770. Graduated at Brown University. He married (1) Hannah Betts; (2) Sarah Otis. He was a doctor of medicine, and practised at Canajoharie, N. Y., where he died Dec. 6, 1853. They had:

    i.   Jane A., b. March 8, 1808; m. Jarvis N. Lake.
    ii. Maria L., b. April 15, 1814; m. G. H. Platner, Rockford, Ill.
    iii. Sarah O., b. April 3, 1825; d. Feb. 14, 1862.
    iv. George K., b. July 24, 1801; d. 1870.

37. Joseph[4] (*Stephen,[3] Joseph,[2] John[1]*), was born Nov. 22, 1758; married (1778) Mary Cole, of Middleboro', Mass.; died Oct. 13, 1838. She died Aug. 9, 1854. They had:

    i.   Sylvester (M.D.), b. Aug. 9, 1799; d. 1840, unm.
    ii. Joseph, b. Sept. 4, 1800. Living (1872) at Hartland, Vt.
    iii. Mary, b. June 8, 1802; m. Job Richmond.
    iv. Eleanor, d. young.
    v.   Eliza Throop, b. Jan. 20, 1805; m. Lewis Merritt.

38. Stephen[4] (*Stephen,[3] Joseph,[2] John[1]*) (M.D.), b. Jan. 1, 1760; married Lucy Jackson (1783). She died Jan. 13, 1844. He practised medicine at Plymouth, Mass.; died March 24, 1804. They had:

    i.   Hannah, b. Sept. 9, 1784; m. Joseph Sanger, of Bridgewater.
    ii. Stephen (M.D.), b. March 11, 1786; d. 1870.
    iii. Charles ("Capt."), b. May 13, 1787; m. Abby Jackson.

iv. JOSEPH, b. Jan. 8, 1789 ; d. 1790.
v. JOSEPH, b. April 5, 1791 ; m. Charlotte Eaton.
vi. WILLIAM, b. July 28, 1792 ; d. at sea.
vii. LUCY, b. May 9, 1794.
viii. EDWARD, b. April 9, 1796.
ix. MARY, b. Sept. 19, 1798 ; d. Aug. 18, 1801.
x. THOMAS J., b. April 12, 1800 ; d. 1801.
xi. MARY T , b. Jan. 5, 1803 ; m. Horace H. Rolfe.

39. ALFRED⁴ (*Nathaniel,³ Joseph,² John¹*), married Rebecca Perrin. Farmer in Woodstock, Ct. ; died Jan. 31, 1855, aged 91. They had :

i. JAMES LORENZO, M.D., m. Frances Browning (1817). Physician at S. Woodstock. Member of Legislature, 1835. Son, Lorenzo J., optician, Philadelphia.
ii. HANNAH G., m. Benjamin Alpine ; d. in Ohio.
iii. SANDFORD, b. March 1, 1804 ; m. Lydia A. Chandler.
iv. ESTHER, d. Aug. 14, 1814, aged 19.

40. NATHANIEL⁴ (*Nathaniel,³ Joseph,² John¹*), born 1775 ; married Amy Bradway ; died May 12, 1854. They had :

i. ORRIN, b. May 26, 1799 ; m. Ann J. Fisher, Pomfret.
ii. GURDON, b. Oct., 1802 ; m. Fidelia Parsons ; d. 1850.
iii. JUSTIN, b. July 18, 1804 ; m. Hannah Powell ; d. in Canada.
iv. EDWIN, m. (1) Belding ; (2) Adeline Wetherell ; d. Dec. 24, 1867, aged 65.
v. ALFRED, ⎫ m. Barbara Albee.
vi. ALVIN, ⎬ twins, b. May, 1807 ; d. 1832.
vii. NANCY ANN, b. Oct. 12, 1809. Killed by log, 1835.
viii. CHARLES GROSVENOR, b. Nov. 12, 1815 ; m. Hough.

41. GROSVENOR⁴ (*Ichabod,³ Joseph,² John¹*), born October 10, 1771 ; married Lucy Bartholomew ; died in Thompson, Ct., April 23, 1867. They had :

i. EBENEZER, b. Sept. 7, 1798 ; m. Damoris Aplin.
ii. LUCRETIA, b. April 15, 1800 ; d. 1867.
iii. RELECTA, b. Nov. 1803 ; d. 1871.
iv. ABIAL, b. Nov. 15, 1805 ; d. young.
v. POLLY, b. Aug. 14, 1807.
vi. MARY, b. Dec. 17, 1809 ; m. Benjamin Town.
vii. NOAH P., b. June 11, 1814 ; m. Eddy.

42. THOMAS⁴ (*Ichabod,³ Joseph,² John¹*), born in Woodstock, Ct., Aug. 27, 1778 ; married Anna, daughter of Andrew and Thankful (Norris) Henry, of Leyden, Mass., by the Rev. Asa Hibbard, Sept. 2, 1806. She was born Sept. 2, 1788, and died in Leyden, Aug. 6, 1865. He died in Coleraine, Mass., July 26, 1828. They had :

i. ANDREW HENRY, b. May 1, 1807 ; m. Lovilla Peck.
ii. GROSVENOR, b. Aug. 12, 1809 ; m. (1) Eliza A. Hastings ; (2) Mrs. Abigail (Liswell) Goudy ; d.
iii. ICHABOD (Rev.), b. July 16, 1811 ; m. Sarah Gill ; graduated at Wes. Univ., Middletown, Ct., 1839. Clergyman in the M. E. Church.
iv. THOMAS (Rev.), b. Aug. 24, 1813 ; m. Lucy Flagg. Clergyman in the M. E. Church.
v. MARY ANN, b. April 29, 1815 ; m. Rev. Asa Niles, son of William H., Prof. in Mass. Inst. Technology, Boston.
vi. JOSEPH, b. Oct. 7, 1818 ; d. young.
vii. OLIVER, b. Feb. 13, 1820 ; m. Elizabeth E. Smith ; graduated at Middletown, Ct., 1846 ; LL.D. Univer. Chicago, 1873 ; Prof. Northwestern University, Evanston, Ill.
viii. ELVIRA, ⎫ m. Geo. Childs.
ix. ALMIRA, ⎬ twins, b. Jan. 7, 1822 ; m. Calvin Peck ; d. May 2, 1860.

x. NANCY MARIAH, b. Sept. 13, 1825; m. Dr. A. S. Flagg.
xi. FANNY E., b. Aug. 15, 1827; m. E. C. Cross, M.D.

43. ICHABOD[4] (*Ichabod,[3] Joseph,[2] John[1]*), was born July 5, 1780. He married Betsey Waterhouse, of Leyden, Mass., where he lived most of his life; d. July 29, 1860. They had:

i. ELIZABETH, b. July 29, 1816; m. Brown.
ii. WILLIAM G., b. April 6, 1818; m. Laura Sumner; lives in Minnesota.
iii. GEORGE W., b. May 13, 1824; unm.; d. Jan. 29, 1849.

44. HOWLAND[4] (*Smith,[3] Joseph,[2] John[1]*), was born in Woodstock, Ct., April 11, 1767; married (1) Jemima Phelps; (2) Esther Southward. They had (1 m.):

i. HADLOCK.
ii. BETSEY.
iii. REBECCA.
iv. NATHANIEL.
v. JEMIMA.
vi. EMILY (2 m.).
vii. ARETHUSA.
viii. JOSEPH.
ix. NATHAN.

45. LAWTON[4] (*Smith,[3] Joseph,[2] John[1]*), born Sept. 27, 1768; married ———; died at Tyringham, Mass., 1846. They had:

i. PATIA L., b. Sept. 27, 1796.
ii. MARY F., b. April 18, 1798.
iii. ALICE T., b. Feb. 26, 1800.
iv. JOHN F., b. March 9, 1802.
v. CLARISSA, b. April 6, 1804.
vi. LUTHER, b. June 21, 1806.
vii. CELINDA, b. Sept. 13, 1809.
viii. BRADFORD R., b. Nov. 29, 1810.
ix. CALVIN L., b. June 31, 1813; unm.
x. SALLY, b. Oct. 27, 1815.

46. THOMAS[4] (*Smith,[3] Joseph,[2] John[1]*), was born in Woodstock, Ct., Feb. 19, 1770. Moved with his father to Otis, Mass., where he lived till 1828, when he went to Freedom (Western Reserve), Ohio. He travelled with his own team 34 times (17 round trips) between the two places, a distance of 600 miles, or in all 19,000 miles, most of the way through an unsettled wilderness, for the purpose of transporting his neighbors and friends to the Western Reserve. He died in Freedom, Jan. 12, 1860, aged 90 years. He married Elizabeth M. Lawton, who died in Freedom, 1842. They had:

i. SMITH, b. Aug. 1, 1795; m. Fanny Gibbs; d. Aug. 10, 1846.
ii. ELIJAH LYON, b. Feb. 4, 1798.
iii. NANCY ALMIRA, b. Oct. 21, 1802; m. Isaac J. Norton.
iv. SALLY, b. Oct. 4, 1807; m. John Johnson.
v. ELIZA ANN, b. Nov. 15, 1809; m. ——— Scott, Windham, Ohio.
vi. THOMAS MELVIN, b. Oct. 30, 1817; m. Almira Percy.

47. CALVIN[4] (*Benjamin,[3] Benjamin,[2] John[1]*), married Abigail Vinton. They had:

i. DAVID, m. Rhoda James.
ii. CALVIN, b. March 30, 1808; m. Elvira Clark; d. April 26, 1868.
iii. MERRICK.
iv. PLYMPTON.
v. FREEMAN.
vi. MARY ANN.

48. BENJAMIN[4] (*Asahel,[3] Benjamin,[2] John[1]*), married Hannah Starks, of Springfield. They had:

i. CHAUNCY, b. March 2 (?); m. Joanna Atkins; d. at Truro.
ii. LABAN, b. April, 1802; unm.; d. 1827, at Greenwich.
iii. ANDREW A., b. Sept. 15, 1804; m. Clementine Town, Dudley.

iv. Galen, b. April 12, 1807; lives in Mornana, Ill.
v. Marietta, b. June 11, 1810; m. Austin Tenney.
vi. John Judson, b. June 2, 1815; m. Amy Tucker.

49. Asahel[4] (*Asahel,[3] Benjamin,[2] John[1]*), was born Oct. 1, 1778; married Persis Burley, June 28, 1800. They had:

i. Mary Eliza, b. March 9, 1801; m. Turner Sears.
ii. Rinaldo B., b. Jan. 11, 1803; m. Chamberlin.
iii. Caroline P., b. Dec. 20, 1809; m. Willard Bugbee, of Ashford.
iv. Ransom D., b. May 10, 1814; m.; lives in Brownsville, Pa.
v. Calistus A., b. Sept. 30, 1819; d. at Brownsville, Pa.
vi. Lucius L., b. Sept. 30, 1831; m. Diana Chapman.

50. Laban[4] (*Asahel,[3] Benjamin,[2] John[1]*), was born March 7, 1780, in Woodstock, Ct. He was educated at Woodstock Academy; studied law with Judge Barnes, of Tolland, and with the Hon. Ed. Dickinson, of Amherst, Mass.; lived and practised his profession in Greenwich, Hampshire co., Mass., for 50 years; was 20 times elected a member of the Legislature of Massachusetts; was a member of the constitutional conventions in both 1820 and 1853. He married Fanny Howe, of Sturbridge, a woman of fine personal appearance and of vigorous intellect. He died October 11, 1860. They had:

i. Randolph Barnes (Inspector Gen. in U. S. A.), b. April 9, 1812; graduated at West Point, 1832; stationed at Green Bay; in the battles of Palo Alto and Resaca de la Palma, May 8–9, 1846. In 1857 served against the Seminoles; Utah exped., 1857–8; paymaster, 1859; inspector gen., 1861; brig. gen., Sept. 23, 1861; on the staff of Gen. G. B. McClellan during his campaigns; author of "Explorations of the Red River in 1852," 1853; "Prairie Traveller, 1859;" "Personal Recollections, 1866;" m. dau. of Gen. Mann, of Syracuse, N. Y. His dau. m. Gen. Geo. B. McClellan.
ii. Erastus Edgerton (M.D.), b. Dec. 9, 1815; graduated at Amherst College, 1837; Jeff. Med. Col., 1840; practised medicine in Hartford, Ct., and in New-York city; editor N. A. Homœopathic Journal, quarterly; editor of "Hahnemann's Lesser Writings, 1854;" "Theory and Practice of Medicine, 1852;" "Homœopathy vs. Allopathy, 1854." Married Emeline B. Kilbourn, of Hartford, Ct.
iii. William Ainsworth, b. July 20, 1818; m. Julia F. Colburn.
iv. Marsia Ann, b. June 20, 1822; m. David Patten, D.D.
v. Mary A., b. Aug. 11, 1824; m. Andrew J. Wilkinson, Boston.
vi. Fred A., b. July 28, 1829; m. Ann S. Jillson.

51. Jedediah[4] (*Jedediah,[3] Moses,[2] John[1]*), was born July 26, 1757; married Ruth Larned, March 1, 1782; died Aug. 14, 1811. They had:

i. Rhoda, b. Aug. 21, 1782; m. Steven Healy.
ii. Joseph, b. June 10, 1784; m. Abigail Shumway.
iii. William Larned, b. Dec. 12, 1786; m. (1) Dolly Newell; (2) Cornelia Knower; graduated at Brown University, 1808; recorder of Troy, N. Y., 1816; adj. gen., 1821; comptroller of New-York, 1823; justice of supreme court, 1829; U. S. senator, 1831; governor of New-York, 1833–9; sec. of war, 1845–9; sec. of state, 1853–7. Died July 4, 1857.
iv. Hannah, b. Jan. 14, 1789.
v. Jedediah, b. Oct. 19, 1791; m. Esther Healy.
vi. Caroline, b. Oct. 11, 1798; d. aged 4 years.

52. Daniel[4] (*Jedediah,[3] Moses,[2] John[1]*), married Elizabeth Larned, of Dudley, June 21, 1787; died May 14, 1833, aged 69. They had:

i. Bradford, b. Oct. 10, 1787; m. (1) Phipps; (2) Cynthia Stevens.
ii. Betsey, b. Jan. 14, 1789; m. Jonathan Stevens.
iii. Darius, b. July 19, 1790; unm.

iv. DANIEL, b. Feb. 2, 1792 ; m. Mary O. Kingsbury.
v. BARBARA, b. Dec. 18, 1793 ; m. Eliot Edmunds.
vi. AUGUSTUS, b. Feb. 16, 1796 ; m. Sally Carter.
vii. LARNED, b. Feb. 5, 1798 ; m. (1) Harriet Perry ; (2) Lydia Chamberlain.
viii. WILLIAM, unm.

53. ELIJAH[4] (*Elijah,*[3] *Moses,*[2] *John*[1]), married Mary Hobbs. He died in 1806, aged 42. They had :

i. SARAH, m. Eli Bush ; d. March, 1869, aged 87, in Montgomery, Vt.
ii. MERIAM, m. Jona. Barnes, Bakersfield, Vt.
iii. ELIJAH, m. Sarah Clemence ; d. 1855.
iv. LUCINDA, m. Amos Oakes.
v. MATILDA, b. Oct. 14, 1792 ; m. William McKinstry.

54. MORRIS[4] (*Daniel,*[3] *Moses,*[2] *John*[1]), married Sally Morse, of Sturbridge. They had :

i. DANIEL G., m. Betsey Lloyd, Springfield.
ii. ADELAIDE M., m. Daniel M. Hodges, Warren.
iii. JAMES L., unm. ; d.
iv. SARAH M., m. John P. Stockwell, Webster.
v. LYDIA H., m. H. Halcomb, E. Bloomfield, N. Y.
vi. OLIVER M., unm. ; d.

55. MARVIN[4] (*Daniel,*[3] *Moses,*[2] *John*[1]), married Christiana Richards, of Boston. Kept a hotel in Cambridge. They had :

i. CHRISTIANA, m. Horace Williams, of Boston.
ii. MARVIN, unm.
iii. MARY, m. Joseph Ford, of Boston.
iv. SUSAN.   vi. WILLIAM.
v. HOWARD.   vii. LYDIA.

56. CHESTER[4] (*William,*[3] *Samuel,*[2] *John*[1]), was born in Woodstock, 1760. Lived and died in Hartland, Vt. Served in the war of the revolution at Fort Bethel, Vt., after the burning of the town of Roystown by the Indians, for which he received a pension. He married Matilda, widow of Dr. S. A. Waldo. Died Oct. 25, 1845, aged 85. They had :

i. SALLY, d. young.
ii. RUFUS, killed in battle at Plattsburg, Sept. 11, 1814.
iii. CHESTER, lives in Michigan.
iv. WILLIAM ——, lives at Allen, Hillsdale co., Michigan.
v. HENRY K.,   "   "   "   "   "

57. GARDNER[4] (*William,*[3] *Samuel,*[2] *John*[1]), was born June 12, 1762. At the age of 18 took the place of his father, who was conscripted into the army from Belchertown, Mass. ; was stationed at West Point ; drilled by Baron Steuben ; " was sold to the British by Arnold ; " saw Arnold go on board the Vulture ; was present when Washington arrived. He settled in Hartland, Vt., where he was a farmer, tanner and dealer in West India goods. He was justice of the peace 14 years, overseer of the poor 6 years, selectman 11 years, captain of a company of infantry. He married Elizabeth Danforth, Dec. 4, 1791 ; died Oct. 8, 1837. They had :

i. SULLIVAN, m. Sarah Waldron.
ii. GARDNER, m. Matilda Walker ; d. Dec. 23, 1848, aged 54.
iii. BETSEY, m. Zenas Hopkins, 1816.
iv. SQUIRE, m. Eliza Bradstreet, now a lawyer and judge in Hartland, Vt.

58. WILLARD[4] (*William,*[3] *Samuel,*[2] *John*[1]), was born Oct. 3, 1764 ; married Lydia, daughter of Ebenezer Pike, of Cornish, N. H. He lived in Hartland, Vt., where he died Jan. 31, 1849. They had :

i. WILLARD, m. Asenith Phelps.

ii. MAHITABEL, m. Elias Hoadley.
iii. CLINTON, m. Cynthia Blanchard.
iv. ADOLPHUS, m. Betsey Kendall.
v. BUCKLEY, b. Sept. 14,1796; m. (1) Mary Hadlock; (2) Amarilla Dutton.
vi. HARRIET, m. John Vaughan.
vii. HIRAM, m. Parthenia Blackwell.
viii. MARY, m. Asahel Bagley.
ix. JAMES, unm., lives in Penn.
x. LUCINDA, m. Israel Gilbert.

59. WINTHROP[4] (*William,*[3] *Samuel,*[2] *John*[1]), was born June 17, 1769;
married (1) Abigail Sargeant; (2) Olive Ayers; (3) Catharine Rawson;
(4) Sophia Keyes; died March 20, 1849. They had (1 m.):

i. OLIVE, m. Elijah Hoisington.
ii. RUTH, m. Elijah Grow.
iii. GEORGE, m. Emily Hoisington.
iv. LEVI, m. Mary Ann Kendall.
v. (2 m.) WINTHROP, m. Maria Stone.
vi. ITHAMAR, m. Mary Smith.

60. LEVI[4] (*William,*[3] *Samuel,*[2] *John*[1]), was born Sept. 3, 1774; married
Ruth Sargeant; died May 15, 1847. They had:

i. SALOME, m. Willard Moore.
ii. NANCY, m. Jason Darling.
iii. ABIAL B., m. Pamelia Bailey.
iv. HANNAH, m. Ira Wood.
v. LUCY, m. James A. Gates.

61. ZEBEDIAH[4] (*Zebediah,*[3] *Samuel,*[2] *John*[1]), was born in Woodstock,
Ct., in 1760. He resided in Willington, Ct., where he died in 1851. He
married (1) Phœbe Pearl, (2) Polly Britt. They had:

PRISCILLA, PHOEBE, LOIS, ELIZABETH, LUCY, HANNAH, THOMAS, TIMOTHY,
ZEBEDIAH, LUCINDA, NEWMAN, JOHN, MARY, LOUISA.

62. ALVAN[4] (*Samuel,*[3] *Samuel,*[2] *John*[1]), married Polly Bunce; lived in
Woodstock, Vt. They had:

i. THOMAS.
ii. JOHN S., b. March 7, 1779; m. Rebecca Vorse, of Walpole, N. H.
Attorney and judge; lives in Windsor, Vt.
iii. MARTHA.   iv. FRANCES.

63. OREN[4] (*Samuel,*[3] *Samuel,*[2] *John*[1]), b. April, 1774; married (1) Polly
Work; (2) Lucy Work; lived in Ashford, Ct.; died July 21, 1828. They
had:

i. (1 m.) JOSEPH W., b. Nov. 18, 1798; d. May 2, 1842.
ii. JOHN S., b. March, 1801; d. June 7, 1856.
iii. MARY, b. in Ashford, 1806; m. Thomas J. Olney, Jan. 10, 1826; d.
March 3, 1850.
iv. OLIVE, b. Dec. 30, 1808; m. Henry Packer, Eastford.
v. STEVEN H., b. Jan. 22, 1813; m.; lived at New-Haven, Ct.
vi. DANFORD S., b. May 21, 1816; lives at Quasqueton, Iowa.
vii. (2 m.) HANNAH H., b. Feb. 28, 1821; m. H. B. Burnham.
viii. ESTHER, b. Feb. 14, 1826; d. Sept. 13, 1829.

64. EBENEZER[4] (*Ebenezer,*[3] *Ebenezer,*[2] *John*[1]), was born July 10, 1780;
married Susannah Adams. He lived in Pittston, where he died, Aug. 9,
1850. They had:

i. JONATHAN, b. Jan. 31, 1803; d. Jan. 5, 1851.
ii. EBENEZER, b. Sept. 2, 1804; d. Dec. 4, 1828.
iii. ABRAHAM, b. Sept. 16, 1806; d. Oct. 26, 1828.
iv. THANKFUL, }   d. Feb. 14, 1833.
v. SPENCER,   } twins, b. July 17, 1808; m. Harriet Pruner.

vi. ELIJAH, b. Sept. 4, 1810 ; d. Sept. 23, 1823.
vii. ELBERT, b. May 28, 1812 ; m. Mary Anne Reddin.
viii. SARAH, b. Feb. 15, 1814.
ix. JARED, b. Jan. 15, 1816.
x. JOSEPH, b. Jan. 22, 1818.
xi. JOHN SAGER, b. Nov. 1, 1821 (Reverend).
xii. MARTHA, b. Sept. 29, 1823.

65. JARED[4] (*Ebenezer,[3] Ebenezer,[2] John[1]*), was born in the Wyoming Valley, Penn., June 6, 1782. He married Sarah Bennett; lived at Pittston where he died, Dec. 18, 1816. They had :

i. LORINDA, b. March 18, 1805 ; d. 1848.
ii. IRA, b. April 20, 1807 ; m. Ann Teeter.
iii. REUBEN, b. Sept. 7, 1809 ; m. Lucy Ann Wrenton.
iv. AVERY, b, Jan. 29, 1811 ; m. Lucinda Blackman.
v. ELMIRA, b. March 18, 1813.

66. JOSEPH[4] (*Ebenezer,[3] Ebenezer,[2] John[1]*), was born in Luzerne co., Penn., Feb. 19, 1787 ; married Delilah Nichols, of Beekman, N. Y. ; lives (1874) at Moscow, Penn. They had :

i. NICHOLS, b. May 1, 1821.
ii. ABEL, b. Feb. 15, 1823. Sup. pub. schools, Wyoming co.
iii. MARTHA R., b. Feb. 3, 1826 ; m. Wm. Ryan.
iv. HENRY F., b. April 28, 1828 ; d. April 9, 1847.
v. WILLIAM L., b. July 4, 1833 (M.D. at Castleton, Vt.), practises in Waymart, Wayne co., Penn.

67. NICHOLSON[4] (*Zebulon,[3] Ebenezer,[2] John[1]*), was born Nov. 3, 1773; married Hannah Hutchinson, daughter of Col. Hutchinson, of Danvers, Mass., who was at the "Tea party" in Boston harbor, and fought at Bunker Hill. They lived at Tunkhannock, Penn. He died Jan. 30, 1827. She died April 8, 1857. They had :

i. WILLIAM N., b. April 16, 1808.
ii. ZEBULON CONANT, b. May 2, 1809.
iii. SUSAN, b. May 22, 1811 ; m. J. Q. Caudry.
iv. ALBERT NICHOLSON, b. Nov. 3, 1813 ; m. Kate S. Lohmer.
v. ISRAEL HUTCHINSON, b. Nov. 17, 1815.
vi. OLIVER H. PERRY, b. Feb. 2, 1818 ; m. Mary Burgess, proprietor of the Tunkhannock Republican.
vii. HARRIET NEWELL, b. Nov. 27, 1819 ; m. Linton Seeley.
viii. EUNICE H., b. Nov. 10, 1821 ; m. Adam Stevens.
ix. PORTER, b. Feb. 22, 1824 ; m. Eliza 11. Cassiday ; lives at Tunkhannock.
x. MARTHA CURTIS, b. July 3, 1826.

GENEALOGICAL SKETCH

OF THE

DESCENDANTS OF REINOLD AND MATTHEW MARVIN, WHO CAME TO NEW ENGLAND IN 1635.

[Compiled from authentic sources, by T. R. MARVIN, Boston.]

The following sketch is necessarily imperfect, from the fact that the records to make it complete are not within the reach of the compiler. It was originally commenced by him with the hope of tracing the direct line of his ancestry to the first emigrant to this country; in this he has been entirely successful. If those of the name will communicate to the compiler correct lists of their families, he will hereafter make use of them.

In some of the following records there are apparent discrepancies in regard to the ages of persons, arising from the fact that their *birth* was recorded for *old style,* and their *death* for *new style.*

The first family by the name of MARVIN, who came to New England, consisted of two brothers, *Reinold* and *Matthew,* and one sister, *Hannah,* who probably came over from England with her brother, Reinold. I have not been able to ascertain in what year Reinold came to New England. Matthew, and his family, came in 1635, as will be seen by the following statement:

During the summer months of 1842, Hon. James Savage of Boston, Mass., who was on a visit to England, was chiefly occupied with searching for materials to illustrate the early annals of New England. He was richly compensated for his toil. The result of his investigations was published in the 8th vol. *Mass. Hist. Coll.,* 3d series, under the title of 'Gleanings for New England History.' From this article I extract the following:

"Perhaps the acquisition most valuable, in the opinion of our local antiquaries, is my copious extracts from a MS. volume in folio, at the Augmentation Office (so called), where the Rev. Joseph Hunter, one of the Record Commissioners, presides, in Rolls Court, Westminster Hall. It contains the names of persons, permitted to embark at the port of London, after Christmas, 1634, to the same period in the following year, kept *generally* in regular succession. This was found a few months since, and may not have been seen by more than two or three persons for two hundred years."

Under date of 15th April, 1635, is the following entry in the above named volume:

"Theis parties hereafter expressed, are to be transported to New England, imbarqued in the Increase, Robert Lea, master, having taken the oath of allegiance and supremacy, as also being conformable, &c. whereof they brought testimony per certif. from the Justices and ministers where there abodes have lately been."

The following names are included in the list above referred to:

488

Husbandman	Matthew Marvyn,	35 yrs.
uxor	Elizabeth Marvyn,	31
	Elizabeth Marvin,	11
	Matthew Marvyn,	8
	Marie Marvyn,	6
	Sara Marvyn,	3
	Hanna Marvyn,	$\frac{1}{2}$

The brothers Matthew and Reinold were among the original settlers of Hartford, Conn., and both were proprietors of land in that ancient town.

MATTHEW resided on the corner of Village and Front streets, Hartford, for some years. He was among the pioneers in the settlement of Norwalk, which town he represented in the General Court in 1654. Matthew, his son, represented that town in 1694 and 1697; Samuel, his grandson, in 1718, and John, his grandson, in 1734 and 1738. He died at Norwalk, in 1687.

REINOLD* sold his land in Hartford and removed to Farmington, and was probably among the first settlers of that town. About 1648, he sold his property in Farmington to John Warner. The property sold to Warner consisted of a homelot of five acres, a new house, and other lands, which are recorded at Farmington. This " was a prominent homelot, having Mr. Willis of Hartford, on one side, and Mr. Hopkins on the other; it was on the west side of the main street." From Farmington he removed to that part of Saybrook, which is now Lyme, where he died in 1662. He had two children, Reinold and Mary. His daughter Mary married William Waller of Saybrook; they had sons William, John, Samuel and Matthew. The early town records of Saybrook have been unfortunately destroyed by fire,—and the Farmington town records do not extend back farther than 1646; so that it is only by collateral evidence that some of the foregoing dates and conclusions have been arrived at. His will is recorded on the Colony Records at Hartford, in which he directs that to each of his grandchildren, " there be provided and given a Bible as soon as they are capable of using them." The inventory of his estate amounted to over £800.

HANNAH married Francis Barnard, at Hartford, in 1644; and removed from thence to Hadley, Mass. She died in 1676. Farmer says, that Francis Barnard is the ancestor of all the divines of the name of Barnard, who have graduated at Harvard, excepting John of Marblehead, and Jeremiah of Manchester, N. H.

REINOLD MARVIN (son of Reinold, preceding), born about 1634, married, about 1663, Sarah Clarke, daughter of George Clarke, Jr., of Milford, Conn., husbandman. She was baptized Feb. 18, 1644. He is known on the town records as *Lieutenant* Reinold Marvin. He was one of a committee appointed to divide the town of Saybrook, in the year 1665. That part of the town lying east of Connecticut river, was named *Lyme*, from Lyme Regis, in the south-west of Eng-

---

* This name is spelled in different ways—Reginold, Reinold, Renold, Reynold. I have used Reinold, in these records.

land. Lieut. Marvin was a large landholder, and a prominent man in the town. He represented Lyme in the General Court in 1670, and from 1672 to 1676. He had three sons,—John, born 1664–5; Reinold, born 1669; and Samuel, born 1671: and two daughters, Mary and Sarah. Mary married Richard Ely of Saybrook. He died in 1676, aged 42 years. His widow, Sarah Marvin, married Capt. Joseph Sill, Feb. 12, 1677–8. She was his second wife, and had children—Joseph, born Jan. 6, 1678–9; and Zechariah, born June 1, 1682. Capt. Sill had formerly lived in Cambridge—his first wife was Jemima Belcher, daughter of Andrew Belcher, by whom he had several children. He had distinguished himself in Philip's Indian war. He died Aug. 6, 1696, aged 60.

REINOLD MARVIN, second son of *Lieutenant* Reinold, was born in 1669. He was famous as *Lyme's Captain*. He was a deacon in the Congregational Church. He represented Lyme in the General Court from 1701 to 1728. He was first married in 1695, to Phebe ——; she died Oct. 21, 1707; married the second time in 1708, to Martha Waterman, daughter of Thomas Waterman of Norwich; she died Nov. 1753, aged 73. He died Oct. 18, 1737, aged 68 years. The following is inscribed on his tombstone:

> This Deacon, aged sixty-eight,
> Is freed on earth from serving;
> May for a crown no longer wait,
> Lyme's Captain, Reinold Marvin.

The above inscription, as also that on the gravestone of his first wife, was executed by an illiterate artist, and with bad spelling, and the effects of time, is now rather obscure. The following is the inscription on the gravestone of his first wife:

> Here lies the body of
> PHEBE MARVIN,
> wife of
> REINOLD MARVIN,
> who died October 21, 1707,
> in the
> 31 year of her age.
>
> Her body only resting here,
> Her soul is fled to a higher sphere.

SAMUEL MARVIN, third son of *Lieutenant* Reinold, represented Lyme in the General Court, in 1711 and 1722.

REINOLD MARVIN, first son of *Captain* Reinold, was known and spoken of as *Deacon* Marvin. A great many anecdotes are related concerning this *Deacon* Marvin—which have generally been attributed to *Captain* Reinold. I am fully convinced, however, that they all belong to *his son* Reinold; both being Deacons, and both having the same Christian name, the mistake could easily be made. This son Reinold was unquestionably the *poet* who composed the epitaphs on his father's and mother's tombstones, and the *odd genius* of whom a multitude of anecdotes and queer sayings and rhymes, are still related; the most of them are positively known to apply *only to the son* of Captain Reinold.

REINOLD MARVIN, first son of *Deacon* Reinold, graduated at Yale College, 1748; studied law; resided in Litchfield. He left a daughter who married Ephraim Kirby, who prepared the first volume of Law

Reports published in the United States. Major Reinold Marvin Kirby of the U. S. Army, son of Ephraim Kirby, was twice breveted for gallantry in the war of 1812, and died in the service in 1842.

RICHARD PRATT MARVIN, a great-grandson of *Deacon* Reinold, was a Member of the 25th and 26th Congresses of the United States. Is at this time one of the Judges of the Supreme Court of the State of New York.

WILLIAM MARVIN, brother of Richard P., is a District Judge in the U. S. Court for the District of Florida, and resides at Key West.

DUDLEY MARVIN, a great-grandson of *Lyme's Captain*, was twice elected a Member of Congress from Ontario county, N. Y., and in 1846, a Member from Chautauque county, N. Y.

WILLIAM MARVIN, another great-grandson of *Lyme's Captain*, was for several years a Judge of Probate, for the District of Lyme, Conn.

DESCENDANTS IN THE LINE OF REINOLD MARVIN, ONE OF THE FIRST SETTLERS.

FIRST GENERATION.

I. REINOLD MARVIN came to New England about 1635. The date of his birth and the name of his wife, are not known. He had two children, and probably no others. He d. at Lyme, Conn., in 1662.

> *Children:*

1. Reinold, b. about 1634.
2. Mary, m. William Waller of Saybrook, Conn. Had sons—William, John, Samuel, Matthew.

SECOND GENERATION.

1.

Lieut. REINOLD MARVIN, m. Sarah Clark, dau. of George Clark, Jr., husbandman, of Milford, Conn., about 1663. He d. at Lyme, in 1676, a. 42. His wid. m. Capt. Joseph Sill, Feb. 12, 1677–8. She was his 2d wife, and had children—Joseph and Zechariah.

> *Children:*

3. John, b. in Lyme, 1665.
4. Mary, b. 1666, m. Richard Ely of Saybrook.
5. Reinold, b. 1669.
6. Samuel, b. 1671.
7. Sarah, b. 1673.

THIRD GENERATION.

3.

JOHN MARVIN m. Sarah Graham of Hartford, Conn., May 7, 1691. She was the dau. of Henry Graham and Mary his wife. He d. Dec. 11, 1711, a. 47 yrs. His wife d. the relict of Mr. Richard Sears, at Lyme, Conn., Dec. 14, 1760, a. 91 yrs.

> *Children:*

8. Sarah, b. in Lyme.
9. Mary.
10. John, b. Aug. 9, 1698.

11. Elizabeth.
12. Joseph, b. about 1703.
13. Benjamin.
14. Mehitable.
15. Jemima.

5.

REINOLD MARVIN (*Lyme's Captain*), was twice m. 1st, to Phebe ——, in 1695; she d. Oct. 21, 1707, a. 31. 2d, to Martha Waterman, dau. of Thomas Waterman of Norwich, Conn., 1708. Reinold M. d. at Lyme, Oct. 18, 1737, a. 68 yrs. His wid. d. at Lyme, Nov. 1753, a. 74 yrs.

Children by first wife:

16. Phebe, b. in Lyme, Dec. 3, 1696.
17. Reinold (Daniel on the town records), b. Jan. 1702.
18. Lydia, b. Jan. 12, 1704, m. Philip Kirkland.
19. Esther, b. April 3, 1707, m. Thomas Lord, Jr.

Children by second wife:

20. Martha, b. April 3, 1710.
21. Elisha, b. Sept. 26, 1711, d. in infancy.
22. James, b. May 26, 1713.
23. Sarah, b. March 8, 1716.
24. Elisha 2d, b. March 8, 1718.
25. Miriam, b. March 1720, m. Samuel Beckwith.

6.

SAMUEL MARVIN m. May 5, 1669, Susannah Graham, dau. of Henry Graham of Hartford, and sister to the wife of John Marvin, No. 3. He d. at Lyme, March 15, 1743, a. 72.

Children:

26. Samuel, b. in Lyme, Feb. 10, 1700.
27. Zechariah, b. Dec. 27, 1701.
28. Thomas, b. March 4, 1704.
29. Matthew, b. Nov. 7, 1706.
30. Abigail, b. Sept. 13, 1709.
31. Elizabeth, b. June 1, 1712.
32. Nathan, b. Nov. 21, 1714.
33. Nehemiah, b. " at the time the great snow-storm commenced," Feb. 20, 1717.
34. Mary, } twins, b. April 15, 1721. The son d.
35. A son, }

FOURTH GENERATION.
10.

JOHN MARVIN, m. Mehitable Champion, Feb. 24, 1725–6.

Children:

36. John, b. in Lyme, Jan. 30, 1726–7.
37. Mehitable, b. June 27, 1729, m. (?) Stephen Lee, Jr., Sept. 25, 1744.
38. Adonijah, b. March 1, 1732.

39. Elizabeth, b. Aug. 21, 1734.
40. Esther, b. April 15, 1737.

12.

JOSEPH MARVIN, m. Jane Lay, May 28, 1730. He d. in Lyme, April 7, 1791, a. 88 yrs. His wid. d. Oct. 21, 1795, a. 89 yrs.

Child:

41. Hepzibah, b. March 11, 1731, m. (?) Enoch Lord, Dec. 31, 1748.

13.

BENJAMIN MARVIN, m. Deborah Mather, dau. of Samuel Mather of Lyme, Nov. 11, 1742. He d. Jan. 21, 1775.

Children:

42. Benjamin, b. Nov. 7, 1743.
43. Mehitable, b. Oct. 4, 1745.
44. Azubah, b. Dec. 23, 1748.

17.

REINOLD MARVIN, was twice m. 1st, to Mrs. Sarah Lay (originally Sarah Marvin, 8, dau. of John Marvin), Dec. 23, 1725. 2d, to Mrs. Mary Kellogg, originally Mary Niles (?) of Colchester, Conn., July 7, 1746. He d. in Lyme, Feb. 24, 1761, a. 60 yrs.

Children by first wife:

45. Reinold, b. Oct. 23, 1726.
46. Phebe, b. March 18, 1729.
47. Dan, b. Jan. 2, 1732.
48. Lydia, b. Sept. 14, 1733.

Children by second wife:

49. Ann,
50. Eunice, } twins, b. Sept. 30, 1748. Ann, d. Jan. 9, 1749.
51. Esther, b. Feb. 14, 1755.
52. Judith, b. April 16, 1757.

22.

JAMES MARVIN, m. (?) Ruth Mather, dau. of Timothy Mather of Lyme. (If this should meet the eye of any of the descendants of James Marvin, they would oblige the compiler of this Genealogy, by communicating to him what they can, respecting this family.)

Child:

53. Moses, b. in Lyme.

24.

ELISHA MARVIN, m. Catharine Mather, dau. of Timothy Mather, 1738. He d. in Lyme, Dec. 3, 1801, a. 84 yrs., 8 mos. and 14 days. His wife d. Dec. 4, 1799, a. 82 yrs., 10 mos. and 12 days.

Children:

54. Pickett, b. 1739, d. Nov. 23, 1762.
55. Elisha, b. June, 1742.
56. Timothy, b. 1744.
57. Enoch, b. 1747.

58. Elihu, b. Dec. 1752.
59. Joseph, b. Feb. 14, 1755.
60. Catharine, b. Jan. 20, 1757.

26.

SAMUEL MARVIN, m. Mary Wege [? Wedge], April 2, 1740. He d. at Lyme, April 18, 1786, a. 86.

Children:

61. Sarah, b. Jan. 27, 1741.
62. Martha, b. May 2, 1743.

27.

ZECHARIAH MARVIN, m. Abigail Lord, March 29, 1732. He d. in Lyme, Sept. 12, 1792, a. 91.

Children:

63. Elisha, b. Feb. 13, 1733.
64. Zechariah, b. Aug. 11, 1735.
65. Thomas, b. Oct. 12, 1737, d. Oct. 15, 1737.
66. Susannah, b. Nov. 12, 1738.
67. Thomas 2d, b. May 29, 1742.
68. Daniel, b. May 2, 1745, d. Jan. 30, 1751.
69. Joseph, b. Jan. 8, 1748, d. in infancy.
70. Silas, b. July 19, 1750.
71. Joseph 2d, b. June 22, 1751.

28.

THOMAS MARVIN, m. Mehitable Goodrich. He d. about 1763.

Children:

72. Joseph, " a sea captain in the West India trade, and supposed to have been lost at sea, not long before the Revolution."
73. Lois.
74. Mehitable, b. Nov. 19, 1738, m. Benjamin Marvin, great-grandson of Matthew Marvin of Norwalk, the original settler, brother of Reinold of Lyme.
75. Samuel, who d. " in the service," in the old French war.
76. Susannah, m. Hezekiah Frisbie; lived and d. at Duanesburg, N. Y.
77. Elizabeth, m. Wm. Roberts.
78. Matthew, b. in Simsbury, Conn., June 7, 1754, d. at Walton, N. Y., Sept. 22, 1846, a. 92.

29.

MATTHEW MARVIN, resided in Lyme, Conn., m. Mary Beckwith, April 20, 1732. " They both d. the same day, of the small-pox, taken from a transient person who came to their house—which was turned into a hospital, and all the children were inoculated, and recovered, as well as several neighbors."

Children:

79. Seth, b. July 12, 1733, " killed in a skirmish with the Indians, on the Susquehannah."
80. Eunice, b. Dec. 2, 1735, m. Judge William Noyes of Lyme.
81. Matthew, b. about 1742, m. Elizabeth Deming.

82. Ezra, b. July 15, 1744, m. Susanna Peck.
83. Elizabeth, b. ———, m. Rev. George Griswold.
84. Mary, b. ———, m. Samuel Griswold.
85. Abigail, b. ———, m. Marshfield Parsons, his second wife.
86. Rhoda, b. ———, m. William Mather.
87. Phebe, b. ———, m. Thomas Lee.
88. Joseph, b. ———, d. in youth.

31.

ELIZABETH MARVIN, m. Richard Waite of Lyme, Nov. 8, 1733. She d. May 27, 1755.

Children :

89. Phebe, b. in Lyme, Sept., 1734.
90. Lois, b. 1735, m. Marshfield Parsons.
91. Richard, b. 1739.
92. Elizabeth, b. 1741.
93. Sarah, b. 1745.
94. Marvin, b. 1746.
95. John, b. 1749.
96. Daniel, b. 1751.

32.

NATHAN MARVIN, m. Lydia Lewis, May 17, 1743. He d. in Lyme, March 15, 1755.

Children :

97. Samuel, b. in Lyme, Feb. 14, 1744.
98. Henry, b. Dec. 21, 1745, d. March 15, 1755.
99. Martin, b. May 6, 1750.
100. Lebbeus, b. Feb. 10, 1752.
101. Nathan, b. Feb. 9, 1754.
102. Henry, b. March, 1755.

33.

NEHEMIAH MARVIN, m. Hester Lord of Lyme, Jan. 9, 1746.

Children :

103. Phebe, b. in Lyme, Oct. 15, 1746.
104. Anne, b. Dec. 29, 1748.

FIFTH GENERATION.

36.

JOHN MARVIN, m. Sarah Brooker of Saybrook, Feb. 10, 1747. He resided in Lyme, Conn., until 1767, when he removed to " Guilford, or Surrey," New Hampshire.

Children :

105. Sarah (or Hepzibah), b. in Lyme, Nov. 7, 1747.
106. Giles, b. Dec. 23, 1751.
107. Lois, b. May 12, 1754.
108. Esther, b. Sept. 12, 1756, d. Nov. 22, 1759.
109. John, b. May 6, 1759, d. June 14, 1759.

110. Lydia, b. Nov. 4, 1760.
111. John 2d, b. Dec. 15, 1763.
112. Mary, b. March 2, 1766.
113. Adonijah, " b. in Guilford or Surrey, N. H.," April 16, 1769.

38.

ADONIJAH MARVIN, m. Diadema Miller, Aug. 20, 1755. He d. at Lyme, April 20, 1758, a. 26.

Children :

114. Elizabeth, b. in Lyme, June 30, 1756.
115. Diadema, b. April 5, 1758.

42.

BENJAMIN MARVIN, was twice m.; first to Phebe Rowland of Lyme, Oct. 29, 1767; and second to Abby Smith. He d. in Lyme, June 14, 1823, a. 79. His first wife d. Dec. 27, 1812, a. 67; his second wife d. Sept. 28, 1840, a. 73.

Children :

116. Abigail, b. in Lyme, Aug. 29, 1768, d. Dec. 5, 1776.
117. Uriah, b. Aug. 8, 1770, m. Olive Ingraham.
118. John, b. June 8, 1772, m. 1st Amy Stevens; 2d Lucia M. Lee.
119. William, b. April 5, 1775, m. Julia Ann Taber, June 29, 1820— resided at New London, Conn., where he d. in 1849. He had no children.
120. Abigail 2d, b. March 27, 1777, m. Ichabod Smith.
121. Phebe, b. May 18, 1779, m. Uriah Benedict.
122. Lois, b. May 2, 1781, d. Aug., 1781.
123. Lois 2d, b. July 21, 1782, m. David E. Gregory.
124. Alexander, b. Jan. 31, 1785, m. Mary E. Pepoon.
125. Richard, b. April 19, 1787, d. Aug. 20, 1840.
126. Edward Lee, b. Aug. 16, 1789, d. Oct. 16, 1820.

45.

REINOLD MARVIN, was b. Oct. 23, 1726. He resided in Litchfield, Conn., at which place he d.

Child :

127. A dau., who m. Ephraim Kirby.

47.

DAN MARVIN, m. Mehetable Selden, Oct. 14, 1762. He d. at Lyme, Dec. 30, 1776.

Children :

128. Reinold, b. in Lyme, July 21, 1763, d. Dec. 10, 1767.
129. Dan, b. Oct. 15, 1765, m. Huldah Mather.
130. Reinold 2d, b. March 21, 1769, m. Mabel Bushnell of Saybrook. He resided at Fairfield, Herkimer co., N. Y., where he d. in 1812.

131. Sarah, b. Sept. 21, 1771, m. Joel Pratt.
132. Selden, b. Nov. 24, 1773, m. 1st Charlotte Pratt; 2d Mrs. Elizabeth Vandenburg. He resided in Herkimer co., N. Y.
133. James, b. May 16, 1776, d. Nov. 6, 1779.

53.

Moses Marvin, m. Zilpah Gillett, at Lyme, March 30, 1780. He removed to Genesee co., N. Y.

Children:

134. James, b. in Lyme, Jan. 24, 1781, d. June 4, 1811.
135. Daniel, b. Feb. 18, 1783, d. Oct. 17, 1801.
136. William, b. 1784, d. Nov. 27, 1793.
137. Moses.
138. John.

55.

Elisha Marvin, m. Elizabeth Selden, at Lyme, July 10, 1766. He d. at Lyme, Oct. 21, 1817, a. 75 yrs. His wife d. July 24, 1825, a. 78. She was the dau. of Samuel Selden of Lyme, and Elizabeth Ely, his wife.

Children:

139. Elizabeth, b. July 6, 1767, m. Judah Colt.
140. Elisha, b. Nov. 22, 1768, m. Minerva Prendergast.
141. Selden, b. March 2, 1770, d. Oct. 23, 1794.
142. Phebe, b. Nov. 28, 1772, m. Seth Ely.
143. Enoch, b. Oct. 19, 1774, m. Eliza Hull; d. at Beaver, Pa., March 31, 1840.
144. Deborah, b. July 11, 1779, d. May 28, 1802.
145. Mary, b. April 1, 1784, d. April 30, 1841.
146. Dudley, b. May 29, 1786, m. Mary Whalley.
147. Emila, b. Nov. 25, 1789, m. Geo. Selden.
148. Elihu, b. Aug. 1, 1791, m. Anna Humphreys; resides in Erie, Pa.

56.

Timothy Marvin, was thrice m. His 1st wife was Sarah Perkins dau. of James Perkins of Lyme, m. May 30, 1765. She d. Oct. 23, 1795. 2d wife, Mrs. Azubah Sill. 3d wife, Mrs. Prudence Lewis. Timothy Marvin d. at Lyme, Feb. 27, 1808, a. 64.

Children, all by first wife:

149. Lucy, b. in Lyme, March 14, 1766, m. Daniel Fuller.
150. Picket, b. Feb. 5, 1768.
151. Asahel, b. Sept. 16, 1769, m. Azubah Sill.
152. Timothy, b. Aug. 3, 1771, m. Rachel Crosby.
153. Sarah, b. July 7, 1773, m. Elisha Gould.
154. Huldah, b. May 31, 1775, m. Matthias Fuller.
155. Seth, b. March 17, 1777, d. April 23, 1799.
156. Abijah, b. April 6, 1779, m. Susan Barker.
157. Catharine, b. June 10, 1781, m. Henry Crittenton.

158. Calvin, b. June 1, 1784, m. 1st, Alice M. Ransom. 2d, Deborah W. Gibbs.
159. Elizabeth, b. Sept. 25, 1786, m. Samuel Parsons.
160. Mather, b. June 25, 1789, m. Matilda Vreeland, resided in Michigan, d. April, 1862.

57.

ENOCH MARVIN, m. Ruth Ely, dau. of Wells Ely of Lyme. He d. in the State of Missouri, about 1842, a. upwards of 90 yrs.

Children:

161. Elizabeth.
162. Catharine.
163. Elisha, m. Laura Foote of Pittsfield, Wis.
164. Rebecca, m. Christopher Lee of Lyme, Conn.
165. Sarah.
166. Ruth, } twins.
167. Rhoda, }
168. Mary.
169. Wells Ely, m. Mary Davis, resided in Missouri, d. 1856, a. 64.

58.

ELIHU MARVIN, m. Elizabeth Rogers, dau. of Dr. Theophilus Rogers, and Penelope Jarvis, Dec. 25, 1780. He resided at Norwich, Conn., where he d. of the yellow fever, Sept. 13, 1798, a. 45 yrs. His wife d. Dec. 30, 1808, a. 51.

Children:

170. Sarah Rogers, b. Oct. 4, 1781, m. George W. Trott, d. Sept. 13, 1807.
171. Elizabeth, b. June 1, 1783, d. Aug. 24, 1802.
172. Penelope Jarvis, b. June 9, 1785, m. John S. Pearson, d. July 16, 1833.
173. Susannah, b. Oct. 1, 1788, d. Feb. 26, 1827.
174. Catharine Mather, b. Jan. 27, 1793, m. Rev. Luther F. Dimmick, d. Dec. 8, 1844.
175. Theophilus Rogers, b. Feb. 23, 1796, m. Julia A. C. Coggeshall.

59.

JOSEPH MARVIN, m. Phebe Sterling, dau. of William Sterling of Lyme, 1783. He d. at Lyme, Nov. 18, 1839, a. 84¾ yrs. His wife d. Nov. 6, 1822, a. 59 yrs.

Children:

176. Fanny, b. at Lyme, Oct. 7, 1784, m. Ezra Pratt.
177. Phebe, b. June 7, 1786, m. 1st, Rev. Leverett I. F. Huntington. 2d, Rev. Urban Palmer.
178. William, b. May 12, 1788, m. Sophia Griffin.
179. Jemima, b. March 28, 1791, m. Abraham Blatchley.
180. Joseph, b. Feb. 8, 1793, m. Elizabeth Hopkins, d. Feb., 1830.
181. Clarissa, b. May 5, 1795, m. Horace Ely.

60.

CATHARINE MARVIN, was m. to Abner Brockway of Lyme, Sept. 7, 1775. He d. at Lyme, Sept. 6, 1808. She d. at Lima, N. Y., 1831.

Children:

182. Catharine, b. at Lyme, July 6, 1776, m. Lazarus Church, d. at Rockford, Ill., Dec. 14, 1851, a. 75½ yrs.
183. Lucina, b. Sept. 17, 1778, d. March 26, 1779.
184. Marvin, b. July 8, 1780.
185. James, b. May 23, 1782, d. Jan. 25, 1806.
186. Abner, b. Aug. 19, 1785, d. Sept. 3, 1808.
187. Pickett, b. April 10, 1788, m. 1st, Rhoda N. Clark; 2d, Nancy Stevens, d. Jan. 20, 1833.
188. Temperance, b. Dec. 10, 1792, m. James Cowles, d. Feb. 9, 1820.
189. David C., b. May 2, 1794, d. Aug. 12, 1806.
190. Samuel, b. Sept. 2, 1795, d. Aug. 12, 1814.
191. Alice, b. May 8, 1798, d. June 3, 1823.
192. Elisha Marvin, b. Aug. 3, 1801, d. Nov., 1848.

64.

ZECHARIAH MARVIN, m. Mrs. Ann Lee, July 23, 1761. She d. at Lyme, March 1, 1777.

Children:

193. Eunice, b. at Lyme, May 22, 1766.
194. Lee, b. Sept. 16, 1768, d. April 21, 1777.
195. Zechariah, b. June 5, 1771.
196. Lucinda, b. Sept. 23, 1773.

67.

THOMAS MARVIN, m. Sarah Lay, May 23, 1784. He was the son, as I suppose, of Zechariah Marvin (No. 27), and if so, he was b. May 29, 1742. He may have been the son of James (No. 22).

Children:

197. Lucy, b. at Lyme, Feb. 11, 1785, d. July 1, 1785.
198. Thomas, b. July 7, 1787.
199. Abigail.

78.

MATTHEW MARVIN, m. Mary Weed, resided in Walton, Delaware co., N. Y. He d. Sept. 22, 1846, a. 92¼ yrs. His wife d. Feb. 25, 1846, a. 88¼ yrs.

Children:

200. Abigail, b. Aug. 5, 1785.
201. Joseph, b. May 1, 1787, m. Mary Tiffany.
202. Jared, b. March 4, 1789, m. Frances Almira Rogers.
203. William W., b. Sept. 26, 1793, m. Frances Cornwall.
204. Thomas, b. April 20, 1795, m. Deney Tiffany.
205. Lewis, b. Oct. 13, 1796, m. Mary Weed.

MATTHEW MARVIN, m. Elizabeth Deming, May 30, 1771. He d. at Lyme, Aug. 29, 1806, a. 64 yrs. His wife d. June 22, 1839, a. 92 yrs.

Children :

206. Joseph, b. at Lyme, March 26, 1772, m. Temperance Miller.
207. Mehetable, b. Oct. 26, 1773, m. Lynde Lord.
208. Mary, b. Nov. 16, 1775, m. William Colt.
209. David, b. Nov. 2, 1777, m. Alpha Bates.
210. Elizabeth, b. Nov. 12, 1779, d. Sept. 19, 1825.
211. Abigail, b. Dec. 31, 1782, m. John L. Higby.
212. Rosalinda, b. Jan. 26, 1781, m. Noah Stone, d. Sept. 16, 1859.
213. Lurana, b. April 18, 1786.
214. Jonathan Deming, b. Sept. 11, 1789, m. 1st, Maria R. Bloom; 2d, Henrietta Andrus; 3d, Mary Seaver.

82.

Capt. EZRA MARVIN, m. Susanna Peck, at Lyme, about 1766. He removed to Granville, Mass., in the year 1773, at which place he resided until his death.

Children :

215. Mary, b. in Lyme, Feb. 25, 1767, m. Israel Parsons of Granville.
216. Jasper, b. 1770, m. Comfort Munson.
217. Matthew, b. 1772, m. Mary Morgan.
218. Nathan, b. June 7, 1775, m. Judith Gates.
219. Sylvanus, b.
220. Henry A., b. Oct. 15, 1782.
221. William-Noyes, b. April 10, 1784, m. Vashti Clark.

MARY E. MARVIN, dau. of William Noyes Marvin, m. Ammi Filley, 1831. Their son, William, b. in 1832, was lost among the Indians, an interesting account of which, and his recovery, prepared by a gentleman in Granville, Mass., was published in the newspapers of the day, and is here subjoined.

In 1835, Mr. Ammi Filley of Windsor, Conn., having in 1831 m. a dau. of Capt. William Marvin of Granville, Mass., removed with his family to the town of Jackson, in the state of Michigan. In this town, then a wilderness, he located himself, and by his industry, economy and perseverance, he soon found himself in possession of a productive and profitable farm, and by the accession of settlers, the town from an uncultivated desert, became a flourishing and populous village. Although in the vicinity of numerous hordes of savages, and often visited by wandering families of the natives with whom the citizens occasionally traded, yet no hostility was ever manifested, all was peace and quietness, and every thing conspired to render their abode pleasant and happy.

On the 3d of August, 1837, his little son, then a child of five years old, went out to a swamp in the vicinity of their dwelling with a hired girl to gather whortleberries. The swamp was in the direction from Mr. Filley's to the dwelling of a Mr. Mount, the father of the girl, whither they expected to go to spend the night, and the scene of their amusement was about a mile from the house of the former and some twenty or thirty rods from the dwelling of the later.

Having satisfied himself with picking berries, the child discovered a desire to return, whereupon the girl conducted him to the road and placed him in the direction to the house of Mr. Mount, not doubting, as the house was in plain view, and only a few rods distant, but the little fellow would reach it in perfect safety. The girl returned to the swamp, and after completing her supply of fruit, went home to the house of her father, and found to her astonishment, as well as that of the family, that William had not arrived. Notice was immediately communicated to the parents and an alarm given through the settlement, and the whole population rushed at once to the assistance of the almost distracted family. Day and night, for weeks, witnessed the praiseworthy exertions of his neighbors, and the whole country in every direction to an extent of more than twenty miles, was searched with untiring vigilance. Every stream of water and pond was examined and dragged, and every rod of ground scrutinized for many successive days, and no trace could be discovered of the absent child. As an inducement to continue the search, notice of the event was published in the papers, and Mr. Filley offered a reward of two hundred dollars for a recovery of the child, either dead or alive.

As suspicions were entertained that foul play had been practised by the Indians, inquiries were made of the different tribes and families in the vicinity, and pecuniary offers tendered to their chiefs and head men, and Mr. Filley himself traversed for months, the wilds of Michigan, Wisconsin and Iowa, but his efforts proved ineffectual; no discovery could be made and no tidings received, and he returned to his heart-broken family with the sad conclusion that their *little William was lost!*

For seven long years this stricken family endured the agony of an affliction which seldom falls to the lot of humanity to experience. "Months of vanity and wearisome nights were appointed to them." If the shaft of death had smitten down their first-born while under their fostering care, and they had seen him laid in the grave of their own churchyard, time would have tempered their grief and mitigated the anguish of their bereavement, but the painful suspense, the awful uncertainty that hung over his fate, was an abiding sorrow which time could not soften and earth had no balm to heal. As time rolled on, hope became more and more extinguished, *William was not forgotten.* The mournful event, with its aggravating circumstances, was a corroding canker upon every comfort of the family—a fatal disease seized the mother and she sunk into an untimely grave.

Since the decease of his wife, Mr. Filley has visited Connecticut, the place of his nativity, and while here, by a mysterious course of events beyond the comprehension of human wisdom to fathom, his long lost child has appeared and been restored to his fond embraces.

It seems that the lad before reaching the house of Mr. Mount, was overtaken and kidnapped by a band of Indians, who in their wanderings, happened to pass that way at that time. In this family he lived, and traveled with them in all their migratory movements from the time he was captured until the autumn of 1843. About this time, this family visited Albany, N. Y., and while there this white child was discovered among them.

The municipal authorities of the city becoming acquainted with the circumstance, at once caused their arrest, and took measures to compel them to disclose the means by which they became possessed of the child. They were alternately flattered and threatened, but no disclosure could be obtained. They manifested their native obstinacy and resolved to submit to any punishment rather than make any communication by which the paternity of the child could be ascertained. They were therefore discharged, the child retained, and very humanely placed in their Orphan Asylum.

Subsequently, in the spring of 1844, Mr. L. Cowles of Tolland, Mass., being in want of a boy in his family, was recommended to this place, and was furnished with this lad, whom he brought home with him to his residence in Tolland.

In the month of Dec. 1844, by a series of events unequivocally bespeaking the intervention of Divine benevolence, the facts that transpired at Albany in relation to this boy, came to the knowledge of the Rev. Dr. Cooley of Granville. The Doctor having frequently heard the circumstances under which the child was lost, immediately communicated the intelligence he had obtained to Mr. Marvin, the grandfather of the child, and he made known the tidings to Mr. Filley, who was then with his friends in Connecticut.

From the knowledge thus obtained, Mr. Filley was prompted to call without delay on Mr. Cowles, and examine the child—although time and exposure had changed his countenace and somewhat obliterated his youthful features, yet in his personal appearance he found a correct counterpart of the other members of his family. Hio size, his age, the complexion of his eyes and hair, and all his prominent characteristics, resembled those of his child, and upon appealing to a known scar upon his head and an indubitable mark in the hair of his head, his identity was plainly recognized, and with emotions of unspeakable joy he pressed to his bosom his *long lost Son.*

From the story of the boy, it appears he has constantly continued in the same family, consisting of four Indians, *Paul Pye* and *Phebe Ann Pye* his wife, *Martha Ann Pye* their daughter, and *Thomas Williams,* who seemed to be an inmate in the family. They adopted him as their son, and he was taught and believed that *Paul* and *Phebe* were his parents, and *Martha* his sister. He supposed himself an *Indian boy,* and was not aware of any difference of complexion or distinction of nation until his deliverance at Albany. It seems he felt an instinctive repugnance to their manners, and attempted once or twice to run away, in consequence of which they cut off one of his toes, by which means they could more readily reclaim him by his track. He has an indistinct recollection of attending school, but when or where, he knows not. This seems to be the only remaining fact in his memory that he can recognize as having transpired prior to his capture, and he does not seem to associate this with any other fact indicative of his home, except that *he did not go to school with Indians.*

The first place which he remembers to have visited was Green Bay, of the scenery of which he gives a faint, though correct description. In traveling to that place they probably either went or returned by water, as he remembers sailing in a steamboat. He was compelled to accompany them in all their migrations, and was used as a mendicant to beg clothes at the white settlements through which they passed, and furnish the family with food when their indolence prevented their obtaining it in any other way.

In the summer they made their peregrinations back and forth through the states of Michigan and New York, and sometimes visiting Connecticut, and at one period encamped themselves for several weeks in Stonington. In the winter they generally quartered themselves in wigwams in the vicinity of some village, and lived on small game, such as rabits, skunks and bullfrogs, the latter of which they deemed a *sumptuous repast.*

Occasionally they made a few baskets and taught the trade to the boy, and also instructed him into the *art and mystery* of bartering the commodity for whiskey.

He recollects living near Detroit, Utica, Brothertown, Catskill and Hudson, and several months at Hillsdale, N. Y.

In all their rambles, in summer and winter, he traveled barefoot, suffering in winter from the cold, and at all times from hunger and fatigue. His little *Indian sister* was his only solace, and like a second *Pocahontas,* her tender assiduities contributed essentially to render his captivity endurable.

Although he can not recognize his new friends, he rejoices in the felicity of a civilized and permanent home, and all parties feel a grateful sense of the kindness of the Author of all good for this marvelous display of his benevolence in *" redeeming us from our enemies, for his mercy endureth forever."*   C. J.
Granville, Mass., Jan. 22, 1845.

DESCENDANTS IN THE LINE OF MATTHEW MARVIN, ONE OF THE FIRST SETTLERS.

FIRST GENERATION.

II. MATTHEW MARVIN came to New England in 1635. He was one of the original proprietors of Hartford, Conn., and was also among the pioneers in the settlement of Norwalk, Conn. He d. in 1687. The Christian name of his 1st wife, who came with him from England, was Elizabeth. Late in life he m., for his 2d wife, Mrs. Alice Kellogg of Norwalk.

Children, all by first wife:

1. Elizabeth, b. about 1624, came to New England, with her father, in 1635, m. Dr. John Olmstead of Hartford and afterwards of Norwich. She d. at Norwich, without issue, at an advanced age.
2. Matthew, b. about 1627, came to New England, with his father, in 1635. He was also one of the original proprietors of Norwalk, which town he represented in the General Court in 1696 and 1697. His wife's Christian name was Mary.
3. Mary, b. about 1629, came to New England with her father in 1635. She d. in Norwich, March 29, 1713, a. 84. She was m. 1st, in 1648, to Richard Bushnell of Saybrook. Their children

were: Joseph, b. in Saybrook, May, 1651, m. Mary Leffingwell
of Norwich, 1673, d. Dec. 23, 1748, a. 97; Richard, b. Sept.,
1652; Mary, b. Jan., 1654-5; Maria, b. 1657. She was m. the
2d time in 1660, to Dea. Thomas Adgate of Saybrook, and was
his 2d wife. Their children were: Abigail, b. in Norwich,
Aug. 1661, m. Daniel Tracy, 1682; Sarah, b. 1663-4; Rebecca,
b. June, 1666; Thomas, b. March, 1669-70, d. 1761, a. 91.

4. Sarah, b. in 1632, m. 1st, William[1] Goodrich of Weathersfield,
Conn., Oct., 1648. 2d, Capt. William Curtis of Stratford,
Conn., son of John Curtis, one of the first settlers of the
town, by whom she had no children. She d. at Stratford, near
the close of 1702. Children by 1st husband: Sarah, b. 1649,
m. John Hollister, Jun[r].; William, b. 1651, d. young; John, b.
May 20, 1653, m. Rebecca Alden; Elizabeth, b. 1658, m. Robert Welles; William 2d, b. Feb. 8, 1661, m. 1st, Grace Riley,
2d, Mrs. Mary Ann Ayrault; Ephraim, b. June 2, 1663, m. 1st,
Sarah Treat. 2d, Mrs. Jerusha Welles; David, b. May 4, 1667,
m. 1st, Hannah Wright. 2d, Prudence Churchill; Mary, m.
Joseph Butler; Abigail, m. Thomas Fitch.

5. Hannah, b. in 1634, m. Thomas Seymour of Norwalk, Conn., Jan.,
1653. Children: Hannah, b. Dec. 12, 1654, m. Francis Bushnell, Oct. 12, 1675; Abigail, b. Jan. 1655-6; Mary and Sarah,
twins, b. Sept. 1658; Thomas, b. Sept., 1660.

6. Abigail, b. at Hartford, Conn., m. John Bouton of Norwalk, Jan.
1, 1656, being his 2d wife. Children: John, b. Sept. 30, 1659;
Matthew, b. Dec. 24, 1661; Rachel, b. Dec. 15, 1667; Abigail,
b. April 1, 1670; Mary, b. May 26, 1671.

7. Rachel, b. at Hartford, Dec. 30, 1649, m. Samuel Smith of Norwalk. Children: Rachel, who m. Thomas Benedict; Lydia,
who m. James Lockwood.

SECOND GENERATION.

2.

MATTHEW MARVIN, m. Mary ——.

Children:

8. Sarah, b. in Norwalk, about 1660, m. Thomas Betts of Norwalk,
Jan. 1680-81. He was the son of Thomas Betts of Guilford,
Conn. Children: Thomas, b. Jan. 17, 1681-2; John, b. July
7, 1684; Sarah, b. Jan. 21, 1686-7; Matthew, b. Jan. 10, 1691-
92; Mary, b. March 31, 1694; Elizabeth, b. Oct. 23, 1699.

9. Matthew, b. in Norwalk.

10. Samuel, b. in Norwalk.

11. Hannah, m. Epenetus Platt.

12. Elizabeth, m. Joseph Platt, Nov. 6, 1700, d. April 9, 1703.

13. John, b. Sept. 2, 1678.

THIRD GENERATION.

9.

MATTHEW MARVIN, m. Rhoda St. John, dau. of Mark St. John, d. in
1691.

Child :

14. Mary, b. in Norwalk, Oct. 7, 1689.

10.

SAMUEL MARVIN, b. in Norwalk; name of wife not ascertained, or date of death.

Children :

15. Matthew, b. Oct. 1702.
16. Samuel, b. in Norwalk.
17. Josiah.
   There were other children, probably.

13.

JOHN MARVIN, b. at Norwalk, Sept. 2, 1678, d. 1774. He was a Representative in the General Court, in 1734 and 1738. He m. 1st, Mary Beers of Fairfield, March 22, 1704. She d. April 17, 1720. His 2d wife was Rachel St. John, dau. of Matthias St. John, m. April 27, 1721.

Children by first wife :

18. John, b. July 22, 1705.
19. Nathan, b. March 4, 1708.
20. Seth, b. July 13, 1709.
21. David, b. Aug. 24, 1711.
22. Elizabeth, b. Oct. 23, 1713.
23. Mary, b. Dec. 29, 1716.
24. Elihu, b. Oct. 10, 1719.

Children by second wife :

25. Hannah, b. Dec. 4, 1722.
26. Joseph, b. May 29, 1724.
27. Rachel, b. Dec. 24, 1725, d. Dec. 26, 1725.
28. Benjamin, b. March 14, 1728, d. March 17, 1728.
29. Rachel 2d, b. March 27, 1729.
30. Sarah, b. May 18, 1733, d. May 21, 1733.
31. Ann, b. Sept. 7, 1741.

FOURTH GENERATION.
15.

MATTHEW MARVIN, m. Elizabeth Clark. He d. about 1746.

Children :

32. Hannah, b. in Norwalk, Sept. 30, 1732, d. 1806.
33. Matthew, b. Oct. 21, 1734.
34. Ozias, b. Jan. 29, 1737.
35. Barnabas, b. Dec. 25, 1739.
36. Silas, b. 1741.
37. Uriah, b. Feb. 17, 1744, d. 1824.
38. Ichabod, b. Dec. 15, 1745.

16.

SAMUEL MARVIN, m. Deborah Clark, Nov. 25, 1735.

Children:

39. Esther, b. in Norwalk, Aug. 22, 1736.
40. Rebecca, b. March 19, 1738.
41. Samuel, b. Feb. 7, 1740.
42. Elizabeth, b. Jan. 12, 1744.

17.

JOSIAH MARVIN, d. about 1780. The name of his wife or date of m. not ascertained.

Children:

43. Daniel, b. in Norwalk, about 1739.
44. William, b. March 24, 1741.
45. Jared.
46. John, who d. in Nova Scotia, a refugee in the Revolution.
47. Josiah, who d. on Long Island, in the British army, during the Revolutionary war.
48. Samuel.
    (Had four daughters besides the above sons.)

18.

JOHN MARVIN, m. Abigail St. John. He d. Aug. 25, 1775.

Children:

49. Mary, b. in Norwalk.
50. Abigail.
51. John.
52. Stephen.
53. Rebecca.
54. Sarah.
55. Benjamin, b. Sept. 30, 1737.
56. Mary.
57. Ebenezer.
58. Lydia.
59. Ephraim.
60. Esther.
61. Jedediah.
62. Susannah.

19.

NATHAN MARVIN, m. Hannah Betts.

Children:

63. Nathan, m. Mary Marvin, dau. of David Marvin.
64. Jesse.
65. Elizabeth, m. Zophar Betts.
66. Hannah, m. Jonathan Perry.
67. Rachel, m. 1st, J. W. Comstock. 2d, Aaron Holley.
68. James.

69. Julia, m. David Herrick.
70. Anna, m. 1st, —— Willard. 2d, —— Adams.
71. Patty, m. Eben Comstock.
72. Esther, m. —— Howard.

20.

SETH MARVIN, m. Phebe Lee, resided in Norwalk.

Children:

73. Seth, b. Dec. 21, 1749.
74. Eleazer, b. March 20, 1752.
75. Moses, b. Aug. 25, 1754.
76. Elihu, b. June 8, 1756.

21.

DAVID MARVIN, m. Hannah Gregory.

Child:

77. Mary, who m. Nathan Marvin, No. 63.

24.

ELIHU MARVIN, m. Abigail Yelverton. He resided in Orange co., N. Y., during the Revolutionary war, through the whole of which, he and his oldest son, Seth, took an active part—the father as Colonel and General, and the son as Captain and Colonel. He d. in Blooming Grove, N. Y., Aug. 17, 1803, a. 83 yrs. 10 mos. 4 dys.

Children:

78. Seth, b. Feb. 15, 1745.
79. Abigail, b. June 28, 1747.
80. Elihu, b. July 2, 1749.
81. John Yelverton, b. March 21, 1751, d. young.
82. Elizabeth, b. April 16, 1753.
83. Hannah, b. June 12, 1755.
84. John 2d, b. April 8, 1757.
85. James, b. Nov. 11, 1759.
86. Keziah, b. March 18, 1762.
87. Anthony, b. Nov. 10, 1764, m. Abigail Paine.

26.

JOSEPH MARVIN, m. Catharine St. John.

Child:

88. Joseph.

MATTHEW MARVIN AND HIS SECOND WIFE, WIDOW ALICE BOUTON.

By WILLIAM T. R. MARVIN, A.M., of Boston, Mass.

IN the Genealogy of the Marvin Family, printed in the REGISTER (Vol. XVI., p. 250 *et seq.*), which was furnished by my father, the late Theophi- * lus R. Marvin, and in the Marvin portion of the "Family Memorials," published by Mr. and Mrs. Edw. E. Salisbury, of New Haven, and compiled by myself, it is stated (p. 91) that the first Matthew Marvin, who came to New England in the "Increase," Capt. Lea, in 1635, and settled in Hartford, and later in Norwalk, Ct., married as his second wife " Mrs. Alice Kellogg." I have recently found that this was an inference made by one of his correspondents,—whether based on an inspection of the will of Alice Marvin, or from some other source, cannot now be determined. The discovery of this will by the late Allyn S. Kellogg, while searching for his own ancestry—he being a descendant of Alice Marvin—seems to show that the inference was made from the will, because it mentions her " daughter Briggit Kellock," who was the wife of Daniel Kellogg, and it was known that Bridget was the daughter of a John Bouton ; and no other John being known than the husband of Abigail Marvin, then living, it was thought that Daniel was her *own* son, and not her son-in-law. This will, of which I give an abstract, is recorded in the Fairfield Probate Records, Vol. III. (1675–89), page 61. It is so important as bringing to light facts hitherto unknown, and as completely disproving the statements concerning the man supposed to be the first John Bouton in New England, which are given in the " Bouton-Boughton Family," that it seems desirable to place these facts in the hands of genealogists, and to correct the errors noted.

The abstract is as follows:

Will of " Alce (*sic*) Marvin of Norwocke . . . . being aged seaventee years or thereabouts."

" Imprimis, I doe will and bequeath the sum of twenty pounds to my sonn John Bowton and to my daughter Bridgit Killock, to be equally devided between thos two : That is to say, ten pounds apiece."

" Item, I doe give after my decease, to my daughter Briggit Kellock my scarfe and my best cloath waskcot and my best serg coat and my best green apron and the best of my two under cotten coats and my spectacles."

" Item, I doe give unto my daughter Abigal Bowton my best hat and my best cloke and my serge wastcoats and my under cotten wastcoat and a pair of lether gloves, 2 brass small wayts."

" Item, I doe give to my daughter Rachell Smith my penne (stone?) coat and my flannel wastcoat, and to my grandchild Sarah Brinsmead my Cheast; and to my grandchild Ruth Bowton my brass kettle 3 old pewter dishes and a brass Chafendish and a gilpot : and to my grandchild Rachell Bowton my Bible."

Remainder ; " my will is shall be devided between my two dafter (*sic*) Brigget Kellock & Rachell Smith. The hetchell my will is, half to my sonn John Bowton and half to my daughter Brigget Kellock, etc."

Witnesses.
RICH OLMSTEED
CHRISTO. COMSTOCKE.
Dated December 1, 1680.
Inventory, " Last of January, 1680." (1681.)
    Amount; 36. 2. 8.

The Marke of
ALCE X MARVIN.
[*So written.*]

*Pages 503-507, this volume.

It is to be noticed first, that the testatrix remembers with gifts of money her "sonn, John Bowton" (who married Abigail Marvin), rather than his wife, and her "daughter Briggit Kellock," who it is certainly known was Bridget Bouton when she married Daniel Kellogg, rather than her husband ; thus giving to those who were her children by blood, and not by marriage, legacies amounting to £20 which had been the property of Alice before she married Matthew Marvin, as I shall presently show, while Daniel Kellogg is not named.

In the will of Matthew Marvin, dated Dec. 20, 1678 (Fairfield Probate Records, III., p. 58, *et seq.*), who died before his wife, he first of all bequeathes "unto my dearly beloved wife Alice Marvin, the sum of twenty pounds as her owne true and proper estate: for her to will and order as she pleaseth, etc." Clearly we have here the £20 which she gives to her sole surviving children by her first husband, and which she felt in duty bound to leave them. She remembers her son's wife, Abigail, and Rachel Smith, who I believe was her daughter by her second husband, Matthew Marvin, as there were at least four and probably five of Matthew's daughters by his first wife living when Alice's will was made, but not mentioned therein, viz: Elizabeth Olmstead, Sarah Curtis, Mary Adgate, Hannah "Semer," and Rebecca Clarke. (The latter is not named in either of the articles on the Marvin Family named above, but I have lately obtained information concerning this daughter and she is mentioned in Matthew's will.)

We may well believe that the reason why Rachel received no more was because she and her husband, Samuel Smith, had already been provided for by Matthew; on Dec. 23, 1674, about four years before his death, he gave her "50 pounds worth of my comonage lot, halfe my home-lot, etc." (See Norwalk Land Records, folio 61; the volume has no index, and is badly out of binding.)

The next person mentioned in Alice's will is her grandchild, Sarah Brinsmead, the married daughter of Bridget,* who does not concern us, and finally we have "my grandchild, Ruth Bowton." This last Mr. Kellogg aptly calls "a most illuminating reference." This Ruth was the posthumous daughter of Richard Bowton and Ruth Turney; the latter was a daughter of Benjamin Turney, of Concord and Fairfield, born Jan. 28, 1643-4. The reference therefore proves that the said Richard Bowton was the son of Alice Marvin by her previous husband. As both Bridget and John are called on different Norwalk records the children of a John, and on Fairfield records Abigail's husband John is called the "uncle" of Ruth, we have the name of Richard's father, and the proof that Alice's first husband was a John Bowton, facts hitherto unknown. These facts are corroborated by other documents on the Fairfield Probate Records, which I will next cite.

I. On page 1, Vol. II., is the "Inventory of Richard Bowton, lately deceased," dated June 27, 1665, in which we find "Coopers Tools, 3: 5: 0." He left no will, but on the day he died said to Joseph Middlebrook and his wife Mary (who I believe was the widow of Benjamin Turney and if so was Richard Bowton's mother-in-law), that he "would give his estate to Ruth, his wife, excepting his tools." The Court approved this as his will; "Only it is provided that if the said Ruth shall now be with child, the said child shall have its part of the estate as the Courte shall hear after think

* An inspection of the dates of birth of Bridget's children, in Hall's "Norwalk," p. 187, shows manifest errors.

meet, yf there be occasion. And yf ther be no issue of the deceased, then it is ordered by the Courte that *John Bowton, sonn of John Bowton*, shall have the said deceaseds tools, the Court apprehending it was the will of the deceased it should be so."

Here we find that John[2] Bowton who married Abigail Marvin, was the "son of John," for although John[2] had a son John[3] in 1665, he was then a mere child (born Sept. 30, 1659), and it is hardly supposable that Richard[2] in dying would have passed over his brother and left his tools to a boy six years old, or that the Court would have approved such an act.

II. Richard's widow, Ruth, died shortly after, leaving an infant child Ruth, of whom more hereafter, who is the Ruth mentioned in Alice's will. The inventory of widow Ruth is given under date of November 7, 1666; it amounts to £91: 06: 7, and mentions "meadow and uplands, £10." (Ibid, II, 16.) Reference to this land appears below.

III. On page 17 is still a more important document. It is an agreement signed by Matthew Marvin, Senr., Rob: Turney, and John Bowton,[2] November 8, 1666, the day after the inventory was entered; I have a full copy of this, but it is too long to quote in full: it begins "Wee whose names are underwritten being Realations to Ruth Bowton, the daughter of Richard Bowton and Ruth his wife, late of ffairfield, deceased, etc." It goes on to provide for the care of the infant child, and her support out of the estate left by her mother; in case of her death the land was to "rearturn to Benj. Turney of ffairfield:" £7: 17: 6 was to go to Thomas Morehouse, and the rest of the estate to be divided. Ruth was to be placed with Matthew Marvin (husband of her grandmother) until she was eighteen; if he died before that time she was "to be put to John Bowton of Norwocke, the childs Unkle, etc."

This proves my statement above, that John[2] was her uncle, and hence her father's brother: that this is the Ruth whom Alice calls her grandchild is also proved by several other documents on record, of which I have copies, and to which brief reference will be made below, but not necessary to quote in full. That this is the Ruth who survived her grandmother is further shown by the inventory of Matthew Marvin's estate; the "meadow-land etc.," is mentioned on III., 59, of Fairfield Probate Records, which say that July 13, 1680, the land in Fairfield was not valued, "but remains to be prized. This land as we understand did formerly belong to the estate of Richard Bowton." Again, on page 60, "The land at Fairfield is found to be in Ruth Bowton's Inventory to be (*sic*) Ten pounds." I have traced it further, but it seems needless to give its history here: it is constantly recognized as belonging to Alice's grandchild.

From the foregoing documents I think these points are fully established, viz:

I. That the second wife of Matthew[1] Marvin was not a Widow Alice Kellogg, but the widow of John[1] Bowton, who has hitherto escaped the knowledge of genealogists entirely.

II. That by her first marriage to John[1] Bowton, she was the mother of the Richard[2] Bowton who married Ruth Turney and died in 1665; of Bridget Bowton, who married Daniel Kellogg; and of John[2] Bowton who married Abigail Marvin.

III. That her first husband's name was John Bowton appears not only from the Agreement cited concerning the infant Ruth, but from the Norwalk Records cited by Hall, p. 187, which say Bridget Bowton, wife of Daniel Kellogg, was daughter of John. This latter statement is what has misled previous writers into believing that John who married Abigail had been previously married, and that Bridget was his daughter (instead of being his sister) by that earlier marriage.

IV. That by her second marriage to Matthew Marvin, Alice became the mother of his youngest child, Rachel, who married Samuel Smith, baptized Sunday, Dec. 30, 1649, at Hartford, and probably of Samuel, baptized Sunday, February 6, 1648, at Hartford, who is supposed to have died young, no further reference to him having been discovered. I mention here that between this Samuel and Abigail who was born about 1636, we should place Rebecca, who married John Clarke, of Farmington, and had John, Matthew, Elizabeth, Rebecca, and probably others; Mr. W. S. Porter also mentions a "Lidia," but I have been unable to learn on what authority. These dates may however help us to approximate the date of the marriage of Matthew and Alice.

If the first John Bowton was the one who sailed for Virginia in the "Assurance" (see Hotten, p. 111, and Savage, etc.), and the first husband of Alice Marvin (and no evidence whatever has been adduced that I can discover, to show that such was the case), he must have died before 1647, and left nothing by which to identify him as such. It is clear, however, that the John of the "Assurance" is not the John who married Abigail Marvin. On the title-page of the "Bouton-Boughton Family" the claim is made that that John was "a native of France, who embarked from Gravesend, England, and landed at Boston in December, 1635, and settled at Norwalk, Conn." He seems from Hotten to have sailed July 25, 1635, aged 20, and therefore, if the theory of the compiler of that book were true, was five months on the ocean, and was a widower of over 40 when he married Abigail Marvin, a girl of about 18! What authority that compiler has for his further statements, that "the Government of England were offering to send emigrants to America, on condition that they would swear allegiance to the crown of England," I know not; it has been generally believed that instead of offering to send them, they did their best to prevent many from coming. I think the liberal *offer* here announced will be news to most of your readers. The author continues: "A registry of such emigrants was kept at London, a copy of which has been examined by the compiler of this work [The B.-B. Family], and as only one person by the Bouton name is found on that registry, embracing a period of one hundred years from 1600 to 1700, it is supposed that said person [the John who sailed from Gravesend] is the John Bouton of whom this account is traced." That is, the John who married, as he believes, Abigail Marvin, is the same as the emigrant, for he knew nothing about the John who was Alice's first husband. The "copy examined" was probably Hotten, which as every genealogist knows, is very incomplete.

But I have neither time nor inclination, nor have you the space to waste in pointing out the numerous errors in the "Bouton-Boughton Family" concerning the person there given as the first of the name. I content myself with showing that the attribution of the children Bridget and Richard to the husband of Abigail Marvin, by an earlier marriage with one "Joan Turney," not mentioned elsewhere so far as I have been able to discover, and said to have died in Norwalk (B.-B. Fam., p. 7), is proved false by the documents cited above: that his statement that Abigail died at Norwalk about 1672, is shown to be an error by the will of Alice: and that his further statement that John "married as his third wife at Norwalk, about 1673, Mrs. Mary, widow of Jonathan Stevenson, who was killed in the

Swamp-fight with the Indians near Norwalk," is rubbish, first, because Abigail was living in 1680; second, the Swamp-fight was in Rhode Island, December, 1675; and third, because Jonathan Stevenson was alive in 1677, on Feb. 20 of which year land was granted him for his services in that fight! (See Hall's Norwalk.)

But the compiler has mixed up three Johns—the first, the husband of Alice; the second, the husband of Abigail, and the third, the son of John[2] and Abigail, who died in Danbury, before his father, and made a will in 1700; while the will of the second John, the copy and the original of which I have examined at Fairfield, is dated Dec. 25, 1706, and the year is written out in words in the instrument. But enough of this. Some of the errors are those of carelessness in copying, by one not familiar with the writing of the period; some are due, like one just mentioned, to ignorance; and some to the confusion caused by the identity of names; while the statement that the John who came in the "Assurance," aged 20 in 1635, was the son of Count Nicholas Bouton, of France, said in the "History of Fairfield County" to have been born in 1598, is as absurd as it is impossible, if the date of the birth of Nicholas given in the "History" be correct. It is at least equally probable that he was a relative of John Bowghton, of Colchester, Essex, who was summoned before the Vicar-General, March 2, 1527. (See Annals of Non-Conformity in Essex, by Rev. T. W. Davids, London, 1863, and Strype, Ecc. Mem., I., 119.) Finally, for amusement, in this dreary waste of blunders, let the reader familiar with French heraldic terms peruse the farrago concerning the Bouton arms [in the B.-B. Family], and the explanation given of the blazon.

MARVIN-BRADLEY.—Knowing that corrections of genealogical matter in the REGISTER are desired, I send the following. My informant was Judge Ulysses L. Marvin, son of the lady.

In vol. 57, page 138, Elizabeth *Clara*,[5] dau. of Arba[4] and Esther (Chamber- * lain) Bradley, should be Elizabeth Chloe, and she married, not *John*, but Ulysses Marvin. One of her daughters was Chloe Bradley Marvin.

I have the same name from several sources, and Judge Marvin is good authority. I have full particulars of the whole family. Elizabeth Chloe died 28 June, 1884.   W. T. R. MARVIN.
Longwood, Mass.

*Page 216, Vol. I of this work.

MASON FAMILY.

Some of the descendants of Major John Mason, the Conqueror of the Pequots.

[Communicated by Hon. REUBEN H. WALWORTH, of Saratoga Springs.]

I Gen. Major JOHN MASON, born in England, about 1600, was a Lieut. in the army, and served in the Netherlands under Sir Thomas Fairfax. He emigrated to America about 1630, settled in Dorchester, and represented that town in the General Court. In Oct. 1635, he removed to Windsor, Ct., in company with the Rev. John Warham, Henry Wolcott, Esq., and others of the first settlers of that town ; where he was elected an Assistant or Magistrate of the colony in 1642. In May, 1637, he commanded the successful expedition against the Pequots, near New London. He m. about 1640, Anne ——, and in 1647 removed his family to Saybrook. In 1660 he became one of the first settlers of Norwich ; where he was Deputy Governor and Major General of the forces of the colony. He d. 30 Jan. 1672, at Norwich, where his widow d. very shortly afterwards.

Their children were :—(1)*Priscilla*,[†] b. Oct. 1641, at Windsor, m. Rev. James Fitch ;—(2) *Samuel*,[†] b. July, 1664, at W., m. 1, —— ; 2, Elizabeth Peck ;—(3) *John*,[†] b. Aug. 1646, at W., m. Abigail Fitch ;— (4) *Rachel*, b. Oct. 1648 at Saybrook, m. 12 June, 1678, Charles Hill of New London, son of George Hill of Derbyshire, Eng., and d. 4 April 1679, at N. L., in giving birth to twins, who d. with her ;—(5) *Anne*,[†] b. June, 1650, at S., m. Capt. John Brown, of Swansey ;—(6)*Daniel*,[†] b. April, 1652, at Saybrook, m. 1, Margaret Denison, 2, —— ; 3, Rebecca Hobart ;—(7) *Elizabeth*, b. Aug. 1654, at S., who prob. d. unm.

II Gen. 1. PRISCILLA MASON, m. Oct. 1664, Rev. James Fitch, first minister of Norwich, b. 24 Dec. 1622, at Bocking in Eng., came to America in 1638, and was ordained as the minister of Saybrook in 1646. She was his second wife. [By his first wife Abigail Whitfield, who d. 9 Sept. 1659, at S., he had 6 children ; James, b. 2 Aug. 1649, who m. twice, and d. at Canterbury ; Abigail, b. 5 Aug. 1650, prob. m. Capt. John Mason ; Elizabeth, b. 2 Jan. 1652, m. Rev. Edward Taylor ; Hannah, b. 17 Sept. 1653 ; Samuel, b. April, 1655, and Dorothy, b. April, 1658, m. Nathaniel Bissell.] Rev. James Fitch d. 18 Nov. 1702, at Lebanon. His children by his last wife, Priscilla Mason, were :—(8) *Daniel*, b. Aug. 1665, at Norwich. He m. and settled at New London North Parish, now Montville, and had a family of children. My information as to most of his family and descendants is very imperfect, but I have ascertained that he had at least three children ; 1. *Daniel*, who m. Sarah ——, and d. in 1755, leaving a property worth from forty to fifty thousand dollars, and leaving a widow surviving him, and two sons and 7 daughters, who were living at the date of his will, in May, 1755 ; to wit : Samuel Sherwood, James, Abiah, Rachel, Eleanor, Sarah, Mary, Anne, and Abigail ; 2. *Capt. Adonijah*, of Montville, who m. twice. I have not been able to ascertain his first wife's name, or all his children by her. For his second wife he m. 22 April, 1744, Anne (Hyde) Gray, dau. of Samuel Hyde and Elizabeth Calkins of Lebanon, and wid. of Simon Gray of L. Anne Fitch, dau. of Capt. Adonijah, by his first wife, m.

1 Jan. 1750, her second cousin, Samuel Hyde (162), eldest son of Samuel Hyde and Priscilla Bradford of Lebanon, (*See No.* 55). Sarah Fitch, another dau. of Capt. Adonijah, by his first wife, m. 7 April, 1751, Thomas Rogers, son of Daniel Rogers of N. L. N. P., (now Montville,) and had 7 children recorded to them at N. L. ; Elizabeth, b. 25 June, 1751 ; Parthenia, b. 8 Nov. 1752 ; Adonijah, b. 18 Nov. 1754 ; Sarah, b. 10 April, 1757 ; Andrew, b. 24 July, 1759 ; Azel, b. 27 Jan. 1765 ; and Frederick, b. 11 April, 1767 ; 3. *Mary*, b. about 1706, who m. 18 Jan. 1726, Rev. James Hillhouse, first minister of Montville, b. about 1688, at Freehall, Londonderry co., Ireland, son of John Hillhouse and Rachel his wife. He d. 15 Dec. 1740, and she had by him four children ;—Esquire John, b. 18 Dec. 1726, d. 9 April, 1735 ; William, b. 25 Aug. 1728, m. 1 Nov. 1750, Sarah Griswold, and had by her 7 sons and three daughters ; James Abraham, b. 12 May, 1730, grad. at Yale, 1749, and d. 1775, s. p . ; and Rachel, m. 4 April, 1753, Deacon Joseph Chester, and d. 11 June, 1765, and had one dau., Mary, b. 1754, d. 1765. After the death of her first husband she m. 17 Nov. 1744, Rev. John Owen of Groton, and d. 1768, at the age of 62 years. She was probably the ancestress of all who inherit the Hillhouse blood in the United States ;—(9) *John*,[†] b. Jan. 1668, at N., m. Elizabeth Waterman ;—(10) *Jeremiah*,[†] b. Sept. 1670, at N., m. Ruth —— ;—(11) *Jabez*, b. April 1672, at N., grad. at Harvard, 1694, was a Congregational clergyman, settled as Minister at Ipswich, 1703, and at Portsmouth, N. H., about 1725, where he d. 22 Nov. 1746 ;—(12) *Anne*,[†] b. April 1675, at N., m. Joseph Bradford ;—(13) *Nathaniel*,[†] b. Oct. 1679, at N., m. 1, Anne Abel ; 2, Mindwell Tisdale ;—(14) *Joseph*.[†] b. Nov. 1681, at N., m. 1, Sarah Mason ; 2, Anne Whiting ; —(15) *Eleazer*, b. 14 May, 1683, at N., m. his first cousin Martha Brown, (26) second dau. of Capt. John Brown of Swansey and Anne Mason, (*See No.* 5.) They settled at Lebanon where he was a Deacon of the church, and d. about 1747, s. p., and by his will left his property to his wife, who survived him.

II Gen. 2. MAJOR SAMUEL MASON, m. ——, and settled at Stonington, where he was a Major of Militia, and an Assistant of the colony, where she died. His children by her were:—(16) *John*, b. 19 Aug. 1676, at S., d. 20 March, 1705, unm. ;—(17) *Anne*,[†] m. her first cousin Capt. John Mason (22), son of Capt. John Mason (3) and Abigail Fitch ; (18) *Sarah*, who m. her first cousin Joseph Fitch, (*See* No. 14.)

Major Samuel Mason then m. 4 July, 1694, Elizabeth Peck of Rehoboth, and d. 30 March, 1705, at S., and was buried at Lebanon. She survived him and m. Gershom Palmer of S. Major Mason's children by her were :—(19) *Samuel*, b. 26 Aug. 1695, at S., d. 28 Nov. 1701 ;—(20) *Elizabeth*,[†] b. 6 May, 1697, at S., m. Rev. William Worthington ;—(21) *Hannah*, b. 14 April, 1699, at S., d. Nov. 1724, unm.; and her will, dated 4 Nov. 1724, at S., was proved 10 Dec. 1724.

II Gen. 3. Capt. JOHN MASON, m. Abigail, prob. dau. of Rev. James Fitch of Norwich, by his first wife. He settled at Norwich, and represented that town several times in the colonial legislature, and was one oi the Assistants of the Colony. He commanded a company in King Philip's war, and was mortally wounded in the swamp fight at Narraganset, 19 Dec. 1675 ; was carried to New London, where he lingered until 18 Sept. 1676, when he died. Their children were :—(22) *John*,[†] m. 1, Anne

Mason (17) ; 2, wid. Anne (Sanford) Noyes ;—(23) *Anne*,[†] m. John Denison.

II Gen. 5. ANNE MASON, m. 8 Nov. 1672, Capt. John Brown of Swansey, b. Sept. 1650, son of John Brown of S., who d. there in March, 1662, and grandson of Mr. John Brown of Rehoboth, born in England, who was one of the assistants of the Plymouth Colony, and d. 10 April, 1662, at Rehoboth. Capt. John Brown and wife settled at Swansey, and prob. both died there. Their children were :—(24) *John*, b. 28 April, 1675, at S., m. 2 July, 1696, Abigail Cole ; was called Capt. John Brown, and d. about 1752, at S., aged 77 years ;—(25) *Lydia*, b. 16 May, 1679, at S., prob. m. 15 March, 1705, Joseph Wadsworth of Lebanon, Ct., and d. 27 Dec. 1759, at L., and had 3 children ; John, b. 15 March, 1706, at L.; Mary, b. 29 Nov. 1707, at L., and Martha, b. 1 April, 1710 ;—(26) *Martha*, b. 20 Nov. 1681, at S., m. her first cousin Deacon Eleazer Fitch of Lebanon, (*See No.* 15);—(27) *Daniel*, b. 29 Oct. 1683, at S., d. in infancy ;—(28) *Ebenezer*,[†] b. 15 June, 1685, at S., m. Sarah Hyde;— (29) *Daniel* 2, b. 26 Sept, 1686, at S.;—(30) *Stephen.*[†] b. 29 Jan. 1688, at S., m. 1, Mary Risley ; 2, Abigail ——, and 3, Mary Jacobs ; and (31) *Joseph*, b. 19 May, 1690, at S.

II Gen. 6. DANIEL MASON, m. Margaret Denison of Roxbury, b. 15 Dec. 1650, dau. of Edward Denison, and Elizabeth Weld of R. He had by her one child (32), *Daniel*,[†] b. 26 Nov. 1674, at Stonington. During King Philip's War, Daniel Mason sent his wife and child to her friends at Roxbury, where the child was bap. 9 May, 1676, by the apostle Eliot, & where she prob. died. DANIEL MASON then m. ——, and lived for a time at Stonington, where she prob. died. He had by her one child ;— (33) *Hezekiah*,[†] b. 3 May, 1677, at S., m. 1, Anne Bingham ; 2, Sarah Robinson. DANIEL MASON was the school-master at Norwich in 1679, & for his 3d wife, he m. 10 Oct. 1679, Rebecca Hobart, dau. of Rev. Peter Hobart, minister of Hingham, Mass. She d. 8 April, 1727, at Stonington, where he d. about 1737. His children by her were :—(34) *Peter*,[†] born 9 Nov. 1680, at S., m. Mary Hobart ;—(35) *Rebecca*, b. 10 Feb. 1682, at S., m. 6 Feb. 1707, Elisha Cheeseboro of S. ;—(36) *Margaret*, b. 21 Dec. 1683, at S.;—(37) *Samuel*,[†] b. 11 Feb. 1686, at S.; 1, Elizabeth Fitch ; 2, Rebecca Lippincot ;—(38) *Abigail*, b. 3 Feb. 1689, at S.;— (39) *Priscilla*, b. 17 Sept. 1691, at S.;—(40 *Nehemiah*,[†] b. 24 Nov. 1693, at S., m. Zerviah Stanton.

III Gen. 9. JOHN FITCH, m. 10 July, 1695, Elizabeth Waterman, b. Aug. 1675, at Norwich, eldest dau. of Thomas Waterman and Miriam Tracy of N. They settled at Windham, where he was J. P., town clerk, and Capt. of militia ; and where he d. 24 May, 1743, and she d. 25 June, 1751. Their children were :—(41) *Elizabeth*, b. 1 June, 1796, at W.;—(42) *Miriam*, b. 17 Oct. 1699, at W., m. 16 Oct. 1740, Hezekiah Ripley, b. 10 June 1695, at W., second son of Joshua Ripley and Hannah Bradford of Hingham, and afterwards of W., and d. 9 Dec. 1744, s. p.;—(43) *Priscilla*, b. 5 Feb .1703, at W.;—(44) *John*,[†] b. 18 March, 1705, at W., m. Alice Fitch.

III Gen. 10. JEREMIAH FITCH, m. Ruth ——. They settled at Lebanon, and removed to Coventry, where he. d. 1736. His will, dated 8 March, 1736, at C., was admitted to probate 23 June, 1736. Their children were :—(45) *Lucy*, b. 18 Sept. 1699, at L., not named in will ;

prob. d. unm. ;—(46) *Ruth* (twin), b. 18 Sept. 1669, at L.;—(47) *Hannah*, b. 18 Jan. 1701, at L.;—(48) *Abner*, b. 8 July, 1703, at L.;—(49) *Jeremiah* ;—(50) *Gideon* ;—(51) *Elisha* of Coventry, 1736, named as Executor ; and (52) *James*. All these children, except Lucy, named in their father's will as then alive.

III Gen. 12. *Anne Fitch*, m. 5 Oct. 1698, Joseph Bradford, only son of Major William Bradford of Plymouth, by his second wife the wid. Wiswall. They settled at Norwich, and removed to Lebanon, where she d. 17 Oct. 1715. She had these children :—(53) *Anne*, b. 26 July, 1699, at N.;—(54) *Joseph*,[†] b. 9 April, 1702, at N., m. Honoretta Swift ;—(55) *Priscilla*, (twin), b. 9 April, 1702, at N., m. Samuel Hyde ;—(56) and (57) *Alithea* and *Irene*, b. 6 April, 1704, and d. same month ;—(58) *Sarah*, b. 21 Sept. 1706 ;—(59) Hannah, b. 24 May, 1709 ;—(59) *Elizabeth*, b. 21 Oct. 1712 ;—(60) *Alithea 2d*, b. 19 Sept. 1715, m. about 1740, David Hyde, bap. 22 March, 1719, at Lebanon, fifth son of Samuel Hyde and Elizabeth Calkins of Lebanon. They settled at L., where he d. 1741. They had one child, *David*, bap. 11 Jan. 1741 ;—(61) *Irene* 2d, (twin), b. 19 Sept. 1715, m, 18 March, 1736, Jonathan Janes of Lebanon.

III Gen. 13. Capt. *Nathaniel Fitch*, m. 10 Dec. 1701, Anne Abel, b. 2 April, 1681, at Norwich, second dau. of Joshua Abel and Mehitable Smith of N. They settled at Lebanon, where she d. 3 July, 1728. His children by her were :—(62) *Anne*, b. 5 Nov. 1702, at L.;—(63) *Joshua*, b. 13 Feb. 1704, at L., m. *Mary*, ——, and had 3 children at L.; 1, *Jonathan*, b. 1 Dec. 1730 ; 2, *Mary*, b. 25 April, 1732, and 3, *Joseph Trumbull*, b. 28 May, 1734 ;—(64) *Nathan*, b. 29 March, 1705, at L., m. Hannah Huntington, who d. 1 Feb. 1738, and he d. 12 June, 1750. They had 5 children ; 1, *Ebenezer*, b. 22 March, 1731, who prob. m. 20 March, 1750, Lydia Fish, and had 7 children, one of whom Ebenezer, b. 29 May, 1755, grad. at Yale, 1777, and was President of Williams College ; 2, *Simon*, b. 24 Aug. 1733, d. 14 Dec. 1736 ; 3, *Cyprian*, b. 16 March, 1734, d. 12 Dec. 1736 ; 4, *Nathan*, b. 26 June, 1736, prob. m. 9 Jan. 1755, Dinah Higby, and had 9 children ; 5, *Abraham*, b. 22 Jan. 1738, m. Elizabeth ——, and d. 1 April, 1821, at Lebanon ;—(65) *Nehemiah*, b. 10 Feb. 1708, m. 3 Nov. 1731, Elizabeth Vetch of Lebanon, and had a son Ezra, b. 5 Sept. 1732, and other children ;—(66) *James*, b. 15 Oct. 1709, at L., m. Ann Abel, and had by her two children ; 1, *Anne*, b. 28 Feb. 1729, and 2, *Elizabeth*, b. 28 June, 1731, at Lebanon, who m. her third cousin Col. Jeremiah Mason (204) of Lebanon, second son of Jeremiah Mason (110) and Mary Clark. James Fitch prob. m. another wife and had a son *William*, b. 18 Sept. 1734, at L.;—(67) *John*, b. 7 Jan. 1712, at L., prob. m. 5 Nov. 1734, Hannah Scott, and d. 7 Jan. 1742, and had 5 children ; 1, *Anne*, b. 6 Oct. 1735 ; 2, *Hannah*, b. 15 June, 1737 ; 3, Benjamin, b. 26 Jan. 1739 ; 4, *Tryphena*, b. 10 Aug. 1740 ; and 5, *Azuba*, b. 7 April, 1742, who m. 7 Feb. 1760, Oliver Wells ;—(68) *Nathaniel*, b. 14 May, 1714, at L.;—(69) *Mehitable*, b. 3 Feb. 1717, at L.;—(70) *Elizabeth*, b. 26 May, 1718, at L., d. 18 Dec. 1747, unm.;—(71) *Rachel*, b. Oct. 1720, at L., d. 23 May, 1721 ;—(72) *Abel*, b. 22 Nov. 1722, at L.;—(73) *Caleb*, b. 17 June, 1725, at L., prob. m. 4 April, 1747, Ruth Woodworth of Bozrah, who d. 19 March, 1751, and had by her two children ; 1, *Anne*, b. 7 Jan. 1748, and 2, *Caleb*, b. 23 March, 1750. Capt. Nathaniel Fitch (13) then m. 17 Sept. 1729, Mindwell Tisdale of Lebanon, and d. 4 May, 1759, at L., aged 79 years. His children by her were :—(74) *Jabez*, b. 4 Oct. 1730, at L., d. 14 Nov. 1736 ;—(75) *Ezekiel*, b. 11 March, 1732, at L.;—(76) *Isaac*, b. 10 May, 1734, at L.

III Gen. 14. *Joseph Fitch*, m. 2 Nov. 1703, his first cousin *Sarah Mason* (18), youngest dau. of Major Samuel Mason (2) of Stonington, by his first wife. They settled at Stonington, and she d. previous to 1721. His children by her were :—(77) *Sarah*, b. 24 Jan. 1705, at S.;—(78) *Mason*, b. 11 Sept. 1708, at S., grad. at Yale, 1729, and d. 10 March, 1734 ;—(79) Capt. *Joseph*, b. 14 Feb. 1711, at S., m. 28 Dec. 1738, Zerviah Hyde, b. 16 Oct. 1721, at Lebanon, eldest dau. of Capt. Daniel Hyde and Abigail Wattles of L., she d. s. p. JOSEPH FITCH (14), the first, then m. 29 Dec. 1721, Anne Whiting, b. 2 Jan. 1698, at Windham, eldest dau. of Rev. Samuel Whiting, minister of W., and Elizabeth Adams, a descendant of Gov. Bradford of the Mayflower. They settled at Lebanon, where he d. 9 May, 1741, and she d. 23 Sept. 1778, at Windham. His children by her were :—(81) *Samuel*, b. 16 Jan. 1724, at L., grad. at Yale, 1742, was a lawyer, settled at Boston, m. Elizabeth Lloyd, was Attorney Gen. of Massachusetts, and d. 1784, in London ;—(82) *Eleazer*,[†] b. 29 Aug. 1726, at L., m. Amy Bowen ;—(83) *Asahel*, b. 7 Nov. 1728, prob. d. in Canada, unm.;—(84) *Ichabod*, b. 17 May, 1734, at L.;—(85) *Anne*, b. 12 July, 1737, at L.;—(86) *Thomas*, b. 11 June, 1739, at L., d. 27 Feb. 1747.

III Gen. 20. ELIZABETH MASON, m. 13 Oct. 1720, Rev. William Worthington, b. 5 Dec. 1695, at Hartford, son of William Worthington and Mehitable (Graves) Morton of Colchester, and grandson of Nicholas Worthington of Hartford, and his first wife Sarah (Bunce) White. He grad. at Yale, in 1716, and was a Congregational minister. They settled at Stonington, where she d. 1 Jan. 1725. His children by her were :— (87) *Mary*,[†] b. 18 Aug. 1721, at S., m. Aaron Elliot ;—(88) *Sybil*, b. 9 Nov. 1723, at S., d. 23 Feb. 1724. After the death of his first wife, Rev. William Worthington m. 20 Sept. 1726, Temperance Gallup of S., and was minister of the Westbrook Society in Saybrook, where he d. 16 Nov. 1756, and had by his last wife 6 other children.

III Gen. 22. Capt. *John Mason* m. 18 July, 1701, his first cousin Anne Mason (17), eldest dau. of Major Samuel Mason (2) of Stonington. They settled at Lebanon—removed to S. about 1703, where she was received into the church 24 Feb. 1706, and died. His children by her were :—(89) *John*, b. 13 Sept. 1702, at L., bap. 19 May, 1706, at S.;— (90) *Rachel*, bap. 19 May, 1706, at S.;—(91) *Samuel*, bap. 30 Aug. 1707, at S.;—(92) *Jemima*, bap. 7 Aug. 1709, at S.;—(93) *James*, bap. 13 May, 1713, at S., m. 22 Nov. 1738, Sarah Denison of S.;—(94) *Elijah*, bap. 12 June, 1715, at S., m. his second cousin, Martha Brown (103), bap. 9 Sept. 1722, at Lebanon, dau. of Ebenezer Brown (28) and Sarah Hyde of L. They settled at L., where he d. 27 March, 1798, aged 83, and she died 27 March, 1805, s. p.

Capt. JOHN MASON (22) then m. 15 July, 1719, Mrs. Anna (Sandford) Noyes, wid. of Dr. James Noyes of Stonington, and dau. of Gov. Peleg Sandford of R. I., and grand-dau. of Gov. William Brenton of Newport. They removed to New London, N. P. (Montville), where he was a teacher of the Indians at Mohegan. He d. Dec. 1736, at London, where he had gone, with Mahomet, grandson of Oweneco, to obtain recognition by the crown, of the right of Mahomet to the Sachemship of the Mohegans. His child by his last wife was :—(95) *Peleg Sandford*,[†] b. 6 April 1720, at S., m. Mary Stanton.

III Gen. 23. ANNE MASON, m. John Denison, b. 1669, at Stonington, son of John Denison and Phebe Lay, and grandson of Capt. George Denison the first, of Stonington, and his second wife Anne Borradill. They settled at Stonington and removed to Saybrook, where they had 4 children recorded to them ;—(96) *John*, b. 30 March, 1692, at S.;—(97)*Daniel* b. 13 Oct. 1693 ;—(98) *James*, b. 16 Feb. 1695, at S.;—(99) *Abigail*, b. 25 May, 1696, at S.

III Gen. 28. EBENEZER BROWN, m. 25 Feb. 1714, Sarah Hyde, b. 20 Dec. 1696, at Windham, eldest dau. of Samuel Hyde and Elizabeth Calkins, and grand-dau. of Samuel Hyde and Jane Lee of Norwich. They settled at Lebanon, where he d. His will is dated 18 May, 1755 ; she d. 1 March, 1797, at L., aged 100 years. Their children were :—(100) *John*, b. 20 Dec. 1714, at L.;—(101) *Joseph*, b. 30 June, 1717, at L., m. 13 Dec. 1736, Eunice Allen of New London, and had 4 children recorded to them at Lebanon ; *Elisha*, b. 11 Jan. 1744; *Abiah*, b. 9 Sept. 1741 ;(?) *Sarah*, b. June 1753, and *Rachel*, b. 14 Aug. 1755 ;—(102) *Daniel*, b. at Lebanon, m. 17 Jan. 1745, Lucy Owen, and d. before the distribution of his father's estate. Their only child was *Ebenezer*, b. 23 Aug. 1745, at L.;—(103) *Martha*, bap. 9 Sept. 1722, at L., m. her second cousin Elijah Mason (94), youngest son of Capt. John Mason (22), by his first wife Anne Mason (17), and d. s. p.;—(104) *Lydia*,[†] b. 19 Mar. 1720, m. Ichabod Robinson ;—(105) *Anne*, bap. 24 April, 1726, at Lebanon, m. —— Bissel, and d. s. p. previous to 1779.

III Gen. 30. STEPHEN BROWN, m. June, 1729, Mary Risley, and settled at Windham, where she d. 1730, s. p. He then m. Abigail ——, who d. Nov. 1731, at W. His child by her was :—(106) *Abigail*, b. 2 Nov. 1731, at W. He then m. Nov. 1734, Mary Jacobs, and d. Oct. 1766, at W. His children by her were :—(107) *Mary*, b. 8 April, 1738, at W.; —(108) *Stephen*, m. Mary Shattuck, and had 11 children at W.;—(109) *John*, b. 18 June, 1742, at W., m. 22 Dec. 1763, Sybil Barrows, and settled at W., where he d. Dec. 1825, and she d. Jan. 1837, aged 92 years. Their 7 children were :—1, *Roswell*, b. 12 March, 1765, at W., d. unm.; 2, *Lydia*, b. 4 Nov. 1767, at W., m. William Spafford; 3, *John*, b. 16 Nov. 1769, at W.; m. 1, 10 Oct. 1793, Olive Martin ; 2, Elizabeth Palmer, and 3, Elizabeth Fitch, and had by them 14 children ; 4, *Eunice*, b. 11 March, 1772, at W.; 5, *Asenath ;* 6, *Sybil ;* and 7, *Lucinda*.

MASON FAMILY.

Some of the Descendants of Maj. John Mason the Conqueror of the Pequots.

[Communicated by Hon. REUBEN H. WALWORTH, of Saratoga Springs.]

III Gen. **32.** DANIEL MASON, m. 19 April, 1704, Dorothy Hobart, b. 21
Aug. 1679, at Topsfield, Mass., third-dau. of Rev. Jeremiah Hobart
and Elizabeth Whiting,* and grand dau. of Rev. Samuel Whiting, minister of Lynn, Mass., and his second wife Elizabeth St. John.
[This Elizabeth St. John, who m. 6 Aug. 1629, Rev. Samuel Whiting,
and came with him to America in May, 1636, and d. 3 March, 1677, at
Lynn, was a sister of Sir Oliver St. John, who was Chief Justice of the
Com. Pleas in Eng. in the time of the Commonwealth. She was a g. g.
dau. of Oliver St. John, Baron of Beauchamp, who upon the coming of
his third cousin, Queen Elizabeth, to the throne, was created Lord St.
John of Bletshoe. (*See Gen. Reg.* xiv. **61.**) Through her ancestress
Margaret Beauchamp, grandmother of Henry Seventh, she was descended
from Gundred, (fourth dau. of William the Conqueror,) who m. William
De Warren, the first Earl of Surry. Through her ancestress Joan Plan-
tagenet, b. in 1272, in Palestine, who m. Gilbert Le Clair, Earl of Gloucester, and her ancestress Matilda of Scotland, wife of Henry first of
Eng., and niece of Edgar Atheling, she was descended from Alfred the
Great and other Anglo-Saxon kings. And through her ancestress Maud,
wife of William the Conqueror, and dau. of Baldwin the 7th, Count of
Flanders, she was descended from Lewis the Fair and Charles the Bald
of France, and from Charlemagne, Emperor of the West, and Hilde-
garde of Swabia, his wife.]
Daniel Mason and Dorothy his wife settled at Lebanon, where he d. 7
May, 1705, and was buried at Stonington. His only child was:—(110)
Jeremiah,[†] b. 4 March, 1705, at L., m. Mary Clark.
[After the death of Daniel Mason(32) his widow married, 1 October,
1707, Hon. Hezekiah Brainard of Haddam, and d. 11 Mar. 1733. She
had by him 9 children. One of them, the Rev. David Brainard, was the
distinguished missionary to the Indians. Another was Martha Brainard,
b. 1 Sept. 1716, who was the first wife of Major General Joseph Spencer,
of the army of the Revolution, and was the grandmother of Elizabeth
Spencer, the late wife of Gov. Lewis Cass of Michigan.]

III Gen. **33.** HEZEKIAH MASON, m. 7 June, 1699, Anne Bingham, dau.
of Thomas Bingham and Mary Rudd of Windham. They settled at W.,
removed to Lebanon and returned to W., where she d. 2 Aug. 1724. His
children by her were:—(111) *Rachel,* b. 12 April 1701, at W., d. 14
Apr. 1701;—(112) *Hannah,* b. 14 June, 1702, at W., united with the
church at W. in 1738, and prob. d. unm.;—(113) *Anne,* b. 1704, m. 9
Nov. 1720, Thomas Dimmock of Barnstable, and settled at Mansfield.
He was an Ensign in the king's service, and d. 7 Oct. 1747, at Cuba.
They had 9 children recorded to them at Mansfield; 1, *Silas,* b. and d. Dec.
1721 ; 2, a *son,* b. 3 Oct. 1722, d. 6 Oct. 1722,; 3, *Jesse,* b. 6. Feb. 1726,
d. 25 Nov. 1726 ; 4, *Anne,* b. 22 Feb. 1728 ; 5, *Thomas,* b. 27 March
1730 ; 6, *Desire,* b. 23 Jan. 1732 ; 7, *Lott,* b. 14 Feb. 1734 ; 8, *Seth,* b.

---

* Not Dorothy Whiting, as Farmer has it. See record of deed from her to her son-
in-law, Hezekiah Brainard, dated 22 Jan. 1717, on Haddam records.

1 June, 1736, d. 4 July, 1748 ; and 9, *Hezekiah*, b. 3 Dec. 1739 ;—(114) *Mary*,[†] m. David Huntington ;—(115) *Rachel*,[†] b. 31 Aug. 1707, at Lebanon, m. Charles Mudge ;—(116) *Daniel*, living 24 Nov. 1731, prob. d. unm.;—(117) *Jonathan*, b. 30 July, 1715, at W., united with church at W. 1738 ;—(118) *Lydia*, d. 7 Oct. 1727, at Mansfield ;—(119) *Abigail*,[†] m. Jacob Lincoln. Hezekiah Mason(33) then m. 15 Nov. 1725, Sarah Robinson, and d. 15 Dec. 1726, at W. without issue by her.

III Gen. 34. PETER MASON, m. 8 July, 1703, Mary Hobart. They settled at Stonington and removed to New London, N. P. Their children were :—(120) *Peter*, b. 25 Aug. 1704, at S., d. 9 Sept. 1704;—(121) A dau. b. 13 Sept. 1705, at S., d. unnamed ;—(122) *Daniel*, b. 25 March, 1707, m. 19 Dec. 1734, Hannah Chappel of N. L., and settled at Stonington, where he d. 5 Feb. 1750. They had 4 children ; Joseph, b. 9 Jan. 1736 ; Alithea, b. 23 Jan. 1739; Priscilla, b. 29 March, 1746 ; and Daniel, b. 28 Dec. 1749 ;—(123) *Japhet*, b. 28 Dec. 1709, at N. L., d. 11 July, 1711;—(124) *Mary*, b. 31 May, 1711, at N. L.;—(125) *Japhet*, 2d,[†] b. 30 Sept. 1713, at N. L., m. —— Chappel ;—(126) *Abigail*, b. 3 Sept. 1715, at N. L., m. 11 Dec. 1737, Samuel Lester of Groton ;—(127) Peter,[†] b. 28 Dec. 1717, at N. L., m. Margaret Fanning ;—(128) *Alithea*, b. 9 Dec. 1720, at N. L.

III Gen. 37. SAMUEL MASON, m. 15 April, 1712, Elizabeth Fitch, and settled at Stonington, where she d. 8 Feb. 1715. His child by her was :—(129) *Mehitable*, b. 15 Sept. 1713, at S., d. 6 Oct. 1713. He then m. 22 Feb. 1720, Rebecca Lippincott. They settled at S., where the following children were recorded to them ;—(130) *Elizabeth*, b. 16 October, 1720, at S.;—(131) *Rebecca*, b. 2 June, 1722, at S., d. 29 Aug. 1723 ;— (132) *Rebecca*, 2d, b. 21 March, 1724, at S., d. in infancy ;—(133) *Samuel*, b. 25 May, 1726, at S.;—(134) *Rebecca*, 3d, b. 3 June, 1728 ;— (135) *Prudence*, b. 2 April, 1730, at S., had an illegit. child, Ianthe, b. 6 Oct. 1752, and d. 12 May, 1759, unm.;—(136) *Elnathan*, b. 16 June, 1732, at S.;—(137 and 138) *Mehitable* and *Eunice*, (twins), b. 1 June, 1734, at S.

III Gen. 40. NEHEMIAH MASON, m. 9 Jan. 1722, Zerviah Stanton, b. 20 Sept. 1704, at Stonington, third dau. of Joseph Stanton and Margaret Cheeseboro', and g. g. dau. of Thomas Stanton the first, of Stonington, and Anne Lord his wife. They settled at S. and owned Mason's Island. He d. 13 May, 1768, and she d. 12 Oct. 1771. Their children were :— (139) *Hobart*,[†] b. 6 Oct. 1722, grad. at Yale, 1748, m. Margaret Copp ; (140) *Andrew*, b. 12 Oct. 1724, d. 28 March, 1728 ;—(141) *Hannah*, b. 10 June, 1726, at S., m. 4 Oct. 1750, Henry Gallup of Groton, Ct.;— (142) *Andrew*, 2d,[†] b. 3 Feb. 1730, at S., m. Mary Gallup ;—(143) *Jared*, b. 29 July, 1733, at S., m. 23 Jan. 1755, Hannah Parke of Groton ;—(144) *Zerviah*, b. 26 Aug. 1735, at S., m. —— Holmes, and at date of her father's will, July 1765, had 2 daus., Zerviah and Mary.

IV Gen. 44. Capt. JOHN FITCH, m. 25 Jan. 1731, Alice Fitch, and settled at Windham, where he d. 19 Feb. 1760. Their children were :— (145) *John*, b. 14 July, 1732, at W., prob. m. 7 Nov. 1753, Mercy Lathrop, and settled at Windham, where he d. 5 June, 1757. He had 2 children ; 1, *Alice*, b. 1 Jan. 1755, and John, b. 11 Jan. 1756 ;—(146) *Alice*, b. 7 Oct. 1734;—(147) *Ebenezer*, b. 30 Nov. 1736, at W., m. 4 May, 1760, Chloe Kingsbury, and d. at Salisbury. Had 2 children recorded to them at W.; 1, *Cynthia*, b. 19 Nov. 1761, and 2, *Elijah*, b. 10 Dec. 1763 ;—(148) *James*, b. 9 April, 1739, at W., prob. m. 23 May, 1763, Anne Hulbert, and had 2 children recorded to them at W.; 1, *Anna*, b. 16 Oct. 1765, and 2, *James*, b. 11 March, 1767 ;—(149) *Miriam*. b. 9 June, 1741, m. Isaac Canada ;—(150) *Elizabeth*, b. 4 Oct. 1743, m. Sandford Kingsbury ;—(151) *Elijah*, b. 8 Jan. 1746, at W., m. 17 April, 1766, Hannah Fuller, and had 1 child recorded to them at W., Elijah Lord, b. 12 Dec. 1766 ;—(152) *Jabez*, b. 2 March, 1748, at W., m. 7 Oct. 1773, Olive Ripley, and settled at W., where he d. 23 June, 1789. They had 5 children ; 1, *Anna*, b. 11 Jan. 1776, at W.; 2, *Elizabeth*, b. 19 May, 1777 ; 3, *John*, b. 5 Jan. 1779 ; 4, *Olive*, b. 26 Sept. 1780 ; 5 *Lucy*, b. 9 Nov. 1783 ;—(153) *Eunice ;—*(154) *Lucy*, b. 26 March, 1753.

IV Gen. 54. JOSEPH BRADFORD, m. March 1730, at New London, N. P., (Montville) Honoretta Swift. Their children were :—(155) *Elizabeth*, b. 17 Jan. 1731, at N. L.;—(156) *Anne*, b. 23 July, 1732, at N. L.;—(157) *William*, b. 13 April, 1734, at N. L.;—(158) *Honory Swift* (son), b. 21 Aug. 1736 ;—(159) *Robert*, b. 21 July, 1739 ;—(160) *Hannah*, b. 10 March, 1741 ;—(161) *Joseph*, b. 10 Jan. 1745.

IV Gen. 55. PRISCILLA BRADFORD, m. 14 Jan. 1725, Samuel Hyde, b. 10 Sept. 1691, at Windham, eldest son of Samuel Hyde and Elizabeth Calkins, and gr. son of Samuel Hyde the first and Jane Lee of Norwich. They settled at Lebanon, where he d. 14 Feb. 1776, and she d. 14 May, 1778. Their children were :—(162) *Samuel*, b. 24 Oct. 1725, at L., m. 1 Jan. 1750, his second cousin Anne Fitch, dau. of Capt. Adonijah Fitch of New London, N. P., (*See No. 8.*) They had 5 sons and 2 daus. ;— (162) *Dan*, b. 7 May 1733, at L., m. Mary Wattles, dau. of William Wattles and Abigail Denison of L., and had 2 children ; 1, *Mary*, who m. 24 June, 1784, James Benjamin of East Hartford ; and 2, *Priscilla*, who m. 19 Oct. 1794, John Pitkin of E. H.;—(163) *Anne*, b. 22 Oct. 1727, m. 2 Oct. 1755, Jared Hinckley of Lebanon, and had 4 sons and 2 daus.; —(164) *Priscilla*, b. 16 April, 1731, d. 5 Oct. 1732 ;—(165) *Sybil*, b. 16 April 1731, (twin), m. 11 Dec. 1753, Jabez Metcalf, b. 30 Nov. 1718, at L., son of Ebenezer Metcalf and Hannah Abel. She d. 5 Nov. 1790, and he d. 15 Nov. 1794. They had 2 children ; 1, *Joseph*, who m. Clarissa Thomas ; and 2, *a dau.* d. unnamed ;—(166) *Priscilla*, 2d, b. 4 June, 1735, at L., d. 4 July, 1759, unm.;—(167) *Hannah*, b. 19 July, 1738, at L., m. 4 Nov. 1760, Lieut. Daniel Moulton of Mansfield, who d. 17 April, 1767, and had by her 2 sons, 1, *Gurdon*, b. 29 Sept. 1763, and 2, *Daniel*, b. 18 Dec. 1765 ;—(168) *Zerviah*, b. 15 Dec. 1740, at L., m. 20 Sept. 1758, Dr. Andrew Metcalf, b. 5 Dec. 1736, at L., son of Benjamin Metcalf and Sarah Abel. They had 2 sons and 3 daus.; 1, *Jabez H.*, b. 26 Aug. 1761, m. Violata Thomas ; 2, *Luke*, b. 4 May, 1764, m. —— Frink, and removed to Oxford, N. Y.; 3, *Priscilla*, b. 29 July, 1759, m. Samuel Robinson, son of John Robinson and Thankful Hinckley of L.; 4, *Sarah*, who d. unm.; 5, *Hannah Hyde*, who m. Chandler Woodworth, and d. s. p.; (169) *Abigail*, b. 4 Nov. 1744, at L., d. 20 Dec. 1830, at the age of 86 years, unm.

IV. Gen. 82. Col. ELEAZER FITCH, grad. at Yale, 1743, and was a lawyer. He m. 4 April, 1746, Amy Bowen of Providence. They settled at Lebanon and removed to Windham, where he was a colonel of militia and sheriff of the county. He refused to take a part against the British government, in the war of the Revolution, and at the close of the

war he went to St. Johns, L. C.,(?) where he died. Their children were :—
(170) *Anne*, b. 18 April, 1747, at Providence, m. 29 Nov. 1767, her
father's second cousin, Major Ebenezer Whiting, b. May, 1735, youngest
son of Lieut. Charles Whiting and Elizabeth Bradford, a descendant of
Gov. William Bradford, and of John Alden and Priscilla Mullins, of the
Mayflower. They settled at Norwich, and he was an officer in the Rev.
and d. 6 Sept. 1794, at Westfield, Mass., she d. 27 June, 1827. Their
children were :—1, *Augustus*, m. Elizabeth Hoes ; 2, *Edward*, m. Nancy Perkins ; 3, *Henry*, m. Nancy Goodwin, and was brevet Brigadier
Gen. in U. S. army, and d. 10 Sept. 1851 at St. Louis ; 4, *Nancy*, m. ——
Gordon ; 5, *Charles*, m. Margaret Regis and lived at Kinderhook, N. Y.;
6, *Bowen*, m. Nancy McKinstry, and was a lawyer and settled and d. at
Geneva, N. Y., and was circuit judge for the 7th circuit ; 7, *Elizabeth ;*
5, *Charlotte*, and 9, *Bernice ;*—(171) *Elizabeth*, b. 12 Feb. 1749, at L.,
m. 7 Jan. 1767, Ebenezer Backus, b. 17 Aug. 1747, at Norwich, only
son of Ebenezer Backus, Esq., of N. by his 2d wife Eunice Dyer. They
settled at N., and had 5 children ; 1, *Eunice*, b. 5 May, 1768, at N.; 2,
Eleazer Fitch, b. 13 Jan. 1770, at N., m. Harriet Whiting, b. 14 Sept.
1779, youngest dau. of Col. William Bradford Whiting and Amie Lathrop of Canaan, N. Y. They settled at Albany, where she d. 13 July,
1804, leaving one child. He then m. 8 June, 1807, Elizabeth Chester, b.
10 Nov. 1774, at Weathersfield, eldest dau. of Col. John Chester and
Elizabeth Huntington, and had by her three children ; Rev. Jonathan
Trumbull Backus, D. D., Presbyterian clergyman at Schenectady, N. Y.,
Rev John Backus, D. D., Presbyterian clergyman at Baltimore, Md., and
Mary the wife of James Bayard, Esq., of Philadelphia ; 3, *Elizabeth*, b.
22 March, 1775 ; 4, *Alexander*, b. 5 May, 1777 ; 5, *Lydia*, m. 21 Oct.
1801, Nathan Whiting, b. 16 May, 1772, son of Col. William Bradford
Whiting and Amie Lathrop of Canaan, N. Y., and d. 1 Dec. 1832, at
New Haven, had 4 sons and 3 daus.; 6, *Julia*, m. 1, Ebenezer Jones of
Troy, N. Y., and 2, Samuel Cheever, and had children by each ;—(172)
Amy, b. 20 June, 1751, at W., m. 12 April, 1781, William Temple of
Boston, and had by him one son, Robert, who settled at Rutland, Vt., and
had a family. After the death of her first husband, Mrs Amy (Fitch)
Temple m. 29 March, 1790, Isaac Clark of Castleton, Vt., who was a
Col. in the army of the U. S. in the war of 1812, and had children by
him ;—(173) *Thomas Mason*, b. 9 Oct. 1753, at W.;—(174) *Philena*, b.
4 July, 1755, at W.;—(175) *Henry*, b. 12 Oct. 1757, at W.;—(176)
Sarah, b. 18 Jan. 1760, at W., m. 1784, Hezekiah Perkins of Norwich,
son of Jacob Perkins and Jemima Leonard, and grandson of Jabez Perkins the first and Hannah Lathrop of N. They settled at Norwich and
had 6 children ; Francis Asher ; Eliza Leonard d. in infancy ; George
Leonard ; Charlotte ; Henry Fitch ; and a dau. who d. in childhood ;—
(177) *Mary*, b. 22 Nov. 1761, at W.;—(178) *Christopher*, 23 April,
1763, prob. m. 29 April, 1784, Lydia Ripley, of W., and had 4 children
recorded to them at W.; 1, *Thomas Mason*, b. 18 Jan. 1785 ; 2, *Henry*,
b. 15 March, 1787 ; 3, *Lucy*, b. 17 July, 1789 ; and 4, *Erastus Ripley*,
b. 9 May, 1792 ;—(179) *Frances*, b. 27 Aug. 1765, at W., m. 1782,
Bela Backus of W.;—(180) *George*, b. 7 March, 1768, at W.,;—(181)
Lucy, b. 20 May, 1771, at W., m. 1790, Lebbeus Larribee of W.

IV Gen.   87. MARY WORTHINGTON, m. 14 Feb. 1745, Aaron Elliot, b.
15 March, 1718, at Killingworth, second son of Rev. Jared Elliot, D. D.

and Elizabeth Smithson, and g. g. son of John Eliot the apostle. He was a physician, and they settled at K., where he was Col. of militia, and was frequently elected to the general assembly. She d. 28 June, 1785, and he d. 30 Dec. 1785, at K. Their children were :—(182) *Hannah*, b. 31 Aug. 1746, at K., m. 23 Nov. 1773, Gen. Reuben Hopkins, b. 1 June 1748, at Amenia, N. Y. He was a lawyer, and they settled at Charlotte and removed to Goshen, N. Y., where he was a Brig. Gen. of militia and commanded a brigade of militia in the service of the U. S., at Plattsburgh, in the war of 1812, and d. about 1819, in Ill. They had 8 children; 1, *Elliot*, b. 12 Sept. 1774, m. Julia Howell, 16 Jan. 1815, at Cincinnati, and had 6 children ; 2, *Benjamin Bronson*, b. 16 March, 1776, married, and 26 Sept. 1852, d. at Augusta, Ga., and had a family of children ; 3, *Mary*, b. 2 Dec. 1777, d. in 1820 at Cincinnati, unm.; 4, *Adelaide*, b. 3 March, 1780, m. at Goshen, N. Y., where she d. 3 March, 1846, and left children ; 5, *Rebecca*, b. 16 Jan. 1782, m. and 3 April, 1816, d. in Ontario co., N. Y.; 6, *William Hector*, b. 12 Nov. 1784, m. and in 1840 d. at St. Louis, Mo., leaving a large family ; 7, *Hannibal Mason*, b. 8 Aug. 1788, m. and settled at Goshen, N. Y., s. p.; 8, *Delinda*, b. 25 March, 1792, m. and 28 May, d. 1823, at Madison, Ga.;—(183) *Mary*, b. 11 July, 1752, at K., m. about 1798, Dr. Christopher Ely of Lyme, son of Daniel Ely. She was his 3d wife, and d. s. p.:—(184) *Samuel Smithson*, b. 2 July, 1753, at K. He m. 17 March, 1779, Margaret Williams, b. May 1753, dau. of Judge John Williams of Sharon. They settled at Sharon, where she d. 27 Oct. 1802. He had by her 8 children, 1, *Samuel Williams*, b. 31 March, 1780, m. 31 Jan. 1809, Sarah Canfield, b. 27 Dec. 1787, at New Milford, settled at Northampton, N. Y., and removed to Penfield, where he d. 30 Aug. 1831, and had 6 sons and 4 daus.; 2, *William Worthington*, b. 21 April, 1782, at S., m. Jan. 1809, Eunice Thomas of Ballston, N. Y., settled at Northampton, N. Y., removed to Ballston Spa, and in 1836 to Niles, Mich., and d. 13 Oct. 1839, and had 3 children ; Eunice Harriet m. Allen G. Kellogg; William Sidney m. Oct. 1836, Louisa Carrington, and 30 Nov. 1844, Caroline Morse, and had 5 children ; and Caroline Elizabeth, m. John Orr, of Niles, Mich.; 3, *Hannah*, b. 12 May, 1784, at S., m. 1814, Daniels B. Stowe of Claverack, N. Y., and had one child, and d. 12 May, 1830 ; 4, *Margaret*, b. 19 June, 1786, at S., m. 6 Sept. 1811, Salmon Hunt of Sharon, removed to Northampton, N. Y., and then to Rochester, where she d. 4 Nov. 1836. She had 3 sons and 3 daus.; 5, *John Aaron*, b. 16 Oct. 1788, at S., m. 4 June, 1809, Joanna Bailey of S., removed to Redhook, N. Y., and afterwards returned to S., where she d. 11 Jan. 1848. He had by her 6 sons and 4 daus. He then m. 8 Nov. 1848, Hannah Eliza Janez ; 6, *Mary Ely*, b. 13 April, 1791, at S., m. Festus Demming of Goshen, N. Y., and removed to Goshen, O., where she d. Dec. 1827. He had by her 3 sons and 3 daus.; 7, *Joseph Benjamin*, b. 23 July, 1794, at S., m. 1814, Hannah Waldo of Chatham, N. Y., and removed to Northampton, N. Y., and d. 20 Dec. 1820, and had 2 children ; Hannah Cornelia, m. Sylvester Reynolds of Chatham, and Samuel Waldo; 8, *Elizabeth*, b. 22 July, 1799, at S., m. 28 May, 1838, Rev. Noah Cook of Bertrand, Mich., and was living at Woodville, Ill., s. p.

After the death of his first wife, Samuel Smithson Elliot m. 17 July, 1803, Sarah Bailey, b. 19 Dec. 1765, at Sharon, and d. 22 April, 1812. He had by her two other children ; 9, *Isaac*, b. 9 July, 1806, at S., m. 11 March, 1834, Sarah Hurd, b. 28 Jan. 1816, dau. of Arba Hurd of Pittsfield, Mich., and had 2 sons and 4 daus.; and 10, *Sarah*, b. 14 April, 1808, at S., d. 1822 ;—(185) *William*, b. 26 June, 1755, at K., grad. at Yale, 1774, and was a physician. He m. his first cousin Ethelinda Ely, b. about 1764, at Saybrook, dau. of Col. John Ely and Sarah Worthington of S. They settled at Killingworth, and in 1801 removed to Goshen, N. Y., where she d. 14 Aug. 1829, and he d. Sept. 1829. They had 6 children; 1, *Horace William*, b. 1788, m. about 1825, Charlotte Westcott, dau. of Col. David M. Westcott and Keziah Gale of Goshen, N. Y. They settled at G., where he was a druggist and postmaster, they had 6 children ; 2. *Sarah Ethelinda*, b. 1790, m. 1817, Rev. Benjamin Gildersleeve of Milledgeville, Ga., and d. 1820, had one child William Elliot, who d. at age of 4 years ; 3, *Charlotte*, b. 1792, d. 1820, at Milledgeville, unm.; 4, *Elizabeth*, b. 1794, m. 1826, Zechariah N. Hoffman of Redhook, N. Y., who was judge and postmaster, and removed to New York, and had 4 children; 5, *Henry William*, b. 14 Aug. 1797, m. 1 Feb. 1843, Sarah Wickham Hulse, and settled at Elmira, N. Y., and had several children; 6, *Frances Maria*, b. 1798, m. Dr. Hudson Kinsley of New York ;—(186) *Aaron*, b. 15 Aug. 1758, at K., m. 15 Jan. 1782, Gloriana Austin, b. 18 Dec. 1758, sister of Moses Austin of Texas. He was a physician and removed to St. Genevieve, Mo., and d. 5 Aug. 1811, and she d. 9 Sept. 1811. They had 4 children; 1, *Henry*, b. 5 Oct. 1782, m. 31 Jan. 1813, Mary Lewis Elliot, b. 18 Jan. 1792, at Killingworth, 2d dau. of Jared Elliot and Clarissa Lewis of K. They settled at St. Genevieve, and he was Capt. of a steamboat on the Mississippi, and d. 16 Sept. 1826, on his passage up from New Orleans, and had 3 sons and 3 daus.; 2, *Elias Austin*, b. 12 April, 1784, d. 25 Aug. 1822, at Genevieve, unm.; 3, *Charles*, b. 15 Dec. 1786, d. 12 Feb. 1811, at S. G., unm.; 4, *Anne Maria*, b. 31 Aug. 1788, m. 17 Nov. 1807, William Chiles Carr of St. Louis, Mo., b. 15 April, 1783, in Albemarle co., Va. She d. 11 Aug. 1826, and had 2 sons and 3 daus.;—(187) *Joseph*, b. 9 Nov. 1760, at K. He m. —— McKinstry, and settled at Montgomery, N. Y., where he was a physician in extensive practice, and d. about 1798, without issue living ;—(188) *Benjamin*, b. 9 Dec. 1762, at K., m. Frances Panca. He was a physician, settled in Ulster co., N. Y., removed to Virginia and d. Nov. 1848, at Little Rock, Ark. He had 4 children, 1, *Mary Worthington*, who was the first wife of General Chester Ashley of Little Rock, U. S. Senator from Arkansas, and had 2 children ; William Elliot, who m. his third cousin Fanny Grafton ; and Henry C.; 2, *Eliza*, who m. —— Henderson; 3, *Louisa*, who m. Edward Cross of Missouri, and had 5 children ; and 4, *Charles William*, who m. and d. in Missouri, and had 3 children ;—(189) *Elizabeth*, b. 9 Dec. 1762, at K., d. at her brother Aaron's at St. Genevieve, unm.

IV Gen. 95. PELEG SANDFORD MASON; m. 4 Nov. 1742, Mary Stanton of Charlestown, R. I.., settled at Stonington, and removed to Lebanon about 1745. Their children were:—(190) *Anne*, b. 7 Nov. 1743, at S.;—(191) *Peleg Sandford*, b. 5 May, 1746, at L., d. 23 March, 1787, unm.;—(192) *Esther*, b. 12 Nov. 1748, at L., prob. m. 9 Dec. 1768, Daniel Tilden of Lebanon, and had 10 children recorded to them at L.; 1, *Stephen Daniel*, b. 3 May, 1769 ; 2, *Mason*, b. 7 May, 1771 ; 3, *Lucy*, b. 20 Sept. 1773 ; 4, *Esther*, b. 23 Feb. 1777 ; 5, *Mary*, b. 12 March, 1779 ; 6, *Lucretia*, b. 22 Oct. 1781 ; 7, *Sabina*, b. 22 April, 1785 ; 8, *Lydia*, b. 27 April, 1787 ; 9, *Josiah*, b. 23 June, 1789 ; and 10, *Harriet*,

b. 31 July, 1792;—(193) *Mary*, b. 22 March, 1751, prob. m. 12 Sept. 1771, John Terry, at Lebanon;—(194) *Lucy*, b. 2 Dec. 1753, at L.;—(195) *Elijah*, b. 26 Sept. 1756, at L., prob. m. his second cousin Mary Marsh,(266) b. 8 Feb. 1759, at L., fourth dau. of Joseph Marsh and Dorothy Mason(205) of L., and afterwards of Hartford, Vt., and had by her five childen, Clarissa. Mary, Roswell, Peleg, and Miranda ;—(196) *James*, b. 7 April, 1759, at L.

IV Gen. 104. Lydia Brown, m. 16 Jan. 1752, Ichabod Robinson, b. 12 Dec. 1720, at Duxbury, Mass., youngest son of Rev. John Robinson, minister of D., and Hannah Wiswall his wife. He was a merchant, and they settled at L., where she d. 23 Aug. 1778, and he d. 20 Jan. 1809. Their children were :—(197) *Joseph*, b. 4 Nov. 1752, at L., where he d. 27 Aug. 1813, unm.;—(198) *William*, b. 15 Aug. 1754, at L., grad. at Yale, 1773, and was a Congregational clergyman, and was minister of Southington. He m. 8 Feb. 1780, Naomi Wolcott, b. 28 Sept. 1754, at East Windsor, dau. of Capt. Gideon Wolcott, by his second wife Naomi Olmsted. She d. 16 April, 1782, at S., and had one child, 1, *William*, b. 12 April, 1781, at S., d. 16 April, 1781. Rev. *William Robinson* (198) then m. 16 Sept. 1783, *Sophia Mosely*, b. 7 Oct. 1760, at Westfield, dau. of Col. John Mosely and Hannah his wife. She d. 31 Dec. 1784, at S. His child by her was, 2, *William*, 2d, b. 31 Aug. 1784, at S., grad. at Yale, 1804, and d. 14 Nov. 1804, unm.; Rev. *William Robinson*(198) then m. 13 Aug. 1787, Anne Mills, b. 11 June, 1761, at West Simsbury, dau. of Rev. Gideon Mills and Elizabeth Higley. She d. 10 July, 1789, at S., and his child by her was, 3, *Naomi Sophia*, b. 30 May, 1788, at S., who m. 24 March, 1811, James Woodruff, and d. 21 Nov. 1849, at Brooklyn, N. Y., and had 2 children, Anne Mills, and Elizabeth. Rev. *William Robinson* (198) then m. 10 Aug. 1790, Elizabeth Norton, b. 13 Jan. 1761, at Farmington, dau. of Col. Ichabod Norton and Ruth Strong. She d. 20 Dec. 1824, at S., where he d. 15 Aug. 1825. His children by her were : 4, *John*, b. 29 Nov. 1791, at S., d. 25 Jan. 1792 ; 5, *Edward*, b. 10 April, 1794, grad. at Hamilton Col. 1816, and was a clergyman. He is the distinguished Edward Robinson, D. D., the oriental scholar, now of N. York, Professor of Biblical Literature in the Union Theological Seminary. He m. 3 Sept. 1818, Eliza Kirtland, youngest dau. of Rev. Samuel Kirtland, missionary to the Indians, and she d. 5 July, 1819, s. p. He then m. 7 Aug. 1828, Therese Von Jakob, dau. of Prof. Von Jakob of the University of Halle, and has by her 4 children ; 6, *George*, b. 10 Sept. 1796, at S., d. 20 Jan. 1799 ; 7. *George*, 2d, b. 3 Dec. 1798, at S., m. 30 Nov. 1820, Sarah G. Cowles, who d. 20 Feb. 1833, and had by her 5 children ; and then m. 7 Jan. 1835, Harriet Whiting Bradley of New Haven and had by her 10 children ; 8, *Charles*, b. 10 Feb. 1801, at S., grad. at Yale, 1821, and was a lawyer, m. 13 March, 1826, Nancy Maria Mulford of New Haven, and had 8 children ; and 9, *Elizabeth*, b. 25 July, 1803, at S., d. in 1859, at New Haven, unm.;—(199) *Mary*, b. 28 Dec. 1755, at L., where she d. 11 Oct. 1780, unm.;—(200) *Lydia*, b. 20 Oct. 1757, at L., where she d. 23 April, 1825, unm.;—(201) Rev. *John*, b. 26 April, 1760, grad. at Yale, 1780, was a congregational clergyman and was minister of Westborough, Mass., from 1789 to 1807, m. Abigail Durry, who d. 29 Dec. 1816, at Lebanon, and had by her two children : 1, *John Augustus*, now of the city of New York; and 2, *Laurinda*, who d. June, 1823, unm. He then m. 15 Feb. 1824, Elizabeth S. Tiffany, and d. 2 May, 1832, at L., without issue by her ;—(202) *Earnest*, b. 11 Oct. 1763, at L., d. 13 Jan. 1765.

IV Gen. 110. JEREMIAH MASON, m. 24 May, 1727, Mary Clark, b. about 1704 at Haddam, dau. of Thomas Clark of H. and g. dau. of Wm. Clark one of the first settlers of H. They settled at Norwich, W. F., (now Franklin,) where he d. 1779 and she 11 April, 1799, aged 95 yrs. Their children were :—(203) *Daniel*, b. 1 July, 1728, at N., d. 13 Nov. 1730 ;—(204) *Jeremiah*,[†] b. 1 Feb. 1730, at N., m. Elizabeth Fitch ;— (205) *Dorothy*,[†] b. 6 April, 1735, at N., m. Joseph Marsh ;—(206) *Daniel*, 2d, b. 10 April, 1735, at N., d. 11 March, 1752 ;—(207) *Mary*, b. 22 Dec. 1736, at N., m. 15 April, 1756, her second cousin, Nathan Huntington (211) fourth son of David Huntington and Mary Mason (114) ; (208) *Anna*,[†] b. 3 March, 1739, at N., m. William Whiting ;—(209) *David*, b. 2 Nov. 1742, m. Susanna ——, and lived on the homestead, and had a family ; his dau. Wealthy, d. 16 April, 1779, at Lebanon, aged 24, unm.;—(210) *Elizabeth*, b. 27 Aug. 1744, m. Theodore Sedgwick, bap. May, 1746, at West Hartford, third son of Deacon Benjamin Sedgwick and Anne Thompson. He grad. at Yale, 1765, and was a lawyer, settled at Sheffield, and removed to Stockbridge, Mass., was a M. C. and U. S. Senator, and a Judge of the Supreme Court of Mass. She was his first wife and d. s. p. about three years after her marriage.

IV Gen. 114. MARY MASON, m. 30 June, 1725, David Huntington, b. 6 Dec. 1697, at Windham, fourth son of Joseph Huntington and Rebecca Adgate of W., and g. son of the first Deacon Simon Huntington, and of the first Deacon Thomas Adgate of Norwich. They settled at Windham, where they had the following children recorded to them :—(211) *Nathan*, b. 22 July, 1726, at W., m. 2 Oct. 1752, Mary Burleigh, who d. 24 Nov. 1754, and had by her one child, 1, *Olive*, b. 8 Nov. 1752, at W., d. 29 July, 1755. He then m. 15 April, 1756, his second cousin Mary Mason, (207) second dau. of Jeremiah Mason (110) and Mary Clark of Norwich, and had by her 4 children recorded at W., 2, *Olive*, 2d, b. 19 July, 1757 ; 3, *Ednah*, b. 14 Jan. 1760 ; 4, *Anna*, b. 2 Jan. 1762 ; and 5, *Daniel*, b. 13 Dec. 1763 ;—(212) *Hezekiah*, b. 3 Oct. 1728, at W., m. 28 Nov. 1754, Submit Murdock. They settled at W. where he is called Major H. H., on the records ; where they had 8 children recorded to them : 1, *Eunice*, b. 3 Jan. 1756 ; 2, *Submit*, b. 29 March, 1758, d. 18 Oct. 1759 ; 3, *Gamaliel*, b. 28 Nov. 1760 ; 4, *Gurdon*, b. 30 Oct. 1763 ; 5, *Submit*, 2d, b. 8 Aug. 1765 ; 6, *Sybil*, b. 22 Nov. 1768 ; 7, *Lydia*, b. 7 Aug. 1775 ; and 8, *Jerusha*, b. 7 March, 1780 ;—(213) *Anne*, b. 14 Nov. 1730, at W., m. 25 Dec. 1755, Samuel Roundy ;—(214) *David*, b. 24 Oct. 1733, d. 25 Oct. 1733 ;—(216) *Mary*, b. 2 April, 1735, at W., prob. m. 3 Sept. 1750, Ebenezer Fitch ;—(217) *Lydia*, b. 29 Aug. 1737, d. 30 Aug. 1737 ;— (218) *David*, 2d, b. 27 Feb. 1743.

IV Gen. 115. RACHEL MASON, m. 3 Oct. 1727, Charles Mudge and settled at Windham. Their children were : (219) *Lydia*, b. 31 Dec. 1728, at W., m. 10 Nov. 1748, Samuel Bingham of W., where she d. 15 Jan. 1768, and had 4 children, Lydia, Martha, Samuel, and Martha, 2d ;—(220) *Mary*, b. 5 March, 1732, at W., m. 2 Oct. 1761, Napthali Webb of W., and had 8 children ;—(221) *Anne*, m. 28 April, 1754, Samuel Kimball of W., and had 4 children, Charles, Sarah, Anne, and Samuel ;—(222) *Rachel*, b. 26 June, 1738, at W.;—(223) *William*, b. 9 Feb. 1741, at W., m. 10 June, 1762, Mary Spencer, and had 4 children : 1, *Charles*, b. 30 March, 1763 ; 2, *Prudence*, b. 22 Nov. 1764 ; 3, *Ichabod*, b. 31 Aug. 1767 ; and 4, *Lydia*, b. 14 Jan. 1773.

MASON FAMILY.

Some of the Descendants of Maj. John Mason the Conqueror of the Pequots.

[Communicated by Hon. REUBEN H. WALWORTH, of Saratoga Springs.]

IV Gen. 119. ABIGAIL MASON, m. 28 April, 1736, Jacob Lincoln, b. 10 May, 1696, son of Samuel Lincoln and Elizabeth Jacobs of Windham. They settled at W., and their children were : (224) *Jacob*, b. 31 Jan. 1737, at W. ;—(225) *Daniel*, b. 31 Aug. 1738, at W. ;—(226) *Abigail*, b. 22 June, 1741, d. 1769, unm. ; (227) *Joseph*, b. 24 June, 1743, d. 25 May, 1753 ;—(228) *Nathan*, b. 11 May, 1746, at W. ;—(229) *Hezekiah*, b. 7 May, 1748, at W. ;—(230) *Anne*, b. 24 April, 1750, d. 16 May, 1750 ;—(231) *Elijah*, b. 23 Jan. 1752, at W., was a soldier of the revolution, and was in the battles of Brandywine, Monmouth, and at Yorktown ; and was afterwards in the indian battles on the western frontier, and was always foremost in action. He was a pensioner, and d. unm. ;—(232) *Anne* 2, b. 26 Jan. 1756, at W.

IV Gen. 125. JAPHET MASON, m. ——— Chappel. Their children were : ,(233) *Japhet*, b. 19 Aug. 1742, m. 1767, Patience Hempstead, b. 31 May, 1744, and had 8 children ; 1, *Mary*, b. 20 Feb. 1768, d. unm. ; 2, *Daniel*, b. 18 June, 1771, d. 11 Aug. 1827, unm. ; 3, *John*, b. 2 April, 1774, m. 22 Nov. 1795, Elizabeth Keeney, and was living at New London in 1860 and had 4 children, 1, *John Hempstead*, b. 3 Feb. 1798, 2, *Silas Keeney*, b. 8 March, 1800, 3, *Elizabeth*, b. 20 July, 1804, and 4, *Charlotte*, b. 27 June, 1806 ; 4, *Amos*, b. 5 May, 1776, m. Sarah Holdredge of Ledyard, and settled at Mystic and had 6 children, Amos, Phinehas, William, pres. of Machinists Bank of Taunton, Japhet, Thompson, and Mary ; 5, *Sarah*, b. 30 May, 1778, m. George Hempstead, and was living at New London in 1860 ; 6, *Guy*, b. 25 July, 1782, d. 1783 ; 7, *Elizabeth*, b. 29 July, 1784, m. Lyman Peck, and 8, *William*, b. 30 Aug. 1786, m. Elvina Keeney, and settled at N. L. ;—(234) *Amos*, m. Naomi Bolles, and had a son Eliphalet ;—(235) *Samuel*, m. 10 June, 1774, Elizabeth Rogers, and settled at New London, where they had 5 children recorded : 1, *Elizabeth*, b. 7 Feb. 1775 ; 2, *Samuel*, b. 23 March, 1778 ; 3, *Peter*, b. 28 April, 1785 ; 4, *Lucretia*, b. 22 April, 1788 ; and 5, *Wilson Lee*, b. 18 March, 1795 ;—(236) *Naomi*, m. 16 Dec. 1779, Amos Thorp, and settled at N. L., where thay had 5 children recorded ; 1, *Eunice*, b. 14 Jan. 1782 ; 2, *Amos*, b. 26 Oct. 1784 ; 3, *Frances*, b. 4 Nov. 1787 ; 4, *Naomi*, b. 5 Nov. 1791 ; and 5, *Japhet*, b. 25 Dec. 1793 ;—(237) *Wealthy*, m. James Davenport of New London.

IV Gen. 127. PETER MASON, m. 1741, Margaret Fanning, b. 23 Nov. 1724, at Groton, Conn., dau. of Jonathan Fanning and Elizabeth Way. They settled at Groton, where he d. about 1765. She d. 19 Oct. 1803, at Castleton, Vt. Their children were : (238) *Abigail*, b. 5 Aug. 1742, at G. ; m. Rufus Branch of Castleton, and had several children, one of whom was Col. Darius Branch of Castleton ;—(239) *Rufus*, b. July, 1745, at G., m. and had 2 sons. He was drowned, 16 Dec. 1778, while on a visit at Castleton, and one of his sons was drowned with him ;—(240) *Robert*, b. 1748 at G., m. Chloe Case ;—(241) *Peter*, b. 1 Aug. 1752 at G., m. Elisheba Farnam ;—(242) *John*, b. 11 Nov. 1764 at G., m. Sarah Woodward.

IV Gen. 139. HOBART MASON, grad. at Yale, 1748, m. 10 Nov. 1748, Margaret Copp and settled at Stonington, removed to Groton, and, at the date of his mother's will, Sept. 1770, was living at Dublin, Nova Scotia. His children by her were: (243) *Margaret*, b. 17 June, 1750, at S.;— (244) *Lois*, b. 29 April, 1752, at G.;—(245) *Elnathan*, b. 17 March, 1754, at G., d. in infancy;—(246) *Elnathan*, 2d, b. 29 Dec. 1755;— (247) *Henry*, b. 3 April, 1758;—(248) *Zerviah*, b. 26 Jan. 1760, named in her grandmother's will;—(249) *Eliphalet*, b. 29 Sept. 1761, d. 25 Nov. 1763;—(250) *Hobart*, b. 15 Nov. 1764;—(251) *Luke*, b. 7 May, 1767. Hobart Mason's first wife died, and he then m. again, and had by his last wife two other children: (252) *Dudley*, b. 24 Sept. 1775, and (253) *Nancy*, b. 22 Feb. 1778.

IV Gen. 142. ANDREW MASON, m. 20 March, 1754, Mary Gallup, and settled at Stonington, where she died 13 May, 1797. They had a son, (254) *Nehemiah*, b. 10 April, 1757, prob. grad. at Harvard, 1780. He m. 6 Nov. 1782, Mrs. Bridget Denison, and settled at Stonington, where they had 8 children recorded : 1, *Mary*, b. 5 June, 1783, m. Amos Miner of Stonington, and had a son Amos, who, at the age of 19 years, went to New Orleans and prob. died unm. ; 2, *Mehitable*, b. 19 Sept. 1784, m. Alexander Latham of S., and d. 2 April, 1806 ; 3, *Bridget*, b. 9. April, 1786 ; 4, *Andrew*, b. 2 June, 1788 ; 5, *Joseph*, b. 4 April, 1790 ; 6, *Daniel*, b. 23 July, 1792 ; 7, *Peleg*, b. 30 Aug. 1794 ; and 8, *Nehemiah*, b. 4 Nov. 1800.

V Gen. 204. Col. JEREMIAH MASON, m. 9 May, 1754, his third cousin, Elizabeth Fitch, b. 28 June, 1731, second dau. of James Fitch (66) and Anne Abel. He was a wealthy farmer, and they settled at Lebanon, where he d. 16 April, 1813. Their children were: (255) *Abigail*, b. 22 Jan. 1755, prob. m. 17 May, 1781, Andrew Fitch, b. 21 Nov. 1748, youngest son of Pelatiah Fitch by his second wife ; he d. 22 Aug. 1811, and had four children ; 1, *Mason*, b. 7 March, 1782 ; 2, *Jabez*, b. 19 Feb. 1784 ; 3, *Gurdon*, b. 16 Feb. 1786 ; and 4, *Abigail*, b. 26 March, 1794;—(256) *James F.*, b. 13 Dec. 1756, at L., d. 26 Sept. 1759 ;— (257) *Elizabeth*, b. 20 Jan. 1759, at L., m. 1786 her third cousin, Judge John Griswold Hillhouse, b. 5 Aug. 1751, at New London, N. P., eldest son of Judge William Hillhouse and Sarah Griswold, and grandson of Rev. James Hillhouse and Mary Fitch, (see No. 8.) They settled at Montville, where he was a member of the Legislature, and Judge of the county court, and died 9 Oct. 1806, and she d. May, 1835. They had 5 children; 1, *Elizabeth*, b. 22 Nov. 1787, at M., d. 13 Dec. 1807, unm. ; 2, *Sarah Griswold*, b. 31 Jan. 1790, at M., m. 4 Nov. 1813, Joseph Bellamy, Esq., b. 1786 at Bethlehem, son of David Bellamy and grandson of Rev. Joseph Bellamy, D. D., minister of Bethlehem. He grad. at Yale in 1808, and was a lawyer. They settled at B., where he d. 1 Nov. 1848, and where she was living in 1858, and had 2 sons and 2 daus., John Hillhouse, and David Sherman who d. in childhood, Charlotte who m. Rev. N. W. Monroe of Cambridge, and d. Dec. 1857, and Elizabeth Mason, m. Rev. Aretas Loomis, minister of Bethlehem ; 3, *Mary Ann*, b. 9 Oct. 1796, at M., m. April, 1823, Dr. Elias W. Williams, youngest son of Rev. Joshua Williams and Mary Webb of Harwinton. He grad. at Yale 1819, was a physician, and died Sept. 1828 at Bethlehem, where she was living in 1860. They had 2 children, Mary E., b. Jan. 1825 at B., m. 14 Oct. 1857, William Fitch, Esq. of Bozrah, youngest son of Col. Asa Fitch by his first wife Susannah Fitch, and John G. H., b. Aug.

1827, d. Feb. 1829; 4, *Harriet*, b. 28 May, 1792, at M., m. 24 May, 1814, David Buel, b. 22 Oct. 1784 at Litchfield, son of David Buel and Rachel McNeil of Troy, N. Y. He grad. at Williams Col. in 1805, and was a lawyer. They settled at Troy, where he was a member of the constitutional convention of 1821, a judge of the county court, and a regent of the University of the State of New York, and d. 16 Aug. 1860, at T., where she is still living. They had 9 children. 5, *John Griswold*, b. 4 Nov. 1802 at M., d. 28 Oct. 1808;—(258) *James Fitch*, 2d, b. 19 Feb. 1761, at L., m. Nancy ——, and d. 7 May, 1835, at L.;—(259) *Anna*, b. 27 June, 1763, at L.;—(260) *Jeremiah*, b. 27 April, 1768, at L., grad. at Yale, 10 Sept. 1788, and was a lawyer, admitted to the bar in Vermont in June, 1791, soon after moved to Westmoreland, and thence to Walpole, N. H.; in the summer of 1797, to Portsmouth, in that State. He m. 6 Nov. 1799, Mary, dau. of Col. David Means ot Amherst, N. H. He had four sons and four daughters, viz., George, Mary E., Alfred, James, Jeremiah, Jane, Robert M., Charles, and Maryanne, of whom five are now (Jan. 1861) living. In 1802 Mr. Mason was appointed Attorney General of N. Hampshire. In 1813, June 21st, he entered the Senate of the U. S., in which he had a seat till 1817. He removed to Boston in 1832, in which city he followed the practice of the law for many years. Mr. Mason enjoyed a high reputation in his profession, and occupied a place in the front rank of the Bar of Massachusetts, where a Webster, a Choate, with many other eminent men in the same profession, had attained an eminence which has probably not been surpassed in any age. He died 4 Oct. 1848, aged 80 years;—(261) *Daniel*, b. 13 Sept. 1770, at L., m. 8 Jan. 1798, Eunice Huntington of Lebanon, where he d. 26 May, 1828. They had 7 children, Eunice Elizabeth, Mary Lyon, Rhoda Louisa, Julia Anna, Wealthy Fitch, John G. Hillhouse, and Abby Jane.

MASON FAMILY.

Some of the Descendants of Major John Mason, the Conqueror of the Pequots.

[Com. by Hon. REUBEN H. WALWORTH, LL. D., of Saratoga Springs, N. Y.]

V Gen., 205. DOROTHY MASON, m. 10 Jan., 1750, Joseph Marsh, b. 12 Jan., 1727, at Lebanon, son of Joseph Marsh and Mercy Durkee of Lebanon, Conn.; they settled at Lebanon, and about 1774, removed to Hartford, Vt., where he was the first lieüt. governor of the state, and was for several years judge of the county court; he d. 9 Feb., 1811. Their children were: (262) *Lydia*, b. 5 Nov., 1750, at L.; m. *Josiah Rockwell* of L. and had six sons and 3 dau.: Lathrop, Asahel, Daniel, Joseph, Erastus, Jabez, Lydia, Clarissa and Rhoda. (263) *Dorothy*, b. 20 April, 1752, at L.; m. Eliphalet Bill, and had 5 sons and 4 dau: Benajah; Eliphalet; Mason, who m. his first cousin Rhoda Pitkin, and was a physician; Roswell; Noadiah; Mary who m. her first cousin Thomas White Pitkin; Dorothy; Elizabeth and Almira. (264) *Rhoda*, b. 20 July, 1754, at L.; m. Thomas White Pitkin, son of Thomas Pitkin and Martha White, and removed to Vermont where he d., 1785. She had by him 6 children: 1, *Thomas White*, b. 1772; who m. his first cousin Mary Bill, dau. of Dorothy Marsh (263) and Eliphalet Bill and was living in 1860. 2, *Rhoda*, b. 1774; who m. her first cousin Dr. Mason Bill; and d. 1858. 3, *Rebecca*. 4, *Ruth*. 5, *Samuel*, m. Elizabeth Hamlin, step dau. of Robert Ellis of Saratoga Springs; and was a physician; and settled at Ballston Spa, N. Y., and removed to Saratoga Springs, where he d. March, 1823, and she d. some few years later. They had 6 children: Erasmus Darwin, b. 1808, m. Frances Wilcox, and d. Oct., 1860, at S. S., and had a family; Caroline b. 1810, m. James Slocum, and d. s. p.; Pamelia, b. 1812, m. the same James Slocum and settled at Brownsville, Pa.; Samuel who was post master at Saratoga Springs, and d. unm.; Elizabeth, who d. unm.; Lucy, b. 1823 (posthumous) and d. unm. 6, *Lucy*, b. 8 Feb., 1784; m. Robert Ellis, Junior, of Saratoga Springs, N. Y., who d. there. She had by him two sons: Robert and Timothy Pitkin. She then m. Joseph Bishop Abrams; and had by him two dau.: Lucy Ellis, who m., 1859, James Sanford, merchant of Mobile; and Mary Pitkin, who m. —— Stevens, and was living at Philadelphia in 1860. After the death of her first husband, Rhoda (Marsh) Pitkin m. Rev. Thomas Gross, and had by him two sons. 7, *Pitkin*, a physician living at Kingston, C. W., in 1860. And 8, *Horace*, who d. unm. (265) *Joseph*, b. 1 Jan,, 1757, at L.; m. Erepta Weld, and settled at Hartford, Vt., where he d. 16 April, 1837; and she d. 5 Sept., 1843, aged 83 years. They had two children: 1, *Gratia*, b. about 1785; d. 25 April, 1858, unm. 2, *Mary*, who m. Ira Hazen of Hartford, Vt., and had 6 children: Asa, who m. Clementine Porter; Louisa, who m. John Paul, and d. 1854; Susan J. who m. Francis Boardman of Newport, N. H.; Joseph M., b. 1830, d. 1855, unm.;

Ellen, b. 1830; and Walter, b. 1835. (266) *Mary*, b. 8 Feb., 1759, at L.; m. her 2d cousin, *Elijah Mason* (191), eldest son of Peleg Sanford Mason (95) and Mary Stanton. (267) *Daniel*, b. 2 Jan., 1761, at L.; m. Marion Harper, and settled at Hartford, Vt., where he d. 11 Dec., 1829; and she d. 18 March, 1851. They had 8 ch.: 1, *Roswell*, a lawyer at Steubenville, O., in 1860. 2, *James*, b. 19 July, 1794, at H., grad. at Dartmouth, 1817, and was congregational clergyman and D. D.; he m. 14 Oct., 1824, Lucia Wheelock, dau. of John Wheelock of Hanover, who d. 18 Aug., 1828; he was professor in Hampden Sidney College and President of the University of Vermont. He had by her 2 ch.: Sidney, grad. at University of Vt., and was President of the University of Oregon, 1860; and James, grad. at U. of Vt.; was Superintendent of Public Instruction at the Sandwich Islands, where he d. 1858. President *James Marsh* then m. 7 Jan., 1835, Laura Wheelock his first wife's sister, who d. 15 Aug., 1838; and he d. 3 July, 1842; and had by her one son: Joseph, b. 1838, a teacher in Canada in 1860. 3, *Percy*, b. about 1797, d. 1844, unm. 4, *Leonard*, grad. a Dartmouth, 1827, where he received the degree of M. D., 1832; m. Mary Foote of Burlington, Vt., and in 1860, was Professor of Natural History and Physiology in the U. of Vt.; and had a family. 5, *Louisa*, m. George Udal of Hartford, Vt.; and had a family. 6, *Arabella*, m. Chauncey Goodrich of Burlington, and left two daughters. 7, *Emely*, m. Thomas Read of Colchester, Vt.; and had a family. And 8, *Daniel*, m. Lucinda Hall of Hartford, Vt.; she d. and he was in Wisconsin in 1860; and had several children. (268) *Roswell*, b. 25 March, 1763, at L.; d. 30 June, 1784, unm. (269) *Charles*, b. 10 July, 1765, at L.; grad. at Dartmouth, 1786, and was a lawyer and LL. D.; he m. 1789, Anne Collins, b. 17 May, 1768, at Litchfield, Conn., second dau. of John Collins and Lydia Buel and grand dau. of Rev. Timothy Collins the first minister of L. and Elizabeth Hyde his wife; they settled at Woodstock, Vt., where he was U. S. Attorney, Member of Congress, and was a trustee of Dartmouth College for 40 years. He had by her 2 ch.: 1, *Charles*, b. 1790, at W., grad. at Dartmouth, 1813; m. 24 Nov., 1816, his second cousin Mary Leonard, b. 3 Dec., 1795, at Granville, N. Y., fourth dau. of Timothy Leonard and Mary Baldwin of Lansingburgh; she d. 21 Dec., 1817, s. p.; and he d. July, 1818, near Louisville, Ky. 2, *Anna*, b. 10 June, 1793, at W.; m. 4 June, 1816, Dr. John Burwell a physician of W., who d. 1846; and she d. 1855; and had one child: Mary Leonard, b. about 1820, who d. 1841, unm. *Hon. Charles Marsh, LL. D.*, then m. 3 June, 1798, Mrs. Susan (Perkins) Arnold, b. 9 Oct., 1776, at Plainfield, Conn., dau. of Dr. Elisha Perkins and Sarah Douglas of P., and wid. of Josias Lyndon Arnold, Esq., of St. Johnsbury, Vt.; he d. 11 Jan., 1849 at W., where she d. 3 Jan., 1853. He had by her 5 children. 3, *Lyndon Arnold*, b. 1799 at W., grad. at Dartmouth, 1819, and was a lawyer; m. 5 Nov., 1829, Lucy Gay Swan, dau. of Benjamin Swan and Lucy Gay of W., where they were living 1860; and had one child: Benjamin Swan, b. 1830, at W., grad. 1849 at Dartmouth College. 4, *George Perkins*, b. 15 March, 1801, at W.; grad. 1820, at Dartmouth College, and was a lawyer; m. 10 April, 1828, Harriet Buel, dau. of Ozias Buel of Burlington, Vt., they settled at Burlington, where he was 4 times

531

elected to Congress, and in 1849 was U. S. Minister to Constantinople; she d. and he had by her 2 children: Charles, who d. in childhood; and George Ozias, b. 24 Aug., 1832, a lawyer at New York in 1860. *Hon. George Perkins Marsh,* then m. Caroline Crain of Berkley, Mass. [He is now (1862) U. S. Minister to Turin.] 5, *Joseph,* b. 16 April, 1807, at W.; received the degree of M. D. at Dartmouth, 1830, and was a physician, and settled at Burlington, where he was Professor of the Theory and Practice of Medicine, in the U. of Vt., and d. 7 Nov., 1841, unm. 6, *Sarah Burrill,* b. 5 June, 1809, at W.; m. 1 Oct., 1828, Wyllis Lyman of Hartford, removed to Burlington, Vt., where she d. i Sept., 1841; and had 4 children: two d. in infancy; Wyllis, b. 4 April, 1830, a lawyer at New York in 1860; and Susan Marsh, b. 19 Oct., 1831; m. 1852, George F. Edmonds, lawyer of Burlington and Speaker of the House of Representatives of Vermont, And 7, *Charles,* b. 1821, living at Woodstock 1860, unm. (270) *Roger.* b. 17 Aug., 1767, at L.; m. Mary Chapman, b. 5 Oct., 1773, at East Haddam, dau. of Timothy Chapman and Sarah Fuller of E. H.; they settled at Hartford, Vt.; and had 4 children: 1, *Levi,* who went west and d. unm. 2, *Charles Chapman,* grad. at Dartmouth in 1828, and was a lawyer at New York in 1860. 3, *Edward Warren,* grad. at U. of Vt. in 1836, and was a lawyer at New York in 1860. And 4. *Franklin,* who was a successful merchant at New York, and d. 1855; (271) *Parthenia,* b. 3 Nov., 1769, at L.; m. Elijah Brainard; and had 9 children: Nancy; Parthenia; Lavinia; Mary; Susan; Henry; William; Columbus; and Joseph. (272) *William,* b. 1 Oct., 1772, at L.; m. Sarah Marshall, who d. s. p.; and he was living at Paulet, Vt., in 1860, s. p. (273) *Elizabeth,* b. 18 April, 1776 at Hartford, Vt., m. Robert Ham; and had 3 children: 1, *Ida.* 2, *Sylvia,* who m. 1st James Snow of H., who d. s. p.; and 2d James Benson of South Royalton, Vt. 3, *Oral,* who d. unm.

ADDENDA.

J. Hammond Trumbull has given me the name of the first wife of Major Samuel Mason; and furnishes me with evidence that Elizabeth the youngest dau. of Major John Mason was the first wife of Major James Fitch; and that the clerk at Stonington was incorrect in stating that Hezekiah Mason was a son of the *second* wife of Daniel Mason. This, with information from other sources and a memorandum I have of the children of Major James Fitch, &c., enables me to make, to my notes of the *Mason family,* the following addenda and corrections.

1. *Major Samuel Mason* (No. 1) m. June, 1670, Judith Smith of Hingham, Mass. (2 *N. E. Hist. Gen. Reg.,* 253). And he brought her home to Stonington, 22 June, 1670; and he had by her, two dau. (who died in childhood) in addition to the children mentioned before (*Miner's Diary*).

2. *Hezekiah Mason,* b. 3 May, 1676, at Roxbury, was a son of Margaret Denison, the first wife of Daniel Mason (No. 6) who was sent to her mother's at Roxbury, to be delivered, in March, 1676 (2 *Col. Rec. of Conn.,* 418). Daniel Mason's first wife died, and was

buried at Stonington, 13 May, 1678 (*Miner's Diary*). Rebecca Hobart
was therefore the *second* wife of Daniel Mason.

3. *Elisabeth Mason* (No. 7) b. Aug., 1654, at S.; m. Jan., 1676,
Major James Fitch, b. 2 Aug., 1649, at Saybrook, eldest son of Rev.
James Fitch, the first minister of Norwich, by his first wife Abigail
Whitfield, they settled at Norwich, where he was elected one of the
assistants of the Colony of Conn. in 1681; and where she d. 8 Oct.,
1684. He had by her 4 children: 1, *James*, b. Jan., 1678; died when
a week old. 2, *James* 2ᵈ, b. June, 1679, died early and unm. 3, *Jedediah*, b. 17 April, 1681; who was living at Nantucket in 1736. And
4 *Samuel*, b. 12 July, 1783; who m. Mary ——, and removed to
Maidenhead, N. J., where he died previous to 1736, and she was
living at Flushing, N. Y., in 1736; and they had 7 children, James,
Samuel, and Sarah, who were then living at Maidenhead; and Mary,
John, Esther and Elizabeth, who were then living with their mother
at Flushing.

After the death of his first wife, Major James Fitch removed to
Canterbury, Conn., and m. 8 May, 1687, Mrs. Alice (Bradford) Adams,
dau. of Major William Bradford of Plymouth, and his first wife Alice
Richards; and grand dau. of Gov. William Bradford of the Mayflower, and his second wife Mrs. Alice Southworth. She was the
wid. of Rev. William Adams, minister of Dedham, Mass., who d. 17
Aug., 1785, and was the mother of Elizabeth Adams the wife of Rev.
Samuel Whiting the first minister of Windham (see No. 14). Major
James Fitch d. 10 Nov., 1727, at Canterbury. By his second wife
he had 8 children: *Abigail*, b. 22 Feb , 1688; *Ebenezer*, b. 10 Jan.,
1690; *Daniel*, b. Feb., 1693; *John*, b. 1695; *Bridget*, b. 1697; *Jerusha*,
b. 1699; *William*, b. 1701; and *Jabez*, b. 1703.

I was wrong in supposing that Ebenezer Fitch d. 29 May, 1755,
grandson of Nathan Fitch (No. 64), was the President of Williams
College, as that Ebenezer Fitch was born a year too early. President Fitch removed to Bloomfield, N. Y., where d. 21 March, 1833,
aged 77, as Allen states. He should have said in his 77 year; for
for President Fitch was b. 26 Sept., 1756. He was a son of Dr.
Jabez Fitch and Lydia Huntington of Canterbury, and grandson of
Col. Jabez Fitch above named, who was b. 1703, youngest son of
Major James Fitch, by his last wife, Alice (Bradford) Adams.

4. I have also became satisfied that Capt. John Mason (No. 3) m.
Abigail Fitch, b. 5 Aug., 1650, at Saybrook, the eldest sister of
Major James Fitch; though I have not been able to find any conclu-
sive evidence of the fact.

5. The name of Major Mason's first wife, to whom he was m. July
July, 1639, was Anne Peck. From the statement of Savage, I think
Major John Mason had, by his first wife, a daughter named Judith,
who m. 17 June, 1658, John Bissell of Windsor, who afterwards removed to Lebanon, and they had 8 children: 1, *Mary*, b. 1659; 2,
John, b. 4 May 1661; 3, *Daniel*, b. 1663; 4, *Dorothy*, b. 1665; 5, *Josiah*, b. 1670; 6, *Hezekiah*, b. 1673; 7, *Anna*, b. 1675; and 8, *Jeremiah*,
b. 1677. (*See* 1 *Sav. Dic.*, 187.)

Saratoga Springs, 30 March, 1861.

MASON FAMILY.

Some of the Descendants of Major John Mason, the Conqueror of the Pequots.

[Com. by Hon. REUBEN H. WALWORTH, LL. D , of Saratoga Springs, N. Y.]

V Gen. 208. ANNA MASON, m. 27 Sept., 1759, William Whiting, b. 8 April, 1730, at Norwich, Conn., fourth son of Col. William Whiting of Norwich, by his first wife Anna Raymond, and grandson of Rev. Samuel Whiting, Minister of Windham, and Elizabeth Adams (a descendant of Gov. William Bradford of the Mayflower); he was a physician and they settled at Hartford, and in 1766, removed to Great Barrington, Mass., where he was a magistrate, and was a member of the Gen. court at Salem, which formed itself into a provincial congress to resist British aggressions; and he afterwards took a very active part, personally as well as by his pen, in quelling Shays's rebellion. He d. 8 Dec. 1792, at Great Barrington, and she d. 13 Nov. 1821, at New Milford. Their children were: (274) *Samuel*, b. 14 Aug. 1762, at H., m 1803, Sarah Betts, dau. of Stephen Betts, Esq., of Reading, Conn., and d. 29 Jan. 1832. They had three children: 1, *William*, who m. 1833, Aurelia Sherman of Newtown, Conn., lived at New Haven, and had four children: Stephen Betts; Sarah Maria; William Samuel, and Edward Sherman. 2, *Stephen*, b. May, 1806, grad. at Medical College, New Haven, 1830, and was a physician, and was killed 14 Oct. 1833, by the bursting of the boiler of the steamboat New England, near Essex, Conn.; and 3, *Maria*, who m. 1840 Rev. Thomas Dutton of Mendon, Ill., and had three children: Anna Dorcas, Aaron Samuel and Thomas. (275) *William*, b. 7 Nov. 1764, at H.; m. Ann Ransom of Great Barrington, where she d. about 1st Dec. 1840, s. p., and he was living at New Milford in 1849. (276) *Mary Ann*, b. 19 Oct. 1767, at H.; m. 25 Sept. 1792, Hon. Elijah Boardman, b. 7 March, 1760, at New Milford, Conn., third son of Sherman Boardman and Sarah Bostwick, and gr. s. of Rev. Daniel Boardman, the first minister of New Milford and his second wife, Jerusha (Sherman) Seelye. He was a merchant and they settled at New Milford, where he was a member of the legislature and one of the assistants of the state; state senator; United States senator. (While the writer of this article was a member of the 17th congress he had the pleasure to become acquainted with the excellent Elijah Boardman, then in the U. S. senate, and became much attached to him, and had the honor of being frequently addressed with him with the appellation of " my young friend," and parted with him to meet no more on earth, on the 3d of March, 1823.) He d. 18 Aug. 1824, at Boardman, O., where he had gone with his wife on business; and his remains were brought to New Milford for interment, and where she d. 24 June, 1848. They had six children: 1, *William Whiting*, b. 10 Oct. 1794, at New Milford, grad. at Yale, 1812, and was a lawyer. He settled at New Haven, where he was judge of probate, member and speaker of the house of representatives, and of the senate of the state, and member of congress. He was living at New Haven in 1859. 2, *Henry Mason*, b. 4 Jan. 1797, at New Milford; m. 13 Dec. 1818, Sarah Hall Benham, dau. of Rev. Benjamin Benham, pastor of St. John's Parish, New Milford. They settled at Boardman, O., where he d. 17 Dec. 1846, by the dislocation of his neck on being thrown from his buggy. He had four children: Frederick Alexander, b. 1 Sept. 1820, who m. Mary Ann Williams of New Milford; Elijah George, b. 30 July, 1829; William Jarvis, b. 15 April, 1832; and Henry Whiting, b. 7 Feb. 1837. 3, *George Sherman*, b. 17 Oct. 1799; grad. at Union College, 1818; and d. 18 Jan. 1825, unm. 4, *Caroline Maria*, m. 22 May, 1825. Rev. John Frederick Schroeder, D. D., grad. at College of New Jersey, 1819, and was an Episcopal clergyman. They settled at New York where he was assistant minister of Trinity church and Rector of the church of the Crucifixion, and had eight children: Caroline Maria, b. 11 June, 1826; d. 25 June, 1826; John Frederick, b. 1827; George Boardman, b. 20 May, 1829; d. 22 May, 1829; Mary Ann Boardman, b. 2 October, 1830; d. 26 March, 1841; Cornelia Elizabeth; Eliza Margaretta; William Henry, b. 1840; d. 1841; and Henry Hermann. 5, *Mary Anna*, b. 19 Nov. 1805; d. 7 April, 1822, unm.; and 6, *Cornelia Elizabeth*. (277) *Abraham*, b. 1 Sept. 1769, at Great Barrington; m. 1793, Carrence Wheeler and was a physician. He settled at Great Barrington, and had six children: 1, *Harriet;* 2, *Emma;* 3, *Theodore;* m. 15 March, 1820, Amelia Ann Robbins, and had two children: Harriet Amelia, who m. W. S. Brown of Rochester, and Frederick Theodore. 4, *Truman*, who m. and d. in Illinois. 5, *Huldah*, who m. Edward Hills and settled in Ohio; and 6, *Gideon* m. 27 Nov. 1833, Louisa Rood, and settled at Great Barrington, and had five children: Cornelia E. Boardman; Martha Cordelia; Mary Louisa; Geo. Boardman and Ruth Emma. (278) *Elizabeth*, b. 15 Jan. 1772, at Great Barrington; lived at New Milford at the age of 30 years and d unm. (279) *Mason*, b. 8 May, 1774, at Great Barrington; m. 26 April, 1800, Mary Edwards, b. 11 Oct. 1770 at Stockbridge, sixth dau. of Judge Timothy Edwards and Rhoda Ogden of Stockbridge, and gr. d. of Rev. Jonathan Edwards President of the College of New Jersey, and Sarah Pierpont. He was a lawyer, and they removed to Binghamton, N. Y., where he was a member of the legislature, and district attorney, and where he d. 11 Jan. 1849. They had eight children : 1, *Mary Elizabeth*, m. John T. Doubleday, and had two children: John Mason and William Edwards. 2, *William Edwards*, m. Ann Lyell Post. 3, *Caroline*, m. Richard Mather, b. 31 Oct. 1798, at Lyme, second son of Sylvester Mather and Elizabeth Waite, and settled at Binghamton, and had seven children: Elizabeth Waite; Rhoda Ann Lester; Frances; Nancy Louisa; Caroline; Mary Whiting; and Mason Whiting. 4, *Rhoda Ann*, m. Ralph Lester, and had one child: Caroline Mather. 5, *Frances*, m. Henry Mather, b. 9 July, 1803, at Lyme, fourth son of Sylvester Mather and Elizabeth Waite, and settled at Binghamton, and had two children: Richard Henry and Elizabeth Radcliffe. 6, *Mason*, m. Eliza Vandewater, and had five children: Eliza Vandewater; Amelia; William Mason; Henry Vandewater, and Jonathan Edwards. 7, *Catherine Spencer*, m. U. M. Stowers of Binghamton, and had three children: Mary Whiting; Catharine, and Morris. 8, *Amelia Ogden*, m. William S. Tyler of Amherst; had three children: Mary Whiting; William;

and Henry Mather. (280) *Fanny*, b. 1 Dec. 1778, at Great Barrington was educated at the Moravian school, at Bethlehem, Pa.; m. Frederick Abbot, and removed to Medina, O., and had five children: Cornelia; Caroline; Frances; Mary Ann, and Mason.

V. Gen. 240. ROBERT MASON, m. 1774 Chloe Case, b. 19 July, 1756, at Simsbury, second dau. of Charles Case and Phebe his wife; they settled at Simsbury, where she died 17 May, 1815, and he d. 5 Feb. 1835, aged 76 years. Their children were: (281) *Chloe*, b. 22 July, 1775, at Simsbury; m. 23 Nov. 1793, Levi Whitlock of Castleton, Vt., and had 9 children: 1, *James*, b. 26 Jan. 1795. 2, *Sarah*, b. 10 April, 1798; d. 23 June, 1799. 3, *Sarah*,2d b. 9 April, 1800. 4, *Samuel S.*, b. 25 May, 1802. 5, *Chloe Mason*, b. 17 Jan. 1805. 6, *Phebe*, b. 26 Aug. 1806; d. 23 March, 1810. 7, *Daniel Mason*, b. 28 Nov. 1809; d. 23 March, 1810. 8, *Levi*, b. 28 Feb. 1811; d. 15 April, 1813; and 9 *Simeon L.*, b. 23 August, 1813; d. 8 March, 1814. (282) *Margaret*, b. 31 May, 1777, at Simsbury; she d. 21 April 1781. (283) *Peter*, b. 6 July, 1779, at Simsbury; m. Nov. 1802, Mercy Case, b. 13 July, 1785, at Simsbury, eldest dau. of Amasa Case and Mercy Hillyer. They removed to New Hartford Centre, Conn., in 1816, where he d. 11 Oct. 1841. They had seven children: 1, *Hilpa*, b. 28 July, 1803; m. 22 Dec. 1831, Milo Watson of New Hartford, and had three children: Albert, b. Nov. 1835; Stephen, b. Sept. 1838, and Stanley, b. June, 1844. 2, *Chloe*, b. 31 Jan. 1805; m. 29 Nov. 1827, Roman M. Butler, and had children: Charles R., b. May, 1834; m. 1858, Cynthia Bunnell of Burlington; Henry, b. 6 March, 1836; m. 1857, Jane Hulbert of New Hartford. 3, *Aurora*, b. 18 July, 1808. 4, *Stephen*, b. 9 May, 1814; m. 2 Oct. 1842, Amanda Attleman of Granby and had five children: Stephen Henry, b. 29 July, 1843; Marian Amanda, b. 21 Nov. 1846; Isabel, b. 10 April, 1848; Loretta Jane, b. 13 April, 1854, and Walter Dwight, b. 13 June, 1857. 5, *Luke*, b. 9 Oct. 1818; d. 19 Jan. 1839, unm. 6, *John C.*, b. 2 Nov. 1820; m. 22 Oct. 1843, Adelia Alderman of Granby, and had four children: Charles John, b. 27 Nov. 1844; Fayette Stephen, b. 17 Aug. 1846; Luke Henry, b Dec. 1848; and Frank, b. June, 1853; and 7, *La Fayette N.*, b. 9 Nov. 1831; d. 19 Dec. 1838 (284) *Robert*, b. 31 March, 1781, living at Clarksburgh, Va., in 1859. (285) *Shubael*, b. 23 Dec. 1783, at Simsbury; m. 21 Nov. 1811, Elizabeth Roberts, and d. 1 June, 1831, at Braceville, O., and had ten children: 1, *Mindwell B.*, b. 7 Sept. 1812; m. 3 Dec. 1841, —— ——. *Robert L.*, b. 22 Aug. 1814; m. 22 Dec. 1841, —— ——, and had three children: Andrew W., b. 21 Oct. 1844; Wesley F., b. 25 Sept. 1852; Charles A., b. 6 Sept. 1859. 3, *Margaret*, b. 4 Sept. 1816; d. Sept., 1816. 4, *Mary Anne*, b. 23 June, 1818; d. 1 Jan. 1845, unm. 5, *Madison S.*, 2 Feb. 1820; d. same month. 6, *Washington S.*, b. 6 Aug. 1822; m. 15 Nov. 1846, and d. 18 Aug. 1853, and had 3 children; Mary Paulina, b. 6 Dec. 1847; Isaiah, b. 5 July, 1850, and George W., b. 6 Dec. 1852. 7, *Isaiah P.*, b. 4 Aug. 1824; m. 1 Feb. 1853. 8, *John W.*, b. 21 Nov. 1826. 9, *Benjamin*, b. 28 June, 1829; d. 5 Sept. 1852, unm. 10, *William*, b. 7 Nov. 1831; m. 30 Oct. 1855. (286) *Margaret*,2d b. 3 Jan. 1787; m. Zophar Brown, and d. 17 May, 1816, at Granby, leaving one child, William, b. 1812, and d. 7 March, 1842. (287) *Mary*, b. 3 Aug. 1789, at Simsbury; m. 1, Eleazer Case; 2, Thomas Vining, and d. 19 Nov. 1857, at Simsbury, s. p. (288)

Charles, b. 30 March, 1792, at Simsbury; m. 25 March, 1817, Sophia Burdick, b. 21 June, 1799, and removed to Leonardsville, N. Y., where she d. 19 March, 1852, and he was living in 1859. They had three children: 1, *Cynthia Maria*, b. 26 Feb. 1819; m. 25 Feb. 1839, at Plainville, N. Y., Clark Saunders, b. 16 July, 1815, and had five children: Gilbert Clark, b. 19 May, 1840; Cartha Jane Victoria, b. 11 Sept. 1841; Charles Albertus, b. 20 April, 1843; Seraphema Parthenia, b. 14 Feb. 1845; and Orson Oswald, b. 25 Nov. 1847. 2, *Charles Lewis*, b. 14 Sept. 1824; m. 18 Dec. 1845, at Plainville, N. Y., Desire E. Bass, b. 27 June, 1826, and had six children: Mary Imogene, b. 27 Feb. 1847; Gertrude Eliza, b. 22 Feb. 1849; Edwy, b. 4 Feb. 1851; Emerette, b. 10 Aug. 1853; Ella, b. 17 Dec. 1856; and Edgar Lewis, b. 10 April, 1857. 3, *Elizabeth Anne*, b. 8 May, 1827; m. 20 Dec. 1847, at Plainville, N. Y.. Samuel Noyes Stillman, and had four children: Eliza Cathalina, b. 18 March, 1839; Helen Emma, b. 29 Dec. 1850; Otto Oscioli, b. 12 April, 1854; and Noyes, b. 12 Nov. 1855. (289) *Daniel*, b. 1 Nov. 1794, at Simsbury; killed 1 Jan. 1810, by the falling of a tree. (290) *Anne*, b. 20 March, 1797, at Simsbury; m. 1 Nov. 1822, Jeffrey Wilcox, and they were living at Simsbury in 1859 and had four children: 1, *Chloe*, b. 7 Aug. 1823. 2, *Lucy*, b. 12 Aug. 1826. 3, *Mariette*, b. 1 Sept. 1830; and 4, *Jane*, b. 2 Oct. 1836. (291) *Luke*, b. 19 May, 1800, at Simsbury; m. 12 March, 1831, Diana Higley, d. 21 March, 1840 at Simsbury, and had four children: 1, *Daniel*, b. 21 Oct. 1833; m. 15 March, 1855, Clementina Pelton, and was living at Simsbury in 1860, and had one child: Frank. 2, *Jane A.*, b. 22 Jan. 1835; m. 11 Feb. 1856, Edwin Hamilton, and living at Unionville, Conn., 1859. 3, *Robert*, b. 16 April, 1837; m. 5 July, 1859, Emma Lowell; and 4 *Carlos*, b. 1 May, 1839.

V. Gen. 241. PETER MASON, m. 24 March, 1774, Elisheba Farnam, b. 26 May, 1754. They settled at Salisbury, Conn., where he d. 28 Dec. 1831, and she d. 4 May, 1833. Their children were: (292) *Sylvester*, b. 13 Oct. 1774, at Salisbury; d. 12 Sept. 1776. (293) *Darius*, b. 7 Jan. 1777, at S.; m. Sarah Post. (294) *Stephen*, b. 5 March, 1779, at S.; m. Anna Ely, b. 10 Oct. 1782. He d. 21 Dec. 1841; and she d. 24 June, 1843. They had ten children: 1, *Merrick E.*, b. 16 Nov. 1800; d. 22 July, 1840. 2, *Harriet*, b. 12 Aug. 1806; d. same day. 3, *Orville L.*, b. 29 July, 1807. 4, *Peter L.*, b. 14 Feb. 1809; d. 8 Sept. 1845. 5, *Edgar S.*, b. 16 June, 1811. 6, *Mary Ann*, b. 27 May, 1813. 7, *Stephen A.*, b. 1 March, 1817. 8, *Anna A.*, b. 1 March, 1817 (twin). 9, *Louisa E.*, b. 10 Nov. 1819; and 10, *Charles Ely*, b. 4 March, 1822. (295) *Levi*, b. 1 July, 1782, at S.; m. Mrs. —— Suydam. (296) *Elisheba*, b. 9 Nov. 1784, at S.; m. —— Bennet. (297) *Peter*, b. 16 Oct. 1786, at S.; m. 24 Dec. 1810, Sebra Day, h. 1 July, 1794. They had seventeen children: 1, *Oscar Day*, b. 10 Oct. 1811; m. 15 June, 1836, M. H. Vinal. 2, *Emily E.*, b. 24 Feb. 1813; m. 16 June, 1836, George Hartzell. 3, *Levi*, b. 25 Sept. 1814. 4, *Cyrus A.*, b. 10 Sept. 1816; m. 27 June, 1839, M. A. Craig. 5, *Miriam C.*, b. 27 May, 1818; m. 15 Oct. 1840, Samuel Diver. 6, *Mary E.* (twin), b. 27 May, 1818. 7, *Seth F.*, b. 24 April, 1820. 8, *Sarah M.*, b. 15 May, 1822; m. 25 April, 1844, W. Craig. 9, *Sebra H.*, b. 7 Feb. 1824; d. 30 Sept. 1828. 10, *Lewis L.*, b. 10 March, 1826; d. 7 Sept. 1827. 11, *Lewis P.*, b. 23 Feb. 1828; m. M. M. Lewis. 12, *Cecilia A.*, b. 23 June, 1830. 23, *Au-*

gustus B., b. 12 June, 1832. 14, *Henry M.*, b. 17 Nov. 1833. 15, *Frank-lin M.*, b. 23 Sept. 1835. 16, *Malvina A.*, b. 15 Sept. 1837. 17, *John V.*, b. 10 July, 1839. (298) *Sylvester*, 2d, b. 27 April, 1789, at S.; d. 15 May, 1826. (299) *Cyrus*, b. 24 May, 1791, at S.; d. 15 Oct. 1829. (300) —— ——, b. 23 Aug. 1793, at S.; d. 2 Aug. 1806. (301) *Mi-riam*, b. 8 July, 1795, at S.; m. 30 March, 1818, Israel Bartlett, b. 12 June, 1793, and had nine children: 1, *Peter Mason*, b. 6 Feb. 1820; m. 24 July, 1845, E. M. Higgins who d. 15 April, 1849; and he then m. Julia W. Smedley, who d. 1 Aug. 1860. 2, *Jerusha*, b. 20 Feb. 1822; m. July, 1840, Silas A. Jackson, and had in 1860 six children. 3, *Lucius*, b. 12 Feb. 1824; m. 28 April, 1850, Sarah A. Leroy. 4, *Alex-ander*, b. 5 Feb. 1826; m. 25 Aug. 1853, Laura S. Merrill, and in 1860 had three children. 5, *Mary E.*, b. 2 Feb. 1828; m. 31 Dec. 1854, Henry Leroy. 6, *Harriet L.*, b. 9 July, 1830; d. 19 Oct. 1833. 7, *Emily*, b. 9 Sept. 1832. 8, *Robert A.*, b. 9 Aug. 1836; and 9, *Sidney S.*, b. 3 June, 1841.

V. Gen. 242. JOHN MASON, m. 24 June, 1786, at Castleton, Vt., Sarah Woodward, b. 28 May, 1768, at Canterbury, Conn., dau. of Joseph Woodward and Mary Bradford, and gr. d., of James Bradford and Edith his wife, which James Bradford was the second son of Thomas Bradford and Anne Smith his wife of Norwich, and gr. son of Major Wm. Bradford of Plymouth, and his first wife Alice Richards, and g. gr. son of Gov. Wm. Bradford of the Mayflower. John Mason (242) and wife, settled at Castleton, where he was a magistrate, member of the state legislature, member of the governor's council, and a pre-sidential elector. She d. 22 Feb. 1826, and he then m. 15 Nov. 1830, Wid. Sarah Noble, and d. 29 July, 1846, at Canterbury, without issue by her, and she d. April, 1851. His children by Sarah Woodward, his first wife, were: (302) *Milo*, b. 24 May, 1787, at Canterbury, grad. at West Point Military Academy, and was a major in the U. S. army, m. 7 Sept. 1815, Maria Louis of Providence, and d. 4 Feb. 1839, at Washington, D. C.; they had seven children, one of whom Col. James L. Mason of the U. S. engineer corps, distinguished himself in the war with Mexico, and particularly in the battle at Molino del Rey. (303) *John Anson*, b. 30 May, 1790, at Canterbury; d. 17 Dec. 1812, unm. (304) *Sarah Malvina*, b. 22 Dec. 1791, at Canterbury; m. 24 July, 1814, Gideon Miner Davison, b. 12 Nov. 1791, at Middletown, Vt., son of Thomas Davison and Abigail Miner. They settled at Rutland, Vt., and removed to Saratoga Springs, where he was a printer and pub-lisher and clerk of the Court of Chancery, and president of the Sara-toga and Washington Rail Road Company, and where they were living in 1860. They had 5 children: 1, *John Mason*, b. 9 March, 1816, at Rutland; m. 31 Aug. 1838, Sarah Simonds Walworth, b. 2 Feb. 1815, at Plattsburgh, second dau. of Chancellor Reuben Hyde Wal-worth of Saratoga Springs, by his first wife Maria Ketchum Averill. He was by trade a printer and settled at Saratoga Springs, removed to Albany in 1839, where he was register of the Court of Chancery until that court was abolished in 1848, when they returned to Sara-toga Springs, where they were living in 1860, and he was then pre-sident and general superintendent of the Saratoga and Whitehall Rail Road Company. She had 5 children: John Mason, b. 18 Dec. 1840, under grad. in Williams College, in 1860; Mansfield Walworth,

b. 13 Jan. 1844; Frances Walworth, b. 14 June, 1845; Sarah Walworth, b. 15 Aug. 1850; and Charles Mason, b. 27 July, 1853. 2, *Clement Miner*, b. 9 Dec. 1817, at Rutland, grad. at Union College, 1838, and was a Presbyterian clergyman; m. 1, Martha Elizabeth Bacon, and 2, Mary Fuller Pomeroy, and was living at Detroit in 1860, and was cashier of a bank, and had two children; 3, *Charles Augustus*, b. 21 May, 1824, at Saratoga Springs, grad. at Williams College, and was a lawyer; m. Mary Anthony Vermilyea and was living at New York in 1860, and had two children; 4, *Sarah Mason*, b. 17 Feb. 1827 at Saratoga Springs, where she was living in 1860, unm.; and 5, *Elizabeth Newman*, b. 7 June, 1829, at Saratoga Springs; d. 14 Oct. 1830. (305) *Altha Stevens*, b. 24 Aug. 1794, at Canterbury; m. 1 May, 1817, Aaron Dana, and had one child who d. young. (306) *Laura*, b. 22 Oct. 1796, at Canterbury; m. 8 July, 1819, Selah H. Merrill, and d. 9 July, 1820, and had one dau. Laura, who m. Noah T. Clark of Canandaigua, N. Y. (307) *Mary*, b. 22 Oct. 1796 (twin), d. 24 Jan. 1797. (308) *Clara*, b. 24 June, 1798, at Canterbury; m. 15 May, 1824, Lieut. Thomas Ingalls of U. S. army, and d. 9 July, 1830, s. p. (309) *George W.*, b. 18 March, 1801, at Canterbury; m. 3 May, 1823, Ruby Brand dau. of his first cousin, Col. Darius Brand of Canterbury (see No. 238); she d. 3 Dec. 1826, and he had by her one child: 1, *Mary Bradford*. He then m. 16 June, 1830, Adaline Eaton, b. 7 Feb. 1806, who d. 15 Sept. 1838, and had by her six children. He then m. 2 May, 1841, Lucinda Stevens, b. 16 June, 1819, who d. 4 Feb. 1858, and had by her five children. He then m. 20 Jan. 1859, Mrs. Caroline (Taft) Orr, and was living at Castleton in 1860. (310) *Samuel*, b. 1803, at Canterbury, d. 19 Feb. 1803. (311) *Margaret Fanning*, b. 7 Feb. 1704, at Canterbury; m. 16 April, 1829, Henry Howe of Canandaigua, N. Y., where she d. 16 Aug. 1844, s. p. (312) *Mary Bradford*, b. 25 July, 1806, at Canterbury; d. 15 Jan. 1823, unm. (313) *Lorenzo*, b. 27 May, 1808, at Canterbury; m. 10 Nov. 1838, Charlotte Luce of Pittsfield, Mass. He was a lawyer, and they settled at Port Huron, and removed from there to Detroit. He was a state senator, and they were living at Detroit in 1860, and had four children. (314) *Elmada Eliza*, b. 23 May, 1810, at Canterbury, where she was living in 1860, unm.

ERRATA.

P. 39, l. 7, *for* Mercy Durkee *read* Mercy Bill. [*]

P. 40, l. 23, *for* Thomas Read of Colchester *read* David Read late of Colchester, now of Burlington.

P. 41, l. 4, *for* Crain *read* Crane.

P. 42, l. 9 from bottom, *for* first wife *read* second wife.

*Pages 530, 531, 532, 533, this volume.

MAYO DEEDS. — Between 1735 and 1745 several families from Barnstable Co., Mass., settled in that part of Middletown, Conn., which in 1767 was set off as the town of Chatham. One of these families was that of Richard Mayo of Eastham. He made his first purchase of lands in Middletown in Mar. 1740 and died there 8 May 1744. Among the papers treasured by his descendants are two deeds of lands in Barnstable County. As the Barnstable County land records were destroyed when the Court House was burned in 1827, the following abstracts of these deeds may be of interest.

"I Thomas Mayo of Eastham In the County of Barnstable In the Province of the Masachusets Bay in Newengland yeoman . . . In Consideration of the sum of sixty & five pounds Currant money of sᵈ Province to me In hand . . . paid by my son Richard Mayo of Eastham . . . Marener . . . have . . . sould . . . unto the sᵈ Richard Mayo & to his heirs & Assignes for Ever the one half part both for quantety & quallity of that parcel of upland being situate In the Township of Chatham in the County of Barnstable above sᵈ at a place Called the great plains & is the one half part as above sᵈ of all that parcel of land there which I bought of Nathaniel Nickason of sᵈ chatham Called by estimation fourty acres be itt more or less as may appear by one Deed Duly Executed baring Date the twenty eight day of february 1720/21 which sᵈ half part of sᵈ parcel of Land is to be laid out to him sᵈ Richard Mayo at the westermost end of sᵈ parcel of Land with the Members Rights privileges & appurtenances to sᵈ half part of sᵈ parcel of Land belonging & appertaining: To have & To hold the Granted Premises . . . for Ever ffree & clere of all entanglements hereby declering that befre & untill the time of signing these presents I was the Lawfull sole proprietor of the Granted. premises & that the same was my absolute Estate In fee simple & I thereby had good Right . . . to Grant & Confarm as above sᵈ & that the sᵈ Richard Mayo is Allredy in the free & Lawfull possesion thereof & May & shall . . . by him self his heirs or assignes for Ever freely vse Occupie possess & Improve the same as a good & absolute Estate In fee simple also I do herby Ingage to warrant . . . & Defend the title & tenure of the Granted premises unto him the sᵈ Richard Mayo his heirs & assignes against all . . . persons Claiming from by or under me or by my Right or title"

This deed, signed 4 Jan. 1726/7 by Thomas Mayo and witnessed by Joseph Doane, Jr., and Jedidiah Higgins, was acknowledged in Barnstable County, on the same day, by the grantor, before Joseph Doane, Justice of the Peace. It was recorded 23 Jan. 1726/7 in Barnstable County Deeds, Book 13, fo. 316, by Jnᵒ Thacher, Register.

"Whereas We Richard Mayo & Israel Mayo both of Eastham In the County of Barnstable In the Province of the Massachusetts Bay In Newengland yeomen do as Joynt Propriators one & hold several parcels of Lands In Eastham . . . (viz) all that Parcell of land which was the home sted of our Decesed ffather Thomas Mayo where he liued & of which he Died seized as also all that his part or parcell of Land which he our sᵈ Deceased ffather Purchased of samuel Cole in sᵈ Town of Eastham at a place Called Jobs guter as it is bounded seperete from the other parts thereof by Division Made with our vncle samuel Mayo and Jospeh Doane Esqʳ Now In Consideration of & to the end & Intent that each of us the sᵈ Richard Mayo & Israel Mayo May have & hold to each of us our Heirs & Assignes forever each ones perticuler part . . . of our sᵈ lands seperate from the other we

540

the s^d Richard Mayo & Israel Mayo have mutually agreed . . . & acordingly Divided all our s^d lands in to two equall half parts or shears to mutual satisfaction & the Dividing buts bounds & parting line betwen s^d two half parts is as follows (viz) begining in the notherly Range of the land of s^d home sted next the cartway that lades into Pochey at a stone set in the Range of s^d land there thence Runing south westerly as the parting fence now stands untill it coms to the orchyard fence then sets off easterly by said orchyard fence twelue feet to a stone set in the ground in s^d orchyard fence thence the s^d Dividing line runs south westerly by the fence as it now stands through s^d orchyard to the notherly side of the swamp to a stone there set in the ground & from thence about south west through s^d swamp to a stone set in the ground a little distance from the south west corner of s^d swamp on the notherly side the way that went to the old house & then from s^d stone the Dividing or range turns away somthing more westerly to a ston set in the ground som distance Notherly from the range of Nathaniel Mayo's land then the Dividing line turns away west notherly to another stone set in the ground laving a sutable pasing way between s^d last Dividing line & Nathaniel Mayo's land & then from s^d last mentioned stone set in the ground to Run on a straight line to the south west corner of our s^d Deceased ffathers s^d land, In which s^d Division the s^d Richard Mayo his half part of the whole is all the land on the easterly & southerly side of s^d Dividing line or range whome to Nathaniel Doane's land & to the cove taking in all the land & medow whome to Nathaniel Mayo's land & medow In consideration of which the s^d Richard Mayo doth take up fully satisfied for his half part of the whole of the lands above specified & doth for him self his heirs exucutors administrators & assigns for ever quit claim to all the other half part of s^d lands Reserving only his third part of the barn that stands on the other half part of s^d land. and In which s^d Division the said Israel Mayo his half part of the whole is all the land on the westerly & notherly side of s^d Dividing line or Range so far as his s^d Deceased ffathers land extended together with all that parcel of land aboue mentioned purchesed of samuel Cole lying at a place called Jobs guter bounded as the fence now stands In Consideration of all which the s^d Israel Mayo doth take up fully satisfyed for his half part of the whole of s^d lands aboue specified and doth for him self his heirs exacutors administrators & assignes for ever quit claim to all the other half of s^d lands always alowing unto the s^d Richard Mayo his third part of the barn with free liberty to pass & repass to & from the same so long as s^d barn doth stand on his the s^d Israel Mayo his land"

This document, signed 28 July 1733 by Richard Mayo and Israel Mayo and witnessed by Elisha Doane and Ebenezer Cook, was acknowledged in Barnstable County, 29 July 1733, by Richard Mayo and Israel Mayo, before Joseph Doane, Justice of the Peace. It was recorded 1 Aug. 1733 in Barnstable County Deeds, Book 15, fo. 249, by Jno Thacher, Register.

Middletown, Conn. FRANK FARNSWORTH STARR.

THE MEIGS FAMILY.

(Copy made April 2, 1835.)

It appears by the Records that Vincent Meigs came with his son John Meigs, from England, with the first settlers of Guilford, Conn^t. There is no record of their ages.

Vincent Meigs died at Hammonasset, in Dec. 1658, as appears by the probate of his will.

Deacon John Meigs sen^r. died   9 Nov. 1713.
Deacon John Meigs 2^d   do. 19 Feb. 1718, aged 48.
Junna Meigs   do.   5 June 1739. He was the first magistrate in East Guilford Society.

The descendants of John Meigs the 1st. were,

John Meigs, born in 1670 ; Junna, 27 Dec. 1672 ; Ebenezer, 19 Sept. 1675 ; Hannah, 25 Feb. 1677 ; Hester, 10 Nov. 1680.

Children of John Meigs 2^d.

John Vincent Meigs, born 10 June, 1697 ; Stephen, 10 Oct. 1699 ; Recompence, 11 Dec., 1701 ; Irene, 10 March 1704 ; Samuel, 22 Aug., 1706 ; Phinehas, 21 Sept., 1708 ; Sarah, 10 Dec. 1713.

Junna Meigs married to Hannah Willard, 18 May, 1698. Their children were : Joanna Meigs, born 17 May, 1699 ; Josiah, 14 May, 1701 ; Zekiel, 11 June, 1703 ; Hannah, 13 Aug., 1705 ; Return, 16 March, 1708 ; Hester, 19 Dec., 1709 ; Silence and Submit, (twins,) 5 Jan., 1711 ; Timothy, Sept. 1713.

Children of Ebenezer Meigs, who married Mercy Weeks of Falmouth, Oct. 7, 1700. Benoni, born 1 June, 1703 ; Mary, 11 Dec., 1705 ; Reuben, 21 Oct., 1707 ; Joseph, 17 Nov., 1709.

Dec. 4 : 1657. — John Meigs was complained of (because he came home from Hammonnasset, late on Saturday evening,) as a Sabbath breaker ; but was forgiven on acknowledging his fault, and promising to declare it, on the next Lecture or Fast Day.

The descendants of Return Meigs the son of Junna Meigs : Return Jonathan Meigs, died in 1820, aged 82. Josiah Meigs, died at Washington city in 1822, aged 66. The last Return Jonathan was father of Return Jonathan, late Postmaster General.

542

SOME DESCENDANTS OF THOMAS MORLEY

By HERBERT S. MORLEY of Newton Center, Mass.

1. THOMAS[1] MORLEY, also spelled Morlow, Marlow, and Marlo, in different records, whose parentage and ancestry are uncertain, was married 8 Dec. 1681, by John Pynchon of Springfield, Mass., to MARTHA WRIGHT, born 29 Nov. 1662, died at Glastonbury, Conn., where her estate was inventoried 2 Jan. 1741, daughter of Lieut. Abel and Martha (Kitcherel, of Hartford) of Springfield. In 1686 he was granted land at Pochasic, now a part of Westfield, Mass., to which he subsequently added by purchase, and was admitted to the church in Westfield 18 Nov. 1702. His wife and daughter Martha were baptized at the church 10 June 1683. Thomas died at Glastonbury, Conn., in Jan. 1712, leaving a will mentioning wife and children.

Children, born at Westfield:

- i. MARTHA,[2] b. 7 Sept. 1682; d. 22 Feb. 1753; m. 13 Jan. 1704, WILLIAM LOOMIS; had ten children.
- 2. ii. THOMAS, b. 14 Sept. 1684.
- iii. MARY, b. 30 Oct. 1686.
- 3. iv. ABEL, b. 18 Jan. 1689.
- v. THANKFUL, b. 28 Feb. 1693.
- vi. MERCY, b. 14 Nov. 1695.
- vii. JOHN, b. 12 Mar. 1699; lived at Glastonbury; inventory of his estate, dated 1 Nov. 1757, in Hartford probate records.
- 4. viii. EBENEZER, b. 22 Mar. 1701.

2. THOMAS[2] MORLEY (*Thomas[1]*), born at Westfield 14 Sept. 1684, died at Glastonbury, Conn., 8 Jan. 1772. He married first, 9 Nov. 1708, ELIZABETH WICKHAM; and secondly MINDWELL LOOMIS.

Children by first wife, born at Glastonbury:

- i. WILLIAM,[3] b. 29 July 1709; records of m. and d. not found; perhaps went to New York state.
- ii. ——, b. 16 June 1711; d. same day.
- iii. ——, b. 30 June 1712; d. next day.
- iv. ELIZABETH, b. 31 July 1715.
- v. JOHN(?), b. 7 Feb. 1717; d. in service in the Revolution, at New York, 31 Aug. 1776.

vi. ENOS, b. 6 Aug. 1719; d. 29 Oct. 1730.
vii. MERCY, b. 24 Oct. 1722.
5. viii. TIMOTHY, b. 15 Feb. 1726.

3. ABEL[2] MORLEY (*Thomas[1]*), born at Westfield 18 Jan. 1689, died at Feeding Hills, now in the town of Agawam, 17 Jan. 1771. He married at Glastonbury, Conn., 9 Apr. 1719, SUSANNAH KILBORN, who died at Feeding Hills 16 Feb. 1782, daughter of John and Susanna. He and his wife joined the Westfield Church, by letter from Glastonbury, 27 Dec. 1741, and they helped form the church at Feeding Hills in 1762.

Children, all but the last two born at Glastonbury :

i. SARAH,[3] b. 23 June 1720.
6. ii. ABEL, b. 23 Feb. 1721-2.
7. iii. THOMAS, b. 6 Mar. 1723-4.
iv. SUSANNA, b. 22 June 1726.
8 v. ISAAC, b. 22 Mar. 1728-9.
9. vi. WILLIAM, b. 3 Sept. 1731.
vii. THANKFUL, b. 19 Mar. 1733-4; d. at Westfield 31 Dec. 1736.
viii: THANKFUL, b. at Westfield 12 July 1737.
10. ix. GIDEON, bapt. at Westfield 9 Nov. 1738.

4. EBENEZER[2] MORLEY (*Thomas[1]*), born at Westfield 22 Mar. 1701, died at Glastonbury, his will being made 16 Sept. 1747, and proved 26 Jan. 1748. He married at Glastonbury, 17 Feb. 1725-6, SUSANNA (PELLET, of Concord, Mass.) WICKHAM, widow of John.

Children, born at Glastonbury :

i. MARTHA,[3] b. 15 Oct. 1726.
ii. SUSANNA, b. 24 June 1728.
iii. PRUDENCE. b. 12 Oct. 1730.
iv. JOHN, b. 19 July 1735; m. ABIGAIL ———; killed in the war at the taking of Savannah, Nov. 1762.

5. TIMOTHY[3] MORLEY (*Thomas,[2] Thomas[1]*) was born at Glastonbury 15 Feb. 1726. He married at Glastonbury, 25 Apr. 1751, MARY WOOD, daughter of Dyer of Hartford.

Children, born at Glastonbury :

i. ELIZABETH,[4] b. 14 Mar. 1752.
ii. MARY, b. 1 June 1753; d. same day.
iii. MARY, b. 23 Apr. 1754.
iv. TIMOTHY, b. 27 June 1755.
v. GEORGE, b. 10 Nov. 1756.
vi. THOMAS, b. 26 Mar. 1758.
vii. EZEKIEL, b. 15 Aug 1759.
viii. PRUDENCE, b. 27 Jan. 1761.
ix. JERUSHA, b. 18 June 1762.
x. DANIEL, b. 2 Dec. 1763.
xi. CHRISTIANA, b 2 June 1765.
xii. RUTH, b. 15 Nov., d. 20 Nov. 1766.
xiii. ELIJAH, b. 4 Jan. 1768.
xiv. SAMUEL, b 30 Apr. 1769.
xv. MOSES, b. 25 May 1771.
xvi. RUTH, b. 23 Aug. 1772.
xvii. AARON, b. 22 June 1774.
xviii. ENOS, b. 29 Sept. 1779.

6. ABEL[3] MORLEY (*Abel,[2] Thomas[1]*), born at Glastonbury 22 Feb. 1721-2, died at Feeding Hills, 31 Dec. 1759, where he was a member of the church. He married, intention recorded 17 Mar. 1753, MARY MILLER of Somers, Conn.

Children, born at Feeding Hills and recorded at Springfield:

   i. MARY,[4] b. 5 Aug. 1754; m. THOMPSON PHILIPS.
   ii. ABEL, b. 4 July 1756.
   iii. DAVID, b. 3 Mar. 1760.

7. THOMAS[3] MORLEY (*Abel,*[2] *Thomas*[1]), born at Glastonbury 6 Mar. 1723-4, married at Westfield, 15 Nov. 1753, SARAH PHELPS, daughter of Isaac, 3d. He probably married secondly at Feeding Hills, 29 Sept. 1779, SARAH CHURCH of Westfield, who died at Brutus, N. Y., 20 Sept. 1795.

   Children, recorded at Westfield:

   i. SARAH,[4] b. 16 June 1756.
   ii. MINDWELL, b. 4 Jan. 1759.
   iii. JOHN, b. 16 Feb. 1761.
   iv. THOMAS, b. 20 Mar. 1765; d. at Brutus, N. Y., 2 Mar. 1813.

8. ISAAC[3] MORLEY (*Abel,*[2] *Thomas*[1]), born at Glastonbury 22 Mar. 1728-9, married first at Springfield, 8 May 1755, HANNAH MILLER, born 1 June 1733, daughter of Ichabod and Hannah; and married secondly RUTH ———, whose will was dated 20 Mar. 1799.

   Children by first wife, recorded at Springfield:

   i. HANNAH,[4] b. 30 Dec. 1755.
   ii. ESTHER, b. 16 Apr. 1757; d. 14 Apr. 1772.
   iii. DORCAS, b. 16 Oct. 1758.
   iv. SABEAH, b. 17 July 1760.
   v. ISAAC, b. 6 Feb. 1762.
   vi. ASAHEL, b. 10 Oct. 1763.
   vii. SIBEL, b. 1 Dec. 1765.
   viii. HULDAH, b. 10 Sept. 1767.
   ix. EUNICE, b. 20 July 1769.
   x. OBEDIAH, b. 30 Nov. 1773.

9. WILLIAM[3] MORLEY (*Abel,*[2] *Thomas*[1]), born at Glastonbury 3 Sept. 1731, married at Westfield, 15 Nov 1753 (at the same time with his brother Thomas), JERUSHA MILLER, daughter of Ichabod and Hannah, and born 19 Mar. 1734-5, according to the record of T. B. Warren of Springfield, or daughter of Samuel of Barkhamsted, Conn., according to the record of Prof. E. W. Morley.

   Children, recorded at Springfield:

   i. DERRICK,[4] b. 18 Sept. 1755.
   ii. WILLIAM, b. 7 or 14 Aug. 1757 (at Westfield).
   iii. JERUSHA, b. 7 Nov. 1759.
   iv. ABNER, b. 8 Oct. 1761.
   v. LUCY, b, 14 May 1764.
   vi. THANKFUL, b. 1 Mar. 1766.
   vii. KILBORN, b. 4 Sept. 1767.
   viii. RUTH, b. 1 Nov. 1769.
   ix. ISRAEL, b. 9 Apr. 1771.
   x. MIRRIAM.

10. GIDEON[3] MORLEY (*Abel,*[2] *Thomas*[1]), baptized at Westfield 9 Nov. 1738, died 24 Aug. 1818. He married, 28 June 1764, MARY MILLER, born 14 Feb. 1742, died 4 Sept. 1814 (gravestone), daughter of Moses and Elizabeth.

   Children, born at Feeding Hills and recorded at Springfield:

   i. WALTER,[4] b. 17 Apr. 1765.
   ii. MARY, b. 14 Sept. 1766; d. 27 Oct. 1769.
   iii. DOSHA (baptized THEODOSIA), b. 10 Jan. 1769.

iv. MARY, b. 11 Nov. 1770.
v. RODERICK, b. 22 Mar. 1773; d. 1777.
vi. ANNE, b. 5 May 1776; d. 1777.
vii. RODERICK, b. 11 Oct. 1778.
viii. NANCY, m. 20 Oct. 1808, DAVID BURBANK.
ix. ANNE, bapt. 12 Sept. 1784.

MORRIS FAMILIES OF WESTERN CONNECTICUT

By DONALD LINES JACOBUS, M.A., of New Haven, Conn.

I. THE THOMAS MORRIS FAMILY OF NEW HAVEN

A BOOK published in 1853 and entitled "Memoranda of the Descendants of Amos Morris, of East Haven, Conn.," gives the line of Amos[4] Morris (*James*,[3] *Eleazer*,[2] *Thomas*[1] of New Haven, Conn.). A more recent compilation, "Genealogy of the Morris Family," purporting to give the descendants of Thomas[1] Morris of New Haven, deals principally with the line of James[3] Morris (*Eleazer*,[2] *Thomas*[1]) and the progeny of female lines. It is the purpose of the writer of the following account of the family of Thomas Morris to correct the inaccuracies of the last-mentioned volume and to set forth the lines omitted therein.

1. THOMAS[1] MORRIS of New Haven,* who died 21 July 1673, married ELIZABETH ———, who died, as his widow, in 1681. He was one of the founders of New Haven, and owned land in that part of East Haven which was named Morris Cove for his family.

Children, recorded at New Haven:
  i. HANNAH,[2] bapt. 14 Mar. 1642 [? 1641/2]; m. in 1662 THOMAS
     LUPTON of Norwalk.
  ii. ELIZABETH, bapt. 10 Dec. 1643.
2. iii. JOHN, bapt. 8 Mar. 1646 [? 1645/6].
3. iv. ELEAZER, bapt. 29 Oct. 1648.
  v. THOMAS (twin), b. 3 Oct. 1651; d. young.
  vi. EPHRAIM (twin), b. 3 Oct. 1651; d. young.
4. vii. JOSEPH, b. 25 Mar. 1656.

2. JOHN[2] MORRIS (*Thomas*[1]), baptized at New Haven 8 Mar. 1646 [? 1645/6], died 10 Dec. 1711 (gravestone at New Haven). He married, 12 Aug. 1669, HANNAH BISHOP, born 29 May 1651, died 12 June 1710, daughter of Deputy-Gov. James and Mary. The "Morris Family" states (p. 74) that prior to this marriage he married first Ann ———, who died 4 Dec. 1664; and secondly, 29 Mar. 1665, Elizabeth Harrison, widow of John [*sic*] Lyne and John [*sic*] Lampson; and that by this second wife he had a son John[3], born 16 Dec. 1666, founder of the Morris family of Newark, N. J. A large section of the book is devoted to the descendants of the Newark family.

* All places mentioned in this article are situated within the present limits of the State of Connecticut, unless another State or region is indicated in the text or may be easily inferred from the context.

But, in reality, it was another John Morris who settled in New Haven and married first Ann ———— and secondly Elizabeth Harrison, widow of *Henry* Lyne and *Thomas* Lampson. With his second wife he removed to Newark, where he died in 1677, leaving two sons, John and Philip. In 1670 John Morris and his wife Elizabeth, of Newark, conveyed to Jonathan Lampson of New Haven land formerly belonging to Thomas Lampson, father to said Jonathan (New Haven Deeds, vol. 1, p. 29). Since this was *subsequent* to the marriage of John[2] Morris (Thomas[1]) to Hannah Bishop, it proves that John Morris of Newark was a separate individual from John[2] Morris of New Haven. That John[2] (Thomas[1]) left only daughters as surviving issue is abundantly proved by probate and land records.

Children, recorded at New Haven:

i. A DAUGHTER,[3] b. 19 June 1670; d. in 1670.
ii. HANNAH, b. 10 Aug. 1671; m. (1) SERGT. JOSEPH SMITH, b. 14 June 1669, d. in 1713; m. (2) 26 Feb. 1717/18 LIEUT. JOSEPH SACKETT, b. 3 Mar. 1659/60, d. in 1729.
iii. MARY, b. 9 Sept. 1673; d. in 1743; m. in 1701 JOHN HEMINGWAY, b. 29 May 1675, d. in 1737.
iv. ELIZABETH, b. in 1675; m. (1) WILLIAM MALTBIE; m. (2) JOHN DAVENPORT.
v. THOMAS, b. 26 Apr. 1679; d. young.
vi. ABIGAIL, b. 22 Aug. 1683; d. between 1721 and 1729; m. 14 Feb. 1705/6 SERGT. JAMES PECK, b. in 1679, d. abt. 1761.
vii. DESIRE, b. 29 Mar. 1687; m. 4 Mar. 1707/8 STEPHEN HOWELL.

3. ELEAZER[2] MORRIS (*Thomas[1]*), baptized at New Haven 29 Oct. 1648, died, according to the "Morris Family," 15 Jan. 1709/10. He married ANN OSBORN, born 6 Apr. 1663, died 10 Dec. 1726, daughter of Jeremiah and Mary.

Children:

i. REBECCA,[3] b. 20 June 1682; d. in 1729; m. 23 Dec. 1702 NATHANIEL HITCHCOCK, b. 28 July 1678, d. 5 Dec. 1726.
ii. JOHN, b. 8 Oct. 1684; d. *s.p.* 19 Nov. 1744; m. 24 Dec. 1713 ELIZABETH ALLING, b. in Nov. 1691, d. in Apr. 1767, who m. (2) 12 June 1754 Isaac Dickerman.
5. iii. JAMES.
iv. ANNA, m. 30 Dec. 1708 SAMUEL SMITH, b. 24 May 1681.
6. v. ELEAZER.
vi. ADONIJAH, removed to Durham, where he d. abt. 1751; m. SARAH MOULTHROP. Children, b. at Durham: 1. *Adonijah*,[4] b. 26 Oct. 1723. 2. *John*, b. 15 Nov. 1725. 3. *Anne*, b. 24 Feb. 1727/8; d. 15 Feb. 1813; m. 16 Jan. 1745/6 Ensign Simeon Coe, b. 22 Mar. 1720/1, d. 23 Sept. 1782. 4. *Timothy*, b. 27 Jan. 1729/30.

4. JOSEPH[2] MORRIS (*Thomas[1]*), was born at New Haven 25 Mar. 1656. He married, 2 June 1680, ESTHER WINSTON, born 11 Nov. 1662, daughter of John. She married secondly Nathaniel Sperry. Joseph's descendants, though very numerous, receive but two pages in the "Morris Family" (pp. 477–478), and therefore they are given below *in extenso*.

Children, born at New Haven:

7. i. THOMAS,[3] b. 23 Mar. 1681/2.
ii. ESTHER, b. 3 Sept. 1684; d. 19 Aug. 1751; m. (1) 30 Jan. 1706/7 JOHN PECK, b. 6 Oct. 1682; m. (2) 14 Feb. 1716/17 JOHN MIX, b.

25 Aug. 1676, d. 10 Dec. 1721; m. (3) ENSIGN JOSEPH SMITH, b. 5 Mar. 1680/1, d. in 1749.

iii. SARAH, b. abt. 1686; m. 3 Aug. 1710 JOSEPH BEECHER, b. 13 Feb. 1683 [? 1683/4], d. in 1712.

8. iv. JOSEPH, b. abt. 1688.

9. v. EPHRAIM, b. in Jan. 1693/4.

vi. DOROTHY, b. in Sept. 1695; d. in 1751; m. JAMES DENISON, b. 5 Jan. 1683 [? 1683/4], d. in 1751.

10. vii. BENJAMIN, b. in Apr. 1699.

viii. MARY, b. in June 1702; m. 9 May 1727 JOEL MUNSON, b. 18 Aug. 1702, d. after 1775.

ix. SAMUEL, b. in May 1705; m. abt. 1729 MARGARET SMITH of Milford. Records of his family are fragmentary. He was residing at Milford in 1739 and 1755 (Milford Deeds, vol. 11, p. 321; vol. 12½, p. 676). In 1751, calling himself of Milford, he conveyed his right to the estate of his father, Joseph Morris, deceased, and his mother, Esther Sperry, deceased (New Haven Deeds, vol. 18, p. 306). In 1764 he was called of Kent (New Haven County Court Records). Margaret Morris, with two females in her family, was living at Warren according to the Census of 1790. Children (record incomplete): 1. *Ann*,[4] bapt. at Derby (Congregational Church) 20 Feb. 1736/7; m. at Woodbridge, in Sept. 1755, Eliphalet Beecher, b. 29 Sept. 1733. 2. *Samuel*, bapt. at Woodbridge 13 Jan. 1744/5; living at Warren according to the Census of 1790.

5. JAMES[3] MORRIS (*Eleazer*,[2] *Thomas*[1]) resided at East Haven, where he died shortly before Feb. 1733/4. He married, 24 Feb. 1714/15, ABIGAIL ROWE.

Children:

i. JEMIMA,[4] b. 27 Dec. 1715; d. young.

11. ii. DANIEL, b. at New Haven 4 June 1718.

iii. ABIGAIL, b. 10 Jan. 1719/20; m. DAVID GAYLORD of Farmington.

iv. JAMES, bapt. at Durham 21 Jan. 1722/3; d. at Litchfield 6 June 1789; m. 8 Apr. 1751 PHEBE (BARNES) BARNES, b. 1 Aug. 1712, d. 15 Apr. 1793, widow of Timothy. He settled in that part of Litchfield which is now the town of Morris, named for his family. Two children (see "Morris Family," p. 171).

v. AMOS, b. abt. 1726; d. at East Haven in 1802; m. twice, and had twelve children (see "Morris Family," pp. 255–256).

6. ELEAZER[3] MORRIS (*Eleazer*,[2] *Thomas*[1]) died at East Haven in Dec. 1740. He married MERCY BALL, born about 1693, living 10 Jan. 1775, daughter of Alling and Sarah (Thompson). She married secondly, prior to 10 Jan. 1775, Deodate Davenport.

Children:

i. STEPHEN,[4] b. abt. 1718; d. 28 Oct. 1775; m. 18 June 1741 HESTER ROBINSON, b. 7 July 1720, d. 17 Feb. 1790. Children: 1. *William*,[5] d. young. 2. *Hannah*, b. 1 Jan. 1745/6; d. 6 Aug. 1751. 3. *Samuel*, d. young. 4. *Hannah*, b. abt. 1751; d. 17 Feb. 1787; m. Samuel Hemingway of East Haven.

ii. SARAH, b. abt. 1720; m. 19 Dec. 1739 SETH HEATON, b. 29 Oct. 1714, d. in 1796.

iii. MERCY, m. ISAAC HOLT.

iv. JACOB, according to "Morris Family," b. abt. 1730; d. 3 Mar. 1734 [? 1733/4].

v. ELEAZER, d. *s.p.* In 1773 Seth Heaton and wife Sarah, Isaac Holt and wife Mercy, and Stephen and Mabel Morris, heirs of their brother Eleazer, deceased, divided land (New Haven Deeds, vol. 36, p. 344). In 1778 Jehiel and Mabel Forbs conveyed to Samuel and Hannah Hemingway their right to the estate of their sister

Mary, deceased, late wife to Samuel Davenport, that came to her from her brother Eliezer Morris, deceased (*ib.*, vol. 36, p. 515).

vi. MABEL, m. JEHIEL FORBES.

vii. MARY, b. abt. 1740; d. *s.p.* 15 July 1765; m. SAMUEL DAVENPORT.

7. THOMAS³ MORRIS (*Joseph,*² *Thomas*¹), born at New Haven 23 Mar. 1681/2, died there 17 Apr. 1726. He married, 25 May 1708, SARAH GILBERT, born 10 Mar. 1685/6, daughter of Matthew and Sarah (Peck) and granddaughter of Gov. Matthew and Jane (Baker). She married secondly William Johnson.

Children, born at New Haven:

i. ESTHER,⁴ b. abt. 1709; d. 12 Jan. 1788; m. 20 Aug. 1743 ANDREW GOODYEAR.

ii. THOMAS, b. in Mar. 1712 [? 1712/13]; living at Kent according to the Census of 1790; m. ———. In 1752 Asa Morris, Andʳ Goodyear and wife Esther, and Joseph Mix, Jr., and wife Sarah, all of New Haven, conveyed land to their brother, Thomas Morris of Kent (New Haven Deeds, vol. 17, p. 1). Children, bapt. at Kent: 1. *Phebe,*⁵ bapt. 7 Aug. 1748. 2. *Sarah*, bapt. 7 Aug. 1748. 3. *Thomas*, bapt. 28 July 1751; living at Kent according to the Census of 1790; m. 15 Nov. 1774 Rachel Budd. 4. *Elizabeth*, bapt. 5 Aug. 1753. Probably others.

12. iii. DANIEL, b. in Apr. 1715.

iv. AMOS, b. 26 Feb. 1717/18; d. *s.p.* in 1741.

13. v. ASA, b. 20 Feb. 1720/1.

vi. SARAH, b. 20 Dec. 1723; m. 21 May 1752 JOSEPH MIX

vii. ELIZABETH, b. 9 Feb. 1725/6.

8. JOSEPH³ MORRIS (*Joseph,*² *Thomas*¹), born at New Haven about 1688, removed to Branford. He married first, at Branford, 4 Mar. 1712/13, LYDIA HARRISON, daughter of Thomas and Margaret (Stent); and secondly ELIZABETH JOHNSON, daughter of Edward and Esther (Wheaton). The "Morris Family" erroneously states (p. 478) that he married, 3 Feb. 1709, Sarah Hotchkiss. In 1755 Joseph Morris and wife Elizabeth conveyed to Timothy Johnson land from father Edward Johnson, deceased (Branford Deeds, vol. 7, p. 503). In 1759 the surveyors set off to Lydia, wife of Samuel Linsly, to Aaron Morris, and to Mary, wife of Nath'll Whedon, Jr. (children and heirs of Lydia Morris, deceased, late wife of Joseph), a right from the estate of Thomas Harrison the first, deceased (*ib.*).

Children by first wife, born at Branford:

i. JOSEPH,⁴ b. 1 Jan. 1713/14; living in 1736 (Branford Deeds, vol. 6, p. 77); probably d. *s.p.* before 1759.

ii. LYDIA, b. 15 Oct. 1715; m. 27 Nov. 1740 SAMUEL LINSLY.

iii. AARON, b. 13 Mar. 1717/18; d. in 1784; m. 29 Nov. 1744 ELIZABETH MUNROE. Children: 1. *Lovice,*⁵ m. Thomas Wheaton of Southington. 2. *Sarah*, b. in 1747; m. Jonathan Baker of Hudson, N. Y. 3. *Andrew*. 4. *Margaret*, m. 21 June 1767 William Stewart. 5. *Edmund*, m. in 1788 Hannah Parmalee. 6. *Zada*, m. 31 Dec. 1789 Joseph Goodrich. 7. *Aaron*, m. 25 Nov. 1795 Elizabeth Norton.

iv. MARY, m. 20 Nov. 1755 NATHANIEL WHEATON.

Children by second wife, born at Branford:

v. ELIZABETH, d. *s.p.*

vi. TIMOTHY, bapt. 8 June 1735; m. CHLOE ———. Children, bapt. at Branford: 1. *Joseph*,⁵ bapt. 31 Mar. 1765. 2. *Foster*, bapt. 30 June 1765. 3. *Daniel*, bapt. 29 Oct. 1769; m. 16 Dec. 1800 Betsey Stewart. 4. *James*, bapt. 15 Sept. 1771. 5. *Keturah*, bapt. 7 Nov. 1773. 6. *Timothy*, bapt. 9 Feb. 1777. 7. *Elizabeth*, bapt. 22 Aug. 1779; m. 3 Mar. 1799 Amos G. Hull.

9. EPHRAIM³ MORRIS (*Joseph*,² *Thomas*¹), born at New Haven in Jan. 1693/4, died there 15 Feb. 1778 (records of First Congregtional Church). He married, 24 Jan. 1716/17, RUTH SPERRY, born 30 May 1695, died 10 Feb. 1773 (*ib.*), daughter of Ebenezer and Abigail (Dickerman).

Children, born at New Haven:

i. ABIGAIL,⁴ b. 31 Oct. 1717.
ii. RUTH, b. 27 Nov. 1718; d. 23 Aug. 1769 (*ib.*).
14. iii. EPHRAIM, b. 23 May 1721.
15. iv. EBENEZER.
v. ISAAC, m. HANNAH GILBERT, b. 4 Sept. 1733, d. 28 Aug. 1769, dau. of Jonathan and Mary (Chidsey). Children, bapt. at First Congregational Church, New Haven: 1. *Mary*,⁵ bapt. 11 Feb. 1759. 2. *Adonijah*, bapt. 7 Mar. 1762. 3. *Mabel*, bapt. 13 May 1764. 4. *Isaac*, bapt. 21 Sept. 1766; removed to Watertown. 5. *Lydia*, bapt. 25 Sept. 1768.

10. BENJAMIN³ MORRIS (*Joseph*,² *Thomas*¹), born at New Haven in Apr. 1699, was living at Danbury in 1732, but returned to New Haven, and was living at Woodbridge as late as 1786. He married first, 17 Nov. 1731, MEHITABEL MUNSON, born 17 Oct. 1709, died 26 Feb. 1779, daughter of John and Sarah (Cooper); and secondly, 1 May 1783, ABIGAIL ASHBURN of Milford, who was living at Colebrook in 1786, when they were divorced.

Children by first wife, born at New Haven:

i. SARAH,⁴ b. 15 Mar. 1736/7; m. 14 Feb. 1759 JUDAH THOMPSON.
ii. ELIZABETH, b. 10 Apr. 1739; m. 13 May 1759 THOMAS HUMPHREVILLE, b. 23 Nov. 1736, d. in 1772.
iii. JOHN, b. 9 Mar. 1741/2; d. at New Haven 18 Oct. 1820; m. MARY (MACUMBER) TROWBRIDGE, b. in 1748, d. in 1811, widow of Thomas. Only child: 1. *Mehitabel*,⁵ b. abt. 1786; d. 14 Feb. 1849; m. John Gilbert, b. abt. 1782, d. 12 Sept. 1848.

11. DANIEL⁴ MORRIS (*James*,³ *Eleazer*,² *Thomas*¹), born at New Haven 4 June 1718, according to the "Morris Family" (p. 167) "removed to Great Barrington, Mass., in 1762," and "lived to be 94." He was living at Salisbury in 1756–1758, and appears in Litchfield County in the Census of 1790. He married, 15 Oct. 1742, ELIZABETH SMITH, daughter of Thomas and Abigail (Potter).

Children:

i. ABIGAIL,⁵ b. at New Haven 13 Aug. 1742; according to "Morris Family" m. ——— GAYLORD, though this statement is probably due to confusing her with her aunt (5, iii). Perhaps she was the Abigail Morris who m. (intention recorded at Great Barrington, Mass., 23 Feb. 1762) Eliathah Rew.
ii. ELIZABETH, b. at New Haven 19 Oct. 1743.
iii. JOHN, b. at New Haven 12 Oct. 1745; of Great Barrington, Mass., in the Census of 1790; according to "Morris Family" m. LOIS WEED.

iv. JEMIMA, b. at New Haven 25 Aug. 1747.
v. ELEAZER, b. at New Haven 25 May 1749; of Great Barrington, Mass., in the Census of 1790; according to "Morris Family" m. SALLY WELLS.
vi. DANIEL, of Spencertown, Mass., physician, b. in 1754; m. ISABEL GARDINER. Five children.
vii. LOIS, b. at Salisbury 11 Mar. 1756.
viii. SARAH, b. at Salisbury 14 Sept. 1758.

The "Morris Family" adds the following children (order of births uncertain):

ix. ESTHER, m. BENJAMIN DICKSON of Ripley, N. Y.
x. ANNA, m. ——— ELTON of New Haven. [This is not accurate. She m. before 1778 WILLIAM ELTON of Burlington, b. in 1748, d. in 1822. Her gravestone states that she d. 25 Nov. 1802, ae. 50, and that she was dau. of Dea. Daniel Morris.]
xi. LEVI.
xii. MARY, b. in 1760; d. in 1831; m. in 1779 JAMES DICKSON, b. at Cherry Valley, N. Y., 3 Feb. 1756. They removed to Erie Co., Pa.

12. DANIEL[4] MORRIS (*Thomas*,[3] *Joseph*,[2] *Thomas*[1]), born at New Haven in Apr. 1715, removed to the parish of Stratfield (now Bridgeport) in the town of Fairfield, and later to Newtown, where he died 1 Mar. 1792. He married first, 19 July 1741, SARAH (FAIRWEATHER) MACKHARD, who d. 16 Apr. 1761, widow of Matthew; secondly, 29 Dec. 1761, PRUDENCE (SOMERS) CURTIS; and thirdly ELIZABETH ———. In 1740 Daniel Morris of Fairfield, with Amos, Asa, Esther, and Elizabeth Morris of New Haven, conveyed to their brother Thomas their rights to lands of their father Thomas, deceased (New Haven Deeds, vol. 17, p. 3). The town records of New Haven, Stratford, and Fairfield prove conclusively the parentage of Daniel Morris of Fairfield; but, despite this, the "Genealogical and Family History of the State of Connecticut" (1911) states (p. 711) that he was born at Bridgeport 7 May 1715, the son of Daniel and Polly (Benjamin), and that the elder Daniel was born at Boston, Mass., 13 Feb. 1672, and died at Bridgeport in 1749, the son of Dorman and Elinor Morris of Boston. The birth of a Daniel, son of Dorman Morris, is recorded in Boston in 1671,* but there is nothing to prove that Daniel of Boston or any other Daniel Morris settled in the neighborhood of Fairfield until Daniel of New Haven moved to that place about 1740. To him and his descendants their correct ancestry is here for the first time assigned.

Children by first wife, born at Fairfield:

i. MARY,[5] b. 1 Dec. 1742; d. 30 Nov. 1776.
ii. SARAH, b. 1 Sept. 1745; d. 21 Nov. 1771.
iii. AMOS, b. 30 Nov. 1747; d. 7 Dec. 1747.
iv. DANIEL, b. 8 Mar. 1748/9; d. 7 May 1749.
16. v. DANIEL, b. 13 Dec. 1750.

* Mrs. Lucia R. Fellows of Salt Lake City, Utah, has records showing that this Boston family was not a Morris family at all. Its progenitor was Dorman Mahoone, an Irishman who died in Boston in 1661; and members of the family appear on record under the names of Mathue, Maroone, Mareen, and Morris. The publication of these records has given rise to a controversy, the outcome of which cannot affect the validity of the statements in the text above.

vi. James, b. 14 June 1753; m. 19 Feb. 1781 Eunice ———, who
obtained a divorce from him in 1787 for desertion in 1784. According to family tradition he joined the British navy.
17. vii. Matthew Mackhard, b. 25 July 1757.

Child by second wife, born at Fairfield:
18. viii. Amos, b. 28 Sept. 1762.

13. Asa⁴ Morris (*Thomas,³ Joseph,² Thomas¹*), born at New Haven
20 Feb. 1720/1, died at Woodbridge in 1760. He married,
1 Mar. 1758, Hannah Brown, born 19 June 1735, died 1 May
1824, daughter of Eleazer and Sarah (Rowe). She married
secondly Daniel Tolles.
Children:
i. Elizabeth,⁵ b. abt. 1759; d. 11 Feb. 1788; m. Abraham Tolles, b.
abt. 1754, d. 20 May 1793.
19. ii. Asa, b. in June 1760.

14. Ephraim⁴ Morris (*Ephraim,³ Joseph,² Thomas¹*), born at New
Haven 23 May 1721, removed to Danbury, where he died in
1792. He married Eunice ———, who died after 1803. His
will names his wife Eunice and the seven children given below
(Danbury Probate Records, vol. 6, p. 242).
Children (order of births unknown):
20. i. Samuel.⁵
21. ii. Shadrack.
iii. Jachin. In 1802, calling himself of Boston, Mass., he conveyed
land inherited from his father Ephraim, deceased (Danbury
Deeds, vol. 10, p. 429).
iv. Ruth, m. in Dec. 1791 Joseph Mead.
v. Eunice, m. Nathan Stewart of Litchfield (Danbury Deeds, vol. 9,
p. 383).
vi. Lydia, m. 13 Dec. 1774 Matthew Judd of Kent.
vii. Rachel, m. before 1789 Timothy Preston of Dover, N. Y. (Danbury
Deeds, vol. 9, p. 454).

15. Ebenezer⁴ Morris (*Ephraim,³ Joseph,² Thomas¹*), born at New
Haven, resided at Woodbridge, where he died about 1798.
He married first, 28 Nov. 1750, Mabel Carrington, daughter
of Zebulon and Sarah (Johnson); and secondly, 11 Sept. 1766,
Rebecca Thomas.
Children by first wife, recorded at New Haven:
22. i. Major,⁵ b. 16 Oct. 1751.
ii. Hester, b. 28 Feb. 1753.
iii. Abigail, b. 1 Sept. 1754; m. at New Haven, 20 Mar. 1776, Miles
Gorham.
iv. Sarah, b. 17 May 1756.
v. Lydia, b. 1 June 1757; d. 4 Aug. 1765.
vi. Amos, b. 7 Oct. 1759. He removed to Watertown.

16. Daniel⁵ Morris (*Daniel,⁴ Thomas,³ Joseph,² Thomas¹*), born at
Fairfield 13 Dec. 1750, resided at Newtown, where he died
28 Mar. 1828. He married, 12 June 1774, Elizabeth Burritt, born in 1757, daughter of Israel.
Children:
i. Israel B.,⁶ b. 26 July 1775; d. 25 July 1837.
ii. Sally, b. 1 Oct. 1777; m. (1) Abraham Blackman; m. (2) Abel
Curtis.
iii. James, b. 23 July 1779; d. 3 Jan. 1855.

iv. DANIEL, of Monroe, b. 27 Jan. 1781.
23. v. ELI GOULD, b. 6 June 1783.
vi. POLLY, b. 1 Aug. 1786; m. JOHN BLACKMAN.
vii. NANCY, b. 1 July 1790; m. NORMAN GLOVER.
viii. ELIZABETH, b. 30 Jan. 1792; m. FAIRCHILD BURRITT.
ix. EUNICE, b. 6 June 1793; m. JOHN BLACKMAN.
x. WINTHROP, of Roxbury, b. abt. 1796; d. 28 July 1872; m. (1) CORNELIA ——, b. abt. 1798, d. 1 May 1838; m. (2) AMY MALLORY, b. abt. 1802, d. 5 Sept. 1884.

17. MATTHEW MACKHARD[5] MORRIS (*Daniel,*[4] *Thomas,*[3] *Joseph,*[2] *Thomas*[1]), born at Fairfield 25 July 1757, resided at Woodbury, where he died 3 Feb. 1825. He married MEHITABEL JUDSON, born 22 May 1762, died 7 Oct. 1846.
Children:
24. i. JUDSON,[6] b. at Woodbury abt. 1778.
ii. SALLY, m. —— ISBELL.
25. iii. JOHN, b. at Woodbury abt. 1784.
iv. A DAUGHTER, b. abt. 1786; d. 20 Feb. 1794.
v. HARVEY, m. 1 Nov. 1810 MARIA JUDSON, b. abt. 1790, d. 16 June 1871.
vi. A SON, b. abt. 1791; d. 3 Mar. 1794.
vii. ALETHEA, b. abt. 1795; d. *s.p.* 17 Feb. 1861.
viii. JAMES, b. abt. 1798; d. 14 Jan. 1861; m. 16 Sept. 1821 CAROLINE THOMAS, b. abt. 1800, d. 22 July 1848. Children: 1. *Mary O.,*[7] m. 25 May 1842 William Frederick Osborn. 2. *Matthew M.,* b. abt. 1826; d. *s.p.* (murdered) 17 July 1861.
ix. GARRY, b. abt. 1803; d. *s.p.* 15 June 1854.

18. AMOS[5] MORRIS (*Daniel,*[4] *Thomas,*[3] *Joseph,*[2] *Thomas*[1]), born at Fairfield 28 Sept. 1762, removed to Bridgewater, and died at Great Barrington, Mass., 2 Apr. 1841. He married, prior to 29 Mar. 1785, EUNICE CLARK, born about 1765, died 29 Mar. 1841.
Children:
i. LEVI,[6] b. 6 Dec. 1785; d. 24 Sept. 1850; m. 24 Sept. 1807 POLLY H. SMITH, b. abt. 1785, d. 16 Aug. 1862.
ii. ROSWELL, of Newtown, b. 27 May 1795; d. in 1874; m. 27 Nov. 1818 LAURA CANFIELD, b. in 1796, d. in 1872. Children: 1. *Cornelia,*[7] m. Henry B. Young. 2. *Caroline,* m. Peter Wooster. 3. *Mary.* 4. *Arza C.,* of Bridgewater, m. Sarah E. Mallett; three daughters.
iii. CURTIS, of Brookfield, b. 7 Feb. 1797; d. 19 Mar. 1869; m. (1) 2 Nov. 1819 ABIGAIL CURTIS, b. 23 Feb. 1797, d. 8 May 1827; m. (2) 2 Sept. 1827 CYNTHIA J. FINK, b. 1 Oct. 1793, d. 24 Nov. 1871. Children by first wife: 1. *Levi C.,*[7] of Hawleyville, b. 24 Oct. 1822; d. 13 Dec. 1856. 2. *Catharina A.,* b. 1 Dec. 1825; m. 22 Apr. 1845 Andrew Northrop of Brookfield. Child by second wife: 3. *Eli F.,* b. 31 Oct. 1833; d. 27 Oct. 1866; m. 12 Nov. 1856 Emily M. Platt, b. 20 May 1836; two children.
iv. MARTHA, b. 6 Dec. 1799; m. 4 Feb. 1819 ORANGE SMITH, b. 29 Aug. 1797.

19. ASA[5] MORRIS (*Asa,*[4] *Thomas,*[3] *Joseph,*[2] *Thomas*[1]), born in June 1760, lived at Woodbridge, where he died 11 July 1828. He married MARY ——, born about 1762, died 3 Aug. 1840.
Children:
i. ELIZABETH,[6] m. —— NETTLETON.
ii. ASA, of Litchfield, m. 20 Mar. 1818 ANN RIGGS, b. abt. 1790, d. 20 Jan. 1845. Children: 1. *Mary Ann,*[7] b. 3 Apr. 1819; d. 2 Oct.

1844; m. 30 Nov. 1843 Henry Sanford. 2. *Sarah Jane*, b. 28 **Dec.** 1820; d. 3 Feb. 1843. 3. *Joseph Riggs*, b. 26 Apr. 1822. **4.** *Samuel B.*, b. 29 May 1824.

iii. ALANSON, b. abt. 1789; d. 10 Aug. 1812; m. ———. Child: 1. *Alanson.*[7]

iv. NATHAN RUEL, of Bethany, b. abt. 1792; d. 9 Dec. 1848; m. 27 Dec. 1820 LUCY WOODING, b. abt. 1796, d. 9 Aug. 1860.

v. ARVIL, of Waterbury, d. abt. 1866; m. at Woodbridge, in Dec. 1826, CAROLINE CASTLE. Children: 1. *Nelson.*[7] 2. *Lucretia*, b. 25 Apr. 1839; m. 17 Aug. 1859 Seneca L. Munson, b. 29 Apr. 1836, d. 30 Aug. 1894. 3. *Susan.* 4. *Joseph N.*

20. .SAMUEL[5] MORRIS (*Ephraim,*[4] *Ephraim,*[3] *Joseph,*[2] *Thomas*[1]), of Danbury, died in 1792. He married JERUSHA ———, who, with the seven children given below, is named in his will (Danbury Probate Records, vol. 6, p. 213).

Children (order of births unknown):

i. BETHEL,[6] died at Danbury in 1844. His will names children Clara, wife of Thomas P. White [m. 9 Mar. 1828], Sally, wife of John L. Mallory, Samuel, Alfred, George [m. 5 Feb. 1834 Hannah Stevens], Betsey, and Angeline, and grandson Granville W. (Danbury Probate Records, vol. 20, p. 238).

ii. CHAUNCEY, removed to Canaan (Danbury Deeds, vol. 11, p. 220).

iii. EDMUND, removed to Poughkeepsie, N. Y. (Danbury Deeds, vol. 27, p. 397).

iv. AMOS, probably the Amos Morris whose estate was settled in 1886 (Danbury Probate Records, vol. 39, p. 17), the records naming widow Lucy Ann and the following children: Frederick Morris of Danbury (who had sons John and William), William Morris, deceased (who left children Mrs. Mary Rogers of Norwalk, Ohio, Cortland Morris of Inwood, Ind., and Samuel Morris of Monmouth, Iowa), Sarah Ann Blackman of Danbury, Amelia Morris of Southbury, Eli Morris of Anita, Iowa, Philo Morris of Bridgeport, Edmund Morris of Danbury, Clarissa Morris of Danbury, and Elizabeth Morris of Falls Village.

v. REBECCA, m. in 1793 LEVI ANDRUS.

vi. LUCY, m. MILES HOYT. In 1802 she, with her husband, conveyed land from her grandfather Ephraim, set off from the estate of Samuel (Danbury Deeds, vol. 10, p. 489).

vii. ANNA, m. BENJAMIN STILES (Danbury Deeds, vol. 11, p. 398).

21. SHADRACK[5] MORRIS (*Ephraim,*[4] *Ephraim,*[3] *Joseph,*[2] *Thomas*[1]), of Danbury, died later than 1804 (Danbury Deeds, vol. 11, p. 278). The record of his family is incomplete; but he is known to have had at least two sons, for in 1799 he conveyed land to his son Asher (*ib.*, vol. 9, p. 518), and Elijah at the time of his marriage is called son to Shadrack (Danbury Vital Records). Children:

i. ASHER,[6] d. at Danbury in 1811; m. HANNAH STEVENS, b. in 1774. His estate was distributed to his widow Hannah and his four children, Ezra, William D., Mary, and Aaron K. (Danbury Probate Records, vol. 11, pp. 6, 273).

ii. ELIJAH, m. 8 Apr. 1798 OLIVE STEVENS, b. in 1776. Children: 1. *Jachin,*[7] of New York, N. Y., b. 12 Jan. 1799. 2. *John Stevens*, b. 14 Jan. 1801 and probably father of Charles and Ephraim, who appear in Danbury Deeds. 3. *Asher*, of New York, N. Y. Probably also: 4. *Stephen G.*

22. MAJOR[5] MORRIS (*Ebenezer,*[4] *Ephraim,*[3] *Joseph,*[2] *Thomas*[1]), born at New Haven 16 Oct. 1751, removed to Waterbury, where he died 5 Sept. 1811. He married ELIZABETH HINE, daughter

of John and Sarah (Sanford). In the "Genealogical and Family History of the State of Connecticut" (p. 1662) Major is incorrectly given as a son of Amos[4] (5, v).
Children:

26. i. SHELDON,[6] b. abt. 1783.
    ii. MILES (twin), of Waterbury, b. 27 Apr. 1785; m. (1) in 1815 KATY SCOTT of Ashly, who d. in July 1837, ae. 44; m. (2) in Aug. 1845 MARY (CADY) RIGGS, dau. of Arah of Middlebury and widow of Joseph. Child by second wife: 1. *Miles*,[7] b. 30 Oct. 1846.
    iii. NEWTON (twin), of Waterbury, b. 27 Apr. 1785; m. 27 Apr. 1807 MOLLY HOTCHKISS. Children (record incomplete): 1. *Merritt Noyes*.[7] 2. *Henry Newton*, b. in 1810. 3. *Isaac Amos*, b. in 1811. 4. *Sarah Ann*, b. in 1813. 5. *Edwin*, bapt. 10 May 1818. 6. *Eunice Atwater*, bapt. 29 July 1821. 7. *Harriet*, bapt. 20 July 1823. 8. *Jane Elizabeth*, bapt. 1 May 1831.
    iv. MEHITABEL, d. in 1862; m. WILLIAM MORGAN of Waterbury.
    v. AMOS, of Waterbury, d. in 1872; m. (1) 29 May 1816 MARY ATKINS of Southington, b. abt. 1794, d. 30 Aug. 1832; m. (2) 27 Nov. 1833 ANNA (ANDREWS) HINE, dau. of Caleb and Anna (Wolcott) of Bethany and widow of Isaac. Children by first wife: 1. *Elizabeth*,[7] b. 10 Sept. 1817; m. 31 Oct. 1842 F. John Woodruff. 2. *Mary Maria*, b. 10 Feb. 1819; m. 8 Feb. 1842 William Umberfield, b. 18 Apr. 1821. 3. *Ellen Ann*, b. 10 Feb. 1822; m. Sherman Fenn. 4. *Eliza*, b. 25 May 1826; d. young. 5. *Eli A.*, b. 3 Apr. 1830; d. 7 Apr. 1833. 6. *Eunice*, b. 24 Aug. 1832; m. George Nettleton.

23. ELI GOULD[6] MORRIS (*Daniel*,[5] *Daniel*,[4] *Thomas*,[3] *Joseph*,[2] *Thomas*[1]), born 6 June 1783, died 3 Jan. 1856. He married, 21 Mar. 1821, LYDIA BENNETT, born 4 June 1793, died 2 July 1879.
Children:

    i. ELI JAMES,[7] of Newtown, member of the Connecticut Legislature, b. 20 Dec. 1821; d. 10 Nov. 1901; m. 2 Sept. 1850 JANE ELIZABETH CHAMBERS, b. 6 Feb. 1825, d. 4 Oct. 1891.
    ii. LUZON BURRITT, member of the Connecticut Legislature, Judge of Probate (New Haven District), Governor of Connecticut in 1892, b. 16 Apr. 1826; d. 23 Aug. 1895; m. 15 June 1856 EUGENIA LAURA TUTTLE of Seymour, b. 5 Oct. 1833, d. 2 Nov. 1916, dau. of Lucius and Laura. Children: 1. *Robert Tuttle*,[8] of New York, N.Y., student at Cornell Univ., 1876–1879, M.D. (College of Physicians and Surgeons of New York, 1882), surgeon and author, President of the American Association of Obstetricians and Gynecologists, 1907, b. 14 May 1857; m. 4 June 1898 Aimée (Reynaud) Mazergue. 2. *Mary Seymour*, A.B. (Vassar College, 1880), b. 1 Dec. 1858; m. Charles M. Pratt of Brooklyn, N. Y., a director of the Standard Oil Co. 3. *Helen Harrison*, A.B. (Vassar College, 1883), b. 12 May 1862; m. Arthur Twining Hadley, LL.D., President of Yale University. 4. *Emily Eugenia*, A.B. (Vassar College, 1890), b. 26 June 1869. 5. *Charles Gould*, of New Haven, B.A. (Yale, 1895), LL.B. (Yale, 1897), b. 4 Feb. 1871; m. 27 Sept. 1899 Elisabeth Woodbridge. 6. *Ray*, of New York, N. Y., B.A. (Yale, 1901), M.A. (Yale, 1904), banker, b. 4 June 1878; m. 4 Oct. 1906 Katharine Grinnell.
    iii. MARTHA JANE, b. 14 Dec. 1835; d. *s.p.* 12 June 1877.

24. JUDSON[6] MORRIS (*Matthew Mackhard*,[5] *Daniel*,[4] *Thomas*,[3] *Joseph*,[2] *Thomas*[1]), born at Woodbury about 1778, died there 15 Feb. 1846. He married first MEHITABEL PECK, born about 1781, died 8 Apr. 1813; and secondly, 1 Feb. 1814, JERUSHA HOTCHKISS, born 20 June 1785.

Children by first wife:

i. ALMIRA,[7] m. ——— BLOSS.
ii. ELIZA, m. ——— RICH.
iii. MEHITABEL, m. ——— HIGGINS.
iv. MARCUS.
v. SALLY, m. ——— CHURCH.
vi. NANCY, m. ——— WEBSTER.
vii. MARIA H., m. 2 Feb. 1831 HORACE S. ATWOOD.

Children by second wife:

viii. HENRY, d. *s.p.*
ix. HOBART HOTCHKISS, b. 24 Mar. 1817; d. 2 Feb. 1891; m. 18 Oct.
1842 SARAH M. HURD. Child: 1. *George Franklin,*[8] town clerk of
Woodbury for ten years, auditor for six years, representative in
the Connecticut Legislature in 1881 and 1901, b. 21 Sept. 1844;
m. 6 Oct. 1868 Sophronia Dawson; two children.
x. BETSEY, m. ——— CHURCH.
xi. RUTH, m. 21 May 1851 WILLIAM LEGRAND JUDSON.
xii. IMOGEN, m. 16 Feb. 1847 CHARLES S. CRANE of Bethlehem.

25. JOHN[6] MORRIS (*Matthew Mackhard,*[5] *Daniel,*[4] *Thomas,*[3] *Joseph,*[2]
Thomas[1]), born at Woodbury about 1784, died there 25 July
1836. He married first, 30 Dec. 1803, ALTHEA MITCHELL,
born about 1784, died 2 Mar. 1811; and secondly, 26 Jan. 1814,
SALLY BISHOP.

Children by first wife:

i. CHARITY,[7] m. 29 Nov. 1827 ELIZUR BARNES of Roxbury.
ii. MARTHA B., m. 3 May 1835 PHILO TUTTLE.
iii. MALGA M., m. 24 May 1835 ASAHEL TYLER of Middlebury.

Children by second wife:

iv. CLARISSA D., m. 15 June 1841 ENOS HOPKINS of Naugatuck.
v. HARRIET, m. ——— UPSON.
vi. EMILY J., m. 29 Dec. 1844 GEORGE LATHROP.
vii. THALIA J., m. 10 Sept. 1845 CHARLES H. BROUGHTON of Naugatuck.
viii. HARVEY.

26. SHELDON[6] MORRIS (*Major,*[5] *Ebenezer,*[4] *Ephraim,*[3] *Joseph,*[2]
Thomas[1]), born about 1783, resided at Waterbury and South-
bury, and died at Litchfield 6 Feb. 1858. He married ———
HICKOX.

Children:

i. SUSAN,[7] m. 29 Nov. 1821 IRA MALLORY of Middlebury.
ii. JOHN N., of Waterbury, m. 16 Feb. 1825 POLLY CHATFIELD. Children: 1. *Leonard A.,*[8] b. 16 Feb. 1826. 2. *William F.,* of Oakville,
b. 22 Feb. 1828; d. 8 June 1872; m. Elizabeth A. Scott; three
children. 3. *George M.,* b. 7 Oct. 1833. 4. *Catherine E.,* b. 1 Nov.
1837.
iii. SAMUEL M., b. 29 Jan. 1808; m. 12 Oct. 1831 EUNICE UPSON, b.
17 Oct. 1810. Children, recorded at Waterbury: 1. *Marietta,*[8] b.
25 Jan. 1833. 2. *Cornelia,* b. 17 Feb. 1838. 3. *Herbert,* b. 27 Nov.
1845.
iv. SHELDON, b. 8 May 1814; d. 10 Aug. 1897; m. BETSY WILLIAMS, b.
in 1813, d. in 1872. In 1854 he was of Bridgeport, where he
organized the Saving Machine Cabinet Co. In 1869 he removed
to Indianapolis, Ind. Children: 1. *Marshall Eliot,*[8] of Bridgeport, b. 8 May 1837; m. in 1862 Mary Elizabeth Winters; four
children. 2. *Bennett Franklin,* of Bridgeport, b. 20 Feb. 1840;
m. in 1861 Ann Louise Curtis, b. in 1843; no issue. 3. *James
Allen,* m. Mary Hill. 4. *George Seymour,* m. Eliza Beatty; one
son. 5. *Frances L.,* m. Hylon P. Warner of Roxbury.

v. Joseph Lucius.
vi. Mary Etta, m. —— Peck of South Litchfield.
vii. Polly Ann, bapt. 8 July 1828.

II. The Richard Morris Family of Milford

1. Richard[1] Morris first appears at Newport, R. I., and it is believed that his mother was Margaret[3] Painter, daughter of Shubael[2] and Mercy (Lamberton) (cf. Register, vol. 68, p. 275). His father * may have been of the family of Capt. Richard Morris, a man of note in early Newport; but the partial destruction of the records of that town makes anything more than conjecture impossible. According to the records of Trinity Church, Newport, he married first, 22 Dec. 1717, Elizabeth Auxeny; and secondly, 24 May 1721, Jean Eddy, daughter of John. In 1726 he was still of Newport (cf. Register, *ut supra*), but on 30 Apr. 1738 Jane, wife of Richard Morris, joined the Congregational Church at Milford, Conn. In his will, dated 24 Mar. 1759 and proved in May 1759, he named his wife Jane and his son John, and referred to other children, unnamed (New Haven Probate Records, vol. 9, p. 247). In Apr. 1767 administration on the estate of Jean Morrice of Milford was granted to Samuel Basset in right of his wife Susanna, daughter of the deceased (*ib.*, vol. 10, p. 399). Her estate was insolvent, and among the debts was a sum due Mercy Morris for nursing.

Very little pertaining to this family is on record at Milford; and since Samuel Morris (4, ix) of the New Haven family resided there for a time, it is difficult to identify Richard's children with certainty. For the benefit, however, of future genealogists the following brief sketch is appended.

Children:

    i. Susanna,[2] m. Samuel Bassett of Milford.
2. ii. John.
3. iii. Thomas (probably s. of Richard).
4. iv. Joseph (probably s. of Richard).
5. v. George (probably s. of Richard), b. abt. 1731.
    vi. Mercy, d. at Milford 25 Mar. 1778.
    vii. David (probably s. of Richard). On 4 Mar. 1780 a private recorder of Milford mortality noted that he had heard of the death of David Morris in captivity.

2. John[2] Morris (*Richard[1]*) lived in that section of Milford later incorporated into the town of Woodbridge. He married at Woodbridge, 12 Nov. 1750, Sybil Newton. The record of his family is incomplete. Clarania, daughter of a John Morris, was baptized at New Milford in 1769.

Children:

    i. Richard[3] (probably s. of John), d. at Milford in 1825, aged 63; m. Sarah ——, who d. at Milford, as his widow, in May 1847, aged 94.
6. ii. Newton John.

3. Thomas[2] Morris (? *Richard[1]*) died at Wallingford 21 Apr. 1777. He married Sarah ——, who was buried at Wallingford (Cheshire), as his widow, 7 Aug. 1777. He lived in that part of Wallingford which later became the town of Cheshire, and his burial is recorded in the Cheshire church records under

*Page 3, Vol. III of this work.

date of 22 Apr. 1777. On 4 May 1777 the Milford recorder of deaths noted the death of Thomas Morris, "once of Milford," thus proving that he belonged to the Milford family.

Children (record incomplete):

i. WILLIAM,[3] m. at Wallingford, 16 Oct. 1777, REBECCA PERKINS, dau. of John and Dorcas (Brooks). He removed from Cheshire to Waterbury, where he appears in the Census of 1790 with six males under sixteen years of age and two females in his family. About 1800 he removed to Hampton, N. Y. Children: 1. *Thomas*,[4] b. 10 Apr. 1778. 2. *Shubael*, b. 17 Nov. 1779.

ii. SOLOMON, m. at Cheshire, 24 Feb. 1780, KEZIA MOSS. In 1778 he and William Morris bought land in Waterbury (Waterbury Deeds, vol. 17, p. 277), but it is doubtful if he removed thither. He settled at Warsaw, N. Y.

4. JOSEPH[2] MORRIS (? *Richard*[1]) probably married SARAH ———, who married secondly John Marchant of Waterbury. Joseph Morris served in 1762 in the French and Indian War. The death is recorded at Milford of a Joseph Morris at Seabrook, 10 Nov. 1776, and of another Joseph Morris, 3 Jan. 1778. On 9 Feb. 1796 Sarah Marchant of Milford and David Morris of Waterbury conveyed to James Rylee their rights in the house and garden of Joseph Morris of Milford, deceased (Milford Deeds, vol. 19, p. 425). On 10 May 1796 David Morris of Waterbury conveyed to James Rylee the rights that John Morris had in the house and garden of Joseph Morris of Milford, deceased (*ib.*, vol. 19, p. 424). On 14 Nov. 1796 Elisha Morris of Milford conveyed to Bryan Gillett his rights in a house and garden (*ib.*, vol. 20, p. 553). It seems likely that the names of the widow and three sons of Joseph Morris appear in these deeds. It is known that the Sarah Marchant of the first-mentioned deed was mother of David Morris of Waterbury, for on 7 Feb. 1796 (two days prior to the date of this deed) the latter conveyed to his mother, Mrs. Sarah Marchant, the east room in his house (Waterbury Deeds, vol. 25, p. 335).

The death of a wife of a Joseph Morris, aged 22, is recorded at Milford, 12 Apr. 1805; but the identity of this Joseph has not been established.

Children:

7. i. DAVID.[3]

ii. JOHN. In 1791 he conveyed land in Salem (Waterbury Deeds, vol. 23, p. 31), then a parish in Waterbury, now the town of Naugatuck.

iii. ELISHA, m. ———, whose death is recorded at Milford, 27 Aug. 1821, aged 54. The death of a child is recorded in 1812. Children, bapt. at Milford 4 Sept. 1808: 1. *Aaron*.[4] 2. *Jared*. 3. *Melinda*. 4. *Andrew*.

5. GEORGE[2] MORRIS (? *Richard*[1]), born about 1731, died at Milford 10 Mar. 1776. He married EUNICE PLUMB, daughter of John and Kezia (Alling). On 30 Apr. 1754 John Plumm conveyed land to his daughter Eunice, wife of George Morris (Milford Deeds, vol. 12½, p. 555); and he also left to her a legacy in his will, dated in 1762 and proved in 1763 (New Haven Probate Records, vol. 10, p. 51). In Oct. 1773 it is recorded that

George Morris of Milford, by the long illness of his wife, was reduced and had come to want; and that he, his wife, and two small children had been under the care of the selectmen (Colonial Records of Connecticut, vol. 14, p. 200). The death of a Widow Morris is recorded at Milford, 9 Sept. 1781.
Children:

 i. JOHN,[3] b. at Milford 4 Apr. 1754 and bapt. in the Second Church, Milford, 19 May 1754. On 15 Aug. 1804 David Morris of Derby mortgaged his home to John Plumb Morris of New York, N. Y. (Derby Deeds, vol. 17, p. 100); and on 7 May 1819 John P. Morris of New York, with his wife Abigail, quitclaimed this property to the widow and children of David (*ib.*, vol. 22, p. 34).
 ii. WILLIAM, bapt. 24 Aug. 1755.
 iii. DAVID, bapt. 19 Aug. 1759; probably d. young.
8. iv. DAVID, b. 5 Feb. 1761 (family records).

6. NEWTON JOHN[3] MORRIS (*John,*[2] *Richard*[1]) removed from Milford to Waterbury, and later to Warren, where he died about 1829. He married first ABIGAIL ———, who died at Milford 1 Apr. 1792; and secondly, 8 Nov. 1792, EUNICE NEWTON.
Children by first wife:

 i. A CHILD,[4] d. at Milford in 1789.
 ii. ABIGAIL (probably a child by first wife).
 iii. AMY, m. in Mar. 1808 WILLIAM W. PRATT.

Children by second wife:

 iv. GARRY, of Sharon, b. abt. 1793; d. 11 Aug. 1869; m. HESTER ———, b. abt. 1801, d. 2 Apr. 1857. Children (record incomplete): 1. *Mary,*[5] bapt. 15 Aug. 1824; d. in 1827. 2. *Mary Jane,* b. in 1829. 3. *Francis Pratt,* b. in 1833. 4. *Harriet Helen,* b. in 1835.
 v. POLLY, bapt. 14 Nov. 1802.
 vi. JOHN.
 vii. REV. MYRON NEWTON, B.A. (Yale, 1837), b. at Warren 19 Nov. 1810; d. 9 July 1885; m. (1) 10 Jan. 1838 JULIA S. AVERY, who d. 26 Mar. 1854, dau. of Elisha; m. (2) 8 May 1855 EMELINE WHITMAN, dau. of Samuel of West Hartford. Myron Newton Morris was principal of Bacon Academy, Colchester, 1840–1843; studied for the ministry, and was ordained in the Congregational Church at North Stonington, 15 Apr. 1846; was installed at West Hartford 1 July 1852, where he continued as pastor until 27 Apr. 1875. He was elected a fellow of Yale College in July 1867, and was a representative in the Connecticut Legislature in 1872 and 1875. Children by first wife: 1. *Julia Louisa,*[5] b. at Colchester 3 Apr. 1840. 2. *Edward Livingston,* b. at Colchester 19 Sept. 1843. 3. *A son.* Child by second wife: 4. *Rev. Charles Newton,* B.A. (Yale, 1882), M.A. (Yale, 1887).

7. DAVID[3] MORRIS (*Joseph,*[2] ? *Richard*[1]) removed from Milford to that part of Waterbury known as Salem, now the town of Naugatuck. He appears in Waterbury in the Census of 1790. He married LOIS LOOMIS.
Children, baptized at the Salem Church 12 May 1799:

 i. PELEG.[4]
 ii. ALANSON, of Torrington, m. in 1812 LUCY BRACE, who d. 20 Apr. 1871. For descendants see Orcutt's History of Torrington.
 iii. DAVID.
 iv. MARCUS.
 v. JULIUS, of Waterbury, b. 18 May 1796; d. in 1864; m. 15 Apr. 1818 HANNAH SCOVILL, b. 13 Oct. 1796. Children: 1. *Fanny Jennet,*[5]

b. 23 Oct. 1820; d. 22 Feb. 1825. 2. *Julia Ann*, b. 14 Sept. 1823; d. 6 Apr. 1862; m. 28 Oct. 1844 John Hine, b. 23 Feb. 1817, d. 1 Aug. 1855. 3. *William Augustus*, b. 5 Apr. 1825.

8. DAVID³ MORRIS (*George,² ? Richard¹*), born 5 Feb. 1761, died 8 Mar. 1810. He married MARY BARTHELME, born 25 Oct. 1766, died 15 June 1853, daughter of Claude and Susan (Plumb). He was a sea captain of Derby.

Children:

i.   EUNICE,⁴ b. 17 June 1787; m. ABRAM HAWLEY.
ii. KEZIA, b. 8 Feb. 1790; d. 31 Dec. 1874.
iii. BELA D., b. 4 Mar. 1792; d. 10 Oct. 1818; m. JULIA THOMPSON.
iv. SUSAN, b. 25 Jan. 1795; d. 20 Mar. 1879; m. in Aug. 1816 GEORGE LINES of Woodbridge, b. abt. 1792, d. 16 May 1852.
v.   LOUISA, b. 23 Feb. 1797; d. 1 Feb. 1814.
vi. SARAH, b. 28 July 1799; d. 9 Sept. 1804.
vii. SARAH, b. 2 Aug. 1800; m. GEORGE BRONSON.
viii. MARY ETTA, b 6 June 1801; m. JEREMIAH THOMAS.
ix. RITTA ANN, b. 4 May 1803; m. 12 July 1829 RICHARD ATWATER.
x.   JOHN PLUMB, b. 8 Oct. 1806; d. 20 Sept. 1807.

III. AN UNPLACED FAMILY

WILLIAM MORRIS of Oxford was possibly a son of George Morris of the Milford family (5). In 1795 he was chosen as guardian by Leverett Lines of Oxford, whose mother is said by descendants to have been Anna Morris. He married first, 28 Mar. 1792, ELIZABETH THOMAS, born about 1772, died in 1808, daughter of Reuben and Rhoda (Clinton); and secondly AMELIA THOMAS, born about 1771, died in 1853, sister of his first wife.

Children by first wife:

i.   MARIA, m. ———— RANSOM.
ii. LYMAN, bapt. 14 Oct. 1794.
iii. BETSEY, bapt. 1 Apr. 1797; m. ———— ALLING.
iv. WILLIAM, of New Haven, b. 6 Mar. 1799; m. ————. He had issue.
v.   SHELDON, b. 8 Apr. 1801.
vi. ELLIOTT, b. 9 Apr. 1803.
vii. JASON, of New Haven, b. 3 May 1805; d. *s.p.* 28 Mar. 1840; m. CYNTHIA BUCKINGHAM.
viii. ADELINE, b. 9 Oct. 1806; m. ———— DOWNS.

Child by second wife:

ix. AMELIA LUCRETIA, bapt. 6 Jan. 1812.

MORSE, EVERETT, JONES, AVERY.— Abigail[3] Morse, daughter of John[2] and Annis (Chickering) Morse, was born in Dedham, Mass., March 2, 1646-7, and baptized March 8, 1646-7. She married for her first husband Israel[2] Everett, son of Richard and Mary (Winch) Everett, who was born in Dedham July 14, 1651, and died there December 23, 1678. To them were born in Dedham *Tabitha*[3] *Everett* June 11, 1676, and *Josiah*[2] *Everett* August 3, 1678. She was married a second time, October 18, 1687, by Rev. John Bayley of Watertown, Mass., to William Jones, a tailor, then of Watertown. He was a son of Dep. Gov. William and Hannah (Eaton) Jones of New Haven, Conn.; date and place of birth unknown; died May 23, 1700, Guilford, Conn. To them was born in Watertown, *Caleb Jones*, December 20, 1688.

The wife survived her second husband, and died in Guilford, Conn., Sept. 23, 1737.

William Jones, with his wife Abigail, appear to have lived in Watertown from their marriage in 1687 until about 1690, when the family, with the three young children, removed to Guilford, Conn., and thenceforth resided there. The two children by the first marriage retained their father's name under the spelling of " Avered," grew up and were married in Guilford.

Tabitha[3] Avered married January 5, 1705, Benjamin Dudley, a twin son of Joseph and Ann (Robinson) Dudley, who was born June 11, 1671, and died February 20, 1720, in Guilford. She married secondly February 21, 1723, Jasper Saxton, whose birth and death are unknown. Her death is recorded in the Guilford Church records: " Tabitha Avered Saxton, widow Jasper, Sept. 27, 1755." By the first marriage there were four daughters and one son.

Josiah[3] Avered married Dec. 20, 1703, Elizabeth Cook, daughter of Thomas and Sarah (Mason) Cook. She was born in Guilford February 22, 1684. To them were born in Guilford five sons and two daughters: *Elizabeth*,[4] Nov. 5, 1704; *Israil*,[4] May 4, 1708; *Josiah*,[4] Aug. 4, 1710; *Reuben*,[4] Nov. 7, 1712; *Sarah*,[4] July 18, 171—; *Abner*,[4] April 7, 1721; *Timothy*,[4] May 9, 1727.

Josiah[3] Avered, or Everett, the father, removed to the adjoining town of Durham about 1728 or 9, and in 1732 moved again to the adjoining town of Wallingford, where he was living in 1747, when he deeded a farm to his son Abner[4] Avered, in consideration of love and good will to him.

Caleb Jones, the son by the second marriage, likewise grew up in Guilford, and was married there July 15, 1723, to Mary Bishop. He died May 24, 1754.

Israil[4] Avered, born as above stated May 4, 1708, in Guilford, removed as a young man with his parents to Durham, where he was married Aug. 25, 1731, to Abigail Beach. Between the years 1736 and 1740 he removed to Torrington, Conn., where he died about 1794. In his early years of married life he resided in Durham or Wallingford, probably the former, where, on the town records, the name is spelled Avered, Avored, Averd, and Auered. After the removal to Torrington it became Averet, Everit, and Everett, and all of his descendants have followed the last. Their children were: *Mical*,[5] born July 29, baptized Aug. 21, 1732, in Durham; *Abigail*,[5] born March 1, 1733-4, in Durham, and living unmarried in 1796 in Torrington; *Samuel*,[5] born Feb. 6, 1739, and died Nov. 1, 1821, in Granville, Ohio; *Anna*,[5] born Jany. 15, baptized Jany. 18, 1740-1, in Durham, and living unmarried in 1796 in Torrington; *Sarah*,[5] baptized May 6, 1744, in Durham, married a Mr. Green, and was living in 1796 in Clarendon, Rutland Co., Vt.; *Hannah*,[5] born May 7, 1747, in Torrington, and baptized July 26, 1747, in Durham, living unmarried in 1796 in Torrington; *Eunice*,[5] baptized Sept., 1750, in Torrington, and died in infancy; *Israel*,[5] born June 16, baptized July 19, 1752, in Torrington, and died about 1800-10, in Ballston, N. Y.; *Eunice*,[5] born April 16, 1755, in Torrington, married Titus Andrews, and they were living in 1796 in Stillwater, Albany Co., N. Y.

Josiah[4] Avered, the second son, born Aug. 4, 1710, in Guilford, died Feby. 23, 1765, Bethlehem, Conn.; married March 20, 1740, Hannah Hinman, daughter of Andrew and Mary (Noble) Hinman. She was born Dec. 5, 1714, in Woodbury, Conn,, and died May 19, 1803, in Winchester, Conn. To them were born in Woodbury five sons and five daughters, one of whom, Rev. Noble[5] Everett, was the settled pastor in Wareham, Mass., for nearly fifty years. With this branch the spelling of the name changed from Avered to Everett.

Abner[4] Avered, the fourth son, born April 7, 1721, in Guilford, accompanied his parents to Durham and Wallingford, and died in Wallingford about 1804. He married in Wallingford Dec. 5, 1744, Eunice Hall, daughter of Ensign Amos and Ruth Hall. She died there Jany. 21, 1776. To them were born: *Amos*,[5] Sept. 25, 1745; *Abner*,[5] April 21, 1748; *Edmund*,[5] Nov. 22, 1750; *Ambrose*,[5] Dec. 7, 1752; *Eunice*,[5] May 22, 1760. This branch has split in spelling the name; Amos and Ambrose, who removed to the present town of Plymouth, Conn. (formerly part of Watertown and Waterbury), spelling it Averet in 1791, and Everit in 1794, while Edmund and Eunice, who remained in Wallingford, and Abner, who removed to Northampton, Mass., spelt it Avery.

The daughter Sarah[4] Avered was married in Wallingford June 12, 1735, to Ebenezer Lewis.

Of the other sons, Reuben[4] and Timothy,[4] I have no history, and would like information if there is any one to give it.

This statement of the ancestry of Abner[4] Avered shows the incorrectness of the claim put forth in the " Averys of Groton," recently published, where he is called Abner Avery (No. 61, pp. 419-20), the son of a Josiah Avery of Stonington (No. 20, p. 410). My attention during the past year has been given to Josiah and Tabitha Avered of Guilford, Conn., and their descendants, two branches of which, Josiah and Israel, I now have nearly in full. While following the Abner branch, I found, in examining the Wallingford records, that the spelling of the name began to change about 1750 to Avery, and that since 1800 one portion of this branch were all Averys, while another portion were all Everetts. The most complete evidence of this claim is the deed signed in 1785 by the four sons and one daughter, wherein by the beginning Amos Avered of Watertown, Ambrose Avered of Watertown, Edmund Avered of Wallingford, Abner Avered, Jr., of Wallingford, and Eunice Avered of Wallingford, deed land descended to us from our honorable mother, deceased, twelve acres, near where Ensⁿ Amos Hall lately lived, and bounded N. and S. on heirs of Amos Hall, deceased; W. on land deeded this day to Abner Avered, Jr.; E. on land of Bartholomew Andrews. This deed was signed Amos Avered, Abner Avery, Jr., Edmond Avery, Ambrose Avery, Eunice Avered. In 1797 the father made his will, which was presented to the Probate Court in 1804, when all the names were spelt Avery. At the same time Amos and Ambrose wrote their names in 1791 as Averet, while Edmond and Eunice became Avery. This shows clearly that Abner was an Everett and no Avery.

An examination of the records of Guilford, Durham and Wallingford will confirm these points. My abstracts of these, together with other references, are now on file, bound, in the library of the New-England Historic Genealogical Society in Boston, where they can be examined.

Cambridge, Mass.   EDWARD F. EVERETT.

MOSELEY, Rev. Samuel. [*N. E. H. & G. Reg.* Vol. vii. page 329.] Mr. Moseley's fifth child was *Anna*, b. May 23, 1746; m. Dea. Daniel Dunham, Dec. 17, 1767; obt. March 6, 1815, in Manlius, co. Onondaga, N. Y. The writer hereof, her grandson, saw her expire. Deacon Dunham's residence in Connecticut was Lebanon Crank, now Columbia. Their descendants are very numerous all over the Union.

Mr. Moseley's 10th child was *Abigail*, not Elizabeth, was born Nov. 19, 1756; m. Dr. John Clark, of Windham, Dec. 13, 1781; obt. in Lebanon, co. Madison, N.Y., Jan. 28, 1834. Her descendants also are numerous, one of whom resides in Boston, Mrs. A. Smith.   EDWIN W. CLARKE.
Oswego, N. Y.

A GENEALOGY OF THE FAMILY OF MULFORD.*

Communicated by WILLIAM REMSEN MULFORD, Esq., Counsellor at Law, Member of the N. Y. Genealogical and Biographical Society of New York City.

AWAY to the eastward on Long Island, is a region where the waves roll in with unbroken force to the silent and thinly populated shore, and where with diapason roar the wintry blasts from the ocean sweep in to howl and whistle over the wild wastes. Here, to this wilderness, in 1649 came a band of pioneers and founded the old, quaint, traditional East Hampton. The majority came from Salem and Lynn, Mass., via Connecticut, to Long Island, and the land was purchased, of the aborigines, from this place as far east as Montauk, for £38. 4s. and 8d. sterling.

"It was then," says an admiring writer, in a descriptive sketch published in New York some eight years since, " an unbroken wilderness, and the Indians were numerous on every side. On the east, at 'Montaukett,' the royal Wyandanch swayed the sceptre; on the north, at Shelter Island, his brother Poggotacut ruled the tribe of 'Manhassetts;' and a third brother ruled over the 'Shinecocks.' And here in the dark and gloomy forest, in silence unbroken save by the Indian war-whoop, the cry of the wild beasts, or the solemn roar of the ocean, they made their earthly home. * * *

> " ' Amidst the storm they sang,
> And the stars heard and the sea,
> And the sounding aisles of the dim woods rang
> To the anthem of the free.
>
> The ocean eagle soared
> From his nest by the white wave's foam,
> And the rocking pines of the forest roared—
> This was their welcome home.' "

This village was afterwards the birthplace of J. Howard Payne, author of "Home, Sweet Home," and it is thought that when he wrote so affectingly of "home," he had in mind this quaint village, with its wide, grassy main street, and the old shingled Church with its spire pointing heavenward, surmounted by the rusty weather vane, and the picturesque surroundings with their legends relating to the once formidable Montauk tribe.

Among these pioneers were Judge John Mulford and his brother William. They came to Long Island from Salem, Mass.

It is the object of the following sketch to give a brief account of some of the descendants of John and William Mulford, two of the first settlers of East Hampton, Suffolk County, N. Y.

---

* Compiled from MSS. in the possession of Robert L. Mulford, Esq., of New York, Charles Hervey Townsend, Esq., of New Haven, and from other sources.

The English pedigree of the Mulfords will be given at some future time.

I. Descendants of John Mulford.

Prepared by Robert L. Mulford, Esq., of New York City.

John and William Mulford, brothers, probably from Devonshire, England, where the name is often spelled Molford, settled in South Hampton, Long Island, going there via Connecticut, of which colony it was then a part. By the records of South Hampton, published 1874, Vol. I. page 29, May 29, 1643, "it was ordered that John Mulford shall have two acres of land on the plain." On page 55, sold his house in South Hampton, Feb. 8, 1648, and in that or the following year was one of the nine persons who settled East Hampton; his name appears many times in the Council Minutes of Connecticut, Vol. 2, 4, 6, and he was commissioned Judge in 1674. In attending to the town affairs, keeping peace with the Indians, representing the eastern towns in Hartford, and afterwards in New York, he was the foremost man until his death in 1686, æt. 80. John Mulford had:

   2. i. SAMUEL, b. 1644; d. Aug. 21, 1725.
      ii. JOHN, b. 1650; d. 1734.
     iii. MARY, who m. Jeremiah Miller.
     iv. HANNAH, who m. Benjamin Conkling.

   2. Capt. SAMUEL[2] MULFORD (*John[1]*), b. 1644 and d. in East Hampton, Aug. 21, 1725; m. first, Esther, who d. Nov. 24, 1717, æt. 64, by whom he had four children. Second, m. Sarah Howell, d. April 6, 1760, æt. 97. Childless. By first wife had:

      i. SAMUEL, b. 1678; d. 1743; m. Sarah ——.
      ii. TIMOTHY, b. 1681; d. 1741; wife Sarah ——.
     iii. ELIAS, b. 1685; d. 1760; m. Mary Mason.
   3. iv. MATTHEW, b. 1689; d. April 28, 1774; m. Elizabeth Chatfield, Dec. 25, 1712.

Capt. Samuel Mulford was at an early age a town officer, and a member of the Provincial Assembly of New York from 1705 to 1720, from which he was expelled for exposing the abuses of Gov. Hunter's administration, and sent back by the votes of his county. He also served as a captain in the colonial militia. He went to England in 1716, appeared before a committee of the House of Lords, and by his pleading, the duty on whale oil was removed. A long sketch of his career is given in Vol. 1, p. 517, of Hollister's History of Connecticut, 1857; also in Thompson's Long Island, 1843, Vol. 1, p. 315; also in Hedges's East Hampton, 1850.

   3. Capt. MATTHEW[3] MULFORD (*Samuel,[2] John[1]*) and Elizabeth Chatfield his wife, m. Dec. 25, 1712. She died Sept. 11, 1754, æt. 67. He served as captain in the colonial militia;* was a landholder in East Hampton.

      i. ELIZABETH, b. Aug. 22, 1714; d. Oct. 21, 1754, on Gardiner's Island; m. May 26, 1737, to Hon. John Gardiner, who d. May 19, 1764, leaving David, John, Elizabeth—3 children.
      ii. JERUSHA (twin), b. Aug. 22, 1714; m. April 13, 1736, to Jeremiah Hedges. Had one child, David, b. Oct. 23, 1737.

* Among the old papers in possession of his lineal descendant (Robert L. Mulford, of New York), is his commission as captain from John Montgomery, Capt. Gen. and Gov. of New York and New Jersey, dated Nov. 29, 1728, "to Matthew Mulford Gentleman."

iii. ESTHER, b. July 10, 1719; m. first, Jonathan Hunting, who died Sept.
3, 1750, leaving 2 children, Jonathan and Matthew. Second marriage, John Darbe. She died Sept. 24, 1757.
4. iv. DAVID (Col.), b. Sept. 10, 1722; d. Dec. 18, 1778; m. Phebe Hunting, June 16, 1751.
5. v. MARY, b. April 9, 1725; d. June 30, 1729.

4. Col. DAVID⁴ MULFORD (*Matthew,³ Samuel,² John¹*), like his ancestors
John and Samuel, was a leading man in his town of East Hampton. His
descendant Robert L. Mulford, of New York, has now his commission,
signed by Gov. Clinton (colonial governor of New York), dated Oct. 13,
1748, and another dated Feb. 13, 1758, by Lieut. Gov. James DeLancey,
appointing him to offices in the colonial militia. When the colonies commenced to resist the stamp act and other taxation of Great Britain, he was
the guiding star in his part of the state. Onderdonk's Rev. Incidents of
Suffolk Co. (1849) states on pages 13, 14, that Col. M. and others composed a standing committee to correspond with other committees and agree
not to import from Great Britain until the blockade of the port of Boston
was raised. Page 19, July 8, 1775. Appointed muster master of troops
to be raised in Suffolk Co. P. 29, in list of field officers his name appears
as first colonel, and he reported to the Provincial Congress, March 5, 1776,
that his regiment consisted of 670 privates and 98 officers. He was executor of David Gardiner (dec.) of Gardiner's Island, and Aug. 25, '75, complained to Congress of depredations by Gen. Gates's army, made on that
island.

July 22, 1776, the Declaration of Independence was proclaimed at the
several places of parade, and his descendant has the copy from which it was
first read to his regiment. He was on the march to Brooklyn at the head
of his troops when the battle of Long Island decided the fate of that part of
the state, and his men dispersed and went to their homes or to Connecticut, by orders of the commanding General.

On page 43 of Onderdonk it is noted, " After the capture of Gen. Woodhull by the British, Col. Mulford was written to come to Huntington and
take command of the regiments."

On page 46. " Col. Abm. Gardiner surrounded the house of Col. Mulford in East Hampton, Sept. 7, 1776, and forced him to take the oath."
P. 58, after the whole island was possessed by the English 3 casks of powder and 2 boxes of lead were taken from Col. Mulford's house, and via
Sag Harbor carried to Connecticut.

Page 70. " Col. Mulford's negro Jack was permitted to return from
Connecticut to L. Island." Col. Mulford died before the war closed, leaving an unstained reputation. Children, all born in Easthampton, N. Y. :

i. DAVID (Maj.), b. Nov. 7, 1754; m. Rachel Gardiner; d. Jan. 8, 1799.
5. ii. MATTHEW, b. Oct. 22, 1756; m. Mary Hutchinson, Feb. 17, 1778; d.
March 24, 1845.
iii. PHEBE, b. Sept. 20, 1758; m. Henry Pierson, Sept. 19, 1780; d. Feb.
28, 1836.
iv. BETSEY, b. 1760; unmarried; d. 1785.
v. ESTHER, b. 1765; m. Dea. David Hedges; d. 1825.
6. vi. JONATHAN, b. 1770; m. Hamutal Baker; d. 1840.

5. MATTHEW⁵ MULFORD (*David,⁴ Matthew,³ Samuel,² John¹*), b. in
East Hampton, Oct. 22, 1756; d. in Rensselaerville, N. Y., March 24, 1845,
after living there about 45 years; m. Feb. 7, 1778, to Mary, dau. of Dr. Samuel Hutchinson. She was b. Aug. 27, 1757, d. July 31, 1824. Before the

age of 20 he was 1st sergeant in Capt. Ezekiel Mulford's company 12, of 1st Suffolk Reg't, Col. Smith commanding, as appears in printed records, and was present at the battle of Long Island. In Onderdonk's Suffolk Co., pp. 28 and 9, Aug. 12, 1776, Col. S. writes his regiment was on the march. It was engaged while in the fort near Brooklyn, and the writer has heard Sergeant Mulford relate his experience as a soldier, and tell of seeing a comrade's head shot off by a British cannon ball, and of hearing Gen. Washington give orders while both were in the fort. He was in the receipt of a pension from the U. S. government for many years. Children, all born in Easthampton, except John, who was born in Rensselaerville :

    i. HANNAH, b. Oct. 28, 1778 ; m. Col. Isaac Wickham; 1799 ; d. Oct. 20, 1821, East Hampton.
    ii. JULIANA, b. 1781 ; d. 1793, East Hampton.
    iii. PHEBE, b. Jan. 12, 1784 ; m. April 9, 1810, Dea. William Hedges ; d. May 13, 1830, Lansingburgh.
7. iv. CHARLES LEWIS, b. July 1, 1786 ; m. Mille Cook, June 25, 1816 ; d. May 28, 1857, Rensselaerville.
    v. BETSEY, b. July 6, 1788 ; m. Jon. Jenkins, Jan. 1, 1809 ; d. July 4, 1875, Rensselaerville.
    vi. MARY, b. 1790 ; unmarried ; d. 1845, Rensselaerville.
    vii. JULIA H., b. Dec. 7, 1793 ; m. Col. Samuel Miller ; d. Jan. 10, 1866, East Hampton.
8. viii. SAMUEL H., b. March 18, 1796 ; m. Clarissa Griffin, Sept. 18, 1823 ; d. Dec. 1871, Holley, N. Y.
9. ix. EDWARD, b. June 9, 1799 ; m. Sarah Reed, Oct. 25, 1832 ; d. May 17, 1863, Newark, N. Y.
10. x. WILLIAM, b. June 10, 1799, twin ; m. Lucy Stewart, June 6, 1841 ; d. March 2, 1862, Cherry Valley, Ill.
    xi. JOHN H., b. April 22, 1802 ; unmarried ; d. Oct. 20, 1876, Albany.

6. JONATHAN[5] MULFORD (*David,*[4] *Matthew,*[3] *Samuel,*[2] *John*[1]) was born in Easthampton in 1770, and died there Feb. 14, 1840 ; m. Humutal Baker, 1799. Children, born in Easthampton :

    i. DAVID, b. April 16, 1800 ; d. unmarried, Nov. 14, 1876.
    ii. MARY C., b. Dec. 18, 1803 ; m. Isaac Van Scoy. No children.
    iii. JOHN H., b. April 24, 1806 ; unm. in 1879.
11. iv. SAMUEL G., b. Feb. 3, 1808 ; m. Charlotte Van Scoy, April 1, 1847.
    v. HARRY, b. Nov. 7, 1810 ; unm. in 1879.
    vi. GEORGE, b. May 18, 1813 ; m. Wid. Maryett Conkling (née Parsons).
12. vii. JEREMIAH, b. Oct. 17, 1815 ; d. May 23, 1867 ; m. Mary M. Hedges, Nov. 10, 1841.

7. CHARLES L.[6] MULFORD (*Matthew,*[5] *David,*[4] *Matthew,*[3] *Samuel,*[2] *John*[1]), b. East Hampton, N. Y., July 1, 1786 ; d. Rensselaerville, May 28, 1857 ; m. June 25, 1816, Mille (dau. Robert and Deborah Cook), who was born in Massachusetts, June 3, 1791, d. Rensselaerville, Feb. 19, 1875.

At the age of 28 he was a commissioned officer in a N. Y. State Reg't, stationed at Sackett's Harbor during the last war with England. He returned with honor to his home in Albany Co., where for many years he was a manufacturer and merchant. He was made a Justice and elected supervisor of his town for several years, always a man of sterling integrity and highly esteemed by his townsmen. Children, all born in Rensselaerville, N. Y. :

    i. MARY H., b. April 10, 1817 ; m. Andrew Palmer, Sept. 22, 1836.
    ii. ROBERT, b. Sept. 15, 1819 ; d. Feb. 3, 1821.
13. iii. ROBERT L., b. Oct. 24, 1821 ; m. first, Henrietta Lester, Dec. 14, 1846, who d. April 5, 1853 ; m. second, Ellen M. Stone (wid.) (née Morgan), June 6, 1860.

iv. Lucia H., b. May 10, 1824 ; m. George W. Rider, Sept. 10, 1856.
14. v. Charles W., b. Feb. 5, 1827 ; m. Deborah Wickes, Aug. 17, 1853.
vi. Millecent, b. Dec. 23, 1830 ; d. Oct. 29, 1834.
vii. Harriet P., b. April 24, 1834 ; unm. 1879.

8. Samuel H.[6] Mulford (*Matthew,*[5] *David,*[4] *Matthew,*[3] *Samuel,*[2] *John*[1]) was born in East Hampton, March 18, 1796 ; d. in Holley, N. Y., Dec. 1871 ; m. Sept. 18, 1823, to Clarissa Griffin. Their children are :

i. Mary E., b. Oct. 17, 1824 ; m. first, 1843, George H. Buckley ; he d. 1851. 3 children. Mar. second, 1854, Cornelius G. Palmer. 2 ch.
ii. Clarissa, b. Nov. 14, 1826 ; m. Thaddeus Sherwood, 1847. Wid. in 1852. Had 3 children, all d. unm.
iii. Samuel E., b. Dec. 19, 1830 ; m. No children, 1879.
iv. Joseph P., b. May 1, 1834 ; m. Harriet Bassett, Jan. 28, 1858. Has several boys, lives in Kendall, N. Y.
v. Harriet J., b. June 22, 1840 ; unm. 1879.

9. Edward[6] Mulford (*Matthew,*[5] *David,*[4] *Matthew,*[3] *Samuel,*[2] *John*[1]) was born in East Hampton, June 9, 1799 ; d. May 17, 1863, in Newark, N. Y. ; m. Oct. 25, 1832, Sarah Reed. Had one child :

i. Mary A., b. Sept. 19, 1833 ; m. Andrew C. Bartle, May 10, 1854 ; now of Newark, N. Y. No children in 1879.

10. William[6] Mulford (*Matthew,*[5] *David,*[4] *Matthew,*[3] *Samuel,*[2] *John*[1]) was born in East Hampton, N. Y., June 10, 1799 ; d. March 2, 1862, near Cherry Valley, Ill. Was married to Lucy Stuart, dau. of Nathan and Lydia Young Stuart, at Kingston, Ill., June 6, 1841. Their children, born in town of Guilford, Ill., are :

i. Eli H., b. June 3, 1842 ; d. in Georgia, a soldier in an Illinois Reg't, in 1863.
ii. Edward, b. March 31, 1844.
iii. John H., b. Feb. 23, 1846.
iv. William D., b. Sept. 23, 1848.
v. Charles L., b. Oct. 9, 1851.
vi. Mary Ellen, b. Sept. 4, 1853.
vii. Ida Viola, b. Sept. 15, 1856.

11. Samuel Green[6] Mulford (*Jonathan,*[5] *David,*[4] *Matthew,*[3] *Samuel,*[2] *John*[1]) and Charlotte Van Scoy, his wife, born in East Hampton, N.Y., where they now reside. Children are :

i. Amanda H., b. June 25, 1848; m. David E. Osborne, Nov. 11, 1875. Child, *Edward,*[8] b. June 1, 1877.
ii. S muel H., b. Oct. 24, 1850 ; m. Isabel Stratton, Nov. 12, 1878. Child, *Charlotte S.,*[8] b. Sept. 28, 1879.
iii. ravid G., b. May 14, 1853.
iv. John H., b. Jan. 15, 1856.

12. Jeremiah[6] Mulford (*Jonathan,*[5] *David,*[4] *Matthew,*[3] *Samuel,*[2] *John*[1]) and Mary Miller Hedges, his wife, both of East Hampton.

i. Mary Esther, b. Feb. 3, 1849 ; m. Nov. 11, 1876, Elihu Miller, of Wading River, N. Y., by whom she had *Emily M.,*[8] b. May 1, 1878.
ii. Carrie, b. Oct. 3, 1852. Lives in East Hampton, N. Y.
iii. Jeremiah, b. Oct. 18, 1854. Lives in East Hampton, N. Y.

13. Robert L.[7] Mulford (*Charles L.,*[6] *Matthew,*[5] *David,*[4] *Matthew,*[3] *Samuel,*[2] *John*[1]), b. Oct. 24, 1821. By his first wife Henrietta (dau. of Ezra and Harriett Lester) who was born Rensselaerville, N. Y., July 3, 1827, d. there April 5, 1853, had :

i.   HENRIETTA L., b. Nov. 15. 1847, in Rensselaerville, N. Y.; m. June 27, 1878, to Charles H. Fisher, of Lansingburgh, N. Y., by whom she has one son, *Robert Mulford⁹ Fisher*, b. May 4, 1879.

ii. CHARLES JOHN, b. April 18, 1852, in Rensselaerville. Not m. in 1879.

By his second wife, Ellen M. Stone, born in Old Town, Me., wid., dau. John B. and Maria I. Morgan, the following children, born in New York city :

iii. ROBERT, b. April 20, 1863.
iv.   JOHN MORGAN, b. Feb. 28, 1866 ; d. July 20, 1874.
v.   RUFUS KING, b. July 16, 1869.
vi.   MARIA, b. Oct. 7, 1872.

14. CHARLES WILLIAM⁷ MULFORD (*Charles L.,⁶ Matthew,⁵ David,⁴ Matthew,³ Samuel,² John¹*), who was b. Feb. 5, 1827 ; m. Aug. 17, 1853, Deborah Wickes, b. March 29, 1825 (dau. Dr. Platt and Fanny Wickes, of Rensselaerville, N. Y.), now residing in Hempstead, N. Y.

i.   FANNIE A., b. Sept. 20, 1855, in Nevada City, Cal.
ii.   HARRIET, b. July 20, 1859, in Rensselaerville, N. Y.
iii. HELEN, b. July 20, 1859, in Rensselaerville ; died Feb. 11, 1862, in Yonkers.

II. DESCENDANTS OF WILLIAM MULFORD.

By the Compiler.

1. WILLIAM¹ MULFORD, as before stated, was one of the first settlers of East Hampton, L. I., 1649. His name appears on the "Town Records" of South Hampton, L. I., in 1645, which town was settled a few years before East Hampton. Unlike his brother, he seems to have taken no part in the government of the colony, but appears to have turned his attention to agriculture. His name appears on the "Estimate of East Hampton," dated "September ye 8ᵗʰ," 1683. He married Sarah ——. His demise occurred in March, 1687. Issue :

2. i.   THOMAS, d. 1727–31, æt. 77 years ; m. Mary Conkling.
   ii. WILLIAM.
   iii. BENJAMIN. He was a resident of E. Hampton in 1699, but afterwards removed to Cape May, N. J., and left descendants in that state, among whom was Isaac S. Mulford, Esq., M.D., late of Camden, author of a History of New Jersey, published in 1848.
   iv. SARAH, d. April 16, 1790, æt. 95.
   v.   RACHEL.

2. THOMAS² MULFORD (*William¹*), born at East Hampton. He m. Mar·, dau. of Jeremiah and Mary (Gardiner) Conkling. It is an interesti g circumstance that the mother of Mrs. Thomas Mulford was born in the Saybrook Fort. She was the daughter of Lieut. Lyon Gardiner, its valiant commander, and patentee and first Lord of the Manor of Gardiner's Island. Mrs. Mulford was also of the third generation of the Conkling family of East Hampton, her father Jeremiah being the son of Ananias Conkling, who came from Nottinghamshire, England, to Salem, Mass., in 1637–8, and from thence to E. H. Thus the later Mulfords of this branch are descended from Lieut. Lyon Gardiner, renowned in the colonial annals of Connecticut, and from one of the children born in the Saybrook Fort. Thomas Mulford died at E. H. in 1727 or 1731, aged 77 years. In his will, dated Feb. 14, "172⁶⁄₇," he is described as a yeoman. By this instrument, rec. Liber 11 of Wills, p. 511, in the office of the Surro-

gate of the City and County of New York, he gives to his well beloved wife Mary, the use of the east end of his dwelling house and one third of all his lands and privileges situated within the bounds of East Hampton, during widowhood, and one half of all his household goods, his two Indian servants, et cetera, et cetera, to dispose of as she shall "think fitt." Mary (Conkling) Mulford died his widow, June 15, 1743, æt. 85 years. Issue :

    3. i.   THOMAS, d. March 8, 1765, æt. 77 years; first m. Mercy Bell; second wife, Deborah ——.
       ii. RACHEL.
     iii. ABIAH, m. William Hedges.
     iv. WILLIAM.
      v. EZEKIEL, m. Bea Osborn.
     vi. LAWSONS.
   vii. DAVID, bapt. Dec. 31, 1699 ; d. 1722, æt. 23 years.
  viii. JEREMIAH.* One of Jeremiah's sons, Lewis,[4] had a son Lewis,[5] who settled in Union County, New Jersey, and left descendants, among whom is Judge David Mulford, of Roselle, N. J., a Judge of the Court of Common Pleas of Union County, and a member of the New Jersey State legislature during the years 1860 and '61.

3. THOMAS[3] MULFORD (*Thomas,*[2] *William*[1]) m. first, Mercy Bell, June 19, 1712. She d. 1737, æt. 50 years. He m. second, w. Deborah ——. In his will, dated May 28, 1757, and rec. in Liber 25 of Wills, p. 89, in the office of the Surrogate of the City and County of New York, he is described as a yeoman. He died at East Hampton, March 8, 1765, æt. 77 years. Issue :

      i. ELISHA, bapt. March 1, 1713. He left descendants, among whom are the Rev. Elisha Mulford, LL.D., of the Episcopal Church, now at Montrose, Penn., a graduate of Yale, author of "The Nation :" and Sylvanus S. Mulford, Esq., M.D., now of New York city, also a graduate of Yale.
     ii. DANIEL, bapt. June 19, 1715.
  4. iii. BARNABAS, bapt. June 3, 1716.
     iv. THOMAS, bapt. Jan. 16, 1719.

4. BARNABAS[4] MULFORD (*Thomas,*[3] *Thomas,*[2] *William*[1]) returned to Connecticut and settled at Branford in that state, about 1740, where he was married to Hannah, daughter of Edward Petty, of that place, by the Rev. Jonathan Merrick, on the 30th of April, 1740. She was descended from Edward Petty, an early settler of Southold, L. I., and the progenitor of the Pettys after whom Petty's Point, which juts out from the northern shore of Long Island into the Sound near Mulford's Point by Orient, was named. Hannah Mulford died 1781. By her will, bearing date June 6, 1788, after devising lands she bequeaths gold buttons, gold beads and wearing apparel

---

* Among other children Jeremiah had a son, Capt. Ezekiel Mulford, and the compiler feels that he must diverge from the thread of this sketch to give a few facts relating to this remarkable man. He lived to the advanced age of 94 years in perfect health. His eyesight good ; reading his bible and offering family prayer to the day of his death ; and after hearing a sermon could repeat it with verbal exactness, and recite sermons and speeches to which he had listened half a century previous. His judgment was reliable and his decision prompt. In addition to his retentive memory, he was very well educated for the times. He was exceedingly fond of equestrian exercise, insomuch that at the age of 85 years he took pleasure in breaking and subduing a most vicious horse. He was captain of the 12 Co. of Col. Smith's Suffolk Co. Reg't, and while in active service on Long Island, he received directly from Gen. Washington the highest compliment, in leading a dangerous ambuscade, for his daring and fearless intrepidity. He told the father of the late William R. Mulford, of Sag Harbor (who was his son), that his grandfather (William[1]) was one of three brothers who came from England ; one going to Virginia and two settling on Long Island, and that they had been soldiers in the English civil wars in the time of Charles the first.

to her two daughters, Mary and Hannah, and gives her silver shoe buckles to her granddaughter, Lucretia Mulford. Barnabas Mulford died Nov. 1792. Issue:

    i.   EDWARD, b. Feb. 1, 1742.
    ii. DAVID, b. June 13, 1744.
5. iii. BARNABAS, b. Feb. 13, 1745 ; m. Mehitable Gorham, Nov. 10, 1771.
    iv. HANNAH, b. May 21, 1749.
    v.   JOEL, b. Dec. 17, 1754.
    vi. LUCRETIA, b. Aug. 15, 1756; d. Sept. 6, 1775.
    vii. NATHAN, b. July 25, 1759; m. Sabrina Barker, March 26, 1782.
    viii. MARY, b. Sept. 27, 1761 ; m. Thomas Rogers, Aug. 5, 1784.

5.   BARNABAS⁵ MULFORD, Jr. (*Barnabas,⁴ Thomas,³ Thomas,² William¹*) was born Feb. 13, 1745, at Branford, Conn. He was married by the Rev. Dr. Jonathan Edwards, on Sunday evening, Nov. 10, 1771, to Mehitable, dau. of Timothy and Mary (Punchard) Gorham, who was born in 1746. Mrs. Barnabas Mulford, Jr., was a descendant in the fifth generation of Capt. John Gorham, baptized at Benefield, Northamptonshire, England, January 28, 1621, who married, 1643, Desire, eldest dau. of John and Elizabeth (Tilley) Howland of the Mayflower. Elizabeth, dau. of John Tilley, was m. to John Howland, says Gov. Bradford in his History of New Plymouth, and R. Hammett Tilley, Esq., in his " Genealogy of the Tilley Family," published in 1878. But other historical writers say that John Howland married the daughter of Gov. Carver of the Mayflower. As before stated, the daughter of John and Elizabeth Howland, Desire, married Capt. John Gorham. He served as a captain in the King Philip Indian war, and died of fever on service at Swanzey, Feb. 5, 1676. His wife died Oct. 13, 1683. One of the captain's sons, Jabez, born at Barnstable, Mass., Aug. 3, 1656, m. Hannah ———.* He was wounded in the King Philip war, and was one of the early settlers of Bristol, R. I. The Plymouth Court granted 100 acres of the tract called Papasquash Neck, near Bristol, R. I., to the heirs of Captain John Gorham in recognition of his services in the Indian war. Isaac, the son of Jabez, the Bristol settler, b. Feb. 1, 1689, bought land in New Haven. He m. first, Mary ———, who d. Sept. 11, 1716, and secondly Hannah Miles, of New Haven, on the 23d of May, 1717, by whom he had, with other children, a son Timothy, who m. Mary Punchard, by whom he had Mehitable, who m. Barnabas Mulford, Jr., aforesaid. Thus the latter members of this branch of the Mulford family are descended from two of Philip's war heroes, and from two of the Mayflower pilgrims, John Howland and John Tilley or Gov. Carver. Barnabas Mulford was for many years a resident of New Haven. He was one of the signers of the agreement (signed by many N. H. residents) to pay Edward Burke the sum of £3 per month to teach the military exercise, which forms the first entry on the record book of the Second Company Governor's Foot Guards of Connecticut. This agreement is signed by Judge Pierpont Edwards and Benedict Arnold, who was the first captain of that organization. Barnabas Mulford died Aug. 19, 1827, æt. 82 years and 6 mos. Mehitable his wife died April 26, 1835, æt. 89 years 4 mos. and 1 day. The remains of both are interred in the Grove Street Cemetery, New Haven. Issue :

    i.   MARY, b. June 24, 1775 ; d. Dec. 22, 1787, æt. 12 years.
6. ii. HERVEY, b. July 7, 1777 ; d. Feb. 16, 1847 ; m. Nancy Bradley.
    iii. MEHITABLE, b. Jan. 25, 1780 ; d. Sept. 1854 ; m. Chauncey Daggette.

* Does any one know the maiden surname of Hannah ?

iv. ELIZABETH, b. April 14, 1782; d. Jan. 11, 1868; m. Benjamin
   Thompson.
v. BARNABAS, b. April 29, 1784; d. June 22, 1807, on his way home from
   W. I.; m. Elizabeth Lyman.

6. HERVEY[6] MULFORD (*Barnabas,[5] Barnabas,[4] Thomas,[3] Thomas,[2] William[1]*) graduated from Yale, taking his degree in 1794, and became a merchant, carrying on quite an extensive business in New York and New Haven. He lost heavily by seizures on the high seas by French vessels of war during the trouble between France and England, when American commerce was so seriously interfered with. The United States afterwards made a claim for losses sustained by American merchants at that time, which was admitted and duly adjusted by the French government. Nevertheless, these just claims have never been satisfied by our government. Notwithstanding the fact that the appropriation bill has twice passed both houses of Congress, all the efforts of these merchants to obtain what was justly due them have failed through the withholding of the President's signature. The first passage of this bill was largely due to the efforts of Mr. Mulford, who resided in Washington several winters for the express purpose of engineering this matter. His losses with interest amounted to, at a loose calculation, between $60,000 and $100,000. Hervey Mulford was married on Wednesday evening, March 29, 1797, by the Rev. James Dana, to Nancy, daughter of Abraham and Amy (Hemingway) Bradley, born Sept. 19, 1778. Mr. Bradley, the father of Mrs. Hervey Mulford, was a descendant of Isaac Bradley, who first settled at Branford in 1667, but removed to East Haven in 1683. Of others of his name some settled at Guilford and some in New Haven. Family tradition says the Bradleys emigrated from Bingley, in the West Riding of Yorkshire, England. Mr. Bradley was a successful merchant in New Haven, a founder of the New Haven Bank and one of its first stockholders. His wife's remains are interred in the beautiful crypt under the Centre Church at New Haven, prepared by the liberal efforts and at the expense of Thomas Rutherford Trowbridge, Jr., Esq., of that city. Mrs. Nancy (Bradley) Mulford died Aug. 19, 1841, æt. 62 years 11 mos. Her remains are interred in the Grove Street Cemetery, New Haven. Hervey Mulford was married to second wife Hannah B. Barker, wid. (Miss Mulford, his cousin), by the Rev. Leonard Bacon, D.D., on October 22, 1845, by whom he had no family. He died Feb. 16, 1847, æt. 69 years 7 mos. and 8 days. His remains are also interred in the Grove Street Cemetery by those of his first wife. Issue:

 i. AMY BRADLEY, b. Dec. 2, 1797; d. Dec. 6, 1797, æt. 4 days.
 ii. ELIZA ANN, b. Nov. 26, 1798; m. Hon. William K. Townsend, Dec.
  3, 1820.
 iii. NANCY MARIA, b. Nov. 23, 1800; d. Feb. 5, 1863; m. Charles Robinson, March 13, 1826.
7. iv. JAMES HERVEY, b. Dec. 26, 1802; m. first, Rebecca G. Atwater; second wife, Mary M. Porter, wid.
 v. JANE BRADLEY, b. June 8, 1805; d. Feb. 6, 1875; m. Charles B. Whittlesey, May 25, 1828.
8. vi. ABRAM BRADLEY, b. Nov. 3, 1806; m. Charlotte Walden, March 22,
  1844.
 vii. MEHITABLE MARY, b. Oct. 14, 1808; d. March 25, 1828, unm.
 viii. GRACE, b. March 17, 1811; d. Jan. 30, 1813, æt. 1 year 10 ms. 18 ds.
 ix. CAROLINE, b. March 15, 1813; m. Joseph Parker, Feb. 16, 1835.
 x. HARRIET, b. Feb. 22, 1816; m. Sidney M. Stone, Sept. 14, 1843.

xi. GEORGE, b. at New York, Sept. 20, 1818 ; d. June 17, 1843, æt. 24 years, unm.

xii. JULIA FORBES, b. July 13, 1822 ; d. Aug. 31, 1849, unm.

7. JAMES HERVEY[7] MULFORD (*Hervey,*[6] *Barnabas,*[5] *Barnabas,*[4] *Thomas,*[3] *Thomas,*[2] *William*[1]), born in New Haven, Dec. 26, 1802, was married March 14, 1826, by the Rev. Harry Croswell, rector of Trinity Episcopal Church, New Haven, to Rebecca Gorham, dau. of Stephen and Elizabeth (Gorham) Atwater. This lady was lineally descended from David Atwater, one of the original planters of the New Haven colony. James Hervey Mulford settled in New York city, where he became a merchant, being a member of the well-known firm of Atwater, Mulford & Co., of that city. He served as captain in 106 N. Y. Infantry Regiment. His commission bears date July 19, 1827, and is signed by Gov. De Witt Clinton. Rebecca Gorham Atwater, wife of James Hervey Mulford, died in New York, May 17, 1845, æt. 42 years 6 mos. and 20 days. Her remains were interred in the Grove Street Cemetery, New Haven. James H. Mulford was married to second wife Mary Moore Porter, wid. (Miss Cunningham), at New York, Dec. 5, 1849, by the Rev. Mr. G. T. Bedell. Issue by first wife :

9. i. HERVEY, b. May 13, 1827 ; d. April 26, 1866 : m. Fredericka S. Ironside.

ii. MARY, b. March 28, 1829 ; m. J. Henry Coghill, Esq., formerly of Virginia, author of the History of the Family of Coghill.

iii. ELIZABETH ATWATER, b. Dec. 11, 1831 ; d. Feb. 3, 1879 ; m. Charles W. Crosby.

iv. JAMES HERVEY, late of the U. S. Navy, b. April 23, 1836.

Issue by second wife :

v. EMMA S., b. Feb 27, 1851 ; d. in infancy.

vi. ELIZA PHILLIPS, b. Sept. 8, 1852 ; m. John E. Curran, Esq., counsellor-at-law.

8. ABRAM BRADLEY[7] MULFORD (*Hervey,*[6] *Barnabas,*[5] *Barnabas,*[4] *Thomas,*[3] *Thomas,*[2] *William*[1]), b. Nov. 3, 1806 ; m. Charlotte, dau. of Thomas and Esther (Franklin) Walden, on the 22d March, 1844. This lady is descended from the Walden family of New York, whose family vault may be seen in Trinity Church yard in that city, on the south side of the Church, and by her mother from the Franklin family of New York, after which Franklin Square was named, which once formed part of the Franklin estate. Abram early engaged in maritime pursuits, and has filled the position of commander in the merchant service for many years. Issue :

i. JAMES HERVEY, b. Jan. 1, 1845 ; m. Josephine May.

ii. WALDEN, b. March 7, 1847 ; d. Oct. 7, 1874, unm.

iii. DE GRASSE FOWLER, b. Aug. 9, 1849 ; unm.

iv. JOSEPH PARKER, b. May 13, 1857, unm.

9. HERVEY[8] MULFORD (*James Hervey,*[7] *Hervey,*[6] *Barnabas,*[5] *Barnabas,*[4] *Thomas,*[3] *Thomas,*[2] *William*[1]), born at New Haven, May 13, 1827 ; was married to Fredericka S., dau. of William Ironside, Esq., counsellorat-law, late of New York city, and Jane Cornelia Bissett his wife and granddaughter of George Edmund Ironside, Esq., A.M., LL.D., late of Washington, D. C., and formerly of Aberdeenshire, Scotland, June 24, 1856, by the Rev. Samuel M. Haskins, D.D., rector of St. Mark's Episcopal Church of Williamsburgh, L. I., N. Y. Hervey Mulford died April 26, 1866. Issue :

i. WILLIAM REMSEN, b. July 4, 1857 ; unm. (The writer of this sketch.)

ii. DEXTER WALKER IRONSIDE, b. Dec. 26, 1865.

NICHOLAS MUNGER OF GUILFORD (CONN.) AND HIS DESCENDANTS.

Compiled by the Hon. R. D. Smyth and communicated by Bernard C. Steiner.

1. Nicholas[1] Munger was a step-son of Henry Goldam, an early settler of Guilford, and probably came thither with his step-father. He was probably the son of Frances, the wife of Henry Goldam and had a half-sister, Susannah Goldam, who married John Bishop, Jr. of Guilford. Goldam had no other children, and by his will (Town Records, Vol. c., folio 104) dated July 9, 1661, left to Nicholas Munger, his " son in law," " all my land in the Neck, paying myself, if demanded during my life time, one barley corn by the year by way of acknowledgement, and, after my death, if my wife shall survive and shall demand the same, the sum of five bushels of whete by the year, but if she miss demanding in or at the very expiring of the year, then to be free from any payment that present year, and at the death of my foresaid wife, to be to him fully and freely and to his heirs forever." Mrs. Frances Goldham survived her husband and died on January 13, 1671. The land left Nicholas Munger was situated on the north bank of the Neck River on the public road, and he is supposed to have settled thereon as early as 1651. He married Sarah Hull on June 2, 1659, and died on October 16, 1668. His age is not known, but he was probably not beyond middle life. His widow married Dennis Crampton in 1669 and died on January 31, 1689. Munger was one of the poorer planters and seems to have been somewhat disorderly in his youth. The following letter, dated October 4, 1668, is interesting. It was copied by the writer, Dr. Bray or Bryan Rossiter, on a fly leaf of one of his medical books—" Francisci Valesii Covarrobiensis in Libros Hippocratis de Morbis

popularibus Commentaria," which book is now in the library of Trinity College, Hartford, Connecticut. "Deacon George Bartlett : I have been often sollicited to doe for Nico. Monger in his sad condition, and have oft visited him and administered in time of his distemp : since his sores breaking out and running I have seen them, used meanes to clense them and have from time to time informed them that he must have constant attendence, and be under a course of phisick if his life be saved, if meanes be not used he will live long in misery, if much meanes be used it is not for one man to beare the burden neyther is one only called to shew mercy. I have not refused to attend him, but rather desyre some other and I will be double my pportion towards the expence. Whoever attends him, it will be double the charge to attend him in the place where he is, wherever comfortable dyet must be sutable to his weaknes and distress and attendance added beyond wt his wife can doe, a society of Indians ioyne helpfullnes to one of there owne in distress, he must take a course of phisick to Divert the currant of humors if one running sore be healed, the humors will have vent at another place, and prsently will be another swelling they say he is to weake to take phisick, but tis a stronger thing to dy then to take phisick, and if he becomes tenn times weaker, yet then he must take phisick or dy. these things I write to discharge myself and let the loss of life and neglect of mercy ly at the right doore."

In addition to the land on the Neck, Nicholas Munger bought from George Hiland the homelot, containing an acre and an half bought by Hiland or Highland from Thomas Betts, " lying in the Plaine, fronting up to the street near agt Mr. Whitfields rearing back to the swamp, the lands of the sd Mr. Whitfield lying next on the South."

The children of Nicholas and Sarah (Hull) Munger were :

  2. i.   JOHN,[2] b. April 26, 1660; d. Nov. 3, 1732.
  3. ii. SAMUEL, b. 1665; d. March 5, 1717.

2. JOHN[2] MUNGER (*Nicholas[1]*), lived in Guilford, and married Mary Evarts, June 3, 1684. She died June, 1734. He was a weaver and had a list in 1716 of £130 6. 3.

His children were :

      i.   MARY[3], b. Jan. 16, 1685–6; d. young.
  4. ii.   JOHN, b. Aug. 19, 1687; d. Oct. 5, 1752.
     iii. MARY, b. Aug. 19, 1689; d. March 18, 1722; m. Joshua Leete of Guilford, June 26, 1709. He d. April 21, 1742.
     iv. ABIGAIL, b. Feb. 26, 1691; d. Oct. 23, 1760; m. Jonathan Dudley of Guilford, Aug. 6, 1712. He died Jan. 4, 1750.
  5. v.   EBENEZER, b. July 4, 1693; d. June 29, 1729.
     vi. CALEB, b. May 16, 1695 : d. young.
  6. vii. JONATHAN, b. April 14, 1697.
  7. viii. JOSIAH, b. July 20, 1704; d. Feb. 21, 1780.
     ix. RACHEL, b. 1706; imbecile.

3. SAMUEL[2] MUNGER (*Nicholas[1]*), by Andrew Leete, Assistant, married to Sarah Hand, daughter of Joseph, Oct. 11, 1688. She married 2d, Caleb Woodworth, and died August 1, 1751. Samuel Munger lived in East Guilford and had a list of £56 11. 0. in 1716. In 1696 he was permitted to build a Sabbath Day house in Guilford.

His children were :

  8. i.   SAMUEL[3], b. Feb. 7, 1690; d. May, 1728.
  9. ii.   JOSEPH, b. Jan. 19, 1693; d. ——
     iii. SARAH, b. March 16, 1694–5; m. —— Shipman.
     iv. DELIVERANCE, b. March 12, 1697; m. Richard Murough of Coventry.

v. NATHANIEL, b. Feb. 26, 1699.

10. vi. JAMES, b. May 15, 1701; d. Jan. 10, 1781.

vii. ANNE, b. Feb. 1, 1703; m. Daniel Colton of Killingworth, Oct. 18, 1727.

viii. JANE, b. Feb. 27, 1705; m. Caleb Woodworth, probably her step-brother.

4. JOHN[3] MUNGER, Jr. (*John,[2] Nicholas[1]*), of East Guilford, had a list of £47 4. 0. He married Deborah French, 1710. She died March 15, 1761.

Their children were:

i. DINAH[4], b. April 5, 1712, at Durham; m. Dea. David Dudley, Oct. 12, 1733.

ii. LUCY, b. Sept. 10, 1713, at Durham; m. Justus Hall, March 6, 1740.

iii. JOHN, b. May 15, 1715; d. single. Oct. 1, 1787.

iv. JEHIEL, b. Feb. 18, 1717; d. April 3, 1751.

v. REUBEN, b. March 10, 1719; d. young.

vi. HULDAH, b. Jan. 20, 1721; m. Moses Blachley, Jan. 16, 1744.

vii. MARY, b. May 13, 1723; m. John Allis, Feb. 3, 1742-3.

viii. WAIT, b. March 28, 1728; d. 1777. He lived in East Guilford and married Lydia Kelsey, May 21, 1752. Their children were: 1. *Lydia*, b. Nov. 8, 1753; d. July 11, 1827; m. Simeon Dudley, who died March 18, 1836, aged 84. 2. *Lyman*, b. 1755; m. Elizabeth Coe. 3. *Lucy*, b. 1760; d. single, Dec. 20, 1844. 4. *Jehiel*, b. March 24, 1763; d. single, March 31, 1841. 5. *Sarah*, b. 1766; d. Aug. 6, 1843; m. Timothy Dowd, Jr., of East Guilford, who d. May 28, 1836, aged 66.

ix. REBECCA, b. 1731; m. Ebenezer Dudley, Sept. 16, 1750.

5. EBENEZER[3] MUNGER (*John,[2] Nicholas[1]*), of East Guilford, married 1st, Anne Scranton, May 27, 1717. She died April 20, 1725. 2d, Susannah Hubbard of Haddam, July 6, 1726. After his death she married Josiah Crampton of Guilford, Feb. 14, 1733, who died Feb. 12, 1776. She lived until March 25, 1788. Ebenezer Munger's list in 1716 was £34.

By his first wife, his children were:

i. EBENEZER,[4] b. Sept. 3, 1718; d. June 20, 1793; m. Anna Lee, daughter of Jonathan, May 3, 1742. She died Aug. 22, 1788. Their children were: 1. *Anne,[5]* b. Jan. 28, 1743; d. Dec. 28, 1821; m. Caleb Dudley of Guilford, Jan. 18, 1769. He d. Sept. 14, 1802. 2. *Olive*, b. Oct. 10, 1747; d. Dec. 3, 1800; m. Samuel Dudley of Guilford, Oct. 10, 1797. He d. Dec. 17, 1819. 3. *Ebenezer*, b. June 3, 1755; d. April 10, 1834; m. Sarah Graves, daughter of Nathaniel. She d. Jan. 1839, aged 77. 4. *Jesse*, b. Aug. 20, 1757; d. 1840; lived at Bergen, N. Y., and m. Eliza Hotchkiss, daughter of David of Woodbury, who d. aged 89, Nov. 1845.

ii. CALEB, b. Sept. 24, 1722; d. Feb. 15, 1797. Lived at North Bristol (now North Madison), and was deacon in the church there; m. Sarah Stannard, Nov. 5, 1747. She d. July 6, 1817. Their children were: 1. *Sarah,[5]* b. Oct. 19, 1748; m. Miles Munger, her cousin, and d. Nov. 9, 1824. 2. *Azubah*, b. May 23, 1752; m. Benjamin Norton of Killingworth, Rutland(?) and East Bloomfield. 3. *Elias*, b. Feb. 17, 1756, moved to Rutland, Vt., about 1798. 4. *Hannah*, b. Dec. 6, 1757; m. Josiah Munger, her cousin. 5. *Eber*, b. March 10, 1762; d. May 16, 1836; m. July 11, 1791, Clorinda Backus (b. June 25, 1770), daughter of Rev. Simon of North Bristol, who d. 1854. 6. *Bela*, b. June 1, 1766; d. March 15, 1781.

iii. REUBEN, b. March 28, 1725; removed to Norfolk, Connecticut, about 1770; m. June 18, 1748, Elizabeth, daughter of Jonathan Dudley of East Guilford. Their children were: 1. *Nathaniel,[5]*

575

b. Jan. 30, 1749; removed to Norfolk 1769. 2. *Abigail*, b. Aug. 30, 1750. 3. *Reuben*, b. April 22, 1752; d. April 15, 1753. 4. *Reuben*, b. Feb. 26, 1754. 5. *Jonathan*, b. Nov. 30, 1755. 6. *Elizabeth*, b. Jan. 27, 1758. 7. *Elizur*, b. 1760. 8. *Edward*. 9. *Dudley*. 10. *Samuel*.

iv. SIMEON, b. March 28, 1725; d. May 11, 1725.

The only child of Ebenezer and Susannah (Hubbard) Munger was:

v. SIMEON, b. April 6, 1727; d. March 16, 1815; lived in East Guilford; m. Sarah, daughter of Josiah Scranton, July 3, 1751. She d. Dec. 15, 1815, aged 83. Their children were: 1. *Simeon*,[5] b. Dec. 7, 1752; d. Oct. 1833. He was a goldsmith, and lived in Redding, Connecticut; m. Lois Lyon there. 2. *Capt. Josiah*, b. Oct. 16, 1754; d. Aug. 1838; m. 1st, Anne Lee, daughter of Jonathan, March 22, 1780. She d. Nov. 8, 1799, aged 43; 2d, Hannah Coe, who d. June 14, 1837. 3. *Mary*, b. Nov. 3, 1756; d. June, 1840; m. 1st, Andrew Leete Stone of East Guilford, Jan. 4, 1781. He d. Feb. 8, 1785. 2d, Samuel Hoyt of East Guilford, who d. Oct. 5, 1826. 4 *Wyllys*, b. Feb. 9, 1761; d. Jan. 31, 1835; m. Jan. 19, 1785, Hester Hand, daughter of Daniel, who died March 12, 1846, 'aged 85. 5. *Mabel*, b. Dec. 17, 1762; d. Nov. 19, 1833; m. Timothy Graves of East Guilford, May 20, 1785. He d. Jan. 6, 1849, aged 90.

6. JONATHAN[3] MUNGER (*John*,[2] *Nicholas*[1]), lived in Woodbury, Connecticut, and married 1st, Sarah Graves, Jan. 4, 1721, who died Dec. 31, 1725; 2d, Aggephe Lewis, July 10, 1728. She died Feb. 18, 1757.

By his first wife, his children were:

i. JONATHAN,[4] b. Jan. 19, 1722; m. Lois Morse, Oct. 5, 1748, and had *Elihu L.*, of Litchfield.
ii. SARAH, b. Oct. 14, 1723; m. Joseph Wilcox, Sept. 17, 1754.
iii. DANIEL, b. Aug. 26, 1725.

The children of Jonathan and Aggephe (Lewis) Munger were:

iv. BENJAMIN, b. July 2, 1731.
v. CHLOE, b. Dec. 12, 1732; d. young.
vi. CHLOE, b. June 2, 1734; m. Giles Kilbourne of Litchfield, a famous church builder, and d. Oct. 10, 1824. He d. Sept. 13, 1797.
vii. JOEL, b. Dec. 19, 1735.

7. JOSIAH[3] MUNGER (*John*,[2] *Nicholas*[1]), of East Guilford, married Elizabeth Hubbard of Haddam, July 24, 1727. She died March 16, 1778. Their children were:

i. ELIZABETH,[4] b. Nov. 1, 1728; d. Oct. 19, 1736.
ii. JOSIAH, b. March 8, 1732; d. Sept. 1, 1752.
iii. TIMOTHY, b. Sept. 5, 1735; removed to New Durham, N. Y., in 1785; m. 1st, Mabel Stevens, Nov. 20, 1757; 2d, Rebecca Evarts, Aug. 28, 1765; 3d, Lorain Murray. By his first wife he had: 1. *Timothy*,[5] b. Oct. 20, 1758. 2. *Josiah*, b. Oct. 2, 1760; d. Dec. 27, 1822; lived at North Bristol, and m. Dec. 9, 1785, his cousin, Hannah Munger. 3. *Linus*, b. Oct. 30, 1763; m. 1st, Elizabeth Field, who d. April 29, 1792; 2d, Julia ———; lived at Claremont, N. H. By his first wife he had no children. The children of Timothy and Rebecca (Evarts) Munger were: 4. *Rebecca*, b. Dec. 19, 1765. 5. *Mabel*, b. July 9, 1769; d. Aug. 25, 1771. 6. *Titus*, b. Jan. 4, 1772; d. Aug. 25, 1772(?).
iv. MILES,[4] b. May 31, 1739; d. Nov. 13, 1826; m. his cousin, Sarah Munger, and lived in North Bristol. Their children were: 1. *Chauncy*, b. Aug. 16, 1768; d. Dec. 3, 1820; m. Jerusha, daughter of Asa Dowd, who d. aged 63, in Feb., 1835, and lived in North Bristol. 2. *Joel*, b. Sept. 23, 1772; d. Sept. 15, 1838;

m. Mary Blachley, daughter of Joshua, Jan. 3, 1798. She d.
June 17, 1838, aged 63. They lived in North Bristol (now
North Madison). 3. *Chloe,* b. July 21, 1777; lived in Guilford
and d. single. July 21, 1842. 4. *Miles,* b. Feb. 12, 1781; d. Feb.
25, 1858; m. Rachel, daughter of John Grumley, June 26, 1803.
She d. April 6, 1862. They lived in Guilford.

8. SAMUEL³ MUNGER, Jr. (*Samuel,² Nicholas¹*), lived in Guilford until
1726, when he removed to Brimfield, Mass. He married Dorothy,
daughter of James Evarts, April 6, 1710.

Their children were:

   i.   SUBRINT,⁴ b. Jan. 5, 1711.
   ii. SAMUEL, b. Oct. 5, 1712.
   iii. ELNATHAN, b. July 24, 1714.

9. JOSEPH³ MUNGER (*Samuel,² Nicholas¹*), was a shoemaker, and had a
list of £35 in 1716. He lived in Guilford and married 1st, ———
Ingham ; 2d, Miriam Pond, Oct. 6, 1726.

By his first wife he had :

   i.   SAMUEL,⁴ b. ———

The children of Joseph and Miriam (Pond) Munger were :

   ii. BILLY, b. July 18, 1727.
   iii. INCREASE.
   iv. ABNER.
   v.   PHILIP.

10. JAMES³ MUNGER (*Samuel² Nicholas¹*), of East Guilford, married 1st,
Susannah Peyer, Dec. 18, 1723 ; 2d, Hannah.

Of which wife his children were born is uncertain. They were:

   i.   SYBILL,⁴ b. Aug. 2, 1725; m. Nathan Dudley, Jan. 7, 1748.
   ii. SARAH, b. Feb. 10, 1729; m. Joseph Wilcox, Sept. 17, 1754.
   iii. JAMES, b. Feb. 18, 1732; lived in Bergen, N. Y.; m. Irene Hill,
        daughter of Dea. Timothy. Their children were: 1. *Albert.*⁵
        2. *Emeline.* 3. *Irene,* who d. of scarlet fever.
   iv. LEVI, b. July 24, 1736.
   v.   TIMOTHY, b. Aug. 9, 1739.
   vi. SUSANNAH, b. Nov. 24, 1741; d. July 18, 1763; m. Scloh Murray of
        East Guilford, who d. aged 81, April 14, 1820.

WILLIAM MUNROE OF LEXINGTON, MASS., AND DESCENDANTS

Compiled by the late LEE MONROE of Topeka, Kansas

1. WILLIAM¹ MUNROE, a Scotchman, brought to America as a
prisoner of war, reached Cambridge Farms, now Lexington, Mass.,
in 1652 and remained there until his death in 1717. According to
Alexander Mackenzie's comprehensive "History of the Munros",
published in Inverness in 1898, he was a lineal descendant from Donald, founder of the clan Munro, who is said to have come, with his
adherents, from Ireland to Scotland in the year 1025 to assist King
Malcolm in his war with the Danes. His lineage is traced, not only
by Mackenzie but also in "The Munroe Genealogy" by John G.
Locke, "The Munro Clan" by James Phinney Munroe, "The
Genealogy of Josiah Munro" by Rev. G. S. Northrup and Hudson's

"History of Lexington" (first edition) from the above Donald Munro through eleven chiefs of the clan, ten of whom were Barons of Foulis and five succeeding generations of Scottish ancestry down to his birth in Aldie, Scotland, in 1625. His father, Robert Munro, was a great-great-great-grandson of Sir George Munro, tenth Baron of Foulis.

The Battle of Worcester was fought by the adherents of King Charles II, against the forces of Cromwell, in which the latter were victorious, in September 1651. William and three other Munros, Robert, Hugh and John, were shipped from London to America in the *John and Sarah* 1 Nov. 1651. Upon his arrival he was bound out to a farmer in Cambridge Farms for whom he was required to work until he earned and repaid the cost of his passage. It is said of him and his family life in Hudson's "History of Lexington" (first edition), published in 1868, page 147:

"William Munroe, the ancestor of all the Munroes of Lexington and this vicinity, was born in Scotland in 1625 and descended from the Munro Clan in Scotland of which we have already spoken. He came to America in 1652 and consequently was at that time twenty-seven years of age. . . . He settled at the Cambridge Farms about 1660 in the northeasternly part of the town bordering on Woburn. Several of his sons lived with or not far from him at first and it was said by Mrs. Sanderson, his great-granddaughter who died in 1853, aged 104 years, that his old house looked like a rope walk, so many additions had been made to it to accommodate his sons as they settled in life. By adopting the custom of the Scottish clans, he, in a manner, confined the Munroes together, and made them for some time, as it were, a distinct people. . . . Though he came to the country under unfavorable circumstances, and set up for himself rather late in life, he appears to have been quite successful in his worldly affairs, and to have been blessed with a large, prosperous family. . . . He was made freeman in 1690 and the subsequent tax bills from 1693 to 1698 show that in taxable property he was among the first half dozen men of the parish thus showing conclusively he was a man of enterprise and force of character."

William Munroe married first MARTHA GEORGE; secondly MARY BALL; and thirdly ELIZABETH JOHNSON.

According to a booklet entitled "Lexington Epitaphs", published by the Lexington Historical Society, his tombstone and that of his second wife bear these inscriptions: "William Munro Died Jan. 27, 1717–18 Aet. about 92 yrs." "Mary Munro, Wife William Munro Aet. 41 yrs. d Aug. 1692."

He is first noticed in the Lexington records as "William Row" by which surname some of his descendants were subsequently known in Connecticut. While he is generally designated "Munroe" the surname of his descendants appears on the records in Connecticut, New York and elsewhere variously spelled "Munrow", "Monrow", "Mon Row", "Row", "Munroe", "Munro", "Monro" and "Monroe" with no apparent reason for the difference. Since the latter spelling is most commonly used it will be followed generally throughout this sketch.

All of his children were born in Lexington. All of them, except his son David, remained and died there. They are noticed at length in each of the above-mentioned works by Mackenzie, Locke, Northrup and James Phinney Munroe, also in Cutler's "Genealogical and Family History of Connecticut", therefore they will be referred to but briefly here.

Children by first wife, born in Lexington:

    i.   JOHN,[2] b. 10 March 1666; d. 14 Sept. 1753.
   ii.   MARTHA, b. 2 Nov. 1667; d. 27 March 1730.
  iii.   WILLIAM, b. 10 Oct. 1669; d. 2 Jan. 1759.
  iv.   GEORGE, b. about 1671; d. 17 Jan. 1749.

Children by second wife, born in Lexington:

    v.   DANIEL, b. 12 Aug. 1673; d. 26 Feb. 1734.
   vi.   HANNAH, m. 21 Dec. 1692 ———.
  vii.   ELIZABETH, m. about 1690 ———.
 viii.   MARY, b. 24 June 1678.
2. ix.   DAVID, b. 6 Oct. 1680.
    x.   ELEANOR, b. 22 Feb. 1683.
   xi.   SARAH, b. 18 March 1685.
  xii.   JOSEPH, b. 16 Aug. 1687; d. in 1787.
 xiii.   BENJAMIN, b. 16 Aug. 1690; d. 6 April 1765.

2. DAVID[2] MUNROE (*William[1]*), born in Cambridge Farms, now Lexington, Mass., 6 Oct. 1680 and baptized there in 1699, died in Canterbury, Windham Co., Conn., 19 June 1755. He married DEBORAH HOW, born 19 Oct. 1685, died in Canterbury 1 Sept. 1748, daughter of Samuel and Mary (Nutting) How of Concord, Mass.

The Lexington records mention only the birth of David Munroe, but Connecticut was then being settled by emigrants from the colonies of Plymouth and Massachusetts Bay, and in April 1705 he and his wife are found in Canterbury, when their first child was born.

The town of Canterbury contained but ten families when it was endowed with town privileges in 1703. In 1714 Samuel Adams and Obadiah Johnson conveyed a farm of 136 acres to David Monroe, by deed recorded in Canterbury. In 1722 David and Deborah joined the church in Canterbury. In 1723 a division of common lands was made among those residents of Canterbury "who were settled inhabitants and paid to ye building of ye meeting house and minister's home", which were completed in 1711. In this allotment David received one and one-half shares. In 1743 a controversy arose among the members of the Canterbury church over a sermon by its minister which did not meet the views of many of them. A committee recommended the minister's dismissal. David and five others made written protest against the committee's report, severely criticising its motives. The committee retaliated by recommending that David and his associates be expelled from the church. The matter was finally settled by the dismissal of the minister, with David and the other protestants remaining in the church.

The identity of David Munroe of Canterbury as the son of William Munroe of Cambridge Farms was questioned by one writer upon the ground that not being mentioned in William's will it indicated that David probably died young. Later, however, Rev. Mr. Northrup and Dr. Will S. Monroe, author and prominent educator, for many years professor of psychology in the Montclair, N. J., State Normal School, in their preparation of the "Genealogy of Josiah Munroe", after much careful research became convinced, and so stated in their publication, that David of Canterbury was, without doubt, the son of William of Cambridge Farms. Their conclusions were based upon the following, among other circumstances: David, appearing as he did, among the early settlers of Canterbury, must have emigrated there from some other place, but the records of emigrants to New England prior to that time and the published vital statistics of Massachusetts, Rhode Island and Connecticut, disclosed no one bearing that name who could have been identified with him other than William's son David; between the time of his baptism in Lexington in 1699 and the birth of his first child in Canterbury in 1705, he was of the age when one might expect him to marry and establish a home in a new community; also, there was a family tradition that he came from Cambridge; his grandson, John Munroe, who lived and died in Canterbury, left a written family record which passed to John's granddaughter, Mary Munroe Collins, who retained it until it was destroyed by a fire which burned the Collins home in 1890, but she well remembered its contents which told of the coming of William from Scotland to Massachusetts and the settlement of his son, David, in Canterbury, all of which she related to Doctor Monroe when he visited Canterbury in 1912 collecting material for their work. Moreover, it appeared that four of David's seven daughters, viz., Mary, Eleanor, Elizabeth and Sarah bore the given names of four of his sisters; and of his four sons, one, William, bore the name of his grandfather and his uncle. It would be quite unreasonable to presume that such a coincidence of names would occur except in immediately related families. In addition to all this Mrs. Collins told Doctor Monroe and after her death her son informed the writer of this sketch that his mother had told him that David Monroe's wife came from Concord. A search of the published vital statistics of that place disclosed only one woman named Deborah, born there of marriageable age for David, viz., Deborah How, daughter of Samuel and Mary How. Upon further search it was found that Samuel How had joined the tide of emigration to Connecticut. According to the "Howe Genealogies" published by the New England

Historic Genealogical Society he resided in Concord until shortly after 1700 when he moved to Plainfield, a new town in Windham County, Conn. It is also there stated that his daughter Deborah married David Munroe and the Probate Records of Plainfield, where he died, show that David Munroe in 1725 receipted for his wife's share of Samuel How's estate. The same records show the distribution of the estate of Mary How who died in 1727 and refer to Deborah Munroe as her daughter.

If David Munroe had died in Lexington, his death would probably have been recorded in the vital statistics of that town and his remains would have rested in the family burying ground with a tombstone marking his grave as do those of his father and mother. The absence of these is further corroborative proof of the correctness of Rev. Mr. Northrup's conclusion as to the identity of David Monroe of Canterbury as William's son of that name. In 1913 the Lexington Historical Society published a revised edition of Hudson's "History of Lexington" in which David Munroe was shown as a son of William. The correction relating to him, appearing in Vol. II, after the index at page 6 of Additions and Corrections, reads as follows: "Before Joseph No. 6 on p. 461 insert: 'David² Munroe (see G. S. Northrup's "Genealogy of Josiah Munroe", 1912), David² Munroe (William¹) b. Oct. 6, 1680; d. June 19, 1755. He moved to Canterbury, Conn. and bought land Feb. 22, 1715. In 1723, received 1½ shares of land, as one who paid towards the meeting house and ministers' house, which were completed in 1711. His will was probated Sept. 8, 1755.'"

Children, born in Canterbury:

i. DEBORAH,³ b. 22 April 1705; d. 16 Sept. 1705.
ii. MARY, b. 9 Jan. 1707; d. 6 Oct. 1795; m. 23 March 1733 BENAJAH DEANS, who d. in July 1762.
iii. DAVID, b. 23 Dec. 1708; d. 15 July 1762; m. 20 May 1733 MARY VALLET.
iv. ABIGAIL, b. 10 Jan. 1711; d. 17 Sept. 1784; m. SOLOMON ADAMS.
v. DEBORAH, b. 12 Jan. 1713.
vi. ELEANOR, b. 27 Sept. 1715.
vii. ELIZABETH, b. 25 May 1718; m. 6 Jan. 1737 STEPHEN GATES.
3. viii. SAMUEL, b. 9 Sept. 1720.
ix. SARAH, b. 24 July 1723; m. 23 Feb. 1743 JEDEDIAH ASHCROFT.
x. WILLIAM, b. 5 Jan. 1726; d. 6 Nov. 1760.
xi. JOSIAH, b. 11 Sept. 1728. He was a Revolutionary soldier and a complete history of him and his descendants is contained in Rev. G. S. Northrup's "The Genealogy of Josiah Munro".

3. SAMUEL³ MONROE (*David,*² *William*¹), of Canterbury and Willington, Conn., born in Canterbury 9 Sept. 1720 and baptized there 1 April 1721, died 15 Jan. 1777, while serving with Connecticut troops in the Revolutionary War. He married ABIGAIL READ, born 29 April 1723, died in Chenango County, N. Y., 4 June 1817, in her 95th year (gravestone), daughter of Isaac and Abigail (Leonard) Read of Norwich, Conn.

Abigail (Read) Monroe was admitted to the First Church of Christ of Canterbury in May 1745, upon letter of recommendation and later was admitted to the church at Willington, upon letter from the church at Canterbury.

Samuel Monroe served in the French and Indian War in the company commanded by Capt. Jedediah Fay of Ashford, Conn., from 10 April to 3 Sept. 1758, and in the campaign of 1759 under Captain Slap of Mansfield, Conn. In the Revolutionary War he served in the Fourth Company, Eighth Regiment of Connecticut Volunteers, from 8 July to 30 Nov. 1775 and re-enlisted 14 May 1776 for one year in Capt. Oziah Pettibone's company of Colonel Ward's regiment. He died in the service 15 Jan. 1777, as shown by a certificate filed in the Archives in the Connecticut State Library as follows:

"This may certify all whom it may concern that Samll Munrow was in the Continental service the last campaign and in Capt. Oziah Pettibones company in Col. Andrew Wards Regt., was going into the Jersies about three miles over the North River from Kings Ferry, was taken sick and died, the 15th day of January, and there being no officer nor soldiers left with him, nor none of same Regt. within sixty miles of him when he died, his gun and cartouch box, blankets and cloths were left viz: [here follows a list of his clothing and accoutrements with appraised value] Windsor, November 29th, 1777 The above clothing we the subscribers were knowing to the sd Munrow having and were left at the above place. Witness our hands George Griswold 1st Lieut"

His widow, Abigail Munroe, was appointed administratrix of his estate in August 1777. She filed a claim for the above clothing and accoutrements which is also on file in the above archives and bears the following endorsement:

"Alld Wid Abig Munro £12–11–6 March 7, 1778 Loss Ward's Regt"

Afterwards she and her sons Isaac, Leonard and William moved to Chenango County, N. Y., where she died and was buried beside her son William. The headstone marking her grave bears this inscription: "In memory of Widow Abigail Monroe, died June 4, 1817 in the 95 year of her age"

Children:

4. i. ISAAC,[4] b. in 1745.
   ii. DEBORAH, b. in Canterbury 5 Nov. 1747; d. in Delaware County, Ohio, in June 1828; m. in Canterbury, in 1764, JOHN WELCH, who d. in Delaware County in May 1831, son of David Welch. They moved from Connecticut to Chenango County, and afterwards, in 1804, to Delaware County.
   Children (surname *Welch*):
   1. *John*, b. 17 March 1765.
   2. *Bildad*, b. 10 March 1767; d. 28 March 1767.
   3. *Eleanor*, b. 24 Feb. 1768; m. Caleb Plumb.
   4. *Bildad*, b. 3 March 1771; d. 23 Sept. 1825; m. in Chenango County, 25 Aug. 1794, Lucy Aspinwall.
   5. *Samuel Monroe*, b. 26 March 1772.
   6. *Deborah*, b. 19 May 1774; d. 31 July 1776.
   7. *David*, b. 20 June 1776; m. (1) Keziah ———; m. (2) Sabra Sheet; m. (3) in August 1843 Sarah Elliott.

8. *Abijah*, b. 7 July 1778; d. in Delaware County about 1806.
9. *Abizah*, b. 1 Sept. 1780.
10. *Isaac*, b. 12 July 1785; d. in 1803.
5. iii. LEONARD, b. 11 Oct. 1757.
6. iv. WILLIAM, b. 16 May 1761.
v. AMMITTY (or AMITTAI), b. in Willington in September 1763 and bapt. there.

4. ISAAC⁴ MONROE (*Samuel*,³ *David*,¹ *William*¹), born in Connecticut in 1745, died at the home of his son, Dan Monroe, in Plymouth, N. Y., 1 Aug. 1825. He married in Pomfret, Conn., 25 July 1768, SARAH FASSETT, daughter of John and Lydia (Warren) Fassett. Through her mother Sarah (Fassett) Monroe was a descendant of the pioneer families of Bushnell and Leffingwell.

Isaac Monroe was residing in Pomfret from 1768 until after 1785, in Brooklyn, in 1800 and in Greene, Chenango Co., N. Y., in 1818.

He was a soldier in the Revolutionary War, first in 1775. When the Lexington Alarm sounded he responded and served with the militia near Boston for twenty days, afterwards he enlisted in Pomfret, 1 Jan. 1776, and served one year in Capt. Grosvenor's company of Col. John Durkee's regiment.

In May 1798 he purchased a fulling mill in Lebanon, Conn., from his son Dan and sold it to James Sexton the following year by deed witnessed by his son Dan and daughter Lucy.

In 1818 he applied for a pension which was granted in 1820. His application was supported by affidavit of his brother William and his comrade in arms, Jonathan Crane. His own affidavit, sworn to in June 1820, states that he was a saddler by trade, with no family, unable to labor, in indigent circumstances and residing with and supported by his son Joseph in Greene.

His name appears on the records in Pomfret and Brooklyn and on the index to the deed records in Lebanon as Isaac Row. In the body of the Lebanon deeds his surname is spelled Mon Row and Munrow. The latter spelling of his surname appears in his signature, also in that of his son Dan and daughter Lucy, witnessing the deed to James Sexton. Notwithstanding these discrepancies in the spelling of his surname upon the records, his identity is amply proven by the above-mentioned affidavit of William Monroe, stating that he and Isaac were brothers, also by existing family records, among which are his son Joseph's family Bible in the possession of E. L. Monroe in Columbus, Pa., stating that Joseph was born 25 Sept. 1776 and separate family records prepared by each of his grandsons, Dyar Monroe and James Sexton Monroe, the former now in the possession of Dyar's granddaughter, Mrs. Estella Hughes in Plymouth, N. Y., the latter with James Sexton's daughter, Mrs. Ella M. Axline of Ada, Ohio, until her death in 1930. Each of these two records state that their father, Dan, son of Isaac Monroe, was born in Pomfret 22 Aug. 1774. These dates exactly correspond with the dates shown by the Pomfret records when sons named Joseph and Dan were born to Isaac Row.

Children, born in Pomfret:

    i.   DYAR,⁵ b. 29 May 1769.
   ii.   ANNIS, b. 18 Aug. 1770; m. in Pomfret, 22 May 1794, JAMES JANES.
          Child (surname *Janes*):
            1. *Betsy*, b. 10 May 1796.
  iii. ELIJAH, b. 20 Feb. 1773; d. in Rockdale Township, Crawford Co., Pa.; m. LOIS SMITH.
          After 1800 he moved to Chenango County, N. Y., and about 1820, with his brother Joseph, he moved to what is now Freehold Township, Warren Co., Pa., where he remained until 1839. Then he moved to Rockdale Township.
          Children:
            1. *Charles*,⁶ d. in Rockdale Township.
            2. *A daughter*, m. ——— Hubbell.
            3. *Martha*, m. James Austin of Columbus, Pa. Five children.
7. iv. DAN, b. 22 Aug. 1774.
8. v. JOSEPH, b. 25 Sept. 1776.
9. vi. SAMUEL, b. 20 Aug. 1781.
  vii. LUCY, b. 4 July 1784; m. ISAAC RATHBONE, b. 11 July 1781, son of Valentine Rathbone, Jr., of Pittsfield, Mass.
          Children (surname *Rathbone*):
            1. *Daniel*, b. 26 Sept. 1807; m. Hannah Scanman.
            2. *Permelia*, b. 9 Nov. 1810; m. in 1832 J. S. Hodges.
            3. *Rufus*, b. 28 Sept. 1812; m. 29 April 1837 Eleanor Robbins.
            4. *Lucy*, b. 1 Nov. 1814; d. 1 July 1862; m. in August 1835 William Norton.
            5. *Thomas T.*, b. 3 Oct. 1817; m. Hannah E. Davis.
            6. *James J.*, b. 10 June 1819; m. ——— Tiffany.
            7. *Louisa*, b. 22 May 1821; m. Burdiah Bailey.
            8. *Content*, d. in infancy.
            9. *Leguester*, b. 2 July 1824; m. ——— Sheldon.
          10. *Martha M.*, b. 24 Dec. 1826; d. in Adrian, Mich., 12 April 1894; m. in 1849 Aziah Hall.

5. LEONARD⁴ MONROE (*Samuel*,³ *David*,² *William*¹), born in Willington, Conn., 11 Oct. 1757 and baptized there in 1764, died in Delaware County, Ohio, 3 Aug. 1827. He married first, in Pittsfield, Mass., ELIZABETH PECK, daughter of Israel and Sarah (Marsh) Peck. He is reported to have married three times after the death of his first wife. He appears to have been a widower in November 1807 when he conveyed land by deed recorded in Book 1, page 556, Delaware County Deed Records, containing no mention of a wife, while deeds subsequently made by him in 1814 and 1815 recorded in Book 3, pages 185 and 512 were signed by his wife Hannah Monroe.

Leonard Monroe enlisted as a private in Captain Ball's company, Col. Samuel B. Webb's Fourth Connecticut Regiment in East Windsor, Conn., 14 March 1777, was later transferred to Captain Whitney's company, same regiment, where he was appointed sergeant. He remained in the service until honorably discharged in Morristown, N. J., 17 March 1780.

Later he, his mother and his brothers Isaac and William, his uncle David Welch and David's sons, John, Aaron and Ebenezer Welch moved to Chenango County, N. Y. While there Leonard Monroe was commissioned lieutenant in the State Militia in 1793, and captain in 1798. He was placed on the Revolutionary soldiers' pension roll 21 June 1819. His application states that he was a tailor by trade.

In 1804 he and John, Aaron and Ebenezer Welch moved to Liberty Township, then in Franklin, now in Delaware County, Ohio. The Monroe and Welch families were closely related by marriage. David Welch married Ammitty Read, sister of Samuel Monroe's wife Abigail. John Welch married his cousin, Deborah Monroe, sister of Leonard.

Children:

    i.   DEBORAH,[5] m. 31 July 1806 CHARLES CLARK of Ashford, Conn., Norwich, N. Y., and Delaware County, Ohio, son of Israel Clark.
        Children (surname *Clark*):
        1. *Nancy*, m. Marquis L. Plum.
        2. *Alsunores.*
        3. *Mary*, m. Jacob Zimmerman.
        4. *Clarissa*, m. ——— Jackson.
        5. *Charles*, went to California during the early gold excitement and settled in that State.
        6. *Hannah*, m. Carroll Hoddy. Moved to Decatur, Ill.
        7. *James Riley*, m. Elizabeth Free. Moved to Decatur, Ill. A son Riley, b. in Decatur.
        8. *Eliza*, b. in Delaware County in May 1825; d. in 1853; m. 21 Feb. 1843 Charles Henry Boardman, son of Jeremiah Boardman and his first wife.
10. ii.   LEMUEL FRANKLIN, b. 18 May 1790.
11. iii. SAMUEL.
12. iv. ALONZO, b. about 1795.
    v.   ISAAC, of whom little has been learned except that in August 1819 he conveyed land in Delaware County to his father by deed in which no mention is made of a wife. By deed dated 20 Dec. 1823 he and his wife Sarah conveyed land in the same county to Henry Jackson, stating their residence as Washington County, Pa. Under date of 16 April 1824 he entered into a contract with Leonard Monroe, L. F. Monroe, Isaac Welch and others to teach a district school in a schoolhouse near Leonard Monroe's home, stating his residence as Delaware County. He is named executor in the will of his brother Samuel which was admitted to probate in Delaware County 21 March 1843.
    i.   ELSIE, m. ELIAS SCRIBNER.
        Children (surname *Scribner*):
        1. *Leonard* (twin), b. 23 April 1832.
        2. *Samuel Rayno* (twin), b. 23 April 1832; d. at the Soldiers' Home in Kansas 24 Dec. 1894; m. (1) Edith B. Lake; m. (2) ———.
          He enlisted 12 Aug. 1861 in Co. F, Seventh Kansas Cavalry; re-enlisted 1 Jan. 1864; honorably discharged 29 Sept. 1865. He resided in Pine Island, Minn., for some time after the war.
        3. *Hannah*, m. as his second wife Charles Henry Boardman.
        4. *A child*, d. young.

6. WILLIAM[4] MONROE (*Samuel,[3] David,[2] William[1]*), born in Willington, Conn., 16 May 1761 and baptized there in July following, died in Plymouth, N. Y., 30 April 1838. He married first, 5 July 1781, SALLY BARNEY, b. in Swansea, Mass., 9 Sept. 1765, died 19 Feb. 1811, in 46th year, daughter of Benjamin and Hannah (Hix) Barney. Through her mother she was descended from John and Eleanor Billington of the *Mayflower* Party. Her tombstone in the family cemetery in Chenango County, N. Y., bears this inscription: "In memory of Mrs. Sally Monroe, consort of Col. William Monroe, died 19 Feb. 1811 in the 46th year of her age." William Monroe married secondly, REBECCA (FOSTER) PRENTICE, daughter of Rev. Dan Foster.

He served nearly four years as a soldier in the Revolutionary War, first from 6 April to 23 May 1777 under Capt. Edward Griswold in Col. Thomas Bilding's regiment, Connecticut Volunteers, when he was discharged in Peekskill, N. Y. He next enlisted for three years in Captain Harmon's company of Col. John Durkee's Fourth Regiment of Connecticut Volunteers from which service he was honorably discharged in 1780 in Morristown, N. J. During his first year he served as a private, then was transferred to Capt. Seth Phillips' company of the same regiment, in which he served as a fifer for two years. He engaged in the battles of Germantown, Fort Mifflin, Monmouth and Stony Point. After his discharge in 1780 he served for six months as orderly sergeant to his old Colonel John Durkee. Later he served a three months' term on a sloop in New York. His interest in military affairs did not abate with the Revolution.

He subsequently moved in 1792 from Windsor, Conn., to Chenango County, N. Y., and settled on the tract on which the court house in the city of Norwich now stands. He there joined the State Militia, serving as ensign, lieutenant, major and lieutenant colonel between 1797 and 1809. By reason of this service he became generally known as Colonel Monroe.

Later William Monroe moved to a farm in the nearby town of Plymouth, N. Y., where he built a log house and lived until he died. He, his mother and other members of the Monroe family were buried in a cemetery on his farm between Norwich and the village of Plymouth.

He served three terms as sheriff of Chenango County and as the member of the Assembly from that county during the session of 1816.

Children by first wife, all except the second Clarissa, born in Connecticut:

    i.   HANNAH,[5] b. 11 Feb. 1782; d. in Warren County, Pa., 6 May 1864; m. her cousin, JOSEPH MONROE.
    ii. ELIZABETH, b. 1 Oct. 1783; d. in Plymouth 2 April 1799.
13. iii. BENJAMIN BARNEY, b. 9 Jan. 1786.

14. iv. WILLIAM WHEATON, b. 2 May 1788.
   v. CLARISSA, b. 24 Feb. 1791; d. 24 Feb. 1792.
   vi. CLARISSA, b. in Norwich, N. Y., 5 May 1793; d. 21 April 1794.

Children by second wife, born in Plymouth:

   vii. SALLY, b. 10 Aug. 1812; d. in Plymouth in March 1882; m. in 1830 DUDLEY WILLIAMS, son of Ben Adam Williams.
Children (surname *Williams*), b. in Chenango County:
1. *Charles L.*, b. 30 June 1831; d. 21 Nov. 1916; m. (1) Jennie Allen, daughter of David and Sarah (Gibson) Allen; m. (2) Catherine A. O'Hearn, daughter of William O'Hearn.
Charles Williams served three years in the 114th Regiment of New York Volunteers during the Civil War. He was postmaster in Greene, N. Y., and a member of the Masonic Lodge.
2. *Lucy Anna*, b. 27 June 1833; d. in 1901; m. Samual H. Burgess.
3. *Cyrus*, b. 16 March 1835: d. unm. 6 Aug. 1856.
4. *Adelaide B.*, b. 26 Oct. 1839; d. in Plymouth 18 Oct. 1898; m. James Stewart, son of Marvin Stewart.
5. *William H.*, b. 8 April 1842; killed at the second Battle of Bull Run. Unmarried. He enlisted in Co. H, 77th Regiment, New York Volunteers.
6. *Emily S.*, b. 31 July 1845; d. in 1924; m. Augustine E. Townsend, son of William J. and Ann Townsend.
7. *Orin P.*, b. 23 Aug. 1847; d. 16 Sept. 1848.
8. *Ellen May*, b. 21 July 1850; d. 31 Oct. 1927; m. in July 1869 Wallace D. Powell, son of Isaac and Eliza (Baker) Powell.
9. *Eva F.*, b. 9 March 1854; d. 1 Jan. 1922; m. Rufus Dodge, son of Daniel Dodge.
15. viii. PUBLIUS VIRGILIUS BOGUE, b. 16 April 1814.
   ix. EMILY, b. 22 Jan. 1817; d. in Owosso, Mich., 6 Feb. 1909; m. in Plymouth, 4 Sept. 1842, DWIGHT DIMMICK, son of Joseph and May (Green) Dimmick.
Children (surname *Dimmick*):
1. *Guerdon Lewis*, b. in New Haven Township, Shiwassee Co., Mich., 25 Feb. 1844; d. in Owosso 10 Aug. 1925; m. in Medina, N. Y., 10 June 1880, Seraphine B. LeValley, daughter of John and Seraphine LeValley.
2. *Mary Ernestine*, b. in Owosso 18 March 1848; d. in Owosso 31 Oct. 1864.
   x. HARRIET ELIZABETH, b. 12 May 1819; d. in New Berlin, N. Y., 6 June 1886; m. in Plymouth, 14 Jan. 1838, LEWIS BROWN, son of Barnabas Brown.
Children (surname *Brown*), b. in New Berlin:
1. *Charles Lewis*, b. 27 Dec. 1842; d. in Lexington, Ky., 5 May 1896; m. in Newport, Ky., 8 June 1869, Emma L. Firth.
He served with distinction in the Civil War; entered service as a private in Company F, 114th Regiment, New York Volunteer Infantry, 9 Aug. 1862, promoted to first sergeant 1 March 1863, commissioned second lieutenant, Company E, 1 Sept. 1863, promoted to first lieutenant, Company G, 10 Aug. 1864. He was wounded in assault on Port Hudson 14 June 1863 and again in the battle of Opequan-Winchester 19 Sept. 1864. He was discharged 17 June 1865.
2. *Arnold*, b. 13 Nov. 1846; d. in Dayton, Ohio, 25 March 1909; m. 4 Sept. 1877 Sallie M. Crominger.

7. DAN[5] MONROE (*Isaac*,[4] *Samuel*,[3] *David*,[2] *William*[1]), born in Pomfret, Conn., 22 Aug. 1774, died in Plymouth, N. Y., 12 Feb. 1854. He married first, in Colchester, Conn., 15 May 1797, DEBORAH SEXTON, daughter of James and Deborah

Sexton; and secondly, in Plymouth, 25 Nov. 1823, MRS. ESTHER PLUMB.

His first business venture of which we have an account was the purchase of a fulling mill in Lebanon, Conn., which he operated until he sold it to his father in May 1798. He remained in Lebanon until near the close of 1800, when he moved to Berkshire County, Mass., where he remained until 1816, residing first in Pittsfield, next in Sandisfield, and lastly in Tyringham. At Pittsfield he bought, in 1800, from Valentine Rathburn, Sr., an antiquated fulling mill which Rathburn had owned since 1770, of which it is said in Smith's "History of Pittsfield": "It was none of your new-fangled German inventions, but an old fashioned, double-action crank-mill, driven by a three-foot, open-bucket water-wheel, only warranted to run in a high freshet or a long spell of weather." He equipped the mill with new and improved machinery and sold it to Daniel Stearns in 1801. In 1816 he and his family moved to Plymouth, N. Y., where he built and resided in a log house, one of the first dwellings in the town. He built a carding mill there, which he and a partner operated, under the firm name of Monroe & Locke, until after the year 1839. He also built another carding mill at the neighboring village of Sherburne Four Corners.

He served as a soldier in the War of 1812 in Capt. John Wilson's company, Col. Prentice Williams's Second regiment of Massachusetts Volunteers.

Children by first wife:

    i.   ARISTARCHUS,[6] b. in Lebanon 18 July 1798; d. unm. in Oxford, N. Y., 17 Jan. 1863.

16. ii. DYAR, b. in Lebanon 2 Sept. 1800.

17. iii. ISAAC, b. in Pittsfield 1 Sept. 1803.

    iv. FIDELIA, b. in Sandisfield 6 Dec. 1806; d. in Oxford, N. Y., 17 Feb. 1867; m. in Plymouth, 22 April 1830, OBADIAH TOWER, son of Shubael Tower. Five children.

    v. ELEANOR, b. in Sandisfield 2 July 1808; d. in Los Angeles, Calif., 15 March 1896; m. in 1838 JAMES LANE BRADLEY, who d. in Franklin Mills, Ohio, 5 June 1854. Six children.

    vi. ALMEDA, b. in Tyringham 7 April 1811; d. in Brimfield, Ohio, 24 Jan. 1887; m. MARCELLA SABIN. Two children.

18. vii. PHILETUS, b. in Tyringham 17 July 1817.

    viii. JAMES SEXTON, b. in Plymouth 19 Feb. 1818; d. in Ada, Ohio, 19 Feb. 1908; m. ————. Four children.

8. JOSEPH[5] MONROE (*Isaac,*[4] *Samuel,*[3] *David,*[2] *William*[1]), born in Pomfret, Conn., 25 Sept. 1776, died near Lottsville, Pa., 6 May 1851. He married in Plymouth, N. Y., in 1798, their uncle, John Welch, justice of the peace, officiating, his cousin, HANNAH MONROE, daughter of Col. William[5] Monroe.

About 1798 he settled in Chenango County, N. Y. He moved to Warren County, Pa., about 1823, where he served as justice of the peace from 1828 to 1832.

He served as a sergeant major in the 27th Regiment of the

New York Militia in the War of 1812, from 12 Sept. until 19 Nov. 1814, when he was honorably discharged.

Children, born in Chenango County, N. Y.:

19. i. ORSAMUS LEONARD,[6] b. 4 June 1799.
    ii. ELIZA, b. 21 Dec. 1800; m. in Freehold Township, Warren Co., Pa., 21 Dec. 1825, DANIEL HIGBY FULKERSON. Eight children.
    iii. DIANA, b. 7 April 1803; d. 27 Oct. 1812.
    iv. MINERVA, b. 1 March 1805; d. in Freehold Township 9 Oct. 1858; m. 22 Feb. 1824 LEVI BOARDMAN. Ten children.
    v. HAVILLA, b. 4 April 1808; d. 16 Nov. 1809.
    vi. CHRYSANTHIS, b. 18 May 1810; d. 24 July 1810.
    vii. CYRENIUS C., b. 24 Feb. 1814; d. in Freehold Township, Warren Co., Pa., 8 Nov. 1855; m. (1) 12 March 1837 MARY ANN HAMILTON who d. 30 Nov. 1848, daughter of Zeri and Jerusha Hamilton; m. (2) 11 Oct. 1849 LUCINDA HINCKLEY. They are all buried in the Pine Valley cemetery near Columbus, Pa. Three children.

WILLIAM MUNROE OF LEXINGTON, MASS., AND DESCENDANTS

Compiled by the late LEE MONROE of Topeka, Kansas

9. SAMUEL[5] MONROE (*Isaac,[4] Samuel,[3] David,[2] William[1]*), born in Pomfret, Conn., 20 Aug. 1781, died in Chenango County, N. Y., whither he had moved about 1800. He married CHARITY ———, who died 15 March 1848, aged 65 years, and was buried in the Crane Cemetery in Pharsalia, N. Y. Children, born in Chenango County:

    i. SUSANNAH,[6] b. 15 June 1803; d. in Sherburne, N. Y., 8 July 1890; m. ASA COLWELL.
        Children (surname *Colwell*):
        1. *James Monroe,* b. 2 Jan. 1820; d. 14 Dec. 1908; m. 14 Dec. 1842 Louisa Arvilla Slater.
        2. *Spencer Truman,* b. 23 Jan. 1822; d. 12 Aug. 1907; m. 13 Oct. 1847 Elizabeth A. Hendee.
        3. *Clarissa Angeline,* b. 2 April 1824; d. 7 Aug. 1912; m. 15 Dec. 1842 Albert Harris Simmons.
        4. *Charles Henry,* b. 24 March 1826; d. 23 June 1898; m. 13 Sept. 1852 Diana A. Allen. He was a captain in Co. F, One Hundred and Fourteenth Regiment, New York Volunteers, in the Civil War. He resigned on a surgeon's certificate of disability 8 Jan. 1863, and was presented a sword by the citizens of Sherburne.
20. ii. SAMUEL, b. in 1805.
    iii. LUCY, m. RICHARD SAYLES.
    iv. ORSAMUS, m. (1) ——— DANIELS; m. (2) ———. He is reported to have moved from Chenango County to Chittenango, N. Y.
    v. CHARITY, m. ——— WILLIAMS.
    vi. MINERVA, m. AMOS DANIELS.
        Children (surname *Daniels*):
        1. *Austin Elias,* d. in Camillus, N. Y.; m. Minnie Abina Glenn.
        2. *Charity Angeline,* m. Alorence Sullivan.
        3. *Jane Maria,* m. Morgan A. Shafer of Peterboro, N. Y.
        4. *Mary Susannah,* b. 19 Oct. 1836; d. in Kewanee, Ill., 7 Jan. 1911; m. in 1854 Robert Newton Carpenter, son of John Carpenter.
        5. *Laura Ann,* m. Theodore F. Patrick.

10. LEMUEL FRANKLIN[5] MONROE (*Leonard,[4] Samuel,[3] David,[2] William[1]*), schoolteacher and minister of the Universalist faith, born 18 May 1790, died 10 Aug. 1863 and was buried in Cole Cemetery near Hyattsville, Delaware Co., Ohio. He married, 29 Dec. 1814, MARGARET BROWN.

He served in the War of 1812 in Capt. Henry Williams' Co. of McDonald's 1st regiment, Ohio Volunteers. Children:

21. i. ISAAC,[6] b. in Delaware County, Ohio, 17 July 1816.
    ii. NANCY, b. in Marion County, Ohio, 18 Feb. 1818; d. 13 Oct. 1865; m. 14 April 1841 SYLVANUS TERRY.

Children (surname *Terry*):
1. *George F.*, b. 23 March 1842; m. in 1868 Mary Kelly. He served in the Thirteenth Indiana Cavalry during the Civil War. Six sons and one daughter.
2. *William E.*, b. 6 Feb. 1844; m. ———. Two sons, one named George, and two daughters.
3. *Mary Jane*, b. 11 Oct. 1846; d. in Manchester, Okla., 8 Nov. 1930; m. in Stark County, Ind., 13 Dec. 1868, Alfred Thomas Hicks. Six sons and one daughter.
4. *Warren S.*, b. 14 July 1849; m. ———. Four sons and four daughters.

iii. MARRIANNE, b. 16 Jan. 1820.
iv. HANNAH, b. 15 Feb. 1822; m. 5 Jan. 1839 JAMES LINDSAY.
Children (surname *Lindsay*) *:
1. *Andrew R.*, b. in January 1840; d. 26 Feb. 1843.
2. *Elizabeth*, b. 15 May 1842; d. 2 June 1924; m. John Foos.
3. *Margaret A.*, b. in February 1845; d. 13 April 1883; m. Harrison Knowles.
4. *Jeannette*, b. in March 1846; d. 7 Dec. 1923; m. (1) ———; m. (2) ——— Kurtz.
5. *John F.*, b. 14 April 1848; d. in November 1917.
6. *Oliver N.*, b. 4 Feb. 1851; d. 13 Sept. 1916; m. 11 July 1895 Elizabeth Mason.
7. *Mary O.*, b. in January 1853; d. 16 Aug. 1926; m. ——— Henson.
8. *Isadora*, b. in January 1856; d. 10 March 1886.
9. *Zula L.*, b. in 1858; m. 12 May 1881 Gardner G. Curtis.
10. *James M.*, b. 18 May 1860; d. in January 1862.

v. WILLIAM, b. 21 June 1824; d. 21 Aug. 1843.
vi. JANE, b. 25 June 1826; d. in Cardington, Ohio, in February 1892; m. in 1846 NATHAN BETTS of New York State.
Children (surname *Betts*), b. near Cardington:
1. *Hubbard*, b. 15 March 1847; m. (1) 28 Sept. 1872 Ella A. Penell; m. (2) 5 July 1876 Annette Henry.
2. *Helen Anne*, b. 21 Sept. 1848; m. 13 Oct. 1867 Samuel John Wise of Macon County, Ill. Six children.
3. *Oran Patterson*, b. 11 Aug. 1850; d. in January 1853.
4. *Adoniram Judson*, b. 4 Aug. 1852; m. 22 Dec. 1882 Anna Warren. Six children.
5. *Gaylord Francis*, b. 19 Aug. 1854; d. in June 1855.
6. *A child*, b. and d. in 1856.
7. *Melville Clifford*, b. 19 July 1857.
8. *May*, b. 11 June 1861; d. in July 1871.
9. *Nettie Blanche*, b. 16 Oct. 1864; m. in Bethany, Ill., 23 Feb. 1886, Alexander Washington of Macon, Ill. Six children.

22. vii. ADONIRAM JUDSON, b. 6 Dec. 1828.
viii. SILAS, b. 30 June 1831; d. 9 Aug. 1838.
ix. CELIA, b. 30 June 1833; d. in Lena, Ohio, 16 Jan. 1912; m. (1) 27 Feb. 1853 TILLMAN H. YOUTSEY; m. (2) 2 Feb. 1892 JOSEPH MERRETT.
Children (surname *Youtsey*):
1. *Margaret E.*, b. 25 March 1854; m. in Troy, Ohio, 9 Jan. 1878, Caleb Williams.
2. *J. Edward*, b. 17 Feb. 1856; d. in 1929; m. (1) 29 March 1881 Mary Criner; m. (2) in Linn, Kans., 24 Jan. 1892, Addie Jane Masters, daughter of Ross and Mary Masters.
3. *Thomas F.*, b. 5 Feb. 1858; d. in August 1926; m. in 1879 Malissa V. Herman.
4. *Ida M.*, b. 1 May 1860; d. in 1918; m. 9 March 1878 J. W. Garland of Sidney, Ohio.

* In 1905 there were reported, living and dead, thirty-seven grandchildren, twenty-nine great-grandchildren, and two great-great-grandchildren of James and Hannah (Monroe) Lindsay.

5. *Mary Elizabeth*, b. 5 Sept. 1862; d. in 1917; m. in 1900 George Comer. Resided in South Paris, Ohio.
6. *Emma J.*, b. 28 Nov. 1864; d. in October 1928; m. in 1883 William Allen.
7. *Jacob H.*, b. 16 April 1866.
8. *Ivanella*, b. 16 April 1868.
9. *William*, b. 19 March 1870.
10. *David J.*, b. 19 March 1872; m. Jessie Ellsworth.
11. *Leota*, b. 1 June 1874; d. 25 May 1930; m. 10 Nov. **1891** William Lathberry.

x. ELIZA, b. 9 Oct. 1835; d. 16 Oct. 1837.
xi. DELIA, b. 16 Nov. 1838; d. 29 Oct. 1856.
xii. ALVIN, b. 11 Sept. 1840; d. 12 Feb. 1859.

11. SAMUEL[5] MONROE (*Leonard,*[4] *Samuel,*[3] *David,*[2] *William*[1]) probably died early in 1843, as his will was admitted to probate in Delaware County in March of that year. He married HANNAH SMITH.

He is described in a deed to him from his father in 1814 as a resident of West Alexandria, Washington Co., Pa. In a deed by himself and his wife in 1833 his residence is given as Delaware County, Ohio.

Children:

i. LEONARD,[6] d. before his father, who named in his will the following children of his deceased son Leonard:
    1. *Marion.*[7]
    2. *Smith*, m. 9 Oct. 1825 Sally Davidson.
    3. *Samuel L.*
    4. *Amanda*, m. ——— Cline.
ii. JAMES, who had a son named SAMUEL.
iii. MARIA, m. 9 Feb. 1834 DAVID SMITH.
    Children (surname *Smith*):
    1. *Seneca A.*, b. in Westfield, Ohio, 5 Oct. 1836; d. 12 Jan. 1912; m. 10 Oct. 1858 Nancy Ellen West.
    2. *Helen Mae*, b. 11 May 1838; m. Anson Place Oliver.
    3. *Claremont Clareville*, b. 2 Jan. 1841; m. in 1886 Mary Eccles.
    4. *Hannah O.*, b. 11 May 1842; d. in May 1926; m. Edson A. Jenkins.
    5. *Edwin*, d. in infancy.
    6. *Ashley*, d. in infancy.
    7. *Alice A.*, d. unm. aged 29 years 10 months.
iv. KEZIAH, m. 11 June 1835 ANSON WOOD.
    Children (surname *Wood*):
    1. *Mary L.*, m. ——— Smith.
    2. *Rosaltha.*
    3. *Claranelle.*
v. SOPHIA, m. FREDERICK WOOD.
vi. ALONZO DECARTO.
vii. JASPER.
viii. SPENCER.
ix. EVALINE, m. ——— JONES.
x. OSCAR.

12. ALONZO[5] MONROE (*Leonard,*[4] *Samuel,*[3] *David,*[2] *William*[1]), born about 1795, died about 1860. He married RACHEL ———.
He resided on a farm near Cardington, Ohio.
Children:

i. HARRIET,[6] b. in 1828; d. in 1856. She resided with her father during her lifetime.

ii. SAMUEL, b. in 1830; d. in 1856. Residence, Milford, Ind. One son.
iii. ANDREW JACKSON, b. in 1832; d. in 1895. Residence, Portland, Oreg. Three daughters.
iv. LOUISA JANE, b. in 1834; m. (1) JESSE OWEŃ; m. (2) ——— HURLBUT, by whom she had three children, names unknown.
    Children by first husband (surname *Owen*):
    1. *William*, residing in Oregon in 1905.
    2. *Jesse.*
v. ANNIE MARY, b. in 1836; d. in 1855.
vi. JAMES, b. in 1838; killed in battle at Holly Springs, Miss., in 1862.
vii. ANNIS SOPHRONIA, b. in 1840; d. in 1856.
viii. JEANETTE, b. in 1842; d. in 1848.
23. ix. RICHARD JOHNSON MADISON, b. 4 Dec. 1843.
x. BYRON A., b. in 1846; d. in Morrow County, Ohio, early in 1871; m. SARAH ———.
    His will, proved in February 1871, mentions his wife Sarah and three minor children, viz.:
    1. *Mary Viola.*[7]
    2. *Ella Dell.*
    3. *Sarah Jane.*
    Possibly another daughter, named *Jennie.*

13. BENJAMIN BARNEY[5] MONROE (*William,*[4] *Samuel,*[3] *David,*[2] *William*[1]) was born at Windsor, Conn., 9 Jan. 1786. He married ABIGAIL ———.
Children, born in Chenango County, N. Y.:

i. LOUISA.[6]
ii. NAPOLEON W., b. in 1810; d. 29 Jan. 1826.
iii. HAVILLA V., b. about 1815, of whom little is known, except that his father conveyed land to him in 1844, and that, as a single man residing in Plymouth, N. Y., he executed a deed to Ezra Hewitt in 1846 and another deed to William Smith in May 1850.
iv. MARIA, b. in 1820; d. in Frankfort, N. Y., in April 1915; m. (1) HENRY K. SISSON, son of Kingman and Elizabeth Sisson; m. (2) KING EVANS.
    Children by first husband (surname *Sisson*):
    1. *Orrin H.*, b. in Fabins, N. Y., 4 July 1837; d. in Fabins 21 Jan. 1916; m. Sarah A. Pendell, daughter of Oliver and Anna (Hodges) Pendell.
    2. *Emily,* b. in South Plymouth, N. Y.; d. in Allentown, N. J., 4 June 1927; m. (1) Henry Clark; m. (2) Murray Aldrich.
    3. *Virgil,* d. in infancy.
24. v. SALAMAN HARRISON, b. in 1822.

14. WILLIAM WHEATON[5] MONROE (*William,*[4] *Samuel,*[3] *David,*[2] *William*[1]), born in Windsor, Conn., 2 May 1788, died in Otselic, N. Y., 17 Dec. 1857. He married PHYLURAH ———, who died 24 Feb. 1826, in her 34th year, as is shown by the inscription on her tombstone.
Children, born in Chenango County, N. Y.:*

i. WILLIAM,[6] of whom little is known except that he was appointed, 5 July 1858, by the Surrogate Court of Chenango County, administrator of his father's estate. He was then living at or near the village of Homer, in Washington Township, Licking Co., Ohio. A letter written 27 July 1885 by the widow of his deceased brother Alonzo to his brother Lerotus contains the statement: "Your brother William Monroe's family are all gone but his two daughters."
ii. SAMANTHA, b. 28 June 1814; d. in Carbondale, Pa., 8 Jan. 1879; m. JESSE G. THOMPSON, merchant, of Carbondale.

* Philena Pangborn, of full age, living at Otselic, N. Y., is named in the affidavit of death of William Wheaton Monroe by his son William as an heir of the deceased, relationship not specified.

Children (surname *Thompson*), b. in Carbondale:
1. *William Monroe*, b. 26 Aug. 1837; d. 21 Jan. 1884; m. (1) 24 May 1856 Frances Adelaide Simpson; m. (2) 1 Oct. 1866 Maria Catherine Davis, daughter of Richard and Julia Anne (Halley) Davis. He served as sergeant in the signal corps during the Civil War.
2. *Elizabeth*, b. in April 1839; m. Alfred Pascoe.
3. *Lurilla*, m. 22 Oct. 1862 Edward Young Davies.
4. *Fannie*, d. in childhood.
5. *Annie B.*, d. in October 1905; m. Willard Chase. Child (surname *Chase*): (1) Francis Willard, d. in infancy.
6. *Harriet A.*, b. 20 Sept. 1845; d. in Carbondale 28 April 1920; m. in February 1867 Joseph M. Alexander.
7. *Mary G.*, m. 31 Dec. 1879 Riley G. Plopper of Illinois.
25. iii. LEROTUS, b. in 1818.
    iv. LURILLA, b. in 1821; d. in 1871. She resided with her father until his death, and afterwards with her sister Samantha.
26. v. ALONZO.
    vi. A DAUGHTER, d. before her father; m. ——— GILES.
        Children (surname *Giles*):
        1. *John Murray*, living in Sandusky, Ohio, 5 Nov. 1866, when he made a deed for his interest in his grandfather's land.
        2. *Alonzo M.*, living in San Francisco, Calif., 1 Sept. 1870.
        3. *William W.*, living in Caldwell County, Mo., 10 July 1871, when he and his wife Jane executed a deed for land belonging to his grandfather's estate.
        4. *Palmer*.
    vii. SALLY B., d. before her father; m. ——— LAMB.
        Children (surname *Lamb*):
        1. *Lerotus,* ⎰ Minors in July 1858, when they were living in
        2. *Eliza,* ⎱ Kalida, Ohio.

15. PUBLIUS VIRGILIUS BOGUE[5] MONROE (*William,*[4] *Samuel,*[3] *David,*[2] *William*[1]), born upon his father's farm near Plymouth, N. Y., 16 April 1814, died in New Berlin, Wis., 6 Nov. 1861. He married first, in July 1837, MRS. CORDELIA A. (RATHBUN) LEWIS, who died in 1855; and secondly EMILY MORGAN, who survived him.

In 1839 he moved to New Berlin. He was a member of the Wisconsin Assembly from Waukesha County in the session of 1852.

Children by first wife, born in New Berlin:

i. HARRIET,[6] b. in August 1840; d. 15 Feb. 1841.
ii. WILLIAM M., b. 6 Feb. 1842; d. 14 April 1898; m. LUCRETIA ———.
27. iii. JOSEPH ALONZO, b. 20 March 1843.

16. DYAR[6] MONROE (*Dan,*[5] *Isaac,*[4] *Samuel,*[3] *David,*[2] *William*[1]), born in Pomfret, Conn., 2 Sept. 1800, died in Plymouth, N. Y., 25 Sept. 1883. He married in Plymouth, 27 Feb. 1821, LYDIA CUTTING, daughter of Eliphalet Cutting, Jr., and granddaughter of Eliphalet Cutting, Sr.

The Cuttings, father and son, the former forty-two years of age, the latter sixteen years, enlisted in Charlemont, Mass., in February 1781, for service in the Continental Army, for three years.

Children, born in Plymouth:

i. WILLARD BARR,[7] b. 17 Nov. 1821; d. in Plymouth 13 Oct. 1908; m. (1) in Pitcher, N. Y., 28 Dec. 1842, HULDAH FOX; m. (2) POLLY

MARIAH (NEWTON) MONROE, widow of his brother Joseph Marcus Monroe.
Child by first wife:
1. *Polly Mariah*,[8] b. in August 1844; d. 3 Jan. 1847.
28. ii. JOSEPH MARCUS, b. 28 Dec. 1824.
iii. A DAUGHTER, b. 10 Jan. 1827; d. 8 Feb. 1837.
iv. MARTHA JERUSHA, b. 28 Dec. 1828; d. in Edmiston, N. Y., 7 March 1886; m. (1) in Sherburne, N. Y., 1 Nov. 1848, ALBERT J. MERIHEW, who d. in 1857; m. (2) JOHN WOOD.
Child by first husband (surname *Merihew*):
1. *Charles Dyar*, b. 29 April 1850; d. in Binghamton, N. Y., 23 Feb. 1924; m. 29 May 1873 Gustina Nhare.
v. FRANCES H., b. 7 June 1832; d. in Plymouth in 1912; m. in Oxford, 4 May 1854, LYMAN DURAN, who enlisted in Company C, One Hundred and Fourteenth New York Volunteers, 7 Aug. 1862 and was killed in action in Winchester, Va., 19 Sept. 1864.
Children (surname *Duran*), b. in Plymouth.
1. *Willard Adelbert*, b. 2 Feb. 1856; d. in Michigan 9 Jan. 1928; m. 25 Dec. 1877 Meribeth Vernette Miller.
2. *Aristarchus M.*, b. 21 April 1858; d. 27 April 1860.
3. *Estella H.*, b. 6 May 1860; m. (1) in 1878 Will Thayer; m. (2) Griff Hughes. Residence, Plymouth.
4. *Lyman Smith*, b. 23 Aug. 1862; m. (1) in Norwich, N. Y., 29 Sept. 1881, Sophia Martz, daughter of John and Margaret (Voltz) Martz; m. (2) in 1914 Edith E. Hornbeck. Residence, Johnson City, N. Y.
vi. MARY E., b. 21 April 1838; d. in Plymouth 17 Oct. 1870; m. in Plymouth, 8 Nov. 1860, RUSSELL G. SMITH.

17. ISAAC[6] MONROE (*Dan*,[5] *Isaac*,[4] *Samuel*,[3] *David*,[2] *William*[1]), born in Pittsfield, Mass., 1 Sept. 1803, died in Mogadore, Ohio, in 1882. He married in Onondaga, N. Y., in September 1828, ANGELINE MOSS, daughter of Rufus Moss.
Children:

i. NELSON,[7] b. in Syracuse, N. Y., in 1830; d. in infancy.
ii. ALZINA, b. in Syracuse, N. Y., 2 Oct. 1832; d. in 1852.
iii. SARAH, b. 13 Sept. 1834; d. in Mogadore 17 Nov. 1923; m. in 1884 JEREMIAH WISE.
iv. EUGENE BRONSON, b. in Bedford, Ohio, 28 June 1838; d. in Reno, Nev.; m. EUGENIA POTTER.
He served two years as a second lieutenant in Company H, Ninth Iowa Volunteers, in the Civil War.
Child:
1. *Lena*,[8] of Honolulu, Hawaii.
29. v. WILLIAM HENRY HARRISON, b. in Mogadore 25 April 1840.
30. vi. JOHN QUINCY ADAMS, b. in Mogadore 28 Oct. 1841.
31. vii. JAMES MADISON, b. in Mogadore 25 Nov. 1843.
viii. CORDELIA CELESTIA, b. 5 Oct. 1846; d. in 1871.
ix. ADELBERT ALFONSO, b. 5 Oct. 1851; d. 17 Oct. 1926; m. MARY ELY.

18. PHILETUS[6] MONROE (*Dan*,[5] *Isaac*,[4] *Samuel*,[3] *David*,[2] *William*[1]), born in Tyringham, Mass., 17 July 1815, died in Hesperia, Mich., 31 Jan. 1890. He married in Rome, N. Y., 18 May 1841, MARY ANN LARKIN, daughter of Ephraim and Susannah Larkin.
Children:

i. HENRY LEWIS,[7] b. in Mogadore, Ohio, 25 April 1842; d. in Mogadore 28 Nov. 1844.

ii.   ALMEDA ELLEN, b. in Grand Rapids, Mich., 4 Nov. 1844; m. 17 July
      1873 ARETES L. JACOBS.   Residence, Schenectady, N. Y.
      Children (surname *Jacobs*), b. in Grand Rapids:
      1. *Carrie*, b. 7 July 1880; d. in infancy.
      2. *George W.*, b. 7 Nov. 1881; d. in infancy.
      3. *Harry M.*, b. 30 June 1883; m. 27 June 1916 Bessie Louise
          Cornell, daughter of Louis and Mary (Arnold) Cornell.
          Residence, Scotia, N. Y.

32. iii. CHARLES B., b. 26 Jan. 1847.
    iv.   GEORGE B., b. 13 Aug. 1849; d. in Gorham, N. Y., 24 Dec. 1855.
    v.   IDA S., b. in Bethel, N. Y., 9 July 1853; m. 18 April 1902 EDWIN W.
          MILLS.   Residence, Grand Rapids, Mich.
    vi.   LORETTA, b. in Plymouth, N. Y., 23 April 1857; m. 20 July 1899
          EDSON W. MILLS.   Residence, Fremont, Mich.
    vii. MARY ANN, b. in Plymouth, N. Y., 30 Aug. 1861; m. 1 Oct. 1889
          REED GIDDINGS.   Residence, Hesperia, Mich.
          Child (surname *Giddings*):
          1. *D. Emmet*, b. in Hesperia 13 July 1892.   Residence, Hesperia.
              In the World War he served overseas in Company L,
              One Hundred and Twenty-sixth United States Infantry, and
              was with the Army of Occupation in Germany after the
              signing of the Armistice.

19. ORSAMUS LEONARD[6] MONROE (*Joseph,[5] Isaac,[4] Samuel,[3] David,[2]
    William[1]*), born in Chenango County, N. Y., 4 June 1799, died
    in Freehold Township, Warren Co., Pa., 28 Jan. 1877.   He
    married, 22 Oct. 1820, ANNA LOWE, born 17 Aug. 1798, died
    8 Feb. 1864, daughter of Daniel and Charity Lowe.   They were
    buried in the cemetery at Pine Valley, near Columbus, Pa.,
    beside his father and mother, Joseph and Hannah Monroe.
        Soon after 1820 he moved to what is now Freehold Town-
    ship, Warren Co., Pa., where he purchased a tract of wild
    land, which he improved as a farm, upon which he resided
    until his death.
        Children:

    i.   DIANA,[7] b. 8 Nov. 1821; d. in 1892; m. 15 Feb. 1847 JOHN WILSON,
          son of James and Katherine (Engle) Wilson.
          Children (surname *Wilson*), b. in Freehold Township:
          1. *Louisa*, b. 28 Sept. 1848; d. 19 March 1913; m. George E.
              Howles.
          2. *Frank*, b. 31 July 1851; d. near Lottsville, Pa., in November
              1931; m. 14 Aug. 1870 Mary Wilson, daughter of Jacob and
              Mary (Cooper) Wilson.
          3. *Charles C.*, b. 29 Sept. 1857; m. 20 July 1877 Alta J. Ayling,
              daughter of John and Betsey (Dewey) Ayling.   Residence,
              Bear Lake, Pa.
    ii.   EMILY, b. 7 June 1823; d. 27 Nov. 1880; m. CHAUNCEY SPENCER,
          son of Israel and Sally Spencer.
          Children (surname *Spencer*), b. in Freehold Township:
          1. *Mary Ella*, b. 31 Oct. 1846; d. in Warren, Pa., in August 1930;
              m. Erwin A. Allen, son of Robert and Isabella Allen.
          2. *Elton*, b. 11 Dec. 1848; d. unm. 6 June 1871.
          3. *Alice*, b. 14 July 1850; d. 31 Aug. 1861.

33. iii. HIRAM LEONARD, b. near Lottsville, Pa., 22 Jan. 1825.
    iv.   MARIA, b. 30 Jan. 1827; d. in Corry, Pa., 12 May 1903; m. 30 July
          1848 HENRY L. ROWE, son of Edmund and Rachel (Hayse) Rowe.
          Children (surname *Rowe*), b. in Freehold Township:
          1. *Florence Elva*, b. 6 Jan. 1852; d. in 1929; m. 9 Oct. 1871 Wesley
              R. Rhodes, son of Richard B. Rhodes.

2. *Charles Lawrence*, b. 24 June 1856; d. in Columbus, Pa., 21 May 1894; m. (1) Belle Howard, daughter of W. B. Howard; m. (2) in Columbus, 13 Sept. 1885, Sybil Tyler, daughter of George and Anne (Hammond) Tyler.
3. *Fred Monroe*, b. 7 Oct. 1861; d. in Dunkirk, N. Y., 15 Aug. 1932; m. 14 May 1884 Minnie A. Rhodes, daughter of Richard B. Rhodes. Residence, Daytona, Fla.
34. v. CYRUS, b. near Lottsville, Pa., 30 May 1829.
   vi. LOVINA, b. 8 Jan. 1837; d. in Columbus, Pa., 1 Dec. 1896; m. ED. C. BAKER.

20. SAMUEL[6] MONROE (*Samuel*,[5] *Isaac*,[4] *Samuel*,[3] *David*,[2] *William*[1]), born in Chenango County, N. Y., in 1805, died in Chenango County in September 1893. He married SARAH SAYLES.

He resided all, or nearly all, his life in Chenango County. He is listed in the published directory of Chenango County for 1869–1870 as a farmer and proprietor of a sawmill in the town of Norwich.

Samuel Monroe's family was patriotic. The five brothers, Frederick David, George O., Israel Daniel, Samuel, and Charles responded to their country's call to arms and enlisted in Company B, One Hundred and Fourteenth Regiment, New York Volunteers, recruited in Chenango County in 1862. Only Frederick David and Israel D., returned. The former was captured and suffered the horrors of an enemy's military prison; the latter was twice wounded in action and twice promoted. George, Samuel, and Charles died in the service. Of their sister Mary (Mrs. Sayles), in the announcement of her death that appeared in a newspaper published in Norwich, N. Y., it was said: "She had five brothers, who were Civil War Veterans. She was a devoted Christian and intensely patriotic. She invariably displayed the American flag on every holiday. . . . Mrs. Sayles will be remembered as an ardent worker in war charity and Red Cross work during the World War."

Children, born in Chenango County:
35. i. FREDERICK DAVID,[7] b. 23 June 1828.
36. ii. GEORGE O., b. about 1833.
  iii. MARY LOWANA, b. in 1835; d. in Preston, N. Y., 7 Oct. 1929; m. FOSTER SAYLES, a Civil War veteran, who d. in 1912.
37. iv. ISRAEL DANIEL, b. 7 April 1837.
  v. SARAH A., b. in 1838; d. in 1901; m. ROBERT CRANDALL, son of Joseph and Prudence Crandall.
     Children (surname *Crandall*), b. and residing in or near Norwich, N. Y.:
    1. *George Monroe*, b. 19 Jan. 1860; m. Nina Belle Monroe, daughter of Orlando and Anne (Monroe) Monroe.
    2. *Frank*, b. 3 April 1862; m. (1) Ida Wescott, daughter of William and Anne Wescott; m. (2) Ella Sullivan.
    3. *Joseph*, b. 28 Jan. 1870; m. (1) Ann Aldrich, daughter of James H. and Ellen (Crandall) Aldrich; m. (2) Ethel Hopkins, daughter of Charles and Lillian (Fish) Hopkins.
    4. *Latham*, b. 26 Aug. 1873; m. Mary Aldrich, daughter of Mark and Amanda H. (Crandall) Aldrich.
  vi. SAMUEL, b. in 1841; d. in a United States Army hospital in New Orleans, La., in 1863.

vii. CHARLES, b. in 1843; d. in a United States Army camp in Donaldsville, La., 27 June 1863.
viii. SPENCER, b. in 1845; d. 10 July 1914; m. LORETTE ———.

21. ISAAC[6] MONROE (*Lemuel Franklin*,[5] *Leonard*,[4] *Samuel*,[3] *David*,[2] *William*[1]), born in Delaware County, Ohio, 17 July 1816, died in Knox County, Ohio, 28 July 1887. He married MARY VORYS of Washington County, Pa.
Children:
  i. JESSE FRANKLIN,[7] b. 26 Oct. 1841; d. 26 Sept. 1842.
  ii. WILLIAM ALFRED, b. 30 Sept. 1844; d. in Delaware Co., Ohio, 28 Sept. 1847.
  iii. LYDIA OPHELIA, b. 4 Sept. 1847; m. in Westerville, Ohio, 23 March 1865, WILLIAM H. HOOVER.
    Children (surname *Hoover*):
    1. *Ermina Z.*, b. 23 Jan. 1866; m. Eber Ackley. Three children.
    2. *Mary Eleanor*, b. 26 May 1868; m. in Galena, Ohio, 26 Oct. 1887, Francis B. Hanover.
    3. *Addie Estella*, b. 7 Nov. 1871; d. 13 Sept. 1913; m. J. William Seeds.
    4. *Charles Monroe*, b. 15 July 1874; d. in Marion, Ind., in July 1932. Served in the Spanish American War.
    5. *John Willard*, b. 17 March 1879.
  iv. ADONIRAM JUDSON, b. 6 March 1851; d. 1 July 1851.
  v. JOHN HAMILTON, b. 9 Nov. 1852; m. JENNIE ROBINSON.
    Children:
    1. *Della*,[8] m. Elmer Hall.
    2. *Ophia*, of Knox County, Ohio.
  vi. WILLARD URSINO, b. in Shadeville, Ohio, 7 Nov. 1855; m. in Brandon, Ohio, 14 Dec. 1881, BELLE WRIGHT.
    Children:
    1. *Myrtle Olive*,[8] b. in Mansfield, Ohio, 6 Jan. 1884; d. 7 Nov. 1885.
    2. *Mary Belle*, of Wooster, Ohio, b. in Mansfield, Ohio, 4 Nov. 1886; m. Wynne Preston.
    3. *Howard Wright*, of Columbus, Ohio, b. in Galion, Ohio, 27 Sept. 1894; m. Grace Clark.
38. vii. CHARLES FREMONT, b. in Shadeville, Ohio, 18 Oct. 1857.

22. ADONIRAM JUDSON[6] MONROE (*Lemuel Franklin*,[5] *Leonard*,[4] *Samuel*,[3] *David*,[2] *William*[1]), born in Liberty Township, Delaware Co., Ohio, 6 Dec. 1828, died 25 Mar. 1905 and was buried in the Lewiston, Ohio, Cemetery. He married first, 21 Dec. 1852, MARTHA ANN BROWN; secondly, 6 Dec. 1857, SUSAN WAGNER; and thirdly HESTER A. HUSTON.
He enlisted as a private in Co. A, One Hundred and Eighty-third Regiment, Ohio Infantry Volunteers, promoted to corporal, wounded in Franklin, Tenn., and honorably discharged at the close of the Civil War. Later he was admitted to the Bar at the age of sixty years.
Children by first wife:
  i. ALFARETTA,[7] b. 26 Dec. 1853; m. 19 Jan. 1879 SAMUEL J. PATRICK of Lewistown:
    Children (surname *Patrick*):
    1. *Elizabeth M.*, school teacher, b. 19 Nov. 1879. Residence, Lewistown.
    2. *Alexander Judson*, b. 19 May 1881; m. 26 Nov. 1908 Bertha Belle Ritchey.

3. *Herman F.*, b. 11 June 1884; d. 24 April 1889.
4. *Harrison Wells*, b. 5 Sept. 1888; m. 6 Nov. 1910 Lena Blanche Smith.
5. *A son*, d. 28 Sept. 1897.

ii. EMIZETTA, b. 30 March 1855; d. 23 July 1856.
iii. ISADORA, b. 29 June 1856; m. (1) 12 Oct. 1876 J. FRANKLIN WILSON; m. (2) 24 March 1887 JOHN R. RENNICK.
 Children by first husband (surname *Wilson*):
 1. *Carrie Ethlyn*, b. 28 Feb. 1878; m. 16 Nov. 1898 James A. Metcalf, newspaper man, of Adrian, Mich.
 2. *J. Horace*, b. 1 Oct. 1879; d. 1 Nov. 1904; m. 24 Oct. 1900 Margaret D. Knapp of Adrian.

Children by second wife:

iv. SARAH ELSIE, b. 30 Dec. 1860; d. 23 Oct. 1862.
v. JENNIE OPHELIA, b. 15 Jan. 1864; d. 18 April 1882.
vi. FRANK D., b. 10 May 1866; d. 20 April 1878.
vii. EVADENA, b. 8 July 1868; m. in December 1888 GEORGE BAILEY. Residence, Los Angeles, Calif.
 Child (surname *Bailey*):
 1. *Rhenel E.*, b. 24 Nov. 1890; drowned 27 Aug. 1903.
viii. GEORGETTA, b. 6 Sept. ——; d. 14 April 1875.

23. RICHARD JOHNSON MADISON[6] MONROE (*Alonzo*,[5] *Leonard*,[4] *Samuel*,[3] *David*,[2] *William*[1]), born in Cardington, Ohio, 4 Dec. 1843, died 25 Jan. 1926. He married, 9 June 1866, FLORA LOUISA DILTS, daughter of Peter and Sarah Dilts.

He enlisted in 1861 in Company C, Eighth Regiment Ohio Volunteer Infantry, and served until the close of the Civil War. He was engaged in the battles of Gettysburg, Antietam, Wilderness, and the second battle of Bull Run, and was seriously wounded at Gettysburg.

Children, born in Caledonia, Ohio;

i. ADDIE BLANCHE,[7] b. 8 Aug. 1867; d. 8 May 1875.
39. ii. ARTUS JUDSON, b. 31 June 1870.

599

WILLIAM MUNROE OF LEXINGTON, MASS., AND DESCENDANTS

Compiled by the late LEE MONROE of Topeka, Kansas

24. SALAMAN HARRISON[6] MONROE (*Benjamin Barney,*[5] *William,*[4] *Samuel,*[3] *David,*[2] *William*[1]), born in Chenango County, N. Y., in 1822, died in Pharsalia, N. Y., 27 Sept. 1908. He married first BETSY ANN CRANDALL, died in Plymouth, N. Y., daughter of Joseph and Prudence Crumb Crandall; and secondly, in Cattaraugus County, N. Y., ————.

After the death of his first wife he moved to Cattaraugus County, later to Kansas, and then returned to Chenango County.

Children by first wife, born in Plymouth:

    i.   HAVILLA V.,[7] b. in 1844; d. in 1848.
40. ii. ORLANDO, b. 28 March 1845.
    iii. EMILY MARINA, b. 26 July 1848; d. 15 Sept. 1927 and buried in Greene, N. Y.; m. 28 June 1866 HARRISON PHILLIPS, son of Nelson and Emily (Aldrich) Phillips.

        Children (surname *Phillips*):

      1. *Bertha Elnora,* b. 9 Oct. 1867; m. 24 Feb. 1884 Lewis N. Bonner, son of Lewis C. and Malvina (Moody) Bonner. Residence, Greene, N. Y.
      2. *Minnie May,* b. 22 Aug. 1869; m. 14 Feb. 1898 Clinton Cable, son of Theodore and Mary (Lunders) Cable. Residence, Albany, N. Y.
      3. *Arthur Milo,* b. 27 Aug. 1873; m. Leona Myrtle Robbins. Residence, Greene.
      4. *Essie Delta,* b. 14 April 1877; m. Eugene Swartz, son of John and Jennie (Baily) Swartz. Residence, Groton, N. Y.
      5. *Effie Pearl,* b. in 1879; m. Frank Redmond. Residence, Hudson, N. Y.
      6. *Coral Alfred,* b. 17 Sept. 1882; m. Mildred A. Van Slyck, daughter of Franklin J. and Emma G. (Stowell) Van Slyck. Residence, McDonough.
      7. *Myrtle Iva,* b. 8 June 1886; m. 20 Aug. 1917 Paul Lewis Bruno. Residence, Groton.
      8. *Bessie L.,* b. 25 Dec. 1888; d. in 1890.
      9. *Crystal F.,* b. 30 Oct. 1892; m. 22 Sept. 1928 Nelson B. Brookens, son of Harrison and Rexaville (Hall) Brookens. Residence, Norwich.
    iv. DORAH E., b. in 1856; d. in 1858.
    v. BETSEY M., b. in 1858; d. in 1881.
    vi. JOSEPH E., b. in 1861; d. in 1863.

One or more children by second wife (names unknown).

25. LEROTUS[6] MONROE (*William Wheaton,*[5] *William,*[4] *Samuel,*[3] *David,*[2] *William*[1]), born in 1818, died in Plymouth, N. Y., 25 July 1870. He married DEBORAH HOGABONE, daughter of Peter Hogabone.

Children, born in Chenango County, N. Y.:

41. i.   PETER LAFAYETTE,[7] b. 16 March 1841.
42. ii. FRANCIS LEROTUS, b. 25 Jan. 1844.
    iii. ELLEN ARAMINTHA, b. in 1846; d. in 1900; m. 8 March 1868 ABRAM
         BENNETT.
         Children (surname *Bennett*):
         1. *John Sherman*, b. 3 Dec. 1870. Residence, Fultonville, N. Y.
         2. *Cora Estella*, b. 13 May 1872; m. 1 June 1892 Richard Brace.
            Residence, Fultonville.
    iv. ALBERT DELOSS, b. about 1846; d. in 1891 and bur. in Bolton's Land-
         ing, N. Y.; m. (1) ——— FRAZIER; m. (2) JULIA MERRILL.
         Child by second wife:
         1. *Carlton Albert*,[8] m. ———. Residence in 1915, Tacoma,
            Wash. One daughter, Gladys, m. ———.

26. ALONZO[6] MONROE (*William Wheaton*,[5] *William*,[4] *Samuel*,[3] *David*,[2]
    William[1]), born in Chenango County, N. Y., died in Kalida,
    Ohio, 26 June 1853. He married HARRIET ———, who mar-
    ried secondly Henry Weatherby, and was residing in Fulton,
    Iowa, in 1885.
    Children:

    i.   A SON,[7] d. in 1855.
    ii. SAMANTHA, who was a minor living with her mother in Maquoketa,
         Iowa, in 1858, afterwards married and was living in Colorado in
         1885.
    iii. PERLINA, m. in Maquoketa, Iowa, 24 Dec. 1862, HENRY D. EATON,
         son of John and Lucy (Daines) Eaton.
         Children (surname *Eaton*):
         1. *Ernest M.*
         2. *Lester M.*, d. in Des Moines, Iowa, leaving a widow and
            children.
         3. *William W.*
         4. *Lee D.*
         5. *John M.*
         6. *George H.*
         7. *Avis.*

27. JOSEPH ALONZO[6] MONROE (*Publius Virgilius Bogue*,[5] *William*,[4]
    Samuel,[3] *David*,[2] *William*[1]), born in New Berlin, Wis., 20 Mar.
    1843, died in Waukesha, Wis., 28 Dec. 1905. He married
    LYDIA A. KILLIPS.
    He served three years in the Twenty-eighth Wisconsin In-
    fantry during the Civil War.
    Children, born in New Berlin:

    i.   PUBLIUS VIRGIL,[7] b. 10 Feb. 1869; m. 7 July 1901 ORA LEONE GRAY,
         daughter of John C. and Clara A. Gray. Residence, Waukesha.
    ii. FLODA MAY, b. 10 April 1871; m. (1) 8 April 1892 J. R. FLEMING;
         m. (2) 10 Nov. 1910 FRED STACY. Residence, West Allis, Wis.
         Children by first husband (surname *Fleming*), b. in West Allis:
         1. *Laverne May*, b. 23 Aug. 1893; m. (1) Meredith Warner, son of
            Monroe and Kate Warner; m. (2) in January 1930 Edward
            Zernes. Residence, West Allis.
         2. *Marian Evelyn*, b. 6 Nov. 1895; d. in West Allis 6 Oct. 1924;
            m. Frank J. Borda, son of Frank J. Borda.
         3. *Hazel Josephine* (twin), b. 29 Aug. 1899; m. 10 Nov. 1917
            George James Borda, brother of Frank J. Borda, Jr.
         4. *Virgil Raymond* (twin), b. 29 Aug. 1899; d. in October 1899.

28. JOSEPH M.[6] MONROE (*Dyar*,[5] *Isaac*,[4] *Samuel*,[3] *David*,[2] *William*[1]),
born in Plymouth, N. Y., 28 Dec. 1824, died there 21 Oct.
1895. He married in Pharsalia, N. Y., 28 Oct. 1849, POLLY
MARIAH NEWTON.
Children, born in Plymouth:

i. ELERY A.,[7] b. 20 Aug. 1853; d. 30 Aug. 1860.
ii. LOUISE, b. in 1855; d. in Plymouth 16 May 1880; m. 27 Sept. 1877
GEORGE H. BREWER.
iii. SARAH ELIZABETH, b. 30 April 1863; m. 24 June 1880 BOYNTON
SLATER. Residence, Plymouth. Mr. and Mrs. Slater celebrated
the fiftieth anniversary of their wedding at their home 24 June
1930, with 131 guests present.
Children (surname *Slater*):
1. *Barton M.*, b. 11 Nov. 1881; d. 22 Dec. 1899.
2. *Arvine Birt*, b. 30 Nov. 1888; m. in Pitcher, N. Y., 22 June
1910, Alice Irene Sheldon, daughter of Fred C. and Sarah J.
Sheldon. Residence, Plymouth.
3. *Monroe Boynton*, b. 15 Jan. 1893; m. 28 June 1917 Hazel Helen
Henry, daughter of Amasa J. Henry. Residence, Plymouth.
4. *Joseph Newton*, b. 23 Aug. 1896; m. 29 Dec 1915 Clara Mae
Dutcher, daughter of Bert and Estella Dutcher.
5. *A child*, b. 27 June 1899; d. 7 July 1899.

29. WILLIAM HENRY HARRISON[7] MONROE (*Isaac*,[6] *Dan*,[5] *Isaac*,[4]
Samuel,[3] *David*,[2] *William*[1]), of Pleasantville, Pa., was born in
Mogadore, Ohio, 25 April 1840. He married in Shamburg,
Pa., 25 Dec. 1871, REBECCA THOMPSON.
He served three years in Co. A, Forty-second Ohio Volun-
teers, in the Civil War.
Children:

i. CLARA CORDELIA,[8] b. 17 Oct. 1874. Residence, Pleasantville, Pa.
ii. CHARLES SEYMOUR, b. in Petroleum Center, Pa., 5 Jan. 1876; m. (1)
GERTRUDE SMITH; m. (2) 10 March 1925 LUELLA HEMINGWAY.
Residence, Corry, Pa.
Children by first wife:
1. *Florence G.*,[9] b. 5 Dec. 1904; m. 31 May 1929 George L. Mee-
han. Residence, Kirksville, Mo.
2. *Dorothy C.*, b. 2 May 1906.
3. *Mildred M.*, b. in July 1911.
Child by second wife:
4. *Charles Conrad*, b. 13 Aug. 1928.
iii. ISAAC EVERETT, b. 17 July 1879; m. REBECCA ROSS. Residence,
Pleasantville.
Children:
1. *Geraldine L.*,[9] b. 13 April 1904.
2. *Ruth E.*, b. 8 Oct. 1905.
3. *Bernice*, b. 11 March 1907.
4. *Eugene*, b. 10 Nov. 1909.
5. *Karl R.*, b. 16 March 1911.
6. *Rebecca*, b. 28 Dec. 1914.
7. *Maurice*, b. 26 Dec. 1916.
8. *Russell*, b. 6 Oct. 1918.
9. *Helen*, b. 1 Dec. 1925.
iv. VICTOR GARFIELD, b. 8 Nov. 1880; m. LEOLA LYTLE, daughter of
Samuel A. and Mary Lytle. Residence, Pleasantville.
Children:
1. *Harry Lytle*,[9] b. 8 May 1910.
2. *Gladys Marian*, b. 29 May 1913.

3. *Wayne Leroy*, b. 24 Oct. 1915.
4. *Lloyd Raymond*, b. 15 Aug. 1917.

30. JOHN QUINCY ADAMS[7] MONROE (*Isaac,[6] Dan,[5] Isaac,[4] Samuel,[3] David,[2] William[1]*), born in Mogadore, Ohio, 28 Oct. 1841, died in Vinson, Okla., 29 Feb. 1928. He married EMMA HYLE, daughter of Peter Hyle.
He served four years in the First Ohio Artillery in the Civil War.
Children:

43. i. AUGUST WILLICK,[8] b. 30 May 1868.
44. ii. IRVING WILBERT, b. 14 Nov. 1870.
iii. WARREN WALTER, b. in Morristown, Tenn., 20 Nov. 1872; m. in Bonham, Texas, 1 Aug. 1900, BEULAH DAVENPORT, daughter of Amos and Kissie Davenport.
Children:
1. *Rufus,[9]* b. in Bonham 12 May 1902; m. in Kansas City, Mo., 29 Dec. 1929, Clara Wheeler, daughter of Charles Wheeler.
2. *Dorothy,* b. in Vinson 28 Feb. 1907; m. 3 March 1925 Ernest Myers, son of E. H. and Norma Myers. Residence, Wellington, Texas. Child (surname *Myers*): 1. *Wayne,* b. 20 Dec. 1928.
3. *Alta,* b. in Vinson 16 Dec. 1915.
iv. ALONZO WILSON, b. 4 April 1876; d. in 1892.
v. ANGELINE ESTELLA, b. 2 Nov. 1878; d. 8 May 1880.
vi. NELLIE, b. in Bonham 19 April 1881; d. in Vinson 1 Jan. 1918; m. M. W. Eubanks.
Children (surname *Eubanks*):
1. *Edith,* b. in El Paso, Tex., 16 March 1902; m. ———— Chasteen.
2. *Hubert,* b. in El Paso 15 April 1903.
3. *May,* b. in El Paso 5 Aug. 1904; m. B. L. Robbins, son of R. D. and Inez (Boone) Robbins.
4. *Otis,* b. in Vinson; killed in El Paso 27 March 1913.
5. *Ruby,* b. in Vinson 6 May 1911; m. 19 May 1929 Albert Rogers, son of E. E. Rogers. Residence, Erick, Okla.
vii. CLARA, b. in Bonham 7 Nov. 1884; m. in Mangum, Tex., 29 Dec. 1909, CHARLES DARNELL, son of Franklin and Susan Darnell. Residence, Shamrock, Tex.
Child (surname *Darnell*):
1. *Grady,* b. in Vinson 20 July 1911.
viii. CORA, b. in Bonham 1 Aug. 1887; m. in March 1910 JESSE ANDERSON. Residence, Erick.
Child (surname *Anderson*):
1. *Thelma,* b. in Vinson 16 Dec. 1910.

31. REV. JAMES MADISON[7] MONROE, A.M. (*Isaac,[6] Dan,[5] Isaac,[4] Samuel,[3] David,[2] William[1]*), born in Mogadore, Ohio, 25 Nov. 1843, died in Los Angeles, Calif., 23 Feb. 1926. He married, 24 July 1874, CLARA A. HUBBARD of Delphi, Ind.
He served in the Civil War in the Forty-second Ohio Infantry Volunteers, was wounded and lost a foot at Culpepper, Va.
He was a minister for more than fifty years, professor of ancient languages in a college at Santa Rosa, Calif., for several years, and for two years was president of the Southern Pacific College.
Children:

603

     i.   WALTER HUBBARD,[8] b. in Santa Rosa, Calif., 28 Aug. 1875; m. CLARA JANE AUSTIN. Residence, Berkeley, Calif.
          Child:
            1. *James Austin,*[9] b. in Bethany, Nebr., 13 Feb. 1907.
    ii. JAMES DONALD, b. in Bellaire, Ohio, 7 Nov. 1886; m. IRMA ROUSE. Residence, Los Angeles.
          Child:
            1. *Donald Rouse,*[9] b. in Los Angeles 27 Oct. 1916.

32. CHARLES B.[7] MONROE (*Philetus,*[6] *Dan,*[5] *Isaac,*[4] *Samuel,*[3] *David,*[2] *William*[1]), born 26 Jan. 1847, died in Freemont, Mich., 18 Dec. 1928. He married, 9 Nov. 1875, CATHERINE BRITTON.
    Children:
      i.   CHARLES BERTRAM,[8] b. in Hesperia, Mich., 18 Oct. 1874; m. ADDIE JOHNSON.
           Child:
             1. *Katherine,*[9] b. in Greenville, Mich., 1 Sept. 1906.
45. ii. WILLIE ROY, b. 20 Feb. 1876.
    iii. GEORGE LESTER, b. in Hesperia 12 Nov. 1877; m. 5 Dec. 1906 JESSIE LAMOREUX.
           Children, b. in Freemont, Mich.:
            1. *Margaret,*[9] b. 1 Nov. 1909.
            2. *Dorothy Jean,* b. 28 Feb. 1914.
    iv. ORA BELLE, b. in Hesperia 16 Nov. 1881; m. 7 Aug. 1906 ARTHUR ROY SHIGLEY. Residence, Lansing, Mich.
           Children (surname *Shigley*):
            1. *Monroe,* b. 12 May 1909.
            2. *Elizabeth,* b. 11 April 1913.
     v. HARRY BRITTON (twin), b. in Hesperia 9 June 1890; m. in 1912 ELLA PEARSON.
          Child:
            1. *Barbara,*[9] b. 1 May 1915.
    vi. ENCIE (twin), d. in January 1891.

33. HIRAM LEONARD[7] MONROE (*Orsamus Leonard,*[6] *Joseph,*[5] *Isaac,*[4] *Samuel,*[3] *David,*[2] *William*[1]) was born near Lottsville, Pa., 22 Jan. 1825. He married first, 11 March 1851, MARY ANN DEWEY, daughter of Jonathan Rudd and Lucy (Spencer) Dewey; and secondly, HANNAH LOW, daughter of Andrew Low.
    Children by first wife:
      i.   ELNORA,[8] b. 11 Jan. 1852; m. 1 Dec. 1870 JOHN W. BABCOCK, son of Delos and Hulda (Neate) Babcock. Residence, Dunkirk, N. Y.
           Children (surname *Babcock*):
            1. *Maude Rose,* b. in Levant, N. Y., 10 April 1872. Residence, Dunkirk.
            2. *Gertrude Mary,* b. in Levant 28 Sept. 1873; d. 3 Sept. 1874.
            3. *Frederick Monroe,* b. in Silver Creek, N. Y., 26 June 1880; m. Amelia Capell. Residence, Dunkirk.
    ii. ELMER, b. 19 Nov. 1855; d. 26 June 1861.
46. iii. ELMON LAVERNE, b. 11 Sept. 1862.
    iv. A CHILD, b. in November 1864; d. 21 Dec. 1864.

34. CYRUS[7] MONROE (*Orsamus Leonard,*[6] *Joseph,*[5] *Isaac,*[4] *Samuel,*[3] *David,*[2] *William*[1]), born near Lottsville, Pa., 30 May 1829, died in Sigorney, Iowa, 10 April 1901. He married RUTH WOODIN, who died in Topeka, Kans., 17 Aug. 1914, daughter of David and Perthena (Cobb) Woodin.

Child:
47. i. LEE,[8] b. 27 Oct. 1857.

35. FREDERICK DAVID[7] MONROE (*Samuel*,[6] *Samuel*,[5] *Isaac*,[4] *Samuel*,[3] *David*,[2] *William*[1]), born in Chenango County, N. Y., 23 June 1828, died 3 Mar. 1893. He married JERUSHA TYLER, daughter of Thomas and Polly Tyler.
He served in the Civil War in Co. B, One Hundred and Fourteenth Regiment, New York Volunteers.
Children, born in Chenango County:
    i.   MARY LOWANA,[8] b. 1 Dec. 1851; m. (1) PRINCE ALBERT LOVELAND, son of Joel and Matilda Loveland; m. (2) LEE BLEVINS. Residence, Whitesboro, N. Y.
        Children (surname *Loveland*):
        1. *Avanell*, b. 24 Nov. 1870; m. Alexander B. Harker, son of Maj. Garrison Harker, a Civil War veteran, and Mary L. (Noble) Harker. Residence, Ottumwa, Iowa.
        2. *Prince Albert*, b. 22 June 1873; m. Mrs. Edith Pardue.
48. ii.   THOMAS SAMUEL, b. 22 Sept. 1856.
    iii.   HURLEY ANNE, b. 10 March 1859; m. ORLANDO MONROE. Residence, Preston, N. Y.
    iv.   FREDERICK AUGUSTUS, b. 12 Aug. 1865; d. at Pharsalia, N. Y., 4 May 1922; m. (1) MRS. EMMA HICKS, daughter of Delos and Emmaline (Stanton) Hicks; m. (2) MRS. MILLIE (CHURCH) NEWTON, daughter of Franklin L. and Nancy (Bennett) Church.
        Child by first wife:
        1. *Elora B.*, b. in Pharsalia 6 Oct. 1896. Residence, Plymouth, N. Y.
        Child by second wife:
        2. *Vivian F.*, b. 16 June 1908; m. 18 June 1930 Henry Tefft. Residence, Norwich, N. Y.
49. v.   SIDNEY SPENCER, b. 27 Apr. 1871.
    vi.   CHARLES DEVER, b. 7 July 1873; m. EMMA HICKS, daughter of Delos and Emmaline (Stanton) Hicks. Residence, South Plymouth.
    vii. ISRAEL DANIEL, m. Olive Slater of Norwich.
        Child:
        1. *Stella*,[9] b. 8 June 1921.

36. GEORGE O.[7] MONROE (*Samuel*,[6] *Samuel*,[5] *Isaac*,[4] *Samuel*,[3] *David*,[2] *William*[1]) was born in Plymouth, N. Y., about 1833. He married first LAURA ANN SCHROCK, who died 4 May 1857, aged 21 years, according to the inscription on her tombstone in the Crane Cemetery at Pharsalia, N. Y.; and married secondly ARAVILLA ———.
It appears from depositions by Mary Monroe Sayles, sister of George O. Monroe, and Jasper Brown, his grandson, on file in the surrogate's office at Norwich, in the matter of the estate of Spencer Monroe, deceased, that Aravilla, widow of George O. and her two sons, Aristarchus and Havilla moved to Michigan, and that later her daughter Sarah Jane Brown and son Victor followed them.
Children by second wife:
    i.   SARAH JANE,[8] m. FREDERICK H. BROWN.
        Children (surname *Brown*):
        1. *Lucerne*. Residence, Norwich, N. Y.
        2. *Jasper*, d. in Pharsalia.

3. *Laura*, m. ———— Rathbun.
4. *Carrie*, m. ———— Courtney.
5. *Lynn*.
6. *Victor*.
ii. ARISTARCHUS.
iii. HAVILLA.

37. ISRAEL DANIEL[7] MONROE (*Samuel*,[6] *Samuel*,[5] *Isaac*,[4] *Samuel*,[3] *David*,[2] *William*[1]), of Franklin Forks, Pa., was born in Plymouth, N. Y., 7 April 1837. He married first HILE ANN FISHER; and secondly MARY SMITH.

During the Civil War he served in Co. B, One Hundred and Fourteenth Regiment, New York Volunteers. He was promoted to corporal in August 1863, and to sergeant in November 1863. He was wounded in the knee at Cedar Creek, in the abdomen at Port Hudson, and was honorably discharged.

Children by second wife, born in Franklin Forks:

i. FRANCES,[8] b. 28 Sept. 1888; m. ORRA SUMMERS, son of Omer and Lucy (Hill) Summers. Residence, Franklin Forks.
Children (surname *Summers*):
1. *Edwin*, b. 16 Nov. 1912.
2. *Retha*, b. 13 Jan. 1917.
ii. ALPHA, b. 8 May 1891; m. ARTHUR COY, son of William H. and Minnie (Short) Coy. Residence, Franklin Forks.
Child (surname *Coy*):
1. *Eugene*, b. 30 May 1913.

38. CHARLES FREMONT[7] MONROE (*Isaac*,[6] *Lemuel Franklin*,[5] *Leonard*,[4] *Samuel*,[3] *David*,[2] *William*[1]), of Galion, Ohio, was born in Shadeville, Ohio, 18 Oct. 1857. He married in Broadway, Ohio, 21 Dec. 1884, JOSEPHINE BURSON.

Children:

i. FLORENCE OLIVE,[8] b. in Broadway 13 March 1887; m. EDWARD FLICKINGER. Residence, Windsor, Canada.
ii. WILLARD TAYLOR, b. in Broadway 31 July 1891; d. in Galion 7 Nov. 1894.
iii. ROWENA, b. in Milford Center, Ohio, 3 Oct. 1901.
iv. CHARLES FREMONT, b. in Milford Center 8 Dec. 1903; m. 3 June 1926 IDABELLE HELFRICH. Residence, Galion.
Children:
1. *Charles Freemont*,[9] b. 1 March 1927.
2. *Charlotte Ann*, b. 29 Sept. 1931.

39. ARTUS JUDSON[7] MONROE (*Richard Johnson Madison*,[6] *Alonzo*,[5] *Leonard*,[4] *Samuel*,[3] *David*,[2] *William*[1]) was born 31 Jan. 1870. He married, 16 June 1897, CARRIE E. BLAND, daughter of William and Margaret Bland.

Children:

i. ERNESTINE,[8] b. in Urbana, Ohio, 14 May 1898; d. in Galion, Ohio, 22 Aug. 1932; m. GEORGE A. WILSON, son of James and Ora M. Wilson.
Children (surname *Wilson*):
1. *Virginia Jane*, b. in 1920; d. 23 Nov. 1931.
2. *Marjorie Jean*, b. 28 June 1926.

ii. CHARLES BLAND, b. in Marion, Ohio, 5 Aug. 1900; m. 23 April 1927 HELEN CHRISTY, daughter of Jilton and Carrie Christy. Residence, Marion.
Children:
1. *William Christy*,[9] b. 21 July 1928.
2. *John Bland*, b. 20 Sept. 1929.
iii. ISABEL LOUISE, b. 28 June 1910. Residence, Galion, Ohio.

40. ORLANDO[7] MONROE (*Salaman H.*,[6] *Benjamin Barney*,[5] *William*,[4] *Samuel*,[3] *David*,[2] *William*[1]), born in Plymouth, N. Y., 28 March 1845, died in Preston, N. Y., 27 Sept. 1825. He married, in 1875, HURLEY ANNE MONROE, daughter of Frederick David Monroe.
During the Civil War he served in the One Hundred and Fourteenth Regiment, New York Volunteers.
Children, born in Chenango County, N. Y.:
i. ERNEST,[8] d. in infancy.
ii. BLANCHE LAVERNE, b. 19 April 1877; d. 2 July 1930; m. (1) HERBERT COY. m. (2) FRED BOSWORTH.
Children by first husband (surname *Coy*):
1. *Herman*, b. 19 Oct. 1894. Residence, South Plymouth, N. Y.
2. *Ivadell*, b. 30 Oct. 1897; m. Rex Franklin, son of Horace and and Louise (Lewis) Franklin. Residence, Preston, N. Y.
3. *Samuel*, b. 4 Jan. 1900; m. Hazel Bosworth, daughter of Eugene and Nettie Bosworth. Residence, East Pharsalia, N. Y.
4. *Estella*, b. 29 Oct. 1902; m. Clifford Bush, son of John and Catherine (Martin) Bush. Residence, Sidney, N. Y.
5. *Sarah Ann*, b. 15 June 1904; m. Charles Mowers, son of Walter Mowers. Residence, Smyrna, N. Y.
6. *Irena*, b. 25 Jan. 1907; d. 4 April 1926; m. Harold Grover.
7. *Ruby*, teacher, b. 6 Jan. 1910. Residence Beaver Meadows, N. Y.
8. *Waldo*.
9. *William*, b. 14 Aug. 1915.
10. *Leon*, b. 16 March 1919.
iii. IDA MAE, b. in 1880; d. in 1908; m. JIM TEFFT, son of Jim and Julia (Havens) Tefft.
Children (surname *Tefft*):
1. *Willard*, m. Neva Butler, daughter of George and Lilla Butler. Residence, Oneida, N. Y.
2. *Ernest*.
3. *Ralph*, m. Sylvia Case.
4. *Floyd*.
iv. NINA BELLE, b. 6 May 1883; m. GEORGE M. CRANDALL, son of Robert and Sarah Crandall. Residence, Norwich, N. Y. (See 20, v, 1.)
Children (surname *Crandall*):
1. *Gladys May*, m. Raymond Davis, son of A. J. and Minnie Davis. Residence, Norwich.
2. *Lawrence Joseph*, m. Eva Livermore.
3. *Emily Ida*, m. Gregg Moore, son of Harry Moore. Residence, Norwich.
v. HARRY ORLANDO, of Oxford, N. Y., b. 4 April 1886; m. JENNIE ECCLESTON, daughter of George and Nancy Eccleston.
Children:
1. *Leona*,[9] b. 11 April 1911; m. Harold Hackett, son of Joe. and Minnie Hackett. Child (surname *Hackett*): (1) *Willard Harold*, b. 15 Aug. 1929.
2. *Beatrice*, b. 29 July 1913.
3. *Richard*, b. 7 July 1916.

4. *Clifford*, b. 9 July 1918.
5. *Genevive*, b. 3 Feb. 1921.
6. *Lila*, b. 25 Aug. 1923.
7. *Irma Jane*, b. 23 Nov. 1929.
vi. HUBERT, b. in 1889; d., aged 3 months.
vii. LEONA, b. in 1891; d., aged 4 months.
viii. GRACE LUDEENA, b. 29 Dec. 1893; m. (1) in Preston, N. Y., 24 Nov. 1911, HAROLD BOYDEN, son of Zone and Estella (Coy) Boyden; m. (2) RAY SANDERS. Residence, Herrick Center, Pa.
Children by first husband (surname *Boyden*), b. in Plymouth, N. Y.:
1. *Mary*, b. 8 Feb. 1914.
2. *Leah*, b. 29 April 1916.
3. *Mildred*, b. 24 Jan. 1918.
ix. NELLIE, m. (1) JOEL SLATER; m. (2) JOHN SLATER. Residence, Windsor, N. Y.
Children by first husband (surname *Slater*):
1. *Alta*, m. Floyd Townsend. Residence, Norwich.
2. *Elsie*, m. Jack Tryon. One child.
x. ROBERT AUGUSTUS, b. 2 Feb. 1895; m. GLADYS BUSH, daughter of Leroy Bush.
Children:
1. *Robert*,[9] b. 8 Oct. 1918.
2. *Grace*, b. in April 1920.
3. *Mildred*, b. in March 1922.
4. *Carl*, b. in 1928.
xi. DANIEL WILSON, b. 9 Nov. 1898; d. in 1925; m. JENNIE WHITE, daughter of George and Mina White.
Child:
1. *Leslie*,[9] b. in 1922.
xii. GEORGE FREDERICK, of Plymouth, b. 13 Apr. 1900; m. GLADYS ELDRED, daughter of Fred and Lizzie (Purdy) Eldred.
Children:
1. *Myron Frederick*,[9] b. 16 Nov. 1925.
2. *Ida*, b. 6 May 1928.
xiii. BURTON LEWIS, resides with his mother at Preston.

41. PETER LAFAYETTE[7] MONROE (*Lerotus*,[6] *William Wheaton*,[5] *William*,[4] *Samuel*,[3] *David*,[2] *William*[1]), born in Chenango County, N. Y., 16 March 1841, died in Richmond, Va., 6 Feb. 1894. He married MARY SULLIVAN, daughter of Jeremiah and Mary Sullivan.
Children:
i. LEROTUS JEREMIAH,[8] b. 3 April 1866. Residence, Richmond.
ii. THOMAS FRANCIS, b. 23 Jan. 1869. Residence, Richmond.
iii. WILLIAM EDWARD, b. 19 Jan. 1871; d. ———.
iv. PETER LAFAYETTE, b. 27 Aug. 1873; d. ———.
v. MARY ELLEN, b. 7 March 1876; m. THOMAS STALLMAN, son of Frederick P. and Margaret Stallman. Residence, Rochester, N. Y.
Children (surname *Stallman*), b. in Rochester:
1. *Marion Agnes*, b. 28 Nov. 1903; m. Leon Cooley.
2. *Thomas Francis*, b. 27 June 1906.
vi. LILLIAN MAY, b. 1 May 1880; d. ———.

42. FRANCIS LEROTUS[7] MONROE (*Lerotus*,[6] *William Wheaton*,[5] *William*,[4] *Samuel*,[3] *David*,[2] *William*[1]), born in Otselic, N. Y., 25 Jan. 1844, died in Oakland, Fla., 14 June 1923. He married, 15 Aug. 1868, JULIETTE ROGERS.

Children:

i.   EDWARD J.,[8] christened Ezra J., but now known as Edward J., b. in Plymouth, N. Y., 29 Jan. 1870; m. (1) MINNIE DOTY; m. (2) ———. Residence, Port Limon, Costa Rica, Central America.
Child by first wife:
    1. *Roger Edward*,[9] b. in Florence, Colo., 10 March 1913; m. at Shreveport, La., 18 June 1928, Iva May Dean. Child: 1. Richard Edward,[10] b. 17 March 1929.

ii. NELLIE ESTELLE, b. in Norwich, N. Y., 24 Sept. 1872; m. (1) 12 Sept. 1894 CLAYTON H. BROWN; m. (2) in Milford, Conn., 24 Oct. 1905, JOHN F. GIBNEY. Residence, Winter Garden, Fla.
Child by first husband (surname *Brown*):
    1. *Gladys*, b. in Milford 22 March 1896; m. in Orlando, Fla., 17 June 1922, Arnold E. Hall.

43. AUGUST WILLICK[8] MONROE (*John Quincy Adams*,[7] *Isaac*,[6] *Dan*,[5] *Isaac*,[4] *Samuel*,[3] *David*,[2] *William*[1]), born in Mogadore, Ohio, 31 May 1868, died in Vinson, Okla., 8 Feb. 1930. He married in Bonham, Tex., MAGGIE WILLIAMS, daughter of Albert and Rosa Williams.
Children:

i.   ELBERT LORENZO,[8] b. in Bonham 29 Dec. 1891; m. SUE HUMPHREY. Residence, Silica, Kans.

ii. NINA MABLE, b. in Bonham 2 Jan. 1893; m. THOMAS P. RASH. Residence, Brownfield, Tex.
Children (surname *Rash*):
    1. *Thomas P.*, b. 14 Aug. 1909; m. 4 Nov. 1929 ———. Child: (1) Thomas Elmer, b. 19 Sept. 1930.
    2. *Hampton W.*, b. 15 Jan. 1911.
    3. *Desmond L.*, b. 25 Oct. 1913.
    4. *Robert M.*, b. 22 Aug. 1917.
    5. *Ruby Nadine*, b. 24 May 1919.
    6. *Greta Madeline*, b. 28 Sept. 1921.
    7. *Evelyn Lavern*, b. 7 Nov. 1927.

iii. VERGIE CORDELIA, b. 3 June 1895; d. 1 Sept. 1929.

iv. FANNIE LEE, b. in Bonham 17 April 1899; m. in Vinson, O. GEORGE. Residence, Wichita, Kans.
Child (surname *George*):
    1. *Ledrick Erwin*, b. 1 April 1918.

v.   MASSIE BELLE, b. in Vinson 24 Sept. 1901; m. (1) GEORGE A. DAFFIN, son of George Allen and Ida (Sutton) Daffin; m. (2) J. M. LA-COSSE, son of Frank and Ellen LaCosse.
Children by first husband (surname *Daffin*):
    1. *Oletha Belle*, b. 14 Nov. 1917.
    2. *Linnie Helen*, b. 27 Feb. 1919.
Children by second husband (surname *LaCosse*):
    3. *Willie G.*, b. 7 Jan. 1922.
    4. *Francis Aaron*, b. 18 Jan. 1924.
    5. *Melba Lee*, b. 2 March 1926.
    6. *Norma Gene*, b. 5 Nov. 1928.

vi. QUINCY MITCHELL, b. in Vinson 19 Jan. 1907.

vii. TOMMIE, b. 12 Oct. 1910; d. 18 Oct. 1910.

viii. RUIE GLADYS, b. in Vinson 23 Oct. 1911.

ix. ELMER OMEGA, b. in Vinson 23 Oct. 1914; m. 2 Sept. 1930 LILLIE REINES.

x.   GEORGE VERLIN, b. in Vinson 3 Dec. 1918.

44. IRVIN WILBERT[8] MONROE (*John Quincy Adams*,[7] *Isaac*,[6] *Dan*,[5] *Isaac*,[4] *Samuel*,[3] *David*,[2] *William*[1]), of Lone Wolf, Okla., was born in Akron, Ohio, 14 Nov. 1870. He married first, in Bonham, Tex., 23 Dec. 1891, JOSEPHINE CARDWELL, daughter of Andrew Cardwell; and secondly, in Chickasha, Okla., 11 Aug. 1921, ALLIE HOPKINS.

Children by first wife:

i. CLARENCE ONA,[9] b. 3 Nov. 1892; d. 29 Feb. 1896.
ii. CLAUD LEE, b. 6 Sept. 1893; d. 15 Jan. 1919.
iii. CHESTER IRVING, b. 26 April 1896; d. 8 May 1916.
iv. EARLIE WILBERT, b. 19 Feb. 1898; d. 27 Dec. 1898.
v. BENNIE CLEO, b. 29 Oct. 1899; d. 29 May 1919.
vi. ARTIE ROZELL, b. 2 Nov. 1901; m. ARTHUR CARD.
    Children (surname *Card*):
    1. *May*, b. 4 Feb. 1922.
    2. *Mary*, b. 11 March 1925.
    3. *Retta*, b. 14 Feb. 1927.
    4. *Betty*, b. 8 May 1931.
vii. STANLEY MARVIN, b. 26 Dec. 1903; m. LUNDY BROOKS. Residence, Lone Wolf, Okla.
    Children:
    1. *Pauline*,[10] b. 8 Dec. 1925.
    2. *Lorene*, b. 1 April 1927.
    3. *Edgar*, b. 2 Oct. 1928.
    4. *Billie*, b. 20 ———— 1930.
viii. IRENE HILE, b. 21 Jan. 1908; m. ROY BROOKS. Residence, Lone Wolf.

Child by second wife:

ix. FLOYD LAVERN, b. 11 Feb. 1923.

45. WILLIE ROY[8] MONROE (*Charles B.*,[7] *Philetus*,[6] *Dan*,[5] *Isaac*,[4] *Samuel*,[3] *David*,[2] *William*[1]) was born in Hesperia, Mich., 20 Feb. 1876. He married, 3 July 1899, BESSIE STOCKS.

Child:

i. CLAIRE STOCKS,[9] b. in Eau Clair, Wis., 15 Aug. 1900; m. in Bloomsburg, Pa., 8 Feb. 1921, MARY AGNES SMITH.
    Children:
    1. *Marjorie Jean*,[10] b. 24 Nov. 1922.
    2. *Claire Stocks*, b. 26 Sept. 1924.
    3. *Marie Harriet*, b. 22 April 1929.

46. ELMON LAVERNE[8] MONROE (*Hiram Leonard*,[7] *Orsamus Leonard*,[6] *Joseph*,[5] *Isaac*,[4] *Samuel*,[3] *David*,[2] *William*[1]), of Columbus, Pa., was born near Lottsville, Pa., 11 Sept. 1862. He married, 28 July 1887, ANNA MCNAMARA, daughter of Dennis and Anne (Smyth) McNamara.

Children:

i. LOUIS GONZAGA,[9] b. in Ithaca, N. Y., 22 July 1888; m. 12 May 1921 KATHERINE SULLIVAN, daughter of Cornelius and Mary Sullivan. Residence, Fredonia, N. Y.
ii. GERALD ELMON, b. in Coxsackie, N. Y., 8 Jan. 1890; m. 17 Nov. 1929 HELENA D. TRAINOR, daughter of John and Mary Trainor. Residence, Jamestown, N. Y.
    Children:
    1. *Gerald E.*,[10] b. 16 Nov. 1930.
    2. *Mary Ann*, b. 30 March 1932.
iii. GERTRUDE E., teacher, b. in Hammondsport, N. Y., 1 July 1897; m. 11 July 1931 WALTER G. TRESSELT. Residence, Lewistown, N. Y.

47. Hon. Lee[8] Monroe (*Cyrus,*[7] *Orsamus Leonard,*[6] *Joseph,*[5] *Isaac,*[4] *Samuel,*[3] *David,*[2] *William*[1]), of Topeka, Kans., was born near Lottsville, Pa., 27 Oct. 1857, and died in Pecos, Texas, 1 Nov. 1937. He married in Shawnee Mission, Kans., 19 March 1885, Lilla Day Moore, who died 2 Mar. 1929, daughter of Ephraim and Rachael A. Moore.

He was Judge of the Twenty-third Judicial District, Kansas, 1895–1903. Deeply interested in the genealogy of his family he was the compiler of this William Munroe family genealogy. Children:

i. Leonore Moore,[9] b. in Wakeeney, Kans., 27 July 1886; m. 20 Aug. 1917 Clifton Jairus Stratton, son of James L. and Mattie (Hulse) Stratton. Residence, Topeka, Kans.
  Children (surname *Stratton*):
  1. *Clifton Jairus*, b. in Topeka, Kans., 4 Dec. 1918.
  2. *Lee Monroe*, b. in Manhattan, Kans., 12 Feb. 1920.
ii. Day Moore, professor of Home Economics, b. in Wakeeney 19 Oct. 1888.
iii. Cyrus Moore, b. in Wakeeney, 20 Aug. 1890; m. in McPherson, Kans., 1 Oct. 1913, Mary Sawyer, daughter of Thomas C. and Louise (Putnam) Sawyer. Residence, San Diego, Calif.
  Child:
  1. *Lee Sawyer,*[10] b. 16 Jan. 1920.
iv. Cynthia Lee, b. in Hays City, Kans., 29 Sept. 1896. Residence, Topeka.

48. Thomas Samuel[8] Monroe (*Frederick David,*[7] *Samuel,*[6] *Samuel,*[5] *Isaac,*[4] *Samuel,*[3] *David,*[2] *William*[1]), of Preston, N. Y., was born 22 Sept. 1856. He married first Phoebe Button, daughter of Leroy and Rhoda Button; and secondly Fern Johnson, daughter of Charles and Ann Eliza (Pike) Johnson. Children by first wife:

i. Arthur,[9] b. 7 May 1878. Residence, North Pharsalia, N. Y.
ii. Ernestine, b. 18 April 1889; m. (1) Bert Hugaboom, son of Erastus and Nellie Hugaboom; m. (2) William Marston. Residence, South Plymouth, N. Y.
  Child by first husband (surname *Hugaboom*):
  1. *Raymond Leroy*, b. 19 Feb. 1909. Residence, South Plymouth, N. Y.
  Children by second husband (surname *Marston*):
  2. *Clarence James*, b. 21 March 1920.
  3. *George Milton*, b. 8 Jan. 1925.
  4. *Irene Louisa*, b. 12 Oct. 1930.
iii. Porter, b. in Chenango County, N. Y., 13 March 1894; m. Viola Hall, daughter of William D. and Bertha Hall. Residence, New Berlin, N. Y.
  Child:
  1. *Elwin James*, b. 20 Oct. 1917.

Children by second wife:

iv. Anna, b. 22 March 1901; m. Edgar James Fuller, son of Franklin and Vira Fuller. Residence, Cincinnatus, N. Y.
  Child (surname *Fuller*):
  1. *Maurice Edgar*, b. 27 Aug. 1921.
v. Alta, b. 14 June 1902; m. John L. Murray, son of George and Georgiana Murray. Residence, Ohio, N. Y.
  Children (surname *Murray*):
  1. *Lawrence George*, b. 19 May 1921.

2. *Laurena Alta,* b. 26 May 1922.
3. *Marjorie Louise,* b. 28 July 1924.
4. *Leroy Samuel,* b. 29 April 1927.
5. *John L.,* b. 3 Sept. 1929.
vi. RAYMOND, b. 9 May 1905. Residence, Plymouth, N. Y.
vii. LAURENA, b. 26 April 1909; m. WALTER FREDERICK DRACHLER, son of Charles and Catherine Drachler.
Children (surname *Drachler*):
1. *Rolland,* b. 9 May 1927.
2. *Wanda,* b. 12 Jan. 1929.
viii. EARL, b. 13 Dec. 1912. Residence, Preston, N. Y.

49. SIDNEY SPENCER[8] MONROE (*Frederick David,*[7] *Samuel,*[6] *Samuel,*[5] *Isaac,*[4] *Samuel,*[3] *David,*[2] *William*[1]), of North Pharsalia, N. Y., was born 27 April 1871. He married Clara Slater, daughter of Perry and Lydia Slater.
Children:
i. SAMUEL,[9] b. in Chenango County, N. Y., 24 Aug. 1890; m. CORA BENNETT, daughter of Herbert and Belle Bennett.
Children:
1. *Kenneth*[10] (twin), b. 21 Sept. 1915.
2. *Keith* (twin), b. 21 Sept. 1915.
3. *Jerusha,* b. 24 March 1917.
4. *Ruth,* b. 8 Aug. 1922.
5. *Samuel,* b. 7 Aug. 1926.
ii. KITTY, b. 27 Aug. 1892; m. WALTER SISSON, son of Frank and Anna Sisson. Residence, Beaver Meadows, N. Y.
Children (surname *Sisson*):
1. *Gladys,* b. 23 Dec. 1909; m. Arthur Stockley. Child (surname *Stockley*): (1) Edith, b. 30 Apr. 1929.
2. *Ada Belle,* b. 3 Dec. 1912; d. ———.
3. *Floyd,* b. 3 March 1915; d. ———.
4. *Clayton,* b. 9 May 1918.
5. *Anna,* b. 9 Sept. 1919.
6. *Stella,* b. 18 Jan. 1921.
iii. AVERELL, m. (1) MERT CALVERT; m. (2) ERNEST FRANKLIN.
Children by first husband (surname *Calvert*):
1. *Grover,* b. 2 Aug. 1913.
2. *Sidney,* b. 26 July 1916.
3. *Lena,* b. 28 Aug. 1920.
Child by second husband (surname *Franklin*):
4. *Edith,* b. 16 Jan. 1924.
iv. CLARENCE, b. in Chenango County, N. Y., 21 March 1900; m. RUTH SAVAGE, daughter of Herman and Cora Savage. Residence, South Plymouth, N. Y.
Children:
1. *Llewellyn,*[10] b. 20 April 1923.
2. *Jerusha* (twin), b. 4 May 1924.
3. *Josephine* (twin), b. 4 May 1924.

GENEALOGY OF THE WINDSOR FAMILY OF MUNSELL.

By Mr. Frank Munsell, of Albany.

THE first immigrants of this name located in the eastern part of Connecticut, but the time of their coming from England is not well settled. They soon separated, and no communication having been kept up between them, their personal history is only to be gathered from town records and tombstones. Early in the last century, Jacob Monsell, one of their descendants, came to East Windsor, and is the progenitor of the families which have ever since been known in the towns and parishes embraced in ancient Windsor ; and his posterity is now widely scattered over the United States. The orthography of the name is various upon the records and monuments, but is now written Munsell by all the families in America.

Notwithstanding the diversity of orthography in England, the family history, as well as the escutcheons of the different branches, show that they are all of one lineage, originating in Sir Philip de Maunsell, who came from Normandy, one of the companions of William the Conqueror, and on whom was bestowed the manor of Oxwiche in Glamorganshire. His grandson, Sir John Maunsell, was constituted lord chief justice of England in the time of Henry III. ; his eldest son, Sir Thomas, knight bauneret, fell in the Barons' wars, at Northampton, in the 48th Henry III., and was succeeded by his son Henry, who was the ancestor of the extinct Lords Mansell and baronets of Margram. This family omitted the *u* in the reign of Queen Elizabeth, and in 1711 dropped the second *l*. A branch of the family emigrated from the neighborhood of Frome, in England, and settled in Ireland early in the reign of Charles I., and is now known as Monsell of Tervor. The name is written Maunsell, Mansell, Monsell, Munsell, Mansel, Moncil, Munsel, Muncil. Descendants of other branches than this of Windsor are frequently met with. We give the device of one of the English families, by way of illustration, which will probably be a novelty to the descendants here ; and the technical description below exhibits all the difference that exists in the arms of the branches, so far as we have been able to discover.

Arms.—Arg., a chevron between three maunches, *sable*.

Crests.—1st, On a chapeau, *gu.*, turned up *erm.*, a falcon rising, *ppr.* 2d, A cap of maintenance, enflamed at the top, *ppr.*

Mottoes.—Quod vult valde vult ; and, Honorantus me honorabo.

1. THOM S MUNSELL resided in 1683 on the Great Neck in New London. His r me is first found on the record in 1681. He had wife Lydia, and childrea :

> 2. i. JACOB.[2]
>   ii. ELISHA.[2]
>   iii. MERCY.[2]
>   iv. DELIVERANCE.[2]

2. JACOB[2] MUNSELL (*Thomas*[1]), of Windsor, 1723 ; m. first, —— Calkins ; m. second, Phebe Loomis, Feb. 15, 1719, and had children :

> 3. i. CALKINS,[3] b. June 12, 1718.
>   ii. THOMAS,[3] b. April 9, 1720 ; d. April 17, 1720.
>   iii. MERCY,[3] b. Feb. 9, 1721 ; d. young.
> 4. iv. ELISHA,[3] b. Sept. 15, 1723.
> 5. v. JONATHAN,[3] b. Oct. 7, 1725.
>   vi. MERCY,[3] b. Feb. 20, 1728.
> 6. vii. GURDON,[3] b. April 26, 1730.

7. viii. JACOB,[3] b. April 21, 1732.
   ix. JOSEPH,[3] b. Sept. 28, 1734.
8. x. JOHN,[3] b. Sept. 5, 1736.
   xi. DESIRE,[3] b. Sept. 5, 1741 ; m. Isaac Rockwell, July 22, 1764.

3. CALKINS[3] MUNSELL (*Jacob,*[2] *Thomas*[1]), m. Mary Booth, May 19, 1743. He d. May 21, 1858, æ. 40. Had children :

   i. MARY,[4] b. Feb. 5, 1744.
9. ii. ZACHEUS,[4] b. Aug. 17, 1745.
   iii. PHEBE,[4] b. Feb. 2, 1748.
10. iv. ALPHEUS,[4] b. Oct. 12, 1749.
   v. SYBIL,[4] b. May 27, 1751.
   vi. CHARITY,[4] b. May 21, 1753.
   vii. CAROLINE,[4] b. Sept. 14, 1754.
   viii. SUBMIT,[4] b. April 16, 1757 ; d. April 30, 1779.

4. ELISHA[3] MUNSELL (*Jacob,*[2] *Thomas*[1]), m. Kezia Taylor, Dec. 27, 1750. Had children :

   i. HEZEKIAH,[4] b. Dec. 7, 1751 ; d. young.
11. ii. HEZEKIAH,[4] b. Jan, 17, 1753.
   iii. JOEL,[4] b. July 8, 1755 ; d. Nov. 23, 1777.
   iv. MIRIAM,[4] b. Jan. 15, 1757 ; d. young.
   v. NAOMI,[4] b. April 3, 1758 ; m. Jonathan Button.
   vi. BATHSHEBA,[4] b. Dec. 6, 1760 ; d. July 10, 1791.
   vii. KEZIA,[4] b. Oct. 17, 1763 ; d. April 9, 1789.
   viii. MIRIAM,[4] b. Jan. 17, 1767 ; m. James Wolcott.

5. JONATHAN[3] MUNSELL (*Jacob,*[2] *Thomas*[1]), m. Hannah Pascoe (?). He d. Aug. 13, 1787. Children :

   i. HANNAH,[4] b. April 15, 1747 ; m. Ichabod Hatch.
   ii. LYDIA,[4] b. Feb. 9, 1749 ; m. Daniel Bissell.
   iii. JONATHAN,[4] b. May 25, 1751 ; served in the Revolution ; d. Aug. 30, 1780.
   iv. SABRA,[4] b. 1753 ; m. Timothy Smith. She d. Jan. 15, 1815.

6. GURDON[3] MUNSELL (*Jacob,*[2] *Thomas*[1]), m. Lucy Stiles, Nov. 11, 1751. Children :

   i. GURDON,[4] b. Oct. 31, 1752 ; d. Oct. 1754.
   ii. SOLOMON,[4] b. April 3, 1754.
   iii. LUCY,[4] b. Nov. 31, 1755.
   iv. MERCY,[4] b. Sept. 30, 1757.
   v. GURDON,[4] b. Oct. 27, 1760.

7. JACOB MUNSELL[3] (*Jacob,*[2] *Thomas*[1]), m. first, Sarah Bancroft, Jan. 2, 1751. She died Nov. 28, 1783. He m. second, Sybil Ellsworth. Children :

   i. SILAS,[4] b. 1751 ; d. young.
   ii. SARAH,[4] b. April 23, 1754.
   iii. ELICE,[4] b. March 12. 1756.
   iv. SILAS,[4] b. March 27, 1758.
   v. ABIGAIL,[4] b. Oct. 15, 1760.
   vi. EUNICE,[4] b. April 30, 1763 ; m. Timothy Smith.
   vii. THOMAS,[4] b. May 19, 1765.
   viii. RACHEL,[4] b. Aug. 4, 1767.

8. JOHN[3] MUNSELL (*Jacob,*[2] *Thomas*[1]). Children :

   i. MARTIN.[4]
   ii. LUTHER.[4]
   iii. ELIZABETH,[4] m. Solomon Pearl.
   iv. TRIPHOSA,[4] m. Ebenezer Starkes.
   v. TRYPHENA,[4] d. unm.
   vi. CALVIN,[4] b. 1776.
   vii. JOHN,[4] d. unm.

9. ZACHEUS[4] MUNSELL (*Calkins,[3] Jacob,[2] Thomas[1]*), m. Hannah Drake, May 4, 1768; joined the Shakers with his whole family. Children :

   i. HANNAH,[5] b. May 14, 1769.
   ii. ZACHEUS,[5] b. April 16, 1771.
   iii. SUSANNA,[5] b. Aug. 14, 1773.
   iv. LEVI,[5] b. Sept. 9, 1775.
   v. AGNES,[5] b. Feb. 23, 1778.
   vi. SUBMIT,[5] b. June 17, 1780.

10. ALPHEUS[4] MUNSELL (*Calkins,[3] Jacob,[2] Thomas[1]*), m. Eunice Hayden, 1783. He d. Dec. 1, 1807. Children :

   i. DEBORAH,[5] bapt. July 19, 1795; m. Elihu Roberts.
   ii. RODNEY,[5] bapt. July 19, 1795.

11. HEZEKIAH[4] MUNSELL (*Elisha,[3] Jacob,[2] Thomas[1]*), m. Irene Bissell, Jan. 24, 1777. He d. April 14, 1844. She d. March 17, 1847. Children :

 12. i. HEZEKIAH,[5] b. Sept. 17, 1777.
   ii. IRENE,[5] b. Feb. 21, 1779; m. Martin Greene.
   iii. JOEL,[5] d. young.
 13. iv. JOEL,[5] b. Jan. 14, 1783.
 14. v. EZRA,[5] b. March 27, 1785.
 15. vi. TIMOTHY,[5] b. July 1, 1787.
 16. vii. LUKE,[5] b. June 4, 1790.
 17. viii. ELISHA,[5] b. March 13, 1793.
   ix. KEZIA,[5] b. Feb. 15, 1796.
   x. LAURA,[5] b. April 29, 1798.

12. HEZEKIAH[5] MUNSELL (*Hezekiah,[4] Elisha,[3] Jacob,[2] Thomas[1]*), m. Mary Hull, 1814; he d. April 16, 1858. Children :

   i. MARY HULL,[6] b. 1815.
   ii. IRENE STILES,[6] b. 1817; m. William Daniell.
   iii. ADDISON,[6] b. 1822; d. 1824.
   iv. ADDISON TILLOTTSON,[6] b. 1824; m. first, Mary Heath, 1851. She d. 1854. He m. second, Jane Gibbs, 1856.

13. JOEL[5] MUNSELL (*Hezekiah,[4] Elisha,[3] Jacob,[2] Thomas[1]*), m. Cynthia Payne, May 5, 1807. He died April 3, 1865. She died July 12, 1864. Children :

 18. i. JOEL,[6] b. April 14, 1808.
   ii. CYNTHIA,[6] b. June 29, 1810.
   iii. Son,[6] b. Aug. 30, 1812; d. young.
 19. iv. CYRUS,[6] b. June 10, 1813.
 20. v. LUKE,[6] b. Oct. 27, 1816.
 21. vi. ELIJAH BISBEE,[6] b. Sept. 21, 1819.
   vii. MARY EDWARDS,[6] b. Nov. 11, 1822; m. Henry Sutliff.

14. EZRA[5] MUNSELL (*Hezekiah,[4] Elisha,[3] Jacob,[2] Thomas[1]*), m. Chloe Aquires, 1811. She d. Nov. 11, 1857. Children :

   i. HENRY,[6] b. Oct. 30, 1811.
   ii. IRENE BISSELL,[6] b. Sept. 6, 1818; m. Stephen Farnham.
   iii. MARY ANN,[6] b. April, 1825; m. Franklin Beckwith.

15. TIMOTHY[5] MUNSELL (*Hezekiah,[4] Elisha,[3] Jacob,[2] Thomas[1]*), m. Abigail Lad, 1812; he d. Aug. 12, 1859. Children :

   i. TIMOTHY EDWARDS,[5] b. April 24, 1813.
   ii. EVELINE,[6] b. Aug. 1815; m. Charles Starr, 1834.
   iii. CHARLOTTE,[5] b. May 12, 1819; m. Daniel Brown, 1841.
   iv. HEZEKIAH,[6] b. July, 1824.
   v. ELIJAH,[6] b. Jan. 1830.
   vi. ABIGAIL,[6] b. July, 1832; d. Sept. 19, 1834.

16. LUKE⁵ MUNSELL (*Hezekiah,⁴ Elisha,³ Jacob,² Thomas¹*), m. Eliza T. D. Z. U. Sneed, 1820; he d. June, 1854. Children:

    i. ALEXANDER JOHN MITCHELL.⁶
    ii. SARAH.⁶
    iii. ELIZA.⁶
    iv. LAURA.⁶
    v. INDIANA.⁶
    vi. MARIA LOUISA.⁶

17. ELISHA⁵ MUNSELL (*Hezekiah,⁴ Elisha,³ Jacob,² Thomas¹*), m. Polly Hurd, 1818. Children:

    i. SARAH,⁶ b. Dec. 8, 1819; m. W. D. Lee, Jr.
    ii. MARY,⁶ b. March 1, 1821; m. Levi Barker.
    iii. DELIA A.,⁶ b. June 13, 1823; m. Horace H. Dayton.
    iv. JULIA E.,⁶ b. April 23, 1825; m. Cushing B. Morse.
    v. DECATUR S.,⁶ b. Aug. 5, 1827.

18. JOEL⁶ MUNSELL (*Joel,⁵ Hezekiah,⁴ Elisha,³ Jacob,² Thomas¹*), m. first, Jane C. Bigelow, June 17, 1834; she d. June 17, 1854; he d. Jan. 15, 1880. Children:

22. i. WILLIAM AUGUSTUS,⁷ b. May, 1835.
    ii. ANNA,⁷ b. Aug. 1839; d. June 10, 1840.
    iii. JULIA ANNIE,⁷ b. Feb. 13, 1850; m. William Turner, Jr., Aug. 28, 1871.
23. iv. CHARLES,⁷ b. Dec. 29, 1852.

He m. second, Mary Ann Reid, Sept. 11, 1856. Children:

    v. FRANK,⁷ b. June 19, 1857.
    vi. JESSIE,⁷ b. Jan. 2, 1859.
    vii. SATIE,⁷ b. Feb. 18, 1861.
    viii. MINNIE,⁷ b. Dec. 9, 1862.
    ix. LAURA,⁷ b. March 15, 1866.
    x. EMMA,⁷ b. June 14, 1868.

19. CYRUS⁶ MUNSELL (*Joel,⁵ Hezekiah,⁴ Elisha,³ Jacob,² Thomas¹*), m. Diantha Huntoon. Children:

    i. RUSSELL,⁷ b. June, 1840.
    ii. ALPHA WILLARD,⁷ b. March 17, 1858.
    iii. HOMER,⁷ b. June, 1859.

20. LUKE⁶ MUNSELL (*Joel,⁵ Hezekiah,⁴ Elisha,³ Jacob,² Thomas¹*), m. Margaret Ann Johnston, 1851; he d. July, 1875. Children:

    i. FREDERICK WILLARD,⁷ b. June 6, 1853; died.
    ii. ALBERT HENRY,⁷ b. Jan. 6, 1858.

21. ELIJAH B.⁶ MUNSELL (*Joel,⁵ Hezekiah,⁴ Elisha,³ Jacob,² Thomas¹*), m. Martha Covel. Children:

    i. FRANKLIN E.⁷
    ii. GERTRUDE.⁷

22. WILLIAM AUGUSTUS⁷ MUNSELL (*Joel,⁶ Joel,⁵ Hezekiah,⁴ Elisha,³ Jacob,² Thomas¹*), m. first, Maria Beers, Sept. 1856. Children:

    i. JENNIE C.,⁸ b. 1857.
    ii. ALICE,⁸ b. 1859.

He m. second, Lizzie Evans. Four children.

23. CHARLES⁷ MUNSELL (*Joel,⁶ Joel,⁵ Hezekiah,⁴ Elisha,³ Jacob,² Thomas¹*), m. Sarah C. Knower, Sept. 5, 1876. Child:

    i. HATTIE EDITH,⁸ b. June 24, 1878.

617

MUNSON OR MONSON.

By Richard Henry Greene, Esq., of New-York, N. Y.

THIS name, it is said, is made up of " Mon," the abbreviation of Edmund, and son, and therefore means the son of Mon or Edmund: this is not an unusual formation; for instance: Richardson, Dickson, Edmundson, Monson.

1. Thomas¹ *Monson* or Munson, for the name is written in both ways in this family, was the emigrant and ancestor of most of the name in this country. When he landed, or where, is not exactly known; but he is first heard of in New-Haven, June 4, 1639, when he signed the original agreement, of all the free planters of New-Haven. He removed to Hartford, where he resided in 1641; but returned to N. H. the following year. On the 10th of March, 1646, the committee of the First Church seated Thomas Monson and five others in " No. 5 cross seats," and " Sister Munson " was seated in " second of seats on the side for women." Oct. 5, 1669, the Hon. James Bishop, Lt. Thomas Munson, and three others were appointed commissioners to meet five from Branford to establish boundaries between the two towns. In September, 1675, Lieut. Munson commanded the New-Haven troops ordered, by the council at Hartford, to Norwottock and up the river to defend the plantations against the Indians. Susan Munson, who was probably his wife, came in the Elizabeth, to Boston, in 1634, aged 25; from which we may conclude that her husband had preceded her, and probably landed at the same port. Mrs. Munson's maiden name is unknown; but she was born about the year 1609. There are no data by which we have been able to fix the time of his birth; but a trans-Atlantic search would undoubtedly disclose it. He was a representative in the general court 1666, 1669, 1670, '1, '2, '3, '4 and '5, and died ten years later, in 1685. In the division of his estate, three children are named; the births of two of whom appear on the records, and are as follows:

    2. i. Samuel, bapt. Aug. 6, 1643.
    3. ii. Hannah, bapt. June 11, 1648.
    4. iii. Elizabeth.

2. Samuel² *Munson* (*Thomas¹*), lived in New-Haven; married, Oct. 26, 1665, Martha, daughter of William Bradley; was made freeman in New-Haven in 1669; ensign in Wellingford 1675; is called a proprietor in N. H., before his removal, and again in 1685, after his return from Wallingford, which took place in 1681 or '2. Ensign Samuel Munson died in New-Haven 169⅔, and his widow,

618

Mrs. Martha Munson, married Mr. Preston. The children of Ens. Samuel[2] and Martha (Bradley) Munson were:

   i. MARTHA, b. May 6, 1667, in New-Haven.
   ii. SAMUEL, b. Feb. 28, 1668–9. " "
   iii. THOMAS, b. March 12, 1670–1. " "
   iv. JOHN, b. Jan. 2⅚, 1672–3. " "
   v. THEOPHILUS, b. Sept. 1, 1675. " "
   vi. JOSEPH, b. in Wallingford.
   vii. STEPHEN, b. "
   viii. CALEB, b. Nov. 19, 1682, in New-Haven.
   ix. JOSHUA, b. Feb. 7, 1684, " "
   x. ISRAEL, b. March 6, 1686, in New-Haven; the only one not living in 1698.

3. HANNAH[2] *Munson* (*Thomas*[1]), married Joseph Tuttle, Mar. 2, 1667. He was son of William Tuttle, who came to Boston in the Planter, in 1635, aged 26, with his wife Elizabeth aged 23, and three children. They had two more children before 1639, when they removed to New-Haven, and seven born afterward, of whom Joseph, mentioned above, was baptized Nov. 22, 1640, made freeman 1669, a proprietor in 1685, and died 1690, aged 62. Hannah (Munson) Tuttle married second, in 1694, Nathan Bradley, and died the next year 1695. The children were:

   i. JOSEPH TUTTLE, b. March 18, 1668.
   ii. SAMUEL, b. July 15, 1670.
   iii. STEPHEN, b. May 20, 1673.
   iv. JOANNA, b. Dec. 13, 1675.
   v. TIMOTHY, b. Sept. 30, 1678; died young.
   vi. SUSANNA, b. Feb. 20, 1680; " "
   vii. ELIZABETH, b. July 12, 1683.
   viii. HANNAH, b. May, 1685; died young.
   ix. HANNAH, b.

4. ELIZABETH[2] *Munson* (*Thomas*[1]), married Richard Higginbotham, a tailor. He was a proprietor in New-Haven in 1685, but removed before 1692 to Elizabethtown, N. J., and a few years later returned to Connecticut and settled in Stamford. She may have been older than Hannah, or even Samuel, which would account for her birth not being on the New-Haven records. Richard and Elizabeth had one child:

   i. REBECCA.

MUNSON.—*A Stately Record Contradicted.*—The most ancient volume of vital statistics in New Haven is a great blessing to the genealogist, and he is disposed to regard its statements as authoritative. But the writer finds occasion to impeach an important record which has stood unchallenged upon its pages for more than a hundred and fifty years. This error relates to the birth of 'Squire Baszel Munson, who appears to have been the most prominent citizen of that part of New Haven which became Hamden in 1786.

This man was born in 1730. According to the venerable record which I have mentioned, he was the son of Sergeant John Munson, Jr. But it is certain that he was the son of John's brother Joel. Some of the elements of this certainty may be seen in the following facts. 1. The estate of John's widow was distributed (Pro. Rec. vii. 337) to three sons and two daughters, surviving children; there is no mention of a Baszel. 2. Two of the three sons were minors, and the eldest became their guardian (vii. 134); there is no mention of Baszell, aged 17. 3. In a deed (Land Rec. xliv. 528) Baszel mentions " my mother Mary Munson." Joel married Mary Morriss; John, Jr., married Esther Clark. 4. In another deed (xxxviii. 393) Baszel names " my sister Mary Mallery." John had no Mary; Joel had a Mary who married Peter Mallery. Add that Mary Mallery in a conveyance (xxxiv. 217) speaks of " my brother Baszel Munson." 5. In another deed (xxxii. 92) Baszel names " my Hon^rd father Joel Munson." 6. And finally, in yet other deeds (xvii. 315; xviii. 320), Joel makes mention of " my son Baszel Munson."

As the error which I have brought to view relates to the ancestry of a large group of families, and as it has been published in various genealogical works, I have thought it desirable that the correction, and the data which support it, should be made known through the pages of the REGISTER.   MYRON A. MUNSON.

New Haven, Ct.

JONATHAN MURRAY OF GUILFORD (CONN.) AND HIS DESCENDANTS.

Compiled by RALPH D. SMYTH and communicated by BERNARD C. STEINER.

1. JONATHAN MURRAY came from Scotland about 1687; married Ann, daughter of Nathan Bradley, July 17, 1688; and died Aug. 27, 1747. His wife died June 5, 1749. His list in 1716 was £65. 10. 6. He settled in that part of East Guilford (now Madison) which took the name Scotland, from his early home, and was a farmer.

His children were:

     i. THANKFUL,[2] b. Dec. 12, 1690; m. John Meigs of East Guilford, April 7, 1724. He d. Nov. 4, 1767.

2. ii. DANIEL, b. Feb. 14, 1691-2; d. June, 1727.

     iii. ANNA, b. Oct. 1, 1695; d. young.

     iv. JONATHAN, b. Oct. 1, 1695; d. Aug. 19, 1714.

     v. HOPE, b. May 20, 1698; m. (1) Jonathan Lee, Aug. 5, 1719. He d. Feb. 10, 1750. She m. (2) William Judd, son of Thomas of Watertown, Conn., who d. Jan. 29, 1772, æ. 82.

3. vi. SELAH, b. May 8, 1701; d. May 13, 1764.

4. vii. JOHN, b. Oct. 10, 1703; d. Sept. 9, 1789.

5. viii. JEHIEL, b. May 13, 1708.

     ix. HESTER, b. June 17, 1711; d. Oct. 10, 1781; m. Dec. 15, 1737, Josiah Cruttenden, who d. Jan. 22, 1776.

2. DANIEL[2] MURRAY (*Jonathan*[1]) of East Guilford, married Mary ———.
Their children were:

    i. MARY,[3] b. Nov. 19, 1706; m. James Van der Marck, July 27, 1726.
6.   ii. JONATHAN, d. March 3, 1764. His grandfather was appointed his
        guardian on Aug. 1, 1727.

3. SERJEANT SELAH[2] MURRAY (*Jonathan*[1]) of East Guilford, married (1)
Anna Norton, May 14, 1725, who died Dec. 22, 1726 ; married (2)
Lydia ———, in 1738, who died August 20, 1746 ; married (3) Ruth
Squire, Feb. 26, 1747, who died July 1, 1776. She married, after
Selah's death, Moses Blachley of East Guilford, Jan. 8, 1766.
Selah Murray's will was dated July 16, 1760. At that time he had
six living children.
    His children were:

    i. DANIEL,[3] b. Dec. 16, 1726; d. Aug. 29, 1751.
7.   ii. SELAH, b. May 8, 1739; d. April 14, 1820.
    iii. ASAHEL, b. Feb. 18, 1741; d. June 30, 1745.
    iv. LYDIA, b. April 19, 1743; d. Aug. 28, 1749; m. Benjamin Judson of
        Woodbury, who d. Sept. 11, 1811.
8.   v. BERIAH, b. Aug. 17, 1746.
    vi. SAMUEL, b. April 13, 1748; lived in Killingworth in 1764.
    vii. ASAHEL, b. June 19, 1749; d. June 30, 1759.
    viii. NATHAN, b. Sept. 10, 1750; lived in East Hampton, Mass., in 1774.
    ix. RUTH, b. July 12, 1753.

4. JOHN[2] MURRAY (*Jonathan*[1]) of East Guilford, married Sarah, daughter
of David Buell of Killingworth, who died March 1, 1743 ; married
(2) Ruth ———, who died Feb. 8, 1757.
    His children were:

9.   i. JOHN,[3] b. Aug. 13, 1731; d. Feb. 23, 1820.
    ii. SARAH, b. April 1, 1733; d. Feb. 16, 1818; m. Job Buell of Killing-
        worth, June, 1753. He d. March 2, 1791.
    iii. LUCY, b. June 8, 1736; d. Oct. 16, 1756; m. Roswell Redfield of
        Killingworth, June 6, 1755.
    iv. TAMAR, b. Oct. 23, 1738; m. Abraham Brooker of Killingworth, Oct.
        12, 1758.
    v. THANKFUL, b. Sept. 1, 1742; d. May 20, 1826; m. Dudley, son of Capt.
        Elisha White, 1759. He d. March 27, 1811.
10.   vi. JESSE, b. Jan. 25, 1746; d. April 12, 1824.
    vii. PETER WARREN, b. Aug. 15, 1748, in Berlin, Conn.
    viii. DANIEL, b. Nov. 5, 1751.
    ix. SYLVIA, b. Sept. 1, 1753.

5. JEHIEL[2] MURRAY (*Jonathan*[1]) of East Guilford, married Nov. 12, 1733,
Mary Way of Lebanon, who died Oct. 12, 1806.
    Their children were:

    i. ANN,[3] b. March 7, 1734.
    ii. ESTHER, b. Sept. 29, 1735.
    iii. ABNER, b. April 8, 1739.
    iv. EZRA, b. July 11, 1741.
    v. REUBEN, b. Feb. 17, 1744.

6. JONATHAN[3] MURRAY (*Daniel*,[2] *Jonathan*[1]) of East Guilford, married
Dorcas Way of Lyme, April 23, 1740. She died Nov. 24, 1794.
She married (2) Reuben Hill of East Guilford.
    Jonathan Murray's children were:

    i. AMASA,[4] b. Dec. 24, 1741; d. Oct. 29, 1822.
    ii. MABEL, b. July 11, 1743; d. May 10, 1779; m. Elias Grave of East
        Guilford, Feb. 23, 1763. He d. May 31, 1802.

iii. EBER, b. May 1, 1745, was the first permanent settler of Orwell, Vt., removing there in 1783; and was elder of the church established at Orwell in 1784. His brother Stephen went with him.

iv. ASAHEL, b. April 16, 1747; d. Sept. 11, 1784; m. Thankful, dau. of Samuel Plumb, of East Guilford, Sept. 26, 1770. She d. Aug. 14, 1821.

    Their children were: 1. *Thankful*,[5] b. Aug. 13, 1771; 2. *Mabel*, b. Aug. 7, 1773; 3. *Huldah*, b. Jan. 4, 1776; m. Henry Hall of Guilford; 4. *Asahel*, b. Nov. 19, 1778; 5. *Jonathan*, b. Jan. 27, 1781; 6. *Samuel Plumb*, b. Dec. 5, 1783.

v. JONATHAN, b. Aug. 10, 1750; lived in East Guilford, and d. March 1, 1785; m. Abigail ——, who d., æ 72, Sept. 17, 1822.

    Their children were: 1. *Mabel*,[5] b. 1776; m. William Bishop, who d. June 28, 1848; 2. *Abigail*, b. 1778; d. Aug. 11, 1852; m. Abel Hoyt of East Guilford, who d. Sept. 23, 1863; 3. *Polly*, b. 1781; 4. *Elizabeth*, b. 1784; m. (1) Lemuel Bushnell; m. (2) —— Conkling.

vi. DANIEL, b. Sept. 13, 1755.

vii. STEPHEN, b. July 13, 1757.

7. SELAH[3] MURRAY, JR. (*Selah*,[2] *Jonathan*[1]) of East Guilford, married (1) Susannah, daughter of James Munger. She died July 18, 1763, aged 22. He married (2) widow Lois Stevens, 1765. She died July 3, 1826, aged 85.

His children were:

i. LYDIA,[4] b. Sept. 18, 1766; m. Abraham Hill of East Guilford, Sept. 29, 1784. He d. Sept. 10, 1840.

ii. SUSANNAH, m. Benjamin Wright of Killingworth.

iii. LOIS, m. Elias Willard.

8. BERIAH[3] MURRAY (*Selah*,[2] *Jonathan*[1]) removed to Durham, and was admitted to the church there in Feb., 1766. He married Mary Meeker of Durham, July 21, 1765.

Their children were:

i. SABRA,[4] b. Aug. 14, 1765; bap. Feb. 9, 1766.

ii. CURTISS, bap. Jan. 3, 1768.

9. JOHN[3] MURRAY, JR. (*John*,[2] *Jonathan*[1]) of East Guilford, married Mindwell, daughter of Jonathan Crampton of East Guilford. She died, aged 78, June 20, 1816.

Their children were:

i. SEYMOUR,[4] of Norwich Landing, m. ——, and had: 1. *Seymour*[5]; 2. *John*, d. April, 1858; 3. *Philo*, m. —— Tracy of Norwich.

ii. LORRAIN, m. Timothy Munger of East Guilford.

iii. CURTISS, b. 1756; d. 1847; lived in Denmark, N. Y.; m. Catherine, dau. of Timothy Scranton. She d. 1848,

    Their children were: 1. *Jonathan*,[5] b. 1790, of Albion, N. Y.; 2. *Augustus*, b. 1793; 3. *Warren*, b. 1801, of Oneida Co., N. Y.; 4. *Julius*, b. Sept. 8, 1803.

iv. LUCY, b. 1758; d. Sept. 29, 1825; m. Benjamin Field of East Guilford, 1783. He d. June 20, 1824.

v. MINDWELL, m. Jedidiah Griswold, Jr. of Killingworth.

vi. JESSE, m. (1) Rachel, dau. of Nathaniel Allis of East Guilford, who was b. July 5, 1767; m. (2) widow Sally Ann (Buckingham) Post. Their children were: 1. *Hart*,[5] a merchant of Brooklyn, N. Y.; 2. *Horace*, who went to Texas; 3. *Rebecca*; 4. *Pierce*, who went to California; 5. *Susan*; 6. *William Hubbard*; 7. *Mary Ann*.

vii. SARAH, b. 1765.

viii. MABEL, b. 1768; m. Ambrose Dudley of East Guilford, 1794. He d. Dec. 22, 1835. She d. Jan. 24, 1823.

ix. BEULAH, m. Eber Field of East Guilford.

x. CALVIN, b. 1781; d. Nov. 4, 1810; m. Diademia, dau. of Arah Norton. She d. July 10, 1837. He lived in East Guilford.

Their children were: 1. *Dickinson*,[5] b. Dec. 10, 1805; d. Oct. 5, 1873; m. Sally, dau. of Chauncey Munger, April 17, 1831, who d. at East Haven, Feb. 10, 1872; among their children were: Rev. Chauncey D. and Rev. William H. H. (" Adirondack ") Murray; 2. *Calvin Nelson*, b. July 14, 1808; of Madison; m. Emily, dau. of Joseph Dickinson of Haddam, Oct. 22, 1837; 3. *Beulah Maria*, b. Dec. 28, 1810; d. April 13, 1844; m. Jared Whitfield, Jan. 13, 1839.

10. JESSE[3] MURRAY (*John,*[2] *Jonathan*[1]) of East Guilford, married Rachel Norton.

Their children were:

i. WILLIAM,[4] of Albany, N. Y.

ii. ZUBAH, m. Calvin Warner of Albany and Troy, N. Y.

iii. RACHEL, d. March 14, 1849; m. Josiah Willard of Madison. He d. May 22, 1858.

iv. HARVEY, of New Haven; m. —— Wilcox of Middletown.

v. EBER, b. 1784; lost at sea, 1821.

623

NEEDHAMS OF WALES, MASS., AND STAFFORD, CONN.

By GRACE OLIVE CHAPMAN, of Dorchester (Boston), Mass.

1. ANTHONY[1] NEEDHAM, of Salem, Mass., was born in England in 1628. He married, 10 Jan. 1655, ANN POTTER, born in Antrim, Ireland, daughter of Humphrey Potter of Coventry, England, who was killed in the Irish Massacre in Dublin, Ireland, in 1641.

Anthony Needham came to New England and settled in Salem about 1653, and Ann (Potter) Needham came to Salem to live with her father's sister, Mrs. Rebecca Bacon, from whom she receiv'·d a considerable estate, as also from her father or his ancestors. She became an enthusiastic Quaker.

"In the English expedition sent by Oliver Cromwell for the taking of the French fort at St. John about 1654, Henry Kenney, Anthony Needham, John Floyd and Thomas Lathrop served under the command of Maj. Sedgwick" (Perley's Salem, vol. III, p. 140).

"Captain Nicholas Manning of Salem served in Captain Paige's troop in the Mount Hope campaign in June 1675, and was in command of a company which marched to Narraganset to recruit the army after the great swamp fight. Among his soldiers at that time, Feb. 29, 1675/6, were Lt. Anthony Needham, John Beckett, Resolved White and Thomas Fuller, from Salem" (*ibid.*, p. 91).

Children, born in Salem (Salem Vital Records):

   i.   REBECCA,[2] b. 21 Dec. 1656; m. in January 1675 MICHAELL CHAPLE-MAN.

   ii. ANNA, b. 31: 6m: 1658.

  iii. ELIZABETH, b. 1: 10m: 1659.

  iv. PROVIDED, b. 12: 2m: 1661; d. unm.

2. v. ANTHONY, b. 11 April 1663.

  vi. MARY, b. 30: 2m: 1665; d. unm. in 1742.

 vii. GEORGE, b. 26 March 1667; d. unm. young.

viii. ISAACK, b. 15 April 1669; d. in May 1750; m. ———.

       Children:

         1. *George.*[3]   2. *Isaac.*

              3. *John.*

  ix. ABIGAIL, b. 31 May 1671; m. in 1691 THOMAS GOULD.

   x. THOMAS, b. 25 July 1673; m. in 1706 RUTH SIBLEY.

  xi. DOROTHY, b. 25 Aug. 1675; m. WILLIAM BROWN.

 xii. RACHEL, b. 17 March 1677/8; m. in 1712 WILLIAM SMALL.

2. ANTHONY[2] NEEDHAM (*Anthony*[1]), born in Salem, Mass., 11 April 1663, died in 1757/8. He married, 3 Jan. 1695, Rev. Jonathan Corwin officiating, MARY SWINERTON, born in Salem 17 May 1670, daughter of Job and Ruth (Symonds) Swinerton.

Children:
- i. THOMAS[3] b. 4 Feb. 1696.
- 3. ii. ANTHONY*, b. 23 Nov. 1696.
- 4. iii. HUMPHREY*, b. in 1698.
- iv. REBECCA, m. 18 Jan. 1719 JONATHAN FELTON.
- 5. v. JASPER, b. 15 June 1705.
- vi. RUTH, d. in 1748; m. 11 April 1733 BENJAMIN WARNER of Brimfield, Mass.

3. ANTHONY[3] NEEDHAM (*Anthony*,[2] *Anthony*[1]), born in Salem, Mass., 23 Nov. 1696, died in South Brimfield, now Wales, Mass., 2 July 1763, aged 66. He married, 10 June 1722, MARY (MOLLY) MOULTON, born in Salem 30 Sept. 1702, died in South Brimfield in 1790, daughter of Robert[4] and Hannah (Groves) Moulton.

Anthony and Molly Needham are said to have gone to Brimfield about 1722, and are said to have been in 1726 the first white settlers of South Brimfield. The name of South Brimfield was changed in 1828 to Wales in honor of James Lawrence Wales.

Absalom Gardner's "Compendium of Wales", 1873, p. 324, says: "Anthony Needham was one of that band of adventurous pioneers who first made lodgment with a view to permanent settlement in this Town about 1726. He fixed his abode upon what we now call the Orcutt Place described in Mem. 1 No. 3, p. 312. There he lived: there he died."

Children, born in Brimfield, except Hannah, said to have been born in South Brimfield (now Wales):

- 6. i. ANTHONY,[4] b. 18 May 1723.
- ii. MARY, b. 21 June 1725; m. in Brimfield, 14 Feb. 1744/5, as his second wife, BENJAMIN[4] COOLEY, born in Longmeadow, Mass., 5 Nov. 1701. Benjamin and Mary Cooley lived in Brimfield, and then moved to Quabin, which later became Greenwich, Mass.

    Children (surname *Cooley*), b. probably in Greenwich:
    1. *Capt. Benjamin*, b. 30 April 1747; d. in Pittsford, Vt., in 1810/11; m. in 1773 Ruth Beach, b. in Morristown, N. J., in 1756. He served in the Revolutionary War. Child: (1) Ruth, m. Jeremiah Needham.
    2. *Reuben*, b. 25 April 1752; d. in 1823; m. (1), Sarah ———; m. (2), Elizabeth Needham. They lived in Pittsford, Vt., and moved to Genesee County, N. Y., in 1811. Children by first wife, b. in Greenwich: (1) Sarah, b. 29 June 1778; m. a Cobleigh. (2) Reuben, b. 24 March 1780; m. Cynthia Evans. (3) Lydia, b. 22 Feb. 1783. Children by second wife: (4) Benjamin, of Chautauqua, N. Y., b. 16 Aug. 1786. (5) Suzanna, b. 12 March 1788; m. Joshua Park. (6) Arad, b. 9 Nov. 1790; d. in 1851. (7) Elias, b. 11 Sept. 1791. He lived in New York then moved to Kalamazoo, Mich. (8) Col. Anthony, of Paw Paw, Mich., b. 27 Oct. 1793; m. Amanda Stanley. (9) Caleb, b. 10 April 1796. (10) Thomas, b. 25 March 1799; m. Augusta Stratton. (11) Elizabeth, b. 4 June 1806.
    3. *Azariah*, of Greenwich, b. 25 July 1755; m. Mercy ———.
    4. *Naomi*, b. 26 July 1756; m. James Ewing.

*All Brimfield and Wales Needhams are said to have descended from the above Anthony, born in 1696, and Humphrey, born in 1698.

5. *Margaret*, b. 13 Nov. 1757; m. (1), Job Winslow; m. (2), Peter Rice.
6. *Caleb*, b. 12 Feb. 1762; d. in Pittsford, Vt.; m. in 1784 Elizabeth Sanford, daughter of Thomas and Lucy (Kellogg) Sanford of Weybridge, Vt.

iii. HANNAH, b. in March 1727; d. 15 Aug. 1781, in her 54th year; m. 28 April 1743 WILLIAM CARPENTER, b. in Swansea, Mass., 24 Sept. 1721, d. in Stafford, Conn., 9 March 1809, aged between 80 and 90, son of Benjamin and Mary (Barney) Carpenter. William Carpenter served in the Revolution from South Brimfield as a private and as a sergeant.

Children (surname *Carpenter*):

1. *Zebulon*, b. 19 July 1744; d. in Brimfield 20 June 1761 (Brimfield Vital Records).
2. *Daniel* (twin), b. 25 May 1749 (*ibid.*); m. 1 April 1784 Eunice White (Stafford Vital Records), probably daughter of Joseph and Eunice (Snell) White.
3. *Jesse* (twin), b. 25 May 1749 (Brimfield Vital Records); d. in Nelson, N. Y., in 1843; m. there Ruth Streeter.
4. *John*, b. in 1751; m. Lovina Chappelle.
5. *Hannah*, b. 8 Sept. 1757 (Brimfield Vital Records); m. 10 Oct. 1774 James Twing of Wilbraham, Mass.
6. *Rev. Jotham*, first settled minister of Fayeston, Vt., b. in 1760; m. Molly Patterson of Barre, Vt.
7. *Nathan*, b. in 1765; m. Azuba Blodgett of Randolph, Vt. Lived in Vermont, New York, and Ohio.
8. *Reuben*, of Worthingham, Ohio; m. ——— Rood.
9. *Barney*.
10. *William*, b. in 1769; m. Sarah Blodgett. Lived in Ohio and California.
11. *David*.
12. *Powell*.
13. *Anna*, m. Moses Rood of Barre, Vt.
14. *Irving*.
15. *Polly*.

("Carpenter Memorial", by Amos B. Carpenter)

iv. RUTH, b. 16 Jan. 1729; m. in Brimfield, 7 June 1756, ISRAEL KIBBE (Brimfield Vital Records), b. 16 Nov. 1727, son of Israel and Sarah (Horton) Kibbe of Somers, Conn. Her sister Naomi m. Joseph Munger the same day.

Children (surname *Kibbe*):

1. *Ruth*, b. 13 April 1757.
2. *Israel*, b. 29 Dec. 1758; m. 3 Jan. 1783 Ruth Woodworth.
3. *Moses*, b. 7 June 1761.
4. *Nathan*, b. 25 Sept. 1763.
5. *Reuben*, b. 17 May 1766.
6. *Sarah*, b. 23 July 1768.

v. NAOME, b. 5 June 1731; d. in Paris, Oneida Co., N. Y., in 1824, aged 93; m. 2 or 7 June 1756, as his second wife, JOSEPH MUNGER, b. in Hampton, Conn., in July 1719, d. in Paris in 1805, son of Samuel Munger. Joseph served in the French and Indian War as Sergeant in Capt. Ebenezer Moulton's company; in the Revolution in Capt. Anthony Needham's company of Minute Men as Sergeant; served also in Capt. Daniel Winchester's company. Lived in Ludlow, South Brimfield, Mass., and Paris, N. Y.

Children (surname *Munger*) ("The Munger Book", 1915):

1. *Jemima*, b. 24 Aug. 1757; m. in Stafford, Conn., 29 April 1773, Moses Johnson.
2. *Nathan*, b. 13 May 1759; m. in South Brimfield, Lovina Bishop. Settled in Munger's Mills, now Copenhagen, N. Y.

3. *Joseph*, b. 23 Aug. 1760; m. Hannah Fiske, daughter of Capt. Asa and Elizabeth (Knight) Fiske. Moved from Ludlow, Mass., to Paris.

4. *Naomi*, b. 14 Aug. 1763; m. in Glocester, R. I., in 1780, Alverson Wade.

5. *Elijah*, b. 4 May 1767; m. Clarissa Quackenbosh. After he graduated from Yale he moved to Paris and then to Sackett's Harbor, N. Y.

6. *Reuben*, b. 29 June 1769; m. in Ludlow, Mass., Lorinda Chapin. Moved to Paris and then to Chautauqua County, N. Y.

7. *Perley*, physician, b. 11 Nov. 1775; m. (1), in Ludlow, Mass., Susanna Fuller; m. (2), Aureria (Barker) Munger, widow of his nephew, Nathan Munger, Jr. Moved from Ludlow to Paris. He served in the War of 1812.

8. *Asa*, b. 29 Oct. 1777.

7. vi.   NEHEMIAH, b. 4 April 1734.
    vii. ABIGAIL, b. 10 Nov. 1736; d. 11 Dec. 1736.
8. viii. JASPER, b. 31 July 1738.
9. ix.   JEREMIAH, b. 17 June 1741.
10. x.   DANIEL, b. 10 Sept. 1743.
11. xi.   ABNER, b. 17 Dec. 1746.

4. HUMPHREY[3] NEEDHAM (*Anthony*,[2] *Anthony*[1]), of Salem and South Brimfield (now Wales), Mass., was born in Salem in 1698. He married, 4 April 1739, DOROTHY MUNGER, daughter of Samuel and Dorothy (Evarts) Munger.

Children, all but last two born in Brimfield (Brimfield Vital Records):

i.   DOROTHY,[4] b. 30 June 1740.
ii. HUMPHREY, b. 3 July 1742; d. 11 Oct. 1815; m. EUNICE MOULTON, b. 24 June 1749, daughter of John and Ruth (Bound) Moulton.
iii. DESIRE, b. 12 June 1744; m. REUBEN PERRY of Stafford, Conn.

    Child (surname *Perry*):

    1. *Ruhama*, b. in 1780; d. 14 Nov. 1812; m. in 1808 Luke Burley, son of Josiah Burley.

iv. JOSEPH, b. 28 Jan. 1746; d. in Whiting, Vt., 20 Dec. 1808; m. MEHITABLE MOULTON, b. 11 June 1756, sister of Eunice Moulton who married his brother Humphrey. He served in the Revolution.
v.   SARAH, b. 28 Feb. 1748.
vi. RUTH, of Stafford and Willington, Conn., b. 30 March 1750; m. in Stafford, 7 Jan. 1779, DEA. JOSHUA AGARD, b. 28 Dec. 1755, son of Benjamin and Elizabeth (Hall) Agard.

    Children (surname *Agard*), first five b. in Stafford, the last three in Willington:

    1. *Joshua*, b. 16 April ———.
    2. *Mehitable*, b. in February ———.
    3. *Phebe*, b. 14 July ———.
    4. *Tryphena*, b. in December ———.
    5. *Zalmon*, b. 17 Nov. 1790; d. 6 May 1806, aged 19 years 6 months.
    6. *Elizabeth*, b. 7 Nov. 1795; m. in 1828 Jason Bugbee, son of Marcus and Sylvia (Corbin) Bugbee of Union, Conn.
    7. *Polly*, b. 18 March 1799.
    8. *Needham*, b. 6 June 1802.

vii. RACHEL, b. 12 Jan. 1753; d. 18 Oct. 1828, aged 74; m. 14 April 1772 DEA. ELIJAH WALES, deacon of the Baptist Church in Wales, b. 28 Jan. 1748, d. 23 March 1826, aged 78, son of Dea. Ebenezer and Deborah (Ward) Wales.

Children (surname *Wales*) (Lawson's "History of Union"):
1. *Nancy*, b. 16 March 1773; m. in 1826 David Rathbone, a Baptist minister.
2. *Tryphena*, b. 11 Oct. 1774; d. in 1777.
3. *Ebenezer*, b. 4 April 1776; d. in Fenner, N. Y.
4. *Alvin*, a Baptist minister in Fenner, N. Y., b. 6 Nov. 1778; d. in 1810.
5. *Elijah*, physician, b. 2 Dec. 1780; d. in Union, Conn., in 1850.
6. *Linus*, b. 28 Oct. 1782; m. in 1811 Mary Loring.
7. *Philena*, b. 24 April 1785; m. Dea. ———— Seward.
8. *Palace*, b. 21 Sept. 1787; d. 27 March 1790.
9. *Tryphena*, b. 5 Jan. 1790.
10. *Joseph*, a Baptist minister, b. 14 Aug. 1792.
viii. PHEBE, b. and d. in 1755.
ix. MARY, b. 9 March 1760; d. 7 Aug. 1839; m. 1 Feb. 1781 Lt. JAMES SLATE of Mansfield, Conn., b. there 11 Dec. 1751, d. 5 May 1836, aged 84, son of Ezekiel and Mehitable (Hall) Slate. Ezekiel Slate served in the Revolution.

Children (surname *Slate*), b. in Mansfield (Mansfield Vital Records):
1. *Clarissa*, b. 16 Nov. 1782; m. ———— Lull. Lived in Vermont.
2. *Mary*, of Wilbraham, Mass., b. 2 Oct. 1784; m. in 1808 Alvin Bennett, son of Lt. Asa and Mary (Barrows) Bennett.
3. *Sally*, of Mansfield, b. 5 March 1787; m. Christopher Nicholas Spencer.
4. *Mehitable*, b. 10 June 1790; d. in Mansfield; m. Charles Thompson.
5. *Laura (Lora)*, b. 10 May 1792; d. in Coventry, Conn.; m. John Thompson.
6. *James*, b. in 1794; d. in 1797.
7. *Nancy*, b. 11 May 1796; d. in Mansfield; m. in 1818 Thomas Place.
8. *Needham*, b. 6 Aug. 1798; m. in 1825 Fanny Burnham, daughter of Daniel Burnham of Hampton, Conn. 6 children one of whom, Daniel Needham Slate, was b. in 1834.
9. *Phila*, b. 7 Jan. 1801; m. in 1818 Horace Hall of Mansfield. Moved to Pennsylvania.
10. *Armina*, b. 29 Aug. 1803; m. in 1822 Eliphalet Martin of Mansfield.
11. *Sabrina*, b. 30 Dec. 1805; m. in 1829 Charles Martin.
12. x. LT. STEPHEN, b. 6 Dec. 1763.

5. JASPER[3] NEEDHAM (*Anthony*,[2] *Anthony*[1]), of Danvers, Mass., born 15 June 1705, died 3 Oct. 1794. He married, published 20 Nov. 1731, Mary Cook.

Children (Salem, Mass., Vital Records):
i. STEPHEN,[4] bapt. in 1735; d. young.
ii. DANIEL, b. 15 June 1735.
iii. BENJAMIN, b. 6 Aug. 1738.
iv. STEPHEN, b. 15 Oct. 1742; m. in 1758 ELIZABETH MOULTON of Brimfield, b. 23 Sept. 1737, daughter of Robert and Elizabeth Moulton.
Children:
1. *Daniel.*[5]
2. *Jasper.*
3. *Stephen.*
4. *Mary.*
5. *David.*

6. CAPT. ANTHONY[4] NEEDHAM (*Anthony*[3], *Anthony*,[2] *Anthony*[1]), born in Brimfield, Mass., 18 May 1723, died in Hopkinton, Mass., while on a journey to Boston, in 1785. He married, 3

Sept. 1741 (Brimfield Vital Records; another record says 1740), REBEKAH MUNGER, born in 1716, died in 1798 (family record), daughter of Samuel Munger.

Capt. Anthony Needham was a lieutenant in the French and Indian War, and a captain in the Revolution. He was the first representative from South Brimfield in the Massachusetts Legislature; selectman, 1746, 1758, 1759; assessor, 1746; selectman of South Brimfield, 1764.

Children, born in Brimfield (Brimfield Vital Records):

 i. ANNAH,[5] b. 2 March 1742; d. 30 June 1843, aged 101 years 3 months 16 days; m. 19 Sept. 1770 SAMUEL STRONG, b. in 1743, d. 28 Jan. 1828, aged 85, son of Samuel and Martha (Stoughton) Strong. The Barbour Collection of Union, Conn., Vital Records states: Needham "Anna of So. Brimfield m. Samuel Strong of Union Sept. 19, 1770". Samuel served in the Revolutionary War.

  Children (surname *Strong*):

  1. *Martha*, b. 22 July 1771; m. 16 Jan. 1794, Solomon Wales, J.P., officiating, Nehemiah May of Holland, Mass.

  2. *Mary*, b. 28 May 1774; m. 17 Feb. 1803 Walter Rosebrooks of Holland, Mass.

  3. *Chloe*, b. 13 Jan. 1779; m. 12 Oct. 1797 Elisha Needham b. in 1770, son of Jeremiah and Elizabeth (Gardner) Needham.

  4. *Anna*, m. John Whitmore, of Ashford, Conn.

  5. *Phebe*, b. 11 June 1781; d. unm. in Palmer, Mass., in 1854.

  6. *Tryphena*, of Skaneateles, N. Y., b. 4 Jan. 1784; m. Aaron Allen of Sturbridge, Mass.

13. ii. ANTHONY, b. 27 Nov. 1744.

 iii. MARY, b. 9 Dec. 1746; m. (1), ROBERT BROWN, JR.; m. (2), JOHN SHAW.

 iv. SAMUEL, b. 16 April 1748; d. in infancy.

 v. EUNICE, b. 2 Dec. 1749; d. in infancy.

14. vi. DAVID, b. 22 April 1755.

7. NEHEMIAH[4] NEEDHAM (*Anthony,[3] Anthony[2], Anthony[1]*), born in South Brimfield, now Wales, Mass., 4 April 1734, died in New Marlboro, Vt., 14 Jan. 1817, aged 82. ("History of the Town of Marlborough, Windham County, Vermont", by Rev. Ephraim H. Newton.) He married, first, 21 June 1758, EUNICE FULLER, baptized in Middleton, Essex Co., Mass., in 1735, daughter of Jonathan and Hannah (Peabody) Fuller; and, secondly, 10 March 1779, LYDIA BLODGET of Stafford, Conn.

Nehemiah Needham served as a private in Capt. Ebenezer Moulton's company, in Col. Pomeroy's regiment, in the expedition to Crown Point, 11 Sept. to 25 Dec. 1755 (Massachusetts Archives, Box 94, p. 45).

Children by first wife:

 i. EUNICE,[5] b. in South Brimfield, now Wales, 24 June 1759; d. 16 Nov. 1837, aged 78; m. 18 April 1781/2 ROBERT ANDREWS, b. in Coventry, Conn., 17 March 1759, d. 14 Feb. 1838, aged 79, son of Lt. Robert and Delight (Kellogg) Andrews.

  Children (surname *Andrews*):

  1. *Betsey*, b. 18 March 1782; m. Elijah Fosket of Wales, probably the Elijah, b. in 1781, son of Joshua.

  2. *Alanson*, b. 1 April 1784; m. (1), Phebe Green, of Wales, daughter of Daniel and Rebecca (Bond) Green; m. (2), Sally (Gates)

Needham. Moved to Ohio in 1818. A son, Robert Warren,
b. in 1814, lived in Staffordville, Conn., a machinist and in-
vented the famous Stafford loom.
3. *Col. Robert*, b. 20 March 1786; m. 19 Oct. 1808 Lucy Needham,
b. 11 Aug. 1790, daughter of Lt. Stephen and Abigail (Perry)
Needham.
4. *Alvin*, b. 10 Nov. 1788; m. 7 April 1814 or 1818 Mary Brown,
sister of Othniel Brown who married Alvin's sister Annis. A
descendant of Alvin and Mary, Harold Lee Andrews, has
been for many years town clerk and treasurer of Stafford,
Conn.
5. *Eunice*, b. 27 March 1793; d. in Bennington, N. Y., in 1862; m.
Elam Munger of Wales.
6. *Annis*, b. 21 July 1798; m. 16 April 1818 Othniel Brown, b. 1
April 1796, son of Othniel Brown and his second wife, Sibyl
Olney, daughter of Isaac and Lydia (Packard) Olney of
Rhode Island. Othniel, Sr., and his father, Col. Chad Brown,
served in the Revolutionary War. Children (surname
Brown): (1) Eunice, b. 26 April 1819; m. 29 Aug. 1844 Loomis
Agard, son of Benjamin and Fanny (Moore) Agard. Chil-
dren (surname *Agard*): (a) *Albert*. (b) *Mary*. (c) *Philena*.
(d) *Elvira*. (e) *Rosella*. (f) *Adelbert*. (2) Holstein, b. 26
Feb. 1821; m. (1), Lottie Bass, probably Elizabeth Loretta
Bass, daughter of Luther and Betsey Bass; m. (2), Mary
Desire Preston, daughter of Silas Preston. Children by first
wife: (a) *Luther B.* (b) *Othniel*. Children by second wife: (c)
Edward Holstein. (d) *Frances Mary*. (3) Mary, b. 13 Feb.
1823; m. 14 Dec. 1843 Benjamin Monroe Gold of West
Stafford, son of Benjamin and Ruby E. (Dennison) Gold.
Children (surname *Gold*): (a) *Alvin Monroe*. (b) *George
Washington*. (c) *Milo Adelbert*. (d) *Georgianna*. (4) Annis
Maria, b. 24 Sept. 1826; m. 12 April 1843 Rev. Leonard Still-
man Goodell, son of Leonard and Jerusha (Corbin) Goodell
of Woodstock, Conn. Children (surname *Goodell*): (a)
Charles Wesley. (b) *George*. (c) *Mary Jane (Jennie M.)*.
(d) *Henry*. (e) *Lucy Maria*, b. in 1852; m. John Royal Chap-
man, and had two children, Ernest Stanley who married
Esther Ann Kendrick, and Grace Olive, the compiler of this
Needham record. (f) *Edwin*. (g) *Olive Lovisa*. (h) *Frank
Miro*, b. in 1859; m. Letitia Armitage, and had one son,
Chester Raymond, who has the Goodell family Bible. (i)
Julia Emma. (j) *Della Almeda*. (k) *John Gilbert*. (l) *Adel-
bert Warren*. (m) *Milo Ernest (Ernest M.)*. (5) Robert
Othniel, b. 22 Jan. 1837; m. 4 Nov. 1868 Mary A. Scripture
of Stafford, daughter of Dennis and Rosetta (Washburn)
Scripture. (6) Persis E., b. 10 Jan. 1841; m. (1), 6 Feb. 1879,
Friend C. Smith, b. 8 May 1817, son of Dr. John and Mar-
garet (Campbell) Smith, and widower of her cousin, Sibyl
Olney Andrews; m. (2), 16 April 1896, Charles Henry Copp.

ii. MEHITABLE, b. 17 Jan. 1762; m. (1), in 1786, EBENEZER MOULTON,
b. in Brimfield 28 Jan. 1746/7, d. in 1816, son of John Moulton; m.
(2), in 1828, AMOS GREEN. Ebenezer served in the Revolution;
lived in South Brimfield.
Children by first husband (surname *Moulton*):
1. *Catherine*, b. 25 July 1781; m. ——— Munger.
2. *Mary*, b. 25 Aug. 1786; d. two days later.
3. *Mehitable*, b. and d. 16 Aug. 1787.
4. *Needham*, b. 24 Aug. 1788, d. 16 March 1863; m. (1), 19 Aug.
1813, Seba Munger, b. 14 Dec. 1793, daughter of Amasa and
Hannah (Corbin) Munger, and sister of Rev. Washington
Munger of Holland, Stafford, Tolland, Mystic, and Waterford, Conn.; m. (2), Miriam Weld, daughter of Benjamin

Draper Weld; m. (3), 21 May 1841, Nancy Green of Vernon, Conn.

Children by first wife: (1) Cheney, b. in 1813. (2) Cutler, b. in 1815. (3) Amasa, b. in 1817. (4) Mary L., b. in 1819. (5) Porter, b. in 1821. (6) Orrill, b. in 1823. (7) Turner, b. in 1825. (8) Zelotes, b. in 1827, (9) Elvira, b. in 1829. (10) Merrick, b. in 1831. (11) Needham, b. 17 Aug. 1833; m. 5 July 1854 Phebe Needham, b. 1 March 1836, daughter of Darius Munger and Lovina (Nelson) Needham.

15. iii. JONATHAN, b. 21 May 1764.
16. iv. ROBERT, b. 27 Nov. 1766.
    v. SUSANNA, b. 14 Dec. 1769; m. David Brown.
    vi. NEHEMIAH, b. 16 Oct. 1772; m. ——— PEASE, daughter of John Pease of Marlboro, private in the War of 1812.
    vii. ABIGAIL, b. 20 June 1775.

Children by second wife:

    viii. SARAH, b. in Wales 29 Dec. 1779; m. in Marlboro, 10 Nov. 1800, WILLIAM GILBERT, JR.
    ix. SAMUEL, b. in Stafford 22 May 1782; d. 17 Feb. 1813; m. POLLY MILLER, daughter of David Miller of Marlboro.

8. JASPER[4] NEEDHAM (*Anthony,[3] Anthony,[2] Anthony[1]*), born in South Brimfield, now Wales, Mass., 31 July 1738, died 14 Dec. 1821. He married, in November 1758, DEBORAH FULLER, baptized in Middleton, Mass., in 1738, daughter of Jonathan and Hannah (Peabody) Fuller and sister of Eunice Fuller who married Jasper's brother Nehemiah.

Jasper Needham served in the French and Indian War as a drummer under the command of Daniel Burt, William Williams Col., from 13 March to 20 Nov. 1758. He served also in the Revolution, enlisting in the regiment of his brother, Capt. Anthony Needham.

Children, born in South Brimfield:

    i. JOHN,[5] b. 1 Dec. 1760.
    ii. NEOMI, b. 24 Sept. 1762; m. 30 June 1786 JAMES STRICKLAND.
    iii. HANNAH, b. 16 July 1764.
    iv. MARY, b. 16 Sept. 1766.
    v. RUTH, b. 29 Sept. 1768.
17. vi. ABNER, b. 23 Feb. 1771.
    vii. HULDAH, b. 19 March 1773.
18. viii. DANIEL, b. 27 June 1775.
    ix. AZUBAH, b. 3 Feb. 1778; m. in 1795 HEZEKIAH NELSON.
19. x. JASPER, b. 25 Nov. 1781.

9. JEREMIAH[4] NEEDHAM (*Anthony,[3] Anthony,[2] Anthony[1]*), born in South Brimfield, now Wales, Mass., 17 June 1741, died in Wilmington, N. Y., in August 1815. He married, 20 Feb. 1765, ELIZABETH GARDNER (Brimfield Vital Records), born in 1740, died in Ferrisburg, Vt., in 1819, probably daughter of Humphrey and Ann Gardner.

Jeremiah served in the Revolutionary War as sergeant in Capt. Daniel Winchester's company, a private in Capt. John Carpenter's company. He was town clerk in South Brimfield in 1765.

Children:

20. i. JEREMIAH,[5] b. 20 Feb. 1766.
21. ii. ELISHA, b. 5 Sept. 1770.
    iii. ANNA.
    iv. CHARLES (twin).
    v. REBECCA (twin).

10. DANIEL[4] NEEDHAM (*Anthony,[3] Anthony,[2] Anthony[1]*) was born in South Brimfield, which is now Wales, Mass., 10 Sept. 1743 (Brimfield Vital Records). On 2 Aug. 1765 he married THANKFUL CORLEY, say the Brimfield Vital Records. Bowen's Woodstock, vol. II, p. 45, says that Daniel Needham was born 13 Sept. 1743, married 2 Aug. 1764 Thankful Corliss, and moved to Stafford in 1783. The Norwich, Conn., Vital Records give Thankful Corlis, born 27 Jan. 1742/3, daughter of Timothy Corlis Jun[r] of Haverhill and Ann Willoughby of Norwich who were married 2 June 1740. Daniel Needham served in the Revolution.

Child:

    i. MARTHA,[5] b. in July 1776; m. ———— SWEET. "Martha Sweet d. 3 Aug. 1872 a. 95y 11m 23d; widow, Wales; b. Stafford, Conn. d. of Daniel Needham b. Wales and Thankful b. Norwich, Conn." (Mass. Death Records, State House, Boston, Mass.) Doubtless other children.

11. ABNER[4] NEEDHAM (*Anthony,[3] Anthony,[2] Anthony[1]*), born 17 Dec. 1746, died 20 June 1800. In 1778 he married HANNAH HEATON, who married, secondly, in 1805, John Wallis. He served in the Revolution.

Children (Wales, Mass., Vital Records):

    i. FREDERIC,[5] b. 13 Sept. 1780.
    ii. JAMES H., b. 28 April 1783.
    iii. CLARRA, b. 21 Dec. 1784.
    iv. HEATON, b. 19 Aug. 1790.

12. LT. STEPHEN[4] NEEDHAM (*Humphrey,[3] Anthony,[2] Anthony[1]*), born 6 Dec. 1763, died 4 July 1836, aged 72. He married, 15 Dec. 1785, ABIGAIL PERRY, died 17 April 1832, aged 73.

He served in the Revolution; was selectman, 1801, 1805 to 1810, 1813.

Children, born in South Brimfield:

22. i. DANFORD,[5] b. 26 Oct. 1786.
    ii. MELINDA, b. 3 Feb. 1788; d. 20 Jan. 1841, aged 53 years; m., as his third wife, BENJAMIN AGARD, b. in Stafford, Conn., 5 March 1787, d. 18 March 1872, aged 85, son of Benjamin and Sarah (Hiscock) Agard.
    Children (surname *Agard*):
    1. *Philena*, b. 25 April 1825; m. in 1854 Dr. Jeduthan Campbell Eaton, b. in Mansfield, Conn., in 1807, son of Jeduthan and Lydia (Campbell) Eaton.
    2. *Lucius*, b. in Stafford 6 March 1827; m. in 1854 Mary Minerva Corbin of Union, Conn., daughter of Healy and Nancy (Coye) Corbin.
    3. *Stephen*, b. 23 Nov. 1829; m. 23 Oct. 1856 Rebecca Corbin, b. 23 Sept. 1834, sister of Mary Minerva Corbin who m. his brother Lucius.

iii. LUCY, b. 11 Aug. 1789; d. 30 April 1869, aged 78 years 8 months 19 days; m. 19 Oct. 1808 COL. ROBERT ANDREWS, b. 20 March 1786, d. 24 Aug. 1870, aged 85 years 4 months 4 days.

Children (surname Andrews):

1. *Warren*, b. in 1809; d. in 1814 and buried in Wales.
2. *Abigail Needham*, b. 18 Dec. 1810; m. in 1831 Orre Parker.
3. *Eunice*, b. 21 Sept. 1813; m. in 1841 John S. Fosdick.
4. *Horatio*, b. and d. in 1815 and buried in Wales.
5. *Austin*, b. 9 Feb. 1817; m. in 1845 Lorana Barney.
6. *Martha* (twin), b. 18 Dec. 1818; d. 17 March 1819.
7. *Mary* (twin), b. 18 Dec. 1818; d. 19 March 1819.
8. *Miner*, b. 6 Aug. 1820; m. in 1845 Sarah Janes, b. in 1820, daughter of Albon Janes.
9. *Lucy S.*, b. 4 Nov. 1824; m. in 1850 James F. Parker.
10. *A daughter.*
11. *Sarah A.*, b. 31 Aug. 1829; m. in 1849 Benjamin G. Webster.
12. *Charles*, b. 19 March 1833; m. in 1856 Harriet Brown.

iv. STEPHEN, b. 21 July 1791; d. in Wisconsin in 1853; m. MARY FULLER. They moved to Holland Purchase, Erie Co., N. Y., after their marriage, and then to Wisconsin in 1848.

v. DANIEL D., b. 23 Aug. 1794; d. in Lyons, N. Y., in 1840; m. ———. They moved to Lyons after their marriage, where he taught school.

vi. ORIN, b. 4 July 1797; d. 23 May 1861, aged 64 years; m. SOPHIA ———, d. 28 Sept. 1870, aged 75 years.

Children:

1. *Mary M.*,[6] d. in Wales 26 Sept. 18—, aged 6 years.
2. *George H.*, d. 23 May 1883, age 62 years 26 days.

13. ANTHONY[5] NEEDHAM (*Anthony*,[4] *Anthony*,[3] *Anthony*,[2] *Anthony*[1]), born 27 Nov. 1744 (Brimfield Vital Records), died 27 Sept. 1785, in 42d year. He married in Monson, Mass., 31 July 1765, Catherine Warner, born in 1743, died 3 June 1808.

Anthony Needham was a Corporal in the company of his father, Capt. Anthony, on the Lexington Alarm; Sergeant in Capt. Aaron Charles' company at Ticonderoga in Feb. 1776; Sergeant in Capt. Munn's company in 1777; as Anthony "Nedom" a private in Capt. William Richards' company, 1781–1783.

Children, born in South Brimfield (Byrdee M. Needham, Omaha, Nebr.):

i. SARAH,[6] b. 3 Dec. 1766.

ii. SUSANNA, b. 7 April 1768; m. JOS. WALKER.

iii. EUNICE, b. 5 Feb. 1770; m. in 1792 SIMEON MUNGER, b. 10 Jan. 1771, d. in Wales, son of John and Sybil (Parsons) Munger. He was living in Plainfield, Otsego Co., N. Y., before 1804, then returned to Massachusetts.

Children (surname *Munger*) ("Munger Book", p. 267):

1. *Susanna*, b. in Wales in 1793.
2. *Sally*, b. in Wales 6 Jan. 1795; m. Henry Chandler. Lived in Nunda and Portage, N. Y.
3. *Irene*, b. in Wales 2 Dec. 1797.
4. *Delency*, d. young.
5. *Eunice*, d. young.
6. *John*, b. in Plainfield 30 Aug. 1804.
7. *Anthony*, b. in Plainfield 8 April 1807.
8. *Samantha*, b. in Plainfield 15 Feb. 1809.

iv. MARY, b. 25 Oct. 1772.

v. ANTHONY, b. 5 Jan. 1774; d. in January 1858; m. (1), in South Brimfield, 5 Aug. 1798, SOPHIA PRATT, who died after their first child
was born; m. (2), 22 Nov. 1803, ANNA THAYER, d. in December
1857.

Child by first wife, b. in South Brimfield (Byrdee M. Needham
of Omaha, Nebr.):

1. *Anthony Storrs*,[7] b. 26 Feb. 1800; d. in Blue Mounds, Dane Co.,   [1]
   Wis., 4 Aug. 1865; m. in Baltimore, Md., Emma Souder, b.
   4 July 1826, d. 18 Nov. 1881, daughter of George Souder.   [2]
   Resided in Massachusetts, Maryland, Pennsylvania, Illinois,
   and Wisconsin. Children: (1) Georgiana,[8] b. in Baltimore
   8 May 1827; d. in Denver, Colo.; m. Thomas Heeney. (2)
   Anthony Matthias, b. in Philadelphia, Pa., 19 Jan. 1829; d.
   in Madison, Wis., in 1858; m. Sarah Jane Olds, daughter of
   Nathaniel and Sally (Avery) Olds. (3) Mary Elizabeth, b.
   in Illinois 24 Jan. 1835; d. in Milford, Iowa; m. Michael
   Tusler. (4) Ebenezer Brigham, b. in Putnam County, Ill.,
   28 Aug. 1837; m. Amanda Jane Holton. (5) Jane Ann, b. in
   Putnam County, Ill., 28 March 1840; d. in 1901; m. in
   Austin, Nebr., Abel Gates. (6) John Sample, b. in Platte-
   ville, Wis., 1 March 1845; m. Ella Viantha Hiddleson.
   Children (a) *Gabrielle*.[9] (b) *Charlie*. (c) *Pearl Emmerette*.
   (d) *Byrdee M.*, who furnished the information for descendants of Anthony,[5] John Anthony Bruce. (7) Melissa Clarissa,
   b. in Blue Mounds 4 April 1850; d. in Moingona, Iowa, in
   1874; m. Daniel Smith.

Children, by second wife:

2. *Sylvester*, b. 28 June 1804; d. in Caledonia, Ill., 10 Feb. 1874.
3. *Laura*, b. 28 Aug. 1806; d. in Oswego, N. Y., in 1873; m. John
   Wilder.
4. *Annis*, b. 10 May 1809; d. in Hartford, Conn.; m. Edward
   Smith.
5. *Orril* or *Orriel*, b. 15 Nov. 1811; d. 5 Feb. 1898; m. in 1831
   William Howard.
6. *Lyman W.*, b. 10 Nov. 1814; d. in Oshkosh, Wis., in 1893.
7. *Willard M.*, b. 20 Aug. 1817; d. in Utica, N. Y., 21 April 1897.
8. *Orrin*, b. 22 Feb. 1820; d. in January 1840.
9. *Emmerette P.*, b. 22 Dec. 1822; d. in Chicago, Ill., in 1887; m.
   10 Aug. 1847 Enos C. Boynton.
10. *Candace*, b. 19 Sept. 1825; d. in Springfield, Mass.

vi. IRENE, b. 5 Jan. 1776; d. probably in Minneapolis, Minn.; m. WIL-
LIAM MORSE of Rodman, N. Y.

vii. LOVINA, b. 24 May 1778; d. 29 June 1859; m. NATHAN BOND of Brimfield.

viii. ALVIN, b. 23 Feb. 1780; d. 4 Dec. 1847; m. 26 May 1802 ABIGAIL
WALBRIDGE, probably the Abigail b. in 1784, daughter of William
and Rebecca (Moulton) Walbridge.

ix. BETSEY, b. in 1782; d. 12 Sept. 1858, aged 76; m. in 1803 LEONARD
CHAFFEE, b. in Woodstock, Conn., 11 April 1782, die' in Weathersfield, N. Y., 25 Dec. 1857, son of James Chaffee and his second wife
Rhoda Cady. He was wounded in the Battle of Black Rock, N. Y.,
in War of 1812.

Children (surname *Chaffee*):

1. *Hiram*, b. in Massachusetts 3 July 1806; m. Philenda Butler.
2. *Mary Ann*, d. in Attica, N. Y., in 1836; m. Simeon Jones.
3. *Lucy*, d. in Genesee Falls, N. Y., in 1880; m. Foster G. Rogers.
4. *Leonard Leander*, b. 21 May 1826; m. Julia A. Thorpe.

[1] After Md. insert 4 July 1826, and delete b. after Souder.
[2] Delete 4 July 1826.

NEEDHAMS OF WALES, MASS., AND STAFFORD, CONN.

By GRACE OLIVE CHAPMAN, of Dorchester (Boston), Mass.

14. CAPT. DAVID[5] NEEDHAM (*Anthony,*[4] *Anthony,*[3] *Anthony,*[2] *Anthony*[1]), born in Stafford, Conn., 22 April 1755, died 22 Nov. 1815, aged 60. He married, 10 June 1779, MARSYLVIA AINSWORTH, born 26 Aug. 1759, died 21 May 1853, aged 94, daughter of Capt. William and Mary (Marcy) Ainsworth of Woodstock, Conn.

David Needham served in the Revolution, and was selectman in South Brimfield in 1786, 1793, 1796, and 1813.

Children (Lovering's "History of Holland", 1915):

i.   LUKE,[6] b. 27 May 1780; d. 28 May 1780.
ii. POLLY MARCY, b. 12 April 1782; m. in 1803 EZRA ALLEN of Holland, Mass.
iii. ALFRED, b. 15 Feb. 1784; d. 27 March 1853; m. in South Brimfield, 29 April 1807, SALLY PRATT, b. 21 June 1787, d. 24 Feb. 1848, aged 60. He was known as Squire Alfred, and was prominent in town affairs. He was town clerk, 1816–1834; selectman, 1817–1828, 1833–1835; and representative to the Massachusetts legislature, 1833–1835.

Children, b. in South Brimfield, now Wales:
1. *Marcilvia,*[7] b. 4 Aug. 1808; d. 10 Aug. 1842; m. Robert Headley.
2. *David B.,* farmer, of Wales, b. 11 July 1809; d. 6 July 1857.
3. *Mary M.,* b. 21 Nov. 1811; d. in Woonsocket, R. I., 30 Aug. 1851.
4. *Salome.,* b. 10 Feb. 1814; d. in Monson, Mass., 13 March 1871; m. Foster Pepper.
5. *William,* b. 2 Feb. 1816; d. in Cleveland, Ohio, 18 Oct. 1854. Moved to Minnesota in 1834, and later settled in Cleveland.
6. *Alfred Allen,* farmer, b. 1 Aug. 1817; d. 18 May 1881. Moved to Rockford, Ill., in 1856.
7. *Otis,* b. 25 June 1821; d. in Monson, Mass., 12 Feb. 1888; m. (1), in 1841, Olive M. White, daughter of John and Eunice White; m. (2), in 1853, Julia F. Warren, b. in Piqua, Ohio, in 1833. Children by first wife: (1) John A.[8] (2) Sarah P., b. in 1842; m. David Belcher. A daughter Minnie J. Belcher m. Frederick Morgan Smith and had nine children. (3) Otis. Children by second wife: (4) George A. (5) William A. (6) David Besse. (7) Wales Foster. (8) Olive A. (9) Helen M. (10) Fred J.
8. *Wales,* b. 22 June 1823; m. in 1844 Catharine Walbridge, daughter of Samuel and Electa (Moulton) Walbridge of Wales, Mass. He went west in the early fifties.
9. *Sally,* b. 20 Feb. 1826; d. in Wales 5 April 1842.
10. *Luke B.,* b. 14 July 1828; d. 5 Oct. 1830.
iv. ANTHONY, b. 24 Feb. 1786; d. 17 April 1819.
v. OLIVER, b. 8 March 1788; d. in Concord, N. Y., 4 Sept. 1872.
vi. SALLY, b. 4 June 1790; m. 12 May 1811 ADOLPHUS WEBBER.
vii. WILLIAM, b. 18 March 1792; d. 17 Sept. 1794.
viii. REBECCA M., b. 20 May 1794; m. in April 1819 SILAS PERRY, son of Abner Perry.
Children (surname *Perry*):
1. *Oliver A.,* b. in 1820; m. Amy A. ———. Children: (1) Annie, b. in 1868; d. in 1873. (2) Silvie, b. in 1871; d. in 1880.
2. *Winthrop,* b. in 1826.
3. *Marsylvia,* b. in 1828; m. William Shumway Wallis of *Holland,* Mass.
ix. WILLIAM A., b. 5 May 1796; d. in 1860 and buried in Wales; m. ORINDA NELSON.
x. LORINDA, b. 9 Nov. 1798; d. in 1854; m. DANIEL MOORE.
xi. ANDREW A., b. 1 Sept. 1800; d. 17 Nov. 1880, aged 80 years 2 months 16 days; m. (1), in Monson, Mass., 20 Sept. 1821, DEIDAMIA WALBRIDGE, d. 22 Jan. 1822, aged 19, possibly daughter of William and Catharine Walbridge; m. (2), Nancy Belcher, d. 31 Jan. 1881, aged 71 years 9 months 16 days, daughter of David and Chloey (Sawyer) Belcher. Andrew Needham lived in Wales and was selectman in 1847.
Children by second wife:
1. *Chloe M.,*[7] b. 2 Feb. 1830; d. 1907; m. Orsan A. Eaton, b. 25 Oct. 1831, d. 9 Jan. 1902.
2. *David A.,* b. 14 Jan. 1836; m. Lydia A. ———, d. 24 Jan 1866, aged 27 years. Child: (1) Persis,[8] b. in 1859, d. in 1915, m. Charlie M. Greene, b. in 1857, d. in 1895.

15. JONATHAN[5] NEEDHAM(*Nehemiah,*[4]*Anthony,*[3]*Anthony,*[2]*Anthony*[1]), born 21 May 1764, died in Calvert County, Md., 8 Dec. 1811. He married, 30 May 1787, EUNICE FISKE, born 24 Oct. 1768, daughter of Capt. Asa and Elizabeth (Knight) Fiske.

He served in the Revolution, enlisting in Wales 12 July 1780, at the age of 17; discharged in December 1780; re-enlisted in 1782 for three years.

Children:

i. ROSWELL,[6] b. 8 Aug. 1787; d. 8 April 1870; m. SARAH THAYER, d. 30 Dec. 1860, aged 72, buried in Wales, Mass.

Children (Mrs. Leon Thompson of Wales, 1942):
1. *Warren,*[7] b. 29 April 1813; d. 1 April 1883; m. Elizabeth Wilder, d. 13 July 1885, aged 68.
2. *Chandler,* b. 16 May 1816; d. 19 Nov. 1901; m. 25 Nov. 1839, Rev. Washington Munger officiating (Stafford, Conn., Vital Records), Lauretta Howe.
3. *Lyman,* b. 18 Sept. 1818.
4. *Sarah,* b. 4 Aug. 1821; m. Ira Porter Thompson, son of William and Margaret (Nelson) Thompson.
5. *Francis M.,* b. 2 March 1826; d. 3 Oct. 1846.
6. *Roswell,* b. 26 Feb. 1827; d. 6 Feb. 1901, aged 77 years; m. (1), 28 March 1846, Calista E. Belcher, b. in 1830, d. 23 March 1858, daughter of David and Chloey (Sawyer) Belcher, m. (2), 3 May 1857, Loretta A. Corbin, b. 6 April 1834, d. 15 Dec. 1875, aged 41 years, daughter of Hermon and Calista (Knowlton) Corbin. Child by first wife; (1) Belle E., b. in 1848; m. Hiram Rathbun.
7. *Ann E.,* b. 28 June 1831; d. in 1856; m. Linus Albee.

ii. SALLY, b. 29 March 1789.

iii. ASA, b. 18 May 1791; d. in Baltimore, Md.; m. (1), AMANDA COOLEY; m. (2), SALLY COLBURN; m. (3), MARY JANE DAVIDSON.

iv. JONATHAN, b. 21 June 1793; d. 24 Jan. 1862; deacon of Baptist Church in Wales for 20 years; served in the War of 1812; m. in South Brimfield, 21 Dec. 1816, LODISA PRATT, b. 3 May 1799, d. 19 Nov. 1873.

Children:

1. *Asa H.,*[7] b. 6 April 1821, d. in Baltimore 27 April 1849.
2. *Eunice M.,* b. 8 April 1827; d. in Wales 29 Sept. 1843.
3. *Henry Miles,* b. 23 Nov. 1829, d. 12 Aug. 1890; m. in St. Albans, Vt., 6 July 1864, Helen E. Chapman, b. 3 Oct. 1840, d. in Brooklyn 23 Aug. 1903, daughter of Henry T. Chapman, a chemist of Brooklyn, b. in London, England, and his wife, a Curtis of the old New York family of that name. He was educated at Union College and Harvard Law School; lawyer, New York City, lived in Brooklyn, N. Y. Children, b. in Brooklyn: (1) Helen P.,[8] b. 19 April 1865; m. in Brooklyn, 21 June 1892, George C. Flynt of Monson, Mass. (2) Henry Chapman, b. 8 Nov. 1866; received degree LL.B. from Columbia Law School in 1882; a New York lawyer until his death; had a very fine collection of Needham family data, with which he was very generous. (3) George A., b. 12 Sept. 1868. (Cutter's "New England Families", vol. 1, pp. 10 and 100, 1913 ed.; and Henry Chapman Needham).

v. CHESTER, b. 10 Oct. 1795; d. 7 Nov. 1850.

16. CAPT. ROBERT[5] NEEDHAM (*Nehemiah,*[4] *Anthony,*[3] *Anthony,*[2] *Anthony*[1]), born 27 Nov. 1766, died 20 Sept. 1823, aged 54. He married DOLLY ——.
He lived in Stafford, Conn., and was a Captain of the Connecticut Militia.

Children:

i. MATILDA,[6] b. in Stafford 20 Nov. 1790; d. in Windsor Locks, Conn., 11 Dec. 1863; m. in Stafford, 10 March 1813, TIMOTHY CRANE, b. 28 Jan. 1783, d. in Russell, Mass., in 1830, son of Aaron and Mary (Barber) Crane.

Children (surname *Crane*) ("Crain-Crane Genealogy"):
1. *Matilda Amelia*, b. 22 Aug. 1814.
2. *Edwin T.*, d. in 1852.
3. *Lyman Walbridge*, merchant, of Stafford Springs, Conn., d. in 1890; m. Harriet Swift Grant, b. 4 July 1820, d. in 1895, daughter of Billings and Lucy Green (Sanford) Grant.
4. *Mary Jane F.*, d. in 1846.
5. *Catherine C.*, living in Springfield, Mass., in 1897.
ii. ROBERT W., probably m. 9 Dec. 1824 BATHSHEBA FERRY, b. 2 Aug. 1804, d. 18 April 1828, aged 23, daughter of James and Polly (Rogers) Ferry of Staffordville.
iii. SIDNEY F., probably b. 6 March 1798; d. 2 May 1883; m. SARAH ———, b. 26 July 1799, d. 5 May 1883.

17. ABNER[5] NEEDHAM (*Jasper*,[4] *Anthony*,[3] *Anthony*,[2] *Anthony*[1]) was born in South Brimfield, which is now Wales, Mass., 23 Feb. 1771. He married in Pittsford, Vt., ELIZABETH MEAD, daughter of Stephen and Polly (White) Mead.

In 1794 he went to Pittsford with his cousin Jeremiah[5] Needham, son of Jeremiah[4] and Ruth (Cooley) Needham.

Children 12, born in Pittsford, Rutland Co., Vt. (Warren Melvin Packer of Evansville, Ind., a descendant of Abner and Elizabeth Needham):

i. AMY,[6] b. 8 July 1795; m. in Pittsford, 4 July 1821, EZEKIEL ST. JOHN.
ii. SALLY, b. 27 Feb. 1797.
iii. HULDA, b. 7 Nov. 1798.
iv. TRUMAN, b. 3 Sept. 1800.
v. STEPHEN MEAD, b. 5 July 1802.
vi. MELINDA (twin), b. 18 June 1803.
vii. MIRIAM (twin, b. 18 June 1803.
viii. BETSEY, b. 6 May 1805; d. in Medina County, Ohio, in 1846; m. 20 July 1823 JEREMIAH YOUNG of Rutland, Vt., born in New Hampshire in 1795, said ot have been a son of Jeremiah Young, a Revolutionary soldier of Scotch extraction; served in War of 1812.
    Children (surname Young):
    1. *Elizabeth*, b. ca. 1824; to Wisconsin.
    2. *George W.*, b in Rutland County, Vt., in 1825; served in Civil War; to Michigan.
    3. *Charles B.*, b. in 1828/9; m. Almyra Bailey; served in Civil War.
    4. *Jeremiah*, b. in 1832; to Ohio and Michigan.
    5. *Sarah Victoria*, b. ca. 1834; m. ——— Green; to Illinois, to Iowa.
    6. *Lucy Columbia*, b. in Brandon Twp., Franklin Co., N. Y., 29 Oct. 1836; m. in Medina, Ohio, in 1857, Victor Trautman, b. in Alsace-Lorraine, France, in 1829, d. in Dorr, Mich.
    7. *John S.*, b. in St. Lawrence County, N. Y., 3 April 1838; m. in 1859 Hannah Losier.
    8. *A child*, b. in 1840.
    9. *Mary Caroline*, b. in Lawrence Twp., St. Lawrence Co., N. Y., 16 March 1842; d. in Pine River Twp., Gratiot Co., Mich.; m. 27 April 1863 Isaac Mitchell Packer, son of Amos Victor and Elizabeth (Lingle) Packer.
    10. *Daniel*, b. in 1843; d. in 1858.
ix. ANNA, b. 18 Nov. 1806(?).
x. ABNER, b. 10 Jan. 1807.
xi. HARRIET.
xii. HARRY.

18. DANIEL[5] NEEDHAM (*Jasper*,[4] *Anthony*,[3] *Anthony*,[2] *Anthony*[1]), born 27 Jan. 1775, died 11 Sept. 1844 (Tolland and Windham

Co. Biog. Record). The late Henry Chapman Needham gave Daniel's birth as 27 June 1775, and his death as 16 Sept. 1846. He married LUCY GREEN, born in Wales 25 Oct. 1779, died 29 July 1872.

Children:

i. LYMAN,[6] b. 20 Dec. 1802; d. in infancy.
ii. LOVISA, b. 27 Jan. 1804; m. (1), WILLIAM THOMPSON of Wales; m. (2), LUKE CHILDS of Brimfield, Mass.
iii. DARIUS MUNGER, b. 28 March 1807; m. 4 Oct. 1832 LOVINA NELSON, b. 31 May 1808, daughter of Archibald and Lucy (Moulton) Nelson (Nillson, Nilson).
   Children ("History of Brimfield", 1879):
   1. *Wyles*,[7] b. 24 July 1833; d. 27 April 1869.
   2. *Phebe*, b. 1 March 1836; m. Needham Moulton.
   3. *Lyman*, b. 13 May 1841.
iv. ALANSON ANDREWS, of Wales, b. 16 Sept. 1808; d. in Braintree, Mass.; m. CYNTHIA BAXTER of Wales.
v. PHEBE GREEN, of Bloomington, Ill., b. 14 June 1809; m. AMASA MOULTON of Wales.
vi. WILLIAM MERRITT, b. in 1813; d. in 1814.
vii. ABNER, b. 31 Jan. 1817; d. in Stafford Hollow, Conn., 24 Jan. 1898, aged 82; m. (1), in 1843, MARY M. WORTHINGTON, b. in Amherst, Mass., 14 Aug. 1822, d. 29 June 1873, aged 51, daughter of Albert and Lucinda (Moore) Worthington; m. (2), in 1874, HANNAH (GIBBS) NICHOLS, widow of Cyrus Nichols of Stafford.
   Children by first wife:
   1. *Adelbert*,[6] b. in Stafford 5 April 1847; m. (1), 6 Aug. 1872, Josephine Turner, b. in Coventry, Conn., 8 July 1850, daughter of Rufus and Laura (Woodworth) Turner; m. (2), 4 May 1887, Helena Wenberg of Willington, Conn., daughter of Benjamin J. and Julie A. (Bell) Wenberg. 2 sons by second wife, Adelbert Jordan and Howard Chamberlain.
   2. *Isabel* (twin), b. 9 Oct. 1848; d. 22 Aug. 1849.
   3. *Arabel* (twin), b. 9 Oct. 1848; m. in Stafford, 19 Feb. 1873, Chauncey Orcutt of Orcutville, Stafford, Conn., b. there 12 Dec. 1839, son of Harvey and Mary Ann (Billings) Orcutt. A daughter, Gertrude May Orcutt.
viii. WILLIAM MINOT, of Wales, b. 9 May 1819; d. 9 Feb. 1896; m. CHARLOTTE ALAXA PHETTEPLACE, b. 4 May 1823, daughter of Smith and Alaxa (Barrows) Phetteplace. A daughter, Charlotte Adele, m. Eliot Herbert Brown, son of Orin Washington and Mary Ann (Breard) Brown.
ix. LUCY D., b. 20 Aug. 1821; m. 21 Nov. 1847 JOSEPH E. WINTER of Stafford, Conn., son of Zina and Sally (Ellis) Winter.

19. JASPER[5] NEEDHAM (*Jasper*,[4] *Anthony*,[3] *Anthony*,[2] *Anthony*[1]), of Wales, Mass., born 25 Nov. 1781, died 26 Oct. 1847, aged 66. He married in South Brimfield, Mass., in 1809, HANNAH AGARD, born 29 Feb. 1792, died 14 May 1880, aged 88 years, daughter of Benjamin and Sarah (Hiscock) Agard. Hannah was a sister of Benjamin Agard, Jr., who married for his third wife Melinda Needham.

Children, first five born in Stafford, Conn., the last five in Wales, Mass.:

i. BENJAMIN AGARD,[6] b. 26 Oct. 1811; d. 23 Oct. 1864; m. in Stafford, Conn., in 1834, JULIA TIFFANY of Wales, b. 21 March 1808, her mother a Needham; d. 27 Jan. 1894 (part of this information from Etta (Belcher) Duncan of Monson, Mass., a granddaughter.)

639

Children, b. in Wales:

1. *Lucy*,[7] b. 11 June 1836; d. in California 2 July 1926; m. 9 April 1865 Carlos Bond of Monson. 1 son, Elmer.
2. *Monroe*, b. 17 April 1840; d. 26 June 1864.
3. *Mary M.*, b. 12 Feb. 1844; m. (1), 7 March 1865, Prescott M. Belcher, b. 23 March 1847, d. 28 Sept. 1805, son of Norman W. and Sarah (Bradway) Belcher; m. (2), ——— Washburn, and lived in Monson, Mass. (Mary Needham, daughter of Danford, m. Prescott Sawyer Belcher, an uncle of Prescott M.) Children (surname *Belcher*): (1) Ella. (2) Milton. (3) Etta M., m. Clauda A. Duncan.
4. *Miner G.*, b. 4 Sept. 1846; d. 23 March 1911; m. Abbie Pratt of Wales. 1 son, Fayette O., m. Margaret J. Coye.
5. *Julia Jane*, b. 25 Dec. 1848; d. 18 May 1884; m. 17 April 1865 Dr. Harvey H. Converse.

ii. HORATIO, b. 22 Feb. 1814; d. 21 Feb. 1822.

iii. AZUBAH, b. 11 March 1817; d. 27 Feb. 1910; m. 10 Aug. 1834 ELVIN (ALVIN) FERRY, b. in Stafford 23 July 1813, d. 12 Jan. 1884, aged 69 years, son of James and Polly (Rogers) Ferry.

Children (surname *Ferry*):

1. *Henry*, d. in infancy.
2. *Henry J.*, d. in infancy
3. *George L.*, of Staffordville, Conn., b. 11 March 1840; d. 11 May 1900; m. Lucy Root, b. 13 May 1843, d. 11 April 1908. During the Civil War he served in Co. D, 25th Regiment, Connecticut Volunteers. 2 daughters: ———, Mr. Alonzo [1] necticut Volunteers. 2 daughters: ———, m. Alonzo Spelman, [2] and Ella A., m. John Eliot Brown.
4. *Almeda.*
5. *William A.*, b. in 1849; d. 19 May 1933, aged 84; m. 15 Nov. 1871 Susan E. Hatch, b. 24 Dec. 1850, d. 9 Ju.y 1898, aged 47, daughter of John Bliss and Priscilla L. (Chapman) Hatch.
6. *A daughter*, of Windsor Locks, Conn.

iv. HANNAH, b. 28 Oct. 1819; d. 1 July 1902; m. 8 April 1839 DEA. ERASTUS KINGSBURY, b. in Coventry, Conn., 29 April 1812, d. 19 March 1895, son of Jabez and Freelove (Utley) Kingsbury.

Children (surname *Kingsbury*) (Stafford and Coventry, Conn., Vital Records; Kingsbury genealogy.):

1. *Hannah*, b. in Stafford 21 March 1840; m. in 1876 Allyn Kellogg Talcott.
2. *Amelia*, b. in Stafford 16 Sept. 1842; d. in 1864.
3. *Ellen*, b. in Coventry 5 April 1847; d. in 1864.
4. *Andrew*, b. in Rockville, Conn., 8 April 1849; m. in 1880 Mary Laura Hughes.

v. MARY E., b. 19 Sept. 1822; d. 15 Jan. 1901; m. 1 May 1844 JAMES MONROE CHAFFEE, b. in Monson, Mass., 10 Feb. 1820, d. in Staffordville, Conn., 14 April 1908, son of James Austin and Susan (Thresher) Chaffee.

Children (surname Chaffee):

1. *Sarah Amelia*, b. 20 Feb. 1845; m. in 1866 William J. Butterfield, b. in Philadelphia, Pa., 22 Feb. 1844. He served in the Navy during the Civil War.
2. *Eliza J.*, b. 13 Dec. 1849; d. unm. in 1931.
3. *Charles A.*, b. in 1853; d. in 1854.
4. *Ida Gerana*, b. 29 Aug. 1855; m. in 1881, her second cousin, Isaac Merritt Agard, b. in Stafford in 1854.
5. *Frank A.*, b. in 1858; d. in 1859.
6. *George Lincoln*, b. 28 Feb. 1860; m. in 1881 Ida B. Rogers, daughter of Rufus Rogers of Stafford.

---

[1] Delete Mr. Alonzo.
[2] Delete necticut Volunteers. 2 daughters.

vi. SARAH, of Staffordville, Conn., b. 22 Nov. 1826; d. 16 Feb. 1895; m. 8 April 1846 OLIVER FERRY.
    Children (surname *Ferry*):
    1. *Emma A.*, m. 14 Dec. 1881 Charles Leslie Abbe, b. in Enfield, Conn., 30 Oct. 1858, son of Daniel Josiah Abbe. Children (surname Abbe): (1) Ruth Amelia. (2) Ralph A.
    2. *Caroline Emma*, b. 26 Jan. 1853; m. ———— Goodwill.
vii. SOPHIA W., b. 16 Dec. 1828; d. 24 Jan. 1910; m. 10 Sept. 1849 ALVIN TYLER, b. in Staffordville, Conn., 5 Feb. 1825, son of Ara and Abigail (Ferry) Tyler.
    Children (surname Tyler):
    1. *Henry A.*, b. 27 July 1850; m. in 1870 Marietta Maine, b. in Staffordville 6 Feb. 1849, daughter of William Comstock and Belinda (Sessions) Maine. A son, Marshall Henry.
    2. *Abbie Sophia*, b. 26 Oct. 1853; m. in 1869 George Thompson Fiske, son of Calvin and Nancy (Young) Fiske. 2 daughters (surname *Fiske*): May, m. William Clayton. Belle A.
viii. HORATIO G., of Orcuttville, Stafford, b. 12 March 1832; d. 7 Feb. 1907; m. CORNELIA WHITE, b. 8 April 1839, d. 27 Sept. 1909.
    Children:
    1. *Della C.*,[7] b. in 1856; d. in 1863.
    2. *Nettie E.*, b. 6 July 1861; d. in 1937. Lived in Brooklyn, N. Y., Monson, Mass., and Stafford, Conn.
    3. *Nellie*, b. in Orcuttville 31 Oct. 1873; m. 22 June 1891 Charles Irons, b. in Willington, Conn., in 1867, son of William Irons. 1 son (surname *Irons*): Horatio Needham.
    4. *Eva*, living in Orcuttville in 1937; m. Neverson Hemenway.
ix. HENRY, b. in 1834; d. in infancy.
x. CAROLINE AMELIA, b. 25 May 1835; m. 14 Nov. 1852 PAINE CLEAVELAND, b. in Tolland, Conn., in 1831, son of Orange and Hannah (Turner) Cleaveland.
    Children (surname Cleaveland):
    1. *Orange.*
    2. *Charles Fremont.*
    3. *George Alden.*

20. JEREMIAH[5] NEEDHAM (*Jeremiah*,[4] *Anthony*,[3] *Anthony*,[2] *Anthony*[1]), born in South Brimfield, now Wales, Mass., 20 Feb. 1766, died in Vergennes, Vt., 1 Nov. 1846. He married, 30 May 1791 or 31 May 1792, RUTH COOLEY, aged 14, born 31 Dec. 1777, died in Ferrisburg, Vt., 12 March 1858, daughter of Col. Benjamin and Ruth (Beach) Cooley.

In 1794 they went to Pittsford, Vt., and in 1806 moved to Elba, N. Y.

Children ("History of Pittsford, Vt.," p. 716):
i. BENJAMIN COOLEY,[6] b. 17 Aug. 1794; m. (1), 17 March 1814, ACHSAH THAYER, d. in 1820; m. (2), 22 Feb. 1821, LOIS HUNTLEY. He served in the War of 1812 and lived in Wilmington, N. Y., Pittsford, Vt., and later in Parkersburg, Iowa.
    Children (Caverly's Pittsford, Vt., 1872):
    1. *Benjamin*,[7] b. 27 Dec. 1814; m. in 1839 Charlotte Bowers.
    2. *Silas Thayer*, b. 27 April 1817; m. in 1841 Susan Deming.
    3. *Jared Gardner*, b. 19 Feb. 1820; d. in April 1820.
    4. *Achsah*, d. aged 1 year.
    5. *Noah L.*, d. aged 1 year.
    6. *Achsah L.*, m. in 1850 S. H. Taylor.
    7. *Lois A.*, m. in 1851 E. B. Gilbert.
    8. *Eunice*, m. in 1848 John Moore.
    9. *Josephine M.*, m. in 1859 T. B. Bates.
    10. *Lucretia O.*, m. in 1858 Benjamin Connell.
    11. *Lyman H.*, d. in Andersonville Prison 31 Aug. 1864.

ii. JEREMIAH.
iii. HORACE.
iv. CHARLES.
v. AZARIAH C.
vi. RUTH.
vii. EUNICE.
viii. NORMAN G.
ix. EUNICE.
x. ORENDA.
xi. CAROLINE D.

21. ELISHA[5] NEEDHAM (*Jeremiah*,[4] *Anthony*,[3] *Anthony*,[2] *Anthony*[1]), of Union, Conn., born 5 Sept. 1770, died 16 April 1822, aged 52. He married, 12 Oct. 1797, his second cousin, CHLOE STRONG, born 13 Jan. 1779, daughter of Samuel and Annah (Needham) Strong.

Children (Lawson's Union, Conn.; Barbour Collection; Union Vital Records):

i. MARSENA (MASSENA, MARCENA),[6] b. 12 July 1800; d. in Stafford, Conn., 31 Aug. 1831, aged 31; m. 29 Jan. 1823 ABIGAIL Wales, b. 31 Oct. 1798, d. in Monson, Mass., 21 Aug. 1859, aged 61, daughter of Gideon and Abigail (Gallup) Wales of Montville, Conn.
Children:
1. *Esther Burnet*,[7] b. 23 July 1826; m. Abraham B. Rogers of Monson, Mass. Child (surname *Rogers*): (1) Everton.
2. *Abigail G.*, b. 28 March 1829; d. young.
3. *Marsena Wales*, b. in Stafford 4 Jan. 1832; m. Sarah Gage of Somers, Conn. Children: (1) Charles. (2) Mabel.
ii. MARY (POLLY), b. 28 Nov. 1802; m. SYLVESTER ROBBINS of Holland, Mass.
iii. SAMUEL STRONG, b. 10 Sept. 1805; d. 4 June 1886, aged 80 years; m. (1), 13 Dec. 1836, ESTHER WALES, b. 22 Jan. 1805, d. in Union, Conn., 24 Nov. 1839, aged 34, daughter of Gideon and Betsey (Allen) Wales; m. (2), 6 April 1841, MARY FOSTER, d. 11 Jan. 1897, aged 89, daughter of William Foster.
Children by first wife (Stafford Vital Records):
1. *Jane Elizabeth*,[7] b. 19 Aug. 1837.
2. *Esther Wales*, b. 11 Nov. 1839; d. in Monson 21 May 1874; m. Horace Bumstead of Monson.
Child (surname *Bumstead*): (1) William.
iv. ZALMON, b. in Union 20 July 1808; d. 31 July 1892; m. 25 Aug. 1833 MARY ANN TOWN, b. 9 Nov. 1815, daughter of Alvin and Martha (Haskell) Town.
Children:
1. *William*.[7]
2. *Lewis*.
v. LURANCY, b. 3 April 1811; m. CALEDONIA WEST of Albany, N. Y. "Luranny, m. Caledonia West, May 11, 1841 by Rev. Washington Munger".
vi. TRYPHENA, b. 22 Nov. 1813; m. 25 Dec. 1851 DARIUS HILL of Thompson, Conn. No children.
vii. ENOCH GARDNER, b. 1 Feb. 1817; m. Caroline Cook of New Berlin, Wis.
Children:
1. *Martin*.[7]
2. *Chloe*.
3. *Mary*.
4. *Louisa*.
5. *Amelia*.
6. *Julia*.
viii. JANE ELIZABETH, b. 22 May 1820; d. 18 Oct. 1836, aged 16.

22. DANFORD[5] NEEDHAM (*Stephen,*[4] *Humphrey,*[3] *Anthony,*[2] *Anthony*[1]), born 26 Oct. 1786, died in Racine, Wis., 8 Oct. 1855. He married, 28 Nov. 1811, ALICE THOMPSON, born in Wales, Mass., in 1789, died there in 1854, daughter of William Thompson.

Children, born in South Brimfield:

i. MARY,[6] b. 26 Aug. 1812; d. 12 Nov. 1897; m. in 1835 PRESCOTT SAWYER BELCHER, b. in 1811, d. in 1892, son of David and Chloey (Sawyer) Belcher.
   Child (surname Belcher):
   1. *John Henry,* born in Stafford on 29 Nov. 1836; died there 9 April 1915; m. in Wales, 5 June 1867, Julia Ann Royce, b. in Sturbridge, Mass., 22 April 1848, d. in Stafford 14 July 1932, daughter of Joseph Upham and Mary Eliza (Hooker) Royce. Children (surname *Belcher*). (1) Flora Elizabeth, b. in 1869; m. Dawes Perry, son of Samuel. (2) Mabel Julia, b. in 1871; m. in 1899 George Alfred Jenkins of Stafford, b. in Holywell, Wales, in 1862, son of Evan and Eliza (Banford) Jenkins (furnished Needham and Belcher information). (3) William Hooker, b. in 1873; m. (1), Martha Boerner; m. (2), Della Dimmick. (4) Mary Helena, b. in 1876; m. Oscar Norman Colburn, son of Alvin and Chloe Emeline (Belcher) Colburn. (5) Rose Viola, b. in 1878; d. in 1879. (6) Robert Aretas.

ii. LOUISA, b. 19 June 1814; d. in 1836; m. NORMAN W. BELCHER, brother of Prescott Sawyer Belcher.

iii. WILLIAM LORING, b. 12 Nov. 1816; d. in Racine, Wis., 1 Aug. 1899, where he went from Wa.es in 1851; m. CAROLINE WOODWARD. A daughter, *Caroline,* born in Sturbridge, Mass., 16 Aug. 1844.

iv. LUCY D., b. 20 Aug. 1818; d. in Atlantic, Iowa, 18 Dec. 1887; m. in 1837 ALONZO COBURN.

23. v. STEPHEN, b. 4 Nov. 1820.

vi. JAMES FRANCIS, b. 12 June 1828; d. in Lincoln, Nebr., 10 Aug. 1902; to Racine in 1851 with his brother William Loring; enlisted in the 10th Iowa Infantry in 1861; had a daughter Anna Hosick.

vii. STILLMAN, b. 20 Aug. 1831; d. in Grinnell, Iowa, 29 May 1914; m. (1), in Grinnell HESTER ANN HIATT; m. (2), MARY ELIZABETH (GORDON) WELLS. He and his brother Stephen went to Racine in 1855, later to Grinnell.
   Child by first wife:
   1. *Dora A.*[7]
   Children by second wife:
   2. *Ninna N.*
   3. *Ward S.*

23. STEPHEN[6] NEEDHAM (*Danford,*[5] *Stephen,*[4] *Humphrey,*[3] *Anthony,*[2] *Anthony*[1]), born 4 Nov. 1820, died 6 July 1886. He married NANCY E. JANES (Southbridge, Mass., Vital Records), born 23 Jan. 1821, died 28 May 1858, daughter of Levi and Mary (Lumbard) Janes. Stephen's Bible in 1951 was in possession of Alfred C.[8] Needham of Baxter, Iowa. To Wisconsin then to Iowa.

Children (Warren, Mass., Vital Records):

i. FRANCIS A.[7] (twin), b. 28 May 1845; d. in Moline, Ill., 16 March 1905; m. (1), in Jasper County, Iowa, 9 Dec. 1868, GERTRUDE SEARS, b. in New York in 1853; m. (2), in Newton, Iowa, 6 June 1878, DINAH (FOSTER) AMOS, b. in England in 1846. He served in the Civil War.

Children by first wife:
1. *Charles Stillman*,[8] of Eldon, Iowa; m. in 1899 Campbell Gertrude Nickson. Child: Wilma Icle.[9]
2. *Abbie*, m. J. R. Newton.
3. *W. E.*, of Moline.
4. *Gertrude*, m. A. G. Parish of Newton.
5. *Emma*, m. J. C. Smith of Kansas City, Mo.
    Children by second wife:
6. *Frank A.*, of Moline.
7. *John*, of Newton.
8. *Alfred C.*, of Moline.
ii. JAMES (twin), of Meeker, Colo., b. 28 May 1845.
iii. CHARLES OSGOOD, of Salt Lake City, Utah, b. 26 Dec. 1847.

NEEDHAM NAMES IN WALES, MASS., AND STAFFORD, CONN., CEMETERIES

Copied by GRACE OLIVE CHAPMAN, of Dorchester (Boston), Mass.

Cemetery No. 1, the old cemetery, overlooking the Wales lake.

In Memory of M[r] Anthony Needham who died July 2nd 1763 in his 67th year. On the top of the stone is the inscription: First White Settler 1726.

Jasper Needham died Oct 26, 1847 aged 66.

Hannah wife of Jasper Needham died May 14, 1880 AE 88 ys.

Capt. David Needham died Nov 22, 1815 AE 60.

Marcilvia wife of David Needham died May 21, 1853 AE 94.

Orin Needham died May 23, 1861 aged 64 years. Sophia his wife died Sept 28, 1870 age 75 yr.

Mary M daughter of Orin & Sophia Needham died Sept 26, 18— aged 6 yr.

Benjamin A. Needham Oct 26, 1810 Oct 23, 1864. Julia Tiffany, his wife Mar 21, 1808 Jan 27, 1894.

Deidamia wife of Andrew A Needham died Jan 22, 1822 AE 19.

Andrew A. Needham died Nov. 17, 1880 aged 80 yrs 2 mos 16 ds.

Nancy A wife of A. A. Needham died Jan 31, 1881 aged 71 yrs 9 mos 16 ds.

Lieut Stephen Needham died July 4, 1836 aged 72.

Abigail wife of Lieut. Stephen Needham died April 17, 1832 aged 73.

Capt. Anthony Needham May 18, 1723 —— 1785.

Phebe Needham March 30, 1755 In Infancy.

Rebecca Munger wife of Capt. Anthony Needham

Humphrey Needham July 3, 1742 Oct 11, 1815.

Adj. James H. Needham died 28 Nov 1815 AE 32.

Wm. A. Needham died Feb 9, 1860 AE[t] 64.

In Memory of Anthony Needham who died Sept 27th 1785 in the 42[d] year of his age.

Rebecca dau of Alvin & Abigail Needham, died 1 Dec 1818, AE 7.

Cemetery No. 2, located on the main road, really is in the church yard of the old Baptist Church, which building is now the Town Hall. Buried in this cemetery is James L. Wales, for whom the town of Wales was named (formerly South Brimfield), also Absalom

Gardner, town clerk for years, who compiled the "Compendium of Wales".

Lydia A wife of David A. Needham died Jan. 24, 1866 aged 27 yrs.
Alfred Needham died Mar 27, 1853 AE 69. Sally his wife died Feb. 24, 1848 AE 60.
Mary Needham Nov 21, 1811 Aug. 30, 1851.
Mrs. Marsilvia wife of Robert Hadley Died Aug. 10, 1842 AE 35. [Needham]
Mrs. Olive M wife of Otis Needham died Sept. 22, 1852 AE 31.
Charles G. Needham Aug. 29, 1838 Oct. 27, 1910.
Betsey Soule wife of Charles G. Needham Feb 20, 1838 Dec 19, 1898.
Alice wife of Danford Needham died May 5, 1854 AE 65.
Danford Needham died & buried in Wisconsin Oct. 9, 1855 AE 69.
NEEDHAM. Eunice M Apr 8, 1827 Sept 29, 1843. Henry M Nov 23, 1829 Aug 12, 1890. Jonathan June 21, 1793 Jany 24, 1862. Lodisa F May 3, 1799 Nov 19, 1873.
Elvira Miller adopted child of David B. & Eliza Needham died April 7, 1841 AE 9 yrs 8 mo & 3 ds.
David B. Needham died July 6, 1857 aged 48 yrs. Eliza his wife died Feb. 17, 1893 AE 81 yrs.
Sally daughter of Alfred & Sally Needham died April 6, 1842 AE 16 yrs.
Daniel Needham died Sept. 16, 1846 aged 71.
Lucy wife of Dan'l Needham died July 9, 1872 aged 93 yrs.
Oril wife of Wm. L. Needham died June 9, 1813 AE 20 yrs.

Cemetery No. 3, LAUREL HILL CEMETERY, at the end of a short road leading off from the lower Wales-Brimfield road, from a section I think known as Shawville.

Roswell Needham died April 8, 1870 aged 82 yrs. Sally Thayer his wife died Dec 30, 1860 aged 72 yrs. Francis M. Needham died Oct. 3, 1846 aged 20 yrs. Annis E. Needham wife of Linus Albee died Mar. 18, 1856 aged 24 yrs. Chandler Needham died Nov. 19, 1901 aged 85 yrs. Laurette H his wife died Jan. 28, 1899 aged 81 yrs.
W. Eugene Needham. Mary Hopkins his wife died Mar. 10, 1892 AE 50 ys. Children of Warren & Elizabeth Needham Ernest T died Jan. 1, 1856 AE 7 yrs 3 mos & 1 day. George E died Feb. 15, 1846 AE 3 days. Warren Needham died Apr. 1, 1883 AE 70 yrs. Elizabeth Wilder his wife died July 13, 1885 AE 68 yrs.
Helen G. Needham 1844–1910. Carlos D. Needham 1843–1916. [Helen and Carlos on same lot as W. Eugene Needham monument.]
I. Porter Thompson Nov. 4, 1819 — Mar 10, 1892. Sarah Needham his wife Aug. 4, 1821 — Oct. 6, 1900.
Lyman Needham died Dec. 29, 1862 AE 44 yrs. Harriet his wife died May 7, 1880 AE 60 yrs. Their children Ida L died Sept. 18, 1856 AE 6 yrs. Walter H died Sept. 10, 1858 AE 10 mos. Ellen A wife of Frank M. Needham died Aug. 11, 1876 AE 29 yrs.
Henry H. Needham 1835–1876. Sarah J. Thompson 1841–1914. Willie M. Peck 1855–1927. Annie E. Thompson his wife 1859–1930.
Fayette O. Needham 1878–1930.
Margaret J. Coy Needham 1874–   .
Father George H. Needham died May 22, 1883 AE 62 yrs.
WIFE Mary C wife of G. H. Needham died Jan. 26, 1880 AE 53 yrs.
Wm. M. Needham died Feb. 9 1896 aged 76 yrs.
Charlotte A wife of Wm. M. Needham died July 5, 1872 aged 49 yrs.
Edward W. Needham June 22, 1869 — Sept. 22, 1906.
Susan R. Young wife of Watson Needham died May 26, 1882 aged 42 yrs & 6 mos.
Milton W son of W. W. & Susan Needham died Sept. 7, 1869 aged 2 yrs & 7 mos.
John S. Needham May 26, 1825 — Oct. 8, 1898. Sophia Gardner his wife Aug. 20, 1831 — Dec. 20, 1913.
Charlie M. Greene April 21, 1857 — Mar. 10, 1895. Persis Needham his wife 1859–1915.

Cemetery No. 4, the newest cemetery in Wales, is located on a hill next to cemetery No. 3.

Eugene Needham 1839–1925 his wife Mary L. Hopkins 1842–1892. Nancy A. Smith 1808–1895 Caroline Smith wife of W. E. Needham 1843–1934.

George B. Clarke 1847–1905 Ellen E. Needham his wife 1847–1918.

J. A. Needham Co. I 34th Mass. Inf.   [flag]

W. B. Needham Co. I 34th Mass. Inf.   [flag]

[Between 1938 and 1944 I copied the inscriptions in all the cemeteries in Stafford, except the two large cemeteries in Stafford Springs. Needham names were found in only four, given below.]

STAFFORD HOLLOW, HILLSIDE CEMETERY

Mary M wife of Abner Needham died June 29, 1873 aged 51. Isabel twin daughter of Abner & Mary M Needham died Aug. 22, 1849 aged 10 mos 13 ds. Abner Needham died Jan. 24, 1898 aged 82.

STAFFORD STREET, NEWER CEMETERY

In Memory of Capt Robert Needham who died Sept. 20, 1823 AE^t 54.

In Memory of Bashaba wife of Robert W. Needham who died April 19, 1828 AE 23 yrs.

Sidney F. Needham born Mar 6, 1798 died May 2, 1883. Sarah his wife Born July 26, 1799 Died May 5, 1883. Theodore P. Needham Co D 26 Reg Conn Vols Died Apr. 29, 1906 aged 71. Maria A. Sykes wife of T P Needham Died Jan 7, 1928 aged 87. Archie W. Tuthill 1855–1933. Addie Needham his wife 1857–1899. Their children Frank–Milton–Ruth.

Frank son of T P & Maria A Needham Died July 8, 1881 aged 1 yr.

STAFFORDVILLE CEMETERY

Elvin Ferry Died Jan 12, 1884 aged 69 yrs. Azuba Needham Wife of Elvin Ferry Mar 11, 1817 Feb 27, 1910.

Timothy Foskit born June 1, 1822 died Sept 20, 1881. Mary M. Belcher His wife Sept 29, 1820 May 12, 1900. Belle E. Needham wife of Hiram Rathbun born Oct. 6, 1848 died Dec 22, 1884.

Roswell Needham died Feb 6, 1901 aged 77 years. Corlistis wife of Roswell Needham died Mar 23, 1858 aged 28 years. Loretta wife of Roswell Needham died Dec 15, 1875 aged 41 years.

Jane Needham wife of Harvey H. Converse Dec 25, 1848 — May 18, 1884. Miner Needham Sept 4, 1846 — Mar 23, 1911.

Horatio G. Needham Mar 12, 1832 — Feb 7, 1907 Cornelia White his wife Apr 8, 1839 — Sep 27, 1909. Children Della C. Needham Dec 22, 1856 — Dec 15, 1863.

Prescott S Belcher died May 3, 1892 AE 81 yrs Mary his wife died Nov. 12, 1897 AE 84 yrs. [Mary Needham]

Nettie E. Needham 1861–1937.

STAFFORDVILLE, HALL DISTRICT CEMETERY

Melinda Needham wife of Benjamin Agard died Jan 20, 1841 Aged 53 yrs. Benjamin Agard died Mar 18, 1872 Aged 85.

NEWTON, COOKE.—The following notes from Mr. J. T. Newton (see query in REGISTER, vol. 60, p. 316) are based upon memoranda on the fly leaves of an old book, upon graveyard inscriptions, and the two wills mentioned below.

JOHN[4] NEWTON (*John*,[3] *John*,[2] *Roger*[1]), born in Milford, Conn., 1734; died there 21 Dec. 1797; married first MARY MILES, daughter of Stephen and Frances of Milford; married secondly MARTHA COLBRAITH (daughter of Humphrey), who died 10 Feb. 1826, aged 78 y. 10 m. John Newton's will is dated 29 May 1784; and his widow's 6 Jan. 1815, probated 21 Feb. 1826.

Children by first wife:
i.   MARY[5] (Polly), m. ——— Hawley.
ii.   JOHN, d. Oct. 1776.
iii. MILES, b. 1762; d. 1822.
iv. EUNICE, m. 1792, NEWTON JOHN MORRIS.
v.   COMFORT, d. 1799, aged 30.
vi. NATHAN, b. 14 Apr. 1776; d. 1813.

Children by second wife:
vii. SARAH, b. 25 Apr. 1781; d. unmarried 30 May 1843, aged 62.
viii. ELIZABETH, b. 28 Dec. 1782; m. 1809, JOHN BUCKINGHAM; d. 1838, aged 55.
ix. SUSANNA, b. 6 Aug. 1784; d. 10 Feb. 1809.
x.   ESTHER, b. 10 Jan. 1787: m. Dan Fenn.
xi. NAOMI, b. 19 Mar. 1789; m. JAMES HINE of Milford; d. 10 Nov. 1881, aged 93.

Family Record.

The Reverend Samuel Cooke was born Nov[r] 21st 1687 and Died Dec[r] 6th 1747. He married for his 4th wife Mrs. Elisabeth Platt Sept[r] 28th 1727 who was born Dec[r] 2nd 1701 & died May 16th 1732.

Joseph Platt Cooke was born Dec[r] 24th 1729 died 1816
Sarah Benedict was born June 10th 1740
Joseph Platt Cooke & Sarah Benedict were married Nov[r] 22nd 1759
1 Joseph Platt Cooke born Nov[r] 11th 1760 d. June 1841
2 Thomas Cooke born August 4th 1762
3 Elisabeth Cooke born July 23rd 1764 d. Oct. 21, 1834.
4 Daniel Benedict Cooke born Nov[r] 27th 1768.
5 Amos Cooke born Oct[r] 21, 1773, and died Nov[r] 13, 1810.
Yale University Library, New Haven.   M. RAY SANBORN.

NORTHRUP GENEALOGY.

By Hon. A. JUDD NORTHRUP, of Syracuse, N. Y.

1. JOSEPH[1] NORTHRUP, probably from Yorkshire, England, was one of the first settlers of Milford, Conn. The first planters of the town were enrolled Nov. 20, 1639; but, Joseph not then being in church fellowship, his name (with others) appears in the list immediately after the " free planters." A part of the settlers were from Wethersfield, Conn., whither they had come from Watertown, Mass. They were part of Sir Richard Saltonstall's company. Having be-

come attached to their pastor, Rev. Peter Prudden, from Egerton, Yorkshire, England, they accompanied him to Milford. Another part of the settlers were of Eaton and Davenport's company,—"of good characters and fortunes,"—who landed in Boston, July 26, 1637, and settled at New Haven in April, 1638. They were mostly from Yorkshire, Hertfordshire and Kent. The Hertfordshire families seem to have tended to Milford.

The surname *Northrup* was spelled, as here given, in the earliest deeds and records and inscriptions on tombstones, *rup*, sometimes *rupp*. About the time of the Revolution, apparently, many families changed it to North*rop*. (That spelling will be followed in their cases, in the genealogy to be published.) Jan. 9, 1642, Joseph united with the First Church in Milford. Married Mary, dau. of Francis Norton, who came to Milford from Wethersfield with Rev. Peter Prudden. Died Sept. 11, 1669. Will dated Sept. 1, 1669; mentions only Joseph, Samuel, Jeremiah and John. Codicil to will: "My mother shall have a living in my house as long as she lives,"—perhaps meaning Mrs. Norton. His wife survived him, and made her will Jan. 24, 1683; mentions Joseph, Samuel, Jeremiah (omits John, who probably was dead), Zophar, Daniel, William and Mary,—the two latter as being in their minority,—also her mother Norton. Inventory of her estate dated Feb. 28, 1683. Children :

2. i.   JOSEPH,[2] bapt. Aug. 9, 1649.
3. ii.   SAMUEL, bapt. 1651.
4. iii.   JEREMIAH, b. Jan. 1654.
    iv.   JOHN, b. Sept. 1656; probably died before 1683.
5. v.   ZOPHAR, b. June 21, 1661.
6. vi.   DANIEL, b. Aug. 1664.
7. vii.   WILLIAM, b. June 2, 1666.
    viii.   MARY, b. Jan. 1670.

2.   JOSEPH[2] NORTHRUP (*Joseph[1]*), bapt. August 9, 1649, Milford. Freeman, May 12, 1670; married to (?); died May —, 1700. Children born at Milford:

8. i.   JOSEPH,[3] bapt. Oct. 1689.
9. ii.   JAMES, bapt. Jan. 1693.
10. iii.   MOSES, bapt. March, 1695.
    iv.   MIRIAM, bapt. May, 1698.

3.   SAMUEL[2] NORTHRUP (*Joseph[1]*), bapt. 1651, Milford. Freeman, May 11, 1671; married Sarah ———. Inventory dated Jan 30, 1712-13. Children born in Milford:

11. i.   SAMUEL,[3] b. ———.
12. ii.   AMOS, bapt. Sept. 1689.
13. iii.   JOEL, b. Feb. 1691.
    iv.   MARY, b. Sept. 1694; m. April 9, 1717, Josiah, son of Josiah Tibbals (his 2d wife).
    v.   HANNAH, b. Dec. 1696; m. James Smith.
    vi.   ABIGAIL, b. May 1, 1699; m. Jan. 6, 1724, Dea. Jonathan Guernsey, son of Joseph.
    vii.   MARGARET, b. Aug. 1702; m. (prob.) Joseph Gunn, son of Jeboniah, and settled in Waterbury.

4.   JEREMIAH[2] NORTHRUP (*Joseph[1]*), born Jan. 1654, Milford. Married Phœbe ———; died April 11, 1734. Children born in Milford:

14. i.   JOHN,[3] bapt. Jan. 16, 1695.
15. ii.   JEREMIAH, bapt. Jan. 16, 1695.

16. iii. PHINEAS, bapt. Jan. 16, 1695.
17. iv. BENJAMIN, bapt. Oct. 1696.
    v. PHŒBE, bapt. Nov. 1705.

5. ZOPHAR[2] NORTHRUP (*Joseph*[1]), born June 21, 1661, Milford. Married Sarah Tibbals, dau. of Josiah and Mary (Sherwood) Tibbals, of Milford (her parents married July 13, 1670); died 1729. Will made in 1728. Children born in Milford:

    i. ZOPHAR,[3] bapt. Dec. 1696. (Not mentioned in father's will.)
    ii. JOSIAH, bapt. Oct. 1699. (Probably died before 2d Josiah was born.)
18. iii. JOSIAH, bapt. 1702.
    iv. MEHETABEL, bapt. Dec. 1708.
    v. HANNAH, bapt. June, 1712.
    vi. REBECCA. (Mentioned in father's will, 1728.)

6. DANIEL[2] NORTHRUP (*Joseph*[1]), born August, 1664, Milford. Married Sarah ———; died 1728. Children born in Milford:

    i. ROBERT,[3] bapt. 1692.
    ii. DANIEL, bapt. Dec. 1693.
19. iii. GAMALIEL, bapt. May, 1696. Of Ridgefield, 1721.
    iv. EBENEZER, b. May, 1698.
20. v. DAVID, b. Aug. 1701.
    vi. SARAH, b. July, 1702; m. March 6, 1727–8, Samuel St. John, and probably was of Ridgefield, 1734.
    vii. NATHAN, bapt. Aug. 1705. Of Ridgefield, 1734.
    viii. MEHETABEL, bapt. April, 1708; m. Aug. 23, 1733, Josiah Hine, son of Samuel.
21. ix. JABEZ, bapt. Jan. 1710. Of Ridgefield, 1736.
    x. JONAH, mentioned in will. Died March 31, 1736, Ridgefield.

7. WILLIAM[2] NORTHRUP (*Joseph*[1]), born June 2, 1666, Milford. Married Mary Peck, dau. of Joseph; died 1728. Children born in Milford:

22. i. WILLIAM,[3] b. Dec. 1694.
23. ii. EPHRAIM, b. 1696.
24. iii. JOSEPH, b. 1698.
    iv. HANNAH, b, Dec. 1699.
25. v. THOMAS, b. 1701.
26. vi. JOHN, b. 1703.

8. JOSEPH[3] NORTHRUP (*Joseph*,[2] *Joseph*[1]), bapt. Oct. 1689, Milford. Removed to Ridgefield, Conn. Joseph and his brothers James and Moses united with others in the purchase of lands from the Indians in Ridgefield, March 18, 1715, Nov. 22, 1721, and July 4, 1727,— the 2d, 3d and 4th purchases from the Indians. Married Nov. 20, 1713, Susanna Roberts; died 1773. Children recorded at Ridgefield:

    i. SUSANNA,[4] b. Aug. 31, 1714.
27. ii. JOSEPH, b. May 11, 1716.
28. iii. ELI, b. May 1, 1718.
29. iv. AARON, b. Nov. 30, 1720.
30. v. ABRAHAM, b. Sep. 18, 1722. Removed to Lenox, Mass.
31. vi. ISAAC, b. Nov. 10, 1725.
    vii. MIRIAM, b. July 18, 1728.

9. JAMES[3] NORTHRUP (*Joseph*,[2] *Joseph*[1]), bapt. January, 1693, Milford. Bought lands in Ridgefield with brothers Joseph and Moses, 1715, 1721, and 1727, and settled there. Also bought lands of Joseph Benedict for £60, March 29, 1714. Married 1st, Hannah Hine, of Milford, who died about 1737. Children by 1st wife recorded at Ridgefield:

32. i. JAMES,[4] b. Nov. 9, 1719.
    ii. NATHAN, b. May 30, 1721; m. Eunice ———, of Salem, N. Y.
    iii. HANNAH, b. Nov. 16, 1723; d. before 1731.
    iv. STEPHEN, b. Dec. 13, 1725; m. Abigail; d. June 22, 1757.
33. v. THOMAS, b. Dec. 5, 1727.
    vi. HANNAH, b. Aug. 20, 1729; m. Aug. 23, 1747, Stephen Olmstead.
    vii. ANNA, m. Dec. 24, 1754, Jonah Smith, Jr.

JAMES,[3] married 2d, wid. Lydia Mills, and by her had:
    viii. AMBROSE, b. April 30, 1740; d. Oct. 7, 1745.
    ix. JOHN, b. Nov. 28, 1743; d. March 20, 1761.
    x. BENJAMIN, b. Oct. 26, 1747.

10. MOSES[3] NORTHRUP (Joseph,[2] Joseph[1]), bapt. March, 1695, Milford. With his brothers Joseph and James (and others), purchased lands of the Indians in Ridgefield, Conn., in 1715, 1721, and 1727. Described in deed of Sept., 1714, as "of Milford," and in deed of May 11, 1716, as "of Ridgefield." Lived in Ridgefield until some time between Nov. 24, 1733, and August 2, 1734, when he removed to Dutchess Co., N. Y. Described himself in deed dated March 10, 1735, as "lately of Ridgefield . . . . . now living at *Wostershire* in the Province of New York." Again, in 1740, "of *Worcester*, N. Y." Again, Feb. 7, 1744–5, " of *Worstershire*, Dutchess Co., N. Y." In " N. Y. Calendar of Land Papers, 1643–1803," Vol. XIII., pp. 139–140 (State Library, Albany, N. Y.), are two original Petitions, dated April 29, 1743, of Moses Northrup and Abigail his wife and Moses Northrup, Jr., for license to purchase vacant lands in the County of Dutchess, " where their dwelling stands," &c.—10,000 acres. Petitions denied. He married about 1721, Abigail Cornell, who survived him. She quit-claims her dower, &c., by deed Jan. 22, 1759. The sons convey Ridgefield lands of their father by deed Jan. 19, 1759. He died about January, 1759. The children born, some in Ridgefield, some in Dutchess Co. Order of birth not known.
34. i. MOSES,[4] b. Nov. 1, 1722, Ridgefield, Conn.
    ii. JOSEPH.
35. iii. AMOS, b. 1730.
36. iv. BENJAMIN, b. about 1739.
37. v. CORNELL, b. probably about 1740–2.
    vi. ABIGAIL.
    vii. SARAH.

11. SAMUEL[3] NORTHRUP (Samuel,[2] Joseph[1]), b. in Milford. One of the original proprietors—*not* one of the " first 12 settlers "—of New Milford; list dated, Milford, April, 1706. Married Feb. 25, 1714, Sarah Andrews.
    i. MERCY,[4] b. Sept. 1715.
    ii. SAMUEL, b. June, 1718.
    iii. ABIGAIL, b. July, 1723; m. Lawrence Clinton, and had: 1. *Sarah.*[5] b. Aug. 1747; 2. *Simeon*,[5] b. Feb. 1749; 3. *Abigail*,[5] b. Aug. 1751; 4. *Samuel*,[5] b. July, 1754.

12. AMOS[3] NORTHRUP (Samuel,[2] Joseph[1]), bapt. Sept. 1689, Milford. Married Jan. 6, 1713–4, Mary Gunn. It is said he removed to New Milford and died not long after 1726; and that his widow married, 1729, Henry Peck, and removed to Brookfield, where his son Amos[4] was brought up. Will dated Feb. 25, 1726. Ephraim Northrup was one of the witnesses.

38. i.   Amos.⁴
     ii.   Mary, bapt. Sept. 1714; d. young.
    iii. Joan, bapt. March, 1718; d. young.

13. Joel³ Northrup (*Samuel,² Joseph¹*), b. Feb. 1691, Milford. Married Ruth Andrews, dau. of Thomas; died 1752. Children, all born in Woodbridge, Conn.:

    i.   Ruth,⁴ b. 1725; m. Hezekiah Camp, of Salisbury.
    ii.   Sarah, b. 1727.
   iii. Hannah, b. 1728.
   iv. Mary, b. 1730.
39. v.   Joel, b. 1732.
   vi. Abigail, b. 1734; d. young—before 1740.
  vii. Margaret, b. 1736.
 viii. Abigail, b. 1740.

14. Lieut. John³ Northrup (*Jeremiah,² Joseph¹*), bapt. Jan. 16, 1695 (probably when several years old), in Milford. He and his brothers Jeremiah³ and Benjamin³ were among the first settlers of Newtown, Conn., where they took their "pitch" with others for home lots, commencing April 7, 1712, each to have 4 acres of meadow land; and again in 1720, the brothers John³ and Benjamin³ are together allotted 10 acres more. He was appointed Selectman in 1722 and held the office 13 years; was Town Clerk from 1739 to 1752. He was a weaver. Was known as "Lieut. John." Married Jan. 7, 1713–4, Mary Porter, who died March 19, 1786, aged 97 years. Died Jan. 9, 1767, very suddenly, "*aged 80 years.*"

40. i.   Jonathan,⁴ b. March 3, 1715, Milford.
    ii.   Ruth, b. Jan. 15, 1717; m. Nov. 30, 1737, Peter Ferris, son of Samuel, of Newtown. Peter d. 1795, aged 81 years. She died May 28, 1804. Had: 1. *Samuel,⁵* b. May 10, 1740, d. Jan, 12, 1796; 2. *Martha,⁵* b. Nov. 12, 1743; 3. *Joseph,⁵* b. Aug. 2, 1746.
   iii. Mary, b. Oct. 17, 1725, Newtown; m. Aug. 21, 1743, Daniel Sherman.
41. iv. John, b. July 9, 1732.

15. Jeremiah³ Northrup (*Jeremiah,² Joseph¹*), bapt. Jan. 16, 1695, Milford (probably when several years old). Married Hannah ———, who died March 19, 1767, aged 70. He died July 4, 1771, "in the 87th year of his age." Quite probably there was a *Job* in this family, b. in Milford.

    i.   Jeremiah.⁴
    ii.   Joshua.
   iii. Ezra, b. 1724 or 5.
   iv. Amos, b. 1727.
    v.   Waite, b. 1740.
   vi. Enos, b. 1742, Brookfield, Conn.
  vii. Hannah, m. Hawley. He d. May 12, 1790, aged 60.
 viii. Phœbe, m. Weller.

16. Phineas³ Northrup (*Jeremiah,² Joseph¹*), bapt. Jan. 16, 1695. Married Dec. 9, 1732, Elizabeth Brinsmeade, dau. of John.

    i.   Elizabeth,⁴ b. Jan. 1733; m. Enos Baldwin.
    ii.   Phœbe, b. April, 1735.
   iii. Ann, b. March, 1737; m. Beers.
   iv. Susanna, b. March, 1741; m. Sears.
    v.   Rachel, b. Dec. 1743; d. Aug. 22, 1750.
   vi. John, b. Feb. 1746; d. Aug. 21, 1750.
  vii. Phineas, b. Feb. 1749; d. Nov. 1777.

17. Dea. Benjamin³ Northrup (*Jeremiah,² Joseph¹*), bapt. Oct. 1696, Milford. A mason. His name appears on record in Newtown in

1712. Had land set off to him and his brother John³ in 1720. Was Deacon of Cong. Church in Newtown. Married March 4, 1724, Sarah Platt, who died Feb. 25, 1775, aged 75 years. He died Aug. 9, 1775, in a fit, aged 79 years. Children, born in Newtown:

i. BENJAMIN,⁴ b. Feb. 7, 1725; d. Nov. 7, 1727.
ii. SARAH, b. Feb. 25, 1727; m. Wakeley.
iii. PHŒBE, b. Feb. 25, 1727; m. May 14, 1760, Joseph Rockwell, of Danby, Conn.
iv. BENJAMIN, b. Feb. 24, 1729.
v. ABIGAIL, m. Castle.
vi. MIRIAM, m. Bristol.
vii. MERCY, m. Monger.
viii. ALICE, m. Jan. 5, 1760, Joseph Botsford, of Newtown; d. April 5, 1774.
ix. NATHANIEL, b. 1740.
x. EUNICE, bapt. June 3, 1743; m. Nov. 7, 1768, Eben Castle, of Roxbury, Conn.
xi. ELIHU, bapt. Feb. 16, 1747.

18. JOSIAH³ NORTHRUP (*Zophar,² Joseph¹*), bapt. 1702, Milford. Married Mary Sanford, who was born July 5, 1702.

i. JOSEPH,⁴ bapt. Jan. 1728.
ii. SARAH, bapt. Nov. 1728.
iii. ABIGAIL, bapt. Nov. 1728.
iv. MOSES, bapt. June, 1730; m. Elizabeth Baldwin, dau. of Joshua.
v. JONATHAN, bapt. May, 1732.
vi. ANNA, bapt. Oct. 1735.
vii. ISRAEL, bapt. Dec. 1739; d. Aug. 10, 1750.

19. GAMALIEL³ NORTHRUP (*Daniel,² Joseph¹*), bapt. May, 1696, Milford. Married Jan. 2, 1723–4, Mary Dauchy. In deed, Nov. 16, 1717, describes himself " formerly of Milford, now resident in Ridgefield, blacksmith." Dis. of estate July 31, 1783. Children recorded at Ridgefield:

i. ELIZABETH,⁴ b. Oct. 2, 1723; d. March 14, 1725.
ii. MARY, b. May 26, 1726.
iii. SARAH, b. April 29, 1728.
iv. GAMALIEL, b. May 9, 1730.
v. DANIEL, b. July 17, 1733; d. Jan. 18, 1738.
vi. ELIZABETH, b. Feb. 29, 1735–6.
vii. MEHETABEL, b. May 13, 1738; m. Sept. 15, 1756, Jesse Benedict (b. Feb. 2, 1735, d. Sept. 2, 1805, Ridgefield), son of Capt. Matthew and Ruth (Keeler) Benedict. 10 children. She d. Dec. 11, 1804.
viii. RACHEL, b. July 18, 1740.
ix. MARTHA, b. Dec. 2, 1744; m. John St. John.
x. HANNAH, b. May 1, 1747; m. Olmstead.

20. DAVID³ NORTHRUP (*Daniel,² Joseph¹*), born Aug. 1701, Milford. Married Rebecca Downs, dau. of Deliverance Downs (who in her will mentions " Rebecca, wife of David Northrup"). Describes himself in deeds Dec. 12, 1721, and March 8, 1722–3, " of Milford."

i. DAVID, bapt. 1734.
ii. ISAAC, bapt. 1734.
iii. REBECCA, bapt. 1734.
iv. EUNICE, bapt. 1734.
v. SARAH, bapt. 1734.
vi. ELIZABETH, bapt. May, 1735.
vii. JOSIAH, bapt. Feb. 1738.

21. JABEZ³ NORTHRUP (*Daniel,² Joseph¹*), bapt. Jan. 1710, Milford.

Of Ridgefield in 1736. Married March 6, 1735, Sarah ———.
Children, born in Ridgefield:

- i.   EUNICE,[4] b. Oct. 6, 1735.
- ii. JABEZ, b. Aug. 14, 1737.
- iii. SARAH, b. June 21, 1741.
- iv. LOIS, b. Feb. 16, 1743–4.

22. WILLIAM[3] NORTHRUP (*William,*[2] *Joseph*[1]), b. Dec. 1694, Milford.
Signs " of Greenfield," 1736. Died (probably) in 1736 or 1737,
as his children quit-claim in 1737.

- i.   WILLIAM.[4]
- ii. ANNA.
      (Perhaps others.)

23. EPHRAIM[3] NORTHRUP (*William,*[2] *Joseph*[1]), b. 1696, Milford. Married
Nov. 26, 1730, Sarah Gunn, dau. of Samuel. Died Oct. 10, 1787.

- i.   ABIGAIL,[4] b. Aug. 1731; d. March 20, 1790, unmarried.
- ii. EPHRAIM, b. April, 1733.
- iii. LAZARUS, b. June, 1735; d. 1802. (Remembered in Lazarus Gunn's
      will.)
- iv. MARTHA, bapt. July, 1737; m. March 8, 1757, David Lambert, son
      of Jesse.
- v.   MARY, bapt. Dec. 1739; m. Joel Smith.
- vi. ESTHER, bapt. Sept. 1744; m. Feb. 23, 1763, Dr. Elias Carrington,
      son of Noadiah.

24. JOSEPH[3] NORTHRUP (*William,*[2] *Joseph*[1]), b. 1698, Milford. Married
Jan. 10, 1725, Ruth Allen, dau. of Henry.

- i.   MARY,[4] b. Jan. 1729; m. Oct. 3, 1745, David Canfield, son of Jere-
       miah.
- ii.   RUTH, b. March, 1730; m. Joseph Camp.
- iii. JANE, b. May, 1732.
- iv.   ANDREW, b. January, 1736.
- v.   ABEL, bapt. Dec. 1739.
- vi.   ALLEN, bapt. Dec. 1741.
- vii. MERCY, bapt. March, 1743.
- viii. CATHERINE, mentioned in will 1775; m. Ezra Merchant.
- ix.   HETH, mentioned in will as youngest.

25. THOMAS[3] NORTHRUP (*William,*[2] *Joseph*[1]), b. 1701, Milford. Married Abigail Terrill. Removed to Newtown, Conn., and resided
there until the children were grown and settled. His wife died
there, and he went to New Milford and resided with one of his
sons. Residents of Newtown in 1712, Thomas Northrup, Benjamin and Jeremiah and John (brothers) Northrup.

- i.   JOB,[4] b. April 25, 1731; m. April 8, 1756, Violet Peck.
- ii. THOMAS, b. Dec. 2, 1732; m. Aug. 25, 1757, Johanna Leach.
- iii. ISAAC, b. Aug. 6, 1734.
- iv. SARAH, d. at Newtown, aged 96.
- v.   ABRAHAM, b. Aug. 13, 1738; m. twice.
- vi. JOEL, b. March 3, 1742; m. Eunice Marsh.

26. JOHN[3] NORTHRUP (*William,*[2] *Joseph*[1]), b. 1703, Milford. Married
Aug. 14, 1728, Rebecca Roberts, at Ridgefield, whither he had
removed.

- i.   JOHN,[4] b. Jan. 14, 1729.
- ii. WILLIAM, b. Oct. 26, 1730; d. Jan. 14, 1734.
- iii. ENOS, b. Sept. 14, 1733.
- iv. REBECCA, b. Sept. 25, 1735.
- v.   WILLIAM, b. Feb. 6, 1737–8.
- vi. RUTH, b. Jan. 11, 1742–3.
- vii. SAMUEL, b. Feb. 2, 1746.

27. Joseph⁴ Northrup (*Joseph,³ Joseph,² Joseph¹*), b. May 11, 1716, Ridgefield. Married Aug. 9, 1738 (recorded at Ridgefield), Allyn Hayes (dau. of James Hayes of Norwalk, Ct., who had : 1, Eunice, married John St. John; 2, Mary, married Isaac Sherwood, Jr.; 3, Rachel, married Samuel Gates; 4, Allyn, married Joseph⁴ Northrup). She died Sept. 12, 1784, aged 66. He died Sept. 23, 1785. Both buried at Salisbury, Ct.

    i.   Allyn⁵ (dau.), b. May 13, 1739, Ridgefield.
    ii.   Joseph, b. March 20, 1742, Ridgefield.
    iii. Samuel, b. Nov. 26, 1744, Ridgefield.
    iv. Anna, b. Sept. 10, 1745, Ridgefield.
    v.   Elijah, b. April 10, 1750.
    vi. Nathaniel, b. March 26, 1752.
    vii. Jeremiah.
    viii. Marion.
    ix. Eunice.
    x.   Elizabeth.

28. Eli⁴ Northrup (*Joseph,³ Joseph,² Joseph¹*), b. May 1, 1718, Ridgefield. Married Jan. 3, 1738–9, Abigail ———. Gave deed in Ridgefield Dec. 2, 1773. "Of Ridgefield," Feb. 20, 1777. Gave deed in "*Balltown,*" Albany Co., N. Y., Oct. 25, 1779. (Doubtless *Ballston, Saratoga Co., N. Y.,* Albany Co. then extending far to the North.) The deed was given to Josiah Northrup of Ridgefield. Children, born in Ridgefield:

    i.   Eli,⁵ b. Feb. 2, 1742–3.
    ii.   Joanna, b. Aug. 6, 1745.
    iii. Jane, b. Oct. 21, 1747.
    iv. Esther, b. Jan. 18, 1749–50.
    v.   Benajah, b. March 27, 1752. "Loyalist." Removed to New Brunswick 1783; d. May 17, 1838, leaving 14 children, 118 grandchildren and 111 great-grandchildren. (I have a great number of them.)
    vi. Wilson, b. April 7, 1754.

29. Aaron⁴ Northrup (*Joseph,³ Joseph,³ Joseph¹*), b. Nov. 30, 1720, Ridgefield. Married Jan. 25, 1743, Rebecca Hyatt (b. June 20, 1723; d. March 9, 1800). He died March 21, 1802. Resided at Ridgefield and children born there:

    i.   Hannah,⁵ b. Dec. 3, 1744; m. 1st, Elisha Vibbert; m. 2d, Daniel Hoyt; m. 3d, ——— Godfrey.
    ii.   Mary, b. Oct. 13, 1746; m. Ephraim Smith.
    iii. Sarah, b. Aug. 22, 1749; m. Samuel Nash, son of Abraham.
    iv. Aaron, b. June 21, 1751; d. May 21, 1768.
    v.   Rebecca, b. March 7, 1754; m. Joshua Jones, Ballston, N. Y.
    vi. Millicent, b. Feb. 25, 1757; m. John Northrup, of Salem, N. Y., son of Nathan.
    vii. Josiah, b. May 28, 1759.
    viii. Jared, b. Nov. 19, 1761.
    ix. Joseph, b. Oct. 16, 1764.

30. Abraham⁴ Northrup (*Joseph,³ Joseph.² Joseph¹*), b. Sept. 18, 1722, Ridgefield. Married July 13, 1752, Mehetabel Gunn, of Newtown. Removed to Lenox, Mass. Gave deed there Dec. 2, 1773. Covenant—"non-importation," &c.—signed at Lenox, 1774, by Samuel, Elijah and Abraham Northrup, and others. (I have not yet ascertained his children.)

31. Isaac⁴ Northrup (*Joseph,³ Joseph,² Joseph¹*), b. Nov. 10, 1725, Ridgefield. Married 1st, Hannah Gunn; married 2d, Jan. 16,

1752, Elizabeth Lobdell. Lived in Ridgefield until, at least, first six children were born, then in South Salem (giving deed there, Dec. 2, 1773), Westchester Co., N. Y., where he died July 9, 1810. Wife died about 1790. (?)

i. ISAAC,[5] b. Dec. 24, 1752.
ii. DAVID, b. March 20, 1754.
iii. ELIZABETH, b. Oct. 28, 1755.
iv. LOIS, b. July 17, 1757.
v. REBECCA, b. July 13, 1759.
vi. EUNICE, b. Feb. 3, 1761.
vii. PHALLE. x. MOLLY. xii. LEWIS.
viii. SARAH. xi. JONAH. xiii. ISAAC. (?)
ix. RUTH.

These last seven mentioned in dis. of estate May 4, 1791, Ridgefield.

32. JAMES[4] NORTHRUP (*James,[3] Joseph,[2] Joseph[1]*), b. Nov. 9, 1719, Ridgefield. Married Jan. 13, 1742, Rachel Smith, daughter of Samuel, of Norwalk (b. March 27, 1723). Distribution of his estate July 26, 1784. Children, recorded at Ridgefield:

i. JAMES,[5] b. Jan. 22, 1744-5; d. before July 15, 1751.
ii. SAMUEL, b. March 5, 1746; m. Prue Riggs.
iii. MATTHEW, b. April 6, 1749; m. Hannah Abbott.
iv. JAMES, b. July 15, 1751; d. ———.
v. NATHANIEL, b. July 15, 1751; m. Nov. 5, 1772, Chloe Baldwin.
vi. RACHEL, b. Jan. 28, 1754; m. Theophilus Taylor.
vii. HANNAH, b. Feb. 28, 1755; m. Samuel Baldwin, and settled in Aurora, Portage Co., O.; d. about 1826.
viii. STEPHEN, b. Jan. 22, 1759; m. 1st, Betsey Murch; m. 2d, Deborah Robinson.

33. THOMAS[4] NORTHRUP (*James,[3] Joseph,[2] Joseph[1]*), b. Dec. 5, 1727, Ridgefield. Married 1st, March 9, 1747-8, Rachel (b. Feb. 11, 1727, d. Oct. 4, 1759), daughter of Lemuel and Mary Morehouse; married 2d, Jan. 1, 1760, Mehetabel (b. April 11, 1738, d. July 30, 1808), daughter of John and Elizabeth Rockwell. Died Aug. 29, 1799.

i. MARTHA,[5] b. June 8, 1747-8.
ii. THOMAS, b. Sept. 26, 1751.
iii. JACOB, b. Feb. 21, 1762; d. April 28, 1784.
iv. MOSES, b. Jan. 17, 1764.
v. ELIJAH, b. Oct. 8, 1765; m. Aug. 3, 1786, Amy Williams.
vi. JOSHUA, b. July 12, 1777, town of Lee, Mass.; m. 1st, Polly Wade; m. 2d, Harriet Wade.

34. MOSES[4] NORTHRUP (*Moses,[3] Joseph,[2] Joseph[1]*), b. Nov. 1, 1722, Ridgefield. Married Dec. 1749, Patience Beardsley (b. Dec. 22, 1729, d. Oct. 17, 1778). Removed with his father 1733-4 to Dutchess Co., N. Y., and united with him in petitions to purchase vacant lands, April 29, 1743. Had "land troubles" in Pawling, —was "wrongfully driven from his home,"—removed to New Milford, Conn., after Nov. 25, 1760, where he gave deeds in 1768, 1771 and 1774 of lands in Ridgefield. Deeds of division were given between Moses of New Milford and his brothers Benjamin of Hardiston, Sussex Co., N. J., Amos of Tyringham, Mass., and by him and Joseph of Philips Patent, Dutchess Co., N. Y.,—this last, March 14, 1774. Moses[4] was a "loyalist" in the Revolution. Died Oct. 15, 1788.

i. MOSES,[5] b. Jan. 2, 1752; d. July 26, 1778.

 ii. JOHN, b. Nov. 12, 1753; d. March 20, 1755.
 iii. JOSHUA, b. Sept. 10, 1755; m. Olcha Lowe, Nova Scotia.
 iv. JOSEPH, b. April 30, 1757; m. Mary Foster, dau. of Thomas.
 v. ABIGAIL, b. March 25, 1759; m. Elnathan Gunn; d. Jan. 12, 1787.
 vi. EUNICE, b. Feb. 5, 1761; d. Sept. 4, 1788.
 vii. CALEB, b. Dec. 13, 1763; m. July 3, 1785, Silvina Knowles.
 viii. PAUL, b. Oct. 5, 1765; d. May 10, 1791.
 ix. KEZIAH, b. March 8, 1768; d. Oct. 23, 1770.
 x. BENJAMIN, b. Aug. 25, 1770; mar. but had no children; d. April 9, 1796.
 xi. PATIENCE, b. Sept. 7, 1772; m. Nathan Sanford; lived in Kingsbury, Wash. Co., N. Y. Died June 5, 1810.

35. AMOS[4] NORTHRUP (*Moses,[3] Joseph,[2] Joseph[1]*), b. 1730, Ridgefield. Went with his father, 1733–4, to Dutchess Co., N. Y., thence to "Hop Brook," Tyringham, Berkshire Co., Mass., as early as 1771. Gave deed there April 2, 1771, to Moses Northrup of New Milford, of "lands divided or undivided" in Ridgefield. Farmer. Married, 1758, widow Hannah (Calkins) Hatch, who died April 22, 1804, in 68th year of her age. He died Feb. 9, 1810. Children, probably all born at Tyringham:

 i. MIRIAM,[5] b. 1762; m. Dea. Seth Kingsley; d. Jan. 30, 1831.
 ii. MARY, b. 1763; unm.; d. Dec. 16, 1843.
 iii. AMOS, b. April 14, 1765; m. March 10, 1796, Betsey Stedman, dau. of Tristam. She was b. Dec. 18, 1773, and d. Nov. 15, 1852. Amos d. Oct. 12, 1835, Smithfield, Madison Co., N. Y. He had *Rensselaer,[6]* b. Aug. 10, 1804, Tyringham, Mass., d. Aug. 8, 1874; and *Rensselaer[6]* had *Ansel Judd Northrup,[7]* b. June 30, 1833, Smithfield, Madison Co., N. Y.
 iv. BARZILLAI, b. Aug. 15, 1768; m. June 6, 1791, Margery Rockwood.
 v. ANNA, b. Sept. 1769; m. Gideon Hale; d. April 4, 1849.
 vi. JOHN, b. Dec. 2, 1771; m. Jan. 7, 1798, Sarah Miller.
 vii. ABRAHAM, b. April 9, 1774; m. Jan. 17, 1802, Pamelia Jones.
 viii. TIMOTHY, b. Dec. 1779; unm.; d. May, 1820, Pompey, N. Y.
 ix. ENOS, b. June, 1781; m. Sophira Kingsbury.

36. BENJAMIN[4] NORTHRUP (*Moses,[3] Joseph,[2] Joseph[1]*), b. about 1739, Dutchess Co., N. Y. Removed to Sussex Co., N. J., in 1760. In deed Nov. 22, 1760, describes himself "of Bateman's Point, Dutchess Co., N. Y." In deed Nov. 25, 1760, describes "of Newtown, Sussex Co., N. J." In deed May 3, 1768, describes "of Hardiston, Sussex Co., N. J." Married Leonora Holmes (*or* Whitehead) who survived him and married 2d, Peterson. Benjamin d. Sept. 4, 1774, "æ 35 yrs."

 i. BENJAMIN,[5] unm.; d. 1812.
 ii. MOSES, b. 1762; m. 1st, May 1, 1787, Sarah De Witt.
 iii. ABIGAIL, m. John Gauterman. Had 2 children.
 iv. JOSEPH, b. Jan. 7, 1765; m. Feb. 23, 1786, Lucy Price.
 v. MARY, m. Daniel Harker, Sussex Co., N. Y.
 vi. SALLY, m. Samuel Harker, brother of Daniel.

37. CORNELL[4] NORTHRUP (*Moses,[3] Joseph,[2] Joseph[1]*), b. probably *as late* as 1740–2, in Dutchess Co., N. Y. In deed April 27, 1763, describes as "of Beekman's Precinct, in Dutchess County, Province of New York." Nov. 14, 1768, "Cornell Northrup of Sheffield in the County of Berkshire, in the Province of Massachusetts Bay," deeds to "Moses Northrup of New Milford, Yeoman, of Litchfield Co., Conn.," lands in Ridgefield (both divided and undivided.) No record of marriage or death. First 5 children are recorded at Sheffield, Mass.,—the others not recorded. He probably removed

from Sheffield after 1772, and finally to Coeymans, Albany Co., N. Y., where some of the last 4 children are said to have been born.

i. JOHN,[5] b. March 4, 1767; m. 2d, Tamarintha Nichols.
ii. ABIGAIL, b. March 3, 1768; m. Silas Dunham.
iii. SARAH, b. May 29, 1769; m. John Cowel.
iv. ELAM, b. Sept. 7, 1770; m. 1st, Elizabeth Edmunds; m. 2d, Martha Davenport.
v. REBECCA, b. July 20, 1772; m. Peleg Le Valley; d. aged 70.
vi. POLLY, m. Ezra Champions.
vii. BENJAMIN, b. June 4, 1778.
viii. CORNELL.
ix. EUNICE.
x. JAMES. (?)

38. AMOS[4] NORTHRUP (*Amos,[3] Samuel,[2] Joseph[1]*), b. (prob.) 1713–14, Milford. Went to New Milford. Married Dec. 16, 1741, Anna, daughter of Solomon Baldwin of Milford. She joined the First Church in New Milford in 1748, by letter from Amity (Woodbridge). June 30, 1743, he bought of Dea. Job Terrill of New Milford, for £1600, 190 acres of land at (now) Park Lane, East of the road, including 17½ acres with a dwelling house thereon, where he lived and died. His will dated Oct. 1, 1788, and probated July 2, 1790.

i. AMOS,[5] b. Dec. 19, 1742. Recorded at Milford. Grandfather of Hon. Birdsey Grant Northrup, Lecturer, &c.
ii. SOLOMON, b. Dec. 29, 1744; m. Lois Mallery.
iii. DAVID, b. Jan. 27, 1746; m. Rachel Grant.
iv. LOIS, b. Sept. 17, 1748; m. 1771, Rev. Abner Benedict (his 2d wife), son of Peter Benedict. Had 2 sons, distinguished ministers, and 3 daughters, one of whom, Irene, was mother of Hon. Joel T. Headley.
v. ANNA, b. April 3, 1751; m. Aug. 31, 1774, Col. Nathaniel Taylor. Her granddaughter, Mary T., was wife of President Noah Porter, of Yale College.
vi. JOEL, b. July 27, 1753; grandfather of Gen. Lucius Bellinger Northrup, and great-grandfather of Harry Pinckney Northrop, R. C. Bishop at Charleston, S. C.

39. JOEL[4] NORTHRUP (*Joel,[3] Samuel,[2] Joseph[1]*), b. 1732, Woodbridge, Ct. Married Oct. 12, 1756, Abigail Camp. Captain in the Revolution. Died 1786. Children, born in Woodbridge:

i. JOEL,[5] b. Feb. 1758.
ii. ABIGAIL, b. April, 1761; m. Eli Stillson.
iii. ANNA, b. Jan. 1764.
iv. HEZEKIAH, b. April, 1766; died young.
v. MARGARET, b. April, 1771; d. young.
vi. JOHN, b. 1772; d. young.
vii. JOHN, b. 1775.
viii. HEZEKIAH, b. 1778.
ix. MARGARET, b. 1780.
x. ABEL, b. 1781.

40. Capt. JONATHAN[4] NORTHRUP (*John,[3] Jeremiah,[2] Joseph[1]*), b. March 3, 1715, Milford. Removed to Newtown, Conn., with his parents, when quite young. "Captain,"—commanded a Company under Gen. Braddock and afterwards in the Revolution. Married June 2, 1740, Ruth Booth, who died July 25, 1799. He died 1783. Children, born in Newtown:

i. SOLOMON,[5] b. March 8, 1741; had Joseph and Johanna.
ii. GIDEON, b. May 20, 1742; m. 1st, Rhoda Northrup.

iii.   ELIZABETH, b. Sept. 29, 1744.
iv.   MARY, b. June 28, 1746: d. Feb. 22, 1753.
v.   CLEMENT, b. April 15, 1749; m. Jerusha Clark, dau. of Jared.
vi.   GEORGE, b. March 21, 1754; m. 1st, Kimberly; m. 2d, Booth.
vii.   LEMUEL, b. May 31, 1757; m. Lois Woodward.
viii.   AMOS, b. Sept. 7, 1759; married 3 times; had 14 children.

41.   JOHN[4] NORTHRUP (*John,*[3] *Jeremiah,*[2] *Joseph*[1]), b. July 9, 1732, Newtown. Succeeded his father as Town Clerk of Newtown, 1752, and held the office until 1765. Married July 30, 1752, Lois, dau. of William Northrup of Newtown. She died Dec. 3, 1800, aged 68. He died March 11, 1805.

i.   PETER,[5] b. July 3, 1754; m. Lucy Sherman; d. Nov. 27, 1810.
ii.   MARY, b. Jan. 28, 1756; m. Feb. 2, 1773, Solomon Glover.
iii.   NANNY, b. May 14, 1758; m. May 22, 1778, Elijah Sherman.
iv.   AMY, b. Feb. 9, 1760; m. John Sanford.
v.   LOIS, b. Jan. 25, 1762; m. Jacob Wallace.
vi.   BETTY, b. Jan. 15, 1764; m. Daniel Foote.
vii.   HULDAH, b. Oct. 26, 1765; m. Abner Betts.
viii.   RUTH, b. Oct. 5, 1768; m. Solomon Johnson.
ix.   JOHANNA, b. Nov. 10, 1770; d. July 9, 1771.
x.   JOHN, b. Aug. 2, 1772; m. Nabby Baldwin.

REVEREND JOHN NORTON OF MIDDLETOWN.

By ZOETH S. ELDREDGE, of San Francisco, Cal.

1. JOHN NORTON, of Branford, Conn., is believed to have been the third son of Richard Norton, of London, and Ellen Rowley his wife, but this, however, remains to be proven. The name of John Norton appears on the first page of the Branford town records. He married first, Dorothy ———, who died in Branford, January 24, 1652; married second, Elizabeth ———, who died in Branford, Nov. 6, 1657; and third, Elizabeth Clark, who died in Farmington in 1702. He removed to Farmington, Conn., about 1659, and his name appears on record as one of the eighty-four proprietors in the first division of land. He died in Farmington, Nov. 5, 1709.

Children, by first wife, Dorothy, all born in Branford:

 i. ELIZABETH,[2] b. about 1645; m. John Plumb, of Milford.
 ii. HANNAH, b. about 1646; m. Samuel North, of Farmington.
 iii. DOROTHY, b. March 1, 1649.
 iv. JOHN, b. March 24, 1651; d. Jan. 15, 1657.

Child, by second wife, Elizabeth, born in Branford:

2. v. JOHN, b. Oct. 14, 1657.

Children, by third wife, Elizabeth Clark:

 vi. SAMUEL, b. in Farmington, May 13, 1659; d. Aug. 20, 1659.
 vii. THOMAS, b. in Farmington, 1660; m. Hannah Rose.

2. JOHN[2] NORTON (*John*[1]), born in Branford, Oct. 14, 1657; died in Farmington, April 25, 1725; married in Farmington, Ruth, daughter of Dea. Isaac and Ruth (Stanley) More, born in Norwalk, Conn., Jan. 5, 1657. He was deputy for Farmington in 1680, 1681 and 1682.

 Children, born in Farmington:

 i. RUTH,[3] b. about 1675; m. Thomas Seymour, of Hartford.
 ii. ELIZABETH, m. Samuel Catlin, of Hartford.
 iii. ISAAC, b. 1680; m. Elizabeth Galpin, of Hartford.
3. iv. JOHN, b. 1684.
 v. MARY, b. 1686; m. 1st, John Pantry, Jr.; m. 2d, Solomon Boltwood.
 vi. SARAH, b. 1689; m. Samuel Newell.
 vii. HANNAH, b. 1692; m. John Pratt, of Hartford.
 viii. DORCAS, b. 1695; m. Joseph Bird, of Litchfield.
 ix. THOMAS, b. 1697; m. Elizabeth Macon.
 x. EBENEZER, m. Sarah Savage.

3. JOHN[3] NORTON (*John*,[2] *John*[1]), born in Farmington, 1684; died in same place, 1750; married in Farmington, May 6, 1708, Anne, daughter

of Thomas and Elizabeth (Smith) Thompson, born in Farmington, Feb. 10, 1689. Her father, Thomas Thompson, was born in 1651, and after the death of his first wife, Elizabeth Smith, he married Abigail ———. On Dec. 14, 1705, his wife, Abigail, threw a pair of shears at him; the point penetrated the brain, causing his death in a few days. Abigail was convicted of murder, sentenced to death, and after one or two reprieves the sentence was executed. While in prison she gave birth to a posthumous child which she named Mercy. Thomas Thompson was the son of Thomas Thompson of Farmington, and Ann Welles his wife, daughter of Thomas Welles, Governor of Connecticut Colony.

John Norton was called Sergt. John Norton, and John Norton 3d. Children, born in Farmington:

  i. GIDEON,[4] b. Jan. 12, 1709; d. 1712.
  ii. CHARLES, b. Dec. 17, 1710; d. Dec. 24, 1786; m. Rebecca Munson.
  iii. GIDEON, b. Sept. 5, 1713; m. Marella Thompson.
4. iv. JOHN, b. Nov. 16, 1715.
  v. ANNE, b. Jan. 15, 1718; m. Judah Hart, of New Britain.
  vi. JOB, b. Feb. 19, 1720.
  vii. ROGER, b. March 15, 1722.
  viii. RUTH, b. March 28, 1724; m. Josiah Burnham, of Kensington.
  ix. SARAH, b. June 5, 1726; m. Moses Deming.
  x. LUCY, b. March 31, 1728; m. John Kirby, of Middletown.
  xi. MARY, b. May 20, 1730; m. James Bidwell, of Hartford.
  xii. ELIAS, b. March 28, 1732; d. April 9, 1732.
  xiii. THANKFUL, b. Jan. 28, 1734.

4. JOHN[4] NORTON (*John,[3] John,[2] John[1]*), was born in Kensington Society (now Berlin), in the town of Farmington, Nov. 16, 1715; died in East Hampton, Conn., March 24, 1778, a victim to the small pox. He was graduated from Yale College in 1737, studied theology and was ordained Nov. 25, 1741 (at Deerfield), the first pastor of the church at Falltown (now Bernardston) on the northern border of Massachusetts. He remained in charge of this church for some time after the breaking out of the five years French and Indian war in 1744. The new settlement, struggling for existence, exposed as it was to the inroads of the savages, with difficulty supported a minister and in 1745 he severed his connection with the church and accepted the post of chaplain to the three forts, Shirley, Pelham and Massachusetts, built by the Massachusetts government on the north-western boundary of the province, to protect her frontier from the incursions of the French and Indians from Canada, by way of Lake Champlain and Wood Creek. Norton placed his wife and children in Fort Shirley and divided his time among the three garrisons according to their needs.

On August 14, 1746, the chaplain left Fort Shirley in company with the surgeon, Dr. Williams, and fourteen soldiers, and went to Fort Pelham, and on the following day to Fort Massachusetts where he expected to remain about a month. This fort was situated on the Hoosac river in what is now the town of Adams. It was a wooden enclosure formed of squared logs, laid one upon another and interlocked at the angles. This wooden wall rested upon a foundation of stone designated as the "underpinning." A block house, crowned with a tower which served as a lookout and was supplied with means of throwing water to extinguish fire-arrows thrown upon the roof, stood in the north-west corner. There were other buildings in the enclosure, and one—a large log house on the south side—overlooked the outer wall and was probably loopholed for musketry. The commander of the fort, Captain Ephraim Williams (founder of Williams College), with a large portion of his force, had gone to take part in the proposed invasion of Canada, leaving Sergeant John Hawks in charge of the fort. On Saturday, August 16th, Hawks sent Dr. Williams to Deerfield with a detachment of fourteen men to get a supply of powder and lead. This reduced the entire force, including Hawks himself and Norton the chaplain, to twenty-two men, half of whom were disabled with dysentery from which few of the rest were entirely free.* There were also in the fort three women and five children.

On July 23, 1746 (old style), Rigaud de Vaudreuil, town major of Three Rivers, left Montreal with a fleet of canoes carrying a large war party. Their objective point was Fort Frédéric (Crown Point), which was threatened by the English. Rigaud reached Fort Frédéric on the first of August, and in a few days received a reïnforcement of sixty Frenchmen and a band of Indians commanded by the elder of the brothers Du Muy. They had just returned from an incursion towards Albany, and reported that all was quiet in that direction and that Fort Frédéric was in no danger. This left Rigaud free to take the offensive. The question was, where to strike. The Indians held a number of councils and decided upon nothing. Rigaud made them a speech and giving them a wampum belt told them he meant to attack Corlaer (Schenectady). At first this pleased them, and then they changed their minds. Saratoga was proposed, but finally at the suggestion of some of the Indians they decided on Fort Massachusetts. Leaving the canoes at East Bay, just north of the present town of Whitehall, in charge of a guard, they proceeded southward on foot along the base of Skene mountain. The force numbered about seven hundred men, of whom five hundred were French and two hundred were Indians. They reached Fort Massachusetts between eight and nine o'clock on the morning of August 19th. Rigaud had planned a night attack, but was thwarted by the impetuosity of the young Indians and Canadians, who became so excited at the first glimpse of the watch tower of the fort that they dashed forward, firing their guns and yelling. They prudently kept themselves out of reach of the guns of the defenders, however, and surrounding the fort they sheltered themselves behind stumps and opened a distant and harmless fire, accompanied by unearthly yells and howlings. The situation of the little garrison was now a perilous one indeed. Beset by sixty times their effective force and nothing but a log fence between them and the enemy. The men were armed with smooth bore hunting pieces, but so short of ammunition were they that Hawks was obliged to order them to fire only when necessary to hold the enemy in check. Yet so stout was their defence and so effective their fire, that the assailants made no attempt to carry the fort by assault. Norton writes, "about this time we saw several fall to rise no more." Among those who fell was the chief of the St. Francis Indians, shot through the breast by Sergt. Hawks. Rigaud, the French commander, ventured too near

---

* "Lord's day and Monday (Aug. 17 & 18). The sickness was very distressing . . . Eleven of our men were sick and scarcely one of us in perfect health; almost every man was troubled with the griping & flux."—*Norton. The Redeemed Captive.*

the fort and received a shot in the arm which sent him to the rear. In addition to the Indian killed by Hawks, Rigaud reports sixteen Indians and Frenchmen wounded, "which, under the circumstances," says Parkman, "was good execution for ten farmers and a minister; for Chaplain Norton loaded and fired with the rest."*

All that day until nine in the evening the enemy continued their firing and yelling, and then placing a line of sentinels around the fort to prevent messengers from carrying the alarm to Albany or Deerfield, they withdrew to prepare for a night attack. It was Rigaud's intention to open trenches to the foot of the wall, place fagots against it, set them on fire and deliver the fort a prey to the fury of the flames; but a rain coming on he determined to wait till morning.

Hawks filled all his tubs and pails with water and posted his men to repel an assault. Two men had been wounded, thus farther reducing his effective force. Throughout the night they kept the watch, the enemy frequently raising their hideous outcries as though about to attack.

The firing was quickly renewed in the morning, but no attempt was made to open trenches by daylight. About eleven o'clock one of the men in the watch tower, Thomas Knowlton, was shot through the head. The number of effectives was now reduced to eight, including the chaplain. About noon Rigaud sent an Indian with a flag of truce to say he desired to parley. Hawks consented to it, and he with Norton and one or two others met the French commander outside the gate. Rigaud offered honorable terms of capitulation. Hawks promised an answer within two hours and with his companions returned into the fort to consider their means of defence. He found that they had but three or four pounds of powder and about as much lead. Norton prayed for divine aid and guidance. "Had we all been in health or had there been only these eight of us that were in health, I believe that every man would willingly have stood it out to the last. For my part I should," writes the manful chaplain. But besides the sick and wounded there were the three women and five children to be considered. If the fort were taken by assault these would undoubtedly be murdered. Hawks determined therefore to make the best terms he could. Rigaud agreed to the conditions of surrender submitted to him, which were in brief—that all in the fort should be treated with humanity as prisioners of war and exchanged at the first opportunity, and that none of them should be given to the Indians. At three o'clock the gates were opened, the prisoners were conducted to the French camp, the fort given over to plunder and burned to the ground. Notwithstanding his agreement, Rigaud delivered a portion of his prisoners to the Indians, at which Norton made a vigorous protest. The captives were well treated, however, Rigaud having given the Indians presents to induce them to treat their prisoners with humanity. The retreat began the next morning, the force marching back as they had come. They moved slowly, encumbered as they were with the sick and wounded.

The wife of one of the soldiers, John Smeed, was taken in labor. Some of the French made a seat for her to sit upon and carried her

* A Half-Century of Conflict, ii. 245 (Champlain ed.).

662

into camp where about ten o'clock that night " she was graciously delivered of a daughter and was remarkably well. * * * Friday: this morning I baptized John Smeed's child. He called it's name *Captivity.*" The French made a litter of poles, spread over it a deer skin and a bear skin on which they placed the mother and child and so carried them forward.

The march was long and dreary. The prisoners were kindly treated by the victors, some of whom were sorely wounded, and four Indians died within a few days. In due time they reached Quebec, and in course of a year those who remained alive were exchanged and returned to New England. Mrs. Smeed and her infant daughter, Captivity, died in Canada.

Mr. Norton reached Boston, Aug. 16, 1747, where he was received and entertained by Col. Winslow. He published his " Redeemed Captive " in 1748 in Boston. Copies of it are very rare. Drake in his " Particular History of the Five Years French and Indian War," prints it verbatim.

During his captivity his wife and children continued to reside at Fort Shirley and just about the time of his return to Boston his little daughter, Anna, died at the fort and was buried in a field a little to the west of it. The stone which marked her grave is now preserved in the museum of Williams College. His wife applied to the Massachusetts government for the wages due him as chaplain and at one time received one pound sixteen shillings and six pence then due. In October, 1747, the Connecticut Assembly appropriated one hundred pounds to be paid him in consideration of his services and loss and damage, and in February, 1748, the Massachusetts government allowed him £37. 10s. for his services as chaplain to the prisoners while in captivity in Canada.

On Nov. 30, 1748, he was settled minister in the parish of East Hampton, in Middletown, Conn., which position he held for thirty years to the time of his death.

In August, 1755, he was appointed chaplain to the forces sent by Connecticut against Crown Point. In March, 1756, he was again appointed chaplain to the forces sent against Crown Point, and in March, 1760, he was appointed chaplain of the Third Connecticut Regiment in the expedition against Canada, in the campaign which resulted in the capitulation of Vaudreuil by which Canada passed to the British crown.

John Norton was married in Springfield, Mass., August 28, 1738, to Eunice, daughter of Luke and Elizabeth (Walker) Hitchcock. She was born in Springfield, March 2, 1712/3, and died in East Hampton, May 27, 1796.

The children of Rev. John Norton, so far as known, were:

i. ASENATH,[5] b. ———; d. Jan. 2, 1810; m. Dea. James Bill.
ii. ELIZABETH, b. Dec., 1740; d. May 18, 1770; m. Nathaniel Clark.
iii. JOHN, b. 1743; d. May 11, 1808; m. Edey Clark.
iv. ANNA, d. Aug., 1747, at Fort Shirley.
v. JACOB, b. Dec. 15, 1748; d. on prison-ship in New York, Revolutionary war.
vi. ELIAS, b. Oct. 21, 1750; d. Nov. 5, 1750.
vii. ANNE, b. March 29, 1752.
viii. EUNICE, b. Oct. 23, 1754; d. Oct. 12, 1845.
ix. ELIAS, b. Oct. 23, 1754; d. 1825.

REVEREND JOHN NORTON OF MIDDLETOWN.—In my article in the REGISTER *
for January, 1899, the statement is made that the children of John Norton, the
first, iv John, born March 24, 1651, died January 15, 1657, and that the next
child was v John, born October 14, 1657, who became John Norton, the second.
This statement was questioned, and after a careful study of both town and church
records, I am satisfied that a mistake has been made, not only by myself, but
by Mr. Albert B. Norton and by Judge C. C. Baldwin, both of whom have published this family record. The Branford town records do not give the double
dates for the year, between January 1 and March 25, as was customary, and
the above death recorded as of January 15, 1657, occurred in 1657-8, or as we
now write the year, 1658. Much study has been given to the name of the child
born October 14, 1657. It has been pronounced John, Joseph and Joshua. I
am satisfied it is not John, and I am further satisfied that the entry of January
15, 1657-8 records the death of this child. John Norton, the second, was therefore born March 24, 1651-2. His son Isaac married Elizabeth Galpin of Stafford, not Hartford as written, and the wife of his son Thomas was Elizabeth
McIan, daughter of Robert and Sarah (Wilcoxson) McIan.

ZOETH S. ELDREDGE.
Bohemian Club, San Francisco.

THE DESCENDANTS OF THOMAS NORTON OF GUILFORD, CONN.

Compiled by Hon. R. D. SMYTH and communicated by Dr. BERNARD C. STEINER.

THOMAS NORTON came to Guilford with Rev. Mr. Whitfield in 1639,
was a signer of the Plantation Covenant, and served the town as its miller
until his death in 1648. He is stated to have been a church warden of
Mr. Whitfield's parish at Ockley in Surrey, England, and has been thought
to have been connected with the Mortons of Sharpenhow, Bedfordshire.
(REGISTER, vol. xiii., p. 225.) Dea. L. M. Norton of Goshen identified
him with Thomas, son of William Norton and his second wife Dennis
Chelmsby, and put the date of his birth as about 1582. His home lot in
Guilford contained two acres and was on the west side of Crooked Lane
(now State Street). This lot fell to his son John, on Thomas Norton's
death, and afterwards was occupied by Lieut. William Seward, his son-in-
law. Thomas Norton also owned seventeen and one-half acres of upland in
Norton's quarter, a parcel of four and one-half acres of "upland in the
plaine" and a parcel of one and one-half acres of marsh land by the sea-
side. His wife was named Grace and her maiden name is supposed to
have been Wells. [*Note.* In the REGISTER for April, 1897, vol. li.,
p. 221, is a note by Elliot Stone, calling attention to the fact that Thomas
Norton and Grace Wells were married in Shelton Parish, Bedfordshire, on
May 5, 1631, and that their daughter Grace was baptized Jan. 13, 1632,
in the neighboring parish of Deans. A son, John, was baptized Feb. 15,
1634. (See Blaydes' "Genealogica Bedfordiensis.") Mr. Smyth gave
the birth of his children as follows: 1, Anne, about 1625; 2, Grace,
about 1627, and 3, John, in 1640. Also that Thomas Norton of Ockley,
Surrey, married Judith Howell in 1637. No explanation of his tangle can
as yet be given.—B. C. S.]

The children of Thomas[1] and Grace Norton were:

  i.   ANNE,[2] m. John Warner of Saybrook and Hartford, 1649.
  ii.   GRACE, m. William Seward of Guilford, April 2, 1651. (See REGIS-
       TER, July, 1898, vol. lii. p. 323.)
  iii.   MARY, b. about 1635; m. Dea. Samuel Rockwell of Windsor, April
       9, 1658.
2. iv.   JOHN, d. March 5, 1704.

v.   ABIGAIL, b. about 1642; m. Ananias Tryon of Killingworth, Aug. 6, 1667.
3. vi. THOMAS, d. about 1713.

2. JOHN[2] NORTON (*Thomas[1]*), was a miller at Guilford for many years. In 1667 he bought Mr. Robert Kitchel's home lot and removed thither. He married first, Hannah Stone, daughter of William, in 1665, and second, Elizabeth Hubbard, daughter of George, who died February, 1710.

The children of John Norton were:

   i.   JOHN,[3] b. Nov. 18, 1666; d. Jan. 10, 1666-7.
4. ii. JOHN, b. May 29, 1668; d. March 15, 1711.
5. iii. SAMUEL, b. Oct. 4, 1672; d. April 2, 1752.
6. iv. THOMAS, b. March 4, 1675; d. Sept. 21, 1740.
   v.   HANNAH, b. Feb. 24, 1677-8; m. Ebenezer Stone, Jan. 16, 1702.
   vi. MARY, b. 1680.

3. THOMAS[2] NORTON, JR. (*Thomas[1]*) of Saybrook, was a farmer in prosperous circumstances. His education was good for the period. Dea. L. M. Norton thought that he was born as early as 1626. He left Guilford early, never being made a freeman there, and with fourteen others, on Sept. 9, 1662, signed a writing on the records at Saybrook, agreeing to sustain John Clark, Sr., and others in opposing the settlement of Killingworth at the Hammonassett river. He was made free at Saybrook, Sept. 9, 1668. The connection of the Nortons with Saybrook began early and when Mary Norton, his sister, was married in 1658 to Samuel Rockwell of Windsor, she is described in the records of the latter place as of Saybrook. After the death of his wife he lived for a while with his son Thomas in Saybrook, and later with his son Joseph in Durham. By instrument dated May 8, 1706, in the Saybrook records, he appoints Dea. William Parker and Dea. Nathaniel Chapman of Saybrook, and John Parmelee of Guilford, "overseers of all his estate and affairs," as well during life as after his decease, "to see the several settlements of his children performed, etc., on account of his "Inability and Incapacity by reason of old age." He owned extensive tracts of land at Saybrook, Cochinchauge (Durham), Middletown, and probably at Killingworth. He married Elizabeth Mason, daughter of Nicholas, May 8, 1671. She died Jan. 31, 1699.

Their children were:

   i.   ELIZABETH,[3] b. Oct. 13, 1674; d. April 2, 1676.
7. ii.   THOMAS, b. June 1, 1677; d. Aug. 26, 1726.
   iii. ELIZABETH, b. Dec. 26, 1679.
8. iv.   JOSEPH, b. Nov. 6, 1681; d. December, 1756.
9. v.   SAMUEL, b. Nov. 6, 1681; d. July 13, 1767.
   vi.   ABIGAIL, b. Oct. 26, 1683.
   vii. EBENEZER, b. Oct. 26, 1683.
10. viii. JOHN, b. Oct. 3, 1686; d. December, 1768.

4. JOHN[3] NORTON (*John,[2] Thomas[1]*) of Guilford, married Hannah, daughter of Emmanuel Buck, Nov. 14, 1694. She was born at Wethersfield, April 12, 1671, and died Oct. 22, 1739. As second husband she married John Fowler.

The children of John and Hannah (Buck) Norton were:

   i.   ANNA,[4] b. Oct. 16, 1695; d. single, October, 1721.
   ii. MARY, b. Dec. 6, 1697; d. single, 1711.

665

iii. JOHN, b. Dec. 23, 1699, of Guilford. He was a man of strict integrity and piety. His descendants regarded him with high respect and veneration. He retained his physical and mental strength to the close of his long life and d. at the house of his son-in-law, Nathan Chittenden, Jan. 11, 1797. He m. 1st, Elizabeth Robinson, dau. of Thomas, by whom he had no children. She d. 1728. He m. 2d, Mary, dau. of John Morgan Groton, Nov. 14, 1729. She d. Nov. 14, 1769. Their children were: 1. *Elizabeth*,[5] b. 1732; d. single, Oct. 21, 1784. 2. *John*, b. December, 1734; d. Aug. 17, 1804; m. Lucy Lee, Dec. 27, 1758; she d. March 16, 1802. 3. *Ruth*, b. December, 1736; d. Aug. 12, 1814; m. Nathan Chittenden, Oct. 23, 1756; d. June 6, 1819, aged 89. 4. *Zebulon*, b. 1740; removed to Bloomfield, N. Y.; was at South Britain, 1765; d. 1815; m. Naomi Booth. 5. *Abraham*, b. 1742; removed to Wolcott, Conn.; m. ———— Doolittle, and had four sons and nine daughters. 6. *Mary*, b. 1747; d. at Bristol; m. Justus Pierce of Southbury. 7. *Andrew*, b. 1750; d. single, Sept. 2, 1775. 8. *Nathan*, b. 1752; d. March 1, 1785; lived in Guilford, and was drowned at the mouth of the harbor; m. Elizabeth Roberts of Middletown, May 14, 1771. 9. *Huldah*, b. 1754; d. 1748; m. Israel Johnson of Meriden or Wallingford, who d. Oct. 21, 1784.
iv. SARAH, b. Feb. 26, 1702.
v. JOSEPH, b. Oct. 10, 1704; lived in Guilford; d. March 9, 1781; m. Mary Champion of Lyme, April 11, 1728. She d. July 13, 1800. Their children were: 1. *Simeon*[5] of Guilford; b. March 3, 1729; d. Dec. 22, 1772; m. Mary, dau. of Patrick Faulkner, Nov. 20, 1755. 2. *David*, b. Oct. 31, 1730; lived in Waterbury, 1780, and later at Wolcott; killed by lightning, 1802; m. 1st, Submit Benton, Nov. 11, 1752; she d. about 1755. He m. 2d, Suza Bishop. 3. *William*, b. Jan. 22, 1732; d. June 17, 1760. 4. *Hannah*, b. Oct. 1, 1734. 5. *Philemon*, b. June 24, 1736; d. October, 1736. 6. *Noah*, b. June 27, 1740; d. May 31, 1763; m. Mary ————. 7. *Beriah* of Guilford, b. 1742; d. Nov. 10, 1803; m. Rebecca Howd of Branford, Feb. 24, 1760; she d. Jan. 28, 1805.
vi. ELIZABETH, b. Oct. 6, 1706; d. Sept. 21, 1753; m. Daniel Benton, Aug. 8, 1728. He d. Aug. 25, 1756.
vii. HANNAH, b. March 10, 1710; d. single, November, 1724.

5. SAMUEL[3] NORTON (*John*,[2] *Thomas*[1]) of the East River Quarter in Guilford, married first, Abigail Ward, Jan. 25, 1692–3. She died Aug. 10, 1733. He married second, widow Sarah West, who died Aug. 6, 1752. His list in 1716 was £87. 3s. 0d.
His children were:

i. ABIGAIL,[4] b. Nov. 12, 1693; m. Benjamin Griswold, June 17, 1718.
ii. SAMUEL, b. July 10, 1698; lived in Salisbury, Conn., and d. November, 1745; m. Thankful Wilcox, Sept. 6, 1722. Their children were: 1. *Samuel*,[5] b. 1723; lived at Salisbury. 2. *Ishi*, b. 1729; lived at Hammonassett in East Guilford; d. July 21, 1801; m. 1st, Mary Hand, who d. July 6, 1785; m. 2d, Lydia Hill, who d. March 19, 1843, æ. 90. 3. *Asahel*, lived in Salisbury in 1760. 4. *James*, lived in Salisbury in 1765.
iii. KEZIAH, b. Dec. 21, 1700; m. John Grave, the "smith," Aug. 1, 1723. He d. April, 1759.
iv. ANNA, b. July 10, 1703; d. Dec. 22, 1726: m. Selah Murray, May 14, 1725. He d. March 13, 1764.
v. TRYAL, b. Jan. 16, 1706; d. Aug. 19, 1784; m. Richard Bristow, May 11, 1738. He d. April, 1800.
vi. MINDWELL, b. June 6, 1708; d. Sept. 20, 1750; m. Samuel Meigs, Nov. 4, 1731. He d. Sept. 1, 1751.
vii. THANKFUL, b. Sept. 4, 1710.
viii. ISAIAH, b. Jan. 12, 1712; lived in Middletown; m. Joanna Morehouse of Saybrook. Their children were: 1. *Sarah*,[5] b. March 12, 1749. 2. *Aaron*, b. June 13, 1750. 3. *Andrew*, b. Feb. 18, 1752.

6. THOMAS[8] NORTON (*John*,[2] *Thomas*[1]) of Guilford was a miller and wheelwright. His list in 1716 was £109 in addition to a trade rating or "faculty" of £10. He married May 28, 1701, Rachel, daughter of Comfort Starr of Middletown, who died Sept. 30, 1740. Their children were:

i. RACHEL,[4] b. July 12, 1702; d. March 31, 1750; m. Timothy Stone, Esq., Aug. 29, 1720. He d. Sept. 9, 1765.

ii. THOMAS, b. Oct. 1, 1704; A.B. (Yale), 1723; lived in Guilford, and d. Sept. 8, 1768; m. Bethia ——, who d. Sept. 28, 1776. Their children were: 1. *Thomas*,[5] b. 1732; lived in Branford in 1774, and d. May 5, 1797; m. Mercy, dau. of Roger Tyler, March 28, 1761. 2. *Ashbell*, m. Submit Whedon, July 19, 1756; she d. Feb. 15, 1792. He lived in Branford, and d. Sept. 12, 1799. 3. *Jedidah*, lived at Middletown in 1771. 4. *Bethiah*, m. Dea. Pelatiah Leete, June 1, 1767. 5. *Zerviah*, m. Simeon Leete. 6. *Elijah*. 7. *Benjamin* of Rutland, Vt., in 1799. 8. *Martha*.

iii. DANIEL, b. Jan. 17, 1707; lived in Guilford, and d. Dec. 4, 1789; m. 1st, Sarah Bradley, 1730, who d. Nov. 5, 1756; m. 2d, Elizabeth Chittenden, March 9, 1761, who d. Sept. 21, 1802. His children by his first wife were: 1. *Sarah*,[5] b. about 1731; d. Feb. 14, 1761! m. Joseph Chittenden, Jr., 1749. He d. Jan. 8, 1793. 2. *Daniel*, b. about 1733; m. Sarah Stone, Nov. 5, 1756, and lived in Durham. 3. *Leah*, bapt. 1735; m. Thomas Stone, March 27, 1754. 4. *Rachel*, b. about 1737; d. of dysentery, Sept. 18, 1756. 5. *Elon*, b. about 1739; d. of dysentery, Sept. 30, 1756. 6. *Lois*, d. Feb. 28, 1758. 8. *Felix*, lived at Freehold, N. J., 1779; m. 1st, Anna Leete in 1763; she d. May 13, 1773; m. 2d, Hannah Harrison, March 2, 1774. 8. *Hannah*, d. Sept. 22, 1820; m. Solomon Leete, Nov. 3, 1772; he d. at Greenville, N. Y., about 1822. 9. *Anna*, d. Dec. 13, 1834; m. Thomas Leete, June 30, 1773; he d. May 27, 1830. 10. *Charity*, b. 1743; d. Dec. 13, 1824; m. Dec. 10, 1766, Daniel Leete; he d. May 3, 1825. The order of some of the younger children is uncertain.

iv. REUBEN, b. April 6, 1711; lived in Guilford, and d. Nov. 28, 1796; m. Hannah, dau. of Dr. Daniel Hooker of Hartford, Sept. 7, 1738; she d. May 8, 1797, æ. 78. Their children were: 1. *Arah*,[5] b. Aug. 3, 1739: m. Phebe, dau. of Josiah Scranton, March 7, 1764; she d. Aug. 31, 1818; he lived in Guilford, and d. Dec. 3, 1813. 2. *Hooker*, b. Jan. 15, 1741; d. Sept. 9, 1742. 3. *Diadama*, b. Nov. 2, 1742; m. Joseph Dudley, July 21, 1762; he d. December, 1805. 4. *Hooker*, b. 1744; lived in Guilford, and d. July 17, 1827; m. Sibyl Bradley of Vermont, who d. æ. 61, May 4, 1806. 5. *Hannah*, b. May 1, 1746; d. Feb. 13, 1825; m. Nathaniel Allis of East Guilford, Oct. 2, 1766; he d. March 12, 1785. 6. *Reuben*, b. 1748; lived in Guilford, and d. Oct. 18, 1820; m. Lois, dau. of John Cruttenden, who d. June 9, 1839. 7. *Rachel*, b. 1750; m. Jesse Murray, who d. April 12, 1824. 9. *Stanley*, b. July 5, 1754; imbecile; d. Feb. 25, 1817. 10. *Eber*, b. July 5, 1756; lived in Guilford, and d. Aug. 13, 1843; m. Nov. 2, 1789, Mabel Evarts, who d. May 1, 1848. 11. *Anah*, b. May 14, 1759; lived in Guilford; d. Jan. 5, 1847; m. Mary Bidwell of Manchester, Nov. 14, 1791; she was b. Oct. 11, 1759; d. Aug. 21, 1835, æ. 76. 12. *Azubah*, b. 1752; m. Ichabod Bartlett of New Hampshire, Oct. 2, 1772, who d. Aug. 18, 1777.

v. LEAH, b. April 15, 1715; d. Jan. 17, 1783; m. Daniel Stone, 1731. He d. Dec. 23, 1782.

vi. EBER, b. Nov. 8, 1718; lived in Guilford, and d. Feb. 6, 1794; m. Ruth, widow of Ebenezer Evarts, who d. Jan. 20, 1800. Their child was: *Parnel*,[5] m. 1st, Jeremiah Griffing; 2d, Richard Griffing; 3d, —— Hathaway. She d. Nov., 1811, in New Orleans.

vii. TIMOTHY, b. Feb. 3, 1721; lived in Guilford, and d. Oct. 1, 1793; m. Jan. 1, 1748, Elizabeth, dau. of Col. Andrew Ward; she d. Sept. 9, 1787. Their children were: 1. *Clarissa*,[5] and 2. *Eliza-*

beth, twins, b. Feb. 27, 1749; Elizabeth m. Jonathan Vail of Mt. Pleasant, who d. Sept. 11, 1844; she d. April 11, 1841. 3. *Sabrina*, b. Jan. 22, 1753; d. March 25, 1821.

7. THOMAS³ NORTON (*Thomas,*² *Thomas*¹) married Rebecca Neil, Dec. 11, 1701. She died Dec. 1, 1748. They lived in Saybrook.

Their children were:

i. LYDIA,⁴ b. Dec. 25, 1702.
ii. REBECCA, b. Sept. 16, 1704; m. Aaron Lyman of Wallingford.
iii. JOHN, b. Aug. 6, 1706; d. Nov. 4, 1770; m. his cousin Deborah Norton, March 9, 1732. Their children were: 1. *John,*⁵ b. March 1, 1734, at Saybrook; bapt. June 30, 1734, at Durham, whither his father had removed; m. 1st, Hannah Bishop; Dec. 21, 1757; she d. 1773; m. 2d, Sarah Tainter of Branford, March 24, 1774; she d. Feb. 3, 1815. He lived in Durham, and d. July 2, 1807. 2. *Joel*, b. Sept. 20, 1745; d. July 2, 1746.
iv. JEDIDIAH, b. Dec. 3, 1712; d. 1794; m. 1st, Eunice Curtiss of Meriden, 1737; m. 2d, Achsah Norton, his cousin, 1746; removed to Meriden, and later to Kensington, where he died. His children were: 1. *Lydia,*⁵ b. 1739; d. young. 2. *Eunice*, b. 1740; d. young. 3. *Jedidiah*, lived in Berlin and Avon, and d. 1812; m. Elizabeth Kilbourne of Avon, who d. 1825. 4. *Eunice*, m. John Wilcox, Jr., in 1766. 5. *Josiah*, lived in Castleton, Vt. 6. *Samuel*, b. and d. 1757. 7. *Samuel*, b. 1759; m. Phebe Edwards, 1789. 8. *Achsah*, m. John Tilden. 9. *Rebecca*, m. A. Wright. 10. *Lydia*, m. Josiah Thompson. 11. *Ruth*, m. Asa Upson.
v. ANN, b. May 30, 1714; m. Timothy Jerome of Wallingford, 1736.
vi. SAMUEL, b. January, 1717; cripple.
vii. THOMAS, b. January, 1720; drowned in Connecticut river, 1755; m. Martha ——. Children: 1. *Elizabeth,*⁵ b. 1744. 2. *Rebecca*, b. 1748. 3. *Lydia*, b. 1754.

8. JOSEPH³ NORTON (*Thomas,*² *Thomas*¹) resided for a while in Guilford, and later in Durham. He married Deborah, daughter of Isaac Cruttenden, who died in 1756.

Their children were:

i. JOSEPH,⁴ b. 1710; removed to Goshen in April, 1760; d. April 22, 1773; m. 1st, Prudence Osborne, Dec. 16, 1729; she d. May 4, 1768. He m. 2d, Esther Stanley, who d. Feb. 25, 1795. Their children were: 1. *Mehitable,*⁵ b. July 12, 1730; d. Jan. 1, 1767; m. Charles Brooks. 2. *Elihu*, b. Jan. 11, 1732; m. Dinah Snow. 3. *Daniel*, b. March 2, 1736; d. Feb. 4, 1799; m. Elizabeth Howe of Goshen, May 27, 1762. 4. *Esther*, b. Dec. 18, 1738, bapt. at Durham, Dec. 24; m. Miles Norton. 5. *Prudence*, b. 1740, bapt. Aug. 24, 1742; d. June 15, 1825; m. Joseph Howe of Goshen, Oct. 24, 1768; he d. April 17, 1807.
ii. ISAAC, b. Aug. 17, 1712; lived in Bristol, and d. 1793; m. Mary Rockwell (b. 1711) Nov. 12, 1735. Their children were: 1. *Abigail,*⁵ b. Oct. 14, 1736; m. 1st, —— Peck; m. 2d, Samuel Lane. 2. *Mary*, b. June 1, 1738; m. —— Curtiss. 3. *Lydia*, b. March 5, 1740; m. —— Howe. 4. *Sylvanus*, b. July 16, 1742; settled in Norfolk, Ct. 5. *Anna*, b. Oct. 17, 1743; m. —— Scott. 6. *Deborah*, b. 1745; m. —— Blakesley. 7. *Isaac*, b. March 27, 1747; d. at Bristol, 1792; m. Esther ——, who d. 1809, æ. 55. 8. *Aaron*, b. March 26, 1749; removed to Norfolk; d. 1832; m. Rhoda ——; d. 1812, æ. 64. 9. *Joel*, b. May 13, 1753; lived in Bristol; d. 1825; m. 1st, Phebe ——; 2d, Hannah ——, d. 1821, æ. 70. 10. *Zipporah*, bapt. Oct. 26, 1755, at Durham.
iii. JOEL, b. January, 1714; d. single.
iv. THOMAS, b. May 15, 1715; m. Mary Stedman, Nov. 5, 1740. Their children were: 1. *Elisha,*⁵ b. Nov. 12, 1741. 2. *Ebenezer*, bapt. at Durham, Oct. 2, 1743. 3. *Sarah*, b. March 26, 1746. 4. *Phinehas*, b. April 23, 1748. 5. *Hannah*, b. May 22, 1751.
v. DEBORAH, b. 1719; m. her cousin John Norton.

668

9. SAMUEL³ NORTON (*Thamas*,² *Thomas*¹) of Durham, married Dinah Birdseye, widow of Benjamin Beach, March 13, 1713. She had two children by her first husband, and is said to have been "no ordinary woman."

Their children were:

i. SAMUEL,⁴ b. March 20, 1714; d. March 21, 1716.

ii. EBENEZER, b. Dec. 30, 1715; removed to Goshen in 1739, and d. March 15, 1785; m. Elizabeth, dau. of Nathaniel Baldwin in 1740; she d. April 16, 1811. He was one of the most prominent men of Goshen, and represented Goshen twenty-six times in the General Assembly, between 1760 and 1779. He was a strong and decided whig in the Revolution, and held the office of colonel of militia. He was a civil magistrate from 1771, and a deacon in the Congregational Church from 1766 until his death. He was State agent for procuring arms for the soldiers. His grandson, Dea. L. M. Norton, said that "his Christian character was exemplary and uniform." His children were: 1. *Miles*,⁵ b. March 30, 1741; lived in Goshen; d. Sept. 17, 1795; m. 1st, his cousin Esther Norton, Dec. 14, 1758; 2d, Sibyl Andrews; 3d, Anne Agard, April 3, 1777. 2. *Aaron*, b. March 19, 1743; lived in Goshen and East Bloomfield; d. Nov. 30, 1828; m. Martha, dau. of Ebenezer Foote of Cornwall, May 15, 1769; she d. 1828. 3. *Elizabeth*, b. Dec. 19, 1746; d. at East Bloomfield, January, 1814; m. John Dowd of Goshen, June 4, 1763; he d. September, 1824, æ. 86. 4. *Ebenezer*, b. Aug. 12, 1748; lived in Goshen; d. Sept. 24, 1795; m. 1st, Experience Lewis, dau. of Nehemiah, May 4, 1769; she d. Oct. 30, 1781, æ. 30; m. 2d, Charity Nills, dau. of Dea. Joseph, June 5, 1782; she d. July 17, 1843, æ. 84. He was a farmer, and six times sat in the General Assembly. 5. *Rachel*, b. June 26, 1752; d. Dec. 17, 1789; m. Amasa Cook of Goshen, March 5, 1772; he d. Dec. 4, 1821, æ. 72. 6. *Marana*, b. March 13, 1755; m. Capt. Jonathan Buel, Jr., of Goshen, Nov. 20, 1774; he d. Feb. 14, 1847. 7. *Olive*, b. Jan. 31, 1758; m. Dea. Timothy Buel, Nov. 13, 1777. 8. *Nathaniel*, b. Dec. 31, 1760; of East Bloomfield, N. Y.; d. 1807; m. Patty Beebe of Canaan, Ct., July, 1782. 9. *Birdseye*, b. June 30, 1763; d. March 27, 1812. He was a wealthy merchant and several times sat in the General Assembly. He lived at Goshen; m. Hannah, dau. of Ephraim Starr, Sept. 20, 1792; she d. at Litchfield, Sept. 21, 1826; she m. 2d, Theron Beach of Litchfield, March 30, 1815.

iii. SAMUEL, b. March 6, 1718; lived in Goshen, and d. Sept. 19, 1801; m. Molly Lucas of Middletown, Nov. 27, 1740; she d. April 29, 1801. He was a leading man of the town. His wife was so singular that many thought her deranged. Their children were: 1. *Jabez*,⁵ b. Oct. 6, 1741; d. December, 1777; m. 1st, Margaret Beach, dau. of Caleb, Nov. 21, 1765; she d. Aug. 26, 1766; m. 2d, Sarah, dau. of Ebenezer Buell of Litchfield, Nov. 12, 1767. 2. *Lydia*, b. April 3, 1743; m. John Allen of the N. Y. Oblong. 3. *Mary*, b. May 20, 1744; d. Aug. 2, 1748. 4. *Sarah*, b. Oct. 7, 1745; m. Rice Gaylord of Norfolk. 5. *Samuel*, b. May 19, 1747; lived in Goshen; d. Dec. 7, 1826; m. 1st, Elizabeth, dau. of Ebenezer Lewis, Jan. 1, 1772; she d. March 5, 1814; m. 2d, Phebe Squire, Jan. 4, 1816; she d. June 6, 1830. He was a deacon in the Congregational Church. 6. *Abijah*, b. Feb. 26, 1749; lived in Cazenovia, N. Y.; m. Lucy, dau of Walter Cook. 7. *Mary*, b. April 20, 1751; m. Abel Bristow of Lima, N. Y. 8. *Levi*, b. May 12, 1754; d. May 29, 1754. 9. *Levi*, b. May 13, 1759; d. 1823; m. Olive Whister, and lived in Winsted and Canaan.

iv NOAH, b. Jan. 24, 1720; d. young.

v. DAVID, bapt. Aug. 20, 1721; d. young.

vi. DINAH, bapt. Nov. 24, 1723; d. Sept. 6, 1800; m. John Curtiss of Durham, Nov. 18, 1747. He d. July 1, 1800.

vii. DAVID, bapt. Jan. 30, 1726-7; of Durham and Goshen; d. Nov. 2, 1769; m. Anner, dau. of Cornelius Bronson of Southbury, Jan. 29,

1752; she d. Dec. 7, 1816, æ. 90. He was a man of ability, energy, talent. Their children were: 1. *David*,[5] b. March 6, 1753; of Sangerfield, N. Y.; m. Lois Ferguson, who d. 1837. 2. *Eber*, b. July 29, 1755; of East Bloomfield; m. Diantha Dowd, June 1, 1785; she d. Feb. 1, 1838, æ. 74. 3. *Oliver*, b. May 15, 1757; of Sangerfield; d. Jan. 6, 1838; m. Martha Beach of Goshen. 4. *John*, b. Nov. 29, 1758; of Bennington, Vt.; d. Aug. 24, 1828; m. Lucretia, dau. of Capt. Jonathan Buel; she d. Aug. 15, 1852. 5. *Anna*, b. Oct. 29, 1760; d. at Hudson, Ohio, Aug. 31, 1816; m. David Hudson of Branford, Dec. 23, 1783; he d. March 17, 1836. 6. *Alexander*, b. March 10, 1763; of Goshen; d. Nov. 2, 1848; m. Rhoda Collins, May 4, 1786; she d. Aug. 3, 1855. 7. *Andrew*, b. May 7, 1765; d. Oct. 28, 1838; he lived in Goshen; was a goldsmith; m. Laurain Hurlburt, dau. of Elisha, who d. May 27, 1851. 8. *William*, b. May 30, 1767; d. 1840; he lived at Nassau, N. Y., and m. widow Ann Morrison. 9. *Miriam*, b. March 22, 1770; d. May 6, 1843; m. Timothy Collins, Sept. 8, 1791; he d. April 22, 1846, æ. 77.

viii. NOAH, b. Jan. 26, 1728-9; d. 1807; m. Experience Strong of Durham, Dec. 29, 1757; she d. 1811.

10. JOHN[3] NORTON (*Thomas*,[2] *Thomas*[1]) married Elizabeth ———, Dec. 29, 1757. She died in 1811.

His children were:

i. JONATHAN,[4] b. Feb. 18, 1712; of Durham, Killingworth, Bristol, Southington and Norfolk; d. Oct. 27, 1801; m. Ruth ———, who d. Jan. 15, 1809. They owned the covenant at Durham, Feb. 5, 1737-8. Their children were: 1. *Jonathan*,[5] bapt. March 5, 1737-8, in Durham. 2. *Stephen*, bapt. in Durham, June 28, 1741; d. Sept. 11, 1826; lived in Norfolk, Ct.; m. Experience Gaylord, 1762; she d. Sept. 12, 1825, æ. 83. 3. *Ruth*, bapt. in Durham, Aug. 20, 1743; m. Nov. 26, 1770, Edward Scoville of Waterbury. 4. *Jonathan*, b. Aug. 27, 1745; d. single, in the West Indies. 5. *Sarah*, bapt. Feb. 28, 1748, in Durham. 6. *Phebe*, bapt. May 13, 1750, in Durham. 7. *Job*, b. 1752, in Southington; d. young. 8. *Job*, b. 1757; d. in Southington, 1759. 9. *Lucy*, b. 1791; d. young, at Norfolk, whither the family removed in 1774.

ii. JOHN, b. Feb. 26, 1715; m. Mary Griswold, 1742; lived in Durham and Killingworth. Their children were: 1. *Mary*,[5] b. April 13, 1743; m. ——— Hull, a sailor. 2. *Rhoda*, b. Aug. 16, 1745; m. ——— Parmelee of Killingworth. 3. *Moses*, b. Dec. 28, 1746; m. Mary Linn, who d. 1856. 4. *John*, b. Feb. 23, 1748. 5. *Aaron*, b. June 24, 1751; m. widow Rutty. 6. *Anne*, m. 1st, ——— Baker of Lanesboro; 2d, James Nettleton. 7. *Elah*, m. Huldah Hull. 8. *Amos*, b. 1765; of Killingworth and North. Bristol; d. Dec. 4, 1822; m. Sylvia Field, who d. March 5, 1812. 9. *Abel*, b. 1768; d. single.

iii. BENJAMIN, b. Feb. 12, 1719; of Killingworth and Durham; killed in the French war; m. Eliza Seward, dau. of Noahdiah, who d. 1807. They owned the covenant, July 29, 1740, at Durham. Their children were: 1. *Benjamin*,[5] b. July 10, 1746; m. Azubah Munger, Nov. 22, 1771; lived in Killingworth, Rutland and East Bloomfield. 2. *Noahdiah*, b. Aug. 17, 1748; of North Bristol (now North Madison); d. May 15, 1805; m. 1st, Sarah, dau. of Capt. John Hopson; m. 2d, Abigail, widow of Ebenezer Hall, Oct. 22, 1801. 3. *Joel*, b. Sept. 7, 1750; m. Ada, dau. of David Blatchley of Killingworth (now Clinton). 4. *Hannah*, b. Sept. 17, 1752; m. James Davis of Killingworth. 5. *Elizabeth*, b. May 10, 1755; m. Dea. Timothy Hill of East Guilford (now Madison). 6. *Elnathan*, b. May 10, 1755; m. Rachel Camp of Durham; he lived in Hartland and Southington. 7. *Charity*, b. Sept. 28, 1758; m. Samuel Wright of Durham.

iv. EPHRAIM, b. Aug. 20, 1720; m. Mary ———; lived in Durham, and probably in New Durham, N. Y. They owned the covenant, Dec.

4, 1748. Their children were: 1. *Charles*,[5] b. Dec. 8, 1748; of Durham; m. Elizabeth ———. 2. *Elizabeth*, b. June 9, 1751. 3. *Mindwell*, b. Oct. 21, 1756.

v. STEPHEN, b. June 7, 1724; m. Abigail ———, and d. Nov. 3, 1808. They lived in Durham, and owned the covenant there June 11, 1749. Their children were: 1. *Medad*,[5] b. June 30, 1749. 2. *Abigail*, b. July 14, 1754. 3. *Stephen*, b. Jan. 26, 1756. 4. *Ozias*, b. Dec. 31, 1759. 5. *Lyman*, b. June 1, 1763; a physician; m. Olive Weld, July 18, 1795. 6. *Lewis*, b. April 28, 1766; d. Jan. 8, 1770.

vi. ELIZABETH, b. Jan. 15, 1726; m. Joseph Seward, Jan. 14, 1748.

THE DESCENDANTS OF CAPTAIN RICHARD OLMSTEAD, OF FAIRFIELD, CONN.*

By Frederick Stam Hammond, Esq., of Oneida, N. Y.

1. Capt. Richard[1] Olmstead was born in England, perhaps at Fairstead, Co. Essex, in 1608. His parentage has not been learned, but his "cousin" Nicholas[1] Olmstead, who is mentioned in his will, was a son of James Olmstead, of Cambridge, Mass., and Hartford, Conn., and was baptized at Fairstead, Feb. 15, 1612.

Richard Olmstead came to Fairfield about 1639, and probably settled in that part of the town which was incorporated into the town of Norwalk, in 1651. Fairfield originally embraced the territory which is now comprised in several towns, and extended so far north as to take in the present town of Redding, which was set off from it in 1677. His descendants became very numerous, and lived in nearly every town in the county. The records of many of these towns are very incomplete, and much material has been collected relating to this family which could not be used in this article on account of missing evidences of the proper connection.

So far as is known, Capt. Richard had but two children, James and John, but with him came one Nehemiah Olmstead, presumed to have been his brother, who died leaving an only daughter, Sarah. James Olmstead, of Cambridge and Hartford, also had a son named Nehemiah.

No record of the marriages of Capt. Richard has been found. He had large grants of land in Fairfield, which then embraced a considerable territory, and some of his lands were included in what were known as the "Long lots," which were narrow strips of land running from the coast line back some six or seven miles. The north line of these lots was in about the centre of the present town of Redding, and thus his heirs came into possession of lands at Chestnut Hill and Buckingham Ridge. He also had large grants in Norwalk after its incorporation, the record of his first grant being found on page i. of Vol. 1, Norwalk Land Records.

The original of his will, dated Sept. 5, 1684, is on file at Fairfield, but the seal is so nearly obliterated that no copy of it can be made. It is also recorded in Book III, page 217, Fairfield Probate Records. The following is an abstract:

I Richard Olmstead, of the towne of Norwake in ye County of ffairfield in ye Collony of Connecticut, aged Seventy-six years or therabouts.

Unto my sonn John my present dwelling house, houseing, barne, hom lott, orchard, to be to him . . . unless my sonn James shall acord to A writing underhand make exchange of ye present house and homestead with ye sd John within A year and one day.

To my Eldest sonn James Olmstead my fruitfull springlott of meddow, to be to him and to his heirs, . . . also my cowlott of upland, also three acres of plowing land at Sacatuke Plaine, to be added to ye side of what he ther alreddy possessed of, moreover one acre of my fruitfull springlott of upland next my pasture lott.

To my sonn John Olmstead one acre of land in my fruitfull springlott to be added to that which is now his and also ye lott called pine hill lott, also ye remainder of Sacatuche lott after James hath received his three acres.

---

*This genealogy has been compiled entirely from original records and documents in Fairfield County, Conn. No reference has been had to any printed work. The compiler has quite a collection of evidences from land records in the towns of Fairfield County, and also quite a collection of data relating to later generations of this interesting family.

My lott called the house lott all the aforesaid parcels of land I doe give and bequeth unto my sonn John.

To my two sons James and John my meddow lott on ye other side of Norwake River, which shall be equally divided croswise, . . . and to my sonns James and John all my meddow lying in ye great marsh, to each of them an equal share as near as it can be divided. . . . Moreover unto my sonns James and John my lott called Agratuity lott, lying upon ye hill on ye other side of ye river by the land of Thomas Benedict Senr., also my lott at Stickly Playne and my lott yt lyeth above ye Sawmill, some sixty acres of land granted me by ye Gene^ll Court, also, all my right of lands at Pequoiag.

A legacy of my love unto my Cousen Nicholas Olmstead, of Hartford, the sum of twenty shillings, . . . also, unto my Cousen Bazies, his two daughters Elizabeth Pecke and Lydia Baker to each of them the sum of twenty shillings.

Unto Samuel Smith ye bedd yt was my last wives, alsoe one pillow and ye blew rugg and ye great chest yt was my wives.

My two sonns James and John to be sole and joynt executors and administrators, . . . and my trusted and beloved ffriend Squire John Platt to be overseer.

No record of his death or of the births of his sons is found at Fairfield.
    Children :

  2. i.   JAMES,[2] b. about 1645-8.
  3. ii. JOHN, b. about 1650.

2.   LIEUT. JAMES[2] OLMSTEAD (*Richard*[1]) was born perhaps in Fairfield, Conn., before 1650. At the time of his marriage, and for many years prior to 1700, he held the office of Commissioner of Deeds at Norwalk. He married in Norwalk, May 1, 1673, Phebe Barlow of Norwalk, and died there in May or June, 1731. His will, dated Apr. 28, 1731, proved in Fairfield, June 12, 1731, gives to wife Phebe "all ye Real Estate which I am this day possessed of," which his sons Joseph and John were to have at their mother's decease. It adds, "My son Nathan, now deceased, has had his full portion of my estate."

His sons James and Samuel are not mentioned, and they probably died young.

    Children, recorded in Norwalk :

    i.   JAMES,[3] b. Aug. 17, 1675.
    ii. JOSEPH, b. Mar. 10, 1676-7; living in 1731; probably married and had a family.
  4. iii. NATHAN, b. Apr. 27, 1678.
    iv. SAMUEL, b. May 13, 1683.
  5. v. JOHN, b. Aug. 14, 1692.

3.   LIEUT. JOHN[2] OLMSTEAD (*Richard*[1]), perhaps born at Fairfield, about 1650, married first, July 17, 1673, Mary, daughter of Thomas Benedict of Norwalk; and married second, Elizabeth, widow of Thomas Gregory. No record of his marriages, the death of his first wife, or the births of his children, has been found. It is probable that his first wife died soon after the birth of his daughter Eunice, and that Elizabeth was the first child of the second wife. He died in Dec., 1704. His will does not appear on record, but an inventory of his estate was presented by the widow Elizabeth, Dec. 22, 1704, and in this inventory the names of the children appear with approximate ages; but the ages as given are not correct, as for example, the age of Mary is stated as about 18 years, while the

records show that she had been married eight years at the time the inventory was made. The ages undoubtedly do indicate, however, the order of birth. The record of distribution, in Fairfield Probate Records, dated Apr. 17, 1705, shows that the widow Elizabeth was formerly the wife of Thomas Gregory. The others sharing in the estate were Daniel Olmstead, eldest son, Thomas Reed, Benjamin Wilson, Anna Olmstead, Jonathan Abbott, Samuel St. John, Richard Olmstead, John Olmstead, Elizabeth Olmstead, Eunice Olmstead, Deborah Olmstead, and Abigail Olmstead. A Joseph is mentioned, but whether Joseph St. John or not does not fully appear, as the language is rather ambiguous.

Children by first wife:

6. i. MARY,[3] b. about 1675.
   ii. JANE, b. about 1677; probably m. Benjamin Wilson.
7. iii. SARAH, b. about 1679.
   iv. REBECCA, b. about 1681: probably m. Samuel St. John.
8. v. DANIEL, b. about 1683.
   vi. RICHARD, b. about 1685.
   vii. EUNICE, b. about 1687; probably m. Joseph St. John.

Children by second wife:

9. viii. ELIZABETH, b. about 1690.
   ix. DEBORAH, b. about 1693.
   x. ABIGAIL, b. about 1696.
   xi. ANNA, b. about 1698.
10. xii. JOHN, b. about 1700.

4. NATHAN[3] OLMSTEAD (*James,*[2] *Richard*[1]), born in Norwalk, Conn., Apr. 27, 1678, married, Dec. 17, 1702, Sarah, daughter of Ralph Keeler of Norwalk, as shown in the will of Ralph.

Nathan died in Norwalk, Jan., 1716/17. The inventory of his estate, presented to the Probate Court in Fairfield, Jan. 12, 1716–17, by the widow Sarah, names children: Nathan aged 13, Samuel aged 10, James aged 8, Mary aged 6, Hannah aged 4, and Lydia aged 1 year last May.

Feb. 2, 1725/6, Samuel and James, sons of Nathan Olmstead, late of Norwalk, chose their uncle Moses Comstock as their guardian; and Oct. 14, 1757, they discharged their uncle Moses Comstock of Norwalk " from all the cares and concerns yt he did take of us " (Fairfield Probate Records).

Sept. 6, 1727, Mary, Hannah, and Lydia, daughters of Nathan Olmstead, late of Norwalk, chose their brother Samuel Olmstead as their guardian.

Children:

i. NATHAN,[4] b. in Norwalk, Dec. 4, 1703; probably m. before 1727. Nothing has been learned about his family. In 1727, Oliver Arnold, a minor, of Norwalk, chose him as his guardian.
11. ii. SAMUEL, b. 1706.
    iii. JAMES, b. 1708; living in 1750. In 1748 he was on the bond of Hezekiah Deforest, Guardian of the children of David Deforest late of Norwalk. In 1750 he was one of the committee appointed by the Probate Court to make a division of the estate of Joseph Rockwell, late of Norwalk, among his heirs. Nothing has been learned about his family.
    iv. MARY, b. 1710.
    v. HANNAH, b. 1712.
12. vi. LYDIA, b. May, 1716.

5. JOHN[3] OLMSTEAD (*James,*[2] *Richard*[1]), born in Norwalk, Conn., Aug.
14, 1692, married, Feb. 29, 1717/18, Mary, daughter of "Robert
Small, transient, sometime of Norwalk." He died in Norwalk,
Oct., 1748 ; and Nov. 1, 1748, Gardner and Reuben Olmstead, of
Norwalk, were appointed administrators of his estate.

Apr. 4, 1749, Nehemiah Gruman, of Norwalk, was appointed
guardian of John Olmstead ; and on the same date, Reuben Olmstead was appointed guardian of his younger brothers, Ichabod and
Justice.

Jan. 12, 1748/9, in a distribution of the estate of John Olmstead,
late of Norwalk, the following children are named : Sylvanus,
Phebe the wife of Gardner Olmstead, Reuben, David, James, John,
Ichabod, and Justice. It appears that the son recorded as Small
was afterward called James.

Children :
  i. SYLVANUS,[4] b. Nov. 25, 1718.
  ii. PHEBE, b. Aug. 5, 1720; m. Gardner Olmstead.
13. iii. REUBEN, b. Apr. 5, 1722.
  iv. DAVID, b. Feb. 6, 1724-5.
  v. SMALL (JAMES), b. Mar. 2, 1727-8.
  vi. JOHN, b. Mar. 29, 1729.
  vii. ICHABOD, b. June 14, 1733.
  viii. JUSTICE.

6. MARY[3] OLMSTEAD (*John,*[2] *Richard*[1]), born in Fairfield, Conn., about
1675, married, May 9, 1694, Thomas Reed of Norwalk.
Children, recorded in Norwalk :
  i. MARY REED, b. May 2, 1695.
  ii. EUNICE REED, b. Feb. 26, 1696-7.
  iii. THOMAS REED, b. May 7, 1699.
  iv. JOHN REED, b. Aug. 7, 1701.
  v. ELIZABETH REED, b. Oct. 7, 1703.
  vi. ANN REED, b. July 6, 1706; d. Feb. 9, 1709-10.
  vii. TEMPERANCE REED, b. Oct. 16, 1708.
  viii. ELIAS REED, b. Mar. 10, 1711.
  ix. NATHAN REED, b. Aug. 13, 1713.

7. SARAH[3] OLMSTEAD (*John,*[2] *Richard*[1]), born in Fairfield, Conn., about
1678 or 1679, married, June 5, 1696, Jonathan Abbott of Norfolk.
Children, recorded in Norwalk :
  i. JONATHAN ABBOTT, b. Apr. 6, 1697.
  ii. SARAH ABBOTT, b. June 16, 1699.
  iii. EUNICE ABBOTT, b. Jan. 23, 1702.
  iv. MARY ABBOTT, b. July 8, 1704.
  v. DEBORAH ABBOTT, b. Dec. 3, 1707.
  vi. KEZIAH ABBOTT, b. Apr. 17, 1711.
  vii. SAMUEL ABBOTT, b. Mar. 21, 1713-14.
  viii. JANE ABBOTT, b. Oct. 5, 1716.
  ix. MINDWELL ABBOTT, b. Dec. 21, 1718.

8. DANIEL[3] OLMSTEAD (*John,*[2] *Richard*[1]), born in Fairfield, Conn.,
about 1683, married Hannah, daughter of Joseph Ketcham of Norwalk, as shown in the settlement of Joseph's estate. He resided in
Ridgefield, Conn. Nothing has been learned about his children.

9. ELIZABETH[3] OLMSTEAD (*John,*[2] *Richard*[1]), born in Fairfield, Conn.,
about 1690, married, June 14, 1710, Henry Whitney.

Child, recorded in Norwalk :

i. ELIZABETH WHITNEY, b. Aug. 24, 1711.

10. JOHN[3] OLMSTEAD (*John,*[2] *Richard*[1]), born in Fairfield, Conn., about
1700, married Mindwell ———, of Fairfield, who was born Sept.
8, 1696, and was admitted to the Church at Greenfield Hill, Conn.,
by letter from the First Church of Fairfield, Feb. 22, 1729/30.
No. 49 in the Church record of deaths is Mindwell, wife of John
Olmstead, but the date is not given. They probably lived in the
north part of Fairfield, that part which later became Weston. No
record of his death appears on the Church records. The baptisms
of their children are found on Greenfield Church Records. Their
children lived later in Weston, Redding, and Ridgefield.

In Fairfield Probate Records it appears that John Olmstead, of
Fairfield, was chosen as guardian by Benjamin, son of Elijah Crane,
deceased, in 1739, so his wife may have been of the Crane family.
Children :

i. MINDWELL,[4] bapt. Mar. 3, 1727-8; d. young.
ii. SARAH, bapt. May 25, 1729; d. young.
iii. JOHN, bapt. Oct. 10, 1731; probably m. Abigail Munson of Danbury,
who was bapt. at New Haven, Nov. 6, 1739; lived in Ridgefield
in 1768; had sons *John, Jr.*,[5] and *Elijah*, living in Weston in 1788,
and *David* who lived in Ridgefield. (Redding Land Records, Vol.
II, p. 39, and Vol. III, p. 403.)
iv. SARAH, bapt. Mar. 2, 1734-5; d. soon after her mother. Her death
is No. 51 on the Greenfield Church Records, date not given.
v. MINDWELL, bapt. Feb. 17, 1708-9; d. soon after her mother, and
just prior to the death of her sister Sarah. Her death is No. 50 on
Greenfield Church Records.
vi. ELEAZER, bapt. Aug. 9, 1741; m. Jan. 17, 1765, Grace Pickett of
Redding, Conn.; d. before 1769. (Redding Land Records, Vol.
I, p. 144.) His widow m. (2) Ira Shephard of Redding. Redding
Land Records, Vol. V, p. 419.) He left a son *Eleazer, Jr.*,[5] and
a daughter *Polly*, who m. Nehemiah Seeley of Redding. (Redding Land Records, Vol. V, p. 419.)
vii. DANIEL, bapt. Aug. 19, 1744; d. Feb. 15, 1761.
viii. ELIJAH, b. May 10, bapt. July 13, 1755.
ix. JESSE, bapt. Sept. 24, 1758, aged 7 weeks.

11. SAMUEL[4] OLMSTEAD (*Nathan,*[3] *James,*[2] *Richard*[1]) was born in Norwalk, Conn., in 1706. He probably had a family, and lived to old
age.

There were no less than five Samuel Olmsteads living in Norwalk at the same time, prior to 1800, known as Samuel, Samuel[2d],
Samuel [3d], Samuel [4th], and Samuel [5th]. Three of these were
nearly of the same age, and were married within a few years of
each other. Nothing could be found on Norwalk Town Records
to definitely fix the parentage of any of these.

Samuel [2d] married, Nov. 25, 1773, Anne Dunning of Norwalk,
and had: *Samuel*, b. Dec. 17, 1774; *Sarah*, b. July 27, 1776; *Hannah*, b. Feb. 12, 1779; *Stephen*, b. Dec. 7, 1780; and *Noah*, b. Oct.
3, 1786.

Samuel [3d] married, Aug. 9, 1793, Betsey Disbrow of West
Farms. (West Farms Church Records.)

Samuel [4th] married, Mar. 16, 1797, Rachel St. John of Norwalk,
and had: *Marillus*, b. Oct. 15, 1797.

Samuel ⁵ᵗʰ married, Nov. 12, 1795, Mercy, daughter of Rufus Keeler of Norwalk, and had: *Lewis*, b. Feb. 25, 1797; and *Rufus Keeler*, b. Oct, 27, 1799.

Perhaps one of these last two Samuels was son of Samuel ²ᵈ.

12. LYDIA⁴ OLMSTEAD (*Nathan,³ James,² Richard¹*), born in Norwalk, Conn., May 1716, married in Norwalk, Dec. 7, 1738, as his second wife, Matthew Fitch. His first wife was Jemima St. John, who died at the birth of a daughter *Jemima*, Dec. 25, 1735.

Children, recorded in Norwalk:

i.   NATHAN FITCH, b. Oct. 12, 1739.
ii. MERCY FITCH, b. Dec. 27, 1740.
iii. HANNAH FITCH, b. Aug. 24, 1742.
iv. MATTHEW FITCH, b. June 17, 1744.
v.   LYDIA FITCH, b. Apr. 4, 1746.
vi. REBECCA FITCH, July 9, 1748.
vii. SUSANNAH FITCH, b. Aug. 29, 1750.

13. REUBEN⁴ OLMSTEAD (*John,³ James,² Richard¹*), born in Norwalk, Conn., Apr. 5, 1722, married Anne ———, who was bapt. Apr. 11, 1727. A complete record of their children has not been obtained. They lived near Greenfield Hill, and their eldest children were baptized in Greenfield Church.

Children:

i.   STEPHEN,⁵ b. 1746, bapt. Apr. 4, 1747.
ii. PHEBE, bapt. June 13, 1748.
iii. A CHILD, b. 1750, bapt. in infancy.
iv. ANNE, b. 1754, bapt. July 7, 1754.
v.   REUBEN, b. July 22, 1763, in Norwalk, Conn.; m. Nov. 18, 1784, Hannah Bass, who was b. Apr. 23, 1762; lived in Norwalk, where all of their children are recorded. Children: 1. *Charles,⁶* b. May 24, 1785. 2. *Betsey*, b. Jan. 20, 1788. 3. *Stephen*, b. June 10, 1790. 4. *Seth*, b. July 23, 1792. 5. *Esther*, b. Feb. 28, 1795.

JOHN OWEN OF WINDSOR, CONN.,
AND
SOME OF HIS DESCENDANTS

By WILLIAM ARTHUR OWEN of New York City

THE surname *Owen* was borne by several of the early immigrants in Virginia, Pennsylvania, and other American Colonies, most of whom are believed to have come from Wales. Among the Owen settlers in New England, in the seventeenth century, were Thomas Owen, a merchant of Boston and a member of the Ancient and Honorable Artillery Company in 1639, John Owen, who was at Windsor, Conn., as early as 1650, William Owen of Braintree, Mass., a freeman in 1657, whose children were Daniel, born 1 Aug. 1651, Deliverance, born 15 Feb. 1654/5, and Ebenezer, born 1 May 1657, and Samuel Owen of Springfield and Brookfield, Mass., who married in 1681 Ann, widow of John Pettee. It is the purpose of the compiler of this article to present, in genealogical form, an account of John Owen of Windsor, Conn., and some of his descendants.*

1. JOHN[1] OWEN, of Windsor,† born, probably in Wales, about 1622, died 18 Feb. 1698, the inscription on his gravestone in the old cemetery by the Congregational Church in Windsor reading: "John Owen aged 76 years dyed February ye 18th: 1698:" The town records of Windsor, however, state that he was born 25 Dec. 1624, "so that in December 25, 1664 he was 40 years old," and they give his death as occurring 1 Feb. 1698/9, æ. 76. He married at Windsor, 3 Oct. 1650, REBECCA WADE, who died 3 Dec. 1711.

As to John Owen's ancestry, early life, emigration to America, and date of settlement at Windsor no information has been found; but the town records show his presence there in 1650. Since no town records prior to 1650 exist, much information as to the early history of Windsor has been lost. In a list of early settlers at Windsor, with the location of their home lots, prepared for the Hartford County Memorial History in 1883 by Jabez H. Hayden, a reliable list of all

---

*A brief genealogical outline of some of the Windsor families descended from John[1] Owen may be found in Stiles's Ancient Windsor, vol. 2, pp. 544–547.

†All places mentioned in this genealogy are situated within the present limits of the State of Connecticut, unless another State or region is indicated in the text or may be easily inferred from the context.

those persons who can be traced to Windsor before 1650, it is stated that John Owen, 1650, bought a lot, 12 x 29 rods, on the south side of the road leading west from Palisado, bounded east by Hosford's Lane, which was probably a little west of and parallel with the present railroad track, resided on this lot about twenty years, and then removed to a lot granted at the lower end of Strawberry Meadow. His house stood where the late Nathaniel Owen's residence was, the locality being formerly known as Wales, from John Owen's nationality. In the Windsor land records are entered a number of conveyances of land to John Owen and from him to his sons and others. His name is in the list of those who made voluntary contributions for the poor of other Colonies in 1676.

Children, born at Windsor:

2. i. JOSIAH,² b. 8 Sept. 1651.
ii. JOHN, b. 5 Nov. 1652; d. young.
iii. JOHN, b. 23 Apr. 1654; d. 15 Jan. 1670.
3. iv. NATHANIEL, b. 9 Aug. 1656.
4. v. DANIEL, b. 28 Mar. 1658.
5. vi. JOSEPH, b. 23 Oct. 1660.
vii. MARY, b. 5 Dec. 1662; m. 30 Oct. 1681 NATHANIEL WILLIAMS, b. 25 Oct. 1647, second son of John and Mary (Burley) Williams of Windsor.
Children (surname *Williams*):
1. *Mary*, b. in 1682.
2. *Zebedee*, b. 7 Jan. 1697/8.
3. *John*, b. 16 Apr. 1699.
viii. BENJAMIN, b. 20 Sept. 1664; d. 26 May 1665.
ix. REBECCA, b. 28 Mar. 1666; m. 30 June 1692 NATHANIEL GILLETT, JR., b. in Aug. 1655, who m. (2) 30 Mar. 1704 Hannah Buckland, by whom he had six children.
Children (surname *Gillett*):
1. *Isaac*, b. 2 Aug. 1693; m. in 1719 Elizabeth Griswold. Six children.
2. *Dinah*, b. 18 Oct. 1696.
6. x. OBADIAH, b. 12 Dec. 1667.
7. xi. ISAAC, b. 27 May 1670.

2. JOSIAH² OWEN (*John¹*), of Windsor and Simsbury, born at Windsor 8 Sept. 1651, died there 11 Sept. 1722. He married first, 22 Oct. 1674, MARY OSBORN, born 16 Apr. 1655, died 6 Aug. 1689, daughter of John and Ann (Oldage) Osborn of East Windsor; and secondly SARAH ———, who survived him and married secondly, 17 Jan. 1722/3, Nathaniel Holcomb of Simsbury.

Josiah Owen moved from Windsor to Simsbury, where he became one of the proprietors; and from 1679 on numerous grants and conveyances of land to and from him are entered in the Simsbury records. The baptisms in Simsbury in 1698 of Isaac, Mary, Abigail, Elizabeth, John, and Rachel, children of Josiah Owen of Windsor, are recorded in the church records by Rev. D. Woodbridge. About 1697 Josiah Owen returned to Windsor, where he lived until his death, which is recorded there. In his will he names his wife Sarah, Elizabeth, wife of Samuel Case of Simsbury, Mary, wife of Enoch Phelps of Windsor, Rachel, wife of Samuel Phelps of Windsor, Abigail, wife of Samuel Clark of Simsbury, Josiah Owen, and John Owen.

Children by first wife:

8. i. JOSIAH,³ b. 6 June 1675 (Windsor records).
   ii. ISAAC, b. 4 June 1678 (*ib.*); d. 3 Dec. 1709. The Simsbury probate records show the appointment, 6 Mar. 1709/10, of John Owen of Windsor as administrator of the estate of Isaac Owen of Windsor, lately died, intestate.
   iii. MARY, b. 15 Feb. 1679/80 (Stiles's Ancient Windsor); m. 13 Apr. 1704 ENOCH PHELPS, b. 21 Jan. 1675, d. about 1752, son of John Phelps.
   Children (surname *Phelps*):
   1. *Mary*, b. 11 Sept. 1706.
   2. *Abigail*, b. 9 Feb. 1708/9.
   iv. ABIGAIL, b. 8 Dec. 1681 (Simsbury records); m. SAMUEL CLARK, who d. in 1741 or 1749, aged 61, and was bur. at Turkey Hills, son of Samuel Clark.
   Children (surname *Clark*):
   1. *Joel*, b. in 1717; d. in 1777; m. in 1742 Lydia Forbes, who d. in 1796. Four children: Lydia, b. in 1743 (*vide infra*, No. 25), Joel, b. in 1747, Reuben, b. in 1751, Samuel, b. in 1758.
   2. *Abigail*, b. in 1719.
   3. *Samuel*, b. in 1720 (cf. genealogy by Miss Julia E. Clark).
   4. *Hannah*, b. in 1723.
   5. *David*, b. in 1725; m. Rachel Moore. Twenty children.
   6. *Ann*, b. in 1729; d. in 1741.
   v. ESTHER, b. 17 Mar. 1682 (Simsbury records); probably d. young.
   vi. ELIZABETH, b. 19 Nov. 1684 (*ib.*); m. (1) at Windsor, 23 Oct. 1706, SAMUEL THRALL; m. (2) 8 Nov. 1721, as his second wife, SAMUEL CASE, b. 1 June 1667, son of John and Sarah Case of Windsor. He m. (1) Mary Westover.
   Children by first husband (surname *Thrall*):
   1. *Elizabeth*, b. in 1707.
   2. *Samuel*, b. in 1709.
9. vii. JOHN, b. 27 Mar. 1686 (*ib.*).

Child by second wife:

viii. RACHEL, b. 25 Nov. 1692 (*ib.*); m. at Windsor, 4 June 1712, SAMUEL PHELPS, b. 16 Jan. 1690/1, son of Josiah Phelps.
   Children (surname *Phelps*):
   1. *Samuel*, b. in 1716.
   2. *Shadrick*, b. in 1719.
   3. *Tryphena*.
   4. *Mary*, d. young.
   5. *James*, d. young.

3. NATHANIEL² OWEN (*John*¹), of Windsor, was born at Windsor 9 Aug. 1656. He married first, at Windsor, 14 June 1694, MARY GAYLORD, who died 23 Jan. 1695/6; and secondly, at Windsor, 22 Feb. 1697/8; SARAH PALMER, born 12 Apr. 1675, died at Windsor 25 Apr. 1731, daughter of Timothy Palmer.
   Children by second wife, born at Windsor:
   i. HANNAH,³ "daughter of Nathaniel Owen of Windsor was bapt. 11 Nov. 1699, being about eight months old" (Simsbury church records, by Rev. D. Woodbridge).
   ii. SARAH, b. 3 May 1700; m. 29 Sept. 1737 NATHANIEL GILLETT of Windsor.
10. iii. NATHANIEL, b. 31 Dec. 1702.
   iv. ANNE, b. 17 July 1705; probably d. young.
   v. ABNER, b. 17 Mar. 1706/7; d. in 1708/9.
   vi. AMI (or ANNE), b. 3 July 1709.

4. DANIEL² OWEN (*John¹*), of Windsor, born at Windsor 28 Mar. 1658, died 1 Mar. 1682/3. He married, 24 Jan. 1681, MARY BISSELL.

Child:

i. DANIEL,³ b. 25 Nov. 1682 (Wells's Early Land Records of Connecticut).

5. JOSEPH² OWEN (*John¹*), of Windsor, Simsbury, and Lebanon, born at Windsor 23 Oct. 1660, probably died at Lebanon between 1735 and 1746. He married, as various conveyances show, ESTHER ———.

He settled in Simsbury, probably about 1683, when, on 7 May, he was given 20 acres on Samon Brook, the same as other Samon Brook men. He was subsequently given other pieces of land, on Samon Brook, Manatuck, etc. In 1687 he was one of the forty-nine inhabitants of Simsbury who agreed to call and pay Edward Thompson as minister; and for this he and other subscribers received in 1688 grants of land to run from Simsbury east bounds over the mountain, his lot being No. 18. In 1688 he was one of the fifteen men who received land at Hopp Meadow, for agreeing to build there and to settle families there, his lot being No. 11. In 1692 Joseph Owen, then of Windsor, sold his lands on Samon Brook to Samuel Wilcoxen, Jr., of Simsbury; and in 1708 Joseph Owen, Sr., of Lebanon sold his Lot No. 18, from Simsbury over the mountain, to Isaac Owen of Windsor. Joseph Owen's name appears on the Windsor records in several conveyances of land in 1701 and 1703. On 21 Nov. 1703 the land records of Lebanon show conveyance of a tract of land at that place to Joseph Owen of Windsor by Daniel Mason of Lebanon; and in 1707 land was conveyed to Joseph Owen, then of Lebanon. In 1721 a tract of 40 acres on the westerly side of the highway was laid out by the proprietors of Lebanon to Joseph Owen, Sr., for his common right in the village land. In 1735 Joseph Owen of Lebanon, in consideration of good will and the expectation of comforts and support for himself and his wife Esther from his son, Joseph Owen, Jr., conveyed to him certain of his lands and property in Lebanon; and during the same year also he conveyed for good will certain of his lands in Lebanon to his sons Joshua, Moses, Caleb, and Aaron.

It is apparent from the above-mentioned records that Joseph Owen, Sr., was settled in Simsbury from about 1683 to 1692, when he returned to Windsor, and that he settled in Lebanon about 1703. About 1746, probably after the father's death, his son Joseph moved to Salisbury. The births of his children Ann, Joseph, and Moses are recorded in Simsbury. No record of the births of the others has been found.

Children:

i. ANN,³ "first daughter of Joseph Owen," b. at Simsbury 9 Nov. 1683 (Simsbury records).

11. ii. JOSEPH, b. 29 Jan. 1685 (*ib.*).

12. iii. Moses, b. 7 July 1688 (*ib.*).
13. iv. Joshua.
    v. Caleb, of Lebanon, b. probably at Windsor or Lebanon; living in 1762; m. at Lebanon, 20 June 1740, Elizabeth Brewster. In 1735 his father, Joseph Owen, gave to him 60 acres of land in Lebanon; and in the same year he bought from his brother, Joseph Owen, Jr., 20 acres of Lebanon common rights. In 1759 he acquired of Jacob Redington 25 acres in Lebanon. Other conveyances of land to and from him as a resident of Lebanon are dated in 1759, 1760, and 1762. Elizabeth Owen of Lebanon, for a bond executed by her son, Caleb Owen of Lebanon, conveyed 10 May 1773 land which had belonged to her late husband, Caleb Owen, Sr., of Lebanon.
    Child:
        1. *Caleb,*[4] b. at Lebanon 20 May 1741; m. 16 Aug. 1759 Priscilla Thorp. On 6 June 1774 Abigail Smith of Lebanon conveyed land to Caleb Owen, late of Lebanon, then of Halifax, Cumberland Co., N. Y. Three children, b. at Lebanon: Esther,[5] b. 23 Sept. 1761, Martha, b. 20 Aug. 1763, Joel, b. 4 Sept. 1766.
   vi. Aaron, b. probably at Windsor or Lebanon. In 1735 his father, Joseph Owen, gave to him his land in Lebanon, which he sold to David Bates, Jr., of Hingham, Mass., in 1747.
    Children:
        1. *Sarah*[4] (probably daughter of Aaron), b. 21 May 1733 (Lebanon records).
        2. *Aaron* (perhaps son of Aaron), bapt. 13 Sept. 1741 (Lebanon church records), but his parentage is not stated. Bailey's "Early Connecticut Marriages" states that an Aaron Owen and Miriam Wright were m. 11 Jan. 1773. The marriage is also entered in the Lebanon records, without date.

6. Obadiah[2] Owen (*John*[1]), born at Windsor 12 Dec. 1667, died 11 Oct. 1751, in his 84th year. He married, 21 Sept. 1693, Christiana Winchel, who died 10 Jan. 1762, in her 89th year. (Inscriptions, East Granby Cemetery.)

    In July 1695 his father gave to him land (Windsor records); and in Apr. 1697 the father, John Owen, made over to his sons Obadiah and Isaac of Windsor certain lands.

    Children, born at Windsor:

    i. Obadiah,[3] b. 8 July 1694; d. 18 July 1694.
    ii. Eunice, b. 8 Aug. 1696.
   iii. Martha, b. 31 Aug. 1698; m. 21 May 1720 Amos Moore.
   iv. Jemima, b. 18 Nov. 1700; m. 11 May 1725 Thomas Winchell.
    v. Christiana, b. 10 July 1702.
   vi. Obadiah, b. 8 Jan. 1705; d. 11 Dec. 1728.
14. vii. Samuel, b. 3 Aug. 1707.
  viii. Tabitha, b. 6 Feb. 1709/10; d. 7 June 1714.
   ix. Jedediah, b. 22 May 1712; d. 7 June 1714.
    x. Jedediah, b. 21 Apr. 1715; m. 4 Oct. 1735 Ruth Phelps.
    Children:
        1. *Obadiah,*[4] b. 14 Jan. 1736/7; m. Mary Hart of Farmington. His will, dated in 1762 and proved in 1763, was made upon his entry into His Majesty's service.
        2. *Daniel,* b. 7 Dec. 1738.
        3. *Tabitha,* b. 2 Oct. 1740.
        4. *Christiana.*

7. ISAAC[2] OWEN (*John[1]*), of Windsor and Simsbury, born at Windsor 27 May 1670, died at Simsbury 13 June 1736. He married, 20 Dec. 1694, SARAH HOLCOMB, born 1 Feb. 1673, died 22 Jan. 1763, aged 90 (East Granby Cemetery inscriptions), daughter of Benajah Holcomb.

In 1695 his father gave him a parcel of land in Windsor, called Poquonock; and in 1697 the father made over to his sons Isaac and Obadiah other lands. The baptisms of his children, Sarah and Rebecca in 1698, Ann in 1700, and Elijah in 1707, are entered in the Simsbury church records by Rev. D. Woodbridge. In 1708 Isaac Owen of Windsor bought Lot No. 18 in Simsbury from his brother Joseph. In his will he names his wife Sarah, his sons Isaac and Elijah, and his daughters Rebecca, Ann, Sarah Phelps, and Debora Eno.

Children, born at Windsor:

   i. SARAH,[3] b. 17 Feb. 1694/5; m. 30 Dec. 1714 EPHRAIM PHELPS, JR., b. at Windsor 28 Sept. 1692.
     Children (surname *Phelps*):
     1. *Mary*, b. 24 Dec. 1716; d. 13 Feb. 1717.
     2. *Ephraim*, b. 29 June 1718; d. young.
     3. *Asa*, b. 1 Oct. 1720.
     4. *David* (twin), b. 24 May 1723.
     5. *Jonathan* (twin), b. 24 May 1723; probably m. in 1743 Catharine Messinger.
     6. *Sarah*, b. 1 Apr. 1729.
     7. *Elihu*, b. 28 Feb. 1732.
  ii. REBECCA, b. 2 Mar. 1697/8.
  iii. ANN, b. 12 June 1700; m. 3 Apr. 1735 DAVID HIGLEY, son of Brewster Higley.
15. iv. ISAAC, b. 7 Nov. 1702.
  v. DEBORAH, m. —— ENO.
16. vi. ELIJAH, b. 7 Oct. 1706.

8. JOSIAH[3] OWEN (*Josiah,[2] John[1]*), of Windsor and Hebron, born at Windsor 6 June 1675, died at Hebron 15 Aug. 1763. He married at Windsor, 3 Dec. 1698, MARY HOSFORD, who died 11 July 1753, aged 79 (Hebron records).

On 25 Feb. 1712/13 Josiah Owen, Sr., of Windsor, for good will, etc., gave to his son Josiah of Hebron the west half of Lot No. 15 in Simsbury, which had been given to him by the inhabitants of Simsbury in 1692. In May 1713 Josiah Owen, Jr., of Hebron sold this land to Samuel Case, Jr., of Windsor. In his will, dated in 1750 and proved in 1763, Josiah Owen of Hebron names his wife Mary, his sons Noah, Silas, Amos, Isaac, and Josiah, his daughters Mary and Martha, and the children of his son Asahel.

Children:

17. i. ASAHEL,[4] b. 25 Mar. 1699 (Windsor records).
18. ii. NOAH, b. 14 May 1701 (*ib.*).
  iii. SILAS, b. 9 Mar. 1702/3 (*ib.*); d. at Hebron 4 Jan. 1783, aged 80; m. (1) at Hebron, 14 Feb. 1732/3, ELIZABETH HUNT, who d. 18 Mar. 1759; m. (2) 15 June 1763 SUSANNAH DELANA of Lebanon.
     Children, b. at Hebron.
     1. *Silas*,[5] b. 4 Nov. 1734; d. 24 Dec. 1740.
     2. *Elizabeth*, b. 24 Feb. 1736/7; d. 1 Dec. 1740.

3. *Hannah*, b. 29 Dec. 1739.
4. *Elizabeth*, b. 8 Jan. 1742/3; d. 3 July 1748.

iv. AMOS, b. 4 Mar. 1704/5 (*ib.*); m. at Colchester, 3 July 1735, UNIS
WATERS.
Children, b. at Hebron:
1. *Amos*,⁵ b. 25 Mar. 1736; m. 30 Mar. 1757 Mercy Brown of
Windsor. They had a daughter, Sabra,⁶ b. 22 Apr. 1758.
2. *David*, b. 8 Oct. 1737; d. 17 July 1739.
3. *Simeon*, b. 15 Apr. 1739; d. at Lake George 8 Dec. 1755, in
His Majesty's service.
4. *Eunice*, b. 19 Jan. 1741; m. 2 July 1760 Gill Belcher of
Hebron.
5. *David*, b. 7 July 1744; m. 15 Nov. 1765 Lois Post. Children: Mary,⁶ b. in 1765, d. in 1776, Talbut, b. in 1767,
m. in 1792 Mary Young, Molly, b. in 1770.
6. *Abigail*, b. 19 June 1748; m. 6 Aug. 1769 Jonah Case of
Hebron.
7. *Dorothy*, b. 27 July 1751; m. 23 June 1768 Joseph Peters of
Hebron.
8. *Lydia*, b. 16 Mar. 1754.
9. *Simeon*, b. 29 May 1757.
v. MARY, b. 13 Apr. 1707 (*ib.*); m. 28 Oct. 1731 JOSEPH DAVISS of
Hebron.
vi. ISAAC, b. 28 July 1710 (Hebron records); d. at Hebron 30 May
1761; m. 20 July 1738 REBECCA TILDEN.
Children, b. at Hebron:
1. *Elijah*⁵ b. 24 Feb. 1739/40; m. 21 Oct. 1762 Deborah Holdridge of Hebron. They had a daughter, Hannah,⁶ b. 18
June 1763.
2. *Abbe*, b. 3 Apr. 1743.
3. *Elizabeth*, b. 6 Sept. 1749.
4. *Jonathan*, b. 9 July 1754.
5. *John*, b. 22 Jan. 1758.
6. *Isaac*, b. 15 Nov. 1760.
vii. MARTHA, b. 1 Aug. 1714 (*ib.*); m. 10 Dec. 1736 ELIPHALET CASE
of Hebron.
19. viii. JOSIAH, b. 17 Mar. 1716 (*ib.*).
ix. ANNE, b. 4 Apr. 1718 (*ib.*).

9. LIEUT. JOHN³ OWEN (*Josiah*,² *John*¹), of Simsbury, was born at
Simsbury 27 Mar. 1686, and died there. He married HANNAH
———.

In 1712 Josiah Owen, Sr., for good will, etc., conveyed the
east half of Lot No. 15 in Simsbury to his son John of Windsor;
and in Mar. 1719 he, John Owen, then of Simsbury, sold and
conveyed this land to Isaac Owen of Simsbury.
Children:
20. i. JOHN,⁴ b. 18 Mar. 1712.
ii. DAZIER [*sic*, ? DESIRE], b. 26 Feb. 1718; m. 11 Jan. 1738 JONATHAN
HUMPHREY.

10. NATHANIEL³ OWEN (*Nathaniel*,² *John*¹), of Windsor, was born
at Windsor 31 Dec. 1702, and died there. He married, 2 July
1729, MARY GRISWOLD.
In his will, dated in 1774 and proved in 1776, he names his
sons Nathaniel, Jr., and Alvan and his daughter Mary, wife
of Nathan Warner.

Children, born at Windsor:

   i.   KEZIAH,[4] b. 11 Apr. 1730; d. 11 Aug. 1730.
   ii. MARY, b. 12 Sept. 1731; m. NATHAN WARNER of Hatfield, Mass., and removed to German Falls, N. Y.
  iii. ABNER, b. 4 Jan. 1733; d. at Fort Edward, N. Y. He served under Lieutenant Chick in the French and Indian War.
21. iv. NATHANIEL, b. in 1735.
   v. ALVAN, b. 22 Feb. 1737.

11. JOSEPH[3] OWEN (*Joseph,[2] John[1]*), of Windsor, Lebanon, and Salisbury, born at Simsbury 29 Jan. 1685, died at Salisbury 9 Sept. 1758, in his 74th year (Salisbury records; gravestone in Town Hill Cemetery at Lakeville, in Salisbury). He married first MARY ————; and secondly, about 1718, RUTH ————.

His father moved from Simsbury to Windsor about 1692 and from Windsor to Lebanon about 1703, where Joseph, Jr., resided until about 1745, when he moved to Salisbury.

In 1709 Joseph Owen, Jr., bought land in Lebanon, and in Feb. 1726/7 the proprietors laid out to him common rights to land in the village of Lebanon. The records show also other conveyances to him by purchase and by the proprietors. In 1735 he and his brothers received conveyances of land in Lebanon from their father, Joseph Owen, Sr., for good will, etc. In 1739 Joseph, Jr., conveyed land in Lebanon to his eldest son, David, and to his son Jonathan he conveyed land in 1740. On 3 May 1742 Joseph Owen and his wife Ruth of Lebanon sold and conveyed to Samuel Wells of Bolton, Mass., four of six shares and a half of one share of 153 acres laid out in the village common of Lebanon. On 29 Oct. 1745 Joseph Owen of Lebanon sold and conveyed to Thomas Newcomb of Salisbury his farm of about 200 acres, on which he then dwelt in Lebanon. On 2 June 1746 Thomas Newcomb of Salisbury sold and conveyed to Joseph Owen of Lebanon two tracts of land in Salisbury, of 318 and 101 acres, on the dividing line between Salisbury and Sharon, on the southerly side of the Four-Rod Highway. On 10 June 1746 Joseph Owen, late of Lebanon, now of Salisbury, conveyed to his sons David and Jonathan, late of Lebanon, now of Salisbury, 100 acres each in Salisbury. On 30 Oct. 1747 Joseph Owen of Salisbury conveyed 10 acres to Josiah Heath and Mary, his wife, of Sharon, towards the portion of Mary out of his estate. On 18 June 1757 Joseph Owen conveyed to David Owen of Salisbury 300 acres on the south side of the highway from David Owen's dwelling to Canaan and Sharon, and on the same date he conveyed 9 acres to his grandson James Owen, son of his son David. (Lebanon and Salisbury records.) In his will, dated 10 Aug. 1758 and proved in 1758, Joseph Owen mentions a wife (unnamed), his sons David and Jonathan, his daughters Mary Jacobs, Esther Cole, Ann Culver, Rebecca Wright, Ruth Tupper, Mercy Heath, Lydia Tuttle, and Irene Blogget, and a granddaughter, Hannah Heath (Sharon probate records).

Children by first wife:

i. DAVID,[4] b. probably at Lebanon; m. at Lebanon, 14 Oct. 1736, MARGARET TAYLOR. About 1746 he moved with his father from Lebanon to Salisbury, where the land records show a conveyance of land, 15 Feb. 1768, by David Owen, late of Salisbury, now a resident of Panton [sic], N. H.

Children:

1. *Lucy,*[5] b. at Lebanon 28 Dec. 1737; probably d. young.
2. *Absalom,* b. at Lebanon 29 Mar. 1740.
3. *James,* b. at Lebanon 3 Mar. 1741; m. Johanna ———. Children, b. at Salisbury: James,[6] b. 1 Apr. 1765, Pegge, b. 16 Aug. 1767, Johanna, b. 13 Sept. 1769, Cynthia, b. 27 Sept. 1771.
4. *Lucy,* b. at Lebanon 6 June 1744.
5. *Ann,* b. at Salisbury 14 Apr. 1747.
6. *Thomas,* b. at Salisbury 28 Feb. 1748/9.
7. *Rebecca,* b. at Salisbury 30 May 1751.
8. *Daniel,* b. at Salisbury 20 Aug. 1753.
9. *David,* b. at Salisbury 13 Nov. 1756.

ii. MARY, b. at Lebanon 7 Oct. 1706, daughter of Joseph and Mary Owen (Lebanon records); m. 5 Feb. 1736 DAVID JACOBS (Mansfield records and Lebanon church records), who d. at Salisbury 3 Nov. 1758, his wife surviving him. The Lebanon land records show a conveyance of land, 25 Jan. 1742, by David Jacobs to his brother-in-law, David Owen, adjoining land of his father-in-law, Joseph Owen. The land records of Salisbury show conveyances of land to David Jacobs by Jonathan and David Owen in 1748 and 1750.

Children (surname *Jacobs*):

1. *David,* b. at Lebanon 11 Apr. 1742; m. at Salisbury, 31 Aug. 1763, his half first cousin, Ruth Tupper (11, vii, 4), *q.v.*
2. *Molly,* b. 1 May 1748 (Sharon probate records).
3. *Adonijah,* b. at Salisbury 27 Mar. 1751; m. at Salisbury, 24 Jan. 1772, Elizabeth Loomis of Lebanon.

iii. ESTHER, b. at Lebanon 26 Aug. 1708, daughter of Joseph and Mary Owen (Lebanon records); m. at Lebanon EBENEZER COLE.

Children (surname *Cole*), b. at Lebanon:

1. *Ebenezer,* b. 5 Aug. 1734; m. 23 Apr. 1751 Elizabeth Wheeler of Plainfield.
2. *Chloe,* b. 4 Aug. 1736.
3. *Sarah,* b. 4 Jan. 1737/8; m. 13 Oct. 1757 Jonas Wheeler of Plainfield.
4. *David,* b. 30 Aug. 1739.

iv. ANN, b. at Lebanon 18 Oct. 1710, daughter of Joseph and Mary Owen (*ib.*); m. ——— CULVER.

v. RACHEL, b. at Lebanon 30 Dec. 1711, daughter of Joseph and Mary Owen (*ib.*); m. 9 Jan. 1735 BENJAMIN WRIGHT, son of Abel and Rebecca Wright of Lebanon.

Children (surname *Wright*), b. at Lebanon:

1. *Lucy,* b. 15 May 1735; m. 22 Sept. 1757 Benjamin Owen.
2. *Benjamin,* b. 5 July 1737; m. 29 Apr. 1762 Ann Redington.
3. *Mercy,* b. 26 July 1739.
4. *Abel,* b. 18 Aug. 1742.
5. *Mary,* b. 2 Oct. 1744.
6. *Rachel,* b. 13 Feb. 1747.
7. *David,* b. 14 Mar. 1749.
8. *Rebecca,* b. 2 Apr. 1752.
9. *Jonathan,* b. 31 Mar. 1754.

Children by second wife:

22. vi. JONATHAN, b. at Lebanon 27 Oct. 1718, son of Joseph and Ruth Owen (*ib.*).

vii. RUTH, b. at Lebanon; m. at Lebanon, 27 May 1740, THOMAS TUPPER, who d. at Salisbury 13 May 1761. The births of their children are recorded at Salisbury, but probably the older ones were born at Lebanon. In 1742 Joseph Owen, for good will, etc., conveyed land in Lebanon to his son-in-law Thomas Tupper.

Children (surname *Tupper*):

1. *Jerusha*, b. 21 Mar. 1741.
2. *Charles*, b. 31 Mar. 1743; m. Hannah ———.
3. *Mercy* (twin), b. 4 Dec. 1745.
4. *Ruth* (twin), b. 4 Dec. 1745; m. at Salisbury, 3 Aug. 1763, her half first cousin, David Jacobs (11, ii, 1), *q.v.*
5. *Thomas*, b. 16 Nov. 1747; m. 20 Sept. 1768 Parthena Jaqua.
6. *Benjamin*, b. 27 Feb. 1749.
7. *Lydia*, b. 26 Oct. 1750; d. in Nov. 1759.
8. *Archelaus*, b. 3 Oct. 1752.
9. *Darius*, b. 15 June 1754.
10. *Johanna*, b. 19 Mar. 1756.
11. *Zurice*, b. 21 Mar. 1758.
12. *Absalom*, b. 11 July 1759; d. 3 May 1760.
13. *Absalom*, b. 22 Apr. 1761.

viii. MERCY, b. at Lebanon; d. at Salisbury 28 Oct. 1763; m. 2 Oct. 1740 JOSIAH HEATH (Lebanon church records). In 1747 Joseph Owen, for good will, etc., conveyed land to Josiah Heath and his wife Mary, of Sharon.

Children (surname *Heath*), recorded at Salisbury:

1. *Lucy*, b. 20 Mar. 1742.
2. *Nathaniel*, b. 19 June 1743.
3. *Hannah*, b. 3 Sept. 1744.
4. *Mehitabel*, b. 30 Dec. 1745.
5. *Josiah*, b. 5 Dec. 1747.
6. *Levine*, b. 26 Mar. 1749.
7. *Lovis*, b. 22 Mar. 1751.
8. *Abigail*, b. 21 Jan. 1753; d. 26 Oct. 1753.
9. *Mollie*, b. 21 July 1755.
10. *Obadiah*, b. 30 Sept. 1757; d. about 1760.
11. *Jonathan*, d. about 1760.
12. *Elizabeth*, b. 13 May 1761.

ix. IRENE, b. at Lebanon; m. at Salisbury, 7 Dec. 1750 (Rev. Jonathan Lee officiating), ASA BLOGGET.

Children (surname *Blogget*), b. at Salisbury:

1. *Samuel*, b. 26 May 1751.
2. *Artemas*, b. 31 Dec. 1752; m. 4 Aug. 1774 Rebecca Turner.
3. *Sardias*, b. 25 May 1754.
4. *Archelaus*, b. 29 Dec. 1755.
5. *Irene*, b. 26 Aug. 1757.
6. *Sarah*, b. 7 Apr. 1759.
7. *Elisha*, b. 19 Apr. 1761; d. 19 June 1761.
8. *Silva*, b. 5 Nov. 1762.
9. *Asa*, b. 11 Jan. 1765.

x. LYDIA, b. at Lebanon; m. at Salisbury, 1 Feb. 1753 (Rev. Jonathan Lee officiating), THOMAS TUTTLE.

Children (surname *Tuttle*), b. at Salisbury:

1. *Lydia*, b. 18 July 1753.
2. *Thomas*, b. 5 May 1755.
3. *Solomon*, b. 3 Sept. 1757.
4. *Jesse*, b. 24 Aug. 1759.
5. *Martha*, b. 6 Dec. 1761.
6. *Chandler*, b. 19 Sept. 1763.
7. *John*, b. 5 July 1766.
8. *Othnill*, b. 26 Sept. 1769.

12. MOSES[3] OWEN (*Joseph*,[2] *John*[1]), of Lebanon and Ashford, was born at Simsbury 7 July 1688. He married at Lebanon, 4 Feb. 1713/14, HANNAH MAN.

On 8 June 1732 he bought 17 acres of land in the village of Lebanon. On 10 Apr. 1735 land in Lebanon was conveyed to him by his father, Joseph Owen, Sr.; and on that date he sold and conveyed his land in Lebanon to Ezekiel Fuller. He apparently settled soon afterwards in Ashford.

Children, born at Lebanon:

  i. DANIEL,[4] b. 6 Nov. 1714; m. at Ashford, 25 Apr. 1745, ABIGAIL PIERCE.
       Children, b. at Ashford:
       1. *Daniel,*[5] b. 3 Mar. 1746; d. 21 Nov. 1751.
       2. *Lydia,* b. 6 Jan. 1748.
       3. *James,* b. 2 Apr. 1750.
       4. *Hulda,* b. 17 Apr. 1752.
       5. *Abigail.*
 ii. HANNAH, b. 16 Nov. 1718; m. at Ashford, 25 Oct. 1738, ABRAHAM RUSS.
23. iii. ELEAZER, b. 24 Jan. 1720/1.
 iv. BATHSHEBA, b. 13 June 1728; d. 4 June 1732.
24. v. TIMOTHY, b. 18 Apr. 1731.

13. JOSHUA[3] OWEN (*Joseph,*[2] *John*[1]), of Lebanon and Salisbury, was born probably at Simsbury or Windsor. He married at Lebanon, 5 Nov. 1718, MARGARET WOODWORTH.

On 27 Feb. 1734/5 his father, Joseph Owen, gave him land in Lebanon, which he sold 12 Mar. 1750. On 20 May 1751 Timothy Burbank of Salisbury sold and conveyed to Joshua Owen of Lebanon land in Salisbury. On 2 May 1753 Joshua Owen of Salisbury bought land there from Amos Chipman. These two pieces of land in Salisbury he conveyed to his son Leonard Owen on 18 Oct. 1755.

Children, born at Lebanon:

  i. JEMIMA,[4] b. 26 July 1719.
 ii. LEONARD, b. 13 Dec. 1720; living in 1781; m. (1) EXPERIENCE ———, who d. 1 May 1756, in her 24th year; m. (2) at Salisbury, 28 Apr. 1757, MARY STANNARD. He probably moved to Salisbury about 1750. On 12 Sept. 1750 Yale College leased to Leonard Owen of Salisbury a tract of 728 acres for a long term of years. In 1756 he acquired from his brother, Eliphalet Owen, a one-fourth interest in certain iron works. In 1757 he acquired one-fourth of the iron works, and in 1758 he acquired 46¼ acres called the Iron Works Lot. On 8 Sept. 1758 he sold to John Pell of Sheffield, Mass., his one-half interest in the iron works and house and land near the iron works. The Salisbury land records also show Leonard Owen of Salisbury as a party to conveyances in 1762, 1773, 1775, and 1781.
       Children by first wife, b. at Salisbury:
       1. *Eunice,*[5] b. 30 Nov. 1754.
       2. *Leonard,* b. 20 Apr. 1756.
       Children by second wife, b. at Salisbury:
       3. *Sabre,* b. 26 Dec. 1757.
       4. *Mary,* b. 20 June 1759.
       5. *Sibel,* b. 1 Sept. 1761.
       6. *Thadeus,* b. 27 Jan. 1763.
       7. *Lusina,* b. 18 Oct. 1764.
       8. *Abigail,* b. 18 July or 26 May 1766.
       9. *Daniel,* b. 14 Feb. 1768.
       10. *Abel,* b. 26 Feb. 1772.

iii. ELIJAH, b. 29 Jan. 1721; m. (1) at Lebanon, 21 Oct. 1747, PATIENCE. WRIGHT, who d. 19 Mar. 1756, daughter of Abel and Rebecca. Wright of Lebanon and sister of the Benjamin Wright who m. Rachel, daughter of Joseph Owen (11, v); m. (2) at Salisbury, 10 Nov. 1756, OLIVE BEMON. The Salisbury land records show him as a party to conveyances and as a resident there in 1757, 1758, 1761, and 1768.
Children by first wife, b. at Salisbury:
1. *Sarah*,[5] b. 18 July 1748.
2. *Naomi*, b. 19 Feb. 1750; probably d. in infancy.
3. *Naomi*, b. 3 Mar. 1751; m. in 1770 Mordecai Soaper.
4. *Phebe*, b. 1 Mar. 1753.
5. *Hulda* (twin), } b. 28 Jan. 1755; d. in infancy.
6. *Elijah* (twin),
7. *Patience*, b. 14 Mar. 1756; d. in infancy.
Children by second wife, b. at Salisbury:
8. *Patience*, b. 2 Feb. 1758.
9. *Elijah*, b. 27 Apr. 1759; probably d. in infancy.
10. *Elijah*, b. 5 Oct. 1760.
11. *Electa*, b. 3 Jan. 1762.
12. *Esther*, b. 22 Aug. 1763.
13. *Ann*, b. 27 Aug. 1765.
14. *Lois*, b. 28 Feb. 1767.
15. *Julius*, b. 23 Apr. 1769.
16. *Ambrose*, b. 25 Dec. 1770.
iv. KEZIAH, b. 27 June 1723; m. 15 June 1744 CHARLES BREWSTER.
v. JOSHUA, b. 7 Feb. 1724; m. HANNAH ———.
Children, b. at Salisbury:
1. *Jemima*,[5] b. 19 Sept. 1754.
2. *Ruth*, b. 13 May 1756.
3. *Margaret*, b. 4 Aug. 1759.
4. *Meriam*, b. 8 Nov. 1763.
vi. ELIPHALET, b. 26 June 1727; living in 1782; m. EUNICE ———. The Salisbury land records show that in 1755 he acquired a one-fourth interest in iron works, which he sold in the following year to his brother Leonard. In 1761 he acquired of Thomas Lamb of North Carolina 376½ acres in Salisbury, on Tockonnock Mountain, which he, on 8 May 1769, being then a resident of Sheffield, Berkshire Co., Mass., sold to his brother Leonard of Salisbury. His name appears in the land records in 1782, as of Salisbury.
Children, b. at Salisbury:
1. *Irene*,[5] b. 1 Dec. 1760.
2. *Deidamia*, b. 3 Mar. 1763.
3. *Molly*, b. 11 June 1770.
4. *Rhoda*, b. 3 June 1771.
5. *Charlotte*, b. 17 Nov. 1773.
vii. ESTHER, b. 3 Sept. 1730; m. at Lebanon, 1 Aug. 1749, JONATHAN BILL.
Child (surname *Bill*), b. at Lebanon:
1. *Mary*, b. 6 May 1750.
viii. NAOMI, b. 15 Sept. 1740; d. at Lebanon 26 Sept. 1740.
ix. SAMUEL, b. 26 May 1742.

14. DEA. SAMUEL[3] OWEN (*Obadiah*,[2] *John*[1]), born at Windsor 3 Aug. 1707, died 16 Jan. 1787 (East Granby church records). He married first, 19 Nov. 1730, MARGARET GRISWOLD, who died at Windsor 7 Feb. 1783; and secondly, at Windsor, 26 Feb. 1783, MARY TAYLOR, widow.

He was a deacon, and is frequently mentioned in the records of the East Granby church. In his will, dated 19 Sept. 1780 and proved in 1787, he names his wife Margaret, his sons

Samuel and Seth, and his daughter Margaret, the wife of Barnabus Meacham.

Children by first wife, born at Windsor:

i. SAMUEL,[4] b. 24 Feb. 1736/7; m. about 1759 RACHEL STILES, b. 1 Oct. 1740, daughter of Jonah Stiles.

    Children, b. at Windsor:

    1. *Rachel*,[5] b. 29 June 1760.
    2. *Eunice*, b. 24 Nov. 1761; m. 2 Apr. 1782 Shuball Stiles.
    3. *Keziah*, b. 16 July 1763.
    4. *Azubah*, b. 6 Jan. 1765; m. 20 Jan. 1785 Azariah Phelps.
    5. *Sarah*, b. 16 July 1767.
    6. *Pegge*, b. 22 Apr. 1769.
    7. *Alice*.
    8. *Samuel*, b. 11 June 1775.

ii. MARGARET, b. 28 Apr. 1742; m. BARNABAS MEACHAM.

iii. SETH, b. 1 Jan. 1744/5; d. 29 Mar. 1795 (East Granby church records); m. at East Granby church JEMIMA MURPHY. In his will he gives his estate to his two children, and, in case they die before becoming of age, to the support of the Gospel in Turkey Hills.

    Children, b. at Windsor:

    1. *Seth Calvin*,[5] b. 2 May 1783.
    2. *Jerusha*, b. 12 May 1785.

15. ENSIGN ISAAC[3] OWEN (*Isaac*,[2] *John*[1]), born at Windsor 7 Nov. 1702, died 3 Jan. 1775. He married MARY ELLSWORTH, born in 1706, died 1 Feb. 1778, daughter of Jonathan and Sarah Ellsworth. They were buried in East Granby cemetery.

Children, born at Windsor:

i. MARY,[4] b. 13 June 1733; m. 25 Nov. 1752 THOMAS WINCHEL, JR.

ii. ISAAC, b. 24 Sept. 1736; d. 2 Aug. 1816, aged 80; m. ZERVIAH GRISWOLD, who d. 21 Mar. 1817, aged 81. (Inscriptions, East Granby cemetery.)

    Children:

    1. *Isaac*,[5] b. 16 June 1757; d. 18 Jan. 1826; m. 30 Nov. 1780 Zeriah Cornish, who d. 16 Sept. 1834, aged 76. Their son, Isaac Milton,[6] d. 8 June 1801, aged 18 years.
    2. *Zeriah*, b. 24 Sept. 1758.
    3. *Mary*, b. 24 Aug. 1760; probably m. 25 Nov. 1788 Jesse Taylor.
    4. *Sarah*, b. 18 July 1764; d. 3 Sept. 1840.
    5. *George*, b. 21 July 1767; perhaps the George Owen who, according to Stiles, m. Chloe Pinney, resided at Granby, and had eight children.*
    6. *Lydia*, b. 15 Dec. 1769.
    7. *Benajah*, b. 21 Sept. 1771.
    8. *Mindwell*, b. 18 May 1773.
    9. *Joab*, b. 29 Nov. 1775; m. Dorothy ———, who d. 5 June 1856, aged 77 (inscription at East Granby).
    10. *Lucretia*, b. 27 Sept. 1778; d. 16 June 1859; m. Israel Stoughton.

iii. ABIA, b. 30 Dec. 1739.

iv. BENAJAH, b. 1 June 1743.

v. SARAH, b. 28 Sept. 1747; d. 20 Aug. 1764.

*Stiles also states that George C. Owen, son of George and Chloe Owen, married 21 Nov. 1819 Sabra Pinney (East Granby church records). East Granby inscriptions state that Catherine, daughter of George and Chloe Owen, died 30 Aug. 1826, aged 20, and that Sabra, wife of George C. Owen, died 24 Sept. 1830, aged 27.

16. **ELIJAH³** OWEN (*Isaac,² John¹*), born at Windsor 7 Oct. 1706, died 22 Sept. 1741. He married HANNAH HIGLEY, born 17 Dec. 1717, died 26 Jan. 1806, daughter of Brewster Higley. She married secondly, 29 Mar. 1743, Pelatiah Mills, Jr.
Children, born at Windsor:

    i. REBECCA,⁴ b. 28 Nov. 1736; m. 18 Dec. 1761, as his second wife, BENEDICT ALFORD, whose first wife, Jerusha (Ashley) of Hartford, d. in 1761.
        Children (surname *Alford*):
        1. *Rebecca*, bapt. 31 Oct. 1762.
        2. *George*, bapt. 11 Mar. 1764.
        3. *Rosetta*, bapt. 29 Dec. 1765.
        4. *Oliver*, bapt. 1 Nov. 1767.
        5. *Clara*, bapt. 3 Nov. 1771.
25. ii. ELIJAH, b. in 1738/9.
    iii. HANNAH, b. 17 July 1740; d. at Simsbury 18 May 1831; m. 2 Mar. 1758 CAPT. JOHN BROWN, b. in 1728, d. in New York, while serving in the Revolutionary Army, 3 Sept. 1776. In 1755 they moved to West Simsbury. He was elected captain of the Eighth Company, Eighteenth Connecticut Regiment, in the spring of 1776, at the head of which he marched to the Army in New York.
        Children (surname *Brown*):
        1. *Hannah*, b. 24 Dec. 1758; d. in 1825; m. Solomon Humphrey, who d. in 1834, aged 81.
        2. *Azubah*, b. 7 May 1760; d. in 1812; m. Michael Barbour.
        3. *Esther*, b. 4 Mar. 1762; d. in 1838; m. Timothy Case.
        4. *Margery*, b. 25 Jan. 1764; d. in 1820; m. (1) David Giddings; m. (2) Prince Taylor.
        5. *Lucinda*, b. 18 Nov. 1765; d. in 1814; m. Russell Borden.
        6. *John*, b. 31 Aug. 1767; d. in 1849; m. (1) Millicent Gaylord; m. (2) Widow Abia Case.
        7. *Frederick*, b. 14 Aug. 1769; d. in 1848; m. (1) Catherine Case; m. (2) in 1808 Chloe Pettibone.
        8. *Owen*, b. 16 Feb. 1771; d. in 1856; m. (1) in 1793 Ruth Mills; m. (2) Sarah Root; m. (3) Abbe Hinsdale. John Brown, of Ossawatomie and Harper's Ferry fame, was a son of Owen and Ruth (Mills) Brown.
        9. *Thede*, b. 5 Jan. 1773; d. in 1846; m. William Merrell.
     10. *Roxy*, b. 29 May 1775; d. in 1855; m. Alex Humphrey.
     11. *Abiel*, b. 18 Nov. 1776; d. in 1856; m. Anna Lord.

17. **ASAHEL⁴** OWEN (*Josiah,³ Josiah,² John¹*), born at Windsor 25 Mar. 1699, died at Sheffield, Mass., 7 Apr. 1740. He married, at Bolton, Conn., 9 June 1726, as Asahel Owen of Hebron, PATIENCE ROSE of Bolton, who survived him and married secondly ——— Plantin.

The following abstracts of deeds of Hampden County, Mass., and of Berkshire County, Mass., which was created out of the old Hampshire County in 1761, throw light on this family:

On 2 May 1754 Asahel Owen of Windsor, Conn., sold to David Jewell of Salisbury, Conn., 25 acres granted to the heirs of Asahel Owen, bounded on the south by the supposed Colony line (Hampden Deeds, vol. 10, p. 301).

On 15 May 1754 Abram Owen of Sheffield, Mass., sold to David Jewell a one-fourth part of 100 acres west of Sheffield granted to the heirs of Asahel Owen, bounded on the south by the Colony line and adjoining Nathaniel Jewell (*ib.*, vol. 10, p. 300).

On 29 Apr. 1760 Edward Owen of Sheffield [then in Hampshire County, Mass.] sold to Samuel Norton of Salisbury, Conn., 20 acres in Sheffield, adjoining the Colony line and north line of Salisbury, Conn., being the one-fifth part of 100 acres granted to the heirs of Asahel Owen, late of Sheffield, being in partnership with the rest of the heirs of the said Asahel and yet undivided (Berkshire Deeds, vol. 6, p. 6).

On 8 Jan. 1765 Patience Plantin of Sheffield quitclaimed and sold to Felix Powell of Scatticook, N. Y., land granted to her by the General Court at Boston, viz., 100 acres west of Sheffield, bounded on the south by the Connecticut line (*ib.*, vol. 2, p. 558).

On 3 Apr. 1765 Ezra Fellows of Sheffield, Mass., quitclaimed and sold to Joseph Hanmer of Salisbury, Conn., and Edward Owen of Sheffield, Mass., 100 acres that were granted to Patience Owen, now Patience Plantin, and her heirs by the General Court at Boston, lying west of Sheffield line and bounded on the south by the Connecticut line (*ib.*, vol. 2, p. 591).

On 5 Apr. 1765 Israel Dewey of Great Barrington, Berkshire Co., Mass., quitclaimed and sold to Joseph Hanmer and Edward Owen his interest in a one-fourth part of 100 acres in Sheffield, bounded south by the Connecticut line, which was granted to Patience Owen, now Patience Plantin (*ib.*, vol. 2, p. 591).

In 1755 Massachusetts appointed a committee to dispose of Province land west of Sheffield and Stockbridge; and a tract along the Under Mountain road was laid out and sold to Israel Williams, Patience Owen, Samuel Austin, William Drake, and Joseph and John Owen, which was subsequently annexed to Sheffield.

Children:

26. i. ASAHEL,⁵ b. at Bolton 25 July 1726.
 ii. ABDON, b. at Bolton 3 Dec. 1727.
 iii. ABRAM, b. at Bolton 28 Dec. 1729.
27. iv. EDWARD.
 v. PATIENCE, b. at Sheffield, Mass., 10 Dec. 1738.

18. NOAH⁴ OWEN (*Josiah*,³ *Josiah*,² *John*¹), born at Windsor 14 May 1701, died in 1785 or 1786. He married at Hebron, 30 Mar. 1727, MARY WATERS.

In his will, dated in 1785 and proved in 1786, he names his deceased children, Joel, Noah, Anne, and Uzziel, his two daughters, Lois Northam and Rachel Davis, and two granddaughters, Mary Case and Rachel Kellogg.

Children, born at Hebron:

i. JOEL,⁵ b. 28 Oct. 1728; d. about 1777; m. at Hebron, 24 Apr. 1755, ANNE BUEL.
 Children, b. at Hebron:
 1. *Noah*,⁶ b. 5 Feb. 1756; d. in Licking County, Ohio, in 1821.

2. *Lydia*, b. 29 Mar. 1757.
3. *Parnah*, b. 4 Oct. 1758.
4. *Nomah*, b. 28 Oct. 1760.
5. *Chloe*, b. 24 Nov. 1762.
6. *Thalia*, b. 23 June 1764.
7. *Silas*, b. 20 Feb. 1766; d. 29 Nov. 1768.
8. *Silas* (twin), } b. 13 Apr. 1771.
9. *Joel* (twin), } b. 13 Apr. 1771.
10. *Asahel*, b. 19 Jan. 1773.

   ii. NOAH, b. 1 Oct. 1730; d. at Hebron 23 May 1753; m. at Hebron, 20 Apr. 1752, MARY WILLSON, who d. 31 Aug. 1753.
Child:
1. *Mary*,⁶ b. 7 Aug. 1753.
   iii. MARY, b. 3 Mar. 1733; m. ROGER CASE [?].
   iv. ANNE, b. 29 June 1735; m. at Hebron, 2 July 1759, EZEKIEL KEL-LOGG.
Child (surname *Kellogg*):
1. *Rachel*.
   v. UZZIEL, b. 8 Apr. 1738.
   vi. LOIS, b. 25 Aug. 1744; m. ELIJAH NORTHAM.
   vii. RACHEL (twin), b. 11 Apr. 1747; m. at Hebron, 12 Dec. 1775, ZEPHANIA DAVIS.
Child (surname *Davis*):
1. *Rachel*.
   viii. LYDIA (twin), b. 11 Apr. 1747.

19. JOSIAH⁴ OWEN (*Josiah*,³ *Josiah*,² *John*¹) was born at Hebron 17 Mar. 1716. He married first, 28 Jan. 1741, HANNAH WHITE, who died 28 Apr. 1747; and secondly, 25 May 1749, ZERVIAH ROBBARDS of Norwich.
Children:
   i. MARTHA,⁵ b. at Hebron 22 Oct. 1742; m. 2 June 1763 DANIEL SMALLEY, JR.
   ii. HANNAH, b. at Hebron 8 July 1744; d. 10 Dec. 1748.
   iii. SILVANUS, b. at Hebron 19 Aug. 1746; m. 4 May 1768 EUNICE ROBERTS of Coventry.
Children, b. at Hebron:
1. *Andrew*,⁶ b. 22 Apr. 1769.
2. *Lois*, b. 31 Mar. 1771.
   iv. HANNAH, b. at Norwich 19 Dec. 1749; m. 1 July 1773 SAMUEL GROSS of Lebanon.
   v. FREDERICK, b. at Norwich 16 Feb. 1752; d. in 1837; m. 10 Sept. 1778 PEGGY HUBBARD of Windham. He was a soldier of the Revolution. (Cf. Lineage Book, National Society of the Daughters of the American Revolution, vol. 26, p. 77.)
Children, b. at Windham:
1. *Zerviah*,⁶ b. 13 Feb. 1779.
2. *Rainer*, b. 20 Dec. 1780.
3. *Abigail*, b. 16 Jan. 1782.
4. *Eliphalet*, b. 9 May 1784.
5. *David*, b. 14 Jan. 1786.
6. *Polly*, b. 21 July 1788.
   vi. DELLA, b. at Tolland 8 June 1755.

20. JOHN⁴ OWEN (*John*,³ *Josiah*,² *John*¹), born at Windsor 18 Mar. 1712, died at Simsbury 6 Feb. 1783. He married first, 11 Jan. 1738/9, ESTHER HUMPHREY of Simsbury, who died 7 Mar. 1773, aged 50, daughter of Jonathan and Mercy (Ruggles) Humphrey; and secondly, 17 Nov. 1773, SARAH BANCROFT

of East Windsor. He and his family are buried in the cemetery at Simsbury.

He was known as John Owen, Esq., and had been town clerk of Simsbury.

Children, born at Simsbury:

i. ESTHER,[5] b. 27 Oct. 1739; m. 7 Apr. 1757 BREWSTER HIGLEY.
ii. ROSETTA, b. 25 Aug. 1742; m. (1) 10 Aug. 1769 ELISHA PHELPS of Simsbury, merchant, who d. at Albany, N. Y., 14 July 1776; m. (2) 31 Mar. 1778 CALEB HOTCHKISS of New Haven.
   Children by first husband (surname *Phelps*), b. at Simsbury:
   1. *Charlotte Lenora*, b. 4 Oct. 1761; m. Samuel Hall.
   2. *Heepah Rosetta*, b. 7 Oct. 1763.
   3. *Elisha Pitt*, b. 21 Mar. 1765.
   4. *Sylvia Lorinda*, b. 1 Aug. 1768; d. 10 Apr. 1776.
   5. *Rosanna Clarinda*, b. 16 Sept. 1770.
   6. *Laura Roselle*, b. 31 May 1773.
iii. CHLOE, b. 26 June 1746; m. JOHN CASE.
iv. HANNAH, b. 13 May 1749; d. 9 Apr. 1826; m. 9 Feb. 1760 JONATHAN PETTIBONE.
   Children (surname *Pettibone*), b. at Simsbury:
   1. *Martha*, b. 16 May 1770; d. 9 Dec. 1821; m. Austin Phelps.
   2. *Hannah*, b. 9 Feb. 1773; d. 1 Nov. 1830; m. Wait Latimer.
   3. *Jonathan*, b. 31 May 1775; d. 19 Sept. 1829; m. Fanny Phelps.
   4. *Dorinda*, b. 5 Apr. 1778.
   5. *Harlow*, b. 7 Apr. 1781; d. 27 Feb. 1823; m. Lucy Carmack.
   6. *Samuel*, b. 21 Feb. 1784; d. 26 Aug. 1820; m. Catherine Mills.
   7. *John*, b. 22 Oct. 1787.
   8. *Virgil*, b. 2 Apr. 1790.
v. RUTH, b. 16 Oct. 1752; d. 14 May 1782; m. BARTHOLOMEW CASE.
vi. JOHN, b. 21 Oct. 1759; d. 28 Nov. 1759.
vii. SOPHIA, b. 11 Sept. 1760; d. 1 Nov. 1842, aged 82 (gravestone in Simsbury cemetery, which calls her "Sophia Graham, daughter of the late John Owen Esq."); m. ——— GRAHAM.*
viii. THERESA, b. 7 Nov. 1762.
ix. JOHN CALVIN, b. 22 Aug. 1766; d. 10 Apr. 1798, aged 33.

21. NATHANIEL[4] OWEN (*Nathaniel,[3] Nathaniel,[2] John[1]*), of Windsor, born about 1735, died at Windsor 24 Dec. 1821, aged 86, being then the last male member of the ancient Congregational Church at Poquonock. He married, 16 Apr. 1755, MARY PENNEY.

Since his son Aaron, who was called to do military duty in the American Revolution, was in poor health, the father took his place, and was in the Army at the time of its retreat from Long Island.

Children, born at Windsor:

i. AARON,[5] b. 21 July 1756.
ii. ESTHER, b. 12 Nov. 1761; d. unm. 4 Nov. 1852. She lived with her father, and, after his death, with her widowed sister Keziah, in the homestead which, after her death, was left to her brother Hezekiah and was later owned by Hezekiah's sons, Rev. John Jason Owen, D.D., and Edward Hezekiah Owen, Esq., of New York City.

---

*Another inscription at Simsbury states that "Anna M. Graham daughter of William and Sophia Graham, died Sept. 13, 1884, Age 37."

iii. KEZIAH, b. 15 June 1764; m. GIDEON TUCKER. Two sons and one daughter.
iv. HEZEKIAH, b. 1 Sept. 1766; d. in Brooklyn, N. Y., 16 July 1854; bur. at Ogdensburg, N. Y.; m. 21 Sept. 1785 ELIZABETH THRALL, who d. 9 Jan. 1836. He was of Colebrook, Conn., Kingsborough, N. Y., and New York City, and was a volunteer in the War of 1812. Children:
1. *Elizabeth,*⁶ d. unm. 25 Jan. 1816.
2. *Candice,* b. 14 Aug. 1789; d. 2 Apr. 1839; m. Abner Leonard of Kingsborough, N. Y.
3. *Fanny,* b. 7 July 1791; d. 11 Oct. 1849; m. Roger Stilwell of Manlius, N. Y.
4. *Altamira,* b. 1 Feb. 1799; m. Ephraim Burt.
5. *Rev. John Jason,* D.D., b. 13 Aug. 1803; d. 18 Apr. 1869; m. (1) Elizabeth B. Webb; m. (2) Lavinia B. Heath. He was a well-known clergyman, classical scholar, writer, and teacher; and his career is given briefly in Stiles's "Ancient Windsor," vol. 2, p. 547, and in various biographical dictionaries. His first two children by his first marriage died in infancy, and the third, Edward Jason,⁷ b. 28 Nov. 1835, was a lawyer in New York City.
6. *Edward Hezekiah,* of New York City, lawyer, b. 10 Dec. 1808; m. (1) Jane Augusta Livingston; m. (2) Sarah Seymour Nash. Three children by first wife and two children by second wife.
7. *Roger Leonard,* b. at Watertown, N. Y., 2 Apr. 1812; d. unm. at Houston, Tex., 8 Nov. 1839. He enlisted in the Texan war for independence, and served until its close.

22. JONATHAN⁴ OWEN (*Joseph,*³ *Joseph,*² *John*¹), born at Lebanon 27 Oct. 1718, died not later than 11 Sept. 1759, when administration on his estate was granted by the Sharon probate court to Patience Owen, his widow. He married at Lebanon, 1 May 1740, PATIENCE VALLANCE, living 3 June 1777, daughter of William and Joanna Vallance.

Jonathan Owen's father conveyed land to him in Lebanon in 1740 and in Salisbury in 1746, and other conveyances to and from Jonathan Owen are recorded in Salisbury from 1746 to 1757. The Salisbury land records show that Patience Owen of Salisbury purchased in 1767, from Isaac Bentley, a house and small piece of land, which she sold 3 June 1777 to Daniel Bradley. In the deed to Bradley she was described as a resident of Westmoreland Township, Litchfield Co., Conn., a place in the Wyoming Valley, near the present site of Wilkes-Barre, Pa., in the part of Pennsylvania then claimed by Connecticut under the old charter of the Colony. Anning Owen, a son of Eleazer Owen, who fell in the Battle of Minisink (N. Y.) in 1779, is frequently mentioned as a pioneer minister in the early days of the settlement in the Wyoming Valley; but further trace of Patience Owen and her family at Westmoreland has not been found.

Children:

i. WILLIAM,⁵ b. at Lebanon 7 Apr. 1741 (recorded also at Salisbury); m. in Sept. 1766 LOIS CALKINS of Sharon, b. 20 May 1745, daughter of John and Elizabeth Calkins. On 7 Feb. 1760 he chose John Gay of Sharon to be his guardian.

ii. JONATHAN, b. at Lebanon 18 Mar. 1742/3 (recorded also at Salisbury). He chose David Owen for his guardian, 26 May 1761. He is apparently the Jonathan Owen who served in the Revolution in the New York Militia, in the Second Regiment of Ulster County, under Col. James McCloughry.

iii. MARY, b. at Salisbury 16 Apr. 1745.

iv. OLIVER, b. at Salisbury 24 Sept. 1748; d. at Jamesville, Onondaga Co., N. Y., about 1802; m. ———. He chose John Gay, Esq., to be his guardian, 22 Nov. 1762. He served in the Revolution in the New York Militia, in the Second Regiment of Ulster County, under Col. James McCloughry. The United States Census of 1790 gives him as residing in Mamakating Township, Ulster Co., and the Census of 1800 in Manlius, Onondaga Co., N. Y. He was an early settler in Onondaga County, at Jamesville, where he erected a sawmill in 1795. His son, Nathaniel⁶ Owen, administered his estate in 1802. The Onondaga County records show that on 12 Nov. 1794 Lot No. 92 was granted to Oliver Owen of the township of Manlius by Peter Townsend of Goshen, Orange Co., N. Y., and that on 30 July 1817 John B.⁶ Owen, son of Oliver Owen, deceased, was a party to a transaction with George Holbrook of Manlius, N. Y., about this Lot No. 92. It appears that Oliver Owen and his brother Solomon served together in the Revolution, and that both were early settlers in Onondaga County.

v. JOSEPH, b. at Salisbury 20 Feb. 1750/1.

28. vi. AMASA, b. at Salisbury 10 Feb. 1753.

vii. ELEAZER, b. at Salisbury 16 Apr. 1755 (recorded at Sharon). He is probably the Eleazer Owen who served in the Revolution in the New York Militia, in the Second Regiment of Ulster County, under Col. James McCloughry.

viii. SOLOMON, b. at Salisbury 14 Apr. 1757 (recorded at Sharon); living in 1810; m. in what is now Lafayette Township, Onondaga Co., N. Y., in 1793 (the first marriage in the township), Lois ROUNDS, living in 1799, daughter of Comfort Rounds. With several of his brothers he served in the Revolution in the New York Militia, in the Second Regiment of Ulster County, under Col. James McCloughry. He was a resident of Mamakating Township, Ulster Co., N. Y., in 1790, and of Pompey, Onondaga Co., N. Y., in 1810. He settled in Sherman Hollow, in what is now Lafayette Township, Onondaga Co., in 1793, being one of the earliest settlers there. John Wilcox was the first white settler in the town, in 1791, and Comfort Rounds the second, in 1792. The Onondaga County records show that in 1799 Lot No. 75 in Pompey was granted to Solomon Owen and Lois his wife. The land records of Sharon, Conn., show that in 1806 Solomon Owen and Nathaniel Owen (son of Oliver), heirs of Jonathan Owen, sold to Adonijah Morum their interest in 15 acres in Sharon owned by Jonathan Owen at the time of his death and not sold by the order of the Court of Probate by which his estate was settled, the deed being acknowledged before a justice of the peace of Onondaga County in 1809.

ix. SARAH, b. at Salisbury 16 May 1759 (recorded at Sharon). The Sharon probate records, in naming the children for whom their mother, Patience Owen, was appointed guardian on 11 Sept. 1759, name this one as Submit, born 16th of May last. She is recorded in the vital records of Sharon as Sarah.

23. ELEAZER⁴ OWEN (*Moses*,³ *Joseph*,² *John*¹) was born at Lebanon 24 Jan. 1720/1. He married at Ashford, 20 Feb. 1744, JERUSHA RUSS.

Children, born at Ashford:

i. JERUSHA,[5] b. 25 May 1745.
ii. ESTHER, b. 20 Feb. 1747.
iii. BATHSHEBA, b. 30 July 1748; m. 5 Apr. 1767 JOSEPH SHUMWAY.
iv. EBENEZER, b. 13 Feb. 1749/50; m. 1 June 1772 DEBORAH FULLER.

    Children, b. at Ashford:
    1. *James,*[6] b. 30 Oct. 1772; d. 3 Nov. 1775.
    2. *Esther,* b. 11 Feb. 1775.
    3. *James,* b. 14 Mar. 1777.
    4. *Ebenezer* (twin), } b. 26 Oct. 1778.
    5. *Nathaniel* (twin), }
    6. *Polly,* b. 26 Apr. 1781.
    7. *Miriam,* b. 5 Aug. 1782.
    8. *Sally,* b. 2 Aug. 1784.
    9. *Lucy,* b. 3 July 1786.
    10. *Almyra,* b. 30 Aug. 1788.
    11. *Ella,* b. 22 Nov. 1790.
    12. *Rainor,* b. 27 Aug. 1792.
    13. *Deborah,* b. 20 Mar. 1794.
    14. *Daniel,* b. 16 Jan. 1797.
    15. *William,* b. 15 Sept. 1800.

v. MARY, b. 13 Feb. 1752.
vi. MIRIAM, b. 15 May 1754.
vii. TIMOTHY, b. 10 Nov. 1756.
viii. DANIEL, b. 15 Jan. 1759.
ix. ELEAZER, b. 16 Apr. 1761; m. ABIGAIL ———.

    Children, b. at Ashford:
    1. *Ralph,*[6] b. 3 June 1785.
    2. *Betsey,* b. 11 Nov. 1786.
    3. *Leonard,* b. 6 Sept. 1788.
    4. *Willard,* b. 2 Nov. 1791.

x. PRISCILLA, b. 15 May 1763.
xi. JEMIMAH, b. 16 Aug. 1765.

24. TIMOTHY[4] OWEN (*Moses,*[3] *Joseph,*[2] *John*[1]) was born at Lebanon 18 Apr. 1731. He married KEZIAH ———.

Children, born at Ashford:

i. KEZIAH,[5] b. 23 Mar. 1761; m. 23 Nov. 1786 GIDEON WOOD.
ii. HULDA, b. 8 Apr. 1763; d. 18 Apr. 1763.
iii. HANNAH, b. 30 Aug. 1765; m. 13 Jan. 1789 SAMUEL RUSS.
iv. AMASA, b. 12 Aug. 1766; m. 1 June 1794 ELIZABETH DANA, daughter of Jedida Dana of Ashford.

    Children, b. at Mansfield:
    1. *William Dana,*[6] b. 6 Jan. 1795.
    2. *Lucy,* b. 8 Oct. 1796; d. 25 May 1799.
    3. *Timothy,* b. 11 Mar. 1799.
    4. *Hiram,* b. 1 Apr. 1801.
    5. *Roderick,* b. 24 May 1803.
    6. *Jedidah,* b. 28 May 1805.
    7. *Maria,* b. 10 Mar. 1808.

25. ELIJAH[4] OWEN (*Elijah,*[3] *Isaac,*[2] *John*[1]) was born at Windsor in 1738/9. He married, 8 Mar. 1762, LYDIA CLARK, who died at Lee, Mass., 28 Nov. 1838, aged 95, daughter of Joel Clark and granddaughter of Samuel Clark and his wife Abigail, who was a daughter of Josiah[2] Owen. (Cf. 2, iv, 1.)

In her will, made at Otis, Berkshire Co., Mass., in 1835 and proved in 1839, Lydia (Clark) Owen names her son Elijah Owen, his wife Hannah, and their son Harvey, the heirs of her deceased daughter Lydia Adams, her daughter Hannah Sutliff, the heirs of her late sons Shem and Silas Owen, and her sons Daniel, Erastus, Joseph, Pelatiah, Joel, and Oliver.

Children, born at Windsor:

i. ELIJAH,⁵ b. 17 Apr. 1763; d. at Lee, Mass., 12 May 1842; m. HAN-NAH MATHER, who d. at Lee 9 Jan. 1842, aged 76, daughter of Nathaniel Mather.
    Children:
    1. *Harvey*,⁶ named in his grandmother's will.
    2. *Elijah*, b. at East Otis, Mass.; d. in New York; m. Sarah Hunter. They had Henry,⁷* b. in 1791, Elijah,† b. in 1810, and probably other children.
ii. SHEM, b. 9 Nov. 1764.
iii. SILAS, b. 11 Oct. 1766.
iv. DANIEL, b. 15 Dec. 1768.
v. ERASTUS, b. 1 Jan. 1771.
vi. LYDIA, b. 9 Apr. 1773; m. ——— ADAMS.
vii. HANNAH, b. 11 Feb. 1775; m. ——— SUTLIFF.
viii. OLIVER, b. 24 Apr. 1777; bapt. in 1777 (East Granby church records).
ix. JOSEPH, b. 21 June 1779; bapt. in 1779 (*ib.*).
x. PELATIAH, b. 10 Dec. 1781; bapt. in 1782 (*ib.*).
xi. JOEL, b. 6 Sept. 1785; bapt. in 1785 (*ib.*).

26. ASAHEL⁵ OWEN (*Asahel*,⁴ *Josiah*,³ *Josiah*,² *John*¹) was born at Bolton 25 July 1726. He married at Windsor, in 1752, DE-BORAH DRAKE, both being then of Windsor.

The probate records for the Hartford District show that on 2 June 1741 Asahel Owen, a minor, aged 15, son of Asahel Owen, late of Sheffield, Mass., chose Maj. William Pitkin to be his guardian.

Children:

i. ASAHEL,⁶ b. at Windsor 11 Oct. 1752; m. at Westfield, Mass., 6 May 1781, ANNA PERKINS.
    Children, b. at Westfield:
    1. *Cheney*,⁷ b. 8 Apr. 1782.
    2. *Clarissa*, b. 27 July 1783.
    3. *Orilla*, b. 6 May 1785.
    4. *Anna*, b. 24 Apr. 1787.
    5. *Chauncey*, b. 14 Mar. 1789.
    6. *Jason*, b. 8 Jan. 1792.
    7. *Nancy*, b. 8 May 1795.
    8. *Asahel*, b. 25 June 1798.
    9. *Julia*, b. 7 July 1801.
ii. ABIJAH, b. at Windsor 9 Apr. 1754; m. at Westfield, Mass., 25 Nov. 1784, MIRIAM BROOKS.
iii. CARMI, b. at Simsbury 9 Dec. 1755; m. at Westfield, Mass., 26 Aug. 1781, SARAH LINDSIE.
iv. DEBORAH, b. at Simsbury 26 Jan. 1759.
v. HANNAH, b. at Westfield, Mass., 25 July 1762.
vi. SARAH, b. at Westfield, Mass., 21 Aug. 1766.
vii. ABRAHAM, b. at Westfield, Mass., 30 Mar. 1769; m. at Westfield, 20 Feb. 1794, LUCRETIA LEE.
viii. RHODA, b. at Westfield 3 May 1772.

*Henry had children: Mary,⁸ Harvey, and William Henry.
†Elijah had children: Charles H.,⁸ George H., and Edward. The family of Charles Hunter Owen reside at Hartford, Conn.

27. EDWARD[5] OWEN (*Asahel,[4] Josiah,[3] Josiah,[2] John[1]*), born probably at Bolton, Conn., or at Sheffield, Mass. (cf. *supra*, No. 17), died prior to 14 Apr. 1787. He married at Sheffield, Mass., 2 Oct. 1759, ELIZABETH JOY (Sheffield records).*

He moved from Sheffield, Mass., to Pittsford, Vt., in 1774 (Caverly's History of Pittsford). The town records of Pittsford show that Edward Owen of Pittsford purchased 55 acres of land adjoining that of Joshua Woodward, part of the second division of the original right of David Oaks, 23 May 1776 (vol. 1, p. 135). The names of Edward Owen, Abdon Owen, and Abraham Owen appear in the published record of Vermont Revolutionary soldiers. Abdon Owen of Pittsford sold and conveyed, 14 Apr. 1787, to Josiah Eddy his equal part of the 55 acres of land which had been owned by his father, Edward Owen, deceased.

Children:

    i. REBECCA,[6] b. at Sheffield, Mass., 30 Mar. 1761.
    ii. ABDON, b. at Sheffield, Mass., 25 Nov. 1762; m. ———, and moved to Valley Falls, N. Y. (cf. Caverly's History of Pittsford, Vt., p. 717).
29. iii. ABRAHAM, b. at Sheffield, Mass., 26 July 1764.
    iv. AMASA. Caverly (History of Pittsford, p. 717) names a son of Edward, Amasa, who, he states, m. and moved to Troy, N. Y.
    v. URSULA, m. WILLIAM WARD of Pittsford.
    vi. THURSEY, m. ASBOND POLLEY, who was drowned 12 Apr. 1790 (Pittsford records).
        Child (surname *Polley*):
        1. *Ephraim*, b. at Pittsford 19 Jan. 1790.

28. AMASA[5] OWEN (*Jonathan,[4] Joseph,[3] Joseph,[2] John[1]*), born at Salisbury 10 Feb. 1753, died on a farm near Neville, Clermont Co., Ohio, in 1817, and was buried on the one acre of the farm set apart as a burial ground and reserved for that purpose when the farm was sold by his heirs in 1822. He married SARAH OSBORN, born at Salem, Westchester Co., N. Y., 13 June 1763 and baptized there 17 July 1763, second child of John and Eunice Osborn. Sarah (Osborn) Owen married secondly, 3 Jan. 1819, Solomon Dill of Clermont County, who died in 1820. After the marriage of her son Joseph Owen, who went to a farm nearby on Bear Creek, she made her home with him. Her name appeared on the tax rolls of Clermont County until 1846, which was probably the date of her death. She was buried by the side of her first husband, in the burying ground on the farm which had been their home.†

---

*According to Caverly's History of Pittsford, Vt., p. 47, Edward Owen m. at Sheffield, Mass,. Elizabeth Torrey.

†The family tradition that the maiden name of Amasa Owen's wife was Sarah Osborn and that she came from New York State is confirmed by the Osborn family record in her mother's Bible, according to which Sarah Osborn was married to Amasa Owen; but the date of the marriage was not recorded, and the Osborn family appear to have had no further record of Sarah and her husband.

John Osborn, of the Osborn family of Ridgefield, Conn., and his wife Eunice, the parents of Amasa Owen's wife, lived at Salem, Westchester Co., N. Y., just across the line from Ridgefield. He died at Salem in 1782, leaving a widow and twelve children, who, within a few months after his death, moved to Mamakating Township, Ulster Co., N. Y., near the present site of Otisville,

Amasa Owen was left fatherless at the age of six, and his mother, Patience Owen, was appointed guardian for him and her other younger children. Later she moved to the Wyoming Valley (*vide supra*, p. 56). In 1770, when nearly seventeen years of age, he chose for his guardian Elijah Foster of Sharon. The published records of New York in the Revolution show that Jonathan Owen, Oliver Owen, Amasa Owen, Eleazer Owen, and Solomon Owen served in the Ulster County Militia, in the Second Regiment, under Col. James McCloughry, Maj. Moses Phillips, and Capt. Benjamin Vail and Capt. Abraham Cuddeback, and that Amasa Owen served also in the levies of New York under Col. Frederick Wassenfels. The published records of Connecticut in the Revolution do not appear to show that these brothers served from their native State. The information given above about Oliver Owen (22, iv) and Solomon Owen (22, viii) shows that they, who settled in Onondaga County, N. Y., about 1793, were the sons of Jonathan Owen of Salisbury, deceased, and that they came to Onondaga County from Mamakating Township, Ulster Co., N. Y., whence they had served in the Revolution. It therefore seems reasonable to assume that Jonathan, Amasa, and Eleazer Owen, who served in the same regiment, were their brothers. The records of the War Department, in the Adjutant General's office in Washington, show that Amasa Owen's service in the Second Regiment of the Ulster County Militia was during 1778 and 1779. The original manuscript roll (vol. 1, p. 139), in the State files at Albany, N. Y., shows his service in the levies of New York in 1781 under Lieutenant Colonel Wassenfels, Capt. Henry Brewster, Lieut. Charles Stewart, and Lieut. George Harsen.

In the United States Census of 1790 are found the names of Jonathan and Joseph Owen in Cannon Township, Columbia Co., N. Y., Jonathan Owen and Jonathan Owen, Jr., in Walkill Township, Ulster Co., N. Y., Oliver and Solomon Owen in Mamakating Township, Ulster Co., N. Y., William Owen in New Cornwall Township, Orange Co., N. Y., Jonathan Owen in Clinton Township, Dutchess Co., N. Y., and Jonathan Owen in Philipstown, Dutchess Co., N. Y.

In the Old Records Division of the Adjutant General's office, in Washington, was found the payroll of Paymaster Daniel Britt, for the troops of the United States in the Western Department from 1 Jan. to 31 Dec. 1790, the roll of the First Regiment, under Lieut. Col. Josiah Harmar, containing the

in what is now Orange County, N. Y. A list of their children, with their birth dates, is contained in the records of the South Salem Presbyterian Church.

This John Osborn was a descendant of Capt. Richard Osborn, who sailed from London, 17 Feb. 1634, aged 22, in the ship *Hopewell*, bound for Barbados (Hotten's Original Lists, p. 39). In 1635 Richard Osborn was one of the company who met with Rev. Peter Hobart and drew for home lots in the settlement of Hingham, Mass. In the Pequot War in 1637 he was a volunteer from Windsor, and for service in that war the General Court at Hartford, 4 June 1639, granted to him 80 acres of land, which was set off by Peter Burr and another man in the town of Ridgefield.

names of 674 privates, in 12 companies. In Capt. Erkurius Beatty's company one of the 55 names enrolled was that of Amasa Owen, which was on the roll for the full twelve months, indicating that he had apparently enlisted prior to the first of the year and continued in the service after the close of the year. On the cover was written: "This Regiment of Infantry was in the Expedition against The Miami Indians in Sept. and Oct. 1790" (at Fort Washington). Much has been written as to the early settlements at Fort Harmar (Marietta), Fort Washington (Cincinnati), and along the Ohio Valley about this time, and of the forces under General Harmar who were engaged in defense of the settlers against the hostile Indians; but little has been found as to the personal history of those who filled the ranks. It seems, however, that this Amasa Owen is the one referred to above and in the following lines.

Amasa Owen was an early settler in Clermont County, Ohio (about thirty miles east of Cincinnati), where he was an elector in 1803 in Washington Township, in the first election of which the poll books were preserved. A family tradition is that he and his family came West from Pennsylvania, where his home was on Owen's Island, near Fort Pitt, from which he was driven by Indians. In 1806 he bought from John Obannon 101 acres of land near Neville, on what was then called Bear Creek, but is now known as Maple Creek, a little below and on the same side as McKendrie church, now the Longworth farm, being a part of Survey No. 834 for 700 acres, originally made to Alexander Parker 26 Dec. 1787.

In his will, proved in Aug. 1817, Amasa Owen names his wife Sarah, his sons Elijah, Daniel, Amasa, John, Jacob, and Joseph, and his daughters Delilah Gregg, Sarah Crosiar, and Eunice Owen.

Children:*

i.   SOLOMON,[6] b. 26 Nov. 1783; perhaps d. young, as he is not mentioned in his father's will.

ii.   ELIJAH, b. 18 Mar. 1785; died about 1837, when his estate was administered by his widow, Mary Owen; m. (1) in Pendleton County, Ky., 29 June 1811, POLLY HENDRICKS; m. (2) ANN ———, who joined with him in 1822 in conveying inherited land in Clermont County, Ohio; m. (3) in Campbell County, Ky., which until 1840 included Covington and what is now Kenton County (marriage bond dated 9 June 1827, with Platt Kennedy as bondsman), MARY HOLLAND, who survived him, widow of Ashiba Holland. On 8 June 1842 Mary Owen, late Mary Holland and widow of Ashiba Holland, and the latter's daughter, Elizabeth Holland, conveyed to John B. Casey Lot No. 154, on Scott Street, Covington, Ky. (Kenton County records).
       Children, probably by first wife:
       1. *Amasa*,[7] living 3 Jan. 1839; m. Polly ———. On 3 Jan. 1839 Amasa Owen and his wife Polly and James Owen and his wife Sarah conveyed to M. M. Benton property in Covington, Ky., which had been acquired 12 Jan. 1832 by

*The births of these children are recorded in the family Bible of Amasa Owen. *Vide infra*, pp. 69–70, Addendum.

701

Elijah Owen from Stephen Lancaster and which was described as property that had descended to the grantors as children and heirs at law of Elijah Owen, deceased.

    2. *James*, living 3 Jan. 1839; m. in Campbell County, Ky. (marriage bond dated 13 Nov. 1832, with Elijah Owen as bondsman), Sally E. Bright. (Cf. *supra*, 28, ii, 1.)

iii. DELILAH, b. 3 Oct. 1787; m. —— GREGG.

iv. POLLY, b. 3 Nov. 1789; perhaps d. young, as she is not mentioned in her father's will.

v. DANIEL, b. 10 Jan. 1791; living in La Salle County, Ill., in 1850; m. POLLY ——, who joined with him in 1822 in conveying inherited land in Clermont County, Ohio. He is apparently the Daniel Owen who appears in the United States Census of 1840 as head of a family in La Salle County, Ill., consisting of himself, aged 50 to 60, a male, aged 15 to 20, and two females, aged respectively 30 to 40 and 10 to 15. The Census of 1850 gives in La Salle County Amasa Owen, a native of Indiana, aged 30, and head of a family that included a wife, three children, and Daniel Owen, a native of Ohio, aged 61. In the United States Censuses of 1860, 1870, and 1880 this Amasa Owen and family who were in La Salle County, Ill., in 1850 are found in Brown County, Kans., but without the elder man, Daniel Owen. A grandson of Eunice (Owen) Holland (28, i, x), named Isaac Myers, who knew Amasa Owen of Brown County, Kans., states that he was of the family of Owens of Clermont County, Ohio. It is evident, therefore, from the data here assembled, that he was the son of Daniel Owen.

Child:

    1. *Amasa*,[7] b. in Indiana about 1820; living in Brown County, Kans., in 1880; m. Maria ——, b. in Indiana about 1826. Children: Daniel,[8] b. in Illinois in 1845, Eunice, b. in Illinois in 1849, Benjamin, b. in Illinois in 1855, George, b. in Kansas in 1858, Isaac, b. in Kansas in 1861, Alfred, b. in Kansas in 1863.

30. vi. AMASA, b. 26 Mar. 1793.

vii. JOHN, b. 3 Sept. 1795; probably the John Owen who m. in Clermont County, Ohio, 31 Dec. 1817 (Joseph Larkin, J.P., officiating), ANN JAMES (Clermont County records). His wife "Nance" joined him in 1822 in conveying inherited land in Clermont County.

viii. SARAH, b. 15 Feb. 1798; d. at Utica, La Salle Co., Ill., in 1871; m. 29 Jan. 1817 (Joseph Larkin, J.P., of Clermont County, Ohio, officiating) SIMON CROSIAR, b. near Pittsburgh, Pa., d. at Utica in Nov. 1846. He had migrated from Pennsylvania to Ohio in 1815, and with his family went from Clermont County, Ohio, to Illinois in 1819, settling finally in Utica. They were pioneers in that region, and the Crosiar family has since then been a prominent family in La Salle County.*

Children (surname *Crosiar*):

    1. *Amasa O.*, b. in Clermont County, Ohio, 12 Oct. 1817; m. (1) Sarah Brown; m. (2) 16 Oct. 1853 Lavinia Brown, b. at Crawford, Ind., in 1833, sister of his first wife. One daughter by first wife and at least nine children by second wife.†

---

*For a sketch of this family and for the early history of Utica see "The Past and Present of La Salle County, Illinois," pp. 333 and 457–460, published by H. F. Keer & Company in 1877, and also "History of La Salle County, Illinois," by Elmer Baldwin, 1877, pp. 354–360.

†Children of Amasa O. Crosiar: — Child by first wife: 1. Zulekiah, b. 16 Mar. 1852; m. Bedford Fisher, who d. in 1913 in California, whither they moved in 1907. A son, George Amasa Fisher, b. in 1879, lives at Los Angeles, Calif. Children by second wife: 2. Ella, b. 2 Sept. 1854; m. William E. Turner, who d. at Eugene, Oreg., 9 Apr. 1925. Children (surname *Turner*): Charles, b. in 1879, Lovina, b. in 1881, Albert, b. in 1883, Orville, b. in 1887, Annie, b. in 1890, Grace and

2. *Eli*, drowned in the Illinois River, while trying to rescue his
   sister Sarah (*vide infra*), who, with himself and his wife,
   was in a canoe. His sister also was drowned, but his wife
   was saved.
3. *Sarah*, drowned in the Illinois River (*vide supra*).
4. *Asa*, b. about 1835; d. in Brown County, Kans., whither he
   moved about 1868; m. at Utica, Ill., his first cousin,
   Louisa Holland (28, ix, 9), b. in Clermont County, Ohio,
   about 1839, d. in Brown County, Kans., daughter of
   Nathaniel and Eunice (Owen) Holland. They lived at
   Utica, Ill., until about 1868. Eight children.*
5. *William*, m. ———. His daughter, Catherine, m. George
   Lee and moved to Iowa.

ix. EUNICE, b. 26 Feb. 1800; d. at Utica, Ill., in 1867, and bur. there;
m. 19 July 1818 (Joseph Larkin, J.P., of Clermont County, Ohio,
officiating) NATHANIEL HOLLAND, who d. in Clermont County
and was bur. in McKendrie Cemetery. She, with her children,
moved to Utica, Ill., where they are found in the United States
Census of 1850.

Children (surname *Holland*), b. near Rural, Clermont Co.,
Ohio:
1. *Minerva*, b. in 1818; d. near Chilo, Clermont Co., Ohio, in
   1906; m. (1) Moses Clark, a Pennsylvanian who settled
   in Clermont County and d. there; m. (2) in Clermont
   County, in 1851, David Myers, widower, who had settled
   in Clermont County and d. near Chilo in 1895, son of Abe
   Myers of Pennsylvania. She and her second husband
   were bur. in the Odd Fellows Cemetery. After the death
   of her first husband she went about 1849, with her two
   young sons, to Utica, Ill., but soon returned to Clermont
   County, Ohio. In 1864 she and her second husband moved
   to Utica, but returned three years later to Clermont County,
   where they spent the rest of their lives. Two sons by first
   husband and four children by second husband.†

Leroy, b. in 1895. 3. Emma, b. 5 Sept. 1857; m. Joseph Kinzer; lived at Utica, Ill. Children
(surname *Kinzer*): Rawlin, b. in 1878, Ernest, b. in 1882, Jessie, b. in 1884, Ward, b. in 1887,
Dean, b. in 1889, Ethel, b. in 1890, Lawrence, b. in 1893, Lura, b. in 1895, Verna, b. in 1897.
4. Mary Louisa, b. 14 Sept. 1861; d. in 1891; m. Dr. K. W. Leland, who d. in 1920; lived at
Utica, Ill. A son, Pardon Leland, was b. in 1884. 5. William A., b. 17 Jan. 1865; d. in La Salle
County, Ill., where he was highly esteemed, in 1918; m. (1) Susie Conder, who, with their only
child, died when the child, a son, was in his 2d year; m. (2) Anna M. Warwick, who d. in 1921.
6. Annie Jane, of Ottawa, Ill., b. 21 Apr. 1867. 7. Olin Lewis, b. 29 June 1869; d. in 1885.
8. Olive Nancy, b. 9 Aug. 1871; d. in 1908; m. George G. Bower; lived at Galesburg, Ill. Chil-
dren (surname *Bower*): Helen, b. in 1896, Crosiar, b. in 1899. 9. Eli Ives, b. 29 Nov. 1873; m.
Mary Ogen; lives at the old Crosiar homestead. Children: Arthur, b. in 1895, Cecil, b. in 1898,
Ruth, b. in 1903, Earle, b. in 1910, Warren, b. in 1914. 10. Mattie A., b. 15 Jan. 1876; m. Dr.
Clarence J. Miner; lives at Gainesville, Ga. Children (surname *Miner*): Clarence, b. in 1895,
Olin, b. in 1897, Leonard, b. in 1906. Amasa O. Crosiar had other children by his second wife
who d. in infancy.
   *Children of Asa Crosiar, the first six b. at Utica, Ill.: — 1. Eva, b. about 1856; d. young.
2. Simon, b. about 1858; m. ———. No children. 3. Amasa, b. about 1860; d. in 1924; m. (1)
Rose Gordon; m. (2) Henrietta Owen, widow, of Cairo, Ill. Children by first wife: Lillie, Nettie,
Fae, Selma, Earle, William, John. Children by second wife: Gladys, Hazel, and perhaps Robert.
4. Frank (twin), b. about 1862. 5. Mary (twin), b. about 1862; m. ——— Gasson. She had
issue. 6. Hattie, b. about 1867; lives in Oklahoma. 7. Fred, b. about 1875; d. young. 8. Lillie,
d. young.
   †Children of Minerva (Holland) (Clark) Myers: — Children by first husband (surname *Clark*),
b. in Clermont County, Ohio: 1. William R., of Clermont County, b. in 1844 or 1845; d. at
Felicity, Clermont County, in Aug. 1915; m. 15 Oct. 1872 his first cousin once removed, Sarah
Owen (28, xi, 2), b. in Clermont County 19 Nov. 1836, d. at Felicity, Clermont Co., in Oct. 1915,
daughter of Joseph and Eliza Ann (Sargent) (Pigman) Owen. William R. Clark served in Co. K,
Fifty-ninth Ohio Regiment, in the Civil War, and lost an arm at Murfreesboro, Tenn. 2. Wallace,
b. in 1847; d. near Oakley, Thomas Co., Kans., in 1918; m. in 1868 Eliza Boggs of Utica, Ill.
They moved to Shelby County, Iowa, about 1884 or 1885, and thence to Thomas County, Kans.,
settling near Oakley, where the family now lives. Children: Kirt, b. about 1869, William, b. in
1871, Ira, b. in 1873, Nellie, b. in 1875, Edna, b. in 1877, Bowlin, b. in 1878. Children by second

703

2. *Warren.* He went South before the Civil War, and probably served in the Confederate Army.

3. *Augusta,* m. in Clermont County, Ohio, Simon Leach. They went by boat to Utica, Ill., and thence to Texas, where they were living when last heard from. One child at least, and probably other children.

4. *Ellen,* d. in Clermont County, Ohio, in 1862; m. James Carr. They lived in Clermont County. Eight children (surname *Carr*), viz., Alonzo, Greenberry, Ann, Mary, William, Bart, Lott, Marion.

5. *Amelia,* b. about 1827; d. at Council Bluffs, Iowa, in 1854; m. at Utica, Ill., James Kingsley. One son, Albert Kingsley, b. in 1854, who m. in 1878 Blanche Strobel and had three children, Alice, Nettie, and Ralph.

6. *Joseph,* b. about 1833; killed at Fort Donelson, Tenn., about 1862, while in the military service of the United States; m. at Utica, Ill., Lottie Crosiar, who m. (2) David Myers, son of David Myers (*vide supra*, 28, ix, 1) by his first wife, who after her death m. (2) Martha Owen (28, x, 2), *q.v.,* daughter of Jacob and Isabelle (Williams) Owen.

7. *Nathan,* b. about 1836; d. at Sabetha, Brown Co., Kans.; m. at Utica, Ill., Ellen Myers, daughter of David Myers (*vide supra*, 28, ix, 1) by his first wife. Children: Mary, b. in Illinois about 1868, Gustava, b. in Kansas about 1870, Low, b. in Nebraska about 1872.

8. *James Frank* (twin), b. about 1839; m. at Utica, Ill., Maggie Jones.

9. *Louisa* (twin), b. about 1839; d. in Brown County, Kans., whither she and her husband had moved about 1868; m. at Utica, Ill., her first cousin, Asa Crosiar (28, viii, 4), b. about 1835, d. in Brown County, Kans., son of Simon and Sarah (Owen) Crosiar. They lived at Utica, Ill., until about 1868. Eight children, for whom see *supra*, p. 64, first footnote.

10. *Mary,* b. about 1842; d. about 1912; m. (1) at Utica, Ill., John Crosiar, b. in Illinois about 1838, d. in Shelby County, Iowa, about 1892 or 1893, not of the family of the Simon Crosiar who m. Sarah Owen (28, viii) but of a related family; m. (2) ———; m. (3) ———. She and her first husband moved to Shelby County, Iowa, and the United States Census of 1880 lists there John Crosiar, b. in Illinois, aged 42, and Mary, his wife, b. in Ohio, aged 38. Children by first husband (surname *Crosiar*), b. in Illinois: Charles, b. about 1860, m. Louisa Smith, Joseph, b. about 1864, m. Emma Pitzer, Charlotte, b. about 1869, m. twice, William, b. about 1873, Everett, b. about 1877, m. ——— Glancy, Ethel, b. about 1879, Glen, m. Annie Lantz.

x. Jacob, b. 27 Sept. 1802; d. (it is believed) at Corning or Portsmouth, Iowa, about 1887 or 1888; m. Isabelle Williams, b. about 1806, d. probably in Adams County, Ohio. They moved to Adams County, where they lived until about 1862 or 1863. He returned to Clermont County, Ohio, and went thence a few years later, about 1866, to Utica, La Salle Co., Ill., and thence, after 1880, either to Corning or Portsmouth, Iowa.

husband (surname *Myers*), b. in Clermont County, Ohio: 3. Isaac, of Felicity, Clermont Co., Ohio, b. 9 June 1852; m. 8 Nov. 1916 Barbara (Cotes) Brush, widow, of St. Bernard, Ohio. For many years he was employed on steamboats on the Ohio and Mississippi Rivers. 4. James T., b. 21 Mar. 1854; d. in Clermont Co., Ohio, 2 Jan. 1916; m. (1) in 1877 Caroline Mackelfresh; m. (2) in 1904 Anna Strout. Children by first wife: Flora, Clell. 5. Charles A., b. in 1856; d. in 1873. 6. Emma E., of Hamilton, Ohio, b. in 1858; m. William Utter, who d. in 1903. Children (surname *Utter*): William, Edgar, Clifford, Maud, Clyde, Fred, May, Geneva, Grace, Gertrude, Blair.

Children, b. in Adams County, Ohio:
1. *Robert*,[7] b. about 1833; d. at Loveland, Ohio, about 1899; m. ———. Eight children, of whom only four, two sons and two daughters, are living. A son, Henry[8] Owen, b. about 1871, lives in Loveland and has two sons.
2. *Martha*, b. about 1835; living near Los Angeles, Calif., in 1904; m. at Utica, Ill., in Aug. 1867, as his second wife, David Myers, who d. in California, whose first wife was Lottie (Crosiar) Holland, widow of Joseph Holland (28, ix, 6). They went to Corning, Iowa, before her father, and moved from Corning about 1892 to California.
3. *Sarah*, b. about 1837; m. at Utica, Ill., Moses Woods, brother of Rebecca Woods, who m. Sarah Owen's brother, Joseph Owen (*vide infra*). They moved from Utica to Panama, Iowa. They had a son, Arley Woods.
4. *Harriet*, b. about 1839; d. in Iowa about 1898; m. at Corning, Iowa, William Crosiar, from whom she separated and went with her sister Martha to California.
5. *Charles*, b. about 1841; d. in 1866; bur. in McKendrie Cemetery, Clermont County, Ohio. He served in Co. K, Fifty-ninth Ohio Regiment, during the Civil War, from which he returned about 1865.
6. *Joseph*, b. about 1846; d. in California after 1880; m. at Utica, Ill., Rebecca Woods, b. about 1847, sister of Moses Woods, who m. his sister Sarah. He went from Clermont County, Ohio, to Utica, Ill., about 1865, a year before his father. He and his wife went to Shelby County, Iowa, after 1880, and thence to California. Ten children: Spencer,[8] Frank, Wilbur, Esther, and six others.

xi. JOSEPH, b. 29 Oct. 1804; d. 11 May 1879; m. in Clermont County, Ohio, 1 Oct. 1834, ELIZA ANN (SARGENT) PIGMAN, widow, b. 15 Feb. 1808, d. 31 Oct. 1885, daughter of Silas Sargent and sister of Griffith Sargent, who m. Sarah Holland (sister of the Nathaniel Holland who m. Eunice Owen, 28, ix). Two sons by her first marriage were Simpson and Joshua Pigman. Joseph Owen lived with his mother at the Owen homestead on Maple Creek, Clermont County, until he married. Then he lived on his wife's farm, nearby, on Bear Creek. His mother (Widow Dill) lived with them during the latter part of her life. He and his wife were bur. in the McKendrie Cemetery.
Children, b. in Clermont County:
1. *Malissa*,[7] b. 27 June 1835; d. 22 June 1896; m. Frank Frambers. They went to Spencer County, Ind., about 1865 and thence to Missouri. They had issue.
2. *Sarah*, b. 19 Nov. 1836; d. at Felicity, Clermont Co., Ohio, in Oct. 1915; m. 15 Oct. 1872 her first cousin once removed, William R. Clark of Clermont County, b. in 1844 or 1845, d. at Felicity in Aug. 1915, son of Moses and Minerva (Holland) Clark (28, ix, 1). They remained in Clermont County, and after her father's death her mother made her home with them.
3. *William C.*, b. 31 Mar. 1838; killed in the Battle of Murfreesboro, Tenn., 31 Dec. 1862, while serving in the Civil War in Co. A, Fifty-ninth Ohio Volunteer Infantry; bur. in McKendrie Cemetery.
4. *Frances Ellen* (or *Fanny*), b. 23 Dec. 1840; d. 27 Aug. 1909; m. in Clermont County, 27 Jan. 1862, Joseph Richards, b. about 1832. They lived in Indiana, and had children.
5. *Ida A.*, b. 13 Sept. 1843; d. at her father's home in Clermont County, 5 Sept. 1865; bur. in McKendrie Cemetery; m. James Abbott. They moved to Indiana. A son, William C. Abbott, lives at Chrisney, Spencer Co., Ind.

29. ABRAHAM[6] OWEN (*Edward*[5], *Asahel*,[4] *Josiah*,[3] *Josiah*,[2] *John*[1]), of Pittsford, Vt., born at Sheffield, Mass., 26 July 1764, died at Pittsford 14 Feb. 1813. He married at Pittsford, in Aug. 1796,* MRS. NELLIE BOGUE, who survived him, widow of William Bogue, whose son, William Bogue, Jr., was born at Cambridge, N. Y., 12 Nov. 1783.†

Children, born at Pittsford:†

i.   REBECCA,[7] b. 6 May 1787; d. at Brandon, Vt., in 1865; m. SAMUEL B. SMITH.

ii. ISAAC, b. 24 Oct. 1788; d. in Minnesota in 1871; m. ABIGAIL ROOT of Benson, Vt.

iii. ABRAHAM, of Pittsford, b. 19 July 1790; d. 5 May 1872; m. (1) MARY BUTLER, who d. ———; m. (2) 10 Mar. 1836 WEALTHY PALMER of Castleton, Vt.

Children by first wife:
1. *Mary Butler*,[8] b. 22 June 1814; m. Ebenezer B. Beach of Ferrisburgh, Vt.
2. *Laura*, b. 25 Dec. 1815; m. in 1838 James Palmer.
3. *Abraham*, b. 26 Oct. 1817; m. ———, and resided in Iowa.
4. *Hannah*, b. 5 Oct. 1829 [*sic* ? 1819]; m. Alphonso Newcomb.
5. *James Davie*, b. 17 Oct. 1824; d. in Ohio in 1851.

iv. AMASA, carpenter, b. 17 Apr. 1792; living in the West about 1872; m. in New Brunswick, in 1818, MARY McKEEL. He served in the War of 1812, the records of the War Department showing that Amasa Owen, carpenter, aged 20, b. at Pittsford, Vt., enlisted for five years, 8 July 1812, as a private in the Eleventh United States Infantry, and left the Army at Williamsburg 11 Nov. 1813. The facts are that, as a member of Captain Hawley's company, Colonel Clark's regiment, he was at Sackett's Harbor at the time of the British attack, 29 May 1813, and in the Battle of Williamsburg, 11 Nov. 1813, he was wounded in the thigh by a musket ball and was taken prisoner by the enemy. He was taken to Prescott, where his wound was dressed and he remained a short time in the hospital. Then he was taken to Montreal, and thence to Quebec and Halifax, and was confined in a prison on Melville Island. He escaped from prison, lived for some time in New Brunswick, where he married, and came back to Pittsford, with his family, in 1824. He remained there, however, but a short time, and about 1872 was living in the West. (Cf. Caverly's History of the Town of Pittsford, Vt., Rutland, 1872, p. 366.)

Children (Caverly's History of Pittsford, p. 717):
1. *Benajah*.[8]   3. *John*.   5. *Martha*.
2. *Eleanor Ann*.   4. *Joseph*.

v.   MILANDA, b. 6 Jan. 1794; d. in Pennsylvania in 1866; m. ETHAN P. EDDY.

vi. SABRINA, b. 27 Feb. 1800; d. in Wisconsin in 1865; m. ENOS PARDY.

vii. EMILY, b. 5 Jan. 1802; d. in childhood.

viii. JOHN, b. 12 Sept. 1803; m. LORINDA GILKEY. He moved to Brookfield Township, Tioga Co., Pa.

Children, b. at Pittsford, Vt.:
1. *Laura Ann*,[8] b. 17 June 1827.
2. *Maria*.
3. *Sabrina*, b. 10 Mar. 1829; m. William George.
4. *John*, b. 4 Apr. 1831; d. in Pennsylvania 1 Mar. 1894; m. (1) Maria Outman; m. (2) Helen Foote, who d. in 1895. He migrated to Pennsylvania when he was young. Child

*Probably an error (in the records) for 1786.
†For Abraham Owen's dwelling places in Pittsford see Caverly's History of Pittsford, Vt., pp. 214–215. For his children, cf. Caverly, p. 717.

by first wife: Maria,[9] b. in 1857. Children by second wife: Zelma, b. in 1860, Martha, b. in 1863, Myra, b. in 1869, Bert, b. in 1877.

ix. JAMES, b. 19 Sept. 1805; m. ———. He resided in Pennsylvania.

30. AMASA[6] OWEN (*Amasa*,[5] *Jonathan*,[4] *Joseph*,[3] *Joseph*,[2] *John*[1]), born 26 Mar. 1793, died at Stepstone, Pendleton Co., Ky., 16 Dec. 1869, and was buried in Linden Grove Cemetery, Covington, Ky. He married first, in Clermont County, Ohio, 26 Nov. 1812, SALLY BUTLER, who was living in 1822, when she joined with her husband in conveying land in Clermont County; and lastly,* at Covington, Ky., 28 July 1832, JANE (BODWELL) DEARY, widow, who died 30 Nov. 1874 and was buried at Flag Spring, Campbell Co., Ky., near Stepstone, daughter of Joshua Bodwell.†

In the United States Census of 1820 Amasa Owen appears as head of a family in Washington Township, Clermont Co., Ohio, with a wife aged 26 to 45, and one male and four female children under 10 years of age. His name is found on the tax lists of Clermont County in 1826 and 1827; and soon afterwards he probably settled in Covington, Ky., where for many years he was superintendent of the ferries between Cincinnati and Covington, which were owned and operated by Platt Kennedy. In a Covington directory of 1840 and in the United States Census of 1850 he is recorded as a native of Kentucky [*sic*]. In 1853 he moved, with his family, to Foster's Landing on the Ohio River, in Bracken County, Ky.; and a year or two later he settled on a farm a few miles below, at Stepstone, Ky., on the Ohio River.

Children by first wife, born in Clermont County, Ohio:

i. WASHINGTON.[7] When a young man he migrated to the Territory of Nebraska, and took up a land claim there. His half brother, Orvil Ives Owen, who went with him, soon returned to Kentucky. It is believed that Washington Owen went from Nebraska to the Territory of Washington, and thereafter nothing more was heard from him by his family.

ii. LOUISA, b. 6 Jan. 1822; d. in Clermont County, Ohio, 18 Oct. 1887; m. ELIJAH MARRIOTT, who m. (2) in 1890 Allina Downing and d. in Clermont County 10 July 1902. Louisa Owen was reared in the home of Joseph Larkin of Clermont County. She and her husband lived in Clermont County and were bur. in McKendrie Cemetery.

Children (surname *Marriott*), b. in Clermont County:

1. *Edward L.*, b. in 1844; d. at Stone River, Tenn., in 1863, while serving in the Civil War in the Fifty-third Kentucky Regiment.

2. *Joseph S.*, b. about 1846; d. in 1896; m. 20 Dec. 1866 Malinda Prather. They had a son, Edwin Marriott.

3. *Isaac Franklin*, b. about 1848; d. 11 Jan. 1902; m. Elizabeth McKee. Children: Charles, Hubert, Cora, Grace.

4. *George*, b. about 1850; living in Indiana; m. Laura Slater.

*There is a tradition that Amasa Owen had more than two wives.
†This Joshua Bodwell was born at Methuen, Mass., about 1765, settled at Marietta, Ohio, about 1790, and died at Covington, Ky., in 1837. He was a descendant of Henry Bodwell of Essex County, Mass., a soldier in King Philip's War, who was wounded in the Battle of Bloody Brook and who died 1 June 1745, in his 94th year.

5. *Sarah Ellen*, b. 8 Nov. 1851; d. 23 June 1852.
6. *Charles*, living at Santa Maria, Calif.; m. ———.
7. *Anna*, now deceased; m. Joseph McBeth.
8. *Will Clark*, living at Santa Maria, Calif.; m. Adda Heiser. Children: Earl, Oliver.
9. *Walter Scott*, b. about 1860; living at Indianapolis, Ind.; m. Georgie Daughters. Child: Elsie. Probably other children.

Children by last wife, born at Covington, Ky.:

iii. ORVIL IVES, b. 2 June 1833; d. unm. at the home of his brother in Pendleton County, Ky., 3 Nov. 1909; bur. in Mount Auburn Cemetery, in Pendleton County, Ky.

iv. EMMA AMELIA, b. 27 Oct. 1836; d. at the home of her son in Jacksonville, Fla., 14 May 1910; bur. in Jacksonville; m. 24 Feb. 1858 JOHN W. DIGGINS, who d. in Florida 10 Dec. 1883. They lived many years at Covington, Ky.

Children (surname *Diggins*), b. at Covington:

1. *Walter Leroy*, b. 20 Apr. 1859; d. at Jacksonville, Fla., 30 Jan. 1914; bur. at Jacksonville; m. (1) in 1882 May Tennant, from whom he was separated; m. (2) Jennie Amelia White. He lived for many years at Covington, and then settled at Jacksonville. Child by first wife: William, b. at Covington.

2. *Emma Jane*, b. 18 June 1862; living at Lockland, Ohio; m. 8 Dec. 1892 Harry Wood. Child (surname *Wood*): Ethel Amelia, b. 25 Sept. 1894.

v. EUNICE ROWENA, b. 7 July 1838; d. 24 Jan. 1848; bur. in Linden Grove Cemetery, Covington.

vi. ROBERT WALLACE, b. 16 Feb. 1841; d. at Falmouth, Pendleton Co., Ky., 13 Jan. 1925; m. 3 Jan. 1871 THERESA MAINS, b. in Pendleton County 11 Feb. 1843, d. at Falmouth 6 Aug. 1922, daughter of Peter and Catherine Mains of Pendleton County. Both were bur. in Riverside Cemetery, Falmouth. They lived at Stepstone, Pendleton Co., until 1885, and then at Pleasant Hill in the same county until 1917, when they moved to Falmouth.

Children, b. at Stepstone:

1. *Albert Perley*,[8] of Washington, D. C., b. 6 May 1874; m. 19 Oct. 1904 Sarah Abigail Ellis, b. 6 Oct. 1881.

2. *William Arthur*, b. 9 Jan. 1876; living unm. in New York City. He is the compiler of this genealogy.

3. *Nellie*, b. 1 Nov. 1879; m. 30 May 1905 Archibald Thomas Shafer, b. 31 Jan. 1882. They live at Falmouth, Ky. Child (surname *Shafer*): William Albert, b. 12 Aug. 1909.

ADDENDUM

RECORDS IN THE FAMILY BIBLE OF AMASA[5] OWEN OF CLERMONT COUNTY, OHIO*

Lemul Barrett the Sun of Lemul Barrett and Mary his wife was Born March the–3–7–1793 and Dide Novembor the 10th Dy 1793
Lamel Barrett†

Vide supra, p. 60, No. 28.
†No explanation has been found for the presence here of the record of Lemuel Barrett. A Barrett genealogy accounts for one Lemuel, who was born at Littleton, Mass., in 1726. In 1763 Capt. Lemuel Barrett was granted some land at Brownsville, Pa., by the military commander at Fort Pitt, which he held until 1783. He was captain of an independent company in Maryland during the Revolution, and went soon after the War to Harrison County, Ky., which is not far from Clermont County, Ohio. There he died about 1802. His wife's name was Mary, which was also the name of a sister of Amasa Owen (22, iii), born at Salisbury, Conn., 16 Apr. 1745, of whom no further record has been found.

The birth of the Children of Amasa Owen and Sarah his wife and as follows
   to wit

> Solomon was born Nov 26 1783
> Elijah was born 18 March 1785
> Delilah was born 3 October 1787
> Polly was born 3d Novenber 1789
> Daniel was born 10 January 1791
> Amasa was born 26th of March 1793
> John was born 3 September 1795
> Sally was born 15 February 1798
> Eunice was born 26 February 1800
> Jacob was born 27 September 1802
> Joseph was born 29 October 1804

DESCENDANTS OF JOHN OWEN: ADDITIONAL RECORDS.—In an article entitled "John Owen of Winsor, Conn., and Some of His Descendants," contributed to the REGISTER of January 1929 (vol. 83, pp. 39–70), the date of birth only of Timothy[5] Owen (No. 23, vii) is given. The following records add much to the genealogical information about him and some of his descendants.

1. TIMOTHY[5] OWEN (*Eleazer,[4] Moses,[3] Joseph,[2] John[1]*), born at Ashford, Conn., 10 Nov. 1756, died at Hanover, N. H., 24 Aug. 1837, aged 80 years, and was buried in Center Cemetery. He married at Hanover, 11 Sept. 1785, LYDIA PERRY, born about 1767, died 20 Aug. 1816, aged 49 years.

Timothy Owen moved to Enfield, N. H., by 1777. While living there he joined Col. Jonathan Chase's regiment, which "went and reinforced the northern Continental Army at Ticonderoga by Maj. Gen. Folsom's orders." He was discharged 18 June 1777.

In 1784 he moved to Hanover. The "History of Dartmouth College and Hanover, N. H.," by Frederick Chase, p. 377, states: "in Capt. Hendee's Co. of Col. Chase's regiment a number of Hanover men were recognized, and also Timothy Owen . . . who moved to Hanover soon after."

   Children, born at Hanover:

2. i. IRA,[6] b. 16 Aug. 1787.
   ii. TIMOTHY, b. 13 Aug. 1789; d. at Hanover 13 Jan. 1845. Seven children.
   iii. DANIEL, b. 15 Jan. 1791; d. 5 Nov. 1791.
   iv. DANIEL PERRY, b. 26 Aug. 1796.
   v. MINER, b. 6 Apr. 1799; d. 18 Aug. 1800.
   vi. LYDIA, b. 27 July 1801.
   vii. ESTHER, b. 22 Nov. 1805; d. 11 May 1836; m. 8 Apr. 1828 ULYSSES Dow of Hanover.

2. IRA[6] OWEN (*Timothy[5]*), of Montpelier, Vt., civil engineer, born at Hanover, N. H., 16 Aug. 1787, died at Montpelier 27 Oct. 1836 and was buried in Elm Street Cemetery, where his grave is marked as a veteran of the War of 1812. He married (Rev. David Selden officiating) at Middle Haddam, Conn., 19 Jan. 1814, HARRIET MURICH DOANE, born at Middle Haddam in 1793, died at Rutland, Vt., in 1886, aged 93 years, daughter of Nathaniel and Prudence (Smith) Doane.

Ira Owen was a corporal in September 1814 in Capt. Timothy Hubbard's company, Montpelier Volunteers, for the relief of Plattsburg.

He was elected a director of the Vermont Railway Association on 22 Feb. 1830, and was one of the committee which disbanded the Aurora Lodge of Masons in 1834.

   Child, b. at Montpelier:

3. i. WILLIAM HENRY BRADFORD, b. 2 Nov. 1819.

3. WILLIAM HENRY BRADFORD[7] OWEN (*Ira,[6] Timothy[5]*), of Rutland, Vt., mer-

*Pages 678-709, this volume.

chant, born at Montpelier 2 Nov. 1819, died at Rutland 15 Aug. 1890. He married (Rev. John A. Hicks, D.D., officiating) at Rutland, 7 July 1847, MARY ELIZABETH HODGES, who died at Rutland 6 May 1883, daughter of Hon. George Tisdale and Emily (Bliss) Hodges.

Children, born at Rutland:

i. GEORGE HODGES,[3] A.B. (Middlebury, 1870), A.M. (*ib.*, 1873), lawyer, United States consul at Messina, Italy, 1875–1885, for many years secretary of The Navy League, author of short stories in the *New York Evening Post,* b. 6 Aug. 1848; d. at Towson, Baltimore Co., Md., 24 May 1917; m. at the United States consulate, Frankfort, Germany, 3 Jan. 1876, LOUISE E. BRAUN, who d. at New Haven, Conn., 5 Feb. 1932, aged 81 years, daughter of Dr. Gustavus Braun of Hesse-Nassau.

Children, b. at Messina, Italy:

1. *Mary Elizabeth Hodges,*[9] b. 7 Oct. 1876.
2. *Hans Christian,* A.B. (Trinity, 1899), a soldier in the First Connecticut Volunteer Infantry in the Spanish-American War, 1898, a captain in the United States Army in the World War, b. 13 Mar. 1878; m. in New York City, 15 Sept. 1905, Christine Towne Stocker of Newburgh, N. Y. Children: (1) Hans Christian, A.B. (Trinity, 1930), b. at Newburgh 11 Nov. 1906. (2) Josephine, b. at Newburgh 4 Apr. 1909; m. in Paris, France, 6 Sept. 1929, William MacNeil Rodewald, Jr., of New York City. Children (surname *Rodewald*) 1. Loraine Bliss, b. in New York City 4 July 1930. 2. William MacNeil, III, b. in New York City 15 Dec. 1931.
3. *William Henry,* b. 25 Oct. 1879; d. at Nice, France, 21 Jan. 1929.
4. *Margaret,* b. 16 Sept. 1882; m. in May 1927 Bosley Hiss of Baltimore, Md.

ii. EMILY BLISS, b. 21 June 1852; m. at Messina CARL F. BRAUN; d. in New York City 11 Apr. 1900.

iii. WILLIAM DOANE, b. 19 Aug. 1854; d. in Florida in 1918; m. in Chicago, Ill., 30 Oct. 1879, CARRIE CHARLESTON.

iv. JAMES HODGES, b. 11 Jan. 1857; d. in New York City 16 Mar. 1916.

v. MIRRIAM LORAINE, b. 19 Jan. 1854; d. at Rutland 24 Jan. 1864.

New Haven, Conn.   H. C. OWEN.

———

DESCENDANTS OF JOHN OWEN: ADDITIONAL RECORDS.—In a note entitled "Descendants of John Owen: Additional Records," contributed to the REGISTER of July 1935 (*supra,* pp. 288–289) by H. C. Owen, one line only of the * children of Timothy[5] Owen is carried forward. The following records supply much genealogical information about three more of the children of Timothy[6] Owen.

TIMOTHY[6] OWEN (*Timothy[5]*), of Hanover, N. H., inspector of schools for many years, born at Hanover 13 Aug. 1789, died there 13 Jan. 1845. He married SARAH INGALLS, who died 11 June 1882, aged 93 years, daughter of Luther Ingalls of Pomfret, Conn.

Children, b. at Hanover:

i. ZAPHIRA,[7] b. 29 May 1815; d. *s. p* in June 1840; m. as his first wife, 16 Feb. 1840, JESSE MILTON COBURN.

ii. JULIUS LAWRENCE, b. 13 Mar. 1817. The United States Census of 1860 shows him and his wife Affiah living at Hanover with the following named children, Zaphira, aged 10, Charles, aged 7, and Laura, aged 3.

iii. LUCY ANN, b. 25 Sept. 1818; d. unm. 11 July 1863.

*Pages 709-710, this volume.

iv. FREDERICK LANGDON, b. 1 Oct. 1821; d. 7 Aug. 1891; m. (1) REBECCA CHANDLER, b. in 1823, d. in 1855; m. (2) in 1858 EMMELINE E. INGALLS.

Children by first wife:
1. *Timothy,* [6] b. 28 Mar. 1847; m. at Hanover, in 1871, Nancy J. Coburn. Children: (1) Florence L., b. 6 Feb. 1872. (2) Alice M., b. 15 June 1873. (3) Frederick L., b. 15 Mar. 1875. (4) Emily D., b. 19 July .1876. (5) Coburn S., b. 12 Oct. 1877.
2. *Millard Fillmore,* b. 16 Sept. 1850; d. in March 1861.
3. *Emily,* b. 1 Sept. 1852; m. 1 May 1881 Wilbur H. Power, lawyer, of Boston.
4. *Frederick,* of Canton, Mass., high school principal, b. 27 July 1854; m. 28 Dec. 1881 Emma Bense of Canton.

v. SARAH INGALLS, b. 21 Sept. 1824; m. at Hanover, 25 Nov. 1856, ELIAS COBURN of Manchester, Mass.

Children (surname *Coburn*):
1. *Sarah Daisy.*   2. *Katherine Theodosia.*

vi. LYDIA PERRY, b. 6 July 1826; d. in 1869; m., as his third wife, JESSE MILTON COBURN.

Children (surname *Coburn*):
1. *William Plummer,* b. 21 Jan. 1859.
2. *Owen Saunders,* b. 24 Feb. 1863.

vii. TIMOTHY, a student in 1844 at Kimball Union Academy, b. in 1828; d. young.

DANIEL PERRY[6] OWEN (*Timothy*[5]), born at Hanover 26 Aug. 1796, died 15 Mar. 1849. He married, 29 May 1821, MINERVA DOWE, d. 27 Oct. 1887, aged 87 years.

Children, born at Hanover:
i. DANIEL PERRY, a student at Dartmouth, 1845–47.
ii. LEMUEL DOWE, b. 8 Sept. 1824; m. MARY FRANCES BRIDGEMAN and removel to Chicago.
iii. FRANKLIN DODGE, b. 27 Sept. 1832; d. 23 Jan. 1896.

ESTHER[6] OWEN (*Timothy*[5]), born at Hanover 22 Nov. 1805, died 11 May 1836. She married, 8 Apr. 1828, HON. ULYSSES DOWE.

Children (surname *Dowe*):
i. CHARLES, a soldier in the Civil War, b. 4 Dec. 1828; m. 20 Oct. 1853 VINA HALL ROSS.
ii. ELLEN ESTHER, b. 15 Mar. 1832; m. 14 Sept. 1854 ORLANDO CULLEN BLACKMER of Barnard, Vt., and Oak Park, Chicago, Ill.

New Haven, Conn.   H. C. OWEN.

ISAAC OWEN OF HEBRON, CONN.,
AND
SOME OF HIS DESCENDANTS

By Mrs. CLIFFORD J. HUYCK of West Brookfield, Mass.

IN the REGISTER for January 1929 (vol. 83, pp. 39–70) appeared *
an article entitled "John Owen of Windsor, Conn., and Some of His
Descendants," by William Arthur Owen of New York City.

The following article concerns Isaac⁴ Owen (No. 8, vi.) and some
of his descendants.

1. ISAAC⁴ OWEN (*Josiah,³ Josiah,² John¹*), of Hebron, Conn.,
born 28 July 1710 (Hebron records), died at Hebron 30 May 1761.
He married, 20 July 1738, REBECCA TILDEN, born 7 Mar. 1716/17,
daughter of Isaac and Rebecca (Mann) Tilden.

In his will, dated 27 May 1761, Isaac Owen named his dearly beloved wife Rebecca, and his children, Elijah, Abel, Elizabeth, Jonathan, John, and Isaac. The inventory of his estate was made 13 June
1761, the allotment to the heirs was allowed on 23 Dec. 1762, and
the distribution of his estate was made 6 Mar. 1763.

On 4 Apr. 1763 Eliphalet Case, husband of Martha Owen (a sister
of Isaac), was made guardian of Jonathan, John, and Isaac Owen,
the three minor sons of Isaac⁴ Owen. Amos Owen (a brother of
Isaac) became bondsman for Eliphalet Case. (Probate Records at
the State Library at Hartford, Conn.) On 1 Apr. 1773 Eliphalet
Case was acquitted as guardian of the three children and Amos⁴
Owen, brother of Isaac Owen, took the bond and care and trust
into his own hands (*op. cit.*).

"To the Honorable Joseph Spencer, Judge of the Court of Probate
for the district of East Haddam; Sir: This may inform you that
Eliphalet Case was appointed guardian over the three sons of Isaac

*Pages 678-709, this volume.

Owen, viz: Jonathan, John and Isaac Owen, in the year 1763 and continued faithfully therein until the year 1773, at which time I took the bond into my hand and acquitted the said Case of the trust, and so promise to pay said Case whatever your honor shall find to be his due. [Signed] Amos Owen. May 29, 1775" (*op. cit.*).

Children, born at Hebron:

    i.   ELIJAH,[5] b. 24 Feb. 1739/40; m. 21 Oct. 1762 DEBORAH HOLDRIDGE of Hebron.

          Elijah Owen, with his brothers Abel and Jonathan, settled at King's District, later Canaan, Albany Co., N. Y.,* where he bought the Erastus Rowley farm.

          Children:
          1. *Hannah*,[6] b. 18 June 1763.
          2. *Elijah*, m. Mehitable Nash. Child: (1) Augustus Holdridge,[7] b. at Lennox, Madison County.

2. ii.   ABEL, b. 3 Apr. 1743.
    iii.   ELIZABETH, b. 6 Sept. 1749.
3. iv.   JONATHAN, b. 9 July 1755.
    v.   JOHN, b. 22 Jan. 1758.

          "To the Honorable Joseph Spencer, Esquire, Judge of the Court of Probate, for the District of East Haddam, this may certify that John Owen, a minor, in the 16th year of his age, son of late Isaac Owen, of Hebron, deceased, personally appeared this day before me the Subscriber for Hartford County, and made choice of his brother, Elijah Owen of King's District in the County of Albany, for his guardian. Dated Hebron, Oct. 4, 1773. John Phelps, Justice of Peace." (Probate Records at the State Library at Hartford, Conn.)

    vi.   ISAAC, a soldier in the Revolution, b. 15 Nov. 1760.

          On 17 Feb. 1775 Isaac Tilden was bonded in the sum of £200, English money, and was elected guardian of Isaac Owen, a minor, of the town of Hebron, to make a true account of guardianship to ward, when arrived at full age, then this above obligation to be void. [Signed] Isaac Tilden, Richmond, Berkshire Co. Massachusetts; Elijah Buel of Colchester. (Probate Records at the State Library at Hartford, Conn.)

2. ABEL[5] OWEN (*Isaac*,[4]), born at Hebron, Conn., 3 Apr. 1743, died in Cortland County 25 July 1827, aged 84 years. He married first, possibly at Old Canaan, Berkshire Co., Mass., about 1766, ———, who was living in 1777 and probably died at New Lebanon; and secondly, ELIZABETH ABBOTT of Stephentown, daughter of Nathan and Hulda Abbott.

Abel Owen was living at New Canaan, Albany County, as early as 1 Oct. 1777, when Isaac Preston of New Canaan sold for £31 to "Jonathan Owen and Abel Owen of the same County, town and provence" a lot of land. About 1784 Abel Owen sold his share in this lot to his brother Jonathan and went to Stephentown.

Abel Owen served in the Revolution as a soldier "in the Line, 2nd Regiment, Col. Phillip Van Cortland, General Stephen Van Renssalaer." (New York in the Revolution, p. 36.)

*All places mentioned in this genealogy are situated within the present limits of the State of New York, unless another State or region is indicated in the text or may be easily inferred from the context.

Soon after the close of the [Revolutionary] war, Abel Owen, a Revolutionary soldier [then living in New Lebanon] received 200 acres of land in Stephentown from General Stephen Van Renssalaer as an inducement to settle there. (See History of Renssalaer County, p. 547.) He went to Grafton, built a home, and moved his family there.

"Abel Owen, a Revolutionary soldier, is belived to have been the first settler in Grafton." (Landmarks of Renssalaer County, p. 562.)

On 19 Feb. 1790 Abel Owen of Stephentown bought from Matthew Vischer of Albany for £25 lot 76, consisting of 600 acres, in the town of Pompey (then in Herkimer County), a part of the "Military Tract." It was on this land that Solomon Owen, son of Abel Owen, settled the next year.

According to the 1790 Census it is evident that Abel Owen was living at Stephentown in 1790 and that his family consisted of himself, his two oldest sons Solomon and Lewis, both over 16, his daughter Lucy, his son Roderick (under 16), children by his first wife; also his second wife, Elizabeth, whom he had probably married at Stephentown about 1784, and their three children, Hannah Maria, Anna, and Almond, all born at Stephentown. Charlotte his oldest daughter had been married to Ebenezer Hill, Jr., of Grafton, and was living with her family near her father, Abel Owen.

Abel Owen occupied his farm until about 1795, when he sold his place to Lemuel Steward, Esq., and with the rest of the Owens removed to Lysander, Onondaga Co., and settled on a lot which was awarded to him as a Revolutionary soldier. (See History of Renssalaer County, p. 547.)

The Abel Owen home in Grafton is now (1935) Mountain Top House, owned by Mr. and Mrs. J. W. Moon, on the road between Petersburg and Troy. The History of Renssalaer County states: "Abel Owen, being a somewhat prominent citizen, the old road running from Petersburg to Grafton is called in all the old leases 'Owen Road.' It is now a part of the Taconic Trail."

The will of Abel Owen, dated 16 Feb. 1827, mentions "my three children by my present wife, that is to say, Anna Owen, Almond Owen, and Hannah Maria Owen," "my four children, Solomon Owen, Roderick Owen, Charlotte Hill, the wife of Ebenezer Hill, and Lucy Demmon, the wife of Jason Demmon," "my wife Elizabeth" and "Eunice Weld, the daughter of my last wife."

Children by first wife:

i.   CHARLOTTE,[o] b. 31 Oct. 1767; d. at Lafayette 1 July 1830; m. at New Lebanon or Grafton, about 1784, EBENEZER HILL, of Grafton and Pompey, 1795, b. 30 Mar. 1768, d. at Lafayette 15 Oct. 1849.
     Children (surname *Hill*):
     1. *Sally,* b. in 1787; d. in 1829.

2. *Ebenezer,* b. in 1791; d. in 1860; m. Anna Phelps, b. at Lafayette.
3. *Lewis Owen,* b. in 1795; d. in 1878; m. Temperance Dixon.
4. *Lovina,* b. in 1797; d. unm. in 1867.
5. *Purdee,* d. young.
6. *Hiram,* b. in 1801; d. in 1877; m. Hannah Almedia Benjamin.
7. *Milo,* a teacher at the Old Pompey Hill Academy, later a physician at Buffalo, b. in 1803; d. in 1877; m. Ruth Fleming. Child: (1) Rowena Flavia, b. in 1841; d. at Buffalo in 1897; m. Clayton Lewis Hill,* of Buffalo, b. in 1840, d. at Buffalo in 1905, son of Hiram Hill.
8. *Riley,* b. in 1806; d. in 1831.
9. *Lucy,* b. in 1808; d. in 1830; m. Eri Mesuard.
4. ii. SOLOMON, b. in April 1770.
    iii. LEWIS STILES, of Homer, physician, a founder of Cortland, (N. Y.) Academy, trustee of Homer Academy, b. at New Lebanon in 1772; d. at Normal, Ill., in 1849; m. MARY BELL.
        Children:
        1. *Benson,*[7] m. Maria ———.
        2. *Anne Eliza,* m. Rev. ——— Catlin.
        3. *Maria Louisa,* m. George Potter.
        4. *Robert Carter,* of Bridgeport, N. Y., and Normal, Ill., a graduate in 1825 of the Boston Medical College, physician, b. at Homer in 1806; d. at Normal; m. at Homer Charlotte Gleason, b. at Avon, Conn., 9 Oct. 1807, oldest daughter of Thomas and Elizabeth (Curtis) Gleason. Children: (1) Mary Elizabeth,[8] m. Dr. William Elder. (2) Eliza, m. M. A. Livingtson. (3) Lillian. (4) Clarence, m. Ella Templeton. (5) Louisa, m. Andrew Craig Cowles.†
    iv. LUCY, b. at New Lebanon in 1774; m. at Grafton JASON DEMMON of Sullivan, Madison County, a Revolutionary soldier, bur. at Bridgeport.
        Jason Demmon was a Revolutionary soldier in Capt. John Carpenter's company with service from 6 May 1780 to 6 Feb. 1781, stationed at Springfield, Mass.
    v. RODERICK, a settler at Homer in 1794, b. at New Lebanon 20 Nov. 1777; d. at Homer 5 Sept. 1849; m. 9 Nov. 1797 LOVINA DAVISON, of Grafton, daughter of Asa Davison, a soldier in the French and Indian War and in the Revolution.
        Roderick Owen built his home on a part of Lot 26, Homer, which his father had given him in 1799. The Census of 1800 shows that the family of Roderick Owen consisted of himself, his wife, and one son under 16.
        Children, b. at Homer:
        1. *Nathaniel,*[7] b. 1 Mar. 1799; m. ———, living in 1890 at Syracuse.
        2. *Sally,* b. in March 1801; m. A. T. Bowne of Lansing, Mich.
        3. *Alanson,* physician, a settler in the West, b. 12 Mar. 1803.
        4. *Almond,* physician, a settler in the West, b. 4 Apr. 1805.
        5. *Edson,* b. 4 June 1807.
        6. *Lovina Sophronia,* b. 24 June 1809; m. Dr. Daniel Denison.
            Two granddaughters, Miss Mary Denison and Mrs. Cora Stohrer, live at Syracuse.
        7. *Roderick Mandred,* b. in 1812; d. in 1884; m. Sarah Grover of Nanticoke, Pa.
            Two living granddaughters are Florence Lovina (Scoville) Lee of Manlius, and Emma Owen Hill Erickson of Cazenovia.

*A daughter, Florence Hill, and a son, Robert, with wife and two children, live at Lafayette.
†A daughter, Catherine L. Cowles, of Bloomingtno, Ill., owns the family Bible of Dr. Lewis Stiles[6] Owen of Homer, in which is recorded the name of his father, Abel[6] Owen, born at Hebron, Conn., in 1743.

Children by second wife:

vi. HANNAH MARIA.
vii. ANNA.
viii. ALMOND.

3. JONATHAN[5] OWEN (*Isaac*[4]), of Canaan, Columbia County, born at Hebron, Conn., 9 July 1755, died at New Lebanon 26 Mar. 1821, aged 65 years. He married ABIGAIL ————.

Jonathan Owen, a minor, was bound out 18 Oct. 1766 to Ezra Strong. The same year he, together with his brothers Elijah and Abel, and Ezra Strong, John Strong, and Isaac Tilden went to Richmont [now Richmond, Berkshire Co.] in western Massachusetts.

On 1 Oct. 1777 Jonathan Owen and Abel Owen, his brother, both residents of New Canaan, Albany County, bought land there from Isaac Preston. About 1784 Jonathan Owen bought his brother's share in this land.

On 14 May 1791 Abraham Havens of Canaan, Columbia County, sold to Jonathan Owen, of Canaan, for £100, "a certain piece or parcel of Land, lying and being in Canaan, County of Columbia and State of New York, butting and bounding as follows—West on Lands of the said Jonathan Owen, Southerly by said Owen's Land to Land of Ebenezer Darling to a White Oak Tree, then Easterly on said Darling's land to the Land of Abel Mott then northerly to the road, from thence northerly to Joshua Green's Land thence westawardly on the said Green's Land to the first mentioned Bounds to the same, more or less butted and Bounded."

Jonathan Owen served for three months in the Revolution as a soldier "in the Levies, stationed at West Point." (New York in the Revolution, p. 81.)

The will of Jonathan Owen, sworn to in Surrogate Court, Kinderhook, Columbia County, names son Solomon Owen as administrator of estate, and mentions children, Solomon, Anson, Rebecca, and wife Abigail.

Children:

i. ANSON,[6] physician, m. SALLY SEELY.
ii. REBECCA, m. BENJAMIN BUEL.
iii. WILLIAM, m. CHLOE HATCH.
iv. SOLOMON (or SALMON), b. at New Lebanon; d. there 18 Aug. 1861, aged 76 years; m. ————.
    Children:
    1. *Silas*,[7] b. at Boston, Erie County. A daughter, Josephine,[8] m. Dr. William Binford, living (1935) at Davenport, Iowa.
    2. *Willis*.
    3. *Phoebe*, b. at New Lebanon in 1854; d. there in 1928; m. George Temple of Wakefield, Mass. Children (surname *Temple*): (1) Edith M. (2) George M. (3) Cyrus R. (4) Silas A. (5) Carrie O., m. Henry Rhinehart. Child (surname *Rhinehart*): 1. Carl.

4. SOLOMON[6] OWEN (*Abel*,[5] *Isaac*[4]), of Pompey, Lafayette, and Palermo, brickmason, born at Old Canaan, Berkshire County,

Mass., 7 Apr. 1770, died at Palermo 26 Aug. 1855, aged 85 years. He married first, at Pompey, in 1793, LOIS ROUNDS, died 15 Dec. 1824, daughter of Comfort Rounds; and secondly, LUCY ALLEN, born in Massachusetts 20 Nov. 1790, died at Palermo 30 Apr. 1877, aged 87 years.

Solomon Owen went to Pompey in 1792 with James Sherman, a Revolutionary soldier, of Berkshire County, Mass., and later of Stephentown, and built a home on Lot 76, where he raised his family.

He owned a brickyard on his farm between his home and the home of Ebenezer Hill, and made high-grade bricks for building purposes. Two Colonial-style houses built of these hand-made bricks about 1810 for Solomon Owen and Ebenezer Hill by John Woodruff, Sr., contractor, still stand on Lot 76, which is now in the town of Lafayette. The Hill home is owned by Florence H. Hill and Robert Hill, great-grandchildren of Ebenezer Hill, and the Cherry Valley turnpike crosses their beautiful meadow not far from the house.

Solomon Owen and his family lived at their home (which was in that part of Pompey which became Lafayette in 1825) until 1836, when he sold the brick house and 225 acres of land to Calvin Cole, and with his family and married children went to Palermo. The old farm at Lafayette was in 1935 the home of George Palmer.

Solomon Owen was on the tax list and assessment roll of Lafayette on 1 Jan. 1836, and had children on the school roll.

Children by first wife, born in that part of Pompey now Lafayette:

i.   ABEL,[7] of Lafayette and Palermo, b. 18 Oct. 1794; d. at Navoo, Hancock Co., Ill., in June 1848; m. BETSEY DAVIS.
      Child:
      1. *Francis Marion*,[8] b. at Villanova in October 1830.

ii.   ALSON, b. in 1796; d. at Van Dieman's Land (Tasmania), where he was kept as a political prisoner, after being captured in an invasion of Canada by United States soldiers.

iii.   LORINDA, b. about 1797; d. *s. p.* in Cortland County in 1845; m. at Lafayette REUBEN BRYAN of Cincinnatus, Cortland County. He m. (2) ——— Butts. One son.

5. iv.   WASHINGTON, b. 21 Dec. 1799.

v.   NELSON, of Palermo, b. in 1801; d. at Hastings about 1855; m. TABITHA FARR.
      In 1855 Tabitha (Farr) Owen, widow of Nelson Owen, in a petition for administration of her husband's estate, names Homer W. Owen, LeRoy Owen, Eliza Anna Owen, Benjamin Owen, Nelson A. Owen, all residents of Palermo, and Mary A. Owen of Hastings, as heirs. (Oswego Records, Book 32, p. 32.)
      Nelson Owen was on the tax list and assessment roll of Lafayette on 1 Jan. 1836, and also had children on the school roll.
      Children:
      1. *Le Roy*,[8] b. at Lafayette or Palermo; d. at Palermo in 1875; m. Lydia Anna Babcock, d. at Palermo about 1884. Child: (1) Jennie,[9] of Fulton, teacher, b. at Palermo about 1870; m. in Colorado ———.
      2. *Homer.*
      3. *Eliza Ann,* b. at Lafayette or Palermo in 1845; d. at Syra-

cuse, aged 70 years; m. Henry DeWitt of Lafayette, d. at Syracuse 14 Oct. ——, aged 72 years. Child (surname *DeWitt*): (1) Cora, b. in 1870; d. ——; m. —— Crew. One son, b. at Syracuse, living there in 1935.
4. *Benjamin*, b. at Lafayette or Palermo; d. at Schroeppel about 1925; m. Nora ——. Child: (1) Adelbert,* of Syracuse, d. about 1900; m. ——.
5. *Nelson*.
6. *Mary A.*

vi. LOLA, b. at Lafayette 22 Sept. 1804; d. at Palermo 27 Aug. 1872, aged 67 years, 11 months, 5 days; m. JOHN WOODRUFF, a settler about 1836 in School District No. 4, Palermo, about a half mile south of the home of her brother, Washington Owen, b. at Lafayette in May 1804, d. at Palermo 16 Apr. 1881, son of John and Delilah Woodruff of Lafayette.
Children (surname *Woodruff*):
1. *Polly* d. *s. p.* at Fulton; m. Harrison Richardson, d. at Fulton.
2. *Lorinda*, b. about 1838; d. at Syracuse in 1924; m. Horace Plaisted, of Palermo and Syracuse, d. at Syracuse. Children (surname *Plaisted*), b. at Palermo: (1) Ernest, b. about 1868; d. *s. p. at* Syracuse. (2) Myron, b. about 1872; living at Syracuse in 1935; m. ——. (3) William, b. 19 Oct. 1874; d. at Rochester.
3. *Myron*, of Palermo, physician, b. about 1842; d. about 1899; m. Laura ——. Child: (1) Angeline, d. *s. p*; m. ——.
4. *Henry,* d. unm. at East Palermo in 1872.

vii. LOISA, b. at Lafayette in 1806; d. there; m. WILCOX WOODRUFF, b. at Lafayette 6 May 1802; d. at Palermo 6 Sept. 1879. He m. (2) Phoebe Olmstead, by whom he had two children.
Children (surname *Woodruff*), b. at Lafayette:
1. *George*, of New Orleans, La.
2. *Loisa Adell*, b. in 1848; d. at Pennelville, a village in Schroeppel, in 1912; m. Julius Bowman, of Palermo, d. at Phoenix in 1933. Children (surname *Bowman*): (1) George, of Ogdensburg. (2) Frank, of Fulton, m. ——. Several children. (3) Blanche, b. 10 Sept. 1879; m. —— Hirt of Phoenix. No children.
3. *Smith*, b. and d. at Lafayette; m. at Palermo Angelina Hanchett of Palermo, daughter of Squire Hanchett. Child: (1) Ella, m. —— Weideman of Fulton. One daughter, Helen, b. in 1920.

Children by second wife, born at Lafayette:

viii. ARMENIA, b. 6 Dec. 1826; d. unm. at Palermo 5 Jan. 1908.
ix. SOPHRONIA, b. 21 Dec. 1828; d. at Palermo 28 July 1900; m. at Palermo FREEMAN RICHARDSON, d. .ᴛ Palermo about 1901.
Children (surname *Richardson*), b. at Palermo:
1. *Alice*, m. (1) Fairfield Stafford; m. (2) Robert Rhines. Children by first husband (surname *Stafford*): (1) Maude. (2) Daniel, living at Fulton in 1935. Child by second husband (surname *Rhines*): (3) Floyd, living at Fulton.
2. *Edson*, d. at Syracuse; m. Carrie Upson, d. at Syracuse. Children, living at Syracuse in 1935: (1) Nellie May, m. —— Schindler. (2) Lloyd. (3) Frank Owen. (4) Etta, m. —— Blumer.
x. THEODOSIA (twin), b. 1 June 1831; d. unm. 23 Sept. 1882.
xi. THEODORE (twin), b. 2 June 1831; d. in March 1832.
xii. IRA (adopted), of Palermo, b. at Lafayette; m. ——.
Children:
1. *John*, m. Mary Coulter of Port Byron.
2. *Mary Ann*, m. (1) —— Berry; m. (2) Tom Gardner.

Child by first husband (surname *Berry*): (1) Jay.
Child by second husband (surname *Gardner*): (2) Tom.
3. *Martha*, m. —— Snooks.
4. *Theodore*, m. Sarah Dennis. Child: (1) Charles LeRoy of Syracuse.
5. *Lucy*, m. —— Pooler.
6. *Isador.*   9. *Allen.*
7. *Andrew.*   10. *Clinton.*
8. *Alson.*   11. *George.*
                          12. *Almon.*

5. WASHINGTON[7] OWEN (*Solomon,*[6] *Abel,*[5] *Isaac*[4]), of Palermo, born at Pompey 21 Dec. 1799, died at East Palermo 31 July 1865. He married first, at Pompey, 15 July 1823, POLLY DYER, born at Pompey 20 Dec. 1807, died at East Palermo 12 July 1856, daughter of Thomas and Polly (Mallison) Dyer; and secondly, CATHERINE COPELAND, died *s. p.* 26 Mar. 1871.
Children by first wife, first five born at Lafayette:

i.   FLORETTA,[8] b. 10 Feb. 1825; d. at Phoenix in March 1872; m. at Palermo, about 1843, CHARLES OLIVER, d. at Buffalo about 1893. Child (surname *Oliver*):
     1. *Harriet*, b. at Palermo about 1844; d. *s. p.* at Buffalo about 1910; m. John Dagwell, of Phoenix and Buffalo, d. about December 1917.

ii. MARILO PITT, b. 21 Nov. 1827; d. at Syracuse 8 Dec. 1898; m. at Palermo, in 1852, HARRIET MOSHER, of Palermo, b. 23 Oct. 1835, d. *s. p.* at San Joaquin, Calif., in December 1908.
     In 1852 Marilo Pitt Owen built a house at Owen Corners, Palermo, across the road from the home of his father. He also erected a large carriage shop, where he did an extensive business for several years before selling it and moving to the village of Peats Corners, where he continued his business. Later he moved to Syracuse, where he built an apartment house and store.

iii. RANSOM EZRA, b. 1 Feb. 1830; d. at East Palermo 11 Dec. 1908; m. at Palermo, about 1853, PHOEBE KLOCK, b. 15 Oct. 1839, d. at Palermo about 1905, daughter of John and Mary Klock.
     Children, b. at Palermo:
     1. *George,*[9] d. young.
     2. *Albertus,* b. in 1857; d. young.
     3. *Mary,* b. in 1860; d. at Fulton in 1923; m. at Palermo, about 1876, Joseph Hegman, of Baltimore, Md. Children (surname *Hegman*): (1) Florence, b. at Baltimore in December 1878; d. about 1916; m. at Fulton Bert Vinton. Children (surname *Vinton*): 1. Albertus, of Fulton, b. at Palermo in 1884. 2. Phoebe, b. at Palermo in 1888; m. at Fulton Glenn Loomis. 3. James, b. at Fulton in 1895.
     4. *Anna,* b. in January 1867; m. (1) at Palermo, in 1883, William Thompson, d. about 1883; m. (2) Lester Thompson; m. (3) Henry Schilley. Child by first husband (surname *Thompson*): (1) William Owen, b. in May 1886; living in 1935 at Syracuse. One son and one daughter.
     5. *Marilo Harrison,* of Palermo and Syracuse, b. in July 1870; d. in 1932; m. about 1893 Mattie Flint of Palermo. She m. (2) Fred Wing of Syracuse. Children: (1) Rev. Ira Marilo.[10] (2) Clayton Ransom. (3) ——, m. C. R. Wilson, of Syracuse.
     6. *Alice,* b. 21 May 1875; living in 1935 at Palermo; m. Frank Phillips, b. about 1869, d. in January 1934. Children (surname *Phillips*): (1) Anna. (2) Myrtle. (3) Genevieve.

iv. CALPHURNIA, b. 10 May 1832; d. at Bay City, Mich., 30 May 1900; m. at Palermo, 5 July 1851, WILLIAM DANIELS, of Bowen's Corners, b. 3 Nov. 1829, d. at Bay City in February 1910.
Children (surname *Daniels*), b. at Caughdenoy, a village in Hastings:
1. *Charles Wallace,* b. 4 June 1853; d. at Akron, Ohio, in 1933; m. (1) Emma Griffin, d. on same day as son; m. (2) Bertha Lewis. Child by first wife: (1) Frank, b. at Bay City, Mich.; d. aged 2½ years. Children by second wife: (2) Hazel. (3) Francis, of Butte, Mich.
2. *Lettie,* b. in 1855; d. at Bay City, Mich., 6 Dec. 1926; m. there, in January 1874, Robert Tavener. Children (surname *Tavener*): (1) Helen, b. 9 Oct. 1883; m. Carl Fox. (2) Hubert, of Bay City, b. in 1889.
3. *Emma,* b. in 1856; d. at Cleveland, Ohio, 18 Dec. 1931; m. at Bay City, Mich., Milton Henry, d. 26 Mar. 1924. Child (surname *Henry*): (1) Edith, b. 24 Mar. 1880; m. 27 Nov. 1907 Okey Moore.
4. *Lydia Ann,* b. 13 Sept. 1864; d. at New Orleans, La., about 1915; m. Titus Wagner, d. at New Orleans about 1921. Children (surname *Wagner*), b. at New Orleans: (1) Bessie, m. Alexander Roy of Handsboro, Miss. One daughter and two sons. (2) Henry, m. ———. Children: 1. Jessie. 2. Floyd. 3. Esther. 4. Richard. 5. Phillip.
5. *Florence,* b. at Bay City, Mich., 3 Sept. 1872; d. at Cleveland, Ohio, in November 1933; m. at Bay City, 23 Aug. 1892, Fred Discher, b. at Lexington, Mich., 12 Nov. 1869, living in 1935 at Cleveland. Children (surname *Discher*): (1) Eunice, b. at Bay City 20 Aug. 1894; m. 30 Aug. 1924 William Rawlings, living in 1935 in Pittsburg, Pa. (2) Esther, b. at Bay City 26 Aug. 1896; d. at Bay City 17 May 1928. (3) Frederick Elton, b. 11 Aug. 1898; d. 13 Apr. 1902.

v. CONSTANTIA V., b. 17 July 1834; d. at Bay City, Mich., 23 Nov. 1904; m. at Palermo, in 1851, JOHN MARTIN AURINGER, a soldier in the Civil War, b. 10 Aug. 1832, d. in New Orleans, La., 18 June 1863.
Children (surname *Auringer*), b. at Palermo:
1. *Rozella Elnora,* b. 9 May 1852; d. 4 Aug. 1893; m. at Watertown, in 1876, Edward L. Youngs, d. at Flint, Mich., in January 1918. Child (surname *Youngs*): (1) Martin P., b. at Fulton 24 Nov. 1877, d. at Buffalo 10 Dec. 1902.
2. *Ardelia Sophronia,* b. 12 Sept. 1854; living in 1935 at Fulton; m. at Fulton, 11 Sept. 1872, Charles Russell Guile, b. at Fulton 14 July 1850, d. at Fulton 14 Apr. 1930. Children (surname *Guile*), b. at Oswego Falls: (1) Claude Elwin, attorney, b. 6 Jan. 1876; m. at Fulton, 12 June 1901, Clara Terry. Child: 1. Robert Terry, b. at Fulton 9 Sept. 1909. (2) Elsie Goldie, b. 18 Oct. 1880; m. at Fulton, 22 Sept. 1919, Roy Engell, of Schenectady, a graduate of Rensselaer Polytechnic Institute, electrical engineer (1935). Children (surname *Engell*): 1. Richard Guile (twin), b. 1 Nov. 1920; d. 5 Dec. 1920. 2. Elinor Louise (twin), b. 1 Nov. 1920. 3. Theodore, b. 29 Apr. 1924. (3) Jennie Ardelia, b. 24 July 1883; m. 16 Apr. 1913 Clay Beckwith. Child (surname *Beckwith*): 1. Charles Guile, b. at Fulton 19 Apr. 1923. (4) Hazel May, b. 13 June 1886; m. 21 June 1911 Reed William Cady, A.B. (Syracuse, 1907). Children (surname *Cady*): 1. John Gilbert, b. at Seneca Falls 30 Jan. 1914. 2. Russell Guile, b. at North Tonawanda 12 May 1918. 5. Charles Russell, b. 20 Mar. 1889; d. 30 Sept. 1929; m. 10 Feb. 1913 Ruth Elizabeth Switzer, b. 17 Mar. 1892, d. 14

Feb. 1922. Children: 1. Harlan Switzer, b. at Fulton 14
Sept. 1913. 2. Owen Phelps, b. at Canton 14 Aug. 1916.

vi. PARINTHA, b. at Palermo 4 Sept. 1837; d. about 2 Aug. 1905 and
bur. at Saginaw, Mich.; m. at Palermo, 26 Nov. 1859, URB
LADD, of Caughdenoy, d. at Saginaw about 1912.
Child (surname *Ladd*):
1. *Hattie,* b. at Caughdenoy, Hastings, 24 Nov. 1861; d. at
Saginaw, Mich., about 1923; m. at Saginaw, in 1879,
James Fenimore Cooper, d. about 1917. Children (surname *Cooper*), b. at Saginaw: (1) James Fenimore, of
San Francisco, Calif., a lieutenant in the World War, b.
24 Nov. 1884; m. in 1915 Edith ———. Child: 1. Jane
Harriet, b. about 1917. (2) Warner Ladd, a lieutenant
in the Navy in the World War, electrical engineer, b. 11
Dec. 1888; d. at Buffalo 17 Feb. 1920; m. at Buffalo, in
1916, Bessie Madden. Child: 1. Warner Ladd, of Detroit, Mich., b. at Newport News, Va., in July 1918.
(3) Thomas DeWitt, of Flint, Mich., b. in 1890; m. at
Flint, in 1917, Irene ———. Child: 1. Joyce, b. in 1927.
vii. STEARNS P., b. 9 May 1840; d. at Palermo 6 Jan. 1848.
viii. LOVINA ADELL, b. 26 Apr. 1849; d. at Weedsport 12 Feb. 1930;
m. (1) ORIN DARIUS PANGBURN, a Civil War veteran, b. at
Palermo 8 May 1839, d. there 24 Feb. 1908; m. (2) 9 Oct. 1909,
as his second wife, ALVIN FLINT, a Civil War veteran, d. 16
Nov. 1915.
Children by first husband (surname *Pangburn*), b. at Pa-
lermo:
1. *Harriet Amanda,* b. 13 Dec. 1866; living in 1935 at East
Syracuse; m. at Palermo, 22 Mar. 1885, Alexander
Thompson, b. at Roosevelt in November 1856, d. at East
Syracuse in July 1936. Children (surname *Thompson*):
(1) Iva May, b. at Phoenix 5 Apr. 1886; m. at East Syra-
cuse, 21 Oct. 1907, Robert Gleasman, b. at Syracuse 12
Feb. 1886, son of Henry and Mary (Dunn) Gleasman.
Two daughters. (2) Lola Elnora, b. at Baldwinsville 7
July 1891; m. at East Syracuse, 16 Dec. 1914, Charles
Gilbert, b. at East Syracuse 14 Feb. 1890, son of Samuel
and Sarah (Ingerson) Gilbert. Four Children.
2. *Frederick Ransom,* b. 14 Jan. 1869; d. at Caughdenoy,
Hastings, 15 Dec. 1911; m. at Caughdenoy, 25 Dec. 1905,
Floy Campbell, b. at Caughdenoy in November 1882, d. at
Phoenix in 1918, daughter of Milton Campbell.
3. *Elnora Parintha,* of West Brookfield, Mass., compiler of
this genealogy, b. 12 Apr. 1872; m. at Palermo, 10 Nov.
1897, Clifford John Huyck, a student of medicine at the
New York Homeopathic College and Flower Hospital,
New York City, graduate in 1896 from the Cleveland
University of Medicine and Surgery, physician and sur-
geon, a captain in the Medical Corps, United States
Army, stationed at Hospital No. 4, Fort Porter, N. Y.,
in the World War, b. at Exeter 25 Dec. 1873, son of
Robert L. and Margaret (Warner) Huyck. Children
(surname *Huyck*): (1) Freeda Elnora, b. at Acworth,
N. H., 28 Aug. 1900. (2) Margaret Lovina, b. at West
Brookfield 4 June 1912.
4. *Francis Albertus,* b. 19 Oct. 1873; m. at Pennelville,
Schroeppel, May Bowering, b. 11 Sept. 1875, daughter
of William Bowering of Roosevelt. Children, b. at Roosevelt: (1) Anna May, b. 19 Jan. 1901; m. at Belle Isle, in
June 1919, Harold Sadler, b. 16 Feb. 1898, d. in April
1934. Four children. (2) Eva Alberta, b. 28 Dec. 1904;
m. at Weedsport, 16 Dec. 1931, Charles Robert Lawson,
b. at Auburn. (3) Clifford Francis. b. 14 Sept. 1910. (4)
Walter, b. 5 Dec. 1912; d. in January 1914. (5) DeForest
Grant, b. 14 Jan. 1915. (6) Fern Belle, b. 12 Aug. 1917.

Barber (cont.)
Thomas (Lt.) 61
Barbour, Michael 691
Thomas 38
Barden, Frances Eleanor
277
George Nason 277
Bardwell, Abigail Kimberly 361
Ebenezer 65
Ebenezer (Lt.) 65
Elesebeth 69
Elizabeth 64,69
Mary 49
Robert 49,65
Robert (Sgt.) 65
Barker, Aurelia 627
Charles Albrow 102
Elizabeth 131
Hannah 130
Hannah B. 571
Justus 131
Levi 617
Lois 132
Lydia 129
Lydia Harrison 122
Mary 26,126
Sabrina 570
Samuel A. 374
Susan 497
William 121
Barlow, Claude W. (Dr.)
352
Deborah 74
George 74
Phebe 673
Sarah 74
Barnard, Francis 489
Jeremiah 489
John 489
Joseph 42
Barnes, --- 422
--- (Judge) 484
Abigail 437
Abraham 186
Achbel 237
Benjamin 355,438,451
Desire 435
Eliphalet 132
Elizabeth 84,130,
303,449
Elizur 556
Enos 437
Eunice 438,451
Freelove 86
Hannah Abbott 438,451
Israel 471
John 225
Jona. 485
Lois 128,418
Mary 225,471
Mercy 115
Nathaniel 186
Phebe 548
Phoebe 128
Sarah 225
Seth 437
Timothy 128,548
Barnet, Robert 45
Barney, Benjamin 586
Hannah Hix 586
Lorana 633
Mary 626
Sally 586
Barnum, --- 400
Barons, Marie 225
Barrat, James 428
Barret, James 429

Barrett, Lamel 708
Lemuel 708
Lemuel (Capt.) 708
Lemul 708
Mary 708
Rhoda 213
Barrows, Alaxa 639
Mary 628
Sybil 518
Barstow, Charles 261
Barthelme, Claude 560
Mary 560
Susan Plumb 560
Bartholomew, --- 477
Abigail 190
Adonijah 462
Amos Adams 462
Andrew 361
Ann 137
Artemus 462
Clarinda 462
Dan 463
Daniel 292
Hannah 133
Hannah Williams 129
Irene Munson 133
Isaac 455,462
Jehiel 455,462
Jesse Bradley 462
John Brooks 136
Jonathan 137
Juliana 462
Lemi 462
Lucy 482
Lydia 459
Minerva 462
Noah Willis 462
Phebe 455,462
Rachel 130
Rebecca 133
Sabra 455
Samuel 133
Sophrina 462
Susanna 129
Watson Hines 462
William 129
Bartle, Andrew C. 567
Bartlett, Alexander 538
Daniel 170
Deborah 26,38,170
Ebenezer 117,419
Emily 538
Fiske 85
George 306,320
George (Dea.) 574
Harriet L. 538
Ichabod 667
Israel 538
Jerusha 538
Joseph 84
Lucius 538
Mary 419
Mary E. 538
Peter Mason 538
Robert A. 538
Ruth 306
Sidney S. 538
Barton, William 380
Bascom, --- 370
Bass, Betsey 630
Desire E. 537
Elizabeth Loretta 630
Hannah 153,677
J. Lawrence 101
John 153
Lottie 630
Luther 630
Basset, Samuel 557

Bassett, Hannah 317,470
Harriet 567
Samuel 557
Bate, Hannah 327
Samuel 327
Bates, --- 285
A. C. 424
Abigail 135
Albert C. 101
Albert Carlos 101
Alpha 500
David (Jr.) 682
James 13
Mary 312
Samuel 327
T. B. 641
Baxter, Cynthia 639
Bayard, James (Esq.) 522
Bayes, Thomas 223
Bayley, Edith 162
Hannah 434
John (Rev.) 561
Mary 418
Nathaniel 418,434
Zerviah 434
Baylies, Francis (Hon.)
2
Bazies, --- 673
Beach, Abigail 561
Benjamin 669
Caleb 669
Ebenezer B. 706
Elias 450
Elizabeth Wadhams 128
Eunice 188
Hannah 129,311
John 132,311
Margaret 669
Martha 670
Noah 127
Ruth 625,641
Sarah 306
Theron 669
William 306
William G. 331
Zophar 128
Zopher 142
Beadel, Elizabeth 197
Nathaniel (Capt.) 197
Beadles, Elizabeth 197
Nathaniel (Capt.) 197
Bearding, Nathaniel 367
Sarah 367
Beardslee, Abigail 405
Clark S. 33
Claude G. 33
Ephraim 404,405
Lyndon S. 33
Raymond A. 33
Ruth 33
Thomas 404
Beardsley, Hannah 130
Patience 655
Beatty, Eliza 556
Erkurius (Capt.) 701
Joseph M. 443
Beauchamp, Margaret 519
Beaumont, Deborah 8
Beckett, John 624
Beckley, Benjamin 409
Beckwith, Abigail 229
Bethuel 229
Charles Guile 720
Clay 720
Daniel 231
Eleazer 242
Elisha 229
Elisheba Reiner 252

728

Boardman (cont.)
Caroline Maria 535
Charles Henry 585
Chloe 118
Cornelia Elizabeth
535
Daniel (Rev.) 534
Elijah (Hon.) 534
Elijah George 535
Francis 530
Frederick Alexander
535
George Sherman 535
Henry Mason 535
Henry Whiting 535
Israel 354
Jeremiah 585
Levi 589
Mary Anna 535
Sarah 109
Sherman 534
William Jarvis 535
William Whiting 534
Bodge, --- 207
Elizabeth 263
Bodwell, Henry 707
Jane 707
Joshua 707
Boerner, Martha 643
Bogardus, Rebecca 446
Boge, Elisha 238,252
Boggs, Eliza 703
Bogue, John 250
Nellie 706
William 706
William (Jr.) 706
Boleyn, Anne 5
Bolton, C. K. 392
Boltwood, --- 64
L. M. 43
Lucius M. 50
Lucius M. (Esq.) 335
Sarah 336
Solomon 659
Bond, Carlos 640
Elmer 640
John 151
Mary 150,151
Nathan 634
Nicholas 415
Rachel 435
Rebecca 629
Bonner, Lewis C. 600
Lewis N. 600
Malvina Moody 600
Bonython, --- 7
Booge, Elizabeth 263
Boone, Inez 603
Booth, --- 7,658
Elizabeth 79
Mary 615
Naomi 666
Ruth 657
Simon 16
Boras, Lucy 411
Borda, Frank J. 601
Frank J. (Jr.) 601
George James 601
Borden, Elizabeth 226
Russell 691
William 228
Bornson, Gideon (Capt.)
253
Borodell, Ann 394
Borradill, Anne 518
Boss, Ruth 152
Bostwick, John (Sr.) 450
Sarah 534

Bosworth, Abigail Chap-
pel 265
Eugene 607
Fred 607
Hazel 607
Ichobod 265
Nettie 607
Zelinda 265
Botsford, Jabez 405
Joseph 652
Mary Gorham 76
Sarah 405
Bott, Joel 346
Sarah Neal 346
Boughton, --- 508,511
Bound, Ruth 627
Bouton, Abigail 504
Alice 508
Bridget 339,508,509
John 339,504,508,511
Mary 504
Matthew 504
Nicholas (Count) 512
Rachel 504
Bovis, H. Eugene 88
Bow, Alexander 217
Jerusha 426
Bowen, --- 157
Amy 517,521
Daniel 115
Henry 474
Bower, Crosiar 703
George G. 703
Helen 703
Bowering, May 721
William 721
Bowers, Charlotte 641
Ella M. 272
Bowghton, John 512
Bowker, Hannah 369
Tryphena Kendall
368,369
Bowman, Blanche 718
Frank 718
George 718
Julius 718
Bowne A. T. 715
Bowton, Abigail 511,512
Abigal 508
Alice 512
Bridget 509,510,511
John 508,509,510,
511,512
Rachell 508
Richard 509,510,511
Ruth 508,509,510
Boyden, Estella Coy 608
Harold 608
Leah 608
Mary 608
Mildred 608
Boykim, Bethia 122
Boynton, Enos C. 634
Brace, Lucy 559
Richard 601
Brackett, Rachel 377
Braddock, --- (Gen.) 657
Bradfield, Martha 431
Bradford, --- 99
--- (Gov.) 517,570
Abigail 521
Alice 533
Alithea 516
Alithea (II) 516
Anne 516,521
Dan 521
Edith 538
Elizabeth 516,521,522

Bradford (cont.)
Hannah 515,516,521
Honory Swift 521
Irene 516
Irene (II) 516
James 538
Joseph 514,516,521
Julia 522
Mary 521,538
Matilda 270
Priscilla 514,516,521
Priscilla (II) 521
Rebecca 130
Robert 521
Samuel Cheever 522
Sarah 516
Sybil 521
Thomas 538
William 521
William (Gov.) 272,
522,533,534
William (Maj.) 516,
533
Wm. (Gov.) 538
Wm. (Maj.) 538
Zerviah 521
Bradley, Abigail Howd
444
Abraham 571
Amy Hemingway 571
Ann 620
Arba 512
Ashbel 86
Benjamin 188
Caleb 185,187
Chloe 198
Daniel 117,444,695
Elizabeth 362
Elizabeth Chloe 512
Elizabeth Clara 512
Elizabeth Thompson
188
Esther Chamberlain
512
Eunice 189
Gustavus 208
Hannah 470
Harriet Whiting 525
Isaac 207,571
Israel 200
James 204
James (Jr.) 191
James Lane 588
Joel 471
Lois 207
Martha 472,618,619
Mary Merrick 364
Mercy 208
Molly 203
Nancy 570,571
Nathan 619,620
Phoebe 132
Rachel 444
Sarah 186,187,198,667
Sibyl 667
Susannah 188
William 618
Zimra 158
Bradly, William 297
Bradlye, Stephen 163
Bradstreet, --- 11
Eliza 485
Simon (Esq.) 139
Bradt, Merrit B. 403
Bradway, Amy 477,482
Sarah 640
Brainard, Columbus 532
David (Rev.) 519

Brown (cont.)
Thomas 430
Tristram 284
Victor 605,606
W. S. 535
William 536,624
Zophar 536
Browne, --- 289
--- (Rev.) 290
Peter 36,38,44
Browning, Frances 482
Brownson, Prudence 444
Tillotson (Rev.) 194
Bruce, John Anthony 634
Bruen, Hannah 392
John 392
Matthias (Rev.) 392
Obadiah 392
Sarah 141,Sarah 392
Bruno, Paul Lewis 600
Brush, Barbara Cotes 704
Bryan, Reuben 717
Sarah 195
Buck, Dorothy 112
Elizabeth 440
Emmanuel 665
Esther 135
Hannah 665
Henry 440
Samuel 440
Thomas 217
William 440
Buckingham, --- (Eld.) 142
Belinda 208
Cynthia 560
Ephraim 203
John 647
Mary 318
Sally Ann 622
Temperance 375,383
Thomas (Rev.) 375
Buckland, Hannah 679
Buckley, Aaron 433
William 433
Budd Rachel 549
Budlong, Betsy 270
Buel, Anne 692
Bela 373
Benjamin 716
David 529
Dorothy 53,54
Ebenezer 53,54
Ebenr. 53
Elijah 713
Harriet 531
Hiel 118
Jonathan (Capt.) 670
Jonathan (Capt.Jr.) 669
Joseph (Gen.) 118
Lucretia 670
Lydia 531
Ozias 531
Timothy (Dea.) 669
Buell, David 621
Ebenezer 54,669
Elizabeth 127
Job 621
John 54
Lucy 85
Martha 144
P. 29
Peter 144
Peter (Sgt.) 39
Samuel 54
Sarah 621,669
William 54

Bugbee, Annis 271
Elijah 480
Jason 627
Lucy 478
Lydia 275
Marcus 271,627
Sylvia Corbin 271,627
Willard 484
Bulkley, Ann Jeannette 403
Bull, Abigail 412
Ann 399
Anna 397
Edward 397
Esther A. 333
Isaac 46
Issac (Dr.) 46
Jonathan 16
Mary Post 397
Bullock, Lucy Ann 445
Bumstead, Horace 642
William 642
Bunce, Polly 479,486
Sarah 517
Bunel, Joseph 463
Bunnell, Benjamin 447, 448,450
Cynthia 536
Eunice 136
Jacob 192
Joseph 189
Nabby 198
Nathaniel 463
Rebecca 447,448,450
Sarah 450
Sarah Mallory 451
William 448
Durbank, David 546
Timothy 688
Burbidge, Mary 222
Burchard, Betsey 386,387
Sophia 146
Burchsted, John Henry (Dr.) 383
Burden, Abigail 273
Burdick, Bertha May 275
Frances Emma 273
Joel 273
Lucy Tracy 275
Lydia Geer 273,275
Nancy 273
Rowland 273,275
Sally Kenyon 273
Sophia 537
Burgess, Mary 487
Samual H. 587
Burgoyne --- (Gen.) 337, 363,463,464,468
Burke, Edward 570
Burleigh, Mary 526
Burley, Josiah 627
Luke 627
Mary 679
Persis 478,484
Burnap, Mary 371
Burnett, Clarissa 105
Mary 152,415
Sarah 413
Burnham, --- (Rev.) 408
Daniel 628
Elisha 410
Fanny 628
H. B. 486
Isaac 104
Josiah 53,660
Philomena 130
Seymour 479
Burr, Adonijah 144

Burr (cont.)
Benjamin 54
Hannah 53,54
John 54
Martha 372
Nathan 295
Noadiah 53,54
Peter 700
Samuel 54,372
Burrall, Jonathan 338
Burrington, Isabella 324
Burritt, Elizabeth 552
Fairchild 553
Sarah 154,202
Tamar 360
Burson, Josephine 606
Burt, Daniel 631
Ephraim 695
Jonathan 166
Lloyd 480
Sarah 166
Burton, Lydia 387
Burwell, Benjamin 82
John (Dr.) 531
Mary Leonard 531
Busby, Jerusha Kimberly 360
Bush, Catherine Martin 607
Charles 423
Clifford 607
David 423
Eli 485
Gladys 608
John 607
Ruth Hitchcock 167
Susan Thalia 423
Bushell, John 94
Bushnell, --- 583
Abigail 115,399
Eber 399
Electa Ann 419
Elizabeth 299,305
Ephraim 157
Francis 299,504
Francis (Dea.) 315, 321
Hepsibah 378
Jane 156
Jerusha 413
Joseph 504
Lemuel 622
Mabel 496
Maria 504
Mary 315,321,504
Richard 503,504
Samuel 156
Samuel (Dea.) 161
Thankful 378
William 327,328
Zippora 153
Buswell, Jacob 359
Butler, Almon Maro 273
Charles R. 536
Dinah 132
Ellen 29
Eunice 448
Ezekiel 318
George 607
Hannah 92
Henry 536
Hester 159
James 124
Jonathan 131
Joseph 504
Lilla 607
Lulu Alma 273
Lydia 131,134,136

Butler (cont.)
Mabel 346
Neva 607
Philenda 634
Phoebe 131
Richard (Dea.) 92
Roman M. 536
Rosetta Eastman 273
Sally 707
Samuel 159
Sarah 158
Thomas 16
Thomas Harvey 273
Vivian Lenore 273
Zebulon (Capt.) 229,
234,236,240,294
Butterfield, William J.
640
Buttolph, Hannah 147
Button, Jonathan 615
Leroy 611
Phoebe 611
Rhoda 611
Butts, --- 717
Byfield, Nathl. 57
Byington, Benjamin 131
Byles, Mather (Rev.Dr.)
18

--- C ---

Cable, Clinton 600
Mary Lunders 600
Theodore 600
Cadwell, Charles 146
Eliza D. 207
Cady, Arah 555
John Gilbert 720
Lucy 313
Mary 555
Reed William 720
Rhoda 634
Russell Guile 720
Cahoon, Hannah 295
Mary Rathbun 295
Reynolds 295
Caldwell, --- 236
Anna 158
Charles 86,158
Lizzie 251
Mary 251
Calkin, Hugh 420
Calkings, Daniel 261
Calkins, Deborah 420
Elizabeth 513,516,
518,521,695
Hannah 656
John 695
Lois 695
Callender, Eleanor Kel-
logg 338
Joseph 337
Philip 337
Callsey, --- 13
Calver, Caleb 467
Calvert, Grover 612
Lena 612
Mert 612
Sidney 612
Camden, --- 2
Cammock, --- 7
Camp, Abigail 657
Alice 405
Anna 411
Elah 418
Hezekiah 651

Camp (cont.)
Joseph 653
Lemuel 405
Lucy 411
Mary 148,409
Rachel 670
Ruth 413
Samuel (Rev.) 148
Stephen 137
Campbell, Floy 721
John 93
Lydia 632
Margaret 630
Milton 721
Roger 259
Campfield, Margaret Kel-
logg 344
Canada, Isaac 521
Candee, --- 449
Abigail Pinion 359
Hannah 359
Samuel 359
Cane, Rachel 342
Canfield, --- (Capt.)
256
David 653
Jeremiah 653
Laura 553
Matthew 142
Samuel (Capt.) 254,
257
Sarah 523
Canodise, Edward 432
Capell, Amelia 604
Card, Arthur 610
Betty 610
Elisabeth 387
John W. 445
Mary 610
May 610
Retta 610
Cardinal, Jane Amelia
445
Cardwell, Josephine 610
Carew, --- (Capt.) 264
Edm. (Sir) 4
Carey, Joseph 154
Seth 153
Carmack, Lucy 694
Carnes, Anna 187
Rachel 187
Thomas 187
Carpenter, Amos B. 626
Anna 626
Arthur B. 33
Barney 626
Benjamin 626
Champion G. 33
Daniel 626
David 626
Hannah 626
Henry T. 33
Irving 626
Jesse 626
John 590,626
John (Capt.) 631,715
John A. 33
Jotham (Rev.) 626
Katherine E. 33
Mary Barney 626
Mary L. 33
Nancy 271,478
Nathan 626
Polly 626
Powell 626
Reuben 626
Robert Newton 590
Sarah E. 33

Carpenter (cont.)
William 626
Winifred G. 33
Zebulon 626
Carr, Alonzo 704
Ann 704
Bart 704
Greenberry 704
James 704
Lott 704
Marion 704
Mary 704
William 704
William Chiles 524
Carren, Eunice H. 106
Carrier, Andrew 29
Andrew E. 29
Electa 29
Erastus 29
Ernest E. 30
Huldah 437
Mary 29
Mercy 29
Phebe A. 29
Carrington, Elias (Dr.)
653
John (Dr.) 187
Louisa 523
Mabel 552
Mary H. 31
Noadiah 653
Sarah Johnson 552
Zebulon 552
Carroll, Elvin Knight
274
Frank Jackson 274
George H. 274
Carter, Amos 332
Anna Hopkins 130
Eunice Kellogg 344
Joshua 53
Mary 320
Rachel 340
Sally 485
Samll. 52
Samuel 51
Thomas 130
Cartier, Eliza McKay 274
Frank J. 274
Robert 274
Carver, --- (Gov.) 570
Cary, --- 7
Nellie F. 325
Case, Abia 691
Amasa 536
Bartholomew 694
Catherine 691
Charles 536
Chloe 536
Eleazer 536
Eliphalet 684,712
Elizabeth 679
Israel 144
Joanna 144
Job 144
John 680,694
Jonah 684
Mary 692
Mercy 536
Phebe 536
Roger 693
Samuel 679,680
Samuel (Jr.) 683
Sarah 680
Sylvia 607
Timothy 691
Casey, John B. 701
Cason, Margaret 346

732

734

735

736

737

Dexter (cont.)
Emery Frank 274
Franklin B. 101
Frederic 274
Henrietta 274
Ida M. 274
Mary F. 274
Orrando Perry 425
William L. 274
Dibble, Abigail 143
Abraham 144
Charles (Capt.) 458
Ebenezer 144
Elizabeth 160
Hannah 157
Josiah 39
Miriam 26,38
Moses 144
Robert 143
Samuel 39,143
Thomas 38,39,143,144
Thomas (Sr.) 39
Vienna Kellogg 338
Wakefield 39
Dibol, Abigail 143
Dickensen, Nathaniel 66
Dickenson, Hannah 66
Dickerman, Abigail 550
Abraham 185
Elizabeth 187
Esther 194
Isaac 547
Leverett 206
Dickinson, Abraham (Lt.) 298
Agnes 417
Azariah 417
Benjamin 53
Charles 16,17
Ed. (Hon.) 484
Elizabeth 49,66
Emily 623
Frances 48
Hannah 43,48,343
Hepzibah 417
Hesther 49
John 69
John (Jr.) 64
John (Sgt.) 43,48
Joseph 623
Joshua 69
Moses 53
Nathaniel 40,42,47,
60,66,343
Nathaniel (Dea.) 48
Nathaniel (Sr.) 48
Obadiah 60
Samuel 49
Thankful 172
Thomas 16
Dickson, Benjamin 551
James 551
Diggins, Emma Jane 708
Hannah 117
Jeremiah 117
John W. 708
Walter Leroy 708
William 708
Dill, Sarah Osborn Owen 705
Solomon 699
Dilts, Flora Louisa 599
Dimmick, Della 643
Dwight 587
Guerdon Lewis 587
Joseph 587
Luther F. (Rev.) 498
Mary Ernestine 587

Dimmick (cont.)
May Green 587
Dimmock, Anne 519
Daniel 479
Desire 519
Hezekiah 520
Jesse 519
Lott 519
Seth 519
Silas 519
Thomas 519
Dimon, Mary Ann 332
Dinon, John 293
Disberowe, Isaack 382
Disborough, --- 320
Disborow, --- 326
Disbrow, Betsey 676
Discher, Esther 720
Eunice 720
Fred 720
Frederick Elton 720
Diver, Samuel 537
Dixon, Betsey 29
David 331
Jane Betsey 464
Temperance 715
Dixwell, --- (Judge) 71
Doane, Elisha 541
Harriet Murich 709
Joseph 540,541
Joseph (Esq.) 540
Joseph (Jr.) 540
Nathaniel 541,709
Prudence Smith 709
Dodge, Amos 153
Daniel 587
Eunice Marcy 475
Hepsibeth 272
Martha 153
Rufus 587
Dodley, Thomas 178
Dodly, Lucrese 178
Dodson, John 135
Mary 135
Dolan, Prudence Hebert 153
Dolber, Rawkey 36
Robarte 36
Robert 36
Rockye 36
Dolbere, Agnes 36
Cornelius 36
Mary 35,36,Mary 37
Robert 36
Dolbiar, Mary 35,36,37
Dolebeere, Mary 36
Rockye 36
Doolittle, --- 158,666
Hannah 214
Lowly 197
Lucy 159
Martha 29
Mary 310
Ruth 198
Ruth Richardson Hill 160
Doran, Bethiah 253
Dorchester, Benjamin 166
Sarah 166
Dorman, Benjamin 183,
187,299
Edmund 405
Hannah Hull 405
Lydia 187
Mary 405
Ruth Johnson 187
Dorrance, David (Capt.) 264

Doty, Minnie 609
Doubleday, John Mason 535
John T. 535
William Edwards 535
Douglas, --- (Col.) 463
--- (Maj.) 463
Abigail 192,213
Alexander 213
Joseph 260
Mary 260
Mary Thompson 260
Sarah 531
Sarah Ballard 213
William (Capt.) 462,
463
Dow, --- 27
Samuel 82
Ulysses 709
Dowd, Asa 576
Billy 86
Cornelius 116
Desire 174
Diantha 670
Henry 217
Jerusha 576
John 669
Mary 217
Orrin 86
Pinnock 359
Timothy (Jr.) 575
Dowde, Cornelius 434
Hitty 434
Dowe, Charles 711
Ellen Esther 711
Minerva 711
Ulysses (Hon.) 711
Downer, Andrew (Dr.) 154
Anne 246
Edmund 246
Hannah 154
Richard 139
Downing, Allina 707
Downs, Abigail 362
Adeline Morris 560
Deliverance 652
Hannah 357
John 357
Rebecca 652
Sarah 203
Dowse, Jonathan 22
Jonathan (Esq.) 17,22
Dox, Cathalina Lansing 423
Drachler, Catherine 612
Rolland 612
Walter Frederick 612
Wanda 612
Drake, --- 2,7
Deborah 698
Elizabeth Marcy 477
Francis (Sir) 3,4,5
Gillian 470
Hannah 616
Jacob 37
Joan 4
John 4
Lucy Marcy 477
Lydia 141
Mary 350,352
S. G. 379
Simon 38
William 692
Draper, Deborah 94
John 93,94,95
Lydia 94,95
Margaret Green 94
Richard 94,95

Ells, Joshua 258
   Mary 258
   Sarah 258
Ellsworth, Anne 79
   Jessie 592
   Jonathan 690
   Mary 690
   Sarah 690
   Sybil 615
Ellwell, Mark 154
Elmere, Edward 10
Elton, William 551
Elwell, Catharine 435
   Ebenezer 435
   John 463
   Samuel 317
Ely, Anna 537
   Christopher 523
   Daniel 523
   Elisha 259
   Elizabeth 497
   Ethelinda 524
   Horace 498
   Jane 437
   John (Col.) 250,264,
      524
   Mary 595
   Mary Ann 256
   Nathaniel 80
   Richard 490
   Ruth 498
   Sarah 27
   Seth 497
   Wells 498
Emberton, --- 380
Emblem, Margret 15
Emblin, Richard 15
Emerson, Elizabeth 366
Endicott, --- (Gov.) 72
Engell, Guile 720
   Richard 720
   Roy 720
   Theodore 720
Engle, Katherine 596
Enno, James 39
   Sarah 40
Eno, --- 405
   David 39
   Debora 683
   James 39
Ensign, David 52
   Jacob 53
   John 53,413
Erchdecon, --- 4
Errickson, Emma Owen
      Hill 715
Estabrook, Calvin 273
   Calvin Lewis 273
   John 273
   Mary Estabrook 273
   Nathaniel 273
Eubanks, Edith 603
   Hubert 603
   M. W. 603
   May 603
   Otis 603
   Ruby 603
Evans, Cynthia 625
   King 593
   Lizzie 617
   Louisa 285
   Peter 51
Evarts Ambrose 84
   Ann 214
   Daniel 160
   Dorothy 577,627
   Ebenezer 372,667
   James 65,577

Evarts (cont.)
   John 65
   Jonathan 64,65,69
   Lydia 418
   Mabel 667
   Mary 118,574
   Rebecca 576
   Ruth 372,667
   Stephen 85
Everdeen, Mary 458
Everet, Sally 332
Everett, Abigail 561
   Abner 562
   Anna 561
   Edward F. 562
   Eunice 561
   Hannah 561
   Israel 561
   Israil 561
   Josiah 561
   Mary Winch 561
   Mical 561
   Richard 561
   Samuel 561
   Sarah 561
   Tabitha 561
Everit, Ambrose 562
   Israil 561
Everson, Louisa 76
Evets, Hannah 69
   Mary 64,69
Evetts, Mary 64,65
   Nathaniel 64
Ewing, James 625

--- F ---

Fairbanks, Caroline A.
      423
   Charlotte 423
   John 423
Fairchild, Caleb 465
   Ebenezer 358
   Elizabeth 158
   Frances Aurelia 465
   Isaac Maltby 465
   Joseph Lewis 465
   Julia Ann Norton 465
   Mary Elizabeth 465
Fairfax, Thomas (Sir)
      513
Fairweather, Sarah 551
Fake, Kate 333
Falconer, Patrick 322
Falley, Alexander 168
   Anna Lamb 167
   Daniel 167
   Frederick 167
   Lewis 167
   Lovisa 167
   Margaret 167,168
   Richard 167,168
   Richard (Jr.) 167
   Russell 167
   Ruth 167
   Samuel 167
Fallows, Annette Richard
      140
Fanning, Margaret 520
Farmer, John 102
Farnam, Elisheba 537
   Gad 128
   Hannah 128
   Jane Bishop 128
Farnham, Elizabeth 385
   Hannah 386

Farnham (cont.)
   Peter 399,463
   Stephen 616
Farnsworth, Levi 374
Farr, Tabitha 717
Farrington, Desire 124
Fasset, Amos 313
   Betty 312
   Josiah 441
   Josiah (Esq.) 442
   Nabby 442
Fassett, John 583
   Lydia Warren 583
   Sarah 583
Faulkner, Mary 666
   Patrick 666
Faust, William H. (Mrs.)
      293
Fay, Hannah 412
   Jedediah (Capt.) 582
   Orlando P. 148
Fellows, Edmund 338
   Ezra 692
   Lucia R. 551
Felton, Jonathan 625
Fenn, Dan 647
   Isaac 203
   Sherman 555
Fenner, Arthur 393
   John 393
   Sarah 393
   William 393
Fenton, Rebecca 385
Fenwick, --- 394
Ferguson, Lois 670
Fernald, Natalie R. 215
Ferns, Elizabeth 472,473
   James 472,473
   John 472,473
   Martha 189,473
   Samuel 472,473
   Samuel (Jr.) 472
   Samuel (Sr.) 472
Ferris, Joseph 651
   Martha 651
   Peter 651
   Peter (Jr.) 282
   Samuel 651
Ferry, Abigail 641
   Almeda 640
   Alvin 640
   Bathsheba 638
   Caroline Emma 641
   Elias Hitchcock 167
   Elvin 640,646
   Emma A. 641
   George L. 640
   Henry 640
   Henry J. 640
   James 638,640
   Oliver 641
   Polly Rogers 638,640
   William A. 640
Field, Abigail 96
   Alexander 470
   Benjamin 622
   Catharine 86
   Chloe 373
   Ebenezer 115
   Elizabeth 576
   Esther 161
   Jason 418
   Mary 65
   Mary Bishop Hodgkin
      Johnson 171
   Nathan 418
   Sylvia 670
   Zachary 85

Gold (cont.)
Georgianna 630
Milo Adelbert 630
Ruby E. Dennison 630
Sarah 468
Goldam, Frances 573
Henry 573
Susannah 573
Frances 573
Goldhatch, Alice 422
Goldsmith, Frances 72
Walter 72
Goodale, Hannah 472
Goodell, Adelbert Warren
630
Alice Corbin 271
Asa 271
Azabah 271
Charles Wesley 630
Chester Raymond 630
Della Almeda 630
Edwin 630
Ernest M. 630
Frank Miro 630
George 630
Henry 630
Jennie M. 630
Jerusha Corbin 630
John Gilbert 630
Julia Emma 630
Leonard 630
Leonard Stillmann
(Rev.) 630
Lucy Maria 630
Mary Jane 630
Milo Ernest 630
Olive Lovisa 630
Orinda 271
Gooding, George 15
Goodrich, Abigail 356,
504
Chauncey 531
David 504
Elizabeth 504
Elizur 53,464
Ephraim 504
Hannah 402
Jeremiah 358
John 504
Joseph 549
Lewis 332
Martha 135
Mary 372,434,504
Sarah 504
William 504
William (II) 504
Goodsell, Elizabeth 431
Lydia 437
Mary 192,361,437
Samuel 186,437
Sarah 136,437
Goodwill, Caroline Emma
Ferry 641
Goodwin, Abigail 128
Clara Wild 276
Elizabeth Nash 127
Elizard 54
Emma Warren Wild 276
Eunice 410
Hannah Vaille 128
James 127
James Otis 276
Nancy 522
Nathaniel 54
Nathaniel (Capt.) 127
Ozias 54
Ozias (Ens.) 128
Sarah 52,53,54

Goodwin (cont.)
Stephen 45,53,54
William 54,80
Goodyear, --- 7
Andr. 549
Andrew 549
Esther 549
Gookin, --- 9
Goph, --- (Col.) 70
Gordon, Betsey 106
George (Sir) 223
Mary Elizabeth 643
Nancy Whiting 522
Rose 703
Gorges, --- 3,6
Ferdinando (Sir) 4,7
Gorham, Aaron 75
Abigail 74,75,76
Alonzo 76
Amy 76
Barlow 76
Barlow W. (Rev.) 76
Benjamin 74,76
Benton 76
Betsey 75
Betsy 76
Charity 76
Charles 76
Charles T. 76
Chauncey T. 76
Daniel 74,75,76
David 76
Deborah 75
Deming 76
Desire Howland 395
Eli 76
Elizabeth 572
George S. 76
H. S. 285
Hannah 74
Hezekiah 75
Hiram 76
Ichabod 74,75,76
Isaac 74,570
Jabez 74,75,76,570
James 75
Jared 74,75
Jeremiah 75
John 75,76,395
John (Capt.) 74,570
Joseph 74,75,76
Judson 76
Laura 76
Lockwood 74
Lucy 75,76
Mary 74,76
Mary Punchard 570
Mehitable 570
Mercy 395
Miles 552
Phineas 74
Ralph 74
Rebecca 76
Russell 76
Sally 76
Sarah 76
Seth 74,75,76
Shubael 74
Thomas A. 76
Timothy 570
Wakeman 75
William 76
Gosard, Elizabeth 144
John 144
Nicholas 144
Gosnold, --- 2
Goss, Abel 442
Zenas 442

Goudy, Abigail Liswell
482
Gould, Elias 362
Elisha 497
Martha 453
Martha Smith 153
Thomas 624
William 131
Wm. (Dr.) 306
Gozzard, John 144
Grafton, Fanny 524
Graham, Anna M. 694
Chauncey (Rev.) 284
Elizabeth 148
Henry 491,492
John 40
Mary 491
Sarah 491
Sophia 694
Susannah 492
William 694
Granberry, Mary Emeline
405
Granger, Beldad 368
Elijah 368
Gideon 369
Grannis, Alline 437
Isaac (Jr.) 437
Jared 437
Joseph 437
Mabel 299
Mehitable Thompson
437
Olive 437
Russell 434
Thankful 436
Thomas 437
William 436
Granniss, Edward 299
Joseph 299
Mabel 299
Mehitable 299
Grant, --- 21
Abigail 79
Adoniram 79
Anna 79,80
Billings 638
Clara 80
David 79
Ebenezer (Capt.) 79
Elizabeth 80,81,410
Ephraim 79
Grace 79
Hannah 79,80
Harriet Swift 638
Jesse Root 80
John 78,79,80
Josiah 79
Lucy Green Sanford
638
Margaret 80
Martha 79
Mary 79
Mary Frances 80
Matthew 26,78,424
Mehetable 80
Miner 79
Nathaniel 79
Noah 78,79,80
Oliver 79
Ovil L. 80
Peter 80
Priscilla 78
Rachel 80,657
Roswell 80
Samuel 78,79,80
Sarah 79,81
Seth 80,81

749

751

Hayes (cont.)
Abigail 143,144,145,
  146,147
Alice 146
Allyn 654
Alpheus 146
Alson 148
Amasa 146
Amos 146
Andrew 147,148
Ann Coley Kellogg 340
Ann G. 148
Anna 141
Anne 147,148
Ansel 147
Anson B. 148
Anson E. 146
Apphia 148
Asa 148
Asahel 147,148
Asenath 148
Benajah 148
Benjamin 144,146,
  147,148
Benjamin Sheldon 146
Benoni 146
Betsey M. 148
Bruen 141
Calvin 146,148
Casson 148
Cephas 148
Charles W. (Rev.)
  143,148
Chauncey 148
Chester (Dea.) 145
Chloe 147
Cullen 147
Curtiss 146
Daniel 141,144,145,
  147
Daniell 144
David 141,142,146
David A. 141
Dianthy 148
Dorcas 144,147
Doritha 144
Dorothy 144
Drayton 148
Dudley 147,148
Elijah 146
Elisha 146
Elizabeth 141,146,
  147,148,354
Elizabeth A. 148
Elizur 146
Emily 148
Emma L. 148
Enos 148
Esther 141
Eunice 654
Everett A. 146
Ezekiel 143,145,146
Flora 146
Georg 143
George 141,143,144,
  146,147,148
George Edward (Dr.)
  148
Gunilda 148
Guy 148
Hannah 141,148
Harold 148
Hector 148
Henry 148
Henry O. 148
Hilpah 147
Honora 147
Horace 146

Hayes (cont.)
Isaac 141
Jabez W. 141
Jacob 146
James 141,142,654
Jane 146
Jemima 146
Jenny 147
Joanna 144,147
Joel 145,146
Johanna 144
John 141,143
Jonathan 146
Joseph 141,142,148
Joseph B. 148
Joseph M. (Rev.) 148
Judah 147
Lester 148
Levi 148
Levi L. 148
Lewry 148
Lura 148
Luther 146
Lydia 147
Martha 141,142,145,
  146,148
Martin 148
Mary 144,145,146,
  147,148,354,654
Mary Ann 147
Mary M. 148
Mehetabel 147
Melissa 147
Mercy 146
Michael 148
Moses 141,146
Mumford 148
Nancy 148
Nathaniel 142,143,354
Newton 146
Obadiah 145
Oliver 141,148
Oliver Bliss 146
Orlin P. (Rev.) 148
P. H. (Dr.) 148
Patty 146
Philip 146
Phoebe 141
Pliny 148
Pliny (Dr.) 148
Priscilla D. F. 148
R. S. (Dr.) 148
Rachel 141,654
Rebecca 146
Rhoda 146,147
Robert 141
Robert P. 148
Rosanna 146,147,148
Rosetta 147
Roswell 146
Roswell P. (Dr.) 146
Roxy A. 148
Rufus 146
Ruhama 148
Rutherford 146
Rutherford B. (Pres.)
  146,277
Samuel 141,142,144,
  145,146,147,148
Samuel (Maj.) 142
Samuell 144
Sarah 141,144,145,
  146,148
Seth 147
Sheldon 146
Silas 147
Silas (Capt.) 148
Silence 146,147

Hayes (cont.)
Simeon 148
Susanna 147,148
Temperance 148
Temzen 146
Thaddeus 146
Thankful 144,147
Thankfull 144
Theodore 146
Theodosia 148
Thomas 141,142,143
Thomas (Sgt.) 141,142
Warren H. 148
William 144,147,148
William (Jr.) 147
William R. 148
Willis G. 147,148
Zaccheus 146
Zadock 148
Zedekiah 148
Zenas 147
Zilpah 145,146
Zophar 146
Haynes, Jasabell 119
John 52
Jonathan 234,236
Judith 312
Rebecca Green 413
Samuel 98
Samuel (Capt.) 119
Hays, Daniel 143,145
George (Jr.) 143
George (Sr.) 143
Samuel 143
William 143
Hayse, George 143
Rachel 596
Hayward, Sabra 480
Hayz, George 143
Haze, --- 143
Hazen, Asa 530
Ellen 531
George 267
Ira 530
Joseph M. 530
Louisa 530
Susan J. 530
Walter 531
Headley, Joel T. (Hon.)
  657
P. C. (Rev.) 77,78,80
Robert 636
Heale, --- 7
Healy ,Emma 32
Esther 484
Mary 476,478
Rhoda Marcy 478
Steven 484
Heath, Abigail 687
Elizabeth 687
Hannah 685,687
Jonathan 687
Josiah 685,687,687
Lavinia B. 695
Levine 687
Lovis 687
Lucy 687
Mary 616,685,687
Mehitabel 687
Mercy 685
Mollie 687
Nathaniel 687
Obadiah 687
Heaton, Daniel 123
Hannah 632
Sarah 548
Seth 548
Hebard, Abigail 153

753

Hebard (cont.)
Anna 153
Daniel 150
David 153
Deborah 153
Elisha 153
Elizabeth 150
George 153
Gideon 153
Hannah 153
Harvey (Esq.) 149
Jemima 153
Joanna 153
John 150,152
Jonathan 153
Joseph 153
Joshua 152
Josiah 152,153
Martha 150,153
Mary 150,152,153
Mehitabel 153
Moses 153
Nathaniel 153
Paul 153
Robert 150,152,153
Ruth 150,153
Samuel 152,153
Sarah 150,153
Seth 153
William 150
Zaccheus 150
Zebulon 153
Hebart, Joan 150
Robert 150
Hebbert, Daniel 152
Dorothy 152
Ebenezer 152
Elizabeth 152
Esther 152
Henry 152
Jacob 152
Joanna 150
John 152
John (Jr.) 152
Joseph 152
Martha 152
Robert 152
Robt. 150
Ruth 152
Samuel 152
Hebert, Abigail 150,
151,154
Anna 154
Benjamin 152
Calvin 154
Clara 154
Cyprian 154
Deborah 151
Ebenezer 153,154
Ebenezer (Lt.Jr.) 154
Elizabeth 150
Hannah 152
Jemima 152
Jeremiah 152
Joanna 151
Johanna 150
John 150
Jonathan 151
Joseph 150,152
Keziah 154
Lovine 149,154
Margaret 153
Marie 150
Mary 151,152
Nathan 153
Olandina 154
Prudence 153
Reuben 154

Hebert (cont.)
Robert 149,150,151,
152,153,154
Samuel 150,151
Sarah 150,152
Shubael 154
William 154
Ziphron 154
Zipperac 154
Hecock, Martha 146
Hedges, David 564
David (Dea.) 565
H. P. 423
Jeremiah 564
Mary M. 566
Mary Miller 567
William 569
William (Dea.) 566
Heeney, Thomas 634
Hegman, Florence 719
Joseph 719
Heiser, Adda 708
Helden, Pauline 402
Helfrich, Idabelle 606
Hemenway, Abby Maria 101
Neverson 641
Hemingway, Amy 571
Charlotte 209
Hannah 548
John 547
Luella 602
Samuel 548
Heminway, Mary 434
Hemmenway, M. 182
Hemmingway, Joanna 475
Hempstead, Amanda 214
Betsey 214
George 527
Joshua 233,238,239
Patience 527
Hendee, --- (Capt.) 709
Hendee, Elizabeth A. 590
Henderson, Eliza Elliot
524
James 83
Marvin 363
Hendey, Clara Alice 33
Hendrick, Jabesh 475
Hendricks, Polly 701
Hendricksen, Tryntie 309
Henerig, Tryntie 307,309
Henry, Amasa J. 602
Andrew 482
Anna 477,482
Annette 591
Edith 720
Hazel Helen 602
Milton 720
Thankful Norris 482
Henshaw, Benjamin 463
Henson, Mary O. Monroe
591
Hepburn, Aner 207
Heridon, Wm. 480
Herman, Malissa V. 591
Herrick, David 507
Hewes, Richard 216
Hewett, Reuben 331
Hewitt, Ezra 593
Hiatt, Hester Ann 643
Hibbard, Asa (Rev.) 482
Hibbart, Samuel 200
Hibberd, Joan 150
Robert 150
Hibbert, Abigail 151
Bridget 151
Daniel 150
Dorcas 151

Hibbert (cont.)
Elizabeth 150,151
George 150
Jeremiah 151
Joanna 151
John 150
Jonathan 154
Joseph 151
Martha 150
Mary 150,151,154
Rebecca 151
Robert 150,151,154
Ruth 150
Samuel 154
Sarah 150,151
Seth 154
Southwick 154
William 150
Zaccheus 150
Hibbird, Abigail 151
Ebenezer 151
Hannah 151
Joseph 151
Josiah 151
Lydia 151
Martha 151
Mary 151
Nathaniel 151
Robert 150,151
Sarah 151
Hichborn, Thomas 95
Hickok, James 330
Hickox, --- 556
John 129
Samuel 293
Hicks, --- 95
Alfred Thomas 591
Delos 605
Emma 605
Emmaline Stanton 605
John A. (Rev.Dr.) 710
Hiddleson, Ella Viantha
634
Higby, Dinah 516
John L. 500
Martha 146
Ozias 146
Higginbotham, Rebecca
619
Richard 619
Higgins, E. M. 538
Jedidiah 540
Mehitabel Morris 556
Highland, --- 574
Deborah 115,155
Elizabeth 155
George 155,157
Hannah 155,157
Mary 155
Higley, Brewster 683,
691,694
David 683
Diana 537
Elizabeth 525
Hannah 691
Hiland, --- 574
Deborah 155
Elizabeth 155
George 155,157,574
Hannah 155,157
Mary 155
Hilborn, Samuel 148
Hildeburn, Charles R.
101
Hill, --- 3
Aaron 161,162
Abigail 89,96,156,
158,159

Hill (cont.)
Abner 160
Abraham 160,161,165,
  622
Abraham Enoch 166
Abram 161
Ahira 159
Alpha 274
Ann 157,159,164
Anna 156,158,160,161
Anne 159
Benajah 166
Benjamin 158
Benjamin (Dr.) 159
Benjamin S. 163
Bettsy 161
Betty 161
Beulah 86,160,161
Bille 165
Charity 157,159
Charles 96,513
Charles (Capt.) 89
Charlotte 714
Christopher 162
Clayton Lewis 715
Cloe 165
Daniel 157,159,160,
  164,472
Darius 642
David 160
Dorcas 161
Ebenezer 156,165,
  714,715,717
Ebenezer (Jr.) 714
Edward 162
Edwin (Dr.) 393
Edwin A. 318
Edwin A. (Dr.) 400
Edwin A. (Esq.) 163,
  315
Elijah 158
Elizabeth 156,157,
  158,160,161,163,
  164,171
Elizth. 4
Esther 161
Ezra 160
Flora 161
Florence 715
Florence H. 717
George 158,362,373,
  513
Hamilton A. 101
Hannah 157,158,159,
  160,161,164,306,
  359
Henry 158,159,161
Henry (Hon.) 158
Hiland 161
Hiram 715
Huldah 158,160
Ichabod 161
Irena 160
Irene 577
Isaac 156,157,159,
  164,165,166
James 157,159,160,
  161,163,164,165
Jerusha 161
Jesse 160
John 4,156,157,158,
  159,160,161,163,
  164,165,359,471
John (III) 157
John (Jr.) 155,157,
  164
John (Sr.) 156,164
Jonas 161,165

Hill (cont.)
Jonathan 159,160
Joseph 159
Joseph (Col.) 161
Josiah 159
Julius 164
Katharine 164
Keziah 156,165
Leah 158
Lewis Owen 715
Lovina 715
Lucy 158,159,606,715
Luke 156,163,165,166
Luke (Jr.) 156
Lydia 156,160,165,666
Marcy 159
Mary 156,157,158,
  159,160,161,556
Mary Ann 162
Mehitabel 162
Mercy 159,160
Michael 157,161,163,
  164
Milo 715
Mindwell 160,419,471
Molly 159
Moses 159
Nathaniel 157,158,161
Noah 159
Peleg 161
Phineas 165
Purdee 715
Rachel 158
Rebecca 161
Reuben 158,160,164,
  621
Rhoda 159
Richard 161
Riley 715
Robert 4,297,715,717
Rousel 159
Rowena Flavia 715
Roxanna 162
Ruth 158,161
Sally 166,714
Sam (Col.) 158
Samuel 156,157,158,
  162
Samuel (Col.) 158
Sarah 157,159,160,
  161,162,163,164
Selah 159
Seth 166
Sibyl 159
Silas 159
Submit 159,195
Susannah 158,159
Tahan 156
Tapping 164
Thankful 159
Thomas 158,306,373
Timothy 160
Timothy (Dea.) 160,
  419,577,670
Walter 274
William 161
William (Rev.) 161
William Asa 161
Zenas 160,165
Hillhouse, --- (Capt.)
  464
Elizabeth 528
Harriet 529
James (Rev.) 514,528
James Abraham 514
John 514
John (Esq.) 514
John Griswold 529

Hillhouse (cont.)
John Griswold (Judge)
  528
Mary Ann 528
Rachel 514
Sarah Griswold 528
William 514
William (Judge) 528
Hills, Edward 535
John 328
Hillyer, James 144
Joanna 144
Mercy 536
Hinckley, Jared 521
John 27
Lucinda 589
Thankful 521
Walter 418
Hindsdale, Samll. 53
Hine, Adelaide 294
Anna Andrews 555
David 203
Eliphal 203
Eliza Hotchkiss Mun-
  ger 195
Elizabeth 554
Hannah 649
Isaac 555
James 647
John 555,560
Josiah 649
Mary 128
Samuel 194,649
Sarah Sanford 555
Hinkley, Scottoway 341
Hinman, R. R. (Hon.) 2,8
Royal R. 115
Hinsdale, Abbe 691
Jonathan 467
Robert 41
Hinsdell, Mahuma 51
Robert 41
Samll. 48
Hinsdill, Anna 336
Hirt, Blanche Bowman 718
Hiscock, Sarah 632,639
Hiss, Bosley 710
Hitchcock, --- (Dea.)
  336
Abigail 167,202,292
Abigail Merriman 292
Alexander 370
Allen B. 208
Apollos 370
Arthur 167
Betsey Kimberly 364
David 166
Edithha 167
Elias 167
Elihu 203
Elizabeth 167
Elizabeth Walker 663
Eunice 167,663
Experience 369
Gaius 167
Hannah 166
Heman 167
Jacob 437
James 370
Jerusha 167
John 166,167,168,
  292,344,359
Jonathan 166
Lemuel (Dea.) 195
Lois 167
Luke 166,167,168,663
Margaret 167,168
Martha 359

Holton, Amanda Jane 634
  Mary 13
  Samuel 17
Honeyman, James (Rev.)
  359
Hood, John 15
Hoods, Henrietta 136
Hoof, Anne Catherine 99
Hooker, Andrew 409
  Daniel (Dr.) 667
  Hannah 667
  Mary Eliza 643
  Thomas 90
  William 26
Hoover, Addie Estella
  598
  Charles Monroe 598
  Ermina Z. 598
  John Willard 598
  Mary Eleanor 598
  William H. 598
Hopkins, --- 9,489
  Adelaide 523
  Allie 610
  Anna 130
  Benjamin Bronson 523
  Benjamin F. 274
  Bethia 180
  Betsy 181
  Charles 597
  Consider 180
  Consider (Jr.) 24
  Daniel 180,181
  David 181
  Delinda 523
  Dorcas 180
  Ebenezer 180
  Edward (Esq.) 180
  Elias 24
  Elizabeth 498
  Elliot 523
  Enos 556
  Ethel 597
  George Nelson 273
  Hannah 180
  Hannibal Mason 523
  Huldah 180
  Isaac 135
  James 180
  Jane 180
  Joanna 181
  John 180,214
  Joseph 180
  Levi 181
  Lillian Fish 597
  Lois Fuller 130
  Mark 180
  Mary 180,523,645
  Mary L. 646
  Miriam 23,24
  Mirriam 23
  Moses 181
  Rebecca 523
  Reuben (Gen.) 523
  Rhoda 181,214
  Ruth 130
  Ruth Berry 130
  S. 50,182
  Samuel 180,181
  Samuel (Rev.Dr.) 180
  Sarah 180
  Silvanus 130
  Stephen 180
  Timothy 180
  Webster 180
  William Hector 523
  William S. 273
  Zenas 485

Hopson, Abigail 169
  Ann 170
  Deborah 170
  Dorothy 117
  Ebenezer 170
  Elizabeth 169
  Eunice 170
  Frances 169
  Hannah 170
  Huldah 117,170
  John 117,169,170,344
  John (Capt.) 170,
    344,670
  John (Lt.) 117
  John (Lt.Jr.) 169
  Jordan 170
  Mary 170
  Millicent 170
  Nancy 86,170
  Nathan Wilcox 170
  Nathaniel 170
  Samuel 169
  Samuel (Lt.) 169
  Sarah 169,170,670
  Theodore 170
  Timothy 170
  William 170
Horley, Jno. 380
Hornbeck, Edith E. 595
Horsington, John 177
Horton, Abigail 211
  Margaret 138
  Polly 192
  Samuel 211,292
  Sarah 211,626
  Thomas 380
Hosford, Hannah 144
  Mary 683
Hoskins, Alexander 45
  Anthony (Jr.) 46
Hosmer, Robert 96
  Ruth 337
Hossenton, Ebenezer 177
  Elisha 177
  Elizabeth 177
  James 177
  Joab 177
  John 177
  Nathaniel 177
  Sarah 177
  Thankful 177
Hotchkin, Abigail 211,
  306
  Abraham 211
  Alice Rebecca 176
  Amanda Charlotte 211
  Augustine Hall 176
  Beniah 175
  Beriah (Rev.) 175,176
  Beriah Bishop (Rev.)
    176
  Charles 211
  Elias 211
  Elizabeth Alice 176
  Gurdon Beriah (Dr.)
    175,176
  Helen 176
  James (Rev.) 175
  James Henry (Rev.)
    176
  James Hervey 176
  James Hervey (Rev.)
    175
  James Rowland 176
  John 211
  John Niles 176
  Joseph 306
  Lovinia 211

Hotchkin (cont.)
  Mary Ann 211
  Noah 175
  Oliver 211
  Samuel 176
  Samuel Fitch (Rev.)
    176
  Tabitha 211
  William Henry 176
  William Rowland 176
Hotchkiss, Aaron 203
  Abigail 173,183,184,
    186,187,188,191,
    197,200,202,204,
    206,212,213
  Abigail Smith 202
  Abijah 214
  Abner 198,203
  Abraham 184,186,187,
    188,192,193,194,
    202,203,292
  Abraham Barnes 193
  Ada 197
  Adonijah 198
  Albert 201,209
  Amasa 190,212
  Ambrose 211
  Amelia 210
  Amos 174,175,184,
    189,190,191,192,
    197,203,211
  Amos (Capt.) 189
  Amraphel 213,214
  Amy 191
  Amzi 192
  Andrew 210,214
  Andrew T. 208
  Aner 211
  Ann 202
  Anna 184,192,197,203,
    204,206,213,292
  Anna Maria 210
  Apalina 213,214
  Arthur 191
  Asa 189,191,198
  Asahel 192,212,213,
    214
  Asahel Augustus 213,
    214
  Asenath 211,212,213
  Aurelius 199
  Azubah 198
  Bathsheba 186
  Beecher Delos 209
  Bela 202
  Benjamin 184,186,
    189,193,194,197,
    198,202,203
  Benjamin Berkley 214
  Benoni 190,192,200
  Betsey 201,204,206,
    212
  Beulah 213
  Bildad 203
  Briant 211
  Burr 194,209
  Caleb 173,174,175,
    183,185,186,190,
    191,194,198,199,
    201,206,207,394
  Calvin 202
  Candace 195
  Caroline 198,200,
    207,208
  Caroline Lucina 208
  Carver 213
  Charity 213
  Charles 190,210,214

760

Huntington (cont.)
  Samuel 218,219,220,
    221
  Simon 218,219,220,221
  Simon (Dea.) 526
  Solomon 218,220,325
  Submit 526
  Submit (II) 526
  Sybil 526
  Thomas 218,220,221,
    222
  Thomas (Dr.) 222
  William 218,220
Huntley, Aaron 224,225,
    226,227,228,230,
    231,232,233,235,
    237,238,239,240,
    242,243,244,245,
    246,252,253,254,
    255,256,257,258,
    259,260,261,262,
    263,264,265,266,
    267
  Aaron (III) 240
  Aaron (Jr.) 232
  Aaron John 247
  Abel 247
  Abel Lord 260,261
  Abigail 229,239,247,
    248,249,251,258,
    268
  Abner 234,248,249
  Abraham 253
  Acel 265
  Adam S. 260
  Adriel 235,237,251
  Alanson 264
  Albert Phineas 260
  Alden 257
  Alexander 267
  Alice 225,226
  Alice P. 223,234,
    242,254,267,268
  Allen 256
  Almira 262
  Alson 265
  Alvin 258
  Amanda 257
  Amos 229,232,243,
    244,245,255,258
    259,262,263
  Andrew 246,265
  Andrew M. 265
  Ann 243,258,264
  Anna 244,246,265
  Anne 259
  Ansel 249
  Asa 258
  Asahel 265
  Asenath 261
  Asher 248,266
  Augustus 249
  Aurelia 249
  Azuba 242
  Azubah 245,252
  Barnabas 268
  Barnabas B. 264
  Baruck 264
  Benegar 234,249,250,
    254
  Benejah 229,234,268
  Benejah Francis 254
  Benejar 235
  Beniah 252
  Benjamin 230,238,
    239,240,253
  Bethaniel 241
  Bethuel 241

Huntley (cont.)
  Betsy 258,260,262,266
  Bettey 252
  Borden 226
  Calkins 255
  Calvin 246,256,259,
    260,265
  Calvin Wheeler 267
  Caroline 261
  Caroline Mathilde 262
  Caroline Matilda 249
  Catherine 241
  Charles 249,254,261,
    263,267
  Charlotte 258,263
  Christopher Columbus
    252
  Clarenda 256
  Clarissa 265
  Clarry 263
  Curtais 234,240,252
  Curtis 257
  Dan 244,245,255
  Daniel 228,231,232,
    242,243,244,251,
    257,258,258,259,
    260,261,262,263
  Daniel (Jr.) 258
  Daniel (Sr.) 258
  Daniell 228
  Danuel 253
  David 228,232,233,
    239,245,246,247,
    263,264,265,266,
    267
  Davis 253
  Deborah 231,243,264
  Delana 237
  Delia B. 262
  Delight 263
  Demarus 249
  Dennis 249
  Diadema 262
  Dorcas 234
  Duran 253
  Easter 232
  Edmund 246,265
  Edmund B. 265
  Elethere S. 251
  Elias 248,267
  Elias Sanford 267
  Elihu 245,263,264
  Elijah 233,246,247,
    257,264,265,266
  Eliphalet 247
  Elisha 228,233,242,
    246,256,257,259,
    259,261,263
  Elisheba 252
  Elisheby 252
  Eliza 261
  Eliza Ann 267
  Elizabeth 224,224,
    225,226,228,230,
    238,239,244,245,
    258,267,268
  Elkanah 244,262
  Elkanah Allen 262
  Elsie 267
  Ely 226
  Emilie 262
  Emma Way 267
  Enoch 244,251,256,258
  Enoch Hill 251
  Enock 260
  Erastus 249,263
  Erastus Calvin 263
  Erastus S. S. S. 262

Huntley (cont.)
  Ester 231
  Esther 240,255
  Esther Moor 257
  Ethelinda 257
  Eunice 238,239,246,
    253,261
  Eunice Holmes 266
  Eunice Royce 256
  Experience 261
  Ezekiel 233,246,247,
    248,259,266,267
  Ezra 238,248,252,
    255,266,267
  Fanny 254,260
  Florus 261
  Fred 253
  Frederick 236,237,251
  George 229
  Gideon 264
  Giles 255
  Giles B. 262
  Guerdon 256
  Gurden 263
  Hana 231
  Hannah 226,229,231,
    235,238,239,243,
    247,248,250,252,
    254
  Hannah Brown 232
  Harriet 265
  Harriot 261
  Harris 254
  Harvey 241
  Heman 265
  Henry Holmes 266
  Hepsebeth 240
  Hepsibah 240
  Hezekiah 235,238,
    240,254
  Hiram 252,259
  Hoel 235,250
  Hope 253
  Horatio 258
  Howell 235,250
  Hubbard 257
  Huldah 244,249
  Ira 244,260
  Ira (Jr.) 260
  Irena 249
  Irene 244
  Iron 228
  Isaac 243,261
  Isaac Smith 251
  Isaiah 242,256
  Jabez 229,236,237,
    250,251,268
  Jacob 232,243,251,258
  Jacub 258
  James 232,243,244,
    251,258,259,260,
    261,262
  James Calkins 261
  Jane 224,226,228
  Jason 243
  Jasper 238,252
  Jedidiah (Capt.) 247
  Jedidiah Brockway 264
  Jehiel 230
  Jemima 231,232,263
  Jerusha 234
  Jim (Dea.) 261
  Jno. 224
  Joanna 233
  Joel 265
  John 223,224,225,226,
    227,228,229,230,
    232,234,236,237,

Jones (cont.)
324,325,561
William (Dep.Gov.)
315,316,317,318,
453,561
William (Esq.) 72,322
William (Jr.) 323
William (Lt.Gov.)
321,322
William Rosewell 325
William Trowbridge
324
Zachariah 318
Zachariah Hard 323
Jordan, --- 7
Ann 326
Bertha Hessie 274
Catherine 327,328
Dayton DeForest 274
Dennison Palmer 274
Elizabeth 326,327
Hannah 326,327
James 327,328
Joanna 325
John 325,326,327,328
Mary 325,326,327,328
Thomas 326,327,328
Josslyn, Daniel 261
Joy, Elizabeth 699
Judd, Betsy B. 419
Chauncey 192
Elizabeth 407,408
Eunice 408
Hannah Diggins 117
Jesse 408
John 408,411
Jonathan 419
Jonathan (Rev.) 180,
182
Lois 408
Mary 180,408
Mary Maltby Brown 455
Matthew 552
Rachel 407
Rebecca 455
Rhoda 411
Ruth 408
Sylvester (Esq.) 2,
180
Thomas 620
Thomas (Dea.) 180,
407,408
William 408,620
William (Esq.) 416
Judson, Benjamin 621
Maria 553
Mehitabel 553
William Legrand 556
Jurdan, James 328
Jurianse, Laurens 308

--- K ---

Kaye, Ruth Lincoln 348
Keach, Dorcas E. 275
Harriett Young 274
John 274
John Everett 275
John R. 275
Merrill H. 274
Robert Nelson 275
Walter Edmund 275
Keeler, Mercy 677
Sarah 674
Ralph 674
Rufus 677

Keeler (cont.)
Ruth 652
Keeney, Elizabeth 527
Elvina 527
Kelley, --- 3
Elizth. 4
Jo. 4
Kellock, --- 329
Brigget 508
Briggit 508,509
Kellog, Nathll. 344
Kellogg, --- Susanna 339
A. S. (Esq.) 336
Aaron 337,347
Abigail 28,336,337,
338,340,341,344,
346,347
Abigail Ann 332,333
Abner 344,345,347
Abner (Capt.) 345
Adelia 338
Albert 338
Alexander Cyrus 331,
339
Alice 503,508,510
Allen G. 523
Allyn 341
Allyn S. 316,508
Allyn Stanley 341
Alvan 331
Amanda 331
Amasa 338
Amelia L. 333
Amos 337,338,347
Ann 340,344,345
Anna 330,346
Asa 330,331,332,333,
339,345
Augustus 338
Augustus Fake 339
Benjamin 340
Bethiah 347
Burr Smith 334
Butler 346
Calvin Whitwood 332
Caroline 333,338
Caroline Louisa 334
Cassius 339
Catherine 338,348,351
Charles 331,332,338,
339,341,344,346
Charles Annable 332
Charles Augustus 334
Charles Day 334
Charles Dor 339
Charles Harvey 333
Charles White 332
Chauncey 338
Clara Dauchy 333
Clarissa H. 332
Cyrus 339
D. O. 329,335
Dan W. 332,333,339
Daniel 336,337,339,
340,341,344,345,
346,347,508,509,
510
Daniel (Dea.) 337
Daniel (Dr.) 339
Daniel W. 342
David 340,341,345
David (Rev.Dr.) 339
Day Otis 332,334
Deborah 340
Delia 332
Delight 345,629
Donny 338
Dor 332

Kellogg (cont.)
Dorliska 333
Dorothy 348,349,350,
351,352
Dwight 332,339
Ebenezer 336,337,
338,340,341,342,
343,346
Ebenezer (Esq.) 341
Ebenezer (Rev.) 341
Ebenezer Noble 341
Edburgh 338
Editha 344
Edmund B. 341
Edward 333,336,348,
349,350,352,353
Edward (Sr.) 349
Edward Asa 333
Edward H. 333
Edwin 338
Eleanor 330,338,348,
351
Electa 331
Electa Semanthy 333
Eliasaph 340
Elijah 340,344
Elijah C. 341
Eliphalet 340
Elisha 337,338,345
Eliza 333
Elizabeth 197,336,
339,340,341,345,
346
Elizabeth Homer 334
Ellen Maria 334
Ellen Wheeler 334
Emma Louise 339
Enos 330,338
Ensign H. (Hon.)
335,338
Epenetus 340
Ephraim 330,337,338,
348,349,351
Esther 338,340,346
Eunice 341,343,344
Eve 347
Ezekiel 344,345,693
Ezra 330,332,340,
344,345
Ezra Powell 332
Fanny 332
Fanny Louisa 333
Frances 338
Frances Louisa 333
Frances Lucretia 334
Frances Southwick 333
Francis Pelatiah 333
Frederick 330,331,
332,338
George 338,341
George Abel 333
George Dimon 334
George Dwight 332,339
George William 333
Gertrude 332
Gideon 337,340
Hannah 337,340,341,
343,344,345,346,
347
Harriet 332,338
Harriet Odin 333
Henry 333,338,339
Henry Lyman 334
Henry Parmelee 333
Homer Hall 334
Horace 341
Hosmer 338
I. Newton Phelps 333

Kingsley (cont.)
  Albert 704
  Alice 371,704
  Amos 371
  Eldad 371
  Eliza 371
  Isaiah 371
  James 704
  John 371
  Joseph 371
  Lovinia Hotchkin 211
  Lydia 152
  Nathaniel 371
  Nettie 704
  Ralph 704
  Ruth 371
  Ruth Adams 371
  Samuel 371
  Seth (Dea.) 656
Kinney, Elisha 481
  Horace 481
Kinsley, Hudson (Dr.)
  524
Kinzer, Dean 703
  Ernest 703
  Ethel 703
  Jessie 703
  Joseph 703
  Lawrence 703
  Lura 703
  Rawlin 703
  Verna 703
  Ward 703
Kirby, Abiah 355
  Ephraim 490,491,496
  John 660
  Joseph 355
  Reinold Marvin (Maj.)
  491
Kircum, Henry 372
Kirkham, Anna 372
  Anna Forsdick 372
  Anne 455
  Austin Parker 373
  Bedad 373
  Bela Stone 373
  Benjamin 372
  Benjamin Franklin 373
  Benjamin Mortimer 373
  Betsey 373
  Caleb Evarts 373
  Calvin Crampton 373
  Catherine Ward 374
  Clarissa Griswold 374
  Daniel 372,373,455
  Daniel Erastus 373
  Daniel Maltby 373
  David 372,373
  Eber 372
  Eli 372,374,455
  Eli Maltby (Rev.) 374
  Elihu 372,455
  Elijah 372
  Eliza Ann 373
  Elizabeth 372
  Ellen Roselia 373
  Erastus Rodney 373
  Esther 372,455
  George 373
  George Albert 373
  George Anson 373
  Guilford Montgomery
  373
  Harriett Maltby 374
  Henry 371,372
  Isaac Johnson 373
  Jane Amorett 374
  Jane Eliza 373

Kirkham (cont.)
  Joanna 372
  John 372,373,374,455
  John Bates 373
  John Harrison 374
  Laura B. 373
  Levi 372,455
  Lydia 372
  Marietta 374
  Martha 372
  Mary 372,373
  Mary Ann 374
  Mercy 372
  Nancy 373
  Nathaniel 372
  Patience 372
  Philemon 372,373,455
  Rebecca 372
  Richard Monson 373
  Ruth 371
  Samuel 371,372,373,
  373,374,455
  Samuel (Jr.) 372
  Sarah 372,373
  Solomon 372,455
  Susan 373
  Susannah Collins 374
  Thomas 371,372,373,
  374
  Wealthy 372
  William 372,373
  William L. 373
  Zerviah 372,455
Kirkland, Daniel (Rev.)
  379
  Eliza 379
  George Whitfield 379
  Jerusha 379
  John 379,380
  John Thornton 379
  John Thornton (Pres.)
  383
  Joseph 380
  Philip 492
  Saml. (Rev.) 383
  Samuel 379
  Samuel (Rev.) 379,380
  Sarah 379
Kirtland, Abigail 380,
  381
  Abner 376,378
  Ambrose 376,379
  Anne 376
  Asa 377
  Azubah 378
  Benjamin 378
  Billious 378
  Charles 376,378
  Clarinda 378
  Constant 375,377
  Daniel 376,378
  Daniel (Rev.) 375,
  376,380
  Deborah M. 378
  Dorotha 375
  Eleazer 378
  Elias 375,377
  Elisabeth 375
  Elisha 375,377,378
  Eliza 525
  Elizabeth 375,376,378
  Esther 376
  Ezra 375,378
  Francis 380,381
  Fras. 380
  George 378
  Gideon 376,378
  Hanna 382

Kirtland (cont.)
  Hannah 376
  Hester 375,377
  Isaac 378
  Jabez 376
  James 377
  Jared 378
  Jedediah 376
  John 375,376,377,
  378,379,380,381,
  382,383,401
  John (Lt.) 383
  John L. 401
  Joseph 377,380,381
  Lydia 375,376,377,378
  Major 380
  Martha 375,376
  Martin 376,378
  Mary 376,378,380,
  381,382
  Mercy 378
  Nathan 376,378
  Nathanael 375,376
  Nathaniel 379,380,381
  Parnell 375,377
  Phebe 376
  Philip 375,376,378,
  379,380,381
  Priscilla 375,376
  Rachel 378
  Reynold 376
  Ruth 378
  Samuel 375,376,378
  Samuel (Dea.) 378
  Samuel (Rev.) 376,
  379,525
  Sara 382
  Sarah 375,376,378
  Stephen 376
  Susanna 380,381,382
  Sybil 378
  Temperance 375,377
  Turhand 378
  William 377
  Zebulon 378
Kitchel, Robert 83,217,
  665
Kitcherel, Martha 543
Klock, John 719
  Mary 719
  Phoebe 719
Knapp, Alexander 461
  Alexander Horace 461
  Benjamin S. 461
  Elihu 259
  Henry E. 461
  Jesse Maltby 461
  Margaret D. 599
  Samuel Isaac 461
Kneeland, John 92
  Samuel 92,93,96,99
  Stillman Foster 101
Kneelon, Charity Betsey
  Johnson 295
Knight, Elizabeth 627,
  636
  Jonathan 311
  Sarah Fuller 105
Knollys, Hanserd 392
Knolton, Deborah 389
  Joseph 389
Knower, Cornelia 484
  Sarah C. 617
Knowles, Elizabeth 440
  Harrison 591
  John 440
  Mary 433
  Mary McCloud 440

771

776

Marcy (cont.)
Ithamar 486
James 474,475,477,
480,481,486
James L. 485
James Lorenzo (Dr.)
482
Jane A. 481
Jared 480,487
Jedediah 476,478,484
Jemima 483
Jeruiah 475
Jerusha 476,480
Job 477,481
John 474,475,476,
477,478,479,480,
481,482,483,484,
485,486,487
John F. 483
John Judson 484
John S. 479,486
John Sager (Rev.) 487
Jonathan 476,480,486
Joseph 474,475,476,
477,478,480,481,
482,483,484,487
Joseph (Capt.) 475
Joseph W. 486
Joshua 480
Judah 475
Justin 482
Laban 478,483,484
Larned 485
Laura 479
Lawton 478,483
Lebeus 478
Lemuel 271,478
Leonard 480
Levi 479,486
Lois 475,479,486
Loren 481
Lorenzo J. 482
Lorinda 487
Louisa 486
Lovia 475
Lucinda 485,486
Lucius L. 484
Lucretia 482
Lucy 477,481,482,486
Luther 483
Lydia 475,477,480,485
Lydia H. 485
Mahitabel 476,478,
479,486
Maria L. 481
Marietta 484
Marisia Ann 484
Martha 475,476,479,
480,486,487
Martha Curtis 487
Martha R. 487
Marvin 478,485
Mary 475,476,477,
478,481,482,485,
486,635
Mary A. 484
Mary Ann 481,482,483
Mary Eliza 484
Mary F. 483
Mary T. 478,482
Matilda 485
Matthew 477
Matthew (Judge) 481
Mehitabel 475
Mellissa B. 481
Meriam 485
Merrick 483
Michael B. 478

Marcy (cont.)
Miriam 475
Mirriam 476
Molly 479
Morris 478,485
Moses 474,476,478,
479,484,485
Moses (Col.) 475
Nabby 480
Nancy 486
Nancy Almira 483
Nancy Ann 482
Nancy Carpenter 271
Nancy Mariah 483
Nathan 483
Nathaniel 475,477,
482,483
Newman 486
Nichols 487
Nicholson 480,487
Noah P. 482
Olive 478,479,486,486
Oliver 482
Oliver (Dr.) 474
Oliver H. Perry 487
Oliver M. 485
Oren 479,486
Orrin 482
Patia 478
Patia L. 483
Peter 474
Phoebe 486
Plympton 483
Polly 479,480,481,482
Porter 487
Priscilla 271,479,486
Prosper 479
Prudence 477,478,480
Rachel 479
Randolph B. (Gen.)
474
Randolph Barnes 484
Ransom D. 484
Rebecca 477,479,483
Rebecka 475
Relecta 482
Reuben 475,477,481,
487
Rhoda 478,480,484
Rinaldo B. 484
Rufus 485
Ruth 479,486
Sally 479,480,481,
483,485
Salome 479,486
Samantha 481
Samuel 474,476,478,
479,485,486
Samuel Sumner (Dr.)
481
Sandford 482
Sarah 474,475,476,
477,478,479,480,
481,485,487
Sarah M. 485
Sarah O. 481
Simeon 481
Simeon (Dr.) 477
Smith 475,478,483
Sophia 478,479
Spencer 486
Squire 485
Stephen 481
Stephen (Capt.) 475,
477
Stephen (Dr.) 477,481
Steven 479
Steven H. 486

Marcy (cont.)
Sullivan 485
Susan 485,487
Sybell 476
Sylvester 477
Sylvester (Dr.) 481
Tabitha 476
Thankful 480,486
Thomas 475,477,478,
479,482,483,486
Thomas (Rev.) 482
Thomas J. 482
Thomas Melvin 483
Timothy 486
Uriah 475,477
Uriah P. 481
Welthy 480
Willard 479,485
William 476,478,482,
485,486
William Ainsworth 484
William G. 483
William L. (Dr.) 487
William Larned 474
William Larned 484
William N. 487
William W. 481
Winthrop 479,486
Zaviah 476
Zebediah 476,479,486
Zebulon 476,480,487
Zebulon Conant 487
Mareen, Dorman 551
Marks, Levi 28
Marlin, Aeltye 310
Anna 310
Marlo, Thomas 543
Marlow, Thomas 543
Maroone, Dorman 551
Marriott, Anna 708
Charles 707,708
Cora 707
Earl 708
Edward L. 707
Edwin 707
Elijah 707
Elsie 708
George 707
Grace 707
Hubert 707
Isaac Franklin 707
Joseph S. 707
Oliver 708
Sarah Ellen 708
Walter Scott 708
Will Clark 708
Marsh, Anna 531
Arabella 531
Benjamin Swan 531
Betsy 259
Charles 532
Charles (Dr.) 531
Charles Chapman 532
Daniel 531
Dorothy 530
Ebenezer 49,54,127
Ebenezer (Col.) 127
Ebenr. 54
Edward Warren 532
Elizabeth 49,52,53,
54,532
Ely T. 260
Emely 531
Enos 53
Eunice 653
Franklin 532
George Ozias 532
George Perkins 531,

Marvin (cont.)
W. T. R. 512
William 491,496,497,
  498,506
William (Capt.) 500
William Noyes 500
William T. R. 508
William W. 499
Zechariah 490,492,
  494,499
Marvyn, Elizabeth 489
Hanna 489
Marie 489
Matthew 489
Sara 489
Mashupanan, --- 11
Mason, Abby Jane 529
Abigail 515,520,527,
  528
Alfred 529
Alithea 520
Altha Stevens 539
Amos 527
Andrew 520,528
Andrew (II) 520
Andrew W. 536
Ann 534
Anna 526,529
Anna A. 537
Anne 513,514,515,517,
  518,519,524,537
Augustus B. 537,538
Aurora 536
Benjamin 536
Bridget 528
Carlos 537
Cecilia A. 537
Charles 529,537
Charles A. 536
Charles Ely 537
Charles John 536
Charles Lewis 537
Charlotte 527
Chloe 536
Clara 539
Clarissa 525
Cynthia Maria 537
Cyrus 537,538
Daniel 513,515,519,
  520,526,527,528,
  529,532,533,537,
  681
Daniel (II) 526
Darius 537
David 526
Dorothy 519,525,526,
  530
Dudley 528
Edgar Lewis 537
Edgar S. 537
Edwy 537
Elijah 517,518,525,
  531
Eliphalet 528
Elisabeth 533
Elisheba 537
Elizabeth 513,514,
  517,520,526,527,
  528,532,591,665
Elizabeth Anne 537
Ella 537
Elmada Eliza 539
Elnathan 520,528
Elnathan (II) 528
Emerette 537
Emily E. 537
Esther 524
Eunice 520

Mason (cont.)
Eunice Elizabeth 529
Fayette Stephen 536
Frank 536,537
Franklin M. 538
George 529
George W. 536,539
Gertrude Eliza 537
Guy 527
Hannah 514,519,520
Harriet 537
Henry 528
Henry M. 538
Hezekiah 515,519,
  520,532
Hilpa 536
Hobart 520,528
Huldah Perry 271
Ianthe 520
Isabel 348,350,352,
  536
Isaiah 536
Isaiah P. 536
Israel 352
Jacob 478
James 517,525,529
James F. 528
James Fitch (II) 529
James L. (Col.) 538
Jane 529
Jane A. 537
Japhet 520,527
Japhet (II) 520
Jared 520
Jemima 517
Jeremiah 516,519,
  526,529
Jeremiah (Col.) 516,
  528
John 513,514,517,
  527,538
John (Capt.) 352,513,
  514,517,518,533
John (Maj.) 12,513,
  519,527,530,532,
  533,534
John A. 271
John Anson 538
John C. 536
John G. Hillhouse 529
John Hempstead 527
John V. 538
John W. 536
Jonathan 520
Joseph 520,528
Judith 533
Julia Anna 529
La Fayette N. 536
Laura 539
Levi 537
Lewis L. 537
Lewis P. 537
Lois 528
Lorenzo 529
Loretta Jane 536
Louisa E. 537
Lucretia 527
Lucy 525
Lucy E. 271
Luke 528,536,537
Luke Henry 536
Lydia 520
Madison S. 536
Malvina A. 538
Margaret 515,528,536
Margaret (II) 536
Margaret Fanning 539
Marian Amanda 536

Mason (cont.)
Mary 520,525,526,527,
  528,536,539,564
Mary Ann 537
Mary Anne 536
Mary Bradford 539
Mary E. 529,537
Mary Imogene 537
Mary Lyon 529
Mary Paulina 536
Maryanne 529
Mehitable 520,528
Merrick E. 537
Milo 538
Mindwell B. 536
Miranda 525
Miriam 538
Miriam C. 537
Nancy 528
Naomi 527
Nehemiah 515,520,528
Nicholas 665
Noah 271
Orville L. 537
Oscar Day 537
Peleg 525,528
Peleg Sandford 518,
  524
Peleg Sanford 531
Peter 353,515,520,
  527,536,537
Peter L. 537
Phineham 527
Priscilla 513,515,520
Prudence 520
Rachel 513,517,519,
  520,526
Rebecca 515,520
Rebecca (II) 520
Rebecca (III) 520
Rhoda Louisa 529
Robert 536,537
Robert L. 536
Robert M. 529
Roswell 525
Samuel 513,514,515,
  517,520,527,539
Samuel (Maj.) 514,
  517,532
Sarah 514,517,527,561
Sarah M. 537
Sarah Malvina 538
Sebra H. 537
Seth F. 537
Shubael 536
Silas Keeney 527
Stephen 536,537
Stephen A. 537
Stephen Henry 536
Sylvester 537
Sylvester (II) 538
Thompson 527
Walter Dwight 536
Washington S. 536
Wealthy 527
Wealthy Fitch 529
Wesley F. 536
William 527,536
Wilson Lee 527
Zerviah 520,528
Massey, --- 474
Massie, --- 474
Masters, Addie Jane 591
Mary 591
Ross 591
Mather, Anne 368
Caroline 535
Catharine 493

779

783

784

786

Northrup (cont.)
Hannah 648,649,650,
    651,652,654,655
Heth 653
Hezekiah 657
Huldah 658
Isaac 649,652,653,
    654,655
Israel 652
Jabez 649,652,653
Jacob 655
James 648,649,650,
    655,657
Jane 653,654
Jared 654
Jeremiah 648,651,
    653,654,657,658
Joan 651
Job 651,653
Joel 648,651,653,657
Johanna 657,658
John 648,649,650,
    651,652,653,654,
    656,657,658
John (Lt.) 651
Jonah 649,655
Jonathan 651,652
Jonathan (Capt.) 657
Joseph 647,648,649,
    650,651,652,653,
    654,655,656,657,
    658
Joshua 651,655,656
Josiah 649,652,654,
    654
Keziah 656
Lazarus 653
Lemuel 658
Lewis 655
Lois 653,655,657,658
Lucius Bellinger
    (Gen.) 657
Margaret 648,651,657
Marion 654
Martha 652,653,655
Mary 648,651,652,
    653,654,656,658
Matthew 655
Mehetabel 649,652
Mercy 650,652,653
Millicent 654
Miriam 648,649,652,
    656
Molly 655
Moses 648,649,650,
    652,655,656
Moses (Jr.) 650
Nanny 658
Nathan 649,650,654
Nathaniel 652,654,655
Noanna 654
Patience 656
Paul 656
Peter 658
Phalle 655
Phineas 649,651
Phoebe 649,651,652
Polly 657
Rachel 651,652,655
Rebecca 649,652,653,
    654,655,657
Rensselaer 656
Rhoda 657
Robert 649
Ruth 651,653,655,658
Sally 656
Samuel 648,650,651,
    653,654,655,657

Northrup (cont.)
Sarah 649,650,651,
    652,653,654,655,
    657
Solomon 657
Stephen 650,655
Susanna 649,651
Thomas 649,650,
    653,655
Timothy 656
Waite 651
William 648,649,653,
    658
Wilson 654
Zophar 648,649,652
Northrupp, --- 648
Norton, Aaron 666,668,
    669,670
Abel 670
Abigail 665,666,668,
    671
Abijah 669
Abraham 666
Achsah 668
Albert B. 664
Alexander 670
Amos 670
Anah 667
Andrew 666,670
Ann 668
Anna 621,663,665,
    666,667,668,670
Anne 660,663,664,670
Arah 623,667
Asahel 666
Asenath 663
Ashbell 667
Azubah 667
Benjamin 160,575,
    667,670
Benjamin (Sgt.) 463
Beriah 666
Bethiah 667
Birdseye 669
Charity 667,670
Charles 465,660,671
Clarissa 667
Daniel 171,667,668
David 666,669,670
Deborah 668
Diadama 667
Diademia 623
Dinah 669
Dorcas 659
Dorothy 659
Ebenezer 659,665,
    668,669
Eber 667,670
Edward 465
Elah 670
Elias 660,663
Elihu 668
Elijah 667
Elisha 668
Elizabeth 160,525,
    549,659,663,665,
    666,667,668,669,
    670,671
Elnathan 670
Elon 667
Ephraim 670
Esther 668,669
Eunice 663,668
Felix 132,667
Francis 648
George (Capt.) 43,62
Gideon 660
Grace 664

Norton (cont.)
Hannah 201,659,665,
    666,667,668,670
Hannah Buck 665
Henry 465
Hooker 667
Huldah 666
Ichabod (Col.) 525
Isaac 659,664,668
Isaac J. 483
Isaiah 666
Ishi 160,666
Jabez 669
Jacob 663
James 666
Jedidah 667
Jedidiah 668
Job 660,670
Joel 668,670
John 118,416,659,660,
    661,662,663,664,
    665,666,668,670
John (III) 660
John (Rev.) 663,664
John (Sgt.) 660
Jonathan 670
Joseph 664,665,666,
    668
Joshua 664
Josiah 668
Julia 465
Keziah 84,666
L. M. (Dea.) 664,
    665,669
Lea 667
Leah 667
Levi 669
Lewis 671
Lois 667
Lucinda 465
Lucy 660,670
Lucy Hotchkiss 174
Lucy King 370
Lydia 668,669
Lyman 671
Marana 669
Martha 667
Mary 648,659,660,
    664,665,666,668,
    669,670
Medad 671
Mehitable 668
Mercy 62
Miles 668,669
Mindwell 666,671
Miriam 670
Moses 670
Nathan 666
Nathaniel 669
Noadiah 170
Noah 666,669,670
Noahdiah 670
Olive 669
Oliver 670
Ozias 671
Parnel 667
Phebe 670
Philemon 666
Phinehas 668
Prudence 668
Rachel 204,623,667,
    669
Rebecca 668
Reuben 667
Rhoda 670
Richard 659
Roger 660
Ruth 659,660,666,

790

Owen (cont.)
Lucy 518,686,697,
714,715,719
Lucy Ann 710
Lusina 688
Lydia 684,687,688,
690,693,698,709
Lydia Clark 697
Lydia Perry 711
Malissa 705
Margaret 689,690,710
Maria 697,706,707
Maria Louisa 715
Marilo Harrison 719
Marilo Pitt 719
Martha 682,683,684,
693,704,705,706,
707,712,719
Mary 679,680,683,
684,685,686,688,
690,693,696,697,
698,701,719
Mary A. 717,718
Mary Ann 718
Mary Butler 706
Mary Elizabeth 715
Mary Elizabeth Hodges
710
Mercy 687
Meriam 689
Milanda 706
Millard Fillmore 711
Mindwell 690
Miner 709
Miriam 697
Mirriam Loraine 710
Molly 684,689
Moses 681,682,687,
696,697,709
Myra 707
Nance 702
Nancy 698
Naomi 689
Nathaniel 679,680,
684,685,694,696,
697,715
Nathaniel (Jr.) 684
Nellie 708
Nelson 717,718
Nelson A. 717
Noah 683,692,693
Nomah 693
Obadiah 679,682,683,
689
Oliver 696,698,700
Orilla 698
Orvil Ives 707,708
Palermo 717
Parintha 721
Parnah 693
Patience 689,692,
695,696,700
Pegge 686,690
Pelatiah 698
Phebe 689
Phoebe 716
Polly 693,697,701,
702,709
Priscilla 697
Rachel 679,680,686,
689,690,693
Rainer 693
Rainor 697
Ralph 697
Ransom Ezra 719
Rebecca 679,683,686,
691,699,706,712,
716

Owen (cont.)
Rebeckah 53
Rhoda 689,698
Robert 705
Robert Carter 715
Robert Wallace 708
Roderick 697,714,715
Roderick Mandred 715
Roger Leonard 695
Rosetta 694
Ruth 685,686,689,694
Sabra 684,690
Sabre 688
Sabrina 706
Sally 697,709,715,716
Samuel 678,682,689,
690
Samuel (Dea.) 689
Sarah 679,682,683,
689,690,696,698,
701,702,704,705,
709
Sarah Ingalls 711
Sarah Osborn 699
Seth 690
Seth Calvin 690
Shem 698
Sibel 688
Silas 683,693,698,716
Silvanus 693
Simeon 684
Solomon 696,700,701,
709,714,715,716,
717,719
Sophia 694
Sophronia 718
Spencer 705
Stearns P. 721
Submit 696
Tabitha 682
Tabitha Farr 717
Talbut 684
Thadeus 688
Thalia 693
Theodore 718,719
Theodosia 718
Theresa 694
Thomas 678,686
Thursey 699
Timothy 688,697,709,
710,711
Ursula 699
Uzziel 692,693
Washington 707,717,
718,719
Wilbur 705
Willard 697
William 593,678,695,
697,700,716
William Arthur 678,
708,712
William C. 705
William Dana 697
William Doane 710
William Henry 698,710
William Henry Brad-
ford 709
Willis 716
Zaphira 710
Zelma 707
Zeriah 690
Zerviah 693

--- P ---

Pack, Ann 360

Packard, Lydia 630
Mary 273
Packer, Amos Victor 638
Elizabeth Lingle 638
Henry 486
Isaac 479
Isaac Mitchell 638
Warren Melvin 638
Page, Amos (Jr.) 132
Dan 463
Hannah 130
Ichabod 190
John 466
Leah 175
Martha 437
Moses 84
Nathan 274
Reuben (Col.) 131
Ruth 274
Paige, --- (Capt.) 624
Cora 176
Paine, Abigail 331,333,
507
David 313
Job 115
Painter, Herman M. 173
Margaret 557
Mercy Lamberton 557
Shubael 557
Palfrey, John G. 101
Palmer, A. H. 270
Ammi 362
Andrew 566
Betty 132
Cornelius G. 567
Dorothy 8
Elizabeth 132,518
George 717
Gershom 514
Grace 79
Hannah 79
James 706
John 39,124,132
Lydia 417
Mary 153
Rebecca 418
Sarah 437,680
Stephen (Jr.) 123
Timothy 680
Urban (Rev.) 498
Wealthy 706
Panca, Frances 524
Pangborn, Philena 593
Anna May 721
Clifford Francis 721
DeForest Grant 721
Elnora Parintha 721
Eva Alberta 721
Fern Belle 721
Francis Albertus 721
Frederick Ransom 721
Harriet Amanda 721
Orin Darius 721
Walter 721
Pantry, John (Jr.) 659
Pardee, --- 464
Clarissa 464
Mary 173,183
Samuel 185
Pardue, Edith 605
Pardy, Enos 706
Parish, A. G. 644
Park, Joshua 625
Solomon (Lt.) 45
Parke, Abigail 284
Hannah 520
Parker, --- 50
Abigail 185

796

806

--- (no surname, cont.)	--- (no surname, cont.)	--- (no surname, cont.)
Sophronia 209	Susannah 123,150,204	Uroen 56
Susan 305	Tabitha 412	Wyandanch 563
Susanna 384,526	Thankful 132	